"*KL* goes far beyond the familiar sight of overflowing ditches, corpses, the emaciated bodies, towers and wire fences, furnaces and SS guards. It is monumental. Wachsmann covers all fields of the SS from its origins to its final days: a full, full history of the concentration camp system, from the creation of Dachau, the first camp, in March 1933, to Dora-Mittelbau, the last, in the autumn of 1944 (with its Dantesque tunnels dedicated to the manufacture of Nazi rockets). A story that continually gives us the voices of prisoners and guards, victims and torturers, perpetrators and martyrs. One of the most remarkable things about *KL* is that it is an enlightening, precise survey, but is never cold, rather full of names and faces—it provides a true sense of humanity. Wachsmann's narrative skill ensures that *KL* will connect to specialist and general readers alike" *El Pais* (Spain)

"Wachsmann tells the story of the concentration camps with real intellectual honesty, together with colossal research, developed over many years in dozens of archives around the world. *KL* is exemplery. Wachsmann does not provide an impersonal and disembodied description of the Holocaust and its evolution. Instead, the entire narrative is built from individual case studies, written in a captivating and direct style. *KL* was written to be a worldwide bestseller—and will be, deservedly so ... An overwhelming book" *Público* (Portugal)

"[A] monumental study ... a work of prodigious scholarship ... with agonizing human texture and extraordinary detail ... Wachsmann makes the unimaginable palpable. That is his great achievement" Roger Cohen, *New York Times Book Review*

"*KL* is a definitive history ... Mr. Wachsmann's most impressive achievement in this synthetic work is his portraits of individual human beings. It takes hard effort to assemble enough sources on inmates or SS men to sustain them as characters in a book of this length. The prisoners had a range of references to describe their ordeals, from the Book of Exodus through Dante's *Inferno*. In the generations since, their experience has become one of our points of reference in moral discussions, and it is all the more gratifying to see the camp inmates portrayed here with unvarnished humanity. Mr. Wachsmann has in effect united the best of the German and the British schools of grand World War II history: hugely but humbly exhaustive research with attention to character and to detailed narrative" Timothy Snyder, *Wall Street Journal*

"Deeply researched, groundbreaking history" Adam Kirsch, *New Yorker*

t
o
st
Fri
Jew

"Nik
Nazi
schola
dynan
experie
is an i
Ordinar

"Telling the story of the KL means facing up to a formidable challenge: how
to make the camps relatable, as places where real people lived, worked and
died, rather than transcendental symbols of evil? ... [Wachsmann] proves
himself equal to this challenge ... thanks to Wachsmann's skill as a writer, it
manages to . . . . rse of ever-
increasing

A HISTORY OF THE NAZI
CONCENTRATION CAMPS

NIKOLAUS WACHSMANN

ABACUS

First published in the United States in 2015 by Farrar, Straus and Giroux
First published in Great Britain in 2015 by Little, Brown
This paperback edition published in 2016 by Abacus

1 3 5 7 9 10 8 6 4 2

Published by arrangement with Farrar Straus and Giroux LLC,
19 Union Square West, New York, NY 10003, USA

A CIP catalogue record for this book
is available from the British Library.

ISBN 978-0-349-11866-6

Printed and bound in Great Britain by
Clays Ltd, St Ives plc

Papers used by Abacus are from well-managed forests
and other responsible sources.

Abacus
An imprint of
Little, Brown Book Group
Carmelite House
50 Victoria Embankment
London EC4Y 0DZ

An Hachette UK Company
www.hachette.co.uk

www.littlebrown.co.uk

may the world at least behold a drop,

a fraction of this tragic world in which we lived
*—Letter by Salmen Gradowski, September 6, 1944
(discovered after liberation, in a flask buried on the
grounds of the Auschwitz-Birkenau crematorium)*

Contents

Appendix: Tables

List of Maps

Sources: von Götz, "Terror in Berlin" (map 1); *OdT*, vol. 3 (map 6); Długoborski, Piper (eds.), *Auschwitz*, vols. 1 & 5 (map 5 and 7).

Note on place-names: Both maps and text mostly use the official names of camps and cities at the time events described in this book took place, though occasionally the name in use today, or more familiar to readers, has been used instead (or is given as an alternative).

kl

Prologue

Dachau, April 29, 1945. It is early afternoon when U.S. troops, part of the Allied force sweeping across Germany to crush the last remains of the Third Reich, approach an abandoned train on a rail siding at the grounds of a sprawling SS complex near Munich. As the soldiers come closer, they make a dreadful discovery: the boxcars are filled with the corpses of well over two thousand men and women, and also some children. Gaunt, contorted limbs are entangled amid a mess of straw and rags, covered in filth, blood, and excrement. Several ashen-faced GIs turn away to cry or vomit. "It made us sick at our stomach and so mad we could do nothing but clinch our fists," an officer wrote the next day. As the shaken soldiers move deeper into the SS complex and reach the prisoner compound, later that afternoon, they come upon thirty-two thousand survivors from many ethnic, religious, and political backgrounds, representing about thirty European nations. Some seem more dead than alive as they stumble toward their liberators. Many more lie in overcrowded barracks, infested with dirt and disease. Wherever the soldiers turn, they see dead bodies, sprawled between barracks, dumped in ditches, stacked like logs by the camp's crematorium. As for those behind the carnage, almost all career SS men are long gone, with only a ragtag gang of perhaps two hundred guards left behind.[1] Images of this nightmare soon flashed around the world and burned themselves into collective memories. To this day, concentration camps like Dachau are often seen through the lens of the liberators, with the all-too-familiar pictures of trenches filled with bodies, mountains of corpses, and bone-thin survivors staring into cameras. Powerful as these pictures are, however, they do not reveal the full story of Dachau. For the camp had a much longer history and had only recently reached its last circle of hell, during the final throes of the Second World War.[2]

Dachau, August 31, 1939. The prisoners rise before dawn, as they do every morning. None of them know that war will break out the next day, and they follow their usual schedule. After the frantic rush—jostling in the washrooms, devouring some bread, cleaning the barracks—they march in strict military formation to the roll call square. Nearly four thousand men with cropped or shaven heads stand to attention in striped uniforms, dreading another day of forced labor. Except for a group of Czechs, virtually all the prisoners are German or Austrian, though their common language is often all they share; colored triangles on their uniforms identify them as political prisoners, asocials, criminals, homosexuals, Jehovah's Witnesses, or Jews. Behind the rows of prisoners stand rows of one-story prisoner barracks. Each of the thirty-four purpose-built huts is around 110 yards long; the floors inside are gleaming and the bunks are meticulously made up. Escape is almost impossible: the rectangular prisoner compound, measuring 637 by 304 yards, is surrounded by a moat and concrete wall, watchtowers and machine guns, and barbed and electric wire. Beyond lies a huge SS zone with over 220 buildings, including storerooms, workshops, living quarters, and even a swimming pool. Stationed here are some three thousand men from the Camp SS, a volunteer unit with its own ethos, which puts prisoners through well-rehearsed routines of abuse and violence. Deaths are few and far between, however, with no more than four fatalities in August 1939; as yet, there was no urgent need for the SS to build its own crematorium.[3] This was Camp SS terror at its most controlled—a far cry from the lethal chaos of the final days in spring 1945, and also from Dachau's ramshackle beginnings back in spring 1933.

Dachau, March 22, 1933. The first day inside the camp is drawing to a close. It is a cold evening, less than two months after the appointment of Adolf Hitler as chancellor set Germany on the road to the Nazi dictatorship. The new prisoners (still in their own clothes) are having bread, sausage, and tea inside the former office of a dilapidated munitions plant. This building had been hastily converted in recent days into an improvised camp, cordoned off from the rest of the deserted factory ground with its crumbling structures, broken concrete foundations, and derelict roads. In all, there are no more than 100 or 120 political prisoners, largely local Communists from Munich. After these men had arrived on open trucks a little earlier, the guards—some fifty-four men strong—announced that the captives would be held in "protective custody," a term unfamiliar to many Germans. Whatever it was, it seemed bearable: the guards were not Nazi paramilitaries but amiable policemen, who chatted with the prisoners, handed out cigarettes, and even slept in the same building. The next day, the prisoner Erwin Kahn wrote a long letter to his wife to say that all was well in Dachau. The food was good, as was the treatment, though he was getting restless waiting for his release. "I am just curious how long this whole business will last." A few weeks later, Kahn was dead, shot by SS men after they took over the prisoner compound. He was among the first of almost forty thousand Dachau prisoners to perish between spring 1933 and spring 1945.[4]

Three days in Dachau, three different worlds. In a span of only twelve years, the camp changed time and again. Inmates, guards, conditions—almost everything seemed to alter. Even the site itself was transformed; after the old factory buildings were demolished and replaced by purpose-built barracks in the late 1930s, a veteran prisoner from spring 1933 would not have recognized the camp.[5] So why did Dachau transform from its benign beginnings in March 1933 to the SS order of terror, and on to the catastrophe of the Second World War? What did this mean for the prisoners inside? What drove the perpetrators? And what did the population outside know about the camp? These questions go to the heart of the Nazi dictatorship, and they should be asked not just about Dachau, but about the concentration camp system as a whole.[6]

Dachau was the first of many SS concentration camps. Established inside Germany in the early years of Hitler's rule, these camps soon spread, during the Nazi conquest of Europe from the late 1930s, to Austria, Poland, France, Czechoslovakia, the Netherlands, Belgium, Lithuania, Estonia, Latvia, and even the small British Channel Island of Alderney. In all, the SS set up twenty-seven main camps and over 1,100 attached satellite camps over the course of the Third Reich, though numbers fluctuated greatly, as old camps closed down and new ones opened; only Dachau lasted for the entire Nazi period.[7]

The concentration camps embodied the spirit of Nazism like no other institution in the Third Reich.[8] They formed a distinct system of domination, with its own organization, rules, and staff, and even its own acronym: in official documents and common parlance, they were often referred to as KL (from the German *Konzentrationslager*).[9] Guided by SS chief Heinrich Himmler, Hitler's main henchman, the KL came to reflect the burning obsessions of the Nazi leadership, such as the creation of a uniform national community through the removal of political, social, and racial outsiders; the sacrifice of the individual on the altar of racial hygiene and murderous science; the harnessing of forced labor for the glory of the fatherland; the mastery over Europe, enslaving foreign nations, and colonizing living space; the deliverance of Germany from its worst enemies through mass extermination; and finally, the determination to go down in flames rather than surrender. Over time, all these obsessions shaped the KL system, and led to mass detention, deprivation, and death inside.

We can estimate that 2.3 million men, women, and children were dragged to SS concentration camps between 1933 and 1945; most of them, over 1.7 million, lost their lives. Almost one million of the dead were Jews murdered in Auschwitz, the only KL to play a central role in what the Nazis called the Final Solution—the systematic extermination of European Jewry during the Second World War, now commonly known as the Holocaust. From 1942, when the SS started to dispatch deportation trains from across the continent, KL Auschwitz operated as an unusual hybrid of labor and death camp. Some two hundred thousand Jews were selected on arrival for slave labor with the other regular prisoners. The remainder—an estimated 870,000 Jewish men, women, and children—went directly to their deaths in the gas chambers, without ever being registered as inmates of the camp.[10] Despite its unique role, Auschwitz remained a concentration camp and continued to share many features with the other camps, most of which—KL like Ellrich, Kaufering, Klooga, Redl-Zipf, and many more—have long since been forgotten. Together, they occupied a unique space in the Third Reich. They were sites of lawless terror, where some of the most radical features of Nazi rule were born and refined.

Precedents and Perspectives

In April 1941, German audiences flocked to cinemas to watch a star-studded feature film, purportedly based on a true story and released with much fanfare by the Nazi authorities. The climax of the movie was set against an unusual background—a concentration camp. There was to be no happy end for the starved and disease-ridden inmates, all of them innocent victims of a murderous regime: a brave prisoner is hanged, his wife shot, and others massacred by their vicious captors, leaving only graves behind. These chilling scenes bore an uncanny likeness to life in SS concentration camps at the time (there was even a special screening for guards in Auschwitz). But this was not a drama about the SS camps. The film was set decades earlier, during the South African War, and the villains were British imperialists. *Ohm Krüger*, as the film was called, was a powerful piece of German propaganda during the war with Britain, and mirrored a public speech made a few months earlier by Adolf Hitler: "Concentration camps were not invented in Germany," he had declared. "It is the English who are their inventors, using this institution to gradually break the backs of other nations."[11]

This was a familiar refrain. Hitler himself had made the same point before, telling the German people that his regime had merely copied the concentration camps from the English (though not their abuses).[12] Nazi propaganda never tired of foreign camps. During the early years of the regime, speeches and articles routinely harked back to the British camps of the South African War, which had caused much indignation across Europe, and also pointed at present-day camps in countries like Austria, said to be scenes of great suffering for domestic Nazi activists. The real meaning behind this propaganda—that the SS camps were not exceptional—could hardly be missed, but just to make sure that everyone got the message, SS leader Heinrich Himmler spelled it out during a speech on German radio in 1939. Concentration camps were a "time-honored institution" abroad, he announced, adding that the German version was considerably more moderate than foreign ones.[13]

Such attempts to relativize the SS camps had little success, at least outside Germany. Still, there was a grain of truth in the crude Nazi propaganda. "The Camp" as a place of detention really was a wider international phenomenon. In the decades before the Nazi seizure of power, camps for the mass confinement of political and other suspects—outside regular prisons and criminal law—had sprung up in Europe and beyond, usually during times of political upheaval or war, and such camps continued to flourish after the demise of the Third Reich, leading some observers to describe the entire epoch as an Age of Camps.[14]

The first of these sites appeared during colonial wars of the late nineteenth and early twentieth centuries, as brutal military responses to guerrilla warfare. Colonial powers aimed to defeat local insurgents through the mass internment of civilian noncombatants in villages, towns, or camps, a tactic used by the Spanish in Cuba, the United States in the Philippines, and the British in South Africa (from where the term "concentration camp" gained wider circulation). The colonial authorities' indifference and ineptitude caused mass hunger, illness, and death among those inside such internment sites. However, these were not prototypes of the later SS camps, differing greatly in terms of their function, design, and operation.[15] The same is true for camps in German Southwest Africa (now Namibia), run by the colonial authorities between 1904 and 1908 during a ferocious war against the indigenous population. Many thousands of Herero and Nama were imprisoned in what were sometimes called concentration camps, and around half of them are said to have died due to the neglect and contempt of their German captors. These camps diverged from other colonial camps, as they were propelled less by military strategy than a desire for punishment and forced labor. But they did not provide a "rough template" for the SS camps, either, as has been claimed, and any attempts to draw direct lines to Dachau or Auschwitz are unconvincing.[16]

The era of the camps really began with the First World War, which brought them from faraway colonies into the European heartlands. In addition to POW camps holding millions of soldiers, many of the belligerent nations set up forced labor camps, refugee camps, and civilian internment camps, driven by doctrines of total mobilization, radical nationalism, and social hygiene. Such camps were easy to establish and guard, thanks to recent innovations like machine guns, cheap barbed wire, and mass-produced portable barracks. Conditions were worst across central and eastern Europe, where prisoners often endured systematic forced labor, violence, and neglect, and several hundreds of thousands died. By the end of the First World War, Europe was littered with camps, and their memory lingered long after they had been dissolved. In 1927, for example, a German parliamentary commission still angrily denounced wartime abuses of German prisoners in French and British "concentration camps."[17]

Many more camps emerged in the 1920s and 1930s, as much of Europe turned away from democracy. Totalitarian regimes, with their Manichean division of the world into friend and foe, became the strongest champions of camps as weapons to permanently isolate and terrorize alleged enemies. By birth, the KL belonged to this breed of camp and shared some of its generic features. There were even a few direct links. The camp system in Franco's Spain, for example, which held hundreds of thousands of prisoners during and after the civil war, apparently drew some inspiration from the Nazi precedent.[18]

Probably the closest foreign relative of SS concentration camps could be found in the Soviet Union under Stalin.[19] Building on the experiences with mass detention during the First World War, the Bolsheviks had used camps (sometimes labeled as concentration camps) ever since the revolution. By the 1930s, they presided over a vast system of detention—known as the Gulag—which encompassed labor camps, colonies, prisons, and more. The corrective labor camps of the People's Commissariat of Internal Affairs (NKVD) alone held some 1.5 million prisoners by early January 1941, many times more than even the SS camp system. Like the KL complex, the Soviet one was driven by destructive utopianism, aiming to create a perfect society by eliminating all enemies, and its camps followed a somewhat similar trajectory: from haphazard sites of terror to a huge network of centrally directed camps, from the detention of political suspects to the imprisonment of other social and ethnic outsiders, from an early emphasis on rehabilitation to often deadly forced labor.[20]

In view of these parallels, and the prior emergence of the Soviet system, some scholars have suggested that the Nazis simply seized the idea of the concentration camp from the Soviets—a misleading claim, though one that is almost as old as the SS camps themselves.[21] There are two specific problems. First, there were profound differences between both camp systems. Although the Soviet camps were initially more deadly, for example, the KL later took a more radical turn and developed along far more lethal lines, culminating in the Auschwitz extermination complex, which had no equal in the USSR or anywhere else. NKVD prisoners were more likely to be released than to die, whereas the opposite was true for prisoners in the wartime SS concentration camps. In all, some ninety percent of inmates survived the Gulag; in the KL, the figure among registered prisoners was probably less than half. As the philosopher Hannah Arendt put it in her pioneering study of totalitarianism, the Soviet camps were purgatory, the Nazi ones pure hell.[22] Second, there is little evidence of the Nazis copying the Soviets. To be sure, the SS kept an eye on Soviet repression in the Gulag, especially after the German invasion of summer 1941: Nazi leaders considered taking over "concentration camps of the Russians," as they put it, and sent a summary about the organization and conditions in Soviet "concentration camps" to their own KL commandants.[23] More generally, the violence of the Bolsheviks in the Soviet Union, both real and imagined, served as a permanent reference point during the Third Reich. In Dachau, SS officials told the first SS guards in 1933 to act as brutally as the Cheka (security organization) had done in the USSR. Years later in Auschwitz, SS men referred to one of their cruelest torture instruments as the "Stalin Swing."[24]

But a general interest in Soviet terror should not be mistaken for influence. The Nazi regime was not inspired by the Gulag in any major way and it is hard to imagine that the history of the SS concentration camps would have been substantially different had the Gulag never existed. The KL were largely made in Germany, just as the Gulag was primarily the product of Soviet rule. There were similarities, of course, but they were largely outweighed by differences; each camp system had its own form and function, shaped by specific national practices, purposes, and precedents. A study of international comparisons and connections can still provide useful perspectives, but such an analysis lies beyond the scope of this book; what follows is the story of the SS concentration camps, with occasional glances beyond Nazi-controlled territory.

History and Memory

"In the future, I believe, when the word concentration camp is used, one will think of Hitler's Germany, and only of Hitler's Germany." Thus wrote Victor Klemperer in his diary in autumn 1933, just a few months after the first prisoners had arrived in Dachau and long before the SS camps descended into mass murder.[25] Klemperer, a liberal German-Jewish professor of philology in Dresden, was one of the shrewdest observers of the Nazi dictatorship, and his prediction proved prescient. Nowadays the KL really are synonymous with "concentration camps." What is more, these camps have become symbols of the Third Reich as a whole, occupying an exalted place in history's hall of infamy. They have appeared almost everywhere in recent years, in blockbuster movies and documentaries, bestselling novels and comics, memoirs and scholarly tomes, plays and artworks; google "Auschwitz" and you get well over seven million hits.[26]

The urge to understand the concentration camps began early. They took center stage in the immediate postwar period, starting with the Allied media offensive in April and May 1945. The Soviet press had made little of the liberation of Auschwitz a few months before—one reason why the camp initially remained peripheral in popular discourse—so it was not until the liberation of Dachau, Buchenwald, and Bergen-Belsen by the western Allies that the KL made it onto the front pages in Britain, the United States, and beyond; one Australian news report described Germany in April 1945 as "the concentration camp country." There were radio broadcasts, newsreels, magazine spreads, pamphlets, exhibitions, and speeches. And although they lacked historical perspective, these accounts did convey the scale of the horrors unveiled inside; in a May 1945 survey, ordinary Americans guessed that around one million concentration camp prisoners had been killed.

Of course, these media revelations should not have come as a complete shock. Reports about atrocities in the KL had appeared abroad since the early days of the Nazi regime—sometimes written in exile by former prisoners or relatives of murdered inmates—and the Allies had received vital intelligence during the war. But the reality turned out to be far worse than almost anyone expected. As if to make up for this failure of the imagination, Allied leaders encouraged journalists, soldiers, and politicians to inspect liberated camps. For them, the camps proved the absolute righteousness of the war. "Dachau gives answer to why we fought," declared one U.S. army newssheet in May 1945, echoing the sentiments of General Eisenhower. In addition, the Allies used the camps to confront the German population with its complicity, inaugurating a reeducation campaign that continued over the coming months, reinforced by early trials of SS perpetrators.[27]

At the same time, survivors themselves helped to put the KL in the public eye. They were not stunned into collective silence, as has often been said.[28] On the contrary, a loud, polyphonic chorus rose up after liberation. Throughout their suffering, prisoners had dreamed about bearing witness. Some had even kept secret diaries. One of them, the German political prisoner Edgar Kupfer, was probably the most diligent chronicler of Dachau. Taking advantage of his sheltered office job on the SS complex and his reputation among fellow inmates as a loner, he secretly wrote more than 1,800 pages, starting in late 1942. Prior to his detention in 1940 for critical comments about the Nazi regime, the nonconformist Kupfer had worked as a tour guide, and he envisaged his book as a grand tour of Dachau. He knew that the SS would likely murder him if they discovered his secret, but somehow he survived and so did his notes; barely recovered, he typed up his manuscript in summer 1945, ready for publication.[29]

Other liberated men, women, and children were yearning to tell their story, too, now that they were free to speak. Some started straight away, still inside the camps; even the sick would grab the sleeves of passing Allied medical staff to get their attention. Survivors quickly coordinated their efforts. They had to work together to alert "world public opinion," a former prisoner told fellow survivors in Mauthausen on May 7, 1945. Within days of liberation, survivors everywhere had started to collaborate on joint reports.[30] Thousands more accounts followed soon after former prisoners left the camps. Jewish survivors, for example, testified before historical commissions dedicated to commemoration and research, culminating in the first ever international conference of Holocaust survivors in Paris in 1947, attended by delegates from thirteen countries. Survivor testimonies were also encouraged by occupation forces, foreign governments, and NGOs, to help punish the perpetrators and preserve the memory of the camps.[31] Some of these accounts later appeared in journals and pamphlets.[32] Other survivors wrote directly for publication. Among them was the young Italian Jew Primo Levi, who had endured almost a year in Auschwitz. "Each of us survivors," he later recalled, "as soon as we returned home, transformed himself into a tireless narrator, imperious and maniacal." Writing almost everywhere, day and night, Levi completed his book *If This Is a Man* in just a few months; it appeared in Italy in 1947.[33]

During the first postwar years, a wave of memoirs hit Europe and beyond, mostly searing testimonies of individual suffering and survival.[34] Some former prisoners also reflected on wider themes, writing important early studies of the camp system and the inmate experience, from a sociological or psychological perspective.[35] Others produced first historical sketches of particular camps, or expressed their pain in poems and fictionalized accounts.[36] Most of these early works, including Primo Levi's own, sank with few ripples, but a number of books made a splash. Celebrated survivor accounts appeared in several European countries. Amid the ruins of Germany, too, mass-market paperbacks and pamphlets were printed, while other accounts were serialized in major newspapers. Most influential was a general study of the KL system (with Buchenwald at the center) compiled by the former political prisoner Eugen Kogon, which shaped popular conceptions for years to come; first published in 1946, its German print run had reached 135,000 copies a year later, and it soon appeared in translation, as did other early works by survivors.[37]

By the late 1940s, however, when it came to a U.S. edition, Kogon's publisher, Roger Straus, a passionate believer in the book, was concerned about the "apathy on the part of the public to reading about this type of thing."[38] The popular interest in the KL—which had accompanied their liberation, as well as some of the first memoirs and perpetrator trials—was waning on both sides of the Atlantic. In part, this was a simple case of saturation following the spate of graphic early accounts. More generally, public memory of the camps was being marginalized by postwar reconstruction and diplomacy. With the front line of the Cold War cutting right through Germany, and turning the two new, opposing German states into strategic allies of the USSR and the United States, talk about Nazi crimes seemed impolitic. "Nowadays it is bad taste to speak of the concentration camps," Primo Levi wrote in 1955, adding: "silence prevails." Within ten years of liberation, the camps had been sidelined—a result not of survivors unable to speak, but of a wider audience unwilling to listen. Former prisoners still tried to keep the memory of the camps alive. "If we fall silent, who then will speak?" Levi asked angrily. Another survivor who persevered in the face of widespread indifference was Edgar Kupfer, who finally saw the German publication of his Dachau book in 1956, albeit in a greatly abridged version. Despite some good reviews, however, it left little impression and no foreign publisher picked it up, "afraid that the public would not buy it," as the depressed author concluded.[39]

Popular interest in the concentration camps was rekindled in the 1960s and 1970s. Major trials of Nazi perpetrators, such as the 1961 Israeli case against Adolf Eichmann, the SS officer who had overseen deportations of Jews to Auschwitz, and media sensations like the 1978 U.S. miniseries *Holocaust*, broadcast to a vast audience in West Germany the following year, played an important part in confronting the public with the Nazi regime and its camps. In turn, some early KL memoirs were rediscovered, among them Primo Levi's masterpiece about Auschwitz, which has long since entered the canon of modern literature. At the same time, a wave of new survivor testimonies appeared. This wave kept swelling—Edgar Kupfer's complete Dachau diaries, for example, finally saw publication in 1997—and it is only now subsiding, as the last witnesses are passing away.[40] Survivors also continued to explore the development of individual camps, producing source editions and standard historical surveys.[41] And just like in the early postwar period, former inmates went far beyond writing history, creating an extraordinarily rich body of medical, sociological, psychological, and philosophical studies, as well as literary reflections and works of art.[42]

In sharp contrast to survivors, the wider academic community was slow to engage with the KL. A few specialist studies appeared in the late 1940s and 1950s, particularly on medical aspects.[43] But it was not until the 1960s and 1970s that academic historians published preliminary surveys of some individual Nazi camps and the wider KL complex, based on documentary research. Most influential were the works of two young German academics, Martin Broszat's pioneering survey of the camp system's development and Falk Pingel's powerful study of life inside.[44] Such historical analyses were augmented by works from scholars in other disciplines, on themes like the perpetrator mind and the experience of survival.[45]

Despite inevitable shortcomings, these early studies made important contributions to knowledge about the SS concentration camps. But they remained exceptions and could only sketch outlines. To write a comprehensive history of the camps, Broszat himself concluded in 1970, was simply impossible, because of the dearth of detailed research.[46] Paradoxically, this void was created, at least in part, by the misguided belief that there was little more to learn about the camps, an assumption shared by even some otherwise sharp-eyed observers.[47] In reality, scholars were only starting to discover the KL.

Historical knowledge advanced rapidly in the 1980s and 1990s, above all in Germany itself. With grassroots history on the rise, local activists scrutinized the record of former camps in their neighborhood. Meanwhile, camp memorials moved beyond remembrance and developed into places of scholarship. The opening of the archives in Eastern Europe, following the end of the Cold War, provided further momentum for research. Meanwhile, a younger generation of academics untainted by the past was discovering the Third Reich as a subject and established the study of its camps as a distinct historiographical field, producing major works like Karin Orth's account of the KL organization and structure.[48] Having been ignored for so long, the study of the SS concentration camps was now booming, at least in Germany (few studies were translated).[49]

The boom shows no sign of settling, as historical research continues to expand at a rapid rate. New perspectives have come into view as we learn more about individual perpetrators, prisoner groups, and camps, about the beginning and the end of the SS system, about the local environment around the camps, about forced labor and extermination policy. While all the important scholarly studies of the KL published before the late 1970s comfortably fit onto a single bookshelf, one needs a small library to gather the works published since then.[50]

Recent academic research has culminated in two huge encyclopedias—over 1,600 and 4,100 pages long, respectively—that summarize the development of every single main and satellite camp; the entries were penned by well over 150 historians from around the world.[51] These two indispensable works demonstrate the breadth of contemporary scholarship. But they also point to its limits. Most important, the wealth of specialist studies has greatly fragmented the picture of the SS concentration camps. Where it was once impossible to see the camp system as a whole, because so much detail was missing, it is now almost impossible to see how all the different features fit together; looking at recent scholarship is like looking at a giant unassembled puzzle, with additional pieces being added all the time. It comes as no surprise that the conclusions of the new KL histories have generally failed to connect with a wider public.

As a result, popular images of the Nazi concentration camps remain rather one-dimensional. Instead of the intricate detail and subtle shades of historical scholarship, we see broad brushstrokes and vivid colors. Above all, popular conceptions are dominated by the stark images of Auschwitz and the Holocaust, which have made this camp a "global site of memory," as the political scientist Peter Reichel put it.[52] It was not always like this. In the early decades after the war, anti-Jewish terror was largely subsumed under the general destruction wreaked by Nazism, with Auschwitz as one place of suffering among many. The awareness of the singularity and enormity of the Nazi war against the Jews has grown sharply since then, and the Third Reich is now largely viewed through the lens of the Holocaust.[53] The SS concentration camps, in turn, have become closely identified with Auschwitz and its Jewish victims, obscuring other camps and other inmates. A German poll found that Auschwitz is by far the most recognized KL and that the vast majority of respondents associate the camps with the persecution of Jews; by contrast, less than ten percent named Communists, criminals, or homosexuals as victims.[54] In popular memory, then, the concentration camps, Auschwitz, and the Holocaust have merged into one.

But Auschwitz was never synonymous with the Nazi concentration camps. True, as the largest and most lethal camp by far, it occupied a special place in the KL system. But there was always more to this system. Auschwitz was closely integrated into the wider KL network, and it was preceded and shaped by other camps. Dachau, for example, was more than seven years old when Auschwitz was established, and clearly influenced it. Also, despite its unprecedented size, most registered KL prisoners—that is, those forced into barracks and slave labor—were detained elsewhere; even at its biggest, Auschwitz held no more than around one-third of all regular KL inmates. The great majority of them died elsewhere, too, with an estimated three-quarters of registered KL inmates perishing in camps other than Auschwitz. It is important, then, to demystify Auschwitz in the popular conception of the camps, while still emphasizing its uniquely destructive role.[55]

Nor were concentration camps synonymous with the Holocaust, although their histories are intertwined. First, anti-Jewish terror largely unfolded outside the KL; it was not until the final year of World War II that most of the surviving Jewish victims found themselves inside a concentration camp. The significant majority of the up to six million Jews murdered under the Nazi regime perished in other places, shot in ditches and fields across eastern Europe, or gassed in distinct death camps like Treblinka, which operated separately from the KL. Second, the concentration camps always targeted various victim groups, and except for a few weeks in late 1938, Jews did not make up a majority among registered prisoners. For most of the Third Reich, in fact, they formed a relatively small part, and even after numbers rose sharply in the second half of the war, Jews did not constitute more than perhaps thirty percent of the registered inmate population. Third, the concentration camps used many different weapons, in addition to mass extermination. They had multiple purposes, constantly evolving and overlapping. During the prewar years, the SS used them as boot camps, deterrent threats, reformatories, forced labor reservoirs, and torture chambers, only to add further functions during the war, promoting them as centers for armaments production, executions, and human experiments. The camps were defined by their multifaceted nature, a crucial aspect absent from most popular memories.[56]

More philosophical meditations on the concentration camps have often been reductive, too. Ever since the end of the Nazi regime, prominent thinkers have looked for hidden truths, investing the camps with profound meaning, either to validate their own moral, political, or religious beliefs, or to grasp something essential about the human condition.[57] This search for meaning is understandable, of course, as the shock the KL dealt to faith in progress and civilization made them emblems of humanity's capacity for inhumanity. "Every philosophy based on the inherent goodness of man will forever be shaken to its foundations because of them," warned the French novelist François Mauriac in the late 1950s. Some writers have since endowed the camps with an almost mysterious quality. Others have reached more concrete conclusions, describing the KL as products of a peculiar German mind-set or of the dark side of modernity.[58] One of the most influential contributions has come from the sociologist Wolfgang Sofsky, who depicts the concentration camp as a manifestation of "absolute power," beyond rationality or ideology.[59] However, his stimulating study suffers the same limitations as some other general reflections on the camps. In its quest for universal answers, it turns the camps into timeless and abstract entities; Sofsky's archetypal camp is a wholly ahistoric construct that obscures the core characteristic of the KL system—its dynamic nature.[60]

All this leads to a surprising conclusion. More than eighty years after the foundation of Dachau, there is no single, panoptic account of the KL. Despite the enormous literature—by survivors, historians, and other scholars—there is no comprehensive history charting the development of the concentration camps and the changing experiences of those inside. What is needed is a study that captures the complexity of the camps without fragmenting, and sets them into their wider political and cultural context without becoming reductive. But how to write such a history of the KL?

Approaches

To forget the present, SS prisoners often talked about the future, and for several days in 1944 the discussion among a small group of Jewish women, deported from Hungary to Auschwitz, turned around a fundamental question: if they were to survive, how could they convey their fate to outsiders? Was there any medium that would allow them to express what Auschwitz meant? Maybe music? Or speeches, books, artworks? Or perhaps a film about a prisoner's passage to the crematorium, with the audience forced to stand to attention outside cinemas before the screening, without warm clothes, food, and drink, just like the prisoners during roll call? But even this, the women feared, would not give any insight into what their life was really like.[61] Inmates in other SS concentration camps came to similar conclusions. Prisoners who kept secret diaries, for example, frequently agonized over the limits of testimony. "The language is exhausted," the Norwegian Odd Nansen wrote on February 12, 1945. "There are no words left to describe the horrors I've seen with my own eyes." And yet, Nansen kept writing, almost every day.[62] This dilemma—the urge to speak about the unspeakable—became ever more acute after liberation, as many more survivors struggled to describe crimes which seemed to defeat language and defy reason.[63]

The question of how to frame the past is obviously central for historians, too. Writing history is always fraught with difficulty, and such problems are compounded in the case of Nazi terror. For a start, no historical method can hope to capture the full horror of the camps. More generally, it is hard to find an appropriate language, and this has troubled scholars and other chroniclers as much as the survivors themselves. "I have reported what I saw and heard, but only part of it," the CBS broadcaster Edward R. Murrow concluded in his celebrated radio report from Buchenwald on April 15, 1945. "For most of it I have no words."[64] Still, we have to try. If historians fall silent, much of the history of the camps would soon be left in the hands of cranks, dilettantes, and deniers.[65]

The most effective way of writing a comprehensive account of the KL is as an integrated history, an approach advanced by Saul Friedländer to connect "the policies of the perpetrators, the attitudes of surrounding society, and the world of the victims." In the case of the SS camps, this means a history which examines those inside and the wider populace outside; a history which combines a macro analysis of Nazi terror with micro studies of individual actions and responses; a history which shows the synchronicity of events and the intricacy of the SS system by contrasting developments between, and within, individual camps across Nazi-controlled Europe.[66] Weaving together these different strands will produce a nuanced and expansive history, though it can never be fully exhaustive or definitive. However wide-ranging, it remains *a* history, not *the* history of the KL.

To create such an integrated history, this book views the SS concentration camps from two main perspectives, which merge into a single picture. The first perspective focuses, often close up, on life and death inside the camps, examining the foundations of the camp microcosm—conditions, forced labor, punishment, and more—and how they changed over time. To move beyond abstractions, much of this history will be told through the eyes of the individuals who made it: those who ran the camps and those who suffered in them.[67]

Several tens of thousands of men and women—perhaps sixty thousand or more—served in SS concentration camps at some stage.[68] In the popular imagination, guards often appear as unhinged sadists, a picture which draws on their representation in prisoner memoirs, with nicknames such as "beast," "bone breaker," and "bloodhound."[69] Some guards fit these descriptions, but inspired by recent research into Nazi perpetrators this book paints a more complex portrait.[70] The background and behavior of SS staff varied greatly, and it also changed over the course of the Third Reich. Not every guard committed excesses and only a few were driven by psychological abnormality. As Primo Levi recognized a long time ago, the perpetrators were human beings, too: "Monsters exist, but they are too few in number to be truly dangerous. More dangerous are the common men."[71] But how "common" were the guards?

What was the purpose of their violence? What drove some to extreme brutality? What stopped others? Did female guards act any differently from men?

Just as there was no typical perpetrator, there was no typical prisoner. To be sure, SS terror tried to strip inmates of their individuality. But underneath their identical uniforms, each prisoner experienced the camp differently; suffering was universal, but not equal.[72] Prisoners' lives were shaped by many variables, not least when and where they were held (though even inmates in the same place, at the same time, often seemed to inhabit separate spheres).[73] Another crucial factor was the position individual prisoners held. So-called Kapos, who gained powers over fellow inmates by taking over official functions from the SS, enjoyed special privileges—though at the price of participating in the running of the camp, blurring the conventional categories of victim and perpetrator.[74] The prisoners' background—their ethnicity, gender, religion, politics, profession, and age—also greatly influenced their behavior and options, as well as their treatment by the SS and by other inmates. Prisoners formed different groups, and the histories of these groups, and of their relationships with one another and the SS, need to be explored.

When doing so, the prisoners should be viewed not just as objects of SS terror, but as actors. Some scholars have depicted the prisoners as blank and apathetic automatons, drained of all free will. The total domination of the SS had extinguished every spark of life, Hannah Arendt wrote, turning inmates into "ghastly marionettes with human faces." But even in the exceptional surroundings of the KL, prisoners often retained a degree of agency, however small and constrained, and a close look at their actions will highlight chinks in the armor of total SS supremacy. At the same time, we must resist the temptation to make our encounter with the concentration camps more bearable by sanctifying the prisoners, imagining them as united, unsullied, and unbowed. For the most part, the prisoners' story is not an uplifting account of the triumph of the human spirit, but a tale of degradation and despair. "Confinement in the camp, destitution, torture, and death in the gas chamber are not heroism," three Polish survivors of Auschwitz cautioned as early as 1946, in a book bound in the striped cloth of former prisoner uniforms.[75]

The terror inside the KL can only be fully understood by looking outside the barbed wire. After all, the camps were products of the Nazi regime. Prisoner composition, conditions, and treatment were shaped by outside forces, and these forces have to be carefully examined. This forms the second main perspective of this study, which looks—through a much wider lens—at the course of the Third Reich and the place of the camps within it. The history of the concentration camps was bound up with broader political, economic, and military developments. The camps formed part of the wider social fabric, not only as symbols of repression, but as real places; they did not occupy some metaphysical realm, as some studies have suggested, but stood in villages, towns, and cities.

Most important, the SS concentration camps belonged to a wider Nazi web of terror, which encompassed other repressive bodies, such as the police and the courts, and other places of confinement, such as prisons, ghettos, and labor camps. These other sites of detention often had connections to the concentration camps and shared some of their general characteristics.[76] Important as these links were, however, one also has to stress the distinctiveness of the KL and their strong gravitational pull. For many victims, the concentration camps were the final stop on a torturous journey. Countless prisoner transports arrived here from other sites of detention; few ever went in the opposite direction. As the fugitive Adolf Eichmann told Nazi sympathizers in 1957, when reminiscing in Buenos Aires about the SS camps, "It's pretty easy to get inside, but awfully hard to get out."[77]

Sources

Anyone writing about the KL faces a paradox: although the amount of available documentation is overwhelming, it is insufficient. Since its demise, the Third Reich has been examined in more detail than any other modern dictatorship. And few, if any, aspects have generated more publications than the concentration camps. There are tens of thousands of testimonies and studies, and even more original documents, scattered all around the world. No one can fully master this material.[78] At the same time, there are obvious gaps, both in the historical record and the scholarly literature. Despite its daunting size, recent historical scholarship has been selective, overlooking some crucial aspects.[79] As for primary sources, the SS made sure to destroy the bulk of its files at the end of the Second World War, while Himmler and other leading officers died before they could be interrogated, taking some secrets to their graves.[80]

Survivor accounts are inevitably incomplete, too. Ordinary prisoners rarely caught glimpses of the wider camp system. Take Walter Winter, a German Sinto deported to Auschwitz in spring 1943. At the time, he never moved far beyond the small so-called Gypsy enclosure. Only when he returned as a free man, more than forty years later, did he realize the sheer size of the camp complex as a whole.[81] Nor are the available testimonies fully representative. Many inmates did not return. No Jewish prisoner has spoken about life in the Mauthausen subcamp Gusen between 1940 and 1943, for example, because none survived. They belong to the mass of the "drowned," as Primo Levi called them, who will never be heard.[82] Then there are those who were saved, but who had no voice or could not remember.[83] The stigma attached to social outsiders, for instance, meant that only a few spoke openly after liberation. The first memoir by a criminal prisoner was not published in Germany until 2014, posthumously, and even he did not disclose his background, pretending to have been detained on political grounds.[84] Most former prisoners from the USSR were also condemned to silence, long suspected as potential Nazi collaborators by the Soviet authorities.[85]

Still, an integrated history of the KL demands an expansive approach. This book therefore draws on the huge body of scholarship, pulling together its main findings. Only today, thanks to the immense achievements of recent research, is it possible to embark on such a project. But a synthesis of existing studies alone would not be enough. To deepen our understanding of the KL, to bridge remaining gaps in our knowledge, and to give a clearer voice to prisoners and perpetrators, this study also makes extensive use of primary sources. It draws on a wide range of SS and police records, including circulars, local orders, and prisoner files.[86] Some of this material has only recently become accessible, having been locked away for decades in Russian, German, and British archives, and numerous documents are cited here for the first time.[87]

Contemporaneous material produced by prisoners constitutes another invaluable primary source. Prisoners always tried to gather information. First and foremost, this was about survival, since insights into SS intentions could be life-saving. But some prisoners were thinking about posterity, too. Drawings and paintings, for example, documented the lives of inmates and their state of mind.[88] Prisoners also took secret pictures and hid SS photographs.[89] Even more important are the written records. Some privileged prisoners stole or transcribed SS papers. Between late 1939 and spring 1943, for example, the Sachsenhausen inmate Emil Büge copied confidential records onto wafer-thin paper and then glued them into his glasses case (almost 1,500 notes survived).[90] Other prisoners kept secret diaries, as we saw in the case of Edgar Kupfer, and dozens of such records surfaced after the war. Or they wrote secret reports and letters, hiding them on the camp grounds or smuggling them outside.[91] Such accounts can be augmented by testimonies from escaped or released prisoners, recorded before 1945.[92] Contemporary sources such as these are precious because they give a direct glimpse of those trapped inside. Created in the shadow of the camps, they show the immediate fears, hopes, and uncertainties of prisoners, written without knowledge of what would become of themselves and how the KL would be understood and remembered after the war.[93]

The vast majority of inmates, however, could only testify after liberation. Each of their accounts is unique and it would be impossible to capture them all. This study uses a sample of hundreds of published and unpublished memoirs and interviews of survivors from many different backgrounds. For the most part, it draws on testimonies from the first months and years after liberation, when events were still fresh in the survivors' minds and less likely to be superimposed with collective memories of the KL.[94] To give one example for the malleability of memory: as the Auschwitz doctor Josef Mengele gained in notoriety after the war, his face found its way into more and more recollections of prisoners who had never encountered him.[95] But it would be a mistake to discount more recent testimony altogether. After all, the significance of some events only revealed itself with the passage of time. And although many survivors spoke with surprising candor early on, others were only able to recount their most painful memories much later, if at all.[96]

Material gathered for postwar trials provides another important source for this study. Hundreds of Camp SS perpetrators were brought before Allied courts in the immediate postwar period, followed by further trials later on. Prosecutors collected original documents for these proceedings and questioned former prisoners, including some from forgotten groups.[97] Although these survivor testimonies pose their own methodological challenges, they provide more missing pieces for our jigsaw of the KL.[98] Moreover, the trial records are indispensable for an analysis of the perpetrators. As a general rule, SS guards did not write memoirs or give interviews after the war, preferring to lie low and disappear.[99] Only courts could force them to break their silence. Of course, their statements have to be read with care, sifting truth from evasions and lies.[100] Nonetheless, their testimonies illuminate the mind-set of SS foot soldiers, who committed most of the daily violence but left few traces in the historical record.

Structure

The main constant of the KL was change. True, there were continuities from one period to the next. But the camps took an unsteady route, with many twists and turns during little more than a decade. Only a largely chronological narrative can capture their fluidity. This study opens, therefore, with an account of the prewar origins (chapter 1), formation (chapter 2), and expansion (chapter 3) of the KL system between 1933 and 1939. The picture of this first half of the camps' existence—when most inmates were released after a period of suffering—is often overshadowed by the later wartime scenes of death and devastation.[101] But it is essential to examine what "preceded the unprecedented," as the historian Jane Caplan has put it.[102] Not only did the prewar camps leave a baleful legacy for lawless terror during the war. Their history is important in its own right, as it throws fresh light on the development of Nazi repression and the paths that were left untaken.[103]

The Second World War had a dramatic impact on the KL system and forms the backdrop for the remaining chapters of the book, beginning with its descent into mass death (chapter 4) and executions (chapter 5) during the first phase of the war, between the German attack on Poland in autumn 1939 and the failure of the blitzkrieg against the Soviet Union in late 1941. The book then turns to the Holocaust, examining the transformation of Auschwitz into a major death camp (chapter 6), and the daily lives of prisoners and SS staff in occupied eastern Europe (chapter 7). The following chapter covers the same period from a different perspective, exploring the wider development of the KL system in 1942–43, especially its growing emphasis on slave labor (chapter 8). This theme dominates the next chapter, too, which charts the rapid spread of satellite camps in 1943–44 and the exploitation of hundreds of thousands of prisoners for the German war effort (chapter 9). The study then turns to prisoner communities during the war and the often impossible choices inmates faced (chapter 10), before concluding with the destruction of the Third Reich and its camps in 1944–45, in a final paroxysm of violence (chapter 11).

This broadly chronological approach will highlight a fundamental feature of the Nazi regime. Although the Third Reich was propelled by what Hans Mommsen called a "cumulative radicalization," with terror escalating over time, this process was by no means linear.[104] The KL system did not swell like an avalanche, gathering ever more destructive force as it hurtled toward the abyss; its trajectory sometimes slowed and even reversed. Conditions did not always go from bad to worse; occasionally they improved, both before and during the war, only to deteriorate again later on. A close analysis of this development will give new insights into the history of the camps, and indeed of the Nazi regime as a whole. Terror stood at the center of the Third Reich, and no other institution embodied Nazi terror more fully than the KL.

1

Early Camps

"So you want to hang yourself?" SS Private Steinbrenner asked as he entered Hans Beimler's cell in Dachau on the afternoon of May 8, 1933. The tall Steinbrenner looked down on the haggard prisoner in his filthy brown jacket and short trousers, whom he had tortured for days in the camp's lockup, the so-called bunker. "Well, watch closely so that you learn how to do it!" Steinbrenner ripped a long piece of fabric from a blanket and tied a noose at the end. "Now all you have to do," he added in the tone of a helpful friend, "is to put your head through, fix the other end to the window, and everything is ready. It is all over in two minutes." Hans Beimler, his body covered in welts and wounds, had withstood earlier SS attempts to drive him to suicide. But he knew that time was running out. Only an hour or two earlier, Private Steinbrenner and the Dachau SS commandant had shown him into another cell, where he found the naked corpse of Fritz Dressel, a fellow Communist politician, stretched out on the stone floor. Over the previous days, Dressel's screams had echoed through the Dachau bunker and Beimler assumed that his old friend, unable to bear more abuse, had cut his wrists and bled to death (in fact, SS men probably murdered Dressel). Still in shock, Beimler was dragged back to his own cell, where the commandant told him: "So! Now you know how to do it." Then he issued an ultimatum: if Beimler did not kill himself, the SS would come for him the next morning. He was given little more than twelve hours to live.[1]

Beimler was among tens of thousands of Nazi opponents dragged to makeshift camps like Dachau in spring 1933, as the new regime, following

Adolf Hitler's appointment as chancellor on January 30, rapidly turned Germany from a failed democracy into a fascist dictatorship. The early hunt for enemies of the regime focused above all on leading critics and prominent politicians, and for the authorities in Bavaria, the largest German state after Prussia, few prizes were bigger than the thirty-seven-year-old Beimler from Munich, who was regarded as an extremely dangerous Bolshevik. When he was arrested on April 11, 1933, after several weeks on the run with his wife, Centa, local officers at the Munich police headquarters were jubilant: "We've got Beimler, we've got Beimler!"[2]

A veteran of the imperial navy mutiny of autumn 1918, which brought down the German Empire at the end of World War I and ushered in the Weimar Republic, Germany's first experiment in democracy, Hans Beimler had fought single-mindedly against the republic and for a Communist state ever since. In spring 1919, he had served as a "Red Guard" during a doomed Soviet-style uprising in Bavaria. After the brittle German democracy had weathered the initial assaults from the far left and right, the trained mechanic became a fanatical follower of the Communist Party of Germany (KPD). The rough and gruff Beimler lived for the cause, throwing himself into battles with police and opponents (like Nazi storm troopers), and rose steadily through the ranks. In July 1932, he reached the pinnacle of his party career: he was elected as a KPD deputy to the Reichstag, the German parliament.[3] On February 12, 1933, during one of the final Communist mass gatherings before the national election of March 5, 1933 (the first and last multiparty elections under Hitler), Hans Beimler gave a speech in the Munich Circus Krone. To rouse his supporters, he invoked a rare victory from the 1919 civil war, when Bavarian "Red Guards," Beimler among them, had briefly crushed government forces near Dachau. He ended his speech with a prophetic rallying cry: "We'll meet again at Dachau!"[4]

Just ten weeks later, on April 25, 1933, Beimler did indeed find himself on the way to Dachau, though not as a revolutionary leader, as he had predicted, but as a prisoner of the SS. The brutal twist was not lost on him or his gleeful captors. A group of SS men was already waiting in giddy anticipation as the truck carrying Beimler and others pulled up in Dachau that day. The mood among the screaming guards was "electric," Private Steinbrenner later recalled. They jumped on the prisoners and quickly pulled Beimler out for his first beating, together with a few more denounced as "swine and traitors" by the commandant. Forced to wear a large sign saying "Welcome" around his neck, Beimler was marched toward the bunker, which had been set up in the former toilets of the old factory building now used as a camp. On the way,

Steinbrenner hit Beimler so hard with his horsewhip that even prisoners far away could count each blow.[5]

Among the Dachau SS, wild rumors spread about Beimler, their new trophy prisoner. The commandant falsely claimed that Beimler had been behind the execution of ten hostages, including a Bavarian countess, by a "Red Guard" detachment in a Munich school back in spring 1919. This massacre—overshadowed by the subsequent slaughter of hundreds of leftist revolutionaries by far-right paramilitary units, the Freikorps, which crushed the ill-fated Munich Soviet—had fired the imagination of right-wing extremists ever since. Passing around graphic photographs of the murdered hostages, the Dachau commandant told his men that, fourteen years later, they would exact revenge. At first, he wanted to kill Beimler himself, but he later decided that it would be more discreet to drive his victim to suicide. On May 8, however, after Beimler had held out for several days, the commandant had had enough; either Beimler used the noose or he would be murdered.[6]

But Hans Beimler survived Dachau, escaping certain death just hours before the SS ultimatum expired. With the help of two rogue SS men, apparently, he squeezed through the small window high up in his cell, passed the barbed wire and electric fence around the camp, and disappeared into the night.[7] After Private Steinbrenner unlocked Beimler's cell early the next morning, on May 9, 1933, and found it empty, the SS went wild. Sirens sounded across the grounds as all available SS men turned the camp upside down. Steinbrenner battered two Communist inmates who had spent the night in the cells adjacent to Beimler, shouting: "Just you wait, you wretched dogs, you'll tell me [where Beimler is]." One of them was executed soon after.[8] Outside, a huge manhunt got under way. Planes circled near the camp, "Wanted" posters went up at railway stations, police raids hit Munich, and the newspapers, which had earlier crowed about Beimler's arrest, announced a reward for recapturing the "famous Communist leader," who was described as cleanshaven, with short-cropped hair and unusually large jug ears.[9]

Despite all their efforts, Beimler evaded his hunters. After recuperating in a safe house in Munich, he was spirited away in June 1933 by the Communist underground to Berlin and then, in the following month, escaped over the border to Czechoslovakia, from where he sent a postcard to Dachau telling the SS men to "kiss my ass." Beimler moved on to the Soviet Union, where he penned a dramatic account, one of the earliest of a fast-growing number of eyewitness reports about Nazi camps like Dachau. First published in German by a Soviet press in mid-August 1933, his pamphlet was soon serialized in a Swiss newspaper, printed in English translation in London, and secretly circulated inside Germany. Beimler also wrote articles in other foreign papers and spoke on Soviet radio. Furious Nazi officials, meanwhile, denounced him as "one of the worst peddlers of horror stories." Not only had Beimler escaped his punishment, he publicly humiliated his former torturers by telling the truth about Dachau. The decision by the Nazi authorities in late autumn 1933 to strip Beimler of his German citizenship was no more than an empty gesture. After all, Beimler had no intention of ever returning to the Third Reich.[10]

Hans Beimler's story is extraordinary. Few prisoners in the early Nazi camps were targeted as mercilessly as he was; in 1933, attempted murder was still the exception. Even more exceptional was his escape; for many years, he would remain the only prisoner to successfully flee from Dachau, as the SS immediately strengthened its security installations.[11] Still, Beimler's story touches on many key aspects of the early camps: the violence of guards driven by a hatred of Communists; the torture of selected prisoners, partly to intimidate the great mass of other inmates; the reluctance of the camp authorities, who were liable to judicial oversight, to commit open murders, preferring instead to drive selected prisoners to their deaths or to dress up murders as suicides; the high levels of improvisation, evident in the SS use of the broken-down Dachau factory; and the prominent place of the camps in the public sphere, with press reports, underground publications, and more. All these elements shaped the early camps that emerged in the nascent Third Reich in 1933.

A BLOODY SPRING AND SUMMER

In the early afternoon of January 30, 1937, on the anniversary of his appointment as chancellor, Adolf Hitler addressed Nazi grandees in the defunct Reichstag, taking stock of his first four years in power. In a typically rambling speech, Hitler evoked a gloriously resurgent Germany: the Nazis had saved the country from political disaster, rescued its economy from ruin, unified society, cleansed culture, and restored the nation's might by throwing off the shackles of the despised Versailles treaty. Most remarkable of all, Hitler claimed, was that all this had been achieved peacefully. The Nazis had captured power back in 1933 "almost entirely without bloodshed." To be sure, a few deluded opponents and Bolshevik criminals had been detained or struck down. But overall, Hitler boasted, he had overseen a completely new kind of uprising: "This was perhaps the first revolution during which not even one window was smashed."[12]

It must have been hard for Nazi bigwigs to keep a straight face as they listened to Hitler. All of them remembered well the terror of 1933, and in private they continued to revel in the memory of the violence they had unleashed against their opponents.[13] However, fully entrenched as the regime now was, some self-satisfied Nazi leaders might have been keen to forget just how precarious their position had been just a few years earlier. By the early 1930s, the Weimar Republic had been in terminal decline, pulled apart by a catastrophic depression, political deadlock, and social unrest. But it was not yet clear what would replace the republic. Even though the Nazi Party (NSDAP) established itself as the most popular political alternative, most Germans did not yet support Nazi rule. Indeed, even though they were deeply hostile to each other, the two main parties of the Left—the radical Communists (KPD) and the moderate Social Democrats (SPD)—gained more combined votes in the last free elections of November 1932 than did the Nazis. It took the machinations of a small cabal of antirepublican power brokers to install Hitler as chancellor on January 30, 1933, as one of only three Nazis in a cabinet dominated by national conservatives.[14]

Within a few months of Hitler's appointment, the Nazi movement had been swept to almost total control, riding a wave of terror which engulfed, above all, the different parts of the organized working class. The Nazis smashed their movements, ransacked their offices, and humiliated, locked up, and tortured their activists. In recent years, some historians have downplayed the significance of this prewar Nazi terror. Caricaturing the Third Reich as a "feel-good dictatorship," they suggest that the regime's popularity made a major onslaught against its political enemies largely superfluous.[15] But popular support for the regime, important as it was, only ever went so far, and terror was indispensable for silencing the millions who had so far proved resistant to the lure of Nazism. So-called racial and social outsiders were targeted, too, but early repression was directed, first and foremost, at political opponents, and here above all at those standing on the left. It was the primacy of political terror that set the Nazis on the road to absolute rule.

Terror Against the Left

The promise of national rebirth, creating a new Germany out of the ashes of the Weimar Republic, lay at the heart of the popular appeal of Nazism in the early 1930s. But the Nazi dream of a golden future was always also a dream of destruction. Long before they came to power, Nazi leaders had envisaged a ruthless policy of exclusion; by removing all that was alien and dangerous, they would create a homogenous national community ready for battle in the coming racial war.[16]

This dream of national unity through terror grew out of the lessons Nazi leaders had drawn from the German trauma of 1918. The importance for Nazi ideology of defeat in the First World War cannot be overstated. Unwilling to face the reality of Germany's humiliating defeat on the battlefield, Nazi leaders, like many other German nationalists, convinced themselves that the country had been brought to its knees by defeatism and deviance on the home front, culminating in the supposed "stab in the back" of the German army by the revolution. The solution, Hitler believed, was the radical repression of all internal enemies.[17] In a private speech in 1926, a time when the Nazi movement was still consigned to the extreme fringes of German politics, he promised to annihilate the Left. There could be no peace and quiet until "the last Marxist is converted or exterminated."[18]

Extreme political violence had blighted Weimar from the start, and when the Nazi movement grew in strength in the early 1930s, bloody confrontations began to scar the country on an almost daily basis, nowhere more so than in the capital, Berlin. The paramilitary armies of the Nazis—with their huge storm division (SA) and the much smaller protection squad (SS)—were on the offensive, disrupting rival political meetings, assaulting opponents, and smashing their taverns.[19] Crucially, the Nazi movement gained political capital from these clashes with Communists and Social Democrats, reinforcing its image among nationalist supporters as the most dedicated opponent of the much-hated Left.[20]

Following Hitler's appointment as chancellor on January 30, 1933, many Nazi activists were itching to settle accounts with their enemies. But their leaders were still treading cautiously during the first few weeks, mindful about going too far too soon. Then, on the evening of February 27, a devastating fire ravaged the Reichstag in Berlin. As Nazi chiefs started to gather at the scene, they immediately pointed the finger at the Communists (the real culprit was a Dutch loner, perhaps aided by a covert team of SA arsonists). Adolf Hitler himself arrived in his limousine at around 10:00 p.m., wearing a dark suit and a raincoat. After he had stared for some time at the blazing building, he flew into one of his hysterical rages. Blinded by deep-seated paranoia of the Left (and apparently ignorant about the possible involvement of some of his own men), he denounced the fire as the signal for a long-expected Communist revolt and ordered an immediate crackdown. According to one witness, he screamed: "There will be no mercy now. Anyone who stands in our way will be cut down."[21] In Prussia, the ensuing arrests were centrally coordinated by the political police, using older lists of alleged left-wing extremists that had been revised in recent weeks, in line with Nazi ideology.[22]

The Berlin police immediately swung into action, the German capital still bathed in darkness. Among the victims detained over the following hours were leading Communist politicians and other prominent suspects. One of them was Erich Mühsam, a writer, anarchist, and bohemian, who had become a bête noire for the German Right because of his involvement in the Munich uprising of 1919, for which he had been jailed for several years. Mühsam was still asleep when a police car arrived at 5:00 a.m. on February 28 at his flat on the outskirts of Berlin. Earlier that same night, in other parts of Berlin, the police had arrested Carl von Ossietzky, the famous pacifist publicist, and Hans Litten, a brilliant young left-wing attorney who had tangled Hitler in knots during a court appearance in 1931. Within hours, the police prison at Alexanderplatz held much of the liberal and left elite of Berlin. The arrest sheets read like a Who's Who of writers, artists, lawyers, and politicians despised by the Nazis. "Everyone knows everyone else," one of them later recalled, "and every time someone new is dragged in by the police, there are greetings all around." Some were soon set free again. Others—including Litten, Mühsam, and Ossietzky—faced a terrible fate.[23]

Police raids across Germany continued for days after the Reichstag fire. "Mass arrests everywhere," the daily Nazi newspaper *Völkischer Beobachter* announced on its front page on March 2, 1933, adding: "The fist hits hard!" By the time Germany went to the polls three days later, up to five thousand men and women had been arrested.[24] Dramatic as these events were, however, it soon became clear that they had just been the opening salvo in the Nazi war on political opponents.

The full capture of power began after the March 5, 1933 elections. In a few short months, Germany became an all-out dictatorship. The Nazis took control of all German states, every other political party disappeared, the elected Reichstag effectively dissolved itself, and society was coordinated. Many Germans eagerly supported these changes. But terror was indispensable for the swift establishment of the regime, stunning the opposition into silence and submission. The police stepped up its raids and although the spotlight remained on Communists, it widened to other sections of the organized working class, especially after the destruction of trade unions in May and the SPD in June 1933. In the last week of June alone, more than three thousand Social Democrats were arrested, among them many senior functionaries. Some conservative and nationalist leaders found themselves in custody, too.

Important as police persecution was, terror in spring and summer 1933 rested above all in the brawny hands of Nazi paramilitaries, chiefly the hundreds of thousands of SA brownshirts. Some of these men had already committed murderous attacks in the first weeks of Hitler's rule, not least during the night of the Reichstag fire, when brownshirts had conducted their own search for political opponents (using SA arrest lists). But most had been held back by their superiors, who wanted to make a show of taking power legally. Only after the March 1933 elections had given Nazi leaders a flimsy mandate, returning a small majority for the NSDAP and its national-conservative partners, did they finally release the paramilitaries. Determined to create the new Germany by force, SA and SS men now left a trail of destruction. Heavily armed, they occupied and trashed town halls, publishing houses, and party and union offices, and hunted down political and personal enemies. The grim climax on the streets of Germany came in late June 1933, when Berlin brownshirts raided the left-wing bastion of Köpenick. During five bloody days, they murdered dozens of Nazi opponents and badly injured hundreds more; the youngest victim, a fifteen-year-old Communist, was left permanently brain damaged.[25]

Although much of the early terror was driven from below, local Nazi militants acted in tune with their leaders, who openly incited violence against the opposition. Just before the March 1933 elections, Hermann Göring, one of Hitler's top lieutenants, announced that he did not care about legal niceties, only about "destroying and exterminating" Communists. During a mass rally in mid-March, the new Württemberg state president Wilhelm Murr, an old Nazi veteran, went even further: "We don't say: an eye for an eye, a tooth for a tooth. No, if someone knocks out one of our eyes, we will chop off his head, and if someone knocks out one of our teeth, we will smash in his jaw."[26] The violence that followed offers an early sign of the dangerous dynamic that would come to define the Third Reich: Nazi leaders set the direction of policy, and their followers bettered one another with ever more radical attempts to realize it.[27]

Another legacy of early Nazi terror was the rapid blurring between state and party. With Nazi activists pouring into the police force at all levels, it was impossible, as early as spring 1933, to draw a clear line between police repression and paramilitary violence. On January 30, 1933, for example, Hermann Göring had become acting head of the Prussian Ministry of the Interior (from April 1933 he also served as minister president), which brought the Prussian police force under his control. Not only did Göring instigate the subsequent police assault on Nazi opponents, on February 22 he opened the door for SA and SS men to "relieve the regular police" in its fight against the Left. Nazi thugs were delighted. As auxiliary policemen, they could now settle scores with their political enemies without worrying about interference from the police; they had become the police.[28]

As for established police officers, most were broadly sympathetic to the political aims of Nazism and needed no persuading of the dangers of Communism. The German police embraced the regime with little hesitation; no large-scale purge was necessary to turn it into a repressive machine for the Third Reich.[29] In mid-March 1933, on the occasion of his appointment as acting Munich police chief, SS leader Heinrich Himmler, another senior Nazi official who seized a post in law enforcement, used a newspaper article to praise the excellent collaboration between police and party. Many enemies had already been arrested, he added, after SA and SS men had led the police to the "hideouts of Marxist organizations."[30]

Mass Detention

Vast numbers of opponents were rounded up during the Nazi capture of power. In all, up to two hundred thousand political prisoners were detained at one time or another in 1933.[31] Almost all were German nationals, with Communists in the great majority, especially during the early months of Nazi rule. Some of the prisoners—like KPD leader Ernst Thälmann, caught together with close aides in hiding on March 3, 1933—were known across Germany, but most were minor functionaries and ordinary activists; even members of Communist-affiliated sports clubs and choirs were treated like terrorists. Those who now found themselves in Nazi hands were overwhelmingly young working-class men—the demographic that formed the backbone of the Communist movement.[32]

Compared to the captured men, the number of female prisoners was vanishingly small. Again, most were Communists, often prominent party activists or wives of senior functionaries detained as hostages to blackmail their husbands.[33] One of the imprisoned women was the twenty-four-year-old Centa Beimler, a Communist supporter since her teens, who was surprised in hiding by the Munich police in the early hours of April 21, 1933, ten days after the arrest of her husband, Hans. Just one day earlier, she had told him in a secret message that she wished she could take his place. Now they were both prisoners.[34]

Nazi detention in 1933 was unpredictable and confusing. Thousands of police prisoners were handed over as law breakers to the regular legal system, which played a major part in repression in the Third Reich. German judges and prosecutors, like most other civil servants, largely backed the regime.

They wielded old and new laws against Nazi opponents, rapidly filling the judicial state prisons.[35] But most arrested opponents did not end up in court, at least not in 1933, because they were not detained for illegal acts, but for who they were—suspected enemies of the new order.

In their reliance on mass arrests beyond the law, Nazi rulers followed other revolutionaries: they wanted to destroy their enemies before they might strike back. This called for radical action, abandoning legal principles and paperwork. Years later, SS leader Heinrich Himmler boasted that the Nazis had destroyed the "Jewish-Communist asocial organization" in 1933 by pulling people off the streets "completely illegally."[36] In fact, most suspects had formally been taken into the euphemistically named protective custody (*Schutzhaft*), a form of indefinite detention loosely resting on the Decree of the Reich President for the Protection of People and State. This decree, passed by Hitler's cabinet on February 28, 1933, in response to the Reichstag fire, had suspended basic civil liberties. It became, in the words of the émigré German political scientist Ernst Fraenkel, something like the "constitutional charter of the Third Reich," justifying all manner of abuses of power—including the denial of personal freedom without judicial oversight or appeal. True, the use of extralegal detention was not entirely new in modern Germany and the decree borrowed from earlier Weimar emergency legislation. But it went much further: the Nazi practice of lawless detention was unprecedented both in its severity and scope.[37]

During the first wave of terror in March and April 1933, an estimated forty to fifty thousand opponents were temporarily taken into protective custody, mostly by the police, SA, and SS. The next wave in summer caught further victims, and despite frequent releases, there were officially almost twenty-seven thousand protective custody prisoners on July 31, 1933, falling only slowly to around twenty-two thousand by the end of October.[38] The Nazi press occasionally claimed that this form of detention was well organized. In reality, there was a bewildering array of local rules and practices, with protective custody amounting to little more than kidnapping with a bureaucratic veneer.[39]

Many Nazi activists dispensed even with this formal façade and grabbed opponents without any official authorization. Senior civil servants, municipal officials, Nazi leaders, local party bruisers, and many more claimed the right to lock up anyone they deemed an opponent of the new order. The escalating terror from below and the accompanying chaos were summed up by an exasperated SA Gruppenführer in early July 1933: "Everyone is arresting everybody, bypassing the prescribed official procedure, everyone threatens everybody with protective custody, everybody threatens everybody with

Dachau."[40] The result was a free-for-all, as more and more state and party officials exploited the opportunities for virtually unrestrained terror.

But what to do with all the prisoners? Despite all their talk during the Weimar years about crushing their enemies, Nazi leaders had given precious little thought to the practicalities. Once Nazi terror was unleashed in spring 1933, officials across Germany frantically searched for places to hold the victims of lawless arrests. Over the coming months, many hundreds of new sites were set up, which collectively can be called early camps.[41]

The landscape of early Nazi camps created in spring and summer 1933 could not have been more varied. The sites were run by different local, regional, and state authorities, and came in all shapes and sizes. A handful would operate for years, but most closed after just a few weeks or months. Conditions varied enormously, too, ranging from harmless to life-threatening; some prisoners suffered no cruelty, while others were continually violated. Several of the new sites were called concentration camps, but this term was still applied loosely, and many other names circulated, too—among them detention home, work service camp, and transit camp—reflecting the improvised nature of early Nazi terror.[42] Despite their profound differences, though, the early camps shared a common purpose: to break the opposition.

Many early camps were established inside existing workhouses and state prisons; in spring 1933, whole wings were cleared for protective custody prisoners.[43] The authorities saw this as a pragmatic solution to a pressing problem. Tens of thousands of prisoners could be locked away quickly, cheaply, and securely, as most of the infrastructure, from buildings to guards, was already in place.[44] Workhouses were especially easy to convert, since they often stood half-empty anyway, having lost much of their purpose during the Weimar years. The large workhouse in Moringen near Göttingen, for example, had held fewer than a hundred beggars and paupers in 1932, and its director welcomed the arrival of protective custody prisoners, hoping that it would breathe new life into his outdated institution; he was not to be disappointed.[45] The situation was more complicated in state prisons, which were already crowded with regular remand prisoners and convicts. Still, to demonstrate their support for the new regime, the legal authorities agreed to temporarily open up large prisons and small county jails for extralegal detention. The cells in the new wings were soon packed. By early April 1933, Bavarian prisons alone held over 4,500 inmates in protective custody, almost eclipsing the number of regular state prisoners held there.[46]

Protective custody prisoners were subject to strict order inside prisons and workhouses, as well as low-level harassment and a monotonous daily schedule. Worst of all was the uncertainty about their future and the fate of their loved ones. By September 1933, Centa Beimler had already spent more than four months in the cold, gloomy cells of Stadelheim prison in Munich—one of the few state prisons with a wing for both men and women in protective custody—and there was no end in sight. What was more, she had not heard from her husband, Hans, since his spectacular escape from Dachau; a letter he sent from the USSR, full of love and concern for her, would only reach her years later. Meanwhile, the police had arrested her mother and her sister for their Communist sympathies, and the welfare services had taken her stepson to a borstal. Centa Beimler was not the only Stadelheim prisoner tormented by fears for her family. One of her Communist comrades, Magdalena Knödler, whose children were left all alone after the arrest of her husband, hanged herself in despair.[47]

Despite the many hardships, most protective custody prisoners found life inside prisons and workhouses bearable. They were generally held apart from the rest of the inmate population, sometimes inside big community rooms. Single cells, meanwhile, were simple but not Spartan, typically comprising a bed, a table, a chair, a shelf, a washbowl, and a bucket as toilet.[48] Food and accommodation were mostly adequate, despite the overcrowding, and prisoners were not normally expected to work, passing their time by talking, reading, exercising, knitting, and playing games like chess. During his time in Berlin's Spandau prison in summer 1933, Ludwig Bendix, a senior German-Jewish lawyer and moderate left-wing legal commentator, even managed to draft a treatise on criminal law that was published a few months later in a respected German criminological journal.[49]

Most important, prisoners like Ludwig Bendix and Centa Beimler were mostly safe from assaults. Physical violence had long been banned from German prisons and workhouses, and the old guards were drilled to uphold this rule. This accounts for the "mild" and "peaceful" atmosphere in Spandau, as Bendix put it a few years later, where guards had even showed some sympathy to him.[50] In some other prisons and workhouses, inmates were in greater peril, following an influx of SA and SS guards. But while these men committed some assaults, as did police officers during interrogations, they were largely held in check by the regular staff.[51] Also, the legal authorities insisted that protective custody prisoners in their care would generally be treated like inmates on remand, barring the police and Nazi paramilitaries from exerting any major influence.[52]

The Nazi use of the term "protective custody" was supremely cynical. As one daring inmate of a small jail complained to the Prussian authorities in late March 1933, he was "touched" by all the "concern for my person," but did not need any "protection" because "no decent people are threatening me."[53]

Still, protective custody in prisons and workhouses did save some detainees from excesses in more brutal early camps, at least for a while.[54] This prompted Nazi extremists to complain that their enemies were being handled with kid gloves—rehashing an old right-wing myth about prisons as sanatoria—and to demand their immediate transfer to so-called concentration camps, where much tougher treatment would be guaranteed.[55]

SA and SS Camps

On September 4, 1933, the life of Fritz Solmitz, a Social Democratic journalist and local councillor from Lübeck, took a terrible turn. At the time, Solmitz was one of around five hundred men in protective custody in Hamburg-Fuhlsbüttel, the largest German prison complex, with space for thousands of inmates. Since late March 1933, Fuhlsbüttel included a wing for police prisoners like Solmitz. It was initially controlled by restrained older prison officials, but the period of relative calm did not last. In early August 1933 the Hamburg Gauleiter (NSDAP district leader) Karl Kaufmann expressed his outrage at the lenient treatment of the prisoners and vowed to shake things up. Just one month later, he oversaw the opening of Hamburg's first central concentration camp, in another part of Fuhlsbüttel. The new camp, soon known as Kola-Fu (Konzentrationslager Fuhlsbüttel), was essentially the personal fiefdom of Kaufmann, who appointed a close confidant and Nazi veteran as commandant. Kaufmann and his men watched as Solmitz and the other protective custody prisoners were marched out of their old quarters on the early morning of September 4 and lined up in the yard. After a menacing speech by one of the officials—who announced that the inmates would be taught that no one could disrupt Adolf Hitler's Germany— came the first round of systematic violence, with the new guards, some thirty SS men, kicking and punching the prisoners.[56]

The Fuhlsbüttel guards singled out Fritz Solmitz, who was Jewish, for special abuse from the start. After nine days, on September 13, 1933, they moved him from a large community cell into the cellar for solitary confinement, reserved for torturing supposedly recalcitrant prisoners. Solmitz was immediately surrounded by nine men who pounded him with whips, continuing even after he collapsed semiconscious on the floor. When the guards finally let up, they were covered in the blood that poured from their victim's head. After Solmitz regained his senses, he recorded his torment on small pieces of cigarette paper hidden inside his watch. He wrote another note on the evening of September 18, just after a group of SS men had left his cell, threatening him with more torture the next day: "A very long SS man steps on my toes and yells: For me you'll bend over. 'Oi, say yes, you pig.' Another: 'Why don't you hang yourself? Then you won't get whipped!' The seriousness of the threat is not to be doubted. God, what shall I do?" A few hours later, Solmitz was dead, most likely murdered by his torturers. He was one of at least ten prisoners who lost their lives in Kola-Fu in 1933, all the others being Communist activists.[57]

The death of Fritz Solmitz highlights, in the harshest light, the contrast between different kinds of early camps, in particular those dominated by civil servants and those dominated by Nazi paramilitaries. There were hundreds of early camps controlled by SA or SS men. Some were set up to ease overcrowding in state prisons, following calls by legal officials for police prisoners to be moved elsewhere.[58] This suited Nazi hard-liners, as it gave them greater control over prisoners. Adolf Wagner, the new state commissar in charge of the Bavarian Ministry of the Interior—and a close confidant of Hitler—declared as early as March 13, 1933, that, when state prisons ran out of space, arrested enemies should instead be exposed to the elements in "abandoned ruins."[59] In fact, this was exactly what some brownshirts were already doing.

During spring and summer 1933, early camps run by SA and SS men sprang up in the most unlikely locations. Nazi activists occupied whatever space they could, including run-down or vacant hotels, castles, sports grounds, and youth hostels.[60] Even restaurants were converted, like the Schützenhaus in the town of Annaberg in Saxony; its landlord was the local SA Sturmbannführer, who ran the new camp while his wife prepared the prisoners' food.[61] Most common was the use of so-called SA pubs, which often held just a handful of prisoners. For years, the life of local brownshirts had revolved around these pubs, which served as informal headquarters to meet, drink, and plan the next attacks. In the Weimar Republic, violence against Nazi enemies had spilled from these pubs onto the streets. In spring 1933, terror also flowed the other way, moving from the streets inside the pubs.[62]

"The number of Nazi torture dens is countless," the Communist Theodor Balk wrote about Germany in the spring of 1933. "No village or city quarter is without such private martyring dens."[63] Although this was something of an overstatement, camps run by the brownshirts really did cover Germany. Designed as weapons against the labor movement, most of these early camps were established in cities and industrial regions.[64]

The focal point was "Red Berlin." During 1933, SA and SS troops ran more than 170 early camps in Berlin, clustered in districts known for their opposition to Nazism. In the working-class areas of Wedding and Kreuzberg, for example, where the two parties of the Left had still gained an absolute majority in the tainted March election, no fewer than thirty-four early camps were set up

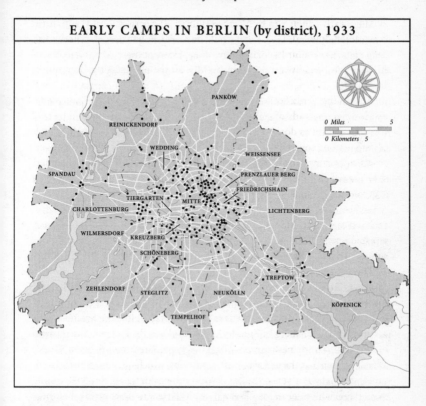

EARLY CAMPS IN BERLIN (by district), 1933

in spring 1933 alone (by contrast, there was just one such camp in leafy Zehlendorf). Because of the density of the new terror network, it often took Nazi thugs just minutes to drag their victims into one of these camps, largely in SA pubs, private apartments, or so-called SA homes, which had offered shelter for unemployed and homeless brownshirts in the final years of the Weimar Republic.[65]

Some prisoners went through several early camps in quick succession. The prominent left-wing lawyer James Broh, for example, was apprehended by a group of local SA men in his home in Berlin-Wilmersdorf on March 11, 1933, and forced into a private-apartment-turned-torture-camp. The next day, he was moved to an SA pub, and a few days later to the house of the local SA leader. After an endless week of extreme abuse, Broh felt that "I would not be able to bear more torture." His ordeal ended only after his transfer to Spandau prison.[66]

Many early camps run by Nazi paramilitaries emerged locally, with little or no direction from above. But it would be misleading to describe them all as "wild camps," as some historians have done. Many of these camps had ties to the state authorities from the start—hardly surprising, given the overlap between police and party officials. Indeed, some SA and SS camps had been initiated by the police authorities, and it was not uncommon for police officials to encourage prisoner abuses and use "confessions" extracted under torture. But even if no such ties existed at first, they soon developed. No SA camp remained isolated from the regional police for any length of time.[67]

Take the camp in the town of Oranienburg, just north of Berlin, which became notorious for its violence. A local SA unit set up the camp on March 21, 1933, on the grounds of a former brewery, to lock up forty of its prisoners. Just a few days later, however, the camp was formally placed under the district state administration. Soon, police and municipal authorities sent alleged opponents of the new order to the expanding camp, still staffed by the SA. By August 1933, Oranienburg was among the largest early camps in Prussia, holding over nine hundred prisoners.[68]

Conditions in early camps run by Nazi paramilitaries were almost uniformly dreadful. Much of the blame lay with the SA and SS guards, but there were also practical problems. Unlike prisons and workhouses, hardly any of the sites had been designed for holding captives. Even basic facilities—toilets, washrooms, heating, kitchens—were lacking, and inmates were forced into bare and cold quarters, such as former storage or engine rooms, some with leaking roofs and windows. In Oranienburg, prisoners initially had to lie on the straw-covered concrete floor of long and narrow cellars previously used for storing beer bottles. Even in the summer months it was dark and damp here, and the inmates "froze like young puppies," recalled the former SPD Reichstag deputy Gerhart Seger, who arrived in Oranienburg in June 1933. Later the prisoners slept on tiny, three-tiered wooden bunks which reminded Seger of "rabbit hutches." The food was no better than the quarters. Just as in many other SA camps, the rations in Oranienburg were small and disgusting, so much so that some prisoners preferred to go hungry.[69] But the defining feature was the guards' brutality, which was no less extreme than in Kola-Fu: at least seven Oranienburg prisoners perished between May and September 1933.[70]

SA and SS Guards

If torture was the essence of National Socialism, as the Austrian philosopher and concentration camp survivor Jean Améry suggested, then the early SA and SS camps stood at the center of the emerging Third Reich.[71] To be sure, not all guards were torturers, not in 1933 and not after. Early on, individual SA and SS men still had to find their roles, and some shied away from hands-on violence against defenseless prisoners. In one exceptional case, an SS guard even protested against the beating of an elderly man—only to be shouted down by his comrades; for them, prisoner abuse was fast becoming second nature.[72]

The violence began on arrival. The breaking of newcomers—stripping them of their dignity and asserting the dominance of the authorities—was a common ritual in "total institutions" everywhere, but it was taken to extremes in early SA and SS camps.[73] From the start, the guards used violence to communicate a simple message: the prisoners were worthless and at their mercy.[74] Screaming men surrounded bewildered newcomers and showered them in abuse. "Get out, you swine!" a Dachau guard shouted in early July 1933 as a truck discharged a group of prisoners. "I'll make you run! For Christ's sake, I will shoot a hole into your noodle."[75] Verbal abuse went hand in hand with physical assaults, as SA and SS men kicked, beat, and whipped their victims.[76] Often, this was followed by punishing exercises and a brief speech from the officer in charge, laced with more threats. Many prisoners had to undergo a bodily search, and occasionally they were photographed and fingerprinted—reinforcing the message that they were dangerous criminals and would be treated as such.[77] All these practices established the template for the prisoner "welcome," an elaborate routine of humiliation and violence that would soon become a permanent feature of the SS concentration camp system.[78]

Every prisoner—young and old, male and female—was fair game for SA and SS guards.[79] They beat inmates with hands and fists, and an array of weapons like truncheons, whips, and sticks. Skin was slashed, jaws smashed, organs ruptured, bones broken. Mock executions were widespread, too, as were other degrading practices. The torturers shaved their victims' body hair, ordered them to beat each other, force-fed them castor oil (a torment copied from Italian Fascists), and made them eat excrement and drink urine.[80] Sexual abuse was frequent in these early camps, at least compared to the later SS camp system. Men were hit on the naked genitals, and some were forced to masturbate each other; in Dachau, one prisoner died in summer 1933 after the SS inserted a hose into his rectum and opened the high-pressure water tap.[81] Female prisoners were targeted, too. Male guards carried out several assaults, beating their victims on the naked thighs, buttocks, and breasts; there were also rapes.[82]

Why this eruption of violence? The authorities did not normally select particularly brutal men to staff SA and SS camps; personnel policy was far too unsystematic in 1933.[83] Most commandants were appointed simply because they headed the local paramilitary unit stationed at the camp.[84] The recruitment of guards was even more haphazard. SS Private Steinbrenner, the man who tortured Hans Beimler, later testified that he had been on his way to a routine assignment as an auxiliary policeman in Munich when, one evening in late March 1933, he happened to walk past an officer from his unit. To Steinbrenner's surprise his superior ordered him to board a bus parked on the street and join other SS men inside; the twenty-seven-year-old apparently had no idea that the bus would head for Dachau and that he had just been seconded as a guard.[85] Like Steinbrenner, most early SA and SS guards were not volunteers.[86] Many must have welcomed their new posts nonetheless, above all those coming from the vast army of the German unemployed—officially numbering around six million in early 1933—who now received pay and free board. Indeed, the Nazi authorities deliberately used appointments to the early camps to reward out-of-work activists (Oranienburg alone employed three hundred brownshirts in June 1933).[87] At the same time, many new guards saw their poorly paid positions as temporary, and almost all moved on after a few weeks or months, as did the commandants. Few men envisaged long careers in the camps.[88]

The casual recruitment policy notwithstanding, many SA and SS guards were primed for violence by virtue of being Nazi paramilitaries. There was no need for the authorities to select especially brutal guards, in other words, because SA and SS men were presumed to be brutal anyway. Most of them were young men in their twenties and early thirties, from working-class and lower-middle-class backgrounds. They belonged to the so-called "superfluous generation"—too young for action in the Great War and hit hardest by the economic upheaval of the Weimar years—which often sought salvation in the radical politics of interwar Germany.[89] These SA and SS men were veterans of Weimar political extremism and many had the scars and criminal records to prove it.[90] In their eyes, the assault on left-wing prisoners in 1933 was the culmination of a civil war that had raged since 1918 against the SPD (as the main defender of Weimar) and the KPD (as the main agent of Bolshevism). "The SA was ready to fight to win the revolution," the Oranienburg commandant, SA Sturmbannführer Werner Schäfer later wrote about the first day in the camp, "just as it had slowly and stubbornly fought to win the [beer] halls, the streets, the villages and towns."[91] Terror inside the early camps, in short, grew directly out of the violent Weimar political culture.

The ferocity of the guards' assault on prisoners also owed much to the peculiar mind-set of Nazi paramilitaries in 1933, which combined euphoria and paranoia into an explosive mix. The guards were celebrating the triumph of Nazism. Intoxicated with their sudden powers, they were anything but magnanimous in victory: they decorated the camps with captured flags of left-wing groups and branded their supremacy onto their enemies' bodies.[92] "Think about what they would have done to you," SA men in Colditz camp were told before they were let loose on inmates in spring 1933.[93] Often, the hatred of prisoners was not abstract but personal. Because of the localized nature of early Nazi terror, jailers and jailed often knew each other well. They had grown up in the same streets and shared a long history of violence and vendettas. Now the time had come for a final reckoning. The worst thing that could happen to an inmate, a former Dachau prisoner wrote in 1934, was to be recognized by a guard from his hometown.[94]

But behind the wild triumphalism of SA and SS guards lurked anxiety. Nazi propaganda had stressed the Communist menace for so long that its crushing defeat seemed to have come too easily. Fear of an imminent counterstrike was widespread in spring and summer 1933, and went well beyond Nazi fanatics; even some deluded KPD prisoners themselves were confident that a workers' uprising was just around the corner.[95] Some Nazi officials feared that the early camps would be attacked by armed gangs, like state prisons had been during the German revolution of 1918–19. Guards were warned to be vigilant at all times about threats from the outside.[96]

The obsession with the Communist specter spurred nervous guards to further attacks, especially during so-called interrogations. There were special torture chambers in many early camps run by Nazi paramilitaries, where guards tried to force prisoners to reveal names, plots, and hidden weapons. In Oranienburg, for example, SA torturers sat in room 16, beating prisoners until their bodies were covered in blood and bruises.[97] Deaths in custody were still rare, however, even in SA and SS camps. Contrary to the picture of early Nazi camps as places of mass extermination, advanced by scholars like Hannah Arendt, the vast majority of prisoners survived.[98] Still, many hundreds lost their lives in 1933, murdered by the guards or driven to suicide. Most vulnerable of all were Jews and prominent political prisoners.[99]

Targeting "Bigwigs" and Jews

On April 6, 1933, a special train left Berlin's Schlesischer Bahnhof for Sonnenburg in the east of Prussia, where SA men had just established a new camp on the grounds of a dilapidated penitentiary, abandoned by the judicial authorities some years earlier after an outbreak of dysentery. On board the train were more than fifty well-known political prisoners ("bigwigs"), including Erich Mühsam, Carl von Ossietzky, and Hans Litten. After their arrest in Berlin in the early hours of February 28, 1933, the three men had spent several weeks in state prisons, describing conditions there as "uncomfortable" but "tolerable."[100] These had been the good days, compared to what was about to follow.

The prisoners were abused and beaten on the special train, and even more so inside Sonnenburg. The SA guards focused much of their attention on Mühsam, Ossietzky, and Litten. Not only were they left-wing intellectuals—a "type" despised as lazy and dangerous by the paramilitaries, who symbolically destroyed Mühsam's glasses—they were famous; even the local newspaper had announced their arrival. The anarchist Erich Mühsam was wrongly held responsible by the Nazis for the notorious execution of hostages in a Munich school during the 1919 uprising (like Hans Beimler). The publicist Ossietzky had previously demanded the disbanding of the Berlin SA Storm 33 (known as the "Murder Storm"), to which many of the camp guards belonged, while the attorney Litten had fought some of its members in court. Now the tables were turned, and at the end of a long day of terror, during which Litten was nearly strangled to death, the three men spent a first terrifying night together in a Sonnenburg cell.[101]

The torture continued during the following days. The two frail older men, Ossietzky and Mühsam, had to dig a grave in the prison yard. Then they had to line up to be shot, only for the SA men to burst into laughter and drop their rifles. Ossietzky and Mühsam also performed humiliating exercises and exhausting menial tasks, at running pace and abused by SA men. Carl von Ossietzky finally collapsed and was taken to the infirmary, pallid, gaunt, and shaking. Erich Mühsam, his clothes covered in blood, broke down on April 12 with "serious heart attacks," as he noted in a diary. Hans Litten, meanwhile, was tortured in a "life-threatening way," as he secretly told his loved ones, and tried to take his own life by cutting his wrists.[102] After just a few days inside Sonnenburg, the SA guards had pushed all three of their trophy prisoners close to death.

Similar scenes took place in other early camps run by Nazi paramilitaries. And it was not just prominent radicals who suffered: senior members of the moderate SPD were exposed, too. On August 8, 1933, for example, the Berlin police took several political celebrities to Oranienburg, among them the longtime SPD parliamentary leader in the Prussian parliament Ernst Heilmann, one of the most powerful politicians of the Weimar era, and Friedrich Ebert, an SPD Reichstag deputy, a newspaper editor, and the son of the deceased first Reich president of the Weimar Republic, a hated figure on the German right. The SA guards were primed for a special "welcome," having been alerted in advance to the transport, as they often were in case of prominent opponents. On arrival, the newcomers had to pose for propaganda pictures. Then they stood to attention in front of all other prisoners on the roll call square, where

a senior SA officer berated them: "Here they are, these seducers! These swin-
dlers of the people! These crooks! These dirty dogs!" he shouted, before pointing out the "red swine" Heilmann, the "bloodthirsty schemer" Ebert, and the
others. The guards forced their victims to undress in public and change into
rags, and then shaved their heads. Later on, Ebert and Heilmann were apparently tortured in the notorious room 16. More abuse followed over the coming weeks. Like other "bigwigs," Heilmann and Ebert had to perform
particularly strenuous, useless, and disgusting work. And whenever Nazi dignitaries visited Oranienburg, the two men were put on show, like dangerous
animals in the zoo.[103]

The guards' violent hatred of prominent political prisoners was further
inflamed by radical anti-Semitism. The fact that some victims—among them
Heilmann, Mühsam, and Litten—had Jewish roots was taken as confirmation of incendiary stereotypes linking Jews to political deviance, summed up
in the mortal threat of "Jewish Bolshevism."[104] At the core of the Nazi worldview stood extreme anti-Semitism, which branded Jews as the most dangerous of enemies. Jews were blamed for all the misfortunes that were said to
have befallen modern Germany, from the "stab in the back" to the corrupt
Weimar regime. So obstinate was the belief that all Jews were political foes,
and vice versa, that Sonnenburg SA guards convinced themselves that Carl
von Ossietzky must be Jewish, too (he was not), redoubling their assaults on
the "Jewish swine."[105]

German Jews constituted a small minority among the prisoner population of the early camps, perhaps some five percent.[106] However, this still
meant that Jews were far more likely to be dragged to camps than the average
citizen, an early sign of things to come.[107] In all, up to ten thousand German
Jews were forced into early camps during the course of 1933.[108] Most were
detained as left-wing activists (although contrary to Nazi propaganda, Jews
were far from dominant among the German Communists).[109] But some eager
officials also arrested Jews primarily for being Jewish, among them numerous
lawyers. In Saxony, the Ministry of the Interior had to remind its policemen
that "affiliation to the Jewish race *alone* is not a reason to impose protective
custody."[110] In Berlin, meanwhile, local SA leaders cautioned their men in
May 1933 that "not everyone running around with dark hair is a Jew."[111] Kidnapping and arrest were part of an anti-Semitic wave that swept through Germany in spring and summer. While the new leaders were busy implementing
a raft of discriminatory measures, trying to make good on their promise to
exclude Jews from German life, local thugs launched their own attacks
on Jewish businesses and individuals. Some victims were forced into early
camps—often after denunciations by neighbors or business rivals—where

they were held for "crimes" such as alleged profiteering or sexual relations with so-called Aryans.[112]

Whether prominent or not, almost all Jewish prisoners faced abuse from Nazi paramilitaries, who subscribed to a wild blend of anti-Semitic fantasies. Not only were Jews seen as deadly political enemies, they were branded as racial threats, capitalist exploiters, and lazy intellectuals.[113] When new prisoners arrived at a camp, guards would often order Jews to make themselves known: "Are there also any Jews?," a young Dachau SS man screamed at newcomers on April 25, 1933, the day Hans Beimler arrived in the camp. With external markings for identifying prisoner groups yet to be introduced, such verbal orders for Jews to step forward became routine. Some prisoners concealed their origins, but this was risky. In Dachau, the Communist prisoner Karl Lehrburger was murdered by Private Steinbrenner in May 1933, shortly after his true identity was revealed by a visiting policeman who happened to know him.[114]

Anti-Semitic abuse in early SA and SS camps took many forms. Like other torturers, Nazi guards oversaw acts of ritual humiliation and desecration. Beatings were accompanied by vile insults. "We'll castrate you so you can't molest Aryan girls anymore," two Jewish men were told as they were tormented in the cellar of a Berlin SA pub in August 1933.[115] In Dachau, Steinbrenner later recalled, there was "much hilarity" among his SS comrades after they shaved a cross on the head of a Jewish prisoner. In Sonnenburg, SA men defaced Erich Mühsam's beard to make him resemble the Nazi cartoons they knew so well.[116] Jewish inmates were also often forced into particularly arduous and revolting jobs. What was reserved as a cruel and unusual punishment for individual non-Jews—mostly prominent political prisoners—became normal for Jews, who found themselves at the bottom of the prisoner hierarchy. Ernst Heilmann, for example, was made "director of the crapper" by the Oranienburg SA, placing him in charge of a group of Jews who had to clean the four toilets—sometimes with their bare hands—used by almost a thousand prisoners. Heilmann took over this post from Max Abraham, a rabbi from Rathenow near Berlin, who was now called "deputy director" by the sneering SA men.[117]

In Oranienburg—and a few other large camps, like Dachau—anti-Semitic terror even led to the creation of separate labor details and barracks (so-called Jew Companies). However, such spatial separation was still unusual in the early camps. Jews mostly worked and slept with other inmates, especially in smaller camps, though even a comparatively large camp like Osthofen near Worms (Hesse), which held well over a hundred Jewish inmates, had no "Jew Company." Osthofen was different from camps like Oranienburg in other ways, too. The local commandant, SS Sturmbannführer Karl D'Angelo, who would later transfer to Dachau, was more restrained than his opposite number in Oranienburg and did not promote violent excesses among the guards.[118]

This highlights, once again, the disparities between early camps, even those staffed by Nazi paramilitaries. As yet, there was no agreement on how Jewish prisoners should be treated. Occasionally, this even led to open conflicts between Nazi officials, as happened in Sonnenburg. Rumors about the torture of Hans Litten and Erich Mühsam had reached Berlin within days. Concerned about the reputation of Sonnenburg, attorney Dr. Mittelbach from Berlin police headquarters carried out an inspection on April 10, 1933. A glance at the prisoners—Mühsam's dentures were smashed and Litten's face grotesquely swollen—quickly confirmed that they had been harmed "in a very serious way," as the civil servant informed his superiors. Mittelbach called together the SA guards and lectured them that abuses were strictly forbidden. When it became clear that his warning was being ignored, he returned to Sonnenburg by car on April 25 to pick up Litten, coming back around one month later for Mühsam. He took both prisoners to state prison wings in Berlin, where their treatment improved immeasurably. "Dr. Mittelbach has saved my life," the beaming Litten told his mother in Spandau prison.[119]

Mittelbach could intervene in Sonnenburg because the camp—though staffed by SA men—came under his authority. It was the first major camp of the Prussian political police and Mittelbach, who had helped to set it up, was soon appointed to an even more influential post: coordinating protective custody across Prussia from inside the secret state police office (Gestapa), established as a new agency under the Prussian Ministry of the Interior in late April 1933. The official task of the secret state police (Gestapo) officers in the Berlin headquarters and its regional branches was to pursue "all subversive political activities in the whole of Prussia." Mittelbach himself did not last long in his new post, perhaps because of his help for Litten. Still, the central state authorities, in Prussia and other German states, were starting to assert greater control over the chaotic network of early camps.[120]

COORDINATION

In early March 1933, at the dawn of the Third Reich, government officials in Thuringia hastily erected a camp for Communist prisoners on the grounds of a former airfield in Nohra near Weimar; within a few days, more than two hundred men were held inside. Just ten weeks later, however, the new camp was abandoned again. Sometimes described as the first German concentration camp to open, Nohra was also one of the first to close down.[121] Many others followed, and by late summer 1933 most early camps had shut their gates.[122] These camps had never been intended as anything more than temporary and their closure reflected a wider shift in Nazi terror. Once the regime had secured its position, its leaders tried to rein in the storm troopers, whose excesses were beginning to cause concern even among staunch Nazi supporters. On July 6, 1933, Hitler unequivocally told senior Reich officials that the Nazi revolution was over.[123] The resulting decline in rank-and-file violence meant fewer prisoners and fewer camps.

Among the remaining early camps were several larger state camps. Attempts to coordinate political terror had already begun in spring 1933 and gathered pace from mid-1933.[124] Just two months after local activists had set up Osthofen in March, for example, the Hesse police commissioner designated it as an official state camp.[125] Senior state officials elsewhere also established large camps.[126] The most significant initiatives came in the two biggest German states, Prussia and Bavaria, where officials formulated ambitious visions for the future of extra-legal police detention. To implement their rival plans, both states operated model camps, in the Emsland and in Dachau respectively. Not only were these the largest sites in the second half of 1933—holding some 3,000 (Emsland) and 2,400 (Dachau) prisoners a day in September—they were the closest the early camps came to prototypes for later SS concentration camps.[127]

"Protective Custody" in Prussia

During the Nazi capture of power, far more political opponents were locked up in Prussia than in any other German state. At the end of July 1933, well over half of all protective custody prisoners were detained there.[128] Many of them were so dangerous, a top Prussian civil servant claimed in summer 1933, that they could not be released for a long time. Over the coming years, he estimated, around ten thousand protective custody prisoners would be held in Prussia on a daily basis. Lawless detention in camps was here to stay.[129]

The conviction that the camps were more than an emergency measure, that they would last beyond the capture of power and become a permanent feature of the Third Reich, galvanized early efforts to create a more ordered system of detention beyond the law.[130] In Prussia, the coordination of the camp system was spearheaded by the Ministry of the Interior. Hermann Göring himself had signed off on its new model by autumn 1933: in the future, there would be four large state concentration camps, in place of the plethora of early camps.[131]

The first Prussian state camp was the infamous one in Sonnenburg, where Carl von Ossietzky was among the approximately one thousand prisoners in late November 1933.[132] About the same number of men was detained in a second state camp in Brandenburg on the Havel River, set up in August inside another run-down former penitentiary. The inmates here included Erich Mühsam and Hans Litten, whose brief refuge in Berlin prisons had come to an abrupt end.[133] Even more men—some 1,675 in late September— were detained in a third camp, Lichtenburg in Prettin on the Elbe, which had opened back in June, again on the grounds of a derelict penitentiary.[134] But the pride of Göring's officials was the largest site, a major complex of camps established from summer 1933 around Papenburg in the Emsland, in north-western Germany near the Dutch border.[135]

Beyond these four main sites, the Prussian state authorities approved a handful of regional camps, among them Moringen, which became the central Prussian camp for women in protective custody; by mid-November, almost 150 women were held here.[136] As for all the other remaining early camps, Hermann Göring's deputy announced in October 1933 that they were "not recognized by me as state concentration camps" and would "shortly, in any case by the end of this year, be dissolved."[137] Several early camps really were closed down around this time and their prisoners taken to the Emsland.[138]

The new Prussian model envisaged a system of large state camps coordinated from Berlin. Instead of different authorities meddling in protective custody, police offices would apply to the Prussian Ministry of the Interior, which would oversee the detention and release of all prisoners in state concentration camps.[139] The individual camps were headed by civil servants from the police service, who reported to the Ministry of the Interior. In turn, these camp directors were in charge of the commanders of local SS guards. The SS monopoly over guard duties in Prussia had been secured by SS Gruppenführer Kurt Daluege, the head of the police department in the Ministry of the Interior. Other senior officials—duped by SS efforts to project a more disciplined public image than the unruly SA—evidently endorsed the move. The decision to put the SS in charge led to the replacement of SA guards in camps like Sonnenburg, and by late August all the main Prussian state concentration camps were staffed by SS units.[140]

But the Prussian model was never fully realized. Its administrative structure proved unworkable. Far from ensuring central control, it was a guarantee for turmoil, as many local SS guards were loath to submit to directors from the civil service.[141] Similar conflicts were played out at a higher level between officials from the Prussian Ministry of the Interior and SA and SS chieftains. In autumn 1933, for example, the ministry had to shelve its plan to close Oranienburg, following furious protests by SA leaders who defended the camp as a bulwark against enemies of the state (more important, perhaps, was their desire to secure the future employment of the local SA guards). In the end, the Prussian Ministry of the Interior grudgingly accepted Oranienburg as a regional state camp run by the SA.[142]

This climb-down was typical of the inability of Göring's officials to bring lawless detention in Prussia fully under their control. Not only did some Nazi paramilitaries continue to arrest prisoners on their own accord; a few defiant SA and SS leaders even struck out on their own to set up new camps.[143] In autumn 1933, for instance, the police president of Stettin, SS Oberführer Fritz-Karl Engel, established a camp in an abandoned wharf building in the Bredow district, which operated until March 11, 1934.[144] When it finally closed down, an exasperated Göring ordered that any other police camps that "bear the character of concentration camps" had to be "dissolved at once."[145] A few days later, during a conference with Hitler, Göring went even further and suggested that an official commission should comb the country for secret SA camps.[146]

The Prussian experiment ended in disarray. No sooner had a comprehensive model for a state camp system been developed, than it came apart. Its unraveling was hastened by the lack of leadership from the top of the Prussian state. Hermann Göring himself began to doubt the purpose of his large camps and pushed for mass releases instead (see below). Further down the hierarchy, Prussian state officials pulled in different directions. In late November 1933, the Ministry of the Interior effectively lost control over the camps, which passed instead to the newly independent Prussian Gestapo, now run as a special agency subordinated directly to Göring. But the Gestapo failed to develop a systematic vision and over the coming months, Prussian policy drifted.[147] The general confusion and conflicts that characterized the Prussian state system was reflected in its flagship camps in the Emsland, during a long year of terror.[148]

Inside the Emsland Camps

Wolfgang Langhoff woke with a jolt one early morning in July 1933, roused from a deep sleep by shrill whistles and screams. He had no idea where he was. Langhoff looked up in a daze and found himself surrounded by beds full of equally bewildered men. In a flash, it all came back to him and he choked with fear: they were prisoners of the Börgermoor camp in the Emsland. Langhoff had arrived on a large transport the previous night. He was already a veteran of the early camps, having been arrested on February 28, 1933, in Düsseldorf, where he was well known as a stage actor, often playing the youthful hero, and as an agitator for the Communist cause. It had been dark when Langhoff passed through the Börgermoor gate, and after the march from the faraway railway station, brutally driven on by SS men, he had collapsed on a straw mattress inside a large building. Now, with the dull morning light creeping through the windows, he had a closer look around. The cheap wooden barrack was some 130 feet long and 30 feet wide, reminding him of a stable. Most of it was crammed full of bunk beds, holding a hundred prisoners in all, with a few narrow lockers for their belongings. Beyond, there was a smaller area with tables and benches for prisoners to eat, and a separate washroom at the far end.

As there was no running water yet, Langhoff and the others were ordered outside to wash. The dense fog, typical of the region, made it hard to see at first, but when it lifted Langhoff realized that he was standing in a small town of barracks. His was one of ten identical yellow prisoner huts, five neat rows of low wooden buildings on either side of a path bisecting the rectangular camp. In addition, there were five administrative barracks, including kitchen, infirmary, and bunker. The compound, which somewhat resembled German First World War POW camps, was enclosed by two parallel double fences of barbed wire, with a narrow corridor inside for patrols. On the other side, near the gate and the watchtower (fitted with searchlights and machine guns), stood yet more barracks, though they looked more comfortable; here the SS guards did paperwork, slept, and got drunk. Beyond these barracks, there was nothing, except for a white pole with a swastika flag, a few dead trees, and a row of telegraph poles lining the flat landscape to the faraway horizon. "Endless moorland, as far as one can see," Langhoff wrote two years later. "Brown and black, broken up and ditches running through." It was hard to imagine a bleaker place than Börgermoor, deep inside the sparsely populated Emsland.[149]

Börgermoor was one of four almost identical state camps—there was another one in Neusustrum and two in Esterwegen—opened by the Prussian Ministry of the Interior between June and October 1933 across a wide stretch of largely uncultivated land in the northern Emsland. The decision to set up this complex was made as early as spring 1933, and ministerial officials soon saw it as the centerpiece of the emerging Prussian state system.[150] The special nature of these camps was obvious at first sight. In contrast to other spaces turned into early Nazi camps, the Emsland camps were not found. Instead of adapting existing buildings, the authorities had planned and purpose-built new ones, forcing prisoners to construct their own camp in the barrack style that would become a standard for the later SS camp system.[151] Not only did the new complex look unlike other Prussian camps, it dwarfed them in size. In autumn 1933, the Emsland camps together held up to four thousand men—half of all prisoners in Prussian state concentration camps.[152]

Forced labor also set the Emsland camps apart. It was not incidental, as in most early camps, but integral. The cultivation of the Emsland moor, which had only advanced fitfully in previous years, promised both economic and ideological gain. Land reclamation would raise German agricultural self-sufficiency and chimed with the Nazi doctrines of "blood and soil" and "living space." Also, it would not upset small businesses worried about cheap competition from prisoner labor. Most important of all, such work was a perfect fit for the propaganda picture of early camps as places of "reeducation" through hard manual labor.

In practice, work in the Emsland camps was all about harassment, as Reichsführer SS Heinrich Himmler acknowledged a few years later, summing up the approach with a revealing pun: "You wait, I'll teach you *mores* [manners], I'm sending you into the moor."[153] The prisoners left their compounds early, before 6:00 a.m. in summer, and normally marched for over an hour. They were often forced to sing on the way, though the SS soon banned the "Song of the Moorland Soldiers," a protest song composed by three inmates (Wolfgang Langhoff among them). On the moor, prisoners had to dig trenches and turn over the soil, at breakneck speed to avoid SS punishment for slacking or for missing the daily quota. After his first day, Wolfgang Langhoff wrote, "My hands are full of blisters. My bones ache, every step hurts." Each day brought more pain, he added, as hundreds of men slaved for weeks on a piece of land that could have been turned over by a couple of tractors in a few days.[154]

Despite their distinct features, the Emsland camps shared key elements with other early camps staffed by Nazi paramilitaries. In the Emsland, too, most prisoners were left-wing political opponents, with German Communists in the absolute majority. And these men faced extreme violence. Although the Emsland camps were headed by a senior police officer as director, the real masters were the SS camp commanders—all of them embittered First World War veterans who had joined the Nazi movement before its electoral breakthrough in 1930—and their brutal guards.[155]

As in other early camps, SS violence reached a terrifying crescendo whenever well-known politicians and Jews arrived.[156] On September 13, 1933, one such transport of around twenty men from Oranienburg reached Börgermoor. Their arrival had been anticipated for days by SS guards, who pounced on the newcomers and soon pulled out the two most prominent prisoners, Friedrich Ebert and Ernst Heilmann. Their "welcome" in the SS camp Börgermoor was even more brutal than it had been in the SA camp Oranienburg five weeks earlier. On arrival, both men were humiliated and beaten with slats and table legs. Later, the two SPD politicians were thrown into a hole, together with three new Jewish prisoners (among them the rabbi Max Abraham), for a "meeting of the parliamentary group," as their tormentors called it. Bleeding profusely and pleading for mercy, Heilmann was briefly buried alive, while Ebert apparently refused an SS order to kick the others and was threatened with execution. Some prisoners felt that Ebert's defiance impressed the guards, who later seemed to go a little easier on him.

Meanwhile, the suffering of Ernst Heilmann in Börgermoor continued. Once, he had to spend an entire day smeared from head to toe in human excrement. Another time, he crawled on all fours into the prisoner barracks, led on a chain by an SS man, barked loudly, and exclaimed "I am the Jewish Parliamentary Deputy Heilmann from the SPD!" before he was maimed by guard dogs. Just before he had arrived in the Emsland, Heilmann had told a fellow prisoner that he could not endure another day like his first one in Oranienburg. But in Börgermoor, every day was like a new "welcome," as guards invented ever more sadistic games to drive him to his grave. Finally, on September 29, 1933, Ernst Heilmann, his body battered and his spirit broken, tried to take his own life, stumbling like a sleepwalker over the sentry line. Several shots missed before a bullet felled him. But Heilmann's suffering was not over yet, not for a long time. He was hit in the thigh, and after a spell in the hospital he came back to the Emsland in 1934, this time to Esterwegen camp.[157]

In the weeks before Heilmann's shooting, the Emsland guards killed three men. Another three prisoners were murdered in early October 1933, among them the former police president of Hamburg-Altona, an SPD official executed on orders of the Esterwegen commander for his alleged part in the death of two storm troopers back in 1932.[158] Details of the SS excesses spread among the local population and soon reached the Prussian Ministry of the Interior, which eventually stepped in. On October 17, 1933, it ordered the immediate transport of all prominent prisoners and Jews out of the Emsland camps. Local SS guards were fuming when almost eighty prisoners, including Friedrich Ebert and Max Abraham, were led away that afternoon by the police. The transport went to Lichtenburg, and despite poor conditions and occasional SS abuses there, the prisoners were greatly relieved to have escaped the Emsland. "Finally," one of the Jewish men recalled, "the special treatment came to an end."[159]

Back in the Emsland, there was no letup. At least five more prisoners died in the second half of October 1933. The outrages inside the camps (widely publicized abroad), and the growing conflicts between brawling SS guards and the local population outside, finally prompted Göring to intervene in spectacular fashion. On Sunday, November 5, 1933, a heavily armed police detachment moved to the Emsland to depose the SS. The camps were surrounded and the army was apparently put on alert in case of a violent confrontation. Following a tense overnight standoff, during which the furiously drunk guards smashed buildings, burned things, threatened to shoot prisoners, and even proposed to arm them for a joint uprising, the hungover SS men meekly handed over their weapons and dispersed without resistance. The exit of the former SS masters could not have been more inglorious.[160]

But life in the Emsland camps did not quiet down for long after the dramatic demise of the SS. Following a more benign interlude of police rule, Göring handed guard duties over to SA units in December 1933. Soon there were more excesses and murders, as many SA men acted just like their SS predecessors.[161] The victims included some new "bigwigs." Among them was Hans Litten, who was taken from Brandenburg to Esterwegen in January 1934; after weeks of torment and draining work, he fainted and fell off a truck that ran over his leg. Around the same time, Carl von Ossietzky arrived, almost a year after his and Litten's arrest in Berlin. He, too, was singled out for more abuses during the work on the moor, and quickly lost hope of ever leaving the camp alive.[162]

Unable to bring the Emsland camps under control, Göring prepared to abandon them. In April 1934, he presided over the closure of Börgermoor and Neusustrum, two camps he had seen as permanent places for extralegal detention only a few months earlier. Now only the two Esterwegen camps were left, holding no more than 1,162 prisoners on April 25, 1934.[163] In faraway Bavaria, Heinrich Himmler must have rubbed his hands with glee at the failure of Göring's project. While the Emsland complex was breaking apart, his own large camp was still going strong.[164]

Himmler's Model Camp

"I became police president of Munich and took over the police headquarters, Heydrich got the political section," SS leader Heinrich Himmler reminisced some ten years later about March 9, 1933, the day that set him on track to become the undisputed master of the Third Reich terror machine, with his faithful lieutenant Reinhard Heydrich by his side. "This is how we started," Himmler added wistfully.[165] His party career had begun before 1933, of course. Born in Munich in 1900, he was one of those angry young men from the war youth generation—too young to serve at the front—who joined radical right-wing groups after the German defeat and revolution of 1918, making up for missing the First World War by fighting a proxy battle against the Weimar Republic. A foot soldier in the nascent Nazi movement, Himmler's big break came in 1929 when he took over the SS. Initially, it was a small bodyguard unit, no more than a peripheral part of the powerful SA under Himmler's mentor, Ernst Röhm. But the sly and ambitious Himmler quickly turned the SS into a paramilitary force in its own right. Himmler, who unlike most Nazi activists came from the educated middle class, positioned the SS as the self-professed racial and soldierly elite of the Nazi movement, allowing him to indulge his frustrated military fantasies. By the time of the Nazi capture of power in 1933, Himmler's SS had grown from a few hundred men to over fifty thousand, and it became ever more powerful as its leader rose through the Nazi state. On April 1, 1933, Himmler had already taken charge of the Bavarian political police and auxiliary police, and set out to build a powerful apparatus of repression in his home state.[166]

Dachau stood at the heart of Himmler's vision. On March 13, 1933, a commission inspected the old munitions factory and approved its use as a camp for protective custody. Preparations began the following day, and on March 20, 1933, Himmler proclaimed the creation of the "first concentration camp" to the press. The self-assurance with which the political novice presented his radical vision was remarkable. The remit of Dachau was not restricted to Communist functionaries, he said, but extended to all left-wing officials who "threaten the security of the state." The police had to be uncompromising, Himmler added, and restrain these functionaries for as long as necessary. And Himmler was thinking big: Dachau would hold some five thousand protective custody prisoners, more than the average prisoner population of all large Bavarian state prisons in 1932.[167]

Himmler's camp soon became the center for lawless detention in Bavaria. Prisoners arrived in Dachau from across the state, once protective custody was centralized in the hands of the Bavarian political police, and in just a few months, prisoner numbers rose from 151 (March 31) to 2,036 (June 30).[168] By then, the camp's appearance had changed, too. The prisoners had moved from the provisional compound into a larger one, which they had helped to build on the old factory grounds. The new Dachau camp compound, enclosed by barbed wire, contained ten one-story barracks made of brick and concrete, which had once housed workshops of the munitions factory. Every barrack was subdivided into five rooms with bunk beds, each designed for fifty-four prisoners (attached to each room was a small washroom with sinks). Also inside the prisoner compound was the infirmary, the laundry, and the roll call square. Right outside was the large SS shooting range—a daily reminder of the guards' dominance—and several more buildings for prisoners, including a canteen and a new bunker. Beyond these huts stood some administrative buildings, workshops, and the guards' quarters. The whole area was surrounded by yet more barbed wire and a long wall with guard towers. To walk around the entire camp complex, one prisoner estimated, would have taken two hours.[169]

The most momentous change in Dachau did not affect its appearance, however, but its staff, as Dachau turned into an SS camp. The first guards had come from the regular state police, but Himmler regarded this as a short-term measure only. Sometime in late March 1933, a small SS detachment was sent to Dachau, officially deployed as auxiliary police, and on April 2, 1933, Himmler effectively ordered Dachau to be placed under the SS. After several days of training by the state police, the SS troop, which had grown to 138 men, stepped up. On April 11, 1933, a select band of SS men took over the prisoner compound. Meanwhile, SS sentries stationed around the barbed wire, some of them barely able to point their weapons in the right direction, continued to be supervised and drilled by a small police force. The police finally departed at the end of May 1933, when the entire Dachau operation fell to the SS.[170] The basic structure of Bavarian lawless terror was now in place: the political police carried out arrests and sent protective custody prisoners to the camp in Dachau, where they were guarded by the SS. Crucially, both SS and police came under the leadership of one man, Heinrich Himmler, who had created the template for the later Germany-wide camp system.

Himmler knew that his SS men would rule Dachau differently from the state police. The first SS detachment had been met on the premises by the Munich SS district leader, Baron von Malsen-Ponickau. In a chilling speech, he pictured the prisoners as beasts who had planned to massacre the Nazis; now the SS would hit back. Private Hans Steinbrenner, who was among the assembled men, recalled that the baron ended his address with an open incitement to murder: "If one [prisoner] tries to escape, you shoot and I hope you don't miss. The more of these types die, the better."[171] These words were still ringing in the ears of the SS men when they took over the prisoner compound on April 11, 1933. They were led by the new commandant, the thirty-three-year-old SS Hauptsturmführer Hilmar Wäckerle, who proved no less belligerent than the bloodthirsty baron. Wäckerle was yet another Nazi activist of the first hour—an ex-combatant of the First World War and of Weimar's virtual civil war—and he played up his brutal persona inside the camp, where he was rarely seen without his bullwhip and his huge dog.[172]

The SS inaugurated its reign over Dachau with an explosion of violence.

On their first day in charge, the SS men battered newcomers, saving their worst for Jews, and at night drunkenly attacked their victims inside the barracks.[173] By the following day, April 12, 1933, they had whipped themselves up into a murderous frenzy. Sometime in the late afternoon, Hans Steinbrenner called out the names of four prisoners. Among them was Erwin Kahn, in Dachau since its inception, who had assured his parents just a week earlier that he had no complaints about his treatment: "I hope!! to be free soon," he wrote in what would be his last letter. The other three men, Rudolf Benario, Ernst Goldmann, and Arthur Kahn, were all in their early twenties and new to the camp, having arrived the previous day. All four men had already suffered terribly at the hands of the SS—a little earlier on April 12, Steinbrenner had whipped them until they were covered in blood—and they feared more torture as he led them out of the compound with a few other SS men, supposedly for punitive labor. After they reached the nearby woods, one of the guards asked the prisoners innocently if the tools they had shouldered were heavy. When Erwin Kahn said that it was not too bad, the guard answered: "We'll soon wipe that dirty smile off your face." The SS men then raised their rifles and fired from behind at the prisoners. After their screams fell silent, three of them lay dead, sprawled facedown. Erwin Kahn survived with a gaping head wound, and an SS man was just about to finish him off when one of the remaining state police officers arrived on the scene. He ensured that the badly wounded prisoner was rushed to a Munich hospital. Erwin Kahn was fully conscious when his wife saw him there three days later and he told her what had happened. A few hours later he was dead, too, probably strangled during the night by the guards who had stood watch outside his hospital room.[174]

The first murders in Dachau were premeditated, designed to demonstrate the new SS rulers' power over the prisoners, now that the police reign was over.[175] But how did the SS select their first victims from among the four hundred or so Dachau prisoners?[176] Strikingly, none of the four doomed prisoners were prominent political opponents. Two had been lowly local left-wing activists, the other two had pretty much stayed out of politics altogether. "In my whole life I never joined a party," Erwin Kahn wrote in his last letter, puzzled by his detention in Dachau. What set Kahn and the other three apart from most other Dachau prisoners was their Jewish descent. All four had been identified by the SS as Jews, and as such they were regarded as the most dangerous enemies of all. As Hans Steinbrenner told one of the other Dachau inmates shortly after the murders: "We'll leave you guys alone, but we'll bump off all the Jews."[177]

Once the Dachau SS men started to kill, they found it hard to stop. After a lull of a few weeks—waiting to see if they would get away with murder—they executed several more prisoners. Hatred of the Communists was clearly an important factor, with some KPD functionaries among the dead (and Hans Beimler only just escaping a similar fate). But extreme anti-Semitism overshadowed everything; at least eight of the twelve prisoners murdered in six weeks from April 12 to May 26, 1933, were of Jewish descent, making Dachau by far the most lethal early camp for Jews in Germany. Most exposed were Communist activists, who embodied the SS hate figure of the "Jewish Bolshevist"; only one Jewish KPD supporter dragged to Dachau in 1933 survived.[178]

Throughout the initial period of SS rule, the Dachau commandant Wäckerle acted as if he were omnipotent. This also affected the special camp regulations he introduced in May 1933. These rules placed the camp under "martial law," exercised by the commandant, and threatened any prisoner with the "death penalty" if he dared to incite others to "deny obedience" to the SS.[179] Although capital punishment was still the monopoly of the regular judicial system, the Nazi veteran Wäckerle believed that Dachau was beyond the law.

Dachau Under Pressure

Early on April 13, 1933, attorney Josef Hartinger from the Munich state prosecutor's office set off for an urgent trip to Dachau, where he was met by Commandant Wäckerle. Having learned about the violent deaths of Rudolf Benario, Ernst Goldmann, and Arthur Kahn the previous day, Hartinger followed standard procedure and inspected the scene. The attorney soon came to question the official SS version that the prisoners had been killed as they escaped and that a fourth prisoner, the seriously wounded Erwin Kahn, had been caught in the line of fire. The suspicion of foul play deepened after Erwin Kahn died mysteriously in the hospital and his widow reported his posthumous account to Hartinger. But the case went nowhere. It was hard to contradict the stonewalling SS men, and Hartinger's own superior initially showed little appetite for a fight with the Dachau SS, mindful perhaps of the demonstrative support it had received from Police Commissioner Himmler: on the very day Hartinger visited Dachau, Himmler announced at a press conference that the four prisoners—whom he described as Communists—had been shot as they tried to flee, coining what would become a standard phrase for concealing KL murders (a few years later, in a secret speech to SS leaders, Himmler made clear that he knew very well that "shot while trying to escape" was a euphemism for execution).[180]

Attorney Hartinger was soon back in Dachau in May 1933, as one suspect prisoner death followed another. The autopsies of victims like Louis Schloss, who had evidently been battered to death, left him and his colleagues in no doubt that they were looking at a spate of murders. They became even more alarmed after reading the homicidal camp regulations introduced by Wäckerle, who blithely told them that the rules had been approved by Himmler. Wäckerle and his men felt invincible, obstructing and taunting Hartinger and his judicial colleagues whenever they showed up inside the camp; some guards barely bothered anymore to camouflage their murders.

The confrontation between the Dachau SS and the law came to a head in early June 1933. On June 1, the Munich state prosecutor's office launched preliminary proceedings against several Dachau SS men; Commandant Wäckerle was named as an accessory. On the same day, Hartinger's superior, the Munich chief public prosecutor, held a lunchtime meeting with Heinrich Himmler, who had to promise his full cooperation with the judicial investigation. Himmler's defeat seemed complete when he was forced, at a hastily arranged conference on June 2 with the Bavarian Reich governor von Epp and several ministers, to cut loose his tarnished commandant. At the time, this seemed like a humiliating setback for Himmler. In the long run, however, he probably regarded it as a blessing in disguise. The judicial investigation petered out after his police officials asked for the case files and then "lost" them. As for Wäckerle's sacking, Himmler may have been quite happy to sacrifice him, having clashed over the commandant's brazen provocation of the legal authorities. Himmler needed a shrewder man to lead his camp and he found the perfect candidate in, of all places, a mental asylum. The patient's name was Theodor Eicke.[181]

On June 26, 1933, Theodor Eicke officially took command in Dachau, and over the coming years this bluff and burly man, who often had a Virginia cigar dangling from his lips, dominated the SS concentration camps. In a quirk of fate, the judicial effort to stop the murders in Dachau had paved the way for the entrance of the man who would mastermind the transformation of Dachau and other early camps into permanent sites of terror. While Himmler set the general direction for the later SS camp system, Eicke became its powerful motor. He was a roughneck, a bully, and a fanatical Nazi. Always spoiling for a fight, this overbearing and vindictive man suspected foes everywhere. Feared by his rivals for his obstinacy and temper, he felt that his destiny would finally be fulfilled under Nazi rule, after years of personal struggle and frustration. But he could hardly have got off to a worse start in the Third Reich.

As a young man in 1909, aged seventeen, Eicke had left his modest family home in Alsace (then part of Germany) without completing school, determined to make a career for himself. He volunteered for the army and quickly took to military life. However, he did not cover himself in glory during almost ten years as a paymaster, and when the German army downscaled after the war, he was discharged without reaching officer rank. Married with a young child and few prospects, Eicke never really adjusted to civilian life. He failed miserably to make the grade as a police officer, a perceived injustice that rankled to the end of his days, and finally found steady but dull employment with the chemical giant IG Farben in Ludwigshafen, working mainly in its security branch. Eicke's humdrum life was shaken up in the late 1920s, when he found the Nazi movement and with it a new calling. In July 1930 he joined the SS, with membership number 2921, and soon gave all his spare time to the cause. Eicke proved himself as an able organizer and leader. He became a powerful regional commander and soon caught Himmler's eye. Eicke's reputation as a desperado grew further when the police discovered dozens of homemade bombs in his flat. Sentenced in summer 1932 to two years' penitentiary, Eicke absconded to Lake Garda in Fascist Italy, entrusted by Himmler with the command over a local terrorist training camp for Austrian Nazis; once, he had the honor of showing the Italian dictator Benito Mussolini around.

After Eicke returned to Hitler's Germany in mid-February 1933, hoping to harvest the fruits of his sacrifices for the cause, he was bitterly disappointed. As he jostled for position, his longstanding feud with the Gauleiter of the Palatinate Josef Bürckel, who branded Eicke as "syphilitic and completely mad," escalated and ended in Eicke's ignominious incarceration, first in prison and then from late March 1933 in a Würzburg mental asylum. In addition, Eicke was stripped of his SS rank. Although the consulting doctor Werner Heyde—later a pivotal figure in the murderous "euthanasia" program—quickly concluded that his prominent patient was not clinically ill, Himmler let Eicke stew, ignoring his desperate pleas. By early summer, the Reichsführer SS finally decided that it was time to bring him back into the fold. On June 2, 1933—the very day that he agreed to dismiss Commandant Wäckerle—Himmler informed the Würzburg asylum that Eicke could be released and might soon find himself in an important position. His selection of Eicke as the new Dachau commandant was a characteristic move for Himmler, who often bought himself the loyalty of failed SS men by giving them a chance for redemption. Sure enough, Eicke repaid his master with blind devotion for the rest of his life.

When Theodor Eicke took up his post in Dachau a few weeks later, now reinstated as SS Oberführer, he knew that, at the age of forty, this might well be his final chance to make something of his botched life. Unlike many other commandants of early camps, Eicke did not see his appointment as a diversion or nuisance, but as an opportunity to build a career. He grabbed it with his customary zeal. The concentration camps, he wrote to Himmler a few years later in one of his self-aggrandizing letters, became his life's work.[182]

During his first days in Dachau, Eicke observed the SS routines, walking around and making notes, as he drew up plans for restructuring the camp. He worked around the clock and even slept in his office. "Now Eicke is in his element," one SS man later commented. Eicke soon changed the face of Dachau and became its real founding father. He oversaw a major overhaul of SS staff, creating a regimented troop loyal to him. Most of Wäckerle's closest aides departed, among them the notorious Hans Steinbrenner. Eicke also got rid of the querulous leader of SS sentries and replaced him with Sturmführer Michael Lippert, who would come to play a particularly malignant part. Finally, Eicke drew up new rules of engagement, to make SS violence appear less arbitrary, and introduced a more coherent administrative structure for the SS staff.[183]

Himmler was delighted by Eicke's progress. On August 4, 1933, he visited Dachau with SA leader Ernst Röhm, still his nominal superior. Following their inspection of the camp, they were guests of honor during the unveiling of a monument (built by prisoners) dedicated to the Nazi "martyr" Horst Wessel, a young SA firebrand killed in a dispute with local Communists in Berlin in 1930, and celebrated by Nazi propaganda as a symbol for the deadly struggle against Bolshevism. During a festive get-together in the large SS mess hall that evening, Himmler and Röhm applauded the discipline of the guards and singled out Commandant Eicke for special praise. In Röhm's case, this would prove a grimly ironic moment, in light of what Eicke would do to him less than a year later.[184]

Behind Dachau's front as a model camp, the torment continued. Eicke did not want to go any easier on the inmates than his predecessor. He just wanted a slicker operation. And so the abuse carried on, with "bigwigs" and Jews still suffering the worst treatment and hardest labor, like pulling a huge rolling barrel to flatten the paths inside the camp.[185] Eicke's approach was summed up in his camp regulations of October 1, 1933, which greatly expanded the list of punishable prisoner offenses, compared with Wäckerle's earlier rules, and pronounced even more savage penalties. They also continued to threaten prisoners with death. Eicke warned all "political agitators and subversive intellectuals" that SS men will "reach for your throats and silence you according to your own methods." Prisoners suspected of sabotage, mutiny, or agitation would be executed on the basis of "revolutionary law": "Anyone who attacks a guard or an SS man physically, refuses obedience or, at his work place, refuses to work ... [or] bawls, shouts, agitates or makes speeches on the march or at work *will be shot dead on the spot as a mutineer* or subsequently hanged."[186]

Armed with this license, Dachau SS guards continued to murder individual prisoners. By the end of 1933, at least ten more inmates had died on Eicke's watch (three of the dead were Jews).[187] And although the murders were better camouflaged than before, they provoked further investigations and political wrangling. Himmler soon found himself in another tight corner and had to be bailed out in December 1933 by Ernst Röhm. Using his considerable political muscle, Röhm stalled a judicial inquiry into three suspicious prisoner deaths by arguing that the "political nature" of the matter made it "presently unsuitable" for legal intervention. Once again, justice was denied.[188]

Dachau was something of an outlier in 1933, standing at the extreme end of a wide spectrum of early camps. From the beginning, SS leader Heinrich Himmler oversaw a particularly radical approach to lawless detention; more prisoners were killed in Dachau than in any other early camp. By comparison, some other large state camps were considerably less brutal. Inside Osthofen in Hesse, for example, not one of the 2,500 or more prisoners died.[189] Nor did all other official camp regulations resemble the radical Dachau ones. The police rules for state camps in Saxony, passed in summer 1933, explicitly banned physical punishment.[190]

But even in Dachau, the epicenter of early terror, death remained the exception; out of 4,821 men dragged through the camp in 1933, no more than twenty-five lost their lives.[191] The other inmates suffered daily drills and humiliations, and were always at risk of hideous assaults. And yet, they survived, and even snatched some moments beyond violence; after lunch, for example, prisoners would normally rest and play chess, smoke, read, and sometimes play an instrument. Dachau—like the other early camps—was not yet consumed by deadly force.[192]

The Roots of the Nazi Camps

On August 11, 1932, the Nazi daily *Völkischer Beobachter* had carried a prophetic story on its front page. More than five months before Hitler was appointed chancellor, the paper predicted that a future Nazi government would pass an emergency decree to arrest left-wing functionaries and put "suspects and intellectual instigators in concentration camps." This was not the first time the Nazis had anticipated the use of camps against their enemies. In an article as far back as 1921, when he was no more than an unusually venomous agitator in Munich, Hitler had promised to "stop the Jews from undermining our nation, if necessary by keeping their bacilli safely in concentration camps."[193] Clearly, the idea of setting up camps had crossed the minds of Nazi leaders long before they came anywhere near power. But there was no direct line from their early threats to the later camps. The scattered references of the Weimar years owed much to the political rhetoric of the time; at most, they were vague statements of intent. The improvisation after the capture of power makes abundantly clear that there was no blueprint in Nazi files. When Hitler took charge of Germany in 1933, the Nazi concentration camp still had to be invented.[194]

This is not to say that the early camps came from nowhere, as has sometimes been suggested.[195] On the whole, Nazi officials took their inspiration less from foreign precedents than from existing national disciplinary discourses and practices, with the most important influences—especially on larger and more permanent state camps, like Dachau and those in the Emsland—coming from the German prison system and from the army.

SS officers like Theodor Eicke often stressed the uniqueness of their camps, denying any resemblance to regular prisons and penitentiaries.[196] But back in 1933, Nazi officials borrowed liberally from the traditional prison service. Indeed, many officials—including Eicke—could draw on personal experiences of the Weimar prison, which had mostly been strict and highly regimented (contrary to later Nazi caricatures). Having been locked up for political extremism during the Weimar years, these men now applied the lessons they had learned to the early camps.

The masters of the early camps copied from the prisons' rigid schedules and rules, lifting some passages directly from existing regulations. Traditional disciplinary punishments from the prison service, like aggravated detention (depriving prisoners for several weeks of their bed, fresh air, and regular food), found their way straight into the early camps.[197] Even flogging, introduced as an official disciplinary punishment under Eicke in Dachau, had its roots in German prisons: until it was abandoned after the First World War as inhumane and counterproductive, men in Prussian penitentiaries could be officially punished with thirty or even sixty lashes.[198]

Another element appropriated from the prison service was the so-called progressive stages system, which had been practiced in all large German penal institutions from the mid-1920s. Prisoners were divided into three groups, with sanctions for supposedly ill-disciplined or incorrigible inmates, and corresponding benefits for more docile ones.[199] In 1933, a similar stages system—with significantly harsher sanctions—was introduced in several early camps, at least on paper. When Hans Beimler arrived in Dachau, for example, the SS immediately put him into stage three, officially reserved for prisoners "whose previous life justifies a particularly severe supervision."[200]

Yet another influence on early camps was forced labor, which stood at the heart of the modern prison, thanks to its easy compatibility with very different conceptions of detention. Traditionalists had long seen hard manual work as a punishment. Prison reformers, meanwhile, regarded it as an instrument of rehabilitation; repetitive labor in their cells would inoculate inmates with a strict work ethic, and toil outside (in farming or land cultivation) would tie deviants to the countryside and help cleanse "degenerate" cities.[201] Similar beliefs had underpinned other institutions of social welfare and discipline in Weimar Germany, like workhouses and the camps of the Voluntary Labor Service, which left their own marks on the early Nazi camps.[202] Drawing on these precedents, forced labor figured fairly prominently in early camps, not least because it could be presented as a means of both repression and redemption. Reporting the opening of the new Prussian state camp in Brandenburg in August 1933, a local newspaper announced that work would force prisoners to "reflect at leisure upon their earlier actions and assertions" and help them "to reform." What readers were not told, of course, was that in Erich Mühsam's case such work meant wiping the floors while SS men kicked and beat him, dragged him by his hair, and forced him to lick the dirty water.[203]

Just as the masters of the early camps tried to differentiate themselves from prison officials, they drew a line between themselves and regular soldiers. But there was no mistaking the influence of military traditions, which were widely copied and perverted inside camps. Again, SA and SS officials could often fall back on their own experience. Many commandants were First World War veterans (some had even spent time in POW camps), and so were some of the guards.[204] Those who had been too young to enlist had often soaked up the army spirit in extremist paramilitary formations like the SA, which was consciously modeled on the army, with its flags, uniforms, and rituals, and had provided its members with comprehensive military training.[205]

"When a new arrival first enters the concentration camp," a former Dachau prisoner recalled, he finds "a kind of military camp."[206] There were many echoes of army life in the early camps, starting with the guards' demeanor. The Dachau SS, for example, greatly prized military bearing among its men, who learned to march in formation in exaggerated goose step, proudly wearing uniforms with army-inspired insignia.[207] Army veterans among the prisoners were also familiar with daily marches (accompanied by military music) and roll calls (with barked commands like "Caps off" and "Eyes right").[208] "As an old soldier I knew that the wisest thing was to say Yes and Amen to everything," an ex-prisoner reported about his time in Esterwegen.[209] During their encounters with guards, prisoners had to offer a salute and "adopt a military stance," Theodor Eicke ordered (similar rules existed inside German prisons). Eicke also insisted that the start of the inmates' work day was marked by an SS trumpeter with the bugle call to arms.[210] The militarization of some early camps even extended to everyday language. In Dachau, each barrack constituted a "prisoner company," made up of five "platoons" (i.e., five rooms) supervised by an SS "company leader."[211]

Violent abuses in early camps were also inspired by military routines, starting with the ubiquitous "welcome," an exaggerated version of initiation rituals common in the armed forces.[212] Then there were all the drills. Exhausting training had been the norm for army recruits in the German Empire, sometimes accompanied by slaps and punches from commanding officers.[213] The amplified counterpart in the early camps was prisoner "sport," a succession of torturous exercises such as slow knee bends and unending push-ups, as well as crawling, hopping, and running. In the army, such drills aimed at fusing recruits into a cohesive unit. In the camps, they were meant to break the prisoners.[214] Mindless discipline continued inside prisoners' living quarters, with the pedantic rules giving guards a ready excuse for more abuse. Once more, many of the routines mirrored military practices, including the daily "bed building," where prisoners had to make their beds perfectly straight, with sharp edges like boxes; prisoners often had to use strings and spirit levels to evade punishment. Again, army veterans were at an advantage. "I had been a soldier," a prisoner in a Berlin camp later wrote. "I know this drill." Some better-off inmates, meanwhile, used food and money to pay skilled colleagues to help them.[215]

The novices behind the early Nazi camps borrowed established disciplinary methods—from the prison, the army, and other institutions—as a matter of convenience and opportunism. This had an unintended, though not unwelcome, side effect. By drawing on familiar customs and ideas, the early camps (and protective custody) did not appear like a complete break with German traditions. To some members of the public, this made the camps seem less exceptional than they really were. As Jane Caplan has said, the inflection with existing practices helped to disguise "the ruthless character of Nazi repression, and eased its official and popular acceptance."[216]

OPEN TERROR

Contrary to the pervasive myth of ignorance about the KL, which dominated German memory for decades after the war, the camps had lodged themselves early and deeply into the minds of the population—so much so that some ordinary Germans already started dreaming about them in 1933. As one local newspaper concluded in May of that year, everyone was talking about protective custody.[217] The regime did not hide the early camps' existence. On the contrary, the press—soon coordinated by the new rulers—carried countless articles, some initiated by the authorities, others by journalists themselves. The Nazi media emphasized that the main targets were political opponents of the new order, primarily Communist "terrorists," followed by SPD "fat cats" and other "dangerous characters." A newsreel, shown in German cinemas in 1933, described prisoners of a camp in Halle as "the main rabble-rousers among the red murderers and incendiaries." The detention of well-known political figures was given particular prominence: a photograph of the arrival in Oranienburg of Friedrich Ebert and Ernst Heilmann, described in the press as "one-time greats," even featured on the front page of the *Völkischer Beobachter*.[218]

Several historians have suggested that most Germans welcomed such reports because they supported the camps and the regime's broader aims.[219] There is some truth in this. Given the pervasive hatred of the Left among Nazi followers and national conservatives alike, the authorities knew that their crackdown was likely to be greeted with applause in these quarters.[220] But propaganda about the early camps was not just about consensus building. Those who rejected Nazism heard a very different message: "There is still room in the concentration camp," one regional paper declared darkly in August 1933, summing up the camps' deterrent function.[221] More generally, one should tread carefully when judging the mood in the Third Reich, because of the evident difficulty of measuring popular opinion in a totalitarian dictatorship, and because official propaganda messages were contradicted by rumors.[222] When we examine reactions to the early camps, we have to address a rather more complex set of questions: who knew what, when, and reacted how, to which aspect of the camps?

Witnesses and Whispers

The Nazi authorities were never in full control of the camps' image. Although the regime dominated the public sphere, its authorized version of the early camps, as disseminated in the media, was often undercut. In 1933, there were still many ways of learning the truth, and a large number of ordinary Germans gained a surprisingly accurate picture of what was really going on.[223]

Many Germans witnessed Nazi terror firsthand. Their first glimpse often came during processions of prominent prisoners through towns toward nearby camps. Along streets and squares lined with spectators, the prisoners, some of them wearing demeaning placards, were cursed, shoved, and spat at

by jeering crowds of SA and SS men. When Erich Mühsam, Carl von Ossietzky, and Hans Litten marched with other prisoners through Sonnenburg to
the camp on April 6, 1933, they were "frequently helped along" by the rubber
truncheons of the guards, a local paper reported the following day.[224]

Such humiliating parades were not the only time locals came face-to-face
with prisoners. Some inmates, for example, were deployed for public works
outside the barbed wire, and their dress and demeanor spoke volumes about
the treatment. Often, their work was designed as a demeaning spectacle, like
in Oranienburg, where Commandant Schäfer once sent a group of left-wing
politicians—among them the former SPD deputies Ernst Heilmann, Friedrich Ebert, and Gerhart Seger—into town to scratch old election posters from
the walls.[225]

Germans who lived in the immediate vicinity of early camps also witnessed abuses inside. With so many early camps in the middle of towns and
cities, it was impossible for the authorities to shut out all observers. In residential areas, neighbors occasionally saw the prisoners or, more often, heard
them; tourists at Nuremberg castle could listen as prisoners were tortured in
the cellars below. Sometimes witnesses tried to intervene. In Stettin, locals
complained to the police about screams and shots fired at night inside the
Bredow camp.[226] Further news spread through encounters with the camp staff.
Although guards were supposed to stay silent, some boasted loudly in local
pubs about beating prisoners or even murdering them.[227]

Before long, many places across Germany were abuzz with news about
crimes in local camps. In Wuppertal in western Germany, rumors about prisoner abuses in Kemna camp circulated widely, as leading Nazi officials conceded.[228] Farther east, a local woman confided to a Lichtenburg prisoner that
the townspeople of Prettin "know everything that goes on inside!"[229] In the
far north of the country, legal officials warned that cases of "serious ill-
treatment" in Bredow were "known among the general public of Stettin and
Pomerania."[230] And around Munich in the south, there was talk about abuses,
too, with sayings like "Shut up, or you'll end up in Dachau!" and "Please, dear
Lord, make me dumb, so that I won't to Dachau come" circulating widely by
summer 1933.[231] But the capital of whisperers must have been Berlin, with its
vast number of early camps. In spring 1933, explained Hans Litten's mother,
Irmgard, it was impossible to step into a café or an underground train without
hearing all about the abuses.[232]

Irmgard Litten herself had more to go on than hearsay when it came to
the early camps. Like many other relatives of prisoners, she received regular
letters from her son—the intervals varied, ranging from a week to a month—
and like many other inmates, Hans Litten smuggled references about his

condition into his correspondence. Writing from Sonnenburg in spring 1933, the lawyer Litten mentioned a fictitious "client" of his who was "on such bad terms with the other residents that they constantly attack him when he comes home at night." He also advised another "client" to make his will because he was dying. Later on, Hans Litten used a special cipher to dupe the censors. In his first coded letter, he asked for enough opium to kill himself.[233]

Many relatives could see for themselves how their loved ones were being treated. In sharp contrast to the later SS camps, the authorities in 1933 often allowed visits, just as in prisons. Some camps permitted bimonthly meetings for a few minutes under strict observation. Others allowed weekly visits lasting several hours, during which prisoners could speak relatively freely.[234] What the visitors saw often confirmed their worst fears, with the marks of abuse and torture clearly visible. When Irmgard Litten met her son in Spandau in spring 1933, shortly after his transfer from Sonnenburg, he was difficult to recognize, with a swollen face and a deformed, strangely crooked head. His whole appearance, his mother noted, was ghostly.[235]

Normally, visits were authorized by the camp officials. But on occasion, relatives talked their way into early camps, almost unthinkable in the later SS system. When Gertrud Hübner learned that her husband was held at the SA camp on General-Pape-Strasse in Berlin, she immediately went to the camp and persisted until the guards admitted her. "My husband made a very run-down and tormented impression," she remembered. "I took my husband into my arms and he started to cry."[236]

On their return from early camps, relatives often shared their impressions with friends and family, starting off a whirlwind of whispers. Some women displayed their husbands' bloodied shirts and trousers, which they had received in exchange for fresh clothing; in May 1933, Erich Mühsam's wife, Kreszentia, even confronted the Prussian civil servant in charge of protective custody, Dr. Mittelbach, brandishing the blood-soaked underwear she had been sent from Sonnenburg.[237] News of deaths also spread fast. Following mass turnouts at burials of prominent political prisoners, the Prussian Ministry of the Interior ordered local authorities in November 1933 to forbid any more funerals "with a dissenting tone."[238]

As popular knowledge of abuses spread, the authorities came under pressure to release individual inmates. Some initiatives came from religious groups.[239] But mostly, it was relatives who lobbied on behalf of prisoners. Within a few months, Irmgard Litten, who was well connected, had contacted the Reich defense minister Blomberg, Reich minister of justice Gürtner, Reich bishop Müller, and Hermann Göring's adjutant.[240] Much to the annoyance of camp and police officers, such campaigns for imprisoned men sometimes caused senior state officials to step in.[241] In Hans Litten's case, his treatment occasionally improved following interventions from above.[242] Yet Litten remained inside the camps, as did other prominent prisoners. Even Friedrich Ebert was not released, despite support from Reich president Hindenburg himself, who had been petitioned by Ebert's mother to spare her son from being abused "as a humiliated laboring prisoner."[243]

Friedrich Ebert was unfortunate. Most other prisoners of the early camps were soon set free again—not because of outside intervention, but because the authorities felt that a brief period of shock and awe was normally enough to force opponents into compliance. As a result, there was a rapid turnover in 1933, with the places of released prisoners quickly filled with new ones. The duration of detention was unpredictable. Prisoners who expected to regain their freedom after a few days were mostly disappointed, but it was rare for them to remain inside for a year or more. Longer spells were served in the bigger, more permanent camps, but even in a large camp like Oranienburg, around two-thirds of all prisoners stayed for less than three months.[244] The result was a constant stream of former prisoners back into German society, and it was these men and women who would become the most important sources of private knowledge about the early camps.

Popular Reactions

Martin Grünwiedl had just been released from Dachau in early 1934, after more than ten months inside, when two of his Communist comrades, who operated undercover in Munich, asked him to write a report about the camp. Despite the risks, the thirty-two-year-old decorator produced a remarkable thirty-page account of SS crimes called "Dachau Prisoners Speak Out," incorporating testimonies from several former inmates. Following painstaking preparations, Grünwiedl and four helpers then copied the pamphlet. Equipped with tents, food, carbon paper, and a copying machine, they cycled to a remote islet in the idyllic Isar River, dressed as vacationers. After several anxious days, the men returned to Munich to complete their work. When all was done, Grünwiedl handed around four hundred copies to underground KPD officials. Some 250 more copies were put into mailboxes or sent to sympathizers and public figures, with instructions to pass on the pamphlet "so that it is read as widely as possible!"[245]

The resisters clearly faced huge obstacles: months of dangerous work involving more than a dozen individuals, several of whom were later arrested (among them Grünwiedl, who found himself back in Dachau), had yielded no more than a few hundred copies. But the production of the pamphlet also demonstrates the determination of left-wing opponents to spread the word about the regime and its camps. Grünwiedl and his friends were not alone. There was still a sizable resistance movement in 1933–34, turning out hundreds of thousands of underground newspapers and flyers.[246] Some publications were hidden inside harmless books, like a Communist pamphlet on the torture of Hans Litten and others in Sonnenburg, distributed inside the cover of a medical textbook about kidney and bladder disease.[247] Several prisoner reports circulated widely in Germany, among them an account by Gerhart Seger, written in Czechoslovakia after he managed to escape from Oranienburg in early December 1933.[248]

When it came to news about the camps, word of mouth was even more important than the written word. Upon release, prisoners often had to vow to stay silent, otherwise, guards threatened, they would be taken back to the camp or beaten to death.[249] But such threats could not stop former inmates from talking to family and friends, who in turn talked to others, in a countrywide game of pass the message.[250] There was so much talk that some observers concluded that everyone "knew or had heard about someone who had been to a concentration camp once."[251]

Even former inmates unable to speak about their experiences—because of fear or trauma—bore witness to the camps.[252] Their broken teeth, battered bodies, and terrified silences were often more revealing than words; it could take months for visible injuries to heal, and some victims never recovered.[253] Doctors and nurses joined the growing circle of German professionals— including lawyers, civil servants, state attorneys, and morgue attendants— who knew about SA and SS crimes. In early October 1933, for example, a Wuppertal hospital attendant made the following case notes about twenty-five-year-old Erich Minz, who had been admitted from Kemna with a fractured skull and obvious signs of abuse: "Patient is completely unconscious. The whole body, especially the back and buttocks, are covered with welts and bruises, some blue-red, others blue-yellow-green. The nose and lips are swollen, blue-red."[254] Talk of torture soon spread outside hospital wards, especially when former prisoners died of their injuries.[255]

At the beginning of the Third Reich, then, Germany was awash with rumors about the early camps. Not only were most Germans aware of their existence, they knew that the camps stood for brutal repression. Camps were held up as the ultimate sanction in private and public disputes, and found their way into popular jokes, too:

"Sergeant," anxiously said a warden in the concentration camp, "look at the prisoner in that bed. His spine is broken, his eyes are put out, and I think the damp has made him deaf. What shall we do with him?"

"Set him free! He is prepared to receive our Führer's doctrine."[256]

Information about the abuses was not spread evenly across the nation, however. There were differences among German regions—with far more early camps in urban than in rural areas—and between social groups. The best-informed Germans often came from the organized working class. After all, the vast majority of prisoners were Communist and Socialist activists, and their supporters—to say nothing of their wives, children, friends, and colleagues—were desperate to learn about their fate. Moreover, left-wing workers were most likely to receive underground pamphlets and to hear from released prisoners, who tended to share their experiences within their traditional milieus. Finally, with so many early camps established in the middle of working-class areas, supporters of the Left often had direct insight into the daily violence.

Class was not all-decisive, of course. There were middle-class professionals who knew all about the camps. Also, some reports by left-wing prisoners reached beyond the organized working class, sometimes circuitously. When the Dresden professor Victor Klemperer heard about the abuse of Erich Mühsam, for example, it was from a friend who had met up with exiled German Communists in Denmark.[257] On the whole, however, the middle classes—who largely supported the Nazis by 1933—knew less about the reality of Nazi terror.[258] They were also more inclined to dismiss rumors about abuses as lies spread by enemies of the new state.[259] Still, Nazi followers were largely aware of the early camps' dark side. So how did they react?

Nazi supporters from all classes and backgrounds hailed the regime's crackdown on the Left. "You have to have order," one factory foreman told his son in spring 1933, regarding the arrests of left-wingers.[260] Many followers also welcomed harsh measures in the early camps; the Left's danger justified brutal means, they believed, and "terrorists" deserved all the violence that came their way. Some even screamed abuse as prisoners were paraded through the streets. In Berlin, spectators egged on the brownshirts, shouting things like: "Finally you've got the dogs, beat them to death, or send them to Moscow." But support for attacks on left-wing organizations did not always translate into support for violent attacks on left-wing activists.[261] Looking back at the prewar years, Heinrich Himmler later admitted that the establishment of the camps had been greatly condemned by "circles outside the party."[262] Himmler may have embellished for effect, but still, some Nazi sympathizers were clearly uncomfortable about reports of abuses. There were various reasons for their unease. Having been drawn to the Nazi movement for its promise to restore public order following the Weimar street fighting, some supporters worried about the growing lawlessness of the early camps.[263] Others were more concerned with Germany's image abroad, as news about atrocities quickly spread across the border, where the early camps became a byword for the inhumanity of Hitler's new Germany.[264]

The View from Abroad

"If they could, they would take us to a concentration camp," the satirist Kurt Tucholsky wrote from the safety of Switzerland about Nazi supporters, in a despairing letter on April 20, 1933, the day Germany celebrated Hitler's birthday. "The reports [about the camps] are horrible, by the way," Tucholsky added.[265] German émigrés like Tucholsky learned about the Nazi camps from contacts inside the country and from the exile press. In France, Czechoslovakia, and elsewhere, German-language publications sprang up. Following the arrest of its editor Carl von Ossietzky, for example, the influential *Weltbühne* was relaunched from Prague, featuring the first of many articles on the camps in September 1933. Exile papers and magazines focused on the most notorious camps, like Dachau, Börgermoor, Oranienburg, and Sonnenburg, which was also featured in a poem by Bertolt Brecht, another famous exile. Meanwhile, German left-wing parties in exile sponsored editions of eyewitness reports, like the Communist Brown Book (*Braunbuch*) on Nazi terror. Printed in August 1933 in Paris and widely translated afterward, this bestselling book of anti-Nazi propaganda called the camps' creation the "worst act of despotism by the Hitler government" and included more than thirty pages on crimes inside.[266]

Some of these exile publications were smuggled into the Third Reich. In exceptional cases, they even found their way into early camps, boosting prisoner morale. But on the whole, their circulation was too small to make much of an impact in Germany.[267] More important was public opinion abroad, with some reports quickly picked up by foreign papers and politicians. On October 13, 1933, barely a week after a German-language paper in the Saarland (under League of Nations mandate until 1935) had printed an article by a former Börgermoor prisoner, the *Manchester Guardian* ran the same story, reporting that Friedrich Ebert had been "struck with rifle butts until his face was covered with blood" and Ernst Heilmann had been "so badly beaten that he was prostrate for several days."[268] The most vocal former prisoner was Gerhart Seger, who lectured, published, and lobbied in Europe and North America in a campaign to draw attention to the Nazi camps.[269]

In 1933, hundreds of articles about the camps appeared in newspapers and magazines around the world. Many of these articles did not originate with German exiles, but came from foreign reporters in Germany; in 1933/34, *The New York Times* alone printed dozens of detailed stories by U.S. journalists. Other foreign papers did the same. As early as April 7, 1933, the *Chicago Daily Tribune* featured an article about a Württemberg camp, with its correspondent describing the "shocking" appearance of the prisoners. Foreign journalists sometimes drew on secret contacts with the German resistance. In this way, a reporter of a Dutch newspaper obtained a sensational letter by Oranienburg prisoners about their torture.[270]

Foreign press reports highlighted the suffering of prominent prisoners, often as part of international campaigns backed by leading public figures. In November 1933, for instance, the British prime minister Ramsay MacDonald made an official inquiry about the fate of Hans Litten. Such pressure benefited some prisoners—despite the Nazi fury about outside meddling—though not Litten. In reply to MacDonald's intervention, the Prussian Gestapo refused to answer any questions about him, while the German foreign office concluded that "provocative" foreign campaigns had to be refuted as part of a wider German PR offensive to improve the camps' image abroad.[271]

The Nazi regime, which closely monitored foreign opinion, was acutely sensitive about critical reports. As articles about abuses inside early camps mounted up, paranoid Nazi leaders suspected an international conspiracy by Jews and Bolsheviks, and drew comparisons to the Allied "atrocity propaganda" of World War I. As a popular Nazi tract explained at the time, the camps were used to defame Nazi Germany in the same way alleged crimes during the invasion of Belgium had been used to slander the German Empire in 1914. "Like in the war!" Propaganda Minister Joseph Goebbels fumed in his diary.[272]

Why were Nazi officials so thin-skinned? They were obviously concerned about critical reports filtering back to the Third Reich (where foreign papers remained on sale), adding more grist to the fast-spinning rumor mill.[273] Even more pressing was their concern about Germany's standing abroad. In 1933, its position was still weak, and Hitler had to tread carefully on the international stage to make other leaders believe his guise as a man of peace—a difficult enough feat even without the stream of reports about atrocities in Nazi camps.[274]

In order to silence criticism abroad, German state officials held press conferences for foreign correspondents and staged visits to selected camps, which were meticulously prepared in advance.[275] This was a high-risk strategy, though, as Nazi officials realized themselves.[276] Several visitors were not tricked and some crude propaganda backfired. When Dr. Ludwig Levy, a former Oranienburg prisoner, used a reader's letter from Germany to refute a detailed eyewitness account in the London *Times* of September 19, 1933—which had named him as an SA torture victim—and praised the "thoroughly good and even respectful" treatment he had received, the author of the original article replied in a letter of his own, offering yet more detail about the abuses:

> Dr. Levy lived in the same room as myself at Oranienburg ... I saw Dr. Levy with his left eye black and swollen and blood running from it. About a fortnight later his right eye was in the same condition. On both occasions he was fresh from an interview with the camp "leaders." I also saw him kicked and knocked about by the guards, like the rest of us, many times.
>
> I do not blame Dr. Levy for making the statement which you have published, as I am well aware of the kind of pressure to which he, still living in Potsdam [outside Berlin], must be exposed.[277]

The Nazi PR campaign also scored some successes, however, especially when it played upon fears of Communism. Some foreign news editors published positive stories, or became wary about running negative ones.[278] Several diplomats were duped, too, among them the British vice-consul in Dresden. In an enthusiastic report on his October 1933 visit to Hohnstein in Saxony—one of the worst early camps, with at least eight prisoner deaths—the vice-consul praised it as "a model from all points of view," with "exemplary" SA guards and prisoners who made a "distinctly satisfied impression."[279]

Nazi propaganda tried to persuade a skeptical foreign audience that the camps were orderly and benevolent institutions, which turned terrorists into worthy citizens.[280] This message was summed up in an extraordinary radio report recorded on September 30, 1933, inside Oranienburg, for broadcast on Germany's international station. During the lengthy report, which aimed to refute "lies and atrocity stories" abroad, a reporter strolled through the grounds, the dining hall, and the sleeping quarters, accompanied by Commandant Schäfer, who extolled his decent treatment of left-wing criminals and the exemplary discipline created by his SA men. The broadcast even featured interviews with prisoners, including the following exchange:

> [REPORTER]: The fellow German standing before me, this incited Communist, doesn't know me and I don't know him, he has not been coached for this but has just been called over to us . . . You don't have to

worry, you will not be punished even if you tell me that you are dissatisfied. You need say nothing more than the truth.

[INMATE]: Yessir.

[REPORTER]: Tell us how you feel about the food.

[INMATE]: The food here is good and plentiful.

[REPORTER]: ... Has anything at all happened to you here?

[INMATE]: Nothing has happened to me.[281]

It is unclear if the report was actually broadcast and if anyone was fooled by its heavy-handed direction. Still, the regime persisted with its narrative of the good camps—not just abroad, but also at home in Germany.

Nazi Propaganda

The Oranienburg camp was less than a week old when local Nazi leaders felt compelled to jump to its defense. The resulting article, published in a local paper on March 28, 1933, included many ingredients that would define the domestic image of the Nazi camps, as authorized for public consumption by the regime. The central message of this article, and many others like it, was that prisoners enjoyed "decent, humane treatment." Sanitary conditions were said to be more than adequate, labor was "neither degrading nor exhausting," and food was ample, with prisoners eating from the same pots as SA guards. The prisoners' military exercises were salutary, no harder than those performed by the guards themselves, and were followed by games in the yard. Then, at the end of the day, prisoners could relax, "lazing comfortably in the sunshine" with cigarettes in hand. Turning to the function of Oranienburg, not only did the camp protect the general public from political enemies, it safeguarded the very same enemies from the fury of the people.[282] This, then, was the alternative reality of the early camps: orderly institutions staffed by selfless guards who treated the captured men (women were rarely mentioned, presumably because their detention was thought unpopular) strictly but fairly, in healthy surroundings and with plenty of leisure time. "They can't complain," ran a typical headline.[283]

This fairy-tale image of the early camps was disseminated in various ways across the Third Reich. Nazi officials praised the camps in public speeches and authorized newsreels shot in camps.[284] But the main medium was the press, including articles with staged photos of prisoners working, exercising, and relaxing.[285] In addition to the template set by the March 1933 article on Oranienburg, such reports typically included one additional feature. They depicted the early camps as places of reform and reeducation, above all through productive labor.[286] Only occasionally did articles acknowledge that certain prisoners were thought to be beyond redemption. "The owner of this or that semi-animal face cannot be anything other than an incorrigible Bolshevist," a regional paper said about Oranienburg in August 1933, concluding that "no instruction can help in these cases"—a hint at the possible long-term future for the camps.[287]

Several accounts were published by senior camp officials themselves, including a full-length book in February 1934 by the Oranienburg commandant Werner Schäfer. As the only such account by a camp commandant, it caused something of a stir. The book sold tens of thousands of copies, was serialized in several regional newspapers, and was read by Nazi leaders. Even Adolf Hitler received a volume, courtesy of Commandant Schäfer. Another two thousand copies were dispatched to German embassies abroad, on the initiative of Goebbels's Ministry of Propaganda.[288] In his book, the verbose Schäfer stuck closely to the official narrative of the camps. He claimed that his men had triumphed over many obstacles—such as poor infrastructure and hostile prisoners—to create a model institution, based on care, order, and labor. Carried away on his flight of fancy, Schäfer described his SA guards as dedicated "pedagogues" and "psychologists," who gave their all to turn former enemies into "useful members of the German national community." To prove his point, Schäfer included several letters purportedly sent to him by former prisoners, including one who praised the "very valuable" experience and another who personally thanked Schäfer "for the good treatment and everything else."[289]

The cynical use of prisoners was a key feature of the Nazi public relations strategy. Testimonies by supposedly satisfied prisoners became a staple of German press reporting.[290] This campaign peaked on November 12, 1933, when the Nazi state held a rigged plebiscite and national election. Prisoners in the early camps were "allowed" to participate, with largely predictable results; according to the Munich press, almost all Dachau prisoners voted in support of the Third Reich.[291] This farcical result was no proof of the regime's popularity among prisoners, of course, but of the brutal effectiveness of SS terror in Dachau. About a week before the election, a senior Bavarian state official had warned the inmates that naysayers would be treated as traitors. On the day of the vote, SS guards reminded them to support the regime if they ever wanted to be free again. This the prisoners did, for they were well aware that the SS had devised a system for identifying individual voters.[292] Prisoner fears of retribution for disobedience were well founded; in the Brandenburg camp, a Communist who cast his vote against the state was tortured to death.[293]

The official rationale for the media blitz across Germany—emblazoning the image of the "good camp"—was the rebuttal of foreign "atrocity stories." The self-important Commandant Schäfer, for one, announced that Oranienburg was the most "defamed" camp in the world and pointedly called his rejoinder the "Anti-Brown Book."[294] But Nazi outrage at foreign criticism was often disingenuous, little more than an excuse for tackling a far more pressing problem—the whispers inside Germany. Early on, the authorities occasionally admitted that their real concern was domestic public opinion. As the glowing article about Oranienburg put it on March 28, 1933, all the "talk of merciless flogging" was just "old wives' tales." In the previous week, Heinrich Himmler had made a similar point as he announced the establishment of Dachau, denying all rumors about abuses of protective custody prisoners.[295] Such reassurances were directed at Nazi supporters, aiming to "dissolve the anxieties of the middle-class followers who feel that illegal acts destroy the foundation of their existence," as the former Dachau prisoner Bruno Bettelheim later put it.[296]

It is hard to judge the popular response to the official narrative of the "good camp." Nazi sympathizers—who were more insulated from knowledge of abuses—may well have been reassured and probably wanted to believe the regime's version. At the same time, many other observers saw through the smoke screen. Victor Klemperer was not alone in greeting the November 1933 reports about prisoners voting overwhelmingly for the Nazis with incredulity.[297] More generally, rumors about violence and torture persisted, chipping away at the official picture.

At times, it was Nazi officials themselves who contradicted the carefully crafted official message. In his sensationalist book, Commandant Schäfer repeatedly let slip his benevolent mask, admitting that prisoners had been beaten.[298] Other publications revealed that for prominent prisoners, the much-vaunted productive labor amounted to degrading work like cleaning latrines.[299] And in Dachau, local papers kept readers informed about deaths inside, with articles about "suicides" and prisoners "shot trying to escape" exposing the fiction of the camp as a benevolent educational establishment. But such revealing reports were the exception in 1933—a time when Nazi propaganda was not yet fully streamlined—and disappeared altogether in later years.[300] On balance, the regime had little to gain by deviations from the official line. Instead of playing up the violence inside the camps, the authorities tried to silence the chorus of whispers.

Fighting "Atrocity Rumors"

On June 2, 1933, a Dachau newspaper printed an ominous directive by the Supreme SA Command. Under the headline "Warning!" it informed the local population that two people were recently arrested as they peered into the camp: "They claimed to have looked over the wall out of curiosity about what the camp looked like from inside. To enable them to satisfy their thirst for knowledge and to provide them with an opportunity to do so, they were kept in the concentration camp for one night." Any other "curious individuals," the directive added, would be given an even "more prolonged opportunity to study the camp." Not for the first time, the residents of Dachau were being warned to stay well away from the camp in their midst.[301]

Despite such threats, officials in early camps like Dachau found it impossible to shut out spectators. Some local authorities responded by taking prisoners to more secluded locations. This is what happened in Bremen in September 1933, where the Missler camp—located inside a residential area—was closed down and most prisoners moved to a new camp on a tug boat beached on the embankment of an isolated stretch of river outside the city.[302]

The Nazi state also continued to threaten whisperers. Since spring 1933, press and radio reports carried warnings that so-called atrocity rumors would be punished.[303] New special courts passed exemplary sentences, using the March 21, 1933, Decree Against Malicious Attacks that criminalized "untrue or grossly exaggerated" statements which could cause "serious damage" to the regime.[304] Among the defendants were locals living near camps, such as a joiner who fell into a nighttime conversation with two men on a Berlin street and told them about abuses in Oranienburg, only to be denounced and sentenced to a year in prison. "Such rumors," the judges found, "have to be rigorously combated in order to deter others from similar deeds."[305] Even some Germans far away from camps were convicted. In August 1933, for example, the Munich special court sentenced several workers to three months' imprisonment for discussing the death of the KPD deputy Fritz Dressel in Dachau—a case widely known in Bavaria, even before Hans Beimler mentioned it in his book—as they sat in a stonemasons' hut in the hamlet of Wotzdorf, some 125 miles east of the camp.[306]

The heavy-handed response by the authorities drew more sarcasm about the regime and its camps, including the following joke about Dachau:

> Two men meet [on the street]. "Nice to see you're free again. How was it in the concentration camp?"

"Great! Breakfast in bed, a choice of coffee or chocolate. Then some sport. For lunch we got soup, meat, and dessert. And we played games in the afternoon before getting coffee and cakes. Then a little snooze and we watched movies after dinner."

The man was astonished: "That's great! I recently spoke to Meyer, who was also locked up there. He told me a different story."

The other man nods gravely and says: "Yes, well, that's why they've picked him up again."[307]

In their eagerness to silence critics, the Nazi authorities targeted relatives of former prisoners, who often knew particularly damaging details. Among the victims was Fritz Dressel's widow, who was apparently taken to Stadelheim.[308] Centa Beimler, meanwhile, was imprisoned for several years, following her arrest in spring 1933, in a bid to stop her escaped husband from making further revelations about Dachau. But the detention of relatives for revenge or deterrence, later known as *Sippenhaft*, only gave further ammunition to foreign critics. The decision of the Dessau political police in early 1934 to force Elisabeth Seger and her baby daughter Renate into Rosslau camp, following the escape of her husband Gerhart from Oranienburg, became a public relations disaster. At a press conference in London on March 18, 1934, Gerhart Seger denounced the reprisals of the Nazi regime. Because of his book, which was circulating inside Germany, the Nazi authorities "have now taken my wife and child from me." There was a public outcry in Britain, which even reached Hitler's ears, and after sustained pressure from the British press and politicians, the German authorities released both mother and daughter, who were reunited abroad with Gerhart Seger.[309]

Undeterred, some Nazi fanatics resorted to murder to suppress rumors. In the new Dachau camp regulations of October 1, 1933, Commandant Eicke had threatened prisoners who collected or passed on "atrocity propaganda about the concentration camp" with execution. Less than three weeks later his guards uncovered an alleged prisoner plot to smuggle evidence of SS crimes abroad, and Eicke made good on his threat. Backed by Heinrich Himmler—who claimed that the guilty prisoners had tried to send material for an "atrocity propaganda film" to Czechoslovakia—the Dachau commandant swore revenge. SS suspicions centered on five prisoners, three Jews and two non-Jews, who were thrown into the bunker. They were all doomed. The first to die were Wilhelm Franz (the Kapo overseeing prisoner correspondence) and Dr. Delvin Katz (an orderly in the infirmary), who were tortured and strangled by SS men the night of October 18–19, 1933. The next day, Eicke announced their deaths to all assembled prisoners and declared a temporary ban (sanctioned by Himmler) on letters and releases. According to an eyewitness, Eicke had a chilling message for the prisoners, which summed up the Nazi double-speak about the early camps: "We still have enough German oaks to string up everyone who defies us," Eicke warned, adding: "There are no atrocities and no Cheka cellars in Dachau."[310]

Such threats were still on the minds of prisoners when they were released from early camps. The camps left many deep and lasting wounds on prisoner bodies. In addition to the visible scars, there was the enduring trauma of fear, humiliation, and shame. Many men found it hard to live with memories that undermined their masculine identity, as when they had pleaded, cried, or soiled themselves in the face of overwhelming terror.[311] In light of these experiences, and the regime's crackdown on "atrocity propaganda," it took great courage for former prisoners like Martin Grünwiedl to write about the camps and continue their fight against the dictatorship. Not surprisingly, many more left-wing activists retreated from resistance. As early as summer 1933, the underground Communist leadership warned die-hard supporters that many released comrades were "renegades" who had broken with the party out of fear.[312] This fear gripped other opponents of the regime, too. Once the reality of Nazi terror was known, they anxiously withdrew into the private sphere.[313] In this way, the whispers about abuses and atrocities in the early camps paved the way for total Nazi rule, fatally weakening the resistance.[314]

Of course, deterrence was just one of many functions of the early camps. From the start, Nazi camps were multipurpose weapons. This left an important legacy for the future, as did the innovations in camps like Dachau, with its specific architecture, administrative routine, and daily rituals. Clearly, some of the essentials of the SS concentration camps had emerged early on. All the same, the later SS system was still a long way off. After one year of Nazi rule, individual German states still pursued rival visions and there was no coordinated national network of camps. Instead, the early camps differed in terms of how they looked, who ran them, and how prisoners fared. In early 1934, their future remained undecided. In fact, it was not even clear if the camps would have any future at all in the Third Reich.[315]

2

The SS Camp System

Murder was the making of Theodor Eicke. More precisely, it was a single shot he fired at around 6:00 p.m. on July 1, 1934, that ignited his career. As he hurried to his murderous assignment that early Sunday evening, striding across a new cell block of the Stadelheim prison complex in Munich, Eicke may already have dreamed about the rewards he would reap. Although he was no experienced killer—as Dachau commandant, he had left most of the dirty work to his men—he betrayed no sign of nerves as he climbed up to the second floor and walked along two corridors lined with armed policemen. He finally stopped outside cell number 474 and ordered the door to be unlocked. Eicke stepped inside, accompanied by his right-hand man Michael Lippert, and came face to face with his former benefactor, now the Nazis' most prized political prisoner—SA leader Ernst Röhm.

Eicke and Lippert had arrived in Stadelheim about an hour earlier from Dachau, heading straight for the governor of the prison. They demanded immediate access to Röhm, who had been arrested for treason the previous morning, together with other senior SA men. After the governor stalled, Eicke announced angrily that he was acting on orders from Hitler. The Führer, barked Eicke, had personally instructed him to give the SA leader an ultimatum to commit suicide; if Röhm failed to comply, Eicke would shoot him. After the governor had made some frantic phone calls to corroborate Eicke's story, the two SS officers were allowed to proceed to cell 474. Here, Eicke handed Röhm a copy of the *Völkischer Beobachter*, with details of the execution of six SA leaders in Stadelheim the previous day, and tersely issued Hitler's ultimatum.

Röhm apparently tried to protest, but his cell was quickly locked again, a gun loaded with one bullet left on a small table. Outside, Eicke checked his watch and after a tense ten minutes, the time span specified by Hitler, he ordered a prison official to retrieve the unused weapon. Eicke and Lippert then raised their own guns and pointed through the open door at Röhm, who had taken his shirt off. After steadying themselves for several seconds, both men pulled the trigger. Röhm stumbled backward. He was bleeding heavily, but he was still alive. The sight of the moaning Röhm may have spooked Eicke, for he ordered Lippert to finish the job. The younger man duly stepped up and fired a third bullet from close range at Röhm's heart. According to one eyewitness, the last words of the dying SA leader were: "Führer, my Führer."[1]

Hitler's reckoning with Röhm had been a long time coming, though few would have predicted such a violent end. Over the previous months, many SA men had ignored Hitler's call for calm. Inspired by their bullish leader Röhm, they had pushed for a "second revolution" and an "SA state." Such violent talk, combined with open acts of disorder and brutality, caused a major political headache for Hitler. Not only did the rowdy SA add to the growing popular dissatisfaction with the regime during the second year of Hitler's rule, it alienated the German army. The generals felt threatened by Röhm's military ambitions and his vast paramilitary force, which had grown to well over four million men by mid-1934. What is more, Röhm had also made enemies among jealous Nazi leaders, who now conspired to eliminate their rival. Himmler and Heydrich, in particular, fed Hitler a diet of lies about a supposed SA coup.

In June 1934, after months of vacillation, Hitler finally made his move. Indeed, Hitler worked himself into such a rage about Röhm's "betrayal" that he acted ahead of the secret schedule. In the early hours of June 30, 1934, he headed straight for the SA leaders' retreat in Bad Wiessee, with little backup, and had Röhm and others arrested. A few hours later, Hitler ordered the first executions, though he spared Röhm until the following day. Meanwhile, police and SS forces struck elsewhere in Germany, using lists of suspects drawn up in preparation. The victims were not only SA men. The purge also provided a cover for silencing national-conservative critics of the regime and other alleged enemies or renegades. In the end, the so-called Night of the Long Knives—which actually lasted for three days—may have claimed some 150 to 200 lives.[2]

During this bloody purge, the Dachau SS proved itself as Hitler's most energetic executioner. Several days before, Eicke had held discussions with leading Dachau SS men, planning raids and arrests across Bavaria. Then, on June 29, the Camp SS was put on alert. Later that night Eicke told his men about an SA plot against Hitler, which had to be put down without mercy;

Eicke was raging and is said to have smashed a photograph of Röhm. It was still dark when several hundred guards, some armed with machine guns taken from the watchtowers, left the camp a few hours later on trucks and buses, led by Eicke. They eventually stopped a few miles outside Bad Wiessee to rendezvous with another SS unit, Hitler's Leibstandarte. However, because Hitler had moved prematurely, the Dachau SS came too late and eventually had to follow Hitler's convoy back to Munich. Here, Eicke met other Nazi leaders in the Party HQ, the so-called Brown House, where a hysterical Hitler railed against the "worst treachery in world history" and promised that all SA rebels would be shot. At this point, Eicke probably received instructions for a state-sponsored massacre in Dachau, and soon after he returned to the camp, later on June 30, the murders began.[3]

One of the first victims, and by far the most prominent, was the seventy-one-year-old Gustav Ritter von Kahr, who was dragged to Dachau after his arrest by SS men in Munich in the evening of June 30. The former monarchist Bavarian minister president was a hated figure on the far right ever since he had helped to put down Hitler's feeble putsch back in November 1923.[4] When the Dachau SS men recognized von Kahr, as he emerged from a black police cabriolet, they almost lynched him. A baying mass of uniformed guards pulled the old man before Theodor Eicke, who had been sitting on a chair outside the commandant's office, smoking one of his cigars. Like a Roman emperor, Eicke apparently raised his right thumb in the air and then pointed downward. The SS mob pushed von Kahr through a nearby iron gate into the new Dachau bunker. Soon afterward, a shot rang out.[5]

The murders continued deep into the night, after cars brought more "traitors" from Munich to the camp. Like von Kahr, most of them died in or around the bunker, but at least two men were executed in the harsh glare of camp searchlights on the SS shooting range. The Dachau inmates, locked into the camp compound, heard the shots, followed by roars of SS men intoxicated by bloodshed and alcohol; on the orders of Eicke, who was in triumphant mood, beer flowed freely in the SS canteen, with loud music playing.[6] The macabre SS party was periodically interrupted by more shootings and beatings; some victims were tortured to death, their faces smashed and their bodies butchered.[7]

Not all the dead had arrived from outside the camp. In their frenzy, the Dachau SS executed five long-term prisoners from the bunker, among them at least two German Jews. In contrast to the other killings—where Dachau SS men had followed superior orders, presumably relayed to Eicke by police and SD (Security Service) leaders—the SS men now acted as judge and executioner; to cover up their rogue action, Eicke and his men apparently told Himmler that the murdered inmates had declared their solidarity with Röhm and incited prisoners to rise up. Word about the prisoner executions quickly reached other inmates of the camp, who were already agitated and now feared that the SS might come for them, too.[8]

After a long night of violence, Theodor Eicke appeared early on July 1, 1934, at the barbed wire of the Dachau camp compound. To quash the panic among prisoners, he informed them about the purge and announced that Röhm would soon be hanged inside the camp.[9] But when Eicke's convoy returned from Stadelheim that evening—driving at top speed, with a loud siren—Röhm was already dead, shot by Eicke and Lippert. Eicke was still determined to put on a murderous performance in Dachau, however. He had brought with him four lower-ranking SA men, who were led to the canteen while the camp was prepared for their execution. SS guards assembled outside the bunker, on the edge of the shooting range. Opposite, the regular prisoners were watching from behind the wire fence, on Eicke's orders. Then the victims were led out, one by one, into the evening sun shining across the range. Eicke pronounced their death sentence and a commando of SS sentries took aim. After each salvo, the crowd of SS guards, some still hungover from the night before, broke into wild screams and shouts of "Heil!"[10]

After yet more murders the following morning—in the forest north of the SS parade ground—the massacre in Dachau finally came to an end. On the same day, July 2, 1934, Hitler officially declared that the purge was over and that calm had been restored across the Reich.[11] By then, more than twenty people had been murdered on the Dachau camp grounds, and several more in the vicinity.[12] The dead were victims of vengeance and vendettas, and included senior SA officers, personal associates of Röhm (such as his chauffeur), the girlfriend of an alleged spy (the only woman among the dead), and several dissident writers and politicians. The SS had also executed a music critic by the name of Dr. Schmid, mistaken by the Bavarian political police for a journalist of the same name; by the time the authorities had realized their mistake and placed an urgent call to Eicke in Dachau, the wrong Dr. Schmid was already dead.[13]

The Röhm purge of summer 1934 was a watershed in the history of the Third Reich. With one stroke, the SA was cut down to size, destroying the greatest internal threat to Hitler's rule. Its demise as a major political force led to the submission of grateful German generals. And it was not just the generals who applauded Hitler. All across Germany the Hitler myth grew, as many Germans praised him for restoring order and decency by dealing a decisive blow against SA thugs and deviants (Nazi propaganda made much of Röhm's homosexuality, previously tolerated by Hitler). The unassailable position of

Hitler was confirmed in August 1934, after the death of President Hindenburg, when he took the title "Führer and Reich chancellor."[14]

The purge was also a crucial point in the history of the camps. It helped to
clear the way for a permanent system of lawless imprisonment in SS concentration camps. And it accelerated the creation of a professional corps of SS
guards, held together by their shared crimes. In Dachau, the massacre claimed
as many lives in three days as had died during the entire previous year, making it a formative experience for many local SS men. "These events greatly
impressed me," recalled Hans Aumeier, then a twenty-seven-year-old rookie
with only a few months' experience in Dachau, who would go on to serve as a
camp leader in Auschwitz.[15]

A PERMANENT EXCEPTION

The Röhm purge was a golden opportunity for Theodor Eicke. He had hyped
his men as more than mere guards. They were the "most loyal pillars" of the
Nazi state, he had boasted a few weeks earlier, ready to "rally round our Führer" and defend him with their "merciless spirit of attack."[16] The purge, Eicke
realized, was the chance to prove himself, and he did not slip up. He reminded
Himmler afterward of the "important task" his men had executed, demonstrating their "loyalty, courage and fulfillment of duty."[17] Dachau had been
the main killing ground, though other SS camps had been involved, too, detaining prisoners under brutal conditions.[18] Most important, Eicke himself
had helped to put away the mastermind of the "plot" against Hitler, Ernst
Röhm. This would become his calling card in SS circles. During a celebration
of the winter solstice in Dachau, some 18 months later, Eicke is said to have
exclaimed: "I am proud that I shot this faggot swine with my own hands."[19]

Hitler did not forget the murderous services rendered by Eicke and his
men. Just days after the purge, he promoted Eicke to SS Gruppenführer, just
three ranks below Himmler. The growing status of the SS as Hitler's favored
instrument of terror was reflected in an order of July 20, 1934, making it a
fully independent force, free from its previous subordination to the SA organization. SS leader Himmler knew that the purge had been a pivotal moment.
Almost a decade later, he still commended his men for the resolve they had
shown by "putting comrades, who had done wrong, against the wall and shooting them." In fact, the greatest beneficiary of these murders had been Himmler
himself. His star had already been on the rise, but the purge hastened his as-
cendancy, which would eventually bring him control over the German police
and the camps, though not before some fierce internal struggles.[20]

The Inspectorate of Concentration Camps

"Like mushrooms growing after rain"—this is how Himmler later described the formation of political police forces during the Nazi capture of power.[21] Initially, German states had directed their own troops. But it did not take long before the forces were coordinated, and the man who did so was Himmler. From late 1933, he moved beyond his Bavarian base, and within a few months, the dogged Reichsführer SS had secured, one by one, control over the political police in virtually all German states. The last major state to fall into Himmler's clutches was the biggest—Prussia, where various rivals had been vying for preeminence over the byzantine terror apparatus. In the end, the Prussian strongman Hermann Göring agreed to appoint Himmler on April 20, 1934, as inspector of the Prussian secret state police. Himmler's trusted chief of staff, Heydrich, became the new head of the Prussian Gestapa, with around six hundred officials in the Berlin headquarters and some two thousand more officers across the state. On paper, Göring remained in control as head of the Prussian Gestapo, and initially still played a significant role. But ultimately, he was no match for his shrewd subordinates.[22]

Himmler's mastery over the German political police—the main authority imposing protective custody—provided him with the perfect launching pad for taking over the camps. This Himmler realized only too well. He had recognized the camps' potential more clearly than any other Nazi leader and had planned for some time, certainly since late 1933, to take the remaining early camps into his own hands.[23] Now that he had gained dominance over the political police, the time had come to act.[24]

To realize his plans, Himmler turned to Theodor Eicke. Sometime in May 1934, just weeks before the Röhm purge, Himmler instructed him to carry out a "fundamental organizational restructure" of the camp system, beginning in Prussia. Himmler wanted to bury the flawed Prussian model and replace it with the SS system he had perfected in Dachau.[25] The first test came in Lichtenburg. Eicke, who now styled himself as "inspector of concentration camps," arrived on May 28, 1934, and took control of the camp from its civilian director, a police official called Faust, who had nominally supervised the Lichtenburg SS guards. One day later, Eicke had Faust arrested on trumped-up charges (the luckless former director soon found himself in protective custody on Himmler's orders, first in Berlin and then in Esterwegen). Eicke also sacked the two police administrators who had worked for Faust. Instead, he put his trust in the murderous commander of the local SS guards. To ensure a stricter regimen, Eicke also introduced new punishment rules for prisoners on June 1, 1934, virtually identical to the Dachau ones.[26] He completed the initial shake-up the following day, with a first written order to the Lichtenburg guards: "Until now your superiors were officials and a corrupt director, from now on soldiers will be in charge of your well-being and your troubles. Together we will place stone upon stone until completion, but cast aside bad stones as worthless."[27]

Encouraged by the retooling of Lichtenburg, which continued apace over the coming weeks, Himmler mapped out the next steps. In June 1934, he trained his sights on Sachsenburg (Saxony) and on Esterwegen, the largest Prussian state camp—a far more ambitious maneuver, since both camps were still guarded by the SA. Esterwegen would be first, and Eicke was already planning his move for the camp—scheduled for July 1, 1934—when he was overtaken by the bloody events of the Röhm purge, which hastened the SS capture of the early camps.[28] In its wake, SS forces not only took over Esterwegen and Sachsenburg, as planned, but two other SA-run camps, Hohnstein and Oranienburg.[29] The SS domain was growing, and over the coming weeks, Theodor Eicke—officially confirmed as inspector of concentration camps on July 4, 1934, three days after he shot Röhm—shuttled between the new sites.[30]

The capture of Oranienburg—the oldest and most prominent SA camp—symbolized the new SS hegemony. On July 4, 1934, a few days after a police unit had disarmed most of the Oranienburg SA, Eicke made his grand entrance. SS troops under his command, some of them drawn from Dachau, surrounded the camp; according to one witness, Eicke had brought two tanks for backup. But there was no resistance from the scared SA men. Eicke curtly announced the SS takeover, telling the assembled SA guards to look for another job. SA rule over Oranienburg ended with a whimper. The new masters, meanwhile, celebrated in SS style by killing their most prominent prisoner, Erich Mühsam. At first, they tried to drive him to suicide. Mühsam resisted, but quietly distributed his belongings among fellow prisoners, knowing that his killers could strike at any time. On the night of July 9–10, 1934, the frail Mühsam was led away. He was strangled with a clothesline, apparently, his body hanged in the camp latrine in a feeble attempt to make his death look like a suicide. Erich Mühsam's funeral was held in Berlin on July 16, attended only by a few brave friends and admirers. His wife, Kreszentia, who had tried so long to save him, was not among them; she was escaping abroad, where she would publish a searing account of her husband's torment.[31]

Himmler and Eicke quickly streamlined their new camps. They had no interest in maintaining Oranienburg and Hohnstein, and closed both.[32] By contrast, Eicke led the conversion of Sachsenburg and Esterwegen into SS camps, along the lines of Dachau.[33] The new Esterwegen regulations of August 1, 1934, for example, were based directly on Dachau.[34] Eicke also looked for officials who would bring the SS spirit to his new camps. Back in Dachau, he had been impressed by Standartenführer Hans Loritz, a belligerent fanatic in Eicke's own image, and he now helped to make him the new commandant of Esterwegen. Loritz did not disappoint. A former prisoner remembered his first address in July 1934: "Today I have taken over the camp. In regards to discipline, I am a swine."[35]

Theodor Eicke initially directed his fiefdom of camps from Dachau and during flying visits to the other SS sites.[36] Then, on December 10, 1934, Himmler gave him a permanent office to go with his title. The choice of location revealed the importance Himmler attached to the camps, for Eicke moved right into the heart of the police headquarters in Berlin. As a part of the state bureaucracy, Eicke's new Inspectorate of Concentration Camps (IKL) was housed in five rooms on the ground floor of the Gestapa, on 8 Prinz-Albrecht-Strasse. Despite their proximity, however, Himmler made sure to keep Eicke's IKL separate from Heydrich's Gestapa.[37] The two men, who had an uneasy relationship, were forced to work closely together. Heydrich enforced the virtual police monopoly over protective custody, sending suspects to the KL and ordering their release; the organization and administration of the KL, meanwhile, was left to Eicke.[38]

Eicke's standing was bolstered further after his guards were removed from their subordination under the general SS (in the same way the Gestapo was removed from the oversight of the regular police). In a significant move, Himmler elevated the camp guards on December 14, 1934, to the status of a separate force within the SS, and as their leader, Eicke garnered yet another title: inspector of SS Guard Troops. To be sure, Eicke was not fully autonomous from the expanding SS administration, especially in regard to financial and staffing matters, and he also still came under the formal authority of the chief of the new SS Main Office (until summer 1939). In practice, though, Eicke often bypassed the chain of command by appealing directly to Himmler.[39]

By the end of 1934, in the space of just a few months, Himmler and Eicke had created the rudiments of a nationwide system of SS concentration camps. There was now a small network of five KL—run along similar lines and staffed by SS Guard Troops—under the umbrella of the new Inspectorate in Berlin.[40] But the future of this SS system remained uncertain, as the KL had not yet been confirmed as permanent fixtures. In fact, it had seemed likely in 1934 that they would soon wither away.

SS Camps Under Threat

Once the Third Reich was established, an internal tug-of-war began over its direction: Exactly what kind of dictatorship would it become? Today, the answer seems obvious. But Nazi Germany did not follow a preordained path to extreme terror. Initially, some influential figures in state and party envisaged a rather different future. They wanted an authoritarian regime, bound by laws enforced by the traditional state apparatus. True, they had accepted, or applauded, the unrestrained repression in 1933 as a means for stabilizing the regime. But they saw the Röhm purge as the last act of the Nazi revolution, clearing the way for a dictatorship based on authoritarian law. Now there would be no more need for arbitrary violence and for extralegal camps, which only damaged the image of the regime at home and abroad.[41]

State officials had made tentative moves to curb the camps as early as spring and summer 1933, while some newspapers assured their readers that these sites would not become a regular feature of the new Germany.[42] Such efforts gathered momentum toward the end of the year, pushed ahead by an unlikely champion: Prussian minister president Hermann Göring. Once the initial wave of Nazi terror had subsided, Göring, always a proponent of a strong state, styled himself as a respectable statesman upholding law and order.[43] Following the "completed stabilization of the National Socialist regime," he announced in the Nazi press in early December 1933, there would be mass releases from the Prussian camps. In all, up to five thousand inmates were freed during this so-called Christmas amnesty, almost half of all the Prussian protective custody prisoners.[44] Most of them were foot soldiers or sympathizers of the Left; others had been held for grumbling about the regime.[45] But the authorities also freed some prominent figures, among them Friedrich Ebert, who kept his head down after his release, running a gas station in Berlin.[46]

The early camps' decline accelerated during 1934. Hermann Göring continued his campaign, both in public and in private, not least with Hitler. He was backed by the Reich minister of the interior, Wilhelm Frick, another Nazi faithful, who sharply criticized the excessive use of protective custody and indicated that the camps would fade away.[47] As the regime consolidated, more prisoners were released (among them Wolfgang Langhoff in late March) and fewer were dragged inside; in Prussia, just 2,267 prisoners were held in protective custody on August 1, 1934, down from 14,906 one year earlier.[48] The early camps were disappearing fast. More than a dozen shut down in Prussia and elsewhere in the first few months of 1934, including Brandenburg, Sonnenburg, and Bredow.[49]

Further camps closed later that year, following a direct intervention by Hitler. In early August 1934, shortly before a plebiscite endorsed him as Führer and Reich chancellor, Hitler made a play for the public gallery, announcing a major amnesty for political and other offenders. Crucially, Hitler extended his grand gesture to the camps. He ordered a speedy examination of all protective custody cases, demanding the release of prisoners held for minor transgressions and those thought to pose no more threat.[50] Despite some resistance from the SS and Gestapo—who refused to free high-profile figures like Carl von Ossietzky and Hans Litten—most of the remaining protective custody prisoners were let go. In Prussia, there were just 437 inmates left after Hitler's amnesty; Esterwegen—the last outpost of the Emsland concentration camp complex, originally built for five thousand prisoners—was down to an estimated 150 men by October 1934.[51] The camps' rapid decline was public knowledge. In late August 1934, Göring authorized a press release about the closure of Oranienburg, adding that protective custody would be "greatly curtailed" in the future, with lawbreakers "immediately transferred to the courts" instead.[52]

The judicial apparatus—with its hundreds of prisons—stood ready to take over the mantle of the camps. The German legal system had undergone a major transformation since early 1933. Although it was still largely run by national conservatives, such as the long-serving Reich minister of justice Franz Gürtner, it became a loyal servant of the Nazi regime. Critical officials were dismissed, fundamental legal principles abandoned, new courts set up and stricter laws applied. German jurists overwhelmingly backed this development. The upshot was a huge increase in the number of state prisoners, from a daily average of around 63,000 in 1932 to more than 107,000 in summer 1935, including at least 23,000 political prisoners. Gürtner and other jurists were sending a clear message to Nazi leaders: enemies of the regime would be punished hard by the law, making measures such as protective custody superfluous. With such a determined legal system, who needed concentration camps?[53]

To support their case, legal officials could point to their harsh prisons. In 1933, senior legal figures promised more deterrence and retribution—turning the prison into a "house of horror," as one put it—and introduced harder sanctions and diminished rations.[54] The showcase for the new prison regime was a network of camps in the Emsland. In a move that summed up their ambition to constrain lawless detention, the German legal officials had taken over the early camps Neusustrum and Börgermoor in April 1934; inside, the places of protective custody prisoners were taken by regular penitentiary inmates. By 1935, the Reich Ministry of Justice ran six camps in the Emsland, holding well over five thousand prisoners. Rules, conditions, and treatment were brutal, with thirteen confirmed prisoner deaths in 1935 alone. The high levels of violence were due, in large measure, to the employment of former

SA camp guards as prison warders. They were led by another veteran of the early camps, none other than SA Sturmbannführer Werner Schäfer, who had been poached by the legal authorities in April 1934 from his post as commandant of Oranienburg. Appointed as a civil servant, Schäfer served in the Emsland prison camps until 1942, by which time several hundred inmates had died inside.[55]

While legal officials generally turned a blind eye to abuses in their own prisons, they began to take more concerted action against atrocities in SA and SS camps. True, there was some collusion; murders committed during the Röhm purge, for example, were out of bounds.[56] Still, now that the early camps seemed to be fading, state prosecutors launched several criminal investigations, touching at least ten camps in the mid-1930s. The biggest case was brought against former SA guards from Hohnstein, following the camps' closure. Flaunting their Nazi credentials, the legal authorities were willing to overlook crimes committed in revenge for Communist "wrongs" or for "political reasons." But the judges drew a line when it came to arbitrary atrocities. In their view, there was no place in the Third Reich for the sadistic excesses that had blighted Hohnstein, and on May 15, 1935, the regional court of Dresden sent twenty-three SA men to prison, with sentences ranging from ten months to six years for the former commandant.[57]

SS men found themselves in the dock, too. In spring 1934, the regional court of Stettin convicted seven SS men from the recently closed Bredow camp for grievous bodily harm and other offenses, with the former commandant sentenced to thirteen years in a penitentiary. The case was widely reported in the German press, as part of Göring's effort to present himself as a guarantor of order. Not to be outdone, Hitler used a speech in the Reichstag on July 13, 1934, after his action against Röhm, to announce that three SS guards (of the Stettin camp) had been shot during the purge because of their "vile abuse of protective custody prisoners."[58] Even the KL now under Eicke came under scrutiny, resulting in the arrest and conviction of senior officers from Esterwegen and Lichtenburg.[59]

The SS was put on the back foot.[60] Its reputation was already poor—"I know there are some people in Germany who feel sick at the sight of this black uniform," Himmler conceded—and the legal investigations only dragged it further down, at the very time when the future of the KL system was in doubt.[61] Eicke railed against "poisonous" attacks that "serve the sole purpose of systematically undermining and shaking the state leadership's confidence" in the camps.[62] Meanwhile, the legal authorities continued to chip away at the KL. In summer 1935, Reich minister of justice Gürtner, whom Eicke regarded as a personal enemy, suggested that all camp inmates should be granted legal representation, a proposal supported by many German lawyers and the leaders of the Protestant Church.[63]

By 1935, then, the SS concentration camp system—only just established—found itself under serious pressure. Greatly depleted, the KL faced a crisis of legitimacy; to many observers, their days seemed numbered. But Heinrich Himmler had different ideas. In December 1934, he warned Göring against "abolishing an institution that at present is the most effective means against all enemies of the state."[64] Himmler would fight tooth and nail for the survival of the KL, to secure and extend his own power, but also, as he saw it, to save the Third Reich.[65]

Himmler's Vision

The mass releases from Nazi camps in 1934 were "one of the worst political mistakes the National Socialist state could have made," Heinrich Himmler seethed in a confidential speech a few years later. It had been sheer "madness" to allow vicious opponents to resume their destructive work. After all, the fight to secure the Nazi regime was far from won. According to Himmler, the German nation was still in mortal danger from shadowy enemies who threatened everything from the foundations of state and society to the moral fiber and racial health of the people. The nation had to fight to the death against the "forces of organized subhumanity," a catch-all term he would use over and over again, meaning Communists, Socialists, Freemasons, priests, asocials, criminals, and above all Jews, who "should not be viewed as humans of our species."[66]

Himmler's beliefs rested on an apocalyptic worldview. In his mind, the all-out battle against Germany's enemies might last for centuries and could never be won with traditional weapons. To annihilate opponents hell-bent on Germany's ruin, Himmler and his supporters argued, the nation had to be put on a war footing. Like soldiers on the battlefields, the troops fighting against the "inner enemy" at home had to act beyond the law. Total victory could only come through total terror, led by Himmler's elite warriors: the police would arrest all individuals harmful to the "body of the nation," and the SS would isolate them in concentration camps.[67]

Himmler's call for unfettered police and SS terror, based on a permanent state of emergency, set him on collision course with those Nazi leaders who merely wanted an authoritarian state.[68] This clash came to a head in spring 1934, and the main battleground was Himmler's home state of Bavaria. Elsewhere, he was still too weak and had to stand by while almost all camp inmates were released. Not so in Bavaria. Backed by his superior, the powerful minister of the interior Adolf Wagner, Police Commander Himmler felt bold enough to challenge calls to empty his model camp at Dachau: "Only I in Bavaria didn't give in then and didn't release my protective custody detainees," Himmler claimed a few years later.[69] But this was only half the truth, as Himmler had been forced to fight a rearguard battle in Bavaria.

In March 1934, the Bavarian Reich governor von Epp launched a full-blown attack on Himmler's approach, alarmed by the news that Bavaria appeared to hold more protective custody prisoners than Prussia (the previous summer, Prussia still outstripped Bavaria by more than three to one). Epp called for a generous amnesty, to coincide with the one-year anniversary of the Nazi capture of power in Bavaria. In a letter of March 20, he argued that the current Bavarian practice was disproportionate, arbitrary, and excessive, undermining "the trust in the law, which is the foundation of any state system." It is worth noting that the sixty-five-year-old Epp was no closet liberal. He was a far-right icon, a former army general and early Nazi supporter, known as the "liberator of Munich" after his Freikorps helped to crush the left-wing uprising of 1919. But Governor von Epp saw the Third Reich as a normative state. Now that the Nazi revolution was over, emergency measures such as protective custody were becoming "dispensable," all the more so since new laws and courts gave the legal authorities ample power to deal with criminal offenses.[70]

Himmler was stung. In a remarkably rude reply, which he drafted for his boss Wagner, he vigorously defended his record. The use of protective custody had driven down political crime and other offenses in Bavaria, he claimed, something that the legal system could not hope to emulate.[71] But Himmler had to give some ground. Even though Governor von Epp was becoming little more than a figurehead of the Bavarian state, his word still carried weight in government circles, and Himmler's Bavarian police grudgingly released almost two thousand inmates from Dachau and elsewhere in March and April 1934.[72]

When the conflict over Bavaria flared up again in autumn 1934, Himmler offered stauncher opposition, reflecting his growing stature in the Third Reich following the Röhm purge. This time it was Reich minister of the interior Frick who challenged him. In a letter to the Bavarian state chancellery in early October, Frick pointed out that Bavaria currently held some 1,613 protective custody prisoners—almost twice as many as all other German states combined. Given the excessive zeal of the Bavarian authorities, Frick asked for a review of individual cases, as a first step for further releases.[73]

Himmler's response was disdainful. Following a "most thorough" review, he noted in mid-November 1934, Bavaria had released another 203 protective custody prisoners, a paltry figure. Any mass releases, Himmler added, were out of the question. He claimed that the recent releases of dangerous Communists from concentration camps had created a serious security threat in Germany—except in Bavaria, thanks to its more stringent approach. Elsewhere, "cheeky" Communists had been emboldened by the "general slackness" of the authorities. Such enemies of the regime saw mass releases as a sign of the "inner weakness of the National Socialist state," and escalated their attacks against the regime. Himmler's conclusion was clear: far from releasing additional inmates, he wanted to take more prisoners inside the camps, proposing to wage a preemptive war against Communism.[74]

In reality, the Communist "threat" was imaginary by autumn 1934, as the Gestapo was well on top of the underground resistance.[75] And although Himmler's fear of Communists—which also gripped many lower-ranking police and state officials—was genuine, he clearly exploited it to advance his policy of preventive policing.[76] But not everyone shared his grim outlook, and Reich minister Frick continued to press for further prisoner releases from Dachau.[77]

Himmler stood his ground in late 1934, but his foothold was far from secure. His new SS concentration camp system, in particular, was still fragile. The camps remained controversial and their impact negligible, at least in terms of prisoner numbers; by autumn 1934, Himmler's camps only held an estimated 2,400 inmates.[78] The KL might well have vanished altogether, had it not been for several decisive interventions in 1935 by the most powerful man in the Third Reich.

Hitler and the KL

As a public figure, Adolf Hitler remained studiously detached from the concentration camps, keeping a careful distance throughout the Third Reich. He was never seen inside a KL and rarely referred to them in public.[79] There was good reason for his reticence, as Nazi leaders knew that the camps' reputation was not the best. "I know how mendaciously and foolishly this institution is being written about, spoken about and blasphemed," Heinrich Himmler acknowledged in 1939.[80] Hitler, acutely aware of his own image, did his best to avoid association with potentially unpopular matters.[81] This, no doubt, is why he stayed clear of the concentration camps—at least in public. In private, it was a different matter. Hitler conferred about the camps with his closest associates from the start, and would become one of the greatest champions of the KL.[82]

Hitler's support had not always been unconditional. As the regime steadied itself, he initially seemed to side with those who envisaged the early camps fading away. Thousands of prisoners had already been released, he said in the *Völkischer Beobachter* in February 1934, and he hoped that even more would follow.[83] Hitler backed up his words six months later. His amnesty of August 1934—widely publicized in Germany and abroad—resulted in the release of some 2,700 protective custody prisoners.[84] But did Hitler really want the camps to disappear? Or was he just biding his time?[85]

In 1935 Hitler revealed his true feelings about the camps, behind closed doors. On February 20, he received Himmler, who showed him a copy of the latest letter by Reich interior minister Frick, urging further releases. Himmler, who had only just returned from inspecting Lichtenburg and Sachsenburg, scribbled Hitler's emphatic verdict on the letter: "The prisoners are staying."[86] Four months later, Hitler went even further. Meeting Himmler on June 20, he confirmed that the KL would be needed for years to come and, for good measure, approved Himmler's request for more SS guards.[87] In the Third Reich, destructive dreams could easily come true, if they were in line with Hitler's wishes. And Hitler backed the extension of Himmler's terror apparatus.

To cement the camps' standing, Hitler agreed to place them on a firm financial footing. Funding had been a contentious issue since the start, with different state and party agencies trying to pass the buck.[88] In autumn 1935, Hitler approved a proposal by Theodor Eicke: from spring 1936, the Reich would pay the SS Guard Troops, while all other KL costs were borne by individual German states.[89] Eicke regarded this as a temporary arrangement only. Now that the camps were fixtures of the Nazi state, he fully expected the Reich to pick up the whole bill.[90] He soon got his way. From spring 1938, the camps and their SS troops were allocated funds within the Reich Ministry of the Interior budget, with almost sixty-three million Reichsmark that fiscal year alone.[91] Thanks to Hitler, the financial future of the KL was secure.

Hitler also confirmed that the SS concentration camps would largely operate outside the law. On November 1, 1935, he told Himmler that protective custody prisoners should not be granted legal representation. On the same day, he brushed away as irrelevant concerns by the legal authorities about suspicious prisoner deaths.[92] Only a few weeks later, Hitler pardoned the convicted Hohnstein SA men, sending a chilling message to the judiciary: even the most sadistic camp guards could count on his backing.[93] On paper, the courts could still investigate unnatural prisoner deaths at the hands of the SS. But in practice, such cases were now generally dropped.[94] Prosecutors knew that there was little chance a sentence would stand, even if they could overcome the usual SS obstruction.[95]

Before long, Hitler added the final piece still missing for Himmler's autonomous terror apparatus: in October 1935, he agreed in principle to unify the entire German police under Himmler's leadership, and after months of wrangling with Frick, Himmler was appointed on June 17, 1936, as chief of German police. The Gestapo—now a nationwide body—gained complete control over protective custody; all decisions about detention and release from the KL were made centrally inside the Berlin HQ.[96] Heinrich Himmler had become the undisputed master over indefinite confinement in concentration camps.

Himmler's rise seems irresistible, but he would have been nothing without Hitler's backing. So why did Hitler offer such unwavering support? For a start, he took a rather dim view of Himmler's competitors. The fortunes of Wilhelm Frick were already fading, while the star of Franz Gürtner (and his Ministry of Justice) never rose at all. Hitler was deeply distrustful of the legal authorities, dismissing jurists as timid bureaucrats who placed abstract laws above the vital interest of the state.[97] Hermann Göring, meanwhile, had gradually withdrawn from his role as police leader, turning his attention instead to the German economy and rearmament.[98]

The stage was clear for Himmler, who had already demonstrated his worth during the Röhm purge in summer 1934. His uncompromising attitude elevated him into Hitler's innermost circle, and once he had Hitler's ear, he never stopped extolling the camps' virtues.[99] His subordinates tried to do the same. Theodor Eicke pinned particularly high hopes on the Nazi Party rally in September 1935, when his KL troops filed past Hitler for the first time. Eicke saw this as an important audition. His men rehearsed for weeks—arriving from different camps for special drills in Dachau—before setting off for Nuremberg in pristine uniforms and freshly painted steel helmets. "We passed our test there," Eicke wrote proudly afterward.[100] Hitler thought so, too. He was impressed by all he saw and heard about the KL and praised their exemplary management during a meeting with Himmler in November 1935.[101]

Hitler came to regard the KL as indispensable, as they allowed him to swiftly settle scores with personal enemies.[102] Most important, Hitler valued the camps as powerful weapons in the all-out assault on "community aliens." The safe detention of dangerous prisoners was essential, Hitler told Himmler on June 20, 1935, and he approved special machine gun units at concentration camps. In case of domestic unrest, Hitler agreed, SS guards could even serve as shock troops outside camps.[103]

Emboldened by Hitler's support, Himmler launched the first of many "preemptive" nationwide strikes. On his orders, issued on July 12, 1935, the

SS CONCENTRATION CAMPS, SUMMER 1935

COLUMBIA HOUSE
400 inmates (estimate)

DACHAU
1,656 inmates, July 1935

ESTERWEGEN
322 inmates, June 10, 1935

LICHTENBURG
706 inmates, June 10, 1935

SACHSENBURG
678 inmates, June 10, 1935

police arrested well over a thousand former KPD functionaries; the mere suspicion of a "subversive attitude" was enough to warrant arrest.[104] But Himmler's sights were set higher, as we have seen, targeting all alleged enemies. Once more, he could count on Hitler's support. When the two men met on October 18, 1935, they discussed not only the attack on Communists, but abortionists and "asocial elements," too.[105] Before long, raids on social outsiders by the criminal police intensified, sending ever more prisoners to the KL.[106]

The triumph of Himmler's model marked a major defeat for the legal authorities. "Only those who still mourn a past liberalistic era," a Gestapo official crowed in the leading legal journal, "will regard the application of protective custody measures as too harsh or even illegal."[107] Jurists now faced a parallel and permanent apparatus of detention outside their jurisdiction, typical for the duplication of powers under the polycratic Nazi system of rule.[108] True, legal officials could console themselves in the knowledge that their prisons remained the main site of state detention, dwarfing the camps; despite Himmler's best efforts, his KL held no more than around 3,800 inmates by summer 1935, compared with well over 100,000 inmates in regular prisons.[109] But jurists had to accept that the camps were here to stay, and just like most Germans, they gradually got used to their existence.[110]

Although there were still flash points in the second half of the 1930s, the legal authorities developed a largely cordial relationship with Himmler's terror apparatus.[111] Their collaboration rested on a division of labor in the fight against suspected enemies of the new order: lawbreakers would be sent to prison by courts, while those who could not be convicted of new offenses ended up in concentration camps.[112] In addition, thousands of state prisoners were transferred to the KL following the completion of a judicial sentence. When the former KPD Reichstag deputy Karl Elgas came to the end of his three-year sentence for high treason in 1936, the Luckau penitentiary governor advocated his transfer to a concentration camp as there was no certainty that "he will leave his seditious activities behind him in the future"; the Gestapo agreed. Occasionally, prisoner transfers also went in the opposite direction, as KL inmates convicted of criminal offenses could be taken to a prison to serve their sentence, before returning to the camp.[113]

The growing complicity of legal officials was summed up in a letter by the Jena general state prosecutor in September 1937. After he informed the Reich Ministry of Justice of the recent opening of a large new camp named Buchenwald, he added: "During the first few weeks seven inmates have been shot dead by the guard posts while trying to escape. The judicial proceedings have been stopped. Cooperation between the camp management and the Public Prosecutor's office has so far been good."[114]

The New KL

On the afternoon of August 1, 1936, after athletes from more than fifty countries had filed into the world's largest sports stadium, during a lavish ceremony watched by more than a hundred thousand spectators, Adolf Hitler stepped up to the microphone and officially opened the Olympic Summer Games. The Berlin Games were a master class in Nazi propaganda. The German capital had undergone a facelift, with gleaming streets and colorful flags greeting foreign visitors, while Nazi leaders were on their best behavior, downplaying the regime's repressive reality and basking in the reflected glory of the games.[115] But Nazi terror was never far from the surface. Even as the

Olympic torch was lit inside Berlin's Olympic Stadium, a group of exhausted prisoners, driven on by SS guards, were clearing a vast pine forest less than twenty-five miles to the north, on the edge of Oranienburg; they were preparing the ground for a new concentration camp called Sachsenhausen.[116]

Heinrich Himmler saw the creation of a big KL near the German capital as an urgent necessity. At the time, there was only one SS camp in Berlin, the Columbia House, a notorious former Gestapo prison taken over by the IKL in December 1934.[117] And this building was far too small for the mass of enemies Himmler targeted. The SS was looking for a suitable location for a large camp, and Oranienburg, the town that had housed one of the biggest early camps, seemed like the perfect spot. Since spring 1936, SS planners had their eyes on a large area of secluded woodland to the northeast of the town, which offered ample space for a new camp, and could be reached easily from Berlin. Following site visits by Himmler and his enforcer Eicke, the SS went ahead in July 1936 with the construction of Sachsenhausen. The new camp quickly took in prisoners from other KL now regarded as redundant. By early September, it had absorbed the remaining inmates from Esterwegen, who later commemorated their move in the "Sachsenhausen Song":

> From Esterwegen we set out,
> away from moor and mud,
> and Sachsenhausen was soon reached,
> the gates were once more shut.[118]

Among the prisoners was Ernst Heilmann, who had somehow survived until now. "I have returned from the moor," he wrote in a first letter to his wife from Sachsenhausen on September 8, 1936. Esterwegen, meanwhile, was hastily closed down and turned into yet another judicial prison camp (the timing was fortunate for the SS, since the Emsland land cultivation project proved largely fruitless). The next camp to shut was the cramped Columbia House, bringing even more inmates to Sachsenhausen in autumn 1936; by the end of the year, the new KL already held some 1,600 prisoners.[119]

Sachsenhausen was the first of many purpose-built KL sites and came to rival Dachau as the new model camp. Its construction was part of the wider consolidation of the concentration camps in 1936–37 by Himmler and Eicke, who remained in close contact during this time. Now that the future of the KL system was secure, they reshaped it, replacing most of the existing camps with two brand-new ones: Sachsenhausen and Buchenwald (in Thuringia).[120]

Himmler and Eicke had already hoped in 1936 to set up a large new KL in

Thuringia, around the same time as Sachsenhausen, but the project only got off the ground the next spring. Following personal inspections in May 1937, they finally approved a suitable site, a large forested area on the northern slopes of the small but steep Ettersberg (a beauty spot favored by the nearby Weimar population). The new camp was provisionally named after the mountain, but when this met with local opposition because of the association with Weimar's most famous citizen, Johann Wolfgang von Goethe (1749–1832), Himmler opted instead for Buchenwald ("beech forest"), a pastoral term that would come to stand for institutionalized inhumanity. The connection with Goethe, however, could not be severed. A large oak tree, under which he had supposedly met with his muse, stood right on the new camp grounds; because it was protected, the SS had to build around it. Prisoners came to see the presence of Goethe's oak in the midst of Buchenwald as a desecration of the memory of Germany's greatest writer, symbolic of the wider destruction of culture under National Socialism.[121]

The first prisoners arrived in Buchenwald on July 15, 1937, and more transports followed over the next weeks. By early September, some 2,400 men had been placed in the new camp. Almost all had arrived from three older KL, which now closed down. There was Bad Sulza, a small camp only recently taken over by Eicke; Sachsenburg; and Lichtenburg, which would reopen a few months later, in December 1937, as the first SS concentration camp for women. Among the prisoners moved out of Lichtenburg was Hans Litten, who had spent three comparatively bearable years there. He found no such respite in Buchenwald. In his first letter to his mother, sent on August 15, 1937, he told her in code that he was once again brutally abused.[122]

The landscape of SS terror was changing fast in the second half of the 1930s. Camps that had been hurriedly set up during the Nazi capture of power were replaced by tailor-made structures meant to last.[123] Of the four camps under Eicke's IKL in late 1937, only Lichtenburg and Dachau had their roots in 1933. And Dachau was already in the midst of a major rebuilding program; much of the old munitions factory was torn down to make way for a permanent new camp.[124] SS leaders saw newly built KL as the future. Himmler and Eicke enthused about such modern camps, as they called them, and over the coming years added another three: Flossenbürg (May 1938), Mauthausen (August 1938), and Ravensbrück (May 1939), the first SS concentration camp specially constructed for women, replacing Lichtenburg.[125]

What made the new camps so novel, in the eyes of Himmler and Eicke, was not their internal organization or the guards' ethos, both of which followed the old Dachau model.[126] Rather, it was their functional design. The new concentration camps were planned as small cities of terror, holding masses of prisoners. At a time when the entire SS system held less than five thousand prisoners, Sachsenhausen and Buchenwald were projected for six thousand men each.[127] In fact, following Himmler's vision of unrestrained police terror, there was no fixed limit on prisoner numbers. In contrast to older camps in narrow buildings, the new KL was designed to be "capable of expansion at any time," Himmler wrote in 1937, shortly after he and Eicke inspected the Sachsenhausen prototype. Boundless terror required boundless camps.[128]

This was one reason why the new grounds were so large: Sachsenhausen encompassed almost eighty hectares of land (1936) and Buchenwald more than a hundred (1937).[129] In the growing camp cosmos, the prisoner compound itself made up only one part, and by no means the biggest. Outside, there were storage rooms, garages, workshops, administrative offices, petrol stations, and water and sewage pumps, as well as large SS quarters and residential settlements, all connected by a network of roads built by prisoners.

Prisoner compounds looked rather similar across the new KL. They were clearly organized and easy to survey. The SS prided itself on strict security and surrounded the sites with wire, fences, towers, ditches, and a no-go zone. Inside stood a few administrative buildings—such as the laundry, kitchen, and infirmary—as well as a large roll call square. Then there were the prefabricated single-story wooden prisoner barracks (in Buchenwald, two-story stone barracks were added in 1938). The barracks resembled the ones Wolfgang Langhoff had seen in Börgermoor back in 1933. Such parallels with the Emsland camps were not accidental, since the SS architect of Sachsenhausen had previously worked there (there was one major change, though: most of the new barracks were longer and split into two wings, with prisoner quarters at each end and washrooms in the middle). Despite many similarities, the new KL compounds were not identical to each other, owing in part to the terrain on which they were built. Also, the SS still experimented with different designs. The Sachsenhausen compound was initially laid out as a triangle, with prisoner barracks forming a half-circle around the roll call square at the base; but this shape impeded the camps' expansion and surveillance, and was later loosened. In Dachau, by contrast, the SS opted for a rectangular design, with rows of symmetrical barracks on either side of the main camp road. This would become standard in most SS concentration camps.[130]

There was one more central feature of the new KL: secrecy. To be sure, even these camps were never completely isolated. Social contacts to locals living outside continued as the SS system grew; by 1939, for example, SS men made up nearly one-fifth of the local Dachau population.[131] Still, the new camps were largely shielded from sight. In contrast to most early camps, they were set up in more remote and concealed locations, keeping curious spectators away.[132] These KL were also more autonomous from the surrounding infrastructure. Many citizens had initially expected economic benefits from a camp in their midst. A few traders did indeed profit, as did some other locals; a Lichtenburg farmer, for example, used prisoner excrement as fertilizer on his fields. But on the whole, hopes for major material benefits were dashed, not least because the new camps became more self-sufficient, with workshops for blacksmiths, shoemakers, tailors, joiners, and others. Dachau even had its own bakery and butcher, leading the way for the other KL.[133] As a result, camps became less visible for the men and women living in nearby villages and towns, just as they did to most other Germans in the second half of the 1930s.[134]

THE CAMP SS

During a speech on German radio on January 29, 1939, to mark the Day of the German Police, Heinrich Himmler made a rare public reference to the SS concentration camps. After reassuring his listeners about the decent conditions in the "strict but fair" KL, Himmler turned to their function: "The slogan that stands above these camps is: There is a path to freedom. Its milestones are: obedience, diligence, honesty, orderliness, cleanliness, sobriety, truthfulness, readiness to make sacrifices, and love of the fatherland."[135] The SS was so taken with Himmler's motto that it was soon displayed in several KL—on signs, roofs, and walls—for all inmates to see; a photo of prisoners before one of the placards featured in the Nazi press.[136] Similar SS slogans had appeared before. Since 1936, for example, the wrought-iron doors leading from the Dachau gatehouse to the prisoner compound bore the words "Work Makes Free," a phrase later added to the gates of Sachsenhausen, Flossenbürg, and Auschwitz.[137] SS men used such cynical phrases to torment prisoners. During the war, guards in Sachsenhausen would direct new inmates to the solemn slogan from Himmler's 1939 speech, painted in huge letters on the barracks around the roll call square, and then point to the nearby crematorium: "There is a path to freedom, but only through this chimney!"[138]

In his own warped way, however, Himmler had been quite serious about the "path to freedom."[139] He liked to think of himself as a strict teacher and regarded camps in general as instruments of mass education—a popular view in Nazi Germany, with its many different types of camps for molding "national comrades." As for his KL, Himmler saw them as part reformatories, and prisoners who had been made to change their "inner attitude," as the SS called it, might be allowed to rejoin the national community.[140] In line with this approach, many prisoners detained during the second half of the 1930s were eventually released again.[141] None of them had been educated, of course; they had been broken. When Himmler talked about SS "methods of education," what he really meant was coercion, punishment, and terror—the only ways to deal with all the deviant, dirty, and degenerate "scum" and "rubbish" in the KL, as far as he was concerned.[142] What is more, Himmler insisted that not all prisoners be freed, even after they were broken. Echoing contemporary criminological thinking, with its division of offenders into reformable and incorrigible, Himmler was certain that one "must never release" the most depraved common criminals and the most dangerous political enemies, those who would infect the German people once more with the "poison of Bolshevism."[143]

Only SS men with special qualities, Himmler claimed, could navigate the dangerous terrain of the KL: "no other service is more devastating and strenuous for the troops than just that of guarding villains and criminals."[144] Some historians have taken Himmler's aspirations at face value, falling for his idealized image of SS guards as a select force of fighters.[145] The prisoners, meanwhile, often reversed the official image and described guards as a freak show of misfits and sadists.[146] In Sachsenhausen, they even made up their own ditty, mocking Himmler's famous slogan: "There is a path to the SS. Its milestones are: stupidity, impudence, mendacity, boasting, shirking, cruelty, injustice, hypocrisy, and love of booze."[147] Although this witticism holds some truth, it offers only a partial picture of the background and actions of men serving in the KL and the IKL. Collectively, these men can be called the Camp SS, though at the time they were known under a far more sinister name. By 1935, they were wearing a badge with a skull and bones on their uniforms: "he who joins our ranks enters into comradeship with death," as the histrionic Theodor Eicke put it. The macabre symbol gave rise to the official name that Himmler bestowed on the Camp SS men in spring 1936—Death's Head units.[148]

Constructing the Political Soldier

An elite unit of political soldiers: this is how Himmler and Eicke liked to depict the Camp SS. In peacetime, Eicke kept telling his men, they were the only soldiers protecting the German fatherland, fighting day and night against the enemy behind the barbed wire of the concentration camps.[149] The figure of the "political soldier" had first been popularized by the SA in the Weimar years.[150] But it was quickly appropriated by Heinrich Himmler and his SS leaders, who loved to style themselves as hard soldiers.[151] Theodor Eicke laid full claim to the term, which became so closely associated with him that after his plane was shot down on the Eastern Front on February 26, 1943, his obituary in the *Völkischer Beobachter* carried the subheading: "Eicke, the political soldier."[152]

The construction of Camp SS men as political soldiers was made up of several components. To start with, there was the "superb esprit-de-corps," as Eicke called it, based on "cordial comradeship." The ideal of military camaraderie—derived above all from the myth of German fraternity in the First World War trenches, with its glorified images of solidarity and sacrifice—had become a powerful political tool in postwar Germany, not least for the mobilization of Nazi activists.[153] The flip side of comradeship was the closing of ranks against others, and Eicke exhorted his men to show no pity to prisoners. The empathy of Camp SS men toward one another, he insisted, had to be matched by their hostility toward inmates. "In service there is only merciless severity and hardness," Eicke reminded his subordinates, "outside service hours there is heart-warming comradeship."[154] The SS men had to show their teeth to prisoners, he demanded, leaving no room for empathy. "Tolerance means weakness," he said, and for Eicke there was nothing worse than compassion for enemies.[155] Weaklings were not cut out for the Camp SS and would be better off in a monastery. "Keep our ranks pure," he told his men: "Tolerate no softies or weak characters amongst yourselves."[156] Behind all this stood a reverence of masculine virtues like military bearing, toughness, physical strength, and cold-bloodedness. Only real men would make the grade in the Camp SS.[157]

But how should SS recruits be molded into political soldiers? Heinrich Himmler tried to show the way. Once he had secured the future of the KL system in 1935, he remained hands-on during its consolidation and expansion. Himmler passed on orders, appointed senior staff, conferred with Eicke, visited new sites, and inspected existing ones. Some of his visits were closely stage-managed, so that the camps came closer to their official image, in order to impress Himmler as well as other dignitaries.[158] Occasionally, however, Himmler appeared unannounced, to the alarm of the local SS. For all his talk of comradeship, Himmler was not popular among his men, who disliked his reserve and feared his fastidiousness; one long-serving Camp SS man later described the SS leader as "a mean-minded pedant" and "petty tyrant."[159]

By contrast, Theodor Eicke enjoyed a good working relationship with his boss, based on their shared vision for the camps, on Eicke's undying gratitude to Himmler, and on Himmler's respect for the man he regarded as the perfect manager of the SS camp system. The decision to give the disgraced Eicke another chance had paid off handsomely for Himmler. He trusted Eicke, and when it came to the creation of the Camp SS, he gave him plenty of leeway, admiring and perhaps even envying the rapport Eicke built with his men.[160]

Eicke quickly put his stamp on the concentration camps. He transformed the Camp Inspectorate from a small backroom operation to an influential agency. His IKL staff increased from five (January 1935) to forty-nine (December 1937), spread across several departments; there was the main (or political) office, as well as separate offices for personnel, administrative, and medical matters.[161] The IKL became the nerve center of the SS camp system. From here, key decisions by Eicke and his officers were transmitted to the individual camps. From 1937, the IKL also printed a monthly newsletter, a set of musings and instructions by Eicke on organizational matters (from staff IDs to weapon maintenance), SS deportment, and prisoner treatment.[162] Demonstrating his independence from the Gestapo, Eicke soon moved the IKL office out of Prinz-Albrecht-Strasse into larger premises, first, in June 1936, to Friedrichstrasse in central Berlin, and then in August 1938 to a brand-new office block in Oranienburg, right next to Sachsenhausen (some prisoners were forced to work on the construction). Because of its shape, the long three-story structure later became known as the T-Building. Eicke himself occupied the most lavish office, overlooking the large landscaped square outside, and in the evenings retired to wine and dine in his luxurious new villa nearby. Commensurate with their growing status, the men from Camp SS headquarters now resided in some style.[163]

But Eicke never saw himself as an aloof manager. Like other Nazi activists, he worried that too much paperwork might turn him into a pencil pusher; he and his followers had to stay true to themselves as men of vigor and action.[164] Eicke led by example and kept up a hectic schedule of meetings and inspections. "For twenty days each month I am traveling and exhausting myself," he wrote to Himmler in August 1936, eager as ever to impress. "I live only to fulfill my duty to my troops that I have come to be fond of."[165] In addition, Eicke held regular conferences with his commandants. On one memorable occasion in late 1936, they all met in a picturesque hotel at the foot of the Zugspitze, Germany's tallest mountain; a snapshot shows Eicke and his officers milling around by the snow, wearing their long black SS coats and caps bearing the skull and bones.[166]

Eicke's authority over his men was absolute, and although it ultimately derived from Himmler, it was fed by the force of his personality. Eicke was a charismatic leader, and many of his men felt bound to him by their belief in his heroic character, his exceptional abilities, and his vision.[167] His followers revered him as Röhm's killer and projected all kinds of other epic deeds onto him, picturing Eicke as a titanic warrior.[168] And although Eicke reveled in the trappings of his office, he made a show of breaking barriers of rank and status, asking his men to address superiors with the informal "Du" and telling them, "I am ready to listen at any time to the youngest comrade and will stand up for any comrade if he proves an open and honest character." In an ostentatious celebration of SS comradeship, Eicke even met with regular guards, carousing, drinking, and smoking late into the night—quite unthinkable behavior for the uptight Himmler.[169]

Many of his men, in turn, worshiped Eicke. They bought into his ideal of the Camp SS as a surrogate family—"My men are dearer to me than my wife and family," he once stated—with Eicke as the omnipotent father figure; his underlings even called him "Papa Eicke" (as Eicke proudly relayed to Himmler).[170] One of these fawning SS men was Johannes Hassebroek, a twenty-five-year-old hand-picked by Eicke in 1936 as platoon leader, after passing an elite SS leadership academy (*Junkerschule*). Hassebroek's devotion to Eicke remained undimmed even decades after the war. "Eicke was more than a commander," the misty-eyed sixty-five-year-old reminisced in 1975. "He was a true friend and we were his friends in the way that only real men can be."[171]

The Janus Face of Punishment

When Heinrich Himmler fantasized about his political soldiers, there was one virtue he prized above all others—decency. Among all the commandments he issued, and there were many, this was paramount. However brutal the fight against the enemy, his men had to remember that they were fighting for the greater German good, not for personal gain or pleasure. Speaking to SS leaders in 1938, Himmler insisted that sadism toward prisoners was just as wrong as compassion: "to be hard, without being cruel" was the guiding principle.[172]

Himmler's call for propriety was echoed in Camp SS orders. As early as October 1933, Theodor Eicke, only a few months into his reign as Dachau commandant, instructed guards that any "maltreatment or chicanery" of prisoners was strictly forbidden. Other SS commandants followed suit.[173] Later on, SS guards were even required to sign a written declaration that they would not "lay a hand" on any opponent of the state.[174] Disobedient Camp SS men were threatened with sanctions. In March 1937, Theodor Eicke warned in a newsletter that Himmler might expel guards for "the least maltreatment (box on the ear)" of inmates.[175] Just a few months later, another newsletter carried this stunning announcement: "SS Oberscharführer Zeidler in the Sachsenhausen concentration camp has, because of sadistic tastes, beaten a prisoner in a most vile manner. He was reduced to the rank of SS man, permanently expelled from the SS and handed over to the criminal judge. This case is being made known as a warning example."[176] What was going on here? Were Himmler and Eicke serious about clamping down on SS assaults in the KL?

What really concerned SS leaders was not prisoner abuse as such, but what one of Himmler's aides, in a telling aside, called "unnecessary torture" that breached decorum or caused disorder.[177] To stop such acts, SS leaders introduced two key measures. First, they issued an approved catalogue of punishments for all KL, largely modeled on practices tried and tested in Eicke's old stomping ground at Dachau.[178] Second, they regulated the execution of these official punishments; only the commandant could impose them. If guards spotted an infraction, they were supposed to follow the rule book. Rather than assaulting the guilty prisoner themselves, they would send a written report up the chain of command.[179] Even the commandants were not fully autonomous. When it came to flogging, the most brutal sanction, they had to send a written application in triplicate to the IKL.[180]

Flogging prisoners was a favorite punishment of the Camp SS, and indeed of Himmler himself. The use of sticks and whips had already been widespread in early camps, as SA and SS men preferred to use torture instruments instead of their bare hands; this way, they could inflict greater damage, at little risk of injuring themselves. Such assaults carried symbolic weight, too, with a long history of masters whipping their slaves.[181] In addition to wild beatings, some early camps had practiced formal flogging. In Dachau, SS men under Commandant Wäckerle staged regular "welcome" beatings of new prisoners, who were pulled over a table and whipped, often until they fainted. Wäckerle also introduced corporal punishment for alleged infractions. "Guilty" prisoners received five to twenty-five blows with a bullwhip or a long willow rod.[182] This torture continued under the new Commandant Eicke, who included the "twenty-five blows" in his official Dachau punishment regulations of October 1933. Later, as camp inspector, he rolled out the same rules to the other KL.[183]

Most ritual floggings took place behind closed doors. But the Camp SS also staged regular performances of cruelty on the roll call squares, to shame its victims and intimidate others (in Buchenwald, well over 240 prisoners were publicly whipped during the second half of 1938 alone). On such occasions, all inmates were forced to stand to attention and watch as the victims, strapped to a special wooden buck, were whipped on the behind, with blood running down their legs; some overeager SS men hit so hard the canes broke.[184] This, then, was Himmler's ideal of "decent" punishment.

An equally gruesome practice was the so-called tying to a post.[185] It was another official form of SS torture—drawing on practices dating back to the Inquisition and beyond—that had been pioneered in Dachau before spreading to other KL.[186] Prisoners, their hands tied behind their backs, were hung from a pole by their wrists. Sometimes they were left to touch the ground with the toes; or they were suspended without any support, often for several hours. To intensify the torment, SS men pulled on prisoners' legs or punched them so that they swayed from side to side. The pain from torn ligaments and dislocated or broken bones was so excruciating that prisoners were soon bathed in sweat and struggled for breath, although some fought hard to keep their composure, to demonstrate to the SS and other prisoners that they would not be broken. Their bodies were marked for many days. An inmate who had been tortured for three hours in Sachsenhausen in summer 1939 testified not long afterward that "for around ten days, I did not know if I still had a pair of arms attached to the shoulders, my comrades had to do everything for me . . . because I could not touch anything, because I had no sense of feeling in the arms." Some victims did not survive; others were so traumatized they tried to kill themselves.[187]

Hanging and flogging were only two of the approved SS torture methods. In addition, Eicke's catalogue of official punishment included penal labor, pack drill (or "sport"), cuts to rations, detention in the dreaded bunker, and transfer to a special penal company (or penal block).[188] Most of these sanctions remained in force until the end of the Third Reich, one of the many pernicious legacies of the prewar camps.

By the late 1930s, the SS had built up an elaborate bureaucracy of torture: before a prisoner was officially punished, reports were written and forms were signed. SS leaders saw several advantages in this formal system. To begin with, it imposed some oversight. The leadership principle applied to the camps just as it did to other parts of the Nazi state, and some central control was deemed necessary to prevent chaos.[189] Also, the new system had the desired effect of terrorizing prisoners. Since every behavior could be construed as an infraction of the rules, every prisoner was at risk of punishment—and prisoners knew what this meant. As for the victims, the pain of torture was preceded by another torment. They had to wait for days or weeks, following their initial "infraction," to find out how they would be punished.[190] Finally, torture-by-the-book protected the Camp SS. Its leaders were still concerned about the reactions of other Nazi agencies and used the official catalogue of punishments to erect a façade of orderliness around the KL. As Eicke told his men, he had plenty of sympathy for those who hit "cheeky detainees," but he could not openly condone it "or we would run the risk of being described, by the Ministry of the Interior of the German Reich, as incapable of dealing with prisoners."[191]

But the official KL regulations did not put an end to other excesses. Nor were they meant to. SS guards saw violence as their birthright. They continued to torment prisoners and found ways to aggravate regular punishment, for example by flogging prisoners more than officially allowed.[192] This happened with the support of local Camp SS officers, who knew that wild assaults added yet another layer of fear for prisoners. Indeed, most commandants led from the front: at the same time as they signed official torture orders, they abused inmates without recourse to the written rules.[193] It was this duality of regulated and spontaneous violence that created the unusual potency of SS terror in the camps.

The Janus face of Nazi terror—with its normative and prerogative side—reflected the wider beliefs of Himmler and Eicke.[194] In normal circumstances, they expected their men to respect the rules of engagement and the lines of command. But in an emergency, no political soldier could wait for written permission to strike. If the enemy behind the barbed wire went on the offensive—and prisoners were always suspected of being on the brink of insubordination—then guards had to throw out the rule book. In the moral universe of the Camp SS, almost all attacks on inmates could be justified as acts of necessity. This had pragmatic advantages, too, as it would thwart judicial investigations. In a secret order, the leader of the Dachau sentries reminded his men that all prisoner abuses should officially be recorded as self-defense.[195]

Only in exceptional circumstances did SS leaders discipline abusive guards. This is what happened to Paul Zeidler, mentioned in Eicke's newsletter above. However, Zeidler was not expelled for torturing a prisoner, as Eicke suggested; if prisoner abuse had been a ground for dismissal, most SS guards would have been fired. Zeidler's real crime, as far as his superiors were concerned, was that he had let himself be caught by the judiciary. Zeidler had been part of a gang of SS guards who murdered the prisoner Friedrich Weissler in February 1937 in the Sachsenhausen bunker: after slowly beating Weissler to a pulp, they had strangled him with his own handkerchief. During the ensuing routine investigation, the local Camp SS covered up the crime. But it did not go away. Weissler had been a leading official in the Protestant Confessing Church—he was arrested after a petition to Hitler, critical of the regime and the camps, was leaked to foreign newspapers—and his death caused alarm in

German church circles and abroad. Moreover, Weissler was a former colleague of the Berlin state prosecutors; until he was dismissed in 1933 because of his Jewish heritage, he had been the presiding judge at a regional court. This prompted a more persistent investigation than usual, quickly unraveling the SS lies. Only then, after the case threatened to engulf the Sachsenhausen SS more widely, was Paul Zeidler cut loose. By sacrificing the shifty Zeidler, who was later sentenced in a secret trial to one year of imprisonment, SS leaders managed to protect other implicated Sachsenhausen officials—men like Commandant Karl Otto Koch, who would go on to become a dominant figure of the prewar KL.[196]

Death's Head Careers

The Death's Head SS expanded fast during the second half of the 1930s, growing from 1,987 men (January 1935) to 5,371 (January 1938).[197] In each KL, these men were divided into two main groups. A select few, easily identifiable by the letter "K" on their uniforms, joined the so-called Commandant Staff and controlled most key aspects of the camps, including the prisoner compound itself.[198] The rest belonged to the so-called Guard Troop sentries, with one Death's Head battalion (later regiment) stationed at every concentration camp for men. The Guard Troops were responsible for external security. They patrolled the camp perimeter and manned the watchtowers, and shot prisoners who crossed the sentry line. They also guarded prisoners working outside, offering them the opportunity for hands-on violence.[199] Although there were many points of contact between Guard Troops and Commandant Staff, the SS tried to maintain a division of duties; normally, sentries were not even permitted inside the camp compound. This separation between running a camp and guarding it—a separation already in place in early camps like Dachau—became the basic organizational feature of the KL.[200]

The great majority of Camp SS men served as sentries in the Guard Troop, outnumbering Commandant Staff personnel by a ratio of over 12:1 in late 1937.[201] Like other SS members at the time, these sentries had gone through a selection process, essential for maintaining the elite image of the SS. All recruits had to be healthy and at least 5 feet, 6 inches tall, with physical prowess equated with manliness and character. And they had to conform to Himmler's crank ideas of racial purity, tracing their "Aryan" heritage back to the eighteenth century.[202] Beyond these general requirements, selection for the camps had initially been haphazard. But with the coordination of the KL system in the second half of the 1930s, Theodor Eicke pursued a more systematic recruitment strategy for the Guard Troop, focusing on two aspects—youth and voluntarism.[203]

Eicke was after "bright-eyed" and "brawny" sentries. He welcomed even sixteen-year-olds into the fold, while he considered anyone much over twenty "only a burden." The "boys," as Himmler called them, were thought to be easily malleable into political soldiers. A more pragmatic motive, given the tight purse strings of the SS, was that single young men came cheap.[204] Eicke's obsession with youth changed the Camp SS, with the average age dropping to around twenty by 1938; many new recruits had enrolled straight out of the Hitler Youth.[205] But Eicke did not welcome all applicants. They were supposed to show passion for their chosen path and be eager to devote their lives to the SS. Here, Eicke was drawing on the ideal of the volunteer soldier, a figure long associated in nationalist circles with dedication and self-sacrifice.[206]

Although Eicke could not afford to be too selective, given the fast expansion of his troops, he achieved his primary aim. By the late 1930s, the Camp SS was made up almost entirely of volunteers, and mostly of teenagers.[207] What had drawn many of them to the Death's Head SS was its image as a crack military formation. SS recruitment material painted parallels to the army and alluded to special missions for the Führer, holding out the promise of playing at war while Germany was still at peace. By contrast, the camps and their prisoners were not mentioned at all. Most applicants must have known where they would be stationed, but recruiters did not consider the KL a selling point.[208]

The training of Guard Troop recruits—with continuous parades, marches, obstacle courses, and weapons exercises—was hard. The newcomers were at the mercy of older SS officers, some of them First World War veterans, who harassed and humiliated their charges at every turn. "They drilled us," one SS man later recalled, "till we howled with rage." This brutal induction was designed to weed out "weak" men, and more than a few recruits collapsed or broke down in tears; they had signed up for four (later twelve) years of service, but did not even last the three months of probation. Others, by contrast, positively enjoyed the hazing—the harder, the better—as a showcase for their toughness.[209]

Recruits who endured the initiation rituals were taken over into the Guard Troop. But their daily lives bore little resemblance to the adventures some had expected. By the late 1930s, Guard Troops worked on strict rotation. Most of the time was taken up with routine military exercises and training, interrupted by one week of sentry duty each month, which often proved tiring and tedious. Most men lived regimented communal lives and some grumbled that they were no more than "prisoners with rifles." The sentries envied other SS formations bearing arms, like the Leibstandarte, which were better equipped and paid. These were the real elite units, while the Guard Troops were mocked as dull watchmen.[210] "Morale among the comrades is not very good," one guard admitted in 1935. There was a great gap between the heroic self-image of the Camp SS and their mundane lives, a gap that even Eicke's bombastic oratory could not always bridge. "I am aware of your hardships and am striving every day to remove them," he assured his men, "but this can only be done one step at a time."[211]

There were plenty of Guard Troop recruits who believed Eicke, despite the privations, and such men could reap rich rewards. The Camp SS offered rapid advancement toward better pay and other perks. Nowhere else in the SS could men with a modest education go further; it was not uncommon for recruits to ascend from private to officer in just a few years.[212] Their rise often led them to the Commandant Staff. In the eyes of their superiors, they had proven themselves as political soldiers and were now allowed to rule the lives of prisoners inside the compounds.[213]

One of these fast risers was Rudolf Höss. Born at the turn of the century, he dreamed of becoming a soldier, and during the First World War, he escaped from his stifling home into the army, still in his teens. Even the German defeat could not dim his devotion to a martial male lifestyle. He spent most of the hated Weimar years among far-right paramilitaries, fighting vicious battles in the Freikorps and then joining isolated rural communities of like-minded men. He never lost his taste for violence, either, and in 1924 Höss was convicted for his part in the slaughter of a supposed Communist traitor (he served four years in a penitentiary). The radical right-wing connections Höss forged during the Weimar years would later bring him to the SS concentration camps. He had joined the Nazi movement in the early 1920s, when he met Himmler for the first time. Their paths would cross again over the coming years, and in summer 1934, during an inspection of the regular SS (Höss had joined up the previous year), Himmler advised him to enter the Camp SS. Höss accepted, tempted not least by the prospect of rapid promotion. He joined the Dachau SS as a sentry in December 1934. Just four months later, Eicke plucked him from the Guard Troop and transferred him to the Commandant Staff, the springboard for his later meteoric rise.[214]

Höss would advance faster and further than almost any other new recruit, but his background was similar to many others in the KL Commandant Staffs. Like Höss, they were largely in their late twenties and thirties, far older than the youngsters from the Guard Troop. Most had gained their first military or paramilitary experiences prior to 1933, often showing early enthusiasm for the Nazi movement; in spring 1934, eight of the eleven officers in the Dachau Commandant Staff carried prestigiously low SS membership numbers of ten thousand or lower.[215]

Among the most experienced Camp SS men were the commandants. Almost all prewar SS commandants had seen action during the First World War—around half of them as professional soldiers—and had later drifted to the Nazi movement, joining the SS before 1932 and reaching officer rank by early 1933.[216] These commandants reported to Eicke's IKL, but inside their camps they exercised the ultimate authority over prisoners and SS men; to do so, commandants relied on their staff office, above all on their adjutants, who often became powerful figures in their own right.[217] Commandants had authority over the Guard Troops on sentry duty.[218] And they controlled the Commandant Staff, passing on orders and directives during large assemblies, and supervising officers from the various KL departments.[219]

From the mid-1930s, the Commandant Staff included five main departments, a basic division—based on the organizational structure of Dachau—which would remain largely unchanged until the end of the war.[220] In addition to the commandant's staff office (Department I), it included the so-called political office (Department II), which registered prisoner arrivals, transports, releases, and deaths, keeping files as well as photographs of inmates. In addition, it was in charge of the bunker and prisoner interrogations, using a range of torture methods. This was why a summons to the political office "was quite likely to induce a heart attack in a prisoner," a former Buchenwald inmate wrote after the war. Crucially, the leaders of the political office reported not just to the commandant but to the police, as well. They were career policemen appointed by the police authorities, and as a sign of their special status frequently wore civilian dress.[221]

The chief camp doctor, who headed the medical office (Department V), stood under dual subordination, too. In addition to the commandant, he answered to the chief medical officer in the IKL, Dr. Karl Genzken, a former navy doctor and old Nazi activist, who in turn reported to the SS Medical Authority (which posted the doctors to the camps) and the SS Reich physician. Camp doctors were in charge of all medical matters, supervising the provision for both SS troops and prisoners, for whom basic infirmaries existed.[222] These doctors loomed large in the lives of inmates, in contrast to the bureaucrats from the administration office (Department IV), who operated largely hidden from view. In many ways, though, the administration office proved no less important. Not only were the officials overseeing the camp budget, they were in charge of food, clothing, and lodging (for prisoners and the SS), as well as maintenance in the camp, working closely with the SS Administration Office under Oswald Pohl.[223]

The most powerful figure in the Commandant Staff, with the exception of the commandant, was the camp compound leader, who headed the protective custody camp (Department III). A more visible presence than the commandant, for whom he deputized, he was a key figure for inmates and SS men alike. Rudolf Höss called him the "real ruler over the entire life of prisoners." This was reflected in the location of his office, in the gatehouse directly overlooking the prisoner compound. The camp compound leader directed the largest department in the Commandant Staff. His personnel included one or more deputies at the top, a report leader (responsible for prisoner discipline and roll calls), a work service leader (supervising SS commando leaders in charge of prisoner labor details), and the block leaders (in charge of prisoner barracks). Dedicated SS men quickly moved up the ranks, sometimes all the way to the top.[224]

Rudolf Höss was among the brightest stars of the Camp SS. In the Dachau Commandant Staff, he was soon fast-tracked from block leader to report leader, and after a visit in 1936, Heinrich Himmler himself promoted him to Untersturmführer; just three years after joining the SS, Höss was now an officer. He moved to Sachsenhausen in summer 1938, first as adjutant, then as camp compound leader. These two posts were the main gateways for striving SS men to become commandants, and sure enough, when his superiors searched for a dynamic officer to head one of their new KL in 1940, Höss was their choice. He packed his bags and traveled east to a place "way back in Poland," as he wrote, as commandant of a camp called Auschwitz.[225]

Camp SS Professionals

Theodor Eicke never tired of conjuring up the SS Death's Head "spirit"—the mortar, as he called it, which bonded his men.[226] But Eicke's rhetoric could not smooth over the cracks in the Camp SS. For all his bluster about breaking down barriers, for example, there were many formal and informal hierarchies separating leaders, NCOs, and ordinary men, both in the camp and off-duty; officers often lived in spacious and well-appointed houses in newly built SS settlements, while their men slept in large and shabby huts which sometimes faced the prisoner barracks, separated only by the barbed wire.[227]

Instead of a unified community of SS comrades there were rival groups, an inevitable consequence of drafting so many ruthless and hard-nosed men.[228] Conflicts also erupted over the daily duties, with plenty of men failing to live up to Eicke's ideals. Camp SS leaders frequently reprimanded their men for slovenly dress and poor posture, for chatting with inmates, for stealing from SS stores, and for reading, or worse still, for falling asleep on duty.[229] A few errant guards even ended up as prisoners themselves, after Himmler introduced a new sanction for disgraced SS men in summer 1938: on his personal orders, they would be placed into protective custody in Sachsenhausen. By September 1939, seventy-three ex–SS men—including former guards—were held here in the so-called Education Platoon, under comparatively lenient conditions. Their former SS comrades regularly set them upon fellow prisoners, who greatly feared these "bone men," a nickname derived from the crossbones on their prisoner uniforms, a daily memento of how they had fallen.[230]

Despite Eicke's exaggerations, the SS Death's Head spirit was not entirely imaginary. Like a true corporate leader, Eicke did impress a distinct organizational identity onto the Camp SS—with its own traditions, values, and vocabulary—and the hard core among his men fully embraced it. "We in the KL were a completely isolated clique," one of them recalled proudly after the war. They signed up for Eicke's ideal of the political soldier and pursued long-term careers as concentration camp professionals. There may not have been more than a few hundred of them in the prewar years, mostly inside the Commandant Staff, but it was these men who ultimately dominated the KL.[231]

Life as a political soldier was a full-time commitment. The core members of the Camp SS spent much of their free time together on the grounds. They met up in SS canteens and celebrated festive occasions together. In Dachau, SS men mingled at their own private swimming pool, bowling alley, and tennis courts; there was even a nature reserve with wild animals. Senior officials socialized outside the camp grounds, too. Most of them were married with two or more children—another signifier of masculine SS identity—and their families often lived together in the nearby SS settlements. In this way, the private and professional lives of dedicated Camp SS men merged into one.[232]

At the center of their lives stood violence. This was the real mortar binding together the Camp SS professionals, as their shared practice of abuse created close bonds of community and complicity.[233] So strong was the violent energy at the core of the SS, it spread beyond the camps, leading to scuffles and brawls between guards and locals; the worst incident occurred in April 1938 in Dachau, when an SS man used his ceremonial dagger to stab two workers to death, apparently after an argument about his uniform and golden Nazi Party badge.[234]

Violence was the essence of the Camp SS spirit, and it was soaked up by the SS professionals. In addition to official prisoner punishments, they practiced many other forms of violence, starting with slaps. For prisoners the first slap in the face was a humiliating reminder of their servitude—slaps were commonly used by German men to discipline minors and inferiors—but it was preferable to many other abuses.[235] Punches and kicks, for example, caused real bodily harm, as did another violent SS ritual, the raid, when screaming guards would descend on prisoners, followed by carnage and torture.[236]

By contrast, murder was still unusual in the mid-1930s. On average, around five prisoners died monthly in 1937 in each of the big SS camps for men (Dachau, Sachsenhausen, and Buchenwald), which held a daily population of some 2,300 prisoners each.[237] In all, perhaps three hundred prisoners perished in the KL between 1934 and 1937, most of them driven to suicide by SS men or killed outright.[238]

Violence came easy to the hard core of the Camp SS, justified (as in early camps) as the only way to hold down dangerous inmates. True, the fiction of the savage prisoner was more difficult to maintain, now that the Third Reich was fully entrenched. But Camp SS leaders worked hard to fan the flames of hatred. New recruits received ideological instruction, which continued throughout their service. In lectures, leaflets, and directives, SS leaders painted prisoners as dangerous enemies, never to be trusted, never to be left alone, never to be spared. These slogans often stuck, partly because the KL were staffed by self-selected National Socialist believers, partly because prisoners began to resemble the stereotypical image of convicts, with shaved heads and striped uniforms (see below). SS revulsion against prisoners became so intense, Rudolf Höss wrote, it was "unimaginable for outsiders."[239] Not every slap or kick was prompted by burning hatred, however. SS men found many practical reasons for assaults, to punish infractions or to maintain discipline. And sometimes, they simply assaulted prisoners out of sheer boredom, to liven up their dull days.[240] Whatever the motive, however, all attacks grew out of a deep disdain for the victims.

To make his men even harder, as Theodor Eicke put it, they were ordered to attend official prisoner floggings. The first time, Rudolf Höss recalled, he was shocked by the screams, but he got used to it, just like his comrades, some of whom appeared to enjoy the suffering of their "enemies."[241] Professional Camp SS men were more than passive observers, of course. A few of them received specialist training in torture methods.[242] But most men learned on the job, copying the behavior of more experienced colleagues and superiors.[243] They could deaden any remaining scruples with alcohol, which fueled violent excesses; some men got so drunk they hurt themselves as they stumbled around the camp.[244]

Violence not only united Camp SS hard-liners, it propelled their careers. In a community based on the veneration of the political soldier, brutality brought valuable social capital. Ambitious SS men knew that a reputation for ruthlessness would impress superiors and boost their prospects. This was one reason why block leaders attacked prisoners and volunteered to carry out floggings. Senior officials, meanwhile, did not want to be outdone by their men. "I could not ask block leaders to do more than I was willing to do myself," the former Sachsenhausen report leader testified after the war. "That is why I personally punched and kicked." To maintain their status, Camp SS men had to reaffirm their brutality, over and over again. Unlike prisoners, who were desperate to lie low—a common motto was "don't be conspicuous"—committed SS men were eager to stand out, impressing their SS audience with theatrical displays of cruelty; the ensuing competition ratcheted up the spiral of terror.[245] In sum, the SS perpetrators did not simply commit violence for its own sake.[246] Rather, their actions were driven by an explosive mix of ideological and situational factors.

Camp SS men who failed the test of violence were marginalized and mocked. Just as Eicke had demanded, they were shamed as weak and effeminate. This created significant group pressure on individual men to "toughen up." Rudolf Höss, for one, was terrified of ridicule. "I wanted to become notorious for being hard," he wrote, "so that I would not be considered soft." Those written off as failures were sidelined into office jobs, punished, or dismissed— "for the Death's Head strikes its wearer," Eicke wrote in his inimitable style, "if ever he deviates from our prescribed course." Eicke's drive to remove "soft" men claimed several prominent casualties, none more so than the commandant of the largest SS concentration camp.[247]

The Dachau School

When Heinrich Himmler cast around for a permanent new Dachau commandant to replace Theodor Eicke, he turned to one of his oldest followers. Born in 1890, Heinrich Deubel had returned from Allied captivity in the First World War as a decorated lieutenant and settled into a steady job as a customs official. His real passion, however, was for far-right politics. He joined the fledgling SS in 1926 as member number 186, rising fast through its ranks. By 1934, Oberführer Deubel was commanding a regiment of Austrian SS men, stationed on the same grounds as the Dachau camp. As an army veteran and passionate SS officer, with a violent temper to boot, Deubel seemed as good a choice as any to succeed Eicke and took over as Dachau commandant in December 1934.[248] His appointment was rather typical of the haphazard personnel policy in the early phase of the KL, when so-called old Nazi fighters, some of whom had fallen on hard times, were rewarded with posts for their early dedication to the movement, often on the spur of the moment.[249]

But impeccable Nazi credentials were no guarantee of a successful Camp SS career. Like several other Nazi veterans, Heinrich Deubel failed the expectations of his superiors. It quickly became clear that in terms of terror, he was anything but Eicke's double. Dachau remained a brutal SS camp, to be sure, with thirteen known prisoner deaths in 1935. But these were still better days for most inmates. They faced less severe punishment, worked less hard, and mingled more freely. Supported by his camp compound leader Karl D'Angelo (who had shown himself as a more moderate officer in the early camp Osthofen), Deubel championed new methods of prisoner reform, including lessons in math and foreign languages in a so-called camp school. He even suggested sending a Communist on a Nazi-sponsored cruise to win him over for the national community.

Significant as the Deubel era was, as early evidence that the KL did not move inexorably from bad to worse, it was short-lived. Eicke soon attacked Deubel for compromising the flagship KL, and inside Dachau, too, hard-line guards complained about the "disgusting humane treatment" of inmates. In late March 1936, Eicke had enough and removed Deubel. As with other failed officers, the principle of SS comradeship dictated that he would get another chance. But after Deubel spent a few unhappy months as commandant of the Columbia House, Eicke kicked him out as "completely unsuitable." Soon after, Deubel found himself back in his old job in the customs office.[250]

His place in Dachau was taken by the forty-year-old Oberführer Hans Loritz, who would become a pivotal figure in the Camp SS. His background was remarkably similar to Deubel's. Here was another First World War veteran and former POW, whose humdrum life as a civil servant in the Weimar years had become secondary to his SS career (he had joined in 1930). In one crucial respect, however, Loritz was different. He had volunteered for the KL, professing a deep admiration for Eicke, and had already proven himself as uncompromising during his tenure as commandant of Esterwegen.[251]

Loritz, a coarse and barrel-chested man with small dark eyes and a black Hitler moustache, did not disappoint after he arrived in Dachau in spring 1936. In several letters to Eicke, he posed as the defender of the Camp SS spirit. He banned the camp school and denounced Deubel's "lazy" regime, with its almost "comradely" treatment of prisoners, vowing to clean up the "muck." Loritz started as he meant to go on, and supervised a mass flogging during his first prisoner roll call. Nicknamed Nero by the prisoners, he even laid hands on prisoners himself.[252] Those officers who followed his lead prospered. They included the new Dachau camp compound leader Jakob Weiseborn—another notoriously brutal Camp SS man—who succeeded the "soft as butter" D'Angelo (as Eicke put it when he dismissed him). This was part of a major reshuffle, as Loritz purged men tainted by Deubel's regime and brought in veterans from other KL. The result was a sharp rise in the Dachau death rate.[253]

The appointment of Hans Loritz in Dachau signaled the beginning of a more coherent SS personnel policy. Following the consolidation of the KL system in the mid-1930s, several hastily appointed "old fighters" like Deubel were dismissed as commandants. They were replaced by a new breed of SS men, who had learned their trade inside the camps. The system became more stable as a result; Loritz, for example, served for more than three years in Dachau, followed by more than two years in Sachsenhausen.[254]

Dachau remained the most promising springboard for ambitious Camp SS men. Seven of its ten prewar camp compound leaders were later promoted to commandant, among them Jakob Weiseborn, who headed Flossenbürg from 1938. Prior to his appointment, he had been dispatched in 1936 from Dachau as camp compound leader to Sachsenhausen, highlighting another element of the emerging SS personnel policy: through the transfer of committed officers, Eicke exported the Camp SS spirit from established KL to new ones.[255] Like Weiseborn, most of the senior Sachsenhausen staff were KL veterans; the leader of the Guard Troop, for example, was none other than Eicke's old confidant Michael Lippert. The same process repeated itself in summer 1937, when Buchenwald was established. This time, trusted SS men arrived from Sachsenhausen, including Lippert, Weiseborn, and the commandant Obersturmbannführer Koch, who would dominate the new camp for over four years.[256]

Karl Otto Koch was the leading SS commandant of the prewar years, together with Hans Loritz. Another keen soldier, he had experienced the German defeat in the First World War in British captivity. Koch struggled through a succession of white-collar jobs during the Weimar years and became unemployed in 1932. He then devoted himself fully to the Nazi movement, having joined the SS one year earlier. His official KL career began in October 1934, when, aged thirty-seven, he became commandant of Sachsenburg. Over the following months, he held the same position in Lichtenburg, Columbia House, and Esterwegen, before his appointment as Sachsenhausen commandant in September 1936. The flabby and balding Koch, who had once been a bank clerk, now modeled himself as the ideal political soldier. He even got married in the forest around Sachsenhausen, wedding his second wife

Ilse in a ghostly nighttime ceremony surrounded by uniformed Camp SS men holding torches.[257]

Koch was a cruel commandant and unforgiving superior. Not content with terrorizing the prisoners, he micromanaged the lives of his staff. Some of his SS men, in turn, were weary of Koch. The prisoners, meanwhile, despised him. It was hard to decide, a Buchenwald survivor wrote in 1945, which was Koch's most evil trait, "his sadism, his brutality, his perversity, or his corruption."[258] For now, none of these features slowed his career. On the contrary, Koch's brutality strengthened his standing. Eicke relied on him, as he did on Loritz, and sought their opinion when it came to the appointment of other senior Camp SS officials.[259]

By the late 1930s, Theodor Eicke had molded the Camp SS into a rather cohesive corps, more uniform than ever before or after. Close networks had formed, bound together by patronage, comradeship, and nepotism, rather than formal hierarchical structures. However, the Camp SS was far from united. There was plenty of disaffection at the fringes and infighting at the core. What is more, the KL failed to attract the cream among SS recruits, leaving Eicke with limited choice when it came to senior positions. He was stuck with some men he regarded as utterly unsuitable, like Karl Künstler. A senior officer in the Dachau Guard Troop, Sturmbannführer Künstler fell out of favor after a drunken rampage. Künstler had behaved "like a brewer's drayman," Eicke fumed, adding that the miscreant was a bad influence on his men. As punishment, Künstler was sent into the wilderness, serving from January 15, 1939, in a Death's Head reserve regiment in eastern Germany, on reduced pay. But Eicke immediately recalled him. Following the unexpected death of Jakob Weiseborn on January 20, 1939, Eicke urgently needed an experienced officer to fill in as Flossenbürg commandant. Installed just a few days later, Künstler would oversee the camp's descent into mass death during the following years, which claimed the lives of thousands of inmates.[260]

PRISONER WORLDS

In the wake of SS coordination, a more standardized concentration camp system had emerged in the mid-1930s. The outlines of different camps began to resemble one another, as did the background and careers of the staff. The SS also imposed greater uniformity on prisoners. Inmates even began to look alike: by 1936, most male prisoners had their hair shorn on arrival and at regular (often weekly) intervals thereafter.[261] Later on, from around 1938, they wore identical uniforms, too. Instead of the assorted clothes of earlier

years—a colorful jumble of civilian outfits, old police garments, and more—
prisoners were dressed in the same striped clothing, the so-called zebra uniform, blue and white in summer, blue and gray in winter, with numbers sewn
on jackets and trousers. In the small early camps, guards had often addressed
inmates by name; in the large KL of the late 1930s, prisoners were reduced
to numbers.[262]

Newcomers often felt lost among the sea of seemingly identical inmates.
But when they looked more closely, they soon noticed different prisoner
groups and hierarchies. Some prisoners were better dressed, housed, and
groomed than others, for example, and it was they who often wore signs that
identified them as so-called Kapos.[263] There were also badges for different
prisoner backgrounds. Pioneered in some early camps, such insignia were
standardized around 1937–38, when the Camp SS placed colored triangles on
trousers and jackets to differentiate inmates according to the grounds for
their detention.[264] The color of the triangle had a profound impact on prisoner lives in the camps, and so did their gender, with men and women facing
very different treatment.

Daily Lives

No day was ever the same in the KL. Schedules varied, depending on the
camp, the season, and the year. Also, the SS men, masters over time in the
camp, did not want life to become too predictable, keeping inmates in a state
of suspense. Every day, prisoners woke up dreading the terror of the known
and of the unknown, aware that their repetitive daily grind might be interrupted at any moment by a spell of unscripted SS abuse.[265] Still, the stream-
lining of the camps created similar routines. In all camps, days were split into
distinct segments, marked by sirens or bells sounding across the grounds—
yet another element borrowed from the regimented life in the army and
the prison.[266]

An average day in a concentration camp for men began very early, when it
was still dark outside; during the summer, the inmates had to rise around
4:00 a.m. or even earlier. Prisoners splashed some water on their faces and
bodies, wolfed down breakfast (bread or porridge, with tea or ersatz coffee),
hastily washed tin cups and plates, stored them in lockers, and attended to
the "bed building." Then prisoners left their quarters and marched to morning
roll call, in a "silent, speedy, and military manner," as the Buchenwald camp
compound leader demanded in 1937. Weak and sick inmates were supported
by others, as the roll call was obligatory for all (except those in the infirmary).
Once all prisoners were assembled, the SS report leader verified the total

number; if there were mistakes, prisoners had to stand for a long time, some-times hours. During roll call, SS officers also made announcements over loudspeakers and ordered brief military drills, while block leaders punished alleged infractions such as poor posture and dirty shoes. Finally prisoners split into their labor details and marched away at double time, often for work outside the compound.[267]

Forced labor took up most of the prisoners' daytime hours, only briefly interrupted by lunch.[268] Lunch was generally bland, often some kind of veg-etable stew with bread. Stomach complaints were frequent and so was hunger, with some prisoners suffering sharp weight loss. But overall, the food was just about bearable. From the vantage point of prisoners who went through the wartime KL, it was positively rich in retrospect, not least because inmates were allowed to augment their daily rations. Although relatives were now banned from sending food (or any other goods), they could transfer small sums of money to prisoners for additional supplies in SS-run canteens. In Dachau, an inmate who received four Reichsmark a week in 1938 could pur-chase half a pound of butter, half a pound of biscuits, a tin of herring or sar-dines, some artificial honey, a few personal goods like soap, shoelaces, or toothpaste, a few dozen cubes of sugar, and two packs of cigarettes (in-mates were allowed to smoke after meals and also used cigarettes as an unof-ficial currency).[269]

The early evening roll call, following the return of all external labor de-tails, was particularly feared by prisoners. Exhausted, they had to stand to attention, irrespective of the weather, until the SS determined the final tally. SS men liked to prolong the prisoners' agony, forcing them to sing songs or making them watch the execution of official punishments. Finally prisoners went off for dinner in their quarters, eating some more soup, or bread and cheese. Afterward, they sometimes endured more forced labor inside the com-pound or performed chores like cleaning their uniforms. However, prisoners also snatched some spare time. Private conversations were officially forbid-den for much of the day, but now prisoners came together and talked; others read Nazi newspapers (which they paid for). Then taps sounded—between 8:00 p.m. and 9:00 p.m.—and prisoners had to move inside their quarters. Some spent a few more minutes reading, but soon the siren sounded for lights off. Prisoners were now forbidden to leave their quarters, at the threat of death, and fell into a fitful and uneasy sleep, never long enough before they had to face another day in the KL.[270]

Most prisoners looked forward to Sundays, which followed a different rhythm. While prisoners occasionally worked, for once labor did not take center stage. SS men still dictated life in the compounds, of course. Sometimes they insisted on longer roll calls and forced prisoners to polish their quarters. Or they would blast speeches by Nazi leaders and approved music from loudspeakers (as they did on some weekday evenings), or oversee orchestra performances. Following the establishment of the first official prisoner orchestra in Esterwegen in 1935, several KL set up similar ensembles, whose main function was to perform for SS and prisoners.[271] At first, there were also religious Sunday services, as in regular prisons. Even in Dachau, the SS initially allowed a local priest to celebrate mass on the roll call square. During the wider Nazi confrontation with the churches in the mid-1930s, however, such services petered out and were eventually banned altogether by Himmler.[272]

Despite their dominance, the SS stranglehold over the KL was never absolute. Although some guards hated the idea of prisoners "idling," reduced staffing levels on Sundays meant that SS control had to be relaxed, leaving more space for prisoner initiative. Occasionally, they were permitted to play sports outside their quarters. More often, they sat inside and played board games or read. Initially, some inmates had been allowed to keep their own books, though this changed later on. When Hans Litten was moved from Lichtenburg to Buchenwald in 1937, he had to send home his entire collection. "You can well imagine what that means to me," he wrote to his mother in despair. Litten now had to rely on rudimentary camp libraries that had sprung up since 1933, sometimes funded with monies extorted from prisoners. Though the SS purchased plenty of propaganda tracts, there were enough books—almost six thousand titles in Buchenwald by autumn 1939—to include the occasional gem.[273]

Inmates also used their spare time to write to loved ones. Prisoners could send a brief letter or postcard every week or two, though they had to stay clear of any topic that could be construed as criticism; the ideal letter, one prisoner recounted, would have read something like this: "Thanks for the money, thanks for the mail, I am fine, all is well, your Hans." Bland as most messages inevitably were, they gained added significance, as visits were now only allowed in exceptional circumstances. Delayed or withheld letters could therefore cause alarm among relatives, who were already under great strain. Sometime in 1938, the wife of a Dachau prisoner contacted the commandant's office, asking bluntly: "Have you shot my husband, because no mail is arriving anymore?"[274]

In principle, all prisoner activities took place within a narrow space demarcated by the SS. In practice, prisoners often used this space to undermine

SS control. They smuggled hidden references into letters, as we have already seen. Similarly, prisoners from early on subverted artistic performances sanctioned by the SS. Take the "Circus Concentracani" in Börgermoor. One Sunday afternoon in August 1933, a group of prisoners directed by the actor Wolfgang Langhoff put on a show of acrobatics, dance, and music, including the premiere of the defiant "Song of the Moorland Soldiers." They made jokes at the expense of SS men, too, who watched in amusement and some disbelief. Such daring displays were very rare, however, especially after the SS tightened its grip on the camps. In the later 1930s, the SS allowed only a few cabaret performances, wary of blurring the boundaries between oppressors and oppressed. Of course, prisoners did not always seek SS permission to act, and also asserted their identities during illicit cultural, religious, and political meetings.[275]

Kapos

One of the secrets of the success of the KL, Heinrich Himmler told German generals in summer 1944, was the deployment of prisoners as surrogate guards. This ingenious scheme for "holding down subhumans," he added, had been pioneered by Theodor Eicke. A few select inmates, Himmler explained, forced others to work hard, keep clean, and make their beds. These prisoner supervisors were known, Himmler added, as "so-called Kapos."[276] Himmler was right to regard the Kapo, a word widely thought to derive from the Italian capo (head or leader), as a central cog in the Camp SS machinery of terror. Indeed, it had proven so effective in the prewar KL—allowing a small gang of SS men to dominate large camps and driving a wedge between prisoners—that Nazi officials later introduced a similar mechanism of "divide and rule" in Jewish ghettos and slave labor camps.[277]

The origins of the Kapo system, however, were very different from the airbrushed picture Himmler presented in 1944. To start with, there was nothing new about co-opting prisoners.[278] In German prisons, inmates had long been appointed to menial positions as "trusties" (back in 1927, for example, Rudolf Höss became a clerk in the Brandenburg penitentiary, following his conviction for homicide). Since many KL inmates had previously spent time inside Nazi prisons, they were already familiar with the idea of assuming influential posts. "We arrived from the penitentiary," one Communist activist later described his arrival in Buchenwald, "and were used to a comrade serving as a trusty."[279] What distinguished the KL was not the deployment of prisoners as such, but the powers some Kapos gained.

Neither was Theodor Eicke the creator of the Kapo structure, as Himmler claimed in his bid to depict the KL as products of intelligent SS design. In truth, such purpose and planning had often been lacking during the birth of the camps. In some early camps, it had been the prisoners themselves—well versed in the practice of political organization—who selected representatives for overseeing order and taking grievances to the authorities. Shortly after Wolfgang Langhoff arrived in the protective custody wing in Düsseldorf prison in spring 1933, the inmates, mostly Communist workers, elected a young KPD functionary called Kurt as their leader. In other early camps, such appointments were initiated by the SS or SA, but it was still the prisoners who selected their own spokesmen. When Langhoff was transferred to Börgermoor in summer 1933, the deputy commandant told the new arrivals to pick a block elder; following lengthy discussions, the prisoners elected the same man who had led them back in Düsseldorf, Kurt, who then gave a brief speech, recorded in Langhoff's memoirs. The most important thing, Kurt told the others, was "to demonstrate to the SS, by our impeccable order and discipline, that we are not subhumans"—inadvertently summing up the appeal of the Kapo system for the captors.[280]

The Kapo system was firmly entrenched by the mid-1930s and continued to grow as the KL expanded. At the end of 1938, for example, when Buchenwald held around eleven thousand prisoners in all, there were over five hundred Kapos.[281] Senior Kapos were now appointed by the SS—though the officers often listened to proposals by prominent prisoners—and formed a parallel organizational structure to the SS.

Broadly speaking, Kapos fell into three functional groups. The first were the work supervisors, with larger labor details—sometimes holding hundreds of inmates—having several prisoner foremen in addition to a chief Kapo. Such Kapos had various duties, like reporting delays and preventing escape. Above all, they had to be "good slave driver[s]," as one survivor put it. SS expectations were summed up in an internal manual: "The Kapo is responsible for the strictest implementation of all orders and for all incidents in the labor detail."[282]

Second, there were Kapos who supervised prisoner life inside the quarters. Each barrack (or block, as it was often called) was led by a block elder, supported by a few block service inmates, room elders, and table elders. In the absence of SS guards, who only entered the barracks intermittently, the block elder held full authority. Each morning, he supervised the rigorous routine after reveille. Then he led his prisoners to the roll call square, where he reported the tally to the SS. After the others had left for work, he would inspect the barrack, to ensure—as SS regulations demanded—that beds were made "impeccably" and no "work-shy prisoners" were hiding inside (only the block elder and his men were allowed into barracks during the day). Come evening, he controlled the distribution of food, reported missing prisoners, initiated new arrivals, and prepared for lights-out. Afterward, he was "responsible for quiet at night," as the SS regulations stated.[283]

Finally, more and more inmates served as Kapos in the camp administration. Prisoners had already been drafted as orderlies into infirmaries of some early camps, a practice that would become more widespread from the late 1930s.[284] Kapos also worked in the prisoner kitchen, storeroom, and bunker, and as clerks in various SS offices. At the top of the hierarchy stood the camp elder (often with two deputies), who supervised the other Kapos and reported to the SS, acting as the main conduit between oppressors and oppressed. Few prisoners were mightier than the camp elder. However, it was a dangerous post, and by no means all inmates aspired to it. The political prisoner Harry Naujoks, for instance, initially resisted attempts by others to install him in Sachsenhausen, until some of his Communist comrades—who dominated Kapo positions in the prewar concentration camps—persuaded him to accept. His general strategy, Naujoks wrote in his memoirs, was to make Kapos indispensable by ensuring the smooth operation of roll calls and labor details, thereby keeping the SS at bay. But he knew that the SS wanted more, aiming to use Kapos as auxiliaries of terror. How individual Kapos reacted to these pressures and how they used their "small room for maneuver," as Naujoks called it, determined their standing among the rest of the inmates. Some became the scourges of prisoner lives; others, like Naujoks, won a reputation for decency.[285]

All Kapos gained a measure of influence over other prisoners, and some enjoyed great powers, issuing commands and hitting out.[286] This led some inmates to speak of the Kapo system as a form of "self-administration," a term widely adopted in the historical literature.[287] But the term is misleading, implying a level of autonomous decision-making absent in the KL.[288] After all, Kapos had to serve, first and foremost, the wider interests of the SS; block elders reported to SS block leaders, medical orderlies to SS doctors, labor supervisors to SS commando leaders, and so on. A Kapo who failed to fulfill SS expectations faced punishment and dismissal.[289] Despite the privileges that came with being a Kapo, then, it was a precarious existence. Even Harry Naujoks, who was more adept at playing the SS than most, did not last. After he had spent three and a half years as Sachsenhausen camp elder, the SS one day threw him into the bunker, accusing him of a Communist conspiracy, and then dispatched him to another camp.[290]

Inmate Groups

"The camps were a veritable circus, as far as colors, markings, and special designations are concerned," the Buchenwald survivor Eugen Kogon wrote shortly after the war, ridiculing the SS obsession with emblems, acronyms, and badges.[291] Triangles—which came in eight colors, with various additional markings—became the main visual markers to differentiate the prisoner population. Of course, the classification by the camps' political office was often erratic. Some Communists who had fought the Nazis were designated as asocials, while some Jews who had broken anti-Semitic laws were labeled as professional criminals.[292] Nonetheless, Camp SS men relied on the triangles for initial guidance, and prisoners, too, used these SS symbols to distinguish one another. The color of the triangle shaped each inmate's identity, whether they liked it or not.

Until 1938, the majority of inmates were classified as political prisoners, mostly wearing red markings on their uniforms.[293] In November 1936, for example, the authorities identified 3,694 of all 4,761 concentration camp inmates as political prisoners.[294] Among them was a hard core of political activists, first and foremost Communists.[295] Many were veterans of the early camps. Following their release in 1933–34, they had often rejoined the underground resistance and soon found themselves back in the KL.[296] On Himmler's orders, issued in March 1936, such prisoners, held for a second time, faced extra punishment and were only considered for release after a minimum of three years (not three months, as in the case of other inmates).[297] In Dachau, there were an estimated two hundred so-called second-time-rounders by early 1937, wearing special markings. Their barrack was fenced off from the rest of the compound, effectively creating a camp inside the camp. For the first time, an entire group of inmates was isolated from the others, setting an inauspicious precedent. These second-time-rounders received no books, fewer letters, and less medical care, while facing the most exhausting work. One of the prisoners was the German-Jewish lawyer Ludwig Bendix, whose time in Dachau in 1937 was a far cry from his first spell in protective custody back in 1933. Bendix, who was now weak and ill, experienced Dachau as a martyrdom "which I feared I would not survive and which I could only bear by mobilizing all my strength."[298]

Despite Himmler's obsession with left-wing opponents, the overall proportion of underground activists among KL inmates decreased in the mid-1930s, reflecting both the gradual demise of the resistance and the general shift to policing other forms of deviance. When it came to opposition against the regime, the police now cast its net wider than before. Grumbling and dissent probably accounted for some twenty percent of all protective custody cases in 1935–36; in some months, as many individuals were detained for jokes or verbal attacks as for Communist activities.[299] It did not take much to be branded a dangerous enemy of the state. Magdalene Kassebaum, for example, endured two spells in Moringen, first for singing "The International," then for burning a picture of Hitler.[300]

The police also detained some clergymen, part of the wider Nazi confrontation with Christian churches in the mid-1930s. Although the number of arrests remained very small—no more than a few dozen Catholic and Protestant priests were held in the KL in 1935—they carried symbolic weight and caused some disquiet within German society.[301] The clergymen, who had to wear the red markings of political prisoners, were frequently singled out for violent abuse. The Camp SS was militant in its anticlericalism, even more so than the general SS, and most men renounced the Church, goaded by the fanatical Eicke, who summed up his views as follows: "Prayer books are things for women and for those who wear panties. We hate the stink of incense."[302] Eicke's hatred erupted spectacularly in 1935, after the Berlin Cathedral chaplain Bernhard Lichtenberg had privately questioned the conditions in Esterwegen. Responding to the accusations in a note to the Gestapo, Eicke blasted the interference of "Rome's black agents," who "leave their excrement on the altars," complained about the stain of "poisonous state-eroding saliva" on his SS uniform, and called for Lichtenberg to be sent to Esterwegen himself.[303] Many guards emulated Eicke when they encountered imprisoned priests. So brutal were the verbal and physical assaults that even the wives of some Camp SS men expressed sympathy for the plight of clergymen.[304]

By far the largest group of religious prisoners in the mid-1930s was Jehovah's Witnesses, who, having pledged their allegiance to God, resisted the total claim of Nazism. Their persecution had started early in the Third Reich and soon intensified, after they refused to serve in the new German conscript army, continued to proselytize after their religious association was banned, and distributed critical leaflets. The regime tried to stamp out such defiance, with some paranoid Nazi officials picturing the Witnesses as a mass movement in cahoots with Communists (in reality, they only had some twenty-five thousand members). Several thousand believers were arrested in the mid-1930s. Most ended up in regular prisons, but others were taken to the KL. At the height of repression in 1937–38, more than ten percent of all men in Sachsenhausen and Buchenwald were Jehovah's Witnesses. So large was this prisoner group that the Camp SS gave them a special insignia: the purple triangle.[305]

Prisoners with the purple triangle endured great hardship. "The Jehovah's

Witnesses are the daily targets for every kind of persecution, terror, and brutality," one of them wrote in 1938, not long after his release. Some abuse was ideologically motivated, with Camp SS men mocking their victims as "heaven clowns" and "paradise birds." Asked after the war why he had buried one of the prisoners up to the neck, the former report leader in Sachsenhausen replied: "He was a conscientious objector. As such he had no right to life, in my view."[306] What really enraged the SS men, however, was not the prisoners' religious beliefs but their "obstinate" behavior, as Jehovah's Witnesses refused to carry out certain orders and even tried to convert other prisoners.[307] The leaders of the passive resistance were hit with great venom. One of them, the miner Johann Ludwig Rachuba, was punished by the Sachsenhausen SS between 1936 and 1938 with more than 120 days strict detention, more than one hundred lashes, four hours hanging from a post, and three months in the punishment company (he later died in the camp). Such brute tactics rarely worked, however, as many prisoners saw the torture as a test of their faith. Only later in the war did SS officials become shrewder, realizing that many Jehovah's Witnesses made reliable workers as long as they were not deployed in ways that conflicted directly with their beliefs.[308]

Just as the German police continually expanded the circle of political suspects, so, too, did it widen its assault on social outsiders. The main victims were those pursued since 1933 as asocial or criminal, identified in the camps by black or green triangles. They were joined in the mid-1930s by another group: men arrested as homosexuals, who had to wear pink triangles. Following the murder of Ernst Röhm, the regime cracked down hard on homosexuality. Existing legislation became stricter in 1935 (though women were still exempt) and the police stepped up its raids, led by the obsessively homophobic Himmler; it was regrettable that gay men could not be killed, Himmler told SS leaders in 1937, but at least they could be detained. Again, the vast majority of arrested men were sent to prison, but some found themselves in the KL.[309] In 1935, these men were briefly concentrated in Lichtenburg—in June, 325 of all the 706 inmates here were classified as homosexual—but mostly they were distributed across the SS camp system.[310]

Men detained as homosexuals suffered unusually harsh treatment in the KL. The SS saw them as perverts deserving special punishment. To "protect" others, some officials put men with the pink triangle into isolated barracks. And to "cure" them, guards often forced them into particularly hard labor details, like the latrine and punishment company.[311] In addition, several prisoners were castrated. Under Nazi law, homosexuals had to consent to such operations, but Camp SS officials forced some into submission. Among them was the Hamburg tailor Otto Giering, who, having been convicted repeatedly for homosexual acts, was taken to Sachsenhausen in early 1939, at the age of twenty-two. In mid-August 1939, Giering was called to the infirmary and sedated. When he woke up, with a heavy bag of sand on his stomach, he was told that he had just been castrated. A few days later, the commandant himself walked in and triumphantly pointed to a glass: "You can have one more look at your balls, but as a conserve."[312]

SS men watched homosexual prisoners with great suspicion, and those accused of sexual contacts inside the KL were tortured to extract "confessions"; occasionally, the men were then handed over for criminal trials to courts.[313] Some of the suspects had been denounced by other inmates. Given the force of SS homophobia, accusations of homosexuality proved a potent weapon against competitors and antagonists. More generally, many fellow inmates shared the social prejudices against homosexuals and ostracized them; even sympathetic prisoners kept their distance. As soon as he received the pink triangle on his uniform, Otto Giering recalled, he was "subjected to mockery and harassment" by prisoners "of all categories"—just one example of the many rifts between inmate groups.[314]

Solidarity and Friction

Harry Naujoks felt at home inside the Communist movement. He had been born in 1901 into a poor working-class family, not far from the ships on the Hamburg docks, and the small and sturdy man even looked like a sailor, with his strangely swaying gait. He had actually trained as a boilermaker, leaving school early, and quickly became politicized in his local union. In March 1919, not yet eighteen years old, he joined the recently founded KPD and later led the party's Hamburg youth wing. Naujoks was a loyal local functionary and in 1933 joined the resistance against the Nazis. He would pay a heavy price: detention in several early camps in 1933–34, more than two years in a penitentiary, and well over eight years in the KL. Throughout, Naujoks remained devoted to the cause and was repaid with support from other Communist inmates. From the moment he set foot inside Sachsenhausen on November 11, 1936, his comrades took him under their wing. As he entered the camp, he was shown to the storeroom by a fellow Hamburg Communist; his block elder, another Hamburg comrade, told him about the most important rules of camp life; then yet another former KPD functionary from Hamburg took Naujoks to get food from the camp kitchen. At the end of his first day in Sachsenhausen, Naujoks later wrote, he already felt a sense of belonging.[315]

Newcomers from other large prisoner groups—such as Social Democrats and Jehovah's Witnesses—could count on friends and comrades for moral and material support, too.[316] Solidarity within these groups was often close and could pave the way to better positions inside the camp, as in the case of Naujoks, who was transferred in early 1937 (with the help of another old Hamburg associate) from the exhausting forest clearing detail to a coveted post as a joiner. "There are no [more] screams, no beatings, not even any pressure to work fast," Naujoks wrote. Prisoners united by a shared past maneuvered trusted individuals into Kapo positions to gain greater influence. The Communists proved particularly adept at this, thanks to their large numbers and tight discipline. Harry Naujoks himself was installed in late summer 1937 in the storeroom, beginning his rise to camp elder.[317]

Since members of the same prisoner group spent much of their free time together—because the SS tended to assign barracks based on triangle colors—these groups became focal points for collective self-assertion. In the evenings, prisoners would conduct illicit discussions and lectures about politics, religion, history, and literature. In Esterwegen, the much-weakened Carl von Ossietzky seemed to revive when he engaged fellow prisoners in debate. "It was always quite an experience to listen to him, to argue with him, to ask him questions," a former Communist prisoner recalled reverently.[318]

There were some bigger meetings, too. In Sachsenhausen, Harry Naujoks and his comrades held a first large gathering in December 1936, as SS guards were getting drunk at their staff Christmas party. The covert meeting was organized by a former KPD Reichstag deputy, who gave a brief speech, followed by the recitation of poems and songs of the labor movement. "Each one of us at that event was touched by the power of the collective, giving us the strength to withstand the terror," Naujoks wrote in his memoirs.[319] Communist prisoners were not alone in fostering a community spirit. Jewish prisoners held cultural events in their barracks—with music, poetry, and plays—and Christians came together to pray on festive days.[320]

Any more direct challenges to SS dominance remained extremely rare. In the early camps, prisoners had occasionally stood up to protest, emboldened by their belief in the imminent demise of the Third Reich.[321] But there was no sign of the Nazi regime crumbling, and by the mid-1930s SS guards took great pleasure in crushing even hints of defiance. Only a few individuals still dared to confront the SS. Among them was the Protestant pastor Paul Schneider, held in Buchenwald since late 1937. The following spring, Schneider was dragged into the bunker, where he was starved and abused for months, after he had refused to salute a new swastika flag hoisted above the main gate. But Schneider was not deterred. On Sundays and holy days, he sometimes shouted brief words of encouragement from the bunker to prisoners on the roll call square, before furious SS guards silenced him with whips and fists; his voice finally fell quiet in summer 1939, following a deadly injection by the SS doctor.[322]

The bold defiance of prisoners like Pastor Schneider briefly united inmates of all backgrounds in admiration. Such unity was rare, however, as the KL bred much division and discord. The most pronounced chasm, at least until the late 1930s, existed within the large group of left-wing prisoners, between German Communists and Social Democrats. The long history of antagonism between the parties—with each accusing the other of betraying the working class and enabling the rise of the Nazis—often crippled closer contacts in the camps.[323]

In the early camps, Communists and Social Democrats were still sore from their recent clashes during the Weimar Republic. True, there was some solidarity across party lines, especially among the rank and file. But many revolutionary Communists had not forgotten their suppression at the hands of the pro-democratic forces in Prussia and elsewhere, and openly snubbed SPD-affiliated prisoners. Some Social Democrats, in turn, were dismayed at being sidelined by the more numerous and better organized Communists; one complained that Communists in his barrack treated him "like a leper," while another lamented the absence of even "a minimum of comradeship." On occasion, Communist inmates even denounced SPD prisoners to the camp authorities, or attacked them physically.[324] Former SPD leaders, ridiculed as "bigwigs" by Communists and Nazis alike, endured the greatest hostility. Ernst Heilmann, for example, had been known for his uncompromising opposition to the KPD and did not change his views in captivity, earning him the lasting contempt of Communists in all the camps he was dragged through; no one had a trace of sympathy or compassion for him, the Communist Wolfgang Langhoff recalled. Apparently, guards also ordered KPD inmates to assault Heilmann, typical of SS attempts to inflame existing tensions between left-wing prisoners.[325]

The conflicts between left-wingers continued into the mid-1930s and beyond. The scars of the Weimar battles healed only slowly, if at all, and there were repeated clashes over the distribution of Kapo posts, with Social Democrats complaining about Communist domination. Some individual friendships evolved, as they had done in the early camps, and open-minded prisoners like Harry Naujoks reached out and supported others irrespective of political differences. But the dominant mode was still that of mutual distrust, and the Left never formed a united front in Nazi captivity.[326]

Women in the Camps

It seemed a day like any other when, one Friday morning in early 1936, a guard unlocked Centa Beimler's cell in Stadelheim. She expected to be escorted to work, as usual, but there was exciting news: she was about to leave the prison. Beimler began to hope that she would finally be set free, almost three years after her arrest. But the Gestapo had other plans. As long as her husband Hans remained at large, following his spectacular escape from Dachau, his wife would stay put. Rather than being released, Centa Beimler was moved from Stadelheim to the Moringen workhouse, which had become the central German protective custody camp for women.[327]

Fortunately for Centa Beimler, Moringen was a world away from the camps for men. Moringen was not even an official SS concentration camp, as it was still controlled by the Prussian state, not by the IKL; its civilian director—a rule-bound bureaucrat from the civil service—was the antithesis of Eicke's "political soldier." Compared to the KL, inmate numbers were much smaller, with a monthly average of no more than ninety women on the protective custody wing. These women wore their own clothes, not uniforms, and faced monotonous but bearable labor; most of them knitted or mended clothes, working for less than eight hours a day. Most important of all, there were no physical assaults by the staff.[328]

On the whole, Moringen resembled a regular prison, with many of the related hardships, like rigid schedules, bland food, and poor hygiene. However, the Moringen women—divided into several communal rooms and dormitories, according to their backgrounds—could mingle relatively freely. After her long time in a tiny cell in Stadelheim, Centa Beimler was grateful for the company of other Communists, including her own sister. The women played games and sang together, and held political discussions. "You could talk about everything, and that made it easier for all of us," Beimler later wrote.[329]

Centa Beimler was a leading figure among the Communist women of Moringen. Her husband, Hans, was a hero of the resistance, while Centa impressed even prisoners of different beliefs with her strength of will, unbowed by her long imprisonment.[330] But the women around Centa Beimler did not dominate Moringen in the same way Communist men did in the KL. For a start, female Kapos gained far less power and influence.[331] Moreover, the prisoner population in Moringen was more diverse. Jehovah's Witnesses made up a sizable proportion already in 1935, reflecting the high level of female activists, and during 1937 they became the largest prisoner group; by November, around half of the protective custody prisoners were Jehovah's Witnesses.[332]

These changes in Moringen went hand in hand with sharply rising prisoner numbers, up from 92 in early January 1937 to around 450 in November 1937.[333] Centa Beimler herself was no longer among them, having been released in February under tragic circumstances. Several months earlier, the Communist women in Moringen had heard that Hans Beimler was fighting with the International Brigade during the Spanish Civil War, further boosting his reputation. Then rumors spread that he had been killed during the defense of Madrid. Centa Beimler was tormented by uncertainty—she "walked around more dead than alive," one fellow inmate recalled—until the director confirmed the news. Soon after, she was set free. Now that her husband was dead, the Nazis no longer needed her as a hostage; her sister followed a few months later.[334] Most other inmates, however, stayed behind until the entire protective custody wing in Moringen was closed down and all remaining prisoners were transferred to Lichtenburg.

Opened in December 1937, Lichtenburg was the first KL for women. It had taken Theodor Eicke three years to establish such a camp, highlighting the peripheral place of female prisoners in his vision; for him, the "enemies behind barbed wire" were men. Still, he finally felt forced to act. Not only was the detention of protective custody prisoners outside the IKL an anomaly, but the numbers of female inmates just kept on rising. Moringen was becoming too small, as Himmler himself had seen during an inspection in late May 1937, while the bigger Lichtenburg stood empty after its closure as a camp for men. It was quickly redesignated and soon filled up again; by April 1939, 1,065 women were held inside.[335]

Upon arrival in Lichtenburg, Erna Ludolph—a Jehovah's Witness from Lübeck—immediately realized that the premises were much bigger than Moringen. Soon, Ludolph and the others saw further differences, almost all for the worse. As an SS camp, Lichtenburg was run along far more military lines, with roll calls in the corridors and the yard. Leisure time was cut back and forced labor extended by about two hours. The SS also made far greater use of Kapos. Above all, the women endured harder punishment and occasional violence. Jehovah's Witnesses made up the largest prisoner group, and conditions were particularly grim for those, like Erna Ludolph, who were isolated as "incorrigible." One day in 1938, after these women refused to line up to a radio speech by Hitler, the guards attacked them and sprayed them with high-pressure water hoses.[336]

Although the local SS staff ensured the stricter treatment of female prisoners, they stopped well short of running Lichtenburg like a KL for men. It developed a distinct identity all its own, removed from the other SS concentration camps. The differences started with the camp's appearance. The old castle in Lichtenburg, with its large dormitories, was a long way from the SS ideal of a modern barrack camp. More generally, the Lichtenburg women faced less terror than male KL prisoners. Forced labor was not yet all-consuming, violent excesses were infrequent, and punishments were less severe (according to the official regulations, there was no flogging, for example). As a result, the death rate was very low, with two confirmed prisoner deaths—both of them Jehovah's Witnesses—between late 1937 and spring 1939, when the SS closed down the KL Lichtenburg.[337]

"In the middle of May 1939," Erna Ludolph recalled after the war, "we Jehovah's Witnesses, all 400 to 450 of us, were brought by truck with the first mass transports to Ravensbrück." Expecting the number of female prisoners to grow further, SS officials had decided sometime in 1938 to establish an entirely new camp for women. After plans to build it near Dachau fell through, attention soon turned to a secluded site by the town of Fürstenberg, some fifty miles or so north of Berlin. Once a small detachment of men from Sachsenhausen had erected the first barracks and buildings in the early months of 1939, the new camp, called Ravensbrück, was ready.[338]

The prisoners' living conditions deteriorated after the move from Lichtenburg, just as they had done after the prior move from Moringen. "Everything escalated to an unbelievable degree," Erna Ludolph recalled. Roll calls in Ravensbrück were more torturous, forced labor more exhausting, punishment more severe, and life more rigid, with women now wearing identical dresses with blue and gray stripes, as well as an apron and headscarf.[339] Still, terror remained gender-specific, as the Camp SS continued to reserve its most violent abuse for men. Although flogging was introduced as an official punishment in Ravensbrück, some other excesses, including hanging from a post, were still absent. Instead of brutal assaults, the local SS relied more heavily on guard dogs, because Himmler believed that women would be particularly scared of them.[340]

The special status of Ravensbrück shaped its staff, too. When the SS first decided to open a concentration camp for women, it faced a dilemma. Until now, the Camp SS had been conceived as an exclusive male club, resting on hypermasculine values. But the deployment of men in a women's camp was problematic, as the sexual abuses in early camps had shown. In the end, Himmler opted for a compromise. In Lichtenburg and Ravensbrück, SS men acted as sentries and occupied the senior positions in the Commandant Staff, starting with the commandant himself. The guards inside, however, who had most day-to-day contacts with prisoners, were women, though Himmler balked at admitting them into the SS; although female guards were part of the Camp SS, they were never full SS members. Even during the war, when they came under the jurisdiction of the SS, these women merely belonged to its retinue (*Gefolge*), wearing special field-gray uniforms.[341]

The female guards of Ravensbrück differed from their male counterparts in other SS camps. True, most of them were volunteers, too, often in their mid to late twenties, but they normally had no previous history of political violence; the brawls of the Weimar and early Nazi years had been a male domain. Also, only a fraction of the female guards were NSDAP members, while the bulk of SS men had signed up with the party. What attracted most female recruits to the KL was not any ideological mission, but the prospect of social advancement. Many were poor and unmarried, with few professional qualifications, and the camp promised regular employment with decent pay and other benefits, such as comfortable quarters and even (from 1941) an SS kindergarten.[342] Once inside Ravensbrück, the lives of the female guards were strictly regimented, though they were never subject to the same drill as male "political soldiers"; indeed, the frustrated Ravensbrück commandant repeatedly reprimanded his female guards for breaches of military decorum.[343]

For now, women remained marginal in the KL system, both as guards and as inmates. True, the overall proportion of female prisoners was rising fast—from around 3.3 percent in late summer 1938 to 11.7 percent one year later—but Ravensbrück still lagged far behind concentration camps for men, both in size and severity.[344] Nonetheless, its creation was significant, concluding the shift from the more traditional detention of women to the new forms of SS domination.[345]

The camps for women were late additions to the KL system, which had been created and cemented in the mid-1930s. Toward the end of 1934, it seemed as if the camps might disappear. Just three years later, they were firm fixtures of the Third Reich, outside the law, funded by the state and controlled by a new agency, the IKL. The SS had also developed a basic blueprint for the KL, drawing on its first camp at Dachau. Its key features were a uniform administrative structure, a common architectural ideal, a professional corps of SS men, and a systematic brand of terror. The simultaneous extension of the SS system—the prisoner population rose from around 3,800 in summer 1935 to 7,746 at the end of 1937—points to another key aspect of the KL, first highlighted by Hannah Arendt shortly after the Second World War. In a radical totalitarian state like the Third Reich, terror did not decrease after the regime established itself. Nazi leaders pursued ever more extreme aims, and so the KL expanded, even as domestic political opposition diminished.[346] This extension was not yet over by late 1937; it was only just beginning.

3

Expansion

Friday the thirteenth of May 1938 was a date etched into the memory of Buchenwald prisoners. The day had begun balmy and bright; spring was in the air and the countryside around the camp glowed vibrantly. It was still early in the morning, with the sun rising fast across the clear sky above the Ettersberg, but a large prisoner detail was already hard at work in the forest outside the camp, digging trenches for sewage pipes. At around nine o'clock, two of the prisoners, Emil Bargatzky and Peter Forster, went to collect coffee for the others, as usual, walking along a secluded path when they suddenly attacked the guard who escorted them. Before he had time to fire his rifle, SS Rottenführer Albert Kallweit was hit over the head with a spade. The two prisoners, who had long planned their escape, dragged the guard's body into the undergrowth, grabbed his weapon, and ran for their lives.[1]

The killing of Rottenführer Kallweit sent shock waves through the SS. Successful breakouts were extremely rare since Inspector Eicke exhorted his men to shoot at fleeing prisoners without warning. And a deadly attack on the SS was unprecedented.[2] Heinrich Himmler flew to Weimar the next day to inspect the camp and Kallweit's corpse, accompanied by Theodor Eicke. He also ordered a manhunt for the escaped prisoners. Regional papers carried sensational reports about the killing of the SS man and announced a hefty reward of one thousand Reichsmark for information leading to the fugitives' capture; for weeks, the incident was the talk of the town in Weimar and beyond, a rare moment when the camps penetrated public consciousness in the late 1930s.[3]

On May 22, 1938, after Emil Bargatzky had spent nine days on the run, the police found him hiding in a brick factory some 140 miles north of Buchenwald. Within a week, he faced a hastily arranged show trial before the Weimar Special Court. Reporting on the trial, the regional press made much of his criminal record. Born into a poor family in 1901 as one of fifteen children, Bargatzky had struggled to hold down a job during the calamitous Weimar years—working as a carpenter, butcher, and coachman—and committed several offenses. The press pounced on these transgressions as further proof of his subhuman nature. The Weimar state prosecutor, meanwhile, commended the KL guards who protected the national community from dangerous asocial elements like Bargatzky. He also spoke out in favor of the "preventive" policing against social outsiders, which was intensifying during the late 1930s and swept many thousands into overcrowded concentration camps—among them Emil Bargatzky, who had been held since 1937 because of his criminal past.[4]

The judges at Bargatzky's murder trial on Saturday, May 28, took less than two hours to pronounce the death penalty. He was now on death row and faced execution by the legal authorities behind prison doors. But his fate was to take a final twist after Heinrich Himmler asked Hitler for permission to have Bargatzky hanged in Buchenwald instead, near the scene of the crime. Hitler approved.[5] Early on the morning of June 4, 1938, the Buchenwald prisoners lined up on the roll call square. SS guards surrounded them, some pointing machine guns at the crowd. Shortly before 7:00 a.m. the main gate opened and the manacled Emil Bargatzky was led onto the square, past rows of SS men. He walked as if in a trance and some prisoners speculated that the SS had drugged him. After a judge dressed in a black robe read out the death sentence, Bargatzky stepped onto a wooden box on the newly erected scaffold and put his head through a noose. On the word of Commandant Karl Otto Koch, the box was pushed away and a prisoner, designated as the executioner, pulled the rope; Bargatzky twisted and turned for several minutes until he died. The SS left his disfigured corpse dangling for some time on the roll call square, as a grisly warning to all prisoners.[6]

The SS staged this first official execution of a concentration camp inmate, which echoed ritual German executions in the early modern era, as a demonstration of might, attended by high-ranking dignitaries like Theodor Eicke, who eagerly reported the details to Himmler.[7] SS leaders brazenly turned an ignominy—two escaped inmates and a dead guard—into political capital, presenting it as proof of the barbarity of the prisoners and the fundamental importance of the camps. Already before Bargatzky's hanging, a popular SS periodical had tried to boost the status of the Camp SS in a graphic article, complete with mug shots of the two fugitives and a photo of the slain guard in heroic pose. The article, which drew heavily on Eicke's worldview, claimed that the "cowardly attack" by the two "racially inferior criminals" showed just how dangerous the mission of the political SS soldiers really was (in reality, Camp SS men were far more likely to be injured by friendly fire from other guards than by prisoners). Under the headline "He died for us!" the influential SS weekly waxed lyrical about the pasty Rottenführer Kallweit, hoping to elevate him into the pantheon of Nazi martyrs, and also praised the other unsung heroes of the Death's Head SS, who were "permanently facing the enemy" while the rest of Germany was "peacefully going about its daily business."[8] The image of SS guards as valiant guardians of the nation was meant to strike a chord at a time when Eicke was in the midst of a major recruitment drive, greatly expanding the size of the Camp SS in the run-up to war.

Most important, the Camp SS saw the death of Rottenführer Kallweit as a signal for more violence. Even in distant Dachau, guards threatened prisoners with brutal retaliation.[9] In Buchenwald itself, SS men went on a rampage. Collective punishment was common after escapes, but it reached new heights on Friday, May 13, 1938. Screaming guards beat the remaining prisoners from the sewage plant detail back to the compound, where a mob of SS men whipped and punched them until some maimed victims collapsed. The guards murdered at least two Buchenwald prisoners that day. All others, Commandant Koch demanded, would face much greater hardship in the future.[10] He was true to his word, as one assault followed another. During one such attack, some three weeks after Bargatzky's execution, SS men smashed several windows in prisoner barracks, tore up dozens of bed covers, ripped apart hundreds of straw mattresses, and left three inmates dead.[11]

SS leaders supported this hard line. In a paean to the killed guard in the *Völkischer Beobachter,* Theodor Eicke threatened that "enemies of the state" would face "iron hard" discipline.[12] Himmler said much the same during his visit to Buchenwald on May 14, 1938, and two days later, he repeated his demand for tough action in a letter to Reich minister of justice Gürtner. Earlier that spring, Himmler claimed, he had responded to a complaint by Gürtner about excessive SS shootings by ordering his men to use their weapons more sparingly, with "devastating" results. This attempt to blame Gürtner for the killing in Buchenwald was absurd—Rottenführer Kallweit had walked too closely to the two prisoners, in breach of SS protocol—but this did not stop Himmler from announcing that guards would now reach more readily for their rifles, preempting future judicial criticism.[13]

Himmler's swagger reflected his rising status in the late 1930s. To be sure, his SS was not yet all-powerful. The presence of a judge during the execution of Emil Bargatzky in Buchenwald was a reminder that a court had pronounced the death sentence, not the SS. Moreover, the execution remained an exception in the prewar KL. Still, it was a sign for the growing confidence of SS leaders and for their desire to usurp legal powers like the judicial monopoly over the death penalty. In practice, the SS already did so: Camp SS men murdered far more prisoners during the late 1930s than ever before. In Buchenwald, the SS conducted a major killing spree in the weeks after the death of Rottenführer Kallweit; in June and July 1938, 168 prisoners lost their lives, compared to seven prisoners during March and April.[14] In other camps, too, the SS stepped up its violence in the final years before the Second World War, which also saw a great expansion of KL sites and of slave labor. The relentless rise of the concentration camp complex seemed unstoppable.

SOCIAL OUTSIDERS

Heinrich Himmler had big plans for his camps. In a secret speech in November 1937, he told SS leaders that he expected the three KL for men—Dachau, Sachsenhausen, and Buchenwald—to hold twenty thousand prisoners in all, and even more in the case of war.[15] This was an ambitious aim, at a time when his camps held fewer than eight thousand prisoners. But Himmler's target was quickly reached and exceeded in 1938–39, during a frantic period that saw the foundation of the three camps in Flossenbürg, Mauthausen, and Ravensbrück. Thanks to large-scale police raids, prisoner numbers climbed fast, and by the end of June 1938, there were already twenty-four thousand or more inmates in the camps, a threefold increase in just six months.[16] Even that was not enough for police and SS leaders, who soon envisaged a further rise to thirty thousand inmates and more.[17]

As the size of the prisoner population changed, so did its composition, moving ever further away from the preponderance of left-wing German prisoners that characterized the camps early on. Camp SS officials struggled to keep up with all the new prisoner groups. In Sachsenhausen, for example, five separate prisoner categories (early 1937) became twelve (late 1939).[18] Among the new prisoners were thousands of foreigners, after Nazi leaders began to flex their muscles on the international stage. In March 1938, the Third Reich invaded and annexed Austria, and the new rulers quickly arrested tens of thousands of alleged opponents. On the evening of April 1, 1938, the new criminal police office in Vienna dispatched a first transport of Austrian prisoners—among them many members of the old political elite, including the mayor of Vienna—to Dachau; the men suffered extreme abuse on the train, which continued after their arrival the next day. "For a long time, we

Austrians were the main attraction in the camp," the nationalist politician Fritz Bock recalled. In all, 7,861 Austrian men were taken to Dachau during 1938 (almost eighty percent of them Jews).[19]

Prisoners from Czechoslovakia were next, after Hitler bullied French and British leaders into accepting the German annexation of the Sudetenland at the Munich conference. In October and November 1938, well over 1,500 prisoners from the Sudetenland arrived in Dachau, including many ethnic Germans.[20] The isolated Czechoslovakian government also succumbed to German pressure to extradite Peter Forster, who was in their hands after his escape from Buchenwald. Unlike his accomplice Emil Bargatzky, Forster had evaded the German police and managed to cross the border in late May 1938. Forster, a committed left-wing opponent of the Nazi regime, pleaded for asylum and defended the killing of the SS guard. "We acted in self-defense," he was quoted as saying, "because every prisoner in that camp lived in danger of being killed." Despite an international campaign to save him, Forster was handed over to Nazi Germany in late 1938. His fate was the same as Bargatzky's. Sentenced to death on December 21, he was hanged later that day in Buchenwald, the only other prisoner officially executed in a KL before the war.[21] After the German invasion of the remaining Czech territory in March 1939, which was designated as the Reich Protectorate of Bohemia and Moravia, the German police dragged further victims to the KL, among them numerous German émigrés and Czech Jews. However, in view of the international condemnation of Nazi aggression, the police moved rather cautiously and did not repeat the mass deportations that had followed the incorporation of Austria one year earlier.[22]

The arrival of prisoners from abroad foreshadowed the dramatic later changes in the concentration camps. Before the war, however, the number of foreigners generally remained small. In the late 1930s, the regime still saw the KL primarily as weapons against its own people, including Austrian nationals subsumed into the Third Reich (and largely classified as German by the SS). Above all, the authorities were homing in on social outsiders, who were fast becoming the main target.

Early Attacks on "Criminals" and "Asocials"

The pursuit of social deviants was a major part of the Nazi policy of exclusion, aimed at removing all those who did not (or could not) fit into the mythical national community. The motives of the officials in the welfare services, the courts, and the police were as diverse as the men and women they targeted, and often reflected demands which predated the Nazi rise to power.

Some officials had utopian visions of rooting out all social ills; some placed their trust in the teachings of racial hygiene; some hoped to stimulate the economy by terrorizing the jobless. The ensuing offensive against Germans on the margins of society led to benefit cuts and surveillance, as well as to detention, not just in traditional state institutions like prisons and work-houses, but in the concentration camps, too.[23]

The fate of social outsiders in the KL was widely ignored after the Second World War, when these prisoners joined the ranks of other forgotten victims. If writers mentioned their persecution at all, it was in a derogatory manner, describing it as a tactical maneuver by the Nazi authorities to gain popular support or to besmirch the reputation of political prisoners.[24] Only in recent decades have historians recognized the assault on social outsiders as a key Nazi policy in its own right.[25] Many historians now argue that the police and SS turned to a policy of "racial general prevention" from 1936, attacking social outsiders in a bid to "cleanse" the "body of the nation" of alleged deviants and degenerates.[26] Important as this new research has been in revealing the ideological drive behind the mass detention of social outsiders in the late 1930s, it neglects previous Nazi attacks on the same groups. While the early camps in 1933–34 were primarily about political opponents, the authorities had also used them to detain and punish social outsiders.[27]

As soon as Heinrich Himmler became Munich police president in March 1933, he declared the "eradication of the criminal class" as a priority.[28] Over the coming months, he developed his vision of policing as social cleansing, with the early camps as places of detention, retribution, and correction.[29] Himmler's approach altered his model camp Dachau already from summer 1933, when the police dragged the first alleged criminals and vagrants inside.[30] Their numbers soon increased, after the police arrested tens of thousands of beggars and homeless in nationwide raids in September 1933. Although the authorities quickly released most detainees, some ended up for longer in camps and workhouses.[31] Just a year after the SS had set up Dachau, the composition of its prisoner population had changed markedly. Political prisoners still accounted for the great majority of all Bavarian inmates in protective custody, but their proportion had fallen to around eighty percent by April 1934, with social outsiders making up the rest; among them were 142 "work-shy" men, 96 "national pests," and 82 men accused of "asocial behavior."[32]

The detention of social outsiders in Dachau did not escape the attention of the Bavarian Reich governor von Epp. During his general drive to reduce prisoner numbers, Epp protested in March 1934 that the arrest of alleged criminals and asocials violated the "meaning and purpose of protective custody."[33]

Himmler was undeterred. In the rude reply he drafted (see chapter 2), he dismissed any criticism and spelled out his wider convictions: "The observation that imposition of protective custody for alcoholism, firewood theft, embezzlement of moneys belonging to organizations, immoral lifestyle, work shirking, etc., does not quite correspond to the letter of the valid regulations, is entirely accurate. It does, however, correspond to National Socialist sentiment." In Himmler's mind, Nazi "sentiment" trumped everything, including the law. Because the courts did not deal swiftly and firmly with asocials and criminals, he argued, the police had to take the suspects to Dachau. The results, he added, were impressive: the arrests played "the most essential part in the decline of criminality in Bavaria." Himmler saw no reason to change course.[34]

Heinrich Himmler may have faced some internal critics, but he was not alone in his aggressive pursuit of social outsiders.[35] All over Germany, state and party officials placed social outsiders into protective custody during 1933–34, with the initiative often coming from below. In Hamburg, the police temporarily arrested hundreds of beggars, pimps, and homeless in 1933, as well as several thousand female prostitutes. Elsewhere, too, Nazi officials moved against so-called asocials, especially after the "beggar raid" in September; on October 4, 1933, the *Völkischer Beobachter* reported on the "first concentration camp for beggars" in Meseritz (Posen).[36]

As for the fight against crime, Prussia pursued an even more radical policy than Bavaria in 1933, inspired by a nationwide offensive against persistent criminals. German jurists had pushed for years for indefinite sentences against dangerous re-offenders and their wish finally came true in the Third Reich. Under the Habitual Criminals Law of November 24, 1933, judges could punish defendants with custodial sentences followed by open-ended security confinement (*Sicherungsverwahrung*) in a prison or penitentiary; by 1939, judges had passed almost ten thousand such sentences, chiefly against minor property offenders.[37] However, senior Prussian police officers saw the new law as deficient, since it only targeted those found guilty of new crimes. To wipe out the criminal underclass, they argued, it was also necessary to detain "professional criminals" who could not be brought to court due to insufficient evidence. Hermann Göring shared this view and had introduced preventive police custody (*polizeiliche Vorbeugungshaft*) by decree on November 13, 1933. From now on, the Prussian criminal police could hold so-called professional criminals in state concentration camps without trial or sentence. The main targets were ex-convicts with long criminal records for property offenses; but even someone who had never been tried before could be detained if the police alleged "criminal intent."[38]

At the time, the Prussian criminal police did not envisage mass arrests.

Senior police officials believed that a small hard core of offenders was responsible for the great majority of property crime, and that their selective detention would suffice to deter the others. The Prussian Ministry of the Interior initially set an upper limit of 165 prisoners, soon raised to 525; at first, the arrested men were gathered in Lichtenburg, where they soon made up the majority of inmates.[39] Despite the relatively small number of arrests, the Prussian initiative amounted to a radical new approach to preventive policing and set the stage for the future.

The extralegal detention of social outsiders grew during the mid-1930s. In Prussia, the police arrested more men as professional criminals, focusing on "usual suspects" like burglars and thieves with many previous convictions. In 1935, the police authorities concentrated them in Esterwegen, prompting Inspector Eicke to describe that KL as the most difficult to rule; by October 1935, it held 476 so-called professional criminals, forming the largest prisoner group.[40] Meanwhile, several other German states adopted the radical Prussian policy and placed criminals into preventive police custody in concentration camps, too.[41]

Parallel to the pursuit of criminals, the detention of so-called asocials also continued in the mid-1930s. As before, Nazi officials mainly targeted the destitute. In Bavaria, for example, the political police arrested more than three hundred "beggars and vagabonds" in summer 1936 and sent them to Dachau, in a cynical attempt to smarten up the streets before the Olympics.[42] In addition, the authorities trained their sights on "indecent" individuals. Dozens of female prostitutes were dragged to Moringen, among them Minna K., arrested by the Bremen police in late 1935 as a streetwalker. The forty-five-year-old had been held many times before and was accused of drunken attempts to "capture men" in seedy bars, undermining police efforts "to keep the town's streets and establishments clean in a moral respect," thereby endangering public order and the Nazi state.[43]

By the mid-1930s, then, the KL had become well-established weapons against social outsiders. To be sure, their primary focus was still on political opponents, broadly defined. But social outsiders now made up a significant part of the prisoner population, in Dachau and elsewhere. When a delegation of the British Legion visited Dachau on July 21, 1935, the SS hosts (who included Theodor Eicke himself) told them that of the 1,543 prisoners inside, 246 were "professional criminals," 198 "work-shy," 26 "hardened criminals," and 38 "moral perverts"—in other words, some thirty-three percent of inmates were detained as social deviants.[44] Such figures would rise even further across the KL in 1937–38, as the police centralized and escalated the earlier measures against social outsiders.[45]

The Green Triangle

With the appointment of Heinrich Himmler as chief of German police in summer 1936, the path was clear for the creation of a nationwide criminal police. Over the following years, Himmler oversaw the formation of a large and modern force, centrally coordinated in Berlin.[46] Himmler quickly used his new powers to mastermind a strike against ex-convicts. On February 23, 1937, he ordered the Prussian State Criminal Police Office (the later Reich Office, or RKPA) to conduct the first nationwide raid against "professional and habitual criminals," who would be arrested "abruptly" and taken to concentration camps. Using lists compiled earlier by regional police officials, the Criminal Police Office selected the suspects and instructed forces around the country to strike on March 9, 1937. The raids went ahead as planned and over the coming days, some two thousand prisoners—the target set by Himmler—arrived in the KL, which had been primed by Eicke. Almost all the prisoners were men, among them Emil Bargatzky, who was picked up by the police in Essen and sent to Lichtenburg with five hundred other so-called criminals.[47]

The raids in spring 1937 resulted primarily from Himmler's determination to wipe out the criminal subculture. Earlier preventive police measures had not been as successful as anticipated and Himmler worried that the persistence of serious crime would damage the reputation of the Nazi regime, which had promised to clean up Germany. The time had come, he believed, to extend preventive arrests beyond the few hundred most obvious suspects.[48] Naturally, Himmler was quick to declare his initiative a great success, claiming in a speech to SS leaders a few months later that the crime rate had "dropped quite significantly" as a result. He predicted even greater benefits for the future, since some of the detained criminals could be released after several years, once the SS had broken their will and taught them order.[49] Himmler still believed in the transformative power of the camps, no doubt influenced by the conclusion of German criminologists that certain offenders could be reformed through discipline and labor.[50]

Himmler had some additional motives for the spring 1937 raids, beyond his obsession with crime.[51] Economic factors, in particular, began to influence police and SS policy. By the late 1930s, mass unemployment, which had helped propel the Nazis to power, was becoming a distant memory. Following the rapid recovery from the depression, Germany was beginning to face serious labor shortages, accompanied by growing concerns about workers' discipline.[52] At a meeting of senior government officials on February 11, 1937, chaired by Göring, Himmler floated the idea of forcing some five hundred thousand "work-shy" individuals into "labor camps."[53] His proposal, which he had probably discussed with KL chief Eicke, was too radical even for the Nazi state, so when Himmler met senior civil servants from the Reich Ministry of Justice two days later, he only mentioned plans for the selective detention of the "work-shy." Hard work in a camp for up to fourteen hours a day, he announced (according to the minutes), would "show them, and others, that it is better to seek work in freedom than running the risk of being taken to such a camp."[54] Just ten days later, Himmler authorized the March 1937 raids, ordering the police to detain criminals "not in work."[55] No doubt, Himmler intended these arrests as a warning shot to the so-called work-shy.[56]

As an ambitious empire builder, Himmler also saw the mass raids as a way to enlarge his camps, and thereby his power. Indeed, his purpose for calling a meeting with legal officials in February 1937 had been to poach their prisoners: Himmler wanted to get his hands on thousands of inmates in state prisons. Reich minister Gürtner was still strong enough to brush aside Himmler's advance, but it would not be the last time Himmler tried to add state prisoners to his fast-growing KL empire.[57]

SS concentration camps were soon packed, following the March 1937 raids against alleged criminals; further suspects arrived over the coming months.[58] Meanwhile, the RKPA clamped down on their release, so that the great majority of those arrested in spring and summer 1937 were still inside when war broke out over two years later.[59] The total number of "criminal" prisoners remained high as a result, with several thousands held in the camps during 1937–38.[60] In 1937, most of them ended up in Sachsenhausen and Buchenwald, completely changing the composition of the local prisoner population. Shortly after it opened, the new Buchenwald KL took in over five hundred "professional criminals" from Lichtenburg, among them Emil Bargatzky, who arrived on the afternoon of July 31, 1937, with the same transport as his later accomplice Peter Forster.[61] By January 1938, the Buchenwald SS counted 1,008 so-called criminals, making up more than thirty-eight percent of the camp's prisoner population.[62] Later in 1938–39, most of them would leave for the new camp in Flossenbürg, which together with Mauthausen became the main KL for alleged criminals.[63]

Men arrested as professional criminals often faced the wrath of the Camp SS. Rudolf Höss spoke for many SS colleagues when he described the prisoners as "brute and base" villains devoted to a life of crime and sin. He claimed that these "real enemies of the state" were impervious to normal punishment, however strict, thereby justifying the extreme violence of the Camp SS.[64] A political inmate in Dachau later recalled the relish with which SS camp compound leader Hermann Baranowski greeted so-called criminals in spring 1937:

> Listen up, you filth! Do you know where you are?—Yes?—No, you don't
> know? Well then, I'll explain it to you. You are not in a prison and you are
> not in a penitentiary, either. No. You are in a concentration camp. That
> means you are in an educational camp! You are to be educated here—and
> we'll educate you all right. You may rely on that, you stinking swine!—You
> will be given useful work here. Anyone not performing it to our satisfac-
> tion will be helped by us. We have our methods! You'll get to know them.
> There's no loafing about here and let no one believe he can run away. No
> one escapes from here. The sentries have instructions to shoot without
> warning at any attempt to escape. And we have here the elite of the SS!—
> our boys are very good shots.[65]

Baranowski was not bluffing. Camp SS officers really did regard so-called
professional criminals as masters of escape and warned guards to be vigilant
and to use their weapons without hesitation.[66] And SS men were quick to attack "criminals" inside the KL, too; they were easy to pick out because of special markings on their uniforms, with a green triangle becoming standard in
the late 1930s.[67] In Sachsenhausen, at least twenty-six "criminals" died in 1937,
ten of them in March and April, exceeding the death rate among political prisoners in this period.[68] The same was true in Buchenwald, where at least forty-
six so-called professional criminals died during their first year inside the
camp in 1937–38.[69]

Prisoners with the green triangle could expect little support from other
inmates, whose hostility toward the "BVer," as they were often called (short
for Berufsverbrecher, or professional criminal), sometimes matched that of
the SS men. Just like Soviet political prisoners in the faraway Gulag, many
political inmates in the KL despised so-called criminals as coarse, cruel, and
corrupt—"the dregs of society," as one of them put it.[70] Such loathing grew
from social prejudices against men thought to have been arrested as brutal
thugs and from the daily encounters inside the KL, with political prisoners
claiming that the new arrivals used their criminal energies against fellow inmates and collaborated with the SS.[71]

The picture of the "criminal greens" has long been shaped by these testimonies of political prisoners.[72] But it requires correction. Even in the late
1930s, the vast majority of so-called professional criminals were property offenders, not violent felons; just like Emil Bargatzky, most of those arrested
during the spring 1937 raids were suspected burglars and thieves.[73] Also, the
"greens" forged no united front against other KL inmates.[74] Of course, some
formed friendships and cliques inside, since they often worked together and

slept in the same barrack.[75] These bonds appear to have been looser than those among political prisoners, however, since so-called criminals could rarely build upon a shared past or ideological beliefs.[76] Finally, although the tensions between some "red" and "green" prisoners were real, they did not always arise from the latter group's alleged brutality, but simply from competition for scarce resources, a struggle that would escalate during the war.[77]

Following the 1937 police offensive against so-called criminals, Himmler and his police leaders soon plotted the next move in the war against social outsiders. To coordinate and extend the preventive fight against crime, the RKPA drafted the first nationwide regulations, introduced in a confidential decree of the Reich Ministry of the Interior on December 14, 1937.[78] This decree enshrined preventive police custody of criminal suspects in the KL, drawing on the earlier Prussian regulations. Even more important, it greatly extended the number of suspects. In addition to hardened offenders, it threatened "anyone who, without being a professional or habitual criminal, endangers the general public through his asocial behavior."[79] The scene was set for a massive police crackdown on deviance.

Action "Work-Shy Reich"

Why was a pauper like Wilhelm Müller hounded as an enemy of the German state? Divorced and unemployed, the forty-six-year-old was living hand to mouth in Duisburg, deep in the German industrial heartland. The welfare authorities forced him to perform menial labor, four days a week, in return for a paltry 10.40 Reichsmark, barely enough to get by. He occasionally asked for money on the streets, and on the afternoon of June 13, 1938, a police officer caught him in the act. Wilhelm Müller had been fined twice before for begging. This time, the police took a far more drastic step and placed him into preventive custody as an "asocial human being." Müller found himself labeled as a work-shy beggar and criminal who "cannot accustom himself to the discipline required by the state," and on June 22, 1938, he was taken to Sachsenhausen.[80]

Wilhelm Müller was among some 9,500 "asocial" men arrested during mass raids in June 1938 and dragged to concentration camps.[81] These nationwide raids by the criminal police, its most radical attack yet on social outsiders, had begun in the early hours of June 13 and lasted several days, with officers searching railway stations, bars, and shelters.[82] The raids followed an earlier concerted action: in the last ten days of April 1938, the Gestapo had arrested almost two thousand "work-shy" men, who were then taken to Buchenwald.[83]

Meanwhile, local police forces carried out their own measures against so-called asocials in 1938–39, bringing even more suspects to the camps, including several hundred women accused of moral offenses.[84]

Many of the men rounded up during the 1938 mass raids were shocked and bewildered by their sudden detention.[85] Regional police officials had an almost free hand when it came to arrests, as the definition of "asocial" was left deliberately vague, a catch-all term for all kinds of deviant behavior. According to Reinhard Heydrich, the chief of the security police (which combined the criminal and political police), the targets included "tramps," "whores," "alcoholics," and others who "refuse to integrate into the community."[86] In practice, the mass raids centered on vagrants, beggars, welfare recipients, and casual workers. In addition, the police arrested a number of suspected pimps, some of whom were guilty of nothing more than frequenting bars of ill repute.[87]

German police leaders also extended the attack on "asocials" to men regarded as racially suspect. In his orders for the June 1938 raids, Reinhard Heydrich specifically targeted "criminal" Jews. In addition, he picked out men described as Gypsies, who had a criminal record or "have shown no liking for regular work."[88] Because of their often nonnormative lifestyle, the small minority of so-called Gypsies (today frequently referred to as Sinti or Roma) had long faced official harassment in Germany. State-sponsored discrimination escalated dramatically in the Third Reich, especially from the late 1930s. After the June 1938 raids, hundreds of male Gypsies arrived in the KL; Sachsenhausen alone held 442 by August 1, 1938 (almost five percent of the prisoner population). Many had been arrested as self-employed musicians, artists, or itinerant merchants.[89] One of them was the thirty-eight-year-old August Laubinger, a father of four who had been living in poverty with his family in Quedlinburg near Magdeburg. Although he had no criminal record, had worked for years as a textile trader, and had tried to find a steady job, the criminal police still arrested him on June 13, 1938, as "work-shy," accusing him of having "wandered around the country" without fixed employment. A few days later, Laubinger arrived in Sachsenhausen, where he would remain for more than a year.[90]

There was no single driving force behind the all-out assault on "asocials" in 1938. Nazi leaders were attracted to the chilling vision of the police as a doctor that could cleanse Germany of all deviants and degenerates, a vision increasingly inflected with racism.[91] Meanwhile, regional police officials and others involved in the raids—in German welfare offices and labor exchanges—used the mass raids as a pragmatic opportunity to eliminate men long seen as nuisances and threats, including alleged benefit cheats, welfare clients resistant to state control, persistent beggars, and criminal suspects who could not be legally prosecuted. So enthusiastic were regional police officials about rounding up social outsiders that they far exceeded the minimum arrest targets set by Heydrich for the June 1938 raids.[92]

Economic factors were important, too, even more so than before.[93] The charge of "work shyness" had already featured prominently in early campaigns against social outsiders in the Third Reich. Not only were the "work-shy" seen as biologically inferior, as many scholars and scientists insisted at the time, they failed one of the major demands made on national comrades—the performance of productive labor.[94] The Nazi leaders' desire to force "work-shy" men to work gained added urgency as the German economy was gearing up for war. As Reinhard Heydrich put it, the regime "does not tolerate asocial persons avoiding work and thereby sabotaging the [1936] Four-Year Plan."[95] Adolf Hitler shared these views and strongly supported—and possibly even initiated—the mass detention of the "professional unemployed" and "scum," as he called them.[96] At the same time, SS leaders were beginning to pursue a far more ambitious economic policy inside the KL, and were eager to get their hands on forced laborers. Himmler's hunger for more prisoners clearly influenced the raids in 1938, with the police orders for mass arrests of "asocials" stressing the importance of targeting men who could work.[97]

The concentration camps expanded dramatically in 1938 and social outsiders were soon in the majority. According to one estimate, so-called asocials made up seventy percent of the entire prisoner population by October 1938.[98] This figure would have dropped over the following months, but overall numbers still remained high, as many "work-shy" men waited in vain for their release.[99] On the eve of the Second World War, more than half of all the inmates in Buchenwald and Sachsenhausen were still classified as "asocial," instantly recognizable by the black triangle on their uniform (some Gypsies wore brown markings instead).[100] Initially, Buchenwald had been designated as the KL for all men detained in the 1938 mass raids.[101] But the police arrested so many in June that Dachau and Sachsenhausen threw open their gates, too; in fact, Sachsenhausen took in most detainees, with the total number of "work-shy" prisoners reaching 6,224 by June 25, 1938.[102]

Camp SS men labeled these prisoners "asocial parasites," and dismissed them as dirty, dishonest, and depraved.[103] The SS immediately set out to break them with overwhelming force. On arrival in Sachsenhausen in June 1938, prisoners were greeted with invective, kicks, and slaps. Afterward, Commandant Baranowski, a recent appointment from Dachau, ordered his men to select some victims, who were strapped on a buck and whipped in front of the other horrified newcomers. And just as he had threatened "professional criminals" in Dachau, Baranowski had a word of warning for any "asocials" in Sachsenhausen who thought about escape, loudly announcing the motto of his trigger-happy sentries: "Bang—and the shit is gone!"[104]

The prisoners with the black triangle endured particularly poor living conditions. The mass arrests in summer 1938 had caught the Camp SS off guard, leading to chaotic scenes inside overcrowded camps. In Sachsenhausen, the SS replaced bed frames with straw sacks to press some four hundred "asocials" into space meant to hold 146 men; as an emergency measure, the SS also threw up eighteen new barracks, northeast of the roll call square, which formed the so-called little camp. The new prisoners' uniforms were ill fitting and dirty, and the shortage of shoes and caps caused bleeding feet and sunburned heads.[105] If anything, things were even more harmful in Buchenwald. Not only was it still under construction, but the local SS men were also fired up after the murder of SS Rottenführer Albert Kallweit just a few weeks earlier.[106]

To make matters even worse, the "asos" (as they were known) stood near the bottom of the prisoner hierarchy. Just like those with the green triangle, they faced plenty of contempt from fellow inmates. Unlike them, however, prisoners with the black triangle largely failed to gain influential Kapo positions, despite their much larger numbers. And while there was some camaraderie—with inmates helping others, or diverting them with jokes and with romantic tales of life on the road—their sense of shared identity was weak, as "asocials" had even less in common than so-called criminals.[107] Worst off were those regarded as disabled or mentally unstable, who often found themselves isolated under the most dreadful conditions. In Buchenwald, the SS pressed them into the so-called idiots' company, wearing white armbands with the word "stupid."[108]

Some "asocial" prisoners were butchered in the name of Nazi eugenics. The new German rulers had lost no time in 1933 in introducing a law for the compulsory sterilization of the "hereditary ill." By 1939, at least three hundred thousand women and men (many of them inmates of mental asylums) had been mutilated, owing largely to the prejudices of physicians and judges at newly established Hereditary Health Courts.[109] Professor Werner Heyde supervised the sterilization program inside the KL, having been put in charge of "hereditary monitoring" after a 1936 meeting with Inspector Eicke, whom he had last encountered as a patient in his Würzburg clinic. Apparently, all prisoners were to be screened for possible sterilization, with so-called asocials especially vulnerable, since Heyde believed there to be "quite a few feebleminded" among them. Having initially worked alone, Heyde soon taught Camp SS doctors to complete the formal court applications. In the late 1930s, some otherwise indifferent SS doctors developed a sudden zeal when it came to prisoner sterilizations, which were largely carried out in local hospitals.[110]

Inhumane SS treatment, together with the general deterioration of conditions in the late 1930s, killed prisoners on a scale never seen before in the concentration camps. The first huge rise in the death rate came in summer 1938, after the victims of the June raids arrived. During the first five months of 1938 (January to May), ninety men are known to have died in all the KL. Over the next five months (June to October), at least 493 men perished—almost eighty percent of them "asocials."[111] In Sachsenhausen, at least thirty-three "asocials" lost their lives in July 1938 alone, when one year earlier (in July 1937) the Sachsenhausen SS had recorded just a single death among all its inmates.[112]

Worse was yet to come; if summer and autumn 1938 were already toxic, the following months were truly lethal. From late 1938, the death toll among "asocials" rocketed to new heights. During the six-month period between November 1938 and April 1939, at least 744 "asocial" men perished in the KL.[113] In Sachsenhausen, the most deadly month was February 1939, when 121 so-called asocials died, dwarfing the eleven deaths among all other prisoner groups that month. In total, at least 495 "asocials" lost their lives in Sachsenhausen during a single year, from June 1938 to May 1939, accounting for a staggering eighty percent of all prisoner fatalities. The main causes, one survivor of the camp recalled, were "starvation, freezing, shooting, or the effects of abuse."[114] Clearly, death became far more commonplace in the KL during the late 1930s, and men arrested as asocial bore the main brunt: between January 1938 and August 1939, well over 1,200 "asocial" men died across all the SS concentration camps.[115] Even today, it is widely unknown that these men from the margins of society made up the largest group of KL victims in the final period before the war.

Propaganda and Prejudice

The shift from browbeating political opponents to terrorizing social outsiders shaped the public presentation of the KL. To be sure, the regime never drew a strict line between its opponents, and the longer it stayed in power, the more the criminal, racial, and political enemy categories merged in the minds of Nazi leaders; by the end of the war, Heinrich Himmler spoke of having faced a "Jewish-communist asocial organization" in 1933.[116] Still, the early camps had concentrated on the destruction of the left-wing opposition, as we have seen, and this target had also dominated reports and rumors at the time.[117] As the function of the KL changed, however, so did their official image in

Nazi Germany. Already in the mid-1930s, media reports placed growing emphasis on the detention of social outsiders.[118] Most prominent was a five-page story on Dachau, published in late 1936 in a glossy Nazi magazine, with twenty pictures of the camp and its inmates. Right from the beginning, the article stressed how much the prisoner population had recently changed:

> These are no longer the political inmates of 1933, of whom only a small percentage is still in the camp while the rest have long since been released, but for the most part a selection of asocial elements, recidivist political muddle-heads, vagabonds, work-shy persons, and drunkards . . . émigrés and Jewish parasites on the nation, offenders against morality of every kind, and a group of professional criminals on whom preventive police custody has been imposed.

Said prisoners were now learning strict military discipline, rigorous cleanliness, and hard labor, "which many of them have shunned all their lives." Lest anyone worried about SS abuse, the article reassured readers that prisoners were healthy and well fed. Indeed, some of the inmates "from totally wrecked social circumstances" had never had it any better. This was just as well, since it was clear that many of them would never be allowed to taste freedom again—locked up for good to protect the national community.[119] Other Nazi propaganda underscored this last point, stressing that the permanent detention of social outsiders was driving down crime.[120]

Such claims found a receptive audience inside Germany. Weimar society had been fixated on crime, especially during its final years, with an ever-louder chorus clamoring for harsher measures against deviants.[121] The Third Reich could build on this noxious legacy, with even some political prisoners supporting the indefinite detention of selected social outsiders.[122] Nazi media reports about the KL exploited existing prejudices, with staged photos of prisoners in menacing poses and covered in tattoos. "On our walk through the camp," the 1936 magazine feature about Dachau declared, "we often encounter the typical face of the born criminal," playing on popular beliefs in physiognomic theories.[123] Such stories had some impact in the Third Reich, perpetuating the image of the camps as places full of dangerous deviants and strengthening the common conviction that Hitler had made the streets safe again, a myth that long outlived the Nazi regime inside Germany.[124]

Nevertheless, the camps were not foremost in the minds of ordinary Germans in the second half of the 1930s; the strong emotions of 1933—curiosity, acclaim, anger, fear—had given way to greater indifference; even among former supporters of the Left, the novelty of the KL had long worn off. In addition, the detainees now largely came from the margins of society, and were often arrested away from the public eye. Even the mass raids against so-called asocials and criminals, despite their propaganda potential, went largely unreported in the German press.[125]

This was part of a wider trend, as the KL gradually faded from view. Many factors were in the mix. To start with, hundreds of semipublic early camps had been replaced by a handful of secluded sites. At the same time, eyewitness accounts by victims—the main source of popular knowledge about the camps in 1933—largely vanished. There were fewer prisoners, and those who returned were often too scared to say much at all.[126] The ones who did speak, meanwhile, could barely make themselves heard, now that the organized resistance was in tatters. Most important, perhaps, the audience for critical reports was smaller than ever, as the Nazi dictatorship grew in popularity. The German population did not forget the KL, of course, nor did it forget earlier stories of terror inside; in the public mind, the camps remained associated with violence and abuse—to the irritation of some local notables, like those in Dachau, who realized that the bad reputation of the camp was driving away tourists from their town.[127] Still, for the great majority of Germans—content with the regime or at least resigned to it—fears about the KL were now at most dim and abstract.[128]

As for the Nazi dictatorship itself, it was content to let the KL blend into the background, with only occasional reminders of their existence for deterrence. Beyond that, the regime showed no desire to push the KL back into the media limelight. There was no more need for rescuing their reputation, now that rumors about abuses were less virulent.[129] What is more, the Nazi authorities were still unsure about the popularity of the KL, despite their alleged contribution to the Nazi fight against crime. Barely a week after the big Dachau photo spread had appeared in 1936, the authorities even issued a secret order to cut down on press reports about incidents inside camps; such reports, Reich press chief Otto Dietrich announced confidentially, "are apt to trigger damaging effects at home and abroad."[130]

Dietrich's reference to foreign opinion was telling. While the regime had become more adept at managing public knowledge about the camps inside Germany, foreign opinion inevitably proved much harder to manipulate. Not that the Nazis didn't try. To improve the image of the KL abroad, the Camp SS continued to use both pressure and deception.[131] Among those who were fooled were members of the British Legion, who came away from their 1935 tour of Dachau convinced that every SS man "was out to help any prisoner to make the best of himself and of the situation," as they put it in a memorandum to the more skeptical British Foreign Office.[132] Similar apologetic accounts sometimes found their way into the press abroad.[133] But they were far out-weighed, at least in the mid-1930s, by reports about terror, abuse, and murder in the KL, which continued to appear in German émigré papers and the foreign media.[134]

Foreign criticism of the KL still coalesced around the fate of individual political prisoners. In Britain, for example, the ongoing public appeals for Hans Litten led the German ambassador to conclude that his discharge would significantly improve the image of the Third Reich. However, the Nazi regime rebuffed all demands for Litten's release; at a speech at the Nuremberg Rally in September 1935, Propaganda Minister Joseph Goebbels himself denounced Litten as one of the main Jewish enemies behind a global Communist conspiracy.[135] In another, even more high-profile case, however, Nazi leaders partially gave in to foreign pressure.

The pacifist writer Carl von Ossietzky was easily the most famous concentration camp prisoner in the mid-1930s, at least outside the German borders, where a campaign to award him the Nobel Peace Prize was gathering strength. Ossietzky's health had deteriorated dramatically since his arrest in February 1933. He was still in Esterwegen, gravely ill with pulmonary tuberculosis and barely able to speak; a visiting Red Cross official regarded his condition as "desperate." Theodor Eicke, who knew that Ossietzky could die at any moment, still advised Himmler to ignore the clamor for his release, concerned that Ossietzky's iconic stature and insights into SS crimes would make him the "chief witness against Nazi Germany." Heydrich took a similar view, but Hermann Göring overruled them both, evidently worried that the affair would overshadow the forthcoming Olympics. In late May 1936, Ossietzky was moved out of Esterwegen and spent the rest of his life under strict police guard in Berlin hospitals. It was here that he learned that he had won the Nobel Prize. Despite intense Nazi pressure, he accepted the award in a last show of defiance, but the German authorities prevented him from leaving the country to accept the honor. Ossietzky never recovered from the KL and died on May 4, 1938, aged forty-eight.[136]

Although the campaign for Ossietzky momentarily lifted the Nazi camps into the international news, general media interest abroad was on the wane, partly because details were harder to obtain, and partly because of what one historian has called "compassion fatigue," following several years of reports about Nazi atrocities.[137] One cause célèbre that briefly punctured the growing silence in the late 1930s was the detention of the Protestant pastor Martin Niemöller.[138] A right-wing nationalist and one-time sympathizer of the Nazis, Niemöller had become increasingly critical of the regime's pressure on the Protestant Church and emerged as a leader of the breakaway Confessing Church. Niemöller was arrested in 1937; his trial before a Berlin special court in March 1938 ended in a shambles, after the judges found him not guilty of malicious attacks on the state and set him free. Hitler was furious, accusing the legal system of yet another blunder, and ordered Himmler to take the pastor to Sachsenhausen. The police arrested Niemöller inside the court building and took him away, causing worldwide condemnation. Nazi leaders had anticipated this furor, but regarded it as a price worth paying. In contrast to their earlier attempts to pacify foreign critics with their cynical show of compassion for Ossietzky, they ignored all calls for Niemöller's freedom, even when it became widely known that his health was failing; he would spend the next seven years in Sachsenhausen and Dachau.[139]

The obstinacy of the Third Reich reflected its growing strength in the late 1930s. As Nazi leaders became more aggressive and steered the country toward an open confrontation with the West, foreign opinion seemed to matter less and less. The drive to war was transforming Germany's international standing, and also left a mark on the Camp SS.

SS Military Ambitions

Himmler liked to see the Camp SS as soldiers. By presenting his men as warriors fighting "the scum of Germany," he hoped to boost their profile and elevate them above mere prison guards.[140] But Himmler's use of military imagery was more than rhetoric. From early on, he envisaged his guards as paramilitaries, who patrolled not only the make-believe battlefields inside camps, but who would also serve beyond the barbed wire during national emergencies, as the Dachau SS had done during the Röhm putsch in 1934. Hardened by the confrontation with "enemies" in concentration camps, he argued, his special forces could be trusted to fight terrorists outside.[141]

The transformation of the SS Guard Troops into a paramilitary force began early, already in the mid-1930s.[142] Sentry service around the KL was just one of their duties. As we have seen, the men spent considerably more time on military drills. Initially, Guard Troop commanders struggled with poor equipment; in Dachau, they did not even have enough reserve munitions. This changed after Hitler agreed to fund the Death's Head SS from the Reich budget. More weapons for combat now poured into the Guard Troops, which set up additional machine gun formations. In Dachau, the dilapidated old barracks were replaced by a vast training camp, symbolizing the military intentions of the SS. In Sachsenhausen, too, a big new complex was built (by prisoners) near the camp, as a base for SS excursions. In Sachsenburg, meanwhile, prisoners constructed a new and modern shooting range, complete with movable targets. Most significantly, the SS continued to recruit far more

Guard Troops than it needed for running the camps; SS personnel rose from an estimated 1,700 in January 1935 to 4,300 three years later, keeping the staff–inmate ratio well below 1:2. Although the force was still small, there was no mistaking the ambitions of its leaders.[143]

The creeping militarization of the Camp SS was part of a bigger plan by Himmler: the creation of independent SS formations for deployment at the front. The German army, ever since its conflict with SA leader Ernst Röhm, was paranoid about the military aspirations of Nazi leaders, and in Himmler's case, the generals were right to worry. Despite his hollow denials, Himmler was not content with establishing the SS and police as a force inside Germany. He was gunning for the army's monopoly of military might. Speaking to senior SS commanders in 1938, he claimed that it was their solemn duty to stand tall on the battlefield: "Were we not to bring blood sacrifices and were we not to fight at the front, we would lose the moral right to shoot at shirkers and cowards at home." Using all his guile, his direct line to Hitler, and his talent for bureaucratic sparring, Himmler won the upper hand in the turf war with the army. Initially, his hope of creating an SS division centered mainly on the new SS Troop for Special Duty (Verfügungstruppe), formed in autumn 1934 out of different smaller armed units. But he also began to consider the use of SS Guard Troops beyond the German borders, erasing the boundary between internal and external front.[144]

The military role of the SS was cemented in the late 1930s, as a European war loomed ever closer. One landmark was Hitler's secret decree of August 17, 1938, drafted by Himmler, which confirmed that SS formations would be deployed on the battlefield. As for the Death's Head units specifically, they would greatly expand to serve as a "standing armed SS troop" for "tackling special duties of a police nature." This cryptic phrase still pointed to a domestic deployment of Camp SS men. However, a few months earlier, members of the Dachau Guard Troop had already engaged in a first foray onto foreign soil, marching into Austria in March 1938 under the command of the German army. Soon, another opportunity presented itself. In autumn 1938, four Death's Head battalions took part in the occupation of the Sudetenland; they were led by Theodor Eicke, who presented his men during a first review on Czech soil to Hitler. The following May, soon after Death's Head troops had participated in the takeover of the rest of the Czech territory, Hitler issued yet another decree, officially recognizing the military role of SS Death's Head units: in wartime, some Camp SS men would join the front line.[145]

If there was anyone more delighted about the combat status of the Camp SS than Himmler, it was his lieutenant Theodor Eicke. Having fancied himself for some time as a general (commensurate with his SS rank), Eicke was able to realize his dream through the militarization of the Camp SS. In the late 1930s, he threw himself into the expansion of the Guard Troops—even at the expense of the KL, as a resentful Rudolf Höss noted. Eicke showed "incredible generosity" when it came to the Guard Troop, Höss complained, always demanding the best equipment and the biggest quarters.[146] In addition, Eicke pushed hard for new recruits. The criteria for enlistment were relaxed and Eicke even ordered SS "head hunters," as he called them, to poach enlisted soldiers from the armed forces: "Bring them from the bars, bring them from the sports clubs, bring them from the barber. As far as I'm concerned, you can bring them from the brothels. Bring them from every place you meet them."[147]

While this particular scheme probably met with little success, Eicke still managed to attract many new recruits. During the course of 1938, the size of the Death's Head SS more than doubled, reaching 10,441 men in November. By the following summer, the figure had grown further, to around twelve or thirteen thousand full-time staff.[148] At the same time, the Death's Head SS stockpiled weapons. According to Eicke, his units possessed over 800 machine guns, almost 1,500 machine pistols, and nearly 20,000 carbines by mid-1939.[149] Eicke and his political soldiers were ready for a war beyond the camps.

FORCED LABOR

When an esteemed German encyclopedia described the Nazi concentration camps, a new entry within its pages in 1937, it explained that prisoners were "formed into groups and made to perform useful work."[150] It was almost inevitable that the dictionary would highlight forced labor, since labor featured in almost all official Nazi accounts of the KL; no article or speech seemed complete without it. And although these references were all about propaganda, they pointed to a larger truth—that work dominated daily KL life and the thoughts of the prisoners, as this extract from the "Sachsenhausen Song" illustrates:

> Behind barbed wire is our work,
> our backs are sore from bending,
> we're turning hard, we're turning tough,
> our work is never-ending.[151]

The Third Reich did not invent forced labor for captives, of course. It was central to traditional conceptions of prisons and workhouses, as we have seen, promising many practical benefits. On the most basic level, labor was a useful organizing principle for keeping inmates occupied. Moreover, productive labor was said to drive down the cost of detention. As for its wider purpose, some officials regarded it as rehabilitative, preparing deviants for a life on the straight and narrow, while others championed it as an instrument to inflict the right amount of pain, for retribution or deterrence.[152]

This last aspect dominates postwar accounts of the KL, exemplified by the study of Wolfgang Sofsky, who describes the primary function of forced labor as "violence, terror, and death."[153] This conclusion certainly captures a key aim of the Camp SS: the use of work to humiliate and harm prisoners. But this is not the whole story. Reducing camp labor to a demonstration of absolute power oversimplifies SS policy, which was also guided by other ideological, economic, and pragmatic considerations.

Work and Punishment

Although all-out forced labor became an essential element of the KL system, it was not one of its founding principles. In the early camps, labor had played a far less dominant role. In their rush to set up temporary sites, some officials simply disregarded it. Those who did emphasize the importance of labor, meanwhile, were often frustrated by the difficulty of finding any, given the mass unemployment across the country. More generally, there was still uncertainty (especially in protective custody wings of state prisons) as to whether the inmates should be forced to work at all, given the long German tradition of treating some political prisoners as honorable offenders (one beneficiary had been Adolf Hitler, who used his time in Landsberg fortress in 1924, after his failed putsch, to write parts of his opus, *Mein Kampf*). In the end, it was not unusual for prisoners in 1933 to be entirely without work. Some guards in early camps forced these unemployed inmates to perform military drills. Elsewhere, however, the prisoners were left idle in their cells, barracks, and dormitories.[154]

Camp inmates who were compelled to work in 1933 faced two main types of labor. First, there was work on the outside, which enhanced the visibility of Nazi terror. Prisoners were deployed in large-scale projects for the supposed benefit of the nation (like moor drainage in the Emsland) or to improve the local infrastructure, by building paths, roads, and canals, or helping to bring in the harvest; in Breslau, prisoners even had to drain a muddy pond so that locals could use it as a swimming pool. Second, many prisoners, especially at larger sites, were forced into camp construction and maintenance, putting up or repairing the different buildings, and installing the barbed wire that surrounded them. Others had to provide essential services such as cleaning rooms and corridors, preparing food or distributing it.[155] In theory, this captive labor served a practical purpose, but in reality, abuse often took center stage, as guards used the occasion to torment those prisoners they despised the most. These inmates were also most likely to endure pointless labor; in Heuberg camp, for example, prominent political prisoners had to fill baskets with pebbles, only to tip them out and start all over again.[156]

During the coordination of the KL in the mid-1930s, the general approach to labor changed. To start with, the Camp SS would not tolerate "idleness" and made work compulsory for all. As Theodor Eicke's regulations for Esterwegen put it: "Anyone refusing to work, evading work, or, for the purpose of doing nothing, feigning physical weaknesses or sickness, is regarded as *incorrigible* and is made to answer for himself."[157] Meanwhile, the SS put an end to much of the labor outside the KL. Trying to shield its camps from prying eyes, it scaled back work for the wider community, epitomized by the abandonment of moor cultivation in Esterwegen.

When the Camp SS looked at the economic use of prisoners in the mid-1930s, its gaze turned inward, to the construction and maintenance of the KL. All five concentration camps set up between 1936 and 1939, starting with Sachsenhausen, were built on the backs of prisoners, and the first weeks and months in a new camp always ranked among the worst; afterward, the Buchenwald survivor Eugen Kogon wrote, "misery at least consolidated itself." In summer and autumn 1937, the first Buchenwald prisoners had to fell trees, erect barracks, dig trenches, and carry stones and tree trunks, struggling for twelve hours a day or more as the camp slowly grew. Illness and injuries were frequent, and prisoners who could not keep up, like the frail Hans Litten, faced slaps, kicks, and worse. What is more, the prisoners had to endure the primitive conditions typical of new camps. In the beginning, there were no beds, blankets, or running water in Buchenwald; mud was everywhere, clinging to the prisoners' shoes, uniforms, and faces. These conditions, combined with SS terror and exhausting labor, had fatal consequences. Between August and December 1937, fifty-three prisoners died in the new camp at Buchenwald (over the same period, fourteen prisoners died in Sachsenhausen, which was already up and running). Of course, heavy construction work did not cease after the foundations had been laid. None of the large camps were ever finished, and the SS continued to exploit prisoners for repairs and extensions; during the prewar years, around ninety percent of all Buchenwald prisoners worked on the camp itself.[158]

Beyond the building of the growing KL complex, the Camp SS pursued few serious economic activities in the mid-1930s. Himmler and other SS leaders had no real long-term strategy and showed little desire to enter large-scale production. Instead, the SS ran a patchwork of small and obscure businesses outside the KL, among them a porcelain factory producing tawdry statuettes of sausage dogs and Hitler Youths. As for the most valuable resource in the hands of the SS, its prisoners, their deployment was generally overseen locally, by the commandants.[159]

The commandants, in turn, left much of the initiative to guards, who often continued to see labor as an excuse for abuse; however pressing a project was, there was always time for torture. Many years later, Harry Naujoks still remembered the day in 1936 when an SS man had suddenly forced him and other Sachsenhausen prisoners to stop flattening some cleared woodland and dig deep holes instead, at an ever-increasing pace. "We are only robots now," Naujoks recalled. Driven on by kicks and punches, the prisoners shoveled manically until the area they had just leveled resembled a moonscape. "All our earlier work is being destroyed, completely pointlessly."[160]

Overall, then, SS economic ambitions for the KL remained modest in the mid-1930s—with one exception: the prisoner workshops at Dachau. These were not only the earliest SS economic ventures, but one of the most significant of the prewar years. It had all started in 1933, when the Camp SS set up workshops to cater for the immediate needs of the new camp. Despite some protests from local businesses about SS competition, the complex grew quickly over the coming years and soon started to supply SS troops elsewhere; by 1939, 370 prisoners in the big carpentry workshop produced bed frames, tables, and chairs for general SS use.[161] Of course, SS terror still trumped economics. But the success of the Dachau venture—the most profitable SS business of the prewar years, thanks to forced labor—also demonstrated that prisoners could be exploited without compromising the general mission of the KL. SS leaders realized that effective production was compatible with terror. This paved the way for a much more aggressive economic policy in the late 1930s, spearheaded by one of the rising stars of the SS, Oswald Pohl.[162]

Oswald Pohl and the SS Economy

Looking for a manager to professionalize the expanding SS organization in 1933, Heinrich Himmler's eyes fell on Oswald Pohl, at the time a navy paymaster. The two men met for the first time in May that year in the garden of the Kiel navy mess, and Himmler was immediately taken with the tall and imposing Pohl, eight years his senior at forty years of age. Pohl had exactly the kind of résumé Himmler was looking for, combining managerial expertise with ideological fervor. He came from a middle-class family and had joined the navy as a trainee paymaster in 1912, specializing in budgetary and organizational matters. At the same time, he was a far-right activist and Nazi veteran. After the German defeat in the First World War, Pohl served in the Freikorps and then the nascent Nazi movement. He claimed to have joined the party as early as 1923, "following the call of the blood," as he later wrote, and became an SA member in 1926, rising to Obersturmführer by 1933. Himmler had found the right man to build up the SS administration, and apparently offered him a free hand to do so. Pohl jumped at the chance. An impulsive man burning with ambition, he felt trapped in the backwater of the navy. He was desperately seeking an "outlet" for his "lust for work," he wrote to Himmler two days after they met, and promised to serve him "until I drop." Pohl started his new job as chief of the SS Administration Office, with a pay raise and promotion, in late February 1934.[163]

Over the coming years, Pohl accumulated more and more power. He centralized large parts of SS administration and finance, negotiated budgets with the Nazi Party and the Ministry of Finance, and audited SS branches. Pohl also began to reach beyond his original brief, gaining control over SS construction work and the fledgling economic ventures. Pohl's ascent to the top echelons of the SS was swift, and in 1939, following a major restructure of SS operations, he was appointed as head of two separate main offices—administration and business, as well as budget and buildings.[164] Pohl's rise was accelerated by his ruthlessness, which hit both rivals and subordinates, and by his unwavering loyalty to Himmler, who backed him all the way.[165]

The KL system was not immune to Pohl's pull. The stronger he became, the more he drew the camps into his orbit. Pohl was closely involved with the Dachau workshops from 1934—he lived and worked nearby (the SS construction office was based in Dachau in 1933–34) and frequently inspected the sites, before taking sole charge in the late 1930s. He had his hand in other matters, too. By 1938, Pohl controlled the financial and administrative affairs of the camps and the SS Death's Head troops, and supervised various building programs inside.[166]

Pohl's inroads into Camp SS territory set him on a collision course with Theodor Eicke. They held the same SS rank, following Pohl's promotion to Gruppenführer in early 1937, and had a certain grudging respect for each other, using the informal "Du" even in official correspondence. Both men occupied special positions inside the SS, answerable directly to Himmler, and both were determined to make the most of their powers. They were "brutal characters," Rudolf Höss later wrote, and probably recognized each other as kindred spirits.[167] However, their relationship was far less amicable than some historians have suggested.[168] They clashed over the camps' administration, budgets, and buildings, and Eicke must have also begrudged Pohl's occasionally taking credit for the KL; when Himmler conducted an official tour of Dachau in April 1939, for example, it was Pohl who gave the introduction, not Eicke.[169]

Pohl's position strengthened in the late 1930s, after Himmler ordered the massive expansion of the SS economy. Having long neglected economic matters, Himmler displayed a sudden zeal and oversaw the establishment of several major SS enterprises in 1938. It was a landmark year in the development of the SS economy, although historians still disagree about Himmler's intentions; most likely, he sensed another opportunity to enlarge his SS empire, this time at the expense of private industry.[170] Whatever Himmler's motives, the thrust of his policy was clear enough: concentration camp labor would become the main capital of the burgeoning SS economy, and Oswald Pohl its overall manager. In autumn 1938, Pohl bragged that it was his task "to find employment for the very numerous layabouts in our concentration camps," a claim endorsed by Himmler.[171] In practice, however, Pohl was not yet fully in charge, as commandants and the IKL also had their say.[172] But there was no denying Pohl's growing influence, and his control over the SS economy would prove the key to his takeover of responsibility for the entire KL system later on in the war.

By far the most significant SS economic initiative in 1938 was the creation of the German Earth and Stone Works (Deutsche Erd- und Steinwerke GmbH, or DESt), which became Pohl's first significant enterprise. The catalyst was Hitler's monumental construction program for German cities, masterminded by the young architect Albert Speer, who had recently been appointed as inspector general of building for the Reich capital, Berlin, the biggest prewar building site of the Third Reich. As Hitler's megalomaniac vision required far more bricks and stones than German industry could ever deliver—Speer estimated an annual need of around two billion bricks—the SS stepped in. During a meeting in late 1937 or early 1938, Hitler, Himmler, and Speer agreed that KL prisoners would supply vast amounts of building materials. Himmler saw this as an attractive proposition, a first step toward large-scale SS production. Not only would it boost the status of the SS, but Speer provided much of the startup costs, offering an interest-free advance of almost ten million Reichsmark to DESt.

The SS, which had already begun a search for suitable quarries and clay reserves back in 1937, greatly accelerated its efforts from spring 1938 onward, at the same time that the nationwide police raids started to drag more forced laborers into the camps. By summer 1938, Oswald Pohl was overseeing several DESt projects. Prisoners were feverishly building two new brick works, a small one in Berlstedt, some five miles from Buchenwald, and a much larger one near Sachsenhausen. Elsewhere, prisoners were setting up two entirely new KL, near quarries that were meant to provide blue-gray granite for building the Germany of Hitler's dreams; these two new camps were Flossenbürg and Mauthausen.[173]

The Quarry Camps

Sometime during the second half of March 1938, Oswald Pohl and Theodor Eicke set off on a business trip across the south of the German Reich, accompanied by an entourage of SS experts. They were scouting locations for KL suitable for the planned economic ventures.[174] Around March 24 the group traveled through the impoverished and inhospitable landscape of eastern Bavaria, near the Czechoslovakian border, with its dense forests and barren soil. What had brought them to this remote corner of Germany, sometimes jokingly referred to as the Bavarian Siberia, were the quarries around the village of Flossenbürg, which had operated there since the nineteenth century. Thanks to the building mania in the Third Reich, production had recently increased, and Pohl and Eicke agreed that there was an opportunity for the SS to join in. Later the SS search party crossed what had until recently been the Austrian border, heading toward Linz to inspect the nearby granite quarries around Mauthausen. Here, too, Pohl and Eicke found what they wanted and lost no time. Within days of their visits, the establishment of the two new camps was under way.[175]

Flossenbürg opened first, receiving its first prisoners on May 3, 1938, and the camp continued to grow over the coming months. The SS leadership regarded it as an important project. Himmler himself visited on May 16, together with Oswald Pohl, and Theodor Eicke even spent his summer holidays there, sending pictures to Himmler; one snapshot showed an armed guard looking toward a large SS flag, with a white skull on dark ground, fluttering high above the heads of prisoners toiling below.[176] In Mauthausen, meanwhile, the first prisoners arrived on August 8, 1938. The SS initially forced them into provisional quarters in the Wiener Graben quarry (recently leased by DESt from the city of Vienna), and later moved them to a permanent compound on the hill above the quarry.[177]

The SS quickly put its stamp on the two new concentration camps. Their general layout followed the template of other KL, and the core of the SS staff, arriving from Dachau, Sachsenhausen, and Buchenwald, imported proven methods of terror and domination.[178] Still, Flossenbürg and Mauthausen were different: for the first time, economic concerns had dictated the choice of KL locations.[179] The focus of both camps on quarrying even shaped their appearance, with big granite watchtowers rising up; in Mauthausen, these towers joined up with vast granite walls that enclosed much of the compound, making it look less like a camp than a forbidding castle.[180] Initially, Flossenbürg and Mauthausen were also much smaller than other KL for men, in terms of their prisoner numbers; by the end of 1938, Flossenbürg held 1,475 men and Mauthausen 994, at a time when Sachsenhausen, Buchenwald, and Dachau held over eight thousand inmates each.[181] Ambitious SS plans to enlarge the two new camps showed little immediate effect.[182] Only during the Second World War did they catch up with the other KL.

There was another striking difference—the makeup of the Flossenbürg and Mauthausen prisoner population. In 1938, the Camp SS launched its most ambitious attempt yet to gather the same prisoner groups in the same location, reserving the two new camps almost exclusively for social outsiders, especially so-called professional criminals. Mass transports of selected prisoners, rounded up in the big three KL for men, began as soon as the new camps opened.[183] As a result, almost all Flossenbürg prisoners before the war wore the green triangle. In Mauthausen, too, the "greens" made up the largest group, closely followed by "asocials," who arrived from other KL in 1939, with many Gypsies among them.[184] More than a hundred so-called criminals died in Flossenbürg and Mauthausen before the war broke out, more than in the other three KL for men taken together.[185]

Why did the SS concentrate "professional criminals" in the two new quarry camps? Forced labor in quarries was regarded as particularly punishing, and many Nazi officials believed that the worst prisoners deserved the hardest labor. When a senior SS officer suggested in late 1938 that concentration camp prisoners should be sent to lethal radium mines, Himmler responded enthusiastically, proposing to make "the most serious criminals" available.[186] Although this particular plan came to nothing, the SS later adopted the principle of sending "criminally recidivist and asocial" inmates to the KL with the worst working conditions.[187] Heinrich Himmler made no secret of his hatred for prisoners with the green triangle. In a speech in 1937, he described them as dangerous and violent born criminals, who had spent much of their lives behind bars. Himmler painted a terrifying picture of murderers, robbers, and sex fiends, like a seventy-two-year-old man who had committed sixty-three indecent assaults. "It would be an insult to animals to call such a person an animal," Himmler raged, "because animals don't behave that way."[188] When it came to filling the quarry camps in spring and summer 1938, Himmler and other SS leaders felt that it was these prisoners who should suffer.[189]

The prisoners who arrived in the two new camps bore little resemblance to the gargoyles of Himmler's imagination. Typical for men wearing the green triangle, they mostly were persistent but petty property offenders, from especially deprived social backgrounds, who fell back on small-time theft, fraud, and begging for subsistence and survival.[190] One such man was Josef Kolacek, who had been living in poverty with his parents, whom he supported on his own, in a large working-class district of Vienna. Kolacek, who was suffering from tuberculosis, was detained by the criminal police on June 14, 1938, shortly before his thirtieth birthday. When he arrived in Dachau, he was still wearing the cheap jacket and collarless shirt with a missing button that he had been arrested in the previous day; the SS also noted with great interest the tattoos on his arms. Although the police had apparently picked him up during the nationwide raid on the "work-shy," he was classified as a "professional criminal" in the KL. But Kolacek was no dangerous convict. Although he had been sentenced eight times by the courts, the first time in his teens, almost all sentences were for trivial property offenses, punished with no more than a few days' or weeks' detention. Only his last conviction in 1937, for attempted burglary, had merited a longer term of eight months in a penitentiary. And yet, the SS labeled him a criminal menace, and on July 1, 1938, he was transported with many dozens of other "professional criminals" from Dachau to Flossenbürg, where he faced brutal forced labor and abuse. As one SS official noted ominously a few months later, Kolacek "is lazy and sluggish during work and has to be reproved all the time."[191]

The early months in the quarry camps of Flossenbürg and Mauthausen were especially hard. As in other new camps, prisoners had to build the infrastructure—exhausting and perilous work aggravated by the primitive living conditions in makeshift compounds. Meanwhile, hundreds of other inmates were already toiling in the quarries. Work began early in Flossenbürg, where three quarries were operational at the end of 1938. In Mauthausen, too, labor in three different quarries began in 1938, soon the largest such complex controlled by DESt. Prisoners had to carry out the most arduous jobs, preparing the ground with pickaxes and drills, and hauling huge granite blocks.[192] Adolf Gussak, an Austrian Gypsy who came to Mauthausen on March 21, 1939, on a large prisoner transport from Dachau, later recalled the days in the Wiener Graben: "In the quarry we had to carry heavy stones. With them on our backs we had to climb the 180 steps up [toward the compound]. The SS beat us. As a result there often was some pushing: everybody wanted to escape the blows. If anyone fell down he was finished off by a bullet in the back of his neck."[193]

Death was frequent in Mauthausen. In the first year between August 1938 and July 1939, at least 131 prisoners perished, divided almost evenly between so-called criminals and asocials.[194] Relative to the small size of its prisoner population—there were only 1,431 inmates on July 1, 1939—Mauthausen may well have been more lethal than any other KL during this period. In other camps, inmates began to dread a transfer to Mauthausen, after returning prisoners described the huge quarries as hell on earth.[195] Those in Flossenbürg had a better chance of survival: fifty-five prisoners perished before the outbreak of war (almost eighty percent of them so-called professional criminals).[196] Among the survivors was Josef Kolacek from Vienna, who was eventually released after more than nine months in Flossenbürg.[197]

A High-Tech Factory

No project better sums up the economic hubris of the SS in the late 1930s than its giant new brick works at Oranienburg. In summer 1938, on the wooded banks of a canal little more than a mile from Sachsenhausen, the SS began to build what would have been the world's largest brick factory, with a projected annual output of 150 million bricks, around ten times more than large factories normally produced. The project—probably initiated by Albert Speer, who advanced the necessary funds to DESt—was heavily promoted by the SS as a showcase for its economic prowess. Determined to prove its ability to harness modern technology for the Nazi regime, the SS opted for the most costly and cutting-edge equipment, so-called dry press machines, which promised both speed and efficiency. SS managers staked their reputation on a successful outcome. Heinrich Himmler apparently attended the ceremonial laying of the foundation stone on July 6, 1938, and remained keenly interested in progress at the building site.[198]

The entire project rested on forced labor. Although the SS used some civilian contractors for the brick works, the bulk of the labor force came from Sachsenhausen. In the prewar years, a daily average of 1,500 to 2,000 prisoners was deployed, making it the largest labor detail in any SS concentration camp at the time. After the prisoners had cleared many of the trees on site, they began the building work, excavating a dock area, moving and leveling the ground, and constructing the main factory building. Another labor gang worked on a railway line for transporting clay, from its source a few miles away, to the plant.[199]

The contrast between the plant's high-tech design and the primitive conditions on the construction site could hardly have been greater. Prisoners performed the most strenuous labor with the most basic tools or no tools at all. Large groups of inmates carried piles of sand in their uniforms, worn back-to-front so that the back of jackets formed a kind of apron. Others moved large mounds of earth on rickety wooden stretchers or shifted sacks of cement on their shoulders. Elsewhere, prisoners climbed scaffolds and poured down cement, barely clinging on in their wooden clogs. There were many accidents—severed limbs, crushed bones, and the like—but no respite. SS terror was as abundant as facilities were scarce; the latrine, for example, was no more than a beam across a ditch, and SS guards liked to push exhausted inmates into the pool of excrement below.[200]

The Sachsenhausen inmates feared the brick works as a particularly destructive labor detail.[201] In the mornings, they faced a long march to the building site, moved along with clubs and whips by SS men, only to stagger back to the compound in the evenings, carrying the sick, the wounded, and the dead. On site in Oranienburg, the prisoners spent the entire day without shelter; after the glistening heat of summer 1938, they braved the bitter winter, always working at a ferocious pace. Because the deluded SS managers had agreed on an impossibly tight schedule for their flagship plant, guards and Kapos drove prisoners with a brutality unusual even for a KL.[202]

Countless prisoners perished on the desolate Oranienburg building site, succumbing to exhaustion, accidents, and abuse; there were some suicides, too.[203] The worst period came in winter 1938–39, when a renewed SS push to complete the project coincided with a cold snap across the Berlin region. Prisoners worked in thin uniforms and without gloves as the temperatures fell below freezing for almost three months; often, the soup they ate for lunch would turn to ice.[204] Between December 1938 and March 1939, at least 429 Sachsenhausen prisoners died at the brick works and elsewhere in the camp, more than in any other KL during this period.[205] The great majority of the dead were so-called asocials, who made up the largest prisoner group at the Oranienburg building site and often faced special harassment by SS and Kapos.[206]

One victim was the fifty-five-year-old agricultural laborer Wilhelm Schwarz, who was part of a fifty-man-strong earth-leveling detail—all of them, like him, "asocial" prisoners—toiling at the brick works. Schwarz died on the morning of March 21, 1939, some nine months after he had arrived in Sachsenhausen as a "work-shy" prisoner. According to the responsible Kapo, who was interviewed during a routine investigation, Schwarz had been crushed to death as he tried to empty a dump truck filled with sand. This may not have been the whole story, but whatever the truth, the Kapo, a political prisoner, clearly had no sympathy for inmates like Wilhelm Schwarz, even in death: he complained bitterly that the "asocials" in his unit were extremely "lazy" and "unreasonable," refusing to "make the slightest effort during work."[207] The SS guards cared even less about the gruesome death of Wilhelm Schwarz, or any of the other fatalities at Oranienburg. The dead could be replaced straightaway, as there was no shortage of prisoners, and so the Camp

SS worked more prisoners to death, in an early display of lethal disregard for its forced laborers.[208]

But even with a boundless supply of forced labor, the Oranienburg brick works would not have become the expected triumph, as SS ambitions far exceeded SS abilities. The brick works turned into a giant disaster, reminiscent of some vast and pointless state projects pursued by the Soviets in the Gulag. The decisive moment came in May 1939, during the first proper trial run, with the plant already months behind schedule. SS officials watched in disbelief as their dreams turned to dust, quite literally: the bricks that left the brand-new kilns just crumbled and fell apart. In their ignorance and haste, SS managers had committed a litany of elementary errors. Most grievously, they had never bothered to check whether the local clay was suitable for dry press production. It was not. The vast new factory, which had claimed so many lives, would never produce a single usable brick.[209]

The debacle at Oranienburg was a devastating indictment of SS incompetence. Clearly, the SS was in no position to run a large high-tech factory.[210] The reaction of Oswald Pohl was equally telling. Instead of scaling back SS ambitions, he pressed ahead with brick production in Oranienburg, whatever the price. Obstacles would not stop the SS; they had to be overcome. To save face, and his own career, Pohl moved fast in the summer of 1939, hoping to keep Himmler in the dark about the true scale of the disaster. Looking for scapegoats, he got rid of the private building contractor and the hapless chief executive of DESt. Pohl handed control of DESt to younger men with a greater understanding of modern management, who combined opportunism, drive, and professionalism with commitment to the Nazi cause. Soon, prisoners had to tear down structures they had only just erected in Oranienburg; they demolished kilns and ripped out machines and concrete foundations. Meanwhile, a huge rebuilding program added new parts, this time using the more reliable wet press process. All this cost yet more lives and money, and the SS still had little to show for it. In 1940, after production had restarted on a small scale, the plant barely produced three million bricks, almost all of which were needed on site. And although the output rose in the following years, it never even came close to the original targets.[211] However, SS hubris remained unchecked, as SS managers stubbornly clung to the belief that any plans, however far-fetched or deadly, could be willed into reality.

Illness and Death

The KL of the late 1930s were no full-scale slaughterhouses. Living conditions were not lethal for most prisoners, and systematic mass extermination was not yet on the SS agenda. As a result, the bulk of the inmate population survived, at least for now. This was true, above all, for female prisoners, only a handful of whom perished during the late 1930s.[212] Although the prospects for men were bleaker, the great majority of them pulled through, too. True, death was no longer the exception; but it was not yet the norm, either. Of the well over fifty thousand men taken to concentration camps sometime between January 1938 and August 1939, 2,268 are known to have lost their lives inside. Despite the immense hardship of the camps, then, survival remained by far the most likely outcome.[213]

Still, many more men died in KL than in the mid-1930s, especially during the most lethal phase, between summer 1938 and spring 1939. To some degree, this reflected the general growth of the prisoner population at the time. But the death rate rose much faster than inmate numbers. In Dachau, for example, the average prisoner population doubled in the late 1930s, while the number of deaths increased more than tenfold.[214] There were several causes. Daily forced labor became more ruinous than before, as we have seen, with most prisoners forced into heavy construction. At the same time, basic living conditions declined due to shortages and overcrowding. Another important factor was the poor medical care for ill and injured prisoners, a crucial aspect of the KL that requires further scrutiny.

The Camp SS generally neglected the prisoners' health, focusing instead on security, punishment, and labor. In the absence of firm direction from above, the medical infrastructure varied from camp to camp. And although the different infirmaries expanded during the late 1930s, adding more space and technical equipment—in Sachsenhausen, there was now a regular operating room and an X-ray department—the overall standard of care remained woefully inadequate.[215]

The biggest threat were the Camp SS men themselves. It was a basic SS tenet that ailing inmates were still dangerous enemies. SS men automatically suspected sick prisoners of being cheats and stopped many of them from receiving medical help altogether. When an ill Dachau prisoner dared to approach camp compound leader Hermann Baranowski for permission to see the doctor, one day in 1937, he provoked a wild tirade: "So what! During the [First World] War, people marched for hours with their guts in their hands! You have to learn to endure pain! I will make sure of it! Dismissed!"[216] SS doctors, meanwhile, actively searched for supposed malingerers, following orders from Theodor Eicke. "Prisoners trying to avoid work by unfounded or prissy sick-reporting," Eicke insisted, "are detailed to the 'penal work' section."[217] KL doctors were also complicit in countless other acts of terror. They routinely declared prisoners "fit" to be whipped, denied them care for wounds, and covered up murders by forging autopsy reports and death certificates.[218]

SS doctors were in short supply, and although it is hard to generalize, it seems that those who ended up inside the KL were often inexperienced, incompetent, or both. As graduates, they stood out from other Death's Head SS officers, almost none of whom had set foot inside a university, except perhaps to beat up left-wing students in the Weimar years. Many KL doctors had only recently qualified and saw the camps, and the harsh treatment of prisoners, as a springboard for their medical careers. One of this breed of young SS physicians was Dr. Ludwig Ehrsam, the head of the Sachsenhausen infirmary. Not yet thirty years of age, Dr. Ehrsam rarely bothered to examine his patients. Instead, he would force them to perform physical exercises, supposedly to determine whether they were ready to return to work. His callousness cost numerous prisoner lives, earning him a fitting nickname among the Sachsenhausen prisoners: Dr. Gruesome.[219]

There were exceptions, of course. A few SS doctors tried to improve the treatment in the KL and occasionally even sent inmates to specialists in proper hospitals.[220] Mostly, though, sick prisoners could expect poor provision, neglect, and abuse. It would have been easy to improve things, if only the SS had wanted. After all, there were experienced physicians among the prisoners who could have assisted in infirmaries, as they had done in some early camps.[221] Camp SS men knew very well that these inmates were often much better qualified than SS doctors were.[222] However, by the late 1930s, the SS often refused to draw on prisoner doctors, some of whom now helped their fellow inmates in secret.[223] Instead, it left most daily duties in the infirmaries to prisoners with little or no medical training. These Kapos worked under SS orderlies, who were often even more ignorant, and SS doctors, who rarely deigned to deal with routine matters.[224]

The indifference of SS doctors threatened the entire prisoner population. Poor hygiene created a breeding ground for infectious diseases, and several epidemics spread through KL in the late 1930s. Buchenwald was hardest hit, following an outbreak of typhoid fever in the overcrowded camp in late 1938. The epidemic soon spread beyond the compound, after wastewater contaminated a nearby stream. Alarmed municipal officials placed several villages under quarantine and blamed the Buchenwald SS for its negligence. By the time the SS medical staff finally took action—isolating sick prisoners in a special barrack and banning the use of the open latrine—it was too late. The epidemic in the camp raged for weeks, killing scores of inmates.[225]

One of the last victims was Jura Soyfer, a young poet and writer arrested as a left-wing opponent in Austria after the Nazi takeover in spring 1938. The

Buchenwald SS had forced him to work as a corpse carrier and it was here that he caught typhoid fever. Jura Soyfer died on February 16, 1939, only days after he had learned that the SS was about to release him. He was mourned by other inmates, who had been inspired by the witty parodies of the SS he had secretly performed in the barracks. As his wooden coffin left the camp on the back of a van, on its way to the Weimar crematorium, a fellow prisoner wondered "how many unwritten poems, how many unfinished works have we locked inside with him!"[226]

Jura Soyfer was one of around one thousand men who perished in Buchenwald between January 1938 and August 1939, making it, in absolute terms, by far the most deadly KL at the time. In Dachau, by contrast, just over four hundred prisoners lost their lives over the same period, even though it admitted slightly more men than Buchenwald.[227] How do we account for Buchenwald's wretched record? It was the most recent among the big SS camps, and sanitary conditions were worse there than in Dachau and Sachsenhausen, epitomized by the typhoid epidemic. And the Buchenwald SS was particularly violent, whipped up by the traumatic killing in May 1938 of SS Rottenführer Albert Kallweit. But there was another crucial factor, perhaps the most important of all. Buchenwald held far more Jewish prisoners than any other KL at the time, and Jews remained the favorite victims of the Camp SS; of all the Buchenwald prisoners who died in the late 1930s, almost half were Jewish, Jura Soyfer among them.[228]

JEWS

"I would not like to be a Jew in Germany," Hermann Göring quipped on November 12, 1938, at a top-level Nazi meeting on anti-Jewish policy, only days after a devastating state-sponsored pogrom had engulfed Germany, with Nazi mobs razing thousands of synagogues, shops, and houses, and humiliating, robbing, and assaulting tens of thousands of Jews; hundreds had died, murdered during the storm of violence or driven to suicide.[229] The pogrom was the climax of years of Nazi persecution, which saw the gradual but relentless exclusion of Jews from German social, cultural, and economic life, pursued by radical forces from below and above. It was becoming impossible for Jews to live in Germany, and around half of the estimated five hundred thousand Jews left their fatherland during the prewar years, despite the uncertainties of life abroad, the Nazi levies on emigration, and the difficulties of securing visas. The remaining Jews—impoverished, isolated, and deprived—faced a desperate future trapped inside the Third Reich.[230]

The history of Jews in prewar Nazi Germany has been told before, though rarely with more than a passing glance at the concentration camps.[231] There is an obvious explanation for this oversight: except for a brief moment after the pogrom, only a fraction of the Jewish population was held in the camps. In the prewar years, the focal point of anti-Jewish policy was elsewhere—in schools, at work, in courts, on the streets. And yet, the persecution of Jews in the prewar camps was important, too, as the KL spearheaded anti-Semitic terror and pioneered several radical measures that later hit all Jews under Nazi rule.[232]

Take racial legislation. It was an article of faith for Nazi leaders that sexual relations between Jews and non-Jews were a monstrous sin. But even though there had been talk of an official ban since 1933, the regime initially bided its time. From spring 1935, local Nazi thugs across Germany, frustrated with the general direction of the dictatorship, took matters into their own hands and attacked "mixed" couples. The police, in turn, dragged numerous "race defilers" to concentration camps in summer 1935. German courts could not yet punish them; the police and the SS could. "To put an end to his sensual greed," the Magdeburg Gestapo noted in one such case, involving a Jewish man accused of sex with his "Christian" housekeeper, it was "absolutely necessary to confine him in a concentration camp."[233] Such cases declined only after the promulgation of the Nuremberg Laws in September 1935, which formally made Jews into second-class citizens, and outlawed extramarital relations and future marriages, threatening culpable men with prison or penitentiary (women did not fall under this provision). From now on, the Gestapo reserved protective custody for "race defilement" largely for men suspected of "particularly serious" offenses, and later some Jewish women, too (or "Jewish whores," as one police officer put it).[234]

The KL also broke new ground when it came to driving Jews out of the country. Forced emigration only emerged as the primary aim of Nazi anti-Jewish policy in the late 1930s.[235] But the police had already gained extensive experience inside concentration camps. From 1935, the Gestapo had routinely taken German émigrés who came back home into protective custody, suspecting them of "atrocity propaganda" abroad.[236] Among them were many hundreds of Jews. Before they were released again, normally after around six months, the Gestapo insisted that they would have to leave the country, preferably for Palestine or beyond. Before long, the release of other Jewish prisoners had become conditional on emigration, too, pushing even more of them out of Germany; anyone returning once more to German soil was threatened with lifelong detention in a concentration camp.[237]

The prewar camps foreshadowed the later all-out assault against the Jews in many ways. Not only were KL prisoners the first Jews under Nazi control to be marked with the yellow Star of David, but the prewar camps functioned as a "motor of radicalization" for anti-Semitic policy more generally, as the historian Jürgen Matthäus put it, driving forward the isolation, forced labor, and murder of Jews in the Third Reich.[238] The transmission of these measures from the KL across German society was aided by senior SS personnel, starting at the top with Heinrich Himmler, who not only steered the camps, but also helped to propel anti-Jewish policy.

Coordinating Anti-Jewish Abuse

Before 1938, few Jews were taken to the KL. Despite the detention of Jewish "race defilers" prior to the promulgation of the Nuremberg Laws, there were still no more than a few dozen Jewish prisoners in each camp during the mid-1930s; even a large KL like Sachsenhausen only held around fifty Jewish men by early 1937.[239] Despite the small size of the Jewish prisoner population, it always loomed large in the minds of Camp SS men, who eagerly anticipated their arrival, just like some guards in the early camps had done.[240]

Radical anti-Semitism was part of the Camp SS code, a wild mix of traditional prejudice, racial mania, perverse fantasies, and political paranoia. Many SS men had been steeped in anti-Semitism long before they entered the camps, and once inside, their hatred was fanned daily, in word and deed. So deeply ingrained was this mind-set that even an SS guard formally questioned about his part in the murder of a Jewish prisoner (the attorney Friedrich Weissler in Sachsenhausen) saw no cause to conceal his feelings. "[Scharführer Christian] Guthardt acknowledged that he is a fanatical Jew-hater," a Berlin state prosecutor noted after an interrogation in 1937, "and declared that for him, a Jew was less than a head of cattle."[241]

Almost every day in the mid-1930s, SS guards made Jews run the gauntlet. They showered their victims in invective and made them debase themselves with humiliating tasks, like singing the Buchenwald "Jew Song," which ended as follows:

> But now at last the Germans know our nature
> And barbed wire hides us safely out of sight.
> Traducers of the people, we are fearful
> To face the truth that felled us overnight.
>
> And now, with mournful crooked Jewish noses,
> We find that hate and discord were in vain.
> An end to thievery, to food aplenty.
> Too late, we say, again and yet again.[242]

At the center of SS abuse stood, once more, forced labor. The guards, who derided Jews as lazy cheats, were determined to teach them a lesson about labor they would never forget.[243] Just like in the early camps, Jews had to perform particularly heavy and revolting jobs. The infamous latrine squads—widely mocked by the SS as "4711 commandos" (after a German eau de cologne)—almost always included Jews. The same was true for the most exhausting labor details. As they were breaking boulders with heavy hammers, Sachsenburg prisoners had to shout things like "I am an old Jewish swine" or "I am a race defiler and should peg out."[244]

Such work was often accompanied by blows and kicks, as SS guards stayed especially close to the Jewish commandos. In Sachsenhausen, for example, Jews who cleaned the guardhouse regularly suffered "broken ribs, knocked-out teeth, and other physical injuries," two survivors wrote after the war.[245] The guards also tortured Jews with senseless work, even more so than others. In Esterwegen, SS men repeatedly forced Jewish prisoners to pile up a large mound of sand. Once they had finished, they had to pull an iron cart to the top, climb inside, shout "Comrades, a new age is dawning, we're setting off for Palestine!" and ride down; the cart would inevitably crash, causing serious injuries.[246] In view of such excesses, it is not surprising that Jews were far more likely to die than the average inmate during the mid-1930s.[247]

Even so, most Jewish prisoners survived the concentration camps during this period. The SS did not reserve its worst violence exclusively for Jews, at times hitting other prisoner groups just as hard. And Jewish prisoners still received some of the privileges open to others, like permission to buy additional goods with small sums sent by relatives; a few Jews also gained access to Kapo positions, giving them added influence.[248] In Moringen, Jewish women were even allowed to celebrate Chanukah in late 1936—lighting the menorah, exchanging small gifts, and singing hymns—after they were granted two days off work by the senior guard.[249] This would have been unthinkable in camps for men, where conditions were far worse and would soon deteriorate further.

In the second half of the 1930s, the SS increasingly coordinated its anti-Jewish abuse across the KL. Whereas earlier assaults had originated with local Camp SS men, SS leaders now tried to guide terror from above. From August 1936, all releases of Jews from protective custody required the personal approval of Heinrich Himmler, who had discussed the question of releases with Hitler himself.[250] An even more important initiative came in February 1937, when Himmler designated Dachau as the central camp for all male Jewish prisoners.[251] Nazi policy had been moving in this direction for some time. From 1936, the Camp SS had separated Jewish prisoners more systematically from others, forming additional Jewish blocks and labor details in the KL. Now segregation was taken to the next stage.[252]

Dachau seemed the obvious choice as the central camp for Jews. It already held the largest number of Jewish prisoners and had pioneered their separation into a special "Jew company" as long ago as spring 1933. Following Himmler's decision, some eighty-five men arrived from other camps in early spring 1937, bringing the total number of Jewish prisoners in Dachau to around 150, rising further to an estimated three hundred by the end of the year (around twelve percent of the Dachau prisoner population).[253] The prisoners faced a familiar catalogue of SS abuses and occasional murder—like in summer 1937, when an SS block leader forced a prisoner accused of "race defilement" inside a running cement mixer.[254]

The segregation in Dachau made it easier for SS leaders to impose collective punishment against all male Jewish prisoners. On November 22, 1937, for example, Heinrich Himmler announced a general ban on releasing Jews from Dachau, which apparently remained in place for well over six months.[255] Another collective punishment was the isolation of Jewish prisoners in their barrack. This seclusion was enforced at least three times in Dachau in 1937, the first time in March, just as Jews from other camps arrived. It was imposed centrally by the Camp Inspectorate in Berlin, and although Eicke took credit as its inventor, the orders probably emanated from Himmler himself.[256]

SS leaders pronounced such collective punishment as a penalty for "atrocity lies" about the camps, which they blamed, in their fanatical belief in a Jewish world conspiracy, on the collusion between prisoners and Jews abroad. Many regular Camp SS men agreed. "At the time," Rudolf Höss recalled, "I thought it was right to punish Jews we held in our hands for the spread of horror stories by their racial brethren." By using the Jews as hostages—an idea that had preoccupied Nazi leaders for some time and became more virulent in the late 1930s—the Camp SS hoped to put an end to foreign criticism.[257] The Dachau SS also forced the prisoners to send protest letters about "lying reports" in foreign papers. Hans Litten, who had arrived in Dachau from Buchenwald on October 16, 1937, informed his mother on November 27, 1937, that he and the other Jewish prisoners were punished with isolation and that she should try to "influence the emigrant Jews . . . to abstain in the future from such idiotic lies about the concentration camps, since the Jews in Dachau as racial comrades will be held responsible for them." Such crude SS blackmail did not fool anyone, of course, and was quickly exposed by the press abroad.[258]

During those periods when the Dachau Jews were isolated, their seclusion was nearly total. For several weeks at a time, they were cut off from all other prisoners. Except for a brief spell of "sport," they spent day and night in their barrack, with doors locked and windows painted over, allowing only dim light inside; the air was stale and humid, especially during the hot summer months. Prisoners spent most of their time lying on their sacks of straw, lethargic and tense, as well as hungry, since they could not supplement their rations with food from the canteen.[259] Worst of all, perhaps, was the mail embargo, which hit the prisoners as hard as their relatives outside. In late August 1937, after she had waited in vain for more than a month for a letter from her husband in Dachau, Gertrud Glogowski, herself imprisoned in Moringen, sent a desperate plea to the camp authorities: "So far, his letters have held me up. Now, because there is no news at all, I am completely done for."[260]

Cruel as the Dachau isolation was, it had some unintended benefits for the victims. Since Jewish prisoners were excluded from roll calls and forced labor, they temporarily escaped some of the worst SS excesses. To pass the days in the barrack, they made music, discussed politics, and organized talks. In the midst of it all was Hans Litten, who was temporarily reenergized, almost cheerful, sharing his knowledge of art and history, and reciting literature and poems. But this would be Litten's last stand. Once the SS lifted the last isolation in late December 1937, normal life resumed, and Litten was pressed into the grueling snow-clearing commando. After almost five years in Nazi hands, he was haggard, listless, and frail, and he walked with a cane like an old man, belying his youth. The end came in early 1938. Following the death of the Jewish Kapo in his Dachau block—tortured by SS men suspecting a conspiracy—Litten was interrogated by Standartenführer Hermann Baranowski and afterwards lost all hope. Shortly after midnight on February 5, his body was found hanging in the latrine. He was only thirty-four years old, one of forty men who lost their lives in Dachau between January and May 1938; at least half of them had been detained as Jews, like Hans Litten.[261]

Dark Months

The year 1938 was a fateful one for Jews in the Third Reich.[262] In the months leading up to the November pogrom, the authorities launched a frontal assault on the remaining Jews, incited by Hitler and other Nazi leaders. Legal discrimination and state-sponsored robbery of Jewish businesses and property intensified, as did attacks on Jews and their belongings. Meanwhile, the Anschluss of Austria, accompanied by looting, violence, and humiliation on a grand scale, gave further momentum to anti-Semitic policy.[263] And as Nazi terror against Jews escalated, the KL began to play a more prominent role in their persecution.

Austrian Jews were hit first, during a wave of arrests in spring of 1938, following the German invasion. Initially, the police focused on political opponents and prominent men, many of Jewish descent; the first transport of 150 Austrian detainees, arriving in Dachau on April 2, 1938, included sixty-three Jews.[264] The new Nazi rulers quickly extended their reach beyond prominent Jews, encouraged by the Gestapo raids across Germany against the "work-shy" in April 1938. While these raids had not specifically targeted Jews, the authorities in May 1938 launched a major action in annexed Austria specifically against Jews described as "asocial," "criminal," or otherwise "disagreeable." Armed with these open-ended orders, SS and police carried out random raids, swooping on parks, public squares, and restaurants, and arrested Jews simply for being Jewish. In late May 1938, the up-and-coming SD officer Adolf Eichmann, recently posted to Vienna, expected that some five thousand Jews, mostly from Vienna, would be dispatched to Dachau over the coming weeks. Although this target proved too ambitious in the end, the authorities did direct three special trains to Dachau, arriving between May 31 and June 25 with 1,521 Jewish men on board.[265]

The suffering of these Austrian Jews began well before they reached Dachau. Unusually, the trains from Vienna were guarded by SS men from Dachau, not by police officials, and the men with the Death's Head on their uniforms battered their victims during the grueling journey. Several Jewish prisoners were dead by the time the transports arrived at a new track inside the Dachau complex, where the trains were greeted by a baying SS mob, who kicked and punched the survivors with rifle butts until they panicked and ran toward the camp, protecting their heads. The new arrivals were chased along the way by the frenzied guards, who were cheered by off-duty colleagues watching from their quarters; left behind on the road were the hats, scarves, clothes, and shoes of the Jewish men. So excessive was the violence—SS officers estimated that on one transport, around seventy percent of the prisoners had been assaulted, some suffering deep stab wounds—that representatives from the state attorney's office came to the camp to investigate, though to no avail.[266]

The Austrian Jews arrested in spring 1938 were still streaming into Dachau when police leaders moved to the next round of mass arrests, this time across the whole of the Third Reich. The initiative apparently came from Hitler himself, who demanded the detention of "asocial and criminal Jews" in late May 1938, perhaps inspired by the raids in Vienna.[267] Heydrich quickly added a special provision to his orders for the forthcoming mass action against "asocials," instructing regional criminal police officials to take male Jews "who have served a prison sentence of no less than one month" into preventive police custody as well. Although the arrest orders against Jews and asocials went out in the same directive in June 1938, the motives behind them were clearly different. In the case of Jews, the authorities were not interested in forced labor; rather, they wanted to pressure more Jews into giving up their property and leaving the country. This was why subsequent police orders stressed that it did not matter if the arrested Jews were fit for work. All that mattered was that they were labeled as criminals—one of the most enduring anti-Semitic stereotypes—and therefore unwanted in Germany.[268]

The action began in mid-June 1938, as planned. Simultaneous with the arrest of so-called asocials, the police rounded up Jews in their homes and in public places like bars, cafés, and cinemas. Petty offenders, many of whom had fallen foul of Nazi anti-Semitic laws, were dragged away like dangerous criminals; in Berlin, these arrests were accompanied by open violence and destruction on the streets. Members of the wider Jewish community were left deeply shaken and more terrified than ever of the KL—with good reason.[269]

There were far more Jews than ever in the concentration camps. The June 1938 raids forced almost 2,300 Jewish men inside, bringing the total number of Jewish inmates to around 4,600 (late June 1938), an estimated tenfold increase since March. Jews now made up almost twenty percent of the prisoner population across the concentration camp system. Faced with this sharp rise, the Nazi authorities abandoned the near-exclusive use of Dachau, already overcrowded, as the collection camp for Jews. Instead, the largest group of "criminal" Jews arrested during the June raids, some 1,265 Jewish men, was sent to Buchenwald, a camp that only a few weeks earlier had held only seventeen Jewish prisoners. In the blink of an eye, Buchenwald turned into the most lethal KL for Jews.[270]

The general conditions in Buchenwald in summer 1938 were appalling, but they were worst for the Jewish victims of the June mass arrests. As there were not enough barracks, the SS forced hundreds of new arrivals, among them many Jews from Berlin, into a sheep pen; for months, prisoners slept on brushwood spread across the bare ground. And although all the recently arrested "asocials" were assaulted by the SS, the guards singled out Jews for the most vicious abuse. Many Camp SS men were fired up about their first encounters with large numbers of Jewish "enemies"; some screamed things like: "At last we have you here, you Jew pigs. You shall all die a miserable death here." Often, SS men would abandon assaults on other prisoner groups to concentrate their energies on Jews. As always, labor was the greatest torture. "The Jews shall learn how to work," the Buchenwald SS leaders announced, and pressed them into the worst jobs, such as hauling limestone in the quarry, at running pace, for ten or more hours a day; even the sick and old had to carry boulders until they collapsed under the weight.[271]

Jewish prisoners in Buchenwald were soon decimated. Between June and

August 1938, at least ninety-two men lost their lives, making Jews far more vulnerable than other inmate groups. There were so many deaths that Camp Inspector Eicke, as early as June 21, 1938, proposed the construction of a crematorium in Buchenwald, to spare his SS men the frequent transfer of corpses to the municipal facilities in Weimar.[272] The Buchenwald death toll would have been higher still had the police not released hundreds of Jewish prisoners within weeks of their arrest, often conditional on their emigration. Those who returned from Buchenwald were broken and fearful, an underground report explained: "In general, the men start to cry as soon as you ask them anything."[273]

Not every KL was like Buchenwald, however. Despite all the Nazi efforts to coordinate anti-Jewish terror, major differences remained. While Buchenwald was unusually lethal in summer 1938, Dachau proved much less so, with Jewish men around seven to ten times less likely to die.[274] Even Buchenwald did not sustain its ferocity. In September 1938 the inmate population grew further, after the transfer of around 2,400 Jews from Dachau made it the undisputed SS center for Jewish prisoners.[275] On October 4, 1938, Buchenwald held 3,124 Jewish men (some thirty percent of its total inmate population), putting even more pressure on resources in the packed camp.[276] Yet the number of deaths among Jewish prisoners fell sharply, from forty-eight in July to eight in October, after some of the most abysmal lodgings, like the sheep pen, were finally abandoned.[277] This would prove no more than a brief lull in anti-Jewish terror, however, soon to be shattered.

Pogrom

On the morning of November 7, 1938, a Jewish teenager from Hanover, Herschel Grynszpan, walked into the German embassy in Paris, drew a revolver, and fatally wounded a German diplomat. This lone and desperate act of protest—Grynszpan's parents and siblings had just been deported from the Third Reich to the Polish border, together with some eighteen thousand other Jews of Polish nationality—was the spark that set off the pogrom. Two days later, Nazi leaders, who had gathered in Munich for the ritual celebration of the anniversary of Hitler's failed 1923 putsch, seized on the German diplomat's death to launch a nationwide orgy of destruction, later called the "night of broken glass" (*Kristallnacht*) by sarcastic Germans. It was instigated on the evening of November 9, 1938, by Joseph Goebbels, backed by Adolf Hitler, who agreed that the time had come for Jews "to feel the fury of the people," as the eager Goebbels noted in his diary. Senior Nazi officials frantically sent instructions to their underlings across the country, and within hours, local Nazi thugs were on the rampage everywhere.[278]

The pogrom was accompanied by mass arrests, after Hitler ordered the urgent detention of tens of thousands of Jews.[279] Just before midnight on November 9, Gestapo headquarters instructed its forces to prepare the arrest of twenty to thirty thousand Jews, especially prosperous ones. More detailed orders followed less than two hours later, this time directly from Reinhard Heydrich: police officers should arrest as many Jews—above all wealthy, healthy, and younger men—as they could detain locally and then ensure their rapid transfer to concentration camps.[280]

In the days after November 9, 1938, more than thirty thousand Jews of all ages and backgrounds were rounded up in German villages, towns, and cities. SA and SS fanatics, drafted in as auxiliaries, abused their victims during the arrests. Regular policemen, by contrast, often acted in a more detached manner. As a middle-aged Frankfurt doctor, whom I shall call Dr. Julius Adler, recalled a few weeks later, the police officer who had detained him at his home on the morning of November 10, 1938, behaved "not particularly friendly but perfectly proper." Like many other prisoners, Dr. Adler was moved to a temporary holding center, in his case a large hall in the Festhalle, the Frankfurt convention center, where Jews had to hand over valuables and endure occasional harassment and assaults by SS men who mingled among the police.[281] Several thousand Jewish prisoners were spared the KL as the authorities released women and also some men (among them seniors and army veterans) from protective custody within a matter of hours or days.[282] Many other elderly and weak men, however, had to join the other male Jewish prisoners on mass transports to one of three KL—Dachau, Sachsenhausen, and Buchenwald.

Much of the pogrom unfolded before the eyes of ordinary Germans, and the mass arrests and deportations of Jewish men to the KL took place in plain view, too. In many cities, triumphant Nazis publicly humiliated the prisoners; in Regensburg, the victims were paraded through town with a large placard reading "Exodus of the Jews," before they boarded a train to Dachau. Popular reactions are hard to gauge, but there was at least some sympathy for the plight of the prisoners. As one regional SD office complained, "hardened democrats" showed great pity for the imprisoned Jews and spread rumors about suicides and deaths in the camps. There were also some anonymous protests to Nazi leaders. But only a few Germans dared to voice open criticism, while hard-liners loudly applauded the deportations.[283]

The transports were terrifying. When Dr. Adler and other Jews were locked into a special train in Frankfurt, late on November 10, they were warned that they would be shot if they tried to open the windows. Although they were not abused during the journey—unlike prisoners on some other transports—the men were greatly worried about what would happen next. Screaming SS guards met them at Weimar train station and pushed them onto waiting trucks. At Buchenwald, the prisoners had to run into the camp, past more guards who kicked and punched them. "Then we moved at the double across the assembly ground of the camp," Dr. Adler later wrote, "with those who were too slow being again spurred on by blows with sticks." During those dark November days, an endless stream of prisoners spilled onto the Buchenwald roll call square, where they faced hours of torment during registration. Some prisoners arrived drenched in blood, with swollen heads and broken bones, following the SS "welcome" at the gate. "I was hit in the eye," one man later reported, "and as a result lost the sight in that eye."[284] Similar scenes unfolded in Dachau and Sachsenhausen in mid-November 1938, as the SS pressed a total of around twenty-six thousand Jewish men into its three big KL.[285]

Almost overnight, the SS concentration camps had dramatically changed. Never before had they held more inmates: within days, the prisoner population doubled from twenty-four thousand to around fifty thousand.[286] Never since the inclusion of female prisoners in the KL system had there been so few women: as there were no mass transports of Jewish women to Lichtenburg, the overall proportion of female prisoners in the camps fell to under two percent.[287] Never before had there been as many Jews in the KL: at the start of 1938, they had made up only around five percent of the prisoner population; now they were suddenly in the majority. And never before did as many prisoners die in the KL as in the weeks following the pogrom.

The KL after Kristallnacht

"One of the bloodiest and most horrible chapters in the history of Buchenwald"—this is how two veteran prisoners later described the period after the pogrom.[288] The SS was largely unprepared for the huge influx of Jewish prisoners in November 1938, plunging the camp system into even greater chaos than after the June raids against "asocials." In Dachau, barracks that had been cleared for Jews were soon so overcrowded that some new arrivals were forced into a vast tent instead. In Sachsenhausen, the SS used the makeshift barracks of the little camp, first set up after the summer raids against "asocials," and they, too, were bursting.[289] But Buchenwald proved the greatest ordeal.

The first so-called November Jews arriving in Buchenwald were crammed into a primitive barrack erected a few weeks earlier for Austrian prisoners. Meanwhile, other inmates had to build, at frantic pace, four more provisional barracks out of thin wooden boards, with no floors, right on the muddy soil. The entire new area, at the far corner of the roll call square, was cut off from the rest of the compound with barbed wire. At night, each barrack was filled with almost two thousand prisoners, who slept on tiny wooden bunks, more like shelves, without mattresses or blankets; the men were pushed so tightly against one another that it was impossible to move. "Our accommodation was such," the Frankfurt doctor Julius Adler wrote a few weeks later, "that we always felt like cattle locked into a dirty cowshed." One night, two of the barracks caved in under the weight of the bodies inside.[290]

Every day in Buchenwald, the Jews suffered from dirt and disease, thirst and hunger. Food was only handed out at irregular intervals, as the SS struggled to maintain any semblance of order, while the persistent water shortages caused terrible dehydration. The men could not wash either, or change their damp and soiled civilian clothes; "one was covered up to one's knees with a thick crust of clay," reported Dr. Adler. Inside the barracks, the stench soon became unbearable, especially after a mass outbreak of diarrhea. There were no sanitary facilities to speak of, just two overflowing ditches, where murderous SS men tried to drown several Jewish men. Inevitably, many Buchenwald prisoners suffered from infections and injuries, including frozen limbs, as well as mental illness, but the SS initially refused them any medical care. Instead, the sick were dumped in a rickety shed—"a hovel stinking of excrement, urine, and pus," as a prisoner orderly remembered; it was nicknamed the "barrack of death."[291]

The Camp SS did not quite know what to do with the "November Jews" and never fully integrated them into the regular routines. In Buchenwald, as well as in Dachau, these inmates were not pressed into forced labor, watching as other prisoners marched off to work outside the compound. Instead, they spent most of the day sitting, standing, or running on the roll call square, enduring endless drills, parades, and punitive exercises. Only in Sachsenhausen did the SS decide, after a week or so, to draft Jews into work, often at the brick works, where accidents were frequent, and medical treatment scarce. "For Jews, I only sign death certificates," the Sachsenhausen SS camp doctor is said to have exclaimed.[292]

The special status of the so-called November Jews was reinforced by their separation from the other KL inmates, including all other Jews. Despite SS threats, some prisoners—both Jews and non-Jews—passed food and water to the desperate new arrivals, and offered vital advice on how to behave.[293] Such support for the "November Jews" remained rather rare, however, not just because of the obvious dangers, but also because of long-standing prejudices against Jews. "Among the prisoners," an underground SPD report about Dachau concluded, "there are many who despise the Jews."[294]

The "November Jews" had to look to one another for help. Inevitably, there were many obstacles to solidarity, starting with the general deprivation. Many of the new prisoners had yet to adjust to the camps, and were bewildered by the daily torment. Moreover, while the SS may have seen all Jews as alike, things looked very different from the perspective of the prisoners themselves, who were acutely conscious of all the barriers of class, religion, nationality, and politics. The so-called November Jews were German and Austrian, secular and orthodox, young and old, Communist and conservative, intellectual and uneducated, Zionist and assimilated, bourgeois and proletarian. Often, they had nothing in common except for being victims of Nazi racial mania. Such divisions were hard to overcome, especially in the face of extreme suffering.[295] And yet, there were acts of mutual aid, especially among men who had known each other already before their imprisonment.[296]

Solidarity could only achieve so much, however, and prisoners were helpless against SS assaults. While Nazi leaders called off the pogrom outside within a day, the looting and violence inside the KL continued for weeks, effectively extending the pogrom. Whenever an SS man approached, Jewish prisoners feared verbal abuse and worse. "Words like Jewish pig are the order of the day," Dr. Julius Adler recalled, adding: "Woe unto him who was driven to protest."[297] Camp SS men used all their well-honed methods of humiliation, though some were still unsure about how far they should go. When Dr. Adler first arrived in Buchenwald, a guard knocked the glasses off his face; when Adler could not find them, however, the same SS man picked them up for him and handed them back. Other guards had no second thoughts, though, and assaulted the new inmates at every turn, on the roll call squares during the day, and inside the barracks at night. All this violence, as Jewish prisoners recognized only too well, laid bare the true intentions of the Nazi regime. "They have declared war against us," a Buchenwald prisoner later wrote, "having rendered us defenseless for years."[298]

The Camp SS men did not stop at abuse. They also robbed the "November Jews," on a grand scale. Corruption was as old as the camps; it was not exceptional, it was endemic. In the early camps, for example, officials often blackmailed prisoners, forcing them to pay a ransom to regain their freedom.[299] Corruption continued after the SS coordination. Guards forced inmates to carry out household chores in their own homes, ordered prisoners to make goods for them, stole their money, and diverted SS supplies into their own pockets. Few SS men could resist the temptations of near-total power. Almost

the entire Camp SS was on the make, from rank-and-file men to leading officers; even Theodor Eicke, who periodically reproached his men for dishonesty, ran a secret account, spending the funds at his discretion.[300]

SS corruption reached new heights in November 1938. The pogrom outside had involved mass looting, followed by more state-sponsored theft; in
the most cynical move, the regime ordered German Jews on November 12
to pay one billion Reichsmark as "atonement", in effect forcing them to pay
for the damage done by the Nazi mob.[301] The Camp SS enriched itself, too,
above all in Buchenwald. Here, SS men ordered incoming "November Jews"
to throw their valuables into open crates, never to be returned. Prisoners
who had kept back money were robbed later on, in various other ways. SS
guards sold them basic goods—like water, food, shoes, sweaters, and blankets—at exorbitant prices, and also forced them to make "donations" to escape more violence. The Buchenwald SS was not shy about flaunting its
ill-gotten gains; even NCOs were seen around town wearing fancy clothes
and driving luxury cars.[302]

While the Camp SS reveled in its newfound wealth, the balance sheet for
Jewish prisoners was grim. After just a few days in the camps, almost all of
them carried serious wounds, both physical and psychological. There was a
spate of suicides. Several Jewish men, unable to bear their torment, ran into
the electrified fence or crossed the sentry line. In the past, the Camp SS had
sometimes prevented suicide attempts. Not this time. "Just let them get on with
it," Theodor Eicke told his men.[303]

In all, at least 469 Jewish men died in the KL in November and December
1938. Buchenwald was by far the most lethal site, accounting for almost two-
thirds of these deaths; 297 Jewish prisoners are known to have lost their lives
here. Sachsenhausen claimed at least another 58 lives, and Dachau 114. To
put these figures into context: in the five years between 1933 and 1937, 108
men (of all backgrounds) are known to have died in Dachau, an average of
fewer than two fatalities per month.[304]

The Pogrom in Perspective

When Dr. Julius Adler was released from Buchenwald on November 18, 1938,
after eight days inside, he walked toward the next village with some other
freed Jewish men. Famished, they entered a tavern, where the friendly landlord and his wife served them plenty of coffee, water, and sandwiches. Then
the former prisoners drove to Weimar and boarded an express train back to
Frankfurt, still dressed in the filthy clothes they had worn inside the camp.
On his return home, Dr. Adler was grateful for the warm welcome from many

non-Jewish acquaintances. But looking back at Buchenwald, he had learned two critical lessons: "Make every effort to get out those who are still in Germany, or in the camp, and second, to tell oneself in every situation: Anything is better than the concentration camp!" By the time he wrote these lines in January 1939, Dr. Adler had already left Germany.[305]

Many other German Jews did the same. Almost every family had been hit by the mass arrests, in one way or another. And although not all released men would, or could, share their experiences—"My husband does not talk about it," the wife of Erich Nathorff noted on December 20, 1938, after his return from Sachsenhausen—their suffering was written on their faces and bodies. And so the horror of the KL, together with the devastation of the pogrom itself, led to a desperate scramble to escape the Third Reich—exactly what Nazi leaders had wanted.[306]

The pogrom was a watershed for Jews in Nazi Germany. But was it a watershed for the KL, too? The answer seems obvious. The camps changed dramatically in November 1938, after all, becoming bigger and deadlier than ever before, while the acts of theft and violence fused the Camp SS even closer together. Also, the camps proved themselves once more as versatile tools of Nazi terror. By quickly locking away tens of thousands of Jews, and terrorizing more into leaving the country, the men of the Camp SS passed another test in the eyes of Nazi leaders, just as they had done during the Röhm purge more than four years earlier.[307] And yet, one should not overstate the lasting impact of the pogrom on the KL system. In many ways, it marked an exceptional moment in the prewar years, and the camps soon returned to their prior state.

To start with, Jewish prisoners did not remain in the majority for long. Nazi leaders had wanted to shock them, not to lock them away for good, and most so-called November Jews were quickly freed, far more quickly than previous victims of police raids. Mass releases set in around ten days after the pogrom and continued for weeks, as Heydrich's office issued various orders for the discharge of elderly, sick, and disabled Jews, as well as First World War veterans. Of course, the ensuing releases were tied to certain conditions. Some men had to sign over their businesses to non-Jews. Many more had to promise to leave Germany. As early as November 16, 1938, Heydrich had ordered the release of Jews "whose date of departure" from Germany was "imminent"—men like Julius Adler, who had long prepared his exit. Emigration thus became closely tied to the release of "November Jews," with prisoners signing written pledges to get out of the country. "Are any of you not emigrating?" the Dachau commandant Loritz would ask Jewish men, just before they left the camp. But at least the prisoners were released, and at a rapid rate. In Buchenwald, the total number of "November Jews" dropped from almost ten thousand in mid-November 1938 to 1,534 on January 3, 1939, to just twenty-eight on April 19, 1939.[308] With the departure of these so-called November Jews, the total number of Jewish KL prisoners declined to pre-pogrom levels. From the regime's perspective, the camps had served their function—forcing many Jews out of Germany—and there was no need for further mass arrests. Only a few hundred new Jewish prisoners arrived between January and August 1939, and like those Jews still inside, they had largely been detained as asocials, criminals, or political opponents. When war broke out in September 1939, the Nazi regime held no more than 1,500 Jews in its concentration camps, out of a population of 270,000 to 300,000 Jews still living on the territory of the Third Reich.[309] The pogrom, in short, did not turn the KL into places for the permanent mass confinement of German Jews.

Neither did it lead to a permanent extension of the KL system. Following the dramatic growth after the pogrom, prisoner numbers quickly dropped again after most of the "November Jews" departed, falling to around 31,600 by the end of 1938.[310] Numbers continued to fall over the coming months. True, there were some major police actions—including mass arrests of Austrian Gypsies in summer 1939—but not on the scale of the raids in the previous year; overall, far fewer new prisoners entered the camps.[311] Meanwhile, the police continued its prisoner releases. Most surprisingly, given his previous hostility to mass releases, Heinrich Himmler agreed to mark Hitler's fiftieth birthday on April 20, 1939, with a major amnesty, extended to various long-term political prisoners and social outsiders. On the instructions of Himmler and Eicke, the inmates were told that they had reached "the road to freedom" (though their fate would be dependent on their future behavior). Thousands of prisoners were freed in late April 1939, among them the petty criminal Josef Kolacek from Vienna and the beggar Wilhelm Müller from Duisburg, whom we encountered earlier on. Because of the amnesty, which was not publicized in the press, KL prisoner numbers fell to around twenty-two thousand in late April 1939, slightly below the mark for summer 1938.[312] This figure was virtually unchanged when Germany went to war four months later; on September 1, 1939, the KL system held around 21,400 prisoners.[313]

The camps' seemingly irresistible rise had stalled in the run-up to war. This was not what SS and police leaders had envisaged. In late 1938, Himmler and his men had hoped to use the momentum of the pogrom to enlarge the camps even further. More construction was urgently needed, they argued, so that thirty-five thousand prisoners could be accommodated at any one time. However, the call for an injection of 4.6 million Reichsmark for new build-

SS CONCENTRATION CAMPS, SEPTEMBER 1, 1939

DENMARK
SWEDEN
LITHUANIA
Memel

Baltic Sea

Königsberg

North Sea

EAST PRUSSIA

DANZIG

Hamburg

RAVENSBRÜCK □

SACHSENHAUSEN □

Hanover •
• Berlin
Oder R.

Elbe R.

0 Miles   100   200

0 Kilometers   200

GERMANY

POLAND

BUCHENWALD □

Breslau

BELGIUM
Frankfurt
Prague

LUX.
BOHEMIA AND MORAVIA
(GERMAN PROTECTORATE)

FLOSSENBÜRG □

Rhine R.

Danube R.

FRANCE
DACHAU □
MAUTHAUSEN □

Munich •
Vienna •

SLOVAKIA

HUNGARY

SWITZERLAND

ITALY
YUGOSLAVIA

□ DACHAU	4,000 inmates
□ SACHSENHAUSEN	6,500 inmates
□ BUCHENWALD	5,300 inmates
□ MAUTHAUSEN	1,500 inmates
□ FLOSSENBÜRG	1,600 inmates
□ RAVENSBRÜCK	2,500 inmates

ings met with staunch opposition from Reich minister of finance Count Schwerin von Krosigk, backed by Hermann Göring. Von Krosigk wanted to prevent the unchecked growth of the concentration camps. Every time they were extended, he warned, the police would fill them with more prisoners, and then demand further extensions, setting off an endless cycle of arrests. Instead of enlarging the KL system, he proposed the release of thousands of work-shy prisoners and others who posed no real threat to the state.[314] Even in the late 1930s, leading Nazi figures still questioned the radical direction of Himmler's terror apparatus and saw no need for bigger camps.

What, then, about the long-term impact of the SS assault on the "November Jews" on life inside the KL? In the history of the prewar camps, the weeks after the pogrom stand out as the most deadly by far, in terms of the total number of dead. This is not to say, however, that the Camp SS had suddenly moved to new extremes of violence, as historians have often suggested.[315] Rather, the weeks after the pogrom marked a deadly peak in a much longer lethal spell, which began in summer 1938 and lasted until spring 1939, and which claimed many victims in addition to the Jewish men arrested after the pogrom.

As we have seen, the expansion of terror and the deterioration of conditions began several months prior to the pogrom, in summer 1938. Following the raids against the "work-shy," prisoner mortality across the concentration camp system shot up, from a monthly average of around eighteen deaths between January and May 1938 to around 118 deaths between June and August 1938.[316] The main victims were "asocial" men, with the Jews among them being the most vulnerable of all—sometimes even more vulnerable than the so-called November Jews who arrived months later.[317] As far as Jewish prisoners were concerned, at least, SS terror in the camps did not suddenly intensify after the pogrom. It had started to escalate before.

And the terror carried on for several months after the pogrom. From late 1938, inmates were at greater risk of death than before; on average, 323 prisoners perished each month between November 1938 and January 1939.[318] Nearly half of them were Jews arrested after the pogrom. The remaining victims came from other prisoner groups, who were also hit by the rise in SS terror.[319] This was especially true, once more, for so-called asocials.[320] Crucially, mass mortality in the KL persisted well into spring 1939, long after the release of almost all so-called November Jews.[321] Despite a drop, the death rate initially remained extremely high; on average, 189 inmates lost their lives each month between February and April 1939. Almost two-thirds of the dead were "asocial" prisoners, for whom lethal SS repression continued almost unchanged into 1939.[322]

Only later that year did the KL death rate decline more markedly, at a fast pace. Soon, prisoner mortality had fallen well below the highs of the preceding months. During the summer of 1939, the last period of calm before the outbreak of the Second World War, an average of thirty-two prisoners died each month in the camps—far fewer even than in summer 1938, although overall prisoner numbers were almost identical.[323] This serves as another reminder that the Nazi camps did not head straight into the abyss. Instead, just like the Soviet Gulag, periods of rising terror were followed by greater moderation. There were structural reasons for the turnaround in summer 1939: the weather was much better, prisoner quarters were less crammed, and other elements of the infrastructure improved, too, such as the water supply at Buchenwald. At the same time, the SS also pulled back from some of its most violent excesses.[324]

Inmates were grateful for the respite in summer 1939, after the horrors of the previous twelve months. "If we were not prisoners," the Sachsenhausen camp elder Harry Naujoks wrote, "one could almost describe our life at the moment as peaceful."[325] Long-term prisoners like him were not deceived, however. They had seen enough of the KL to know that their course could change again at any moment, in a far more deadly direction.

One of these veteran prisoners was Ernst Heilmann, who had suffered all the pains of the camps, many times over. Back in summer 1933, as we have seen, he had been beaten and degraded as the "director of the crapper" in the early camp Oranienburg. Later, he was tortured in the Prussian "model" camp Börgermoor, where guards shot and wounded him during a suicide attempt. His abuse had continued after the coordination of the KL system in Sachsenhausen and Dachau, and from September 1938 in Buchenwald, the new central camp for Jews, where he was pressed into a transport detail, carrying heavy stones and earth. It was in Buchenwald that another prisoner, who had known Heilmann in his glory days as a leading Weimar politician, met him in one of the barracks reserved for Jewish inmates, sometime after the November pogrom. Heilmann was unrecognizable; his clothes were soiled and ripped, his face furrowed, his mustache cut off, his hands chapped, his back bent, his spirit broken. "He was no longer the human being Heilmann," his acquaintance later wrote, "he was just the wreck Heilmann." After they exchanged some news about mutual friends and politics, Heilmann told him about his torment at the hands of the guards. Asked about the future, Heilmann gave a stark reply: "There will be war. You Aryans will still have a chance, because they will need you. But we Jews will probably all be beaten to death." This chilling prediction soon came true for Heilmann himself, who died in the early months of the Second World War, as the KL descended into terror on an unprecedented scale.[326]

4

War

On the morning of September 1, 1939, Adolf Hitler, wearing a simple gray military uniform, addressed the hastily convened Reichstag in Berlin. Unusually tense and nervous, Hitler announced to millions of Germans listening on the radio—among them KL prisoners lined up on roll call squares—that war with Poland had broken out. In his speech, Hitler played the victim. Germany was forced to act because of Polish provocations and border violations, he claimed, including no fewer than three serious incidents during the previous night. "Tonight," Hitler announced, "Poland has for the first time fired on our territory with regular troops. Since 5:45 a.m., fire is being returned!"[1] There had indeed been trouble on the German-Polish border in Upper Silesia. But it had all been staged by the Nazis themselves: dramatic political theater—devised by Hitler and Himmler, directed by Heydrich, performed by special Nazi forces—to give an excuse, however flimsy, for German aggression. "The victor," Hitler had bluntly told his military commanders a few days earlier, "will not be asked whether he told the truth or not."[2]

The sinister plot had been prepared for some time, and on August 31, in anticipation of the imminent German attack, Heydrich gave the final go-ahead to his men in Upper Silesia. That evening, a covert commando stormed a radio station in the German border town of Gleiwitz. The men brandished pistols and announced over the airwaves that the station was in the hands of Polish freedom fighters; for effect, shots were fired in the background. Later that night, other Nazi special commandos staged the "Polish assaults" on German territory that Hitler later referred to in the Reichstag. The SS and policemen involved had trained for weeks at secret locations, even learning to sing Polish songs and growing beards and sideburns to look the part. The most elaborate mock attack came at Hochlinden, where one group, wearing Polish army uniforms and screaming in Polish, attacked and demolished the German border post, before another group, dressed as German guards, overpowered them.

To make this farce look more convincing, the conspirators decided that bodies of killed "insurgents" were needed. Looking for men who could be executed on cue, their eyes fell on KL prisoners. Sometime in mid-summer 1939, Heinrich Müller, who headed the central Gestapo department for domestic matters, arranged for top-secret transports of prisoners—or "supplies," as he apparently called them—from Sachsenhausen, Flossenbürg, and other concentration camps to a police prison in Breslau, where they were placed in solitary confinement. On August 31, 1939, some of these prisoners were taken out of their cells. An SS doctor apparently drugged them, before their lifeless bodies, dressed in Polish uniforms, were driven to Hochlinden in black Mercedes limousines with drawn blinds. After the staged attack began, the bodies were dragged out, dumped at the border post, and shot. To obscure the identity of the dead, the killers smashed their faces with hammers and axes. Then they took photos of the slain at the scene, which were sent to Berlin as "proof" of the Polish attack. The following morning, as the actual German troops were advancing into Poland, the special commando hastily buried the prisoners' corpses in the forest near Hochlinden.[3]

It could be said that the first victims of the Second World War were concentration camp inmates. Many more casualties would follow, and when the war finally ended, six years later, more than sixty million men, women, and children were dead, including more than 1.7 million KL victims.[4] Nazi leaders had long despised the prisoners, their savage mind-set summed up in spring 1938 by Joseph Goebbels, following a private conversation with Hitler and Himmler about the concentration camps. "There is only scum inside," he noted in his diary. "It has to be annihilated—for the benefit and welfare of the people."[5] This was no empty talk. During World War II, mass death engulfed inmates in almost all the camps. And although the great majority of victims died during the second half of the war, the lethal turn of the KL system began early, in the years between 1939 and 1941.

THE CAMP SS AT WAR

"War came," Rudolf Höss wrote in early 1947, looking back on the Nazi invasion of Poland, "and with it the great turn in the life of the concentration camps."[6] Höss was right, at least up to a point. The prisoner population doubled in little more than a year, reaching around fifty-three thousand at the end of 1940, and it continued to rise. A year later, by early 1942, around eighty thousand men and women were locked up, many of them crammed into new concentration camps. Because just as inmate numbers grew, so did the KL system. In autumn 1939, the SS had controlled six main camps; by early 1942, it was thirteen.[7] Considered in isolation, the expansion of the concentration camps might seem exceptional. But the KL system remained part of the wider Nazi web of terror, which also grew much denser during the early war years; existing sites flourished and new ones sprang up everywhere, with camps, jails, ghettos, prisons, and dungeons holding millions of men, women, and children. And yet, the war did not change everything; it did not revolutionize the Third Reich.[8] As far as KL terror was concerned, there was no immediate break with the past. The SS remained in overall charge and saw no need to redraw the basic outlines. The ability of the concentration camp system to absorb change and to adapt, without losing its core mission, would prove to be one of its most terrifying strengths over the coming years.

Eicke's Legacy

Hitler envisaged the war with Poland as more than an ordinary military campaign. His view of the Polish people as racial enemies—"subhuman" Slavs who had to be enslaved or destroyed—helped to make the Polish campaign the first of the Nazis' racial wars.[9] This was Himmler's moment. Since summer 1939, his deputy Reinhard Heydrich had overseen the formation of special SS and police task forces, primed to follow the army and fight against "anti-German elements."[10] After the invasion, these task forces wreaked havoc in Nazi-occupied Poland, targeting politicians, state officials, priests, and noblemen, as well as local Jews. Other troops went on a rampage, too, and by the end of 1939, after the German victory, tens of thousands of Polish civilians had been murdered, including at least seven thousand Jews.[11]

Among the fiercest killers in newly occupied Poland were Death's Head SS troops, led by none other than Theodor Eicke. Eicke had long styled himself as a "political soldier" and now moved from the imaginary inner front of the camps to the real front line. During the invasion, he commanded three SS Death's Head regiments, giving some of his orders from the safety of Hitler's armored train. For weeks, his men laid waste to villages and cities, robbing, arresting, torturing, and murdering many of the locals. As a reward, the insatiable Eicke was entrusted with the formation of the SS Death's Head division, which gradually developed its own organizational structure, separate from the KL, as Eicke's move from the camps to the front became permanent. He was joined by thousands of SS sentries as well as several senior KL officials, who came to occupy almost all leading positions in the new division (some later returned to the Camp SS). Once more, Eicke drummed his core values—brutality, racism, ruthlessness—into his men, and they did him proud. The SS Death's Head division was responsible for countless war crimes and became one of the most feared units during the Second World War.[12]

The SS men chosen for Eicke's division initially assembled for training on a site many of them knew well—Dachau. Eicke had started his career there as commandant in 1933 and now returned, six years later, as a general. On November 4, 1939, Himmler himself came to check on Eicke's progress, finding the whole complex much changed; to make room for the SS troops, Dachau had been cleared of almost all prisoners in late September 1939, with some 4,700 men transported to Mauthausen, Buchenwald, and Flossenbürg. The survivors returned after January 1940, once Eicke and his SS troops had left for another training ground.[13]

With Eicke gone, the Camp SS had lost the headmaster of its school of violence. But Eicke's spirit remained; the essence of his teachings had entered the core of the Camp SS. Also, Eicke never fully severed his ties to the camp system, acting as its elder statesman. His family still lived in the SS settlement in Oranienburg, and whenever he was on leave, he was welcome at the nearby IKL office, where he was more than happy to share his thoughts with his successor as inspector of the concentration camps, Richard Glücks.[14]

A sturdy man in his early fifties—born on April 22, 1889, just two days after Hitler—Richard Glücks had spent most of his adult life in uniform. During the First World War, he mainly fought in France, participating in the battles of Verdun and the Somme. Following a brief interlude in a Freikorps after the German defeat, the decorated soldier served in the much-reduced German army, aiding its illegal rearmament. Glücks eventually lost his post in 1931, during the depression, and was briefly unemployed. He was already a member of the Nazi Party by then, having joined in March 1930, and in November 1932, he entered the SS: the professional soldier became a professional SS officer. Glücks quickly moved ahead and caught the eye of Theodor Eicke, who appointed him on April 1, 1936, as his chief of staff, the second most powerful position in the IKL. The querulous Eicke was difficult to please, but Glücks was a man after his taste. Efficient and energetic, he was devoted to his boss, a key quality for advancing in an organization built on personal connections and favoritism. Eicke duly secured Glücks an early promotion to Oberführer, and as his boss got increasingly bogged down in military schemes in the run-up to war, it was Glücks who took over much of the day-to-day management in the IKL, well before his appointment as inspector in October 1939. He would head the KL administration for more than five years, longer even than Eicke, right up to the collapse of Nazi Germany.

Ideological commitment Glücks had in abundance; but of charisma he had none, and he was always destined to remain in the shadow of his mentor, Eicke. Compared to the overbearing Eicke, who led from the front, Glücks appeared indecisive, a serious character flaw in SS circles. And while Eicke had sought the company of his men, Glücks was a more remote figure. The intense male world of SS camaraderie was not really for him. "I live very frugally, don't drink, and have no passions," he wrote in 1935. Some senior Camp SS members viewed him with suspicion because he had never served an apprenticeship inside a KL, complaining that he was just a desk-bound bureaucrat. His superiors were more positive, but even here Glücks could not emulate Eicke. Although he was directly subordinate to Himmler, the two men were never close and rarely met.[15] Himmler had promoted Glücks not for his initiative or leadership skills, but because he stood for continuity, promising to consolidate his predecessor's legacy.

The same message was sent by the appointment of Arthur Liebehenschel as Glücks's second-in-command. More than ten years Glücks's junior, he had also been a career soldier, leaving the German army after twelve years in late 1931 as an NCO. Just a few months later, he enlisted in the SS, and in summer 1934 he joined the Camp SS, which he served for almost all of the Third Reich. As adjutant in Lichtenburg, Liebehenschel gained hands-on experience and then moved to the IKL in summer 1937. Here, he headed the political department and worked closely with Glücks, who valued his managerial skills. Some of his other colleagues, by contrast, saw Liebehenschel as a weak figure, describing him as "sensitive," "quiet," and "kind"—damning words in the martial world of the Camp SS. Rudolf Höss, his former neighbor in the genteel SS settlement in Sachsenhausen, where their children had sometimes played together, pictured him as a man "who could not even hurt a fly." In reality, Liebehenschel was deeply implicated in the increasingly murderous IKL policies, and he later got a chance to prove himself as commandant of Auschwitz.[16]

In the early war years, then, the camp administration was headed by two old hands, Glücks and Liebehenschel, who had learned their trade under Eicke. Continuity was the watchword in the individual camps, too, at least inside the Commandant Staffs, where key positions, from senior officers down to block leaders, were largely held by Camp SS veterans. Most of the eleven men promoted by Glücks to camp commandant between 1939 and 1942, for example, had previously held senior KL positions, and they, too, had internalized Eicke's values.[17] Take Martin Weiss, appointed in April 1940 as commandant of the new SS camp Neuengamme. Weiss was a first-generation member of the Camp SS, having started his career in April 1933, aged twenty-seven, as a sentry in Dachau. He later moved to the Commandant Staff, and by 1938 had risen to adjutant. An electrical engineer, Weiss was better educated than most of his comrades, but like them, he had frequented radical nationalist circles in the Weimar years and had been active early on in the nascent Nazi movement. Weiss was part of the new breed of technocrats of terror, graduates of Eicke's school who came to the fore during the Second World War. Above all else, Weiss saw himself as a professional: just as other people became army or police officers, he had become a camp commandant, and he was so proud that he used his job title even on his private notepaper.[18] In the daily running of their KL, commandants like Weiss needed little prompting from above. Inspector Glücks was not looking for administrators but for men of action who knew the rules of the game, and he was generally happy to let them get on with it. According to Rudolf Höss, Glücks often dismissed questions from commandants: "You all know much better than me what's going on."[19]

And yet, the early war-time commandants were never autonomous, despite their considerable might. Glücks and his IKL managers were in constant contact with individual camps, ruling on requests and issuing instructions about labor, punishment, transfers, promotions, discipline, and much else besides; the IKL also updated Eicke's old camp regulations.[20] Some commandants grumbled about "unrealistic" directives sent by Oranienburg pencil pushers.[21] But although they could sidestep some central rules, local camp officials implemented most orders. They also sent a stream of statistics to the IKL, including daily updates on inmate numbers and categories, and monthly figures of fatalities and causes of prisoner deaths.[22] Of course, the managers at the IKL gained no complete picture from this data, thanks not least to cover-ups by individual commandants. "What the camps really looked like," Rudolf Höss cautioned, "could not be seen from the correspondence and the files."[23] But the IKL officials had more than reports to go on. They inspected camps and called local officials for regular meetings to Oranienburg, keeping up the informal contacts so important in the Camp SS.[24] Overall, then, the IKL kept a watchful eye on its camps.

Other agencies and individuals interfered with the concentration camps, too. The police continued to hold great sway; in charge of arrests and releases, it regulated the prisoner flow to and from the KL system, and involved itself in many internal matters.[25] Other branches of the SS were shaping the camps as well, none more so than Oswald Pohl's buoyant business and administration empire. Finally, some of the most critical choices were still made at the top of the Nazi state. The personal power of Heinrich Himmler grew enormously during the war; among all the pretenders to Hitler's throne, it was Himmler who gained the most, outflanking more senior rivals. And despite his increasingly hectic schedule, he retained an intense interest in the KL, his own creation. Himmler continued to involve himself on all levels, from trivial minutiae to pivotal decisions, sometimes bypassing the police and the Inspectorate altogether.[26] In fact, SS officials could barely keep him away; in 1940 alone, his itinerary included at least nine trips to KL and associated sites.[27] The camps were still very much Himmler's camps.

Changing the Guards

While there was much continuity at the top of the Camp SS, the situation was different further below. After the invasion of Poland, a large number of sentries, who had long trained for military duties, departed. In all, an estimated 6,500 to 7,000 Camp SS men joined the SS Death's Head division in autumn 1939.[28] The gaps were filled with new recruits, who were quickly trained and deployed, generally as sentries in the Guard Troop.[29] Camp SS veterans passed on the basics. Shortly before he left to take up his military command, Theodor Eicke assembled SS men in charge of training in Sachsenhausen. They had to teach the novices to treat prisoners with absolute severity, Eicke ordered, as all foes and saboteurs had to be exterminated.[30] SS publications reminded new recruits of their duties, too, rehashing the old story of guards performing a soldier's job.[31] The fictional parity with the combat troops was upheld in other ways, as Camp SS men were soon subsumed under the large umbrella of the Waffen SS (Armed SS), which included all the militarized sections of the SS.[32]

The longer the war lasted, the more diverse the Camp SS became. This trend was set already in autumn 1939. The replacements arriving in the KL were far older than Eicke's "bright-eyed" youngsters had been. Many were in their forties or fifties, judged unfit for frontline duties and drafted from the regular SS.[33] The Buchenwald prisoner Walter Poller remembered most of these recruits as "elderly SS men with minor physical ailments."[34] It was not just their appearance that counteracted SS ideals. Many of the new men were markedly less enthusiastic than the prewar volunteers had been. And although some had previously received basic training as sentries, or had gained military experience during the First World War, they were frequently lambasted for their incompetence by Camp SS veterans.[35] A few newcomers even committed the sin of showing a human face to prisoners. Having lived through the German Empire and the Weimar Republic, they had retained some sense of right and wrong, and were not cut out for the KL.[36] In Dachau, for example, an older SS man on sentry duty confessed to prisoners that he was disgusted by his job and did not want to shoot at "helpless and desperate people."[37]

The new recruits were pushed hard to fall into line. Camp Inspector Glücks signed a thundering directive in early 1940, threatening anyone guilty of "sentimental humanitarianism" with severe consequences; newcomers had to handle all prisoners as "enemies of the state of the worst kind."[38] More reminders kept on coming.[39] Such interventions probably had some effect, as did the passage of time; what had first seemed unbearable to some novices quickly became acceptable. Many new guards soaked up the spirit of the Camp SS and became inured to the violence, just as members of Nazi killing squads in occupied Europe found that their bloody task became easier over time.[40] In a private letter soon after his arrival in Flossenbürg, one new recruit expressed his "pride" in protecting the German public from all the "bums and public enemies" inside the KL.[41]

Camp commandants piled added pressure on their men, old and new. The most domineering figure in the early war years was the Buchenwald commandant Karl Otto Koch, as the following directives from autumn and winter 1939 demonstrate. Again and again, Koch blasted his men for being lazy, stupid, and useless. Prisoners were not worked hard enough, he ranted: building sites were dirty, output "pretty much zero," and discipline "rotten."[42] It was no better inside the prisoner barracks, thanks to "indifferent" SS block leaders, who were practically "asleep."[43] His men showed no initiative, Koch railed, leaving everything to him. "It won't be long," he sneered in October 1939, "before I will have to make sure that everyone wipes their own asses."[44] Worst of all, some SS men colluded with inmates. Rather than punish or shoot prisoners who foraged for food in the camp's no-go zone, guards had asked the prisoners to fetch some vegetables for them, too. "Truly a charming way," Koch remarked acidly, "to fraternize and cooperate with criminals."[45]

Punishment was never far from Commandant Koch's mind. His main targets were prisoners, of course.[46] But the failings of SS men called for strict sanctions, too, like special drill exercises.[47] Koch habitually spied on his men through SS confidants, and in late November 1939, he took the drastic step of grounding all block leaders for two weeks; even married SS men who lived outside the camp complex were forbidden to leave.[48] The final punishment for miscreant SS men, Koch said more than once, would be their own detention in the KL: "He who gets involved with prisoners will be treated like a prisoner."[49]

Other Camp SS officers made similar threats and occasionally followed through; in Sachsenhausen, an SS man was publicly whipped because he had been bribed (by prisoner relatives) to treat some inmates better.[50]

Koch's tirades infuriated many Buchenwald SS men. To them, Koch's posing as a paragon of propriety must have smacked of grand hypocrisy, for the commandant was corrupt to the core. Not for him the small-scale scams of most SS men; as greedy as he was brutal, Koch had bigger ambitions. He had already demonstrated his ruthlessness after the 1938 pogrom, when he systematically robbed imprisoned Jews, and he became ever more brazen during the war, squirreling away tens of thousands of Reichsmark in secret bank accounts and hoarding gold ripped from the mouths of dead prisoners. He spent his loot on food and drink and on his mistresses in Weimar; he also bought himself a motorboat and extended his lavish villa. Koch lived like an SS king. His greatest extravagance was the massive indoor riding hall, complete with mirrors, which he had commissioned in February 1940 for himself and his wife, who often took her turns in the morning, accompanied by music from the camp orchestra. The prisoners paid for her pleasure with their lives; dozens had died during the breakneck construction of the riding hall, which stood near the prisoner canteen.

Eventually, Koch's crimes caught up with him. He had alienated too many SS men inside the camp and outside, including the regional higher SS and police leader, who ordered Koch's arrest in late 1941 (he was succeeded as Buchenwald commandant by Hermann Pister, who had previously run the small SS special camp Hinzert). But Koch was not finished yet. As a key member of the Camp SS, and a protégé of Eicke's, he still had powerful friends, and following an intervention from Himmler, Koch was swiftly released.[51] On probation, he was sent in January 1942 to one of the new camps in Nazi-occupied Poland. Luckily for Koch, the camp system was expanding quickly during the war, affording him another opportunity for violence, theft, and abuse.[52]

New Prisoners

Adolf Hitler always saw the Second World War as a conflict fought on two fronts. On the battlefield, he believed, Germany waged a life-and-death struggle for survival. But there was another war going on, at the home front, where Germany had to face down its remaining internal enemies. Hitler had been obsessed with the home front ever since the defeat of 1918, which he (like many Germans) blamed on the collapse of civilian morale and the "stab in the back" by Jews, Communists, Social Democrats, criminals, and others.[53] Lessons had been learned, Hitler swore in the Reichstag as he announced the attack on Poland: "A November 1918 will never be repeated in German history!" This was a rallying cry he would return to again and again during the Second World War.[54]

Policing the home front was Himmler's domain. His terror apparatus was consolidated on September 27, 1939, when the security police and the SD merged into the Reich Security Main Office (RSHA), led by Heydrich. The RSHA became the center of Nazi repression. Over the coming years, all the most radical measures were coordinated in the RSHA, a new type of Nazi institution without limits and restraint, run by young, ambitious, and educated fanatics.[55]

The police swung into action at the start of the war, pulling many more Germans into the KL. Using up-to-date databases of potential "enemies of the state," Gestapo raids caught several thousand political suspects, mainly former activists from the KPD and SPD.[56] Some were veterans of the prewar KL and now returned to the place they feared the most.[57] The criminal police, meanwhile, wanted to use the cover of war to cleanse Germany of deviants. In autumn 1939, its targets included the "work-shy," "Gypsies without fixed residence," and "criminal psychopaths," as well as homosexual men and female prostitutes.[58] As a result, the number of social outsiders in concentration camps gradually increased once more; by the end of 1940, there were over thirteen thousand prisoners in preventive police custody, slightly more than two years earlier.[59] German Jews were on the police radar, too. As early as September 7, 1939, the criminal police ordered that former Jewish camp inmates should be rearrested if they had made no real effort to leave the country—never mind the fact that escaping Germany was fast becoming impossible. Jews working "productively" were supposed to be exempt from imprisonment, as were elderly and ill Jews, at least for now.[60]

This detention of German Jews, political opponents, and social outsiders could build on prewar practices. What was new, during the war, were mass arrests of foreign nationals. As Nazi Germany staked its claim on Europe—following the conquest of Poland in 1939, Denmark was occupied in April 1940, Holland and Belgium capitulated in May, and France and Norway followed in June—more and more people from abroad were dragged to the KL. At the beginning of the Third Reich, the camps had been conceived as weapons against Germans; a decade later, they threatened the people of Europe.

Foreigners began to arrive in larger numbers in concentration camps from autumn 1939. Among the first were further Czech nationals. At the start of the war, the Nazi occupation authorities arrested hundreds of politicians and officials as "hostages" to deter resistance. But the Czech population was not cowed, resulting in large demonstrations at universities in Prague and elsewhere. The Nazi authorities quickly crushed these protests, apparently on Hitler's orders, and forced more prisoners into the KL.[61] The largest transport, with some 1,200 Czechs, arrived in November 1939 in Sachsenhausen. Among them was Jiri Volf, arrested with fellow students in his hall of residence, who later recalled the SS reception: "We were immediately beaten with truncheons, so that I lost four teeth."[62]

Other foreign political prisoners, such as those who had been on the side of the doomed Republic during the Spanish Civil War, fared even worse. Many left-wing veterans had fled Spain after Franco's victory and sought refuge in France, together with their families. It was here, often fighting for the French army, that they fell into Nazi hands. Reinhard Heydrich ordered that they should normally be taken to the KL, with Mauthausen, the most punitive camp at the time, set as the main destination. The first prisoners arrived on August 6, 1940, and within a year, more than six thousand men had been taken to the camp. Some were Germans and Austrians who had fought in the international brigades, but the great majority of the "Red Spaniards," as the Nazis called them, were Spanish.[63]

Despite the arrests across Nazi-controlled Europe, the KL did not become truly international overnight; in all, foreign prisoners still made up a rather small group until summer 1941. There was just one exception—Polish prisoners. The Nazi invasion of Poland was accompanied by extreme violence, as we have seen. The German forces started as they meant to go on, and over the coming months a brutal occupation regime was set up, aimed at the destruction of the Polish nation, the plunder of its economic resources, and the enslavement of its people. One radical project was the ethnic cleansing of the western Polish territory, which was incorporated into the Reich; by the end of 1940, more than three hundred thousand Poles had been deported from here to the so-called General Government, the eastern part of Nazi-controlled Poland, under German civilian administration (headed by Hans Frank).[64] At the same time, the occupation of Poland also radicalized Nazi anti-Jewish policy.[65]

Terror was ever-present in German-controlled Poland. Mass arrests had been in the cards well before the invasion; in late August 1939, Reinhard Heydrich envisaged that his task forces would take some thirty thousand people to the KL, far more than the entire camp population at the time.[66] The first Polish prisoners duly arrived in autumn 1939, among them resistance fighters and members of the intelligentsia, including 168 academics from Krakow University.[67] But the number of prisoners from the newly occupied Polish territory initially remained much smaller than the SS had anticipated.

Far more Poles were detained inside the old German borders in autumn

1939; above all, police leaders wanted to remove Polish Jews, sanctioning the arrest of men who had often lived in Germany or Austria for decades.[68] Police terror against Poles inside the German heartland expanded further during the following year, after the mass influx of civilian workers. The Nazi regime was determined to place most of the war's burden on other shoulders and increasingly exploited foreign workers. In the early war years, most of them were Poles. Some came voluntarily, deceived by Nazi promises of a rosy life, while many more were dragged westward by force. Conditions were poor and discipline harsh, and the police were never far away. Prejudice and paranoia were ingrained in the minds of the policemen, who saw Polish foreign workers as potential thieves, saboteurs, and rapists. Infractions of the strict rules—written and unwritten—were severely punished, not least with transfer to the concentration camps.[69]

Mass arrests in occupied Poland were stepped up, too, and in line with Himmler's wishes, countless prisoner transports set off for the KL from spring 1940. Often, the Gestapo offered no more than a stereotypical phrase to justify their detention, such as: "Belongs to the Polish intelligentsia and harbors the spirit of resistance." In Dachau alone, 13,337 Polish men arrived between March and December 1940, mostly from the incorporated Polish territories; among them were hundreds of Polish priests, after Dachau was designated as the central concentration camp for arrested clergymen.[70]

In some of the older KL for men, the number of Polish prisoners soon began to rival that of German inmates.[71] The Ravensbrück women's camp was affected, too; in April 1940, more than seventy percent of all new arrivals were Polish. As they watched Ravensbrück fill up with even more Polish women over the coming months, other prisoners began to wonder whether Hitler had decided "to wipe out the Polish people altogether."[72]

Extending the KL System

Heinrich Himmler had never expected his camp system to stay still. Speaking candidly in November 1938, he told the top brass of the SS that during a war "we won't be able to make do" with the existing concentration camps. He was worried about another so-called stab in the back, no doubt, and his prescription was clear: more people would be arrested, more space would be required.[73] Himmler's vision soon came true, though even he did not foresee what would become of his terror apparatus—a sprawling, squalid maze of hundreds of camps.

This apocalyptic final stage was still some years off. Nonetheless, the wide-ranging arrests after the outbreak of war quickly led to overcrowding; by late 1939, the KL population had already risen to around thirty thousand prisoners, and SS leaders cast around for more camps.[74] It was around this time that Heinrich Himmler ordered a survey of provisional prisoner camps set up since the start of the war. Primarily, he wanted to stop regional Nazi officials from running their own private camps, as they had done in 1933. "Concentration camps can only be established with my authorization," he insisted in December 1939. But Himmler was also thinking about adding one of these provisional sites to his official KL portfolio.[75]

Several of his lieutenants, including Camp Inspector Glücks, championed a new KL "for the East," to hold down the Polish population.[76] After much deliberation, the SS settled on a site in the provincial Polish border town Oświęcim, southeast of Katowice (Kattowitz). Oświęcim, part of the Habsburg Empire until 1918, had been occupied in the first days of the Second World War, and incorporated into the German Reich in late October 1939, together with the rest of east Upper Silesia. Even before then, the occupiers had taken the symbolic step of renaming the town, reverting to its old German name—Auschwitz.[77]

The origins of the Auschwitz camp go back to the First World War, when a temporary settlement for seasonal workers laboring in nearby Germany had been set up just outside the town. Most of the grounds, containing brick houses and wooden barracks, were later used by the Polish army, before being taken over by the Wehrmacht in September 1939 as a POW camp. But it was quickly closed down again and by the end of the year the site was almost empty, if only for a short time.[78] In the early months of 1940, SS experts repeatedly inspected the location, weighing up the pros and cons of its use as a KL. In their eyes, it was not perfect; the buildings were run down and the groundwater of poor quality. Worst of all, two rivers, the Soła and Vistula, met nearby, creating a flood-risk area infested with insects. At the same time, the SS noted several advantages. The site was already established, lay close to a railway hub, and could easily be shielded from prying eyes. In the end, these arguments won the day, and in April 1940, work on the grounds began.[79] Faced with new demands in wartime, the Camp SS was willing to improvise; contrary to its recent policy of purpose-building new camps, it returned to the old practice of converting existing structures.

Auschwitz officially operated from June 14, 1940, when the first mass transport of Polish inmates arrived: 728 men from Tarnów prison near Krakow, across the border in the General Government. Most of them were young men, including students and soldiers, accused of a wide range of anti-German activities.[80] On arrival, they were assaulted by SS men and by some of the thirty German Kapos who had come from Sachsenhausen more than three weeks earlier. Soon, the shirts and jackets of the Polish prisoners were covered in sweat and blood. One of them was twenty-one-year-old Wiesław Kielar, who received inmate number 290. Once he and his fellow prisoners had lined up on the roll call square, they were addressed by the new camp compound leader, Hauptsturmführer Karl Fritzsch, previously stationed at Dachau and one of around 120 SS men in Auschwitz, who told them that this was not a sanatorium but a German concentration camp. "We were soon to experience," Kielar wrote later, "what that meant, a concentration camp!"[81]

The Auschwitz commandant was another old hand of the Camp SS. Rudolf Höss was officially appointed (by Himmler) on May 4, 1940, having recently inspected the site. As commandant, the tireless Höss was eager to apply what he had learned in Dachau and Sachsenhausen. For over a million prisoners, Auschwitz was death. For Höss, it was his life. When he arrived, he envisaged a new model camp, with himself at the helm. But the dilapidated place he took over was far removed from his dreams. There was not enough wood or bricks during the initial construction, and Höss could not even put up a fence around his camp: "So I had to steal the urgently needed pieces of barbed wire."[82]

Auschwitz remained a wasteland, as even the SS acknowledged, though this did not stop its rapid expansion into one of the largest KL.[83] At the end of 1940, just half a year after it opened, nearly 7,900 prisoners had been transported to Auschwitz, where they were held in one-story and two-story brick buildings on the former army barrack grounds.[84] Many more arrived over the following year, as the grounds were extended. By early 1942, Auschwitz had become the largest concentration camp of all (except for Mauthausen), with nearly twelve thousand men locked up inside. More than three-quarters of these men were Poles, as the camp's main purpose remained the battle against the conquered population.[85] Today Auschwitz is synonymous with the Holocaust, but it was built to impose German rule over Poland.[86]

In addition to Auschwitz, the SS established four other KL for men between spring 1940 and late summer 1941.[87] The first was Neuengamme, close to Hamburg. Previously a satellite camp of Sachsenhausen, it was now turned into a main camp, a few months after an inspection by Himmler in January 1940. The SS transferred more prisoners from Sachsenhausen, who had to build the new main camp, working for up to sixteen hours a day in frost and rain. One inmate recalled that, early on, the ground had been completely frozen: "We had to dig the foundation for the barracks. The pickaxes were heavier than we were." On June 4, 1940, survivors and recent arrivals were finally relocated to the new compound, which was far from ready; around eight hundred prisoners were crammed into three half-finished barracks. Nonetheless, the camp grew quickly; at the end of 1941, Neuengamme held 4,500 to 4,800 prisoners.[88]

Gross-Rosen, another of the new main camps, had started out as a satellite camp, too. Situated in Lower Silesia, on a hill near the town of Striegau, it had operated as an outpost of Sachsenhausen since early August 1940, when the first prisoners were taken to two provisional barracks surrounded by a fence. Himmler himself visited in late October 1940, and in the following spring, on May 1, 1941, Gross-Rosen was designated as a main camp. At first, it remained rather small, however, as there were no funds for its enlargement, and by October 1, 1941, no more than 1,185 prisoners were held inside.[89] Its moment as a place of mass detention and death was still to come.

At the same time as Gross-Rosen, another main camp was founded—Natzweiler, in idyllic surroundings on a steep hill in the Vosges Mountains in Alsace. It also started out as a small camp, with the first three hundred prisoners arriving toward the end of May 1941. As in the other new camps, the SS was forced to improvise during the construction phase. At the outset, inmates were held on a temporary site, while the SS administration was housed in a hotel, the Struthof.[90] And just as in Gross-Rosen, the camp grew more slowly than the SS had anticipated; the initial target figure of 2,500 prisoners was only approached at the end of 1943.[91]

The final new SS concentration camp, located near Paderborn in Westphalia, was Himmler's private folly. Devoted to mysticism, he wanted to create a spiritual home for the SS. He selected the renaissance castle Wewelsburg in Niederhagen, and from 1934 turned it into an enormous SS shrine. In May 1939, during a time of severe labor shortages in Germany, Himmler drafted KL prisoners to help with his pet project. Soon they were held in a small labor camp on a hill opposite the castle, run as a satellite camp of Sachsenhausen, but on September 1, 1941, Himmler turned it into a main camp, called Niederhagen. On paper, it was a regular SS concentration camp. Given its specific focus, however, it remained the smallest of all the main camps, holding no more than around six hundred prisoners in early 1942. And yet, it was no less lethal than other KL. Some prisoners died in quarries, others during the construction of the "crypt" (presumably designed for worshipping SS leaders) under the northern tower of the castle. In the end, Himmler's eerie plan was never fully realized. In early 1943, as Germany diverted more and more resources to total war, even he could not justify the project anymore. The surviving prisoners were transferred elsewhere and the main camp closed down on April 30, 1943; in all, Niederhagen had existed for less than two years.[92]

Despite its hurried expansion during the early war years, the KL system did not fragment. Before long, life inside the new camps largely resembled life in the old ones. There were structural reasons for this: all camps received orders and directives from the IKL and RSHA. And there were personal links, too. In all the five new camps, the first Kapos had arrived from Sachsenhausen, the springboard for the expansion of the KL system, and they quickly fitted into the routines they knew so well.[93] Many of their SS masters, too, had breathed the air of the camps for years. Among the new commandants were ambitious young officers like Höss. SS leaders also gave another chance to veterans judged to have failed elsewhere, as in the case of Karl Koch. Another beneficiary was the first Gross-Rosen commandant, Arthur Rödl, who had previously held senior positions in Lichtenburg, Sachsenburg, and Buchenwald. Wherever he went, Rödl had offended his superiors; he was incompetent and barely literate, they complained, and had been promoted way above his station. Even Theodor Eicke regarded him as an embarrassment, but had been unable to get rid of him; as a highly decorated stalwart of the Nazi movement who had participated in the 1923 putsch, Rödl could count on Himmler's protection. His promotion to Gross-Rosen commandant in 1941 would be his final opportunity to prove his worth in the Camp SS.[94]

The new camps contributed to the spread of wartime terror. As we have seen, Auschwitz was designed to combat dissent and opposition among the Polish population. And three of the other new KL—Neuengamme, Gross-Rosen, and Natzweiler—had a political function, too. All three were located close to the German border and helped to subjugate occupied peoples. Neuengamme was situated near Denmark and Holland and grew into the most important camp in northwestern Germany; Natzweiler lay in territory recently annexed from France; Gross-Rosen lay in eastern Germany, between incorporated Poland and the Protectorate of Bohemia and Moravia, and already at the beginning some forty percent of its prisoners were Polish and Czech.[95] And yet, the early wartime expansion of the KL system was not about terror alone. It was also about forced labor, with SS economic ambitions growing fast as the German army went from strength to strength.

Bricks and Stones

Following the crushing victory over France, Adolf Hitler fulfilled an old dream: he embarked on a brief tour of the country he had fought against more than two decades earlier, returning as the avenger of the traumatic

German defeat of 1918. The highlight of his trip came on the morning of June 28, 1940, when his Mercedes motorcade entered Paris. The French capital glowed in the early summer sun as Hitler surveyed his new possessions, ticking off the tourist itinerary. He played the guide during his tour, impressing his entourage with details about history, art, and architecture he had gleaned from books. One of the sycophantic hangers-on was Albert Speer, who had been invited to share in his mentor's triumph.

Returning to his temporary headquarters that night, a euphoric Hitler ordered Speer to intensify the monumental plans for rebuilding Berlin and the other so-called Führer Cities (Hamburg, Linz, Munich, and Nuremberg), which had been put on hold after the war broke out. Hitler called it the "most important building project of the Reich," lasting a full ten years. But why restrict himself to just a few cities? Germany would dominate Europe for centuries, Hitler believed, and needed to show a proud face to the world. By early 1941, he had designated more than twenty German cities to be remodeled, fantasizing about new streets and squares, theaters and towers.[96]

The SS was just as eager as Speer to make Hitler's wishes come true, and its cooperation with Speer's office, inaugurated before the war, became closer than ever. Speer needed building materials, and the SS pledged to deliver through its company DESt. Speer was more than happy to bankroll it, and by mid-1941 he had made at least twelve million Reichsmark available to DESt, which grew into a midsize company.[97] The main burden of the work would be borne by KL inmates. In September 1940, in a speech to SS officers, Himmler stressed that it was essential for prisoners to "break stones and burn stones" for the Führer's great buildings.[98]

The entire SS economy was expanding, not just DESt, and the early years of the war saw its greatest period of growth.[99] It was still overseen by Oswald Pohl, who promoted several skilled managers to the top, more determined than ever to turn his ramshackle outfit into a professional operation.[100] Not all the businesses relied on forced labor, at least not early on. Still, the exploitation of prisoners was the backbone of the SS economy, and because private industry was not yet showing any real interest, the SS had a more or less free hand over its inmates.[101]

Forced prisoner labor bolstered the growth of the German Equipment Works (DAW), an SS enterprise that incorporated many of the camp workshops and produced a range of goods, from bread to furniture. Set up in May 1939, DAW came into its own during the war. By summer 1940, the workshops in Dachau, Sachsenhausen, and Buchenwald had been swallowed up, and by early 1941, some 1,220 prisoners worked for DAW in these three camps; numbers were set to rise sharply over the next years, as DAW expanded into the largest of all SS-run companies.[102] Another major SS operation was the grandly titled German Experimental Institution for Nutrition and Provision (DVA). Founded in January 1939, it grew quickly during the war, too, spearheaded by the gardening and herb cultivation on the Dachau plantation, which became one of the largest work details inside the camp; in May 1940, some one thousand Dachau prisoners toiled here every day.[103] The SS authorities had even bigger plans for agricultural production in Auschwitz (largely independent from DVA), keenly watched by Heinrich Himmler, who expected major breakthroughs for the German settlement of the east.[104]

Himmler's attention was soon diverted by an even more ambitious project in Auschwitz, a pioneering collaboration between the SS and private industry. In early 1941, the chemical giant IG Farben decided to build a vast factory by the Polish village of Dwory, a couple of miles from Auschwitz town. The company was primarily attracted by nearby natural resources and good transport links, though it also welcomed the availability of forced laborers from the local KL (at a rate of three or four Reichsmark per prisoner per day). Himmler jumped at the chance of cooperating with industry, hoping to advance the economic standing and expertise of the SS. After his first visit to Auschwitz on March 1, 1941, accompanied by Richard Glücks, he ordered the extension of the main camp, partly to provide more workers for IG Farben. Soon after, in mid-April of 1941, the first prisoner commando commenced work around the new IG Farben construction site, which was designated for a vast factory complex aimed at the production of synthetic fuel and rubber. By early August 1941, more than eight hundred Auschwitz prisoners worked on the site, under terrible conditions, with numbers rising further in the autumn.[105]

Enthusiastic as Himmler was about the budding chemical plant near Auschwitz, his main focus in the early war years was still on bricks and stones. In 1940, some six to seven thousand KL prisoners worked in six different DESt businesses daily; demonstrating his priorities, Himmler personally inspected all six sites in 1940–41.[106] Building materials had been very much on the mind of Himmler and his SS managers as they established their new concentration camps. Neuengamme was all about bricks from the start. It had been set up as a satellite camp in December 1938 on the grounds of a disused brick factory, recently purchased by DESt, though the work did not really get off the ground before the war. Production was pushed ahead when Neuengamme became a main camp, and gained further momentum after the German victory over France; bricks were needed urgently, especially for buildings in nearby Hamburg.[107]

In Gross-Rosen and Natzweiler, the eyes of SS officers were drawn to granite, not brick. In Gross-Rosen, it was black-and-white granite that attracted their attention; DESt bought the quarrying works in May 1940, and the later decision to make Gross-Rosen a main camp was partially influenced by the expectation that this would increase output. In Natzweiler, too, the exploitation of KL prisoners in quarrying was part of SS plans from early on. The DESt work there was established after Himmler inspected the local quarry on September 6, 1940; apparently, Albert Speer had spotted some rare red granite that was perfect for the new German Stadium in Nuremberg.[108]

Existing concentration camps were also affected by the SS building boom, with extra workshops, machines, and prisoners boosting DESt production. On Speer's initiative, stone-processing works were set up from late summer 1940 in Oranienburg. Nearby, other prisoners from Sachsenhausen were still rebuilding the failed Oranienburg brick works. Himmler kept a close watch on progress, just as he did elsewhere; having promised massive deliveries of bricks to Speer, he inspected the troubled Oranienburg factory twice in 1940–41. In Flossenbürg, meanwhile, the SS developed an additional quarry from April 1941, following the example of Mauthausen. Here, quarrying had expanded for some time, especially after the creation of a new subcamp in Gusen, a couple of miles west of Mauthausen (officially operational from May 25, 1940). As a result, Mauthausen remained the largest of all the SS granite works, deploying an average of almost 3,600 prisoners across its three main quarries in July 1940.[109]

The SS looked to prisoners to boost its output and DESt managers even championed the training of KL inmates as stonemasons. Following a meeting with commandants in Oranienburg on September 6, 1940, it was announced that the participating prisoners would be offered privileges such as money, fruit, and separate quarters. In addition, prisoners were to be lured by the prospect of freedom; if they did well, they had the "best prospects" of being freed before long.[110] But these were empty promises. In practice, most bonuses were typically limited to cigarettes and extra rations. Moreover, hardly any prisoners benefited; by early 1941, fewer than six hundred inmates were training as stonemasons in the different KL.[111] Nonetheless, the SS initiative was a sign of things to come. True, this was not the first time the Camp SS had offered rewards. But in the past such benefits were largely restricted to Kapos responsible for order and discipline. During the war, in recognition of the growing importance of forced labor, the SS was prepared to extend preferential treatment to some productive prisoners.

The overall balance sheet of the SS economy in the early war years was mixed. State subsidies and cash infusions by Speer were always welcome, and the SS also gained from corporate scams.[112] Turning more closely to the flagship company DESt, its quarries, heavily reliant on manual work, proved profitable. Above all, DESt benefited from the extremely cheap labor, since SS businesses paid the state no more than a nominal 0.30 Reichsmark per prisoner per day. It was cut-rate forced labor that made the SS quarries lucrative.[113] Despite this competitive edge, other DESt enterprises filed losses. In particular, the SS continued to struggle with more complex technologies, with the calamitous brick works in Oranienburg posting bigger losses than ever.[114]

Looking at Germany as a whole, the early wartime SS ventures remained insignificant. To be sure, they provided some materials for Hitler's megalomaniac building plans. But DESt, like the whole SS economy, never delivered what it promised: production lagged behind targets, prisoners achieved only a fraction of the output of free laborers, and the quality of the stones remained inferior.[115] By the summer of 1941, the SS was no closer to being a significant economic player than it was at the start of the war. While the economic turn of the SS had a negligible effect on the German economy, its impact on life behind barbed wire was dramatic, bringing more death and destruction than ever to KL construction sites and quarries.

ROAD TO PERDITION

"[If] I could enclose all the evil of our time in one image," Primo Levi wrote in his memoir of Auschwitz, "I would choose this image which is familiar to me: an emaciated man, with head dropped and shoulders curved, on whose face and in whose eyes not a trace of thought is to be seen." Such prisoners were still moving, but they were no longer alive, Levi added, "the divine spark dead within them." Before long "nothing will remain of them but a handful of ashes in some nearby field." Levi called these doomed prisoners, who died without anyone remembering them, the "drowned."[116] In the wartime KL, such men and women had been known by other names, such as "cripple," "derelict," or, with heavy sarcasm, "jewel." Most common of all was a term used in Auschwitz and several other concentration camps—*Muselmänner* (sometimes *Muselweiber* for women).[117]

The *Muselmänner* (Muslims) were the living dead. Exhausted, apathetic, and starved, they had lost everything. Their bodies were no more than bones and dry skin covered in sores and scabs. They could barely walk, think, or talk, and stared ahead with a hollow, blank gaze. Other prisoners dreaded them as a harbinger of their own fate, for it did not take much—a cold, a beating, a sore foot—to set a prisoner on the road to perdition. The yearning for food, which still animated the *Muselmann* early on, was the last sign of life to be extinguished. Some died while eating, their fingers gripping a last piece of bread.[118] Life had lost its meaning for the *Muselmann*, and so did the camp's survival strategies. Exercise, washing, mending, barter, and keeping a low profile—none of this was possible anymore. How could he follow orders he no longer heard? How could he obey rules he no longer understood? How could he march when his feet no longer supported him?

In the years after liberation, the *Muselmann* has come to embody the horror of Nazi concentration camps, a harrowing and heartbreaking figure closely associated with the Holocaust and the final stages of the KL system.[119] However, the doomed prisoners had actually appeared much earlier. From autumn 1939, conditions in the camps deteriorated to such an extent that thousands of prisoners joined the ranks of the dying. It was the early wartime period that gave birth to the *Muselmann*.

Hunger and Disease

The last thing new prisoners expected to see in concentration camps, after the brutal SS "welcome," was flower beds. But during spring and summer, blooming flowers and well-tended lawns were everywhere, outside the barracks, around SS buildings, and alongside the main paths. In the early war years, the Camp SS still insisted on decorum and order, cladding the camps in a thin veneer of normality, both for themselves and for visitors. "Sometimes when I was thinking about the loving care the Gestapo henchmen lavished on these flower beds," a prisoner who had come to Sachsenhausen in autumn 1939 recalled, "I thought I was going to go mad over it."[120]

The contrast between the blossoms outside the barracks and the misery inside could hardly have been greater. Once prisoners entered, they were often overwhelmed by a stench of dirty and diseased bodies crammed together.[121] Although the SS continued to insist on barracks being cleaned, as part of the abusive drill that passed for education, this did little to overcome the often dreadful conditions.

Overcrowding was a massive problem early in the war. Buchenwald grew the quickest. In just four weeks, it virtually doubled in size, from 5,397 (September 1, 1939) to 10,046 prisoners (October 2, 1939).[122] The inmate population in Sachsenhausen, too, nearly doubled before the year was out.[123] All aspects of life were affected. Uniforms, soap, bedding, and more were in short supply. Barracks were packed, exceeding their already unviable maximum capacity by two or three times. Only later in 1940 did conditions in Buchenwald and Sachsenhausen ease, after their prisoner populations declined; in Buchenwald, the peak of 12,775 prisoners (October 31, 1939) was not passed again until spring 1943.[124] Now it was other KL that absorbed the general rise in inmate numbers: the reopened camp at Dachau, the extended camp at Mauthausen, and new camps such as Auschwitz. These camps, too, were soon crowded, forcing more and more prisoners to fight over space to sleep, wash, and dress.

The prisoners also faced starvation, as soups became thinner and bread portions smaller. While some shortages were caused by growing pressures on resources during war, the SS deliberately aggravated the situation. On September 1, 1939, the Sachsenhausen SS marked the outbreak of war with cuts to inmate rations, perhaps on orders from above; war meant sacrifice, and prisoners should be the first to suffer. The same reasoning informed the official rations set centrally by the Nazi regime in January 1940. KL prisoners (and inmates in state prisons) were now entitled to much less meat, fat, and sugar than the general public, even though they often worked much harder.[125] To make matters worse, the prisoners received less than their due, as SS men and Kapos continued to siphon off supplies. Often, only the worst food found its way onto the tin plates of ordinary prisoners. As it arrived, a former Sachsenhausen inmate later testified, "the smell of foul vegetables filled the room"; some prisoners gagged and threw up.[126]

Hunger haunted the barracks. Many inmates could only think about food, and some even fantasized about cooking the dogs of SS men. Often, prisoners talked about lavish meals, seasoning and frying imaginary steaks; inmates kept notes on these elusive dishes, collecting books of delicious recipes. Even their nights were marred by hunger. As he was lying in his Flossenbürg barrack one night in late 1939, Alfred Hübsch (a prisoner temporarily transferred from Dachau) dreamed about the butcher shop in his hometown; it was filled with sausages and the butcher told him: "Have a good look around; I'll give you all the ones you want."[127]

Prisoners supported themselves as best they could. There was a burgeoning black market, while those with nothing to trade scavenged scraps of rotten vegetables and kitchen waste, risking food poisoning and SS punishment. Inmates who took from camp supplies were in even greater peril; in Sachsenhausen, a young French prisoner was battered to death in 1941 by an SS block leader for taking two carrots from a sheep pen.[128] More and more prisoners, including inmates known as good comrades, stole from one another. Bread thefts became so common that block elders obstructed or patrolled prisoner lockers, and threatened brutal punishment. But hunger was sometimes greater than the fear of getting caught.[129]

Starvation was often the beginning of the end. Exhausted prisoners quickly fell behind at work, and SS men, in turn, punished them as work-shy, pushing them even closer to their graves. In Flossenbürg, all "lazy" prisoners had to stay away from the big pots of soup as other inmates ate their fill. Only when the others had finished were the starved allowed to approach. A horrified Alfred Hübsch watched as the desperate men fought over the scraps, seemingly numb to blows and kicks by Kapos: "They used their spoons to scour the pots and their fingers to scrape the last bits of food from the sides."[130]

Emaciated prisoners were also more susceptible to illnesses, which spread fast in the early war years. Many prisoners already arrived in a poor state from workhouses, jails, and forced labor camps, as the police had few qualms about dropping ailing prisoners at the camp gates; in Sachsenhausen, the transports included an eighty-year-old blind Serbian man who, though he could barely stand upright, was classified as a dangerous habitual criminal.[131] Whether they arrived healthy or not, almost all nonprivileged prisoners fell ill. Extreme malnutrition, in particular, had dire consequences for prisoners' skin, tissue, and inner organs; hunger edema grew rapidly, as did large ulcers.[132] Frostbite and colds were common, too, often followed by pneumonia. Conditions were already critical in the bitter winter of 1939–40, which covered Germany for months in frost and ice. Some of the barracks had no heating at all. Where there were stoves, prisoners tried to steal—or "organize," as it was called in the KL—more wood. Others stuffed blankets or paper bags under their uniforms. But no matter what they did, they could not escape the cold and dreaded each new day. The Camp SS, meanwhile, did little to help and much to harm, holding back or withdrawing warmer clothes.[133]

Epidemics were rife, too, far more than before the war. Harmful contagious diseases such as scabies were widespread; in January 1941, at least one in eight prisoners in Sachsenhausen were afflicted.[134] Filth and poor sanitation led to mass outbreaks of dysentery, which caused violent diarrhea and extreme dehydration. Many prisoners already suffered from hunger diarrhea and soiled themselves on a daily basis. Michał Ziółkowski, one of the first prisoners in Auschwitz, recalled that at night, sick prisoners who walked to the latrines defecated on others sleeping on the floor.[135] Another constant threat was typhus, a typical disease of mass confinement; it spread through lice, and lice were ever-present in the concentration camps.[136]

The main SS response to the growing misery in the KL was telling. Instead of pushing for improvements and allowing more than a fraction of ill inmates into infirmaries, the Camp SS created additional spaces to isolate the sick and dying in 1939–40.[137] Individual barracks were reserved for prisoners with tuberculosis, open wounds, scabies, and other diseases. The inmates had their own names for these places: the dysentery barrack in Dachau was known as "shit block" and the block for invalids was called "cretin club."[138] Many healthier inmates—afraid of infection and deprived of sleep by the sick—welcomed this isolation. In fact, some of them had already taken similar measures on their own initiative, forcing sick comrades from shared dormitories into the freezing washrooms.[139]

Conditions in the special areas for the sick were shocking even to veterans of the KL, who generally avoided going anywhere near them. The blocks, often empty except for beds or sacks of straw, were crowded with skeletal figures, whose long days and nights were occasionally interrupted by violent outbursts from Kapos. Worst of all was the gnawing hunger. It was no coincidence that the Sachsenhausen barracks for invalid prisoners, established around late 1939, were known as "hunger blocks." Here, and in other spaces for the ill, the Camp SS cut back further on the small rations, hoping to speed up the process of "natural selection" among the sick.[140]

Work and Death

After setting eyes on the devil, Dante in his *Divine Comedy* finally leaves hell on the epic journey that will take him to the heights of paradise. First, though, he climbs through purgatory, where his guide, Virgil, soon draws his attention to an eerie procession of men, barely recognizable as human beings, bowed to the ground by heavy rocks. Even the one "who bore himself most patiently seemed, weeping, to say: 'I can stand no more.'"[141] The horrors conjured up in Dante's medieval poem were a frequent reference point for KL prisoners (and even some SS men), and it was the infernal image of men carrying rocks that came to the minds of Buchenwald survivors, when they tried to explain the prisoners' suffering in the quarries to their U.S. liberators. "Even the name of the stone quarry detail," one of the survivors recalled, "was enough to fill the strongest men with the greatest fear."[142]

Prisoners everywhere dreaded the quarries.[143] After the war, the Polish prisoner Antoni Gładysz still vividly remembered the day in 1941 when he was forced for the first time to climb down the precarious ladders into the Gross-Rosen excavation site. With three other prisoners, all wearing flimsy wooden shoes, he hauled heavy rocks through the grounds. "It was a dreadful day," Gładysz recalled. "We injured our hands. We tried to support ourselves with our knees. We worked in a trance, almost unconscious, without thinking about the day's end."[144] When the prisoners finally did march back to camp, they bore the signs of the quarry all over their bruised bodies.

The Camp SS had long seen the quarries as particularly torturous, and the RSHA agreed. In 1940, with Himmler's blessing, the KL for men were divided into three groups (mirroring the stages system for individual prisoners in early camps, which had been abandoned by Eicke). Each group of camps would hold different prisoner types, based on their "personality" and "threat to the state." Men judged "definitely reformable" would be taken to camps in stage 1 such as Dachau and Sachsenhausen (which had no quarries). Camps in stage 2, like Buchenwald, Flossenbürg, and Neuengamme, were reserved for "more heavily damaged" men who were, however, still "reformable." The lowest rung, stage 3, was to accommodate "heavily damaged" men, especially those who were "asocial and criminally recidivist" and therefore "barely reformable." Initially, there was only one such camp—Mauthausen, which had the largest and most lethal quarry. A former Mauthausen guard later admitted that in practice, stage 3 meant that inmates were "not intended to leave the camp alive"; among the prisoners, the camp became known as *Mordhausen*.[145]

On paper, the SS took the new classification scheme seriously.[146] Its actual impact was limited, however. From the beginning, a camp's grade was no true guide to conditions inside. In 1940, for example, more than twice as many prisoners lost their lives in Sachsenhausen (stage 1) than in Buchenwald (stage 2).[147] Later on, the scheme lost all relevance: although Auschwitz was officially categorized as a stage 1 and 2 camp, it had by far the highest death rate of all KL.[148] In the end, other factors—such as the colors of the inmates' triangles—were far more decisive in determining their fate than the camp's official classification.

Still, the attempt to create a hierarchy among the camps gives an intriguing insight into the thinking of SS and police leaders in the early war years. In the first place, they evidently responded to the growth of the KL system by trying to differentiate more clearly between individual sites. More surprising, perhaps, was their continued emphasis on prisoner reform. This was not about propaganda, as the classification of camps was kept secret. Rather, the officials were deceiving themselves: they still wanted to believe that the camps had another function, beyond terror. In reality, this pedagogical mission was even more fanciful than before the war. Any new skills prisoners learned were about naked survival—how to endure lashes without losing count; how to make a small piece of bread last for days; how to conserve energy by pretending to work hard.

Backbreaking physical labor characterized all KL in the early war years, whether they had quarries or not. Building work was most prominent, and threatened exhaustion, torture, and death. In new concentration camps, nearly all prisoners were forced into construction, erecting their own camp; they built the paths they walked on, the roll call squares they stood on, the barracks they slept in, and the fences separating them from the outside world.[149] Construction work was not limited to the new sites, of course. There was hectic activity at the older ones, too, as prisoner numbers expanded. The Camp SS was forever building and rebuilding, with prisoners paying the price. Many of the around 1,800 inmates who died in Mauthausen between December 1939 and April 1940, for example, lost their lives during the construction of the new Gusen subcamp. As a Gusen prisoner noted in a secret diary on March 9, 1940: "Nothing special. Here, the dead are no news, they appear daily."[150]

In Sachsenhausen, a daily average of two thousand men worked on the construction of the brick works in 1940, still the most feared detail in the camp. Many prisoners were forced to demolish the failed old factory, a massive task that claimed hundreds of lives. Other inmates were erecting a new subcamp in Oranienburg to cut out the daily march from the main compound (it opened in late April 1941). Yet more inmates worked at the few furnaces which now produced bricks. Finally, there were the nearby clay pits, dubbed "hell inside hell"; prisoners had to stand up to their knees in water and mud, and shovel clay onto carts. "In ancient times," concluded the German political prisoner Arnold Weiss-Rüthel, "the slaves of the pharaohs erected the pyramids under much better conditions than Adolf Hitler's slaves did the Oranienburg brick factory."[151]

While the economic ambitions of the SS shaped the general direction of forced labor, they did not make it any more efficient. Most local SS men still showed little interest in output. In their eyes, the camp remained, first and foremost, a battleground against enemies of the Nazi state. This was evident in all the petty rules designed to torment prisoners during work. In Gusen, for instance, inmates had to toil without gloves and coats in 1939–40, despite the bitter cold, and were barred from coming near the fires lit by SS and Kapos.[152]

The priorities of the Camp SS become even clearer when looking at prisoners who did not work because they were too weak, because they had not yet been assigned a labor detail, or because of bad weather and job shortages. Since no ordinary prisoner (apart from the dying) was allowed to be idle, the Camp SS looked for other ways to occupy them. As before the war, some guards used pointless labor and abusive drills. But the SS also invented new forms of torment. In Sachsenhausen, it introduced so-called standing commandos for the unemployed and ill in autumn 1939, having already used "standing still" as a punishment before the war. Hundreds were crammed into barracks where they had to stand all day, with just a brief break at lunch.

"We stood pressed together like sardines," one former prisoner later wrote. For eight or nine hours, they were not allowed to move, talk, or sit; they could not even lean against the walls. Soon, every part of their bodies was aching. But any motion was out of the question: real or imagined infractions were swiftly punished by Kapos and SS.[153]

This was part of the wider escalation of Camp SS terror in the early war years, when deadly violence lurked all around. Among the spaces most closely associated with murder were the infirmaries and, above all, the bunker, which had long stood at the center of violence. But guards now killed almost everywhere, and crucially, they killed far more frequently. Previously, they had often stopped short of murder. Why was there no more holding back after the outbreak of the Second World War?

Executions

Shortly before midnight on September 7, 1939, a police car pulled onto the Sachsenhausen grounds. Inside, flanked by police officers and held in shackles, sat a muscular man with thick, curly hair. His name was Johann Heinen and he only had an hour left to live. Heinen, who looked younger than his thirty years, was a man who had known little good fortune in his short life. In the turbulent Weimar years, the trained metalworker had lost his job, and in the early Nazi years, he was locked away for his Communist sympathies. After his release, he had worked for the Junkers factory in Dessau, but shortly before the Second World War broke out, he was arrested once again, this time for refusing to dig a trench for German air defenses. His resistance proved fatal, as Nazi leaders decided to make an example of him. Having received the go-ahead from Hitler himself, Heinrich Himmler sent a telex to Heydrich in the evening of September 7, 1939, ordering the immediate execution of the "Communist Heinen" in Sachsenhausen. The commandant alerted Camp Inspector Theodor Eicke, who was still in Oranienburg and rushed over. Heinen himself was informed of his fate after he arrived in the camp. He spent his last moments smoking feverishly and writing a farewell message to his wife: "Please be brave and think about our boy; you *have* to live for him. I think the hour is up soon. Please forgive that this letter is so rambling and incoherent. I think I am already dead." Rudolf Höss, then the Sachsenhausen adjutant, led the prisoner to the industry yard, stepped back, and ordered three NCOs to open fire. Heinen collapsed immediately, but Höss stepped up anyway and shot him once more at close range. Afterward, the SS men walked to the officers' mess. "Strangely, there was little conversation," Höss recalled, "as everyone was caught up in his own thoughts."[154]

The killing of Johann Heinen inaugurated a momentous new Nazi procedure. A few days earlier, on September 3, 1939, the day France and Britain
declared war against Nazi Germany, Hitler had publicly announced that anyone undermining the home front would be "destroyed as an enemy of the
nation."[155] He apparently reiterated this point privately to Himmler the same
day, asking him to take any measures necessary to maintain security inside
the Reich.[156] Himmler quickly translated Hitler's general wish into policy. In
a typical case of working toward the Führer, to use a concept advanced by Ian
Kershaw, he launched the regime's execution program, with the KL as semi-
official execution sites for men (later also women) condemned without trial.[157]

The administrative basis for the new policy was laid in a directive by
Reinhard Heydrich, on the same fateful September 3, 1939. Following their
arrest of dangerous suspects, regional Gestapo staff were told, Heydrich's
office could seek "the brutal liquidation of such elements"; it was understood
that the victims would normally be killed in the nearest KL.[158] But the new
measure was not implemented as SS leaders had hoped. After four days, Heydrich sent an urgent telex to regional Gestapo officers, demanding that many
more offenders be reported for execution. Just twelve hours later, Johann
Heiden was shot in Sachsenhausen. However, Heydrich was still not satisfied.
After two weeks, he cabled again, insisting that anyone guilty of dangerous
acts—such as sabotage or Communist activities—had to be "mercilessly
eradicated (that is, through execution)." Once more, Heydrich spoke openly
to his subordinates. Only later, as Nazi murders mounted, did officials use
camouflage language to cover their bloody tracks in internal documents.[159]

The SS executions of Johann Heinen and two other men in September
1939 alarmed officials in the Reich Ministry of Justice, who learned about the
killings through headlines in the press like: "Saboteur shot dead: There is
no place in the community for people like that."[160] Such lawless executions
challenged the judiciary's hold over capital punishment and Reich minister
Gürtner pleaded with Hitler to change course, arguing that the regular court
system was perfectly capable of dispensing punishment without SS interference (indeed, the number of judicial death sentences shot up during the war,
already reaching 1,292 in 1941).[161] But his intervention backfired. When the
head of the Reich Chancellery, Hans Heinrich Lammers, raised the issue on
October 13, 1939, Hitler not only took responsibility for the earlier killings in
the KL, he ordered the execution of two bank robbers who had been legally
sentenced to ten years in a penitentiary, in a much-publicized trial.[162] SS executions were here to stay, and as the war got bloodier, Hitler condemned dozens more Germans convicted of sex offenses, theft, fraud, and arson.[163]

Registered KL prisoners fell under the new execution policy, too. Once again, Sachsenhausen was the testing ground. The first victim was August Dickmann, a twenty-nine-year-old Jehovah's Witness and veteran inmate, who had resisted Camp SS pressure to declare his willingness to serve in the army. After his case reached Nazi leaders, Himmler ordered his execution, with Hitler's agreement. In the early evening of September 15, 1939, all prisoners assembled on the roll call square where the commandant announced the death sentence and then screamed at Dickmann: "Turn around, you swine." An SS commando shot him in the back and Rudolf Höss delivered the coup de grâce. As the SS had intended, the other prisoners—among them Dickmann's brother, who had to put the corpse into a coffin—were terrified. But Himmler also had an eye on wider deterrence and once more sanctioned reports in German papers and on radio.[164]

Himmler also condemned prisoners when he visited camps, as he did in Sachsenhausen on November 22, 1939. After inspecting the bunker that morning, he ordered the guards to murder one of the inmates, the Austrian teenager Heinrich Petz, to whom he had briefly spoken. Petz had been involved in several highly publicized killings during car robberies—the fourteen-year-old was not charged because he was underage—and had recently been dragged to Sachsenhausen. The local Camp SS acted straightaway. In the yard of the bunker, Petz was told to walk toward the fence and was shot as he did so. Since this was no legal killing, the SS draped the youth's body over the barbed wire to "pretend that it had been a failed escape," as one of the perpetrators later admitted.[165]

Early on, some Camp SS men grumbled that such prisoner executions were not worthy of them. But before long, killings on the orders of Himmler and the RSHA were routine, although Rudolf Höss exaggerated when he claimed that he had "lined up almost every day" with his Sachsenhausen firing squad.[166] Still, KL executions became so frequent that detailed guidelines were issued, fixing the procedures in writing.[167] Normally, prisoners were executed out of sight, often at the shooting range, the bunker, or the infirmary. In exceptional cases, when the SS wanted to teach the others a lesson, all inmates had to watch.[168] The job of hangman—traditionally regarded as a dishonorable profession—was often left to specially selected prisoners, who were rewarded with cigarettes, and sometimes coffee, alcohol, or food.[169]

Once the Nazi leadership had designated the KL as execution sites for individual men, it did not take long before the policy was extended. From 1940, the Camp SS executed groups of Germans and foreigners, sometimes killing dozens of victims together.[170] At times, these executions were coordinated across several camps. The first such bloodbath was committed in November 1940, when more than two hundred Poles were murdered in Sachsenhausen,

Mauthausen, and Auschwitz, on the orders of Himmler and Heydrich. Some of the dead had been regular prisoners, others had arrived only for their execution. The exact reason for this killing spree remains unclear, though it was clearly connected to Nazi occupation policy in Poland, which was shifting from open to more covert executions of opponents.[171] Among the victims was the distinguished doctor Józef Marczyński, who had been deputy director of the Warsaw municipal hospitals. After the German invasion, he had joined the resistance and was arrested during a Gestapo action against the Polish intelligentsia. In May 1940, he was transported from Pawiak prison in Warsaw to Sachsenhausen. Six months later, on the morning of November 9, he was led out of his barrack, together with thirty-two other Poles who had arrived via Pawiak. Apparently, the men expected to be released. Instead, the SS wrote the inmate numbers on their foreheads, for easy identification of the corpses, and drove them to the nearby industry yard; after they had partially undressed, they were all shot. In the evening, the other Polish prisoners in Sachsenhausen held an impromptu memorial with prayers and hymns, singing quietly to avoid detection.[172]

Mass executions of Poles in the KL continued over the following months and years.[173] Some inmates were executed as "hostages" for supposed crimes by Polish civilians.[174] Others were already doomed when they arrived, sentenced to death by police summary courts. Operating in occupied Poland since 1939, these were courts in name only; they were really police tribunals beyond the law, handing out death sentences at every turn.[175] The summary courts worked closely with the Camp SS, particularly in Auschwitz, where proceedings eventually moved inside the camp itself, so that the SS could execute the defendants straight after the farcical trials.[176]

Camp SS Killers

The execution policy had a profound impact on the local Camp SS. As state-ordered executions mounted, SS men on the ground felt emboldened to dispense their own brand of justice. Their moral compass was already defective, and once Nazi leaders had set the precedent of lawless executions, an upsurge in murderous initiatives by local Camp SS men was almost inevitable. Such unauthorized killings remained officially prohibited, to be sure, as SS leaders sought to keep a grip on the camps.[177] But it was impossible to draw a line between "right" and "wrong" murders.

Some commandants led from the front, none more so than the indomitable Karl Otto Koch in Buchenwald, who oversaw a first unauthorized mass execution in autumn 1939. The background was the unsuccessful attempt on

Hitler's life on November 8, when a bomb planted by a lone resister detonated in the Bürgerbräukeller in Munich. It killed seven spectators on the spot, but Hitler had left just before the blast, boosting the belief in his divine mission (the would-be assassin, Georg Elser, was murdered in Dachau in 1945).[178] Hitler was riding a wave of popularity at the time and many Germans were appalled by the attempt on his life.[179] Few were more determined to exact revenge than the men in the Camp SS, who launched brutal attacks on imprisoned Jews. The claim that Jews were behind the attack—too far-fetched even for Nazi propaganda—was enough for obsessive anti-Semites to justify vicious assaults, exactly one year after the 1938 pogrom. In Sachsenhausen, SS men tormented Jewish men during the night of November 9 while Jewish women in Ravensbrück were locked into their barrack for almost a month, at the mercy of a particularly abusive female guard. "Our hearts raced as soon as she appeared," one prisoner testified later.[180]

All this was overshadowed by events in Buchenwald, where so many Jews had already suffered before the war. On the morning of November 9, 1939, all prisoners assembled as normal for roll call. But it soon became clear that this was no normal day, for the SS forced the men back into their barracks. Then the Jews were ordered to return. Among them, the SS picked out a group of German and Austrian men, mostly in their twenties and thirties. The others went back inside, where they were isolated for days in complete darkness, without food and drink. Meanwhile, the selected men walked to the camp gate, where they waited anxiously while the SS guards—some still drunk from the previous night—commemorated the anniversary of the 1923 Nazi uprising. After a small parade, the SS returned and lost no more time. On orders of Commandant Koch, the twenty-one Jews were marched from the gate toward the quarry. When they reached flat terrain, SS men drew their weapons and shot the prisoners from behind; anyone who tried to run was quickly hunted down.[181]

This massacre was unparalleled. Never before had the local Camp SS murdered as many prisoners in broad daylight, and without any instructions from above. Perhaps the fanatical Koch felt entitled to act because his camp compound leader Rödl had been slightly wounded in the Bürgerbräukeller blast. Whatever Koch's motives, he had no problems finding willing executioners among his Buchenwald men.[182] And although his SS superiors were suspicious about the cover story he had concocted—that the Jewish prisoners were shot during a mass escape—an internal investigation came to nothing. Koch got away with murder.[183]

Commandant Koch, already drunk with power, soon became fully intoxicated, selecting more and more prisoners for execution. Among his victims were dozens of new arrivals who somehow caught his roving eye. One was killed simply because Koch had met him before in other KL. "Now this bird won't follow me around anymore," Koch joked. Others were murdered for disciplinary offenses or because they knew too much about SS corruption. The condemned men were taken to the Buchenwald bunker, run by the fearsome Martin Sommer. It is easy to see why Sommer became the unofficial camp executioner. A longtime Nazi activist (he had joined the NSDAP in 1931, when he was just sixteen years old), Sommer was a man of exceptional cruelty. He dispensed the official punishments like whipping, and took part in other outrages, starving and choking prisoners, sexually abusing them, and crushing their skulls; on some days, he later admitted, he had dished out more than two thousand beatings in the bunker. Although Sommer was not the only Camp SS man to graduate with ease from torture to murder, his cold-bloodedness was remarkable even among the SS; after his deadly deeds, he sometimes slept in his office, with the prisoner's corpse stowed under his bed.[184]

Among Sommer's victims were some well-known prisoners. Perhaps the most prominent was Ernst Heilmann, the former Prussian SPD leader. Just as he had foreseen, his suffering came to a terrible end soon after the outbreak of the war. On March 31, 1940, after almost seven years inside the camps, Heilmann was called to the Buchenwald bunker, where he was murdered a few days later. Some of Heilmann's comrades suspected that he had been denounced by a fellow prisoner for some infraction and avenged his death by murdering the alleged traitor. The climate of the camp was becoming more severe among the prisoners, too.[185]

The lethal atmosphere, with all the official and unofficial executions, was highly contagious for the local Camp SS. From 1940, more and more SS men turned murderers. Take an officer like Rudolf Höss. Having participated in sanctioned executions in Sachsenhausen from September 1939, he soon initiated his own killings. On January 18, 1940, a freezing winter day, the prisoners from the "standing commandos"—more than eight hundred of them—had to assemble outside, on the orders of Höss. An icy wind was blowing over the roll call square, and after several hours, the camp elder Harry Naujoks asked Höss for mercy. In his autobiography, Naujoks describes how he had used the expected military address: "Camp Leader, request permission to dismiss [prisoners]." When Höss did not respond, Naujoks tried again, more urgently: "Camp Leader, the people are finished." Höss replied: "They are not people but prisoners." When the action finally ended, the shivering prisoners huddled around stoves in the barracks. Others were carried to the infirmary. Left behind on the snow-covered square were the corpses of the dead, with many more weakened prisoners dying over the next few days.[186] The Camp SS had long regarded invalids as a nuisance, but Höss went much further than he would have dared before the war. And he was not an outlier. Elsewhere, too, SS men began to systematically kill selected ill inmates, using lethal injections and other methods, at a time when casual murders in the concentration camps escalated.[187]

The Sachsenhausen Death Squad

It was during the early months of the Second World War that Gustav Sorge, the twenty-eight-year-old deputy report leader in Sachsenhausen, became a mass murderer. Sorge had killed before, participating in the shooting of inmates soon after joining the Camp SS in Esterwegen in autumn 1934. His education in the school of violence had continued over the coming years, but only during the war did he turn to mass killing. Unlike some of his fellow SS guards, Sorge had been no underachiever; he had done well in school and trained as a metalworker. Like a disproportionate number of Nazi killers, he had grown up as an ethnic German abroad after his Silesian hometown fell to Poland after the First World War. He was infused with radical German nationalism in his early teens and finally left for Germany in 1930, where he was further embittered by his unemployment. Sorge threw himself into the Nazi cause, joining the NSDAP and SA in 1931, aged nineteen, and the SS in the following year. Although he did not appear brawny, with a puny physique and high voice, he became a feared bruiser in the street brawls of the dying days of the Weimar Republic. It was during one such fight that he gained the nickname "Iron Gustav" (after a German celebrity of the time), which he later carried as a badge of honor in the KL.[188]

In the early war years, Gustav Sorge led a small band of Camp SS killers in Sachsenhausen, which acted as an informal death squad; an escaped prisoner, speaking to British agents, described Sorge as the "high priest" over life and death, "whose helpers and aides were constantly competing with each other in shameful and murderous deeds." The group was largely made up of block leaders, the men who supervised prisoner barracks and labor details. As we have seen, only SS men committed to cruelty could make the grade as block leaders. The rest—judged by their superiors, like Sorge, as "too weak" and "too slack"—moved to less prominent posts or sentry duty; in early 1941, one Sachsenhausen block leader was even committed to a ward for mentally ill SS men because he was plagued by nightmares.[189]

No single path led to the Sachsenhausen death squad. In all, there were perhaps a dozen men, mostly NCOs in their twenties. The youngest was Wilhelm Schubert, who had joined the Hitler Youth in 1931, aged fourteen. He volunteered for the Camp SS in 1936 in Lichtenburg, joined the Sachsenhausen Commandant Staff in spring 1938, and became a block leader the following summer, aged twenty-two. Mocked by his SS colleagues as immature and erratic, Schubert sought their acceptance by public displays of brutality. He was always quick to reach for his weapon, earning him the nickname "Pistol Schubert" among prisoners. True to form, when he was promoted to Oberscharführer in 1941, he celebrated by beating up prisoners at random and shooting at their barracks.[190]

Perhaps the most feared member of the death squad was Richard Bugdalle, nicknamed "Brutalla" by prisoners. At twenty-nine years of age, he was slightly older than his colleagues when he became block leader in 1937. But, like them, he was a seasoned Nazi activist, having joined the SS in October 1931, and he was also a veteran of the KL. In Sachsenhausen, Bugdalle directed the notorious penal company. In contrast to Schubert, who became agitated when torturing inmates, the burly Bugdalle was calmness personified. His specialty was punching prisoners; a keen amateur boxer, he could kill with a few well-aimed punches in the ribs and stomach. "If a man had to be liquidated," Gustav Sorge later testified, "Schubert and I always took Bugdalle with us."[191]

The men of the death squad sometimes acted on superior orders. But they also set themselves up as judge and executioner, condemning prisoners for any number of "crimes." Several men were killed on arrival, after Sorge's gang stepped up the long-established "welcome" procedures; others were hounded for weeks "with a view to slowly liquidate [them]," as Sorge confessed after the war.[192] Some newcomers were murdered as suspected sex offenders or homosexuals.[193] Prominent political prisoners and other opponents were targeted, too. After the Austrian state prosecutor Karl Tuppy—who had tried the Nazi murderers of the Austrian chancellor Dollfuss in 1934—arrived in Sachsenhausen on November 15, 1939, the SS went into overdrive. For about twenty minutes, Tuppy was battered in the political office. When the prisoner Rudolf Wunderlich was called in to drag the body away, he recoiled: "I had never seen anything like it. His face was gone. Just a piece of completely undefined meat, full of blood, cuts, the eyes completely swollen up." He left Tuppy at the gate, where Sorge and Schubert took turns in beating him. He died later the same day.[194]

The death squad pursued prisoners not just for who they were, but also for what they did in Sachsenhausen. Over a brief period in 1940, Sorge killed an inmate who did not greet him fast enough, one who had stumbled, and one who had left ink stains on a letter (the SS suspected a secret code). Anyone who challenged the SS—mostly new prisoners who did not know better—was in grave danger, too. When Lothar Erdmann, a distinguished former union official, arrived in autumn 1939, he was shocked by the violence. After he was beaten himself by Wilhelm Schubert, he dared to answer back: "What, you're hitting me? I was a Prussian officer in the First World War and now have two sons at the front!" Erdmann was a marked man; mocked as "the officer," he was battered for days, especially by Schubert and Sorge, until he could barely move. He died on September 18, 1939, around two weeks after his arrival in the camp.[195]

Although the violence of Sachsenhausen guards built on prewar practices, their sustained campaigns of murder were greatly heightened by the war. The guards must have been encouraged by the introduction of a perfunctory SS court system in October 1939, which finally removed Camp SS men altogether from the grasp of the regular judiciary.[196] Also, the dehumanization of prisoners by the spread of illness and starvation made it easier for the SS to treat its victims as "the scum of all scum," as one Sachsenhausen block leader put it.[197] Even more important was the escalating SS execution policy. The guards knew that their superiors pushed for the murder of individual prisoners, so why should they hold back?

Finally, there was the general eruption of violence during wartime. Hitler's genocidal rhetoric and the brutal reality of German warfare from autumn 1939 made clear that a new era had begun, and the guards were bound to participate. Prisoners speculated that success on the faraway battlefields brutalized the Camp SS; as the German army vanquished its enemies abroad, guards felt empowered to do the same on the "inner front."[198] This echoes the view of some historians that extermination policy in the Third Reich was radicalized by the Nazi leaders' elation over apparent victories.[199] But just as some SS men murdered because they felt that the Third Reich was untouchable, others got carried away after setbacks and defeats; it is striking how often KL murders were committed in "revenge" for supposed attacks on Germany.

Before long, local Camp SS men like Gustav Sorge claimed the right to murder on their own initiative. Although they knew that killings officially required authorization from above, the perpetrators were convinced that they did the right thing, as Sorge later testified in court: "We believed that we were helping state and leadership when we abused prisoners and drove them to their deaths."[200] To some extent, this was a self-serving lie; after all, Camp SS men sometimes tortured just for fun.[201] Nonetheless, the killers did feel that they were realizing the general wishes of their superiors, as Sorge later explained: "Personally, I now believe that orders to act, in so far as they were given, were only meant to point lower-ranking officials in a certain direction, so that they would then try to act, of their own accord, as the top leadership wished."[202] In this way, SS killers saw themselves as working toward their leaders.[203] The result was a lethal dynamic, with murderous orders from the top and local initiatives from below radicalizing each other and plunging the KL into a maelstrom of destruction.

SCALES OF SUFFERING

The odds for survival fell dramatically in the early war period. On some days, inmates in KL workshops produced nothing but coffins, just to keep up with all the dead.[204] In 1938, the deadliest year before the war, around 1,300 prisoners had perished inside.[205] In 1940, at least 14,000 prisoners lost their lives; 3,846 are known to have died in Mauthausen (around thirty percent of its inmate population), making it the most lethal KL at the time.[206] Hunger and disease were the greatest killers—most of the dead were emaciated, haggard, and hollow-eyed—followed by SS violence and executions.[207] Prisoner suicides shot up, too. In Sachsenhausen, twenty-six prisoners are said to have killed themselves in April 1940 alone; some died in a fit of despair, running into the electrified fence, and some had meticulously planned their demise. The other inmates soon got used to the presence of death; on occasion, they even ignored the corpses sprawled beneath their feet as they used the latrines. Pity was becoming an increasingly rare commodity in the early wartime camps.[208]

Camp SS officers regarded the growing mountain of corpses with some concern. What troubled them was not their conscience, though, but the disposal of the bodies. In the prewar years, prisoner corpses had normally been taken to nearby towns or cities for incineration. This was no longer viable. Not only was it too time-consuming to store and transfer all the dead, the SS had no desire to advertise the lethal turn of the KL. The solution was simple— the SS would operate its own crematoria inside the camps. Although such plans had been mooted before, they were only realized from late 1939 onward, in cooperation with two private contractors (Heinrich Kori GmbH and Topf & Sons). By summer 1940, all prewar KL for men were equipped with incinerators, and similar machinery was set up in new camps, too; the Auschwitz crematorium went into operation in August 1940.[209] Other practical measures followed. From 1941, for example, registry offices were established inside the camps, so that fatalities could be recorded by SS men, not by regular civil servants outside; inevitably, the SS officials classed almost all prisoner deaths as natural or accidental.[210]

There was no sure way to survive the KL during the war, but there were countless ways to die. Some groups were in much greater danger than others, however. Suffering inside the camps was never indiscriminate, and the gulf between prisoners became even wider during the early part of the war. The political and racial hierarchies imposed by Nazi rulers were crucial; in general, Poles were more likely to die than Germans, and Jews more likely to die than Poles.[211] Gender was decisive, too, as the KL system remained a mostly male construct; at the end of 1940, female prisoners only accounted for around one in twelve inmates, and the fate of these 4,300 women was still very different from that of their male counterparts.[212]

The Ravensbrück Women's Camp

When Margarete Buber-Neumann arrived in Ravensbrück on August 2, 1940, she came to the end of an arduous journey that had begun six months earlier, and more than three thousand miles away, in the Karaganda Gulag. Born in Germany in 1901 into a bourgeois family, she had joined the KPD as a young woman. By the late 1920s, she had dedicated herself full time to the cause, working in the Berlin office of the Comintern magazine. Here she met her husband, Heinz Neumann, the high-flying editor of the incendiary newspaper *Rote Fahne* (Red Flag). When he fell from grace in the early 1930s, after internal party intrigues, Margarete followed him abroad. After moving like fugitives from one European city to another, they finally arrived in Moscow in early summer 1935. By then, the witch hunts were already under way. The Great Terror—fueled by Stalin's obsession with spies and saboteurs— claimed a million or more victims in 1937–38, including thousands of German Communists. Having escaped the Nazis, they fell to their Soviet heroes instead. Among them was Heinz Neumann, jailed, tortured, and executed in late 1937. A few months later, his wife was arrested, too. Sentenced to five years' imprisonment, Margarete Buber-Neumann was taken to Karaganda in the Kazakh steppe, one of the largest Soviet labor camps, where around 35,000 prisoners faced harsh labor under appalling conditions. In early 1940, she was suddenly taken back to Moscow, and soon farther to the west. The Soviet authorities, whom she had once revered, delivered her to the Nazis, as one of around 350 prisoners handed over between November 1939 and May 1941, during the time of the Hitler-Stalin pact. Many were released, once they had been pumped for intelligence. Not so Buber-Neumann. The Gestapo accused her of high treason and placed her in protective custody.[213]

One of the prisoners to suffer both Stalin's and Hitler's camps, Margarete Buber-Neumann immediately saw glaring differences with the Gulag.

Karaganda had been a vast complex of camps spread across an area as large as a midsize European country. Ravensbrück, by contrast, held around 3,200 prisoners in less than two dozen barracks, surrounded by a high wall with electrified barbed wire. Also, Ravensbrück was a camp exclusively for women, as there was still strict gender separation in the SS system. And Buber-Neumann was struck by the SS drills and exercises; everything was done with Prussian thoroughness, she thought. Painful as it was, such strict order also had its benefits. The new purpose-built barracks, with beds, tables, lockers, blankets, toilets, and washrooms, "seemed a palace" compared to the filth of Karaganda.[214]

Unbeknownst to Margarete Buber-Neumann, Ravensbrück was also unlike other SS concentration camps at this time. The prewar delay in terror against female prisoners continued into the early war years, as SS leaders persisted with differential treatment. Heinrich Himmler still saw female prisoners as less dangerous than male ones, and more susceptible to reform.[215] Obsessed with corporal punishment, Himmler demanded more than once that female prisoners should only be whipped as a last resort; he eventually ordered all such cases to be referred to him personally.[216] Such interventions were less important for their specifics than for their message: women, as the "weaker sex," should be treated with more moderation than men.

Basic living conditions in Ravensbrück were considerably better than in other early wartime KL. Clothes and bedding were changed regularly in 1940, and there was just about enough food. Margarete Buber-Neumann, for one, was surprised by the size of her first meal, which included fruit porridge, bread, sausage, margarine, and lard. As for the treatment of the sick, seriously ill prisoners could still be taken to hospitals on the outside and some were released altogether.[217]

Ravensbrück was also set apart by forced labor, which was hard, but not yet destructive. While many women worked in construction, there were no quarries or brick works, which claimed so many lives in KL for men. Instead, the Ravensbrück SS increasingly focused on the mass production of uniforms in large tailors' workshops, since women were "best suited for this kind of work," as one SS manager noted. Provisional production started in late 1939, spurred on by Himmler, and in summer 1940 the workshops became part of a newly created SS enterprise, the Company for Textile and Leather Utilization (Texled). Prisoner productivity almost reached civilian levels, and because female forced labor was even cheaper than men's, Texled was probably the only SS business profitable from the start. The Ravensbrück tailors' workshop produced some seventy-three thousand prisoner shirts between July 1940 and March 1941, as well as other garments, and for a long time, Texled remained the main employer in Ravensbrück. By October 1, 1940, almost seventeen percent of inmates worked for the SS company, rising to an all-time high of around sixty percent by September 1942. The women feared the SS supervisors and the hard work. But it was nowhere near as exhausting as building work; the workshops were partially mechanized, with sewing and knitting machines, and prisoners were sheltered from the elements.[218]

Most important of all, physical violence was less endemic and lethal than in the KL for men, as the Ravensbrück guards exercised a far less brutal regimen. True, the top posts were occupied by uncompromising Camp SS men, such as Commandant Max Koegel. A grizzled war veteran and right-wing extremist, Koegel had come to Dachau as a guard in April 1933 and never looked back. Before Ravensbrück had even opened, he had already demanded the construction of a large cell block in the new camp to break the defiance of "hysterical women," as he put it.[219] But the leading female officer in Ravensbrück was cut from a different cloth. Johanna Langefeld, the senior camp supervisor, had not signed up with the Nazi Party until her late thirties, in 1937. From a deeply religious family, she worked in social care and the prison service before joining Lichtenburg in 1938. In contrast to Koegel, Langefeld really did see reeducation as an important goal and opposed some of his more violent initiatives. This mattered, because Langefeld set the tone inside the camp and did not push her female guards to excesses.[220] While most new female guards quickly got used to slapping prisoners, or even kicking them, they rarely went further in the early war years.[221] Their behavior was influenced, no doubt, by the fact that the state execution policy, which had boosted violence levels in the KL for men, was not initially extended to Ravensbrück; the first execution of a woman did not take place until February 1941, apparently, and only in 1942 did such killings become the norm.[222]

As a result, almost all women survived Ravensbrück during the early war years. Over two years (1940–41), around one hundred female prisoners lost their lives—less than two percent of the prisoner population and a fraction of the deaths in KL for men; only in 1943 did the Ravensbrück SS feel the need to operate its own crematorium. The contrast between the sexes was plain to see even inside Ravensbrück itself. From April 1941, a separate compound for men was set up here, to supply forced labor for the extension of the camp. This was an important development in itself; in the future, more and more camps would become mixed, though male and female prisoners were still held in separate compounds. By the end of 1941, around one thousand men had arrived in the new Ravensbrück subcamp, where conditions soon resembled the other KL for men; in the last three months of 1941 alone, more than fifty male prisoners died here. Proportionally, about as many men died in Ravensbrück in a single month as women did in two years.[223]

In many ways, the women's camp in Ravensbrück was still stuck in the prewar period; for the inmates, the real break came not in 1939, but 1942. This is not to say that the camp was unaffected by wider developments. Living conditions deteriorated after the outbreak of war. Food cuts, combined with the freezing temperatures, caused widespread illness during the first winter, and with some 6,400 women arriving in 1940–41, many barracks were overcrowded.[224] Then there were the daily hardships and humiliations. The local SS established a particularly degrading ritual on arrival, when women had to undress, shower, and endure a bodily examination; many were also shaved. Any "feeble attempts at modesty had to be abandoned," Buber-Neumann wrote. These assaults on women's bodies and their gender identities—"with our bald heads, we looked like men," another prisoner noted in her diary— had not been common before the war. The trauma was greatly intensified by the presence of SS men, who ogled the naked women, made lewd remarks, or slapped them.[225]

Like in the other KL, there were scales of suffering within Ravensbrück, too. German political prisoners enjoyed some benefits; their barracks, for example, were often less packed. Meanwhile, Polish women, who apparently replaced German "asocials" as the largest prisoner group in 1941, initially faced added discrimination; in the infirmary, some SS doctors refused to see prisoners who could not speak German.[226] And Jewish women—around ten percent of the prisoner population (1939–42)—remained at the bottom of the hierarchy, singled out for the worst labor and abuse.[227] In these respects, at least, Ravensbrück moved in line with general SS terror, as the abuse of Poles and Jews escalated across the whole of the KL system in the early war years.

War and Retribution

During the first weeks of the Second World War, the Third Reich was awash with rumors about Polish atrocities. Having blamed Poland for the outbreak of war, Nazi propaganda now accused Poles of gruesome war crimes, in another reversal of reality. From the first days of the invasion, German soldiers sent paranoid reports about ambushes by "snipers." Such rumors spread fast, amplified by Nazi leaders.[228] In particular, Nazi propaganda seized upon events in the Polish city of Bydgoszcz (Bromberg), where several hundred ethnic German civilians were killed in clashes with Polish forces in early September 1939 (German units, among them two Death's Head battalions, later massacred large numbers of local Poles). For days, Nazi papers carried lurid articles and even fantasized about ritual killings. According to the *Völkischer Beobachter* of September 10, Poles had "cut off the left breast of an old woman, ripped out her heart, and threw it into a bowl, which had been used to catch her blood"; similar articles were illustrated with graphic photos of maimed body parts.[229] A few days later, Hitler himself stoked the flames further. In a frenzied speech in occupied Danzig on September 19, he claimed that Polish enemies had butchered thousands of ethnic Germans "like animals," among them women and children, and mutilated countless captured German soldiers "in a bestial way, gouging out their eyes."[230]

Many Germans bought into this atrocity propaganda and demanded swift retaliation.[231] Poles taken to the KL felt the full force of public outrage. On September 13, 1939, when 534 Polish Jews were assembled at a Berlin railway station en route to Sachsenhausen, they faced a mob baying for the blood of the "Bromberg murderers" (in fact, the prisoners were residents of Berlin); more spectators waited at the station in Oranienburg, throwing stones and excrement.[232] Much worse was to follow, as Camp SS men were itching for brutal retribution and hounded the Poles as soon as they arrived.

The epicenter of KL violence was in Sachsenhausen and Buchenwald, which held the vast majority of Polish prisoners in the early months of war. The Buchenwald SS improvised, just as it had done after the 1938 pogrom, and forced the newly arriving Poles and Polish Jews into a compound next to the roll call square, cordoned off with barbed wire. This so-called special (or little) camp, set up in late September 1939, became an island of extreme suffering. Among the first prisoners were 110 Poles arrested in the border regions during the German advance. The fact that a few of them really came from Bromberg proved their death sentence. Labeled as "snipers," the SS pressed them into a small cage of planks and barbed wire, where they slowly starved to death; by Christmas Day, all but two of the 110 men inside the cage were dead.[233]

The other prisoners in the Buchenwald special camp were also fighting for survival. Exposed to freezing temperatures, hundreds of Poles and Polish-born Jews suffered inside a wooden barrack and four large tents. At first, the prisoners still had to work in the quarry. Jakob Ihr, who had been arrested in Vienna, remembered that the "despair was so great, after only a few hours, that a number of our comrades beseeched the SS to shoot them dead."[234] Labor was eventually halted in late October 1939, when a dysentery epidemic spread through the special camp. "The prisoners now dropped like flies," another witness said after the war. Those who tried to escape to the relative safety of the main compound were whipped by the SS.[235] The men in charge formed a terrifying double act. Hauptscharführer Blank, a Camp SS veteran, gained a reputation as a cold-blooded executioner, while his colleague, Hauptscharführer Hinkelmann, a violent drunk, channeled his energy into new forms of prisoner abuse. Apparently, he particularly enjoyed beating hungry prisoners during the distribution of the watery soup. On other days, Hinkelmann and Blank handed out no food at all.[236]

The Buchenwald special camp was eventually closed down in early 1940. By then, around two out of three prisoners were dead.[237] As the last survivors entered the main camp compound in January and February 1940, even long-time inmates, like the camp elder Ernst Frommhold, were shocked: "17-year-old boys barely weighing 50–60 pounds, not a gram of fat on their bodies, only skin and bones. Even today, I cannot understand how such emaciated men could still be alive, and yet they were."[238] In all, well over five hundred Polish-born Jews and three hundred Poles had died in the special camp.[239]

In Sachsenhausen, too, Polish-born Jews fared the worst in the early months of World War II. About a thousand men arrived between September and December 1939, some from Poland, but most from inside Germany itself. Around half of them came on the very first transport from Berlin on September 13, which had met with such public outrage. Among them was Leon Szalet, a middle-aged estate agent brought up in Warsaw, who had lived in Berlin since 1921. Just before war broke out he had made a daring bid to leave: he managed to board a flight to London without a visa on August 27, but was turned back on arrival by zealous British immigration officials. Two weeks later, he was greeted in Sachsenhausen by a mob of screaming SS men, who "jumped on us like wild beasts." Szalet himself was beaten unconscious by one of the block leaders. In the evening of their first day, after hours of abuse, he and the other new prisoners fell on sacks of straw in their barracks. But few found sleep: the horror of the past few hours and the dread of what would follow kept most of them awake for a long time.

Leon Szalet and the other Polish Jews were held in the Sachsenhausen little camp, first established for "asocials" in summer 1938. As a special punishment, the SS had the barrack windows nailed shut with planks, an extreme form of isolation already familiar from prewar Dachau. There was no light and no ventilation. "Some men were close to suffocating," Szalet recalled, "others literally died of thirst." The SS forced prisoners who begged for water to drink their own urine. By September 29, when the action was called off after the capitulation of Warsaw, some thirty-five men had died.[240] The torment of the others continued over the following months. Initially, Polish Jews only left their barracks for roll calls and "sport." The rest of the time was spent inside, at the mercy of Kapos and SS block leaders like Wilhelm "Pistol" Schubert, who regularly raided the barracks at night. Among their many vicious games, SS men forced prisoners to fight each other for bread; those who refused were beaten or killed.[241] Later, many of the inmates were pressed into forced labor, frequently at the Oranienburg brick works. "Our daily routine," Leon Szalet wrote, "involved freezing, being chased, carrying snow or sand wrapped in our coats, stumbling, falling and being chased again."[242]

Before the Holocaust

Soon all Jewish men in the KL were in mortal danger. In the first months of the Second World War, the SS still differentiated, directing its greatest fury against Polish Jews. But such distinctions soon disappeared, as the police extended its persecution of German Jews—suspected as supporters of the enemy—and the Camp SS extended its terror. "The struggle against the Jews," the Sachsenhausen death squad leader Gustav Sorge testified after the war, "was a racial struggle."[243] Even the hearts of some guards considered humane hardened when it came to Jews. The Ravensbrück camp supervisor Johanna Langefeld, for example, was a fanatical anti-Semite and let Jewish prisoners feel her hatred.[244]

A crucial moment came on March 9, 1940, when Heinrich Himmler banned all further releases of Jews; only Jews who held valid visas and could emigrate before the end of April would still be freed.[245] The flow of releases of Jews, already small, became a trickle and then dried up altogether.[246] One of the lucky few to escape at the last moment was Leon Szalet, thanks to the dogged persistence of his daughter, whom he had brought up alone, as a widower. In early 1940, the mood among Polish Jews in the camp had fluctuated between hope and despair. When Szalet heard that he might be released, some comrades could not hide their envy. When it looked as if his plans would fall through, one gleeful prisoner broke into a popular tune, changing the lyrics: "A ship leaves for Shanghai, and Szalet won't be nigh."[247] But on May 7, 1940, he really was set free, to the surprise even of SS block leaders. After eight months in Sachsenhausen, he was sick, starved, and depressed, and he never really recovered.[248] But at least he escaped more SS torment. This was the fate of the Jews who were left behind, and now faced near-certain death.

Sachsenhausen and Buchenwald, which initially led the way in early wartime terror against Jews, claimed the lives of many Jewish prisoners; in Buchenwald alone, almost seven hundred died during 1940.[249] Men accused of intimate relations with "Aryan" women, and marked on their files and uniforms as "race defilers," were particularly vulnerable, as the combination of sex and race remained irresistible to the SS. On May 3, 1940, for example,

Gustav Sorge beat and kicked to death an elderly Jewish prisoner who had just arrived in Sachsenhausen; before Sorge broke his victim's bones, he screamed: "Oh, you swine, you're a Jew and fucked our Christian women!"[250] Like this inmate, many Jewish men died within days or weeks of their arrival. Those who survived a little longer carried the deep marks of SS excesses. Crushing forced labor was accompanied by extreme violence, wiping out several members of the same families. The Camp SS also continued to cut rations, holding regular "fasting days," when Jews received no food at all, and occasionally banned all Jews from entering the infirmaries. Young and strong men soon looked old and infirm, and even the most resilient among them fell into despair. "In Sachsenhausen, I did not know whether I was still human," the Polish-born boxer and mechanic Salem (Bully) Schott remembered. "I did not feel anything anymore, except hunger."[251]

In other camps, too, Jewish men lost all hope. In Dachau, the most feared site was a new extension of the plantation, called Freiland II, which was cultivated from spring 1941.[252] Karel Kašák, a privileged Czech prisoner who worked as an illustrator on the plantation (the SS planned a publication about the different plants), secretly documented the abuses: "21 March [1941]. [Commando leader] Seuss ordered the Jews to immediately take off their bandages from the infirmary, under which they have horrific wounds, and to work without them in the soggy and muddy ground. All 200 Jews are terribly miserable, shattered, abused, and utterly emaciated figures; 90 percent can barely keep on their feet."[253] Almost every day, there were murders or forced suicides on the plantation, as this extract from Kašák's notes illustrates:

> May 9 [1941]. Again a Jew shot in Freiland II. He started to run. The sentry told us that although he has instructions to shoot without warning, he shouted twice. The [prisoner] stopped and just exclaimed: "I want to go there" and fell after two shots . . . Again they have put a group of lifeless and unconscious Jews on the cart. Human flesh, the bodies of these sons of God, stacked like logs, arms and legs swaying limply—a horrendous picture that we witness daily . . .
>
> May 14. In the afternoon they again shot a Jew in Freiland II . . .
>
> May 15. Again a Jew shot. They threw his cap behind the sentry and the Kapo forced him with a truncheon to fetch it. Complete exhaustion has made [the Jewish prisoners] unrecognizable, like in a trance, with a far-away gaze . . .
>
> May 16. At nine in the morning two more Jews shot in Freiland II. They threw the exhausted men into the water and held them under water until they had almost lost consciousness, and definitely lost their minds,

and Kapo Sammetinger hit them with the spade until he had forced them to cross the sentry line, whereupon they were immediately shot.[254]

Dreadful as Dachau was, conditions were even worse in Mauthausen. This KL, which had not held any Jews in the prewar period, gradually filled up in the early war years, with almost one thousand Jewish men arriving in 1940–41. The vast majority of them were doomed.[255] Most of the victims were Jewish men arrested in the occupied Netherlands. A first large group had been rounded up there in February 1941: after the German authorities and their local allies had met growing resistance to their persecution of Dutch Jews, Himmler ordered mass arrests in retaliation. Their initial destination was Buchenwald, where some 389 young Jewish men arrived as so-called hostages on February 28, 1941.[256] "Unbearable conditions soon arose," one of them testified later, and by May 22, 1941, over forty men had died. That day, almost all the survivors, some 341 men total, were forced on a train to Mauthausen on orders of the IKL; most likely, SS leaders had decided that they should die.[257] The prisoners arrived in Mauthausen around midnight and the SS guards set upon them straightaway; within three months, more than half had perished. Most of them died in the quarries, crushed by rocks, beaten to death, or forced over the sentry line. Some committed suicide and threw themselves to their deaths, holding hands; on October 14, 1941, for example, the SS recorded that sixteen Jews had perished by "jumping [in the] quarry." Whether they had been pushed or not, the SS men were guilty, a responsibility they bore lightly. When further transports of Jews arrived in Mauthausen, SS officials jokingly welcomed their new "battalion of paratroopers."[258]

By 1941, concentration camps had become death traps for Jewish prisoners. The sharp rise in the death rate, compared to the prewar years, owed much to the unrestrained rank-and-file guards. But their superiors were involved, too, and several prisoners reported that KL commandants had given explicit orders to kill Jewish prisoners.[259] Clearly, the Camp SS was influenced by the general course of Nazi anti-Jewish policy, which turned far more lethal between 1939 and 1941, with the SS in the driving seat. Still, the transition to systematic murder came particularly early in the KL, well before Nazi policy as a whole moved in this direction. While the immediate extermination of European Jews had not yet been decided by early summer 1941, the death of Jews in concentration camps was an almost foregone conclusion by then.

This is not to say that the Nazi Final Solution started earlier than we thought. Despite isolated calls by radical Nazi activists for deporting all Jews to the KL, the camps remained on the periphery of anti-Jewish policy in the early war years.[260] Instead, the authorities relied on other sites of mass detention, setting up hundreds of forced labor camps and ghettos in Poland, Germany, and elsewhere; the largest ghetto in Warsaw held some 445,000 Jews by March 1941, suffering mass starvation, disease, and death.[261] By contrast, the KL were reserved for selected Jews only, above all men seen as particularly dangerous criminals or terrorists. They were arrested for punishment and deterrence, as in the case of the Jews rounded up in the Netherlands, whose fate was common knowledge among the Dutch Jewish community.[262] If the only "crime" of Jewish men, women, and children was being Jewish, however, they were far more likely to suffer elsewhere.

Attacking Polish Prisoners

On August 13, 1940, the daily routine in Mauthausen was briefly disrupted when two middle-aged Polish prisoners, Victor Lukawski and Franc Kapacki, slipped away from the Gusen subcamp. Escapes were still extremely rare, and after the guards realized that two men were missing, they ran amok. As collective punishment, all eight hundred prisoners (almost all Poles) in the escaped men's work detail were forced to move heavy rocks in the quarry at running pace; those who broke down were battered by Kapos and SS. After they returned to the camp, they had to stand to attention all night without any food. The balance sheet of the day of violence was stark: in all, fourteen Polish prisoners died in Gusen on August 13, 1940. The two escapees met a gruesome end, too; they were dragged back a couple of days later and beaten to death.[263]

From the beginning, the new Gusen subcamp had been earmarked as a "reeducation camp" for Polish prisoners. The first transport with 1,084 Polish men came on May 25, 1940, the day the camp officially opened, and others soon followed. In all, some eight thousand Poles, many of them members of the Polish intelligentsia, arrived in late spring and summer 1940, mostly from other KL like Dachau and Sachsenhausen. By the end of the year, more than 1,500 had lost their lives in Gusen, where the average monthly mortality stood at five percent.[264] The inferno was overseen by SS camp leader Karl Chmielewski. A trained woodcarver from Hesse, he had come to the SS in 1932, after he lost his workshop during the Great Depression. He prospered after joining Himmler's personal office, and in summer 1935, at the age of thirty-one, he was initiated into the Camp SS; he trained in the Columbia House camp under Karl Otto Koch, one of the best teachers in cruelty, and in the following year he moved to Sachsenhausen, where he was groomed for higher office. Chmielewski's moment came in 1940, when he was transferred to Gusen to lead some sixty SS men in the Commandant Staff. Under his reign, which lasted until late 1942, one in every two prisoners perished. A tall and strong man, Chmielewski led from the front, showing his men how the prisoners should be beaten, kicked, whipped, and killed. His superiors were duly impressed, with the Mauthausen commandant Franz Ziereis praising his "especially pronounced" personal toughness.[265]

Murderous violence also surrounded Poles in the other KL, after prisoner numbers shot up in 1940–41. In Sachsenhausen, thousands of Poles were isolated in the little camp, now cleared of Jews and known as the "Polish quarantine camp," where they were tormented like the Jewish prisoners before them.[266] Extreme terror characterized the smaller camps, too. After a Polish inmate escaped from Flossenbürg in summer 1941, the local Camp SS made the other Poles stand to attention for three days and nights without food—perhaps the longest roll call in the history of the KL; some prisoners who fell unconscious were murdered by a Kapo, who forced a hose with running water down their throats.[267]

Nowhere was the SS assault on Polish prisoners more deadly than in Auschwitz, where Poles made up the great majority of inmates in 1940–41. Prisoner numbers had grown rapidly after the camp was set up and so did the dead. The ingredients making up camp life were the same as elsewhere: violent and often senseless labor, never-ending roll calls, hunger, disease, and dirt. "In the camp, one lived from one day to the next, just to be still alive tomorrow," Wiesław Kielar recalled.[268] In its first twelve months, several thousand men died in Auschwitz, and things only got worse. During a twelve-week period from October 7 to December 31, 1941, SS bureaucrats recorded the dispatch of 2,915 prisoner corpses from the main camp's morgue to the crematorium.[269]

The rage of the SS extended to other prisoner groups, too, in addition to Poles and Jews. German-speaking Gypsies were often targeted during the early war years, partly owing to deep-seated prejudices among SS men (Rudolf Höss, for one, was convinced that Gypsies had tried to abduct him as a child). In Buchenwald, some six hundred Austrian Roma arrived via Dachau in autumn 1939. They faced extreme hardship and hunger, and around two hundred died during the first winter. Many had suffered frozen limbs and were brought for amputations to the infirmary; SS doctors had no hesitation about killing some with deadly injections. "None of my comrades want to go to the infirmary anymore, because no one comes back," one young inmate told a fellow prisoner. "I think all of us Gypsies will die in Buchenwald."[270]

The SS also selected some political opponents for "special treatment." In the first half of 1941, the great majority of new arrivals in the Gusen subcamp were veterans from the Spanish Civil War. Among the other inmates, these men quickly gained a reputation for bravery and solidarity. This only confirmed the fears of the SS, who saw them as battle-hardened enemies and singled them out for the hardest punishment. In 1941, almost sixty percent of prisoners classified as "Red Spaniards" or "Spaniards" perished in Mauthausen; many of the 3,046 victims were murdered in the quarries. The steep steps the prisoners had to climb every day, with huge blocks of granite on their backs, resembled "a long cemetery," one of the survivors wrote.[271]

Prisoner Relations

The dealings between different inmate groups became more strained than ever as conditions deteriorated. The basic principles of the camp pitted them against one another, and their backgrounds, beliefs, and experiences were too diverse to unite them against the SS. Many Polish prisoners, for example, felt hostile toward prisoners from Germany, the enemy nation. Their dislike extended even to dedicated opponents of the Nazi regime like German Communists. Many Poles despised them as atheists and, even more so, as friends of the Soviet Union, which had invaded the eastern half of Poland in mid-September 1939, under the ignominious Hitler-Stalin pact, and arrested, deported, or executed many tens of thousands of Polish civilians and soldiers.[272]

German prisoners, meanwhile, were not immune to Nazi racism, which tapped into a long history of chauvinism toward Slavs. In Neuengamme, a German Kapo warned newcomers about Poles: "We know that riffraff: lazy, dirty, and most of them also bread thieves."[273] Jews continued to suffer at the hands of some German inmates, too. In Sachsenhausen, Leon Szalet had briefly worked with political prisoners from the penal company. It was heavy building work and the forty-eight-year-old Szalet, new to the job, could not keep up: "My work colleagues used this to furiously insult me. I was lazy like all Jews, they screamed." Then they beat Szalet until he collapsed.[274]

By no means were all German prisoners blinded by racism, of course. Szalet himself praised the Sachsenhausen camp elder Harry Naujoks for helping as much as he could, and he greatly admired his courageous block elder, another left-wing German prisoner.[275] Other Polish and Jewish inmates received help from German prisoners, too. In the savage world of the camps, even small gestures meant a lot, and were still remembered decades later.[276] Nonetheless, the friction between prisoner groups increased under the pressure of war.

Tensions were exacerbated by the preferential SS treatment for selected

German prisoners.[277] Across the KL system, most of the coveted Kapo posts went to Germans, and the contrast between these inmates and the rest was stark. In the unforgiving winter of 1939–40, hundreds of Sachsenhausen prisoners died in outside labor details and freezing barracks. At the same time, privileged inmates like Emil Büge, who worked as a prisoner clerk, had a desk in a heated office. Together with the other German clerks, Büge enjoyed extra sandwiches, milk, and cigarettes, and celebrated the birthday of one comrade with cake and coffee, a delicacy most other prisoners only dreamed about.[278]

Not only did German Kapos enjoy better conditions, they often held the fate of foreign inmates and Jews in their hands. Take Johann Brüggen, a German political prisoner who terrorized two hundred men on a large Dachau building site in 1940, pursuing Jews with particular vengeance. One of his victims was Gerhard Brandt, a twenty-seven-year-old graphic designer who arrived in Dachau on May 24, 1940, and joined Brüggen's commando a few days later. When Brandt fell behind, Kapo Brüggen was all over him, screaming "Dirty Jew," "Jewish pig," and "You're not even human." On June 5, 1940, the seriously injured prisoner was admitted to the Dachau infirmary; here, he confidentially described the torture he had suffered: "When I fell, Brüggen would always trample over my body. I was also beaten every day on the head and the face with a wooden cudgel. With his hands, too, Brüggen pushed into my face, so that I always bled very heavily from the nose. The handkerchief was so blood-soaked I could not use it anymore for drying off." A few hours after he gave this account, Gerhard Brandt died.[279]

Kapo Brüggen was no exception; hundreds of German Kapos were guilty of violent excesses in the early war years. But the other prisoners did not see all such violence as taboo. Quite the contrary. There was widespread agreement that slaps and kicks were in order if a prisoner had stepped out of line. Emil Büge recorded such a case in winter 1939–40. One night, a Polish prisoner moaned and pleaded for water, and grabbed the covers of other inmates in his barrack. Tired of the commotion, a block service prisoner eventually hit the man with a truncheon. "We all approve that he is beaten," Büge wrote, "and he duly becomes 'sensible' and no longer disturbs us." In fact, the prisoner was dead. In the darkness of the night, no one had realized that he was no troublemaker; he was dying.[280]

This unknown Polish prisoner was one of many thousands of victims in the early war years, a period of change inside the KL. Many key features of the wartime camps emerged early on: bigger compounds, new camps outside the German heartland, masses of foreign prisoners, lethal living conditions, murderous everyday violence, and planned executions. The terror would intensify in later years, but it had started early in the war. And yet, even during the worst days, victims were still counted in their dozens, not hundreds or thousands. The transition from mass death to systematic mass extermination did not take place until spring and summer 1941, when Nazi leaders took the next steps on the road to genocide in the KL.

5

Mass Extermination

On the morning of Friday, April 4, 1941, two German doctors, Friedrich
Mennecke, a dapper thirty-six-year-old, and the dumpy Theodor Steinmeyer,
seven years older and sporting a crude Hitler mustache, arrived at Oranienburg train station and made their way to the nearby Sachsenhausen concentration camp. Except for their looks, the two psychiatrists had much in
common. Ambitious and ruthless, they were both committed to radical racial hygiene and had risen at a young age to become asylum directors in the
Third Reich, assisted by their early dedication to the Nazi cause (Steinmeyer
had joined the party in 1929, Mennecke in 1932). During their half-hour walk,
the two men, who would become firm friends, probably talked about their
first trip to the camp on the previous day, when their superior, Professor
Werner Heyde, had initiated them into a secret mission: they would examine
around four hundred prisoners, selected by the Camp SS from among all the
twelve thousand Sachsenhausen inmates.[1]

On arrival, Dr. Mennecke and Dr. Steinmeyer set themselves up in the
camp's infirmary to see the selected prisoners. The two physicians worked all
day, interrupted only by lunch in the SS officers' mess. They finished at 6:00
p.m., having each examined several dozen prisoners. Steinmeyer then returned to his hotel in Berlin, while Mennecke retired to a luxurious double room
in the posh Hotel Eilers in Oranienburg. Buzzing with excitement, he fired off
a letter to his wife. "Our work is very, very interesting," he told her. At 9:00 a.m.
the next day, after a good night's rest and a rich breakfast, Dr. Mennecke
met up again with Dr. Steinmeyer at Oranienburg station and returned to

Sachsenhausen for more prisoner examinations, breaking off at lunchtime for the weekend. They resumed their duties on Monday morning, when they were joined by a third psychiatrist, Dr. Otto Hebold. They worked even quicker now and on the following day, Tuesday, April 8, 1941, after seeing the last remaining eighty-four prisoners, they had completed their mission.[2]

The doctors departed from Sachsenhausen as suddenly as they had appeared, leaving behind the prisoners they had examined. Most of them were little more than skin and bones. "They were so weak," Dr. Hebold recalled later, "they could barely stand upright"; many were unable to work and had been in the infirmary for some time, suffering from a range of debilitating illnesses. Others had been selected by the SS inside their barracks. One was Siegbert Fraenkel, a refined fifty-seven-year-old art and book dealer from Berlin. Fraenkel had made many friends among the other Jewish prisoners in the torturous standing commando, diverting them during their interminable days with talks about paintings, literature, and philosophy. "Through his lectures," one inmate later remembered, "he gave us back a bit of dignified, human life." The corpulent Fraenkel was still in reasonable health after more than five months in the camp. Still the SS presented him to the visiting physicians in spring 1941, presumably because of his deformed spine.[3]

The doctors' examinations in Sachsenhausen were a short, sharp ordeal. For several minutes, they interrogated each inmate about his background, health, and family; repeatedly, local Camp SS officials intervened, adding further details about alleged misconduct and poor work performance. Worst of all was the uncertainty about what the doctors wanted. Under the extreme conditions of the camps, inmates were always second-guessing their captors, trying to read the SS runes, and the doctors' visit to Sachsenhausen in early April 1941 was no different. The most persistent rumor, encouraged by the SS, was that the physicians selected infirm inmates for easier work in Dachau. Other prisoners suspected more sinister motives, though no one was sure. But after several weeks had passed without further incident, many prisoners must have forgotten all about their examination by the mysterious doctors. None of them knew that their fate had already been sealed.[4]

Dr. Steinmeyer, Dr. Mennecke, and Dr. Hebold were no ordinary doctors. They were veterans of the "euthanasia" action, the Nazi program for the mass murder of the disabled. These physicians had long broken their Hippocratic Oath and came to Sachsenhausen not to heal but to kill: they judged most of the prisoners they examined as "life unworthy of life," as the doctors called them, and reported them to the headquarters of the "euthanasia" program.[5] After the files had been processed there, a final list of names was sent back to Sachsenhausen. Early on June 3, 1941, exactly two months after Steinmeyer and Mennecke had first visited the camp, the SS assembled the first ninety-five victims in the infirmary. Here they were injected with a sedative and forced onto a large truck, covered with a tarpaulin. Another 174 prisoners followed on two further transports a few days later. Among them was Siegbert Fraenkel, the Jewish art dealer, who feared the worst. Shortly before he left Sachsenhausen on June 5, he told the camp elder Harry Naujoks: "It is obvious; we're being treated like doomed men." Fraenkel was right. The truck brought him and the others to Sonnenstein asylum in Saxony, where they were all murdered on arrival.[6]

These murders were no one-off. When he came to Sachsenhausen in April 1941, Dr. Mennecke knew that this trip was only the beginning of his lethal service in the KL. By the time Siegbert Fraenkel and the other Sachsenhausen prisoners were murdered two months later, Mennecke had already completed his next round of selections, this time in Auschwitz, and over the coming months he would travel to Buchenwald, Dachau, Ravensbrück, Gross-Rosen, Flossenbürg, and Neuengamme.[7] Thousands of prisoners were killed as a result.

The year 1941 was when the KL moved from mass death to mass extermination. From early autumn, with the killing of infirm inmates still in full swing, the Camp SS embarked on an even more radical program, murdering tens of thousands of Soviet POWs. The concentration camps turned into killing fields and annihilation became a way of life for the perpetrators, inaugurating a new period in the camps' history: for the first time, Camp SS men participated in the coordinated slaughter of prisoners on a grand scale.

KILLING THE WEAK

The Nazi "euthanasia" action had taken shape just before the outbreak of the Second World War, when Hitler authorized a secret program for the murder of the disabled. The men in charge were Hitler's personal doctor Karl Brandt and Philipp Bouhler, the head of the Chancellery of the Führer. A marginal figure in the Nazi hierarchy, Bouhler saw mass murder as a chance to boost his standing, and entrusted the day-to-day management to his right-hand man Viktor Brack. Soon, the perpetrators had established an effective organization, working from headquarters in a Berlin villa on Tiergartenstrasse 4 (hence the code word of the "euthanasia" program, Operation T-4). German asylums were asked to submit special forms about their patients, with details about their condition. These forms were then dispatched to specially recruited

doctors like Dr. Mennecke and Dr. Steinmeyer, who made the initial decision
about the patients' fate, cursorily reviewed by a senior physician like Professor Heyde. Their main focus was on the patients' ability to work: anyone
regarded as unproductive would be killed. But how?

The murderers considered several methods. Initially, they thought about
lethal injections. But this was soon abandoned in favor of a different approach.
Apparently backed by Hitler, the fateful decision was taken to kill the disabled with poison gas. In late 1939–early 1940, the SS set up a trial gassing in
a former jail outside Berlin. Several disabled men were locked into a sealed
room pumped full of carbon monoxide; they died under the watchful gaze of
the top brass of the "euthanasia" action. Before long, the newly recruited T-4
staff ran several killing centers (mostly converted mental asylums), each with
a gas chamber. Mass gassings of patients from across Germany only ceased in
summer 1941, on Hitler's orders, following growing public anxiety about the
killings, which had become an open secret (the murders continued less conspicuously inside local asylums). By this time, some seventy to eighty thousand people had been murdered inside gas chambers, the "unique invention
of Nazi Germany," in the words of the historian Henry Friedlander, that would
become central to the genocide of European Jews. Its first victims, though,
were patients from asylums, and they were soon followed by KL inmates.[8]

"Euthanasia" and the Camps

Heinrich Himmler must have been appalled when he stepped inside Dachau
on January 20, 1941, some nine months after his last visit, to lead a delegation
of senior SS officials and Dutch Nazis.[9] Anxious Camp SS officers always
tried to gloss over difficulties during his inspections, but there was no way of
hiding that his favorite camp was in crisis. The problem, as far as the local
Camp SS was concerned, had started several months earlier, when Camp
Inspector Richard Glücks, faced with an ever-growing number of ill and
weak prisoners across the KL system, had designated Dachau as a collection
point for *Muselmänner*. Previously, individual camps had isolated the sick
inside special zones. Now Glücks planned to relieve other camps by concentrating the greatest misery in Dachau.[10] Following Glücks's order, thousands
of sick men had arrived in Dachau from late summer 1940 onward. Between
August 28 and September 16 alone, four large transports left Sachsenhausen,
bringing four thousand invalid prisoners (mostly from the standing commandos) to Dachau; in exchange, the Dachau SS dispatched up to three thousand healthier inmates in the opposite direction.[11] Smaller transports also
came from other camps. On October 24, 1940, for example, the Buchenwald

SS sent a special train to Dachau; the SS described all 371 men on board as "ill prisoners and cripples" who were "unfit for work."[12]

Dachau turned into a nightmare. Bodies of *Muselmänner* who had died en route were dumped at the train station. Those who made it into the compound lay sprawled across the roll call square or inside specially cleared barracks. They were emaciated, often with frostbitten hands or feet, and covered in lice, edema, and pus-filled wounds; passing SS guards were surprised when these half-dead men still showed signs of life, crying, whimpering, and begging for mercy, or when they screamed in pain as others ripped off clothing that stuck to their scabs. Many suffered from acute dysentery and an infernal stench soon filled Dachau. The prisoner Alfred Hübsch vividly recalled the arrival of one of the "horror transports" from Sachsenhausen in early September 1940: "We saw dozens [of new prisoners] with excrement running out of their trousers. Their hands, too, were full of excrement and they screamed and rubbed their dirty hands across their faces. These soiled and sunken faces, with their protruding cheekbones, had something terrifying about them." Too weak to walk and eat, many had come to Dachau only to die.[13]

In all, more than one thousand prisoners perished between September and December 1940; in four infernal months, around twice as many men had died in Dachau as in the seven prewar years. Then conditions got even worse. In January 1941, the month when Himmler visited, Dachau reached a new deadly record, as at least 463 prisoners lost their lives.[14] At the same time, the camp was ravaged by scabies. An estimated four to five thousand men were infected in early 1941, almost half of the entire prisoner population. Many were isolated with no medical help, little food, and only bags of straw to sleep on. The prisoner Adam Kozlowiecki, a Polish priest who saw the sick on their way to their weekly bath, recorded their appearance in a secret diary: "Yellow skeletons with big, sad eyes. They looked at us. Some glances expressed a plea for help, others complete apathy."[15]

The dirt and disease in Dachau dented Himmler's ideal image of the KL, even if his subordinates shielded him from the worst during his visit on January 20, 1941. Himmler's vision was about all-out order and cleanliness, and filthy invalids had no place in it; they were a drain on resources, a health risk, and an economic liability. Many Camp SS men agreed. As one of them explained in early 1941, all prisoners "who cannot work" and all "cripples" posed a "colossal burden" for the KL.[16] By then, Camp SS leaders must have realized that the decision to turn Dachau into a dumping ground for the sick had backfired. Not only had it turned the old model camp into a pit, the situation in the other KL was little improved. True, prisoner mortality had fallen temporarily after sick prisoners left for Dachau.[17] But their numbers soon grew again, and by early 1941 all SS concentration camps for men were full of dying inmates.[18] Something had to be done.

Around the time of his trip to Dachau, Heinrich Himmler settled on a radical solution: invalid prisoners would be systematically exterminated.[19] Mass murder was already in the air. Across the Third Reich and its newly conquered territories, Nazi leaders and their followers were getting used to murder as a solution to all kinds of "problems," from political resistance to mental illness. As for weak and sick prisoners in the KL, many SS men were more than happy to see them die. According to a former inmate, the views of Dachau SS leaders about invalids in 1940 could be summed up as follows: "Let them croak—then we'll be rid of them."[20] In fact, as we have seen, some local Camp SS men had already started to go further, murdering some weak and sick prisoners on their own initiative. In another case of "cumulative radicalization," such unauthorized and ad hoc killings by overzealous local Camp SS men must have given an added spur to the new centralized program of murdering the infirm, with Himmler reasserting his authority as the final arbiter over life and death.[21]

To implement his plan, Himmler turned to the T-4 killing experts. Rumors that the "euthanasia" program would be extended to the KL had circulated in Germany since 1940.[22] But Himmler did not settle things until early 1941, during discussions with Bouhler and Brack from the Chancellery of the Führer.[23] It was convenient for Himmler to latch on to the "euthanasia" action. Here was a well-oiled machine that had already delivered tens of thousands to their deaths. Moreover, Himmler knew that he could trust the T-4 officials, many of whom were SS veterans (including several former Camp SS men who had been transferred from Sachsenhausen and Buchenwald to T-4 in late 1939). Some he knew personally: Viktor Brack had once worked as Himmler's driver and Werner Heyde had overseen prisoner sterilizations in the prewar KL.[24] Once Himmler had made his decision, he moved fast. After a further meeting with Brack on March 28, 1941—and possibly the final go-ahead from Hitler himself—the operation began, and just one week later, Dr. Mennecke and Dr. Steinmeyer set to work in Sachsenhausen.[25]

It is significant that Himmler decided to outsource the first extermination program of his prisoners to the T-4 killers, rather than leaving it to the Camp SS. We can only guess at his motives. Perhaps Himmler wanted his SS men to learn from the T-4 professionals before they turned their own hands to large-scale executions. Or perhaps he worried that mass slaughter inside the camps themselves might trigger prisoner uprisings, whereas killing invalids in far-away "euthanasia" centers meant that the remaining inmates might be deceived about the murderous turn of SS policy.[26]

Selections

Local Camp SS officers were initiated into the program by their superiors, who told them about Himmler's orders to kill the invalids and the infirm. Although the local Camp SS did not act as executioner, it still had a crucial role to play: picking out inmates for the T-4 selections. The most important task, the IKL stressed, was to single out those "who are no longer able to work" (echoing provisions of the "euthanasia" program); among those who were specially targeted, a senior Auschwitz official recalled, were "cripples," "incurables," and "infectious prisoners."[27]

Although the IKL issued some quotas for the total number of prisoners to be presented to the T-4 doctors, local Camp SS men had plenty of leeway when it came to their initial selections. In Dachau, for example, the SS forced prisoners from the various labor details to assemble on the roll call square; Camp SS leaders then noted the names of particularly weak and emaciated men, as well as those with disabilities, such as missing limbs or club feet. The Dachau SS chose yet more prisoners from so-called invalid blocks and the infirmary, forcing some Kapos to cooperate. Walter Neff, a prisoner orderly on the Dachau tuberculosis block, later acknowledged that he had picked out bedridden prisoners.[28]

Following the SS preparations, the T-4 doctors traveled to the camps, alone or in small groups. After the inaugural trip to Sachsenhausen in April 1941, the physicians visited most other camps, including Auschwitz (May 1941), Buchenwald (June and November–December 1941), Mauthausen (June–July 1941), Dachau (September 1941), Ravensbrück (November 1941 and January 1942), Gross-Rosen (January 1942), Flossenbürg (March 1942), and Neuengamme (April 1942).[29] In all, a dozen or more T-4 doctors were involved.[30] They were led by the senior medical "euthanasia" experts, Professor Werner Heyde and Professor Hermann Paul Nitsche, who occasionally participated in the selections themselves. The others were mostly veterans from the T-4 program. Previously, men like Dr. Steinmeyer and Dr. Mennecke had visited mental asylums to select patients to die. Now they came to the camps.[31]

On arrival, the T-4 doctors were met by senior members of the local Camp SS—the commandant, his adjutant, or the camp physician—who briefed them about SS preparations.[32] The T-4 physicians, who could move freely around the compound, sometimes demanded to see more prisoners than the

SS had picked. The doctors' power was a potential cause of friction with local Camp SS chieftains.[33] But in practice, their relationship was largely cordial. They worked together and sometimes socialized, too, going for walks around the grounds to aid their digestion after lunch in the SS officers' mess.[34]

During their selections, the T-4 doctors briefly studied the prisoner files. Then they completed a registration form for each inmate, which had been prepared by the SS, using the standard criteria developed for the "euthanasia" program. Most questions concerned the prisoner's condition, asking about "Diagnosis," "Main Symptoms," and "Incurable Physical Ailments."[35] Normally, the doctors also took a cursory glance at the inmates, just as Dr. Mennecke and Dr. Steinmeyer had done in Sachsenhausen. One at a time, the prisoners, often undressed, were paraded before them; those unable to walk were carried. The doctors scribbled some notes on the forms; occasionally, they would also ask inmates about their background.[36] Then the doctors turned to their next victims.

The selections were swift—like a "conveyor belt," Dr. Mennecke noted in Dachau—and sped up as T-4 doctors gained experience. By November 1941, Mennecke needed less than three minutes to pass judgment on a prisoner, down from an average of eight minutes back in April. "The work is going with a real swing," he informed his wife.[37] Apparently, the T-4 doctors only spared a few of the prisoners they saw. It is not clear what swayed them, though it is likely that some First World War veterans were among those given a temporary reprieve.[38] In the end, the decision by Mennecke and his colleagues came down to a snap judgment they entered into a box on the bottom left-hand corner of the form.[39] The fate of each prisoner was determined by a quick stroke of the pen: "+" meant death, "-" meant life.[40]

The forms were reviewed by officials at T-4 headquarters in Berlin, who approved the final list of victims.[41] This list was then dispatched to one of three "euthanasia" killing centers (Hartheim, Bernburg, or Sonnenstein) that liaised with the respective KL to organize the prisoner transports.[42] When the day came—often several months elapsed between selections and transports—Camp SS men accompanied the prisoners to the killing centers; the Mauthausen SS used a Mercedes omnibus and two yellow postal buses to ferry the victims to their deaths.[43] The prisoners' departure was reported by telex to the IKL in Oranienburg, which kept abreast of the whole operation.[44]

By the time the death transports arrived at the killing centers, many prisoners on board were suspicious and scared; the smell of burning flesh that sometimes hung over the institutions added to their alarm. As local T-4 staff took over from the SS men and checked the paperwork, some prisoners lied about their health or background, hoping that this might help them. A few others tried to run, only to be wrestled to the ground by SS men. There was no way out. Soon, the prisoners were led away, supposedly to the showers. After they had undressed and entered the gas chamber, the T-4 staff locked the door and pumped poison gas inside, from carbon monoxide steel cylinders supplied by IG Farben. Some victims began to vomit, shake, or scream, and struggled for air. After several minutes, the last ones fell unconscious, and some minutes later all were dead. After a while, the gas chamber was ventilated and the bodies dragged out by T-4 staff. They burned the corpses in an adjacent crematorium, but not before ripping out all gold fillings (prisoners had been marked before they went to their death). The gold was sent in batches to T-4 headquarters, which arranged for it to be melted down and sold on. According to one former official, this more or less covered the costs of the killings. The murder machine was self-financing, as victims paid for their own extermination.[45]

Doctors as Murderers

Like other T-4 doctors, Friedrich Mennecke reveled in his role. It has sometimes been suggested that enthusiastic henchmen like Mennecke led double lives to cope with their grisly deeds. Mass murderers in the camps and loving husbands at home, they are said to have erected an impenetrable barrier between professional and private lives.[46] Nothing could be further from the truth in Mennecke's case, as his copious correspondence reveals. Whenever he was away from home, he bombarded his wife with postcards and letters; like an obsessive bookkeeper of his own life, no detail was too small to ignore, from his bowel movements in the morning to his choice of dessert wine after dinner.[47] The letters dating from his time in the camps show that SS Hauptsturmführer Mennecke saw no reason to deceive his wife, who, like him, was a committed National Socialist. He even joked about his murderous mission: "Let the next happy hunt begin!!" he scribbled one morning in November 1941 as he set off for Buchenwald.[48] Far from drawing a line between his work and private life, Mennecke pleaded with his wife to join him—and she did, more than once, accompanying him on his trips to Buchenwald, Ravensbrück, and Gross-Rosen.[49]

Friedrich Mennecke took great pride in his work, which allowed him to rub shoulders with eminent doctors and senior Nazi officials; he proudly informed his wife whenever his superiors praised him.[50] And he was fiercely competitive, rejoicing whenever he managed to finish more forms than his colleagues ("He who works fast saves time!"). Throughout his time in the KL,

Mennecke did not suffer any obvious pangs of conscience, sleeping soundly and eating well. If anything, the selections of starving prisoners seemed to whet his appetite. "This morning, we worked really hard again," he reported about his stint in Buchenwald on November 29, 1941. By eleven o'clock, he had completed seventy forms and felt hungry. He walked over to the SS canteen and devoured "a huge meat dumpling (not a burger), salted potatoes and cabbage, plus sauce."[51]

His verbosity aside, Dr. Mennecke cut no exceptional figure among the T-4 physicians. Mass murder seems to have come easy to them. Like Mennecke, the others saw the killings as an opportunity—an important step for the Third Reich and an important step for their own careers. What is more, they did not have to execute the death sentences they signed, quickly moving on to the next KL. The general atmosphere during these trips was friendly and collegial, as the T-4 men often shared the same hotels and socialized, drawing on their expense accounts. From the outside, they must have appeared like salesmen on a business trip. And this impression was not entirely wrong; it was just that their business was death.

The mood of T-4 doctors was particularly buoyant in early September 1941, when they met in Munich for their biggest mission yet, in nearby Dachau. The situation inside was largely unchanged since Himmler's visit in January: no other KL held more sick and dying men. This was why, presumably, the camp was only targeted now, after the murderous operation was fully up and running.[52] In late summer 1941, the Dachau Camp SS selected two thousand prisoners to be presented to the T-4 commission; many of them had arrived on "invalid transports" from other camps. To guarantee the speedy examination of these prisoners, T-4 managers mobilized at least seven physicians, headed by Professors Heyde and Nitsche themselves; the latter was determined to make the most of his trip to southern Germany and brought along his wife and daughter, who went on an excursion to the Alps. The T-4 officials, meanwhile, paid a preparatory visit to Dachau on September 3, 1941. Because the SS had not yet completed all its paperwork, the doctors stayed only briefly and took the rest of the day off. Dr. Mennecke, Professor Nitsche, and a few others took advantage of the sunshine and strolled along the scenic Lake Starnberg. They did some more sightseeing back in Munich, before moving on to dinner. Afterward, the group split; most doctors went to the movies, while Mennecke and his friend Steinmeyer carried on drinking in a popular wine bar. The next morning, the group went back to Dachau to begin the selections.[53]

Inside Dachau, the T-4 doctors acted professionally, corresponding to their self-image as men of Nazi science. To deceive the prisoners about their ultimate fate, they put on a farce, just as they had previously done in other camps. They approached the inmates calmly and politely, in deliberate contrast to the Camp SS. One T-4 official even made a show of chastising a young Dachau block leader for his brutality, to the amazement of onlooking prisoners. The doctors behaved in "a very odd and completely unprecedented" manner, Karel Kašák wrote in his secret notes in September 1941—perhaps the beginning of a better life for the prisoners, he speculated.[54] Such hopes were raised further after the T-4 doctors promised the selected prisoners that they would be taken to a camp with light work and better conditions.[55] This chimed with claims by Camp SS men, who also painted a rosy picture of transfers to sanatoria, hospitals, and recuperation camps.[56] All these lies were designed to make the doomed prisoners compliant. Just as during the general "euthanasia" action, the plan was to leave the victims in the dark until the moment they were killed; even the gas chambers were disguised as washrooms, complete with tiles, benches, and showerheads.[57]

It was not just the prisoners who were deceived. The whole operation was shrouded in secrecy to prevent the spread of public rumors of the kind that had disrupted the general "euthanasia" program.[58] In line with this covert nature, T-4 doctors like Mennecke received most of their instructions during face-to-face meetings and telephone calls.[59] Meanwhile, SS officials inside the camps had to sign a written pledge to keep silent about the operation.[60] There was no more open talk of murder in the internal correspondence either, as there had been during the first KL executions in September 1939. When it came to the mass murder of invalid prisoners, the officials used a code name, Action 14f13 (insiders immediately recognized its significance: on Camp SS paperwork, the prefix "14f" always referred to the death of prisoners).[61] Naturally, the rule of secrecy applied to the victims' relatives, too. Camp SS doctors sometimes wrote letters with fake medical details, adding condolences about the sudden deaths and assurances that everything had been done to save the deceased (there was no such subterfuge in the case of Jewish prisoners; here, a curt notification of death was considered enough).[62]

Despite these provisions, Action 14f13 did not proceed as smoothly as the perpetrators planned. There was plenty of improvisation and confusion, as the following example of selections in Ravensbrück shows. On the afternoon of November 19, 1941, Dr. Friedrich Mennecke—seen by his T-4 superiors as the concentration camp specialist—arrived in the town of Fürstenberg near the camp. He came straight from Berlin, where he had met with Professors Heyde and Nitsche to confirm his itinerary for the coming weeks. After dropping off his suitcase in a local hotel, Mennecke walked to the camp and briefly talked with the adjutant, who told him that the SS had identified a total of 259 prisoners for the examination. Afterward, Mennecke discussed the next steps with Commandant Max Koegel over coffee and beer in the SS mess hall, and then strolled back into town.

Early the next day, Mennecke called Heyde in Berlin to tell him that he would carry out his assignment without the help of other T-4 doctors. He then returned to Ravensbrück and examined the first ninety-five women, who had to appear naked before him. He also held another meeting with Koegel and the camp doctor, convincing them that a further sixty to seventy prisoners should be included. All seemed to be going according to plan, and Mennecke was even more pleased with himself than usual as he returned to his hotel. But later in the evening, he was surprised by the arrival of two colleagues who brought news from Berlin: T-4 leader Viktor Brack had given instructions for a vast two thousand prisoners to be examined in Ravensbrück—around one in every four inmates. Mennecke immediately dispatched a letter to his wife to complain about the administrative chaos. "Nobody cares if that many [prisoners] actually fall under the general guidelines!" he grumbled.

Next morning, the three physicians went to Ravensbrück for a meeting with the commandant about the new directives. Before the expanded selections really got started, however, Heyde called and ordered the two doctors, who had only just arrived, back to T-4 headquarters. The two men were furious and Mennecke, who worked alone again, also fumed about the "height of Berlin *in*competence." One day later, on November 22, 1941, Mennecke received yet another call from the headquarters, informing him that Heyde now expected the Ravensbrück Camp SS to prepare the paperwork on some 1,200 to 1,500 prisoners by mid-December—the fourth target figure in three days. He dutifully passed the message to Commandant Koegel during a final meeting on Monday, November 24, 1941, before leaving for Buchenwald. By then, Mennecke had examined almost three hundred women. Once the Ravensbrück SS had picked out the additional prisoners (including men from the local subcamp), Mennecke returned on January 5, 1942, to finish the job. He selected hundreds more to die, completing 850 forms in little more than a week. The first transport left the camp in the following month, probably for the killing center in Bernburg.[63]

Dr. Mennecke's murderous mission to Ravensbrück highlights the ad hoc aspects of Action 14f13. At the same time, it marked a significant moment in the treatment of female prisoners. Previously, the women in Ravensbrück had been spared some of the most deadly SS excesses. Now they were included in the KL extermination policy, although some differences between the sexes remained. Proportionally, the Ravensbrück SS presented far more male prisoners to Mennecke than female ones, probably a reflection of the devastating conditions inside the small compound for men. This highlights another important element of the murderous program: its divergent impact on different prisoner groups. Once again, suffering in the KL was not equal.[64]

Extending Action 14f13

Did Ferdinand (Faybusch) Itzkewitsch have any idea—as he boarded a truck with ninety-two other Buchenwald prisoners in mid-July 1941—that he only had a few hours to live? A forty-nine-year-old Russian Jew who settled as a shoemaker in Germany after the First World War, Itzkewitsch had been held in Buchenwald since 1938, following a prison sentence for "race defilement" (he was convicted for his long-term relationship with his German partner). He had hoped in vain to be released and to emigrate, suffering untold horrors in the camp. But in a letter of June 29, 1941, he still tried to sound upbeat, telling his teenage son that "I am doing well, health-wise" and asking for a quick reply. He probably expected that he would soon leave the camp. Two weeks earlier, he had been among around two hundred prisoners selected by T-4 doctors (Itzkewitsch was presumably picked because of a physical disability). Many Buchenwald inmates had been alarmed by these examinations, after one of the T-4 doctors, Bodo Gorgass, had deviated from the usual script. As Dr. Mennecke noted when he came to Buchenwald a few months later, his coarse colleague "is said to have behaved like a butcher, not like a doctor, damaging the reputation of our action." To calm the prisoners, Buchenwald SS men promised that there was nothing to fear, as the selected men would be taken to a recuperation camp. Not all inmates were fooled. But there were plenty who wanted to believe the lies; the weaker the prisoners were, the harder they clung to the SS fairy tales. In the end, many men who left Buchenwald in mid-July 1941, on two separate transports, must have still had some hope of being saved. But all of them, including Ferdinand Itzkewitsch, were gassed in Sonnenstein.[65]

As Action 14f13 continued, the wall of deception inside the concentration camps began to crumble. Some prisoners heard about the murders from SS men who could not bite their tongue.[66] Several Kapos, meanwhile, learned the truth after the SS brought back the victims' clothes and other possessions. Not long after the lethal transport of Ferdinand Itzkewitsch to Sonnenstein, Rudolf Gottschalk, a prisoner clerk in the Buchenwald infirmary, saw the SS return with dentures, spectacles, and crutches. Later Gottschalk was ordered to prepare death certificates for all the departed men. When he asked about their cause of death, the Camp SS doctor handed him a medical dictionary and said "just pick out what you need"; in Itzkewitsch's case, he chose "pneu-monia."[67] The news about the prisoners' true fate quickly made the rounds in Buchenwald, just as it spread through other KL after the first transports. Many inmates were shocked. The Camp SS, they felt, had crossed a threshold. Prison-ers knew their captors to be capable of heinous crimes, but few, it seems, had expected them to turn to systematic mass murder.[68] From now on, no one volunteered for transports to the so-called sanatoria, as had sometimes hap-pened in the past, and those who were selected desperately tried to get struck off the lists, though with little hope of success.[69]

Just as prisoners' awareness of Action 14f13 grew over time, so did T-4 selections. In line with Himmler's original orders, selections initially focused on sick, weak, and disabled prisoners—all those written off as unproductive. The victims' national backgrounds varied from camp to camp, depending on the local makeup of the prisoner population. In Gusen, for example, Poles and Spaniards were in the great majority when the T-4 commission arrived in summer 1941, and consequently accounted for almost all the victims.[70] Dachau, by contrast, still held a large number of German men, and they made up almost half of those selected to die by the T-4 doctors in September 1941.[71]

Although every infirm prisoner was threatened by Action 14f13, some were more likely to be killed than others. Sick and weak "asocials" and "crim-inals" were specially targeted, it seems, perhaps because the SS saw their inability to work as confirmation of their "work-shy" nature.[72] Criminality figured prominently on the official forms, and the T-4 doctors, who had al-ready considered deviance an aggravating factor during earlier "euthanasia" selections in asylums, now appeared to apply similar rules to the KL.[73] Sum-ming up his impression of the inmates he had selected in Sachsenhausen in April 1941, Dr. Mennecke informed his wife that they were all, without ex-ception, "'antisocials'—to the highest degree."[74]

The hunt for the infirm hit many prisoners at the bottom of the SS hierar-chy, since they were generally in the worst state of health. This was true for social outsiders, and it was even truer for Jewish inmates, outcasts in all the concentration camps. Since the war began, Jews had swelled the ranks of the dying, and by 1941, only a few men with the yellow star were not injured, ill, or starving. Once Himmler launched Action 14f13, the weakest Jewish pris-oners, and those with disabilities, like Ferdinand Itzkewitsch and Siegbert Fraenkel, were doomed.[75] They were conspicuous not only because of their physical condition. T-4 doctors had already become used to racial mass mur-der, overseeing the killing of all Jewish patients during the general "euthana-sia" program. When it came to the selection of invalids in the KL, a prisoner's

Jewish background must have often tipped the scale.[76] Consequently, Jews made up a disproportionately large number of victims; forty-five percent of the 187 Buchenwald prisoners gassed in Sonnenstein in mid-July 1941 were Jews like Ferdinand Itzkewitsch, even though Jews only made up seventeen percent of the camp's prisoner population.[77]

Still, during the initial T-4 selections in the concentration camps in spring and summer 1941, medical matters generally outweighed ideological ones. The fact that a prisoner wore a yellow, green, or black triangle—marking him as Jewish, criminal, or asocial—was an aggravating factor, but what counted above all else was his state of health, as we can see when looking more closely at the summer 1941 selections in Buchenwald: although Jews were far more likely to be picked out than most other prisoners, the T-4 doctors sentenced only a fraction—around six percent of all Jewish inmates, many of them elderly—to death.[78] The other Jews in Buchenwald were left untouched by the killing program, though not for very long.

Sometime in autumn 1941, the leaders of Action 14f13 stepped up the murder of Jewish prisoners: from now on, almost all Jews in the KL would be assessed by the T-4 doctors.[79] This new approach was no doubt linked to the recent escalation of general Nazi anti-Jewish policy; in summer 1941 Himmler's SS and police units had begun to murder hundreds of thousands of Jewish men, women, and children in the occupied east, and the regime was closing in on Jews elsewhere.[80] In turn, the terror against Jewish KL prisoners intensified, too. Several months before the Nazi regime embarked on the systematic extermination of European Jews, almost all Jews held inside concentration camps were regarded as candidates for the T-4 gas chambers.

The new priorities of T-4 doctors were revealed when they returned to Buchenwald for a second round of selections in November 1941.[81] During their first visit, five months earlier, the doctors had only examined a small proportion of the prisoner population. This time, Dr. Mennecke told his wife on November 26, things were different. In addition to the regular selections, the doctors would determine the fate of 1,200 Jewish men—more than eighty-five percent of all Jewish prisoners in Buchenwald.[82] To save time, the doctors abandoned the individual assessments of Jews. Mennecke explained that "none of them will be 'examined'"; he would base his judgments solely on prisoner files.[83] In the end, 384 Buchenwald prisoners were taken to the Bernburg gas chamber between March 2 and 14, 1942. Every single one of them was Jewish; in less than two weeks, more than a quarter of all Buchenwald Jews were murdered, setting the standard for future T-4 selections.[84]

How did Mennecke and other T-4 doctors choose their Jewish victims in late 1941–42? Physical condition continued to play a part: many prisoners were elderly and infirm.[85] But T-4 doctors also included a number of Jews who could still work.[86] In these cases, the physicians were guided by other criteria. As Mennecke admitted after the war, he condemned some Jewish prisoners who had still been in reasonable health; their selection had nothing to do with medical matters and everything to do with racial policy.[87]

Dr. Mennecke's thinking can be reconstructed from notes he made on the back of prisoner photographs (he was planning a publication on Nazi racial science). Recovered after the war, all the photos appear to show Jewish KL inmates, several of whom are known to have died in T-4 gas chambers.[88] None of Mennecke's comments referred to their health. Instead, he made copious notes on their anti-Nazi views, especially in the case of foreigners; "extraordinarily impertinent and spiteful comments about Germans," he remarked in one case. Mennecke was even more exercised by "asocial" behavior, particularly by what he saw as moral deviance. Most Jewish women selected by Mennecke for his photo collection were accused of sex with German men ("race defilement with German soldiers, like on a conveyor belt") and around half of them were labeled as prostitutes ("pure-bred Jewish whore with venereal disease"). He regarded these women with leering revulsion, cataloging their supposed promiscuity and degeneracy ("sexually impulsive and insatiable Jewess"). Mennecke applied his moral judgments to men, too; in Buchenwald, almost all Jewish men presumed to be homosexual were sent to the gas chambers.[89] Finally, Mennecke took note of the Camp SS verdict on the prisoner's conduct. Eduard Radinger, for example, a thirty-four-year-old tailor's assistant from Vienna, was accused of "gambling, laziness, impertinence." This may well have helped to condemn him to death, as Mennecke apparently placed a "+" next to his name. On March 12, 1942, after having spent almost three years in the KL, first as a "work-shy Jew" and later as a Jewish "protective custody" prisoner, Radinger was deported from Buchenwald to Bernburg, together with 104 other Jewish men, and gassed.[90]

The Camp SS Takes Charge

Not long after the extension of Action 14f13 in late 1941, the Nazi authorities cut it back. Dr. Mennecke, accompanied by other T-4 doctors, made his final trip to the KL in spring 1942, calling at Flossenbürg and Neuengamme; the last transport of victims left Neuengamme for the Bernburg killing center in June 1942. This marked the end of the operation in its original setup, twelve months after the first prisoners—Siegbert Fraenkel and the other men from Sachsenhausen—had been murdered.[91] Inside a year, some 6,500 or more concentration camp prisoners had died in the T-4 gas chambers.[92]

The commandants were informed about the curtailment of Action 14f13 on March 26, 1942, in a secret communication. Arthur Liebehenschel from the IKL announced that the slaughter, which he referred to as "special treatment," had to be scaled down. The general rules of the program had been disregarded, he claimed, with the SS presenting too many prisoners to the T-4 commissions. From now on, Liebehenschel stressed, only prisoners who were permanently unable to work should be sent to their deaths. All others—including the sick who could regain some strength—would be held back to "carry out the labor tasks given to the concentration camps."[93] At first glance, this apparent reversal of policy was caused by a recent shift in SS priorities; in spring 1942, Heinrich Himmler demanded that the KL make a greater economic contribution to the German war effort (chapter 8), prompting Camp SS managers like Liebehenschel to scramble to stay on message.

In reality, however, the demise of Action 14f13 was not about economics at all.[94] Rather, the marriage of convenience between Camp SS and T-4 had come to an end. The focus of the T-4 organization had shifted to a far bigger program of mass extermination—the Holocaust. By spring 1942, many officials had already relocated to occupied eastern Europe, where they were in great demand for the new death camps at Belzec, Sobibor, and Treblinka; in comparison, the murder of KL prisoners in the "euthanasia" killing centers inside Germany lost its significance.

The Camp SS, meanwhile, did not need the T-4 killers anymore. In recent months, SS men had proven themselves as professional mass murderers in their own right, with *Muselmänner* among their prime targets. While thousands of weak and sick prisoners were being selected for the T-4 gas chambers, local Camp SS men had started to murder many more on the spot during the second half of 1941.[95] Previously, such SS murders of invalid inmates inside the KL had been sporadic. Now they became systematic and soon superseded Action 14f13. Although some more prisoner transports still went to the external T-4 gas chambers later in 1942, before they closed down, most murders now took place inside the concentration camps.[96]

Why did local Camp SS men embark on mass executions of infirm prisoners, in parallel to the coordinated T-4 program? Partly because they could. Their initial experiences during Action 14f13 had taught them that it would be safe to move to executions inside the KL. Fears about prisoner unrest had proved unfounded; the T-4 selections continued without a hitch, despite the growing prisoner awareness of the murders. Also, the local Camp SS must have seen practical benefits; murdering *Muselmänner* inside the KL meant no more doctors' commissions, deportations, and delays. Furthermore, SS men believed that they had the right to kill. Once Himmler had sanctioned the mass murder of the infirm by launching Action 14f13, the local Camp SS saw little reason to hold back. The dynamic had been the same in autumn 1939, when Himmler's central execution policy set off a spate of local killings. Once again, radical actions taken at the top of the SS state triggered a radical response from below, ratcheting up terror inside the camps.

The scene of the first Camp SS massacre of *Muselmänner* was Buchenwald. Following the arrival of two prisoner transports from Dachau in July 1941, Buchenwald SS men felt overwhelmed by infirm inmates and feared that some of the newcomers carried infections. The local SS decided to kill the invalids, and rather than wait for the return of the T-4 commission, went ahead on its own. Several hundred exhausted prisoners were isolated in the infirmary, as suspected carriers of TB, and murdered by an SS doctor with lethal injections.[97]

Other concentration camps followed suit during the second half of 1941. SS men in different camps explored different killing methods, as the spirit of lethal experimentation became all-pervasive. In Gusen, for example, hundreds of weak and emaciated prisoners were killed during so-called bathing actions. Directed by the terrifying camp leader Karl Chmielewski, the Gusen SS forced the prisoners under freezing showers for thirty minutes or more; some drowned in the standing water, others succumbed to hypothermia, with the screams of the dying men echoing across the compound.[98] Camp SS men elsewhere used other ways to murder the infirm, with lethal injections—either intravenously or straight into the heart—emerging as the SS favorite. The main drug of choice was phenol; when it was unavailable, SS doctors often injected air instead. The Ravensbrück camp doctor Rolf Rosenthal recalled that, when he witnessed the lethal injection of a female prisoner after his arrival in January 1942, he was told that "this was always administered when people were very ill and incurable."[99]

By 1942, the systematic murder of exhausted, weak, and ill prisoners had become a permanent feature of the KL. Sometimes local Camp SS officials would pick their victims within days of arrival.[100] More commonly, the prisoners were pulled out during regular selections in infirmaries. Doctors played a major role here, just as they had done during Action 14f13; but this time it was Camp SS physicians who sent the prisoners to their deaths, not outsiders like Dr. Mennecke.[101]

Although the mass murder of *Muselmänner* was decentralized, it was sanctioned and probably encouraged by senior IKL managers. Previously, the Oranienburg officials had insisted on steering such killings—as during Action 14f13. But in view of the growing number of sick prisoners, they must have concluded that managing all murders was impossible and relaxed the rules. According to an internal SS document, camp doctors were now authorized to kill "on their own initiative" those prisoners who were "incurably ill," "ridden with epidemics," or "suspected of suffering from an epidemic disease."[102]

To retain some central control, Camp SS managers in October 1942 revived the plan of turning Dachau into a collection camp for "physically weak prisoners who are not fit for use"; this time, all these prisoners were slated for extermination.[103] Over the coming weeks and months, many *Muselmänner* from other KL arrived in Dachau to die.[104] Some perished in transit.[105] The most appalling transport arrived on November 19, 1942, with several hundred men on board. It had set off days earlier from Stutthof and the prisoners, crammed into cattle cars, had received almost no food since. When the doors opened at the Dachau SS compound, dozens of corpses lay inside. The dead were dumped inside the camp, together with the soiled survivors, some so starved that their shoulder blades protruded like wings. Even the cruelest SS block leaders "turned away in disgust," Karel Kašák wrote in his notes. Dozens of the new arrivals are said to have died within hours; at least one of them was killed by an SS guard, who stepped on his throat until he suffocated.[106]

Few prisoners who arrived in Dachau on so-called invalid transports in 1942 lived for very long. Those who defied illness, hunger, and neglect were killed after SS selections, apparently by lethal injection.[107] Another method of mass murder considered by the Dachau SS was poison gas. The construction of a gas chamber was under way since spring 1942, and its primary purpose, it seems, was the extermination of weak and sick prisoners, though it remains unclear whether this facility was ever put to use.[108] Dachau would not have been the first KL to kill invalid inmates with gas; by autumn 1942, SS men in several other camps had already done so.[109] The main target of these experiments with poison gas had not been *Muselmänner*, however, but Soviet prisoners of war, who began to arrive in the thousands from late summer 1941 onward.

EXECUTING SOVIET POWS

Early on June 22, 1941, German troops invaded the Soviet Union—Operation Barbarossa, the biggest and most devastating military campaign ever, had begun. German forces, more than three million men strong, initially advanced rapidly and left death and destruction in their wake.[110] Hitler had long dreamed about this moment, picturing a decisive showdown with "Jewish Bolsheviks" that would determine Germany's destiny. More than two months before the invasion, he told his generals to prepare for an all-out war of extermination.[111] From June 1941, the German army realized Hitler's order, flanked by specially trained SS and police killing units, such as the task forces. At the same time, the German authorities were drawing up plans for the long-term occupation of the Soviet Union, which were gigantic in scale and genocidal in intent, condemning many millions of civilians to death by starvation.[112]

There was no mercy for captured Soviet soldiers either. Hitler regarded them as no better than animals—dumb, dangerous, and depraved—and the German Army High Command decided even before the invasion that the conventional rules of warfare would not apply to them (in contrast to POWs on the Western Front).[113] Entire armies of Soviet prisoners perished in German hands. "The more of these prisoners die, the better for us," crowed some senior Nazi officials. In all, an estimated three to five hundred thousand Soviet POWs died each month between October and December 1941. Most of them wasted away in POW camps, starving and freezing to death in makeshift tents and muddy holes. Other Soviet soldiers were murdered elsewhere, including concentration camps, after the Nazi war of extermination entered the KL.[114]

Searching for Commissars

Hitler and his generals were obsessed with Soviet commissars; among all the enemies they saw lurking in the east, the commissar was one of the fiercest, an almost mythical figure. Nazi leaders were convinced that savage and fanatical commissars, as the personification of "Jewish Bolshevism," would force their troops to fight to the end and commit untold acts of cruelty against German soldiers. To preempt such atrocities and to break the Soviet resistance, the German Army High Command on June 6, 1941, ordered the execution of all "political commissars" who acted against German troops. This order, which found widespread support among the fiercely anti-Bolshevik German officer corps, was applied very widely—on the battlefields and in the rear, against combatants and captives—and thereby contributed to the erosion of the boundaries between front line and occupied territory.[115]

Himmler's police and SS apparatus was closely involved in the executions. To make sure that no commissars slipped through the net, the RSHA dispatched special police units to search for "unacceptable" Soviet prisoners in

POW and labor camps. The list of suspects was as long as it was vague, including not just alleged commissars and party officials, but also "fanatical Communists," "the Soviet-Russian intelligentsia," and "all Jews." After these enemies had been identified among the mass of POWs, Reinhard Heydrich ordered in mid-July 1941, they would be exterminated.[116]

Armed with Heydrich's order, police commandos swarmed all over POW camps. The policemen briefly interrogated suspects about their identity and activities; if they did not get the right answers, the officials would turn to violence and torture. In addition, they used intelligence provided by prisoner informers who hoped to save their own lives. Grigorij Efimovitsch Ladik, for example, was betrayed by one of his comrades. Interrogated by his captors in a POW camp, Ladik admitted that he had previously lied about his background: "I gave a wrong account of my personal details because I was frightened that I would be recognized as a political leader and shot" (he was executed soon after). Such confessions were rare, however. Far more often, Heydrich's policemen relied on guesswork and prejudice. Most of them did not even understand the term "intelligentsia." But they did know how to abuse and humiliate their victims. Soldiers suspected of being Jewish, for instance, were forced to strip to determine if they were circumcised, sealing the fate of many Jews, as well as Muslims.[117] After the policemen completed their selections inside a POW camp, they reported all suspects—sometimes more than twenty percent of all examined prisoners—for execution, with Jewish POWs, widely suspected of being synonymous with commissars, more likely to be murdered than non-Jews.[118]

The doomed men were isolated while the perpetrators awaited further instructions.[119] Most of the victims were young, largely in their twenties, and came from a wide range of backgrounds. The vast majority were regular soldiers, including many peasants and industrial workers—a far cry from the satanic commissar of the Nazi imagination.[120] To pick just one example: among a group of 410 Soviet POWs selected for execution, the Gestapo described only three as "functionaries and officers." The rest were rank-and-file men; 25 were classed as "Jews," 69 as members of the "intelligentsia," 146 as "fanatical communists," 85 as "agitators, troublemakers, thieves," 35 as "escapees," and 47 as "incurably ill."[121]

When it came to the execution of "commissars" (as I will call all those deemed "unacceptable") in the occupied east, the RSHA was rather relaxed; a few more massacres hardly mattered. The only rule was that killings were carried out in some seclusion, away from the POW camps themselves.[122] The situation was rather different inside the Third Reich, where the authorities had established additional POW and labor camps. So as not to alarm the German public, Gestapo chief Heinrich Müller ordered on July 21, 1941, that selected prisoners should be killed "inconspicuously in the nearest concentration camp."[123] Continuing the SS practice of camouflaging programs of mass murder, the new program was code-named Action 14f14.

The first Soviet POWs arrived in concentration camps in early autumn 1941. Most transports were rather small, consisting of around twenty prisoners or so; others were much larger, however, taking hundreds to their deaths. Many victims never even reached the KL. After weeks or months in German army camps, they did not survive the long hours shackled together inside freight trains; others collapsed during the march from railway stations to the camps.[124] In Sachsenhausen, the deadliest such train arrived on October 11, 1941, from a POW camp in Pomerania, nearly two hundred miles away; out of some six hundred prisoners on board, sixty-three had perished.[125]

The deaths during transports caused concern among the Camp SS, and in autumn 1941 a complaint by commandants that between five and ten percent of Soviet POWs were dead or dying on arrival reached Gestapo boss Müller. The commandants feared that the semipublic deaths of POWs would sully the SS reputation among the local population.[126] These concerns were not entirely unfounded, for popular reactions were quite different from the whipped-up frenzy during the arrival of Polish "snipers" back in autumn 1939. Some ordinary Germans were shocked by the lethal treatment of Soviet prisoners. In November 1941, a German teacher wrote in his diary what he had heard about the arrival of Russians in Neuengamme: "They were completely starved, so much so that some fell off the truck and staggered limply toward the barracks."[127] Heinrich Müller was worried enough about public opinion to order an end to the transports of Soviet POWs who were, as he put it, "about to die anyway."[128] This did not save the "commissars," of course. They had already been condemned. The only question was where they would die—in a POW camp, in transit, or in a KL.

Most Soviet "commissars" who made it to the concentration camps were executed within days. Unlike other new prisoners, they were not even properly registered. In the eyes of the Camp SS, there was no need; they were already dead. Most KL turned to mass killing in autumn 1941 and continued until the following spring or summer, when the German authorities officially rescinded the commissar order, for tactical reasons, and scaled down selections in POW camps; by then, forty thousand or more Soviet soldiers had been dispatched to the concentration camps for execution.[129] Almost all of them were men, with the women's camp in Ravensbrück among the few untouched KL.[130] The systematic mass extermination of Soviet "commissars" was a cataclysmic moment in the camps' history, dwarfing all previous killing campaigns. For the first time, the Camp SS carried out executions on a vast scale. Sachsenhausen stood at the center of the slaughter: during a frenzied two-month period in September and October 1941, SS men executed around nine thousand Soviet POWs, far more than in any other KL.[131]

Death in Sachsenhausen

Sometime in August 1941, a group of leading Camp SS men came together for a secret meeting in the Sachsenhausen office of Hans Loritz, the longest-serving SS commandant. Loritz and some of his men were joined by Inspector Richard Glücks from the nearby IKL and his chief of staff Arthur Liebehenschel, who took the minutes. But all eyes were on the special guest of honor— Theodor Eicke.[132] As commander of the SS Death's Head division, Eicke had been involved in heavy fighting during the German attack on the Soviet Union and was wounded in Latvia on the night of July 6–7, 1941, when his car hit a mine.[133] Recovering at his villa on the edge of the SS grounds in Oranienburg, Eicke had made the short trip to Sachsenhausen, where his former subordinates—who idolized him even more now that he was a decorated military commander—welcomed him with open arms. They also knew that he still had a direct line to Himmler. The Reichsführer SS regarded Eicke as one of his "most faithful friends" and met him twice in late summer 1941, just as the killing of Soviet commissars in the KL was getting under way. In fact, it was probably Himmler who had authorized Eicke to initiate the Sachsenhausen SS.[134]

At the meeting in Sachsenhausen in August 1941, Eicke took the floor to announce the program to murder Soviet POWs. Typically, Eicke presented the Third Reich as the victim of a subhuman enemy who had left it no choice but to strike back. Gustav Sorge, the leader of the Sachsenhausen death squad, later summarized Eicke's speech: "In retaliation for the shooting of German soldiers in Soviet captivity, the Führer had approved a request by the Wehrmacht High Command and agreed to a retaliation action . . . by shooting prisoners, namely commissars and supporters of the Soviet Communist Party." The words were given added weight by the reference to Hitler and by the wounds Eicke had sustained on the Eastern Front, still visible to all.[135]

After Eicke's general introduction, the talk turned to practical matters. The Camp SS leaders apparently discussed various ways of mass killing, trying to surpass one another with ever more ingenious proposals.[136] In the end, they chose a new method, which required the construction of a special execution chamber, and designated Sachsenhausen block leaders to carry out the killings; it seems that the men were inducted into their tasks that day, followed by a round of drinks to mark the occasion.[137] The preparation for mass murder in Sachsenhausen quickly began. Supervised by SS men, prisoners from the joinery workshop turned a barn on the so-called industry yard into an execution barrack, using plans supplied by Commandant Loritz.[138] Once it was completed, the SS made two trial runs, murdering a small number of Soviet prisoners.[139] Then the apparatus went into full operation.

The first mass transport of Soviet "commissars" arrived in Sachsenhausen on August 31, 1941, from the Hammerstein POW camp (Eicke met up with Himmler on the same day). The transport was made up of well over four hundred soldiers, mostly from around Minsk, and included a large number of Jews. Thousands more men followed over the coming weeks.[140] The new prisoners were confused and scared; far from home on enemy soil, they did not know where they were and what would happen to them. Despite their youth—some soldiers were no more than fifteen years old—many looked utterly worn out. They were clad in dirty and torn clothes, with trousers held up by string, and soiled bandages covering their wounds. Instead of shoes, many had rags on their feet or went barefoot.[141]

Some Sachsenhausen guards saw the endless procession of misery as proof of the prisoners' savage nature. SS officials even took pictures for propaganda purposes (a practice established in the prewar camps); a few of the images were later reprinted in the SS publication *The Subhuman*, which pointed its readers to the "caricatures of human faces, nightmares that have become reality."[142] In reality, the SS men were the savages. Block leaders dished out brutal beatings and locked the prisoners into bare barracks cut off from the rest of the camp by barbed wire. To increase the isolation, the windows were painted over.[143]

After the recent arrivals spent a grim spell in these isolation barracks, lasting no more than a few days, SS block leaders collected them, usually in small groups of a few dozen men, and drove them on canvas-covered trucks to the execution barrack, which was shut off from the rest of the camp by a wooden fence. Taking their cue from Action 14f13, the Camp SS left its victims in the dark until the end. Following a medical exam, the SS told the prisoners, they would be taken to a better place. But the victims went straight to their deaths. Inside the barrack was a large room, where the SS ordered all prisoners to undress, before leading the first man to an adjacent, smaller room, furnished like a doctor's office; it looked like a small stage set, complete with medical instruments and anatomical charts. Here an SS man dressed in a white coat was waiting, posing as a physician. While he pretended to carry out a brief physical examination, he checked whether the prisoner had any gold fillings; those who did were marked with a cross (another practice borrowed from the "euthanasia" killings). Then the prisoner was led next door to an even smaller room, which resembled a bathroom with shower heads on the ceiling. An SS man ordered the prisoner to stand with his back against a measuring pole fixed to the wall. A small gap in the pole allowed another SS man—hidden in an adjoining booth—to aim his gun at the prisoner's neck. Once the prisoner was in place, the killer received a signal and pulled the trigger. Judging by the gaping holes in the victims' skulls, the SS used special dumdum bullets.

After the body slumped to the floor, another door opened. Kapos from the crematorium commando appeared and dragged the corpse to the make-shift morgue in the barrack's last room. Wearing rubber gloves, they ripped out gold teeth; any prisoner who still showed signs of life was finished off by an SS block leader. Later the Kapos threw the corpses into the oven of mobile crematoria, stationed just outside the barrack. Back inside the execution chamber, the perpetrators sprayed the floors and walls with a hose to wash away all the blood, tissue, and bone splinters. Then the next prisoner was led in. Some of them sensed that they would die. Many others were oblivious to their fate. Illness and exhaustion clouded their minds, and they were fooled by the SS theater. The SS also muffled the gunshot sounds. Not only was the killers' booth soundproof, a gramophone played in the room where the other naked men were waiting. Cheerful tunes flowed through the barrack, the last sound a Soviet soldier would hear before he was shot from behind.[144]

The Sachsenhausen SS quickly became used to these assembly-line murders. Until mid-November 1941, when the operation was suspended because of a typhus epidemic, mass shootings took place several times a week. According to a former SS block leader, such actions lasted from early morning until late at night, with a prisoner being shot every two or three minutes, claiming around 300 to 350 lives a day.[145] The Kapos worked nonstop, too, burning more than twenty-five bodies per hour at the crematoria.[146] The smoke and stench soon spread outside the camp, alerting the local Oranienburg popula-tion. There was much talk behind closed doors about the murders and some bold children even approached passing SS men to ask when the next Russians would be burned.[147]

One evening in mid-September 1941, after the neck-shooting apparatus had operated for around two weeks, the Sachsenhausen SS proudly demon-strated it to two dozen SS grandees.[148] The visitors were led through the execu-tion barrack and watched as several Soviet POWs were shot and then "thrown with great brutality onto heaps," as one of the SS officers later testified. Among the visitors were Inspector Glücks and his staff, who toasted their murderous invention with alcohol. Also present was Ernst Grawitz, the SS Reich physician, who had long been involved in Nazi mass murder. Most important, Theodor Eicke once more graced the Camp SS with his presence, just before he went back to the Eastern Front. Eicke addressed the Sachsenhausen SS men, encouraging them to keep up their grisly work. The grateful men sent off their hero with cheers and presents, including three cakes and a card addressed to "Papa Eicke."[149]

Before Eicke returned to the front, he also took leave from Heinrich Himmler, meeting him on the evening of September 15, 1941, just a few hours after Reich physician Grawitz had seen Himmler. There can be little doubt that the Reichsführer SS was updated that day about the Sachsenhausen murders.[150] After all, SS leaders knew that Himmler was actively looking for new methods of mass extermination. The daily massacres in the occupied Soviet Union, where Jews were lined up and shot into mass graves, had revealed that not all Nazi killers could stomach the pools of blood, the piercing screams of the wounded, and the cries of those next in line.[151] This had prompted Himmler to look for more humane ways of mass murder—more humane for the killers, that is. Grawitz or Eicke, or both, must have reported back to Himmler about the new Sachsenhausen method, which promised some "advantages" over conventional mass shootings. After all, the killers did not have to look at their victims when they pulled the trigger, and most victims went to their deaths unaware, without protest or panic.

Experiments in Mass Murder

One of the SS officers invited to watch the demonstration of the Sachsenhausen neck-shooting mechanism in mid-September 1941 was the Mauthausen commandant Franz Ziereis. The IKL had invited him, together with other commandants, to learn "how to liquidate the Politruks and Russian Commissars," he later testified. Ziereis was duly impressed. Upon his return to Mauthausen, he oversaw the construction of a similar apparatus in his own camp, ready for the first execution of Soviet officers on October 21, 1941.[152] He was not the only commandant inspired by his Sachsenhausen colleagues. In Buchenwald, Karl Otto Koch also set up an execution chamber that closely resembled the Sachsenhausen prototype.[153] Others went in a different direction, however. Inspector Glücks still valued local initiative and allowed his commandants to choose their own methods. As a result the KL turned into testing sites for mass execution in autumn and winter 1941.

In Dachau, the murder of Soviet "commissars" started in early September 1941, just like in Sachsenhausen. But instead of elaborate new techniques, the

Dachau SS used the very method that Nazi killers elsewhere sought to abandon—open mass shootings. At first, the Dachau SS killed outside the bunker, as it had done on previous occasions, but as the number of victims increased, it moved the executions to its shooting range in Hebertshausen, about a mile and a half away. Here, Camp SS men forced the Soviet soldiers to strip naked and line up. Everything happened at great speed. A commando of SS men pounced on those in the first row, with five SS men grabbing one prisoner each, dragged them around a corner, and shackled them to posts. Then an SS squad opened fire, often shooting wildly at the helpless victims. The remaining POWs knew exactly what awaited them; they heard the salvos and saw the growing mountain of corpses. Some of the doomed men were paralyzed, some cried, some struggled, some screamed, some held up crosses, some pleaded for their lives. But the shootings only stopped when every prisoner had been executed. Afterwards, the killers would clean the mud and blood from their uniforms, using fresh towels and hot water brought over from the camp.[154]

Twenty-eight-year-old Ignat Prochorowitsch Babitsch was one of around 4,400 Soviet POWs murdered in Dachau between September 1941 and June 1942. A married man from a small village in northern Ukraine, Lieutenant Babitsch had served in an infantry division when he was captured in July 1941 near Berdychiv. He initially stayed in the occupied east, in Stalag 325 in Zamosc, before being moved to the Hammelburg camp in Germany. The army mug shot taken on arrival in mid-March 1942 shows a man with delicate features, a shaven head, and a quizzical expression. Just two weeks later a Gestapo commission selected him for extermination, presumably because Babitsch, a teacher, was regarded as a member of the intelligentsia. The RSHA approved his execution on April 10, 1942. A few days after that he was deported to Dachau and executed on the shooting range.[155]

The corpses of Soviet POWs murdered in Hebertshausen, like Ignat Babitsch, were brought to the Dachau camp crematorium. When one of the Kapos there asked SS camp compound leader Egon Zill where to store the ashes, he was told to just dump "the dirt of these Bolshevik swine."[156] It is not clear why Dachau Camp SS leaders continued with these massacres, when they could have employed the more clinical method practiced in Sachsenhausen and Buchenwald. Perhaps they felt too proud to follow the lead of another camp—Dachau, after all, had been the first model KL. Or maybe they wanted to show that they were tough enough to kill without deception, in a gruesome display of what passed for manliness within the Camp SS.

The Dachau SS was not alone in favoring mass shootings. In Flossenbürg, the SS also mowed down Soviet "commissars" on its shooting range from early

September 1941. These executions were hastily abandoned a few months later, however, apparently after blood and body parts had been swept by a nearby river into Flossenbürg village, leading to complaints from locals. In Gross-Rosen, too, rumors among the local population put an end to mass shootings of Soviet POWs, which had initially been carried out near the crematorium; the Camp SS had forced other prisoners to sing at the top of their voices, but this had not masked the sounds of the shootings.[157]

In both Flossenbürg and Gross-Rosen, the Camp SS replaced mass shootings with lethal injections. SS men subjected Soviet "commissars" to fake medical exams, measuring and weighing them, and then gave the deadly injection; the murderers tried various poisonous substances, including prussic acid, carbolic acid, and petrol.[158] This method of killing proved more effective, though it was hardly new; as we have seen, the Camp SS had already begun to use deadly injections during its earlier murders of *Muselmänner*. As a result, the wider significance of the killings in Flossenbürg and Gross-Rosen was limited. The same cannot be said for the executions of Soviet POWs in another KL, farther to the east. Here, the experiments in autumn 1941 produced devastating results that would affect the very nature of Nazi mass extermination. The site of these trials was Auschwitz.

Inventing the Auschwitz Gas Chamber

One day in early September 1941—probably on September 5—a train from the Neuhammer POW camp in Lower Silesia arrived at Auschwitz. Hundreds of prisoners spilled out of the railcars. All of them were Soviet POWs identified by the police as "unacceptable."[159] By the time they marched through the Auschwitz compound, it was dark. The silence was punctured by barking guard dogs and the screams of the prisoners, beaten and whipped by cursing SS men. The noise stirred some inmates who had been asleep inside their barracks. Breaking strict SS instructions, they peered through the windows and saw the columns of POWs, illuminated by searchlights, disappear into block 11. Of all the places in Auschwitz, this was the most feared: it was the bunker, the SS center for torture and murder. Prisoners called it the "death block," and Camp SS men associated it with death, too, which is why they had turned it into a makeshift gas chamber for Soviet POWs.[160] The Auschwitz SS was about to carry out the first mass gassing inside a concentration camp.[161]

Inspired by the earlier murder of prisoners in the T-4 gas chambers (during Action 14f13), Auschwitz SS officials had decided to experiment with poison gas as well.[162] They chose prussic acid—more commonly known by its trade name, Zyklon B—which had been used in the KL for some time to fumigate vermin-infested buildings and clothes. SS orderlies were trained in handling this delousing agent and knew how dangerous it was. It was also easier to deploy than the carbon monoxide used in T-4 killing centers, as there was no need to install pipes or gas cylinders—the murderers just had to drop Zyklon B pellets into a sealed chamber.[163] A first lethal test had taken place around late August 1941, when the Auschwitz SS executed a small group of Soviet prisoners. The action was supervised by camp compound leader Karl Fritzsch, a Camp SS veteran who later bragged to colleagues that he was the inventor of the Auschwitz gas chambers.[164] Commandant Rudolf Höss quickly agreed to a larger trial. In preparation, the SS cleared the bunker; doors were sealed and the cellar windows filled with cement.

It was into this cellar—a series of small cells and corridors—that the Auschwitz SS led the Soviet "commissars" that fateful night in early September 1941. As they were forced down the stairs, the POWs saw some 250 other prisoners sprawled across the floor, invalids from the infirmary who had been selected to die with them. Once the last Soviet prisoner had been crammed into the cellar, the SS threw Zyklon B crystals inside and locked the doors. On contact with the warm air and the captives' bodies, highly toxic prussic acid was released and desperate screaming started, carrying all the way to the adjacent barracks. The gas quickly destroyed the victims' mucous membranes and entered their bloodstream, asphyxiating them from within. Some dying men stuffed bits of clothing in their mouths to block the gas. But none survived.[165]

Commandant Rudolf Höss, who had watched outside with other SS men, took off his gas mask and congratulated himself; hundreds of prisoners had been killed without an SS man firing a single shot.[166] Still, the practical-minded Höss saw room for improvements. For a start, block 11 was too far away from the Auschwitz crematorium: the corpses had to be dragged through the whole camp for disposal. Moreover, there was no built-in ventilation in block 11. The building had to be aired for a long time before the SS could force other inmates inside to recover the bodies. By then, the corpses—swollen, entangled, and stiff—had started to decay and proved hard to dislodge. One witness, the Polish prisoner Adam Zacharski, saw everything: "The scene was truly eerie, because one could see that these people had scratched and bitten each other in a fit of madness before they died, many had torn uniforms . . . Although I had already got used to some macabre scenes in the camp, I became sick when I saw these murdered people and I had to vomit violently."[167]

To make mass murder more efficient, the Auschwitz SS soon relocated gassings to the morgue of the crematorium. It lay outside the camp compound, which meant that there would be fewer unwelcome witnesses among the regular prisoners. The morgue could hold hundreds of victims and already had an effective ventilation mechanism, making its conversion into a gas chamber easy; the doors were insulated and holes were hammered into the ceiling, so that Zyklon B could be dropped in from the flat roof above. Afterward, the corpses would be burned in the adjacent crematorium ovens. The Auschwitz SS had stumbled across the prototype of the death factory.[168]

Its first lethal test came in mid-September 1941, when the SS gassed some nine hundred Soviet POWs in the Auschwitz crematorium.[169] As the prisoners arrived, SS men told them to undress and then forced them into the morgue, supposedly for delousing. SS men now slammed the doors shut and threw in the gas pellets. Commandant Rudolf Höss watched once more: "After the insertion, some screamed 'gas,' followed by mighty howling and pushing toward the two doors. But they withstood the pressure." It took several days, he added, to burn all the bodies.[170]

Höss was convinced that the Auschwitz SS had made an important discovery. True, his men continued to use other methods to kill.[171] But when it came to large-scale murder, Höss much preferred gassing over shooting, because it was less stressful for the SS. "Now I was relieved indeed," he noted later, "that all of us would be spared these bloodbaths." Höss also claimed that gassings were kinder on the victims, blanking out the terrible death struggle of all those crammed into the gas chamber.[172]

After the Auschwitz SS pioneered the use of poison gas in concentration camps, other KL followed, just as they had imitated the Sachsenhausen neck-shooting apparatus. Camp SS officers, already familiar with the principle of gassings (from the T-4 centers), were keen to test the latest innovations in mass murder. Once again, Franz Ziereis in Mauthausen was especially eager. From late autumn 1941, he oversaw the construction of a gas chamber, converting a cellar near the crematorium. The first large-scale gassing here took place in May 1942, killing 231 Soviet POWs with Zyklon B.[173] Meanwhile, the Mauthausen Camp SS doctor requested a mobile gas van, developed by the Criminal Technical Institute (KTI) of the Reich Criminal Police Office. The local SS used such a van, probably from spring 1942, to murder hundreds of Mauthausen prisoners, among them sick inmates and Soviet POWs.[174]

Mobile gas vans had originally been developed during the Nazi search for more effective ways of murdering Jews in the Soviet Union. Before the vans were deployed in the occupied east, however, the KTI had tested them inside Germany in autumn 1941. The location of these lethal tests was Sachsenhausen, and the victims were Soviet POWs, who were gassed instead of being shot. Camp SS men would force the naked prisoners into the van, customized to pump carbon monoxide from the engine into the hold. Then the van drove off. When it came to a stop outside the Sachsenhausen crematorium, all prisoners inside were dead, their bodies turned pink by the fumes.[175] These experiments must have piqued the interest of the Sachsenhausen SS officers, though it was not until later, probably summer 1943, that they constructed their own stationary gas chamber; the first victims were once again Soviet POWs.[176] Several other concentration camps added gas chambers in 1942–43, too, following in the footsteps of Auschwitz. The Neuengamme SS, for example, murdered some 450 Soviet POWs in autumn 1942 by dropping Zyklon B pellets into its converted bunker.[177]

Although many concentration camps used poison gas, it never became the main weapon of choice of the Camp SS: it was just one among many in its deadly arsenal. The main exception was Auschwitz, where the victims of the gas chambers were soon counted in the hundreds of thousands.[178] The separate path of Auschwitz was due to its transformation, in 1942, into a camp of the Holocaust. Commandant Höss himself had briefed Adolf Eichmann from the RSHA about his experiments with Zyklon B, and both men agreed to use it for the genocide of Jews. Less than a year after the first gassings in Auschwitz, many thousands of Jews from across Europe were exterminated there each month.[179] However, although the Auschwitz gas chambers have long since become synonymous with the Holocaust, their origins lie elsewhere.[180]

SS Executioners

The mass extermination of Soviet POWs in 1941–42 turned hundreds of Camp SS men into professional executioners.[181] Most were low-ranking members of the Commandant Staffs who had served in the KL since the prewar years and had long become used to terror and destruction.[182] Several Sachsenhausen killers, for example, had earned their spurs as block leaders in the notorious death squad; a man like Wilhelm Schubert had become a murderer long before he started shooting Soviet soldiers in the neck.[183] And yet, the mass extermination of the POWs broke new ground, even for the most experienced SS men. Instead of occasional murders, they now participated in serial killings. Organized mass murder became part of the daily routine.

Many Camp SS men quickly adjusted to the new demands. Their self-image as political soldiers—the cornerstone of their collective identity—must have helped them to construe the killing of defenseless men as a valiant act of warfare against the "Jewish Bolshevik" enemy; it was their contribution to the war in the east, continuing the Nazi campaign of extermination behind the barbed wire of the camps. Such thinking was encouraged by widespread talk about Soviet atrocities. After the start of Operation Barbarossa, Nazi propaganda swamped the Third Reich with graphic reports about beastly Bolshevik crimes. Camp SS officers, too, told their men that Soviet "commissars" were savage insurgents and partisans, guilty of heinous crimes against German soldiers, and praised the SS executioners for performing an important duty for the fatherland.[184] The feeling that the Nazi leadership had entrusted them with such a vital mission must have filled many Camp SS killers with pride and a sense of purpose.[185]

In addition to these ideological factors, the executions provided SS perpetrators with their biggest stage yet to impress comrades in the camps' theater of cruelty. Participation in the mass killings, which some SS men belittled as a "shooting match," was seen as a test of character, and those who passed it without flinching received respect from their peers and praise from their superiors. Just as German air force pilots bragged to other soldiers about the number of enemy planes they had downed, Camp SS killers would boast about the number of Soviets they had finished off.[186] Some SS men also demonstrated their cold-bloodedness by mocking the dead and violating their bodies. What passed for SS humor knew no bounds of decency. On the Dachau shooting range, an SS man once grabbed a long wooden stick and aimed a swing at the genitals of a murdered Soviet prisoner, shouting to his colleagues: "Look here, he is still standing!"[187]

Other Camp SS men, however, felt far less comfortable about all the bloodshed. Some were scared of infection, since Soviet "commissars" were widely suspected as carriers of dangerous diseases. SS killers in the neck-shooting barracks wore protective clothing and cellophane masks, but despite these precautions, several of them contracted typhus, brought inside from the abominable POW camps; one block leader died as a result.[188] A number of SS men harbored doubts about the righteousness of the whole operation. A Sachsenhausen official, who was not directly involved in the killings, warned that the Red Army would retaliate by executing German soldiers (a fear shared by some Wehrmacht officers). The mass murder in the Nazi camps was wrong, he told the camp elder Harry Naujoks in autumn 1941, and it meant that the Third Reich had already lost the war, at least morally. Meanwhile, over at the shooting ranges and the execution barracks, several killers could not stand the carnage and fainted or broke down (just like some task force men in the occupied east). Others were very reluctant participants and tried to get out of the massacres; after their superiors announced the roster of designated killers for the next execution, they reported late for duty, or quietly stole away when the execution commando assembled.[189]

But it was hard to do the right thing. The concentration camp was an inverted world, where those who showed courage—by challenging the murderous status quo—were branded as cowards. Several unwilling executioners cracked under pressure from gung-ho comrades, with group conformity continuing to fuse Camp SS men into a large criminal gang. Any hesitation was seized upon with alacrity by the others. In Sachsenhausen, Wilhelm Schubert openly derided another SS block leader as a "wet blanket" for killing fewer POWs. SS men who tried to duck out altogether faced even more mockery about their manliness, and often caved. In the end, their fear of shame was stronger than their fear of killing. Nobody wanted to be seen as a "limp dick," one Sachsenhausen killer later conceded (using a revealing phrase).[190] If social pressure was not enough, SS superiors brought reluctant killers into line.[191] Only a handful of SS men continued to refuse. A few of them were probably excused, though punishment was another realistic prospect.[192] Oberscharführer Karl Minderlein, a member of the Dachau SS since 1933, stubbornly rejected calls to participate in the executions. Following a heated confrontation between Minderlein and the commandant, an SS court sentenced the disobedient SS man to imprisonment; he spent several months in solitary confinement in Dachau, before being transferred in summer 1942 to a penal company on the Eastern Front.[193]

Senior Camp SS officials were well aware that numerous killers struggled with the murderous tasks, reflecting general concerns by SS leader Heinrich Himmler that his men might "suffer damage" when executing prisoners in concentration camps.[194] In the case of the Soviet "commissars," SS leaders could have limited the circle of perpetrators by assigning a few expert executioners (as they would later do at the Auschwitz gas chambers). Instead, they often roped in as many men from the Commandant Staff as possible. "Almost all block leaders of the camp participated," a Sachsenhausen SS man admitted after the war, and their duties in the neck-shooting barrack rotated, as another killer testified: "Each block leader did, at different times, shoot through the gap, play the doctor, clean away the blood, and so on."[195] In this way, the burden of the killings was widely shared, leaving many Camp SS men with blood on their hands. Their shared complicity bound the killers ever closer together and made it harder to step outside the group.

To help the killers forget their grisly experiences, Camp SS leaders held regular comradeship evenings. After a long day of mass shootings in Sachsenhausen, the leaders would say "Come on, let's grab some food," and head for the SS canteen, where delicacies like pork schnitzel with fried potatoes were waiting.[196] Free schnapps and beer was even more popular.[197] Alcohol had fueled outrages in the camps since the early days. There was always plenty to drink, especially for younger and unmarried rank-and-file men, who spent much of their spare time in the canteen. On weekdays, alcohol was served at lunchtime and again in the evenings until late, and on Sundays the tap often ran all day.[198] Not only was alcohol an enabler of violence, it helped to deaden scruples after the deed. Just as Nazi murderers on the Eastern Front dulled their conscience with drink, so, too, did Camp SS men who murdered Soviet POWs.[199] But some killers continued to struggle with their conscience, however hard they tried to silence it. The Sachsenhausen block leader Max Hohmann, who was known as a reluctant killer, once drunkenly asked a political prisoner whether he looked like a murderer. When the prisoner answered in the negative, Hohmann replied: "But I am one!" and unburdened himself about the shootings.[200]

To lift the morale of their executioners, Camp SS leaders promised riches and glory. To show the appreciation of the fatherland, IKL bosses distributed a one-off payment in November 1941; the SS killers in Gross-Rosen, for instance, shared the tidy sum of six hundred Reichsmark between them. In the same month, the IKL asked commandants for the names of all "SS members involved in the executions," so that they could be awarded military decorations. In the eyes of Heinrich Himmler, shooting Soviet POWs in the neck, gassing them, or giving them lethal injections merited an award for bravery, the Kriegsverdienstkreuz 2nd Class with Swords—an honor previously reserved in the Camp SS for commandants.[201]

The biggest reward for the executioners was a holiday abroad, an unheard-of luxury for most SS men. Their destination was Italy. In spring 1942, more than two dozen Sachsenhausen killers set off for a trip to the south; two months later, a party from Dachau went the same way, heading for the Isle of Capri. The killers celebrated in SS style; some Sachsenhausen guards trashed their hotel rooms in a drunken stupor, causing considerable damage. In the small town of Sorrento, the men found time to pose for a German magazine, which later printed one of the photos on its title page: an Italian girl dances the tarantella, while several Sachsenhausen block leaders—in full regalia, with hats, black leather gloves, and ceremonial sabers—relax in the background, slumped into wicker chairs. Even a holiday in the sun could not clear the minds of all killers, however. On his return, at least one of the Sachsenhausen shooters confessed to a colleague that he was still plagued by nightmares about the murdered POWs.[202] In the end, mass murder proved harder than some SS men had imagined. Coming face-to-face with their helpless, naked victims, they had struggled to live up to the ideal of the merciless political soldier.[203]

Even so, the murderous operation largely proceeded as planned. Occasional

SS scruples did not create any real obstacles, and neither did the growing awareness of the killings by regular prisoners. Within weeks, well-informed inmates knew what was going on. Kapos in camp laundries received truckloads of Soviet army shirts, coats, and uniforms, and Kapos in the crematoria, who helped to burn the bodies, found Soviet medals and coins among the ashes.[204] Soon the murders were an open secret inside the KL. "We are all shattered by these mass murders, which have already claimed more than a thousand [Red Army soldiers]," political prisoners from Sachsenhausen wrote in a secret note on September 19, 1941. "We are currently unable to help them."[205] Once more, prisoners were confronted with their helplessness. And they also feared for their own lives. Now that the SS had moved to mass murder inside the camps, who would be next? Rudolf Wunderlich, a Communist Kapo in Sachsenhausen, recalled not long after that all prisoners were "gripped by impotent fury, also fear and depression."[206] The Camp SS leaders, meanwhile, saw their first foray into mass extermination as a success and soon turned to even more expansive programs of abuse and mass murder.

MURDEROUS UTOPIAS

There was a time, in the early years after the Second World War, when historians showed little real interest in Hitler's worldview. Writing him off as a madman or an opportunist, they overlooked his core convictions. Of course, Hitler's rambling writings and speeches, and his interminable monologues over lunch and dinner, never added up to a systematic body of thought, and there continues to be some debate about the extent to which his views dictated the course of the Third Reich. Nonetheless, Hitler clearly held strong political beliefs that guided him and shaped the new Germany he wanted to build.[207]

At the very center of Hitler's worldview—together with his fanatical hatred of Jews and Bolsheviks—stood the belief that Germany could not survive without the conquest of living space. Hitler had already made up his mind about this in the mid-1920s, when he still seemed destined for political obscurity. Germany needed to expand, he believed, and its future lay in the east, above all in the Soviet Union, with its vast stretches of land and rich agricultural resources. Hitler remained fixated on this goal for the rest of his life. Even as he was cowering in a maze of bunkers under the garden of the bombed Reich Chancellery, not long before his suicide in April 1945, he talked feverishly about the German mission to secure living space in the east.[208]

Back in summer 1941, right after the start of Operation Barbarossa, Hit-

An SA guard threatens recently arrested political prisoners in the early camp on Friedrichstrasse in Berlin on March 6, 1933, a day after the national elections. (akg-images, courtesy of ullstein bild)

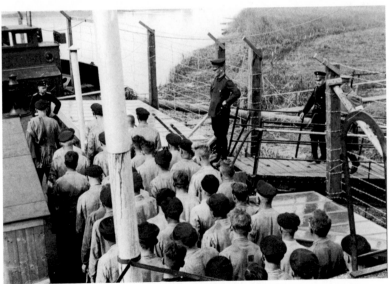

Among the many improvised camps set up for political opponents in 1933 was this old tugboat on the Ochtum River near Bremen. (Staatsarchiv Bremen)

A caricature about concentration camps in the German satirical magazine *Kladderadatsch* from April 30, 1933: left-wingers perform hard labor using symbols of the Communists (hammer and sickle) and of pro-democratic paramilitaries (three arrows), while another prisoner contemplates the Soviet red star.
(bpk/*Kladderadatsch*)

Photograph from the front page of the Nazi daily *Völkischer Beobachter* from August 10, 1933, recording the arrival in the Oranienburg camp of prominent political prisoners, including (suited, from left) the Social Democrats Ernst Heilmann and Friedrich Ebert (akg-images)

Propaganda image of "productive" labor in the Dachau camp, May 1933. The heavy road roller was pulled mainly by Jews and well-known left-wingers. (Bundesarchiv, picture 152-01-24)

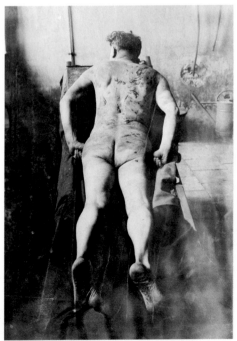

Autopsy photograph from the Munich state prosecutor's files on the suspicious death of the Jewish prisoner Louis Schloss in Dachau on May 16, 1933, which triggered legal proceedings against the camp's commandant (Staatsarchiv Munich)

The overbearing inspector of concentration camps, Theodor Eicke (center), during a trip to the Lichtenburg camp in March 1936 (United States Holocaust Memorial Museum [USHMM], courtesy of Instytut Pamięci Narodowej)

Eicke's more reserved successor, Richard Glücks (center, with briefcase), during a visit to the Gross-Rosen camp in 1941 (USHMM, courtesy of Martin Mansson)

SS leader Heinrich Himmler confronts a political prisoner in the Dachau workshops during an official inspection of this "model" camp by Nazi grandees on May 8, 1936. (Bundesarchiv, picture 152-11-11/Friedrich Franz Bauer)

Propaganda photograph of prisoners walking along the main path of the rebuilt and extended Dachau camp, June 28, 1938 (akg-images, courtesy of ullstein bild)

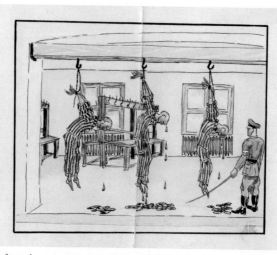

Hanging from the arms was among the worst of the official SS punishments. This scene in the Dachau baths was drawn by a survivor in 1945. (KZ-Gedenkstätte Dachau)

Mutter mit Britta bei der Dressur

This photograph, taken outside the walls of the Ravensbrück camp circa 1939–40, comes from an album the guard (center) made for her son. The inscription reads: "Mother with Britta [her guard dog] during training." (Mahn- und Gedenkstätte Ravensbrück/Stiftung Brandenburgische Gedenkstätten)

Commandant Karl Otto Koch with his wife, Ilse, and their children outside his Buchenwald office, December 1940 (Gedenkstätte Buchenwald)

SS snapshot of Commandant Koch and some of his men at work, towering over a prisoner in Sachsenhausen, 1937 (Archive of the Federal Security Service of the Russian Federation, Moscow, with the kind assistance of the Gedenkstätte und Museum Sachsenhausen)

Theodor Eicke (center, with cigarillo) presides over an SS comradeship evening in Dachau in 1934. (Hugh Taylor Collection)

SS men at leisure, at the newly built swimming pool just outside the Esterwegen camp, in 1936 (Archive of the Federal Security Service of the Russian Federation, Moscow, with the kind assistance of the Gedenkstätte und Museum Sachsenhausen)

Prisoner "workout" in Esterwegen, 1935. The photograph appeared in an SS album presented to Karl Otto Koch and was captioned, tellingly, "At the double, or there'll be trouble." (Archive of the Federal Security Service of the Russian Federation, Moscow, with the kind assistance of the Gedenkstätte und Museum Sachsenhausen)

Private SS photograph of young Buchenwald sentries showing off their physical prowess and camaraderie, 1940 (Gedenkstätte Buchenwald/personal album of Gerhard Brendle)

"Political recidivists" featured in a cover story about Dachau in the Nazi weekly *Illustrierter Beobachter*, December 1936. The prisoner on the right is Karl Kapp, the future camp elder. (KZ-Gedenkstätte Dachau)

Dachau mug shot of the petty criminal Josef Kolacek, one of almost ten thousand "asocial" men rounded up across the Third Reich in June 1938 (International Tracing Service, Bad Arolsen)

In this staged SS photograph, female camp inmates—small in numbers until the later war years—make straw shoes in Ravensbrück, 1941. (Mahn- und Gedenkstätte Ravensbrück/Stiftung Brandenburgische Gedenkstätten)

Roll call in Buchenwald, November 1938, with some of the 26,000 Jewish men forced into concentration camps after the Kristallnacht pogrom (USHMM/American Jewish Joint Distribution Committee, courtesy of Robert A. Schmuhl)

Polish prisoners outside a tent of the Buchenwald special camp in autumn 1939, after the outbreak of the Second World War; within a few months, most inmates in the camp were dead. (USHMM/American Jewish Joint Distribution Committee, courtesy of Robert A. Schmuhl)

Czech prisoners use basic tools to break up the concrete foundations of the failed SS brickworks near Sachsenhausen, 1940. (Gedenkstätte und Museum Sachsenhausen, Mediathek)

Dachau SS men gather near the body of Abraham Borenstein, one of the Jewish prisoners "shot trying to escape" on the camp's plantation in May 1941. (Gedenkstätte und Museum Sachsenhausen, Mediathek)

Slave labor in the SS quarry at Flossenbürg, circa 1942 (Beeldbank WO2—NIOD)

Heinrich Himmler (second from right in the group of uniformed Nazi dignitaries) in Mauthausen in 1941, passing a prisoner carrying a rock from the quarry (Museu d'Història de Catalunya/Fons Amical de Mauthausen)

Dachau mug shot of the Austrian Jew Eduard Radinger, who was murdered in 1942 during the "euthanasia" program. On the reverse, one of the doctors responsible, Friedrich Mennecke, recorded the prisoner's alleged crimes (e.g., "theft") and misconduct in the camp (e.g., "laziness"). (Staatsarchiv Nuremberg, ND: NO-3060)

Taking a break from their murderous task: Dr. Mennecke (third from right) and other "euthanasia" physicians unwind at Lake Starnberg on September 3, 1941, upon their return from Dachau. (Bundesarchiv, B 162 picture-00680)

As epidemics such as typhus spread through the camps, naked prisoners wait in the Mauthausen courtyard during a mass disinfection in June 1941. (BMI/Fotoarchiv der KZ-Gedenkstätte Mauthausen)

Hans Bonarewitz (on the cart), an alleged "professional criminal" recaptured after an escape, is led to the Mauthausen gallows in a macabre SS spectacle on July 30, 1942. (BMI/Fotoarchiv der KZ-Gedenkstätte Mauthausen)

Propaganda picture showing Soviet POWs arriving in Sachsenhausen in September 1941. Over the following months, the SS executed some forty thousand "commissars" in the concentration camps. (Národní archiv, Prague)

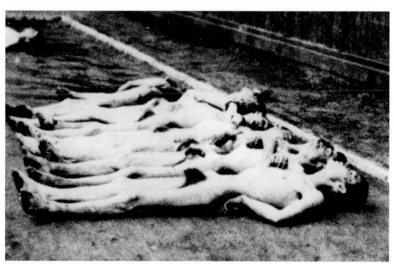

Some of the nine thousand Soviet POWs murdered in Sachsenhausen in September and October 1941. The image was smuggled out of the camp by an inmate. (Národní archiv, Prague)

ler's dream appeared to be within his grasp. Germany was on course for a crushing victory over the Soviet Union, or so it seemed; within a month of the invasion, the Wehrmacht had crossed the Dnieper, taken Smolensk, and closed in on Kiev. On July 16, 1941, in a top-level conference, Hitler laid out his vision. All the European areas of the Soviet Union would remain in German hands, Hitler announced: "We have to turn the newly gained eastern territories into a Garden of Eden."[209] Over the coming weeks and months, Hitler fantasized again and again about the glorious future awaiting Germany in the east. His mind kept wandering over his new dominions, daydreaming about all the towns and cities he would build. In three hundred years, Hitler mused, the bare and empty expanses would be flowering landscapes. Lording over the remaining Slavic population, the German rulers would live in opulent settlements, connected by a huge network of roads. "If only I could give the German people an idea," Hitler sighed in private in early September 1941, "of what this space means for the future."[210]

Settlements in the East

One man who needed no convincing was Heinrich Himmler, who was infatuated with the idea of living space. Soon after the German victory over Poland in autumn 1939, he had traveled across the occupied territory with his friend Hanns Johst, who afterward wrote how the Reichsführer SS, who had studied agriculture as a young man, got out of his car, gazed across the fields, and picked up some earth: "Thus we stood like ancient farmers and we smiled at each other with twinkling eyes. All of this was now German soil!"[211] Himmler made it his mission to colonize this soil, after Hitler charged him in autumn 1939 with "shaping the new German settlement areas" through major population transfers, replacing dangerous "racial aliens" with ethnic Germans.[212] Himmler took his cue from Hitler. Backed by a large new organization, he oversaw the brutal deportation of hundreds of thousands of Poles and Polish Jews eastward, as well as the influx of ethnic Germans into the western parts of Nazi-occupied Poland.[213]

After the German invasion of the Soviet Union, Himmler lost no time in staking his claim on these possessions, too. As the head of the Nazi terror apparatus, Himmler was in charge of policing the newly conquered areas.[214] And as the Reich Commissioner for the Strengthening of the German People, he tried to transform this territory along the lines of Nazi racial thinking. On June 24, 1941, just two days after the German invasion, Himmler charged his chief planner, Professor Konrad Meyer, with drawing up a blueprint for "new settlement planning in the East."[215] Himmler's men set to work on the so-called General Plan East, which gained, over the coming weeks and months, truly monstrous proportions. It aimed to reconstruct the entire face of eastern Europe. The SS planners did not advocate cosmetic changes but butchery, with whole cities razed, vast regions Germanized, and tens of millions of civilians deported, enslaved, and killed.[216]

These plans for Germany's colonial future required a gigantic construction effort, an assignment tailor-made for the expanding SS economy under Oswald Pohl. By early 1942, Himmler had put Pohl in charge of all SS peacetime building projects in the east, a huge task that included the construction of dozens of new bases across the former Soviet Union.[217] Back in mid-December 1941, Pohl had already presented Himmler with a comprehensive postwar building program for Germany and much of Nazi-controlled Europe. The estimated cost was a staggering thirteen billion Reichsmark, with almost half of it earmarked for SS and police structures on former Soviet territory. But in January 1942 Himmler rejected these plans, not because they were too outlandish, but because they were too cautious. One had to think even bigger, Himmler lectured Pohl, to create the "mammoth settlements" with which "we will make the east German." At Himmler's insistence, the SS building program went through ever more gargantuan drafts over the coming months.[218]

Much of the projected building work was supposed to be carried out by concentration camp prisoners. This made economic sense, as far as the SS leaders were concerned. The war had severely strained Germany's financial resources, Himmler reminded Pohl, and the German state would have to spend prudently after the victorious war. At the same time, the SS plans could not wait. Himmler's solution was simple: costs would be kept down by upping production in SS quarries and brick factories.[219] This vision was grounded in the colonial euphoria and genocidal utopianism that gripped the SS, from the highest echelons down to foot soldiers like the Mauthausen Hauptscharführer who ordered prisoners to draw detailed plans for a castle in Crimea.[220] Like all true zealots, the SS believers wanted to turn their dreams into reality as fast as possible. Even though their most ambitious plans were scheduled for after the war, they felt that construction should start straightaway; after all, they expected a swift victory. And because prisoners were critical to their plans, they set out to transform the KL system.

There was no mistaking the stronger emphasis of Camp SS leaders on forced labor. To begin with, they launched one of their periodic restructures of KL labor. In late September 1941, the ineffectual bureau for prisoner labor, set up the previous year in Pohl's SS Main Office for Budgets and Building, was incorporated directly into the IKL, together with its local representatives in camps, the so-called labor action leaders (*Arbeitseinsatzführer*). Although the immediate impact was negligible, the move demonstrated the growing preoccupation of the Camp SS with "major visionary, economic and war-essential tasks," as Inspector Richard Glücks put it.[221]

The main focus of SS leaders was not on organizational matters, but on the prisoners themselves. Himmler zeroed in on their training. Earlier SS initiatives to teach practical skills had not amounted to much. Now Himmler demanded the creation of an army of skilled inmates. In early December 1941, he ordered Pohl to have at least fifteen thousand concentration camp prisoners trained as stonemasons and bricklayers. Himmler added that this program should be completed by the end of the war, so that the prisoners were ready for deployment in "large-scale construction which would then be undertaken," such as Hitler's monumental city building projects, which had been the main stimulus of the SS economy since the late 1930s.[222] But Himmler's gaze had already shifted from rebuilding Germany to settling the conquered east, which would require even more inmate labor. And so prisoner training became an idée fixe for Himmler and his managers. One senior IKL official stressed in late 1941 that *every healthy inmate* had to become *a skilled worker.*[223] Like many of Himmler's favorite projects, this remained a pipe dream. Proper training would have required decent treatment, adequate food, and reasonable conditions—the exact opposite of what the KL stood for. If Himmler's plans had been realized, the camps would no longer have been the camps, and no SS manager was willing to contemplate this. In any case, prisoner training alone would never be enough to create the workforce required for the SS construction program. What the SS leaders really needed were masses of new slave laborers.

Soviets as Slaves

With his planners busily redrawing the map of Europe, turning entire countries upside down, Heinrich Himmler did not hold back when it came to forced labor, either. He envisaged huge concentration camps filled with slaves to realize his monumental vision; new settlements in the east would be erected on soil soaked with the sweat and blood of KL inmates. Himmler's main push came in September 1941, when his eyes fell on Soviet POWs.[224] At the time, there seemed to be an infinite supply of Soviet prisoners. Vast numbers had fallen into German hands, with many more on their way (by mid-October 1941, the Wehrmacht had captured more than three million men), and Himmler identified them as an untapped resource. Nazi leaders had previously banned their deployment for the German economy, so they had often remained idle in the hands of the Wehrmacht. When this resolve to shut out

Soviet POWs was weakening in late summer 1941, Himmler saw his chance: Why not exploit some as forced laborers in concentration camps?[225]

Himmler moved fast for Soviet POWs, supported by Hitler.[226] On September 15, 1941, he evidently discussed his plans with his closest confidant, Reinhard Heydrich, and with Oswald Pohl; he probably also raised them with the godfather of the KL, Theodor Eicke, that same day. The following morning, he telephoned Pohl once more; we do not know the details of their conversation, but Himmler's notes reveal the magnitude of his plans: "100,000 Russians take over into concentration camps."[227] Enormous as these figures were, Himmler soon doubled them. On the drawing boards of the SS, radical plans were quickly torn up and replaced by even more radical ones. By September 22, 1941, when Himmler met with Camp Inspector Glücks (who had been briefed some days earlier), he wanted two hundred thousand POWs for the KL.[228] Discussions were already under way with the Army High Command, and it did not take long to reach a deal: in late September the army agreed to leave up to one hundred thousand Soviet POWs to Himmler.[229] It seemed as if the Reichsführer SS had reached his initial goal with speed and ease.

Even before the negotiations with the army were concluded, the Camp SS prepared for the influx of Soviet soldiers. Some of these prisoners, Himmler decided, would be diverted to existing camps. On September 15, 1941, the same day he talked to Heydrich, Pohl, and Eicke, the IKL sent an urgent telex to commandants, asking them how many POWs they could accommodate. The plan was to put them in new barracks—as basic as possible—but to speed things up the local Camp SS also cleared some old barracks of other inmates. By October 1941, special areas, separated from the rest of the compounds and identified by signs such as "Prisoner of War Labor Camp," had been hastily completed in Neuengamme, Buchenwald, Flossenbürg, Gross-Rosen, Sachsenhausen, and Dachau, as well as in Mauthausen, which was earmarked as the largest such site within the prewar German borders.[230]

The bulk of Soviet POWs, however, were assigned elsewhere, after SS planners decided to build two massive new concentration camps on occupied Polish soil. The first was established in Lublin, some one hundred miles southeast of Warsaw, and became known as Majdanek (from the Majdan Tatarski district to the north). Majdanek was the first KL in the General Government. In the early phase of the occupation of Poland, Nazi leaders had decided against such a camp. As governor Hans Frank told senior German police officials in May 1940, it would be redundant: "Any suspects on our patch should be liquidated straightaway." But during a visit on July 20, 1941, Himmler selected Lublin as the site of a big new concentration camp, to help turn the region into a major outpost for German settlements. His order was not immediately implemented, perhaps because it was not yet clear where all the prisoners would come from. Only two months later, during Himmler's quest for Soviet POWs, did the SS push ahead with the plan. On September 22, 1941, Dr. Hans Kammler, recently appointed as the head of the construction office in Pohl's SS Main Office for Budgets and Building, ordered the erection of the camp on the edge of Lublin, with a projected capacity of fifty thousand prisoners; construction began on October 7, 1941. But the blueprint for Majdanek was outdated as soon as it had been drawn up. As Himmler's appetite for Soviet POWs grew, so did the projected prisoner figures for Majdanek. By early November 1941, Dr. Kammler already expected some 125,000 POWs, rising to 150,000 by early December.[231]

The second major new camp in occupied Poland was set up on land already controlled by the Camp SS. On September 26, 1941, just days after the construction order for Majdanek had gone out, Dr. Kammler ordered the building of a huge new camp near the town of Auschwitz. During a local inspection on October 2, 1941, Kammler chose the location of the new POW camp, less than two miles west of the main Auschwitz camp, to which it was subordinated. The spot was slightly moved a few days later, on the insistence of Commandant Höss: the new camp would grow on the site of a village called Birkenau (Brzezinka), inside the large SS interest zone that had been cleared of all inhabitants several months earlier. Construction began on October 15, 1941, and just like in Majdanek, the SS planners set their sights high. In late September 1941, the SS already expected fifty thousand prisoners, a figure revised within weeks to a hundred thousand.[232] There were no signs yet that Birkenau would one day stand at the center of the Holocaust.[233] The new subcamp was not built to murder the Jews of Europe, but to exploit vast numbers of Soviet POWs in the quest for German living space. In part, the SS hoped to turn the city of Auschwitz into a model settlement. More important, no doubt, were the plans for settlements elsewhere. As the most easterly established KL, Auschwitz would be a good base for the expansion of the SS, following in the footsteps of the revered Teutonic Knights.[234]

Similar motives stood behind the creation, later in 1941, of a third new camp in occupied eastern Europe, near a small village called Stutthof (Sztutowo), near Danzig. In contrast to Majdanek and Auschwitz-Birkenau, a camp already existed here. The Stutthof camp, surrounded by thick forests, swamps, and canals, had initially been set up by a local SS unit on September 2, 1939, just after the German attack on Poland, to terrorize the local population. In early 1940, SS leaders briefly considered turning the site into a concentration camp. But after some discussion, Himmler decided against it. In autumn 1941, he changed his mind. During a visit on Sunday, November 23,

1941, he concluded that it should become a KL proper. His order was implemented in early 1942.[235] The new camp was designated as a regional provider of forced labor for German settlements in Danzig and West Prussia. Because the plans were more modest than for Majdanek and Birkenau, Himmler was thinking of allocating fewer Soviet POWs than to the other two new camps; in late 1941, he envisaged sending some twenty thousand men. Plans for a new compound on the site were duly drawn up in Berlin and sent to Stutthof in early March 1942, at a time when the building work in Birkenau and Majdanek was already under way.[236]

It is worth pausing to reflect on the magnitude of Himmler's plans for Soviet POWs. What he was proposing in autumn 1941 was the greatest shake-up of the KL system since the mid-1930s. He envisaged a colossal increase in prisoner numbers. At a time when the entire camp system held fewer than eighty thousand prisoners, Himmler wanted to add some two hundred thousand or more. The great majority would work in gigantic new camp complexes, towering over the existing KL. The main camp in Auschwitz (with some ten thousand prisoners, currently one of the largest camps) would be dwarfed by the attached new camp in nearby Birkenau.[237] And with so many Soviet POWs earmarked for new camps in occupied Poland, the balance of the entire concentration camp system would tip sharply eastward. This focus on the east pointed to the new function of concentration camps: the colonization of German living space. Making prisoners perform productive labor was nothing new. Neither was their use in construction projects. But the plans in autumn 1941 were of a different order. Himmler envisaged an enormous program of forced labor, harnessing vast numbers of prisoners for a vital Nazi building program overseen by the SS. The KL would grow, the SS economy would grow, and Germany would grow. Once again, Himmler saw himself as acting in the best interests of both the SS and the nation.

KL Graveyards

On October 7, 1941, a freight train pulled up at a ramp near the Auschwitz main camp and slowly came to a halt. Inside were 2,014 men, the first Soviet POWs dispatched to the camp for forced labor. The doors were flung open and the prisoners, dazed and dirty, staggered out of the stifling carriages into the bright light, gasping for air. Among them was the twenty-eight-year-old infantry lieutenant Nikolaj Wassiljew from Moscow. "We did not know where we had arrived," he said later, "and what kind of camp this was." The SS guards soon showed them: screams and blows rained down on Wassiljew and the others. Some feared that they would be shot straightaway. Instead, the SS forced them to strip and jump into a vat filled with disinfectant. Wassiljew recalled that those "who did not want to jump were kicked and pushed in with sticks." Then the bone-thin POWs had to crouch naked on the floor.[238]

The newcomers had barely caught their breath when the Auschwitz SS ordered them to march to the camp. It was an icy autumn day, with frost on the roofs and patches of snow on the ground, and the Soviet soldiers were shivering with cold as they arrived inside the compound, where more SS men lay in wait. Some pointed their cameras at the POWs and took trophy photographs. Others battered the prisoners and then forced them to line up. There were further disinfections, which spread more terror, and also more disease since they were performed ineptly. "Then we were chased into the barrack[s]," remembered Nikolaj Wassiljew. The new POW section in the Auschwitz main camp consisted of nine completely bare blocks. "We remained without clothes for several days," Wassiljew added, "we were always naked." For warmth, the prisoners would huddle together in groups. The weakest leaned against the walls or lay on the concrete floors.[239]

More and more transports arrived over the coming days, and the small POW enclosure was soon desperately overcrowded; between October 7 and 25, 1941, almost ten thousand Soviet soldiers were pressed inside, doubling the Auschwitz prisoner population in just eighteen days.[240] All this was the result of Himmler's deal with the army. Following the general agreement in late September, the High Command of the Wehrmacht had started to make good on its promise to hand over Soviet POWs. On October 2, 1941, it ordered the transfer of twenty-five thousand prisoners for labor inside the Third Reich; the ensuing transports to the KL started within days—mostly heading for Auschwitz—and were completed by the end of the month. An additional two thousand Soviet POWs were dispatched to Majdanek in the General Government.[241]

The incoming Soviet POWs faced infernal conditions, not just in Auschwitz. In Sachsenhausen, they were also crammed inside empty barracks. There were "no beds, no cots, no chairs or tables, no blankets," recalled Benjamin Lebedev, who arrived with 1,800 other Soviet soldiers on October 18, 1941. "We slept on the ground, our wooden shoes as a cushion."[242] In Gross-Rosen, the first arrivals were not even allowed inside their barracks and had to spend several nights outside; between two hundred and three hundred men are said to have lost their lives during the first night alone.[243] In Majdanek, too, some Soviet POWs had to sleep out in the open, as there were not yet enough barracks; desperate for shelter, the prisoners dug holes in the hard ground.[244]

In line with Himmler's plans, the Camp SS soon pressed some of the POWs into forced labor. In Auschwitz, Soviet prisoners had to prepare the new

Birkenau compound from autumn 1941 onward. They cleared woods, dug trenches, and dismantled old farmhouses to gather bricks for the new camp buildings. Toiling with their bare hands in icy temperatures, many prisoners collapsed and died. "They froze en masse," a Polish resistance fighter wrote in a secret note; other POWs were shot or beaten to death during work. As the survivors dragged themselves back each evening from the Birkenau building site to their quarters in the main camp, they were accompanied by a cart that carried the corpses of their comrades.[245]

The majority of Soviet POWs were too weak to work at all. In Flossenbürg, it took several months before the Camp SS deployed any of the 1,700 POWs who had arrived in mid-October 1941.[246] In Gross-Rosen, the SS sent only 150 of the 2,500 Soviet men into the camp's quarry, and even they produced almost nothing, as the local DESt office complained in mid-December 1941: "These Russians are in such bad physical shape that one can barely demand any labor from them. They are worse than the worst prisoners so far."[247] Having already suffered at the noxious hands of the German army, the Soviet soldiers were in a desperate state even before they entered the concentration camps. "I was already ill when I arrived," recalled Nikolaj Wassiljew. "I had a kidney infection, pneumonia, and dysentery." After a week in Auschwitz, he was moved to an infirmary for Soviet POWs, which resembled a morgue more than a hospital. There was almost no hope of treatment, with prisoner orderlies reduced to using toilet paper as bandages.[248]

Most Soviet POWs joined the ranks of the dying—such were the conditions in most concentration camps. Many starved to death, since the Camp SS had reduced their rations well below those of other prisoners, until there was almost no food left at all; probably for the first time in the history of the KL, some inmates became so desperate they resorted to cannibalism. In Auschwitz, Commandant Rudolf Höss viewed the death struggle of Soviet soldiers like an anthropologist, as if it had nothing to do with him. "They were no longer human beings," he wrote in 1946. "They had become animals, only on the hunt for food." Some Camp SS men amused themselves by throwing bread into the POW enclosures, watching the frantic prisoners fight for every scrap.[249] Starvation soon bred more illness.[250] And epidemics were rampant, too; by late November 1941, half of all Soviet soldiers in Majdanek were suffering from typhus and its aftereffects.[251]

The Camp SS did not hesitate to kill ill, infectious, and weak Soviet soldiers, perhaps aware that Himmler approved such murders as a radical solution to epidemics and supply shortages.[252] In Auschwitz, Nikolaj Wassiljew, who worked in the infirmary after his health had improved, witnessed a large SS selection among POWs in early 1942. Stripped naked, they had to run past

SS men, sitting behind a table, who singled out the weakest ones. The victims were led, one by one, into the operating room and murdered by lethal injection.[253] In other camps, too, SS men routinely murdered sick POWs (just as they started to murder other so-called invalids, too). In Majdanek and Mauthausen, for example, SS men responded to typhus outbreaks by killing large numbers of Soviet soldiers in autumn and winter 1941; murder was seen as the surest method of disease control.[254]

Camp SS men also executed Soviet POWs on political grounds, even though they had been sent for work. Within weeks of their arrival in October 1941, the RSHA, still obsessed with the danger of commissars, apparently dispatched Gestapo commissions to concentration camps to root out supposed enemies hiding among the new arrivals. In Auschwitz, Gestapo officials screened all Soviet slave laborers, and selected one thousand "fanatical communists" and "politically unacceptable [elements]" for execution; the Camp SS shot and gassed the victims from late 1941 onward.[255]

The line between Soviet POWs who came to concentration camps for forced labor and those who came for execution became ever more blurred. In November 1941, Heinrich Himmler even agreed to temporarily exempt "commissars" from execution if they were fit for work. From now on, the local Camp SS could pick out physically strong men from execution transports for labor in quarries; soon these prisoners would be dead, too, but not before the SS had harnessed their last strength.[256] This was an early appearance of the concept of "annihilation through labor," which SS leaders were also considering as a weapon against Jews, and which would claim countless lives in the KL over the coming years.[257]

But this was still in the future. Back in autumn and winter 1941, the Camp SS gained almost nothing from the suffering of Soviet soldiers who arrived as slave laborers. The scale of death was stunning. In Majdanek, hardly any of the two thousand Soviet POWs were still alive in mid-January 1942.[258] In Auschwitz, too, the young soldiers "dropped like flies," as Commandant Rudolf Höss noted. Around eighty percent—some 7,900 men or more—were dead by early January 1942, less than three months after the first transport had reached the camp; the worst day came on November 4, 1941, when 352 Soviet POWs died in Auschwitz.[259] The mass death of Soviet soldiers in late 1941 was not confined to the KL in the occupied east. In Sachsenhausen, almost thirty percent of Soviet POWs are said to have perished within their first month inside (not counting "commissars" executed in the neck-shooting barrack).[260] And in Gross-Rosen, just 89 out of 2,500 Soviet POWs were still alive on January 25, 1942.[261]

At the time, the local Camp SS saw these deaths, which far exceeded all previous Camp SS records, largely as a logistical problem. This was true above all in Auschwitz, which claimed the lives of more Soviet slave laborers than any other KL. The Auschwitz SS initially struggled to identify all the dead, as army tags were lost in the chaos of the POW enclosure and numbers written on bodies quickly rubbed off. To prevent cases of mistaken identity, the SS took a drastic step. From November 1941 onward, Soviet slave workers had their prisoner number tattooed onto their skin. A special metal stamp was punched into the prisoner's chest, with ink wiped into the wound; the men were so weak they were propped against a wall, lest they collapse under the blow of the stamp. The notorious Auschwitz tattoo was born and later extended to most inmates in the camp (no other KL used tattoos, though some had used ink stamps in the past).[262]

The Auschwitz SS also searched for new ways to dispose of the dead. The existing crematorium in the main camp could not burn all the dead POWs, and as corpses were piling up all over the enclosure, a sickening smell of decomposing bodies began to spread through the camp and beyond. On November 11, 1941, the recently appointed head of the Auschwitz SS building office, Karl Bischoff, sent a cable to the camp's furnace supplier in Germany: "Third incinerator urgently needed." Because it would take months before the new oven was installed, the Camp SS in the meantime decided to dump the bodies in ditches in Birkenau, hastily dug by other POWs. Birkenau became a vast graveyard for Soviet soldiers.[263]

Himmler Thwarted

In autumn and winter 1941, a gulf opened up between Himmler's megalomaniac plans for the mass deployment of Soviet POWs, which envisaged their exploitation for gigantic German settlements, and the reality inside his concentration camps, which was all about death. Even a few Camp SS men were alert to the apparent contradictions of SS policy. Their doubts were summed up by a Sachsenhausen official, who asked himself out loud: "So have these people come here to die or to work?"[264] As an advocate of "annihilation through labor," Himmler's answer would have been "both." But in the case of the Soviet POWs who arrived for slave labor in October 1941, the SS succeeded only in part; the soldiers were annihilated all right, but long before most of them could be exploited. The RSHA warned the Camp SS not to confuse POWs arriving "for labor deployment" with those destined "for execution."[265] Not all local SS men could see the difference; after all, Nazi propaganda had long painted all Soviet soldiers as dangerous subhumans.[266]

And so the death of Soviet POWs continued. When the Sachsenhausen block leader Martin Knittler, a seasoned killer from the camp's neck-shooting barrack, was informed one day in November 1941 that nine Soviet slave laborers had perished, he replied: "What? Only nine deaths today? We'll see to that." Knittler then ordered the remaining Soviet soldiers, who had just showered, to stand for hours outside their barrack in the freezing cold. The next day, thirty-seven of them were dead.[267] SS men like Knittler could rationalize their murders as economically beneficial. Following Nazi social-Darwinist thinking, the lethal conditions they helped to create led to a natural selection; those Soviet soldiers who survived would be the fittest and hardest workers.[268]

Camp SS leaders in Oranienburg were well aware of the slaughter of Soviet slave laborers. But Richard Glücks and his men were neither surprised nor alarmed.[269] In fact, they fostered the lethal atmosphere inside the KL. When it came to the construction of new barracks, Arthur Liebehenschel had been implacable from the start. The Soviet POWs, he announced in mid-September 1941, had to be housed "in the most primitive manner."[270] What this meant becomes clear when studying the SS plans for the new camp at Birkenau, drawn up in mid-October 1941. Disease and death were built into the plans, which envisaged 125,000 POWs packed into 174 barracks; the surface space allocated to each prisoner was, appropriately enough, the same size as a coffin. Seven thousand prisoners were supposed to share a latrine hut and 7,800 prisoners a wash hut. These provisions were worse, far worse, than the standard design for concentration camps. But in the eyes of SS planners—who subscribed to Himmler's views of Soviets as resilient "human animals"—they were just right.[271]

At first glance, the treatment of Soviet POWs in late 1941 seems baffling: Why were so many men, who had been earmarked for KL slave labor, pushed to their graves? From the perspective of the SS, however, these murders were less contentious. The deaths would have raised concerns only if the lives of Soviet slave laborers had held any real value. They did not. Underlying the murder and neglect by the Camp SS was the conviction that the twenty-seven thousand soldiers who had arrived in October 1941 were just the vanguard; far more Soviet POWs would follow and take the place of the dead. Caught up in the hubris of Nazi domination, the Camp SS counted on an infinite surge of Soviet prisoners.[272]

But the reinforcements did not come. Not long after the SS had staked a claim on captured Soviet soldiers, Hitler made a decisive intervention. On October 31, 1941, faced with growing labor shortages, he ordered the mass deployment of Soviet POWs for the general German war effort; soon, SS claims were sidelined by the more urgent demands from state and private industry. What is more, there were far fewer captives than expected. Never again did the Wehrmacht take as many prisoners as it did in the early months of Operation Barbarossa. Afterward, the blitzkrieg predicted by Hitler's cocksure generals turned into an unceasing war of attrition. The German advance stalled outside Moscow, followed by the first major counteroffensive in December 1941. By then, most of the captured Soviet soldiers were already dead or dying, victims of the fatal conditions in Wehrmacht compounds and the merciless hunt for "commissars."[273] Himmler's huge wave of Soviet POWs never hit the concentration camps.

As a result, his grandiose plans for the expansion of the KL system—with the giant new camps in Birkenau and Majdanek as the main base for Soviet soldiers—failed to materialize, at least in the way he had intended. On December 19, 1941, SS buildings supremo Hans Kammler sent Himmler a sobering update about progress in Birkenau and Majdanek. Hard as he tried to apply a positive gloss, Kammler conceded that the construction of both camps—now projected at one hundred and fifty thousand prisoners each—was well behind schedule; so far, only twenty-six barracks had been built in Majdanek, and fourteen in Birkenau. The main problem, apart from subzero temperatures and shortages of building material, was the sheer lack of manpower. As conceived in autumn 1941, the building project relied on the influx of huge numbers of Soviet soldiers. But the POWs who had arrived so far were of no use to the SS. The plans to make the POWs build their own barracks, Kammler admitted, had to be dropped, because the prisoners "are in such a catastrophic physical state that it is currently not possible to contemplate a successful labor deployment."[274]

In the end, Majdanek never grew into a major hub for forced labor. The provisional compound was still far from finished in summer 1942. There were only two barracks for SS guards, the watchtowers were incomplete, and building material was scattered all over the grounds.[275] Majdanek did not come close to its projected size. Most of the time, it held no more than around ten to fifteen thousand inmates, and none of them laid any foundations for German settlements in the east.[276] SS progress in Birkenau remained slow, too. Only in March 1942, half a year after the initial construction order, had work progressed far enough for the surviving POWs to be transferred from their enclosure in the main camp to Birkenau. These Soviet soldiers now numbered fewer than one thousand, and most of them soon perished, too. In mid-April 1942, a young Jewish prisoner who had just been deported from Slovakia (a German puppet state) to Birkenau found the last remnant of the Soviet soldiers "in a terribly neglected state," living on the "unfinished building site, without any protection against cold and rain, and dying in droves."[277]

Heinrich Himmler's first bid for Soviet slave laborers ended in failure and misery. Rather than turning the KL into gigantic reservoirs of forced labor, the arrival of Soviet soldiers opened a new round of carnage in the camps. In spring 1942, when most of the remaining POW compounds were closed down—with the prisoners now officially classified as concentration camp inmates—no more than perhaps five thousand of the twenty-seven thousand Soviet soldiers who had arrived for forced labor in autumn 1941 were still alive.[278] One of the survivors was Nikolaj Wassiljew, who was among the Auschwitz prisoners transferred to Birkenau in March 1942. Asked after the war about the fate of his comrades, Wassiljew gave a blunt answer: "Shot. Killed during work. Died of hunger. Died of illness."[279]

Taking Stock

Looking at the KL in late 1941 and early 1942, a great deal had changed since the outbreak of the Second World War. While they were still recognizable as concentration camps, the system had undergone a major makeover in barely two years. In early 1942, there were thirteen main camps, not six, with four new ones in occupied Nazi Europe: Auschwitz, Majdanek, and Stutthof in Poland, and Natzweiler in France.[280] Prisoner numbers had shot up, too, from just over twenty thousand to around eighty thousand, with most new prisoners coming from occupied Europe, above all from Poland and the Soviet Union. And while prisoners in 1939 might have imagined that their treatment could not get any worse, it quickly had. Nazi terror escalated during the war, inside and outside the KL. The camps' towering death rate tells its own story, as do the weapons deployed by the SS. By 1942, the Camp SS practiced almost every conceivable form of murder: beating, hanging, shooting, starving, drowning, gassing, and poisoning.

The pivotal year was 1941, as the concentration camps moved from the lethal conditions of the early war period to mass extermination, developing a dual function. As before, the Camp SS exploited, abused, and killed individual prisoners. But the camps now also became sites of systematic mass murder, with central programs to kill infirm prisoners and so-called Soviet commissars. Take Sachsenhausen, one of the model camps of the SS. During 1941, an average of maybe ten thousand regular prisoners were held here. Every day was torture for them, dominated by forced labor, drills, crammed barracks, hunger, illness, and extreme violence. Death from malnourishment and disease was common, especially among Poles and Jews. Still, the Camp SS had no plans to kill all these prisoners and the majority survived.[281] The opposite was true for the ten thousand "unacceptable" Soviet POWs who came to the camp between September and November 1941 and rarely lived longer than a couple of days; Sachsenhausen was an extermination camp for these men.

Systematic mass killing turned to genocide in 1942, as the Holocaust entered the KL. But this change did not come out of nowhere. It is striking how many structural elements of the Holocaust had emerged inside concentration camps before the SS crossed the threshold to genocide. This included the deportation of victims straight to their deaths; tight transport schedules; the elaborate camouflage of mass murder, with fake showers and doctors' offices; the use of poison gas, including Zyklon B; the construction of new crematoria, which were adapted, repaired, and extended to keep up with all the dead; the regular purges among prisoners to kill those "unfit for work"; the violation of prisoners' bodies after death, with gold teeth broken out. All this predated the Holocaust. Even the selection of prisoners on arrival—sending the weaker ones straight to their deaths and working the others until they, too, perished—had been pioneered in autumn 1941, targeting Soviet "commissars." Simply put: the essential mechanics of the Holocaust were in place by the end of 1941—a KL like Auschwitz was ready for the genocide of European Jewry.

And yet, the mass murder of invalids and Soviet POWs was no dress rehearsal for the Holocaust. This would be reading history backward. These killings were driven by their own terrible logic, without the murder of the Jews in mind. Indeed, when the decision for these earlier killing programs was taken in spring and summer 1941, the Nazi regime had not yet settled on the immediate extermination of European Jews as state policy. No KL was designated as a place for killing large numbers of Jews until 1942. This shift came only after momentous decisions by Nazi leaders ushered in a new chapter in the history of the SS concentration camps, and the Third Reich as a whole.

6

Holocaust

Shortly after three o'clock on the afternoon of July 17, 1942, a plane carrying SS leader Heinrich Himmler and his small entourage touched down at Kattowitz airport. Waiting on the ground were high-ranking party and SS officials, among them the Auschwitz commandant Rudolf Höss, who had busily prepared his camp for Himmler's impending visit. Höss accompanied the SS leader and the other dignitaries on the drive south, heading for Auschwitz, where Himmler was formally welcomed over tea and coffee in the officers' mess.[1] The whole camp complex had grown enormously since Himmler's inaugural visit in spring 1941. The SS had greatly extended its local zone of interest. The main camp was also much changed and now included a makeshift section for thousands of female prisoners, who were poised for transfer to the huge new compound in Birkenau. Another major development was under way at the nearby IG Farben site, where a satellite camp (Monowitz) was being built. Most significant of all, Birkenau had recently become a camp for the systematic mass extermination of European Jewry.

During his two-day visit, Himmler was given a comprehensive tour of the Auschwitz complex. He was keen to check on various economic ventures, both agricultural and industrial. To discuss his ideas about farming, the trained agronomist Himmler set time aside for the dynamic local SS director of farms, Joachim Caesar, and he also visited agricultural projects, apparently stopping at a cowshed for a glass of milk poured by a prisoner.[2] Himmler also toured the IG Farben building site. Though impressed by the modern construction methods, he was impatient for the production of synthetic fuel and rubber to begin. Not for the last time, he pushed the company to speed things up.[3] Inside the main camp, Himmler inspected the overcrowded women's compound and watched as one female prisoner was whipped during corporal punishment.[4] He was standing not far from the camp's crematorium, where the gassing of Soviet POWs had taken place back in autumn 1941. By the time of his visit, however, the center of mass murder in Auschwitz had already shifted, away from the main camp to the new extension in Birkenau.

Well beyond the first nearly complete Birkenau prisoner sectors stood a couple of innocuous-looking farmhouses—a few hundred yards apart and hidden among the trees—that had lately been converted into gas chambers. Here, according to Rudolf Höss, Himmler closely observed the mass murder of a newly arrived transport of Jews: "He did not say anything at all about the extermination process, he just watched in silence."[5] The SS leader was a dispassionate observer, just as he had been during a massacre of Jewish men and women near Minsk, one year earlier.[6]

But Himmler was not silent for long. On the evening of July 17, 1942, he attended a festive dinner with the leading Auschwitz SS officers—all in full uniform—and made small talk about their jobs and families. Later he relaxed, during an informal get-together with Höss and his wife, and a few select others, in the modern mansion of the Nazi Gauleiter in a forest near Kattowitz, complete with golf course and swimming pool. Himmler was uncharacteristically lighthearted that night, even exuberant, though he avoided any direct references to the events of a few hours earlier. Still, the murder of European Jewry must have been on his mind and he even allowed himself a few glasses of red wine and a smoke. "I had never known him like that!" recalled Rudolf Höss.[7] The following morning, back in Auschwitz, Himmler made a point of calling on Höss before his final departure. Visiting the commandant's villa, Himmler was at his most affable and posed for the cameras with Höss's children, who called him "Uncle Heini" (Höss later proudly displayed the pictures in his home).[8] Perhaps he felt that such displays of civility were especially important in a place like Auschwitz, where his men were engaged in daily assault, plunder, and mass murder.

The visit of the Reichsführer SS to Auschwitz coincided with major developments in the Third Reich. Since spring 1942, Himmler had been pushing for forced labor in the KL to redouble, reflecting the new Nazi priorities. Following the failure of the rapid offensive against the Soviet Union and the United States' entry into the war, the regime faced a lengthy battle and had to urgently boost war production. For his part, Himmler had decided in early March 1942 that the entire KL system—previously only loosely integrated into the wider SS organizational chart—would become part of the SS Business and Administration Main Office (WVHA), with the Camp Inspectorate forming Office Group D. The WVHA was the newly created organizational and economic hub of the SS, led by the single-minded Oswald Pohl, who had now reached the top echelon of the SS.[9]

But when Heinrich Himmler traveled to Auschwitz in July 1942, it was the Nazi Final Solution, not the SS economy, that was foremost in his mind. Himmler, the master of the KL, also oversaw the annihilation of European Jewry, which escalated in summer 1942. Just days before his trip to Auschwitz, he had met with Hitler and afterward pushed to speed up the genocide. And immediately following his inspection of Auschwitz, Himmler flew to Lublin to plot the extermination of Polish Jews in three new death camps in the General Government—Belzec, Sobibor, and Treblinka. He visited Sobibor on July 19 and later that evening issued an order from Lublin for the rapid "resettlement of the entire Jewish population in the General Government"; except for selected forced laborers in the few remaining ghettos and camps, all local Jews had to be exterminated by the end of the year.[10]

So Himmler's trip to Auschwitz in July 1942 came at a crucial moment. Productive labor was becoming more important than ever, at the same time as the program of deportations and mass killings of Jews from across Europe got under way. Himmler's visit touched on both aspects, as Auschwitz was a focal point for SS economic ambitions *and* a center of the Nazi Final Solution. Before he left the camp on July 18, 1942, Himmler told Höss to push ahead with the economic exploitation of prisoners and the mass gassings, with deportations set to increase month by month. At the end of their meeting, Himmler spontaneously promoted Höss to Obersturmbannführer, in recognition of Auschwitz's significance for Nazi plans.[11] But how had the camp become part of these plans in the first place? And what function did it and the rest of the KL system have in the Holocaust?

AUSCHWITZ AND THE NAZI FINAL SOLUTION

Auschwitz has long been *the* symbol of the Holocaust. The Nazis murdered almost one million Jews here, more than in any other single place. And only in Auschwitz did they systematically kill Jews from all across the continent, deported to their deaths from Hungary, Poland, France, the Netherlands, Greece, Czechoslovakia, Belgium, Germany, Austria, Croatia, Italy, and Norway. In part, Auschwitz was so lethal because it operated so much longer than other killing sites. In late spring 1944, when the three death camps in the

General Government had long closed down again, Auschwitz was only just beginning to reach its murderous peak. And after Soviet troops finally liberated the camp in January 1945, much of the infrastructure of murder remained on-site, in contrast to Belzec, Sobibor, and Treblinka, where the traces of genocide had been carefully concealed. This is one reason why we know so much more about Auschwitz than about the other death camps. Another is the abundance of testimony. Several tens of thousands of Auschwitz prisoners survived the war and many of them told their story. By contrast, hardly anyone left the other death camps alive, since they functioned purely as extermination sites; only three survivors ever gave testimony about Belzec.[12]

In view of Auschwitz's preeminence in Holocaust memory, it is worth recalling once more that the camp was not created for the annihilation of the Jews. Nor was this ever its sole rationale. Unlike the single-purpose death camps in the General Government, Auschwitz was always a site with multiple missions.[13] What is more, it was incorporated late into genocide. Contrary to some suggestions, it did not become a death camp for European Jews as early as 1941.[14] This function gradually emerged during 1942, and only from summer of that year did the camp play a more prominent role.

Death Camps in the General Government

The genesis of the Holocaust was lengthy and complex. The days are long gone when historians believed that it could be reduced to a single decision taken on a single day by Hitler. Instead, the Holocaust was the culmination of a dynamic murderous process, propelled by increasingly radical initiatives from above and below. During World War II, the Nazi pursuit of a Final Solution moved from increasingly lethal plans for Jewish "reservations" to immediate extermination. There were several key periods of radicalization. The German invasion of the Soviet Union in June 1941 marked one such moment, as mass shootings of Jewish men of military age soon grew into widespread ethnic cleansing, with daily bloodbaths of women, children, and the elderly. At the end of 1941, some six hundred thousand Jews had been murdered across the newly conquered eastern territory.

By then, the Nazi regime was already moving toward the extermination of European Jewry as a whole. Autumn 1941 saw the first systematic mass deportations from Germany to the east, following Hitler's decision to remove all Jews from the Reich. Even though most of these victims were not yet murdered on arrival, it was clear that they would not live for long. At the same time, the slaughter of Jews expanded beyond the Soviet Union to Serbia and parts of Poland. Meanwhile, plans were made for several regional gassing facilities on occupied Polish and Soviet soil, targeting eastern European Jews, especially those judged "unfit for work." Chelmno, in the Warthegau (the western Polish territory incorporated into the Reich), was the first such death camp to start up, on December 8, 1941. Within four months, more than fifty thousand people, mostly Polish Jews from the Lodz ghetto (some forty miles away), were murdered here in gas vans. Farther east, in the General Government, construction of the first stationary exter-mination camp in Belzec (Lublin district) began in early November 1941, followed by the establishment of a second death camp in Sobibor (also Lublin district) from February 1942.

It was around this time that the genocidal program was being finalized. From late March 1942, deportations from western and central Europe slowly expanded, with the first transports of selected Slovakian and French Jews to occupied Poland. SS managers started to prepare a comprehensive plan for Europe-wide deportations, which was launched from July 1942. Mean-while, the killing in eastern Europe intensified, too. In the occupied Soviet Union, ghetto clearances and massacres were stepped up, and in occupied Poland, too, more and more regions were pulled into the inferno. The perpe-trators moved with great speed, emptying one ghetto after another. Accord-ing to Nazi figures, of the two million Jews who had once lived in the General Government, just three hundred thousand were still alive at the end of 1942.[15]

Most Jews murdered in the General Government in 1942 died in the three new death camps. Mass extermination in Belzec started in March, followed by Sobibor in early May; around the same time, construction began on a third camp, Treblinka (Warsaw district), in the north of the General Government, which was set up primarily for the murder of Jews from the Warsaw ghetto and operated from late July.[16] In the historical literature, the mass extermi-nation of Jews in the General Government is commonly referred to as "Op-eration Reinhard," and these three death camps as "Reinhard camps," after a Nazi code word chosen in memory of Reinhard Heydrich (assassinated in summer 1942).[17] However, this terminology is misleading. The Nazi authori-ties did not restrict the code name "Operation Reinhard" to Belzec, Sobibor, and Treblinka, but also applied it to the extermination of Jews and the plunder of their property at the SS concentration camps Auschwitz and Majdanek (the two KL operating simultaneously as death camps).[18] Despite their shared his-tory, however, the three new death camps in the General Government did exist independently from Auschwitz and Majdanek (and the rest of the KL system), and to signify this distinctiveness, Belzec, Sobibor, and Treblinka will be referred to here as the "Globocnik death camps," after the SS and police leader in Lublin district, Odilo Globocnik.

Perhaps Himmler's most obsequious follower and ferocious executioner, Odilo Globocnik had cut his teeth as a violent young fanatic in the illegal Austrian Nazi movement. His brief reign as Vienna Gauleiter after the Anschluss ended ignominiously, mired in suspicions of corruption. But as he did with many "old fighters," Himmler gave him another chance, and Globocnik grasped it eagerly. In late 1939, after he was posted to Lublin, he quickly made his name as a champion of radical anti-Jewish policy. Since autumn 1941, he coordinated the mass extermination of Jews in his district, a task later extended to the entire General Government. "Globus" (globe)—as Himmler jokingly called him—was delighted when his master ordered him in July 1942, after his trip to Auschwitz, to oversee the immediate annihilation of Jews in the General Government. "The Reichsführer SS was just here and has given us so much new work," he gushed. "I am so very grateful to him, that he can be certain that these things that he wishes will come true in no time." As Rudolf Höss recalled, Globocnik's hunger for deportations to his death camps became insatiable: "He could never get enough."[19]

In the second half of 1942, the Holocaust unfolded with unremitting force inside the General Government. Train after train carried hundreds of thousands of Jews to Globocnik's death camps. Few survived for more than a few hours; once they were crammed into the gas chambers, powerful engines started up, pumping carbon monoxide inside. The deportations were coordinated from Globocnik's Lublin office. The death camps, meanwhile, were staffed with the experienced killers from the "euthanasia" program. Starting in autumn 1941, more than 120 T-4 veterans—mostly men in their late twenties and thirties—were transferred to the General Government to set up and run the new death camps. At the top stood Christian Wirth, a former police officer who had become the main troubleshooter during the "euthanasia" action. Wirth now used his murderous know-how as the local T-4 representative and inspector of the Globocnik death camps, earning himself the nickname "Wild Christian." From summer 1942, as the Holocaust accelerated, he oversaw major changes in Belzec, Sobibor, and Treblinka, including the extension of the killing facilities, to ensure the smooth running of the genocide.[20] The same aim was pursued farther west, in Auschwitz. Here, too, SS men were hard at work, refining and enlarging the machinery of death for the Holocaust.

"Jews into the KL"

In the early years of the Second World War, the concentration camps had stood on the sidelines of Nazi anti-Jewish policy; the present was largely about ghettos and forced labor camps, and the future about deadly reservations. Concentration camps, by contrast, were marginal. Even when the Third Reich began to move toward the systematic extermination of European Jews, there were no signs yet that the KL would become more prominent anytime soon. Their peripheral role was reflected in prisoner numbers: by early 1942, Jews made up fewer than five thousand of the eighty thousand KL inmates.[21]

On January 20, 1942, a crucial conference took place in the leafy Berlin suburb of Wannsee. At lunchtime, a group of senior party and state officials gathered to coordinate the Nazi Final Solution, under the overall control of the RSHA. The meeting was chaired by Reinhard Heydrich, who laid out the general direction. Some aspects were still in flux, but the overall aim was now clear: European Jews would be concentrated in the occupied east and murdered there, either straightaway or by working them to death. The vision of "annihilation through labor" was an important element of these plans. As Heydrich put it at Wannsee—according to minutes compiled by Adolf Eichmann, the RSHA desk officer who managed the deportations from western and central Europe—large labor gangs would be formed in the east for heavy road construction: "undoubtedly a large number of them will drop out through natural wastage."[22] Although the specifics remained vague, there was apparently no place for the concentration camps in these genocidal plans, neither as extermination centers nor as hubs for lethal labor. The KL were not on the agenda at Wannsee, and no representative of the concentration camp system had been invited to the gathering.

Within days of the Wannsee conference, however, SS leaders changed their tune. The trigger, it seems, was their final acceptance that the grandiose settlement plans in the east would never be realized with Soviet POWs; too few had arrived in the KL, and too many of those who had were already dead.[23] The SS now looked for replacements and soon found them: instead of Soviet soldiers, Jews would build the gigantic settlements. On January 26, 1942, just six days after Wannsee, Himmler telexed Glücks to outline the change in direction. Since no more Soviet POWs could be expected in the near future, Himmler explained, he had decided to send large numbers of Jews to the KL: "Get ready to accommodate 100,000 male Jews and up to 50,000 Jewesses in the KL within the next four weeks."[24]

The decision to substitute Jews for Soviet POWs was taken impulsively at the top of the Nazi state. On January 25, one day before he informed Glücks, Himmler had evidently discussed the use of Jewish workers with Oswald Pohl. Immediately afterward, Himmler had apparently raised his plan in the Führer's headquarters. During lunch, Hitler ranted about the need to make Europe free of Jews: "If [the Jew] gets wrecked along the way, I cannot help it. I see only one thing: total annihilation, if they don't go voluntarily. Why should I look at a Jew with different eyes than a Russian prisoner?" Soon after the meal, Himmler put Heydrich in the picture, calling him in Prague. The note for this call in Himmler's office diary reads: "Jews into the KL."[25]

SS Camp Inspector Glücks and his men were caught unawares by Himmler's new scheme. In recent weeks, the IKL had devised its own, far more modest plan to exploit some Jewish prisoners. After it became evident that the colossal designs for Majdanek could not be achieved with Soviet POWs, the IKL ordered other concentration camps on January 19, 1942, to send Jewish prisoners "fit for work" to Majdanek. Just one week later, however, Himmler's sudden message that huge numbers of Jews were on their way from elsewhere forced a volte-face. The IKL managers in Oranienburg immediately abandoned the small-scale transports from other camps to Majdanek and focused instead on preparing the KL system for the mass arrival of Jews from outside.[26]

But Himmler had jumped the gun when he announced the imminent influx of up to one hundred and fifty thousand Jewish prisoners. Not for the first time, his ambitions outstripped the SS and police abilities, and two months passed before the first transports got under way. During this time, several key decisions were made. One concerned the victims. Initially, Himmler had targeted German Jews for immediate deportation to the KL, but this plan was dropped.[27] Instead, SS attention turned to Jews regarded as "fit for work" from two other countries, Slovakia and France.[28] Meanwhile, the IKL confirmed the destination for the forthcoming mass deportations—Majdanek and Auschwitz.[29] This was an obvious choice. Both camps had previously been designated for huge numbers of Soviet POWs; as Jews would replace them as forced workers, SS logic dictated that they would be taken to the same camps. In practice, Auschwitz became the primary destination for deportations of Jews from western and central Europe, because of its greater proximity, better transport links, and superior infrastructure.

The new role of Auschwitz prompted the SS authorities to take two major initiatives toward the end of February 1942. First, it resolved to build a large crematorium in Birkenau, capable of disposing of eight hundred bodies in twenty-four hours. The plans for a big crematorium were not new. Back in autumn 1941, with an enormous new camp for Soviet POWs scheduled at the Auschwitz complex, SS planners had decided to erect a high-capacity crematorium in the main camp, in order to deal with the anticipated surge in prisoner deaths. This location was now changed to Birkenau, during a local inspection on February 27, 1942, by the SS construction chief Hans Kammler.[30] Large numbers of Jewish prisoners were expected to arrive in Birkenau soon, and all would eventually die through "annihilation through labor." Why haul their corpses all the way back to the main camp, Kammler must have thought, when they could be burned in Birkenau?

Second, Auschwitz prepared for the mass influx of women, who were part of Himmler's deportation plans. Himmler turned to his in-house experts in female detention in Ravensbrück. He visited the camp on March 3, 1942, and then briefed Pohl the following day, setting off a flurry of activity.[31] On March 10, 1942, the IKL ordered two Auschwitz officers to head for Ravensbrück to "get acquainted with the running of a women's concentration camp."[32] Soon after, Johanna Langefeld, the senior Ravensbrück camp supervisor, traveled in the opposite direction to oversee the new women's compound in Auschwitz; she was joined by more than a dozen female guards from Ravensbrück. When Langefeld arrived, the Auschwitz SS was already preparing the new compound for women, initially in blocks 1 to 10 of the main camp. On Höss's orders, a wall was hurriedly erected to separate it from the men's section.[33] The scene was being set for the huge increase in female prisoners during the second half of the war.

Destination Auschwitz

Systematic mass deportations of Jews to Auschwitz began in late March 1942. The first RSHA train, carrying 999 women from Slovakia, arrived on March 26; the next transport from Slovakia, with another 798 women, came two days later. Then, on March 30, the first mass transport from France, holding more than 1,100 men, pulled up near the camp.[34] The men on board had set off several days earlier, packed into freight cars with little food or drink; several died before the train reached its destination. Among those who arrived on the morning of March 30 was Stanisław Jankowski. Like many other Jews deported from France, the thirty-one-year-old carpenter was a Polish émigré. Jankowski had grown up in poverty in the city of Otwock, where he dedicated himself to the Communist movement. In 1937, he had traveled to Spain to fight in the civil war. Following the defeat of the Republican forces, his unit retreated over the French border in early 1939, where he was arrested. This was the beginning of more than two years of squalid internment on French soil, interrupted after Jankowski managed to escape from a camp in Argelès-sur-Mer and reached Paris. But he was quickly rearrested by the French police. First he was held in Drancy—a new internment camp for Jews in a Parisian suburb, from where the great majority of French transports to Auschwitz would depart—and later as a "hostage" of the German military authorities in Compiègne. It was here that Jankowski was isolated one day in

March 1942, together with other Jewish prisoners, and told that they would be sent for heavy labor to the east.

In Auschwitz, Jankowski and the other men marched in rows of five toward the main camp, driven forward by the sticks of SS men. They faced more violence inside the compound—including their first taste of SS "sport"—and received a pitiful portion of food. Soon they went on the move again. Surrounded by SS men on horses, they marched in double time to Birkenau, dragging their wooden shoes through the marshy soil. At the gate of the new enclosure, SS men and Kapos armed with clubs were waiting for them. Several prisoners were beaten to death, Stanisław Jankowski recalled, so that "the next ones had to jump over them to run inside the camp." Here, they assembled for their first roll call in Birkenau, exhausted, bleeding, and terrified, with mud all over their new uniforms. These uniforms held special significance. Just like the Slovakian women who had arrived a few days earlier, the Jewish men from France wore the clothes of the murdered Soviet prisoners of war. The Camp SS probably saw this as a convenient solution to the endemic shortages of clothing. But it also symbolized the fate of the new arrivals: they had come to Auschwitz to replace the POWs and, like them, they, too, would soon be dead. This symbolism was not lost on the Jewish prisoners themselves, who learned about the fate of Soviet POWs; there were even rumors that thousands of soldiers lay buried right underneath the Birkenau barracks that now housed the Jewish men.[35]

In spring 1942, Auschwitz was still a long way from becoming the "capital of the Holocaust," as the historian Peter Hayes has called it. To be sure, the camp was now involved in the emerging pan-European extermination program.[36] But the number of Jewish inmates still lagged far behind the figures announced by Himmler back in late January. By the end of June 1942, after RSHA deportations had been going on for three months, sixteen transports from France and Slovakia had brought no more than around sixteen thousand Jews to Auschwitz.[37] Also, none of these prisoners were supposed to be killed on arrival. They had been earmarked as forced laborers and the Auschwitz SS was meant to provide some minimal provision. Presumably, IKL managers were hoping to prevent a repeat of the rapid deaths of Soviet POWs; already a few months earlier, Arthur Liebehenschel had reminded commandants that "everything has to be done to preserve the Jews' ability to work."[38]

The reality turned out very differently. Even if Auschwitz was not yet a full-fledged death camp, it was already deadly for Jews; it is likely that two-thirds or more of all Jewish prisoners newly registered in spring and summer 1942 were dead within eight weeks.[39] Some RSHA transports were almost completely wiped out; three months after their arrival on April 19, just seventeen of 464 male Jews from the transit camp Žilina (Slovakia) were still alive. Among the dead were some boys, after the Slovakian authorities had begun to include families in the deportations; the youngest victim was seven-year-old Ernest Schwarcz, who had survived for barely one month.[40]

The Jewish men suffered dismal conditions, lethal violence, and draining labor in Birkenau. The local SS saw Birkenau as a camp for those condemned to die and oversaw a huge procession of death during spring 1942. The compound was still under construction and few of the primitive barracks were finished. Everything was caked in dirt and excrement, and even rudimentary facilities were lacking, as were medical supplies and food. Many Jewish men were forced into camp construction, though there was plenty of pointless labor, too. Prisoners who survived these rigors were shot, beaten to death, or killed in some other way, with selections of weak and unproductive inmates commencing in Birkenau around early May 1942.[41]

Less than two miles away, Jewish women in the Auschwitz main camp also faced a dreadful fate in spring 1942. They made up the great majority of prisoners in the new women's compound, which rapidly grew in size. Provisionally run by the Ravensbrück administration (only in July 1942 was it organizationally integrated into the Auschwitz complex), it soon outstripped its parent camp. By the end of April 1942, over 6,700 women were held in Auschwitz, compared to around 5,800 in Ravensbrück; within a month, Ravensbrück had been surpassed by the hastily improvised site in Auschwitz—an early sign of the Holocaust's impact on the wider SS camp system. More female prisoners arrived over the coming months, leaving the Auschwitz compound hopelessly overcrowded; by late June 1942, the SS had erected additional wooden barracks, squeezed between the old stone ones.

The women's compound was a sanitary disaster. Dysentery, pneumonia, and open wounds were widespread, and typhus was on the rise, too, as were injuries sustained during heavy labor in agriculture and construction. Many sick and weak women were selected for extermination; some were gassed, others injected with phenol. The ensuing mass death of women in Auschwitz was unprecedented in the history of the KL. By the time the surviving women were transferred to the new sector BIa in Birkenau in August 1942, perhaps one-third of the fifteen to seventeen thousand women who had been forced into the main camp since late March were dead.[42]

A Regional Killing Center

The Holocaust started to change Auschwitz. The camp complex grew and prisoner numbers soared, from around 12,000 in early January 1942 to around

21,400 in early May, and included thousands of women.[43] But Auschwitz was not transformed overnight; mass death, after all, had already marked the camp before, especially from autumn 1941, when Soviet POWs arrived and the extension in Birkenau was planned. And Auschwitz was still rather peripheral for the Holocaust in spring 1942. Its route to genocide took several months, with three key steps along the way. The first was the start of RSHA mass deportations from late March 1942, as we have just seen. The next one followed just a few weeks later.

In May 1942, Auschwitz became a regional death camp for the systematic slaughter of Silesian Jews.[44] Just as nonworking Jews from the Warthegau were being killed in Chelmno, Silesian Jews selected as unfit for work were killed in Auschwitz.[45] The Auschwitz SS now applied both elements of the Nazi Final Solution—immediate extermination and murderous forced labor—depending on where prisoner transports came from: "unfit" Silesian Jews would be murdered on arrival, while other Jews would be registered as regular inmates and worked to death. Again, such a parallel policy had precedents, mirroring the lethal approach of Auschwitz SS men to Soviet POWs in autumn 1941.[46]

The details of the development of Auschwitz into a regional Holocaust killing center remain shrouded in uncertainty. Original documents are missing, and postwar testimonies by key players like Rudolf Höss and Adolf Eichmann are inconsistent and inaccurate.[47] What is known is that Eichmann repeatedly visited Auschwitz to coordinate the so-called Final Solution. He built a close relationship with his "dear comrade and friend" Höss, whom he admired for his "exactness," his "modesty," and his "exemplary family life." The taciturn Höss recognized Eichmann as a kindred spirit, too, addressing him with the informal "Du," and after a long day's work, inspecting the camp or driving to one of the new buildings, these two zealous managers of mass murder would relax in each other's company, smoking and drinking heavily, followed by a joint breakfast the next morning.[48] It is likely that Eichmann first visited Auschwitz in spring 1942, probably in March or April. The RSHA deportations from France and Slovakia—which he masterminded—were getting under way, and he appears to have traveled to the camp to confer with Commandant Höss about these transports and about the next moves. Eichmann probably told him that transports of Jews, selected for immediate extermination, would soon arrive from Upper Silesia.[49] This was just one of many meetings, of course. Over the coming months, Eichmann held frequent conferences with Höss and senior Camp SS managers, prior to mass deportations, to determine the "capacity" of Auschwitz; "after all," Eichmann explained years later, the Auschwitz SS had to know "how much human material I was planning to send."[50]

The growing significance of Auschwitz for the Nazi Final Solution must have been on the agenda during a visit of WVHA boss Oswald Pohl around early April 1942, his first official visit to the camp since he had taken charge of the KL system.[51] Pohl was in close touch with Himmler during this period—meeting him repeatedly in mid-April—and he was no doubt in the picture about the general plans of Nazi leaders, who were finalizing the outline of their pan-European extermination policy.[52]

The death transports of Silesian Jews began soon after Pohl's visit to Auschwitz. During May 1942, around 6,500 Jews—selected as unfit for work—arrived from several towns in Upper Silesia. Many of them came from Będzin, just twenty-five miles away, where the first victims were rounded up by the German police and Jewish ghetto militia in a large "action" on May 12, inside the desolate and overcrowded Jewish sector of the small town, which had previously been an important hub for Jewish cultural and economic life in the region. During the following month, another estimated sixteen thousand Jews were deported from Silesia to Auschwitz, leading Nazi officials in several localities to proudly declare themselves "free of Jews."[53]

The Little Red House

The mass murder of Silesian Jews was witnessed by Filip Müller, a twenty-year-old Slovak Jew who had come to Auschwitz on April 13, 1942, and soon joined a special prisoner detail at the main camp crematorium, which had doubled as a gas chamber since autumn 1941. After the war, Müller testified to the arrival of several transports of Polish Jews in May and June 1942, including many elderly men and women, as well as mothers with children and babies. SS men led the prisoners into the yard outside the crematorium and told them to undress for a shower. Then they locked the victims into the dimly lit, windowless gas chamber inside the crematorium. Panic soon spread among the trapped prisoners. SS men shouted back: "Don't burn yourselves in the bath." Loud engine noises were supposed to drown out the sound of the death struggle, but those standing close to the crematorium, like Filip Müller, caught everything: "We suddenly heard heavy coughing. And the people screamed. You could hear the children, and all of them screamed." After some time, the screams died down and then they stopped altogether.[54]

The mass murder which began in the gas chamber of the main camp crematorium (later called crematorium I) soon continued in new killing facilities in Birkenau.[55] On a secluded spot near the birch forest, the SS turned an empty farmhouse into a gas chamber. Known as bunker 1, or the "little red house," the small building was easily transformed; windows were bricked up, doors insulated and reinforced, and small holes (concealed by flaps) drilled in the walls for the insertion of Zyklon B pellets. Hundreds of prisoners could be forced into two rooms, with wood shavings on the floor to soak up blood and feces.[56] Bunker 1 probably went into operation sometime in late May 1942, and gassings in the main camp crematorium ceased a few months later.[57]

The SS killers saw the relocation of mass gassings to Birkenau as a solution to the practical problems of genocide. Mass murder and the disposal of corpses was proving increasingly cumbersome in the creaking and overused old crematorium, and it attracted too much attention in the main camp; moving the gassings to the isolated Birkenau farmhouse would be more efficient and covert.[58] Moreover, as Birkenau became a large camp for doomed inmates—with many more on their way—mass selections among the registered inmates there grew more widespread. From the perspective of the SS men, it would be far easier to kill these selected prisoners in Birkenau itself, rather than transport them back to the gas chamber in the main camp. And so Birkenau was designated as the new center for mass extermination in the Auschwitz complex.

"FACTORIES OF DEATH"

On June 11, 1942, several SS managers of genocide, led by Adolf Eichmann, met in the offices of the RSHA Jewish Department in Berlin to discuss details of their Europe-wide deportation program. Their mood was grim. Just two days earlier, Reinhard Heydrich, Himmler's closest accomplice, had been buried during a bombastic state funeral, following his assassination by two British-trained agents from Czechoslovakia. Nazi leaders were already wreaking brutal vengeance against the Czech population and agreed that Jews would have to pay, too. During his eulogy for Heydrich on June 9, Himmler told SS generals that the time had come for "a clean sweep" against Jews: "We will wrap up the mass migration of the Jews within a year, no doubt; afterward, none of them will be migrating anymore." Auschwitz figured large in Himmler's thinking. As Eichmann explained two days later, during the meeting in the RSHA, Himmler had ordered the deportation of large numbers of Jewish men and women for forced labor to Auschwitz. The SS managers then hammered out the details: starting in mid-July 1942, some one hundred and twenty-five thousand Jewish men and women would be taken by train from France, Belgium, and the Netherlands to the camp. Himmler still envisaged most of these prisoners as slaves; the bulk of Jews deported to Auschwitz, he ordered, should be young (between sixteen and forty years) and ready for work. But he made a crucial exception: the transports could also include a smaller proportion of Jews—some ten percent—who were unfit for work. Their fate was clear to Eichmann and the other SS managers. They would be murdered on arrival.[59]

Preparing for Genocide

In Himmler's eyes, Auschwitz was ready to play a major part in the Holocaust. It had been designated as a large forced labor camp for Jews in early 1942, and he now decided that it could also become a sizable death camp. It was isolated enough for secretive mass murder, but close enough to receive deportations from western and central Europe, thanks to its good railway links.[60] What is more, the basic infrastructure for genocide was already in place, following the mass gassing of alleged commissars from the Soviet Union and of Jews from Silesia. After Auschwitz had proved itself as a regional extermination camp, it was promoted to the first rank of Nazi death camps. As Commandant Höss proudly put it the following year, the Auschwitz SS had been given an important new task: "the solution of the Jewish question."[61]

The new plans for Auschwitz triggered hectic activity among the Camp SS in June 1942. It was no coincidence, surely, that the head of the company distributing Zyklon B was called to Berlin around this time; the orders of gas deliveries for Auschwitz soon increased dramatically.[62] Inside the WVHA, key discussions involved Oswald Pohl, who was at Himmler's side on June 18 and 20, 1942.[63] Just a few days earlier, his KL manager Richard Glücks (now chief of WVHA office group D) had traveled to Auschwitz for face-to-face talks with the local executioners. Rudolf Höss complained after the war that Glücks did not like to hear about the so-called Final Solution.[64] This may have been true later on, when Glücks was increasingly sidelined, but initially he was hands-on, keeping in close touch with Adolf Eichmann and holding regular talks with his own opposite number in the RSHA, Gestapo head Heinrich Müller.[65] What is more, he was keen to impress his new boss, Pohl, with whom he met regularly to confer about the Holocaust.[66]

Glücks arrived in Auschwitz in the late afternoon of June 16, 1942, and probably stayed until the following day. He must have talked about Nazi extermination policy, since the death rate of registered Jewish prisoners shot up dramatically right after his visit.[67] Glücks also toured the camp. His itinerary apparently included the old crematorium in the main camp (now undergoing repairs) and the storeroom for the clothes of murdered prisoners.[68] Glücks must have been especially keen to see the new extermination facilities in

Birkenau. Bunker 1 was already in use. Meanwhile, a few hundred yards away, SS men were turning a second, slightly larger farmhouse—the "little white house"—into another gas chamber, almost certainly as a result of the recent decision to make Auschwitz a European death camp. Bunker 2 probably went into operation in late June or early July 1942.[69]

Just one week after Glücks's trip to Auschwitz, Rudolf Höss traveled to the WVHA headquarters in Berlin-Lichterfelde, where Pohl had called a meeting of all camp commandants for the evening of Thursday, June 25, 1942. The impending mass deportations to Auschwitz were no doubt on Höss's mind as he set off for the German capital. Not long before he left the camp on June 24 to catch the overnight train to Berlin, his staff sent a secret cable to Glücks, asking for a private appointment the following morning or afternoon, so that Höss could "discuss urgent, important matters with you, Brigadeführer." Glücks's staff quickly scheduled a meeting in the office of SS engineer Hans Kammler, who was intimately involved in all the major building projects in Auschwitz.[70] We do not know what the SS officers plotted during this meeting. But they must have touched on the preparation of Auschwitz for the arrival of vast numbers of Jewish deportees destined to die in the concentration camp.

Mass Deportations

Deportation trains from across Europe started to arrive in Auschwitz, as planned, from July 1942. In previous months, mass transports of Jews had still been more sporadic. Now, especially from mid-July 1942, they became routine. The transports, usually carrying around one thousand people, arrived on a daily basis; occasionally, two trains came on the same day. In all, more than sixty thousand Jews were taken to Auschwitz during July and August 1942, from France, Poland, the Netherlands, Belgium, Slovakia, and Croatia.[71] Determined to kill as many Jews as quickly as possible, the RSHA pushed for even more deportations. During a meeting in Berlin on August 28, 1942, Adolf Eichmann told his men to step up transports from Europe over the coming months. This must have been news to Commandant Rudolf Höss, who had been summoned from Auschwitz to attend the meeting (the following day, Höss briefed Glücks about it). From autumn 1942, regular transports rolled from the Greater German Reich, initially from Theresienstadt (Terezín) and Berlin. Then, in spring 1943, trains from Salonika arrived; the first four transports in March brought ten thousand Greek Jews to the camp. And in October 1943, after German forces had poured into Italy following its defection, the first RSHA train left from Rome for Auschwitz, with some 1,031 Jewish prisoners on board. Despite the geographical extension across Europe, however, Polish Jews still made up the largest group among the 468,000 Jews deported to Auschwitz during 1942–43.[72]

While the reach of the RSHA steadily grew, the number of death trains fluctuated wildly, rising and falling in line with the general pace of the Holocaust. In July 1943, for example, the RSHA deported fewer than 7,200 Jews to Auschwitz. One month later, more than fifty thousand arrived, after a renewed push to destroy ghettos in east Upper Silesia.[73] Most trains arrived from such ghettos and from transit or internment camps. As in the case of Stanisław Jankowski, the prisoners had often been shunted from one camp to another, with the KL the last link in a long chain. There were many Jewish camps across Europe, some like Westerbork (Netherlands) still well known, others like Žilina (Slovakia) long since forgotten.[74] Not all these sites were staffed by German authorities. Drancy, for example, was guarded by French policemen until the SS took over in summer 1943.[75] Conditions in the camps varied greatly; though they were often poor, they were generally not lethal. Crucially, none of these transit camps were run by the WVHA as SS concentration camps, except for Herzogenbusch (Vught) in the Netherlands.

Herzogenbusch, in the district of Noord-Brabant, was not initially conceived as a KL. In summer 1942, Hanns Albin Rauter, the higher SS and police leader in the Netherlands, decided to set up an additional large camp for Jews: before they "depart for the East," they would be held there during the "general cleanup in the Netherlands." But in December 1942, the site was placed under the WVHA as an official concentration camp (Rauter still stayed in the picture, though, resulting in repeated conflicts with the WVHA). The so-called transit camp for Jews was opened on January 16, 1943, with "many buildings only half-finished," recalled Arthur Lehmann, a German Jewish lawyer in his early fifties. The new camp quickly filled and by early May 1943, more than 8,600 Jewish men, women, and children were detained here. Many had been officially exempted from immediate deportation, giving them false hope that Herzogenbusch would become a regular ghetto in all but name.[76]

At this time, Herzogenbusch bore only superficial similarities to a KL like Auschwitz. True, there were purpose-built barracks, roll calls, SS guards, and work. But here the resemblance ended. To deceive the Jewish inmates about their ultimate fate, the Herzogenbusch SS acted with far more restraint. For a start, prisoners were allowed to keep their own clothes and belongings; Arthur Lehmann, with his glasses and tussled hair, looked more like a professor than a prisoner. Conditions during labor—which later included work for the Philips electronics company—were mostly bearable. And although prisoners were divided by gender, with children joining their mothers, the men and women were allowed to visit each other regularly. Most important, much of the internal organization lay in the hands of imprisoned Jews themselves, just like in Nazi ghettos. Jewish leaders like Lehmann, who became chief of the internal administration, controlled funds for purchases from the canteen, organized food distribution, and maintained links with lawyers and relatives outside the camp. There was also a Jewish camp police (*Ordnungsdienst*), which patrolled the camp and its storeroom, and met new arrivals at the railway station. Inmates accused of theft and other infractions came before a prisoner court, headed by a former judge, rather than facing SS punishment. Overall, there was little abuse inside the camp, and the Camp SS maintained a low profile. All this was reflected in the comparatively small mortality rate, with around one hundred deaths—almost all of them infants or elderly—among all the twelve thousand Jews who passed through the camp.

Jews arriving in the Herzogenbusch transit camp were relieved that conditions were better than they had feared. When Helga Deen, an eighteen-year-old from Tilburg, came to the camp on June 1, 1943, she noted in her secret diary that "until now, it is not as bad as all that," adding: "there is nothing dreadful here." But the lethal SS intentions were merely masked; terror lurked and it soon raised its head. In July 1943, after barely one month in the camp, Helga Deen and her family were deported to the east and murdered. This was part of a larger SS action in summer 1943, during which the great majority of Jewish prisoners in Herzogenbusch—more than ten thousand—were sent to their deaths in Sobibor; for them, life in the KL had been no more than a brief lull on the road to a death camp. Among the small number of prisoners left behind, who now had their privileges cut, were some skilled workers at the Philips factory and a few Jewish leaders, such as Arthur Lehmann. The truth about Nazi intentions was slowly dawning on them, but their special status in the camp could not save them from deportation, and in early June 1944, the SS removed the last group of Jews from Herzogenbusch. "I am very melancholic," one of them scribbled in a note on the train to Auschwitz. Lehmann himself had already been taken away in March 1944, and eventually ended up in the Auschwitz satellite camp at Laurahütte. Compared to a KL like Auschwitz, he later wrote, conditions in Vught had been "extraordinarily good."[77]

Although Auschwitz played an increasingly important part in the Holocaust from summer 1942, it was a junior partner early on, far surpassed by other sites of terror. The main hubs for lethal Jewish forced labor were still located elsewhere. At the end of 1942, just 12,650 Jewish prisoners were registered in Auschwitz. By comparison, nearly three hundred thousand Jews were still alive in the General Government, according to the SS, most of them toiling in large ghettos like Warsaw (fifty thousand inmates). Ghettos in other parts of Nazi Europe, such as Lodz (eighty-seven thousand) and Theresienstadt (fifty thousand), also held far more Jews than Auschwitz. Even in Silesia itself, Auschwitz was still outstripped by regional forced labor camps for Jews under SS Oberführer Albrecht Schmelt.[78] As for Auschwitz as a death camp, it was eclipsed by Globocnik's death camps. In 1942, around 190,000 Jews died in Auschwitz, the great majority of them in the Birkenau gas chambers.[79] By contrast, the three Globocnik death camps claimed around 1,500,000 victims that year; more than 800,000 were murdered in Treblinka alone, a small number of Gypsies among them.[80] It was only during 1943—when Belzec, Sobibor, and Treblinka were wound down, having fulfilled their mission of murdering most Jews in the General Government, and when most of the remaining ghettos and labor camps were eradicated, too—that Auschwitz moved into the center of the Holocaust.[81]

Arrival in Auschwitz

One freezing morning in late 1942, a large column of Polish Jews set off from a square outside the gates of Mława ghetto (Zichenau district) and marched through sludge and snow on the open roads toward the town's railway station. The men, women, and children were cold and exhausted, having spent the previous night among the dark ruins of a large mill on the ghetto grounds. But belligerent German guards set a brisk pace and the Jews stumbled forward, carrying rucksacks, suitcases, and bundles with their last possessions. Among them was Lejb Langfus, a religious scholar in his early thirties, his wife, Deborah, and their eight-year-old son, Samuel. Like many others on the march, they had recently been deported to Mława from the small ghetto Maków Mazowiecki, which was liquidated by the Nazi authorities during the second half of November 1942. Bathed in sweat, Langfus and the others eventually arrived at the railway station, where police and SS men forced them to line up alongside a train and then pushed them inside. Some families were separated in the confusion, but Langfus apparently held on to his wife and son, and they squeezed into one of the boxcars. After all the doors were sealed, sometime around midday, the train slowly pulled away. It was heading for Auschwitz.[82]

Conditions inside were unbearable, as on most trains to death camps from eastern Europe. After mass deportations of Jews intensified in summer 1942, the German authorities in the east relied on closed, windowless freight trains, which quickly filled with the stench of the sick, urine, and excrement on the floor. Lejb Langfus and the others were standing upright, pressed together so tightly that they could not sit, kneel, or lie down, or reach the provisions in their bags. Soon, everyone in the stifling car was desperate for something to drink. "Thirst ruled everything," Langfus later wrote in secret notes in Auschwitz. An eerie silence settled over his car. Most people were only half-conscious, too drained to talk. The children were listless, too, with their "cracked lips and completely dried-out throats." There was only one moment of respite: when the train briefly stopped, two policemen appeared at the door and gave prisoners some water, in exchange for their wedding rings.[83]

In addition to hunger and thirst, there was crippling fear. Most men, women, and children on this and other deportation trains did not know that they were heading to Auschwitz, and to their deaths. But many Polish Jews had heard of the camp. Langfus, for example, knew it as a notorious punishment camp and a destination for Jewish transports. There were also rumors about mass extermination inside. Jews who lived closer to Auschwitz even heard about prisoners being thrown into "furnaces" or "gassed to death," as a local girl from Będzin noted in her diary in early 1943. Despite such rumors, some deported Polish prisoners remained defiantly upbeat. "We are off to work. Think positive," declared a letter thrown from another train en route from a Polish ghetto to Auschwitz in late 1942. But there was no way of masking the underlying anxieties. While Jews deported from central and western Europe had lived far from the epicenter of the Holocaust and often remained more hopeful that all that awaited them was hard labor (as German officials had promised them before departure and as postcards by friends and relatives, written under duress from the SS, seemed to confirm), Polish Jews had already suffered many months of misery and violence in the ghettos. Langfus and his family had lived through shortages and epidemics, and had witnessed beatings, slave labor, public executions, and murders. Like elsewhere in occupied Poland, talk about Nazi massacres in ghettos and camps had spread during 1942, and when the inhabitants of Maków Mazowiecki were told that they, too, would soon be deported, they were gripped by anxiety. Little Samuel Langfus sobbed inconsolably, screaming again and again: "I want to live!" His distraught father feared the worst, too. Shortly before he boarded the train to Auschwitz, Lejb Langfus spent a restless night in Mława, agonizing with others about their fate: "We were thinking about what would await us at the end of this journey: death or life?"[84]

The Auschwitz SS knew the answer. The camp authorities were routinely alerted about impending transports—by the responsible local police authorities or the RSHA (or both)—so that preparations could be made.[85] Once a train approached, which could happen at all hours, the well-oiled SS machine got into gear. The officer on duty blew a whistle to alert the Commandant Staff, shouting: "Transport is here!" SS officers, doctors, drivers, block leaders, and the rest quickly took their positions. Medical orderlies sometimes drove straight to the gas chambers in Birkenau. Meanwhile, dozens of SS men climbed on trucks and motorcycles, and headed for the "Jews' ramp" (*Judenrampe*), part of a new freight station between the camps of Auschwitz and Birkenau (from May 1944, transports arrived at another ramp inside Birkenau itself). As the train pulled up along the lengthy wooden platform, SS guards formed "a chain around the transport," SS officer Franz Hössler testified in 1945; then the order was given to open the doors.[86]

The shock of arrival in Auschwitz was overwhelming. Lejb, Deborah, and Samuel Langfus, and the other Jews from Mława, had been in a daze for over a day when their train came to a sudden halt, late on December 6, 1942. Then everything seemed to happen at once. The doors flung open, and SS men and some inmates in striped uniforms hurried the Jews off the trains. To speed things up, they screamed and pushed those who hesitated. There were kicks and blows, though the guards rarely went further. Restraint was more likely to guarantee order and compliance, since it helped to deceive the victims about their fate. In great haste, the 2,500 or so Jews from Mława spilled onto the platform, clutching each other and their belongings; left behind were the bodies of old people and children who had been crushed to death during the journey.

Emerging from the dark train, the dazed prisoners blinked into harsh lights that "clouded their minds," Lejb Langfus wrote some months later, in secret. Lampposts illuminated the large area around them, teeming with SS men with weapons and guard dogs. Amid the turmoil and terror, the bewildered Jews were forced to move away from the train and leave behind their bags, bundles, and suitcases, which were then piled up by inmates from the so-called Canada Commando. The loss of their possessions paralyzed the new arrivals, but they had no time to think before the SS told them to line up in two groups, men on one side, and women and most children on the other. The order left many prisoners numb. They had arrived in large families, but the guards quickly drove them apart, as siblings and spouses, sons and daughters, frantically tried to embrace one more time. "Dreadful crying could be heard," noted Lejb Langfus, who had to let go of his wife and son. As the two columns formed, several yards apart, many prisoners lost sight of their loved ones and never saw them again. The columns, with five prisoners in each row, soon moved forward toward a small group of SS men who, as Langfus learned, decided their destiny: "The selection began."[87]

In Auschwitz, regular SS selections of Jews on arrival had started in summer 1942, following Himmler's decision that Jews unable to work should join the RSHA deportation trains.[88] Since all Jews on board were doomed, Himmler had apparently approved selections as a means to determine when and how they would perish. Some would be registered for murderous forced labor; the rest would be gassed straightaway. By the time Lejb Langfus and the others from Mława arrived in Auschwitz—on one of the more than a dozen deportation transports in December 1942—such selections had long become routine.[89] SS men were in a hurry and acted "pretty haphazardly," according to the postwar confession of Rottenführer Pery Broad from the Auschwitz political office; often, the selections were over in one hour. As individual Jews stumbled forward to the head of the ramp, the SS officer in charge—mostly the camp doctor on duty, supported by other senior officials like the camp compound leaders and labor action leaders—had a quick glance, asked some of them about their age and occupation, and then gave a nod or wave, casually pointing to the left or the right. At the time, few prisoners knew that this brief gesture meant immediate death or temporary reprieve.[90]

The Auschwitz SS officials agreed on broad benchmarks for the selection of Jews, going beyond the criteria they had established during the earlier selections of suspected Soviet commissars.[91] Dr. Fritz Klein, one of the Auschwitz SS physicians, put it succinctly: "It was the doctor's job to pick out those who were unfit or unable to work. These included children, old people, and the sick."[92] Like everywhere else during the Nazi war on Jews, children were most vulnerable. Between 1942 and 1945, around 210,000 were deported to Auschwitz. Those under the age of fourteen were almost all gassed on arrival; so, too, were most of the older ones. In all, fewer than 2,500 Jewish children survived the initial selections.[93] Many Jewish women were in great danger, too, even if they were in good health, as the SS murdered most mothers with younger children, rather than separating them at the ramp.[94] Some mothers, meanwhile, abandoned their children with the best of intentions. After Olga Lengyel arrived in Auschwitz, she was determined to protect her son, Arvad, from what she feared would be hard labor. When she was asked by Dr. Klein how old her boy was, she insisted that he was under thirteen, although he looked older. Dr. Klein duly sent Arvad to the gas chambers. "How should I have known," Lengyel wrote in despair after the war.[95]

Some new arrivals learned the truth just in time. As they climbed off the trains or waited at the ramp, inmates from the Canada Commando defied SS orders and told them three basic rules for the selections: act strong and healthy, claim to be between sixteen and forty years old, hand young children to elderly relatives.[96] Such advice saved a number of Jews, at least temporarily.[97] But it also caused dreadful dilemmas. Mothers, in particular, faced a split-second decision. To abandon their children on the barely comprehensible advice of a stranger? Or to join them and stand with a group ominously made up of the elderly and frail? There was no right decision based on ordinary moral norms. Instead, it was one of the "choiceless choices" in Auschwitz, as the scholar Lawrence Langer called them.[98]

Most Jews were murdered within hours of the selections at the ramp. In general, Commandant Höss always wanted more slaves; when SS Oberführer Schmelt interrupted deportation trains bound for Auschwitz and pulled out Jewish men for his own labor camps, Höss and Eichmann agreed to foil such preselections, which deprived Auschwitz of the best workers.[99] When it came to selections at the Auschwitz ramp, however, Höss was adamant that "only the very healthiest and very strongest Jews" should be spared. Otherwise, the camp would be overburdened by needy prisoners, creating worse conditions for everyone.[100] Although there was some internal criticism of Höss's hardline approach, many Auschwitz SS men shared it. Despite all the talk of forced labor, Rottenführer Pery Broad testified, these men saw "the annihilation of the largest number of 'enemies of the state' as their primary task."[101] Some senior SS officers agreed, among them Reich physician Ernst Grawitz, who observed the mass murder in Auschwitz and supported extensive gassings as a radical weapon against illness in the KL.[102] By contrast, Oswald Pohl and senior WVHA managers repeatedly reprimanded Höss, arguing that the Auschwitz SS should select as many Jews as possible for forced labor, including weak ones who could be deployed for a short period of time only.[103] SS leader Heinrich Himmler, the ultimate authority, wavered between both sides of the argument.[104]

In the end, the default option for SS officers at the Auschwitz ramp was to point toward the gas chambers; on average, only around twenty percent of Jews were selected for forced labor and registered as Auschwitz prisoners (though there were significant variations between transports and over time).[105] The SS applied a similar measure on the night of December 6, 1942, to the transport from Mława. Only 406 young and strong men were temporarily spared (unusually, the SS condemned all women on board). Among the chosen few was Lejb Langfus. His wife, Deborah, and his son, Samuel, disappeared into the other group, more than two thousand people strong. Langfus watched intently as women and children calmly climbed on board large SS trucks, illuminated in the bright lights. Many prisoners were deceived by the sight of polite SS men aiding ailing Jews onto the trucks, mistaking it as a sign of charity. Other SS men reassured the remaining Jewish men that they would soon meet their loved ones again; Langfus was told that he would see his family once a week. Then the trucks drove off and made their way to the gas chambers.[106]

Fire and Gas

The other Jews selected for the gas normally followed the same road as the trucks, marching for one and a half miles from the ramp, past the Birkenau camp and across a meadow, toward the converted farmhouses. "This is a one-way street," Charlotte Delbo (who arrived from France in early 1943) later wrote, "but no one knows it." During the march, SS men normally kept the prisoners in line with guard dogs. But they also kept up the deception, casually asking Jews about their jobs and background, and telling them that they were heading to the baths, for disinfection. Some prisoners were relieved to notice that they were followed by an ambulance, which was driving slowly at the rear of the column; occasionally, it even carried Jews unable to walk. But the ambulance was not meant to provide medical care. Its real purpose was to carry the SS doctor to oversee the gassing. The tins of Zyklon B were also on board. "Nobody was bothered in the slightest," Commandant Höss recalled, "about profaning the sign of the Red Cross by driving to the extermination facilities."[107]

When the final destination came into view, the first impression was reassuring: a little farmhouse and two wooden barracks (for undressing), surrounded by fruit trees. On site were more SS men and a group of inmates from the so-called Special Squad (*Sonderkommando*), who had to assist in mass murder. By the time the prisoner column had come to a halt, those who had earlier arrived by truck were often already inside the farmhouse. Before long, the others had joined them. Those who moved too slowly were hit by SS men and attacked by the dogs. As they stumbled inside, the last thing they saw was a sign on the open doors: "To the Baths." Once the rooms had been crammed full of men, women, and children, the heavy doors were locked and the SS physician ordered the medical orderly to throw in the gas. SS doctor Johann Paul Kremer, who supervised numerous gassings in autumn 1942, later testified that he drove off after the "screams and noise of the victims" had died down.[108] The gas chambers remained off-limits for some time, often overnight, as there was no mechanical ventilation in bunkers 1 and 2 to draw out the fumes.[109]

Once the doors were opened, prisoners from the special squad set to work. One of them was Lejb Langfus. After the SS had separated him from his wife and son at the ramp on December 6, 1942, he had marched into the Birkenau compound, together with the other Jewish men selected that day for slave labor. The next morning, they had been led from their barrack to the so-called Birkenau sauna for the usual admissions procedure. After a shower, they had their heads shaved and received striped uniforms; then they were tattooed. Two days later, on the evening of December 9, 1942, SS men led by Hauptscharführer Otto Moll suddenly appeared in the prisoners' barrack and announced that they would choose some strong inmates for a special assignment in a rubber factory. Each prisoner stepped forward and Moll took his pick. None of the three hundred or so Jewish men knew that they had really been selected for the Special Squad. Neither did they know that at the same time the corpses of their predecessors—the first Birkenau Special Squad—were burning inside the old crematorium.

The following day, December 10, most men from the new Special Squad were escorted out of the Birkenau compound, not to any rubber factory, but to the gas chambers, which were operating at full capacity that day (with almost 4,500 Jews arriving on transports from Holland, Germany, and Poland). Surrounded by SS men with guard dogs, Moll addressed the new Special Squad prisoners. They did not yet know that this small, blond man, who looked rather amiable, with his round and freckled face, was feared across the camp. Not only was he exceptionally brutal, Moll was also one of a small group of Camp SS experts in mass murder and cremation. After he had instructed the prisoners about their real task, he threatened anyone who refused to participate with beatings and wild dogs.[110]

The prisoners of the two Special Squads—one for each of the converted farmhouses—now split into different groups. Among the dozen or so prisoners who had to pull bodies out of the gas chambers on December 10, 1942, was a burly twenty-year-old with broad shoulders called Shlomo (Szlama) Dragon. Born in a small Polish town, he had lived for more than a year in the Warsaw ghetto, where his father and sister were to die, before escaping together with his older brother, Abraham. Exhausted, after hiding for months without papers, the two brothers eventually joined a transport to what they assumed was a forced labor camp. On December 6, 1942, they arrived in Auschwitz, on the same train that brought the muscular Lejb Langfus to the camp; like Langfus, the Dragon brothers were selected for the Special Squad.[111]

Wearing masks, Shlomo Dragon and the other men from his commando had to enter the gas chambers after they were opened on December 10, 1942; "it was very hot" inside, he testified a few years later, "and one could feel the gas." Next, they had to drag out the entangled corpses. Complaining that the prisoners from the Special Squad were moving too carefully, Moll showed them how it was done. "He rolled up his sleeves," Dragon recalled, "and threw the corpses through the door into the yard." Here, other Special Squad members stripped the dead of anything the SS regarded as valuable. Some prisoners had to cut the hair of the dead, while so-called dentists pried open the corpses' foaming mouths to rip out gold teeth (some "dentists" took regular breaks to vomit). Once the building was empty, Special Squad prisoners had to wash the floors, scatter more wood shavings, and touch up the white walls, until the bunker was ready for the next transport.[112] From now on, this would be the life of Shlomo and Abraham Dragon, Lejb Langfus, and the others from the Special Squad.

Like many mass murderers before them, the Auschwitz SS men soon realized that it was easier to kill than to dispose of the victims. In their haste to create a large death camp, SS planners had given little thought to the corpses. When the mass extermination transports began in summer 1942, there was no working crematorium: the old one was out of commission, while the new one in Birkenau was not yet built. As the bodies of Jews gassed in Birkenau mounted up, the SS resorted to the same makeshift solution it had used months earlier, during the mass deaths of Soviet POWs, and buried the bodies in ditches in the Birkenau forest (together with thousands of deceased registered prisoners). But this soon proved impractical. By the time Himmler visited in mid-July 1942, the camp was engulfed in a sickening smell. In the heat of the summer, rotting body parts spilled out of mass graves, and there were concerns that the groundwater would be contaminated, threatening the whole region. With more extermination transports on the way, the Camp SS hurried to accelerate the completion of the new crematorium in Birkenau.[113]

Looking ahead, the WVHA construction experts around Hans Kammler agreed that a single new crematorium would no longer suffice, given the role of Auschwitz in the Holocaust. By August 1942, they had settled on three additional crematoria for Birkenau; together, the four new buildings would be able to burn one hundred and twenty thousand corpses each month. Soon, SS planners added an additional feature to the emerging Birkenau crematorium complex—gas chambers. Moving the gassings from the converted farmhouses into the new crematoria would allow the SS to murder and burn the victims in the same location (just like in the main camps' old crematorium). Genocide would become more efficient. The almost identical crematoria II and III were now redesigned for mass murder, by turning the morgues in the basement into undressing rooms and gas chambers; mechanical ventilation was fitted to draw out the gas, and a lift was added for moving corpses to the incinerators on the ground floor. By contrast, the smaller crematoria IV and

V had simpler structures, as they were designed from the start to accommodate mass gassings; both were long above-ground brick buildings, with undressing rooms, gas chambers (naturally ventilated), and incinerators, all on one level.[114]

Until this new cremation complex in Birkenau was operational, the SS decided, the dead would be put into flaming pits. Shortly after his mid-July 1942 visit to Auschwitz, Himmler decreed that all the rotting corpses in Birkenau had to be dug up and burned. Standartenführer Paul Blobel, an SS expert in open-air cremation, was sent to teach the Auschwitz guards. A former commander with the murderous task forces in the occupied Soviet Union, Blobel had recently been appointed to run a secret SS unit devising the most efficient way of destroying corpses of Holocaust victims. Experimenting in the Chelmno death camp, where huge numbers of corpses had accumulated, Blobel quickly arrived at an effective procedure: burning the dead in holes, grinding their bones, and scattering the remains. On September 16, 1942, shortly after Blobel's visit to Auschwitz, Commandant Höss himself traveled to Chelmno to watch the mass cremations in action. He was so impressed that he immediately placed an order for the necessary equipment, including a heavy bone-crushing machine. Within days, the new procedures were in place, largely modeled on Chelmno.

For several weeks in autumn 1942, the SS forced Special Squad prisoners to unearth all the corpses buried in Birkenau, working day and night with their bare hands. By the end, the prisoners had pulled out more than one hundred thousand bodies (by the estimate of Rudolf Höss). One of the Special Squad prisoners, Erko Hejblum, later described the task: "We waded in a mix of mud and decaying bodies. We would have needed gas masks. The corpses seemed to rise to the top—it was as if the earth itself was turning them back." Many Special Squad prisoners could not bear the nightmare. After one week, Hejblum "felt like I was going mad" and decided to kill himself; he was saved by a friend who engineered his transfer to a different work detail. Several prisoners who refused to carry on were shot point-blank. The others had to continue to stack the decomposing bodies for burning, first in huge pyres, later in long rectangular ditches. Meanwhile, the bodies of new victims deported to Auschwitz for mass extermination were cremated in other pits, near the bunkers. Ash and bone fragments were dumped into rivers and marshes. They were also used to fertilize the surrounding fields, where Himmler's cherished agricultural experiments were under way. The roots of Germany's future settlements were supposed to grow from the remains of its slaughtered victims.[115]

The Birkenau Killing Complex

The new facilities in Birkenau—four huge crematoria with integral gas chambers—promised state-of-the-art genocide. But the construction of the new killing complex took much longer than anticipated. The Camp SS continued to push for its completion, blaming the persistent problems on Topf & Sons, the private contractors building the incinerators. After months of delays and recriminations, the four crematoria became operational between March and June 1943.[116] At the end of June 1943, the head of the Auschwitz SS construction authority, Sturmbannführer Karl Bischoff, reported to his superiors in Berlin that the four crematoria could turn 4,416 corpses into ash within twenty-four hours.[117] So pleased was Bischoff, he even displayed pictures of the crematoria in the Auschwitz main building, for all visitors to see.[118] Senior SS officials were proudly shown around the new site. In March 1943, WVHA officers apparently attended the first incineration in crematorium II, and once the entire complex seemed ready for use, SS tours often included the new facilities. When Oswald Pohl came to Auschwitz in August 1943, for one of his regular visits, he carried out a thorough inspection of the new crematoria area. Himmler also sent leading party and SS men to watch and learn. "They were all deeply impressed," Rudolf Höss recalled.[119] Following the hurried initial conversion of Auschwitz into a death camp, the SS had now created more lasting and methodical procedures. In the words of Primo Levi, the camp became an inverted factory: "trains heavily laden with human beings went in each day, and all that came out was the ashes of their bodies, their hair, the gold of their teeth."[120]

This image of Auschwitz as a factory of death evokes its modern nature, with the reliance on bureaucracy, railways, and technology.[121] The use of machinery even extended to the bookkeeping of the dead. After each selection on arrival, an SS man from the Auschwitz political office—which oversaw the process of mass extermination at the crematoria—established how many Jews had been sent to the gas chambers. He then raced back by motorcycle to his office to prepare a statistical report noting the transport's date of arrival and place of departure, the total number of Jews on board, and the number of men and women selected for forced labor and for "special accommodation" or "special treatment" (the Camp SS continued to use camouflage language in documents, with only rare slips). The Auschwitz political office then transmitted these details by telex to the RSHA and the WVHA, mostly within a day of the killings; sometimes the officials added a brief explanatory note, such as the following from a February 1943 telex: "The men are specially accommodated because of excessive frailty, the women because most of them were [with] children."[122] In this way, SS managers in Berlin, such as Adolf Eichmann and Richard Glücks, gained an immediate picture—almost in real time—of the progress of the Holocaust in Auschwitz.

But assembly-line mass murder was not smooth, automatic, and clean, as some historians have suggested.[123] The Birkenau killing complex was less efficient than the SS men had hoped.[124] And however much routine they developed, killing did not become a purely mechanical process, devoid of agency and emotion. Every victim had perpetrators.[125] The doomed prisoners' last hours—between arrival and death—were marked by exhaustion, fear, and torment. Following the traumatic separations by the SS at the ramp and the transfer to Birkenau, the doomed faced humiliation and violence outside the gas chambers. Women who refused to undress were assaulted, the clothes ripped from their bodies. Anyone who refused to enter the gas chamber was shot on the spot or beaten inside.[126] What happened next, when dim suspicion became horrible certainty—with prisoners squeezed against one another in the darkness of the gas chambers, barely able to breathe even before the gas pellets were inserted—cannot be described. Standing outside, inmates from the Special Squad could hear that the death struggle lasted for several minutes; some of the dying threw themselves against the doors, sometimes smashing the glass peepholes and grilles protecting them, and crushing others who already lay on the ground.[127] On occasion, the gas chambers were so packed that the SS forced some prisoners to wait nearby until it was their turn. They listened to the agony of those inside and waited for hours for their own deaths, suffering "the most terrifying pain in the whole world," as Lejb Langfus wrote in his secret notes. "If you have not experienced it, you cannot picture it, even remotely."[128]

Another myth—also attached to the image of Auschwitz as a factory of death—is that of wholly passive victims.[129] Here, the doomed appear like inert objects, drifting to their deaths without disrupting the steady flow of industrialized mass murder. This view was taken to the extreme by the psychologist Bruno Bettelheim, himself a survivor of the prewar KL (having been held in Dachau and Buchenwald between June 1938 and May 1939). In a brief paper written in 1960, still unsettling decades later, he launched an all-out attack on the victims: the Jews of Europe had given up the will to live and then, "like lemmings," voluntarily walked "themselves to the gas chambers."[130]

Bettelheim was grievously wrong. To start with, only a small number of Jews arriving at the Auschwitz gas chambers were certain that they were about to die. The burning ditches and smoking chimneys of the crematoria were ominous signs, but even those who feared the worst often clung to hope. Such hopes were continually fanned by SS men. Despite flashes of violence, the Camp SS tried to deceive its victims to the end, in order to prevent any defiance by the doomed. Before the killings began, SS officers normally made a brief announcement outside the gas chambers, along the following lines: "Stay calm, you are about to take a bath—so get undressed, fold your clothes neatly and then walk into the shower-room. Afterwards, you will receive coffee and something to eat."

To further reassure the doomed, prisoners from the Special Squad generally repeated the same story, well aware that anything else might lead to their own death (in summer 1943, a Special Squad prisoner, who had informed a young woman that she would be gassed, was burned alive in front of his comrades). Racked by their helplessness, the Special Squad prisoners concluded that telling the truth would only add to the agony of the victims.[131] "It was all lies, what we said," one of them told an interviewer after the war. "I always tried not to look into [people's] eyes, so that they wouldn't catch on."[132] Some inmates elsewhere in the Auschwitz complex understood only too well the impossible dilemma of the Special Squad.[133]

Even when prisoners were told about their impending death, an organized uprising was impossible. They were disorientated—tired, famished, hurried along by guards—and had no time to think or confer. After a transport of Jews from Tarnów ghetto heard from Special Squad prisoners at the gas chambers that they were about to be killed, they "became serious and silent," according to one of the Special Squad. Then, with broken voices, "they started saying the Vidui" (the ritual confessional prayer before death). Not everyone could believe that they had been condemned, though; a young man stepped on a bench to calm the others, telling them that they would not die, as the wholesale slaughter of innocents, in such barbaric fashion, could not happen anywhere on earth.[134] All this anguish—which would sometimes turn into spontaneous defiance—was a long way from "a voluntary walk into the Reich's crematoria," as Bettelheim had claimed.[135]

GENOCIDE AND THE KL SYSTEM

The Holocaust transformed the concentration camp system as a whole in 1942–43. Geographically, it was split in two. In the western KL, there were soon hardly any Jewish prisoners left at all, after the SS made its camps inside Germany's prewar borders almost entirely "free of Jews." In the eastern KL, by contrast, Jews selected for murder through labor (instead of immediate extermination) now often made up the largest group among registered inmates. By autumn 1943, many tens of thousands of Jews were held in the east (hundreds of thousands more had already been murdered), not just in Auschwitz, but also in Majdanek and in several new concentration camps, which had been established solely for Jewish prisoners.

The Majdanek Death Camp

Majdanek in the General Government was the only other KL, apart from Auschwitz, which also operated as a Holocaust death camp. Its conversion followed a rather similar trajectory. Just as in Auschwitz, mass deportations of Jews began in spring 1942, initially to replace Soviet slave laborers for the projected SS settlements. In all, around 4,500 young Slovak Jews came to Majdanek between late March and early April 1942. One of their first tasks was to flatten the mass graves of Soviet POWs who had died during the previous months—a grim harbinger of the Jews' own impending fate.[136] Over the coming months, thousands more Jewish men arrived from Slovakia, as well as from the General Government, occupied Czech territory, and the German Reich.[137] Majdanek now grew at a rapid rate. On March 25, 1942, the camp had stood almost empty, with little more than one hundred prisoners, none of them Jewish. Just three months later, on June 24, 1942, some 10,660 men were held inside, almost all of them Jews. Soon, they were joined by women. Following the example of Auschwitz, Himmler ordered in July 1942 that a camp for female prisoners should be set up in Lublin; the WVHA attached it to Majdanek. The first prisoners arrived in October 1942, and by the end of the year, some 2,803 women were held in the camp, again overwhelmingly Jews.[138] As Majdanek was pulled into the current of the Holocaust, it turned into a concentration camp for Jews.

Majdanek was still a big building site, spread across dirty fields. There was no electricity, sewer system, or proper water supply, and many prisoners were packed into bare, crowded, windowless wooden barracks, freezing in winter, baking hot in summer (only in 1943 did the situation improve somewhat). One of these prisoners was Dionys Lenard, a Slovakian Jew who had been deported to Majdanek in April 1942. After a few months, he fled and recorded his experiences later that same year. Lenard writes graphically how the prisoners were forced to build the camp, erecting more barracks, leveling the ground, and performing other grueling tasks, always hounded by the SS. The frantic pace was set by Commandant Karl Otto Koch, who had arrived in early 1942; he was joined by trusted SS veterans from the Buchenwald Commandant Staff, fresh from participating in the mass execution of Soviet "commissars." It says much about slave labor in Majdanek that prisoners volunteered for the "shit commando" to escape from the construction details; in Majdanek, heaving buckets full of feces from the latrines was still better than being chased across the yard while carrying heavy loads of brick or wood.

Prisoners like Dionys Lenard were forever tormented by hunger and thirst. The food in Majdanek was as disgusting as it was meager, often consisting of thin soup with weeds. There was barely anything to drink, either, since inmates were initially forbidden to use the only well, which stood right next to the overflowing latrines and was said to be contaminated. The desperate water shortage also meant that prisoners could only clean themselves once a week. Lenard did so more often by using the warm liquid (so-called coffee) prisoners received in the mornings: "one could not use it for anything else, anyway." Fleas and lice spread everywhere, and half the inmates, Lenard observed, were suffering from diarrhea. And then there was the dirt. As soon as it rained, even a little, the whole camp was submerged in sludge. "Anyone who has not seen the mud in the Lublin camp, has no idea what mud really looks like," wrote Lenard. He could barely walk across the soggy fields without getting stuck with his wooden clogs. A slip could be fatal. Once, an old Slovakian Jew tripped and brushed the trouser legs of a passing SS man, who instantly "drew his gun and shot him."[139]

Lenard was one of a small number of registered Jews who survived Majdanek in 1942. Most succumbed to neglect and abuse; that year, more than fourteen thousand registered Jewish prisoners died in the camp, as well as around two thousand other inmates. As a WVHA official noted after an inspection in January 1943, the two incinerators in Majdanek could "barely keep up" with all the dead.[140] Many prisoners were murdered after SS selections in the infirmary and the main compound. As typhus spread in summer 1942, for example, thousands (mostly Slovakian Jews) were isolated and shot by the SS. In a secret message dated July 14, 1942, following the mass selection of some 1,500 prisoners, a Polish inmate noted that the victims had been driven to a nearby forest, killed, and buried. "This is how the typhus epidemic is fought in Majdanek," he added.[141]

Even though death was ever-present by mid-1942, the SS did not yet use Majdanek as a death camp (hence there were no selections on arrival). When it came to the so-called Final Solution in the General Government, the SS looked to Globocnik's death camps instead, even if this meant longer transports. As the SS decimated the Lublin ghetto in spring 1942, leading away some thirty thousand of the thirty-six thousand inhabitants, it routed the transports not to Majdanek, just a short march away, but by train to Belzec. Over the following months, the functional separation between Majdanek (detention and lethal forced labor) and Globocnik's death camps (immediate extermination) continued. In fact, deportation trains en route to Belzec and Sobibor occasionally interrupted their journey in Lublin. Here, Jewish men considered fit for labor were pulled out and sent to Majdanek for construction work; the others remained on the trains to death camps.[142]

The position of Majdanek only changed during the second half of 1942. Since summer, the local Camp SS had planned to build gas chambers, and the new building was completed around October. Despite the secrecy of the SS, which designated the small stone building by the camp entrance as "baths," everyone soon knew what really was inside. Unusually, the gas chambers were equipped for both Zyklon B (like Auschwitz) and carbon monoxide (like the Globocnik death camps). In the first months, most of those murdered inside were typhus-ridden registered Majdanek prisoners. But the Camp SS also murdered "invalid" Jews from Lublin labor camps and carried out its first selections on arrival, picking out weak and sick Jews from the local Majdan Tatarski ghetto (which had replaced the old Lublin ghetto).[143]

The transformation of Majdanek into a death camp was completed from late 1942. This was linked, apparently, to the sudden end of mass deportations to Belzec, in mid-December 1942.[144] Over the next two weeks, until December 31, many thousands of Polish Jews were taken to Majdanek instead and murdered in its gas chambers.[145] Further extermination transports arrived from spring 1943, bringing the first children to the camp, as the SS stepped up the liquidation of the remaining ghettos. Entire families from Warsaw and elsewhere were deported to Majdanek, where SS men now carried out regular selections upon arrival. First and foremost, the SS sent children, women, and the elderly to the gas chambers, as in Auschwitz. Rywka Awronska came in spring 1943 from Warsaw with a transport of several hundred women and children. In the baths, they had to undress. The SS then picked out those "who looked healthy enough for labor," registered them, and escorted them to the camp; the others, Awronska recalled, "were immediately taken away; I think they were gassed." In all, at least sixteen thousand Jews died in Majdanek between January and October 1943, many of them in the new gas chambers. Their corpses were often burned in pyres in a forest, some distance away. To learn how this was done, the Majdanek crematorium chief, SS Oberscharführer Erich Muhsfeldt, had traveled to Auschwitz in February 1943 to seek inspiration from his SS colleagues.[146]

But Majdanek never rivaled Auschwitz. As a camp for slave labor, it remained insignificant. The SS focused its resources and prisoners on Auschwitz, the KL showcase in the conquered east. Majdanek, by contrast, was regarded by Inspector Glücks as a "difficult camp"—dilapidated, distant, and dirty. Inmates, too, were struck by the difference between the two camps.

When Rudolf Vrba looked back in April 1944 to his transport from Majdanek to Auschwitz, nearly two years earlier, he recalled that "after the filthy and primitive barracks in Lublin, the brick buildings [in the Auschwitz main camp] made a very good impression. We thought we had made a good deal." While Auschwitz pushed ahead with economic prestige projects, most prisoners at the far smaller site at Majdanek continued to work on the construction and maintenance of the camp itself; despite the high death rates, there were normally more prisoners than jobs.[147] As a Holocaust death camp, too, Majdanek stood in the second rank. The WVHA and RSHA managers regarded Auschwitz as a far more convenient target for transports from western and central Europe, while most Jews rounded up in the General Government were deported to Globocnik's death camps.[148]

The Operation Reinhard Camps: An Anatomy

Historians tend to draw a clear line between the Globocnik death camps (Belzec, Sobibor, and Treblinka) and the two SS concentration camps most closely involved in the Holocaust (Auschwitz and Majdanek). There were indeed fundamental differences between these two types of camps, both structural and organizational. To begin with, they came under different authorities, Globocnik's office (in Lublin) and the WVHA (in Berlin) respectively. The Globocnik death camps were staffed by the Chancellery of the Führer with key personnel from the "euthanasia" program, and these men mostly stuck together, even after their murderous mission in the east was completed in autumn 1943. Camp SS officers, meanwhile, as the self-styled shock troops of Nazi terror in the KL, looked down on Globocnik's motley gang of killers as a "true selection of total failures," in the words of Rudolf Höss.[149]

Just as the perpetrators of the two types of camp differed, so did their victims. The great majority of Jews murdered in Belzec, Sobibor, and Treblinka came from the General Government, while the great majority of those murdered in Auschwitz came from more western and southern parts of Europe.[150] And their operation differed sharply, too. Globocnik's death camps were built for one purpose only: the rapid mass extermination of deported Jews. By contrast, Auschwitz and Majdanek continued as slave labor reservoirs, even after they had become Holocaust death camps; their hybrid nature was epitomized by the mass selections of deported Jews on arrival. There was no real equivalent in Globocnik's death camps; selections had taken place before the transports departed—in ghettos and elsewhere—and all those on board were destined for extermination. The SS authorities in Belzec, Sobibor, and Treblinka only needed a very small number of prisoners to keep the camps running; it has been estimated that one out of every hundred prisoners survived for more than a few hours. Even at the height of mass murder in autumn 1942, the three death camps together held no more than 2,500 so-called "work Jews," who maintained the sites, assisted in mass extermination, and sorted the belongings of the dead. Consequently, these camps were small in size. The grounds of Sobibor, for example, initially measured about 600×400 yards; its core staff included twenty or thirty German officials, some two hundred foreign helpers (so-called Trawniki men), and perhaps two or three hundred Jewish prisoners temporarily spared for labor. By contrast, the so-called interest zone of the Auschwitz SS measured around twenty-five square miles (excluding several more far-flung satellite camps); at the end of January 1943, some 40,031 prisoners (including 14,070 Jews) were held across the Auschwitz complex, surrounded by several thousand SS guards.[151] Compared to Auschwitz, terror was greatly compressed in Globocnik's death camps, down to its very essence.

And yet, the links between the two types of death camp were closer than is commonly assumed. To begin with, there were parallels in the mechanics of mass murder. As with the WVHA death camps (and Chelmno), Globocnik's camps relied on a combination of deception, speed, threats, and violence. When Eliasz Rosenberg, one of the few survivors of Treblinka, arrived in the camp in August 1942, on a deportation train from Warsaw, he saw a large sign telling Jews that their "way leads to the bath. Receipt of fresh clothes there and then transfer to another camp." There were neat flower beds and reassuring speeches, with SS men telling the victims that they would move to a work camp as soon as they had washed and their clothes were disinfected (some of this trickery was later abandoned, after knowledge of the mass extermination had spread among Polish Jews). Separated by gender, the victims had to undress in a special barrack and were forced, at breakneck speed and with frequent blows, into the gas chambers. After each mass killing, a group of Jewish prisoners, held in isolation from the rest of the camp, was forced into action. Just like the wretched Special Squad in Auschwitz, they had to dispose of the corpses, rip out gold fillings, and prepare the next gassing. In Treblinka, one of these prisoners was Eliasz Rosenberg. At running pace, he and another inmate had to carry the dead to huge mass graves (later, railway trolleys were used instead). From late February 1943, the SS supervised the exhumation of these rotting corpses, which were thrown on iron rails above shallow ditches and burned.[152] The similarities with Auschwitz and Majdanek are evident, and owed much to the influence of SS cremation experts like Paul Blobel and of the mass killing techniques pioneered during the "euthanasia" program.[153]

As for life inside the small labor compounds of Belzec, Sobibor, and Treblinka, many of the basic structures were borrowed directly from the KL system, probably by some of the former Camp SS men who had arrived via the T-4 operation and now occupied leading positions in Globocnik's death camps. There were daily roll calls, for example, as well as strict prisoner hierarchies, with camp elders, work supervisors, and block elders. Prisoner punishments were familiar from the KL, too. One Sobibor NCO testified after the war that "work Jews" were frequently whipped, enduring ten to twenty-five lashes in front of the assembled prisoners, in order "to maintain discipline in the camp."[154]

The connections between the WVHA and Globocnik's apparatus extended well beyond such structural similarities. There were operational links, too, resulting from the participation of both of these agencies in the Holocaust. In summer 1942, Himmler put the WVHA in charge of processing all the valuables amassed during Operation Reinhard, including the goods plundered in Globocnik's death camps; senior WVHA officials inspected the death camps to ensure that central orders about the plunder were implemented.[155] In addition to stealing from the dead, both agencies cooperated in the exploitation of Jewish forced workers.[156] The closest contacts existed in Majdanek. Regional Nazi chieftains often meddled in the affairs of the nearest concentration camp.[157] But Globocnik's endless interference in Majdanek was quite exceptional. He got closely involved in construction projects, and even diverted some cash, plundered from Jews, to fund Majdanek's extension.[158] And although the concentration camp came under the authority of the WVHA, he was allowed to enter the grounds without formal identification, and frequently dropped by, sometimes at night; his main area of interest, it seems, was the new gas chambers, which he had apparently initiated.[159] At times, Globocnik treated Majdanek like one of his own camps, giving orders directly to the Camp SS and even proposing its commandant, Hermann Florstedt, for promotion.[160]

This is not to say that the various parts of Operation Reinhard added up to a seamless whole. As we have seen, the Holocaust camps run by the WVHA and by Globocnik, respectively, had separate identities and structures. There were also rivalries between officials on both sides, competing to kill and plunder more effectively. Globocnik's main adversary was Rudolf Höss in Auschwitz, who recalled after the war that his rival "was absolutely determined to be at the top with 'his' exterminations." But Höss saw himself as the real master of genocide and dismissed Globocnik as a loudmouth and dilettante who hid the "utter chaos of the Lublin Action Reinhardt [*sic*]" behind a façade of distortions, exaggerations, and lies.[161]

These personal tensions were exacerbated by visits to the rival death camps. Höss toured Treblinka, Globocnik's most lethal camp, and left unimpressed. He regarded the use of carbon monoxide as not "very efficient," as the motors did not always pump enough gas into the chambers to kill straightaway. "Another improvement we made over Treblinka," Höss noted, "was that we built our gas chambers to accommodate 2,000 people at one time"; even in Allied captivity, Höss was bursting with professional pride about his murderous inventions.[162] For his part, Odilo Globocnik and his men apparently resisted pressure to switch their gas chambers from carbon monoxide to Zyklon B, as pioneered in Auschwitz.[163] Globocnik also used the occasion of a visit to the new crematoria and gas chamber complex in Birkenau to disparage the local operation, much to Höss's irritation. Far from being impressed with the up-to-date machinery of mass murder, as other visitors had been, Globocnik claimed that his men worked much faster, and lectured Höss about the greater killing capacities of his own camps. He "exaggerated outrageously, at any opportunity," Höss wrote after the war, still seething about Globocnik's attempts to outdo him as the greatest mass murderer of the Third Reich.[164] This genocidal competition between Höss and Globocnik illustrates once more the entanglement of their camps. Looking at these and all the other points of contact, it is no longer possible to suggest that there were no institutional and organizational connections between Globocnik's camps and the KL system.[165] The Holocaust in the different Nazi death camps of eastern Europe was a collective SS endeavor.

New Camps for Jews

The longer the Holocaust lasted, the more closely involved became the concentration camps. The role of the KL system in Nazi genocide grew during 1943, as the focus of mass extermination began to shift from the killing fields of eastern Europe and Globocnik's death camps to the new killing complex in Birkenau and, to a lesser extent, Majdanek. At the same time, the KL system became a bigger hub for Jewish slave labor. Back in October 1942, Himmler had informed Oswald Pohl and other SS leaders that remaining Jewish forced workers in the General Government should be pressed into KL enterprises, until these Jews, too, would "disappear some day in accordance with the Führer's wish." During the following year, Himmler relentlessly pushed for the liquidation of labor camps and ghettos on occupied Polish

SS CONCENTRATION CAMPS (main camps), SUMMER 1944

and Soviet soil. To ensure that work on essential projects could continue, the SS set up several new KL in former ghettos and labor camps, extending its control over the remaining Jewish forced workers.[166] Oswald Pohl had contemplated the construction of new concentration camps almost as soon as his WVHA had taken control of the KL system.[167] From spring 1943, expansion became reality, at a brisk pace. Within a few months, the WVHA had opened four main camps in eastern Europe (Warsaw, Riga, Vaivara, Kovno), as well as dozens of satellite camps. Unlike other SS concentration camps, these new camps were set up explicitly for the exploitation of Jewish slave labor.

One of these new concentration camps in the occupied east was opened in

July 1943 in Warsaw, among the ruins of what had once been the largest ghetto. After a German attempt to round up Jews for deportation in January 1943 met with an armed response, an incensed Himmler had ordered the destruction of the entire ghetto. The German assault began on April 19, 1943, against desperate resistance. After four weeks of carnage, the uprising was crushed, leaving many thousands of Jewish men, women, and children dead. Himmler then ordered the WVHA to flatten what was left of the ghetto. This scheme included plans for a new KL (such plans had been on the table since autumn 1942), whose prisoners would help to demolish the remaining buildings. Despite some large prisoner transports, however, the Warsaw camp remained smaller than anticipated; instead of 10,000 men, just 2,040 were working in demolition by February 1944. The camp itself was set up in a former military prison, extended with materials from the destroyed ghetto. The work in the ruins—breaking down walls, collecting scrap metal, stacking bricks—was hard and dangerous, and having to toil in a ghost town haunted by Nazi mass murder weighed heavily on the prisoners. "The streets of the ghetto were a dreadful sight for us," recalled the Polish Jew Oskar Paserman, who had arrived from Auschwitz in late November 1943. Months after the uprising, Paserman still stumbled over decaying bodies. "It stank of corpses, which were lying in the bunkers and under ruins. The streets were covered with pieces of furniture and burned clothes."[168]

In the wake of the Jewish resistance in Warsaw, SS leaders redoubled their attempts to wipe out the remaining labor camps and ghettos in the occupied east. Much of their focus turned to the Reich Commissariat of the Eastern Land, that is, the territory under German civilian administration that included parts of Belorussia as well as Latvia, Lithuania, and Estonia, the three Baltic States annexed by the Soviet Union after the Hitler-Stalin pact. On June 21, 1943, Heinrich Himmler ordered the closure of all ghettos in the Eastern Land. The surviving Jews would be forced to work in concentration camps instead, while those who were superfluous to slave labor would be killed. Despite some objections from German officials in the army and the civilian administration, who worried about losing "their" Jewish workers and possible repercussions for war production, the order was implemented over the coming months.[169]

The first new KL complex in the Baltic region emerged in Latvia. Local SS officials had lobbied for a concentration camp for Jews around Riga since the German invasion of summer 1941. According to an internal SS memorandum that autumn, such a local camp promised several advantages over a ghetto: prisoners could be exploited more fully for forced labor, and the separation of men and women would "put an end to the further procreation of the Jews."[170] But it was not until the SS extended its hold over Jews in the Baltic territories that it finally established a KL. In March 1943, around the time of a visit by Himmler to Riga, five hundred prisoners from Sachsenhausen arrived to erect the camp in the small suburb of Kaiserwald (Mežaparks), known in the interwar years as an exclusive seaside resort. The early dimensions of the new camp were modest by SS standards, with four prisoner barracks for men and four for women, separated from each other and the outside world by electrified fences. The camp filled up with Jewish inmates from July 1943 onward, including large numbers of German and Czech Jews who had been deported to the Baltic region back in 1941–42. The prisoners initially came in large columns, with their remaining belongings, from the nearby Riga ghetto, which had been emptied by November 1943; later transports arrived from other Baltic ghettos farther afield and from Hungary (via Auschwitz). But most inmates did not stay put for long. The SS quickly realized that it would be impractical to move all local sites of Jewish forced labor into the small Riga main camp, and set up satellite camps near these sites instead. In all, at least sixteen such camps were established, most of them in Riga itself. The main camp in Kaiserwald now functioned primarily as a transit hub; after registration, new inmates were quickly shunted to one of the satellite camps. By March 1944, the various satellite camps of Riga held around nine thousand prisoners, compared to an estimated two thousand in the main camp.[171]

This imbalance was even more pronounced in another new Baltic concentration camp, Vaivara, a settlement in northeast Estonia. A small contingent of SS men had to improvise here, Richard Glücks conceded, setting things up "completely from scratch." Officially opened on September 19, 1943, after hasty preparation, the KL complex grew within weeks to include at least eleven satellite camps; several of them—such as Klooga, some one hundred and fifty miles to the west—rivaled or surpassed the Vaivara main camp in size. Among the prisoners were many families, and it was the young and the elderly who succumbed most quickly to the SS regime of violence and exhausting labor, which included construction work, the production of explosives, and the extraction of oil shale from marshy terrain. In November 1943 alone, at a time when 9,207 prisoners were held across the Vaivara KL complex, some 296 prisoners died. Hundreds more followed during the bitter winter.[172]

A third main concentration camp in the Reich Commissariat of the Eastern Land was set up in the Lithuanian city of Kovno (Kaunas). Just as in Riga, regional SS forces had already proposed a KL for Jews here in summer 1941, but it was established only in autumn 1943. During the final SS push for the liquidation of ghettos, it turned the Kovno ghetto into a main concentration camp, which held some eight thousand Jewish prisoners at the end of the year. Other former ghettos and labor camps in the region became satellites of Kovno. Among them was the largest Lithuanian ghetto, Wilna. Suspected by the SS as a hotbed of Jewish unrest, it was decimated in summer and autumn 1943. Some fourteen thousand Jews were deported, mostly as KL slave laborers for shale extraction in Estonia, a priority project for Himmler. One of the deported prisoners sent a letter from Vaivara back to the ghetto in Wilna: "We are still alive and working . . . It rains hard here and it's very cold. Conditions are hard enough . . . Good that you stayed." In fact, those left behind faced lethal violence as the Camp SS established itself in the former ghetto. By late 1943, just 2,600 Jews were still alive in Wilna, spread across four satellite camps.[173]

There was something novel about the new eastern European concentration camps. Already at first sight, the compounds looked very different from the KL model devised in the 1930s. Many prisoners were still wearing civilian clothing, and sometimes whole families lived together. In a former ghetto like Kovno, they even continued to occupy the same houses as before (the Jewish Council initially remained in place, too). Another contrast to older KL complexes was the rapid proliferation of satellite camps across the Baltic lands, where prisoner numbers began to outstrip the main camps. Turning to the new camps' administration, they did not adhere to the strict division of the SS Commandant Staff into five departments, which had been the standard in the KL since the mid-1930s. Instead, the internal SS organization was significantly pared down.[174] The local Camp SS staff was also supervised in a novel way; while the ultimate power still rested with WVHA headquarters, the commandants in the Baltic region reported not only to Berlin but to a regional WVHA office in Riga, led by a so-called SS economic officer (SS-Wirtschafter), which was responsible for the KL and other economic and administrative matters in the area.[175]

But the new camps in the occupied east were not alien bodies in the KL cosmos. For a start, the camps still belonged to WVHA, and most rules and staff were drawn from the regular Camp SS. Moreover, the whole KL system was changing from autumn 1943, becoming far more disparate and decentralized, epitomized by the shift away from main camps to a vast network of satellite camps. From this perspective, the new sites in the east embodied the improvised type of concentration camp that would characterize the KL system toward the end of Nazi rule, when the grip of the central authorities weakened and some established practices were thrown overboard in a desperate attempt to shore up the sinking Third Reich.

Action "Harvest Festival"

At the same time as the Camp SS was putting down roots across the Baltic, it continued its expansion in occupied Poland. Numerous new camps were added to the KL portfolio in the incorporated Polish territory. From September 1943, the WVHA began to take over the remaining large forced labor camps in Silesia from SS Oberführer Albrecht Schmelt; around twenty camps were turned into Gross-Rosen satellite camps, and several more into satellite camps of Auschwitz. Among the largest was Blechhammer (Blachownia): when it was attached to Auschwitz in April 1944, more than three thousand prisoners were toiling there on the grounds of a synthetic fuel factory.[176] Farther to the east, in the General Government, former labor camps for Jews came under the WVHA, too. Details of their takeover were settled in a high-powered meeting on September 7, 1943, between Pohl, Glücks, and Globocnik, who agreed that his labor camps in the Lublin district, around ten in all, would turn into satellite camps of Majdanek. In addition, larger labor camps elsewhere in the General Government would also become KL, all "in the interest of a general clearing-up," as Pohl put it; a few weeks later, following local inspections by his men, Pohl signed off on a list of prospective new KL sites, including Radom and Krakow-Plaszow.[177]

The WVHA expansion plans were abruptly disrupted in early November 1943 by a vast bloodbath in the General Government. In the Lublin district alone, SS and police forces slaughtered some forty-two thousand Jews in camps. Apparently, Himmler had ordered this action in response to a recent prisoner uprising in Sobibor, the only one of Globocnik's death camps still operational. Mass murder in Sobibor had continued at a lower pace in 1943 than during the previous year, and once Himmler had abandoned his plan to turn it into a KL (following an intervention by Pohl and Globocnik), it was only a question of time until the camp and its last remaining prisoners were liquidated. Before the SS could implement its plans, however, the prisoners rose up. On October 14, 1943, they attacked and killed twelve SS men and two Ukrainian auxiliaries, and more than 350 prisoners attempted to escape, many successfully. SS leaders were already on edge, following a similar revolt in Treblinka two months earlier and the Warsaw uprising in spring, and amidst mounting SS hysteria about the dangers of the last ghettos and labor camps, Himmler ordered the large-scale mass murder of Jewish forced workers in the eastern parts of the General Government.[178]

Majdanek stood at the center of the slaughter. Under the idyllic code name Action "Harvest Festival," some eighteen thousand Jews were murdered here on November 3, 1943. That morning, the eight thousand Jewish prisoners in the camp had been isolated; those who tried to hide were pulled out by SS men and guard dogs. Driven on by the Camp SS, the prisoners were marched along the main camp street, joined by some ten thousand prisoners from nearby Lublin labor camps. They stopped behind the building site of the new crematorium (under construction since September 1943), at the far corner of the camp. Here, the men, women, and children were forced to undress and lie in large ditches; then they were shot in the back of the head or mown down by machine guns; any wounded survivors were buried alive under the bodies of those shot after them. Most of the killers were SD and policemen, who had been specially dispatched to Majdanek. After the war, one of the killers, Johann B., casually talked about the victims to a film crew, in his jovial Bavarian accent: "Well, they did do some griping. They griped, some came up to us with raised fists. And 'Nazi pigs,' they screamed. You couldn't really blame them, we might have done the same, if we'd got it in the neck."

In an effort to camouflage the salvos, the Majdanek Camp SS piped light music—Vienna waltzes, tangos, and marches—across the ground, using specially set-up loudspeakers. Finally, in the evening, the shots and the music fell silent, after the last prisoner had been executed. Several volunteers from the Camp SS who had participated in the shootings returned to their quarters and held a wild party, drinking much of the vodka they had received as a special reward; some did not even bother to wash off the blood from their boots before they reached for the bottle.[179] What they celebrated was the largest single massacre ever in an SS concentration camp. More people were murdered in Majdanek on November 3, 1943, than any other day in any other KL, including Auschwitz. The massacre also marked the end of Majdanek as a Holocaust camp. Mass gassings had already stopped in September 1943, and now all the remaining Jewish slave laborers were dead; at the end of November, there was not a single Jewish prisoner left inside the main camp.[180]

The wave of mass murder in early November 1943 affected the KL system more widely. Several Jewish labor camps destined for WVHA takeover were effectively wiped out, among them Globocnik's large camp at the old airport in Lublin, which had functioned as a central collection point for the clothes of murdered Jews.[181] Several other labor camps were still incorporated into the KL system from early 1944 onward, though this process now took longer than the SS had anticipated: some camps were established as late as spring 1944, just months before they were abandoned again in the face of the Soviet advance. Among the new camps were three larger former labor camps in

Bliżyn, Budzyń, and Radom, which became satellite camps of Majdanek, as did a smaller camp on Lipowa Street in Lublin itself. By mid-March 1944, these four new satellite camps held some 8,900 prisoners (mostly Jews), almost as many as the Majdanek main camp.[182]

Only one of the Jewish labor camps absorbed by the WVHA in early 1944 was turned into a main concentration camp—Plaszow (Płaszów), the third main KL in the General Government and the last to be established in occupied eastern Europe. In autumn 1942, the German authorities had started to set up a forced labor camp in the Plaszow district on the outskirts of Krakow, mainly for Jews from the local ghetto that was about to be liquidated. Only in January 1944 was this camp transferred from the authority of the regional SS and police leader to the WVHA. By March 1944, Plaszow had overtaken Majdanek in size, holding some 11,600 Jewish men, women, and children (as well as 1,393 Poles in a separate compound). Several thousand prisoners were detained in six attached satellite camps; unlike at Riga and Vaivara, however, the focal point of forced labor remained the main camp itself, with prisoners pressed into workshops, construction, and a quarry.

Plaszow's conversion into a concentration camp resulted in various administrative changes, including the introduction of the WVHA camp rules. The inmates themselves, some now wearing the typical striped uniforms, had initially placed great hopes in the new rulers, the former prisoner Aleksandar Biberstein wrote after the war. But these hopes were soon dashed. Instead of better conditions, terror became more efficient under the auspices of the Camp SS. "The random murders and shootings of Jews ceased," Biberstein recalled, only to be replaced by the systematic "extermination of the rest of the Jewish camp inhabitants," with frequent selections and some transports to Auschwitz.[183] Here, the victims may well have encountered some of the last Jewish survivors of the older KL within the Third Reich's prewar borders, who had been deported to Auschwitz back in autumn 1942.

SS Exceptions: Jewish Prisoners Inside Germany

On September 29, 1942, Heinrich Himmler inspected Sachsenhausen, guided by Inspector Richard Glücks and Commandant Anton Kaindl, who tried to impress him with various economic ventures. Although Auschwitz had already grown into the largest KL, Himmler retained an interest in his older camps, and he probably knew that just a few months earlier the Sachsenhausen SS had committed the bloodiest anti-Semitic massacre inside the German heartland since the 1938 pogrom. In "revenge" for the assassination of Reinhard Heydrich, SS men had executed around 250 Jews on May 28–29, 1942, apparently inside the neck-shooting barrack built for Soviet POWs. Most victims had been rounded up in Berlin for execution. The others were prisoners randomly selected in Sachsenhausen itself, who begged for mercy as they were dragged away. The massacre had been observed by senior SS and RSHA officials. Other Nazi leaders applauded from afar. "The more of this dirty scum is eliminated," the Berlin Gauleiter Joseph Goebbels noted in his diary, "the better for the security of the Reich."[184]

When Himmler came to Sachsenhausen on September 29, 1942, there were only a few hundred Jewish prisoners left inside. Murder and lethal conditions had decimated the already small group of Jews in concentration camps within Germany's prewar borders; overall, there were no more than around two thousand Jewish prisoners left across these KL, mostly German and Polish Jews.[185] But even such a small number was too large for Himmler. At the time, Hitler was pushing for the complete removal of all Jews from the German Reich, and Himmler was keen to comply; during his visit to Sachsenhausen, he ordered the deportation of Jews from all the KL on German soil.[186] Written directives followed a few days later; apart from inmates in important positions (who could be temporarily exempted), all Jewish prisoners would be taken to Auschwitz or Majdanek. In this way, concentration camps in the Reich would finally become "free of Jews," the WVHA informed its commandants.[187] Meanwhile, it ordered the Auschwitz SS to dispatch some Polish prisoners as replacements.[188]

Deportations trains to the east soon started to roll. Gross-Rosen was among the first camps to realize Himmler's wishes, dispatching its last group of Jewish prisoners on October 16, 1942.[189] In Sachsenhausen itself, the deportations triggered an unprecedented mutiny. When the Camp SS rounded up Jewish prisoners on the evening of October 22, 1942, and ordered them to hand over their belongings, panic spread as inmates feared a repetition of the May massacre. A small group of young Jewish men ran onto the roll call square, pushed over some of the SS guards, and shouted: "Just shoot, you dogs!" The Camp SS quickly restored control, though there were no immediate repercussions. The SS men were determined to keep the deportations on schedule, and for once refrained from punishing rebellious prisoners. That same night, a train with 454 Jewish men departed for Auschwitz, including the former boxer Bully Schott, whom we encountered earlier. Arriving on October 25, the prisoners were led to the Auschwitz main camp and registered. But they were not spared for long. Just five days later, the SS carried out a large-scale selection among prisoners recently deported from the westerly KL. Some eight hundred of them, among them Bully Schott, were sent to the IG Farben building site near Dwory for murder through labor. Hundreds more were taken straight to the Birkenau gas chambers.[190]

Before long, almost all Jewish prisoners had been deported from concentration camps inside the German heartland; by the end of 1942, the KL in the Reich (excluding Auschwitz) imprisoned fewer than four hundred Jews.[191] The majority of them were held in Buchenwald, which continued to receive some more arrested Jews from the Gestapo, much to the irritation of the local commandant.[192] In late 1942, there were 227 Jewish men left in Buchenwald. Most of them had been trained as bricklayers and were needed for urgent construction work. Their status as skilled laborers protected them from deportation and from some of the worst SS excesses. For the time being, they were safer than almost any other Jewish prisoners in the KL system. The twenty-eight-year-old Austrian Jew Ernst Federn, for example, worked on an SS prestige project outside the camp. Prisoners here received double the rations of ordinary Buchenwald inmates, while SS guards acted "in every way humanely and correctly," as Federn recalled, because they were restrained by the presence of civilians around them.[193]

In Sachsenhausen, too, a few skilled workers were saved from deportation. Back in summer 1942, the WVHA had begun to assemble a small group of Jewish draftsmen and graphic designers in barrack 19, for a project of national importance, though none of them knew what it could be. Then, in December 1942, a senior SS officer from the RSHA foreign desk, Bernhard Krüger, came to initiate them into a top-secret mission ordered by Himmler and backed by Hitler. Code-named Operation Bernhard (after the shameless Krüger), the prisoners would forge foreign banknotes and stamps.

The Sachsenhausen counterfeiting commando eventually grew from 29 to more than 140 Jewish men. Most of them had arrived from Auschwitz. One of them, Adolf Burger, felt "as if I had come from hell into heaven." The prisoners were no longer beaten and enjoyed sufficient food, worked in heated rooms, had time for reading, cards, and radio, and slept in proper beds. Their main task was forging British currency (attempts to copy U.S. dollars never went past the experimental stage). Overall, the prisoners later estimated, they produced banknotes to the value of over 134 million pounds. The RSHA only deemed a fraction of this to be good enough to buy gold and foreign goods, and to pay off spies; some of the remaining banknotes were dropped over England to destabilize its currency. For this outlandish plan to succeed, the whole of Operation Bernhard had to remain secret. This was why the forgers remained almost completely isolated from the rest of the Sachsenhausen camp (though their secret still leaked out). And this was why the RSHA had selected only Jews, since they could be killed at any time. In the end, through a series of flukes, the prisoners survived the KL. The products of their labor, which had ultimately saved their lives, also endured, as many of the forged banknotes remained in circulation for years to come.[194]

The story of the Sachsenhausen counterfeiting commando was exceptional. But such exceptions matter, not only because they saved Jews like Adolf Burger, but because they demonstrate that the Nazi authorities could be pragmatic if they had to—in this case by partially suspending Himmler's autumn 1942 directive to remove Jewish prisoners from the Reich. This points to a wider truth about the Holocaust: in their pursuit of the wholesale extermination of European Jewry, SS leaders were always willing to consider "tactical retreats."[195] This willingness was nowhere more obvious, perhaps, than in the 1943 order to set up a new KL for Jews, right inside the German Reich.

As the genocide of European Jews reached a frenzied climax during the second half of 1942, the leaders of the Third Reich decided to spare a few victims and exploit them as "valuable hostages," as Heinrich Himmler called them. Obsessed by global conspiracy theories, Nazi leaders had long contemplated the use of Jewish "hostages" as leverage against enemy nations supposedly ruled by Jewish politicians and financiers. Now both the SS and the German Foreign Office agreed that some selected Jews and their families— those with connections to Palestine or the United States, for example—might be exchanged for Germans interned abroad or else for foreign currency and goods. With Hitler's agreement, Himmler in spring 1943 ordered the establishment of a collection camp for Jews who might be used in these prisoner exchanges. He made clear in another directive that conditions should be such that the Jewish prisoners "are healthy and remain alive."[196]

The new camp was set up in Bergen-Belsen, between Hanover and Hamburg in northern Germany, on the half-empty grounds of an existing POW camp.[197] Despite its unusual mission, reflected in the official title "residence camp" (*Aufenthaltslager*), Himmler designated it as an SS concentration camp run by the WVHA. It was initially staffed by SS men from Niederhagen, the camp at Wewelsburg castle that had just closed down. The first large prisoner contingent came from Buchenwald, on April 30, 1943, to prepare the site for the so-called "exchange prisoners," who arrived from July 1943 onward; by December 1944, a total of around fifteen thousand Jewish prisoners had been taken to Bergen-Belsen, where they were held in different sectors, depending on their backgrounds. The proliferation of compounds added to the camp's confusing layout, which turned into a shantytown of barracks and tents. To further complicate matters, the SS later added a KL compound for regular protective custody prisoners, though numbers here remained small, at least initially; during 1943 and 1944, Bergen-Belsen was predominantly a camp for Jews.[198]

The Jewish prisoners in Bergen-Belsen dreamed about leaving on exchange transports. Fanny Heilbut, who had arrived with her husband and two sons (a third son had died in Mauthausen) from Westerbork in February 1944, recalled that the hope of freedom "went a long way to keep us going." But this dream only came true for a small proportion of Jewish inmates. By the end of 1944, only some 2,300 prisoners had been allowed to exit the Third Reich. Fanny Heilbut and her family were not among them. One of the lucky few was Simon Heinrich Herrmann, who departed from Bergen-Belsen on June 30, 1944, with 221 other prisoners bound for Palestine (in exchange, a group of ethnic German settlers from the Protestant Templar sect, who had been interned by the British in Palestine, were sent to Germany). As the former prisoners left Bergen-Belsen behind, Simon Herrmann later wrote, "an invisible hand removed the shackles from our bodies and souls, opening the doors and windows in our hearts." Herrmann and the others safely landed in Haifa on July 10, 1944. Not many other transports left the camp in 1943–44, and by no means all of those headed for freedom. In fact, more than two thousand Polish Jews were deported from Bergen-Belsen to Auschwitz. The German authorities had deemed them unsuitable candidates for exchanges, unwilling to recognize their prospective Latin American citizenship certificates (so-called *Promesas*). By far the largest such transport, with some 1,800 inmates, left on October 21, 1943; all of them were murdered two days later in Auschwitz.[199]

Most Jews remained trapped in Bergen-Belsen, tormented by their receding hopes of freedom. Conditions varied across the different sectors. In 1943 they were worst in the so-called star camp, the largest compound of the exchange camp, named after the yellow stars the Jews had to wear. There was never enough food (official rations were identical to other concentration camps) and all adults, except for the elderly, had to work hard, often in camp maintenance. But even in this compound the authorities initially allowed privileges unheard of elsewhere in the KL system, except for Herzogenbusch, the other camp for "privileged" Jews. In the star camp, inmates wore civilian clothing and kept some of their belongings. Families met up during mealtimes and evenings (there were hundreds of children). As in ghettos, some of the internal administration was left to a Jewish Council and a camp police. And just like in Herzogenbusch, there was a Jewish prisoner court. As for SS guards, they were instructed to address prisoners by name, not number. There were some SS abuses, but nothing like the daily orgies of other KL. Overall, conditions were poor but sufferable, until they began to deteriorate from spring and summer 1944; over the following months, Fanny Heilbut's husband and one of her sons perished, as did many thousands of others.[200]

Bergen-Belsen was an anomaly in the KL system during the middle of World War II. At the time, it was the only concentration camp inside Germany's prewar borders that held large numbers of Jewish prisoners, and the only KL for Jews not geared toward their eventual death. Virtually all other Jewish concentration camp prisoners found themselves in eastern Europe, which meant likely death. This was true, above all, for Auschwitz, the largest of all the Holocaust camps. From summer 1942, most Jews deported to this camp were murdered within hours of their arrival, as we have seen. It is the fate of the others, those selected as SS slaves in Auschwitz and other KL in eastern Europe, to which we must turn next.

7

Anus Mundi

On September 5, 1942, a few SS men marched into block 27 of the Birkenau women's infirmary to assist the camp doctor during a selection. For the SS, such selections were part of their working life. For the prisoners, they were the worst torment. The sick women knew their probable fate and some desperately tried to hide. But to no avail. That day, hundreds of Jewish women were condemned to death and herded onto trucks. Near the gas chambers, they had to undress in broad daylight. Unlike Jews who had just been deported to Auschwitz, these prisoners understood what would happen inside the converted farmhouses. Some silently stood or sat in the grass, others sobbed. Among the supervising SS officials was a physician, Dr. Johann Paul Kremer, who later testified that the women had "begged the SS men to spare their lives, cried, and yet all were driven inside the gas chamber and gassed." Sitting in his car outside, Dr. Kremer listened as the screams died down. A few hours afterward, he recorded a conversation with another Auschwitz doctor in his diary: "[Dr. Heinz] Thilo was right, when he told me today that we are at the *anus mundi* (the anus of the world)."[1]

It is easy to picture the balding, fifty-eight-year-old Dr. Kremer smirking at this expression (the diaries reveal his crude sense of humor). But he recognized some deeper truth in Dr. Thilo's words. After all, Kremer had never planned to be in Auschwitz. Nor was he keen to stay. A professor of anatomy at the University of Münster, he had joined the SS medical service during the summer break, and to his surprise was posted to Auschwitz in late August 1942 for a number of weeks to replace a sick colleague. "There is nothing to excite one here," he wrote on the day of his conversation with Dr. Thilo. The selections and gassings—he participated in more than one per week—certainly gave him little satisfaction.[2] What is more, Dr. Kremer struggled with the climate. He complained about the humidity and the "masses of vermin," including fleas in his room at the SS hotel in town. Then there was the "Auschwitz illness." Within days, Kremer was struck down by this gastric virus, not for the last time. But what he really feared were other diseases, and for good reason. Earlier that year, an Auschwitz SS doctor had died of typhus, and during a ten-day period in October 1942, when Kremer was stationed in the camp, the SS counted some thirteen more suspected cases of typhus among its men, while the officer in charge of agriculture, Joachim Caesar, caught typhoid, which had just killed his wife (Caesar recovered and remarried a year later, wedding his laboratory assistant in the Auschwitz registry office).[3] Conditions for the Camp SS elsewhere in the occupied east were no better. Female guards in Majdanek, too, were in and out of the hospital with infections. The frustrations felt by the SS staff—disgusted by the primitive sanitary conditions and afraid of catching diseases from inmates—only increased their proclivity for violence.[4]

At the same time, the Camp SS found much to like in the east. Dr. Kremer, for one, made the most of his inadvertent posting to Auschwitz. His grim tasks in the camp did not spoil his love of the outdoors. In his spare time, he joined other SS men on sun loungers at his hotel and took a bicycle tour across the vast SS-controlled territory, marveling at the "absolutely beautiful autumn weather." A man with a big appetite, Kremer devoured the generous helpings in the SS officer mess, dutifully recording all the delicacies in his diary, from goose liver and roast rabbit to the "glorious vanilla ice cream." And he liked the entertainment in the camp. One Sunday afternoon in September he listened to a concert by the prisoner orchestra, and he also enjoyed the regular variety shows for the Camp SS in the evenings, sometimes with free beer; Kremer was particularly smitten by a performance of dancing dogs and small hens who could crow on command. Other times, Kremer made social calls on colleagues. After he spent the afternoon of November 8, 1942, at the Birkenau gas chambers—supervising the murder of some one thousand Jewish men, women, and children who had just arrived from ghettos around Bialystok—he relaxed in the evening with Dr. Eduard Wirths, the chief SS garrison physician, sampling Bulgarian red wine and Croatian plum schnapps. In addition to fun and food, Kremer found time to boost his career. He was delighted to get his hands on "virtually alive material of human liver and spleen" for his studies of the effect of starvation on human organs. Kremer apparently later published a paper on the topic in a medical journal.[5]

But the biggest bonus of Dr. Kremer's brief stay in Auschwitz was financial. The belongings of murdered Jews filled the camp, and corrupt SS men like Kremer freely helped themselves. After he was initiated into the tricks of the trade, he took as much as he could from a storeroom near the ramp. The five bulging parcels he sent back home for safekeeping included soap and toothpaste, glasses and pens, perfume and handbags, and much else besides, to a total value of 1,400 Reichsmark. In just five weeks, Untersturmführer Kremer stole goods worth more than half the annual salary of a full-time SS officer of his rank.[6] Many other Camp SS officials were on the make, too, in Auschwitz and elsewhere. In the end, corruption became so endemic that a special police commission was sent to the KL. In Auschwitz, the investigation was triggered in 1943 by an unusually heavy package that an SS man had sent to his wife; when suspicious customs officials opened it, they found a huge lump of gold, as big as two fists, melted down from the dental fillings of murdered prisoners.[7]

By this time, Auschwitz had become the center of the KL system, just as Dachau had dominated the first period of Nazi rule, and Sachsenhausen the early war years. Not that Auschwitz was entirely different; in other KL, too, there was hunger and abuse, selection and mass murder. But everything was more extreme in Auschwitz. No other camp held more staff and prisoners. The mass deportations of Jews had quickly put Auschwitz into a league all its own. During September 1942, the average daily prisoner population across all the KL stood at one hundred and ten thousand. An estimated thirty-four thousand of these prisoners were held in Auschwitz alone, of whom around sixty percent were Jews. They were ruled by some two thousand Auschwitz SS staff, and many of these officials, as we shall see, felt similar ambivalence about their lives in the east as Dr. Kremer.[8]

The shadow of Auschwitz looms even larger when we turn to prisoner fatalities. According to secret SS figures, a total of 12,832 registered prisoners died across the KL system in August 1942; almost two-thirds of them—6,829 men and 1,525 women—perished in Auschwitz (excluding an estimated 35,000 unregistered Jews who were gassed that month after SS selections on arrival).[9] In total, around 150,000 registered prisoners died in Auschwitz during 1942–43 (again excluding Jews murdered on arrival).[10] Their deaths were recorded on various official papers, mostly giving fictitious causes, though rarely as blatant as in the case of the three-year-old Gerhard Pohl, who was recorded as having died in Auschwitz on May 10, 1943, of "old age."[11] Some of the forms ran to around twenty pages, with prisoner clerks typing day and night to keep up. Auschwitz SS doctors, meanwhile, complained about cramps in their hands from signing all the death certificates; to make

THE AUSCHWITZ KL COMPLEX, c. 1944

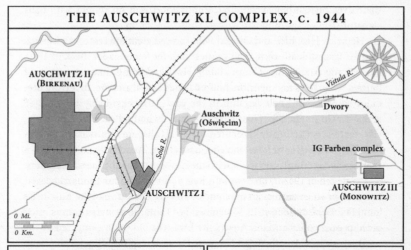

AUSCHWITZ II
(BIRKENAU)

Vistula R.

Auschwitz
(Oświęcim)

Dwory

Sola R.

IG Farben complex

AUSCHWITZ I

AUSCHWITZ III
(MONOWITZ)

0 Mi. 1
0 Km. 1

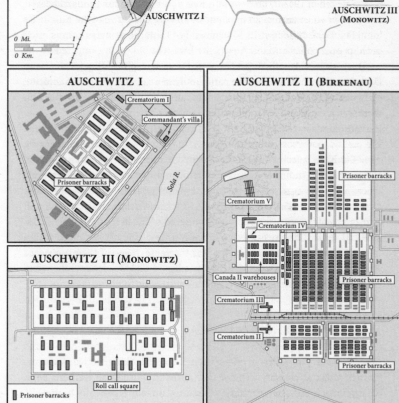

AUSCHWITZ I

Crematorium I

Commandant's villa

Sola R.

Prisoner barracks

AUSCHWITZ III (MONOWITZ)

Roll call square

Prisoner barracks

Prisoner tents

AUSCHWITZ II (BIRKENAU)

Prisoner barracks

Crematorium V

Crematorium IV

Canada II warehouses

Prisoner barracks

Crematorium III

Crematorium II

Prisoner barracks

their lives easier, they eventually commissioned special stamps with their signature.[12]

Heinrich Himmler and Oswald Pohl showed great interest in Auschwitz, as their largest death camp and greatest hub for forced labor. Back in 1940, when it was first set up, Commandant Höss had had to hunt for scraps of barbed wire. Now his superiors poured funds into the camp, diverting precious resources to their flagship in the east. "I was probably the only SS leader in the entire SS," Höss later bragged, "who had such a comprehensive carte blanche for the procurement of all that was needed for Auschwitz."[13] Earlier KL had resembled small cities; Auschwitz turned into a metropolis. By August 1943, it held some seventy-four thousand prisoners, at a time when there were two hundred and twenty-four thousand registered KL prisoners across all the camps.[14] In view of the size of the Auschwitz complex, Pohl divided it in November 1943 into three main camps, each with its own commandant. Auschwitz I was the old main camp, led by the most senior local SS officer (who retained overall responsibility for the camp complex); Auschwitz II was the camp in Birkenau (with the gas chambers); and Auschwitz III contained the satellite camps dotted around eastern Silesia (fourteen by spring 1944), above all Monowitz.[15]

Conditions varied greatly across the vast Auschwitz complex, as we will see, just as they differed in the other KL in occupied eastern Europe during 1942–43. One Auschwitz prisoner likened his summer 1943 transfer from the main camp to Birkenau to a move from a major city to the countryside where everyone wore shabbier clothes. Another prisoner put it more starkly: the Auschwitz main camp—with its brick buildings, washrooms, and drinking water—was like paradise compared to the hell of Birkenau.[16] Despite all their differences, though, the ultimate aim of SS concentration camps in occupied eastern Europe was the same. None of their registered Jewish prisoners—those who had been selected for slave labor rather than immediate extermination—were supposed to survive in the long run.

JEWISH PRISONERS IN THE EAST

More than a year after her liberation from the Nazi camps, Nechama Epstein-Kozlowski lived with her new husband in a Jewish cooperative in a castle near Lake Como in Italy, where they waited impatiently to move to Palestine. It was here, on August 31, 1946, that the twenty-three-year-old Polish woman, pregnant with her first child, talked to the American psychologist David Boder, who had recently arrived in Europe to interview displaced persons. Before their conversation, which was taped on a wire recorder, Boder noted that Epstein-Kozlowski seemed cheerful; but her story, which unfolded over the next ninety minutes, was one of unremitting horror.

Even before she was dragged to the concentration camps, Epstein-Kozlowski had cheated death several times, escaping from a train bound for a death camp and surviving the ghettos of Warsaw and Meseritz (Międzyrzec). In spring 1943, by which time her whole family had been killed, she was taken to Majdanek and began a two-year odyssey through the KL system, which led her to Auschwitz, back to Majdanek, to Plaszow, back to Auschwitz, to Bergen-Belsen, to the Buchenwald satellite camp of Aschersleben, and finally, following a two-week death march, to the Theresienstadt ghetto, where she was liberated on May 8, 1945.

When Epstein-Kozlowski had first arrived in Birkenau, on June 26, 1943, on a transport with 625 other women from Majdanek, they were forced into a road construction commando known as the Death Detail; within a month, she recalled, 150 of the women were dead. Many of those who survived were later murdered. Epstein-Kozlowski herself lived through several selections, including three in the Birkenau infirmary, where, delirious with malaria, she hid in the bunks of non-Jewish prisoners. Jewish children were most vulnerable to such selections, but for several months during 1944, Epstein-Kozlowski helped to protect an eight-year-old orphan called Chaykele Wasserman: "That child was very dear to me. I loved it very much. That child could not go anyplace without me." Chaykele survived a selection in Plaszow by hiding in the latrine, and she also survived the later move to Auschwitz. But after Epstein-Kozlowski was chosen for a transport to Bergen-Belsen, they were finally separated: "And that child cried very much. When she saw that I was being taken, she cried very much and screamed, 'You are leaving me. Who will be my mother now?' But, alas, I could not help any . . . I cried very much. And the child was crying. And I parted from the child and left."[17] Chaykele probably died before the war ended, just like most other children in Auschwitz. Similarly, Nechama Epstein-Kozlowski's experience was shared by most other Jewish adults registered as KL prisoners in eastern Europe during the Holocaust, who faced destructive labor, violence, and constant selections. In one respect, though, her fate was unusual—she survived.

Slaves for IG Farben

Historians have long argued that the Holocaust highlights a sharp contradiction at the heart of Nazism: despite the desperate need for forced labor to feed the German war machine, the regime still went ahead with the mass extermination of European Jewry.[18] But for Nazi hard-liners there was no contradiction. Economics and extermination were two sides of the same coin; both were needed for victory. Winning the war required the ruthless destruction of all perceived threats *and* the mobilization of all remaining resources for the war effort. In the case of Jews judged capable of work, the authorities fused both of these aims into the policy of "annihilation through labor." Forced labor meant temporary survival for the selected Jews; but almost all of them were dead men and women walking, as far as the SS was concerned.[19]

KL labor in occupied eastern Europe varied enormously. At times, most notably in Majdanek, it was designed only for suffering.[20] More often, the authorities pursued aims that included, but also went beyond, the desire to inflict pain. Typically, Jewish prisoners were exploited during the deadly construction phase of new camps, as well as during their extension and maintenance; in Auschwitz, around half of all employed female prisoners worked in the service of the camp itself.[21] Beyond that, prisoners worked for SS enterprises, private companies, and the Nazi state. The experience of slave labor depended on many variables, such as the type, size, and supervision of the work details (few prisoners stayed for long in the same detail, moving frequently and often randomly elsewhere). Still, most Jewish KL laborers faced the same overall threat—labor and death.

This policy was pursued most consistently, perhaps, at the IG Farben site near Dwory. The only living things here, Primo Levi wrote, "are machines and slaves—and the former are more alive than the latter." Auschwitz prisoners had worked on the site since spring 1941. Initially, they still slept in the main camp, so they had to march every day for several hours along muddy roads to and from the building site, around four miles away (later, trains were used, too). IG Farben managers blamed these exhausting transports for the prisoners' poor output and lobbied for a satellite camp right next to the factory grounds. SS officials agreed after some hesitation, swayed by the WVHA's growing emphasis on productivity. Construction of the Monowitz concentration camp (or Buna camp) began in summer 1942, using the standard SS barrack model, and it opened in late October 1942. Built on the ruins of Monowitz village, the new camp cost some five million Reichsmark to construct; the sum was paid by IG Farben, which provided food and other supplies as well. The SS, meanwhile, was in charge of prisoners inside the camp and outside.

The new KL Monowitz belonged to a bigger complex on the grounds. It was one of eight compounds on the huge IG Farben construction site, which together provided around twenty thousand workers by November 1942. Some of them, like German civilians, enjoyed comparatively good conditions, while others, like forced workers from the Soviet Union (both POWs and others), suffered deprivation. But the KL, the only compound around Dwory run by the Camp SS, was the worst. "We are the slaves of the slaves," Primo Levi wrote, "whom all can give orders to." The new concentration camp quickly grew in size, following mass arrivals from the Auschwitz main camp. At the beginning of 1943, there were already 3,750 prisoners, increasing to around 7,000 a year later. The great majority of them—around nine out of ten— were Jews.[22]

Initiated by IG Farben, the KL Monowitz aimed to feed the industrial giant's appetite for labor. Work inside the compound itself was reduced to the bare minimum, so around four out of five prisoners toiled on the factory's building site outside, a "huge entanglement of iron, concrete, mud and smoke," as Levi described it. The great majority of prisoners ended up in large construction gangs. These commandos were all about unrelenting labor, largely performed without gloves, coats, or any other protection, even in winter. Prisoners erected huge concrete slabs and carried bricks, trees, and iron pipes across the site. Among the worst details was the cement commando—"a veritable murder commando," one survivor called it—where prisoners had to run from trains to warehouses with bulging cement sacks on their backs; weighing 110 pounds, the load was heavier than many of the prisoners. In the eyes of the authorities, the men in these labor details were easily replaceable and counted for almost nothing. Only a few trained prisoners in sought-after positions fared better: Bully Schott, for example, survived until his escape in August 1944, because of his abilities as a mechanic. But even skilled inmates like him often faced ruinous labor in Monowitz. After Primo Levi joined a small commando of trained chemists, he had to carry heavy phenylbeta sacks: "our strength," he feared at the time, "will not last out." Only in the final weeks of Auschwitz did he actually work inside the sheltered laboratory.[23]

General disdain for the prisoners shaped conditions inside Monowitz. Overcrowding was endemic—around 250 men were crammed into barracks originally designed for fifty-five civilian workers—as was dirt and disease. The SS aggravated the suffering at almost any opportunity. For example, Jewish prisoners—and only Jewish prisoners—had to exchange their leather shoes for ill-fitting wooden clogs, which soon cut gaping wounds into their feet. Worst of all was the slow starvation, "that chronic hunger unknown to free men," Levi wrote, "which makes one dream at night, and settles in all the limbs of one's body." The regular KL rations were pitiful and the additional Buna soup, which prisoners received courtesy of IG Farben, contained dirt and "plants which I have never seen growing before," according to another inmate. Starvation and strenuous work led to extreme weight loss, on average between four and nine pounds per week. After three or four months at the IG Farben site, the former prisoner doctor Berthold Epstein testified in April 1945, "most people died as a result of exhaustion and overexertion." Overall, around twenty-five thousand of all the thirty-five thousand prisoners sent to Monowitz lost their lives.[24]

Violent excesses hastened their deaths. One of the leading guards in Monowitz was report leader Bernhard Rakers, a brutal Camp SS veteran (he had signed up back in 1934). His violent record was long and he added to it every day, even though inmates tried hard to stay clear of the man they called the "Buna lion."[25] Then there were the Monowitz Kapos. Among the most notorious was the camp elder Josef ("Jupp") Windeck, a middle-aged German petty criminal. On the day Monowitz was first opened, he gave a speech to the assembled prisoners. According to one survivor, he said: "You're not here for fun, you'll all get wrecked anyway, and you'll all go through the chimney." True to his word, Windeck—who used to parade around in riding boots, brandishing a dog whip—frequently beat other prisoners to a pulp.[26]

SS guards and Kapos were the usual suspects when it came to tormenting prisoners at work. But in Monowitz, the IG Farben paymasters had their say, too. Keen to wring as much labor power from prisoners as they could, company officials demanded strenuous efforts and strict discipline from the frail prisoners. While chief engineer Max Faust opposed some SS excesses—such as "shooting prisoners on the building site or pounding them half-dead," as he put it in 1943—he still insisted on "punishment of a moderate kind," which in practice often meant more violence, either beatings by Kapos and company officials or official whippings by the SS.[27]

IG Farben was an active partner in the policy of "annihilation through labor." Instead of improving prisoner provisions and the treatment of the sick, the company received an assurance from the WVHA that "all weak prisoners can be deported" to be replaced by others fit for work. This was the basis for constant selections in Monowitz. They were most frequent in the camp's infirmary, where an SS doctor came about once a week to "empty the beds," as the SS called it. Walking briskly through the rooms—individual decisions often took no more than a few seconds—the physician picked out those who had already spent two or three weeks inside and others who were not expected to return to work anytime soon. In this way, thousands of prisoners—almost all of them Jews—were selected in the Monowitz infirmary and transported to Birkenau.[28] Here, most were driven straight to the crematoria complex; as a former Birkenau block leader put it after the war, the doomed prisoners were "practically no longer alive" even before they were gassed.[29]

The Selection

"To relieve the camp, it is necessary to remove simpletons, idiots, cripples, and sick people as quickly as possible through liquidation."[30] This is how an SS officer summed up, in late 1942, the purpose of selections in a concentration camp like Auschwitz. By then, such prisoner selections had become routine. But things were about to change. As economic imperatives became more pressing, the SS made half-hearted efforts to curb the enormous death rates in the KL system (chapter 8). This included restrictions on selections, at least in some camps.[31] As early as December 1942, the Auschwitz camp compound leader Hans Aumeier complained to a colleague about a ban on gassing Polish invalids, who were supposed to die a "natural death" (as he put it) instead.[32] This did not apply to registered Jewish prisoners, however. Murderous selections remained a hallmark of the KL for Jews in occupied eastern Europe. In mixed camps like Auschwitz and Majdanek, which held both Jewish and non-Jewish inmates, the SS now introduced a two-tier system. Whereas most other registered prisoners were spared the lethal injections and the gas chambers, countless ill, injured, and emaciated Jews were still murdered after selections.[33]

There was no set pattern, as the Camp SS conducted routine selections and impromptu ones, mass selections and individual ones. In general, the period immediately after arrival was particularly perilous. In Auschwitz, some Jewish prisoners had only just survived the initial selection at the ramp when they, too, were condemned: as they stripped naked inside the camp baths, their clothes no longer concealed injuries and illnesses.[34] Many more Jews followed over the coming days, picked out from the quarantine sectors that awaited most new inmates. Murders of selected new arrivals had slowly spread across the whole KL system during the early war years, as part of the wider SS assault on invalids. In summer 1942, the WVHA coordinated matters, ordering that new prisoners should be isolated in special blocks for four weeks after arrival; anyone who was sick would be removed and "treated separately."[35] Camp SS officials in eastern Europe understood this as an open invitation to mass murder in the quarantine sectors.[36]

Mass selections of Jews continued inside the main camp compounds. In the second half of 1943, for example, selections took place at least once a week during roll call in the Riga main camp. One survivor later described the SS man in charge: "He pulled women out of the ranks whose faces he somehow did not like, who wore glasses, had a spot on the face, even an injured finger, and gave orders for their extermination." There were further actions during baths and before or after labor.[37] Such SS selections often turned into grotesque spectacles. The Polish political prisoner Danuta Medryk, who witnessed several selections in Majdanek, described how the Jewish women had to hold up their skirts to expose their legs, as SS doctors picked out those with swollen and bleeding limbs; emaciated buttocks were also regarded as a sure sign of starvation. Those prisoners selected to die ripped off bandages and held their heads up as high as possible, even appearing to smile at their executioners, in the vain hope of a final reprieve.[38]

The conditions in eastern European KL often made it impossible to escape selection and death. Jewish prisoners everywhere were slowly starving to death; in Klooga, for example, the daily ration was thin soup with a piece of bread, partly baked with sand. Add maddening thirst, crippling labor, extreme violence, and the sanitary catastrophe, and it is clear why tens of thousands became *Muselmänner* within weeks of their arrival, and thus prime targets for the selections.[39]

Normally, the SS reflex was to blame prisoners for squalor and disease. But the state of the camps in the east was so appalling that even local officers called for improvements. In a meeting with SS construction boss Kammler, Auschwitz commandant Höss and his chief physician Wirths complained in May 1943 that the situation in Birkenau (still without central water supply) was woeful, lacking the most basic hygienic and medical standards. Höss had not suddenly turned into a humanitarian; he had more pragmatic concerns. From his point of view, too many prisoners died in the wrong way—that is, from illness, not economic exploitation—resulting in a "huge wastage of manpower."[40] Until conditions improved, local Camp SS leaders promoted murderous selections as the most effective defense against the danger of epidemics to themselves and their families. The gassing of sick and weak Jews, Höss assured his men, was necessary to prevent the spread of illness. In this way, local SS officials rationalized the slaughter of prisoners as an act of disease control and self-preservation, and contributed to the escalation of Nazi terror from below.[41]

In reality, SS selections actually helped to spread epidemics, by making the sick even warier of reporting to doctors. Most Jewish prisoners knew about the selections among patients. In Auschwitz, the initial selection came right after a prisoner was admitted to the infirmary; those judged too weak or sick to recover soon were isolated and killed.[42] As for the others, the infernal conditions in most infirmaries offered little hope for recovery. The French prisoner doctor Sima Vaisman later described her first impression of the infirmary at the Birkenau women's camp in early 1944: "A smell of corpses, of excrement . . . And the sick, skeletal beings, covered almost entirely in scabies, in boils, bitten to pieces by lice, all completely naked, shivering with cold under their disgusting blankets."[43] The infirmaries meant death for most Jewish prisoners; reporting for admission was a last resort, an enormous risk, like a game of Russian roulette with an almost fully loaded gun.

Among the infirmary personnel, lower-ranking officials, so-called SS orderlies (*Sanitätsdienstgrade*), played a key role in selections and were often decorated for their murderous deeds.[44] One of these men was Oberscharführer Heinz Wisner. An eager SS activist, born in Danzig in 1916, Wisner worked for several years as a shipping clerk before joining the SS full-time during the war as a medic. In summer 1943, he was transferred from Flossenbürg to the Riga main camp, where he dominated the small infirmaries for women and men.[45] Unlike the elderly SS camp doctor Eduard Krebsbach, who only appeared occasionally, the pompous Wisner made his rounds more than once a week. Wearing a white coat over his uniform, the would-be doctor pushed military discipline to perverse extremes; even the dying had to lie straight on their backs as Wisner moved from bed to bed, inspecting each inmate. After he had made his decision, he frequently marked the bed frames of the doomed with a large "X." These inmates were then either shot in nearby woods or murdered in their beds by lethal injection (there were no gas chambers in Riga). Although he often left these injections to prisoner doctors, it was Wisner who became known in the camp as "the man with the syringe."[46]

Of course, death could come anywhere and anytime, not just after selections; it was the ever-present shadow of Jewish prisoners. One of the first things he was told as he entered Birkenau in late 1942, a Polish Jew wrote not long after, was that no one survived the camp for more than three weeks.[47] The sight of dead bodies—in beds and latrines, on trucks and building sites—was familiar to all, as was the smoke from the crematoria; Renate Lasker-Allais, a young German Jew deported to Birkenau in late 1943, threw up constantly because of the nauseating stench of burning bodies.[48] Even though most Jewish prisoners clung to faint hopes of survival, they knew that few, if any, would get out alive. They even speculated about the relative merits of the different deaths the SS had in store for them: How long before one suffocated in a gas chamber? How painful was death by injection? Better a swift blow to the head, or to waste away in the infirmary?[49]

The Auschwitz Special Squad

In the eyes of Primo Levi, the creation of the Auschwitz Special Squad—the prisoner detail that led the doomed to the gas chambers, burned their bodies, and scattered their remains—was "National Socialism's most demonic crime."[50] Forcing prisoners to assist SS terror was nothing new, and the more strenuous and disgusting the work, the keener the Camp SS usually was to leave it to prisoners. This rule applied, above all, to work in the crematoria. In Dachau, for example, the small cremation commando was made up of German, Russian, and Jewish prisoners. Some of them were expected to do more than burn bodies. Soon after the German prisoner Emil Mahl joined the Dachau commando in early 1944, he was forced to participate in executions. "As a walking corpse," Mahl later testified, "I had to do horrible things here."[51]

But nothing compared to the Special Squad in Auschwitz. Initially, just a handful of prisoners had worked in the old Auschwitz crematorium. But after Auschwitz turned into a death camp in 1942, the SS established a large, permanent prisoner commando at the Birkenau killing complex. Their work temporarily saved these inmates from extermination, though often not for long. While the SS did not murder all Special Squad members at regular intervals (as some survivors and historians suggest), there were selections just as elsewhere in the camp; weak and sick prisoners—sometimes as many as twenty or more a week—were killed with phenol injections in the infirmary. Moreover, the SS occasionally killed a proportion of the prisoners, to reduce the relative size of the Special Squad, during periods when fewer deportation trains arrived. In the end, only a few survived from 1942 through to 1945, among them the brothers Shlomo and Abraham Dragon, whom we encountered earlier.

Overall, more than 2,200 men were forced into the Auschwitz Special Squad during its existence. There were some Polish and German supervisors, like the chief Kapo August Brück. A German prisoner with a green triangle, Brück had worked in the Buchenwald crematorium from 1940, before the SS transferred him to Auschwitz in March 1943 to oversee the Special Squad at the newly built Birkenau crematoria; in contrast to some other supervisors, Kapo August, as the others called him, was regarded as decent (his privileges as a prominent prisoner could not protect him and he died of typhus in late December 1943). Almost all the rest of the Special Squad was made up of Jewish prisoners. They lived apart from the rest of the inmates, first in isolated blocks in Birkenau and later, from early summer 1944, on the grounds of the crematorium complex itself. Like other KL inmates thrown together as Jews, their backgrounds varied widely in terms of education, religion, and age; the oldest was in his fifties, the youngest not yet twenty. The men came from more than a dozen countries and often formed loose groups along national lines. Communication proved difficult across cultural and linguistic barriers, especially for those, like Greek Jews, who spoke neither Yiddish nor German, the two main languages used by the Special Squad prisoners.[52]

In a morbid twist of fate, it was the Jewish prisoners closest to the inferno of the Holocaust who enjoyed the best living conditions. Looking back in early November 1944 on his life in the Special Squad, in a secret letter to his wife and daughter that never reached them, the forty-three-year-old Chaim Herman, a Polish Jew, wrote that prisoners like him had everything but freedom: "I am very well dressed, housed and fed, I am in the best of health" (he was murdered by the SS three weeks later).[53] The prisoners could help themselves to possessions left behind by those who had gone to the gas. They were dressed in warm clothes and proper underwear, and rarely suffered hunger. Among the effects of the dead, they found not only coffee and cigarettes, but delicacies from all across Europe: olives from Greece, cheese from Holland, goose meat from Hungary.[54] And unlike other Jewish inmates in Auschwitz, Special Squad prisoners could move rather freely around their quarters. After the transfer to their new sleeping quarters under the roof of crematoria II and III, they had heated rooms, running water, and proper toilets—unimaginable luxuries for any other Jewish prisoners in the camp. Their quarters were furnished with the goods of the dead: tables covered with porcelain plates and tablecloths, and comfortable bedding and blankets on the bunks.[55]

The Special Squad prisoners also shared an unusual relationship with the SS, as working side by side inside the "death factory" created a certain bond. Prisoners still greatly feared the SS, and with good reason. But they built up personal relationships, which tended to lessen arbitrary violence. These prisoners were not part of a faceless mass but familiar to SS men by name. On some Sundays, when they were off-duty, the guards even played soccer against the prisoners, right by the crematorium. Other SS men and inmates watched, clapped, and shouted their support, Primo Levi wrote, "as if, rather than at the gates of hell, the game were taking place on the village green."[56]

This close relationship with the SS only added to the loathing some other Jews in Auschwitz felt for the Special Squad. Its duties were widely known— details spread via the few non-Jewish Kapos, for example, who slept in regular barracks—and there was plenty of talk about its alleged brutality toward the doomed.[57] There were also rumors that the SS selected only the most violent criminals for the Special Squad. Such hostile feelings were summed up by two Slovakian Jews in 1944: the men of the Special Squad were shunned by others, they wrote, because they "stink terribly" and were "completely degenerate and incredibly brutal and ruthless."[58] Even some of the doomed, on their way to the gas chamber, called the Special Squad "Jewish murderer[s]."[59] The indicted prisoners knew that they were infamous. When Filip Müller met his father in the Birkenau compound, he was too ashamed to admit that he was part of the Special Squad.[60] The stigma remained after liberation and has not vanished even today.[61]

But we must remember that the Special Squad members were caught in a hell made by the SS. None of them had volunteered and many felt, at first, that they would be unable to adapt. "I thought I was going insane," one survivor recalled. Initially, they often worked in a trance, like robots. In secret papers buried in a jar near crematorium III in autumn 1944, Salmen Lewental, a Polish student who had arrived in Auschwitz in December 1942 with his family, wrote that during his first day in the Special Squad "none of us were fully conscious."[62]

The men selected for the Special Squad soon realized that their only options were obedience or death. A few committed suicide. Others were murdered for insubordination; when five Jewish inmates reported sick after their first day in the crematorium, sometime in 1943, the SS killed them straightaway. Even small mistakes could prove lethal; at least one prisoner "dentist" was burned alive by the SS for sabotage because he had overlooked a gold tooth inside a corpse's mouth.[63] Most prisoners chose to comply and to live, at least for the moment. In his secret notes, Salmen Lewental captured the anguish of the Special Squad in an existential cry: "And the truth is that one wants to live at any cost, one wishes to live, because one is alive, because the whole world is alive."[64]

Choosing life in the Birkenau Special Squad was one of the most impossible "choiceless choices" facing prisoners in Auschwitz.[65] What kind of life was this, amidst all the dead? Some men became inured to the suffering, acting indifferent and cruel, and focused only on the material benefits. Others suffered from the daily corrosion of their souls, and escaped into drink. It was not just the horror of mass murder—the pleas, the screams, the bodies, the blood—that haunted them, but their deep sense of guilt, having been deprived by the SS "of even the solace of innocence," in Primo Levi's words.[66] But there were also acts of kindness and courage. As they did not expect to survive, several Special Squad prisoners documented the crimes they witnessed, knowing that no other inmates would come closer to the Nazi heart of darkness. Writing such secret notes required bravery, teamwork, and ingenuity. The great personal risk was worth it, the prisoners felt, to preserve their voices for future generations. Nine different documents, buried on the grounds of the Birkenau killing complex, were recovered after liberation. Among them was a brief message by one of the last surviving members of the Special Squad—he has never been identified—written on November 26, 1944. Certain that he was about to be murdered, he added a final note to several others he had buried earlier in boxes and receptacles near crematoria II and III. At the end of his message, he made this last plea: "I am asking for everything to be arranged together and published with the title 'Amidst a Nightmare of Crime.'"[67]

Women and Men

During the Holocaust, women moved from the fringes toward the center of the concentration camp system. For years, female prisoners had been marginal. But the 1942 decision to use camps in occupied eastern Europe for the "annihilation through labor" of Jewish prisoners irrespective of their gender changed everything. In Majdanek, Jewish women accounted for over one-third of all prisoners by spring 1943.[68] In Auschwitz, the ratio of female to male inmates fell to less than 1:2 by the end of 1943; and the vast majority of the imprisoned women were Jewish.[69] Back in Ravensbrück, female prisoners had initially remained insulated from some of the worst SS excesses. Not so in eastern Europe. From the moment they first set foot in Auschwitz in spring 1942, women faced dreadful conditions, ruinous labor, and extreme violence. Official SS statistics confirm the deadly reality of their lives. During July 1943, registered female prisoners were more than twenty times more likely to die in Auschwitz than in Ravensbrück.[70] In all, an estimated fifty-four thousand registered women lost their lives in Auschwitz in 1942–43.[71]

Of all the female prisoners in the hands of the SS, Jewish women faced the gravest danger. Inside eastern European KL, their mortality rate was broadly similar to that of Jewish men.[72] In fact, it was even higher, if one includes those killed without formal registration (since more Jewish women than men were singled out for immediate extermination on arrival). Overall, the gender-determined delay in Camp SS terror came to an end in 1942–43, at least for Jewish women in eastern Europe. However, this did not mean that their experiences were now identical to those of Jewish men. Many gendered differences remained, while others, such as pregnancy, gained new significance.

Previously, prisoner pregnancies had been regarded as a peripheral problem by the Camp SS. Overall numbers of female prisoners had been relatively small anyway, and there was also a ban (at least on paper) on sending pregnant women to state prisons and concentration camps.[73] But as the war continued, this ban became increasingly meaningless, especially during the mass deportations of the Holocaust: the Nazi Final Solution targeted all Jews. In Auschwitz, visibly pregnant Jewish women were selected on arrival and gassed; a few were subjected to atrocities at the ramp, like a Greek woman who was kicked so hard in the stomach by an SS man in summer 1943 that she immediately aborted.[74] Jewish prisoners whose pregnancy was discovered later on, after they had joined the ranks of registered slave laborers, were also regularly gassed, either before or after giving birth, and their newborns were killed, too. "Jewish children were immediately exterminated," the former Birkenau camp compound leader Johann Schwarzhuber admitted after the war. In other KL in the east, too, babies born inside were murdered; in Riga, SS men even preserved the corpses of a few infants in a special solution. Meanwhile, some women returned to work after they had suffered a stillbirth or after prisoner doctors had carried out a secret abortion.[75] In Auschwitz, prisoner doctors and orderlies even conspired to kill newborn children to save the mothers. "And so, the Germans succeeded in making murderers of even us," Olga Lengyel, who worked in the Birkenau infirmary, wrote after the war. "To this day the picture of those murdered babies haunts me."[76]

Male prisoners in Auschwitz had been incredulous when they heard about the new women's compound.[77] But contacts remained sporadic, at least in Auschwitz-Birkenau, where the prisoners were strictly separated by sex.[78] For the most part, encounters with the opposite sex did not go beyond brief glimpses from afar, which often caused pity and horror. The destruction of masculine and feminine traits—reducing prisoners to bald and gaunt figures—demonstrated the powers of the SS. In the absence of mirrors, it was also a brutal reminder of each prisoner's own desexualization and dehumanization.[79] Occasionally, men and women in Auschwitz-Birkenau managed to exchange a quick word at the fence or to throw some food across. A few husbands and wives even corresponded by letter, carried by civilian workers and non-Jewish inmates. But such contacts were rare, and their impotence to fulfill gendered expectations—protecting female friends or relatives—deepened the anguish of some Jewish men.[80]

The situation was rather different in the new main concentration camps and satellites established in eastern Europe in 1943–44. Here, too, Jewish prisoners were normally separated by gender—in different compounds, barracks, or rooms—but the layout of these camps made strict isolation more difficult. The closer contact between men and women also reflected the previous use of some of these sites as ghettos or forced labor camps. In KL Plaszow, for example, men and women were still allowed to meet up in the evenings, walking through the unlocked gate that separated their compounds. Elsewhere, men and women worked in the same labor commandos.[81] Once again, SS rules regarded as immutable in established concentration camps were eroded in the new camps for Jews.

The detention of male and female prisoners in the same camps soon gave rise to salacious stories among both prisoners and SS.[82] After the war, the obsession with sex in the camps grew further, spawning a perverse pornography of pain. Following a spate of sadomasochistic films in the 1970s, Primo Levi pleaded: "Please, all you cinema producers, leave the women's camps alone."[83] In reality, sexual activity had largely been the preserve of a few privileged prisoners. In the short lives of most Jewish KL prisoners during the Holocaust, it had played little or no role: starvation killed their sex drive before it killed them.[84] An Austrian Jew, who had come to Auschwitz in 1942, recalled that his sexual urges had simply vanished.[85] Most women experienced the same. A Jewish teacher deported from Hungary to Auschwitz in 1944 noted in her diary that she "ceased to be a sexual being" (for many younger women, such feelings were intensified because they stopped menstruating in the camps).[86] Any encounters that did occur often involved an element of exploitation or force, at least in the case of Jewish prisoners. Most common was probably sex for survival, with prisoners making pragmatic decisions to become intimate with privileged inmates, mostly non-Jews, in exchange for essential goods like food or clothing.[87] Instead of flowers, one survivor recalled, a man might bring a woman a piece of margarine. In this way, sex became another commodity to be exchanged in the camps' flourishing underground economy.[88]

Children

The Holocaust was unprecedented, it has often been said, because of the Nazis' intention to annihilate an entire people, "down to its last member" in the words of Elie Wiesel.[89] The program of all-out mass extermination meant that countless families were dragged to SS concentration camps together. On arrival, they were almost always ripped apart, and most were dead within hours, at least in a death camp like Auschwitz. The survivors suffered a dual trauma. In addition to the shock of Auschwitz, which hit all new prisoners, they soon learned that their wives, husbands, mothers, fathers, or children had already been killed in the nearby gas chambers.

After Salmen Gradowski was taken to a barrack in Birkenau, having just survived the initial selection following his deportation from Grodno ghetto (Bialystok district) in late 1942, he and other men on his transport immediately asked the more experienced inmates about the fate of their families:

What had happened since their separation at the ramp? The veterans answered with brutal honesty, as Gradowski recorded in secret notes buried on the grounds of the camp: "They are already in heaven," the veterans said, and: "Your families have already been let go with the smoke." Auschwitz was an extermination camp, the newcomers were told, and the first rule was to "leave behind all sorrow about your families."[90]

Many other recent arrivals were initiated similarly, but once the awful truth sank in, they reacted in very different ways. Some tried to repress their grief; when Dr. Elie Cohen, a thirty-four-year-old Dutch Jew who arrived in Auschwitz from Westerbork in September 1943, learned that his wife and son had been murdered in the gas chambers, he just wanted "to keep it up"—to go on living (as he later wrote).[91] Other men and women broke down. Magda Zelikovitz remembers that she went "completely mad" after she realized that her seven-year-old son, her mother, and the rest of her family (with whom she had just been deported from Budapest) had been gassed: "I did not want to live anymore." Other prisoners stopped her several times from throwing herself into the electric fence.[92]

The shock of Auschwitz was greatest for children who suddenly found themselves abandoned. Although the vast majority of Jewish children were murdered on arrival, thousands were registered as prisoners, here and in the other KL for Jews in the east. Albert Abraham Buton was just thirteen years old when he was separated from his mother and father at the Auschwitz ramp in April 1943, after their deportation from Salonika. His parents were taken straight to the gas chambers, leaving Albert and his brother behind. "We couldn't think, we were so stunned," he recalled, "we were unable to grasp what was happening."[93] As more child prisoners like Buton were registered (both Jews and non-Jews), the average age of the prisoner population fell. In Majdanek, the authorities responded by creating a new position in the prisoner hierarchy: in addition to the camp elder, there was now a camp youngest, who received special SS privileges.[94]

The SS was partially blind to the age of its prisoners and forced the younger victims to undergo many of the same hardships as adults. Many children, too, suffered abuse, hunger, and roll calls, as well as hard labor. Mascha Rolnikaite was sixteen years old when she had to carry heavy rocks and push carts full of stones and sand on construction sites near the Riga satellite camp Strasdenhof. Other youths worked as gardeners and bricklayers. As for those judged too young to work, small children in Majdanek had to march in circles all day.[95] Nor were child prisoners exempt from SS beatings and official punishments like the penal companies.[96] Some suffered an even worse fate.

In the Vaivara satellite camp Narva, for example, ten-year-old Mordchaj was strung up, after a failed escape, by the SS commando leader as a warning to all others (the SS man later cut him down and he survived).[97]

Selections posed a constant threat, as the children learned only too well. After one of the periodic selections among Jews in the Birkenau quarantine camp, a prisoner doctor briefly spoke to a small boy from Będzin called Jurek, who was among those chosen to die. When the doctor asked him how he was, the boy answered: "I am not afraid, everything is so dreadful here, it can only be better up there."[98] Some SS sweeps targeted children only. In Majdanek, Jewish children and babies were taken to a special barrack, cut off from the women's compound by barbed wire. At regular intervals, SS men emptied this barrack, driving the victims into the gas chambers. Some children escaped, only to be pulled out of hiding by guard dogs. Others struggled with the guards. "The children screamed and did not want to go," the Majdanek survivor Henrika Mitron testified after the war. "The children were dragged around and thrown on the truck."[99]

There was no room for innocence in the KL. Children had to live by the rules of the camp and were often forced to act like adults.[100] Terror even seeped into the games they occasionally played, such as "Caps off" and "Roll call," where older children pretended to be Kapos or SS guards and chased the younger ones. In Birkenau, there was a game called "Gas chamber," though none of the children wanted to enact their own deaths. Instead, they used stones to represent the doomed, throwing them into a trench—the gas chamber—and mimicking the screams of those pressed inside.[101]

No child could survive alone. Occasionally, adult prisoners tried to protect those who had been separated from their parents, acting as their so-called camp mothers or fathers. "We were . . . really well taken care of," recalled Janka Avram, one of the small number of Jewish children to survive Plaszow, "because the thousands of Jewish women who had lost their children to the death camps treated us like their own."[102] More commonly, children stayed with one of their own parents, though their relationships invariably changed. While younger children were terrified of being separated, older ones often grew up fast; as their parents' authority was eroded by helplessness and illness, they sometimes assumed the role of protector and provider.[103]

Several camps in the east, in addition to Majdanek, had special barracks for isolating Jewish children.[104] In Vaivara, they were placed in the lower part of the Ereda satellite camp, together with sick prisoners. Conditions were dreadful. Built on marshy ground, the primitive huts offered no protection from the elements; in winter, it was so cold that the prisoners' hair sometimes froze to the ground as they were sleeping. Among the children languishing here was a five-year-old girl who had been deported to Estonia in summer 1943 with her mother from the Wilna ghetto. Her mother was held in the upper part of Ereda, less than a mile away, and although it was forbidden, she tried to sneak past the SS guards every day to visit her daughter. When her girl became gravely ill, she smuggled her out of the children's compound and hid her in a barrack for adults. But the girl was discovered by the SS camp leader just before a death transport left the camp. "I cried for a whole night," the mother later wrote, "fell to his feet and kissed the boots of the murderer, he should not take my child from me, but it was no use." The next morning, the girl was taken away with many other children, and she was murdered some days later in Auschwitz-Birkenau.[105]

Close to the Birkenau extermination complex, where these children from Ereda were gassed and burned, lay one of the most unusual compounds in any of the concentration camps: the so-called family camp, a special sector for Jewish families deported from Theresienstadt, the dismal Nazi ghetto for elderly and so-called privileged Jews in the Czech Protectorate, which shared some similarities with the KL.[106] The Birkenau family camp had been set up after the arrival of two transports from Theresienstadt in September 1943, carrying some five thousand Jewish men, women, and children, almost all of them Czech Jews; in December 1943, further mass transports from the ghetto arrived in the family camp (this was not the only such compound in Birkenau, as the SS also forced families into the so-called Gypsy camp). Inside, Jewish men and women were divided into barracks on opposite sides of the path dissecting the compound, but they could meet before evening roll call or secretly in the latrines during the day.

Conditions in the family camp were appalling—around one in four Jews perished within six months of their arrival in September 1943—but they were still better than in some other parts of the Auschwitz complex. Compared to other Jews in Birkenau, the prisoners enjoyed numerous privileges. They kept some of their possessions and clothes, even their own hair, and received occasional food packages from outside. Most strikingly, Jews were not subjected to SS selections, neither on arrival nor over the following months. The reason for these exceptions is not clear. Most likely, Himmler wanted to use the Birkenau family camp as a propaganda showcase in case of a visit by the International Committee of the Red Cross (just as the SS planned to deceive the Red Cross with the "model" ghetto Theresienstadt). Whatever the reason, other Jewish prisoners in Auschwitz looked with disbelief and envy upon the family camp.[107]

Among the prisoners in the Birkenau family camp were several thousand

children. During the day, many of those under the age of fourteen were allowed into the children's block, run by Fredy Hirsch, a charismatic twenty-
eight-year-old German Jew who had already played a leading role in youth
welfare in Theresienstadt. While there were barracks for children in other
parts of Birkenau, too, the one in the family camp was unique, reflecting the
compound's special status. Despite shortages of everything, from paper to
pens, Hirsch and the other teachers drew up a full curriculum. There were
songs, stories, and German lessons, as well as sports and games. Older children wrote their own newspaper and painted the walls of the barrack. And
the children put on plays, including a musical based on the Disney cartoon
Snow White. But such eerie moments of normality in the midst of terror—
epitomized by Jewish children dancing and singing jolly tunes, just a few
hundred yards from the Birkenau gas chambers—did not last long. In the
night from March 8 to 9, 1944, barely a week after Adolf Eichmann had inspected the family camp, the SS murdered some 3,800 inmates, who had arrived the previous September, in the gas chambers of crematoria II and III.
Among the dead were many of the children; their mentor Fredy Hirsch had
committed suicide hours earlier, after another prisoner had told him about
the SS plans.[108]

The survivors included some twins spared for human experiments.
Among them were Zdeněk and Jiři Steiner. When the two boys surveyed the
compound after the murders in March 1944, which had claimed their parents, it seemed eerily empty; all they saw were "flames flickering from the
chimney of the crematorium." The remaining inmates of the family camp
were soon joined by thousands of new arrivals from Theresienstadt, following another wave of deportations in May 1944. But few of them would live for
long, either. In July, following the selection of some 3,200 prisoners for slave
labor, the remaining 6,700 inmates—mostly women, children, the elderly,
and the infirm—were murdered in the gas chambers. In the eyes of the SS,
the Birkenau family camp had outlived its purpose and was abandoned.[109]

Some Auschwitz SS men felt uneasy about the eradication of the family
camp. It was not unusual for guards to hesitate when it came to the abuse and
murder of prisoners whom they had come to know personally.[110] This was
especially true for the Jewish children in Birkenau, many of whom had spent
several months inside. During that time, individual SS men had developed a
soft spot for them, bringing them toys like footballs, and enjoying their
theater performances. When the orders came through to liquidate the
camp, a few SS staff apparently tried to intervene with their superiors to
save the children.[111] But they still carried out their murderous orders, leaving
them full of self-pity about the difficult tasks they had to perform for the

German fatherland in the Nazi-occupied east. It was a complaint that had been heard many times before.

SS ROUTINES

Early on Wednesday, September 23, 1942, WVHA leader Oswald Pohl and other senior SS officers, including his trusted construction chief Hans Kammler, arrived in Auschwitz for a day packed full of meetings and inspections.[112] Just one week earlier, on September 15, Pohl and Kammler had met with Armaments Minister Albert Speer, who signed off on ambitious plans for the extension of Auschwitz (projected cost: 13.7 million Reichsmark), reflecting its increasing prominence in the Holocaust. The budget included more funds for the Birkenau killing complex, additional barracks, and other facilities. When all was done, Pohl expected Auschwitz prisoner numbers to reach one hundred thirty-two thousand, effectively quadrupling the current capacity.[113] Pohl immediately informed Himmler about his deal with Speer, and then met him in person on September 19, once more accompanied by Kammler, to review some of the details.[114]

During their visit to Auschwitz four days later, Pohl and Kammler talked over the plans with SS experts from the local construction office. This was just one of many items on their agenda. Pohl also chaired a large meeting with party and state officials to resolve thorny issues about the place of the camp within the wider local community. In addition to the never-ending problem of the camp's water supply and waste disposal, the officials discussed the ongoing efforts to turn the city of Auschwitz into a model settlement. The architect Hans Stosberg offered some particulars about the SS neighborhood and received Pohl's permission to build a leisure park for local residents not far from the camp.[115] On the afternoon of September 23, 1942, Pohl then embarked on a lengthy tour across the SS interest zone itself, including the main camp, Birkenau, and the IG Farben building site. Pohl's trip took longer than expected and he returned just in time for a lavish dinner in the officers' mess, serving the best beer and as much fish as the men could eat.[116]

After the meal, Pohl spoke to the assembled senior members of the Auschwitz Camp SS. He thanked them for turning Auschwitz into the most important SS concentration camp, and reassured them that their work was no less important than frontline service in the Death's Head division (to whom the Camp SS felt chronically inferior). Himmler's orders for the KL were extremely important for victory, Pohl stressed, whatever the strain on individual officers. He was thinking, not least, about the mass murder of

European Jewry, which he alluded to as "special assignments, about which no words have to be lost." An inspection of bunker 2 in Birkenau had been on Pohl's agenda during the previous afternoon, and he cannot have missed the dark plumes of smoke rising from the nearby open ditches, where the SS was burning corpses. Considering the so-called Final Solution, Pohl lauded his men for their dedication and their commitment to the cause.[117] Straight after his speech, Pohl demonstrated his appreciation by offering a special reward. He approved the construction of a brothel for the Auschwitz Camp SS, the first of its kind, so that his men could seek some diversion after a long day of mass murder.[118]

Foreigners in the Camp SS

During his speech on September 23, 1942, Oswald Pohl praised the exemplary comradeship of the Auschwitz SS, firmly united under Commandant Rudolf Höss. But this was just an empty phrase: it was well known in the WVHA that there was plenty of friction within the Auschwitz ranks.[119] The acrimonious tone was set by the unforgiving Höss himself, who clashed frequently with his men. His disdain remained undimmed after the war. Sitting in his prison cell in Krakow, he wrote withering pen-portraits of Auschwitz officials who had crossed his path, dismissing them as devious, duplicitous, or plain dumb.[120] The loathing between Höss and some of his men was mutual. There was much bickering behind his back, with subordinates complaining about his cold, prim, and ruthless manner.[121] Of course, the Camp SS had never been a band of brothers; the picture of close comradeship was always a projection of SS leaders, covering up conflicts between Guard Troop and Commandant Staff, between officers and rank-and-file. Still, the spirit of the Camp SS became ever more fractured as the war wore on, especially in occupied eastern Europe.

The conflicts had much to do with personnel changes and shortages. Although the number of Camp SS men grew during the war, it never caught up with the huge expansion of the prisoner population. In March 1942, there had been around 11,000 prisoners and 1,800 SS men in Auschwitz (6:1). Two years later, there were some 67,000 prisoners and 2,950 SS personnel (23:1).[122] The WVHA was well aware of the resulting strain on its staff. One solution was to reduce demands on them, by handing more powers to Kapos, by rationalizing procedures, and by using more guard dogs.[123] The WVHA also tried hard to recruit new officials, especially for its expanding camps in eastern Europe. Expectations were low. Since he was no longer allowed to recruit men fit for frontline service as sentries, Camp Inspector Glücks was resigned to receiving "more and more physically disabled and cripples," as he put it in 1942.[124]

Some vacant posts in eastern Europe were filled with experienced KL staff from inside Germany; in Auschwitz, around a hundred SS men arrived in 1941 from other concentration camps farther west. Such transfers to the east promised rapid advancement, since the SS had to fill many senior positions. The NCO Hans K., for example, moved in spring 1943 from a lowly position in Sachsenhausen to become labor action leader in Riga.[125] Nonetheless, many German KL staff resented such transfers. They complained about being stuck in primitive backwaters and saw their new posting as a punishment (there was some truth in this, as Camp SS managers often reassigned officials to the east as a disciplinary measure).[126] Additional men arrived from Waffen SS divisions, including injured fighters and invalids, though not all local commandants welcomed these veterans with open arms. Rudolf Höss, for one, complained about Eicke dumping men on the camps for whom he had no use anymore.[127]

The WVHA knew that it could never fill its needs with German nationals alone. Among the foreign associates of the Nazi regime during World War II were many tens of thousands of men who joined the ranks of the Waffen SS. As German losses at the front mounted from 1942, SS efforts to recruit from abroad redoubled, and before long, foreigners made up a large proportion of the Waffen SS.[128] Many thousands of them became KL staff; often, they were deployed in the camps after no more than two or three weeks' perfunctory training.[129] The vast majority of them hailed from eastern and southeastern Europe.[130] Most were "ethnic Germans," an amorphous term applied to those foreigners who were embraced by the Nazi authorities as part of the German people, though they were not normally German citizens. By autumn 1943, around seven thousand such "ethnic Germans"—around three thousand from Romania, the others largely from Hungary, Slovakia, and Croatia—served as sentries in the SS Guard Troops, accounting for almost half of their total strength.[131] In addition, the KL recruited so-called alien auxiliaries, who joined not the Waffen SS but the SS retinue. Among them were several thousand men—mostly Soviet POWs—who had gone through the notorious SS training camp in Trawniki near Lublin. Many of these Trawniki men had first served in Globocnik's death camps and were later redeployed, after the closure of these sites, as KL sentries in the occupied east and inside the old German borders.[132]

The transformation of the Camp SS into a multinational force—most pronounced in the eastern European camps—hastened its fragmentation, with deep rifts between German staff and foreign recruits.[133] All across the occupied east, German officials held their foreign helpers in barely concealed contempt, and it was no different inside the KL. German superiors widely regarded the new Camp SS recruits as simpletons, brutes, or potential traitors.[134] The newcomers' poor command of German was held against them as well, and resulted in numerous dismissals. Despite half-hearted appeals by SS leaders to treat the foreigners as comrades, regular German staff were not afraid to vent their frustrations. When SS Private Marschall, who worked in the Birkenau administration, was stopped one day by block leader Johann Kasaniczky, an ethnic German, at the entrance of the women's camp and asked why he wanted to enter, he gave him a sharp dressing-down: "That's none of your damn business, and you better learn to speak proper German first if you want to talk to me."[135]

Not surprisingly, foreign Camp SS men often felt alienated. For a start, many of them were not volunteers but had been drafted or pressed into SS service.[136] Once inside the KL, they stood at the bottom of the staff hierarchy. In addition to the derision by their German colleagues, who occupied almost all positions of authority, they had few prospects of promotion. SS managers even canceled the leave of ethnic Germans, afraid that they would not return to the camps.[137] Frustration must have been widespread among foreign guards, and in early July 1943, it boiled over among a company of Ukrainian sentries in Auschwitz. Not long after their arrival, fifteen of them escaped from the camp, armed with weapons and ammunition; the ensuing firefight left eight Ukrainians and three SS pursuers dead.[138]

It is hard to gauge what all this meant for the prisoners. Foreign SS men generally joined the Guard Troops around camps and work sites, and therefore had less direct contact with inmates. Some of the sentries still committed acts of extreme violence; prisoners suspected that ambitious ethnic Germans wanted to prove themselves as "real Germans" through displays of violence.[139] On the whole, however, foreign SS men may have acted somewhat less maliciously than most of their German colleagues.[140] Some openly pitied the inmates and admitted their own dissatisfaction with the Nazi regime and their miserable duties in the camps.[141] Prisoners were always delighted to see such cracks in the SS armor, not least because it raised their hopes of striking deals for extra food and privileges. Such illicit contacts were eased by the fact that foreign guards and prisoners often spoke the same language.[142] A shared language could also be dangerous, however. In Gross-Rosen, an eighteen-year-old prisoner from Kursk, who had taunted a Ukrainian guard as a traitor, was hanged in front of all assembled prisoners; the aggrieved guard watched the execution from the front row.[143]

Female Guards

Foreign men were not the only new faces among the Camp SS. As more and more Jewish women were detained during 1942–43, SS managers dispatched German women as guards to all main camps in eastern Europe and to many satellite camps as well; some were veterans from Ravensbrück, while others had been hurriedly trained for their new roles. Although the SS still drew the line at admitting these women to the ranks (they were consigned to the SS retinue), and although the total number of female German guards sent to the occupied east was small (in Majdanek, around twenty women worked opposite 1,200 men), their influx changed the Camp SS. Many male veterans saw the arrival of armed and uniformed women as an affront to their all-male paramilitary ideals. The fact that some female guards did not back down in conflicts with male superiors only heightened the anger of SS men.[144] Insubordination and ill discipline of female staff were punished frequently by male commandants, so strictly that the WVHA called for more restraint.[145] Rudolf Höss spoke for many chauvinistic Camp SS men when he dismissed the new female colleagues as lazy, dishonest, and incompetent, running around the compounds like "headless chickens."[146]

Höss himself engaged in a particularly bitter dispute with the first senior supervisor of the Auschwitz women's camp, Johanna Langefeld. In Ravensbrück, Langefeld had overseen the daily life of female prisoners. She expected similar powers in Auschwitz but met with strong opposition. In July 1942, Himmler waded into the row during his visit to Auschwitz, siding with Langefeld. But Höss had the last laugh, as Himmler's order that a women's camp should be led by a woman, assisted by a male SS officer, was torpedoed by Camp SS men. After all, Höss asked acidly in his memoirs, which male officer would subordinate himself to a woman? As for Langefeld, she was eventually ordered back to Ravensbrück and reprimanded by Pohl; in spring 1943, she was kicked out of SS service altogether and arrested.[147]

There was another side to the relationship between men and women in the service of the Camp SS, beyond spats and quarrels. The SS staff also enjoyed plenty of fun and banter, and just as in Ravensbrück and other mixed camps, romance blossomed in the eastern European KL. In Majdanek, the wooden barrack for female guards stood conveniently opposite the compound for male Guard Troops, and the official ban on illicit meetings could not put a stop to intimate liaisons. The young female guards enjoyed unusual liberties, compared to their more restricted lives back home (as did the few young women who had volunteered as SS telegraph and radio operators). In the end, four female guards ended up marrying SS men in Majdanek. There were also broken hearts, of course; one jilted Oberscharführer is even said to have attempted suicide in the Majdanek gas chamber.[148]

Prisoners often talked about the private lives of the SS guards. This was more than idle gossip, since these entanglements could have serious repercussions for the inmates. After all, SS violence often carried a theatrical element, as we have seen, and such performances were particularly pronounced in mixed camps, with male and female guards trying to impress each other through terror. Female guards often showed added venom in the presence of male colleagues, keen to prove that they were as tough as the men. This gendered dynamic went the other way, too. In a working environment where a cold heart and an iron fist were seen as essential parts of the male anatomy, SS men were all the more determined to appear hard in front of the supposedly weaker sex. The chief of the Majdanek crematorium, Erich Muhsfeldt, one of the Camp SS experts in the disposal of corpses, often indulged in macabre jokes, waving body parts of corpses at passing female guards. Such acts could be described as monstrous deeds of a sadistic madman. Or they could be read differently: as an attempt to get a rise out of "weak" women and a demonstration of what passed for masculine strength within the Camp SS.[149]

Camp SS men tried to demarcate some strictly male spheres. Traditionally, the use of firearms had been a male preserve, and this custom was jealously guarded in the KL. While uniformed female guards carried guns, too, social practice dictated that their use was left to SS men. In addition, female guards were excluded from the business of gassing and burning prisoners in Birkenau and Majdanek; apparently only men were thought to have the stomach for mass murder. Nonetheless, female guards in eastern European KL participated in selections and committed violent excesses—more so than in Ravensbrück—by slapping, hitting, whipping, and kicking the prisoners on a daily basis.[150] Some of these assaults were so extreme that superior officers took the unusual step of issuing reprimands.[151]

Violence

Kurt Pannicke looked like a poster boy of Nazi propaganda. He was an attractive young man, tall and slender, with blond hair and blue eyes; the small scar on his cheek only enhanced his dashing looks.[152] Pannicke was also a drunken thug and a thief, a torturer, and a mass murderer. As SS camp leader in Vaivara and several of its satellite camps in 1943–44, he committed countless crimes. This NCO in his mid-twenties saw himself as omnipotent—one of his nicknames was "King of the Jews"—and he knew no limits. Here was a man who would chat casually with inmates and dish out privileges to his favorites, before murdering them. "I shoot my Jews myself!" he told the prisoners over and over again.[153] Pannicke's public persona as a god of virtue and vengeance may have been unusual, but his overall conduct was hardly exceptional. He was one of many young and lower-ranking Camp SS men who basked in their powers, erecting a regime of terror across the KL of occupied eastern Europe.

Violence and murder were part of the daily Camp SS routine in the east. There were many forms of violence, with some, like slaps and kicks, far more common than others, such as sexual abuse. Still, there was sexual violence. In recent years, historians have become more alert to systematic sex crimes during ethnic cleansing and genocide, not least by German soldiers in the Nazi-occupied east.[154] Inside the KL, too, some prisoners were raped by SS men, though other forms of sexual abuse were more widespread. Women were frequently molested upon arrival in the camps and during selections, as SS men—who were strictly forbidden to have intimate contacts with inmates—could always claim that they were just doing their job, such as searching for hidden valuables. In addition, there were cases where inmates engaged in intimate relationships with guards, in exchange for food and other privileges, although this carried considerable risks, not just for the prisoners but for the SS officials, too.[155]

"Every German in the camp was master over life and death, but not everyone exercised this power"—this was how a Majdanek survivor summarized the unpredictable behavior of the Camp SS.[156] Numerous SS officials in the occupied east relished their jobs; even some of their colleagues suspected that these officials had found their true calling inside the KL.[157] Among them was Auschwitz administration leader Karl Ernst Möckel, who announced in 1943 that he was so happy he never wanted to leave.[158] It was not just bureaucrats like Möckel who enjoyed themselves. There was no shortage of enthusiastic torturers and killers—men who laughed after they gouged out prisoners' eyes and urinated on the corpses.[159] A few were pathological killers. Hauptscharführer Otto Moll, for example, the chief of the Auschwitz crematorium complex, clearly took great pleasure in unimaginable acts of cruelty.[160]

By the same token, there were reluctant perpetrators. Just as some Camp SS men had struggled during the killing of Soviet POWs in 1941, others hesitated during the Holocaust; the daily slaughter of women and children, in particular, hit them harder than they cared to admit.[161] A handful of SS officials evaded such murderous tasks or refused outright to participate; in Monowitz, one SS sentry openly told a Jewish inmate that he would never shoot a prisoner: "It would go against my conscience."[162] But few others followed their lead, even though there was little risk of serious SS punishment. In fact, some men had been told by their officers that they could excuse themselves from certain unpleasant tasks.[163]

Even SS officials who put in for transfer away from camps like Auschwitz continued to do their duty until they departed. Among them was Dr. Eduard Wirths, who was appointed as chief garrison physician in September 1942, aged thirty-three, and served until January 1945. An ambitious doctor and committed National Socialist, with a particular interest in racial hygiene, Wirths cut a contradictory figure. He confided in Commandant Höss that he was troubled by the mass extermination of Jews and by prisoner executions, and repeatedly asked to be moved to a different post. At the same time, however, Wirths played a central part in the Holocaust in Auschwitz. He initiated new SS doctors and drew up their rosters, and supervised selections at the ramp and the subsequent gassings.[164]

As we have seen before, the participation in extreme violence can be partly explained by group pressure. This was true for the Holocaust, too: men who stepped outside their comrades' circle of complicity were shunned and excluded from rewards and promotions.[165] In his memoirs, Rudolf Höss claimed that even he had found the carnage hard to bear. However, he made a point of attending gassings and cremations, and of remaining "cold and heartless" throughout, to set an example to his men and to cement his authority as a tough leader. A perverse sense of pride came into play, too. During official inspections, Auschwitz SS men liked to flaunt their toughness by upsetting visitors with the grisly reality of mass extermination. Rudolf Höss took "great pleasure in showing the ropes to a deskbound bureaucrat" like himself, recalled Adolf Eichmann, who claimed that he had shied away from watching the murders close-up.[166]

Camp SS perpetrators also gained tangible benefits from the Holocaust in the occupied east. As lethal as the KL were for Jews, they were safe havens for the SS men, at least compared to fighting at the front. This was one reason why even reluctant perpetrators did not volunteer for deployment elsewhere.[167] Then there were the material advantages. In addition to gaining access to the property of murdered Jews, perpetrators received official recognition, like promotions and rewards (just as they had done during the murder of Soviet "commissars").[168] The troops also got a small bonus for each selection, gassing, and cremation. It did not take much to make men volunteer. The Auschwitz camp physician Dr. Kremer noted in his diary on September 5, 1942, that SS men were queuing up for "special actions" to get their hands on "special provisions": five cigarettes, one hundred grams of bread and sausage, and, most important, seven ounces of schnapps, with the Camp SS once more using alcohol to ease mass murder (drink fueled the perpetrators in Globocnik's death camps, as well).[169] SS Rottenführer Adam Hradil, one of the so-called gas chamber drivers, who steered trucks with old and sick Jews from the Auschwitz ramp to the gas chambers, testified after the war that he found the trips "not a lot of fun." Nonetheless, he liked his job: "I was happy when I received a special ration of schnapps."[170]

Previous experience with torture and abuse made it easier to participate in the Holocaust. The leading concentration camp officers in eastern Europe could look back on many acts of extreme violence. Some had made their mark outside the KL. Before Amon Göth joined the Camp SS as commandant of Plaszow in 1944, he had committed countless atrocities during ghetto clearances and as the commander of Plaszow forced labor camp.[171] But most senior officers were veterans from the Camp SS, for whom the Holocaust was the climax of their cumulative brutalization.[172] Many of them had gone through the school of violence in the prewar SS camps. In the Auschwitz main camp, two of the three senior commandants (Rudolf Höss and Richard Baer) and four of the five camp compound leaders had begun their careers back in Dachau in 1933–34.[173] There are similar biographies among the lower ranks. Gustav Sorge, who had joined the Camp SS in 1934 and became leader of the Sachsenhausen death squad, was transferred to eastern Europe in the second half of 1943. Sorge had frequently demonstrated his propensity for extreme violence against Jews in the past, and as camp leader of several Riga satellite camps, "Iron Gustav" (as he was known here, too) continued his crimes. One former prisoner testified that Sorge had devised a novel way of identifying male prisoners he wanted dead. During roll call, he would kick them with full force in the groin; then they were dragged away by the camp elder, never to be seen again.[174]

For Camp SS men like Sorge, the Holocaust was the crowning moment in a career of violence. But even these men did not commit atrocities mechanically. Experienced perpetrators still acted within the wider moral landscape delineated by their superiors. And although almost all acts were sanctioned during the Holocaust, there were some limits, for the sake of what Himmler called decency and for more tactical reasons. How such restraints affected even hardened Camp SS killers can be illustrated by briefly turning westward, to the Herzogenbusch concentration camp in the occupied Netherlands.

Herzogenbusch was staffed in January 1943 by several Camp SS veterans. The new work service leader was none other than Gustav Sorge (prior to his posting to Riga). He had been transferred from Sachsenhausen with several notorious block leaders, as well as a feared guard from the bunker, who became the new camp compound leader. The first commandant was another hardened SS man: Karl Chmielewski, who had proven himself as the murderous compound leader of the Mauthausen subcamp Gusen, not least during the mass murder of Dutch Jews in 1941.[175] Gathering such violent veterans would seem like a recipe for atrocities. The reality turned out differently, however. As we have seen, the higher SS and police leader in the Netherlands, Hanns Albin Rauter, held considerable sway over the camp and believed that a more moderate regimen in the transit compound for Jews would mislead the inmates about the Nazi Final Solution. He urged similar moderation in the protective custody compound (opened in mid-January 1943), which mostly held Dutch men detained for alleged political, economic, and criminal offenses; conceived by Rauter to showcase the supposedly strict but fair German occupation policy, treatment here was comparatively mild, too.[176]

The unexpected demand for restraint in Herzogenbusch baffled SS veterans like Gustav Sorge, who complained that it went against all the established practices of the Camp SS.[177] Over time, however, most guards adjusted to the unfamiliar requirements. Those who did not faced sanctions for prisoner abuses and other violations. Rauter was serious about preserving the façade of his "model SS enterprise," as he called it, and initiated a number of cases in SS and police courts.[178] The most prominent target was Commandant Chmielewski; after his taste for violence and corruption became open knowledge outside the camp, he was arrested in autumn 1943. The following summer, he was sentenced to fifteen years in a penitentiary and sent to Dachau as a prisoner.[179]

Location really mattered, then, in Herzogenbusch and elsewhere. It was of great importance where concentration camps lay in occupied Europe, with the occupation authorities treading more carefully in the west than in the supposedly "backward" east. In Herzogenbusch, such tactical considerations resulted in more lenient conditions, compared to other KL. In eastern Europe, where the German occupiers ran a far more draconian regime, Camp SS leaders had no such reasons for restraint. Here, deadly violence became so frequent, a former Majdanek sentry testified after the war, that "it did not attract any attention when a block leader murdered a prisoner, by shooting or beating to death."[180]

Colonial Masters

The outlook of the Camp SS in the east rested on the supremacist ideology that shaped the Nazi occupation of Poland and the Soviet Union as a whole.

Accordingly, SS staff stood at the top of the racial hierarchy, towering over Poles, Soviets, and Jews, who made up the great bulk of the prisoner population. The Camp SS had unleashed extreme violence against these groups for some time, and this violence was bound to escalate in the colonial setting of Nazi rule over eastern Europe.[181] Encounters with prisoners reinforced SS prejudices, as the conditions in the camps in the east made some inmates resemble the miserable caricatures of Nazi propaganda.[182] This was still not enough for some SS officials, who snatched any remaining shreds of dignity from prisoners; in Majdanek, inmates were occasionally forced to walk around the mud in ball gowns, high heels, or children's clothes.[183] The prisoners' dehumanization often had the desired effect, making it easier for the Camp SS to commit genocide. As the SS man Pery Broad wrote in 1945, his colleagues in Auschwitz "simply did not see a Jew as a human being."[184]

It has been argued that hands-on Nazi killers were untroubled by their actions because they believed them to be necessary.[185] There is some truth in this. Rudolf Höss, for one, saw himself as something of an expert on Jewish matters—he had apparently even been to Jerusalem during the First World War—and regarded Jews as existential threats who had to be exterminated.[186] But the mass slaughter in camps like Auschwitz and Majdanek also sowed doubts in the minds of some officials, prompting their SS superiors to reaffirm the moral right of the Final Solution. In Auschwitz, Höss and other SS leaders gave regular pep talks, telling their men that Jewish prisoners deserved to die because they had sabotaged the German war effort by blowing up bridges and poisoning wells (reviving old anti-Semitic tales).[187] The murder of Jewish children was equally essential, Höss reassured his men. Echoing Himmler's views, he explained that the children who looked so innocent would otherwise turn into the most dogged avengers. Höss illustrated his point with a revealing image: if little piglets were not slaughtered, they would grow into proper pigs.[188]

Such vicious propaganda must have fallen on fertile ground. It also added to the residual fears of Camp SS officials, for whom the initial shock about the basic living conditions in the east often gave way to general anxieties about their safety. They might have felt like colonial masters, but their sense of supremacy was undercut by the alien surroundings, fretting about partisan attacks from outside, and prisoner assaults and illness inside.[189] The fear of epidemics, in particular, continued to haunt the Camp SS, despite partial vaccinations. The paranoid Unterscharführer Bernhard Kristan, for example, always pressed the door handle to the office of Jewish clerks in the Auschwitz political office with his elbow, rather than his hand, to avoid any contact.[190]

From this perspective, Jewish prisoners posed not just a general threat to Germany's future, but a more immediate risk to the well-being of local SS officials.[191]

Especially important for the making of Holocaust perpetrators was their habituation to mass extermination. The Camp SS staff in the occupied east regarded bloodshed and murder as part of the job, with shifts and breaks, training and specialization.[192] Genocide became routine, and even Camp SS officials not at the forefront of mass murder became immersed in it.[193] It is particularly striking how quickly novices fit in. Take the SS physician Dr. Kremer. During ten weeks in Auschwitz in autumn 1942, he participated in the murder of Jews on thirteen RSHA transports, as well as other prisoner selections and experiments; he also attended corporal punishments and executions. For a man like Kremer, extreme violence turned into an everyday event.[194]

Even SS officials who were initially shaken by mass murder generally fell into line. A German soldier who spent a few days in Auschwitz in summer 1944 told an SS man that he could never participate in mass extermination. The man replied: "You will get used to it, too, everyone here becomes obedient and eats humble pie."[195] How this worked in practice becomes clear in the case of Dr. Hans Delmotte. A young SS physician, Delmotte suffered a breakdown after witnessing his first selection at the Auschwitz ramp. He appeared paralyzed and had to be escorted to his quarters, where he got drunk and vomited. The next day, still dazed, he demanded to be transferred to the front, as he could not participate in mass slaughter. But Delmotte soon calmed down. He was placed under the wing of his experienced colleague Dr. Josef Mengele, who gradually persuaded him of the necessity of mass extermination in Auschwitz. Delmotte was also reunited with his wife and before long, he had settled into his job, carrying out selections and even drawing praise from his superiors.[196] The presence of his wife in Auschwitz may well have helped him to perform his murderous duties, turning the spotlight on another important aspect—the private lives of the Camp SS in the east.

Happy Days in Auschwitz

In early 1947, as he was writing his memoirs in the Krakow prison, filling 114 double-sided pages with his small and neat script, Rudolf Höss looked back nostalgically at his family life in Auschwitz. Although he himself had been preoccupied with the camp, his family had enjoyed a great time, he remembered. "Every wish of my wife, of my children, was met." They lived together in a spacious villa adjacent to the main camp, mostly furnished in natural wood, the favored SS style. Here, Höss and his wife hosted many dinner parties for local SS men and other dignitaries. His children "could live free and easy," Höss reminisced, while his wife "had her paradise of flowers." Her gardener was a Polish prisoner, Stanisław Dubiel, who grew exotic plants for her, and Frau Höss used numerous female prisoners (including Jews) as personal tailors, hairdressers, and servants. Meanwhile, the four children (a fifth was born in September 1943) became attached to two female prisoners, elderly Jehovah's Witnesses from Germany, who looked after them. Höss's children liked to play with horses and ponies, and with animals caught for them by inmates, like turtles, cats, and lizards. But their greatest pleasure, Höss remembered, was a swim "with daddy" in the Sola River or the paddling pool in the garden, no more than a stone's throw from the main camp.[197]

The social life of the Auschwitz SS largely turned around the camp. Sports were particularly popular, reflecting the SS emphasis on physical exercise and competition. On July 14, 1944, Höss even used his staff circular to congratulate an Unterscharführer Winter who had just been crowned the Upper Silesian champion in the shot put, discus, and javelin. Camp SS men also competed against teams from outside. On the afternoon of September 6, 1942, for example, they played a soccer match on the local athletic field against visitors from the Oranienburg SS (just a few hours after the game, hundreds of Jews arriving from Drancy were gassed in nearby Birkenau). To relax after physical exercise or after a day inside the camp, SS men of all ranks could frequent the Commandant Staff sauna. And there was plenty of entertainment. An old theater on the camp grounds was used for shows featuring dancers, actors, acrobats, and jugglers (some of whom toured through different concentration camps). As late as December 1944, just weeks before the camp was abandoned, Jupp Hussels, famous across the Third Reich as a film comedian and the sunny voice of German breakfast radio, arrived to entertain the Auschwitz SS troops.[198]

Music played an important part, too. There were several orchestras in the Auschwitz complex, including an eighty-strong symphonic orchestra and the only women's ensemble in a concentration camp (led by the prisoner Alma Rosé, the daughter of a famous Viennese violinist). While their main role was to play as the prisoner commandos departed for work (and returned), setting the tempo for all the marching columns, they put on regular concerts, as well. Many SS officials valued these occasions, not just for the music itself but also as signs of the supposed ordinariness of Auschwitz. In addition, prisoners had to give private performances, just as in other KL, ranging from classical music for more high-minded officials to renditions of popular songs and dance music. The Dutch prisoner Richard van Dam, for instance, was frequently ordered to the Auschwitz political office, the scene of so much gruesome torture, where he had to sing jazzy American tunes like "I'm Nobody's

Sweetheart Now," accompanied on the accordion by Rottenführer Pery Broad, an SS official known as much for his sly interrogations as his musical skill.[199]

Diversions beyond the camp complex included a cinema in Auschwitz town, though the favorite stomping ground of the Camp SS and their guests was the Haus der Waffen SS, near the railway station, which offered rooms to visitors and a large Germans-only bar and restaurant; female KL prisoners were forced to work as chambermaids and cooks. SS officers, meanwhile, had their own exclusive building, a little closer to the main camp, where they met in the evenings to eat, drink, and play cards. As a special treat, they could visit the Camp SS weekend retreat, the so-called Sola-Hütte. The rustic log cabin, built by prisoners on an idyllic spot some twenty-five miles away from the Auschwitz main camp, accommodated around twenty people, who could swim in an adjacent lake in summer or go skiing in winter.[200]

Then there were the brothels for Camp SS men. Inside the German heartland, SS men normally frequented existing municipal brothels. As there were no equivalents in Auschwitz, the authorities set up a new brothel with German prostitutes, in line with the order Oswald Pohl had given during his September 1942 inspection of the camp. SS leader Heinrich Himmler generally approved of such establishments, as he feared that his troops were becoming sex starved. But the new Auschwitz brothel was not open to all Camp SS men. Nazi racial thinking dictated that Ukrainian SS men had to visit another site, set up for IG Farben foreign workers.[201]

Although the Auschwitz SS largely kept to itself, it did build up local contacts outside the camp. Told to avoid the Polish population, SS officials developed social contacts with other Germans in town, who arrived as part of the general "Germanization" program. The plans for Auschwitz town were vast, with big apartment complexes, major roads, parade grounds, and several stadiums. As the Holocaust unfolded inside the camp, the nearby town was turned into a major building site (only a few projects were completed by the time the Germans fled in early 1945). The makeup of the local population was transformed, too. Nazi ethnic cleansing had led to the deportation of thousands of Poles and Jews and the influx of some seven thousand Germans by autumn 1943; most of them had been attracted by the financial rewards of employment in the east and worked for IG Farben. The new civic elite built ties to the Camp SS, mingling during theater and variety evenings, Christmas celebrations, and dinner parties.[202]

The SS presence in Auschwitz town was hard to overlook. The SS settlement grew into a district of its own, as SS managers grabbed more and more buildings to accommodate the swelling ranks. The nicest houses were reserved for senior officers, with most of the rank-and-file staff living in large barracks. Married officials received visits from their families, often for several weeks at a time. Sometimes whole families relocated to Auschwitz. Among them were children who had spent all their life in the Camp SS entourage. The son and daughter of the first Auschwitz camp compound leader, Karl Fritzsch, for example, had been born in the Dachau SS settlement; after seven years, during which the children had attended the local SS nursery, the Fritzsch family packed up and went to Auschwitz, soon moving into the first floor of a large house. They met some familiar faces, including former neighbors from Dachau. In fact, so many families moved into town that the local SS leadership put a stop to it in summer 1944.[203]

What made Auschwitz so attractive to the families of SS staff? Apart from the desire to be reunited with their loved ones, married SS men were keen to move from barracks into private accommodation. Their wives and children, meanwhile, often enjoyed greater peace of mind after relocating, as they felt safer from Allied bombing than deeper inside Germany. Besides, life in the shadow of the camp often meant social advances: nobodies became somebodies. The families of Auschwitz SS officers occupied an elevated social status, and enjoyed a lifestyle well beyond their normal means. Men and women from humble backgrounds lived like members of the upper middle class back home, in lavish villas set in large gardens full of flowers and fruit trees, waited on by servants.[204]

The presence of their families also made the job easier for some Camp SS officers, as we saw in the case of Dr. Delmotte. The company of children and wives provided stability and emotional support—some officers hurried home from the Auschwitz camp to eat lunch with their family—and helped to normalize their actions inside the camp. After his family moved out of the SS settlement, leaving him behind, chief garrison physician Dr. Eduard Wirths wrote to his wife in December 1944: "When you and the little ones were with me in Au[schwitz], one could feel nothing of the war!"[205]

The camp was not taboo in the homes of the Auschwitz SS, despite an official ban on discussing their duties.[206] True, there were some limits. When Rudolf Höss found his children playing "Kapo and Prisoner" in the garden, he angrily ripped the colored triangles off their clothes; seeing his children enact the camp in his own private sanctuary was too much for him.[207] Still, Auschwitz SS men frequently spoke about the camp to relatives and friends, just like SS officials in the other KL.[208] Even Commandant Höss himself ignored his own orders and discussed the Nazi Final Solution with his wife, who apparently referred to her husband as the "special commissioner for the extermination of Jews in Europe."[209]

The lives of local SS families were inseparable from the camp. Food, furniture, clothes, and even toys came from the Auschwitz compounds, as did prisoners used as servants and handymen. The wives and children of SS men also attended official Camp SS functions, such as Christmas parties, films, and puppet shows.[210] As for the crimes in the camp, the smoke and stench from the Birkenau crematorium "permeated the entire area," Höss later noted, including the SS settlement; when SS men returned home in the evenings, their uniforms and shoes gave off the camp's distinctive smell of decay and death.[211]

Even the Auschwitz compounds themselves were open to relatives of the Camp SS staff. Although it was forbidden, SS men regularly showed their wives or girlfriends around, perhaps to satisfy their curiosity.[212] SS families made use of the SS medical facilities inside the camp—one located opposite the old crematorium, the other near the so-called Gypsy camp—and treated the prisoners as a source of entertainment. In summer 1944, Birkenau camp compound leader Johann Schwarzhuber forced Soviet prisoners to dance at the electric fence, for the amusement of his family, who watched from the other side. Some children of SS men also entered the compounds, despite attempts by their mothers to protect them from witnessing abuses. In fact, such visits became so widespread that in July 1943 Commandant Höss banned unaccompanied children of SS staff from the camp and its labor commandos. Any direct contact with prisoners, Höss noted sternly, was morally indefensible.[213]

In short, the truth about the camp was well known among Auschwitz SS families. This did not stop the wives from supporting their husbands and from enjoying their time in the SS settlement. In some cases, at least, such support was ideologically rooted. Several wives were fervent followers of the Nazi cause. Frau Höss, for one, had met her husband on the far-right fringes during the 1920s. Several of these women may have treated individual prisoners rather humanely, but they stood behind the camps and condoned their husbands' crimes, tacitly or openly. By performing their role as SS wives and creating a semblance of normality at the *anus mundi*, these women became complicit in the atrocities.[214]

Part of the attraction of Auschwitz for the wives of SS officers was material gain; few, if any, of them ever lived in greater style and luxury. The same was true for SS wives in other KL in occupied eastern Europe. Talking frankly in the late 1970s, the widow of the former Plaszow commandant Göth looked back at her time in the camp with great sorrow—not sorrow for the crimes, but for the "beautiful time" that had long since passed: "My Göth was the king, and I was the queen. Who wouldn't have traded places with us?"[215] Frau Höss, too, felt so happy that she stayed behind in Auschwitz with her children after her husband was transferred to WVHA-D headquarters (formerly the

Camp Inspectorate) in Oranienburg in autumn 1943. Her lavish lifestyle was fed with riches taken as a matter of course from local SS supplies and from Jews killed in Birkenau. Her wardrobe was filled with murdered women's handbags and shoes, and her pantry was bulging with sugar, flour, chocolate, meat, sausages, milk, and cream. Even the gardening supplies for her exotic flowers had arrived from the camp. When the time finally came to leave the commandant's villa in late 1944, as the Soviet troops approached, the Höss family needed a couple of railway trucks to transport all their possessions to safety.[216] Of course, they were not the only pilferers in the Camp SS; corruption was rife across the KL, and nowhere more so than in occupied eastern Europe.

PLUNDER AND CORRUPTION

Heinrich Himmler was a mass murderer greatly concerned with decorum. He had long cultivated an image as a deeply principled man, and during the Second World War he became a prominent preacher of a new kind of Nazi morality that saw mass killing as a sacred duty to protect the German people from its mortal enemies.[217] Contrary to the views of some historians, Nazi perpetrators like Himmler did not see themselves as nihilists.[218] Himmler regarded the Nazi Final Solution as a righteous act, committed out of necessity, idealism, and "love for our people," as he put it in a notorious speech to SS group leaders in Posen in the early evening of October 4, 1943. That the killers had remained unblemished and "decent" during the mass slaughter of Jews was a truly "glorious page in our history," he told himself and the other SS grandees.[219]

In his Posen speech, Himmler also outlined the rules governing the use of the murdered Jews' property. On his orders, Himmler said, all the "riches" were going to the Reich, via Oswald Pohl's WVHA: "We did not take any of it for ourselves." In Himmler's moral universe, state-sponsored mass murder and robbery was just, but individual theft was a sin: "We had the moral right, we had the duty towards our people, to kill this people [the Jews] which wanted to kill us. But we do not have the right to enrich ourselves with so much as a fur, with a watch, with a Mark or with a cigarette or with anything else." The handful of SS men who had broken this hallowed rule, Himmler shouted, briefly betraying some emotion, would be punished "without mercy" and executed on his own personal orders. After all, they had not stolen from Jews but from the Nazi state, which owned all the loot.[220]

Himmler knew only too well that this vision of the SS as a virtuous order was deeply disingenuous. He and his judges were in fact rather sympathetic to thieves within the SS ranks and regarded the tempting availability of valuables belonging to murdered Jews as an extenuating circumstance; even big-time thieves were sentenced to no more than detention (often on probation). Moreover, theft and corruption in the SS was not rare, as Himmler suggested, but rampant: in 1942, property offenses accounted for almost half of all convictions by SS courts (a far higher proportion than among soldiers in the German armed forces, who had fewer chances to enrich themselves). Theft was particularly widespread in the KL, above all in those at the forefront of the Holocaust. In a camp like Auschwitz, where the WVHA was engaged in a gigantic operation of robbery on Himmler's orders, his insistence on the "sanctity of property" was bound to fall on deaf ears: if it was right for the state to rob the Jews, local SS officials asked themselves, why should it be wrong for them to do the same?[221]

Looting for Germany

Official SS plunder was meticulously arranged during the Holocaust. In Auschwitz, a well-rehearsed routine was followed as soon as a deportation train reached the camp. The Nazi authorities allowed Jews to bring some luggage for the promised "new life" in the east, including clothes, food, tools, and other personal items. These possessions were seized at the ramp by a special prisoner unit, piled up, and put on trucks to be sorted. Meanwhile, edible goods were taken to a food warehouse. Once the ramp was empty, another prisoner unit scoured the area for money and valuables discarded before or after the selections.[222]

A second phase of plunder followed near the gas chambers. Here, prisoners from the Special Squad gathered up clothes, shoes, and other personal effects, such as glasses and watches, after the victims had undressed. Following the gassings, the Special Squad also searched the dead for valuables hidden on their bodies. The hair of women, shorn after they were dead, was collected and dried in rooms above the crematoria, and later used for the production of felt and threads (contrary to rumors, no soap was made from human fat). Gold teeth were cleaned and melted down in a special workshop, together with other precious objects, such as jewelry. According to a secret report compiled by Auschwitz prisoners, some ninety pounds of gold and white metal were extracted from the teeth of murdered Jews in the second half of May 1944 alone (at the height of the extermination of Hungarian Jewry).[223]

Most loot in Auschwitz ended up in a special section of the camp known among inmates (and later the SS) as Canada, named after the faraway country associated with great riches. As the Holocaust had gathered momentum, Commandant Höss asked in early June 1942 for the urgent assembly of wooden barracks to store the property of murdered Jews. In the end, six barracks near the main camp were used, but these warehouses (Canada I)—inspected by Oswald Pohl during his visit on September 23, 1942—soon proved too small. The Camp SS killed faster than it could process its plunder, and despite the use of additional huts, the bags and suitcases kept mounting up. Eventually, a much larger compound of thirty barracks was opened in Birkenau (Canada II) in December 1943. But it, too, could not keep up with the pace of genocide, and luggage piled up between the new barracks or had to be moved to other sites.[224]

Inside the Auschwitz storage areas, hundreds of male and female prisoners from the so-called Canada Commando worked around the clock to sort the spoils. The largest labor details were combing through the mountains of clothes, which were fumigated, searched for valuables, separated, and stacked. As they emptied jackets and coats, prisoners from the Canada Commando sometimes found letters or photos. "I never dared to look at them," the Polish Jew Kitty Hart wrote after the war. "Only a few meters away from us—and perhaps at the very same moment—the people, to whom all this had belonged, were burned." Meanwhile, a specialist SS unit sifted through the banknotes and other valuables; German money was deposited in a designated WVHA account, and the rest was itemized and packed up.[225]

Some of the loot stayed inside the camps. In Majdanek and Auschwitz, the SS supplemented its stock of prisoner clothing with suits, shoes, and hats of murdered Jews.[226] But the bulk was shipped elsewhere in Poland and Germany. The transports of human hair, for instance, went to the Reich Economic Ministry and to private companies, some of them hundreds of miles away; in a wool combing plant in faraway Bremen, workers one day discovered small coins inside thickly woven plaits cut from the heads of Greek girls back in Auschwitz. Human hair arrived from other concentration camps as well. From summer 1942, the WVHA had issued instructions to several KL to collect the hair of registered prisoners (including men), for the production of socks for submarine crews, among other things, though the plan to make some of their goods in an SS workshop was soon dropped.[227]

Most garments amassed during the Holocaust in Auschwitz and Majdanek were sent to agencies designated by the Reich Economic Ministry. Other shipments of clothes went to the Ethnic German Liaison Office (VoMi), an SS office that facilitated the settlement of ethnic Germans in the Nazi-occupied east. Under the new Nazi Order, German settlers would not only take over some houses and farms of murdered Jews, but also their clothes. By early February 1943, Auschwitz and Majdanek had sent 211 railway carts of clothing to VoMi, including 132,000 men's shirts, 119,000 women's dresses, and 15,000 children's overcoats. The new owners were not supposed to know about the murderous provenance, so the SS leadership gave strict instructions to remove all yellow stars from the clothing.[228]

At the center of SS plunder in the concentration camps stood the WVHA. As we have seen, it masterminded the looting of property amassed in all Operation Reinhard camps (the two WVHA camps Auschwitz and Majdanek, and the three Globocnik death camps). In the words of the U.S. judges who sentenced WVHA chief Oswald Pohl to death in 1947, his office had become the "clearinghouse for all the booty."[229] In addition to issuing detailed directives for the processing and dispatch of the spoils, and supervising the accounts, the WVHA handled many of the goods.

By autumn 1942, SS couriers regularly dropped crates full of watches, alarm clocks, and fountain pens at the WVHA-D office in Oranienburg. They were repaired in a special workshop in Sachsenhausen by around 150 skilled prisoners, some two-thirds of them Jews; like prisoners in the camp's counterfeiting commando, these men lived under privileged conditions (SS plans to set up a similar workshop in Auschwitz never came to pass). The finished goods were then distributed via WVHA-D—on Himmler's orders—to officers and men from the Waffen SS; the navy and air force benefited, too. Indeed, different agencies competed for the spoils, with gold watches and pens in particular demand; one SS Obergruppenführer asked Himmler in 1943 for "large quantities" to give "real pleasure" to wounded SS men at Christmas time. The ongoing genocide meant that the supply did not dry up, and as late as November 1944, the WVHA-D officials still sat on more than twenty-seven thousand watches and clocks, as well as five thousand fountain pens. (When he later heard about this scheme, Adolf Eichmann could not believe that the "weirdos" in the WVHA had wasted their precious time on such "bullshit.")[230]

Meanwhile, jewelry, foreign currency, dental gold, and other precious metals amassed in the Operation Reinhard camps were delivered to the central WVHA headquarters in Berlin; Odilo Globocnik frequently appeared in person to hand over valuables from his camps. The goods were then taken by SS Hauptsturmführer Bruno Melmer in locked crates to the German National Bank (Reichsbank).[231] Melmer was a busy man: between summer 1942 and late 1944, he made no fewer than seventy-six trips. Normally, the National Bank deposited the equivalent value of the goods in a special account. Purified gold was melted into bars by the Prussian Mint, while other metals were supposed to be sent on for further refining.[232] At the same time, the National Bank handled gold extracted in other KL. In the early war years, dental gold of dead prisoners had been used for the fillings of SS men and their families. But by autumn 1942 the SS had stockpiled enough supplies to last for several years, and so the WVHA decided to deposit the surplus with the National Bank.[233]

The total value of the SS booty in Auschwitz and Majdanek is impossible to determine, but it is likely to have amounted to several hundred million Reichsmark; some was retained by the SS, but most went into the coffers of the German Reich.[234] Still, this was only a fraction of the property seized by the Nazi regime from its victims across the occupied continent—European Jews had been systematically stripped of their belongings long before they reached the KL—and it was rather insignificant for the wider German war effort.[235]

Above all else, the plunder in the KL reveals the murderous utilitarianism of SS managers. Everything had to be harnessed for Germany, they believed, including the dead—even in the face of cold economic logic. There was no profit to be made from human hair, after all, which had to be laboriously collected, dried, packaged, and shipped, only to be sold off at bargain prices: 730 kilograms of hair shaved off the heads of Majdanek prisoners between September 1942 and June 1944 netted just 365 Reichsmark, less than the value of a single gold cigarette case looted during Operation Reinhard.[236] It was not enough for the SS to murder the Jews and steal their property; all traces of Jewish life had to be erased. Once the Nazi Final Solution was complete, nothing would be left behind: the dead turned to dust, their belongings into booty.

Robbing the Doomed

Corruption was a structural feature of Nazi rule, based as it was on patronage and nepotism.[237] And it burgeoned at all levels during World War II. Inside Germany, a rampant black market developed as a result of shortages and rationing.[238] Elsewhere, the Nazi plunder of Europe fueled personal corruption, with the Holocaust offering the greatest profits for the German occupiers, their foreign supporters, and local opportunists.[239] The Treblinka commandant Franz Stangl later recalled that when he had first arrived in the camp in September 1942, local SS men had told him that "there was more money and stuff around than one could dream of, all there for the taking: all one had to do was help oneself."[240]

The Camp SS in the east made the most of these opportunities, lining its pockets with the riches of murdered Jews. Compared to the "gigantic corruption in Auschwitz," wrote the Jewish survivor Benedikt Kautsky, who experienced several KL following his arrest in 1938 as a prominent Austrian Socialist, the regular thefts by SS men in older camps like Buchenwald were negligible.[241] Some rank-and-file SS men became jealous of the riches amassed by their commanding officers, but corruption was all-inclusive; most Camp SS staff in the east were on the make.[242]

The centers of corruption were Auschwitz and Majdanek, the two KL most closely involved in the Holocaust. SS men working near the crematoria, the storage rooms, and the ramps had the easiest access to money and valuables. Georg W., a sentry stationed near the Majdanek gas chamber complex, later confessed that he used to walk "over to the places where jewelry was lying" to take it. Ordinary SS members became wealthy overnight; an Auschwitz official by the name of Franz Hofbauer once pocketed ten thousand Reichsmark in a day. Even train drivers who had steered the deportation transports used to linger nearby—pretending to fix the train engine—after Jews had marched off to their deaths, in the hope of finding some discarded valuables.[243] Living in an upside-down world, some perpetrators saw the Nazi Final Solution as their lucky break.

The Camp SS in the east stole from registered prisoners, not just from new arrivals. Goods earmarked for distribution inside the KL were regularly sold for profit. In Plaszow, most prisoner rations were exchanged by the SS on the local black market, with the blessing of Commandant Göth, who liked to feed the meat intended for prisoners to his dogs instead. SS men also seized prisoner clothing. In Warsaw, for instance, the Camp SS sold underwear to local Poles, leaving the prisoners without a change of clothes.[244] Although such deals with civilians were a profitable way for the SS to market stolen goods, most of its exchanges took place inside the KL, with prisoners.

Each concentration camp had its own underground economy, where inmates offered pretty much anything up for sale. Black markets, vital in all the camps, gained added importance in occupied eastern Europe. Since conditions were more ruinous than elsewhere, survival turned even more on the prisoners' ability to improve their lot through barter. They had to "organize" to stay alive, and the spoils of the Holocaust provided them with the opportunity to do so. In Auschwitz, the prisoners in the Canada Commando were the envy of the camp, because they had ready access to food and clothes—not just for their own use, but for barter on the black market. The members of the Birkenau Special Squad also used their unique position. The "dentist" Leon Cohen, for instance, traded golden teeth with an SS man for schnapps, chicken, and other food.[245] Barter was always on the minds of prisoners, even if they had nothing to trade. As they walked around Auschwitz, they often kept their eyes fixed on the ground, hoping to see something—perhaps a button or a piece of string—that could be exchanged later.[246]

Deals were made at all times and places. In many KL, the black market actually existed as a physical space. In Klooga, it was located in the lower hall, which started to resemble "a market fair in a shtetl," as one Jewish inmate noted in his diary, where one could get milk, fruit, honey, cans of food, and much more.[247] In Monowitz, it could be found in the corner farthest away from the SS barracks. Primo Levi recalled that it was "permanently occupied by a tumultuous throng, in the open during the summer, in a wash-room during the winter, as soon as the squads return from work." Among the crowds were starving prisoners, who hoped to trade a small piece of bread for something better, or to exchange their shirt for food (prisoners who "lost" their shirts were invariably beaten by Kapos). At the other end of the scale were professional traders and thieves with access to the SS kitchens or storage rooms. The main currency among prisoners was bread and cigarettes, with prices for items in regular stock (such as the daily soup) fairly stable, while others fluctuated in line with supply and demand.[248]

Most exchanges on the black market were made between prisoners. But their most prominent customers were SS officials, and the greatest riches inevitably ended up in their hands. After all, what good was a gold coin to a prisoner who was starving to death? Greedy SS men exploited desperate prisoners, who had little choice but to make deals. In Majdanek, where Jewish inmates were going mad with thirst, Lithuanian sentries gave them small cups of water in return for their clothes and shoes.[249] SS men offered many other services, too, if the price was right, including transfers to privileged prisoner squads and delivery of secret letters. Some SS men also blackmailed prisoners, promising to spare them violence or death as long as they could pay.[250]

The illicit encounters between SS and prisoners blurred the lines between them; for a brief moment, they were united by shared interests. But they were far from being equal partners. For a start, the SS staff often cheated prisoners. In one spectacular case, an SS man helped an Auschwitz prisoner to escape, only to shoot him point-blank after he had been paid for his services.[251] Inmates who knew too much about SS deals were sometimes murdered as well, as were inmates who had resisted advances by corrupt SS officials. And if a deal went wrong, prisoners knew better than to name the guilty SS party; otherwise, the inmate was liable to be beaten to death or shot before he could make any more damaging revelations.[252]

SS officials found plenty of uses for all their ill-gotten gains. On occasion, they shared the riches. The Auschwitz SS, for example, ran a secret account—replenished with tens of thousands of Reichsmark stolen from its victims—to pay for alcohol-fueled parties.[253] Many more individual perpetrators smuggled their spoils out of the camps and posted them back home, just as Dr. Kremer had done. Local SS officers also relied on continual thefts to maintain their family's lavish lifestyle in the occupied east. Dinner parties in Auschwitz would not have been the same without all the wine and delicatessen, the linen tablecloths and stylish evening dresses. But greed could be dangerous. When the wife of SS report leader Gerhard Palitzsch, who had lived in a house about five hundred yards outside the main camp, died of typhus in autumn 1942, prisoner rumors had it that she had been infected by lice from clothes stolen from the Canada depot. Following his wife's death, Palitzsch himself lost his last inhibitions; he stole even more brazenly and forced himself on female guards and prisoners. His crimes eventually caught up with him and he was locked into the same bunker in which he had tortured so many inmates. Like other Camp SS veterans, he later got a second chance as the leader of an Auschwitz satellite camp, but Palitzsch was eventually kicked out of the SS and sent to the front (he died in Hungary in December 1944).[254] His fall from grace was far from unique. He was one of a number of corrupt Camp SS men arrested in the second half of the war, during an SS campaign to restore the "decency" of Himmler's black order.

The SS Investigates Itself

In summer 1942, the world of the Camp SS was briefly shaken from within, after two senior commandants were sacked for corruption. Obersturmbannführer Alex Piorkowski, who had succeeded Hans Loritz as Dachau commandant, was suspended for orchestrating a major racket in the camp; Himmler promptly demanded that the SS courts take action against the sickly Piorkowski, who had already fallen out of favor before.[255] An even more prominent casualty was Oberführer Hans Loritz himself, the highest-ranking KL commandant. Back in March 1942, it had come to light that several Sachsenhausen SS men had systematically embezzled food from the camp kitchen, storerooms, and gardens. Such thefts were run of the mill, and so was the response of Loritz, who quickly put a lid on the affair, blaming one of the prisoners. But this strategy failed, for once. A disgruntled SS man informed the Gestapo, pointing directly at Loritz: everyone in the camp knew the commandant to be the "greatest racketeer of all," a claim backed by a long list of indiscretions. Meanwhile, an anonymous letter with further allegations—by the wife of a Sachsenhausen guard, as it turned out—was sent to Heinrich Himmler.[256]

The Reichsführer SS promptly initiated an official investigation. Amid the endemic corruption it exposed—with prisoners forced to make carpets, paintings, vases, furniture, and even a sailing boat for Loritz—perhaps the most damaging revelation concerned a villa under construction near Salzburg. Back in 1938, Loritz had bought a large piece of land in the sleepy village of St. Gilgen on the Wolfgangsee, and ordered prisoners to build his dream house there, complete with terraced gardens and water features. By the time Loritz came under scrutiny in 1942, most of the work was done, and his wife and sons had already moved in, watching from the windows of their new villa as prisoners put on the finishing touches.[257] Asked to explain himself, Loritz protested in June 1942 with great pathos that his honor as an SS officer was being sullied, laying bare the inordinate sense of entitlement of Camp SS officers; Loritz simply could not understand why he, of all people, was pulled up for conduct that was tolerated elsewhere. He was not even the only Camp SS leader who liked to live large on the Wolfgangsee. Not far from his home on the lake, KL prisoners were building another private residence, for Arthur Liebehenschel from the WVHA.[258]

So why did the SS leadership move against Loritz in summer 1942? During the second half of the war, when hardships for many ordinary Germans grew, the Nazi leadership became less tolerant of corruption in the ranks, concerned that criticism of crooked officials could erode the already brittle popular mood. In spring 1942, Hitler announced that leading figures of the regime had to demonstrate an exemplary lifestyle, and in summer 1942, Himmler acknowledged that corruption cases caused outrage among the wider public (though his own family continued to live in considerable luxury).[259] In this spirit, Himmler decided to make an example of Loritz, whose transgressions had become known beyond Sachsenhausen.

WVHA chief Oswald Pohl had his own reasons for cracking down on Hans Loritz. Following the recent incorporation of the KL system into his domain, Pohl was keen to establish his authority. And what better way to demonstrate it than to sack a man like Loritz, a stalwart of the Camp SS since its early days and a protégé of Pohl's old rival Theodor Eicke?[260] At the same time, Pohl used the opportunity to present himself as incorruptible, which may account for his theatrical sacking of Alex Piorkowski; apparently, Pohl ordered the Dachau commandant to Berlin and demoted him on the spot, even though he had no authority to do so, completing Piorkowski's humiliation by stripping him of his ceremonial dagger, the very symbol of virility among the SS.[261]

But SS leaders like Pohl were reluctant to tackle the real roots of corruption. Although the WVHA knew that a large number of concentration camp guards were guilty of misconduct, few allegations were taken seriously.[262] And even cast-iron cases like the ones against Loritz and Piorkowski were only pursued cursorily, perhaps because they did not become all-too-widely known beyond SS circles. Though Himmler eventually threw Piorkowski out of the SS, the threat of criminal proceedings was not followed up.[263] As for Loritz, he kept his SS rank and was redeployed to a new post, setting up a network of forced labor camps in Norway; his family, meanwhile, continued to live in the villa on the Wolfgangsee.[264]

Heinrich Himmler was still conscious of appearances, however, and in 1943 he sanctioned another, more concerted push against corruption, triggered by the investigation of another Camp SS veteran, Karl Otto Koch. Koch was one of the most prominent prewar commandants, but his career went off the rails during the war, and his fall would be the most spectacular of any Camp SS official. Spared by Himmler in late 1941, following his first arrest for corruption, Koch was given another chance as commandant of Majdanek, as we have seen. But he soon failed again. On the night of July 14, 1942, more than eighty Soviet POWs fled the camp, climbing over the barbed wire and disappearing into the night. To cover up the ease with which these prisoners had vanished, Koch ordered the immediate execution of dozens of Soviet POWs who had stayed behind, informing his superiors that the slaughtered men had participated in the mass breakout. He also tried to shift the blame for the escape, denouncing the provisional state of the camp, the poor quality of the guards, and the two hapless sentries at the scene, one of whom was the appropriately named Gustav Schlaf (his surname translates as "Sleep"). Unimpressed, Himmler, who visited Lublin days after the escape, ordered on July 25, 1942, that Koch be recalled and investigated for negligence by the SS courts. Koch moved back to his old Buchenwald home to await the outcome. In the end, the case against him was dismissed, though he was not reinstated.[265]

Koch soon found himself in more trouble. In March 1943, Himmler visited Buchenwald and was surprised to find Koch and his wife still living in the opulent commandant's villa. Himmler asked for the "tired and lazy" Koch, as he called the man who was just three years his senior, to be kicked out and sent to the front.[266] His order had not yet been implemented when further evidence for Koch's corruption came to light, prompting Himmler to sign off on a new investigation. Koch's villa was searched the next day, and on August 24, 1943, he was arrested together with his wife, Ilse, and taken to the Gestapo prison in Weimar.[267]

The case against Koch was led by an arrogant young SS jurist named Konrad Morgen, who spent several months in Buchenwald from summer 1943, gathering incriminating material. Born into a poor family in 1909, Morgen had worked his way up to university to study law. He briefly served in a regular Nazi court, and then pursued a career in the SS, joining the newly established SS Main Office for legal matters as a judge in 1940. Sent to the General Government, Morgen gained a reputation for tackling SS corruption and deviance, and following his transfer to the RSHA in late June 1943, on Himmler's personal orders, he took charge of the Koch case.[268] After the war, the canny Morgen testified against some former Camp SS men, portraying himself as a tireless campaigner for law and order. Several historians have fallen for this pose, as did some judges.[269] But his postwar testimony was self-serving, riddled with omissions and brazen lies.[270] Konrad Morgen had been a committed SS officer. During his investigation of Koch, he condoned RSHA executions, the killing of prisoners in medical experiments, and the murder of supposedly sick and infectious inmates. His main aim was not to stop prisoner abuse but to root out personal corruption (and other cases of insubordination).[271] In short, Morgen was no champion of common decency, but a crusader for Himmler's peculiar brand of SS morality, which tried to exorcise any blemishes from the uniforms of "virtuous" SS killers.

While Koch stood at the center of Morgen's investigation, which spanned the former commandant's reign over both Buchenwald and Majdanek, many other SS men were soon implicated, too. For example, Morgen found that almost all NCOs under Koch in Majdanek had become "completely corrupt," openly stuffing valuables into their pockets. In the end, though, only close associates of Koch were prosecuted.[272] Among them was Hauptscharführer Gotthold Michael, who was accused of running some of his master's fraudulent operations, as well as stealing prisoner property for his own use, including valuable leather suitcases.[273] A more senior defendant was Hermann Hackmann, who had risen in the slipstream of his patron Koch to adjutant in Buchenwald and camp compound leader in Majdanek, in a typical example of Camp SS nepotism. Hackmann was sentenced to death by an SS court on June 29, 1944, for persistent theft, but the judgment was not carried out and he was released after half a year in Dachau to fight against the advancing U.S. troops.[274]

Meanwhile, the case against Karl Otto Koch dragged on. Himmler had authorized the use of torture to break those who might know about SS corruption, and in March 1944 Koch was forced into a partial admission of guilt—the blind support from his superiors had turned him into a megalomaniac, he said—only to recant his confession.[275] Koch's trial finally began in

September 1944 before an SS and police court in Weimar, but it was quickly adjourned and only resumed on December 18, 1944. Ilse Koch, who had been accused of involvement in the corrupt dealings, was found not guilty. But her husband was sentenced to death. SS leaders hesitated to carry out the sentence. Then, in early April 1945, just before the war ended, Koch was taken from the Weimar police jail to Buchenwald and executed by an SS firing squad. In a final gesture of bravado, he refused a blindfold, clinging to the macho spirit of the Camp SS to the very end.[276]

A Judge in Auschwitz

As evidence for large-scale corruption in Buchenwald mounted up in 1943, Heinrich Himmler authorized the extension of the internal SS investigation into several other KL.[277] By early 1944, a few dozen officials were working under Konrad Morgen, who led the investigative teams, and a special SS and police court had been established to deal with the more complex cases.[278] The reach of the corruption probe was limited, however, and Morgen's team investigated no more than half a dozen concentration camps.[279] Much of the focus was on the occupied east, where the ready availability of "Jewish property" had resulted in "familiar manifestations of corruption," as Morgen wrote in 1944.[280] A number of Camp SS men were arrested, including two commandants. Hermann Florstedt, who had led Majdanek since November 1942, had initially been praised by his superiors for turning the camp around after Koch's chaotic reign. By and by, Florstedt turned out to be no less crooked than his predecessor, and in autumn 1943 he was arrested on suspicion of embezzlement, among other charges. His case never came to court, though, and in late March 1945 he was still held on remand in a Weimar police jail; his subsequent fate remains unclear.[281] Meanwhile, the Plaszow Commandant Amon Göth—notorious for his lust for gold—was arrested in September 1944, but like Florstedt, he was never sentenced by the SS.[282]

From around autumn 1943, Konrad Morgen and several members of his team worked in Auschwitz to investigate SS larceny and fraud, following the aforementioned discovery of dental gold posted by a medical orderly.[283] To stop Morgen's investigation in its tracks, the Auschwitz SS leadership reminded its officials "one last time" that prisoner property—including gold and valuables—was out of bounds; all those who "sullied themselves with such a dirty deed" as theft would be kicked out and prosecuted.[284] But corruption was too deeply ingrained to cease on command. After several months in Auschwitz—searching lockers and barracks, examining paperwork, and interrogating suspects—Morgen's men arrested several people (twenty-three

NCOs and two officers, according to a former investigator). Once more, how-ever, the threat of draconian sanctions evaporated. Even major offenders got away with a few years of detention or less. Others were punished even more lightly. Franz Wunsch, for example, an NCO in the Canada storage area who was caught carrying stolen gloves, knives, cigarettes, and more, only received five weeks in solitary confinement.[285]

The SS investigation in Auschwitz continued well into 1944. There was even talk of broadening its remit: in June, Morgen expected that Himmler would appoint him to head a major inquiry leading "from Hungary to Auschwitz." Apparently, the mass murder of Hungarian Jews in Birkenau, which had recently begun, yielded less bounty than the SS authorities ex-pected, raising renewed suspicions of embezzlement; it is unclear, however, if this new inquiry ever got off the ground.[286] Ultimately, the most high-profile victim of Morgen's corruption investigation was the head of the Auschwitz political office, Maximilian Grabner. The role of political offices, which were closely involved in mass death and executions, grew sharply across the KL system during the Second World War, and nowhere more so than in Aus-chwitz, where its many tasks included the supervision of the crematoria and gas chamber complex. Grabner, who had joined the Camp SS from the Vi-enna Gestapo, carved out a powerful place for his office, almost independent of Commandant Höss, and became perhaps the most feared SS man in the camp.[287] Using his privileged position, Grabner helped himself freely to the property of murdered Jews, sending home whole suitcases stuffed with loot.[288] His schemes eventually caught the eye of Morgen's investigators, and on December 1, 1943, he was removed from his post.[289]

Grabner's trial before the special SS and police court in autumn 1944 soon took an unusual turn, revealing the full absurdity of SS justice. Grabner was not only charged with corruption, he was the only Auschwitz SS man also to be indicted for arbitrary prisoner killings, outside the chain of com-mand.[290] To Grabner, this must have seemed like a preposterous accusation: Had he not acted according to the general principles of Nazi terror? Some of his old Auschwitz colleagues, called as witnesses, duly came to his defense. Rudolf Höss argued that Grabner's deeds were hardly worth mentioning, in view of the daily mass murder all around the camp. One of Grabner's former subordinates, Wilhelm Boger, went even further and is said to have ex-claimed: "We have killed far too few for Führer and Reich!"[291] Such radical sentiments were probably shared by Heinrich Himmler, who normally backed autonomous acts of Camp SS violence. Even on the rare occasion when he reproached individual SS officials for having gone too far, he was willing to accept that they had acted in the right spirit.[292] Predictably, given Himmler's views and the all-out terror in the KL, it was impossible to prove that Grabner had overstepped his authority. The trial against him was adjourned, amid general confusion, and never resumed.[293]

Keeping Up Appearances

The fanatical Wilhelm Boger spoke for many of his Camp SS comrades, in Auschwitz and elsewhere, when he described Konrad Morgen's investigation as "a ridiculous theater."[294] And yet, most Camp SS officials did not feel like laughing, as Morgen's commission was a potential threat; they relied on thefts and fraud as a second income and were in no mood to compromise their lifestyles. These men feared and hated Morgen and did their best to obstruct, sabotage, and undermine his team.[295] It was surely no accident that, one day in December 1943, the Auschwitz barrack that held much of the evidence gathered by Morgen's team mysteriously went up in flames.[296]

Compared to most Camp SS men, Heinrich Himmler's stance on corruption was more ambiguous. He always presented himself as a paragon of propriety. And he was instrumental in launching the investigation into the KL, following the Holocaust-related rise in larceny. Himmler personally approved Konrad Morgen as the head of the anticorruption force and continued to back him, despite opposition from senior Camp SS officials. As late as summer 1944, Himmler expressed his appreciation for the special SS and police court and asked for Morgen's promotion to Sturmbannführer.[297] At the same time, Himmler's threat of unforgiving punishment for corrupt Camp SS men was empty; behind the scenes, he was reluctant to push for harsh sentences. Himmler also had no desire to broaden Morgen's small-time operation, since he must have realized that a more systematic probe into SS sleaze would destabilize the entire KL system; after all, corruption was the glue that helped to hold it together. So why did Himmler support Morgen at all? Primarily, it seems, the investigation served a symbolic function. With other Nazi leaders only too aware of the allegations of corruption in the concentration camps, the Reichsführer's willingness to castigate a few Camp SS offenders was offered as proof of the purity, rigor, and decency of the SS.[298]

If Heinrich Himmler was two-faced about corruption, his chief of the KL system was even more duplicitous. Officially, Oswald Pohl and his WVHA managers had no choice but to back the campaign against theft and fraud.[299] Pohl was even willing to sacrifice individual SS officers—especially if this strengthened his own hand, as in the case of Loritz. But Pohl balked at a more far-reaching investigation of the KL and repeatedly torpedoed the anticorruption drive, complaining that it undermined prisoner discipline and war production.[300]

There was an obvious reason for Pohl's obstructionism: like other SS leaders, he was hugely profiting from Nazi terror. Divorced in 1938, Pohl had remarried on December 12, 1942, in Himmler's East Prussian headquarters (Himmler had handpicked the much younger bride, Eleonore von Brüning, a rich heiress).[301] The couple enjoyed a feudal lifestyle. In Berlin, they occupied a large villa, "aryanized" from a Jewish woman who later died in Ravensbrück. The Pohls lived rent-free and made themselves comfortable in their new home; it was rebuilt by prisoners from Sachsenhausen, and five inmates remained on hand as servants.[302] Pohl joined the new Nazi nobility, which included other pompous leaders like Hermann Göring.[303] To announce his arrival, he even made up his own coat of arms, depicting a knight's helmet with closed visor and a proud horse on its hind legs.[304]

Above all, Pohl fancied himself as a landed nobleman—he lied to Himmler, claiming that he came from a long line of farmers—and duly acquired not just one but two manors in the country. His wife had brought into the marriage a beautiful property in the Bavarian countryside, which was renovated by prisoners from Dachau, though the couple did not make much use of it until the closing stages of the Third Reich.[305] Instead, they spent time on the Comthurey estate in northern Germany, with its vast grounds and roaring fireplaces. The estate encompassed a satellite camp of Ravensbrück, six miles or so away, with dozens of prisoners serving as slave laborers; some worked in agriculture, others waited on the Pohls, and still others landscaped the gardens and rebuilt the manor house, adding a sauna and other comforts. The bill for Pohl's extravagance came to several hundreds of thousands of Reichsmark, paid for by the SS.[306]

His growing property portfolio also included a splendidly appointed apartment on the Dachau SS plantation, which he used during his wartime trips to southern Germany (Pohl was no stranger to Dachau, having lived in the SS settlement with his first wife in the prewar years). He was a workaholic, but in Dachau, of all places, he sometimes relaxed. Lounging on a deck chair, he was served by prisoners, including a waiter wearing a white jacket; he also sampled meals prepared by his private cook and went on hunting trips, accompanied by his personal master of the hunt.[307]

Oswald Pohl's entire existence was enmeshed with the KL. To him, the camps were not remote abstractions. He lived and breathed them. During meetings and inspections, and during his charmed private life, he was surrounded by prisoners, violence, and death. The Dachau inmate Karel Kašák, who observed Pohl close-up, described him as a typical Nazi upstart who acted like "a god and emperor." Setting an example for local Camp SS men, Pohl treated prisoners as his personal property and thought nothing of walking around in his dressing gown while ordering them to shine his boots.[308] For him, prisoners were slaves to be exploited at will.

8

Economics and Extermination

Shortly after Heinrich Himmler put him in charge of the KL system, Oswald Pohl summoned the top Camp SS officials to a major two-day conference at his WVHA headquarters in Berlin-Lichterfelde. Brimming with confidence, Pohl used the meeting on April 24 and 25, 1942, to set out his agenda. His reign would be all about economics, he announced, with the immediate goal of kick-starting armaments production. The only way to reach this goal, he added, was to drive prisoners until they dropped: working hours would be unlimited and lunch breaks reduced to the bare minimum. "To attain the utmost performance," Pohl concluded, "this action must literally be exhausting." Underscoring the order's importance, Pohl put the responsibility for its implementation onto the shoulders of individual commandants.[1] But his message went beyond economics. He also wanted to impress and intimidate his new subordinates. Facing a gathering of Camp SS veterans—led by Richard Glücks, and including commandants of all fourteen main KL in existence at the time—he was keen to put down an early marker. And although some officials grumbled about his ascent, Pohl swiftly established himself as the overall head of the concentration camp system.[2]

Pohl's close ties to Heinrich Himmler—they corresponded frequently, and also regularly met up or talked on a special phone line installed in the WVHA—strengthened his position; all Camp SS men knew that the Reichsführer held him in great respect. Pohl, in turn, was slavishly devoted to his younger mentor. He treated Himmler's wishes as hallowed commands and lambasted anyone who dared to question them.[3] Himmler was still the true master of the KL: no major initiative went ahead without his approval during the second half of the war. He received updates about prisoner numbers and deaths from the WVHA, and repeatedly demanded additional details.[4] Himmler even found time for further inspections, making at least five trips to concentration camps in 1942.[5] Such visits were not empty ceremonies; Himmler remained an exacting, stern ruler. When he arrived unannounced in Dachau on May 1, 1942, for example, and passed a prisoner detail on a vegetable patch that worked too slowly (to his mind), he jumped out of his car, bawled out the Kapo, the sentries, and the SS commando leader, and ordered the prisoners to continue until nighttime. Told that most of the inmates were priests, Himmler exclaimed: "These bastards shall work until they collapse!"[6]

As the war dragged on, Himmler's inspections and interventions grew less frequent. As a leading proponent of total war, he accumulated more and more power. Himmler became Reich minister of the interior (August 1943) and commander of the reserve army (July 1944), and his new posts absorbed much of his time.[7] Yet he never forgot the KL, and continued to set their general direction. And as we will see, certain pet projects—such as human experiments and the exploitation of prisoners for the German war economy—still brought out the micromanager in him, stirring subordinates like Pohl to ever more radical initiatives.

OSWALD POHL AND THE WVHA

The absorption of the concentration camps into Oswald Pohl's WVHA coincided with major shifts in the German economy. At the beginning of 1942, Nazi leaders stared into an uncertain future. The army had suffered a dramatic setback in the USSR, war production stagnated, and Germany faced an open-ended global war. To increase its armaments output, the regime took several significant steps, symbolized by two key appointments. In February 1942, Hitler installed his protégé Albert Speer as minister for armaments and ammunition, and in March 1942, he named the Thuringian Gauleiter Fritz Sauckel as the new general plenipotentiary for labor mobilization. Their fierce activism and ebullient rhetoric quickly made both men into major players in the German war economy.[8]

This development spelled danger to Heinrich Himmler, who worried that Speer and Sauckel would push him aside.[9] To keep his two rivals at bay, and away from KL labor, Himmler in early March 1942 hastily ordered the incorporation of the Camp Inspectorate into the recently established WVHA.[10]

Mindful of appearances, Himmler justified the restructure on economic grounds. Absorbing the camps into Pohl's WVHA would guarantee the utmost exploitation of prisoners, harnessing "every last working hour of every person for our victory."[11] Hitler was persuaded, at least for now, and personally agreed to the expansion of armaments production in concentration camps.[12]

Putting the camps into Pohl's hands made perfect sense to Himmler. Pohl was no stranger to the KL and had gained major influence over the previous years. And unlike the obscure camp inspector Richard Glücks, who hardly ever got an audience with Himmler, Pohl was a close confidant and SS notable, reflected in his promotion to Obergruppenführer, agreed on in a meeting between Himmler and Hitler on March 17, 1942. He had great ambitions and the WVHA seemed destined to become a major force under his leadership. Deeply committed to the cause—he claimed to be a "National Socialist before there even was National Socialism"—Pohl was single-minded, well connected, and politically astute, and had long cultivated a forbidding image; his subordinates marveled at his resilience and feared his temper. His second wife summed up her husband's image, in a letter to Himmler, as "indestructible, robust, and utterly strong."[13] Clearly, Himmler hoped that other Nazi bigwigs would think twice before pushing Pohl around.

Inside the WVHA

The WVHA was a large outfit, with up to 1,700 officials in five main departments overseeing tens of thousands of workers across Europe. Its remit went far beyond the KL; as its name suggests, it was involved in all aspects of SS business and administration, from the acquisition of real estate to the provision of accommodation for SS troops. Nonetheless, all five WVHA departments had close links to the concentration camps. Office Group A dealt with personnel matters, budgets, and payrolls, and with the transfer of funds to individual camps. Among the duties of Office Group B was the supply of food and clothing. Office Group C, meanwhile, was involved in construction projects, including the gas chambers and crematoria in Auschwitz; it was led by SS Oberführer Hans Kammler, who was poised to become a dominant figure in the camp system. As for Office Group W, headed by Pohl himself, it oversaw SS enterprises such as the German Earth and Stone Works (DESt), which continued to rely heavily on KL slave labor; at its height in 1943–44, the SS economy included around thirty different companies, which exploited up to forty thousand camp inmates.[14] The administrative heart of the KL system, however, was Office Group D, the former Camp Inspectorate, still based in the so-called T-Building in Oranienburg.

Compared to the other WVHA offices, Office Group D was rather small.[15] In early September 1944, it had no more than 105 employees. Among them were nineteen officers; the rest were auxiliary staff, like secretaries, telex and telephone operators, caretakers, and canteen staff, as well as drivers (Camp SS cars had their own registration numbers, running from SS-16 000 to SS-16 500).[16] The atmosphere inside the T-Building reflected the martial values of the Camp SS. Officials normally wore boots and uniforms to work, and put in long hours, until six or seven o'clock in the evening, with some working well into the night; a few officers even slept in private rooms in the T-Building, probably after a meal and some drinks in the local Waffen SS mess hall (other officials lived in Oranienburg or nearby Berlin).[17] Like most concentration camps, the KL headquarters were an almost exclusively male workspace. In September 1944, just one woman, a Frau Bade, was listed among the staff members; working as a personal assistant, she was also the only civilian employee and non-SS member.[18]

Office Group D had four departments.[19] Every two weeks or so, the four department heads would meet in the large office of Richard Glücks on the first floor of the T-Building. Glücks's deputy Arthur Liebehenschel ran department D I, the so-called central office. Most of the correspondence went through this office. It collated statistics about prisoner numbers, transfers, releases, and deaths, and ruled on applications by commandants for official punishments of individual prisoners. Department D I also transmitted many other orders—from Office Group D, the RSHA, Pohl, and Himmler—to the KL, and kept some oversight of executions and systematic killings inside.[20] For example, the officials in D I received the figures of Jews sent to Auschwitz, divided into those gassed on arrival and those selected for labor; Glücks regularly presented a summary of these figures to Pohl.[21] The Nazi Final Solution was common knowledge among WVHA officials, and so were many other crimes: "down to the last little clerk," Pohl testified after the war, "they all must have known what went on in the concentration camps."[22]

Department D II managed KL slave labor, and as the camps' economic significance increased, so did its status. Its remit was enormous: to oversee the deployment of prisoners across all concentration camps. The D II officials supplied prisoners for SS-owned enterprises, operating as the "labor exchange" of the SS economy, as one former manager put it. Later on, the Oranienburg officials allocated hundreds of thousands of prisoners to state and private industry. To keep track of its slave labor force, D II regularly collected data from the KL about prisoners no longer available for work—because of death, illness, exhaustion, or other reasons—and about the current deployment of their prisoners; executive summaries went to Glücks and Pohl.[23]

Health matters in the KL were coordinated through department D III. Its officials liaised with Camp SS doctors—several hundred SS physicians worked in concentration camps at one time or another—by sending orders and checking reports; a monthly summary of prisoner illnesses and casualties by D III was presented to Pohl.[24] Dr. Enno Lolling, the chief of D III, frequently traveled to the camps and initiated doctors into various killing programs that required their participation.[25] Despite his tough demeanor, however, Lolling's position was weak. He had the fewest staff in Office Group D, and his Oranienburg colleagues repeatedly encroached on his turf.[26] What is more, his department held an outsider status inside the WVHA, because it also reported to the medical office of the Waffen SS (based in the SS Leadership Main Office), which provided the camps with equipment and medical supplies.[27] The standing of D III was further damaged by Lolling himself. His superiors showed some goodwill toward him, but other Camp SS officials were less charitable about his abilities. To boot, a scandalous reputation preceded him. Stories about his morphine and alcohol addiction were legend, and he was said to suffer from syphilis. "He was so easy to deceive during inspections," Rudolf Höss later wrote, "especially, as happened most times, when he had been plied with alcohol."[28]

The fourth and final department, D IV, dealt with administrative issues, including budgets and accommodation. Collaborating with Office Group B, it was also involved in the supply of food and clothes to Camp SS troops and prisoners.[29] Initially led by Anton Kaindl, D IV was later headed by Wilhelm Burger.[30] Born in 1904, Burger had trained in business and joined the SS in September 1932. Before long, he worked full time as an SS bureaucrat, eventually in the administration of the Death's Head troops (his rise was not impeded by an ideological blot on his SS résumé: until his divorce in 1935, Burger had been married to a woman of Jewish descent). Following a spell with the Death's Head division in the early war years, Burger moved to the KL. In June 1942, he became director of administration in Auschwitz, just as the camp turned into a major site of extermination. Burger proved himself there—he was one of the few senior officials to gain unreserved praise from Commandant Rudolf Höss, who commended his "organizational abilities," "ruthless zeal," and "hard will"—and after less than one year, on May 1, 1943, Burger was promoted to his new post in the WVHA.[31]

This was no exceptional move: several SS officers gained senior positions in Office Group D after first serving in concentration camps. The most prominent was Höss himself, who left Auschwitz in November 1943 to head department D I. Known as "Rudi" to his colleagues, he was one of the zealous officials who often slept in the T-Building. As a hugely experienced practitioner of terror from the largest KL, Höss had much to offer the WVHA and became Pohl's main troubleshooter.[32] Conversely, many men from Office Group D moved in the opposite direction, with two senior managers leaving Oranienburg to take up the top position inside camps. Arthur Liebehenschel became commandant of Auschwitz (in November 1943), effectively swapping jobs with Höss, while Anton Kaindl became commandant of Sachsenhausen (in September 1942), next door to the T-Building. Senior posts within the WVHA may have been better remunerated, but Kaindl's move still advanced his career. Little more than a year after his transfer, he was promoted to Standartenführer, climbing one rank above Höss in the SS hierarchy.[33]

There were pragmatic reasons for moving SS managers like Kaindl from headquarters to the camps. KL staff were in short supply and it made sense to plug sudden gaps with experienced officers.[34] However, the rotation of staff—which affected more than half of all the officers working in the Oranienburg T-Building—was about more than expedience.[35] Oswald Pohl dreamed of "soldierly officials" who combined bureaucratic skills with experience on the battlefields of the Third Reich, and was keen to employ KL veterans as managers; many of his Oranienburg officials had served apprenticeships inside the camps.[36] As for the men transferred from WVHA-D to the concentration camps, there was an expectation that they would prove themselves anew as "political soldiers" at the "front," lest they become "comfortable, fat, and old" in their office jobs, as Theodor Eicke had once put it.[37] Just like the terror experts in the RSHA, the Camp SS managers saw themselves as part of a "fighting administration," wielding both pen and sword in the name of the SS.[38]

Managing the KL

Immediately after the collapse of the Third Reich, the mighty Oswald Pohl fled from his wife's Bavarian manor before U.S. soldiers could catch him. He set off on foot to northern Germany, at the other end of the country, where two daughters from his first marriage (both married to SS men) hid him.[39] After British soldiers finally arrested him in May 1946, Pohl had another stab at escaping his past. Facing the gallows at his forthcoming trial at Nuremberg, he disowned any responsibility for the crimes in the camps. He had had little involvement, he protested, even after the KL system had come under his WVHA. Apart from labor deployment, which Himmler had asked him to supervise, it was Richard Glücks who had continued to direct "the whole internal operation"; this was why, Pohl added, the Camp Inspectorate had been left unchanged, except for its new name as Office Group D.[40] Although some historians have since echoed this claim, presenting Pohl as a rather peripheral character, his self-serving account had little basis in fact.[41]

Oswald Pohl was far more than the remote figurehead of the concentration camps. True, there were continuities in the operation of the KL system. Most of its managers came from the old Camp Inspectorate, among them Richard Glücks and three of his four department heads, who effectively continued their previous jobs in the WVHA.[42] If we probe more deeply, however, a different picture emerges. Changing the doorplate of the T-Building from "Camp Inspectorate" to "WVHA Office Group D" was more than an exercise in rebranding. The camps really did become part of the WVHA, and Pohl their energetic leader. He may have left day-to-day matters to Glücks and his staff in Oranienburg, but Pohl's fingerprints were all over the major decisions regarding the camps. His focus on camp labor certainly did not limit his engagement with other matters. After all, by the second half of the war, slave labor touched on most, if not all, aspects of the KL—in line with Himmler's wishes, who urged Pohl to ensure the "total priority of labor."[43]

And so Pohl's involvement stretched from medical matters to construction, from prisoner privileges to mass extermination. In addition to a constant stream of reports and statistics from Office Group D, Pohl held weekly meetings with Richard Glücks, and regularly saw other senior Camp SS managers.[44] Pohl also summoned the KL commandants for face-to-face conferences; following the inaugural meeting in April 1942, they came together every few months in the German capital.[45] Meanwhile, the physical distance between Pohl's headquarters (in Berlin-Lichterfelde) and the T-Building (in Oranienburg) was bridged by telephone and a designated SS courier.[46] All these contacts contributed to the gradual integration of the camp administration into the WVHA.

Much as Pohl learned about the KL from his vantage point in Berlin, he was no born bureaucrat. Contrary to the image of the efficient desk-bound perpetrator, so popular among some historians of Nazi terror, SS managers like Pohl were often hands-on.[47] Modeling himself as the ideal "soldierly official," he went on the road to impose his vision, ruling on many local issues. His master Heinrich Himmler drove him to ever more vigorous action, demanding in March 1943 that Pohl or Glücks should travel each week to a different camp to push everyone to work harder. "I believe that at the present moment we have to spend an enormous amount of time in person in the enterprises out there," Himmler told Pohl, "to crack with the whip of our words and to help on the spot with our energy."[48]

These words were Pohl's mantra. Like Eicke before him, he was always on the move and became a familiar face in many KL, from small satellites to huge complexes like Auschwitz, which he visited at least four times between April 1942 and June 1944.[49] Local officials must have dreaded his arrival—like Himmler, he sometimes appeared unannounced—for Pohl was hard to please and quick to punish. He inspired fear in his men, just as Eicke had done, though far less affection. His memory was unforgiving and his zeal unsurpassed. Even the single-minded Rudolf Höss had finally found his match. During joint inspections, Pohl, who was in his early fifties, would hasten from one stop to the next, wearing out the younger man. "Having to join him on a business trip," the weary Höss concluded, "was no pure pleasure."[50]

Pohl's ascent over the KL system eclipsed Richard Glücks. To be sure, as the head of Office Group D, Glücks was still an influential figure, supervising the everyday operations and participating in personnel and policy decisions; in November 1943 he was rewarded for his long service in the Camp SS with promotion to Gruppenführer. But there was no doubt that Pohl was in overall charge, as even Glücks himself accepted.[51] Crucially, Glücks's position was also eroded from below by one of Pohl's protégés, Gerhard Maurer, who joined Office Group D in spring 1942 to head department D II (labor action of prisoners). In the past, the Oranienburg managers had only paid limited attention to forced labor.[52] But there was no overlooking Maurer's new department, which grew into a dominant force, as did Maurer himself; in charge of camp labor until the end of the war, he became the most powerful man inside the T-Building.[53]

In many ways, Gerhard Maurer was typical of the SS managers who thrived under Pohl: ambitious young men who combined experience of modern business administration with firm commitment to the Nazi cause, allowing them to harness SS economic activities for the Nazi national community.[54] Born in 1907, Maurer apprenticed in business after leaving school and worked as an accountant. Like so many others, he drifted to the radical right as the Weimar Republic crumbled. Maurer signed up with the Nazi Party in December 1930, days shy of his twenty-third birthday, and joined the SS the following year. Soon after the capture of power, Maurer married his political beliefs and professional skills, first as chief accountant of a Nazi publishing house and then, in 1934, as a full-time SS official. Maurer never looked back. He rose through the burgeoning SS bureaucracy, gaining glowing reports along the way, and was poached in summer 1939 by Oswald Pohl for the new SS Main Office Administration and Business. He had reached one of the top managerial positions, with the rank of Sturmbannführer, by the time he moved to Oranienburg to take up his new post.[55]

Although Gerhard Maurer came from outside the Camp SS, he was no freshman. His previous work had brought him into close contact with the concentration camps, and he hit the ground running in spring 1942; as Pohl's point man, he was in a strong position to impose his will. Maurer accompanied Richard Glücks to the weekly meetings with Pohl, which were mostly about labor allocation, and he had direct access to Pohl at other times. Uncompromising, unflappable, and untiring, Maurer quickly gained the respect of other SS men in the Oranienburg HQ and inside the camps. He often spent half the week on the road, traveling from camp to camp, sometimes accompanied by other senior colleagues like Wilhelm Burger and Enno Lolling.[56] In the KL, Maurer built up especially close relations with the labor action leaders, who now became powerful figures. These men were his local enforcers, and he regularly summoned them to Oranienburg for conferences to discuss new initiatives.[57] Maurer also liaised with many outside agencies, including Speer's ministry and private industry, cementing his status as the principal SS manager of forced labor. When Speer scheduled a central planning meeting for late October 1942, Pohl immediately recalled the indispensable Maurer from an inspection to Auschwitz, rather than send another SS official to the meeting.[58]

The more intense the SS fixation on slave labor, the higher Maurer's star rose over the KL system. Maurer was officially appointed as Glücks's deputy in autumn 1943 (following Liebehenschel's departure for Auschwitz), and the other Oranienburg officials knew that he was the real power behind Glücks's throne. Compared to the dynamic Maurer—just thirty-four years old when he joined the Camp SS staff—the portly Glücks, almost twenty years his senior, seemed like a spent force. Even Glücks's sidekick Liebehenschel saw that "the old man," as he called him, was out of touch. For his part, Glücks was ready to take a backseat, though he still enjoyed the trappings of his job. Many of the key decisions, however, were now taken two doors down from his lavish room in the T-Building, in Maurer's small office.[59]

Pohl's Commandants

As the commandants fanned out from Berlin back to the concentration camps across Nazi-controlled Europe, following their inaugural conference with Oswald Pohl in late April 1942, they wondered what the new era would bring. All of them must have been struck by Pohl, who came across as a "brute force of nature," in the words of Rudolf Höss; there was no doubt that Pohl was serious about changing the KL system.[60] But none of the commandants could have foreseen just how soon they would be affected personally. Pohl was not content with remaking the Oranienburg HQ. He was determined to put his stamp on the individual camps, too, and in summer 1942, he made sweeping changes among the commandants, with Himmler's approval. A minor restructure was already on the agenda, after several officers had become embroiled in scandal. Pohl's ambitions went further, however, and when the dust had settled in October 1942, all but four concentration camps had a new commandant.

Pohl's shake-up started further down the Camp SS hierarchy, when the WVHA ordered individual camps in early May 1942 to report long-serving SS block leaders for relocation.[61] The resulting rotation of low-level staff disrupted set routines and old cliques, as the WVHA had evidently intended. In Sachsenhausen, for example, the death squad was broken up and several members moved to another KL (only a few indispensable experts in torture and death stayed behind).[62] Others left the camps altogether, after SS leaders stepped up transfers to the Death's Head division, which had suffered huge losses during ferocious fighting on the Eastern Front since early 1942.[63] Among the Sachsenhausen block leaders who departed for military training were Wilhelm Schubert and Richard Bugdalle. Schubert later fought in Poland, Hungary, and Austria. Bugdalle, by contrast, did not last long as a soldier. He was unable to control the violent urges that had served him so well in the camps, and was thrown in an SS prison camp for beating up a commander who had found fault with his military salute.[64]

The Camp SS entered a major period of flux under Pohl, as new staff joined and experienced men moved on. Although all ranks were affected, it was his summer 1942 reshuffle at the top of the KL that caused the greatest upheaval. Of fourteen commandants, five were kicked out of the Camp SS altogether. In addition to Piorkowski (Dachau), Loritz (Sachsenhausen), and Koch (Majdanek), Pohl also sacked Karl Künstler (Flossenbürg) and Arthur Rödl (Gross-Rosen); a sixth commandant, Wilhelm Schitli, left after the closure of the Arbeitsdorf KL. Of the remaining eight commandants, four kept their old jobs—Hermann Pister (Buchenwald), Franz Ziereis (Mauthausen), Rudolf Höss (Auschwitz), and Adolf Haas (Niederhagen)—while the remaining four were transferred to a different KL: Martin Weiss moved from Neuengamme to Dachau, Max Pauly from Stutthof to Neuengamme, Egon Zill from Natzweiler to Flossenbürg, and Max Koegel from Ravensbrück to Majdanek. Finally, five SS officers were newly appointed as camp commandants: Fritz Suhren (Ravensbrück), Wilhelm Gideon (Gross-Rosen), Anton Kaindl (Sachsenhausen), Paul Werner Hoppe (Stutthof), and Josef Kramer (Natzweiler).[65] When the KL commandants assembled for their next conference with Pohl in Berlin, it became clear just by looking around the table how much had changed since April 1942.

The scale of Pohl's reorganization is not in doubt; but what about its significance? After the war, Pohl claimed it was all down to his kindness: he had wanted to establish a more humane spirit, he said, by removing "roughnecks" educated in "Eicke's school."[66] No credible historian would buy this tale of compassion. But the depiction of the reshuffle as a break with the Eicke era has gained some traction, as has the argument that Pohl was aiming to mobilize forced labor by appointing better managers.[67]

Pohl clearly had high hopes for his five new commandants. They were comparatively young men, thirty-seven years old on average, and had all previously served in the Camp SS. Josef Kramer, for example, had gained almost all his professional experience inside, serving on the Commandant Staff of six different concentration camps between 1934 and 1942.[68] Three of the new commandants had belonged to the Death's Head division, with both Hoppe and Gideon wounded at Demjansk in 1942.[69] They could boast some administrative skills, too, none more so than the new Sachsenhausen commandant, Anton Kaindl, the chief administrator in the Camp SS (as the former head of WVHA-D IV). Kaindl was a manager through and through, and with his round, horn-rimmed glasses, the slight man looked a breed apart from beefy thugs of the prewar years like Hans Loritz. Born in 1902, Kaindl had served for twelve years in the Weimar army as an accountant and paymaster. In the Third Reich, he put his skills into the service of the SA and then Pohl's SS Administration Office. In 1936, he joined Eicke's staff and soon became chief administrative officer of the Death's Head troops. He took the same post in the Death's Head division in autumn 1939, before returning to the Camp Inspectorate some two years later. Pohl had long admired Kaindl's organizational talent and hoped that he would bring it to Sachsenhausen in 1942.[70] Likewise, Pohl's vision of productive KL influenced his dismissal of commandants.[71] With Germany's victory no longer a foregone conclusion, incompetence became a threat to the war effort. Koch's time was up after he messed up one time too many, leaving Majdanek in a shambles. Künstler, too, finally had to go. A chronic drunk, he had failed to mend his ways, and when news of yet another bacchanalia at Flossenbürg made the rounds, SS leaders lost patience; a failure like Künstler was out of step with the Pohl era.[72]

Despite its far-reaching changes, however, we must not exaggerate the impact of Pohl's 1942 reshuffle. For a start, he was no more adept than his predecessors at imposing a fully coherent personnel policy. Some new commandants like Kaindl may have approached Pohl's ideal of the soldierly official, but most did not. Indeed, many appointments were makeshift, the result of chance and connections.[73] Just as in the early years of the Camp SS, there was a high turnover of staff. Some of Pohl's commandants fell fast, proving themselves just as inept and corrupt as the men they had replaced. Wilhelm Gideon, for example, lasted barely one year at Gross-Rosen. Perhaps Pohl's most unusual appointment, Gideon had been chief administrative officer in Neuengamme, and was the first such official to rise to commandant. He was also the last; more devoted to alcohol than to his job, Gideon was sacked in autumn 1943.[74] Pohl proved no more sure-footed in his other appointments, with three commandants anointed by him at later dates—Karl Chmielewski, Hermann Florstedt, and Adam Grünewald—arrested by the Nazi authorities for violence and corruption.[75] And far from provoking a rupture with the Eicke era, Pohl drew heavily from the "talent pool" filled by his old adversary. Most commandants who stayed on—experienced men like Höss, Koegel, Weiss, Ziereis, and Zill—had thrived during Eicke's time; they were experts in terror, first and foremost, not in business. The same was true for new commandants. Even Anton Kaindl had been taken under Eicke's wing back in 1936 and remained one of his closest associates until 1941.[76]

In the final analysis, then, Pohl's reshuffle was meant to refresh the camps, not to reinvent them. Clearly, Pohl wanted to pave the way for more effective slave labor. At the same time, though, he wanted to retain the spirit of the Camp SS and continued to put his trust in veterans of violence. In a pattern repeated elsewhere, Pohl expected radical change without making radical changes. More generally, his reshuffle was not just about economics; it was also about power.[77] Pohl was a master of gesture politics and wanted to prove to Himmler that he would fight corruption and incompetence. Simultaneously, he gave notice to the Camp SS staff that he would be no pushover like Glücks. The message was understood, and by autumn 1942, Pohl's authority over the KL had been cemented. As a piece of political theater, then, his reshuffle succeeded. As an economic initiative, it failed, for the concentration camps would never turn into significant hubs for the German economy.[78]

SS Armaments Works

Oswald Pohl was hoping to press more prisoners into the war effort. Previously, SS thinking had been dominated by visions of vast settlements, but these dreams were already fading fast when Pohl took control of the KL in spring 1942, punctured by the harsh reality of a war that would not end. True, SS leaders found it hard to let go of their dreams, which continued to offer relief from the growing gloom enveloping the Third Reich, just as Hitler later lost himself in architectural models of his imaginary cities when much of

Germany lay in ruins.[79] As a practical policy, however, the construction of huge new SS buildings in the east was losing its urgency. In the end, most plans remained in drawers, grim reminders of what might have been.

The attention of SS leaders shifted from the future to the present, from German cities and settlements to weaponry. At a time when the entire German economy was gearing up for the war effort, the SS could not stay on the sidelines. There was widespread agreement among the Nazi elite, starting with Adolf Hitler, that the KL had to focus more intensively on arms production.[80] Oswald Pohl was one of the greatest proponents of the new course. The priority, he confirmed to Himmler in late April 1942, was no longer the SS peacetime building projects; it was the increase of armaments.[81] But how would this be done?

To Himmler, the answer was obvious: it was time to establish the SS as an arms manufacturer. This quickly turned into another of his flights of fancy. By summer 1942, he was fantasizing about arsenals of high-tech weapons such as grenade launchers and machine guns rolling out of KL-factories. Himmler's enthusiasm was contagious. His enforcer Pohl was equally optimistic that SS enterprises in concentration camps could undertake "armaments tasks on the largest scale."[82] Shortsighted though they were, even Himmler and Pohl saw that they could not go it alone, at least not at first; the SS needed help from private industry. Still, Himmler hoped to maintain ultimate control over such joint ventures, and insisted in spring and summer 1942 that all production take place in the KL. While he was prepared to accept (at least in theory) that private companies would retain economic supervision over shared enterprises, his general ruling was clear: arms manufacturers had to erect their factories inside his concentration camps.[83]

Perhaps Himmler's basic rule was a reaction to the first major collaboration between the SS and the armaments industry, which had quickly gone awry. On January 11, 1942, Hitler had signed off on a deal for the SS to participate in the construction of a light alloy foundry on the grounds of the Volkswagen (VW) works in Wolfsburg. On paper, this order put the SS into pole position, as Himmler was in charge of the "completion, extension, and operation" of the foundry, using "manpower from the concentration camps." However, VW was unwilling to cede control on its home turf and the SS soon gave in. VW would run the factory, while the SS would merely supply and guard the prisoners. A new KL—tellingly named Arbeitsdorf (village of labor)—was set up for this purpose on the foundry's building site, and in April 1942 hundreds of inmates arrived for construction work. But their hard labor proved pointless. Albert Speer had undermined the project since his appointment as armaments minister, not least because of its limited relevance for the war effort, and quickly used his influence over production planning and raw materials allocation to bring it down; the Arbeitsdorf camp closed within a few months. When the prisoners were withdrawn in October 1942, they left behind a half-completed and empty shell.[84]

Himmler was unfazed by the failure of Arbeitsdorf. Frustrated that SS armaments production amounted to no more than "peanuts," as he put it, he pressed ahead with more joint ventures, though this time inside existing KL.[85] Himmler was pursuing four key projects: the production of rifles in Buchenwald (working with the Wilhelm Gustloff company), handguns in Neuengamme (Carl Walther company), antiaircraft guns in Auschwitz (Krupp), and transmitters in Ravensbrück (Siemens & Halske). The SS was building all these factories, and Himmler expected them to provide supplies for the Waffen SS.[86] He also tried to impress Hitler, dazzling him with tales of vast armies of slaves churning out weapons in the KL. "The Führer," Himmler informed Pohl in March 1943, "counts so very firmly on our production and our support."[87]

By that time, the momentum behind the SS plans had already stalled. Still, Himmler and Pohl plowed on, determined to establish yet more KL armaments factories. To this end, they were even prepared to transform established SS businesses. In some concentration camps, DESt now moved into war production, gradually shifting from bricks and stones to weaponry. In Flossenbürg, its construction of fighter plane parts began in 1943, with Messerschmitt providing raw materials and technical training; forced labor in the quarry, meanwhile, the symbol of the camp since its inception, came to an almost complete standstill. In SS circles, the Flossenbürg project was hailed as a triumph—Pohl personally inspected the new factory—and it seemed to stick closely to Himmler's blueprint: production took place inside the camp and was supervised (at least nominally) by the SS, which sold the finished goods to Messerschmitt at a profit.[88] Such apparent successes made Himmler bullish about the significance of the SS economy, and he acted as its greatest cheerleader. In October 1943, he bragged to SS leaders about "giant armaments works" run by the SS in concentration camps.[89] But this was just wishful thinking. In truth, the SS had failed to become a serious arms manufacturer.

Among all the SS businesses in concentration camps, DESt was alone in turning to arms manufacturing, and even this move was partial and reliant on unsophisticated production methods. Many SS businesses remained largely untouched by the war. Peacetime production simply continued, despite an explicit order by the WVHA in autumn 1942 to abandon all permanent KL labor details that were not engaged in work important or essential for the war effort. In several camps, even DESt still focused on building materials and other goods. The DESt factory in Berlstedt, for example, staffed by prisoners from nearby Buchenwald, actually stepped up its production of flowerpots, turning out nearly 1.7 million in 1943 alone. SS managers made absurd attempts to designate such work as indispensable, even passing off the production of porcelain as "war essential." In reality, much of the SS output had little to do with the war effort, never mind high-tech weaponry.[90] These shortcomings were plain to see, and in April 1943, Himmler suffered the indignity of being patronized by Albert Speer, who complained that the SS was wasting its resources.[91]

As for the wider SS collaboration with the arms industry, none of the four pet projects pursued by Himmler came to much, hampered by changing military priorities and shortages of adequate machinery. In Ravensbrück, production expanded only slowly; in summer 1943, after one year, no more than six hundred female prisoners were toiling for Siemens & Halske. Elsewhere, the picture was even less flattering to Himmler's ambitions. Rifle production in Buchenwald only got under way in spring 1943, on a much smaller scale than planned. In Neuengamme, the partial production of firearms began even later, with negligible results, while the production of antiaircraft guns in Auschwitz never even started.[92] SS efforts to dominate their business partners ended in defeat, too, as it largely failed to wrest control over production in KL factories. The reason was simple, as Speer pointed out bluntly to Himmler: industrialists were "not keen to build up the SS as competition."[93] For his part, Speer, who had long backed economic ventures in the KL, threw his weight behind industry. While Himmler and Pohl were still dreaming about the SS production of weaponry, he dealt them a fatal blow.

War and Satellites

The future of concentration camp labor was determined not in spring 1942, when Oswald Pohl took over the KL system, but in autumn, at a time when only around five percent of prisoners were working for the war industry.[94] And its future was determined not by Pohl but by Albert Speer, who was fast becoming one of the most powerful men in the Third Reich. During a crucial meeting on September 15, 1942, Speer outwitted Pohl. Blinded by Speer's enticing (but empty) talk of a big SS armaments complex, the giddy Pohl stumbled into a major concession: he abandoned Himmler's rule of moving all production into the camps and allowed that prisoners could be sent to armaments works elsewhere. Speer pounced on this concession and used it a few days later, during a conference with Hitler. After he persuaded Hitler that it would be impossible to set up substantial weapons production inside the KL—Speer highlighted the poor infrastructure—he received backing for the deployment of prisoners in established arms factories, without major SS influence.[95] Instead of moving arms factories *inside* the KL, prisoners increasingly moved *outside* to factories owned by private and state industry. Appointed to strengthen the SS economy, Oswald Pohl had hastened its decline, loosening the grip over its slave labor force.

Hitler's basic decision in September 1942 was a catalyst for the growing cooperation between industry and the SS. From now on, the SS guarded more and more of its prisoners at new satellite camps near arms factories and construction sites. Previously, as we have seen, neither the SS nor industry had shown a burning desire to work together. The SS preferred to use its prisoners for its own schemes while industry preferred more flexible sources of labor. Ambitious projects such as Monowitz (IG Farben) and Arbeitsdorf (VW) had been the exception, not the rule, and further joint ventures had remained sporadic even during the early months of Pohl's stewardship of the KL system.[96] This began to change from late 1942, and so did the function, spread, and size of satellite camps. Though a few small sites had existed before, some going back to the prewar years, it was only now that the systematic spread of KL satellites (administratively attached to main concentration camps) started. The SS established a whole raft of new camps, largely near factories; by summer 1943, there were already around 150 satellite camps (up from around eighty at the start of the year). Some of their inmates worked for the SS, though many more worked for the war industry, often in manufacturing.[97]

Many of the new satellite camps supplied forced labor for the aircraft industry, which faced particularly severe shortages. The two largest camps were connected to state-of-the-art factories run by Heinkel and BMW. The exploitation of Dachau prisoners by BMW had begun as early as March 1942, at its new factory for airplane motors in the Munich district of Allach. Prisoner numbers initially remained small, however, and inmates were transported back every evening to the main camp, some seven miles away. But in March 1943 the SS set up a satellite camp outside the factory gates, and within six months almost two thousand male KL prisoners worked in Allach, together with other forced laborers.[98] Even bigger was the satellite camp at the Heinkel works in Oranienburg, just around the corner from Sachsenhausen, which became a model for the collaboration between the SS and industry. Here, too, the local Camp SS initially supplied only a small prisoner commando, which expanded rapidly after the establishment of a permanent satellite camp on site in September 1942; barely half a year later, 150 prisoners had become some four thousand, producing all the parts for the biggest German bomber, the Heinkel 177.[99]

The mass deployment of KL prisoners for arms production required a rethink from both SS leaders and industrialists, as demonstrated in the case of AFA, Germany's largest manufacturer of batteries (rebranded as Varta after the war). In 1941, the SS had floated the idea of using Neuengamme prisoners at the AFA factory in Hanover, which produced batteries for submarines and torpedoes. However, the stringent SS conditions—including the total separation of the prisoners from other workers—put off the firm, which still had sufficient workers anyway. By spring 1943, however, the situation had changed. After the supply of workers from labor exchanges had dwindled, AFA grew interested in KL prisoners. The SS, meanwhile, was more cooperative than before. Accepting the priority of production, it relaxed its rigid rules and allowed its prisoners to work with other foreign laborers. Chivied along by Speer's ministry, both sides reached an agreement, leading to the creation of the Neuengamme satellite camp Hanover-Stöcken in summer 1943; it stood some four hundred feet away from the factory and held up to one thousand prisoners by autumn 1943.[100]

In addition to satellite camps for war production, the SS established satellites for repairing war damage. Since 1940, selected prisoners (from KL and prisons) had had to defuse unexploded Allied bombs, on Hitler's orders; numerous men were blown to pieces in front of their terrified comrades. As the air raids intensified, the German authorities drafted many more prisoners. Following a tour of devastated German cities in late summer 1942, Heinrich Himmler ordered the urgent dispatch of mobile prisoner squads to clear up the debris. By mid-October, the WVHA had designated three thousand inmates from Neuengamme, Sachsenhausen, and Buchenwald. In close cooperation with Speer's office and other Nazi agencies, these prisoners were stationed in barrack camps and converted buildings in several major German cities. They were forced to clear rubble, gather bricks, wood, food, and roof tiles, build air raid shelters, bury the dead, and rescue survivors. This work was exhausting and dangerous, but the SS and municipal authorities regarded it as a great success, paving the way for the expansion of these so-called SS Building Brigades, which formed some of the largest satellite camps in early 1943.[101]

Although KL labor changed during 1942–43, this was still an experimental phase. It would be wrong to think that almost all prisoners now worked flat-out for the war industry or cleared bomb damage. These pioneering projects were just that, pioneering, and they were not yet representative of the KL system as a whole. By summer 1943, no more than an estimated thirty thousand of two hundred thousand prisoners worked in satellite camps; the vast majority of prisoners remained inside main camps and at the disposal of the SS.[102]

There was a simple reason for the slow pace of change: the German arms industry was still in no hurry to draw on KL labor. Industry managers saw numerous pitfalls of working with the SS. High levels of security and myriad rules could disrupt production; prisoners, widely regarded as dangerous enemies, might engage in sabotage and incite the rest of the workforce; or they might be too exhausted to work properly. As one leading industrialist put it in October 1942, after Speer suggested the redeployment of prisoners from the Mauthausen quarry: "I already looked at them myself; they are no use to me in coal mining." In general, therefore, German industry still preferred other sources of labor power, such as foreign workers. Only after these sources began to dry up did it become more proactive, resulting in a scramble for KL prisoners from autumn 1943.[103]

Even though the full impact of the new direction of concentration camp labor was not felt until later, the earlier developments were significant nonetheless. The groundbreaking cooperation with leading firms like IG Farben, Heinkel, BMW, AFA, and VW provided the blueprint for future agreements between SS and industry. So what did this emerging blueprint look like? The allocation of KL prisoners would be handled centrally by the WVHA, one of the main innovations made by Pohl in spring 1942, following a discussion with Himmler.[104] Typically, companies submitted their requests for forced workers via the local commandants or via the offices of Speer, Sauckel, or Göring (some companies also contacted the WVHA directly). Gerhard Maurer and his men in Office Group D II, who would often meet managers of the interested firms, assessed all applications, and then presented their recommendations to Pohl, who made the final decision. If Pohl gave permission to proceed, local camp officials would work out the contractual details with company representatives. Once the WVHA had approved the contract and all preparations were complete, the prisoner deployment would begin.[105]

When it came to the establishment of new satellite camps, there was a clear division of labor between SS and firms. In addition to the prisoners, and their basic clothing and food, the SS provided the personnel (Guard Troops and Commandant Staff) to oversee sentry duties, prisoner transports, punishment, and medical care. The companies, in turn, were in charge of technical supervision during work, and paid for the construction and maintenance of the compound, which had to conform to strict SS standards.[106] Firms also paid daily rates for prisoner labor, revised in October 1942. In Germany, the daily price for each qualified male prisoner now stood at six Reichsmark, and four Reichsmark for an unskilled one. In occupied eastern Europe, including Auschwitz, the daily rate was reduced to four and three Reichsmark respectively, presumably because less output was expected from the even more ravaged prisoners. There was no such distinction between skilled and unskilled labor in the case of female prisoners, who were regarded as less able workers; instead, there was a flat rate similar to the one for unskilled men.[107] Contrary to the claims of some historians, the SS benefited from most payments only in a roundabout way. Since the prisoners were regarded as the property of the state, most of the income from their labor—perhaps around two hundred million Reichsmark in 1943, rising to around four to five hundred million the following year—officially went into the coffers of the Reich (though this helped to finance the state-sponsored KL system).[108]

If there was little immediate financial gain for the Camp SS, why did it lease inmates to the war industry? For a start, the SS remained subject to outside influence, and as the demand for labor grew, so did the pressure (above all from Speer) to surrender prisoners for war production. But the SS also expected advantages from its collaboration with industry. In addition to tangible benefits, such as the preferential allocation of weapons for SS troops, Himmler, who never quite abandoned his dream of an SS arms complex, hoped that working with industry would enhance the expertise of his own managers. And then there was power and prestige. With labor becoming an increasingly precious resource, the SS could present the KL as vital cogs in the Nazi war economy; the larger the SS army of forced workers, the greater its potential influence.[109] This was one reason, no doubt, behind the strenuous efforts by Pohl and his WVHA managers in 1942–43 to extend the overall number of prisoners in the concentration camps, as well as their output.

SLAVE LABOR

Is it right to call SS prisoners "slaves"? The term is commonplace in many accounts of the concentration camps, but some scholars have questioned its use. Slaveholders, these critics suggest, had an innate interest in their bondsmen's survival, since they represented economic value; prisoners, by contrast, were worthless to the SS, who deliberately drove them to their graves. However, this argument is not fully convincing. After all, the SS always assigned some value to its prisoners. Even at the height of their destructiveness, when some prisoner groups were singled out for annihilation, the camps never aimed at the systematic destruction of *all* their inmates. More generally, there are different definitions of slavery. If used broadly—to describe a system of domination based on force and terror, which aimed at economic gain through the unrestrained subjugation of social outcasts—then the term captures the fate of many KL prisoners in the Second World War, especially during its latter stages.[110]

This is what many prisoners themselves thought when trying to make sense of their suffering. In February 1943, the Dachau inmate Edgar Kupfer described the SS use of inmates for the war effort as "modern slave rental."[111] This verdict chimed with the views of the perpetrators. In March 1942, Himmler himself told Pohl that the SS should feed its KL prisoners cheaply and simply, like "slaves in Egypt."[112] The term seemed so apt to Himmler that he repeated it on further occasions. Just a few months later, he spoke to SS generals about "work slaves" in the camps, who were building the new Germany "without consideration for any losses."[113]

Himmler expected extraordinary results from his slaves, insisting that their output should equal or exceed that of ordinary German workers. "Herein lies the largest reservoir of manpower," he lectured Pohl.[114] One early SS initiative to increase productivity aimed at the reduction of inmates working in maintenance (in KL kitchens, laundries, barracks, and elsewhere). To free more prisoners for other jobs, Richard Glücks announced in early 1942, no more than ten percent of those judged fit for work should be deployed in this way (in early 1944, the target figure was reduced to six percent). However, even if commandants had been willing to implement these orders fully—which they were not—it would have done little to satisfy the economic ambitions of their superiors, who pursued many more measures in 1942–43 to create a more industrious KL slave labor force.[115]

Privileges and Productivity

Most prisoners had known only one main reason for working—fear. Since forced labor was primarily about punishment, not productivity, the Camp SS had not seen any real reason to rewarding diligent prisoners: Why offer carrots if one could use sticks, whips, and boots? As economic imperatives became more pressing, however, SS leaders decided to break with convention and allow incentives. They could build on some precedents; since 1940–41, for example, a few prisoners in SS quarries had received bonuses.[116] Heinrich Himmler was sympathetic to such initiatives. As he told Pohl in March 1942, rewards for hard-working men would guarantee "an enormous increase in the labor performance." Above all, he regarded monetary and carnal bribes as surefire bets: prisoners would step up if promised money and sex.[117] In fact, Himmler had advocated sexual incentives for prisoners before, in October 1941, when he ordered the establishment of a brothel in Mauthausen; the "special building" (*Sonderbau*) opened in June 1942, the first inside any KL.[118]

The Camp SS initially remained reluctant to reward prisoners. Attitudes only started to change in spring 1943, and the impetus came once more from Himmler. Following an inspection of the troubled Wilhelm Gustloff rifle factory in Buchenwald on February 26, 1943, he ordered Pohl to introduce a "performance system" for the KL as an "incentive" for harder work. Himmler pointed to the Nazis' greatest rival, the Soviet Union, and its use of food and financial rewards in driving its people to "the most incredible feats." In his own camps, Himmler envisaged a graded system, with benefits rising from cigarettes and small payments to the greatest reward of all: a visit for male prisoners, once or twice a week, to a camp brothel. In Himmler's mind, it was still sex—not food, drink, or clothes—that the prisoners craved most of all.[119]

Pohl acted straightaway. Within weeks, he agreed to a set of prisoner privileges, valid from May 15, 1943, which would guide the Camp SS in the future (with some later amendments). The aim, Pohl explained, was the urgent increase in prisoner output. Taking his cue from Himmler, he outlined the conditions for earning tobacco and money. He also fleshed out the procedure for entrance to camp brothels, a special prize for "star performers" who had made "truly outstanding efforts." Other bonuses included additional letters to relatives, extra rations, and the privilege of wearing longer hair. Typically, the SS drafted these regulations with men in mind; female prisoners, by contrast, were still banned from smoking, at least in Ravensbrück, and their only way into camp brothels was as forced sex workers.[120]

Camp SS managers no doubt regarded the new privileges as a major concession. In reality, they were far from revolutionary. Token payments for forced labor had long been common in Nazi Germany, even in state prisons.[121] What is more, vast numbers of KL prisoners never received any rewards. Too weak and exhausted to qualify, they were often even worse off than before, as the SS diverted some of the meager rations to "diligent" prisoners.[122] And some of these inmates were left empty-handed, too, after local Camp SS officers delayed the introduction of the rewards system; elsewhere greedy guards and Kapos simply pocketed the bonuses themselves.[123]

Even prisoners who received rewards—an estimated fifteen percent in a camp like Monowitz—were often disappointed.[124] The WVHA had swiftly ruled out the possibility of paying money, since it could easily be used for bribes (from 1942–43, inmates were forbidden to carry cash and to spend money sent by relatives). Instead, the WVHA introduced vouchers, whose monetary value was only redeemable inside the camps. Kapos stood to gain the most; typically, labor supervisors could earn the equivalent of four Reichsmark per week (in vouchers), three or four times more than ordinary workers in the KL. Not only were the authorities often miserly in handing out vouchers, there was little to purchase in KL canteens. True, some prisoners bought cigarettes for barter, and others enjoyed the alcohol-free malt beer. But food was of poor quality and in short supply, as were other essentials.[125] Nicholas Rosenberg, a Hungarian Jew in the Auschwitz satellite camp Bobrek, who worked as a mechanic in a Siemens-Schuckert factory, spoke for many when he described the vouchers as fairly pointless. The canteen was rarely open, and when it was, it "mostly sold nothing but toothbrushes and toothpaste." Hardly surprising, then, that the vouchers never became the main currency on the concentration camps' black markets.[126]

The vouchers also served as admission tickets to the KL brothels, at the equivalent cost of two (later one) Reichsmark per visit. The creation of these brothels caused both excitement and outrage among prisoners, and some red faces among the SS. Even Heinrich Himmler, their chief advocate, was rather sheepish, admitting that the whole affair was "not particularly edifying." Oswald Pohl felt the same and ordered the brothels to be built on the far edge of the compounds; in Sachsenhausen, the new brothel was located right above the morgue.[127] Although the SS strictly regimented brothel visits—male prisoners had to ask in writing for permission and undergo prior health checks—some witnesses later claimed that the establishments had enjoyed great popularity. According to Tadeusz Borowski, large crowds gathered in the Auschwitz main camp: "For every Juliet there are at least a thousand Romeos."[128] In reality, only a tiny fraction of the prisoner population ever set foot inside the brothels. The Buchenwald brothel, for example, recorded no more than fifty-three daily visitors on average during October 1943. Some prisoner groups were barred altogether, on racial or political grounds; although each KL had different rules, Jews and Russian POWs were not admitted anywhere. In fact, the very idea of visiting the brothels never crossed the minds of most prisoners, who only thought about survival. As for the small elite of better-fed prisoners, who still had sexual desires and the means (vouchers) to satisfy them, some refused on principle to frequent the brothels. Old friends and comrades argued bitterly over such boycotts, and in Dachau, the first men to enter were mocked and jostled by hostile prisoners waiting outside. In the end, most regular users came from among the senior Kapos, who used their visits as demonstrations of their privileged status and virility.[129]

The forced sex workers—fewer than two hundred women in all—were themselves prisoners, selected in different concentration camps. Most wore the black triangle of "asocials," and many, though by no means all, had worked as prostitutes earlier in their lives. Although SS officers prided them-selves on picking volunteers, they actually relied heavily on compulsion, ca-joling the women with promises of better conditions (true) and eventual release (false). Selecting a brothel over a lethal labor detail was just another choiceless choice for these women. As one of them put it in autumn 1942: "Half a year in a brothel is still better than half a year in a concentration camp." What they had not expected was the scorn of some fellow inmates. After the war, a Polish political prisoner recounted how she and ten other inmates had assaulted another Polish woman in Ravensbrück, whom they suspected of volunteering as a prostitute: "We cut her hair a bit and cut her, too, a bit as we were doing it." Such assaults remained rare, however. And despite the dread, distress, and degradation of the brothels, the survival chances of the forced sex workers did improve, since they now received better provisions. For the victims, then, sexual exploitation proved a strategy for survival.[130]

Looking at the reward system as a whole, the high hopes of Himmler and Pohl proved misplaced. Bribes prompted few prisoners to work harder. After all, working harder was not a matter of choice for most, given their poor physical condition. As for the group of prisoners that did benefit the most, it largely consisted of Kapos, who were rewarded not for their output but for their already exalted position in the prisoner hierarchy. Instead of a signifi-cant increase in KL productivity, Pohl's initiative led to a further deepening of the gulf between the small upper class of prisoners and the rest. Growing longer hair, for example, became another visual signifier dividing the privi-leged few, with their immaculate clothes, from the great mass of shaven-headed, dirty, and starving inmates.[131]

Growing the Camps

Sergey Ovrashko was still a boy when he was deported in 1942 from his na-tive Ukraine to Nazi Germany for forced labor. Born in 1926 in a small vil-lage near Kiev, he was supporting his family as a cowherd when German troops invaded the Soviet Union. One year later, he found himself toiling in a high-tech arms factory in Plauen (Saxony), some nine hundred miles away. Worse was to come. After a mistake on the assembly line, he was accused of sabotage, arrested by the Gestapo, and sent in late January 1943 as a political prisoner to Buchenwald.[132] Ovrashko was one of more than forty-two thou-sand prisoners arriving in Buchenwald in 1943, part of an unparalleled surge in inmate numbers that affected the entire concentration camp system.[133]

The KL prisoner population never grew faster during the war than in 1943, shooting up from an estimated one hundred and fifteen thousand at the start of the year to an estimated three hundred and fifteen thousand at the end.[134] In terms of their overall size, the main camps (and their attached satellites) fell into three groups by the end of 1943. Auschwitz, with 85,298 prisoners, was by far the largest and in a league all its own. It was followed by a group of camps established before the war: Dachau, Ravensbrück, Mauthausen, Sachsenhausen, and Buchenwald, which now held between twenty-four thousand and thirty-seven thousand prisoners (the new KL Kovno, with some nineteen thousand prisoners, also belongs to this group). Finally, there were the remaining eleven main camps, many less than a year old, which formed the smallest group, with an average of perhaps six thousand prisoners each.[135] To put these figures into perspective: back in September 1939, when war broke out, the largest KL, Sachsenhausen, had held no more than 6,500 prisoners.[136]

Most new prisoners were caught during an unprecedented wave of arrests sweeping across Germany and much of Nazi-occupied Europe from late 1942 onward. Economic motives played a major part here (as we shall see below), but they overlapped with other Nazi measures. Above all, there was the Holocaust. Deportations of Jews to Auschwitz increased sharply in 1943, compared to the previous year, bringing more prisoners than ever to the camp.[137]

Another important factor was the determination of the RSHA to stamp out any whiff of opposition at home and resistance abroad, a resolve that grew more radical as German confidence in victory began to crumble. From 1942, Nazi leaders became ever more obsessed with the stability of the home front, as the distorted memory of the German defeat and revolution of 1918, so crucial for early Nazi terror, once more dominated their minds. Adolf Hitler, in particular, imagined the catastrophe of an internal collapse in the most garish colors. He was personally responsible, he told his entourage on May 22, 1942, for thwarting "the creation of a home front of scoundrels like in 1918."[138] Ruthless action was required against criminals, political enemies, and other deviants who might attack the regime. During a time of crisis, Hitler repeated again and again, one had to "exterminate," "eliminate," "execute," "beat to death," "shoot," or "liquidate" large numbers of "scum," "rats," and "asocial vermin."[139] Hitler saw the concentration camps as the most powerful weapon in this war on the home front. On May 23, 1942, toward the end of a blazing speech to the Nazi top brass, he singled out the KL as the main bulwark against an uprising. If Nazi Germany should ever face an internal crisis, Hitler exclaimed, Heinrich Himmler would have to "shoot the criminals in all concentration camps, rather than let them loose on the German people."[140]

Himmler did not expect to use these emergency powers. Rather than wait until the Third Reich was in danger, his police forces would root out any threats in advance. Facing a sharp rise in common crime, linked to growing deprivation, dislocation, and damage caused by the war, the criminal police stepped up its policy of crime prevention and sent more Germans straight to the KL, sometimes with explicit instructions that their return was undesirable. Looking at prisoners from the territory of the German Reich, Himmler declared in a speech in autumn 1943, those detained as "asocial" and "criminal" far exceeded political prisoners. Among them were ex-convicts and minor property offenders, whose deviant behavior was characterized as a dangerous attack on the home front. On the same grounds, the police arrested several thousand German women, charged with illicit contacts with foreigners; before being dragged to camps, some women accused of sexual relationships were publicly shamed and humiliated.[141]

The German police also targeted Gypsies inside the Third Reich with unprecedented zeal. In autumn 1942, after years of escalating Nazi persecution, including segregation, sterilization, detention, and expulsion, the leaders of the criminal police in the RSHA advocated a systematic solution to the "Gypsy Question." Depicting Gypsies as a criminal and biological threat to the home front, they lobbied Himmler for mass deportations. Himmler agreed. With Hitler's blessing, he ordered on December 16, 1942, that the great majority of Gypsies should be sent to a concentration camp. Police guidelines, passed in the following month, left some leeway for local officials; determined to make their districts "Gypsy free," they generally opted for the hardest approach. Starting in late February 1943, some fourteen thousand men, women, and children—among them many families—were deported from Germany and annexed Austria to Auschwitz-Birkenau; as the biggest Nazi camp, it seemed best placed to absorb a large number of prisoners at short notice (another 8,500 Gypsies arrived from elsewhere, mostly from the occupied Czech territory). Their arrival marked the birth of the so-called Gypsy camp in sector BIIe of Birkenau.[142] One of the first prisoners was the forty-three-year-old trader August Laubinger from Quedlinburg, who arrived on March 4, 1943, together with his wife, Hulda, and four children. This was not his first time in a KL; in summer 1938, as we have seen, the police had sent him as "work-shy" to Sachsenhausen. Back then, he had been lucky to be released, and returned home to his family just before the outbreak of the war. This time, there was no way out. August Laubinger, prisoner number Z-229, died in Birkenau sometime before the end of the year.[143]

The primary focus of police terror on the home front was not on Gypsies or German social outsiders, however, but on foreign workers; in summer 1943, more than two-thirds of all new Gestapo prisoners were foreigners, who were routinely suspected as troublemakers, subversives, and criminals. The growing number of foreigners living in Germany, which swelled because of the merciless pursuit of foreign labor by Fritz Sauckel, only intensified these fears. By the end of 1943, the total number of foreign civilian workers and POWs inside the Third Reich had reached a staggering 7.3 million, turning the Nazi vision of an ethnically unified "people's community" on its head. The great majority of foreign workers came from Poland and the Soviet Union (especially from Ukraine), with many hundreds of thousands more from western Europe, above all from France. Worst off were the hungry and exhausted men and women from eastern Europe, who had to wear special markers, resembling the KL triangles, to identify them in case they broke the draconian rules.

The police habitually handed out brutal penalties. This was true, above all, for Poles and Soviets, whose punishment the compliant legal authorities now largely left to the police. There was no reason to worry about the millions of foreign workers, Heinrich Himmler assured SS group leaders in Posen on October 4, 1943, "as long as we come down hard on the smallest trifles." Most alleged offenses were indeed trivial. Turning up late for work or disagreeing with a German superior was enough to be accused of "loafing" or "obstinacy." The most common police sanction for supposedly grave offenses was a brief spell in a Gestapo camp (so-called Work Education Camps, or AELs, and Extended Police Prisons); these were harsh wartime additions to the Nazi landscape of terror, designed to discipline and deter "recalcitrant" workers through short but sharp detention. The most serious cases, however, were dealt with elsewhere: prisoners accused of sabotage, such as Sergey Ovrashko, and others regarded as especially dangerous, were dragged to the KL, which filled up with many tens of thousands of foreign workers in 1943. In this way, the SS gained more slave laborers and simultaneously increased the pressure on foreign workers outside to conform to Nazi demands. Punishment and deterrence went hand in hand.[144]

Like Ovrashko, many Soviet foreign workers were still in their teens when they came to the KL. In Dachau alone, some 2,200 Soviet youths, aged eighteen or under, arrived in 1942. Their average age soon fell even further, after the German occupation authorities in the east dispatched ever-younger boys and girls for labor to the Reich. The police had no qualms about dragging these children to concentration camps, and in January 1943 Heinrich Himmler officially lowered to sixteen years the minimum age for committing Soviet forced workers.[145] In practice, some were younger still. The Russian prisoner V. Chramcov, himself a teenager when he was forced to Dachau, recalled that one barrack had been packed with more than two hundred children, aged between six and seven.[146] Some veteran prisoners looked on in horror. In his Dachau diary, Edgar Kupfer noted on April 11, 1943, that the "many little Russians in the camp" were "utterly miserable with hunger."[147]

The tentacles of Himmler's terror apparatus also reached far beyond the borders of the Third Reich, pulling even more foreigners into concentration camps from abroad. As the war turned further against Germany in 1943, resistance across Nazi-occupied Europe intensified. So did the Nazi response. Himmler led from the front, insisting on overwhelming force. In northern and western Europe, he authorized selective assassinations of public figures as a form of "counterterrorism," while his men ran wild in eastern and southeastern Europe, using antipartisan warfare as an excuse for blanket executions. When it came to locking up foreign suspects, Himmler often opted for his trusted concentration camps. The call for mass deportations of foreign resisters, deviants, and hostages to the KL became a reflex for him, and contributed to the sharp rise in prisoners from Nazi-occupied Europe. Among them were the so-called NN prisoners, held in almost total isolation. To discourage resistance in northern and western Europe, Hitler had ordered that some suspects should secretly be deported to Germany, never to be seen again by their families; they would disappear in "night and fog" (*Nacht und Nebel*, or NN).[148]

The mass arrest of foreigners in 1943 left its mark on the KL system. In most camps inside the Third Reich's prewar borders, German prisoners had still constituted the largest or second-largest inmate group in early 1943. Now these camps began to change. In Buchenwald, for example, the proportion of Germans among the inmate population fell from thirty-five percent to thirteen percent during 1943 (even though the number of German prisoners still rose by more than one thousand), while the share of east European prisoners increased correspondingly; on December 25, 1943, there were 14,451 Soviet and 7,569 Polish prisoners in Buchenwald, making up almost sixty percent of the prisoner population (37,221). By contrast, there were only some 4,850 Germans, who were almost outnumbered by the 4,689 French, a prisoner group that had been virtually nonexistent one year earlier.[149]

Hunting for Slave Laborers

In late May 1942, Heinrich Himmler sent a word of warning to Oswald Pohl: it was important to avoid the impression "that we arrest people, or keep them inside [the KL] after their arrest, to have workers."[150] He may have been anxious about appearances, but Himmler had long resolved to grow the slave labor force inside his concentration camps. Economic considerations had already influenced the arrest of "work-shy" men back in the late 1930s, and by 1942, Himmler's appetite for forced laborers had become ravenous.[151]

Seizing prisoners from other Nazi authorities was one way of boosting the KL slave labor force. Before the war, Himmler's bids for regular state prisoners had been rebuffed. But the stance of the legal authorities relaxed after the appointment of the hard-liner Otto-Georg Thierack as Reich minister of justice on August 20, 1942. Desperate to shore up the standing of the judiciary—which had reached a low point in spring 1942, following a public broadside from Hitler—Thierack was willing to throw one of the last legal principles overboard: the rule that defendants sentenced by the courts served their time in state prisons. In a meeting with Himmler on September 18, 1942, Thierack agreed to hand over whole groups of judicial prisoners: those sentenced to security confinement, "asocial" German and Czech penitentiary inmates sentenced to more than eight years, convicts at the bottom of the Nazi racial hierarchy (that is, Jews, Gypsies, and Soviets), as well as Poles serving sentences of over three years. Brushing aside the rule of law, or what was left of it, Germany's leading jurist condemned many of his own prisoners to death in Himmler's concentration camps.

The ensuing prisoner transfers accelerated the shift in power between legal and SS terror, and helped the camps finally to outstrip prisons. Although inmate numbers in the latter swelled during the war, too, they could no longer keep up with lawless terror; by June 1943, the KL prisoner population had grown to some two hundred thousand inmates, around fifteen thousand more than German state prisons. Himmler must have been gratified to overtake the much-maligned legal authorities. But this was now a secondary concern, overshadowed by his quest for more slave labor. Like Hitler, Himmler believed that the incoming state prisoners would be in great shape, having been pampered in plush prisons; working them to death in concentration camps could only benefit the SS.

Deportations from German state prisons to Auschwitz, Buchenwald, Mauthausen, Neuengamme, and Sachsenhausen began in November 1942, and were largely completed late the following spring. In all, the legal authorities handed over more than twenty thousand state prisoners. Most of them were German nationals, above all petty property offenders, while Poles made up the largest group of foreigners.[152] Thousands more Polish state prisoners arrived in Auschwitz and Majdanek from prisons in the General Government (run by the police), following a Himmler order in December 1942, that targeted prisoners judged fit for work.[153]

Himmler's efforts to bolster his slave labor force became more frantic from late 1942, as Germany's strategic position deteriorated. Following the encirclement of the Sixth Army in Stalingrad and losses in North Africa, not even Himmler could ignore the whispers of impending defeat. War production became more pressing than ever, increasing demands on the RSHA (still in charge of arrests and releases) to deliver more slaves to concentration camps.[154] Some of this pressure came from the WVHA, with Oswald Pohl insisting in a letter to Himmler on December 8, 1942, that many more prisoners were required for armaments production.[155] Himmler reacted straightaway. On December 12, he attended Pohl's wedding as the guest of honor and used the joyous occasion for a confidential chat about the KL.[156] Only a few days later, Himmler issued an urgent order to Gestapo leader Heinrich Müller: by the end of January 1943, the police had to deliver some fifty thousand new prisoners to the concentration camps for slave labor.[157] Müller grasped the significance of Himmler's demand and exhorted his police forces that *"every single worker counts!"*[158]

The result was a major police operation against Jews and foreign workers from eastern Europe. On December 16, 1942, Heinrich Müller informed Himmler about plans for the deportation of forty-five thousand Jews—thirty thousand from Bialystok district, most of the others from Theresienstadt—to Auschwitz. The great majority of them, he added, would be "unfit for work" (in other words, they would be gassed on arrival), but at least ten to fifteen thousand could be "set aside" for forced labor.[159] Just one day later, Müller ordered mass transfers from German police jails and AELs, targeting Soviet workers and others of "alien blood," who had been arrested for offenses against labor discipline. Müller hoped that this initiative would net at least another thirty-five thousand prisoners "fit for work" for the concentration camps.[160] Meanwhile, Himmler pushed for even more prisoners. On January 6, 1943, he demanded that boys and girls arrested as "suspected partisans" in the General Government and the occupied Soviet Union should become apprentices in KL enterprises in Auschwitz and Majdanek. And just twelve days later, he responded to bomb attacks in Marseilles by calling for the deportation of one hundred thousand members of the local "criminal masses" to concentration camps, an outlandish target that speaks volumes about Himmler's state of mind (in the end, some six thousand persons were arrested).[161]

The manhunts in early 1943 led to a rapid rise in the KL prisoner population. In Auschwitz, the number of registered Polish inmates doubled, from 9,514 (December 1, 1942) to 18,931 (January 29, 1943). Even more significantly, the SS deported more than fifty-seven thousand Jews to Auschwitz in January 1943, a grim record not surpassed until the mass transports of Jews from Hungary in late spring 1944.[162] Not only did the number of KL prisoners increase, but fewer were allowed to leave, as RSHA regulations for releases, already highly restrictive, were tightened further to retain more slave laborers.[163]

Prisoner numbers across the KL system would have risen much higher still had it not been for the dreadful conditions, the murderous violence, and the systematic killings that decimated Himmler's much-heralded workforce. According to incomplete SS figures, almost ten thousand registered inmates lost their lives in January 1943 alone.[164] Mortality figures had apparently been even higher during the preceding months, and Camp SS leaders would no doubt have continued to ignore these deaths had the growing focus on war production not started to drive up the value of slave labor. For the first time in its history, the Camp SS came under sustained pressure to improve conditions. As the RSHA suggested in a biting letter to Pohl on December 31, 1942, what was the point of all the mass arrests if so many new prisoners died so quickly inside the concentration camps?[165]

Reducing Death Rates

Richard Glücks was not a man of many surprises. But on December 28, 1942, he delivered a stunning message to the Camp SS: Heinrich Himmler had ordered that prisoner mortality in the concentration camps "must absolutely become lower" (this phrase was lifted almost verbatim from Himmler's order, sent two weeks earlier to Pohl). Glücks pointed to grim figures. Although some 110,000 new prisoners had arrived during the last six months (June to November 1942), almost 80,000 inmates had died during the same period, 9,258 after executions and another 70,610 from illness, exhaustion, and injury (Glücks did not include Jews gassed in Auschwitz on arrival, without registration). This huge death rate meant that "the number of prisoners can never be brought up to the [right] level, as the Reichsführer SS has ordered." Consequently, Glücks decreed, senior camp doctors had to take all available measures to drive down "significantly" the number of deaths. This was not the first time Camp SS leaders had reminded their men that greater output required at least a minimum of care; but never before had such an order been made with such urgency.[166]

Signaling its seriousness about raising living standards, the WVHA issued several further directives in 1943. In January, taking his cue from Himmler once more, Glücks made local KL commandants and administration leaders responsible for using all available means to "preserve the labor power of prisoners."[167] Oswald Pohl also weighed in, summing up his views in a long letter to commandants in October 1943. Arms production in the camps was already a "decisive factor in the war," he fantasized, but to further increase output, the SS would have to look after its prisoners. In order for Germany to win "a great victory," Camp SS officers had to ensure the "healthiness" and "well-being" of slave laborers in concentration camps. Pohl then outlined a range of practical improvements. To underline their importance, he announced that he would personally supervise their implementation.[168]

After years of endorsing and escalating violence in concentration camps, senior SS officials in Berlin and Oranienburg now seemed to play a different tune, jarring to some guards raised in the school of violence. Of course, SS leaders had not undergone a sudden conversion from cruelty to compassion. His demands owed nothing to "sentimental humanitarianism," Pohl reassured the commandants. It was a purely practical strategy, since the "arms and legs" of prisoners were needed to support the German war effort.[169] The WVHA was not alone in rethinking its approach. As it dawned on Nazi leaders that the supply of labor power would not be limitless, other groups of forced laborers, too, could hope for some improvements of their conditions.[170]

Since starvation was probably the greatest cause of death among registered KL prisoners, a better food supply was the most pressing task—as even Heinrich Himmler recognized.[171] However, SS leaders were reluctant to distribute additional resources and instead promoted measures that came at no extra cost. Some were just an outlet for the eccentric ideas of Himmler, who fancied himself as a visionary nutritionist. Foremost was his preposterous plan to distribute onions and other raw vegetables, an initiative that would have caused more misery for inmates already suffering from intestinal infections.[172] Drawing on expert SS advice, meanwhile, Oswald Pohl circulated his own proposals to the camps, full of banal cookery tips ("Don't boil warm meals to death!") and stern reminders to be thrifty ("There must be no kitchen scraps in the KL").[173]

Another initiative by Himmler proved more significant. In late October 1942, the Reichsführer SS had permitted prisoners to receive food packages from outside, reviving the old practice from the prewar camps. Soon, parcels arrived from relatives, the International Committee of the Red Cross (ICRC), and some national Red Cross societies.[174] Rare luxuries now found their way into the KL; packages by the Danish Red Cross included sausage, cheese, butter, pork, fish, and more. Such parcels were a blessing for inmates and they talked about little else; some even dreamed about the packages. In her secret Ravensbrück diary, the French prisoner Simone Saint-Clair recorded how desperately she longed for mail: "Never before have I waited like this for packages and letters!" Those who received regular supplies were less likely to suffer from edema, diarrhea, tuberculosis, and other illnesses. Helena Dziedziecka from Warsaw, another Ravensbrück prisoner, later testified that the parcels "kept us alive."[175]

But not every inmate benefited, far from it; there were always many more hopeful prisoners than parcels.[176] For a start, the national Red Cross societies restricted the circle of recipients; in Majdanek, for example, packages by the Polish Red Cross went to Polish prisoners only. Moreover, the SS only passed on parcels addressed to individual inmates; prisoners whose names and whereabouts were unknown to welfare organizations and relatives—or who had no more relatives outside—went hungry. Meanwhile, SS staff and Kapos found a new opportunity for corruption and helped themselves freely to the packages; when Anna Mettbach, a German Gypsy in Auschwitz, received a parcel from her mother, she found the original contents replaced by rotten apples and bread.[177] The local Camp SS barred whole groups of inmates from receiving food parcels altogether, above all Soviets and Jews. "All of us are very needy," Edgar Kupfer wrote in his Dachau diary, "especially the Russians, because they get no parcels."[178]

In addition to parcels, some prisoners received extra food from the German state, again at no extra cost for the SS. Although the Reich Ministry for Food and Agriculture had cut official prisoner rations substantially since early 1942, as Germany suffered a general food crisis, most prisoners did qualify for additional food allowances for heavy labor. However, these allowances were not handed out automatically, and local Camp SS officials were slow to complete the necessary paperwork (some of those who did kept back the extra rations). Eventually, more inmates received their due, though it is likely that most prisoners were left empty-handed.[179]

SS leaders knew that efforts to improve conditions could not stop at the food supply. They would have to do something about all the gravely weak and ill inmates. In late 1942, Himmler complained to Pohl that far too many prisoners—some ten percent, by his count—were currently unable to work.[180] In the past, the Camp SS had been quick to kill such invalids. These murderous reflexes were now more restrained, however, as SS leaders aimed to press prisoners who recovered back into work.[181] In some camps, these considerations led to restrictions on local SS selections.[182] Himmler also effectively abandoned the central program for murdering frail prisoners (Action 14f13), scaled down earlier. In the future, the commandants were told in spring 1943, all prisoners "unfit for work" would be exempt from selections by the doctors' commissions (with the sole exception of mentally ill inmates). Instead of killing "bedridden cripples," the Camp SS should force them to work, as Himmler had demanded for some time.[183]

As for the medical treatment of the sick, Camp SS leaders called for a new approach, too. "The best doctor in a concentration camp," Glücks insisted in late 1942, "is not the one who thinks he has to distinguish himself by inappropriate toughness, but the one who keeps the ability to work . . . as high as possible."[184] This demand resulted in at least one notable change: the SS staffed the KL infirmaries with more inmates who were trained doctors, bringing back another custom from the prewar camps. Soon, these prisoner physicians carried out most of the day-to-day duties. In contrast to their often inept SS superiors, they were highly qualified and secured some improvements for patients; the construction of new buildings and the enhanced provision of equipment and medicines also helped, at least in some camps.[185]

Important as these changes were for individual inmates, they did not transform prisoner care as a whole. Any hygienic improvements were often negated by growing overcrowding, a direct result of the SS push for more slave laborers.[186] The infirmaries continued to be characterized by desperate shortages, neglect, and abuse. Describing the hospital barracks in Sachsenhausen, a recently escaped prisoner wrote in summer 1944 that the "stench of rotting flesh, blood, and pus is unbearable."[187] The best care was reserved for a small number of skilled, well-connected, and privileged prisoners.[188] By contrast, the SS still left most seriously ill inmates to die or murdered them outright. In particular, the practice of deporting dying prisoners to other camps continued, with Auschwitz replacing Dachau as the favored destination. Late on December 5, 1943, for instance, a so-called invalid transport from Flossenbürg arrived in the camp. The packed train included the corpses of more than 250 men who had died en route to Auschwitz. Many of the surviving 948 men, some weighing less than ninety pounds, were close to death. The SS threw the weakest onto the snow-covered ground, pouring water over them to hasten their death. The remaining men soon died, too; by February 18, 1944, just 393 were still alive.[189]

But the WVHA did not abandon its overall ambition to bring down the death rate. And because the climate of cruelty inside the KL was another major cause of injury and death, the officials tried to curb some of the most blatant excesses. They cut back on the number and duration of roll calls (a frequent occasion for SS torture) and instructed local guards to leave prisoners in peace at nighttime, to allow them some more rest. The authorities also pressed for a reduction in corporal punishment and abandoned the infamous "hanging from a pole" (at least on paper).[190] More generally, the WVHA reiterated its ban on rogue attacks on prisoners. Further reminders came from local Camp SS officers, some of whom openly rebuked and even punished violent guards.[191]

Again, these measures showed some effect, although much of the day-to-day terror continued. Many local Camp SS officials lived in a world where the most heinous abuse of prisoner bodies was considered normal, even after death (in Buchenwald, SS men produced shrunken heads and objects made from tattooed prisoner skin). It is not surprising that SS veterans steeped in a culture of cruelty would resist even modest efforts from above to reduce the violence.[192] Their immediate superiors often condoned their stance. Some local SS officers told block leaders to keep battering inmates, even as they asked them, with a wink, to sign the official undertaking not to touch any prisoners.[193]

The persistence of local terror owed much to SS leaders. It would be wrong to imagine a simple clash between reformist WVHA managers and local SS torturers.[194] The central orders for the KL in 1942–43 were by no means clear-cut. At the same time that the WVHA demanded better conditions and treatment, it pushed for the brutal exploitation of prisoners, despite the obvious contradictions. Oswald Pohl himself had set the tone in spring 1942 with his call for "exhausting" forced labor. Gerhard Maurer, Pohl's slave driver, tried to realize this demand. In early June 1942, he repeated his master's words, urging KL commandants to "utilize" the labor power of inmates to the "absolute maximum." To this end, Maurer continued, prisoners had to work not only during the week, but all day on Saturdays and on Sunday mornings, too.[195] It was doubtful whether this order brought any economic benefits; some private companies were unable to operate on Sundays, while utterly exhausted prisoners produced less, not more.[196] The WVHA was undeterred, and in November 1943, Pohl reiterated the orders: "The extensive operations which are being carried on today and which are important for our warfare and decisive for victory do not permit under any circumstances that the *net* daily working time amounts to less than 11 hours." In practice, prisoners often worked even longer, driven on by the local Camp SS.[197] The result was more illness, injury, and death.

A New Direction?

Still, Oswald Pohl was triumphant. Prisoner fatalities inside the KL were falling fast, he boasted in a letter to Himmler on September 30, 1943; thanks to all the recent innovations, the WVHA had accomplished the mission set by the Reichsführer SS. The monthly death rate among registered prisoners had fallen steadily, Pohl announced, from eight percent in January 1943 to less than three percent in June. This was not simply a seasonal adjustment, he implied, but a sharp decline in real terms (the figure for July 1942 had stood at 8.5 percent). To drive home his point, Pohl dazzled Himmler with statistics, graphs, and tables, all of which led to the same conclusion. Himmler was delighted by the good news—which reached him amid more military setbacks for the Nazi regime—and thanked Pohl and his men profusely.[198]

Some historians have accepted Pohl's claims wholesale, including his figures.[199] But caution is in order: after all, Pohl was desperate to be seen to reduce prisoner deaths. Looking more closely, it is clear that his numbers do not quite add up. Not only did the Camp SS simply omit many deaths of registered prisoners from the official record, but Pohl's figures did not even tally with other (higher) SS figures. There can be no doubt, in short, that more KL prisoners died than Pohl suggested.[200] This is not to say, however, that the general trend he outlined was a fabrication.[201] Prisoner mortality across the KL system really did decline; overall, inmates had a better chance of survival in autumn 1943 than eighteen months earlier.[202]

This conclusion must be qualified, however, in three ways. First, the KL system was still lethal. Even though the *relative* death rate declined, *total* mortality increased in several camps in 1943, as the inmate population expanded. In the Auschwitz complex, for example, the estimated number of deaths among registered prisoners rose from sixty-nine thousand (1942) to more than eighty thousand (1943).[203] Even though the basic conditions in Auschwitz improved somewhat during this period—one Polish prisoner even suggested that "there was a huge difference between now and then"— they remained deadly. Hermann Langbein, a privileged prisoner with direct access to confidential SS statistics, later reported that the monthly inmate mortality in Auschwitz had fallen from 19.1 percent (January 1943) to 13.2 percent (January 1944). In other words, the SS had prolonged the suffering of prisoners, but most died all the same.[204]

Second, there were enormous differences between camps. Far more prisoners lost their lives in occupied eastern Europe than farther west. According to the figures Pohl presented to Himmler, the most deadly concentration camp in August 1943 was Majdanek, where prisoners were ten times more likely to die than in Buchenwald.[205] Even in established main camps within Germany's prewar borders, however, conditions developed unevenly. In Mauthausen, the situation improved markedly and the annual inmate mortality almost halved, from an estimated forty-three percent (1942) to twenty-three percent (1943). By comparison, there were few, if any, improvements for the women in Ravensbrück or the men in Flossenbürg over the same period.[206]

Third, the geographical imbalance of the KL system owed much to the different mortality rates of individual prisoner groups. In Majdanek and Auschwitz, the two biggest camps in the occupied east, Jews made up the largest prisoner group in 1943; and these registered Jewish inmates rarely lived for much longer than a few months, as the basic SS approach toward them remained unchanged—"annihilation through labor." The Camp SS even extended this policy to some other inmate groups, notably state prisoners arriving under the agreement between Thierack and Himmler. By the end of March 1943, almost half of the 12,658 state prisoners deported since November 1942 were already dead. Most had survived for no more than a few weeks, pursued mercilessly by the Camp SS. In Buchenwald, for example, the monthly death rate of former state prisoners stood at a staggering twenty-nine percent in early 1943—compared to less than one percent among German "greens" (so-called professional criminals).[207]

Even if the overall trend was less dramatic than the triumphant Pohl suggested, the KL system did become less deadly in 1943, as the WVHA initiatives showed some effect. While the impact of each particular measure was limited, their cumulative effect proved significant. The dramatic descent into squalor and death, which had begun with the outbreak of war in autumn 1939, was temporarily arrested and reversed. As we have seen before, the KL did not develop along a straight line. And they were not impervious to directions from above. Just as SS leaders in Berlin had escalated terror in the past, they could also rein it in. Some central orders took time to sink in and others were subverted and ignored, but the WVHA was able to set the general direction for its camps.[208] Although they succeeded in lowering the death rate, however, the SS managers had no desire to transform the whole ethos of the camps. As a result, the main coordinates of the KL system—which rested on neglect, contempt, and hatred—remained largely unchanged.

"GUINEA PIGS"

Siegmund Wassing, a thirty-six-year-old Austrian Jew, arrived in Dachau in November 1941. Five months later, the former film technician from Vienna was condemned to the most dreadful death. On April 3, 1942, he was locked into a pressure cabin, inside a special truck stationed between two infirmary barracks, and wired up to machines measuring his heart and brain activity. Then the air was pumped out of the cabin, simulating a rapid ascent to a height of over seven miles. Within minutes, Wassing, still wearing his striped prisoner uniform, was sweating and shaking and gasping for air; after half an hour he stopped breathing, and SS Untersturmführer Sigmund Rascher, an air force doctor, prepared for the postmortem. The ambitious thirty-three-year-old Rascher had ordered the medical execution as part of a series of air pressure experiments, which had started in late February 1942, and also included simulated pressure loss and ejections from a height of up to thirteen miles. In all, several hundred prisoners were abused during the trials in Dachau; dozens died. But Dr. Rascher was upbeat. In a letter on April 5, 1942, just two days after the murder of Siegmund Wassing, he envisaged "entirely new perspectives for aviation."[209]

The recipient of this letter, Reichsführer SS Heinrich Himmler, who had authorized the experiments, was equally excited. So fascinated was he that he decided to see for himself, just as some air force and SS officers had done before him. With Oswald Pohl in tow, Himmler came to Dachau on the afternoon of May 1, 1942, and observed around a half dozen simulated ejections at high altitude; none of the prisoners died, apparently, but they cried and fainted, while the Reichsführer SS watched intently. Himmler left contented, but not before he confronted a few local SS men for making free with the coffee and cognac he had sent to the victims as a last meal.[210]

It was around the time of Himmler's visit to Dachau that human experiments proliferated in the KL. Although some trials had taken place earlier, they expanded greatly as Germany's military fortunes declined. By 1942, SS leaders were grasping at projects that promised renewed hope, whatever their human cost, and treated the bodies of KL prisoners as commodities to be exploited for final victory—not just during slave labor, but also during experiments. Many of these trials, like the ones in Dachau, were explicitly conducted for the war effort. As losses at the front and at home grew, anxious officials looked to medical science to turn the tide. The abuse of KL prisoners was supposed to generate new treatments to save German soldiers from cold and hunger, injuries and epidemics, and to protect German civilians from infections and burns. "I thought it my duty to do everything to ensure this protection," one doctor later said, trying to justify his part in the murderous experiments, "and to save the lives of thousands of Germans."[211]

KL Experiments

Human experiments accompanied the rise of modern medicine, in Germany and beyond. Firm regulation was a long time coming, but after several scandals shook the Weimar Republic, the German medical authorities in 1931 drafted pathbreaking guidelines for research on humans, banning any coercion of test subjects as well as experiments on dying persons and those endangering children.[212] Just a few years later, however, physicians in the KL threw out these fundamental rules. The first trials using prisoners, which took place before the outbreak of the Second World War, were still small-scale and comparatively harmless.[213] Once Germany was at war, however, the SS supported potentially lethal tests, with events at the front influencing many of these experiments.

Probably the first such experiments took place in the Sachsenhausen infirmary, where two Camp SS doctors poisoned dozens of prisoners with mustard gas between October and December 1939. The order had come from Himmler, gripped by widespread hysteria about possible chemical attacks on German troops, which awakened traumatic memories from the Great War. To determine the effectiveness of two potential remedies, the Sachsenhausen doctors applied mustard gas onto the arms of prisoners, causing burns that spread all the way up to the neck; in some cases, the doctors infected the wounds with bacteria. In the end, the drugs they tested turned out to be useless. The doctors conceded as much in their final reports, forwarded to Himmler by SS Reich physician Ernst Robert Grawitz, who had personally observed the trials.[214]

Many more experiments followed over the coming years, above all during the second half of World War II. In all, doctors abused more than twenty thousand prisoners from over a dozen KL during the war; several thousand of them died.[215] As the number of victims swelled, WVHA managers became concerned about the possible impact on forced labor and asked individual camps in late 1942 how many workers were being lost to the experiments.[216] The doctors, meanwhile, covered their tracks, describing the deliberate infection of prisoners with viruses and poison as "vaccinations."[217] Occasionally they slipped up, however, and spoke their minds, calling their victims "guinea pigs" and "rabbits"—terms appropriated, with gallows humor, by some of the victims themselves.[218]

Heinrich Himmler presided over these experiments, probably with Hitler's backing.[219] Although this was no centrally coordinated program, with many of the most radical initiatives coming from below, Himmler held the keys to the "guinea pigs" and insisted that no KL experiments go ahead without his say-so.[220] Scientists with personal connections like Sigmund Rascher, whose wife was a close acquaintance of Himmler, could appeal to him directly.[221] Another route led via the Ahnenerbe, Himmler's pseudoscientific research institute. Originally set up to uncover the mythical roots of the Germanic race, it drifted into military research during the war, and facilitated the supply of KL prisoners for various experiments.[222] A third path went through SS Reich physician Grawitz, who became a more influential figure during the war and took control of all SS medical services in 1943. Despite Himmler's repeated attacks on the professionalism of his chief physician, Grawitz proved himself no less enthusiastic about experiments in the camps than his boss, for whom he evaluated applications from scientists.[223]

Himmler was an obsessive micromanager of medical torture, devouring reports and suggesting bizarre new treatments. He was dazzled by science and easily captivated by radical schemes of supposed experts, especially when they chimed with his own worldview. The sacrifice of worthless subhumans in the KL would save the lives of German soldiers, he argued, and anyone who objected to this was a traitor. In Himmler's mind, war justified any means, and he opened the door to many lethal experiments, with Dachau emerging as one of the main centers.[224]

Himmler's Favorite Doctor

The history of human experiments in Dachau is closely linked to Dr. Sigmund Rascher, whose murders in the air pressure cabin were the first in a series of often deadly trials. Born into an affluent family in Munich (his father was a doctor, too), he had qualified in 1936 and served as a physician in the air force from 1939. His rapid rise thereafter owed little to his political activism (he only joined the SS in 1939), and even less to his abilities as a physician. Rather, Rascher was propelled by his ambition and his equally determined wife, who made the most of her contacts with Himmler. With the patronage of the Reichsführer SS, who always had time for young firebrands promising scientific breakthroughs by unorthodox means, he became the doyen of human experimentation in Dachau.

Not everyone was taken in by the brash upstart. Professor Karl Gebhardt, the leading clinician in the Waffen SS and a former assistant to Germany's most famous surgeon, Professor Sauerbruch, dismissed Rascher as a quack. Tellingly, his charge was not that Rascher's work was inhumane—Gebhardt himself carried out experiments in Ravensbrück—but that it was useless. Reviewing one of Rascher's reports, Gebhardt told him to his face that if a first-year undergraduate had handed it in, he would have thrown him out of his office. Rascher's superiors in the air force also grew wary. Grateful that he had initiated aviation experiments in Dachau, they became frustrated with the way Rascher used his direct line to Himmler to go over their heads. On Himmler's wishes, Rascher was eventually discharged from the air force in 1943 and now butchered and killed solely for the SS (with the rank of Hauptsturmführer), running an experimental station in Dachau bearing his own name.[225]

As long as he had Himmler's backing, Rascher kept busy. After the air pressure trials ended in May 1942, Rascher and some colleagues quickly moved on to the next experiment, suspending prisoners in icy water. Again, the trials were driven by military considerations. In view of the growing number of German pilots who crashed in the British channel, the air force wanted to learn more about lengthy exposure to water. During the tests, prisoners had to climb into a freezing tank, with pieces of ice floating inside. Some victims wore full pilots' outfits; others were naked. One young Polish prisoner begged his tormentors to stop, over and over in broken German: "Nothing more water, nothing more water." Another Polish prisoner, the priest Leo Michalowski, later testified at the Nuremberg Doctors' Trial about his ordeal, the only survivor to do so: "I was freezing badly in this water, my feet became stiff as iron, my hands too, I was breathing very shallowly. I started again to tremble badly, and cold sweat ran down my head. I felt like I was about to die. And then I pleaded once more to be pulled out, because I could not bear the water any longer."

After several hours, most prisoners were finally dragged out, unconscious, and the doctors then tried drugs, massages, and electric blankets to revive them. Michalowski was saved, but many more succumbed. Others were deliberately left to die in the tank, so that Rascher could study more closely their cause of death. In all, some two to three hundred Dachau prisoners were tortured in the water tank. Many dozens of them died, mostly under Rascher's sole supervision: after the trials were officially called off in October 1942, because the air force had gathered sufficient data, Rascher himself continued, eager to further his career; and just as he had done during the air pressure experiments, he pushed for ever more extreme setups.[226] Following the German catastrophe at Stalingrad in early 1943, he even extended his freezing experiments to dry land. To study extreme frostbite, Dachau prisoners were left to the elements during the winter nights; they were given a sedative to silence their screams. Rascher's ambition, one former Dachau Kapo recalled, literally made him "walk over corpses."[227]

So fascinated was Heinrich Himmler by Rascher's freezing experiments that he became personally involved once more. The most promising way of reanimating prisoners suspended in icy water, he suggested, was human warmth; to test his hypothesis, he asked Rascher to make naked women fondle the unconscious men.[228] Himmler's suggestion was patently pointless. Even if "animal warmth" (as he called it) had made any difference, which it did not, no one, not even Himmler, would have suggested stationing prostitutes on German navy vessels just in case they fished out a downed pilot.[229] But Himmler's word was sacrosanct in the SS. Ravensbrück duly dispatched four women in October 1942—the first female prisoners to arrive at Dachau—and the experiments could begin. Before long, Rascher's sordid sideshow had become a magnet for the local Camp SS and other interested parties.[230]

The voyeur-in-chief was none other than the sexually repressed Reichsführer SS himself. Himmler felt "great curiosity" about the trials and made sure to see for himself, arriving in Rascher's Dachau station on the morning of November 13, 1942. Himmler watched everything close-up. A naked male prisoner thrown into the water; Rascher pressing him under as he struggled to get out; the man being pulled out unconscious; his frozen body placed in a large bed; two naked women trying to have sex with him. Himmler was satisfied, except for a minor complaint he passed on to Pohl: he felt that one of the women, a young German prisoner, could still be saved for the Nazi national community and should not be used anymore as a sex slave.[231]

Everything seemed to be going right for Dr. Sigmund Rascher. With Himmler's help, he had made a name for himself and by early 1944, he was closing in on his ultimate dream, a professorship. Meanwhile, he continued his human experiments. He was particularly interested in a hemostatic drug called Polygal and ordered the execution of several Dachau prisoners to test its effectiveness. The drug had been developed by a Jewish chemist imprisoned in Dachau, and Rascher planned to make a fortune with it, preparing to manufacture it in a factory of his own. Rascher's professional and financial future appeared rosy, and there was good news in his private life, too. His wife—who generated additional income by blackmailing a released prisoner, threatening to have him taken back to Dachau—announced that she was pregnant with their fourth child.[232]

But all was not as it seemed. Following a child-snatching incident in Munich, the criminal police discovered that the Raschers' picture-book family life—which had brought them gifts and goodwill from Himmler—was built on crime and deception. They had no children of their own; Frau Rascher had taken all her boys from other women, with her husband's complicity. The ensuing police investigation also uncovered evidence of her husband's corrupt deals in the camp. The arrogant Rascher had made plenty of enemies among the local Camp SS, and his bright prospects unraveled spectacularly. He was placed into custody in May 1944, and the SS shot him in the Dachau bunker just before liberation, not far from the sites where he had conducted his murderous trials. Around the same time, his wife, who had repeatedly tried to escape, was hanged in Ravensbrück.[233]

The SS experiments in Dachau did not stop with Rascher's fall, however. He may have been the most prominent medical torturer in the camp, but he was not the only one. Since 1942, several other physicians worked on their own trials, infecting prisoners with bacteria to test drugs against blood poisoning and festering wounds, and forcing them to drink seawater to test a substance said to improve its taste.[234] In fact, Dachau was the site of one of the largest KL trials, at the malaria research station run by Professor Claus Schilling, a pupil of the legendary bacteriologist Robert Koch (1843–1910). Schilling was already in his seventies and had spent his long career searching in vain for a vaccine. Given his paltry record, his proposal for human trials in the camps promised little success. Undeterred, Himmler—keen to find a drug to protect troops from malaria in the occupied east—gave him permission to proceed. The experiments began in February 1942 and Schilling, who moved to Dachau, continued until the camp fell apart in spring 1945. In all, around 1,100 prisoners, some already too weak to walk, were infected through injections or mosquito bites, to allow Schilling and his men to test a range of drugs. The prisoners suffered swollen extremities, the loss of nails and hair, high fevers, paralysis, and more. Numerous victims died through drug overdoses, while survivors often endured further experiments.[235]

The Dachau Camp SS participated in these trials, just as it did in others. When Professor Schilling needed new victims, a list of inmates was drawn up in the office of the Dachau camp doctor. This list was sent to the SS labor office; all registered prisoners had to be accounted for, after all, and prisoners held in the experimental stations were officially classified as employed (their job being tortured as a "guinea pig"). Then, the list of names went to the camp compound leader, who often made a few alterations. Finally, it landed on the desk of the commandant for his signature. Only then were the unfortunate prisoners dragged away to Schilling's malaria station.[236] Similar scenes took place in other KL, where the Camp SS assisted doctors as they abused and killed prisoners to aid their careers and help Germany win the war.

Killing for Victory

On August 14, 1942, Władislawa Karołewska, a young and slight teacher who had been part of the resistance in Nazi-occupied Poland, was ordered to report to the Ravensbrück infirmary, together with several other Polish prisoners. Here she was given an injection in her leg, which made her vomit. Then she was carted into the operating room, where she received another injection; pretty much the last thing she saw before she lost consciousness was an SS doctor wearing surgical gloves. When she awoke, her leg was throbbing: "I realized that my leg was in a cast, from the ankle to the knee." After three days, running a high fever and with fluid oozing from her swollen leg, Karołewska was set upon once more by the same doctor. "I felt great pain," she testified after the war, "and I had the impression that something was being cut out of my leg." After Karołewska lay for two weeks in a room filled with the stench of excretions, together with the other Polish women who had suffered a similar fate, her bandages were finally taken off and she saw her leg for the first time: "The cut was so deep that I could see the bone itself." After another week, the SS released her to her barrack, even though pus was still running from her leg and she could not walk. Soon she was back in the infirmary, where the SS doctor operated once more; her leg immediately swelled up again. "After this operation I felt even worse and I was unable to move."[237]

Władisława Karołewska's mutilation was as painful and traumatic as it was incomprehensible. She did not know that it was part of a coordinated series of experiments across several KL, testing drugs against so-called gas gangrene. Army and SS physicians had debated the usefulness of sulfonamide drugs for the treatment of wound infections since late 1941, as fatalities of German troops on the Eastern Front shot up. Following the death of Reinhard Heydrich in early June 1942 from gas gangrene—the explosion from a hand grenade thrown by one of his assassins had embedded parts of the car's upholstery in his body—the issue gained even greater urgency for Himmler, who believed in sulfonamide as a miracle cure.

In Ravensbrück, the experiments began on July 20, 1942, within weeks of Heydrich's death. SS clinician Professor Karl Gebhardt, who ran a sanatorium and SS hospital in nearby Hohenlychen, supervised the trials. To simulate the symptoms of gas gangrene, doctors made deep incisions into the legs of dozens of prisoners, mostly young Polish women like Karołewska, and inserted bacteria, earth, wood shavings, and glass fragments. Eventually, Professor Gebhardt determined that sulfonamide drugs had little effect on treating these infections. In fact, Gebhardt had wanted the drugs to fail all along. As the leading SS surgeon, he had a stake in defending the primacy of frontline surgery. More pressingly, he was fighting accusations that he had bungled Heydrich's treatment (dispatched by Himmler to attend to his wounded lieutenant in Prague, he had opted against the use of sulfonamides). To prove that he had been right all along, Gebhardt needed the drugs trial in Ravensbrück to come to nothing. Several women died after the ensuing operations, and the others bore the physical and mental scars for the rest of their often short lives.[238]

Like Dr. Rascher's murderous high altitude and freezing trials in Dachau, the mutilation of Ravensbrück prisoners was part of the war experiments, ostensibly designed to help save German troops from fatal injuries. In several other KL, too, prisoners were deliberately wounded and killed for this pur-

pose. In Natzweiler, for instance, a Professor Otto Bickenbach supervised lethal trials with phosgene, a toxic gas used during chemical warfare in the
First World War. To study its effects, and to test a drug meant to protect
German troops, well over one hundred prisoners were forced into the small
Natzweiler gas chamber in 1943–44. Within minutes, one survivor recalled,
he felt such pain he could barely breathe: "It felt like someone was piercing
my lungs with needles." Many prisoners suffocated. Others died a long, lin-
gering death over the coming days, coughing up blood and the remains of
their lungs.[239]

Another series of war experiments aimed to safeguard German troops
from infectious diseases, such as hepatitis, tuberculosis, and, above all, typhus.[240] The German authorities regarded typhus, frequently contracted by
German soldiers in occupied eastern Europe, as a grave threat, not only to the
troops but also to the population back home. The most extensive efforts to
find a vaccine came in Buchenwald. Here, some twenty-four different trials
were carried out in a permanent research station under SS Hauptsturmführer
Dr. Erwin Ding (also known as Ding-Schuler), an inept young physician
from the Hygiene Institute of the Waffen SS. His deputy was the Buchenwald
SS doctor Waldemar Hoven, a dropout from a respectable family who had
drifted around the world—including a spell as an extra on the film sets of
Hollywood—before opting for medicine and joining the Camp SS, after less
than five years of studies (Hoven was so incompetent he asked prisoners to
write his thesis for him). The flawed setup of the Buchenwald experiments
rendered them largely futile, scientifically speaking. The most tangible result
was suffering. During one trial in 1943, which tested two drugs developed by
the firm Hoechst, twenty-one out of thirty-nine prisoners died; most survivors developed high fevers, swollen faces and eyes, delusions, and tremors. In
all, the doctors are said to have experimented on well over 1,500 subjects between 1942 and 1944; more than 200 prisoners did not survive the Buchenwald typhus research station.[241]

A final series of war experiments was designed to boost the performance
of German troops, rather than their protection. Physicians carried out several trials along these lines with Sachsenhausen prisoners. In November
1944, a navy doctor administered high doses of stimulants, including cocaine, in the search for drugs that would allow the deployment of submarine
crews for days on end. The Camp SS let him loose on one of the most exhausting labor details, where inmates walked in a circle for up to twenty-five miles
a day, shouldering heavy sand bags, to test the design of new footwear. The
twenty-year-old Günther Lehmann was among the prisoners selected for the
experiments. During the four-day trial with cocaine he slept no more than a

few hours, forever stumbling along the test track, with a rucksack weighing twenty-five pounds on his back. Lehmann survived his ordeal, unlike so many other victims of the Nazis' human experiments.[242]

Auschwitz and Nazi Racial Science

SS Hauptsturmführer Josef Mengele arrived in Auschwitz at the end of May 1943, aged thirty-two, after spending most of the previous two years on the Eastern Front, as an SS battalion medical officer. During his first year in the camp, he was the main SS doctor in the so-called Gypsy enclosure; later he took over the infirmary sector and became the senior SS physician in Birkenau. Just like the other Auschwitz doctors, Mengele performed a range of murderous duties. He supervised prisoner executions and gassings, and became known among the SS staff for his lethal approach to epidemics. Mengele was also a frequent presence during selections of Jews at the ramp, conspicuous by his elegant looks, high spirits, and theatrical manner, dividing prisoners like a conductor into separate groups. In summer 1944, the chief SS physician in Auschwitz, Eduard Wirths, praised the "prudence, perseverance, and energy" Mengele brought to the job. In addition, Wirths was struck by Mengele's zealous use of his spare time, "utilizing the scientific material at his disposal" to make a "valuable contribution in his work on anthropological science."[243] What Wirths pictured here as a sideline was Mengele's chief obsession: the torture of prisoners in the name of Nazi racial science, which formed part of a second area of KL research, different from the war experiments and clustered around Auschwitz in particular.

Dr. Mengele was a disciple of racial biology, putting his faith in science to purify the body of the nation by identifying and removing supposedly inferior races. Although his beliefs were very much in line with Nazi thinking, Mengele (like Dr. Rascher) was no early Nazi fanatic. He came from an affluent national-conservative family and only applied to join the NSDAP and SS in his midtwenties (in 1937 and 1938 respectively). His main calling was racial science. As an eager student, gaining not one but two doctorates, Mengele had specialized early in racial genetics and anthropology. The diligent young scientist was quickly taken under the wing of Professor Otmar Freiherr von Verschuer, one of the doyens of German racial hygiene, who later headed the Kaiser Wilhelm Institute for Anthropology, Human Heredity and Eugenics in Berlin. Mengele became one of his assistants and continued to work with him after joining the SS full-time.

Auschwitz during the Holocaust was a dream for a striving and amoral racial biologist like Mengele. He was free to test any hypothesis he wanted, however repugnant, and there was always a ready supply of "scientific material." Prisoners he claimed for his experiments received special status. Isolated from the others, they were at his personal disposal; their bodies, dead and alive, belonged to Mengele.[244] Among his victims were those with stunted growth and other unusual features, with Mengele and his assistants eagerly taking photographs, measurements, and X-rays. He was particularly excited in May 1944, when a family of traveling performers with diminutive stature arrived from Hungary. Mengele hoped to experiment on them for years and lost no time in getting started, submitting his victims to injections, bloodletting, eye drops, and bone marrow extraction. One of the artists, Elisabeth Ovici, later recalled that "we often felt sick and miserable and had to throw up." She escaped the worst, though, for Mengele had many prisoners with physical abnormalities murdered; after meticulous autopsies, their bones were dispatched to the skeleton collection of the Kaiser Wilhelm Institute. Specially prepared eyeballs were couriered to the same address, as Mengele supplied one of Verschuer's other assistants, Dr. Karin Magnussen, who was researching Gypsies with different-colored eyes.[245]

The specialty of Dr. Mengele was the torture of twins. Racial genetics in Germany and abroad had long focused on twins, piquing Mengele's interest early in his academic studies. After his posting to Auschwitz, he systematically scoured the camp for victims on whom he hoped to build his career. In all, he probably selected more than one thousand twins for experiments. Most of them were boys and girls between the ages of two and sixteen, among them some siblings who had passed themselves off as twins to escape the gas chambers. Mengele subjected them to a battery of tests. First came the obsessive collection of anthropological data, as Mengele, always a pedant, believed that enough facts would inevitably yield important insights; for each twin, a form with ninety-six different sections had to be completed. "Examined, measured, and weighed a hundred times," is how Eva Herskovits later described her ordeal at Mengele's hands. The SS took so many blood samples that some children died of anemia.

Then came the experiments. To change the twins' eye color, apparently, Mengele and his staff injected liquid into their eyes, causing swelling and burns. The SS also infected them with illnesses to test their reactions. In addition, Mengele carried out grotesque surgical experiments, often without anesthetic, to compare the children's susceptibility to pain. Once, two boys, no more than three or four years old, were stitched together like Siamese twins; they screamed night and day before they died. Death offered Mengele yet another opportunity for his research, and he often set lethal injections himself.[246]

Given the magnitude of Mengele's crimes, it is easy to see why he has become the most infamous of all Auschwitz perpetrators. But his notoriety has obscured the deeds of other doctors. Mengele was not a loner. He operated in an environment where medical murders of prisoners were normal. Dozens of physicians carried out racial experiments in Auschwitz, not just other Camp SS doctors like Dr. Wirths, but SS, army, and civilian researchers from outside, as well. As the concentration camp with the largest prisoner population, among them many Jews, Auschwitz proved even more attractive than Dachau for physicians searching for human "guinea pigs," and no other camp would claim more victims.

Among the physicians lured to the east were two rival doctors, Professor Carl Clauberg and Dr. Horst Schumann, who experimented with fast and cheap mass sterilizations. Keen to eliminate unwanted population groups in occupied eastern Europe, Himmler gave the go-ahead for trials in summer 1942. This triggered a macabre race between the two physicians to find the most effective method. In all, they butchered many hundreds of Auschwitz prisoners (overwhelmingly Jews), in the largest series of experiments in the camp.

The first doctor, Professor Clauberg, who discussed his plans for sterilizing Jewish women with Himmler and Glücks over lunch one day in July 1942, injected a chemical substance into the cervix to cause sterility by closing off the fallopian tubes. The procedure caused excruciating pain and numerous women died from complications; others were murdered so that Clauberg could examine their organs. One survivor, Chana Chopfenberg, later recalled that Clauberg had treated them all "like animals." During the injections, she had been blindfolded; she was also threatened with execution if she dared to scream. Unrepentant, Dr. Clauberg claimed after the war that his experiments had been scientifically valuable and saved many women from extermination (he died of a stroke in a German remand prison in 1957).

His rival Dr. Schumann was feverishly working nearby, using extremely high doses of radiation in a careless, hit-and-miss manner (he had no specialist training as a radiologist), followed by operations. The immediate results were deep burns of the sexual organs, serious infections, and many deaths. Unlike his competitor, Dr. Schumann mainly chose male prisoners for his experiments. One of the men, Chaim Balitzki, broke down in tears after the war when he testified about his ordeal. "Worst of all," he said, "I no longer have a future." Undeterred by the human cost, Schumann pressed ahead, but eventually had to admit that surgical procedures were more effective than his X-rays. Professor Clauberg claimed victory. In June 1943, he informed Himmler that his trials were close to completion. With the right equipment and support, he claimed, he would soon be able to sterilize up to one thousand women a day. He was not yet done with his experiments, though, carrying out further trials with chemical injections in Ravensbrück in 1944.[247]

Nazi doctors even selected Auschwitz prisoners for lethal procedures in other KL. The most notorious case involved the skeleton collection at the Reich University of Strasbourg, a hotbed of Nazi race science established in 1941. In February 1942, Himmler received a report from Professor August Hirt, the leading physician of the Ahnenerbe and recently appointed as professor of anatomy in Strasbourg. Hirt's report included a proposal for killing "Jewish-Bolshevik commissars" to fill gaps in existing "skull collections." Himmler agreed, and the plan soon expanded: by murdering selected prisoners in Auschwitz, an entire racial-anthropological skeleton collection would be created. Eventually, three Ahnenerbe officials visited Auschwitz in June 1943. They picked out prisoners from different countries, who were measured, photographed, and filmed. One of them was Menachem Taffel, aged forty-two, who had been born in Galicia and later worked as a milkman in Berlin, from where he had been deported to Auschwitz in March 1943 (his wife and fourteen-year-old daughter were gassed on arrival). In late July 1943, the SS deported Taffel, together with eighty-six other Jewish prisoners, to Natzweiler, where the SS drove them into the new gas chamber (except for one woman who was shot for resisting); Commandant Josef Kramer then personally inserted prussic acid and watched the prisoners die. The corpses were sent to the Anatomical Institute in Strasbourg, about forty miles away. As the Allies approached Alsace in autumn 1944, Hirt and his colleagues tried to cover their tracks. But they failed to destroy all the evidence and when the soldiers entered the basement of the Strasbourg institute, they found vats full of corpses, sawn-off legs, and torsos, which had been preserved for Hirt's skeleton collection.[248]

Scientific Executioners

After the war, the physicians behind the KL experiments were often depicted as solitary and mad scientists like Dr. Frankenstein, laboring secretly on macabre schemes.[249] The truth is less lurid and more disturbing. Most research was inspired by what passed for mainstream scientific thinking, and many perpetrators were respected members of the medical community. Men like Professor Grawitz and Professor Gebhardt belonged to the German medical elite (as well as to the new SS aristocracy).[250] So did Professor Clauberg, who was so well respected as a gynecologist that a senior WVHA officer brought his wife, who had suffered several miscarriages, all the way from Berlin to Auschwitz for an exclusive consultation.[251]

Even the men behind the most gruesome experiments were no rank outsiders. Granted, perhaps Dr. Sigmund Rascher was a psychopath, as several historians have contended. But his experiments were driven, at least initially, by Germany's perceived military needs; hence the eager cooperation of the air force, whose scientists had called for the air pressure, freezing, and seawater experiments in Dachau.[252] As for Dr. Josef Mengele, although his crimes seem to speak for themselves—an Auschwitz prisoner doctor later called him a sadistic "subhuman" who was "veritably insane"—his peers saw him in a different light. Unlike Rascher, Mengele was an academic highflier and he remained associated with his venerable teacher Professor Verschuer. Human organs harvested by Mengele were analyzed at Verschuer's institute, which was part of the Kaiser Wilhelm Society, the elite organization for scientific research in Germany (renamed the Max Planck Society in 1948) that did much to support Nazi racial policy. Mengele also supplied blood samples from "persons of the most diverse racial backgrounds," as Verschuer put it, for a project on protein funded by the highly respected German Research Association (DFG), which supported several other human experiments in the KL, such as Professor Schilling's malaria experiments in Dachau.[253]

Complicity extended far into the wider German scientific community. The experiments were an open secret, at least in some circles, even if it was considered poor form to talk about them. Senior medical officers in the German armed forces were especially well informed, thanks to papers at medical congresses. One such meeting in October 1942 brought together more than ninety leading air force doctors and hypothermia specialists in a plush Nuremberg hotel, where they were initiated into the Dachau freezing experiments. The presentation, led by Professor Ernst Holzlöhner from the University of Kiel, included remarks by Dr. Rascher that left no doubt that some prisoners had died during the experiments; not one physician in the audience raised concerns. Some perpetrators even published details about their work in scientific journals and books. While they remained quiet about the abuse of prisoners, one could read between the lines that the experiments must have taken place in the KL; it did not require forensic skills to figure out that trials on "test persons" in "Dachau" had involved prisoners.[254]

The German pharmaceutical industry was involved as well. As early as 1941, Dr. Hellmuth Vetter, a Bayer employee (IG Farben) who also served as a Camp SS doctor, was testing a range of sulfonamide drugs on Dachau prisoners. He was delighted to be able to "put our new products to the practical test," he wrote to his colleagues in the company headquarters, and he assured them that he enjoyed the food, accommodation, and company of the SS: "I feel like I am in paradise here." Vetter later moved on to other camps, administering potentially lethal drugs (developed by IG Farben) in Auschwitz and Mauthausen. Meanwhile, Buchenwald became a veritable "laboratory of the pharmaceutical industry," in the words of the historian Ernst Klee, as drug companies vied to test their products on prisoners infected by the SS with typhus.[255]

Looking at the enthusiastic participation of physicians in medical torture and murder, it is worth recalling that German doctors were among the most fervent supporters of National Socialism, which promised them a national renewal and a brighter professional future. During the Third Reich, half of all male physicians joined the Nazi Party and seven percent the SS. Nazi biopolitics not only increased the standing of doctors; it also encouraged a shift in medical norms. Measures like mass sterilization made clear from early on that the health of the "national community" was everything and that "community aliens" had no rights.[256]

Once the KL experiments were under way, they created their own dynamic, further extending ethical boundaries. Take the case of Professor Gerhard Rose, the head of the department for tropical medicine at the famous Robert Koch Institute. In May 1943, Rose attended a conference during which Dr. Ding from Buchenwald gave a paper on typhus experiments. To everyone's surprise, Professor Rose openly challenged Ding, attacking his trials as a fundamental break with medical convention. Put on the back foot, Dr. Ding claimed (falsely) that he was only using criminals already sentenced to death. The flustered chairman quickly ended the discussion. But Professor Rose's principled stance did not last; as human experimentation became more commonplace, he wanted his own research to benefit, too. Just a few months after his attack on Ding, he contacted the Hygiene Institute of the Waffen SS and proposed a new typhus vaccine for tests in Buchenwald. Himmler agreed to a trial on so-called professional criminals and Dr. Ding was happy to help his erstwhile critic; the experiment took place in Buchenwald from March 1944, killing six prisoners.[257]

Forced to defend his experiments at the conference in 1943, Dr. Ding had rightly assumed that many of his colleagues would have few objections to killing selected enemies of the state, especially those who were already doomed. There can be no doubt that the use of KL inmates, whose lives counted for little anyway, helped to ease any misgivings about the experiments. The physicians also stressed the utilitarian nature of their trials. Since invalids were being gassed "in certain chambers" anyway, Sigmund Rascher rhetorically asked in summer 1942 (in a veiled reference to Action 14f13), would it not be better to test "our different chemical warfare agents" on them?[258] Similar arguments were heard elsewhere in the Third Reich. State prisoners were abused as "guinea pigs," too, and one doctor collected the blood of guillotined inmates for transfusions in his local hospital; otherwise, he reasoned at the time, the blood just "flows off without use."[259]

The allure of amoral science even captivated some prisoners. Dr. Miklós Nyiszli, an accomplished forensic pathologist, was deported with other Jews from Hungary to Auschwitz in May 1944. The SS spared his life because he was healthy and spoke fluent German, and thanks to his medical skills he soon became a prisoner doctor at the Birkenau crematoria complex. His superior was none other than Josef Mengele, with Nyiszli serving as his pathology expert; he assisted in murders, dissected twins, wrote up reports, and prepared corpses for skeleton collections. Although he knew all about the depravity of Nazi race science, and was appalled by it, Nyiszli's passion for science occasionally carried him away. Writing soon after the war, he referred to the "vast possibilities for research" in the camp, and recalled with excitement the "curious" and "extremely interesting" medical phenomena he had uncovered during autopsies, and which he had discussed at length, like any medical colleague would, with Dr. Mengele.[260]

As for the victims, a few were saved by the experiments, paradoxically. They were butchered, but escaped certain death at the hands of the SS. The two young Czech brothers Zdeněk and Jiří Steiner, for example, survived Auschwitz only because Dr. Mengele had claimed them for his experiments. Once, he apparently struck their names from a list of prisoners selected for the gas chamber. "Luckily, Mengele heard about it and saved us," the brothers testified in 1945, "because he still needed us."[261]

Many more victims, however, were butchered *and* killed. Overall, the SS targeted more men than women, not only because they were more numerous in the KL, but because the war experiments were meant to benefit German soldiers. Most victims stood near the bottom of the Nazi racial scale, with Poles making up the largest national group of victims. At times, the SS could not agree whom to target. When it came to forcing prisoners to drink seawater, different officials proposed different "guinea pigs." Richard Glücks from the WVHA wanted to use Jews; Arthur Nebe from the RSHA suggested "asocial half-Gypsies"; both were opposed by SS Reich physician Ernst Robert Grawitz, who argued that the victims had to "racially resemble the European population." In the end, no inmate groups were safe. After all, Himmler himself had announced in 1942 that one reason for selecting KL prisoners for potentially lethal trials was that they were "deserving of death"—a label that could be applied to pretty much any inmate, as far as the SS was concerned.[262]

Not even children were exempt, and from 1943 more and more were targeted. They stood at the center of Mengele's twin experiments in Auschwitz, as we have seen, and they were also dispatched from there to other concentration camps. In November 1944, for example, the SS sent a group of twenty Jewish children for tuberculosis trials to Neuengamme, where they would meet a terrible fate. Among them was the twelve-year-old Georges Kohn. He had been deported from Drancy in August 1944 together with his father, the director of the Paris Hôpital Baron de Rothschild (the largest Jewish hospital in France), and five other members of his family. By the time the train pulled into Auschwitz, Georges was all alone, except for his eighty-year-old grandmother: an older brother and sister had escaped from the train, his mother and another sister were in Bergen-Belsen, and his father, Armand, was in Buchenwald. His father would be the only one to survive the KL; he returned to Paris after the war, a sick man, and never learned what had happened to his youngest son.[263]

Armand Kohn had been among a vast number of Jewish prisoners deported to Buchenwald and other KL inside the old German borders during the later stages of the war. Their arrival marked a major shift in policy. By 1944, the regime's desire for forced labor had become so all-consuming that it trumped some hallowed principles of Nazi racial thinking. After years of feverish ethnic cleansing had made much of the Reich and its concentration camps "free of Jews," as Himmler had demanded, the regime reversed this course in a bid to build up its slave labor force.[264] The mass influx of Jewish prisoners far into Nazi Germany was part of a wider transformation of the KL system, which saw the emergence of hundreds of new camps and the arrival of hundreds of thousands of new prisoners. The concentration camps were entering a new phase, which probably began sometime around autumn 1943, when an eerie new camp was set up in the Harz Mountains. Its name was Dora.

9

Camps Unbound

Dust was swirling in the long and narrow tunnel, deep inside the Kohnstein mountain. Through the haze, illuminated by five dim lights, one could make out rows and rows of wooden bunks, four tiers high, crammed together on the slimy ground that was filled with pools of water seeping from the walls. Slumped on the low bunks lay gaunt figures in torn uniforms, some covered with thin blankets, others with empty cement bags; the mattresses were full of lice and filth, as were the masses of prisoners. It was the same scene in three adjacent underground chambers, all of them some 250 to 300 feet long and 40 feet wide. Together, these four tunnels were the sleeping quarters for around ten thousand KL prisoners who toiled in the Dora satellite camp in late 1943.

Dora assaulted all the senses. The air in the sleeping tunnels was unbearable, a mix of sweat, urine, excrement, vomit, and rotting corpses. During five months inside the Dora tunnels, the Polish inmate Wincenty Hein recalled, he only had three brief showers; some prisoners urinated on their hands to wash the dirt from their faces. There were no toilets anyway, just open petrol drums that added to the stench. Prisoners gasped for breath, and they were also tormented by hunger and thirst, forbidden to touch the underground water pipes. Sleep was almost impossible inside the chambers, not least because of the deafening noise of machines, pickaxes, and explosions coming from other tunnels nearby, which reverberated through the prisoner quarters. Dora never fell silent, as inmates worked in two shifts around the clock, digging, moving machinery, and laying tracks through the maze of tunnels. Roll calls on the outside had long been abandoned and prisoners lost all sense of night and day. "I felt like I was buried alive," the Dutch prisoner Albert van Dijk later wrote.

The Dora prisoners ate, slept, and worked underground. Before long, they were barely recognizable. When he arrived in early 1944, the Dutch prisoner Hendrikus Iwes was shocked by the sight of men who "were no[t] real persons anymore." Conditions improved somewhat during the following months, as inmates were gradually transferred to a new barrack camp above ground and a growing number of them were used in skilled production jobs. But this came too late for many: by the end of March 1944, more than one in three Dora prisoners were already dead. Most died from illness and exhaustion, though there was also an unusually large number of suicides.[1]

Dora had been established hastily in August 1943, following a British bombing raid on the village of Peenemünde on a small island on the Baltic coast. The central German military testing facility for missiles, Peenemünde was the site of the production plant and development works of the A-4 rocket, later known as the V2, masterminded by the young engineer Dr. Wernher von Braun (recruited by the United States after the war, the former SS officer became the father of NASA's space program). The attack on Peenemünde caused great concern among Nazi leaders, who had invested much hope in their "miracle weapons"; Heinrich Himmler had visited the facilities, where some six hundred KL prisoners toiled, only a few weeks earlier. Just days after the air raid, Hitler, Himmler, and Speer agreed to relocate V2 production to an underground location, with the help of concentration camp labor; this, Himmler promised, would guarantee the program's secrecy. In the end, the new plant became a joint venture between the SS, the army, and Speer's Ministry for Armaments. Himmler carved out a major part for his SS, including the construction of the new underground facility.

The location of the plant was quickly settled: an existing tunnel system in the Harz Mountains near the city of Nordhausen (Thuringia) in central Germany. Under construction since 1936 as an army fuel depot, it offered over one million square feet of manufacturing space in two parallel tunnels, almost a mile long, which were connected by forty-six side tunnels resembling a giant, curving ladder. Using KL labor, this huge tunnel system would now be extended and made operational for rocket production. Dora, a new satellite camp of Buchenwald, was set up on site, and the first prisoners arrived on August 28, 1943, just ten days after the Peenemünde attack. Seven weeks later, Heinrich Himmler appeared for an inspection.[2]

More subterranean concentration camps followed. Nazi leaders saw the underground relocation of arms production as a surefire way to protect key resources from Allied bombing, and the KL system was meant to play an important part: in mid-December 1943, Heinrich Himmler pictured his troops as "new cavemen" who would establish the "only truly protected production sites."[3] By then, several new sites had emerged already. In addition to Dora, more than five hundred prisoners were held in the Mauthausen satellite camp Ebensee (code-named Kalk, later Zement). The prisoners slept inside a former factory building, before moving to a barrack camp, and had to dig two huge underground tunnels for the Peenemünde rocket development works. Another new Mauthausen satellite was set up in Redl-Zipf, some fifteen miles from Ebensee. By the end of 1943, some 1,900 prisoners worked near the camp (code-named Schlier), extending the cellars of a local brewery for an oxygen factory and digging tunnels to connect it to test ranges for V2 engines (produced in Dora) on a mountain behind; in December alone, ninety-three of the prisoners lost their lives here.[4] The German navy also used KL labor for building shelters. In Farge, a new satellite of Neuengamme outside Bremen, prisoners were helping to erect a massive bombproof bunker (code-named Valentin) that would hold a high-tech factory for submarine assembly. By the end of 1943, some five hundred KL prisoners worked on site, sleeping in an empty fuel tank.[5] Pioneering projects like these paved the way for prisoner mass deployment in gigantic and often pointless underground relocation schemes.

Inmate numbers reached staggering heights in 1944, as did inmate deaths. The KL population more than doubled, shooting up from an estimated 315,000 prisoners (December 31, 1943) to 524,286 (August 1, 1944) and then 706,650 (January 1, 1945).[6] Hundreds of thousands were now working for the German war effort. Most inmates were sent to new satellite camps that sprang up at an incredible rate near factories and building sites. Prisoners were constantly on the move, or so it seemed, taken from one site to the next. Everything was in flux, reflecting the camps' breakneck economic mobilization. Recent calls to improve conditions often went unheeded as SS officials focused their energies on the exploitation of slave laborers at any price. It was imperative, Oswald Pohl lectured the Monowitz SS in September 1944, "to report lazy prisoners for punishment."[7]

The wider changes in the KL system in 1944 were exemplified by Dora, the first relocation camp for war production.[8] Not content with the rocket program inside the Kohnstein tunnels, the planners in the Ministry for Armaments, supported by industry, handed many more projects in the region to the SS, which was soon building new tunnels for airplane and motor manufacturing. Losing touch with reality, these plans became ever more outlandish, turning Dora into a big KL complex in its own right. Prisoner numbers reached over thirty-two thousand in late October 1944, and they were still rising. Most inmates worked in the surrounding satellite camps, which eventually numbered around forty, with names like Hans, Anna, and Erich betraying the SS penchant for camouflage; almost all SS Building Brigades were stationed nearby at the time, supporting the gigantic relocation effort. WVHA leaders officially recognized the importance of Dora in autumn 1944. Previously a satellite camp, it was now awarded the status of main camp. Called Mittelbau, it would be the last main concentration camp founded in the Third Reich.[9]

IN EXTREMIS

Sometime in late May 1944, Ágnes Rózsa was deported to Auschwitz, together with her parents, from her hometown of Nagyvárad. The city had been part of Romania between the wars, as it is again today (Oradea), but in 1940 it was annexed by Hungary with the rest of north Transylvania. This is why Ágnes Rózsa, a thirty-three-year-old high school teacher, was sucked into the maelstrom of the Nazi deportations of Hungarian Jews, which began soon after the German invasion in March 1944. Rózsa arrived in Auschwitz on June 1, 1944, during a period when the Birkenau killing apparatus reached its murderous peak. At the same time, the SS pressed more prisoners than ever into the war economy and Ágnes Rózsa was among those spared for forced labor. After several months in Birkenau, she was deported to a small satellite camp of the Siemens-Schuckert works in Nuremberg.[10]

Rózsa belonged to the vast number of Jewish slave laborers who poured into camps deep inside the old German borders during 1944, following the regime's U-turn on the deployment of Jews. For the first time since late 1938, Jewish inmates became a major presence across the KL system as a whole, as several older camp complexes, which had held virtually no Jews since 1942, quickly filled up. The prisoners from occupied Poland brought with them news of the Nazi Final Solution. In camps like Dachau, some veteran inmates already had a general idea of what was happening in the east, after the earlier arrival of clothes, shoes, suitcases, and other belongings of murdered Jews from Auschwitz and Majdanek.[11] But only now did they learn more details about the deportations, the selections, and the crematoria. The truth came out quickly, sometimes at the moment Jewish newcomers were taken to the showers and screamed, "Not gas! Not gas!"[12]

Going Underground

What started in autumn 1943 as a project to move the secret German missile program underground quickly extended to the air industry as a whole, which would eventually occupy more than one-third of all working KL prisoners.[13] When German airplane factories were hit in late February 1944, during a major Allied bombing campaign (the "Big Week"), the Air Ministry was planning dozens of underground projects. Some were already under way, in fact, and many more would soon follow. On March 1, 1944, the so-called Fighter Staff (*Jägerstab*) was formed, one of several powerful new Nazi agencies aimed at overcoming critical setbacks to war production, which added even more layers to the polycratic Nazi dictatorship in its twilight years. The remit of the Fighter Staff was to protect and increase the production of planes for defending German airspace, which was beginning to be penetrated almost at will by Allied bombers, and there was widespread agreement from the start that the best solution was to move the facilities underground. In a conference on March 5, 1944, Hitler himself announced that this was just the beginning of relocating "all German industrial plants under the earth." The scramble for underground construction had well and truly begun.[14]

The KL played an important role in these plans. The Fighter Staff brought together senior officials from the Armaments Ministry, Air Ministry, and private companies. But the SS also sat at the table, greatly raising its profile, as the aviation sector had become the biggest part of the German arms industry by 1944. The main reason for the SS involvement was its mass of slave laborers and its promise of providing even more. Labor shortages were biting harder than ever. Brutal efforts by Fritz Sauckel to capture millions more foreign laborers had failed, as the German stranglehold over much of continental Europe was broken, leaving the SS as one of the last sources of available labor.[15]

The SS was put in charge of special construction orders within the Fighter Staff, having impressed Albert Speer and others with its apparent success in Dora. Soon, the SS oversaw a range of high-profile relocation projects for the air industry, working together with private contractors. Satellite camps were set up near these new sites, and by June 1944 around seventeen thousand prisoners were toiling there, with many more on the way. Some schemes aimed at the speedy conversion of existing tunnels and caves. But the aircraft industry soon realized that this was a dead end, since corrosion and cramped spaces undermined efficient production. Instead, hopes turned to more complex projects: vast purpose-built tunnels, also dug by the SS. The closer the Third Reich came to defeat, the more monstrous these plans became, in terms of their size and speed of construction, and their human cost.[16]

Among the largest schemes was a network of tunnels near the town of Melk in Lower Austria; this was to house a factory (code-named Quarz) of the Steyr-Daimler-Puch AG, which had lobbied hard for the project and was heavily involved in its implementation. To provide the necessary labor, a satellite camp of Mauthausen was set up in Melk in April 1944, holding some seven thousand prisoners by mid-September. Conditions were infernal; there were constant accidents and most of the tunneling and cementing had to be done by hand. In all, almost one in three prisoners deported to the camp lost their lives there—more than the entire civilian population of the adjacent town of Melk.[17]

The manager of the gigantic SS-run underground program was Dr. Hans Kammler, the leading technocrat of terror in the WVHA. The trained architect had joined Pohl's sprawling organization full-time in 1941 to oversee SS construction (from 1942 as chief of Office Group C), having proven himself, during his time as a civil servant in the Nazi Air Ministry, as a capable manager of large building projects. He impressed his new SS superiors with his technical expertise, drive, and ideological commitment (he had joined the Nazi Party in 1931, and the SS two years later), and quickly became a key figure in several major projects, from the vast settlement plans to the killing machinery in Auschwitz. In 1943, his career really took off, propelling him toward the top of the German war industry. The first major step was his commission by Himmler and Speer, in late August 1943, to turn Dora into an underground missile factory. This was followed in March 1944 by an even more prestigious post: managing all SS relocation projects for the Fighter Staff, as the head of a new "Special Staff Kammler." He pressed ahead regardless of prisoner lives; what counted was the rapid completion of building tasks, not how many died in the process. After all, there still seemed to be enough new prisoners ready to be "pumped" into his projects, as Kammler put it.

Kammler quickly gained a formidable reputation. A restless workaholic in his early forties, this gaunt man, with his thin and haggard face, cut an intimidating figure. He spoke resolutely and rapidly, making clear to everyone that he knew what he wanted and how to get it. Heinrich Himmler was an early admirer and frequently met with him, and Hitler placed equally great faith in Kammler. Albert Speer paid his respects, too. Soon after he had inspected the Dora tunnels on December 10, 1943, Speer commended Kammler for the "near-impossible" speed with which he had built the underground factory, "which has no equal anywhere in Europe."

Dr. Kammler became the man for the most difficult SS missions. Heinrich Himmler expected results, whatever the obstacles, and the loyal Kammler promised to deliver. However, ruthlessness did not equal effectiveness, and several of his high-profile projects failed to live up to his hubris. And yet, there was no stopping his rise. After the Fighter Staff folded in summer 1944 into the Armaments Staff (*Rüstungsstab*), Kammler's remit for underground relocation expanded from airplanes to other arms programs. His attention also turned back to rocket production, which gained added urgency after the Allied landings in Normandy in June 1944. More and more missiles were rolling out of Dora, and it was Kammler who traveled to supervise their deployment, with the rank of army general; the first V2s fell on England in September 1944 and the rockets later hit France, Belgium, and Holland. Over the coming months, Kammler accumulated yet more projects—including the construction of an enormous underground headquarters for Hitler in Ohrdruf, a top-priority project where more than ten thousand KL prisoners worked by late 1944—and by spring 1945 he controlled almost the entire arms production for the air force. Kammler was even talked about as a successor to Speer as armaments minister. At this late stage, of course, with the Third Reich already in ruins, there was no more armaments output to speak of, as Speer pointedly noted in his memoirs.[18]

Powerful as Hans Kammler was, he had no monopoly over underground construction for the German air industry. While his SS office oversaw most of the major Fighter Staff relocation projects, the rival Organization Todt (OT) established itself as another key player. This Nazi construction agency, set up along military lines in 1938, had grown rapidly during the war. Relying largely on foreign labor, the OT ran a huge number of building projects all across Nazi-occupied Europe—including bridges, roads, and defensive installations—and it expanded into German domestic construction, as well. This led to tensions with the SS, after Hitler commissioned the OT in April 1944 to build gigantic concrete bunkers for fighter aircraft factories. Even though this urgent project was supervised by the OT, the SS had to supply much of the labor force. Starting in June 1944, a total of fifteen Dachau satellite camps were established around Kaufering and Mühldorf am Inn, where several tens of thousands of prisoners built four huge bunker complexes. The OT, which subcontracted the work to private firms, was now the largest slave driver of the Dachau prisoners.[19]

This was not the only major OT project using concentration camp labor. In April 1944, the OT took over the construction of a big network of bunkers for Hitler and the top echelons of the regime (code-named Riese, or "giant"). Turning a large wooded area of Lower Silesia into a building site, KL prisoners and other forced laborers had to erect huge underground structures and infrastructure. In all, thirteen thousand Jewish men were held in some twelve new satellite camps of Gross-Rosen, known collectively as "Work Camp Riese"; around five thousand of them lost their lives.[20]

Elsewhere, KL prisoners were exploited during desperate Nazi efforts to protect the fuel supply. Following major Allied bombing raids on German hydrogenation plants in May 1944, Hitler invested Edmund Geilenberg, a top official in Speer's Armaments Ministry, with special powers to keep tanks rolling and planes flying. The main aims of the new Geilenberg Staff were the repair of damaged hydrogenation plants, the construction of new plants, and the underground relocation of production. Many of the construction projects were once again run by the OT, but the SS was involved, too, managing some sites and supplying slave labor to others. By late November 1944, an estimated three hundred and fifty thousand workers toiled on the Geilenberg sites, including tens of thousands of KL prisoners, dispersed across several satellite camps. Some of these camps had originally been erected for other purposes; in Ebensee a huge fuel refinery was set up in the tunnels originally intended for the V2 development works. Other sites were hastily set up from scratch. In Württemberg, for example, the SS created three new Natzweiler satellites to push ahead with project "Desert" (*Wüste*), extracting local shale oil for fuel production. Together with inmates from associated satellite camps, over ten thousand KL prisoners were forced into project "Desert," mostly working in construction; thousands died.[21]

The relocation of the German war industry transformed concentration camp slave labor. It is impossible to say exactly how many prisoners were deployed in this way, but numbers were very substantial. At the end of 1944, according to an estimate by Pohl, around forty percent of all the working KL prisoners came under Kammler's authority, the vast majority of them in relocation camps; many more worked on similar projects managed by the OT.[22] In all, hundreds of thousands of KL inmates were forced into the new relocation camps, and while there were many differences between individual sites, all of them placed inmates in mortal danger. To keep alive their hopes of a miraculous German victory, Nazi leaders sacrificed entire armies of prisoners.

War and Slave Labor

Heinrich Himmler liked to sing the praises of KL labor. His boasts about its contribution to the war economy became set pieces in speeches to senior Nazi officials in 1944. Typically, Himmler pictured the concentration camps as brutally efficient modern arms factories, with long hours and strict discipline; after listening to one of his speeches, Joseph Goebbels summed up Himmler's approach as "pretty rigorous." But the Reichsführer SS stressed that there was no reason to pity prisoners: though it was hard to believe, he told an audience of army generals in June 1944, inmates in his camps were better off than "many workers in England or America." As for their output, the prisoners put in millions of hours each month, supposedly turning out a vast arsenal of high-tech armaments. Himmler was particularly proud of the underground factories, where "this race of subhumans produces the weapons for the war." The startling successes were due, Himmler concluded, to the technical brilliance of the SS and the productivity of the prisoners, who worked twice as hard as foreign workers.[23] None of these claims bore any resemblance to reality, though given Himmler's capacity for self-delusion it is possible that he believed his own hype.

Slave labor in the concentration camps was far less effective than Himmler claimed. Many prisoners were not employed at all, either because they were too sick or because there was no work; according to SS figures from spring 1944, more than one in four Auschwitz prisoners were either invalids or ill in infirmaries.[24] As for the majority of working prisoners, they were much weaker than regular laborers. Food rations for KL inmates (and other Nazi prisoners) were cut once more in 1944, by central order of the Reich Ministry for Food and Agriculture, condemning more inmates to exhaustion and death; some prisoners now received no more than around seven hundred calories per day.[25] WVHA efforts to improve matters remained largely cosmetic; empty words could not feed any prisoners.[26]

The overall productivity of KL prisoners fell far behind the expectations of the SS and industry.[27] True, some skilled and better-fed prisoners delivered outputs approaching those of other workers.[28] But this was impossible for the great mass of inmates. Compared with that of regular German workers, their productivity reached an estimated half in industrial production, and even less in construction, perhaps one-third.[29] And despite some exceptions, such as the Heinkel works in Oranienburg, concentration camp labor was not particularly cost-effective, either. Once all the overheads were deducted, it often came no cheaper than free German labor. But it was still useful: Why else would so many firms have pursued KL prisoners so energetically in 1944? The decisive factor here was not that prisoners came cheap, but that they were available, allowing state and private companies to take on additional arms and building projects.[30]

Although it had secured a more prominent place for the KL system in the German arms industry by 1944, the mass exploitation of its prisoners came at a cost to the SS. Internal rivalries broke out within the WVHA, as Hans Kammler pushed aside Gerhard Maurer (from Office Group D) as the main manager of slave labor; in a new camp like Dora, it was Kammler who had the final say.[31] Meanwhile, armaments minister Albert Speer extended his own reach over forced labor, culminating in a decree on October 9, 1944, that put him in charge of prisoner deployment. New requests for KL labor no longer went to the WVHA but to Speer's ministry, a significant loss of power and prestige for the SS.[32] Private industry chipped away at SS control, too, with managers traveling directly to concentration camps to select slaves. Above all, the managers wanted strong and skilled prisoners, ideally with some knowledge of German. "We were chosen like cattle on a market," the Ukrainian prisoner Galina Buschujewa-Sabrodskaja recalled after Heinkel employees descended on Ravensbrück in late 1943: "They even forced us to open our mouths, and inspected our teeth."[33] An ambitious attempt by the WVHA to steer prisoner deployment by creating a modern machine-readable database in 1944, using punch-hole cards and number codes (the so-called Hollerith technology), was soon abandoned and did nothing to help the WVHA regain the initiative.[34] The more the Camp SS became involved in the German war industry, the less control it had over its prisoners.

What is more, the contribution of the camps for the war economy remained marginal, despite Himmler's bombastic claims. In summer 1944, when German armaments production reached its highest output during the war, KL prisoners working in the arms industry made up no more than around one percent of the labor force in Germany. To be sure, the SS presence was more marked in relocation projects.[35] But most of these projects were strategically pointless even before they got under way; the move of war production underground was the last throw of the dice in a game that was already lost.[36] The SS was the perfect partner for such a doomed plan. Undeterred by previous failures, SS leaders like Oswald Pohl still harbored delusions about their economic prowess.[37]

Even the most high-profile projects launched with SS involvement made little difference to the progress of the war. Despite the investment of hundreds of millions of Reichsmark and the abuse of tens of thousands of slave laborers, the huge IG Farben complex under construction in Auschwitz was never completed and failed to produce any synthetic rubber or fuel.[38] Similarly, few projects of the Geilenberg Staff went past the initial stage. The first factories of project "Desert," provisionally operational from early spring 1945, turned out an oily sludge that was useless for the remaining German tanks.[39] And Dora never became the high-tech underground factory of Himmler's dreams, either. The number of the much vaunted V2s manufactured, around six thousand by spring 1945, remained well behind schedule. And although the rockets killed thousands of civilians abroad and proved a potent propaganda tool inside Germany, their strategic impact was negligible. The uniqueness of the weapon lay elsewhere, as the historian Michael J. Neufeld has pointed out: "More people died producing it than died from being hit by it."[40] This verdict sums up the SS involvement in the war economy as a whole. Its main output was not fuel or planes or guns, but the misery and death of its prisoners.[41]

Far more registered prisoners died in 1944 than during the previous year. The general conditions claimed countless victims, and the SS also extended its murderous selections (which had been cut back during the previous year), because the sick were seen as obstacles to effective war production and as threats to the health of other slave laborers. Many died inside satellite camps. Other victims returned to the main camps, after they had been worked to complete exhaustion, and perished in one of the fast-expanding sectors for the weak and ill.[42] Or they were deported to their deaths elsewhere. In Mauthausen, where those isolated in the infirmary sector sometimes outnumbered all other inmates in the main camp, the SS took a particularly radical step. It renewed its links to the Hartheim killing center, dating back to Action 14f13, and sent at least 3,228 *Muselmänner* to the gas chambers between April and December 1944.[43] More commonly, transports of doomed prisoners went to other parts of the KL system. Deportations to Auschwitz, for example, now included weakened Jewish prisoners selected in satellite camps inside the old German borders.[44]

In addition, two other main camps—Majdanek and Bergen-Belsen, both largely untouched by the economic mobilization for war—were designated for dying inmates from other KL. Majdanek had lost much of its purpose in November 1943, following the murder of its Jewish prisoners, and was used from December onward as a dumping ground for men and women from concentration camps inside the Third Reich. Some died en route, thousands more inside; in March 1944 alone, when around nine thousand prisoners were held in Majdanek, the SS registered more than 1,600 deaths.[45] Bergen-Belsen took over from spring 1944 onward, as Majdanek prepared for evacuation in advance of the Red Army. By January 1945, some 5,500 sick prisoners from other KL—judged "an unnecessary burden on the industrial firms" that employed them, in the words of Camp SS leaders—had been taken to Bergen-Belsen.[46] The first transport had arrived in late March or early April 1944 from Dora. The frail men, many of them with bandaged arms and legs, had been thrown into the cattle trucks "like sacks of coal," according to one Dora prisoner; the screams started before the train had even pulled away. After their arrival in Bergen-Belsen, the survivors were left for days inside empty barracks without food or blankets. "We wasted away very quickly," the French prisoner Josef Henri Mulin recalled later.[47]

The Prisoner Population

KL inmate numbers reached record heights in 1944, relentlessly pushed upward by Heinrich Himmler. He promised Kammler as many prisoners as he wanted and became obsessed with statistics charting the growth in inmate figures: Himmler's mantra, Rudolf Höss recalled, became "Armaments! Prisoners! Armaments!"[48] The camps just kept on growing, and even some of the smaller sites now expanded exponentially; the number of prisoners registered in Flossenbürg, for instance, grew more than eightfold, from 4,869 (December 31, 1943) to 40,437 (January 1, 1945).[49] The momentum behind the camps' expansion was only stopped by the Allied armies.

Secret SS statistics reveal two major trends. First, after the balance of the KL system had tilted eastward from 1942, it now swung back again. As the Red Army gained ground, more and more camps in occupied eastern Europe closed down in 1944. Auschwitz was gradually emptied, too, and consequently lost its status as the biggest site. By January 1, 1945, the largest KL complex of all was Buchenwald, in the heart of Germany; 97,633 prisoners were registered there, compared to 69,752 in Auschwitz. Second, the sharp rise in female prisoners, which had begun with the mass deportations of Jewish women during the Holocaust, continued. By the end of 1944, there were almost 200,000 female KL prisoners (up from 12,500 in late April 1942), making up twenty-eight percent of the total prisoner population. They were distributed across the whole KL system. Back in 1939, female prisoners had been confined to a single purpose-built camp, Ravensbrück; now they were registered in every camp complex, except for Dora.[50]

The vast rise in prisoner numbers cannot be reduced to Himmler's hunger for slave laborers alone. Just as in previous years, economic motives coincided with other matters of national interest, as defined by the Nazi regime. Police arrests broadly followed the pattern established in 1942–43. As defeat came closer, Nazi paranoia about the home front grew even more intense. There were further crackdowns on Germans suspected of criminal activity, defeatism, and subversion. In August 1944, shortly after the failed bomb plot on Hitler's life, more than five thousand left-wing activists from the Weimar period, as well as some one-time officials of Catholic parties, were dragged into the KL as part of Operation Thunderstorm; some, like the sixty-six-year-old former SPD Reichstag deputy Fritz Soldmann, had already been tormented in the KL several times before.[51] The police also focused on resistance activities by foreigners inside Germany and expanded its general assault on foreign workers: many tens of thousands were arrested in 1944 for "breach of contract" and often taken straight to concentration camps, in line with Himmler's orders.[52]

Outside the Third Reich, meanwhile, more people were rising up, and the German occupiers answered with extreme force; many resisters were murdered on the spot, and many more deported to concentration camps.[53] Among them were several tens of thousands of men and women arrested inside France.[54] Even more new KL prisoners arrived from occupied Poland, in the wake of the doomed Warsaw Uprising. The insurgency had been triggered on August 1, 1944, by the Polish Home Army, which hoped to drive the German occupiers out just before the seemingly imminent arrival of the Red Army. But the Soviet advance stalled, and the uprising was put down with extraordinary brutality by Nazi troops, who had long seen the city as the hotbed of Polish resistance. After nine terrible weeks, some one hundred and fifty thousand local civilians had been killed and much of Warsaw lay in ruins (among the dead were several hundred prisoners from the local KL, who had briefly tasted freedom during the uprising). As for the survivors, SS officials were determined to add them to their slave labor force; in mid-August, the SS dreamed of four hundred thousand extra prisoners for the concentration camps. In the end, an estimated sixty thousand men, women, and children were deported from the remains of Warsaw to the KL. Among them was a twenty-one-year-old seamstress (her name is unknown), who was forced out of her destroyed building in September 1944 with her husband and neighbors. After several days in packed cattle trucks, the men were dragged out near Sachsenhausen. "Families that were separated screamed and cried," she recalled. Then the train took the remaining women and children to Ravensbrück, where some twelve thousand prisoners from Warsaw arrived in all.[55]

Diverse as the KL population was, there was one prisoner group that grew faster than any other—Jews. In the course of 1944, the German authorities forced more Jewish men, women, and children to the KL than ever before. According to one estimate, almost two-thirds of all new arrivals between spring and autumn 1944 had to wear the yellow star. By the end of the year, more than two hundred thousand were registered as KL inmates; any Jews in German-controlled territory were now most likely held inside concentration camps.[56] Among them were many Polish Jews who had survived outside the KL system until now. Tens of thousands came from abandoned forced labor camps, including the so-called Schmelt camps in Upper Silesia.[57] Others arrived from the last ghettos. During the final liquidation of Lodz in August 1944, almost sixty-seven thousand Jews were deported to Auschwitz; around two-thirds were murdered on arrival.[58]

Auschwitz also continued to receive deportation trains from the rest of Nazi-occupied Europe, as the RSHA pursued Jews who had so far escaped its clutches. Among the largest transports in 1944 were those from France, Holland, Slovakia, Greece, and Italy. One of these trains, which arrived late on February 26 from a camp near Modena, brought Primo Levi to Auschwitz, together with 649 other Jews; 526 of them were gassed on arrival.[59] Further prisoners arrived from Theresienstadt. In May 1944, some 7,500 Jews, many of them old, orphaned, or ill, were deported to Auschwitz during a Nazi effort to put the ghetto into better light for the impending visit by the International Committee of the Red Cross; many thousands more, especially younger prisoners, followed in the autumn.[60]

By far the largest number of Jews deported to Auschwitz in 1944 came from Hungary. After Hungary had distanced itself from its German partner, seeking a separate peace with the Allies, Nazi forces invaded the country in March 1944. The German occupation was a catastrophe for Hungarian Jewry, which had so far been spared from the Holocaust. German troops were accompanied by Adolf Eichmann and his team. Drawing on their experience with round-ups, deportations, and extermination, Eichmann's men proceeded with great speed and efficiency. Mass transports began in mid-May 1944, and by July, when they were stopped after an intervention by the Hungarian regent Horthy, at least four hundred and thirty thousand Jews had been taken to Auschwitz.[61]

After SS units removed Horthy in mid-October 1944, the Nazis renewed their effort to deport the remaining Hungarian Jews. Trains were scarce now, as transport shortages started to bite, so tens of thousands of Jewish men, women, and children were forced on marches to the distant Austrian border. By the end of 1944, an estimated seventy-six thousand Jews had been driven toward Austria. Here, some survivors were forced to build fortifications, while others were taken to the KL. Among them was the teenager Eva Fejer, who eventually reached Ravensbrück. "At first," she later said, "we thought we were coming into a decent camp, not least because we had been made to believe that it would be good as long as one behaved properly." She soon learned the truth.[62]

Nazi leaders and industrialists saw the Hungarian Jews as an important addition to the workforce. Even before the mass deportations began, there were plans—pushed forward by Hitler and Himmler—to send one hundred thousand or more as slave laborers to the KL inside Germany. In particular, the prisoners were earmarked for Fighter Staff relocation projects. When Albert Speer asked in a meeting on May 26, 1944, when these prisoners would arrive, he was assured by Kammler that the transports were already "on their way." But before they reached the building sites inside the old German borders, these Hungarian Jews had to pass through Auschwitz. After all, the SS was only interested in slaves who could work; all those who were too young, old, or weak would be murdered.[63]

The Murder of Hungarian Jews

Auschwitz was never more lethal for Jews than in spring and summer 1944. Among the dead were many regular prisoners, including most inmates from the Theresienstadt family camp.[64] The overwhelming majority of victims, however, had only just arrived. Huge numbers poured into Auschwitz—between May and July 1944, more Jews were deported to the camp than during the entire preceding two years—and nearly all came from Hungary. Their murder marked the climax of the Holocaust in Auschwitz, at a time when most European Jews under German control had long since been killed.[65]

The man who oversaw the extermination of Hungarian Jews was a familiar figure in Auschwitz: Rudolf Höss, the old commandant. Around late April or early May 1944, shortly before the mass deportations started, Höss traveled to Hungary to meet his friend Eichmann at his temporary residence in Budapest (Eichmann, in turn, visited Auschwitz several times in spring 1944). The two men brooded over the deportation schedules to determine how many trains "could be dealt with" in Auschwitz, as Höss put it. In addition, Höss wanted to inform his WVHA superiors how many slave laborers they could expect, once those deemed unfit had been gassed. Höss conducted trial selections in Hungary, and concluded that most Jews had to die; at best, he estimated, twenty-five percent would be selected for labor.[66]

Next, Höss traveled to Auschwitz, returning to the scene of his earlier crimes, and on May 8, 1944, took over temporarily as senior commandant of the Auschwitz camp complex.[67] In view of the scale of the impending genocide, WVHA leaders had dispatched their most experienced manager of mass murder.[68] In their eyes, the reappointment of Höss was all the more pressing because the position of the current senior commandant, Arthur Liebehenschel, had become untenable. Apparently, the reserved Liebehenschel had gained a reputation as a soft touch, though the immediate reason for his removal was a private drama.[69] Back when Liebehenschel had worked in the WVHA, he had fallen for Richard Glücks's secretary, who eventually joined him in Auschwitz after his divorce. But after Liebehenschel sought permission to remarry, his superiors learned a dark secret: early in the Third Reich, his fiancée had been arrested for a relationship with a Jew. Oswald Pohl was horrified. He dispatched his bullish adjutant Richard Baer to tell Liebehenschel to terminate the relationship. After Baer broke the news in the Auschwitz officer mess late on April 19, 1944, Liebehenschel sobbed and got drunk. Then he confronted his pregnant fiancée, who protested her innocence. Two days later, the love-stricken Liebehenschel, his eyes swollen from crying, told Baer that he stood by his lover, adding that the Gestapo must have forced her into a false confession all those years ago. There was no way back now for Liebehenschel, who had broken the SS racial code (by consorting with a suspected "race defiler"), its unspoken rules (by accusing the Gestapo of torture), and its social norms (by acting "anything but manly," as Baer called it). Pohl swiftly removed Liebehenschel and after a brief stint as caretaker of the depleted Majdanek camp, he left the Camp SS embittered and sick.[70]

His fall eased the return of Höss to Auschwitz in late spring 1944. Here was a man SS leaders could trust with the largest extermination program the KL system had ever seen. Höss surrounded himself with a handful of close associates and killing experts, whom he had known for years. Among them was the Camp SS veteran Josef Kramer, who had served as Höss's first adjutant in Auschwitz in 1940, and now returned from Natzweiler to become commandant of Birkenau. Another familiar face was Otto Moll, who had gained plenty of experience at the Birkenau gas chambers in 1942–43, and was called back from a satellite camp to oversee the crematoria complex once more.[71] After Höss and his men had completed some last-minute preparations, the mass deportations from Hungary began. Between mid-May 1944 and mid-July 1944, trains came on an almost daily basis and Auschwitz was soon overwhelmed; on some days, as many as five transports arrived, carrying around sixteen thousand Jews (between January and April 1944, during the Liebehenschel era, a daily average of around two hundred Jews had arrived in Auschwitz). While Adolf Eichmann marveled at the "record performance" of his men, Höss implored his friend to slow things down. But even a dressing down from Oswald Pohl made no difference, with Eichmann pushing for even more transports, citing "force majeure during wartime" (as he told his sympathizers after the war).[72]

As they emerged from the trains, the Hungarian Jews had little idea what awaited them; few had heard of Auschwitz and fewer still of the gas chambers. The Camp SS, meanwhile, swung into action. SS doctors subjected all these new arrivals to selections, in contrast to some other Jewish deportation transports in 1944. In general, the SS applied the same criteria used previously; those classified as unfit for labor included pregnant women, older prisoners, young children, and their accompanying parents. At the end of each day, the Auschwitz SS sent statistics about the selections to the WVHA, to update the managers about newly available slave laborers. Overall, the local SS officers stuck to Höss's forecast and picked out around one in four Jews from Hungary for slave labor. The fate of these approximately one hundred and ten thousand prisoners differed: some were formally registered in Auschwitz, some were sent to other KL, some perished in Birkenau transit compounds. The remaining three hundred and twenty thousand or so Hungarian Jews, declared unfit, were killed straightaway, during a murderous frenzy that lasted until the mass deportations stopped in July 1944.[73]

Rudolf Höss threw himself into mass murder with customary zeal, knowing that he would return to the WVHA once he had completed his mission (he was succeeded as senior commandant of the Auschwitz camp complex on July 29, 1944, by the ruthless Richard Baer, who liked to show off his experience as a frontline SS warrior by wearing his old Death's Head division uniform).[74] During his time in charge, Höss did his best to accelerate the extermination process. Trains from Hungary no longer stopped outside the camp but followed a single track to a hastily completed ramp right inside Birkenau; as they lined up here on arrival, the deported Jews could hear the incongruous tunes of one of the camp orchestras, brought in to lull them into a false sense of security. After the SS selection, the great majority of the newcomers walked directly toward their deaths, carrying small children and supporting the weak as they filed past several Birkenau compounds on the way to the gas chambers. Left at the ramp, after the trains pulled away to collect yet more victims, were all the suitcases, bags, and bundles, gathered up by the greatly expanded Canada Commando.[75]

The Birkenau crematoria burned longer than ever, stoked by the Special Squad, now some nine hundred prisoners strong and working around the clock. The SS also put bunker 2 back into use for gassings and reactivated crematorium V (out of commission since autumn 1943). But because the SS still murdered more Jews than it could burn in the crematoria, it decided to use open-air pits for cremation, as well, just as in 1942. To hide these crimes from new arrivals, Oswald Pohl gave the go-ahead—after an inspection of the camp on June 16, 1944, at the height of the murder—to erect a fence around the crematoria areas.[76] SS men stationed inside the killing complex lost their last inhibitions. They murdered in such a rush that some victims were still breathing when the doors of the gas chambers were unlocked. Sometimes the killers bypassed the gas chambers altogether, shooting Hungarian Jews at the burning pits, beating them to death, or throwing them into the flames alive. This inferno was overseen by Otto Moll, who made Dr. Mengele look human, according to one survivor.[77]

Because of the sheer number of incoming deportation trains in summer 1944, the SS was sometimes unable to carry out its selections at the Birkenau ramp. In such cases, new arrivals were taken to transit compounds, where their ultimate fate would be decided later. The largest of these compounds was a huge, unfinished extension of Birkenau known as "Mexico" (BIII), which held an estimated seventeen thousand Jewish women from Hungary and elsewhere by early autumn 1944. Living conditions were worse than almost anywhere else in the camp. There was no running water and barely any food. Huge vats served as toilets, and instead of clothes, many prisoners wore blankets draped around their shoulders (this apparently reminded some of ponchos, hence the name "Mexico"). Barracks, each holding around one thousand women, were unfurnished, with prisoners lying on the muddy ground; Ágnes Rózsa, the teacher from Nagyvárad we encountered earlier, shared a small urine-soaked sheet with four other women. Some prisoners, like Rózsa, were eventually deported elsewhere for forced labor. But many others wasted away or were led to the gas chambers. This was the perpetrators' preferred solution to the human catastrophe they had created. A former Camp SS man later testified that his colleagues had often talked about murdering the prisoners left in "Mexico." The catchphrase was: "Let them go through the chimney."[78]

The Gypsy Camp

During the Holocaust, Auschwitz turned first and foremost into a KL for Jews, who replaced Poles as the largest inmate group. Numbers shot up further in the wake of the Hungarian deportations; according to one estimate, around seventy-five percent of all the men, women, and children held in Auschwitz in late August 1944 were Jews.[79] In popular memory, the move of the camp to the epicenter of the Holocaust has sometimes overshadowed the fate of other prisoner groups. This is particularly true for Gypsies, the third-largest group in Auschwitz, whose treatment in some ways mirrored that of Jews.[80]

The so-called Gypsy camp in Auschwitz-Birkenau had grown rapidly from late February 1943, as the mass deportations from the German Reich arrived.[81] Within weeks, over ten thousand prisoners were held here, and numbers were still rising. There were thousands of children, making up half of all children registered in Auschwitz. The oldest prisoner, meanwhile, was said to be 110 years old. The Gypsies were held in sector BIIe, at the far end of Birkenau, just below the infirmary sector and close to the crematoria. Like most other sectors in Birkenau, the Gypsy camp was almost two thousand feet long and four hundred feet wide, and contained two rows with barracks on either side of a muddy path. Inside the converted horse stables, it was dark (there were no windows except for small skylights), dirty (most floors consisted of clay), and overcrowded (with whole families crammed onto a single bunk). There was no separation by sex, one of several differences from other Birkenau sectors. Also, the prisoners' hair was not fully shaved and they often kept their clothes, too, marked with a red cross on the back.

When the deportations to Auschwitz started in spring 1943, the Gypsies' fate had not been decided. Even so, the conditions in Birkenau condemned the vast majority to death. In addition to the usual SS tortures such as "sport," many prisoners—labeled "work-shy"—had to perform extremely heavy labor. Boys and girls as young as seven carried heavy bricks. As for sanitation, things were even worse in the Gypsy camp than elsewhere in Birkenau. In the early months, with the compound still under construction, there were no toilets or washrooms. "We washed when it rained," the German Sinto Walter Winter recalled, "making do in the puddles . . . Adults and children had to relieve themselves outside, to the rear of the blocks." Conditions barely improved after the SS added rudimentary facilities; the overflowing latrines were rarely emptied, and water was scarce and contaminated.

Soon, disease ravaged the Gypsy camp. More and more space was set aside for sick and dying prisoners, and by autumn 1943 the infirmary inside the compound had grown from two to six barracks. Perhaps the most terrifying sight was that of boys and girls suffering from Noma, an oral infection, caused by extreme deprivation, which cut deep holes into their cheeks. Hardly any medical treatment was available. Instead, the Camp SS relied on death. When a typhus epidemic spread through the Gypsy camp, with up to thirty prisoners perishing each day, the SS placed it under quarantine and led many of the sick to the gas chambers. Some survivors tried to alert the outside world to their suffering; in a coded message, one of them referred to Baro Nasslepin, Elenta, and Marepin—the Romany words for "great illness," "misery," and "murder."

Entire families died together in the Gypsy camp. Elisabeth Guttenberger, who had been deported from Germany in spring 1943, later testified that she lost around thirty relatives. "The children were the first to die," she said. "Day and night they cried for bread; soon they had all starved." The morgue in the infirmary was piled high with corpses of children, covered with rats. Many of the dead babies had been born inside the Gypsy camp. In all, some 370 children were delivered here, with prisoner numbers tattooed on their tiny thighs; more than half were dead within three months. Most parents soon followed their children. Elisabeth Guttenberger's father starved to death early on, together with her four siblings, and her mother soon lost her life, too. Survival seemed almost impossible; by the end of 1943, around seventy percent of prisoners who had been locked into the Gypsy camp were dead.[82]

The final liquidation of the Gypsy camp came in 1944, as mass murder in Auschwitz reached a fever pitch.[83] The fate of the surviving prisoners became increasingly intertwined with that of the Hungarian Jews. Several Gypsies worked on the extension of the railway spur into Birkenau; and when the new ramp was completed and the trains from Hungary started to arrive, thousands of Jews were taken to the half-empty Gypsy camp, which now doubled as a transit camp. One of the new arrivals from Hungary was Josef Glück, who recalled that the compound was divided "so that Jews were on one side and the Gypsies on the other." Many of these Jews were later murdered in the nearby gas chambers, and the carnage was witnessed by the remaining Gypsies. "What I saw was so dreadful that I fainted," testified Hermine Horvath, who had come from Austria with her family in early April 1943. Many prisoners in the Gypsy camp had premonitions that they would be next, and their fears soon came true.[84]

Late on August 2, 1944, as darkness descended over Birkenau, the SS surrounded the Gypsy camp with a large number of uniformed men. Over the next few hours, all the remaining 2,897 Gypsies were driven by truck to crematoria II and V; first up were the orphaned children, rounded up by drunken SS men. Some prisoners knew they would die; there were scuffles and shouts of "murderers!" To deceive their victims, the SS drove the trucks by a circuitous route. But after the prisoners were finally forced out, they all knew what would happen and their screams echoed across Birkenau all night. Some fought until the end. "It was not easy," Rudolf Höss later wrote, "to get them inside the [gas] chambers." Obersturmführer Schwarzhuber, the Birkenau camp compound leader and an old confidant of Höss, reported that it had been the most difficult mass extermination action so far.[85]

Few Gypsies survived Birkenau. Only a small number of transports had left by the time the compound was liquidated. Between April and late July 1944, the SS had moved no more than around 3,200 inmates to central Germany, mostly men selected for slave labor. Among them were a number of former Wehrmacht soldiers (and their immediate families), several of whom had been decorated for bravery on the Eastern Front prior to their deportation to Birkenau. Some of these war veterans had been incredulous at their treatment. "You coward!" one of them shouted on arrival at an SS man. "You fight here against women and children, when you should be fighting at the front! I was wounded in Stalingrad . . . How dare you insult me!!" Some of the survivors of the Gypsy camp were taken to Ravensbrück. Many more ended up in Dora, the largest of the SS relocation camps. From here, many were sent farther on to a satellite camp in Ellrich. This was no coincidence. The Camp SS often took Jews and Gypsies to lethal satellite camps, and Ellrich was one of the worst.[86]

SATELLITE CAMPS

In early April 1944, Oswald Pohl sent a large map of Europe to Heinrich Himmler, pinpointing all main concentration camps and their attached satellites. There were marks all over the map: the whole Nazi territory was covered in KL, from Klooga at the Gulf of Finland to the Loiblpass camp in occupied Yugoslavia, from Lublin in eastern Poland to the occupied British Channel Island of Alderney. In the accompanying letter to Himmler, Pohl could not resist a dig at his late rival, Theodor Eicke. In a handwritten comment in the margin, he compared his own empire to that of his predecessor: "In Eicke's time, there were a total of 6 camps!" Himmler was duly impressed. Thanking Pohl, he noted with satisfaction "how our things have grown."[87] With the SS desire for ever more prisoners acting as a centrifugal force, many hundreds of satellites soon spread around the main camps and beyond. The climax came in the second half of 1944, when the gigantic relocation projects really took off; over a six-month period, as many satellite camps were erected as in all the preceding thirty months.[88] By the end of 1944, no fewer than seventy-seven satellites were attached to the Dachau main camp alone, several of them located more than 125 miles away.[89] The KL system was changing so fast, with satellite camps set up almost as quickly as they were abandoned, that even the WVHA could not keep count; in January 1945, the officials assumed that there were 500 satellite camps, when the real figure was nearer 560.[90]

A Shifting Landscape

There was no typical satellite camp, just as there was no typical main camp.[91] Satellite camps came in all sizes, from small labor details with no more than a handful of prisoners to vast compounds holding thousands.[92] Set up for specific projects and linked closely to other authorities—such as the OT, military, state, and private companies—most SS satellites focused either on construction (with prisoners digging tunnels and trenches, clearing rubble, building bunkers and factories) or production (with prisoners making batteries and munitions, assembling tanks and rockets). But not every satellite camp was geared for slave labor; a few functioned primarily as sites for dying prisoners or as holding pens for recent arrivals from evacuated KL.[93]

There was no common design. Many satellites took after main camps, with wooden barracks surrounded by barbed wire. Others looked very different, though. In their haste to establish new KL, the authorities used whatever sites they could find, forcing prisoners inside sheds, tents, factories, cellars, ballrooms, and former churches.[94] The same spirit of improvisation governed the search for SS accommodation; in Ellrich, some guards slept in a popular local restaurant, which remained open for business.[95] Some new satellites were even mobile. Between summer 1944 and early 1945, the SS set up eight traveling KL (so-called railway building brigades) for the repair of destroyed tracks; each camp consisted of a long train, with around five hundred prisoners crammed into modified boxcars.[96] By 1944, then, the architectural model of the KL, as it had been developed in the late 1930s, gave way to a random assortment of sites. There were strong echoes here of the emergence of the camps back in 1933. At both ends of the Third Reich, its terror camps were characterized by improvisation. In 1933, the KL system had not yet formed; in 1944, it was starting to fray.[97]

The final decision to set up a new satellite camp was normally made inside the WVHA. Once it was up and running, however, such a new KL rarely reported to Berlin. Instead, relocation camps often coordinated prisoner deployment through regional SS Special Inspectorates (*Sonderinspektionen*), which reported further up the chain to Kammler's office in Berlin. Even closer links existed between satellites and their respective main camp. Many prisoners arrived via the main camp. In addition, SS officials in each main camp took on administrative tasks for its satellites, including the distribution of prisoner clothing and medicine. The result was the emergence of a layer of regional supervision that removed direct control from the WVHA.[98]

Main camps came to resemble huge transit hubs. New prisoners rarely stayed for very long, but were quickly shunted on to one of the satellites. In the Ravensbrück main camp, 12,216 new inmates were registered in September 1944; in the same month, 11,884 moved on to satellite camps.[99] Satellites drew the great bulk of new prisoners in 1944, swelling like a malignant growth. The result was a decisive shift in balance between main camps and their

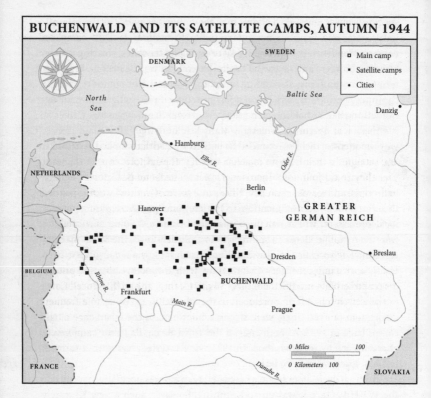

BUCHENWALD AND ITS SATELLITE CAMPS, AUTUMN 1944

satellites. Take the Buchenwald complex. When war broke out in 1939, only a small number of prisoners—less than ten percent—had been held permanently outside the main camp. During the early war years, this figure had increased, but only slowly, and by summer 1943, it was still no higher than fifteen percent. Within a year, however, the picture changed completely, as the proportion of Buchenwald prisoners in satellite camps shot up to thirty-four percent (October 1, 1943), forty-six percent (December 1, 1943), and fifty-eight percent (August 15, 1944).[100] A similar shift occurred in other camp complexes, with striking results: by late 1944, most KL prisoners were held in satellite camps.[101]

Traffic between main camps and their satellites in 1944 was not all one-way. A large number of prisoner transports also went in the opposite direction, as we have seen, bringing seriously ill, injured, and exhausted inmates back to main camps; most of them had worked in construction and were seen as easily replaceable.[102] In addition to the dying, many satellite camps also returned the dead, for incineration in the main camp. Until Dora completed its own crematorium in April 1944, for example, thousands of corpses were driven to Buchenwald, some fifty miles away; later on, the dead were burned in Dora itself, which also began to receive transports of bodies from other satellites nearby.[103] In sum, the general movement of KL inmates often looked something like this: new prisoners departed from main camps to satellites for slave labor, and returned when they were dead or dying.

The gradual disintegration of established KL structures was reflected in the satellites' administrative makeup, which was no perfect copy of the traditional main camp model. There were fewer SS staff and posts, and the internal organization was much simplified, too. Normally, there was no political or administrative department, and in smaller satellites there was not even an SS doctor, an infirmary, or a prisoner kitchen. The most powerful local figure was the so-called camp leader. In charge of the day-to-day running of a satellite camp, he was the de facto commandant, assisted by a report leader. These local SS men enjoyed plenty of autonomy. True, they were appointed and supervised by officers from the respective main camp, or by experienced Camp SS officers in charge of a regional cluster of satellites. But despite frequent inspections and correspondence, these senior officers could not keep a tight rein on all the new sites. As each camp complex expanded, adding more and more satellites, it became ever more difficult to exercise central control, giving greater independence to the local officials.[104]

Soldiers into Guards

The face of the Camp SS changed almost beyond recognition in 1944, with tens of thousands of new guards joining the KL. SS demand was huge. All the new satellite camps had to be staffed, and what was more, they required proportionally more guards than main camps, because of inferior security installations.[105] The need for new staff put great pressure on WVHA managers, who had wrestled with personnel shortages since the war began. The competition for manpower was more intense than ever in 1944, and the KL system was still losing some of its younger sentries to frontline service.[106] Nonetheless, the WVHA managed to bolster its force. By April 1944, the KL staff already numbered more than twenty-two thousand, probably growing to over fifty thousand by the end of the year.[107]

The bulk of the new personnel came from the military. Since KL slave labor was meant to benefit the armed forces, the WVHA insisted that the military should provide soldiers as guards. Supported by Hitler and Speer, it was in constant negotiations with the military authorities, resulting in a massive influx of soldiers from spring 1944 onward. By summer, more than twenty thousand soldiers had joined the concentration camps, and more arrived over the following months. Most of these new recruits were dispatched to satellites, after some brief training in a main camp. By early 1945, more than half the male KL staff was made up of former soldiers; in satellite camps, they far outnumbered seasoned SS officials.[108] Most of them served as sentries, who now came into closer contact with prisoners than before. Not only did they march prisoners to building sites and guard them there, they were more visible inside the compounds, too, as the difference between these Guard Troops and the Commandant Staff became more blurred.[109]

Most of the soldiers had been reservists, only recently called up for active duty. On average, they were probably in their forties—some prisoners called them "grandpas"—and they often struggled with the physical demands of KL service. The initial training was "very rigorous and hard to bear for a man my age," the fifty-six-year-old Hugo Behncke wrote after joining the Neuengamme Camp SS. Men like him had not arrived from the battlefields but from regular jobs on the home front. Behncke had worked as a clerk for a large Hamburg undertaker when he was called up in June 1944. Another new recruit, the fifty-five-year-old Wilhelm Vierke, had been employed as a gardener when he was ordered to report to Sachsenhausen in November 1944. These recruits were less ideologically invested than SS volunteers—Vierke was not even an NSDAP member—and often made more reluctant guards; the end of the war was near and they feared that they would be punished by the Allies for crimes in the camps.[110]

The changes among the KL staff were compounded, in the eyes of Camp SS veterans, by the further influx of female staff. By January 1, 1945, there were almost 3,500 female KL guards, reflecting the recent rise in female prisoners. Like most of the new male guards, these women differed from previous recruits. In the early war years, many female guards had volunteered for service in the camps. But from 1943, the authorities increasingly relied on pressure and coercion, drafting women from labor exchanges or directly from the factories where female prisoners would be deployed.[111] Though the SS rejected some of these women as unsuitable (just as it sent back a number of soldiers), it could not afford to be too demanding. Evidence of ideological commitment, for example, was no essential requirement, and only a fraction of female KL guards were members of the Nazi Party.[112]

The mass influx of new staff in 1944 damaged the Camp SS self-image beyond repair. The propaganda picture of an elite troop of political soldiers was finally destroyed by the realities of total war. Theodor Eicke's principles for recruitment and ideological training had been gradually abandoned ever since 1939, and they were entirely obsolete by late 1944. Instead of bright-eyed SS volunteers, many guards were elderly soldiers who had been drafted into the camps; instead of proven fanatics, the KL employed thousands of women not even eligible for SS membership; and instead of the pride of Germany, there were masses of foreign guards. Eicke's veterans were now in a tiny minority, especially inside satellite camps.[113]

There was plenty of grumbling among the new KL recruits, although tellingly, their discontent largely centered on the rigors of their job, not the fate of the prisoners. They complained about their tedious and regimented lives, their cramped and primitive quarters, and their long hours. The SS was a "club of sadists," the former airman Stefan Pauler wrote in a letter from Ellrich in January 1945, furious about being denied leave. In a glaring breach of protocol, a few female guards even lodged official complaints about their working conditions with SS superiors. More commonly, dissatisfied recruits kept their heads down and sought diversions. "Sunday we received a bottle of wine for 3.80 Mark," Stefan Pauler noted in November 1944. "I drank it up immediately."[114]

On paper, most new recruits became SS members, with some important exceptions (notably female guards and navy personnel). But in practice, sharp divisions remained between the newcomers and the more experienced staff. By no means were all former soldiers eager to swap their military uniforms for the black clothing of the SS. When old SS uniforms were eventually handed out in Ellrich, Stefan Pauler complained that they made ex-soldiers like himself look "like clowns." And Pauler and other military men still stood apart, since they had to wear special insignia on their uniforms to distinguish them from the Camp SS proper. Even an eager supporter of the Nazi regime like Hugo Behncke saw himself primarily as a soldier and kept his distance, admitting privately that the SS colleagues were "at times very unpleasant."[115]

The distrust between former soldiers and hardened Camp SS men was mutual. SS veterans mocked the newcomers as clueless and frail, and worried that their disciplinary failings might cause prisoner escapes or uprisings. Not only did the soldiers engage in conversations with prisoners, blasted Richard Glücks, they even showed them "pity," failing to realize that "every prisoner is an enemy of the state and has to be treated as such."[116] To counter such dangerous tendencies, Glücks looked to the local SS men from department VI. An add-on to KL Commandant Staff since 1941–42, these offices for staff instruction came into their own in 1944. Instead of indoctrination, however, the emphasis was put on basic KL duties, and even such practical lessons were often dropped in favor of entertainment, designed to distract the staff from their daily drudgery and gloomy future.[117]

There was a kernel of truth in the vociferous SS complaints about the new recruits. Compared to experienced Camp SS men, some former soldiers really did treat prisoners a little better.[118] The abbé Jacques Boca, imprisoned in the Wolfsburg-Laagberg satellite camp of Neuengamme, noted in a secret diary how his life had improved after the new camp leader, a former army captain, set up a special barrack for recuperating prisoners: "I spend wonderful days there," he wrote. "I don't freeze, I don't work."[119] Even the treatment of Jewish prisoners, the pariahs of the KL, could be affected. Years after the war, Efim K. still remembered his astonishment when a former German colonel in the Vaivara satellite camp Aseri led him and other prisoners to a table laden with food, and said: "Now dig in, my children, I think you need it."[120]

While individual inmates benefited, the overall impact of the deployment of former soldiers on prisoner lives in satellite camps was surprisingly small. Like main camps, these sites were largely characterized by destitution and abuse, raising the crucial question of how the spirit of the Camp SS was exported to the satellite camps. Apparently, the key role was played by a small group of experienced officials, mostly Camp SS veterans. Even though these men were vastly outnumbered by new recruits, they filled most of the top positions inside the new satellites (just as they did in the Commandant Staff of main camps). Supported by trusted Kapos from main camps, these veterans ruled life inside. They had internalized the values of the Camp SS and knew that satellite camps offered unique career prospects, with more power and pay. Even NCOs could become camp leaders ruling over thousands of prisoners—as long as they ruled with terror.

Camp SS veterans initiated some new recruits by ordering them to perform violent acts. More often, the process of hardening was gradual, and like other guards before them, many newcomers became accustomed to the inverted morality of the KL. After several months as a guard, Hugo Behncke, who rarely mentioned the inmates in his letters home to his wife, made a telling throwaway remark about a recent invalid transport from his satellite to the Neuengamme main camp, describing the prisoners as dirty, sick, and stupid skeletons: "all they were good for was incineration in the Neuengamme crematorium." It required moral fiber to resist the corrosive effects of daily immersion in extreme KL terror. "Worst of all," the unusually self-aware Private Stefan Pauler wrote to his mother in mid-January 1945, "one becomes completely apathetic here with all these figures of human misery."

All that was required for the system to function was for the new KL staff to perform their basic tasks. They may have sometimes done their jobs less brutally than seasoned SS men, but they still did them. In his last long letter to his wife, in early April 1945, Hugo Behncke explained that the best thing was to hope for a change in fortune, "put one's head in the sand," and "continue to fulfill my duty here as a guard."[121] The overall conclusion is chilling: the KL system did not require a vast army of political soldiers, as Theodor Eicke had assumed. In the satellite camps, a small band of Camp SS veterans, deeply committed to violence, was enough to sweep along a much larger group of more ordinary men and women. This highlights one of the most striking aspects about the KL toward the end: the terror continued even as the SS presence diminished.

Production and Construction

Since the beginnings of the KL system, the fate of individual prisoners had been shaped by the work details they found themselves in. Conditions could vary enormously and prisoners were forever scheming to escape the worst jobs or to hold on to more desirable ones. The contrast between labor details became even greater during the war. Moving to another detail was often the difference between life and death, and crucially, so was moving to another camp.

Measured against satellite camps geared toward production, those concentrating on construction generally proved more lethal. The great mass of unskilled slaves in relocation camps was regarded as expendable; during building work, the authorities pushed for maximum output at minimal expenditure, expecting many prisoners to die. The smaller number of prisoners in production, by contrast, were often skilled, and replacing them cost more time and effort. As a result, they could hope for less abuse, more food, and better medical care. A former prisoner of Lütjenburg—a small Neuengamme satellite camp, set up in autumn 1944, where two hundred highly trained prisoners worked on compasses for V2 rockets—later said that conditions had been "like in a sanatorium" compared to other KL.[122]

Production camps were far from benign, of course. Lodgings were poor and slave labor was strenuous, especially in low-skilled posts such as transportation. Neither was there sufficient food. "The soup in Buchenwald was wonderful, compared to the one here," the French resistance fighter Robert Antelme wrote about his transfer to the Gandersheim satellite camp in autumn 1944, where some five hundred prisoners made fuselages for Heinkel fighter planes. "Hunger spread slowly and stealthily," he noted, "and now we are possessed by it." In some production camps, death rates rivaled those of construction camps, especially from late 1944 onward.[123]

Nonetheless, there were often stark differences, leading to a functional division of satellite camps. This division was particularly obvious inside the Dora complex. Here, the SS normally separated new arrivals in the main camp; a small proportion of skilled and strong prisoners were picked for production jobs, while most others were sent to construction details. Prisoners were continually reexamined, and as they weakened they were shunted to camps with worse conditions. In this way, a prisoner might start out in a more desirable production detail in the main camp; as he became exhausted, and less productive, he was sent as a construction worker to a satellite camp; here, the SS tried to press the last remaining labor power out of him, before sending him to yet another camp (or compound) for the dying. As a result, most prisoners at the Dora complex went through more than one camp, and with each move, they came closer to death.[124]

For thousands of Dora prisoners, the final station was the construction camp in Ellrich. The camp—also known as Ellrich-Juliushütte or "Erich," its SS camouflage name—had been hastily established in early May 1944, less than ten miles north of Dora.[125] Always overcrowded, Ellrich quickly held eight thousand men and more, almost twice as many as the surrounding town. Set up on the grounds of two derelict gypsum factories, the site was practically uninhabitable. Everything was covered in mud as soon as it rained, and prisoners had to sleep in wrecked buildings and huts, initially without a roof. There were no sanitary facilities to speak of and the latrines became "a veritable cesspool," a French survivor later wrote. The infirmary was added late and little effort was made to keep prisoners alive; the occasional operations were carried out with dirty instruments and medicine apparently ran out altogether in early 1945.[126]

In summer 1944, a regular day in Ellrich started at 3:20 a.m., when prisoners were woken for the first roll call. Two hours later, they were taken in boxcars to building sites, mostly nearby tunnels for SS relocation projects. Here they toiled for thirteen hours, from 6:00 a.m. until 7:00 p.m. (with a one-hour break), longer than in any other Dora camp. Many men worked deep inside the tunnels, sometimes barefoot. Afterward, they often waited for hours for trains back to Ellrich. This delay, following a grueling day of labor, "was for me personally perhaps the most terribly sad thing I have ever lived through, the most extreme point, not of suffering, but of human distress," the French survivor Jean-Henry Tauzin wrote in 1945. When the prisoners finally returned to Ellrich, often late at night, they had to endure another roll call; at best, they could hope for five hours' sleep on crammed bunks and filthy sacks of straw. Few lasted longer than eight weeks working underground.[127]

Having already written off the Ellrich prisoners, the SS withheld vital supplies. There were chronic shortages of prisoner clothing. Vilmos Jakubovics, a seventeen-year-old Hungarian Jew who arrived in August 1944, never once received fresh clothing during almost eight months in the camp: "We were stiff with dirt and terribly lice-ridden." By autumn 1944, many prisoners were naked and covered themselves with thin blankets. The SS bureaucrats in Ellrich duly added a new category to their internal prisoner statistics— "Without Clothing." In the unheated barracks, inmates often awoke with icy limbs; some froze to death. Others starved to death. Prisoners sometimes went for days without their small ration of bread, with food consisting of no more than coffee substitute and watery soup; on average, they received eight hundred calories a day or less and went almost insane with hunger.[128]

The hell of Ellrich was completed by violent excesses. Almost all guards were former airmen, but the camp was dominated by a handful of hard-line SS men who surpassed one another in brutality, forever hitting, kicking, and beating prisoners. One of the camp leaders was Karl Fritzsch, the self-declared inventor of the Auschwitz gas chambers; by the time he arrived in Ellrich in summer 1944, he was one of the most experienced Camp SS men. Following Fritzsch's departure in autumn 1944, the dominant figure was camp compound leader Otto Brinkmann, another veteran who proved no less cruel. On one occasion, he forced a prisoner to cut off the testicles from a corpse and eat them, garnished with pepper and salt. "I just wanted to find out," Brinkmann said after the war, "if something like that was possible."[129]

Ellrich was all about labor and death. During several months, it had the highest mortality rate within the Dora camp complex and the mass death of its inmates was clearly part of SS calculations. After all, the SS selected prisoners for Ellrich who were already exhausted; the only thing they were still good for, in the eyes of the SS, was a short spell of ruinous labor. "Irreversibly, one [prisoner] after the other has the mark of death branded on the forehead," an inmate noted in his secret diary on December 26, 1944. By then, some three thousand Ellrich prisoners—almost half the inmate population— were so ill or deprived that they could no longer work at all. In January 1945, more than five hundred Ellrich prisoners died, at a monthly mortality rate of around seven percent. When he had first arrived in Ellrich, Vilmos Jakubovics worked with a group of other Jews from Hungary; "out of these 30 from my hometown," he testified in summer 1945, "only I stayed alive."[130]

Not all construction camps were as infernal as Ellrich.[131] Prisoners who moved through several such camps saw major differences. In May 1944, when the sixteen-year-old Hungarian Jew Jenö Jakobovics came to the small satellite camp Erlenbusch, part of the Riese complex, he was probably relieved. Labor was very hard—for twelve hours a day, he worked on a new railway station building—but at least there was food, clothing, and warm water. Conditions were far worse at the nearby Wolfsberg camp, where Jakobovics was transferred in autumn 1944. This was the largest and most important Riese camp, holding 3,012 prisoners on November 22, 1944 (510 of whom were aged between fourteen and eighteen, like Jakobovics). Most had to sleep in flimsy wooden huts and toiled in tunneling and other building work. More than anything, it was the guards' brutality that shocked Jakobovics: "Here, one aimed directly at the extermination of prisoners."[132] This raises a critical issue, for Wolfsberg was a camp reserved for Jews. As we have seen, most registered Jewish KL prisoners had faced murder through labor in 1942–43. Did this SS approach remain in place during 1944, as the case of Wolfsberg suggests, at a moment when vast numbers of Jews were pressed into the war economy inside Germany?

Nazi Racial Hierarchies

The Third Reich was a racial state and many historians believe that for Nazi leaders, the primacy of racism remained unalloyed to the end.[133] Applying this conclusion to the concentration camps, it has been argued that the rigid prisoner hierarchies, based on Nazi ideology, continued to determine the survival of inmates, even as the regime made a last final frantic bid to win the war.[134] Recent research paints a more complex picture, however, suggesting that economic pressures started to dilute the full impact of Nazi racial policy, at least temporarily, as the mobilization of the KL system for total war gathered pace.[135]

The partial "erosion of the ideological," as the historian Jens-Christian Wagner calls it, was evident in many satellites. In Ellrich, and the Dora complex as a whole, survival rates among French and Belgian prisoners were far lower than those of Gypsies, Poles, and Soviets, despite the fact that the latter occupied an inferior place in the Nazi racial hierarchy.[136] Dora was no isolated case. In the Neuengamme satellite camps, too, prisoners from western European countries were often more likely to die than those from eastern Europe.[137]

What caused this apparent breach of Nazi racial orthodoxy? Two aspects were decisive, it seems. First, there was the time of arrival in satellite camps.

In Farge, for example, French prisoners arrived after others had already occupied the key Kapo positions, shutting out the newcomers from life-saving posts.[138] Second, a prisoner's professional background could now count for more than his nationality. French prisoners, in particular, often came from the intelligentsia. Having learned no trade, they were frequently forced into manual labor. A number of Soviet prisoners, by contrast, were skilled and thus more likely to work in production. They were also better equipped to withstand hard work because of their youth, their familiarity with physical labor, and their experience with hunger and shortages back home. The French prisoner Jean-Pierre Renouard recalled a revealing incident at the Neuengamme satellite camp Hanover-Misburg. Ordered to operate a heavy pneumatic drill, he stumbled twice and was beaten unconscious by a furious supervisor; when he came to, a strong and skilled Russian prisoner was doing the job with apparent ease, attracting no blows.[139]

But there were limits to the ideological flexibility of the SS: economic pressures did not turn prisoner hierarchies upside down. German inmates stayed near the top of the pecking order, while Jewish prisoners largely remained at the bottom, and for them, forced labor still often meant death. The lethal exploitation of Jews in satellite camps was already well established in occupied eastern Europe, and from spring 1944, in the wake of the mass deportations to the German heartland, such SS abuse spread westward. In many mixed KL, the authorities singled out Jews for the worst treatment. "When the Jew swallows too much food," the SS camp leader of a Neuengamme satellite camp for men is said to have announced, "he becomes fat, lazy, and, in the end, brazen."[140]

The SS reserved many new satellites almost entirely for Jews. Mostly, these were deadly construction camps like Kaufering in Upper Bavaria, set up from June 1944. Attached to the Dachau main camp, Kaufering was probably the largest satellite complex for Jewish prisoners within Germany's prewar borders, with eleven separate camps. Over less than one year, some thirty thousand KL prisoners were taken here, overwhelmingly Jewish men, to work for the Fighter Staff. Prisoners labored in shifts around the clock, largely on the construction of three huge bunkers (two were later abandoned) for aircraft factories; long lines of inmates carrying bags of cement crossed the sprawling building sites, while others worked the cement mixers. Their suffering continued inside the hurriedly thrown-together compounds. Instead of standard-issue barracks, they slept in wooden huts, set up above holes in the ground, with leaking roofs covered by earth; one prisoner likened the conditions to the darkest Middle Ages. A WVHA directive from late 1944, which permitted urgent operations on Jewish prisoners in nearby civilian hospitals (to bolster the slave labor force), went unheeded. Instead, the local authorities cut the rations of the sick. Salamon Fülöp, a young Hungarian Jew, later noted sarcastically that the perpetrators had relied on "starvation cures" to treat the ill; the inmates ate anything they could find, including grass and dry wood. There were also selections; in autumn 1944, for example, more than 1,300 prisoners were deported to the Auschwitz gas chambers. No one knows exactly how many Kaufering inmates died in all, but estimates of almost fifteen thousand dead—around half of those taken to the site—are probably not far off.[141]

Camp complexes like Kaufering were built on prisoner lives, and for the SS no lives held less value than those of Jews. In many satellite camps, guards continued to indulge in anti-Semitic excesses, seemingly oblivious to the wider economic pressures. As a result, construction camps with Jewish prisoners often had higher death rates than those holding other prisoner groups. This is not the whole story, however. As in the past, some skilled and trained Jewish prisoners were temporarily protected from the worst abuses. Also, senior SS officials did not always send Jews to satellites with the worst conditions. The allocation of slave laborers was often more haphazard, driven not by racial thinking but by the need to fill short-term vacancies. In Neuengamme, for instance, most Jews ended up in production camps, escaping the worst construction sites.[142] Evidently, anti-Semitism was not the only factor determining the fate of Jews in satellite camps. And of all the other factors, none proved more decisive than gender.

Gender and Survival

"Women in the camp," Edgar Kupfer noted in his diary in September 1944, after he heard rumors that French women had been taken to the main Dachau compound: "Unthinkable!"[143] German main camps like Dachau, which had previously held no women at all (with the exception of a few forced sex workers in brothels), were suddenly teeming with female prisoners, even if most of them did not stay for long; once they were registered, the SS normally dispatched them to satellite camps for slave labor.[144] The mass influx of women into the KL system was accompanied by several concessions. The SS discarded its ban on male and female prisoners working together in arms production, and it relaxed its rules for the supply of slave labor, deferring to industry demands for smaller prisoner details; instead of providing only groups of one thousand or more, the SS reduced the minimum "order" to five hundred in the case of women, paving the way for more requests.[145]

Female prisoners were held in satellite camps all across Germany. Until summer 1944, the great majority of such camps were attached to Ravensbrück. But as the satellite camps mushroomed, the WVHA simplified their administration. In autumn and winter 1944, the supervision of around half these Ravensbrück satellites, holding some fourteen thousand women, was handed to other main camps (though some links remained, as camps like Buchenwald and Flossenbürg regularly deported "invalid" women back to Ravensbrück). Because these main camps established yet more satellites, the network of female camps continued to expand. By the end of 1944, there must have been well over one hundred satellite camps holding female prisoners; some were reserved for women only, others held male prisoners, too.[146] Even in these joint camps, however, male and female prisoners largely lived and worked apart.

The most striking difference between the sexes lay in the survival rates. Male prisoners in satellite camps were far more likely to die than women, bringing to mind the gendered delay in SS terror in the years before 1942.[147] It is hard to believe that, as some historians have argued, it was the experience of women as homemakers that put them at a significant advantage over men.[148] It is equally unlikely that closer bonds among female prisoners made a decisive difference.[149] Far more important was the type of labor inmates had to perform: unlike most men, most women worked in production; in the Ravensbrück satellites, the split between production and construction was around 4:1 among women, and the reverse among men. Companies often preferred women for precision work in arms manufacturing, drafting female prisoners to make munitions, gas masks, warships, and fighter planes.[150]

These female prisoners also experienced less extreme abuse from fellow inmates and officials. For the most part, the SS authorities felt that they had less to fear from women. Although some officers warned about their cunning nature, the Camp SS was not overly concerned about violent attacks and escapes. This was reflected in staffing levels; proportionally, the SS often deployed more than twice as many guards at satellite camps for men as it did at camps for women.[151] Moreover, camp compounds for female prisoners were mostly guarded by women.[152] Unlike some male guards, none of them had been brutalized by frontline warfare. And although they often acted harshly and unpredictably, they committed relatively few excesses against female inmates; murderous violence remained the exception.[153] The same was true, apparently, for many of the older male reservists drafted as sentries. Female survivors of satellite camps often described these men as rather humane, allowing them extra breaks and additional food. Even some Jewish women recalled former soldiers as acting "very decently," raising the key issue of anti-Semitic terror in satellite camps for women.[154]

When it came to survival in satellite camps, gender largely trumped race: Jewish women were often more likely to survive than non-Jewish men.[155] True, Jewish women in construction—clearing rubble, swinging pickaxes, digging trenches—often faced terrible odds; more than four thousand women (largely Hungarian Jews) were deported to Kaufering alone, where many joined the men on the deadly building sites.[156] The majority of female Jewish KL prisoners on German soil, however, worked in production, just like most other women in 1944, and their chances of survival were much higher.[157] Jewish women in the Gross-Rosen satellite camps, for example, who mostly worked in textile and arms production, suffered a death rate of around one percent; by contrast, more than twenty-seven percent of Jewish men perished in the Riese construction camp complex.[158] In this way, the manufacture of munitions, weapons, and other goods for the Nazi war effort saved thousands of Jewish women from almost certain death, at least for the time being.

Many Jewish women were held in satellite camps together with groups of other female prisoners, and although they often faced additional abuse, they were not singled out for mass murder. In Leipzig-Schönefeld, a satellite camp of Buchenwald, where more than 4,200 women of different nationalities and backgrounds worked in arms production in autumn 1944, the skilled Jewish prisoners were treated more or less the same as other inmates. One witness recalled that the camp leader, a veteran Camp SS man no less, had assured prisoners on arrival that they would be judged on their performance, not the yellow star on their uniforms.[159]

Other Jewish women found themselves in production camps reserved solely for Jews. One such camp, for the Siemens-Schuckert works, was set up in mid-October 1944 in Nuremberg, opposite the city's large southern cemetery. Among the 550 women was Ágnes Rózsa, whom we encountered at the beginning of this chapter. Like Rózsa, the other female prisoners had been deported from Hungary to Auschwitz, and onwards for slave labor to Nuremberg. Held in two barracks surrounded by barbed wire, Ágnes Rózsa and many of the others used precision tools to make electrical goods. In the world of the Nazi camps, this was a privileged detail and the women knew it. "We are no longer threatened by the daily selection or the fear of the gassings," Ágnes Rózsa wrote on December 6, 1944. "I was dead in Auschwitz," she added a few weeks later. "Only here in Nuremberg, as I started to work, was I reborn." Forced labor was strenuous—Rózsa worked up to fifteen hours a day—but not geared toward destruction. Living conditions were pitiful—prisoners sometimes shook with hunger and cold—but not lethal. Violence was common—with slaps during work and occasional beatings—but not deadly. This made all the difference for the prisoners. Before the camp was closed down, following an Allied air raid on February 21, 1945, the SS recorded no more than three deaths.[160]

For most female Jewish prisoners, then, transfer to a satellite camp far inside Germany was an improvement.[161] But these women only made up a small proportion of all imprisoned Jews. Far more were murdered in Auschwitz as "unfit for labor." Talking to Hitler on April 26, 1944, about the deportations of Hungarian Jews, Joseph Goebbels concluded: "If anything, the Führer's hatred of Jews has grown, not diminished . . . Wherever we can get our hands on them, they won't escape retaliation."[162] As for those Jewish women and men selected for slave labor, one should not forget that Nazi leaders had been swayed by short-term economic or strategic considerations before.[163] Such exceptions did not alter the fundamentals of Nazi anti-Jewish policy, and the survival of some Jews as forced laborers in satellite camps in 1944 was meant to be a temporary stay of execution only.[164] The prisoners themselves were well aware of their perilous existence. "When all is said and done," Ágnes Rózsa wrote in her diary on December 22, 1944, "I am only alive because at the moment no one wants to kill me."[165]

THE OUTSIDE WORLD

Fritz Güntsche was ashamed and angry. Looking back in 1951 at the last years of the Third Reich, the Nordhausen teacher attacked the willful amnesia of his fellow citizens, who often feigned ignorance about the violent history of the nearby Dora concentration camp. "Whoever says that kind of thing is lying!" Güntsche bristled. What about the prisoners who had marched right through the town? What about the corpses driven toward Buchenwald? What about the prisoners who had worked with locals in factories and on building sites? All this was proof enough, Güntsche wrote, "that we knew something about the Dora camp and its browbeaten inhabitants! We did not interfere with things there, we did not dare to kick against the pricks. We are responsible for what happened there." A lone voice drowned out in the stubborn silence about Nazi crimes that enveloped much of Germany in the early 1950s—his unpublished manuscript was kept under lock and key in an East German archive—Güntsche pointed to the many ways in which the camps had become public toward the end of the Third Reich.[166] As more and more satellite camps spread across the country, a vast number of Germans had witnessed the crimes committed in their name. And it was not only the German population that learned more about the camps; the Allies, too, saw SS terror more clearly than ever before.

Out of Sight, Out of Mind?

The KL were never cut off from the outside world, least of all from the communities surrounding them. Having tried to isolate the camps in the late 1930s, the SS could not stop them from becoming more transparent again after the war started. It could not hide completely the murder of Soviet POWs and other Nazi victims, as columns of starved prisoners marched toward the camps, followed by telltale smoke from inside. "The chimney of the crematorium," a Dachau woman recalled after the war, "stank and stank, day and night."[167] Another local point of contact was slave labor. In theory, the SS still tried to stop onlookers; any spectators who failed to disperse, Dachau sentries were instructed around 1942, should be dragged before the camp authorities.[168] But such rules were already impossible to fully enforce in the early 1940s, as the outside deployment of prisoners increased (well before the proliferation of satellite camps).[169] Often, the initiative for such employment had come from local officials and traders. Farmers, in particular, petitioned concentration camps for help with the harvest, a well-established custom in state prisons. One of these farmers was Gretel Meier from Flossenbürg, who asked the commandant in June 1942 for "approval of a prisoner mowing detail of four prisoners" because "my husband is at the front" (the request was granted by the WVHA). Shortages among agricultural workers led the SS to rent out sizable numbers of prisoners; in autumn 1942, around thirteen percent of female prisoners from Ravensbrück worked locally in farming.[170]

Occasionally, KL prisoners also worked for small companies, local towns, and cities.[171] Their presence grew from autumn 1942 onward, following Himmler's decision to deploy the new SS Building Brigades to clear rubble and ruins. In their striped uniforms—long associated in the public mind with criminality—the prisoners were highly visible, as were SS abuses. The former inmate Fritz Bringmann recalled an unusual incident on the streets of Osnabrück in autumn 1942. As an SS man battered a prisoner, a woman stepped from the crowd that had gathered, placed herself before the unconscious prisoner, and berated the SS man; later that evening, the prisoners talked excitedly about this intervention as proof that there were still Germans "who had not forgotten the difference between humanity and inhumanity."[172]

In the minds of the vast majority of Germans, however, the camps and their prisoners remained abstractions during the early years of the war. Direct contacts with prisoners were rare, as were references in the press; even the foundation of a large new camp like Auschwitz was suppressed in local and regional papers.[173] Of course, the KL system was not altogether forgotten. It made occasional appearances in public speeches and popular culture. In the 1941 Great German Art Exhibition in Munich, for example, a large oil painting depicted dozens of KL prisoners—recognizable by their caps, uniforms, and colored triangles—who slaved in the Flossenbürg quarry (the painting was acquired for four thousand Reichsmark in Hitler's name).[174] Local Nazi bigwigs also still threatened "troublemakers" with the camps, so much so that Himmler issued a formal warning in summer 1942. The German people were too decent, he insisted, to put up with constant threats of such harsh punishment.[175] And yet, most Germans still pushed the concentration camps to the backs of their minds, just as they had done in the late 1930s. When they thought about the inmates at all, they probably imagined dangerous criminals and other enemies of the state—an image so firmly entrenched by now that it often endured long into the postwar years.[176]

The role of the camps in the Nazi Final Solution did not fully penetrate public consciousness, either. To be sure, the secrecy surrounding the genocide in Auschwitz was never as complete as the perpetrators wanted.[177] Knowledge must have been particularly widespread within SS circles. After Dr. Johann Paul Kremer participated in his first gassing in September 1942, he noted in his diary: "It is not for nothing that Auschwitz is called the camp of annihilation!"[178] Beyond the SS, some regular German soldiers witnessed the crimes in Auschwitz, and by 1944, several senior army officers were well aware that mass gassings were carried out here.[179] Railway workers and other state employees gained insights, too. In January 1943, Germany's top legal officials—who had kept some distance from the KL in the prewar years—toured the Auschwitz camp, led by Reich minister of justice Thierack.[180] Many local civilians, too, had some knowledge of the mass murder in the nearby camp. Indeed, rumors spread across the whole region, though the main victims were sometimes thought to be Poles, not Jews.[181] Through friends and relatives, and Allied radio broadcasts, word about Auschwitz carried inside the Reich. As for German Jews who had not yet been deported, the reports about the death of friends and acquaintances left little doubt in the minds of some that Auschwitz was "a fast-working slaughterhouse," as Victor Klemperer wrote in his diary on October 17, 1942.[182] Despite all this, Auschwitz was no household name across Nazi Germany. While many ordinary Germans had some general knowledge of the mass murder of European Jews in the east, they mainly heard about massacres and shootings, not about camps. Most Germans only learned about Auschwitz after the war.[183]

Such ignorance owed much to the Nazi authorities' strenuous efforts to hush up KL crimes. Camp SS officials were banned from sending blood-soaked clothes of executed prisoners by regular mail, lest a packet spill open, and from sending death notices to relatives of deceased Soviet forced laborers, after rumors about the high mortality in the camps had spread in the occupied east.[184] In addition, the SS began to use a secret code for disguising the number of deaths recorded by camp registry offices, so as not to arouse suspicion.[185] As for public gossip, the Nazi authorities probably regretted a Gestapo order of October 1939 that had encouraged the spread of "rumor propaganda" about hardships inside the KL to increase their "deterrent effect."[186] In fact, public talk about violence and murder was still punished. Loose-tongued Camp SS officials were let off most lightly, though even they sometimes faced imprisonment. Others were less fortunate. After a Hanover dentist, a Nazi Party member since 1931, told a patient in summer 1943 that he deplored the "medieval torture methods" in concentration camps and the murder of a million Jews, he was sentenced to death by a German court.[187]

To control popular knowledge about the KL, the Nazi authorities continued to enforce stringent rules about prisoner access to the outside world. Letters, which could be posted at best every two weeks (many prisoner groups wrote less often or were barred altogether), were still rigorously controlled. They had to be written in legible German—shutting out most foreign prisoners—and any references to illness, slave labor, and camp life were strictly prohibited. Often, the inmates were even forbidden to mention the fact that they were in a concentration camp.[188]

Despite their enforced blandness, the letters still mattered to prisoners, as did the eagerly awaited replies they sometimes received; knowledge that their loved ones were alive proved a source of great strength. "I read [your letter] again and again," Chaim Herman of the Birkenau Special Squad wrote in November 1944 in a final note meant for his wife and daughter in France, "and won't part from it until my last breath."[189] Meanwhile, prisoners continued to subvert the SS rules. Some allusions—such as questions about how "Uncle Winston" was getting on—were so obvious that only dim-witted censors could overlook them. Other references were more subtle, requiring knowledge of foreign cultures. "Mrs. Halál ["death" in Hungarian] is very busy here," Alice Bala wrote from Birkenau in July 1943.[190] Some prisoners even managed to smuggle secret messages outside, in which they expressed themselves more openly. In his last letter from Auschwitz, written in April 1943, just three months before his death, twenty-year-old Janusz Pogonowski told his family that his best friend had recently been shot dead, and pleaded for more packages from home because "my current food situation is in a very bad way."[191] Messages such as this fed rumors on the outside about the concentration camps. Other details came from former prisoners, following their return from the camps.

Release and "Probation"

Hopes of KL inmates of being freed had faded as soon as war broke out. In autumn 1939, Reinhard Heydrich ordered that prisoners should normally not be released from protective custody during wartime. Exceptions may be allowed, he added, but police officials had to make sure that no committed political activists, dangerous criminals, or "particularly asocial elements" were freed.[192] And just a few months later, as we saw, Heinrich Himmler put a stop to releases of Jews, an order implemented almost to the letter. According to top-secret SS statistics drawn up for Himmler, only a single Jewish inmate was released from Auschwitz between June 1940 and December 1942.[193]

And yet, there was no complete ban on prisoner releases. In 1940, for example, 387 women were discharged from Ravensbrück and 2,141 men from Sachsenhausen. This was only a small proportion of the prisoner population in these camps, but it was enough to keep alive the dreams of others trapped inside.[194] Among the lucky few were individual German prisoners wearing green, black, and red triangles, as well as some foreign prisoners, including Czechs and Poles; one of the largest releases came on February 8, 1940, when one hundred professors from Krakow University were freed with Himmler's agreement, following significant foreign pressure.[195] Some released German men were drafted straight into the army. Since summer 1939, prisoners eligible for army service had been examined by military commissions inside the KL, and could be called up upon their release, to the disbelief of the new recruits themselves.[196]

Releases became even rarer from 1942 onward, as police fears about crime and insurrection redoubled. According to SS figures, an average of around eight hundred prisoners a month were released from the KL system during the second half of 1942.[197] At times, releases came to an almost complete standstill. In the first week of November 1943, for instance, just three of over thirty-three thousand Buchenwald prisoners were set free.[198] Mass releases, meanwhile, rather common in the prewar KL, stopped almost altogether. One of the few exceptions was the quick release of former democratic functionaries rounded up in summer 1944 during Operation Thunderstorm. The police authorities let most of the prisoners go after a few weeks, following some popular disquiet and criticism, coming even from senior Nazi officials, about the seemingly arbitrary arrests of elderly Germans who had not been involved in any oppositional activities.[199]

Not all released KL prisoners actually won their freedom: several thousand men were sent to the Special Formation Dirlewanger, a notorious SS unit that turned some former prisoners into killers. The Dirlewanger Formation had been set up in 1940, after Hitler ordered the creation of a special unit of poachers held in state prisons for illegally hunting wild animals. In May and June 1940, dozens were transported for training to Sachsenhausen (more followed in 1942). The small force was led by its eponymous commander Oskar Dirlewanger, one of the most odious characters in the pantheon of SS villains, who had already attracted attention for his avid criminal appetite, which ranged from extreme political violence to embezzlement and sex crimes. As commander of his own SS unit, he now branched out into pillage, rape, and massacres, specializing in the killing of defenseless civilians in the occupied east.[200]

During 1943–44, around two thousand German KL prisoners joined the ranks of the Dirlewanger Formation, which grew into a larger SS force. They included so-called asocial and criminal prisoners (among them several homosexuals who had recently been castrated because of their "degenerate sex drive"). Not all of them were keen to exchange the familiar surroundings of the KL for the unknown dangers of the front. "By then, we had it reasonably well in the camp," one veteran "criminal" prisoner later wrote, "and we could have just waited for the war to end." Some were soon sent back to the KL; others went into hiding or joined the partisans. But the majority entered one of the Third Reich's darkest areas, which erased the difference between victim and perpetrator. Having suffered for years as social outcasts in the camps, these men now fought for the Nazi cause and committed dreadful crimes, and yet remained subject to SS violence themselves. Dirlewanger deployed extreme terror against his men (Himmler spoke approvingly of "medieval" methods against "our camp ne'er-do-wells"), and deployed the former prisoners as cannon fodder. The "blood sacrifices" of "incriminated people," Himmler believed, would spare the lives of a good few "German boy[s]."[201]

One of the casualties was thirty-five-year-old Wilhelm K. from Munich. A destitute father of five who had started poaching to support his family, he had been imprisoned in Dachau since 1942, following a prison sentence. Despite his Communist sympathies and his hatred of the SS, he saw no choice but to join the Dirlewanger Formation in summer 1944. "You and the children," he wrote to his wife in a secret letter in late August, "need decent support and for the time being I have no other option but to join up, so don't be angry, sweetheart." Just a few weeks later Wilhelm K. was killed during the suppression of the Warsaw Uprising, in which the Dirlewanger Formation played a savage part.[202]

In autumn 1944, the first political prisoners entered the ranks of the Dirlewanger Formation. Desperate to shore up German defenses, Himmler was now willing to deploy open enemies of the regime like German Communists, straight from the KL. The prisoners were rounded up through a mixture of false promises and coercion. Many were dismayed about their fate, as were fellow inmates who stayed behind. "I could have cried when I saw them like this," Edgar Kupfer wrote in his Dachau diary after meeting former comrades dressed in SS uniforms, complete with the Death's Head insignia. In mid-November 1944, almost eight hundred former KL prisoners arrived in Slovakia to join the Dirlewanger Formation. Most aimed to escape as soon as possible, and they succeeded faster than they could have hoped. Within a month, almost two-thirds had crossed over to the Red Army—probably the largest desertion by German troops up to this point in the war. But the euphoria about their flight from the SS was short-lived: most of the escaped German anti-Fascists ended up in Soviet forced labor camps, where many of them would die.[203]

Close Encounters

When Himmler told German generals on May 24, 1944, about the deportations of Hungarian Jews to the Third Reich, he insisted that ordinary Germans would remain oblivious. The SS would lock these prisoners away as invisible slaves in underground factories. "Not one of them," Himmler pledged, "will somehow end up in the field of vision of the German people."[204] But the old SS policy of concealing KL sites—never entirely successful—was unworkable by 1944, thanks to the huge rise in inmate numbers and satellites. Whether Himmler wanted it or not, his camp system became enmeshed in the fabric of German society. In the Linz region, for example, the sprawl of the Mauthausen complex meant that there would eventually be one prisoner for every five inhabitants.[205]

The closest contacts came during forced labor, as most KL prisoners worked near, and under, German civilians. In Dora, the production of V2 rockets in summer 1944 involved five thousand concentration camp prisoners and three thousand German workers, many of them locals.[206] One of the Dora prisoners, the French student Guy Raoul-Duval, later tried to summarize the attitude of these German workers:

Some of them were swine, some were good men, but most often they were stupid bastards, not really malicious but fierce, worn out by an interminable war, . . . terrorized by the police and the engineers, profoundly weary, and convinced of the inevitability of the Reich's defeat, yet not resigned to believing the disaster was imminent, and thus continuing, out of habit, the pace they had acquired.[207]

Among the minority of German civilian workers described as "swine" by Raoul-Duval would have been those supervisors who basked in their powers. They did not even have to lay hands on prisoners; more often than not, they used Kapos as their enforcers. Still, some supervisors joined in themselves, especially in construction camps, where prisoner lives came particularly cheap. Occasionally, the violence became so pervasive that managers issued written prohibitions to their staff: if prisoners stepped out of line, employees should report them instead of beating them.[208] Denunciations to the SS were indeed frequent and could result in swift punishment—as in the Hanover-Misburg satellite camp, where a Belgian and a French prisoner were summarily executed in early 1945 after a German worker complained to the Camp SS supervisor that his sandwich had been stolen.[209]

There were also German civilian workers who came to the aid of prisoners, providing food and other supplies (though this did not stop them from acting more obediently on other occasions).[210] Some of these Germans acted out of self-interest, making profitable deals with desperate prisoners on the black market.[211] Others were moved by kindness. The stench of the camps did not rub off on everyone who touched them; just as some workers hardened over time, others softened as they came to know individual prisoners.[212] A few even defended prisoners against SS suspicions. When the Auschwitz SS accused a Jewish inmate of sabotage because he had ruined precious metal parts by drilling to the wrong depth, his German foreman explained the incident away as an innocent mistake by an otherwise "reliable worker."[213] Most famously, and most exceptionally, the German businessman Oskar Schindler helped to save hundreds of lives, by securing better working conditions for Jewish prisoners in his metal wares and munitions plant, and by protecting them from extermination, first at the Plaszow satellite camp Zablocie (established on the grounds of his factory), and then, following the relocation of the business and many of its prisoners in autumn 1944, at a new satellite camp in Brünnlitz in Moravia (attached to Gross-Rosen).[214]

Beyond terror and support, there was distance and detachment. These were no doubt the most common reactions among the civilian workers. "In fact, we are the untouchables to the civilians," Primo Levi wrote about his encounters with German workers around Monowitz.[215] Uncomfortable about the prisoners' proximity, many civilians tried to ignore the wretched figures in striped uniforms; they literally learned to overlook the inmates. At Gandersheim, Robert Antelme once cleaned the floor in an office full of local men and women. "I did not exist for them," he later wrote. One of the men shifted automatically as Antelme picked up a piece of paper next to him. "The German pulled back his foot, in the way you shoo away a fly from your forehead when asleep, without waking up." Only one woman could not look away; she stared at Antelme and became increasingly agitated. "I weighed on her, I made her lose her composure. Had I brushed against the sleeve of her blouse, she would have been sick."[216]

Such anxieties were fed by prejudice toward members of enemy nations in general and KL prisoners in particular; in the eyes of many German workers, the sight of the shaven-headed and disease-ridden prisoners simply confirmed the stereotypes of Nazi propaganda. The Camp SS added fuel to the flames, warning civilians that the male prisoners really were dangerous criminals and the women prostitutes ravaged by sexual disease.[217] Cultural differences, with the bulk of foreign prisoners unable to speak German, only heightened suspicions. Linguistic barriers were not insurmountable, however. At the Continental rubber works in Hanover, where German civilians worked next to political prisoners in the production of gas masks, the hatred of dictators provided common ground. "Hitler *Scheiße*," some German workers said. "Stalin *Scheiße*," came the prisoners' reply.[218]

Any such collusion was strictly outlawed, of course. Managers warned employees that private conversations with prisoners were forbidden, on Himmler's personal orders; all those who broke the rule would themselves end up in protective custody.[219] These threats were mostly about deterrence, no doubt, but the authorities did back them up with occasional sanctions: a number of German workers really were arrested for talking to prisoners.[220] Even harsher punishment—including detention in Gestapo camps—hit German civilians caught smuggling letters for prisoners or giving them food and drink. As early as February 1942, the Sachsenhausen commandant Hans Loritz informed his officials that he had recently handed over to the Gestapo several civilian workers guilty of such offenses. The remaining workers, Loritz insisted, had to "*regard each prisoner as an enemy of the state*."[221] In turn, many civilians learned to keep their heads down.

But indifference was a major factor, as well. Many civilian workers lost no sleep over the prisoners' plight. They were used to foreigners being exploited for the German economy, with KL prisoners merely the latest contingent in a much larger army of forced workers. More generally, death and destruction were all around as the war raged on, a war in which many Germans saw themselves as victims, suffering rationing, bombing raids, and fatalities at the front. Preoccupied with their own struggles, many civilian workers had no time for the fate of prisoners.[222] This was true for other ordinary Germans, too. "If I remember correctly, I did not think much at all, however pathetic that may sound," a German man later described his feelings as a young soldier, when he had seen some SS men and prisoners at Auschwitz in late 1944. "You wondered about what will happen to you, and had no feeling for others."[223]

Camps in the Community

Redl-Zipf was a sleepy town in a valley of the Upper Austrian countryside, made up of farms and cottages with pretty gardens and orchards, surrounded by open fields and wooded hills. The rural idyll was abruptly shattered in autumn 1943, when the test range for V2 rockets was set up in the mountains nearby. Heavy machinery and high-tech matériel arrived, new concrete buildings were erected, cables and rails were laid, and engine tests caused deafening blasts and tremors. Then there were all the prisoners from the new satellite camp, established just a few hundred yards outside town. Their torment was not hidden from residents, who often watched them marching to and from the camp, and there was plenty of talk about torture and death among engineers, construction workers, secretaries, and SS men, many of whom were quartered with local families. Even the camp itself was not out of bounds: some local children climbed on trees and peered inside. In short, one resident later said, "all the Zipfer knew what was going on."[224]

Similar scenes unfolded in many German towns and villages where satellite camps sprang up late in the war. These camps became part of the local landscape, sharing in the social, administrative, and economic life. Businessmen offered their services, waiters attended to SS men, and local registry officials recorded prisoner deaths. Whether dead or alive, the prisoners could not be overlooked. Some locals could see into the camps, as could some relatives of SS guards; during her visits to the Neuengamme satellite camp Salzgitter-Watenstedt in September and November 1944, the wife of Hugo Behncke caught repeated glimpses of the inmates. Even more encounters took place on the streets outside, as prisoner columns moved past houses and shops. Some details worked in the middle of local communities, clearing snow or rubble from homes and businesses, railway stations, and churches. Open abuse was common, as SS men saw few reasons anymore to hide their brutality. The mass death of prisoners was an open secret, too, as the dead were often taken away in plain sight. In fact, some residents had to assist the SS. In Bisingen, local coachmen were ordered to cart corpses from the satellite camp (part of the Natzweiler complex) to mass graves. "One day, I had to drive 52 dead from the camp to be buried," an elderly man testified after the war; he even knew which of the prisoners had been executed, as blood would leak from their wooden coffins.[225]

In larger German cities, too, KL prisoners became a visible presence. Once again, neighbors living next to the hastily erected compounds gained direct insights. The Buchenwald satellite camp Magda, for example, was established on the edge of a residential area in Magdeburg-Rothensee; from their windows and balconies, residents looked straight into the camp, while their children played next to the electric fence.[226] Satellite camps were scattered all across most major German cities. In Munich, there were at least nineteen such camps by autumn 1944, ranging from tiny sites to huge ones like Allach with more than 4,700 inmates; in addition, more than ten prisoner bomb-clearing squads roamed the city.[227] It was the same in other large cities. "If one traveled past slowly in the *S-Bahn*," recalled a Düsseldorf citizen, who had frequently spotted, from his suburban train, a column of prisoners marching to their camp, "one saw, whether one wanted to or not, the faces of the wretches, their skulls shaved clean, yellowish and emaciated to the bone."[228]

Public reactions to such encounters with the KL were mixed, resembling responses by German civilian workers. Some onlookers, including children, were openly hostile, taunting and swearing at prisoners who marched through the streets. Occasionally, a mob would form and throw sticks and stones. When a group of boys strolled past a building site in Hanover-Misburg in summer 1944 and spotted Jean-Pierre Renouard taking a quick rest from the backbreaking labor, one boy stepped forward and lashed out, egged on by the rest of his gang.[229] Other civilians, by contrast, helped the prisoners. In exceptional cases, they supported underground activities in the KL.[230] More often, locals left some food for prisoners, sometimes using their children as go-betweens. Ella Kozlowski, a Hungarian Jew forced to clear debris in Bremen, told an interviewer decades later how a German passerby and her young daughter had hidden a bottle with hot porridge for her, every day for several weeks: "I cannot even begin to tell you what this meant to us."[231] The motives behind such charitable acts were manifold and could spring from political, religious, and humanitarian beliefs, or from gratitude to prisoners who had rescued locals trapped under rubble.[232]

By far the most common reaction of ordinary Germans, however, was indifference. "I am happy when I hear nothing and see nothing of it," a resident of Melk said, describing her attitude.[233] Prisoners were only too aware of this reticence. During encounters with ordinary Germans, they would closely scrutinize their faces and gestures for small signs of sympathy, and were distraught when cautious glances met with evasion. Alfred Groeneveld, a Dutch resistance fighter who was taken to a Buchenwald satellite camp in Kassel in autumn 1943, was struck by the detachment of locals who passed his prisoner detail on the streets: "It seemed as if the people simply did not want to know anything! They looked as little as possible, as if trying to repress the memory in advance!"[234]

But what was the meaning of this silence? It has been argued that the willed blindness of ordinary Germans marks their complicity in Nazi mass murder, turning them from bystanders into perpetrators.[235] But this mistakes the result of public passivity for its cause. Popular acquiescence made SS terror easier, to be sure, but it tells us nothing about the motives behind it, and it certainly does not follow that KL crimes built on popular consent. While popular opinion during the war is difficult to read, it is evident that many Germans felt more than apathy. Plenty of them still supported the camps as institutions. To them, looking away from prisoner abuses was a way of ignoring the unpleasant reality of a policy they agreed with in principle. It also betrayed their fears of the prisoners. Nazi propaganda had been successful in branding prisoners as dangerous criminals, and popular anxieties only increased with the influx of foreigners and the spread of rumors about thefts and murders by escaped inmates, played up by local Nazi newspapers; occasionally, recaptured prisoners were even hanged in public, before the eyes of the population.[236]

The KL were never universally popular inside Germany, however, and this did not change near the end of Nazi rule. Many Germans were genuinely shocked when they came face-to-face with prisoners for the first time.[237] As German defeat became more likely, such moral concerns were fueled by fears of Allied retribution. "God help us, that we won't suffer vengeance in the same way," a group of women cried in autumn 1943 when they saw a ghostly procession of Ukrainians from the Dachau railway station to the main camp.[238] SS leaders were well aware of the continued unease about the KL. Speaking confidentially to army generals on June 21, 1944, Heinrich Himmler conceded that ordinary Germans thought "very often" about the camps, "greatly pitied" the prisoners inside, and said things like "Oh, the poor people in the concentration camps!"[239]

Himmler and other Nazi leaders regarded such critical views as seditious.

After the failed bomb plot on Hitler's life on July 20, 1944, Nazi propaganda made much of the supposed plans of the conspirators to free prisoners from the KL (for good measure, the authorities dragged many family members of the plotters inside, including relatives of Count Stauffenberg, the would-be assassin).[240] Many German resisters did indeed oppose and abhor the camps, as is evident from their leaflets and private papers.[241] But disquiet about the KL went beyond Germans who fundamentally opposed the Third Reich, and occasionally even reached veteran Nazi supporters.[242]

So why did such reservations about the camps not translate into greater support for prisoners? Fear was clearly a factor, as SS guards openly threatened Germans who tried to help. And just as in the case of civilian workers, the authorities occasionally followed through; in Mühldorf, for instance, a local woman was arrested in August 1944 after she handed fruit to a group of Jewish prisoners.[243] But such cases were rare. After years of Nazi rule, many Germans were fatalistic. Their sense of impotence was summed up by a woman who witnessed exhausted prisoners from Stutthof march to work in summer 1944, driven on by SS guards with whips: "Feeling pity, that was the most one could do."[244] Looking away, then, could be a sign of resignation, too.

The mind-set of many people in Nazi-occupied Europe was different. Although there was plenty of indifference, fear, and collusion, there was far more defiance. The determination to oppose the occupiers was widespread and often led to a clear-cut view of KL prisoners: as victims of the common enemy, they deserved help. Foreign civilian workers, deployed at German factories and building sites, were more likely to come to the prisoners' aid than their German counterparts.[245] POWs, who knew themselves what it meant to fall into Nazi hands, gave some support, as well. Around Monowitz, British soldiers in the local POW camp (set up in autumn 1943) often left some of their Red Cross supplies to KL inmates. Working as a mechanic with a group of British soldiers, the German Jew Fritz Pagel, who spoke a little English, regularly received food from a British gunner; the soldier even wrote to Pagel's brother in London, at grave danger to himself.[246]

Local residents near concentration camps in Nazi-occupied Europe also acted with more courage than their counterparts inside the Third Reich. This was obvious to prisoners from the SS Building Brigades who were transported to satellite camps in occupied France and Belgium in spring and summer 1944 (for setting up launchpads for German rockets). Despite SS threats, many locals gave food, sometimes walking up directly to prisoners in defiance of SS threats. Some residents even supported escaped inmates, offering clothes and shelter; Gerhard Maurer from the WVHA complained that the

French population gave "every help possible" to those on the run. Veteran inmates, like the twenty-four-year-old German Jehovah's Witness Helmut Knöller, were astonished by the generosity of local people in western Europe: "We prisoners had a great life there in Flanders, the most beautiful time in the KL! The Belgian population brought us prisoners *everything*, tobacco in abundance . . . bread and fruit, sweets, sugar, milk and so on." Returning to Germany a few weeks later, in autumn 1944, Knöller was struck by the very different attitude of the local population, which cheered the accompanying troops, not the prisoners.[247]

Hostility to the KL was most vociferous among the anti-Nazi resistance in occupied Europe—hardly surprising, given the camps' prominent role in the war on the political underground. As symbols of Nazi terror, the camps were frequently denounced in leaflets and graffiti.[248] In Vught, locals are even said to have thrown stones at SS guards.[249] Most significant were the systematic efforts to help prisoners, reminiscent of the activities by left-wing activists in Germany during 1933–34, before their networks were destroyed. The Polish Home Army and other resistance organizations managed to smuggle money, food, medication, and clothes to prisoners in Auschwitz. "Thank you for everything. The medicine is priceless," a Polish inmate wrote to the local underground on November 19, 1942. The SS was well aware of the groundswell of local opposition around Auschwitz. Following the first prisoner escape in summer 1940, Rudolf Höss complained to his superiors about the "fanatically Polish" attitude of the population, which was "ready for any action against the hated SS men."[250] Another mission of the organized resistance was the collection and dissemination of information about the KL. Around Auschwitz, the Polish resistance received a large number of secret messages from prisoners, as well as some documents stolen in the camp. The inmates took enormous risks to gather this material, in the hope that it would reach the wider world.[251] Against the odds, some of it did.[252]

The Allies and the Camps

Sometime in late 1940, British secret service agents at Bletchley Park, some fifty miles north of London, made a breakthrough: they cracked one (or more) of the advanced Enigma keys used by the SS to code radio transmissions. Now the British could eavesdrop on Nazi terror as it unfolded, including the highly sensitive traffic between concentration camps and their Berlin headquarters.[253] Over the coming years, British intelligence collected a vast number of decoded messages and, as a look at the material from 1942 reveals, gained astonishing insights into the KL system. The agents could track movements within and between camps, using the daily statistics of prisoner populations; it was clear, for example, that many "unfit" prisoners were sent to Dachau. The messages revealed much about the Camp SS, as well, including staffing levels and transfers, and the influx of ethnic German guards. Regarding the function of the KL, British intelligence was aware of the shift toward slave labor for industry, on Himmler's personal orders, with major factories under construction around Auschwitz, Buchenwald, and elsewhere. In addition, there were many glimpses of terror inside, with reports on epidemics, corporal punishment, human experiments, executions, and prisoners "shot trying to escape." As for the place of Auschwitz in the KL system, it was obvious that huge numbers of Jewish prisoners were arriving in what had become a very deadly camp.[254] Revealing as all this material was, however, it was fragmentary. Not only did the British miss many SS messages, but the most secret exchanges were not sent by radio at all.[255] This meant that the meaning of orders deciphered in Bletchley often remained hazy. It was not immediately obvious, for example, that sick prisoners were sent to Dachau as part of a program of murdering invalids. Neither was it clear that Auschwitz became a destination for the systematic mass extermination of Jews, who were mostly murdered on arrival and hence absent from the figures seen by the British.

To gain a clearer picture, the Allies needed information from other sources, in addition to the decryptions. There was no shortage, even in the early war years, and especially in London, where the British authorities collected more extensive and reliable intelligence than their counterparts in the United States.[256] Some accounts of abuses and atrocities in the KL came from British staff abroad.[257] But the most telling material arrived via outside agencies, such as Jewish groups and the Polish government-in-exile, which collected and circulated numerous reports from the Polish underground. Though sometimes confused and contradictory, and weighted toward the suffering of the Polish population, these reports added crucial details about the camps— including news about the mass extermination of Jews, with isolated references (especially from 1943) to selections, gas chambers, and crematoria in Auschwitz. The Polish authorities in London not only passed confidential material to the British and other governments, they released some reports directly to the media, resulting in newspaper articles in the United States, Switzerland, Britain, and elsewhere. As early as June 1941, the *Times* of London carried a brief piece on starvation, slave labor, and murders of Polish prisoners in the "dreaded Oswiecim [Auschwitz] concentration camp."[258]

As the war drew to a close, the Allies received ever more detailed reports, especially relating to the Nazi Final Solution. Although Allied governments had been aware since the end of 1942 (at the latest) of the systematic mass extermination of European Jewry, the exact role of Auschwitz and Majdanek in Nazi genocide was not yet fully understood. The famous Allied declaration of December 17, 1942, which publicly denounced the wholesale slaughter of the Jews in eastern Europe, made no direct mention of the KL, referring merely to Jews being worked to death in "labor camps." And even this declaration was quickly forgotten by senior government officials in Britain and the United States, who questioned the reliability of eyewitness testimony and worried that excessive exposure of Nazi atrocities might detract from the business of fighting the war.[259] The magnitude of Nazi criminality took a long time to sink in.

But by 1944, the truth became hard to ignore. To be sure, Allied intelligence was still scattered, which accounts for the continuing confusion about aspects of the KL system.[260] And yet, the contours of the KL, above all of Auschwitz itself, came into ever sharper relief. During interrogations, German POWs mentioned mass killings in the camp, and occasionally referred to gassings. German generals secretly recorded in Allied captivity made similar remarks.[261] By far the most important information, and also the most recent, came from escaped prisoners. A first detailed report about the slaughter of Hungarian Jews reached Switzerland in mid-June 1944, just four weeks after it had begun. "Never since the foundation of Birkenau," it concluded with great accuracy, "have so many Jews been gassed."[262]

The most influential survivor account came from two Slovakian Jews, Rudolf Vrba and Alfred Wetzler, who had been deported to Auschwitz in 1942 and escaped on April 10, 1944. After they had crossed the Slovakian border, they found shelter in the Jewish community in Žilina and completed a sixty-page typed report on the camp. Translated into different languages, it offered a thorough analysis of the Auschwitz complex, outlining its development, layout, and administration, as well as conditions inside. Most critically, Vrba and Wetzler gave a thorough account of Auschwitz as a death camp, detailing the arrival of Jews from across Europe and the selections, gassings, and cremations. The sober tone and the mass of details made the report all the more devastating. Over the coming months, copies were distributed to influential figures in Slovakia and Hungary, and also reached the World Jewish Congress in Geneva, the Vatican, the U.S. War Refugee Board, and several Allied governments. Some conclusions featured prominently in the media in summer 1944, and in the United States, whole extracts of the report by Vrba and Wetzler were published a few months later.[263]

Given the growing awareness of genocide in Auschwitz, some survivors and historians have since asked why the Allies did not bomb the killing facilities or the tracks leading up to the camp. "Why were those trains allowed to roll unhindered into Poland?" asked Elie Wiesel, who was fifteen years old when he was deported in May 1944 from Hungary to Auschwitz with his parents, his sisters, and his grandmother.[264] In fact, bombing raids on Auschwitz had been considered for the first time back in 1941 by the British air force, following a request by the Polish government-in-exile. But such proposals only gathered momentum during the mass murder of Hungarian Jews, following urgent appeals from Jewish leaders in May and June 1944 to bomb Birkenau and the connected railway lines.[265] Looking at the Allied response, the lack of urgency is palpable. The USSR showed hardly any interest in the so-called Final Solution, and although the western Allies were more engaged, its military leaders were focused on war strategy—charting the fastest route to victory—not on humanitarian missions. In the end, the pleas were turned down.[266]

This does not mean that the Allies missed a major chance to halt the Holocaust in summer 1944. Railway tracks and yards were hard to hit and easy to repair, and trains could have been rerouted. And while a direct attack on Birkenau would have carried great symbolic weight, it might not have saved many lives. It would have been technically possible for heavy U.S. bombers to attack the site from around July 1944 (the IG Farben factory near Monowitz, which was seen as a military target, was hit for the first time on August 20), but by this time the vast majority of the deported Jews were dead. Moreover, the bombers' inaccuracy makes it unlikely that the killing complex could have been hit without causing carnage in the adjacent prisoner compounds; this was a time before real "precision strikes." But even if such an attack had succeeded, it is hard to see how it would have stopped the mass murder. The determination of Nazi leaders to exterminate the Jews would not have been deflected by bombs on Birkenau (in fact, SS men habitually blamed Jews for Allied air raids and sometimes attacked Jewish prisoners "in retaliation" after KL had been hit). No doubt the SS killers would have found other ways to continue their murderous mission.[267] Indeed, they were already doing so. During the genocide of Hungarian Jews, as we have seen, the Auschwitz SS used not only gas chambers and crematoria, but also shootings and open pits; as the Nazi task forces had demonstrated in the Soviet Union in 1941–42, technically sophisticated facilities were not essential for genocide.

Still, the prisoners who escaped from the KL to warn the world did not risk their lives in vain. Growing awareness of Nazi crimes could save lives. The shock waves caused by the account of Rudolf Vrba and Alfred Wetzler, for example, probably helped to persuade the Hungarian regent Horthy to put an end to the deportations in July 1944.[268] More generally, eyewitness reports by prisoners—those who had fled and those still inside—shaped the picture of the KL in the Allied nations. Articles and radio programs based on inmate testimonies helped to dispel some of the indifference and skepticism that existed. By November 1944, at the time the Vrba-Wetzler report was published, most Americans understood that the KL were sites of mass extermination.[269] Crucially, reports in the Allied media fed back to the Third Reich, as well. By reading foreign newspapers and listening to enemy broadcasts—with millions secretly tuning in to the BBC—more and more Germans learned about the atrocities in Auschwitz and Majdanek.[270] Foreign news even filtered back to the KL. The realization that they had not been forgotten by the outside world gave prisoners new hope, as well as greater determination to resist the SS.[271]

10

Impossible Choices

One day toward the end of World War II, a few Dachau prisoners made a pact. Determined to show that there was an alternative to the usual strife between inmates, they would act like gentlemen; for a whole day, rough and selfish behavior would give way to civility and compassion, as if they still lived regular lives outside. When the agreed day came, the men tried their hardest to stay true to the ideal of common decency, starting with the scramble to dress, wash, and eat in the morning. By evening, all of them had failed, defeated by the harsh realities of the camp. "The beast inside humans gains the upper hand," the Belgian resistance fighter and Dachau prisoner Arthur Haulot noted in his diary on January 19, 1945, after he heard about the experiment. "One does not with impunity live so long outside the norm."[1]

Although survivors drew many conflicting conclusions about the concentration camps after the war, they agreed that the inmates' behavior could not be judged by ordinary standards. This had already been the accepted view inside the camps.[2] The KL, many prisoners believed, had inverted conventional morality. There were times when charity could become suicidal, and deviance—including murder—could be just. Failure to understand this essential truth and adapt to the law of the camp would prove deadly.[3] But what, exactly, was the law of the camp?

Some inmates gave a stark answer: it was the law of the jungle. The conditions caused a relentless battle for goods and positions, they believed, and created an enormous chasm between a small elite, most of them Kapos, and the destitute mass that fought to the death for an extra piece of bread, bedding, or clothing. In this brutish vision, the other prisoners were rivals in the struggle for survival, locked into a war of all against all. Slowly dying in an infernal Neuengamme satellite camp in the last year of the war, an elderly Belgian prisoner wrote a despairing message to his son, himself gravely ill in the infirmary: "The camp is changing, there are only wolves among wolves!"[4] This vision may be too bleak, when applied to the KL as a whole. But we cannot completely wish it away, either. However comforting it would be to cling to idealized images of a prisoner community united in suffering, the conflicts between inmates were all too real, and they turned all the more vicious the more lethal the KL system became.

And yet, prisoner relations were not ruled by aggression and anarchy alone. There were some unwritten rules, for a start. Under the prisoners' informal code, the theft of bread belonging to another was a sin. Saving bread required great self-discipline, as starving prisoners had to fight the temptation to devour their full ration. Every piece of stale bread was a symbol of a prisoner's will to survive; and every theft was seen as an unforgivable betrayal, tantamount to treason. As a Neuengamme room elder told a group of new arrivals: "Stealing bread from a comrade is the worst kind of wickedness; he is stealing his life."[5] This ruling did not put an end to thefts, nor did it result in perfect justice, as some innocent inmates became victims of uncontrolled fury. Nonetheless, such thefts were generally seen as wrong and deserving of punishment.

So there was a moral structure in the KL.[6] Prisoners may have been unable to live by the same ethical code they followed outside, as in the case of the Dachau "gentlemen," but they retained a sense of right and wrong within the warped world of the camps. Not everyone agreed on the same rules, of course, but there were lines most prisoners did not want to cross. Living by these basic rules was not just about survival, it was about self-respect as well. "I am straight with everyone," Janusz Pogonowski secretly wrote to his family from Auschwitz in September 1942, "I have done nothing I need to be ashamed of."[7] Preserving dignity was almost impossible on one's own, and Pogonowski credited two friends for helping him through a severe illness, supporting him materially and morally. It was thanks to them, he wrote, that his soul was "healthy, proud and strong."[8] Such mutual support among KL prisoners was not exceptional, as some observers suggest, but common.[9] It took many different forms, from sharing food to political discussions, and undermined SS attempts at total domination.

Some prisoners saw all such acts as resistance: survival itself was a "form of resistance," Ágnes Rózsa wrote in her diary in early February 1945.[10] Several scholars have taken a similar line, stretching the definition of resistance to cover all nonconformist acts in the KL. As the Italian psychologist Andrea Devoto memorably put it: "anything could be resistance, since everything was forbidden."[11] However, such an all-embracing definition blurs the lines between very different acts. Should we use the same term to describe a prisoner who sabotaged German munitions and a prisoner who fought for his own life, if necessary at the cost of others? Even a narrower definition of resistance can be problematic, when applied to the camps, since prisoners had no hope of working to overthrow the Nazi regime.

In the end, other terms may help us to see the prisoners' choices more clearly, though there are inevitable overlaps between the different categories. There was perseverance, which involved individual acts of self-preservation and self-assertion; there was solidarity, which was directed at the spiritual survival and protection of groups of inmates; and there was defiance, which included protests, and other planned and principled opposition to the Camp SS. Given the immense power of the SS, such direct challenges were rare, and they were not always unambiguous, either. Escaping from the camp, for example, might allow a prisoner to join the partisans or tell the world about Nazi crimes, but it might also condemn other inmates to death, under the SS policy of collective punishment.[12]

COERCED COMMUNITIES

Inmates had to be resourceful to stand any chance of survival during the war, developing what one prisoner called "camp technique."[13] They had to make the most of their existing skills, and acquire new ones, to gain life-saving advantages; a multilingual prisoner might get a privileged position as a translator, while a talented painter might sell his drawings for food.[14] The perseverance of individual prisoners included rituals to preserve their precamp identities. For Primo Levi, his daily wash was less about getting clean—impossible in the filthy surroundings—than about staying human.[15] Other prisoners found solace in religion. God had saved her from losing her mind, a Polish woman testified soon after the war, when she recalled her arrival in Ravensbrück in autumn 1944.[16] Some prisoners also sought strength in art and the life of the mind, recalling old books, poems, and stories. In Ravensbrück, Charlotte Delbo swapped her bread ration for a copy of Molière's Le Misanthrope, and then memorized the lines, a few each day. Silently reciting the play to herself "lasted almost throughout roll call," she later wrote.[17]

Important as individual perseverance was, however, no prisoner could get through the KL alone. The camps were social spaces and inmates always interacted with others. Their fate was shaped, to a large degree, by their place within what the Auschwitz survivor H. G. Adler has called the "coerced community."[18] Without solidarity, an Auschwitz Kapo told a group of new arrivals in late March 1942, they would all be dead within two months.[19]

Some prisoner groups were created by the SS, others by common inmate interests and backgrounds. Some dated back to the prisoners' pre-KL lives; others emerged inside. Some were loose and transitory; others were permanent and closed to outsiders. To complicate matters, prisoners always belonged to more than one group. Primo Levi, for example, was an educated, atheist Jew from Italy, and each of these aspects of his selfhood shaped his social relations in Auschwitz.[20]

Companionship—whether based on sympathy or pragmatism, chance or shared beliefs—was vital for all prisoners. But it was a double-edged sword, since it created discord, as well. Relations between inmates thrown together by fate, like those who found themselves in the same barrack or work detail, often proved volatile. More generally, solidarity among some prisoners could cause conflicts with others. In the end, every prisoner faced the same paradox: how to lead a social life in the unsocial environment of the KL?[21]

Families and Friends

"We depended on each other," Elie Wiesel wrote about the relationship with his father in Auschwitz; "he needed me as I needed him." Sometimes they shared a few spoonfuls of soup or bread, and they gave each other moral sustenance, too. "He was my support and my oxygen, as I was his."[22] Wiesel was not alone. In the inferno of the camps, many prisoners formed close bonds with relatives, since trust was an essential element in their social relations. This was true, in particular, for Jews and Gypsies, who were frequently deported in large families.[23] They had arrived together, and together they hoped to stay alive.[24]

Other small survival networks, sometimes consisting of no more than a pair of prisoners, were made up of close friends.[25] Many had already known one another before the camp. Hailing from the same towns or cities, their common past and culture provided common ground in the camps. Many more were joined together by shared experiences of Nazi terror, on deportation trains and building sites, in barracks and infirmaries.[26] Her friendships with other prisoners had helped her to survive, Margarete Buber-Neumann later wrote, and she never had a closer friend in the camps than Milena Jesenská. She met the Czech journalist, who had been arrested after helping others escape from Nazi-occupied Czech territory, in Ravensbrück in 1940, and the two women quickly bonded. They were kindred spirits and often talked about the past (both had broken with the Communist movement), the present, and the future; Jesenská suggested that they should write a book about camps under Stalin and Hitler, to be called "The Age of the Concentration Camps." In Ravensbrück, the two women cared for each other as best they could. When Buber-Neumann was thrown into the bunker, her friend smuggled sugar and bread inside. When Jesenská became gravely ill, her friend secretly visited her every day for several months.[27]

Such friendships were widespread in the microcosm of the camps. Many women became so close they even referred to each other as sisters. They formed surrogate families, with up to a dozen or so members, sharing food, clothing, and emotional support, and trying to protect each other from selections. Being a "camp sister" was a "very happy and invigorating feeling," Ágnes Rózsa wrote in January 1945. "Whatever happens, we know we can count on each other."[28] It has often been suggested that female KL prisoners were more likely than men to form such intense friendships.[29] But close companionship was not gendered. Primo Levi, for one, forged a deep connection with another Italian prisoner called Alberto, also in his twenties. For months, they slept on the same bunk and they were soon "bound by a tight bond of alliance," Levi wrote, dividing all additional food they could scrape together (they were only separated when Alberto left on the Auschwitz death march in January 1945, from which he did not return).[30] Many male prisoners enjoyed similar friendships, and while some later felt embarrassed to talk about them, other men had no such hesitation, referring to "sleeping brothers" and "comradeship marriages."[31]

In the unforgiving climate of the KL, however, even the closest bonds could be broken, especially among ordinary prisoners, who were always exposed to the full force of the camps.[32] There is no shortage of chilling images from the concentration camps, but few are as disquieting as those of friends and family robbing one another, and of sons denying their fathers when they pleaded for bread.[33] More generally, mutual aid within small collectives, bound by a strong sense of solidarity, often brought harm to others, intentionally or unintentionally. Each set of prisoners primarily fought for itself, in what Primo Levi termed "we-ism" (as a collective extension of egotism) and what we might call "groupness." The success of each individual group in gaining food, cigarettes, or clothing almost inevitably meant that there was less for others to "organize"; sometimes prisoner collectives even stole from one another.[34]

Then there were all those prisoners who could not form any alliances. This was true, above all, for the *Muselmänner*, the lepers of the camps. These doomed men and women haunted the compounds like ghosts, though there was nothing unworldly about their presence, with their festering wounds and stinking rags. "Everyone was disgusted by them, nobody showed any compassion," the Auschwitz prisoner Maria Oyrzyńska recalled. The others stayed away as far as possible, not just out of disgust but for their own self-preservation; because the *Muselmann* was always in the line of fire—stealing food, evading work, ignoring orders—others were afraid of being punished by association. And so the *Muselmann* died the loneliest death.[35]

Most other prisoners knew that uniting with a small group of relatives or friends offered the best hope. Vital as these alliances were, they were always liable to be ripped apart by deportation, illness, selection, and death. After the death of his father, Shlomo, in early 1945 in Buchenwald, Elie Wiesel became indifferent to the hell around him: "nothing touched me anymore."[36] Margarete Buber-Neumann was equally devastated after Milena Jesenská's death in May 1944: "I felt very near despair. Life seemed to have no further point." In the end, she clung on to life, honoring the memory of her dead friend by writing the book about the camps they had talked about back in Ravensbrück.[37]

Comrades

The social ties between friends and relatives were rivaled by those emerging from shared beliefs that predated the camps and endured inside.[38] Individual left-wing inmates were particularly close, perhaps even more so than before the war, and frequently arranged secret meetings; they discussed ideological questions, shared the latest news of the war (gleaned from newspapers and hidden radios), and observed working-class traditions by commemorating significant events and singing protest songs.[39] Some other political prisoners proved equally committed to their cause. In Kaufering, the dreaded Dachau satellite, a few Zionists even put together an undercover Hebrew newspaper that called for unity among Jewish inmates and for the creation of a Jewish state.[40] All such communal activities are best understood as self-assertion; together, political prisoners fought against the eradication of their pre-camp identities and drew strength from their collective convictions.[41]

Some groups went beyond boosting morale and became survival networks. Political prisoners would share essential supplies and use their contacts to save others from punishing labor details or transfers to deadly camps.

And just as before the war, well-placed captives watched out for comrades among new arrivals, to explain the basic rules and to protect them.[42] This was another case of partial solidarity, with any benefits restricted to selected prisoners. Inmates from other backgrounds were often excluded as untrustworthy and undeserving; the basic principle, a former prisoner later explained, had been to "put the politicals first!"[43] Sometimes this meant saving one inmate at the expense of others. Helmut Thiemann, a German Communist and Buchenwald Kapo, testified after the war that he and his colleagues had established a special ward in the infirmary just "for our comrades of all nations." The Communist Kapos did all they could to help these prisoners, providing them with the best available medication. At the same time, Thiemann added, "we had to be ruthless" against others.[44]

The most extreme cases of "groupness" among political prisoners involved so-called victim swaps. This practice took place in several KL and has been documented most fully for Buchenwald. Here, Communist Kapos in the infirmary protected some comrades from human experiments by altering SS lists, substituting their names for those of other prisoners. This was how "we saved each other," Thiemann's colleague Ernst Busse testified after the war, so that "members of our underground organization in the camp could live relatively peacefully." In the same spirit, Communist Kapos in the Buchenwald labor action office altered the composition of prisoner transports to satellite camps. They would spare comrades from transfer to a lethal camp like Dora, and dispatch prisoners considered as undesirable and inferior in their place, including criminals, homosexuals, and other social outsiders. "All these negative elements were selected by the national [Communist] groups," the former prisoner clerk Jiří Žák testified in 1945, "which also identified the positive elements who under no condition were to go on transports." Žák was not the only Communist who vigorously defended this practice after the war. "When I have the opportunity to save ten anti-fascist fighters," Walter Bartel, one of the most senior Buchenwald Communists, insisted in an internal party investigation in East Germany in 1953, "then I will do it."[45]

Not all political prisoners enjoyed the same protection, of course, since the inmates with the red triangle never formed a homogeneous group. Even among the most committed opponents of the Nazi regime there was plenty of tension. The long-standing antagonism between German Social Democrats and Communists was never fully overcome, while other ideological divisions were still more pronounced; French nationalists, for example, shared virtually no common ground with Soviet Communists. There was even strife within the same political factions. German Communists clashed among one another about divisive ideological issues, like the Hitler-Stalin pact, and about the correct tactics in the KL. Dissenters were swiftly accused of deviation and excluded from the collective. When German Communists in Ravensbrück learned that Margarete Buber-Neumann had been a prisoner under Stalin, they branded her a "Trotskyite" and cut her off. Buber-Neumann, for her part, thought that her adversaries were stuck in the past, in the "Communist cloud cuckoo land of 1933."[46]

Believers

Early each morning, before the Auschwitz prisoners had to rise, Elie Wiesel and his father left their bunk and walked to a nearby barrack. Here, a small group of orthodox Jews met to say ritual blessings, sharing a pair of tefillin they had acquired on the black market. Jews faced the greatest obstacles to worship, as they were exposed to the most lethal SS terror. And yet, they found ways to affirm their faith. "Yes, we practiced religion even in a death camp," Wiesel wrote later. "I had seen too much suffering to break with the past and reject the heritage of those who had suffered."[47]

Observant KL inmates knew that it was all but impossible to fulfill their religious duties. They had to work during sacred times and break some dietary rules, and also missed prayer books and spiritual guidance from their leaders.[48] Still they practiced their beliefs, as best they could, forming close-knit groups based on shared beliefs. The observance of Christian rituals was particularly widespread among Polish political prisoners, whose faith was often bound up with their national identity. They held secret Sunday services and even smuggled consecrated Hosts into the camps; at least one prisoner received the Holy Communion in the Auschwitz bunker, after others had lowered a Host, tied to a piece of string, to his cell window.[49]

Many inmates drew strength from religious devotion. Some groups formed close communities of faith, dividing almost everything; in some camps, for example, Jehovah's Witnesses evenly split all the money and provisions sent by relatives. What is more, religious practices provided a lasting link to their pre-camp lives. And it helped them to find meaning in their suffering, seeing the camp as the culmination of centuries of persecution, or as a divine test of faith, or as penance for the sins of mankind.[50] Some atheist inmates felt that the religious believers had an advantage over them, because their faith gave them a fixed point in the universe to unhinge the world of the SS, at least in their minds.[51]

But religious devotion also spelled danger. Prisoners were always at risk during prayer, even on the rare occasion when it was sanctioned. SS and Kapos repeatedly turned religious ceremonies into occasions for torture. In

Dachau, they forced Catholic clerics to drink large amounts of sacramental wine (donated by the Vatican) and dished out special abuse during holy days; in all, close to half of the 1,870 Polish priests dragged to Dachau perished.[52] Even if believers escaped such torment, the act of worship itself could put them at risk. Rising early for prayers deprived them of vital sleep, and fasting weakened them further, as did the adherence to other dietary rules; several orthodox Jews who tried only to eat kosher are said to have quickly died of exhaustion.[53]

The daily rituals of orthodox Jews in particular created frequent flash points. Some prisoners saw the prayers as a disturbance, especially at nighttime, and accused religious Jews of passivity in the face of SS terror. "You can pray as much as you like," Dionys Lenard told an imprisoned cantor, not long before his escape from Majdanek. "I am going to act instead."[54] Other secular prisoners regarded all worship as perverse: how could one suffer in hell and still pray to God? Primo Levi was incensed when, after a selection in Auschwitz, he heard and saw the prayers of an elderly man in another bunk, who thanked God for sparing his life: "Can Kuhn fail to realize that next time it will be his turn? Does Kuhn not understand that what has happened today is an abomination, which no propitiatory prayer, no pardon, no expiation by the guilty, which nothing at all in the power of man can ever clean again? If I was God, I would spit at Kuhn's prayer."[55] The feeling of incomprehension was mutual. A number of orthodox Jews were indignant about the others' lack of religious fervor, and castigated them for questioning, complaining, or abandoning God.[56]

These clashes highlight, once more, the diversity of Jewish prisoners. Although they all wore the yellow star, they formed no unified community, even less so than before the war. The divisions—along religious, political, and cultural lines—became more pronounced, now that all Jewish prisoners had to fight for survival. In addition, there were new national and linguistic barriers; eastern European Jews often spoke Yiddish, which many assimilated Jews from the west did not understand. After many years inside the KL system, Benedikt Kautsky concluded: "One did not see much all-Jewish comradeship."[57] How could it have been different? After all, meaningful support was harder for Jews than for any other group. "We could not help anyone in material terms," Dionys Lenard wrote in 1942, "because none of us had anything."[58] And yet, despite this existential pressure, many Jewish prisoners—including Elie Wiesel, Primo Levi, and Ágnes Rózsa—joined forces with others and formed small support networks.

Notwithstanding the divisions among Jewish prisoners, some other inmates saw them as a cohesive group and an easy target. Jews lived in fear of dangerous encounters, especially with greedy and brutal Kapos. The widespread anti-Semitism among prisoners was palpable, with Kapos screaming abuse like "Dirty Jews have to be exterminated!" as they dealt out blows.[59] Even decades after the war, the former German camp elder of a Neuengamme satellite camp, notorious for his excesses, was open about his motives: "On the whole, I did not like the Jews. In the camp, at least, they were bootlickers and smarmy."[60] But other factors were at play, too, not least the propensity of prisoners to look down on others who were even weaker.[61]

At the same time, Jewish inmates were not universally shunned. Many prisoners treated them in a measured way, ignoring occasional SS threats of punishment for anyone who was too friendly to Jews. In fact, some showed great consideration and courage, extending their compassion beyond their own immediate circle of confidants.[62] In summer 1942, when the Ravensbrück SS punished Jews with a month-long cut in rations, another group of prisoners, led by Czech women, regularly smuggled some of their own bread into the Jewish women's barrack.[63] This was no isolated incident. In Auschwitz-Monowitz, Polish prisoners also occasionally gave some of their provisions to Jews. "They did not have much for themselves," the Hungarian Jew George Kaldore recalled, "but they still shared."[64]

Divided Nations

If one could listen in on conversations in the barracks, late at night near the end of the war, one would hear the prisoners whisper in any number of languages. Take the Buchenwald main camp: by the end of 1944, it held inmates from more than two dozen countries, including small groups from Spain (295 prisoners), England (25), Switzerland (24), and Albania (23). "One is surrounded by a perpetual Babel," wrote Primo Levi.[65] As the prisoner population became more international, nationality became ever more important in shaping this coerced community, bringing some prisoners together and driving others apart.[66]

National solidarity, based on a shared language and culture, could be lifesaving for vulnerable prisoners. In addition, inmates occasionally celebrated their shared national traditions, singing folk songs and telling old tales. Most gatherings inside the barracks were spontaneous expressions of national belonging, after a long day in the camp, though there were organized concerts, too, as well as dances and plays.[67] In addition to stirring the prisoners' patriotic feelings, such performances offered a diversion from their bleak lives. In her Nuremberg satellite camp, Ágnes Rózsa set up a theater group with other Hungarian prisoners, who performed famous songs, as well as parodies of fellow inmates and guards.[68] Reflections on the KL also found their way into prisoner music. Among the songs of Polish inmates in Auschwitz was "Gas Chamber," set to the melody of a popular tango:

> There is one gas chamber,
> Where we will all get to know each other,
> Where we will all meet each other,
> Maybe tomorrow—who knows?[69]

Many acts of national self-assertion took place in an ambiguous area, tacitly tolerated by the SS. This was true, above all, for official cultural events, which carried multiple meanings for the different audiences. When Dachau prisoners put on a "Polish Day" in 1943, complete with choir, orchestra, and dancers, they smuggled patriotic messages into the performance. While the Polish prisoners took great pride in their subversive act, oblivious SS officials sat in the first row and clapped loudly, demanding an encore.[70]

Despite such moral victories, most national prisoner groups did not form close unions. They might have shared the same letter on their uniforms (indicating their country of origin), but issues which had divided fellow countrymen on the outside did not suddenly disappear inside.[71] National discord was most intense, perhaps, among those who wore the letter "R"—prisoners classified as Russian. This term typically covered all prisoners from within the huge territory of the Soviet Union, and hid a great many ethnic and political differences. Above all, there was the antagonism between Russians and Ukrainians, reflecting their often hostile relations back home. Many captive Russian soldiers remained committed to the Moscow regime and branded Ukrainian inmates as traitors and collaborators. For their part, many imprisoned Ukrainian forced laborers saw the Russian POWs as henchmen of Stalin's regime, which had repressed their indigenous nationalism and killed several million Ukrainians through its lethal policy of forced collectivization.[72]

To make matters worse, many Soviet prisoners faced blanket hostility by prisoners from other countries, who denounced them as loafers, thieves, and murderers. Such sweeping judgments were rooted in age-old prejudices, pointing once more to the importance of habits and convictions formed prior to the KL.[73] Other prisoners often felt a sense of superiority over supposedly primitive inmates from the east, and were anxious about Soviets bringing disease into the camps. The pressures of daily survival only exacerbated such fears; on the whole, it is hard to imagine a place less conducive to conquering national stereotypes than the KL.[74]

With Soviet prisoners condemned toward the bottom of the prisoner hierarchy, confrontations with better-off inmates were inevitable. One explosive issue was the uneven distribution of food packages, a constant source of envy and conflict within the prisoner community. In Sachsenhausen, starving Soviets surrounded the blocks of Norwegian prisoners, who enjoyed an abundance of Red Cross parcels. The emaciated men begged for scraps and scoured the floor for crumbs. The Norwegians tried to beat them away. "They're like flies, you can't wave them off, they come back, encamp, and lie in wait for anything that may fall from our luxurious repast," one of the Norwegian prisoners wrote in his diary in autumn 1943. The average Norwegian, he added, treated these prisoners "worse than he would a dog at home."[75]

If Soviets were depicted as brutal and base, the reputation of Germans, who stood near the top of the ladder, was no better. The "dead and the living," three Polish survivors of Auschwitz wrote in 1946, had "boundless contempt and hatred for the Germans."[76] This hostility was rooted in the long-standing antagonism between Germany and its European neighbors, which had greatly escalated after the rise of Hitler; many Polish prisoners saw conflicts with German inmates as a continuation of their struggle against German occupiers outside.[77] The privileges of some German inmates sparked resentment among foreigners, too, as did their casual arrogance. Most noxious was the power wielded by German Kapos. Many foreigners saw abuses by these Kapos as proof of the evil of the entire German nation, erasing the difference between German prisoners and perpetrators. "It does actually seem as if they were all alike, prisoners, SS, or *Wehrmacht*," one foreign inmate noted in Sachsenhausen in October 1944.[78]

Germans and Soviets were not the only ones who faced hostility. Pretty much every national group was mocked, feared, or despised by another, and accused of greed, brutality, and craven submission to the SS. Many French prisoners felt contempt for Poles, for instance, who often returned the sentiment in kind.[79] Relations between Polish and Soviet prisoners were even worse, reflecting the poisonous relations between both countries. When Wiesław Kielar was appointed as a clerk in a block of Soviet POWs in Auschwitz-Birkenau, he did not hide his hostility; his Soviet charges, in turn, answered each of his orders with a curt "Fuck off!"[80]

The SS was no passive observer in all of this. Not only did it create the general conditions that pitted inmate groups against one another, it deliberately exacerbated national hostilities. It bolstered the position of German prisoners, offering them benefits like powerful Kapo posts; such favoritism went so far that some Germans were spared the transfer to a lethal KL like Auschwitz altogether.[81] The SS also fanned the flames between other national groups. Having put prisoners in charge of administering corporal punishment (in place of SS men), Heinrich Himmler ordered that Poles should hit Russians, and Russians should hit Poles and Ukrainians. Rudolf Höss summed up the thinking of SS leaders with customary cynicism: "The more numerous the rivalries and the fiercer the struggles for power, the easier the camp can be led. Divide et impera!"[82]

Elites

The gulf between prisoners grew wider and wider as the war continued. Social differences were at their greatest, Margarete Buber-Neumann recalled, in the final year before liberation:

> Crowds of children hung around the blocks of the better-off prisoners begging for food, whilst ragged, half-starving figures rummaged in the waste-bins for scraps of food. Other prisoners were well dressed and well fed, according to their influence in the camp. There was one woman who might have been strolling along the streets of the West End as she took the greyhound of the SS Camp Leader out for exercise.[83]

Each concentration camp had an elite of privileged prisoners, no more than around ten percent of the population, and admission to this exclusive club depended on an inmate's position in the internal hierarchy, which was determined by myriad factors such as ethnicity, nationality, profession, political beliefs, language, age, and time of arrival in the camp.[84] The specific hierarchies differed from camp to camp, and they shifted over time, as new prisoners arrived or SS priorities changed. And yet, there were some certainties. Skilled workers generally stood above unskilled ones; Jews largely found themselves at the base and Germans at the top; and experienced inmates held an advantage, since seniority translated into know-how and connections, both of which were crucial for cheating death.

Veteran prisoners had some respect for one another, because they knew what it meant to survive, and the "old hands," as they were known, also shared a certain distrust of newcomers. In Auschwitz, Rudolf Vrba recalled, there was a kind of "mafia of the establishment," and in other KL, too, veterans had the edge.[85] The difference from newcomers was visible to all, with experienced prisoners wearing lower numbers and cleaner uniforms.[86] One could even tell them apart in the dark of the barracks at night, as they used peculiar words and phrases—the language of the camps.[87]

Mastering this idiom was essential for survival. Nothing was more important for new arrivals than to learn some basic German, the language of the SS and hence the language of power. Orders were generally given in German, from *"Antreten!"* ("Line up!") and *"Mützen ab!"* ("Caps off!") at roll call to all the exhortations to pick up the pace: *"Schneller!" "Los!" "Tempo!" "Aber Dalli!"* Prisoners also had to answer in German whenever they reported: *"Häftling 12969 meldet sich zur Stelle."* Even when prisoners talked in their native tongue, they used German terms for certain objects, tasks, and spaces.[88] Primo Levi knew that the rudimentary German he had picked up as a student was invaluable: "Knowing German meant life." To improve his chances of survival, he took German lessons from a fellow prisoner, paying him with bread: "I believe that never was bread better spent."[89] Those who understood the language of the camp could hope to become old hands themselves, while incomprehension cast prisoners adrift and exposed them to punishment; it was not for nothing that inmates in Mauthausen referred to the truncheons wielded by Kapos as *Dolmetscher* (translators).[90]

In addition to their peculiar vocabulary, the veterans used a different tone—sharp, coarse, and cruel.[91] Occasionally, they adopted euphemistic SS terms when it came to death and murder, such as "departure," "finish off," and "going through the chimney." But most words left nothing to the imagination. "Shit faster, slut," Kapos shouted at women in the Auschwitz latrine, "or I'll kill you and throw you in the shit." There was no place for decorum. Among the many common terms of abuse among the prisoners, the Czech inmate Drahomír Bárta noted in his Ebensee diary in summer 1944, were "swine" and "shithead."[92]

This vulgar tone reflected the prisoners' debasement, but it also offered an outlet for fears and frustrations. Dark jokes had a similar function, with sarcasm and gallows humor becoming typical traits of KL veterans. "The discovery of this humor," David Rousset wrote later, "enabled many of us to survive."[93] Humor was a defense mechanism that distanced prisoners—however briefly—from the horror of the KL. Nothing was off-limits, neither the food (in Sachsenhausen, a disgusting herring paste was known as "cat shit"), the SS humiliations (in Dachau, a strip shaved across the prisoners' closely cropped hair was known as a "lice motorway"), nor death itself (in Buchenwald, prisoners joked about the shape of the clouds coming from the crematorium). There were plenty of jokes about fellow prisoners, as well, not least the new arrivals. Those who expected that they would soon be released were goaded by more experienced prisoners: "The first fifteen years are the hardest. Then a man gets used to it." In this way, the old hands bolstered their status as hard-bitten veterans, standing above the newcomers, who still had everything to learn about the camps.[94]

After surviving for several years in Auschwitz, following his arrival on the first mass transport in June 1940, Wiesław Kielar (prisoner number 290) was one of these longtimers. Through his contacts to other Polish veterans, he had access to vital goods and extra food, including occasional treats like sausage and ham. When he contracted typhus, he received medicine from friends, and when the SS selected him because he was sick, his experience and connections saved him from the gas chambers. Like other veterans, Kielar escaped the worst labor details; stationed in the infirmary, he was barely working at all by 1943, having perfected the life-saving skill of dodging labor. His fear of daily violence diminished, too, as other Kapos were careful not to tangle with long-time prisoners like him who might have powerful friends; even a few SS men showed respect. Nonetheless, Kielar could never feel secure. He knew that everything he had gained—through chance, cunning, and sacrifice—could be lost from one day to the next. And this day came in November 1944, when Kielar was deported to the Neuengamme satellite camp Porta Westfalica. Privileged prisoners like him dreaded such transfers, because they often fell back down the pecking order; now they were the newcomers who found themselves at the mercy of privileged prisoners.[95]

The prisoner elite sometimes seemed to live in a world apart. Ordinary prisoners had no respite from the daily struggle for survival. Privileged prisoners, by contrast, enjoyed the luxury of leisure. Though limited and regulated, their activities still promised to carry them to a different place, transcending the camp.[96] Among the diversions permitted by the SS was sports, with male prisoners, in particular, participating in a range of activities.[97] Soccer was especially popular, as it was in Nazi ghettos like Theresienstadt, with regular matches between national teams being played in several KL, often on Sundays. Or the privileged few might watch a boxing contest between prisoners, who were rewarded for their efforts with food. Though these spectacles were intended as entertainment for the prisoner elite and SS men, who liked to place bets, some inmates saw something subversive in them, not least when a foreigner sent a German to the canvas.[98]

The SS also sanctioned some cultural activities of privileged prisoners. On Sundays, they could attend concerts by camp orchestras, listening to a varied repertoire from opera to popular music.[99] More solitary pleasures included the reading of books from KL libraries, which grew during the war. "The camp library is superb! Especially in the field of classical literature," the Dutch writer and left-wing journalist Nico Rost noted in his Dachau diary in summer 1944.[100] In several camps, the SS even put on feature films. Some prisoners briefly lost themselves in the drama and romance up on the screen, but terror and death were never far away. In Buchenwald, the hall used as a cinema doubled as a torture chamber, while films in Birkenau were shown near the crematoria complex; returning to his barrack one night, after watching an operetta, Wiesław Kielar passed a large group of Jewish men, women, and children on their way to the gas chamber.[101]

Most incongruous of all were the handful of marriages of well-connected inmates, like that celebrated in Auschwitz on March 18, 1944, when the Austrian Communist Rudolf Friemel wed his bride, who visited from Vienna with their small son. Following the civil ceremony in town and the reception in an SS barrack, the couple walked through the main camp toward the brothel, where they spent their wedding night. The other prisoners talked about little else, well aware that Auschwitz registry officials were normally concerned not with marriage certificates but with death notices—including that of Rudolf Friemel, who was hanged in late December 1944 after a failed escape attempt.[102]

At first glance, the sight of KL prisoners at leisure seems extraordinary. But it was in keeping with the SS vision of the concentration camps. After all, the Camp SS had always maintained traces of normality, and just like fragrant flower beds, a prisoner library projected an orderly image to visitors and staff alike. More pressingly, the SS wanted to win the compliance of selected prisoners through incentives, offering benefits in return for obedience. In turn, the leisure activities added to the already stupendous inequalities between victims of Nazi terror. Few sights capture this gulf more starkly than that of athletic soccer players in bright outfits and studded boots fighting for the ball, while emaciated prisoners in tattered rags nearby fought for their lives.[103] The worlds of the privileged and the doomed often collided, as they did on Sunday, July 9, 1944, in Ebensee. That afternoon, Drahomír Bárta performed his usual Kapo duties as an interpreter, and translated between an escaped Polish prisoner, who begged for mercy, and his captors. After Bárta witnessed the prisoner being beaten by the SS and maimed by a dog, he passed the rest of this day, as he sometimes did on Sundays, by playing volleyball with friends.[104]

KAPOS

Just as the figure of the *Muselmann* is taken to symbolize the destruction of prisoners' bodies, the figure of the Kapo often stands for the corrosion of their souls. Their image as henchmen emerged from many testimonies of fellow inmates who survived the KL. Describing the role of Kapos in Auschwitz, the Hungarian Jew Irena Rosenwasser simply said: "they knew they were on top, because they could beat and kill and send to the gas."[105] The influence of prisoner functionaries did indeed increase dramatically during

World War II. As staff shortages became more acute—with the ratio between SS and prisoners falling from below 1:2 in the late 1930s to around 1:15 by mid-1943—the authorities appointed more prisoners as supervisors and clerks.[106] This was true above all in the new satellite camps, where veteran inmates were indispensable to the largely inexperienced SS staff; the first Auschwitz camp elder, Bruno Brodniewicz, widely regarded by other inmates as a vengeful tyrant, later served as camp elder in the satellites Neu-Dachs, Eintracht-hütte, and Bismarckhütte.[107] Prisoners knew that the status and privileges attached to Kapo positions could prolong their lives—in Ebensee, prisoner functionaries were almost ten times more likely to survive than ordinary inmates—and few turned down such posts when they came their way.[108] The greatest beneficiaries were Germans like Brodniewicz, who occupied many of the coveted posts. To the mass of regular prisoners, they seemed like a breed apart: they were "the demigods of the camp."[109] This description captures the sense of awe felt by other inmates, but it also makes clear that Kapos were not untouchable. The SS men were still the supreme beings and could push anyone from the pantheon without notice.

Power and Privilege

The rise of Kapos during the war seemed unstoppable. Block elders held ever more sway, as SS inspections became less frequent (owing to lack of staff and fear of disease), and the influence of labor supervisors grew, too; as early as 1941, the inmate appointed as chief overseer on the Auschwitz IG Farben building site had more than a dozen Kapos under him, who in turn directed between fifty and one hundred prisoners each.[110] Kapos also performed a range of new functions, gaining access to almost all areas of the KL. As the internal SS organization grew more complex, and paperwork mounted up, additional inmates were drafted into administrative positions. In the orderly room, the statistical nerve center of the main camps, Kapos collated data about inmate numbers and composition, and supervised the assignment of prisoners to barracks. In the political office, too, prisoners were entrusted with clerical duties, from registering new inmates to typing SS correspondence. And in the labor action office, Kapos compiled reports about output and, most crucially, helped to allocate prisoners to labor details and satellite camps.[111]

Many of the new Kapo duties were about coercion and terror, particularly in the second half of the war. When it came to corporal punishment, the SS now relied on block elders and other functionaries to whip fellow prisoners, for a small reward of money or cigarettes.[112] In addition, the SS established Kapo squads, particularly in the larger KL, to extend the surveillance of prisoners by prisoners. Widely known as the camp police, their main function was the maintenance of "order and discipline," in the words of a former Buchenwald squad member. In practice, this meant patrolling the compounds, initiating new inmates, and guarding food depots against prisoner thefts, often with force.[113]

Some Kapos, both male and female, were directly involved in mass murder, selecting weak and sick inmates, escorting condemned prisoners to execution sites, or killing them. Emil Mahl, the senior Kapo in the Dachau crematorium, helped to hang up to one thousand prisoners in 1944–45. "My participation consisted of putting the noose around the necks of the prisoners," he later admitted.[114] It was also not uncommon for Kapos to receive open or thinly veiled instructions to murder certain prisoners on the sly. And Kapos murdered on their own initiative, too, acting far more brutally than before the war. Even pleas from desperate inmates—for food, clothing, or admission to the infirmary—could trigger lethal responses, as in the case of a Polish Jew who asked for bread during a deportation to a Flossenbürg satellite camp in early 1945, only to be beaten to death by a German Kapo.[115]

Such were the powers accumulated by some Kapos that even their SS masters became a little uneasy. In general, any concerns were far outweighed by the expected benefits: here was an easy and effective mechanism for ruling more camps with fewer SS staff. But there was a risk that dominant prisoners would scheme against SS officials and gain too many insights into their criminal and corrupt practices. The KL authorities responded by replacing suspect Kapos with other inmates (or even SS officials), and punishing them with the bunker or worse.[116]

With greater powers came greater privileges. It was easy to spot the Kapos, and not just because of the insignia or colored armbands that signaled their position. The more senior they were, the more they stood out—especially in camps for men, where social differences were particularly pronounced. These Kapos often sported longer hair, instead of shaven heads, and wore clean clothes, complete with leather shoes or boots. Not for them the rags worn by others. Some senior Kapos had their prisoner uniforms altered, wore civilian outfits stolen from SS depots, or ordered made-to-measure suits in the tailors' workshops. "They are better dressed," wrote David Rousset, "and consequently a little more like human beings."[117]

Kapos looked more vigorous, too, the "only healthy people in the camp," as another survivor put it in 1945.[118] They were largely exempt from exhausting manual labor and less exposed to disease. Kapos also often slept separately, sharing an enclosure near the barrack entrance or their own special barrack. For the time being, they had escaped the disease-infected quarters where prisoners were crammed on bunks and straw sacks. They slept in clean beds surrounded by precious reminders of civilization—vases, flowers, curtains—and ate from neatly laid tables laden with food.[119]

Kapos often enriched themselves through corruption and theft. They took from the rations and parcels of others, and from the SS storehouses. "Well, so much stuff came with the Jews, and we filched from it, of course we did," the Auschwitz Kapo Jupp Windeck said after the war, adding that "as Kapos, we always got ourselves the best."[120] Blackmail and profiteering were rampant, as Kapos turned the misery of others to their own advantage. When the starving Haim Kalvo approached his work supervisor in an Auschwitz satellite camp for extra food in November 1943, some six months after his arrival on a deportation train with almost 4,500 Greek Jews, the Kapo promised him a few loaves of bread in return for a gold tooth. The innkeeper from Salonika was so desperate that he offered a golden crown still in his jaw, whereupon the Kapo "took some pliers and, after we had walked aside, pulled out the golden tooth," as Kalvo explained a few days later to the SS, who had got wind of the deal (Kalvo apparently survived the KL).[121]

Sex was also largely the preserve of Kapos, and not only in the camp brothels. In the compounds, too, some of them used their power to get what they wanted. Men forced themselves on female prisoners, though the spatial separation between sexes made same-sex relations far more frequent. Most common were relationships between Kapos and young inmates, known as Pipel, who often submitted for pragmatic reasons, hoping for food, influence, and protection in return.[122] At the same time, sexual violence left deep scars and worse, as a few predatory Kapos tried to murder their victims to avoid detection. After the teenager Roman Frister was raped in his bunk by a Kapo one night in an Auschwitz satellite camp, he realized that his attacker had stolen his cap, without which Frister would face punishment during the next roll call; to save himself, Frister stole the cap of another prisoner, who was executed by the SS the following morning.[123]

Kapos were not shy about parading their power and privilege. Such demonstrative displays—one Mauthausen Kapo insisted on wearing white gloves as he strolled through the camp—reinforced their standing and put other prisoners into place. The disdain some of them felt for fellow inmates is summed up by the gesture of a German Kapo who, without thinking, cleaned his dirty hand on Primo Levi's shoulder.[124] At times, the Kapos' pride in their positions was palpable. For a man like Jupp Windeck, the appointment as Monowitz camp elder in autumn 1942 marked the climax of a staggering social rise. After a miserable life on the margins of German society, with long spells of unemployment and imprisonment for minor property offenses, this unskilled laborer now stood above thousands of inmates. He had been the lord of the manor, Windeck recalled fondly more than twenty years later, when he was tried for his crimes.[125]

The responses by the mass of ordinary prisoners varied. Some inmates ridiculed the powerful and their grand airs, though they normally tried to get out of the way of the most notorious Kapos like Windeck, literally clearing the path for them. There were also hangers-on, who hoped that toadying might elevate them, or at least help them to a few crumbs of food; this is why regular prisoners fought for the privilege of carrying the soup kettle for block orderlies.[126] The most common reaction, though, was envy and loathing, which provoked some Kapos to reaffirm their powers. "I have the authority," one Sachsenhausen Kapo warned his fellow prisoners every morning, "to smash each and every one of you."[127]

Judging a Kapo

It is easy to think of Karl Kapp as a typical Kapo. He had first become a supervisor in 1933, aged thirty-five, during a brief spell in Dachau after his arrest as a union activist and SPD city councilor, but his Kapo career really took off when he returned in 1936 as a recidivist political prisoner. Over the coming years, the trained butcher from Nuremberg, who spoke in the strong local dialect, rose steadily from block elder to labor supervisor (overseeing 1,500 prisoners) and finally to camp elder.[128] During his long spell as a Dachau Kapo, Kapp gained a reputation for severity. Slight but forceful, he was forever screaming at prisoners. He slapped and hit suspected shirkers or reported them to the SS, with potentially lethal consequences. What is more, he killed on command, participating in SS executions inside and outside the camp. The authorities rewarded him with privileges, and like a few other Kapos who had exceeded SS expectations, he finally walked away with the ultimate prize—freedom. Released and reunited with his family in 1944, Kapp spent the final year of World War II as a building contractor for the Ravensbrück SS.[129]

But Karl Kapp was not a typical Kapo, for there was no such thing. Some prisoners, it is true, conformed to the fearsome image of Kapos. They seemed to copy the SS, Margarete Buber-Neumann wrote about the most brutal and greedy supervisors in Ravensbrück, until they resembled them in all but uniform. But there were also their opposites, she added, kind women who made things better for their fellow inmates.[130] And although male Kapos resorted more frequently to violence than their female counterparts, there were decent ones among them, too, including some who refused on principle to lay hands on other prisoners; many more only turned strict when SS guards came near.[131]

Often Kapos struggled with their conscience as they were drawn deeper into SS schemes, suffering what the young Herzogenbusch prisoner David Koker described in his diary in November 1943 as a "moral hangover."[132] SS attempts to turn them into torturers and killers proved a watershed for many. In Dachau, not all Kapos submitted to the order, enforced by Kapp, to dish out corporal punishment. During a heated meeting among block elders, there were cheers for one Kapo who lambasted Kapp's stance and exclaimed that he would rather be beaten himself than hit a fellow prisoner. Like-minded Kapos, in Dachau and elsewhere, subverted SS orders by pretending to whip their victims much harder than they really did.[133] Others openly challenged the authorities. In July 1943, the camp elder in the Dachau satellite camp Allach, the Communist Karl Wagner, refused outright to hit another inmate; he was whipped twenty-five times and thrown into the bunker for several weeks.[134]

Karl Kapp's role in SS executions was particularly controversial among Dachau prisoners and earned him the lasting contempt of several senior Kapos, though when they confronted him, he just shrugged and walked off.[135] Unlike Kapp, some Kapos stood up to the SS: they would not kill. When the Dora SS told the two camp elders, Georg Thomas and Ludwig Szymczak, to hang a Russian inmate on the roll call square, they defied the orders. Furious SS men ripped the Kapo armbands off their uniforms and dragged them away; neither man survived the war.[136] As for Kapos who did succumb to extreme SS pressure—threatened that they would be executed, too, if they did not act as henchmen—not all shrugged off their deeds in the manner of Kapp. In Buchenwald, a Communist Kapo hanged himself after he had been forced to kill another prisoner, unable to bear the guilt.[137]

Even a man like Kapp was a more complex figure than he appears at first sight. There were rational reasons for Kapos like him to do as they were told. In the first place, it was a simple case of self-preservation, as the Camp SS did not think twice about demoting and punishing those who appeared too lenient.[138] The loss of their Kapo positions meant not only the loss of vital privileges, it could also expose them to the wrath of their fellow inmates. Their victims often fantasized about turning the tables and, if they got the chance, exacted revenge. The SS saw such vigilante justice as a bonus, as it forced Kapos into greater compliance. As Heinrich Himmler explained to Nazi generals in 1944: "As soon as we are not satisfied with [a Kapo], he is no longer a Kapo, he sleeps again with his men. He knows that they will beat him to death in the first night."[139] In this way, some Kapos became trapped in a vicious circle. Once other inmates saw them as willing tools of the SS, they felt that they had little choice but to redouble their abuses, lest they lose the life-saving protection of the SS.[140]

But Karl Kapp had his eyes on more than his own survival, and used his powers to aid some fellow prisoners. As camp elder, he allowed prisoners to smuggle food into the penal company and helped some inmates gain better positions.[141] There were limits to what he could do, of course, and his efforts probably involved an element of self-interest, as they created a circle of grateful allies.[142] Nonetheless, Kapp's favoritism was wide-ranging, extending as it did to prisoners from other backgrounds. At great risk, he saved several prisoners he did not personally know and whose political views he did not share.[143]

And like many senior Kapos, Kapp firmly believed that any of his abuses prevented worse. Interrogated after the war, he insisted that he had only ever reported prisoners to the SS as a last resort, if their actions threatened the collective; in all other cases, he had made sure to hand out penalties himself. And what some inmates saw as mindless brutality, Kapp added, had actually been calculated efforts to keep the SS at bay. If he had not enforced strict order during regular barrack inspections, murderous SS block leaders would have descended on the prisoners instead. If he had not hit individuals who were late for roll call, the SS would have made all inmates suffer. If he had not kicked lazy prisoners, the SS would have tortured them and punished the rest of the labor detail, too.[144]

Karl Kapp arrived at a jarring conclusion: to prevent SS abuses he had to play the part of the SS himself.[145] This view was shared by many ordinary prisoners. They agreed that Kapo attacks were the lesser evil, drawing away the attentions of the SS, and they applauded Kapos who punished suspected thieves and traitors.[146] "With his screaming, Kapp kept away the thugs," a pastor who survived Dachau later said. Even some of Kapp's victims defended him. Paul Hussarek, whom Kapp had hit on the neck for talking during the march to roll call, was certain that he had been saved from a far worse fate at the hands of the SS. "I am still grateful to Kapp for this punch," he said years later.[147] Many other survivors spoke up for Kapp, too, and even some of his detractors, who saw him as a bully, conceded that he had averted SS excesses.[148]

The actions of Karl Kapp were dissected in a Munich courtroom in 1960, where he stood accused of murder. In the end, the court found Kapp innocent of all charges. Far from being a willing tool of the SS, the judges declared, he had been loyal to fellow prisoners, protecting them heroically.[149] This was an unduly clear-cut verdict, given the complexities of his case. The judges imposed moral certitude on actions fraught with ambiguity and gave an emphatic reply to a question—"Was Kapp a good man or not?"—that defies an easy answer. After all, had Kapp not reported fellow inmates to the SS? Had he not helped to whip and hang innocent prisoners?

Even those who would have condemned Karl Kapp, however, should remember that he had not made a free choice. He was a victim of Nazi terror, too, trapped for almost nine years inside the KL.[150] The same was true of other prisoners in positions of power. Some of the cruelest Kapos had gone through hell at the hands of the SS. When a prisoner confronted a female Kapo in Auschwitz for beating an inmate who was old enough to be her mother, the woman replied: "My mother was gassed, too. It is all the same to me."[151] The daily exposure to the camps left indelible marks, and so did the corruption by power, as Kapos rose through the ranks; any veteran who retained moral integrity seemed like a saint to other prisoners.[152] This is not to excuse every act, however violent; after all, Kapos had some degree of agency. Nonetheless, even the worst Kapo was still a prisoner, hoping to survive a day at a time. In this respect, at least, all inmates were alike: none of them knew whether they would still be alive the next day.[153]

Hierarchies

The Kapo class was no less stratified than the prisoner population as a whole. There was a vast difference between a mighty figure like Karl Kapp and a lowly inmate in the block service who had to wait on his seniors, shining their boots, cooking their food, and making their beds. Even among Kapos, then, there were masters and servants, leading to a brutal struggle, as David Rousset wrote, to "rise step by step in the hierarchy."[154] Those who made it to the top were known as the notables. It was they who held the senior positions in the orderly room, the labor action office, and the political office, as well as the infirmaries, kitchens, and clothes depots; some prominent block elders and labor supervisors were also among them.[155] These notables were powerful and small in number; few prisoners held Kapo positions, and even fewer gained prominence. In February 1945, for example, at a time when the Mauthausen main camp held some twelve thousand men (excluding the compound for the sick), there were just 184 Kapos senior enough to wear a wristwatch, one of the perks enjoyed by notables; tellingly, 134 of them were German.[156]

As we have seen, the Camp SS pursued a strategy of elevating Germans over foreigners, mirroring social relations across Nazi-occupied Europe. Although the proportion of Germans fell to well below twenty percent of the KL prisoner population in 1944, the top Kapo positions were largely put into the hands of Germans.[157] SS practice was influenced by Nazi racial thinking.[158] Himmler often talked of a sense of loyalty toward "members of our own blood," and even though German prisoners were seen as scum, Camp SS leaders believed that their own countrymen should rise above the flotsam of other nations.[159]

Such preferential treatment was guided not just by dogma, however, but by pragmatism, as well. The fact that German prisoners shared the captors' native tongue was crucial; theirs was the official language of the KL—of documents, signs, and orders—and the SS demanded to be understood. Experience was equally important. The SS was looking for prisoners who knew the KL, and almost all the most seasoned inmates were German.[160] As the demand for Kapos rose during the war, the Camp SS sometimes put such practical considerations above ideological principles and promoted Germans from the most despised prisoner groups to positions of influence. Men detained as homosexuals, for example, had often faced lethal SS violence during the first half of the war, peaking around the summer of 1942.[161] But while there were further murders later on, a growing number of prisoners with the pink triangle now served as clerks, block elders, and labor supervisors; in Bergen-Belsen, a German homosexual was even appointed as camp elder in late 1944, overseeing the compound for regular protective custody prisoners.[162]

Middle and lower-ranking positions often went to prisoners from other nations, and foreign Kapos grew in number and standing as the war continued. In the occupied east, there were never enough German inmates to fill all available positions, so many of these posts went to Poles instead.[163] Elsewhere, too, the SS relied on foreigners, especially during the second half of the war. Prisoners from almost all European countries were promoted, though their prospects varied from camp to camp, depending on the size of national prisoner groups and the time of their arrival. In Ravensbrück, large transports from Poland had come as early as 1940, and Polish women gradually became entrenched in lower and middling Kapo positions, even pushing aside some German "asocials." French women, by contrast, did not arrive in large numbers until 1943–44, and consequently found themselves excluded from posts as block elders or camp police.[164]

As the Kapo class expanded, so did the number of Jews among them, though they were normally restricted to overseeing other Jewish prisoners only.[165] Initially, this development centered on Auschwitz and Majdanek, following the mass deportations to both camps; according to survivors, around half of the Auschwitz-Birkenau block elders in early 1944 were Jews.[166] The number of Kapos with the yellow star increased elsewhere, too, as Jews were forced into new KL in eastern Europe, like in the Baltic region, and into satellite camps inside Germany. In satellites largely reserved for Jewish prisoners, individual Jews were deployed as labor supervisors, doctors, clerks, and block elders, and exceptionally even as camp elders. Some of them were already well versed in negotiating the gray zone between fellow inmates and German rulers, having previously held influential positions in ghettos, where Jewish Councils had been given significant responsibilities for the administration of everyday life.[167]

There was no job security for Kapos, of course, not at the top and even less so lower down, where there were frequent promotions, transfers, and dismissals. Among the greatest powers senior Kapos had was that of anointing others. Officially, appointments were made by the Camp SS. In practice, SS staff were often swayed by experienced Kapos, especially when it came to middling and lower positions. In this way, the notables shaped the composition of the wider Kapo class, creating networks of prisoners bound by patronage and loyalty.[168] This was yet another case of "groupness." Political prisoners, for example, often did their best to reserve Kapo positions for fellow sympathizers. Likewise, foreign Kapos pushed their own countrymen forward; in Ravensbrück, many Polish Kapos owed their posts to Helena Korewina, the influential translator of the SS camp supervisor.[169] The competition over Kapo positions once more pitted different prisoner groups against one another. The battles were fought at all levels, but they were most visible at the top of the prisoner order, and often appeared to pit two groups of German inmates against each other: political prisoners, with the red triangle, and so-called criminals, wearing the green triangle.

Red and Green

When Benedikt Kautsky looked back in 1945 at his seven years as a Jewish Socialist in Dachau, Buchenwald, and Auschwitz, he found harsh words for many of his fellow inmates. But he reserved his greatest condemnation for the "green" Kapos, with their "hideous brutality and insatiable greed." Kautsky pictured them as more animal than human. As serious and incorrigible offenders, he claimed, they had made perfect partners in crime for the SS, who turned them into their most devoted executioners. Wherever the "greens" gained the leading Kapo positions, he reported, the results had been catastrophic, engulfing camps in treason, torture, blackmail, sexual abuse, and murder. The "greens" were the "pestilence of the camps." Only political prisoners, who pursued the good of all decent inmates, could stand up to them. The ensuing struggle for supremacy between the upright "reds" and the wicked "greens," Kautsky concluded, had been a matter of life and death for the other inmates.[170]

Kautsky spoke for many survivors, especially former political prisoners like himself.[171] In their testimonies, they often described the "greens" as deadly threats, who had been unhinged criminals long before entering the KL. According to one German Communist, also writing in 1945, the Nazis had rounded up "thousands of crooks, killers, and so on" after their capture of power, and then filled almost all Kapo positions with these degenerates for whom murder was just a hobby.[172] The same devastating picture of "green" Kapos has been painted over and over again, and has become a fixture in popular works on the KL. But it is no more than a caricature. To be sure, like most caricatures, it draws on some truths. German ex-convicts did gain some leading Kapo positions, especially in camps for men, and a number of them committed hideous crimes inside; Kapo nicknames like "Bloody Alois" and "Ivan the Terrible" speak for themselves.[173] But the sins of some have led to the slander of all.

Contrary to the convictions of so many political prisoners, only a few "greens" had been sent to the KL as violent criminals. Even an observer as astute as Primo Levi was wrong to believe that the Nazis had specially selected hardened criminals in prisons to deploy them as Kapos.[174] In fact, most of those detained in the prewar KL had committed minor property crimes, as we have seen, not brutal excesses. And this did not change during the war. Convicted rapists and murderers did not normally end up in concentration camps, but in state prisons, either locked in dark cells, or led to the gallows or guillotine.[175] The mass of "green" KL inmates were still small-time offenders, if they were guilty of any crimes at all. The reputation of these men and women as savage convicts owed less to their criminal record than the dark fantasies of their fellow inmates, in whose imagination petty criminals mutated into serial murderers.[176] Wild rumors became fact, as the violence of some Kapos was explained by their imagined homicidal past.

The truth was often different, even in the case of some of the most infamous "greens." Take the case of Bruno Frohnecke, a vicious Kapo. Detained since 1941 as a professional criminal, Frohnecke became the scourge of a large Auschwitz construction detail. He abused fellow prisoners at every turn, hitting them with his fist, clubs, and sticks, and kicking them in the abdomen and genitals. "All I can say is that I have never met anyone like him," a survivor told the German police in 1946. "He was not a thug; he was a murderer, in the true sense of the word." But before he had fallen into SS hands, Frohnecke had shown no particular propensity for brutality. He had been an inept conman, not a killer, and had been caught again and again for small scams. Frohnecke, in short, was no natural-born killer: he only became a violent criminal inside the KL.[177] What is more, while Frohnecke's background was typical for "green" Kapos, the same cannot be said for his actions in the camps, as some other "greens" acted in a comradely fashion and took great risks to save fellow inmates, including Jews, from certain death.[178]

The case of the first thirty Kapos in Auschwitz is instructive here. In the literature, these men have sometimes been held up as typical "green" criminals.[179] A closer look reveals a more complex story. Though they were all "green" veterans from Sachsenhausen, and enjoyed many privileges in Auschwitz, not all of them abused their powers. Some did become brutal murderers, like the former safecracker Bernhard Bonitz (prisoner number 6). During his first year or so as a block elder, he is said to have strangled at least fifty Auschwitz prisoners, by throwing his victims to the ground, pressing a stick across their neck, and standing on both ends. He later continued his crimes as the first chief Kapo of the construction commando on the IG Farben site, lording it over some 1,200 prisoners.[180] Several of his "green" Auschwitz colleagues, however, conducted themselves very differently. They shunned Bonitz and other notorious Kapos "because of their behavior toward the prisoners," in the words of Jonny Lechenich (prisoner number 19). Once they even confronted Bonitz directly; he was a prisoner, too, they told him, and should treat his men more humanely. Lechenich himself became active in the camps' underground organization and later fled with two Polish prisoners, joining the Home Army.[181] He was not the only one to make common cause with his charges. Otto Küsel (prisoner number 2), the Kapo in the Auschwitz labor action office, was widely known as decent, and eventually escaped in late 1942 with three Poles, rather than betray their plans to the SS. After nine months on the run, Küsel was rearrested; brought back to Auschwitz, he was tortured for several months in the bunker.[182]

More generally, brutal "greens" like Bernhard Bonitz had no monopoly on violence. Jewish prisoners, for example, were often outraged when they suffered at the hands of others wearing the yellow triangle: "Aren't you a Jew, like us?" Avram Kajzer challenged a Gross-Rosen supervisor, who punched him in reply.[183] The focus on the "greens" has rather obscured the uncomfortable truth that Kapos from all backgrounds colluded with the SS and committed cruel excesses.

Neither did the Camp SS habitually favor "greens" over "reds." Political prisoners had filled positions of authority since the birth of the KL, and this continued during the war. Important clerical posts largely went to politicals, for example, who were more likely to possess the requisite administrative skills, and "reds" also gained other influential positions, above all in Buchenwald, where German Communists held all key posts by 1943.[184]

The pragmatic approach of the Camp SS inflamed tensions between Germans wearing the red and the green triangles.[185] In Dachau, the "reds," who held the upper hand, helped to condemn "greens" to hard labor and human experiments, and restricted their medical treatment. One former prisoner recalled that when he sought treatment for edema in the infirmary, "red" Kapos beat him away, screaming: "Piss off, green swine!" Dachau political prisoners defended their actions as payback for the abuses some of them had suffered at the hands of "greens" in Flossenbürg, early in the war. These Flossenbürg "greens," in turn, had justified their attacks as revenge for even earlier abuses by politicals back in Dachau.[186] The spiral of violence seemed unstoppable, escalating the enmity between the two prisoner groups.

However, the significance of these battles for dominance has been exaggerated. Generally, the outcome only mattered to the small number of prisoners who stood to benefit. "Red" Kapos primarily fought for their own groups.[187] Likewise, most benefits gained by "green" Kapos went to their confidants, excluding many others with a green triangle, even though they often shared the same barrack.[188] All considered, it is likely that a larger number of prisoners benefited when the "reds" were on top.[189] But this was, at best, a matter of degree, as the "groupness" practiced by senior Kapos with "red" and "green" triangles often made it difficult for the mass of ordinary inmates to tell them apart. German political prisoners, a Polish survivor of Auschwitz wrote in 1946, differed "in nothing" from the "greens" and were just as hated by the rest of the inmates.[190]

Wherever possible, the Camp SS encouraged conflicts over Kapo posts, which were fought with equal ferocity by prisoner groups lower down the order.[191] The aim, according to Heinrich Himmler, was to "play off one nation against the other," by putting a French Kapo in charge of Polish prisoners, or a Polish Kapo in charge of Russians. In the same way, the SS sometimes pitted German "reds" and "greens" against each other, to prevent any single group from gaining supremacy and to increase their dependence on the SS.[192]

Some prisoners had different ideas. In autumn 1942, the WVHA sent eighteen Sachsenhausen Communists—almost all of them senior "red" Kapos, including the camp elder Harry Naujoks—to Flossenbürg, because of "seditious activities." Officially, these notables were supposed to be deployed for hard labor there, but the SS must have expected the dominant "green" Kapos in Flossenbürg to drive them to their deaths. Instead, the so-called criminals aided their survival, much to the surprise of the Communist prisoners themselves.[193] Elsewhere, too, prisoners occasionally joined forces. In Buchenwald, for example, a key made by a "green" picklock gave "red" Kapos access to secret documents in an SS safe.[194] More often, though, prisoners did turn against each other. As Karl Adolf Gross concluded in despair in his Dachau diary on June 9, 1944: "How easy it is for our mutual enemies to play the different colors off against each other!"[195]

Inside Infirmaries

The moral ambiguities of being a Kapo were felt most acutely, perhaps, by inmates serving in infirmaries. As the war continued, the Camp SS drafted in more and more prisoners as clerks, nurses, and doctors. Few posts offered greater scope for helping or harming other captives. Exhausted inmates besieged the KL infirmaries on most mornings, but Kapos normally only admitted those whom they expected to quickly recover. "For those I had to reject," one Dora prisoner doctor wrote after the war, "this was usually a death sentence."[196] These doctors also participated in lethal selections, and since they were better qualified than most SS physicians and knew the patients better, their word carried weight.[197] After assisting in his first selection in Auschwitz, Dr. Elie Cohen, a Dutch Jew, broke down; he later took part in further selections, though his sense of shame never left him.[198] Some medical Kapos even gave deadly injections and participated in human experiments, as we saw in the case of Dr. Mengele's assistant Miklós Nyiszli.[199] In fact, almost all experiments required the help of prisoners. In Dachau, well over a dozen Kapos worked on Dr. Rascher's gruesome trials, checking the equipment, making records, conducting autopsies, and selecting some of the victims.[200]

The primary reason for becoming "part of the system," as one prisoner doctor put it, was the same as for other Kapos—survival. Despite the risk of infection, infirmaries were among the safest places of work for KL prisoners, above all for Jews. It was no coincidence that the death rates among trained doctors remained unusually low. "We were so terribly protected," wrote Dr. Cohen, "we really lived a life apart."[201] As so often in the KL, survival came at a heavy price: propping up SS terror. A few months after his arrival with other Slovak Jews in April 1942, Ján Weis became a male nurse in the Auschwitz main camp infirmary. One day in autumn 1942, he had to assist an SS orderly in the routine murder of sick prisoners. As one of the doomed inmates entered, Weis was horror-stricken to see his own father. Afraid for his own life, he said nothing; he watched as the SS orderly gave "father the injection and [then] I carried him, my father, away."[202]

Each day, Kapos had to make dreadful decisions in the infirmaries. Because resources were scarce, saving some inmates meant sacrificing others. "Should I rather help a mother with many children," the Auschwitz prisoner doctor Ella Lingens-Reiner asked herself, "or a young girl, who still had her life in front of her?"[203] Some Kapos made their choice on purely medical grounds. During SS selections, they tried to protect stronger prisoners by condemning weaker ones who might not survive much longer anyway.[204] Other factors came to the fore, too, including the Kapos' national background and political affinity. Take Helmut Thiemann, whom we encountered earlier, a committed Communist imprisoned in Buchenwald between 1938 and 1945. Justifying himself in an internal KPD document written immediately after the war, he argued that he had participated in the SS murder of other prisoners, in order to keep his position in the infirmary and protect Communists. "Because our comrades were worth more than all the others, we had to go along with the SS to a degree, in regard to the extermination of the incurably sick and invalids."[205]

Many other medical Kapos made equally fateful judgments about the worth of individual prisoners. As the senior Kapo in Dr. Rascher's Dachau station, Walter Neff effected "victim swaps" to save some men he regarded as deserving. In place of priests, for example, he put forward alleged pedophiles and other "lowlifes" (as he called them) for the trials. Such practices were contentious among the wider prisoner population, however, not least because some death sentences pronounced by Kapos were based on nothing more than rumor or personal antipathy.[206] In view of their immense powers, it is hardly surprising that some medical Kapos lost their moral bearings.[207]

By contrast, other Kapos in KL infirmaries still saw themselves as healers. Dramatic improvements were beyond them, of course. But fighting against the odds and their own exhaustion—in the Birkenau women's camp, one prisoner doctor cared for seven hundred patients in the winter of 1943–44—they did save lives, drawing on their medical skills, bravery, and ingenuity.[208] They helped to bring down epidemic infections through strict regimens of disinfection, and protected some prisoners from selections by hiding them inside the infirmaries.[209]

One extraordinary rescue was that of young Luigi Ferri, who arrived in Auschwitz with his grandmother on June 3, 1944, on a small transport of Jews from Italy. The SS initially overlooked Luigi and the eleven-year-old boy found himself alone in the Birkenau quarantine camp. SS men would have killed him within hours, no doubt, had he not come to the attention of the prisoner doctor Otto Wolken, a resourceful Jewish physician from Vienna. In tears, Luigi told his story, pleading for help. Dr. Wolken risked his life to protect the boy, whom he soon called his "camp son." Despite repeated SS orders to hand the boy over, Wolken hid him in different barracks for over two months, helped by some confidants. Then, in mid-August 1944, Wolken bribed a Kapo in the political office to have Luigi officially registered. Although the boy could now move more freely around the camp, Wolken still had to protect him, hiding him during selections and letting him sleep in the safety of the infirmary. When Soviet troops reached Auschwitz in late January 1945, both Wolken and Luigi were among the small number of survivors.[210]

DEFIANCE

Defiance is rare in totalitarian regimes, and the KL probably provided the most barren grounds for its growth. During the war, the obstacles were almost insurmountable. Most prisoners were too exhausted to contemplate fundamental opposition to the SS. Meanwhile, those more privileged prisoners who could afford to think beyond their immediate survival had the least incentive for insubordination, because they stood to lose the most. Conflicts between inmate groups further undermined the scope for concerted action, and there was little hope for sustained moral or material support from the outside, either. Given the might of the SS, which tried to crush any seeds of protest, violent confrontations seemed senseless and suicidal. "Resistance is out of the question," Janusz Pogonowski wrote in Auschwitz in summer 1942. "Even the smallest infraction of the camp rules has dreadful consequences."[211] Their inability to take the fight to the SS only increased the inmates' sense of paralysis. They were soldiers "condemned to an unarmed martyrdom," a Polish prisoner exclaimed during a secret memorial service for a dead comrade in Mauthausen.[212] And yet, individual prisoners in every KL challenged the SS, at extraordinary risk. Although most of their acts have been lost to history, some have endured in the perpetrator files and the memories of survivors.

The Prisoner Underground

According to some survivor accounts, political prisoners formed powerful clandestine organizations based on international solidarity, which fought the Camp SS at every turn, saving inmates and sabotaging the war effort. Such depictions feed our craving for heroics by strong and unbowed prisoners, but they appear rather rose-tinted, in light of the huge barriers to opposition in the KL.[213] To be sure, a few prisoners from different nations tried to work together, especially later in the war. However, their efforts inevitably remained limited; in Dachau, for example, a truly international inmate committee only emerged right at the end of the war. Organized opposition was restricted in size and scope, and even at its most daring, it only benefited a small number of prisoners. Many others did not even know that there was an underground movement in their camp.[214]

Among the most audacious acts of organized opposition was the rescue of individual inmates from certain death, by hiding them or giving them false identities. Such operations were dangerous and complicated, as we saw in the case of young Luigi Ferri.[215] And under the laws of the camp, the rescue of one prisoner sometimes condemned another. In Buchenwald, German Communists helped to protect hundreds of children until the end of the war. Among them was the toddler Stefan Jerzy Zweig, barely three feet tall, whom they adopted as a symbol of innocent life (at the age of four, he would become the youngest survivor of the camp). When the boy's name appeared on a transport list to Auschwitz, Communist Kapos managed to get it struck off. But the transport could not leave one prisoner short, so a Gypsy called Willy Blum was chosen to take Stefan's place. The sixteen-year-old boy left Buchenwald on September 25, 1944, and later died in Auschwitz.[216]

The achievements and limits of collective defiance come into sharper focus still when looking at arguably the most spectacular KL rescue mission, also in Buchenwald. In summer 1944, the Paris Gestapo had dispatched a special transport to the camp. On board were thirty-seven Allied agents, among them hardened resistance fighters from France, as well as spies from Belgium, Britain, the United States, and Canada. When it became clear that these men faced execution, a few veteran Buchenwald inmates hatched an ingenious plan. Claiming that typhus had broken out in the agents' barrack, the rescuers spirited away three prominent men—Stéphane Hessel (a French officer working for General de Gaulle), Edward Yeo-Thomas (one of the most intrepid British secret agents, code-named "White Rabbit"), and Henri Peulevé (another longtime British spy)—to the first floor of block 46, the isolation ward for prisoners with typhus, which was closed off from the rest of the camp by barbed wire. Here, they waited for some sick patients to succumb to the disease, so that the identities of the dead and the hidden spies could be switched. After several tense weeks, all three agents finally had their new names. "Thanks to your care, everything has come out all right," Hessel wrote on October 21, 1944, in a secret note to Eugen Kogon, the German medical clerk who had masterminded their rescue. "My feelings are those of a man who has been saved in the nick of time. What relief!" To prevent the three foreigners from being recognized in Buchenwald, other Kapos quickly dispatched them to satellite camps.

This high-wire act could have failed at any moment. It required enormous courage and quick thinking by several powerful Buchenwald Kapos, working together despite personal antipathies and political differences. They tricked SS officers, forged records, stole documents, hid the agents, and even injected one of them with milk to simulate high fever. The risks paid off: all three agents survived. However, an operation such as this pushed organized resistance to the edge and had to remain the exception. The other thirty-four Allied agents who had arrived in Buchenwald together with Hessel, Yeo-Thomas, and Peulevé were all shot or hanged in September and October 1944. As Eugen Kogon wrote, "there simply was no possibility of rescue under the prevailing circumstances."[217]

While the obstacles in the way of rescue often proved insurmountable, it was easier for underground movements to collect evidence about Camp SS crimes. The clandestine groups in Auschwitz, led by Polish soldiers and nationalists, were particularly successful in this respect, after they established links to the Polish resistance outside; extraordinarily, one of the inmates involved, Lieutenant Witold Pilecki, had let himself be arrested by the German authorities, under a false name, to join the prisoner underground in the camps. Using their outside contacts, the Polish prisoners smuggled important material out of Auschwitz, including maps and statistics, as well as reports on SS perpetrators, executions, medical experiments, living conditions, and mass killings. The conspirators even got their hands on SS documents, such as transport lists. "You should make full use of the two original lists of people who were gassed," Stanisław Kłodziński wrote on November 21, 1943, from the camp to a contact in the Polish resistance: "You might send them to London as originals."[218]

To gather material about the Nazi Final Solution, the prisoner underground in Auschwitz needed the help of Special Squad members, who witnessed the daily mass murder close-up. Getting evidence out of the strictly guarded zone of death around the crematoria meant "risking the life of the entire group," one of them, Salmen Lewental, wrote in 1944; but he felt compelled to tell the world about the Nazi crimes "because without us nobody will know what happened, and when."[219] The most daring operation came in late August 1944, when one Special Squad prisoner, helped by others, documented the murder of Lodz Jews with a hidden camera. Concealed inside the gas chamber of Birkenau crematorium V, he photographed the burning of corpses in pits outside; later, he stepped in the open air to capture other victims who had undressed among the trees; four of the images have survived, smuggled out of Auschwitz within days, and they remain some of the most poignant testaments of the Holocaust.[220]

Like other acts of prisoner defiance, the efforts to document KL crimes were extremely courageous. After all, prisoners knew that the SS was hunting everyone engaged in subversive activites. In fact, SS officers even conjured up plots where none existed. "He saw a seditious act of sabotage in every triviality," an SS man from the Auschwitz political office later said about his former boss, Maximilian Grabner.[221] Often, the SS alarm was raised by denunciations from fellow prisoners, as local commandants built up a network of informants (acting on WVHA instructions); the Sachsenhausen SS alone is said to have used almost three hundred "stoolies."[222] Suspects were dragged to the bunkers and tormented by SS men from the political office. And although the evidence they gathered was often negligible, they demanded extreme punishment; when the Dora SS got wind in autumn 1944 of an alleged plot to blow up the tunnel, it tortured hundreds of innocent prisoners and eventually executed over 150 Soviets, as well as some German Kapos, among them four former Communist camp elders.[223]

The authorities were equally uncompromising when it came to suspected sabotage, another SS obsession. Sanctions were swift and severe, even for harmless acts. A joke could cost a prisoner's life, as could purely symbolic acts; in Dora, the SS once strung up a Russian prisoner for allegedly urinating into the body of a V2 rocket.[224] The SS even twisted acts of desperation into sabotage, executing prisoners for using parts of their bedsheet as gloves or socks.[225] In this way, most prisoners were forced into submission. Although they generally hated working for the enemy, there was no widespread obstruction in the KL. "I would have never committed sabotage," a former inmate summed up the feelings of many, "because I wanted to survive."[226]

Insubordination and Escapes

Direct challenges to the SS were madness, most veteran prisoners agreed. It was dangerous enough to charm, bribe, or trick SS officials, but to defy them directly could only lead to disaster. After a Flossenbürg prisoner was beaten senseless during an evening roll call for insulting the SS, Alfred Hübsch wondered what had possessed this "lunatic" to swim against the tide. "Everyone here must have learned a long time ago that any resistance will be broken!"[227] Inevitably, acts of open defiance remained very rare during World War II. When they did occur, they burned themselves deep into the memories of survivors.

Some newcomers stood up to the SS because they did not yet understand the KL.[228] When thirty-nine-year-old Josef Gaschler from Munich was taken to Sachsenhausen, in the early months of the war, and saw SS men punch other new arrivals in the face, he shouted: "What on earth is going on here? Have we fallen among thieves or do you still claim to be cultivated people?" The SS men answered him with feet and fists, dragged him to the penal company, and killed him (the official death certificate stated that he died of "insanity and raving madness").[229] Such assaults were enough to persuade most new prisoners to fall into line. Still, even veterans defied the SS on occasion. Some simply snapped; overwhelmed by despair, grief, or anger, they temporarily lost all self-control.[230] Others were guided by moral or religious convictions. A hard core among the Jehovah's Witnesses, for example, remained firm in their refusal to carry out any work related to the German war effort. The SS fury about their obstinacy, which reached all the way to Himmler, hit these prisoners hard and several lost their lives.[231] These brutal SS responses ensured that prisoner strikes remained exceedingly rare.[232]

One of the most deadly demonstrations of SS resolve came in spring 1944 in the Flossenbürg satellite camp Mülsen St. Micheln, set up a few months earlier in a disused textile plant near Zwickau. Its inmates worked on fighter plane engines on the main floor of the building, and slept in a crowded cellar below. The men never left the factory. Conditions were particularly poor for the hundreds of starving Soviets, who made up the majority of the prisoner population. On the night of May 1, 1944, some of them, delirious with hunger, set alight straw mattresses in the basement, perhaps hoping that this would allow them to flee. SS men made sure that there would be no way out of the inferno. They locked the prisoners inside, shot at those trying to escape, and prevented the local fire brigade from entering. "The smoke was rife with the stench of burning bodies. I could see nothing at all and I struggled for air," one prisoner recalled, who survived by clinging for hours to the bars of a cellar window, with flames scorching his body. When the fire finally died down, around two hundred men lay dead and many more were badly burned. But the SS was not finished yet. Over the following months, it executed dozens of Soviets who had survived the blaze. The message was clear: open defiance would be met with absolute terror.[233]

Given the futility of physical resistance, a couple of bold inmates submitted written protests to the SS instead. In March 1943, several Polish women, who had been mutilated during human experiments, petitioned the Ravensbrück commandant. In their letter, they challenged him to justify the carnage caused by the operations: "We are asking you to grant us a meeting in person or to send us an answer." Predictably, Commandant Suhren never replied. But the women did not give in. When the SS tried to continue the experiments, a few months later, the intended victims hid in their barrack, sheltered by fellow prisoners. "We decided among ourselves that it would be better if they would shoot us," one of them later testified, "rather than have them cut us up all the time." Once again, though, the SS imposed its will. The so-called rabbits were dragged to the bunker, and several were operated on; the other rebels were locked into their barrack for days without food or fresh air.[234]

With open challenges all but impossible, some prisoners came to see escape as their only chance to cheat death. During his imprisonment in Auschwitz, Stanisław Frączysty had a recurring dream, during which he turned into a small animal and slid with ease through the fence around the camp, leaving it and all its horror behind.[235] Escape was on the minds of many inmates, and not just when they were asleep. In the end, though, only a few—mostly men—took the risk of fleeing, though figures were growing during the final years of the Second World War.[236] The number of runaways from the Mauthausen camp complex, for example, rose from 11 (1942) to more than 226 (1944). In the Buchenwald complex, meanwhile, the SS reported the flight of 110 prisoners during a particularly turbulent two-week period in September 1944—though with over eighty-two thousand prisoners held there at the time, this was still an infinitesimal proportion of the inmate population.[237]

The rise in escapes reflects the changes in the KL system during the war. While it remained very hard to abscond from the established main camps—not a single prisoner seems to have managed to flee from Neuengamme until April 1945—the chances of success stood higher in hastily erected and poorly secured satellite camps.[238] The proliferation of prisoner transports also offered greater opportunities for escape, as did the lack of veteran SS guards. As a Polish prisoner explained, after successfully absconding in July 1944, the staff shortages had "caused me constantly to think of escape."[239]

The circumstances of escapes varied greatly. Some prisoners used force, drugging, beating, or killing guards to clear their way.[240] More commonly, they relied on deception, climbing into trucks that left the camp or hiding in safe places until the SS called off its search. Disguises worked, too, with several prisoners dressing up as SS officials. One such escape unfolded in June

1942 in Auschwitz. Sneaking past the guards, four Polish prisoners broke into the SS storerooms, grabbed uniforms and weapons, and then drove off in a limousine. When they were flagged down at a checkpoint, the ringleader, dressed as an Oberscharführer, leaned out of the window and gesticulated impatiently at sentries at the barrier, which was quickly lifted. "A few minutes later, we were driving through the city of Oświęcim," one of the conspirators recalled. After camp compound leader Hans Aumeier found out how his men had been duped, he "went almost crazy, tearing out his hair," according to the Auschwitz underground leader Witold Pilecki.[241]

The ultimate success of escapes depended on many variables, with luck the most important ingredient, followed by outside connections. Once prisoners had left the immediate vicinity of the KL, they needed support, and quickly. In occupied Europe, some fugitives received shelter from members of the resistance, and often joined the underground themselves; following his own escape from Auschwitz, Witold Pilecki fought during the doomed Warsaw Uprising of 1944. Other escapees remained in hiding until the end of the war. After he fled from Monowitz in summer 1944, helped by his girlfriend and a German civilian contractor, Bully Schott changed into regular clothes and traveled on a packed night train toward his hometown, Berlin. Here he survived, as one of a few thousand Jews hiding in the German capital, with the help of old friends, who moved him to different safe houses and provided him with false papers.[242]

A few runaways even crossed enemy lines. Among them was Pavel Stenkin. One of the few survivors of an attempted mass escape of Soviet POWs from Auschwitz-Birkenau in November 1942, he rejoined the Red Army and triumphantly entered Berlin as a liberator in 1945.[243] Another was a Polish lieutenant by the name of Marcinek. Carrying forged papers, a pistol, and an SS uniform, he traveled by train and car from Berlin to the front line in Normandy, where he crossed over to the Allies on July 19, 1944, under heavy artillery fire. A German called Schreck, who accompanied Marcinek, had meticulously prepared their escape. To the surprise of the British troops, Schreck was no prisoner but a Sachsenhausen SS man; entangled in a corruption affair, he preferred Allied captivity to punishment by the SS.[244]

Escapes always prompted manhunts by the Nazi authorities, and although it is impossible to establish how many prisoners managed to evade the clutches of SS and police, the odds were stacked against them, at least until the final months of the war. Take the following example of 471 men and women who fled from the Auschwitz complex between 1940 and 1945. In all, 144 stayed on the run and mostly survived the war. But 327 were arrested and delivered back to the camp, where they faced draconian punishment.[245]

SS Responses

Despite the low number of successful KL escapes, Heinrich Himmler was concerned. Anxious about the safety of the German public, he ordered his men in 1943 to use any means necessary to stem the flow, from planting land mines to training dogs that tore prisoners to pieces. To turn up the pressure, he also insisted that every KL had to inform him personally about escapes.[246] Fearing Himmler's wrath, Richard Glücks—who anxiously asked his managers in the T-Building each morning if any prisoners had run away—made the fight against escapes a priority.[247] His WVHA office exhorted the local Camp SS "never to trust a prisoner" and tightened up procedures.[248] Although official regulations for sentries required them to shout "stop" before discharging their weapons, an internal Camp SS manual instructed guards to shoot without warning.[249] Superiors praised vigilant men who had foiled escapes, awarding furloughs and other bonuses, while they issued threats against negligent ones.[250] The SS had a message for the prisoners, too: anyone who tried to escape would face a terrible fate.

Deterrence was the most important element in the Camp SS fight against escapes. Some recaptured prisoners were maimed by dogs, as Himmler had hoped; afterward, the SS displayed the mangled corpses on the roll call square.[251] More often, the unfortunates were dragged back alive. First the SS tortured them, to find out who had helped them and how they had beaten the defenses.[252] Then they were publicly humiliated, followed by the punishment proper. Some prisoners got away with fifty lashes or transfer to the penal company (apparently, the SS showed such "leniency" to inmates who had run away on impulse).[253] Many more paid with their lives.

Some local SS men took matters into their own hands.[254] At other times, the recaptured inmates were executed in line with official protocol, after commandants applied for, and received, permission to kill from their superiors.[255] Starting in 1942, Camp SS officials carried out numerous such ritualized hangings of condemned prisoners, which resembled the first KL execution, of Emil Bargatzky in summer 1938. The killing of the Austrian prisoner Hans Bonarewitz is a case in point. Bonarewitz had escaped from Mauthausen around noon on June 22, 1942, hidden inside a crate on a lorry. Recaptured some days later, he faced a torturous death. For a week, he was paraded in front of the other prisoners, together with his wooden crate; on it, the SS had written mocking words like Goethe's saying "Why stray far away, when everything good is right here." Then, on July 30, 1942, the SS forced Bonarewitz on the cart used for taking corpses to the crematorium. Some prisoners slowly pulled it toward the gallows on the roll call square, while the others stood to attention. The procession, which lasted more than one hour, was led by a prisoner acting as master of ceremonies, and by around ten inmates from the camp orchestra, who played songs such as the children's classic "All the little birds are back." Along the way, an SS man took photographs, documenting Bonarewitz's final moments. At the gallows, the SS whipped and tortured him, and finally had him hanged; the rope broke twice before he died, accompanied by music from the orchestra.[256]

Prisoner reactions to public hangings—sometimes sarcastically called "German cultural evenings"—varied.[257] Some quietly swore revenge or yelled in protest.[258] Others were unmoved, blaming the executed inmates for the collective SS abuse that often followed escapes. The most common reaction, perhaps, was dread. One former Mauthausen inmate recalled that after the execution of two recaptured German prisoners, one of them so badly wounded he had to be carried to the gallows, he quickly lost any urge to flee himself: "The spectacle has worked: better to kick the bucket in the quarry than to go to the gallows!"[259]

Public executions were not the only SS means of deterrence. Occasionally, the authorities took family members of escaped inmates as hostages to the KL.[260] The Camp SS also punished fellow prisoners in place of escaped ones. From early on, there were torturous roll calls, beatings, and other abuses. Later on, the SS resorted to murder, as well. Following the escape of a Polish inmate in spring 1941, the Auschwitz SS starved ten others to death in the bunker. A few months later, following a further escape, the SS punished another group of prisoners in the same way. To save one of these doomed men, the Franciscan priest Maksymilian Kolbe stepped forward to die in his stead. The SS accepted his sacrifice, but after he had survived for more than two weeks, its patience ran out; Kolbe was administered a lethal injection.[261] Collective executions soon became a regular form of deterrence, in Auschwitz and some other KL. Among the many victims was Janusz Pogonowski, the young Polish prisoner who had remained in touch with his family by secret letters. He was one of twelve prisoners hanged in Auschwitz on the evening of July 19, 1943, in front of rows of other inmates, following the escape of three colleagues from his labor commando.[262]

The SS policy of collective punishment showed some effect, as prisoners thought twice about running away. And they had mixed feelings about the escapes of others. On the one hand, such escapes could boost prisoner morale, as every SS setback did, and offered hope that the world would learn about their fate.[263] On the other hand, inmates dreaded the terror that often followed.[264] The SS was well aware that many prisoners saw escapees as traitors against the community, and sometimes exploited their anger, as in the case of the waiter Alfred Wittig, a "green" prisoner in Sachsenhausen. One afternoon in summer 1940, Wittig went missing. While the SS searched the camp, all prisoners had to stand to attention, deep into the night. When the SS finally dismissed them from the roll call square, several had collapsed. The search for Wittig resumed the following morning and after he was discovered—hidden under a pile of sand—an SS official delivered him to the other prisoners: "Do with him what you want." Seething about their suffering the previous night, dozens of them trampled Wittig to death. For once, the cause of death was recorded accurately on the official paperwork, because the SS had not been directly involved: "Injury to lung and other internal organs (beaten to death by fellow prisoners)."[265]

Resistance by the Doomed

Mala Zimetbaum and Edek Galiński became lovers in Auschwitz, sometime in the second half of World War II. Theirs was one of the few relationships to blossom in the KL, and it has since become a symbol of hope and tragedy in the camps, commemorated in books, films, and a graphic novel.[266] Both were veterans of Auschwitz. Zimetbaum, a Polish Jew, was deported from Belgium in September 1942, while Galiński had arrived more than two years earlier, on the first transport of Polish political prisoners. Over time, both gained privileged posts that allowed them to rendezvous in the X-ray room of the infirmary in the Birkenau women's compound. They often talked about running away together, and after careful planning, they risked everything on the afternoon of Saturday, June 24, 1944. Dressed in stolen SS uniforms, they left the camp, each on their own, and strolled into town, as if they were SS staff on weekend leave. After they were reunited on the banks of the Vistula, they tried to make it to Slovakia. But after they had spent two weeks on the run, exhausted and lost in the Carpathian Mountains, border guards caught them. When they returned to Auschwitz, the SS threw them into the bunker— Galiński's inscriptions on the walls are still legible today—and condemned them to die.

But the day of their execution, September 15, 1944, did not proceed as the SS had planned. Edek Galiński was marched along rows of prisoners in one of the Birkenau compounds for men and led up to the scaffold. Before the SS could read out his sentence, however, Galiński tried to hang himself. Held back by officials, he shouted a rallying cry as the executioner pulled the floor from under his feet. Over in the Birkenau women's compound, Mala Zimetbaum also defied the SS. As she was escorted to the gallows on the roll call square, she produced a razor blade and cut her wrist. When an SS man tried to stop her, she hit him. Stunned officials dragged her away, and she was last seen, more dead than alive, on a cart near the crematorium. Zimetbaum lived on in the memory of the other prisoners. Not only had she escaped from Auschwitz, she had confronted her tormentors, shattering the carefully staged SS spectacle. "For the first time we saw a Jewish prisoner raise h[er] hand against a German," a young survivor later said with admiration.[267]

Defiance by the doomed was unusual, but it was not unprecedented. To stop condemned prisoners like Edek and Mala from addressing the others, SS officials sometimes gagged them before public executions.[268] But the perpetrators knew that executions could still unite the other inmates in their loathing of the SS. This was one reason, no doubt, why most Camp SS murders took place in secret. But even behind closed doors, some prisoners resisted, attacking their killers, or shouting political slogans before they died. SS men tried to laugh off such incidents, but they must have been unsettled, because they had failed to break their victims.[269]

There was defiance at the Birkenau gas chambers, too. Some prisoners—Jews, Gypsies, and others—fought back as the SS pushed them inside, though such desperate resistance was in vain. Others sang political songs or religious hymns on their way to the gas.[270] One of the most celebrated acts occurred on October 23, 1943, when, outside the Birkenau gas chambers, a Jewish prisoner wrestled a gun from the SS and shot at the guards, amid a general commotion. Unterscharführer Josef Schillinger was fatally wounded and another official seriously injured before SS men regained control and slaughtered the inmates; one guard was later commended for helping to "stifle the rebellion" through "determined action." The sensational news of Schillinger's death quickly reached other parts of the camp, and there were many rumors about what, exactly, had happened. In the most popular telling, the killer was a striking young woman, a dancer. As for Schillinger, the word among prisoners was that, as he lay dying, he had whimpered: "O God, my God, what have I done to deserve such suffering." These final words may have sprung from revenge fantasies, but the subsequent SS rage was all too real; at night, guards fired machine guns into the Birkenau camp compound, mowing down more than a dozen prisoners. Of course, these deaths barely registered among the Auschwitz SS, which had long become used to mass murder on a far bigger scale.[271]

An Uprising in Auschwitz

It was just after lunchtime on Saturday, October 7, 1944, a bright autumn day under a cloudless sky, when a small group of SS men entered the yard outside crematorium IV in Auschwitz-Birkenau and ordered some three hundred

Special Squad prisoners to line up. The SS announced a selection, supposedly for transfer to another camp, and began to pick out some men. Not all of them came forward, however, and the situation grew tense. Suddenly, one of the oldest prisoners, the Polish Jew Chaim Neuhoff, lunged forward and attacked an SS man with a hammer. Others joined in. Wielding stones, axes, and iron bars, they forced the SS behind the compound's barbed wire. The air in Birkenau filled with screams, shots, and the sound of sirens, and also with smoke—not from burning bodies, as usual, but from the crematorium building itself, which the prisoners had set ablaze. The uprising of the Birkenau Special Squad had begun.[272]

This moment had been coming for months. "For a long time, we, the 'Special Squad,' wanted to put a stop to our terrible work," Salmen Gradowski wrote in Birkenau in autumn 1944. "We wanted to do something big."[273] There had been talk of an uprising back in spring 1944, probably in connection with the imminent liquidation of the Birkenau family camp (which occurred in March), but in the end nothing came of it. Still, the conspirators started to collect arms, including hand grenades, filled with explosives stolen by female prisoners at the nearby Union armaments works and smuggled into the Special Squad. The clamor for armed action became more persistent from midsummer 1944. Special Squad prisoners thought that most of them would be surplus to SS requirements, once the mass gassings of Hungarian Jews had ended. Given the advance of the Red Army, it also seemed likely that Auschwitz would be evacuated, and the prisoners feared that the SS would execute them before leaving; after all, they bore the darkest secrets of the Nazi Final Solution (similar fears had triggered the uprisings in Treblinka and Sobibor the previous year). The men of the Birkenau Special Squad lived in heightened anticipation, but so volatile was their position that the plan for action had to be repeatedly postponed. Soon, the situation gained even greater urgency. On September 23, 1944, the SS selected two hundred Special Squad members, allegedly for transport to a different KL. The others learned the truth the following day, when they found the charred remains of their comrades in the crematorium. When the SS announced in early October that another selection would follow within days, the prisoners at crematorium IV suspected that this would be their death sentence. They would have to move now or never.[274]

But the Birkenau rebels were poorly prepared. They could not count on the prisoner underground elsewhere in the camp to join them, after these groups had concluded that a violent confrontation with the SS could only end in a massacre. There was an insoluble conflict of interest between Special Squad prisoners, who had nothing to lose, and most other inmates, who hoped to see out the final months. "Unlike us, they did not have to hurry,"

Salmen Lewental noted bitterly in autumn 1944.[275] In fact, the Special Squad itself was divided over the issue of armed action; some prisoners were too exhausted, others wanted to wait for a more opportune moment, when the whole camp would rise up with them. Among those who counseled caution were the main leaders of the Special Squad, who did not face immediate selection on October 7, 1944, and decided against participating in the uprising. Not only were the remaining rebels isolated, they were badly organized. There had been no time to make proper plans, and confusion mired the revolt from the start. Once crematorium IV was on fire, the prisoners could not reach their grenades hidden inside; the strongest weapons were left unused, buried under the collapsing roof of the building.[276]

The uprising was doomed from the outset. Within minutes, SS reinforcements arrived at crematorium IV to shoot at the exposed prisoners, easy to pick out in the bright daylight. One survivor peered into the yard of the compound and saw scores of his comrades "lying very still in their blood-stained prison uniforms," with SS men firing at anyone who still stirred. By then, most of the remaining prisoners had run across the path to the adjacent crematorium V, hiding inside. SS guards soon dragged them out, threw them on the floor, together with other recaptured inmates, and shot many of them in the back of the neck. When the SS had finished, more than 250 corpses covered the grounds of the two crematoria.[277]

Meanwhile, around thirty minutes after Chaim Neuhoff had struck the first blow at crematorium IV, a second uprising broke out at crematorium II. The Special Squad prisoners there had heard the shots fired nearby and seen smoke rising. Following the instructions of their leaders, they initially remained calm. When some SS men came marching toward their compound, however, a group of Soviet POWs panicked and pushed a German Kapo into the burning furnace. The other Special Squad prisoners at crematorium II now had to join them, whether they wanted to or not, and armed themselves with knives and hand grenades. After they cut a hole in the fence surrounding their compound, up to one hundred prisoners escaped. But the SS hunted them all down; some got as far as the small town of Rajsko, a couple of miles away, hiding in a shed until the SS surrounded it and burned it to the ground.

The reprisals were not over yet. Over the coming weeks, the SS executed most survivors of the uprising, among them Lejb Langfus, who was murdered after the last Special Squad selection on November 26, 1944. Just before, he had written a final note: "We are sure that they will lead us to our deaths." Among the other victims were four female prisoners who had smuggled explosives into Birkenau. One of them, Estusia Wajcblum, sent a last letter to her sister from the bunker, after weeks of SS torture: "Those outside of my window still have hope, but I have nothing . . . everything is lost and I so want to live."[278]

In contrast to the revolts at Sobibor and Treblinka, where several hundred prisoners had evaded their pursuers, not a single Special Squad prisoner got away. This was due to the greater SS presence around Auschwitz and the elaborate security arrangements, which had been strengthened earlier that year to thwart an uprising. Within a few hours of the revolt, the SS had slaughtered more than two-thirds of the estimated 660 Birkenau Special Squad members (the SS itself lost three men, who were mourned as heroes). Only those Special Squad prisoners stationed at crematorium III, who did not rise up, were left unscathed and carried on with their duties as if nothing had happened.[279]

Neither did the uprising interrupt the mass extermination of Jews in Birkenau. The burned-down crematorium IV had been out of commission since May 1943, and the Camp SS continued to use its other facilities, gassing an estimated forty thousand men, women, and children after the uprising, in a lethal spurt lasting little more than two weeks. Among the dead were thousands of Jews from Theresienstadt. Although the SS preserved the ghetto to the very end, it deported most inhabitants to Auschwitz in autumn 1944, where the majority were murdered on arrival. The last Theresienstadt transport came on October 30; of the 2,038 men, women, and children on board, the SS sent 1,689 straight to their deaths, in what may have been the last mass gassing in the history of the camp.[280]

The Birkenau uprising throws a light on the terrible dilemma of violent opposition in the KL. Prisoners knew that a revolt would most likely result in their own deaths. Few were willing to take this risk. In general, only those who knew that they were about to be murdered were ready to fight; this was the courage of the doomed in the face of certain death. "We have given up hope that we'll live until the moment of liberation," Salmen Gradowski wrote, not long before his death during the uprising of October 7, 1944.[281] By contrast, inmates who still had hopes of survival, however small, shied away from suicidal rebellions. This was why the main underground groups in Auschwitz decided against joining the armed revolt in autumn 1944, leaving the Special Squad feeling abandoned and alone.[282]

The uprising remains a powerful symbol of prisoner defiance, and much of our knowledge of the events comes directly from survivors of the Special Squad. When the SS abandoned the Auschwitz camp complex in mid-January 1945, some one hundred Special Squad prisoners were among the tens of thousands forced westward. Somehow, almost all of them—including Shlomo

Dragon and his brother Abraham, and Filip Müller—survived until liberation.[283] Such good fortune was the exception, however. The final months of the KL system were among the most lethal, bringing death to several hundred thousand registered prisoners. The closer these men, women, and children came to freedom, the more likely they were to die in the concentration camps.

11

Death or Freedom

On Sunday, February 25, 1945, Odd Nansen followed his usual routine. Since his deportation to Sachsenhausen as a political prisoner almost one and a half years earlier, the forty-three-year-old Norwegian had visited the camp's infirmary on most weekends. Usually he came to help fellow countrymen, but this time he headed straight for one of the youngest patients, a ten-year-old Jewish boy called Tommy, who had been born in Czechoslovakia in 1934, after his parents' emigration from Germany. Tommy was all alone. Separated from his mother and father in Auschwitz in 1944, he had only recently arrived in Sachsenhausen. Nansen had first met him in the infirmary on February 18 and was greatly touched, wondering how a child who had witnessed unimaginable suffering could still be so sweet-natured. Looking at Tommy that day, with his large eyes and his infectious smile, Nansen felt as if an angel had descended into the depths of Sachsenhausen. He desperately missed his own children in Norway and resolved to watch over Tommy, bribing the infirmary Kapo to save the boy from selections. When Nansen came back to visit the following week, on February 25, he brought rare treats like sardines. And as he sat beside the boy, Tommy told him about the evacuation of Auschwitz.

The Camp SS had forced Tommy out of the Auschwitz complex on January 18, 1945, with most of the remaining inmates. Staying close to two other boys from the Birkenau children's barrack, he had joined an endless procession of prisoners dragging themselves westward. Everything was covered in snow and ice, and the roads—littered with dead horses, burned vehicles, and mangled corpses—were submerged by waves of German soldiers and civilians fleeing from the Red Army. Tommy saw many prisoners perish along the way, and soon felt that he, too, would die.

After six months in Birkenau, Tommy was bone-thin, and the boots his mother had left him offered little protection against the winter. More than once, he thought about giving up. Still he pushed himself forward. After three interminable days, Tommy and the other survivors finally reached Gleiwitz, the German border town where Nazi forces had staged the phony attack by "Polish" troops that marked the beginning of World War II. Here they were forced onto open railcars. At first, Tommy was pressed so tightly against the adults that he could hardly breathe, but later death thinned their ranks. The creeping cold tormented Tommy's frozen feet. He had little to eat but snow, trying to imagine that it was ice cream. "And I cried terribly," he told Nansen. After more than ten days, the train arrived near Sachsenhausen. Tommy was soon taken to the main camp infirmary, where two of his toes, black with frostbite, were amputated. "Poor little Tommy, what will become of him?" Odd Nansen thought as he wrote down Tommy's story.[1]

The young boy was one of thousands of Auschwitz prisoners who entered Sachsenhausen in early 1945.[2] Other concentration camps inside the prewar German borders also filled with prisoners from abandoned KL nearer the front line. Faced with the relentless Allied advance, the SS closed camp after camp, forcing hundreds of thousands to leave on foot, trains, trucks, and horse-drawn carriages. The deadly treks led through what was left of Nazi-controlled Europe, sometimes winding over hundreds of miles.[3]

The KL system broke apart rapidly, just as it reached its zenith: climax and collapse went hand in hand. Despite some disruption by the war in 1944, which led the SS to close several main camps and dozens of satellites, its terror apparatus had still been going strong at the end of the year. On January 15, 1945, the eve of the evacuation of Auschwitz, the SS registered a record number of 714,211 KL prisoners in all.[4] Over the coming months, the remaining camps grew into behemoths, bursting with prisoners from evacuated sites, as well as newly arrested inmates. The prisoner population of the Mauthausen complex, for example, exceeded eighty thousand by late February 1945, over fifty thousand more than one year earlier.[5] Not only were the remaining camps inside Nazi Germany now at their largest, they were at their most lethal, too. Starvation and disease were rampant, and the SS went on a last killing spree as the Third Reich went down in flames.[6]

The morale of the prisoners inside was closely tied to the progress of the war, as it had been for years. News of major Allied victories, such as the land-ings in Italy (1943) and France (1944), had been greeted ecstatically, with prisoners smiling, whistling, even dancing.[7] But their hopes of swift libera-tion had been dashed again and again, leading many inmates to seek solace in fantastical rumors and in the stories of spiritualists and fortune-tellers, which flourished in the KL.[8] Only in early 1945 could the prisoners really be sure that the war would soon be over. The Allies were now unstoppable. In the east, Soviet troops penetrated deep into the Third Reich. In the west, the all-or-nothing offensive by the Wehrmacht in December, on which Nazi leaders had pinned their last hopes, quickly stalled, followed by a decisive push from the western Allies, who advanced steadily until they crossed the Rhine in early March 1945. On April 25, 1945, American and Soviet soldiers met on the Elbe, splitting the remnants of the Third Reich in half. The German sur-render came less than two weeks later, in the early hours of May 7, 1945.[9]

Life during the final months and weeks in concentration camps was un-bearably tense. As prisoners heard the detonations from the front come closer, they felt as if "on tenterhooks," one of them wrote in a secret note.[10] The KL resembled beehives, with swarms of inmates gathering to exchange the latest news. Their mood fluctuated wildly between hope and anguish. Some were sure that liberation would come at any moment. Others feared that the SS would execute them before the Allies arrived, or force them out. The prospect of leaving the camp terrified many prisoners, especially after they had wit-nessed the arrival of earlier death marches. But they were also scared of being left behind, especially if they were ill and weak, like little Tommy in Sachsen-hausen. "[If] this camp is evacuated—what then?" the boy asked Odd Nansen in late February 1945. "If I'm still lying here and can't run, what will they do with me?" When Nansen visited Tommy for the last time two weeks later, shortly before Norwegian prisoners like him departed from the camp, he feared that he would never see the boy again.[11]

It is impossible to say how many prisoners perished between January and early May 1945 during the evacuations and inside the KL. However, an esti-mate of forty percent dead—some three hundred thousand men, women, and children—is probably not wide of the mark. Never before had so many regis-tered prisoners died so quickly.[12] Perhaps some four hundred and fifty thousand prisoners came through the final catastrophe, with Jews, Soviets, and Poles making up the largest groups.[13] Most of these survivors were res-cued inside the KL, though some sites stood eerily empty by the time the Al-lies arrived. In the Sachsenhausen main camp, Soviet troops found no more than 3,400 prisoners on April 22–23, 1945, mostly in the abominable sick bays.[14] One of them was Tommy. After the boy limped out of his barrack, he saw Red Army soldiers moving through the big gate and shouting "Hitler kaputt, Hitler kaputt!" Ever since this moment, Thomas (Tommy) Buergenthal has reflected on the reasons for his survival against all odds. "If there is one word that captures the conclusion to which I always returned," he wrote decades later, "it is luck."[15]

THE BEGINNING OF THE END

When Soviet troops reached the Auschwitz main camp and Birkenau, at around three o'clock on the afternoon of January 27, 1945, the site looked nothing like it had just a few months earlier. The SS had dismantled or destroyed many buildings and set fire to the thirty barracks of Canada II, the huge compound storing the property of murdered Jews; the ruins were still smoldering as Soviet soldiers walked among them. Before SS officials had torched these warehouses, they sent some of the most valuable goods back toward central Germany. Building materials had been moved out, too, as had technical equipment like the X-ray machine used for sterilization experiments. The SS had demolished the Birkenau crematoria and gas chambers, as well, beginning in November 1944; crematorium V, the last operational one, was blown up shortly before liberation. Now the Birkenau "death factory" lay in ruins. As for the once overcrowded prisoner compounds, they were largely deserted. Less than five months earlier, in August 1944, over 135,000 prisoners had been held across the camp complex. By the time the Soviets liberated Auschwitz, there were just 7,500 left, mostly sick and weak prisoners abandoned during the final evacuation.[16] But the loss of Auschwitz was still a big blow for the SS, as the camp had been the jewel in its crown: a model for the collaboration with industry, an outpost for German settlements, and its principal death camp.

In recent times, the day of the liberation of Auschwitz has become the focal point for remembrance of the Holocaust.[17] Symbolic as the date is, however, January 27, 1945, marked neither the beginning nor the end of the camps' liberation. The end of suffering was still a long way off for most prisoners; if freedom came at all, it came weeks or months later, often after another round of death marches in April and May 1945. As for the beginning, the first phase of KL evacuations had occurred earlier, between spring and autumn 1944; and although it is widely forgotten today, it foreshadowed much of the horror that was to follow.

Early Evacuations

By early September 1944, the German army appeared to be on the brink of defeat on the Western Front, following the Allied advance after the D-day landings in June. The military situation seemed increasingly hopeless and the popular mood in Germany hit a new low.[18] Anticipating the loss of further territory, the WVHA now ordered the immediate evacuation of its two most westerly concentration camps. On September 5 and 6, 1944, the SS moved all 3,500 prisoners out of the Herzogenbusch main camp in the Netherlands; its small satellite camps were closed down, too.[19] Natzweiler in Alsace was evacuated around the same time. Almost all 6,000 prisoners were deported from the main camp to Dachau between September 2 and 19, 1944; the SS also abandoned around a dozen attached satellites on the left bank of the Rhine, moving out a further 4,500 prisoners. But the Natzweiler complex was not finished yet, as its satellite camps on the right bank of the Rhine continued to operate. In fact, after the German army temporarily stabilized its position, several new satellites were added, and by early January 1945, the camp complex held some 22,500 prisoners. With satellites now turning around an extinct main camp, Natzweiler encapsulated the fragmentation of the KL system toward the end.[20]

Despite their speed, the western European KL evacuations in autumn 1944 proceeded in a fairly orderly fashion. The WVHA closed the camps well before the Allies arrived, which left sufficient time to move the vast majority of prisoners by train, the preferred SS mode of transport. Not only was it easier to guard prisoners on trains, compared to marches, but journey times were much shorter, too. Exhausting as these transports were, they did not cause mass death. "Apart from terrible fatigue, we arrived [in Ravensbrück] in a pretty decent state," a former Herzogenbusch prisoner recalled. As a result, almost all inmates survived the early evacuations in the west.[21]

In the occupied east, events took a very different turn in 1944. Here, too, SS officials had anticipated the loss of camps and prepared for evacuations, hoping to deploy many of the prisoners elsewhere for the war effort. But these plans were often foiled by the size of the task—with five main camps and many dozens of satellites within reach of the Red Army—and the speed of the Soviet advance. Because German military resources were concentrated along the Western Front, the Red Army made dramatic breakthroughs, with the Wehrmacht suffering hundreds of thousands of casualties and losing huge swathes of land.[22]

In the General Government, the SS kept some control and took away most of its KL prisoners in time. WVHA officials prepared for the closure of Majdanek from late 1943 onward, moving many thousands of prisoners out over the coming months. Most others followed in April 1944, when some ten thousand inmates were transported in boxcars to other camps such as Auschwitz. When the SS finally abandoned the main camp on July 22, 1944, with the Red Army closing in fast, it already stood half-empty. The SS left a few hundred sick inmates behind and forced the others, some one thousand or more, westward by foot and train; they were joined by another nine thousand prisoners from the last Majdanek satellites, including the large camp at Warsaw (which had lost its main camp status).[23]

Some of the Majdanek prisoners were taken to Plaszow, the other main camp in the General Government. But it, too, was soon abandoned. Once again, the Camp SS began its preparations early. Prisoners returned from the satellites to the main camp, which was the departure point for deportations. In late July and early August 1944, the SS then dispatched trains packed with prisoners from Plaszow to Flossenbürg, Auschwitz, Mauthausen, and Gross-Rosen, reducing the inmate population from over twenty thousand to less than five thousand. Thousands more left Plaszow in October 1944, which also saw the closure of its last satellite camps. When the regional higher SS and police leader finally ordered the complete evacuation of the main camp on January 14, 1945, there were only some six hundred prisoners left inside.[24]

By this time, the SS had also abandoned all three KL complexes farther north in the Baltic territories—Riga, Kovno, and Vaivara—though these closures unfolded in a far more hectic manner. Riga was closed down between summer and autumn 1944, with the evacuation of the main camp lasting until October 11, shortly before Soviet troops entered the city. During this period, some ten thousand prisoners were driven onto ships heading out to open sea, a prospect they had dreaded for months. Crammed belowdecks for days, the inmates were soon covered in sweat, vomit, and excrement. On arrival in Danzig, the starving survivors were put on barges and taken along the Vistula toward Stutthof, which rapidly filled up with inmates from abandoned concentration camps.[25]

Among the inmates in Stutthof were thousands of Jewish KL prisoners from Kovno, which had been emptied even faster than Riga. All its dozen or so satellites were abandoned in July 1944, and so was the main camp. "Our fate is unknown. Our state of mind is terrible," wrote Shmuel Minzberg, one of the prisoners, just before the evacuation. In all, more than ten thousand Jews were forced out of the complex in little more than two weeks, mostly onto trains and boats; perhaps a quarter of them survived until the end of the war. Before the SS men left Kovno for good, they razed the main camp. Supported by Lithuanian helpers, they burned or blew up the houses, killing hundreds of Jews hiding in bunkers; others were shot as they fled the inferno. Only a few survivors emerged from the ruins after Soviet troops arrived on August 1, 1944.[26]

The evacuation of the far-flung KL Vaivara, the most northerly Baltic camp complex, was the most protracted, spanning seven months. During an initial wave of evacuations in February and March 1944, the SS hastily abandoned some ten sites, including the main camp; on February 3, for example, hundreds of prisoners were rushed out of the Soski satellite camp with the Red Army no more than a few miles away. Prisoners often had to march for days until they reached satellites farther west, where conditions were appalling; in Ereda, sick prisoners were dumped into barracks in the marshes. "About twenty persons died every day," one survivor testified a few months later, shortly before his own death. In mid-1944, the remaining inmates of the Vaivara complex faced a second wave of evacuations. As the Soviet summer offensive made swift headway, the front line was approaching once more. "All around us is noise, pilots are being shot at and do not relent, day or night. A lot of shrapnel over our heads," the Polish Jew Hershl Kruk wrote in the satellite camp Lagedi on August 29, 1944, adding: "What is our destiny, it is hard to tell." In the end, with Estonia virtually cut off from the rest of the German territory, the SS deported most Vaivara prisoners by boat toward Stutthof. After seven days at sea without food, one prisoner recalled, "we arrived in Danzig in terrible condition!"[27]

Murder in the Baltic

Sometime in late September 1944, Soviet troops reached Klooga, which had been the last operational Vaivara satellite camp. Inside were more than one hundred survivors, many of them in shock. "Are we free now? Are the Germans gone?" they asked incredulously. Some touched the red star on the soldiers' uniforms to make sure that they were not dreaming. Only a few days before, these prisoners had been destined to die. Early on September 19, 1944, with Soviet troops just a few days away, the SS had forced the inmates of Klooga—around two thousand men and women—onto the roll call square and split them into groups. Heavily armed SS men then took the first group toward the forest; soon after, the others heard bursts of machine gun fire. Panic spread among the remnant, who tried to flee. Most were slaughtered. Later that night, the SS departed from Klooga, illuminated by the fire of burning pyres and barracks, which had been torched to conceal the evidence of the crimes and to prevent Soviet troops from using the site; left behind were the few survivors who had managed to hide, sometimes among corpses scattered across the grounds and the nearby forest.[28]

This was not the only bloodbath in the Baltic region: one day earlier, several hundred prisoners of Lagedi, Hershl Kruk among them, were driven by truck to a forest clearing and executed.[29] Although such massacres remained unusual, they mark a fundamental difference from the simultaneous KL evacuations in western Europe: in the east, and especially in the Baltic territories, mass death was part of SS calculations from the beginning. The chaotic circumstances were an important factor here; in Klooga and Lagedi, SS men had felt cornered by the rapid Soviet advance and, rather than leave the prisoners behind, resorted to mass killing before escaping.[30] But these last-minute massacres had deeper roots in Nazi ideology. After all, the overwhelming majority of prisoners in the local KL were Jews, and their lives counted for little in the eyes of the SS, especially if they could no longer be exploited for forced labor.

Such murderous convictions had guided the Camp SS already during its preparation for evacuations in the Baltic area. In the months before the Red Army reached the different KL, local SS officials stepped up their selections of weak and sick prisoners: Why save inmates who had little value as slaves and would only be a burden during transports? Children were targeted on the same grounds, and over a frenzied few weeks in spring 1944, Camp SS men murdered several thousand boys and girls; in the Kovno main camp, the action was preceded by a children's party, organized as camouflage by the local commandant. The ensuing deportations were accompanied by dreadful scenes. Parents screamed and pleaded, as the SS dragged the children away. Some joined their children on the trucks, holding hands as they drove to their deaths; other families committed suicide before the SS could part them. Parents left behind were inconsolable. After Wilna prisoners returned from work to their satellite camp one evening in late March 1944, and found that the SS had deported the children, they "did not eat, did not drink and did not sleep," wrote Grigori Schur, who lost his son, Aron. "In pitch-darkness, the Jews cried for their children."[31]

SS murders in the Baltic region continued to the end. In the Riga complex, the last selections in summer 1944 were coordinated by the senior camp physician Dr. Eduard Krebsbach, an SS veteran who had first participated in the mass killing of invalids in 1941 in Mauthausen. Krebsbach and his helpers conducted trials of the prisoners' strength—forcing them to sprint and jump over obstacles—and then condemned the weakest two thousand to die.[32] The SS carried out similar crimes in other Baltic camps. During the "ten percent selections" in the Vaivara complex—as survivors dubbed them, referring to the proportion of prisoners selected to die—the perpetrators loaded the victims onto trucks in July 1944 and later returned with their SS uniforms splattered in blood.[33]

Prisoners who survived the selections and massacres in the Baltic KL headed away from the front line. Unlike the evacuations in the west, these poorly equipped and frenzied transports claimed many more lives in 1944. Hundreds of prisoners must have starved or suffocated on trains and ships.[34] Even worse were the marches across roads, fields, and frozen swamps, which killed several thousand more. The first deaths came as early as February and March 1944, when inmates of abandoned Vaivara satellites like Soski stumbled through the ice and snow; some froze to death, some were shot by panicking SS officials, some were thrown alive into lakes or the sea.[35] More death marches in eastern Europe followed in summer 1944, including one that left Warsaw on July 28, just days before the doomed uprising. Early that morning, the great majority of inmates—some four thousand or more men (almost all of them Jews)—hurriedly set off, surrounded by guard dogs, SS, and soldiers. The sun was beating down on the bedraggled men, some of whom were barefoot. Their mouths became so dry that they could barely swallow the little food they had left; prisoners licked the sweat off their faces, but this only made their thirst more intense. "We prayed to God for rain," Oskar Paserman recalled in 1945, "but none came." Soon the first prisoners broke down; those who lagged behind were shot. After marching some seventy-five miles, for more than twelve hours each day, the survivors reached Kutno, where they were crammed on a train. Just 3,863 prisoners were still alive when it pulled into Dachau five days later; at least eighty-nine men had perished inside the cattle trucks.[36]

The early KL evacuations have long been ignored, overshadowed by the larger death marches in the final months of the Third Reich. But they form an important part of the history of the KL, and contrary to the views of some historians, they anticipated the horrors still to come.[37] They often began with a preparatory phase. During this period, the Camp SS packed its property and loot, and oversaw the partial dismantling of barracks and other equipment. Just like retreating SS units elsewhere, it also tried to destroy the evidence of its crimes: bodies were dug up and burned (sometimes by a special SS unit), together with any incriminating documents. In addition, the authorities reduced the size of the prisoner population through transports or through systematic murders.[38] Then, when it came to the final abandonment of the camp, the SS forced most of the remaining prisoners out, using different means of transport. Much depended on the military situation. In the west, the SS had planned ahead and moved its prisoners by train. In the east, the SS was often caught out by Soviet advances and hastily marched its prisoners away, or tried to murder them all, as in Klooga. This was one reason why the early evacuations proved so much more deadly in the east; the closer the front line came to a KL, the greater the danger for those prisoners still left inside.[39]

The Last Autumn in the East

When twelve-year-old Inge Rotschild arrived with her parents in Stutthof, in the summer of 1944, she had already spent what seemed like an eternity in Nazi ghettos and camps. Deported as German Jews from Cologne to Riga in late 1941, Inge and her family had later been sent to the satellite camp Mühlgraben. It was here that she lost her nine-year-old brother, Heinz, killed in April 1944 during the SS selections of children in the Riga KL complex. A few months later, Inge had been forced onto one of the crowded ships that took the surviving prisoners toward Stutthof, where she would remain until February 1945.[40]

As we have seen, Stutthof emerged as the main destination for prisoners from the abandoned Baltic KL. Inge Rotschild was among more than twenty-five thousand Jewish inmates arriving from these camps in the second half of 1944. Thousands of them, mostly men (among them Inge's father), were soon transported westward for slave labor in satellites like Mühldorf and Kaufering. Many of the women and girls stayed behind. They were joined between June and October 1944 by well over twenty thousand Jewish women from Auschwitz, which was going through the preparatory stages of evacuation. Stutthof changed dramatically as a result, highlighting another effect of KL evacuations: not only did they lead to the closure of camps, they transformed the remaining ones, as well.[41]

One only has to look at the size of the prisoner populations. Stutthof had always been a second-rank KL, holding no more than around 7,500 prisoners in spring 1944. Just a few months later, however, in late summer 1944, it had grown to more than sixty thousand (the SS staff also expanded, following the arrival of guards from the abandoned Baltic KL). The new inmates were mostly Jews, and mostly women. Many of them were sent to Stutthof satellites; between June and October 1944, the Camp SS set up nineteen camps for Jewish prisoners, where they lived under the most primitive conditions, often in tents. Back in the main camp, some 1,200 prisoners or more were crammed into barracks that had previously held just two hundred; prisoners even slept in the latrines. Everything was scarce, not just space. "There were no facilities for washing," Inge Rotschild testified later, "and within a few days we were completely covered with lice."[42]

There were frequent selections in Stutthof, Inge added. Indeed, from summer 1944 local Camp SS officials stepped up the systematic murder of weak, elderly, sick, frail, and pregnant prisoners, just as they did in the Baltic KL. The Stutthof SS initially saw this as a radical solution to the overcrowding of the main camp, where the number of disease-ridden inmates was growing daily, with even more "unfit" prisoners returning from satellite camps. But increasingly, the local SS also used murder to ready the camp for a possible evacuation, preemptively killing those considered a burden for transports (following the example of the Baltic camps).[43]

Several thousand victims of Stutthof selections, largely children and their mothers, were sent by train to Birkenau. Others were murdered in Stutthof itself, especially after the closure of the Birkenau killing complex in autumn 1944. It was around this time that the Stutthof SS began to use a small gas chamber to murder Jews (as well as some Polish political prisoners and Soviet POWs) with Zyklon B. However, the main weapons of the Stutthof SS were deadly injections and shootings. Report leader Arno Chemnitz operated a neck-shooting apparatus in the crematorium, which was modeled on the one he had observed as a block leader in Buchenwald during the 1941 murder of Soviet "commissars." Another Stutthof SS man later described the aftermath of a routine execution of fifty or sixty women: "I did not look closely at the corpses, but I saw drying pools of blood on the floor, also bloodstained faces of corpses and I remember a blood spattered door frame."

Many more Stutthof inmates succumbed to the catastrophic living conditions. Corpses multiplied quickly inside the barracks; some inmates woke up pressed against the cold bodies of those who had perished during the night. In autumn and winter 1944, a typhus epidemic ravaged the camp, the third and worst such outbreak to hit Stutthof. It eventually forced the SS to suspend mass executions, and on January 8, 1945, Richard Glücks placed the entire camp under quarantine, lasting almost two weeks. By this time, around 250 prisoners perished each day, and the dying continued until the camp was evacuated.[44]

Life in the other remaining eastern KL was also overshadowed by the prospect of evacuation in autumn and winter 1944. SS preparations were most intense in the biggest site of all, Auschwitz. Material and machines were moved out, as we have seen, and the families of SS officers finally tore themselves away from their opulent homes (Frau Höss and her children left in early November 1944). SS officials left behind in Auschwitz became increasingly nervous as the front edged closer. Would they manage to escape in time? Would local resistance fighters attack the camp from outside?[45] Would the Soviets get there first? Such fears intensified when SS men heard Allied broadcasts on the BBC in autumn 1944, which named several notorious Auschwitz officials and warned that anyone involved in further bloodshed would be brought to justice. As the mood among the Auschwitz SS darkened, some staff lost their appetite for plunder and excesses.[46]

The demise of Auschwitz was epitomized by the closure of its gas chambers. Sometime in late October or early November 1944, the gassings inside the camp—the last of the Nazi death camps—stopped forever. Soon afterward, the demolition of the Birkenau killing complex began, and prisoners were forced to conceal any remaining ash and bone fragments.[47] Some SS murderers were relieved that this part of their duties had come to an end. "You can well imagine, my beloved," the chief SS garrison physician, Dr. Wirths, wrote to his wife on November 29, 1944, "how nice it is for me that I don't have to do this horrible work anymore, and that it exists no more."[48] The inmates, too, recognized this as a momentous event. As he watched the crematorium walls tumble, Miklós Nyiszli recalled, he had a premonition of the fall of the Third Reich as a whole.[49]

Why did the SS dismantle the Birkenau gas chambers? Many historians have pointed to a supposed Himmler order to stop the mass extermination of Jews.[50] If such an order really existed, it was no more than window-dressing for Himmler's plan to negotiate a secret peace with the west. In practice, the SS never abandoned the Final Solution, and in Auschwitz itself, murders of Jews and other prisoners continued, even after the gassings stopped.[51] The true motives for abandoning the gas chambers were more pragmatic. Mass deportations of Jews were coming to an end because of Germany's deteriorating military position, and the Auschwitz SS was keen to cover its tracks before the Red Army reached the camp.[52] SS leaders wanted to avoid a repetition of events in Majdanek, where the gas chambers had fallen largely intact into Soviet hands.[53] They also hoped to salvage the murderous hardware; many parts of the crematoria were dismantled, packed up, and shipped westward. The final destination was a top-secret location near Mauthausen, where the SS planned to rebuild at least two of the Birkenau crematoria; it also dispatched some of the Birkenau killing experts to Mauthausen. More than likely, this new complex, which was never built in the end, would have included gas chambers for further systematic mass murder.[54]

As the Camp SS gradually prepared to abandon Auschwitz, it preemptively moved many inmates away, following the example of earlier evacuations. This was the main reason why the daily Auschwitz prisoner population almost halved in four months, dropping to seventy thousand by late December. Several compounds were closed down and dismantled, including the huge "Mexico" extension (BIII) in Birkenau.[55] In all, around one hundred thousand prisoners departed during the second half of 1944 from Auschwitz. Previously, the camp had been the final destination for countless prisoners; now the flow was being reversed. Some transports went north to Stutthof, as we have seen, but most went to camps farther west, away from the approaching Red Army. One of them was Gross-Rosen, the only other main KL in Silesia.[56]

Gross-Rosen grew with breathtaking speed in the second half of 1944, following the almost daily arrival of prisoner transports from elsewhere. By January 1, 1945, it held 76,728 prisoners, briefly turning a backwater of the camp system into the second-largest KL; among them were more than twenty-five thousand Jewish women in satellite camps, most of whom had come from Auschwitz. Like Stutthof, Gross-Rosen now operated as a vast reception camp for prisoners from concentration camps farther east. Order started to break down as the overcrowded main camp descended into chaos. Conditions were worst in a new compound, built from autumn 1944 onward with barracks dismantled in Auschwitz. When winter came, the prisoners here were exposed to the bitter cold, as many huts were missing windows and doors; there were no toilets or washrooms, either, and the inmates waded through snow, mud, and feces. Conditions were no better across many of the remaining Gross-Rosen satellites. "Nothing can surprise me anymore," Avram Kajzer noted in his diary in early 1945, after he witnessed two fellow inmates of Dörnhau satellite camp pounce on a bone, after it had been dropped by a guard dog, and then grill it over a fire to eat.[57]

Flight from the Red Army

On January 12, 1945, the Soviet forces launched a devastating offensive that forced the Third Reich to its knees. Tanks broke through along the vast Eastern Front, sweeping past Wehrmacht defenses, and advanced rapidly toward the German heartland. When the Red Army regrouped at the end of the month, the front line had been completely redrawn. The Third Reich had lost its last foothold in occupied Poland, as well as other vital territory—East Prussia, East Brandenburg, and Silesia—as millions of German civilians joined the retreating Wehrmacht in a desperate mass flight.[58]

In the path of Soviet troops had stood three big camp complexes—Auschwitz, Gross-Rosen, and Stutthof—which held over one hundred and ninety thousand prisoners in mid-January 1945, more than a quarter of all KL inmates.[59] Earlier SS discussions about the full evacuation of these camps had involved the respective Gauleiter and higher SS and police leaders, who held significant sway over the evacuations.[60] The WVHA had played a key role, as well. It was Oswald Pohl who had first ordered the Auschwitz SS to plan for retreat, and when he visited the camp one last time, around November 1944, he examined the blueprint drafted by his protégé, Commandant

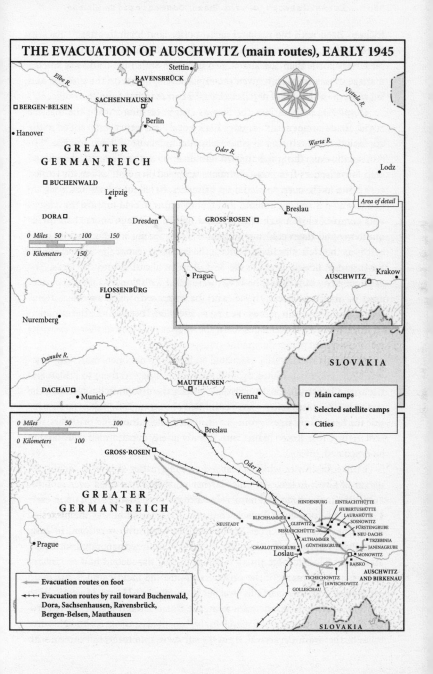

THE EVACUATION OF AUSCHWITZ (main routes), EARLY 1945

Elbe R.

Stettin

RAVENSBRÜCK

□ **BERGEN-BELSEN**

SACHSENHAUSEN

Berlin

Hanover

**GREATER
GERMAN REICH**

Oder R.

Warta R.

Lodz

□ **BUCHENWALD**

Leipzig

DORA □

Dresden

Breslau

Area of detail

GROSS-ROSEN □

0 Miles 50 100 150

0 Kilometers 150

Prague

AUSCHWITZ

Krakow

FLOSSENBÜRG

Nuremberg

Danube R.

SLOVAKIA

DACHAU □

Munich

MAUTHAUSEN □

Vienna

□ **Main camps**

■ **Selected satellite camps**

● **Cities**

0 Miles 50 100

0 Kilometers 100

Breslau

GROSS-ROSEN □

Oder R.

**GREATER
GERMAN REICH**

HINDENBURG EINTRACHTHÜTTE
                     HUBERTUSHÜTTE
BLECHHAMMER   LAURAHÜTTE
         GLEIWITZ   SOSNOWITZ
NEUSTADT BISMARCKHÜTTE   FÜRSTENGRUBE
                          NEU-DACHS
Prague   ALTHAMMER
         CHARLOTTENGRUBE GÜNTHERGRUBE   TRZEBINIA
                               JANINAGRUBE
                      MONOWITZ
Loslau   RAJSKO
              TSCHECHOWITZ   **AUSCHWITZ
                      JAWISCHOWITZ   AND BIRKENAU**
         GOLLESCHAU

Evacuation routes on foot

**←••←•• Evacuation routes by rail toward Buchenwald,
Dora, Sachsenhausen, Ravensbrück,
Bergen-Belsen, Mauthausen**

SLOVAKIA

Richard Baer, with the regional party, police, and SS authorities.[61] Back in Oranienburg, Pohl's managers would decide on the final destination of prisoner transports from the abandoned camps.[62] Still, they could not micromanage events from afar, given the rapid developments on the ground, and left most of the logistical details to local SS commandants and their officers.[63]

Despite its preparations the SS was caught off guard when the massive Soviet attack came in mid-January 1945. Local Nazi leaders only added to the confusion, often refusing to give evacuation orders until it was too late.[64] In Auschwitz, everything was thrown into disarray as the Camp SS abandoned ship. "Chaos; the SS in panic," inmates scribbled on a note as guards rushed across the main camp to round up prisoners, hand out provisions, pack up goods, and destroy documents. Prisoner columns started to leave the Auschwitz complex on January 17, 1945, and within two days, more than three-quarters of all the remaining inmates were on the road. Some were in good spirits as they left Auschwitz behind; the last survivors of the Special Squad, for instance, hoped to evade the SS killers by blending into the treks. The great majority of inmates, however, were filled with dread as they departed, anxious about the snow, the SS, and the unknown. "Such an evacuation," Polish prisoners wrote just as the first treks set off, "means the extermination of at least half of the inmates."[65] In the end, around one in four Auschwitz prisoners would perish during the transports.[66]

Auschwitz was initially evacuated on foot, with prisoners marching westward. The two main routes, around forty miles long, led them to Loslau and Gleiwitz. On arrival, most survivors—among them Tommy Buergenthal, the young boy we met earlier—were crammed onto trains and taken farther inside the Reich. The largest group, an estimated fifteen thousand prisoners, was sent to the Gross-Rosen main camp, already utterly overcrowded and about to be evacuated, too.[67]

Unlike Auschwitz, which was abandoned in a matter of days, the final evacuation of Gross-Rosen, 170 miles farther northwest, stretched over months. While the main camp and numerous satellites were hastily given up in early 1945, the KL complex as a whole continued; because of the way the front line moved, several dozen Gross-Rosen satellites were still operational in early May 1945.[68] Over in Stutthof, the final evacuation was equally protracted. The SS abandoned some thirty satellites during the second half of January 1945, marching many of the prisoners toward the main camp.[69] The main camp itself was then partially evacuated on January 25 and 26, 1945. With the Red Army only thirty miles away, the SS led around half of the twenty-five thousand prisoners on a march to the Lauenburg region, some eighty-five miles farther west. On arrival, it put the survivors into makeshift camps, with virtually no food, water, or heating. When the SS abandoned the Lauenburg camps again, a few weeks later, and forced the remaining prisoners on yet another death march, it left behind hundreds of dead. Meanwhile, the Stutthof main camp was still open. Because of its isolated position, the Soviets had bypassed the area and did not take the camp until May 9, 1945; by then, there were just 150 KL inmates left. Over the preceding weeks, many thousands had died, waiting in vain for the liberation that had seemed so very near. Among the victims was Inge Rotschild's mother, who perished, just skin and bones, on her daughter's thirteenth birthday.[70]

In early 1945, the KL system was in perpetual motion. Fleeing from the Red Army in January and February, the SS had forced more than one hundred and fifty thousand prisoners out of Auschwitz, Gross-Rosen, and Stutthof (several Sachsenhausen satellites were affected, too).[71] When Camp SS officials assembled these transports, the first prisoners were those "fit for work"; as a general rule, probably originating with Himmler and Pohl, these inmates were destined as slave laborers for other KL.[72] Less clear was the fate of invalids. Just as during the earlier evacuations in the east in 1944, there were no definite orders from the top, it seems, leaving the initiative to the local Camp SS. If transport was available, officials sometimes cleared the entire camp, forcing all sick prisoners onto trucks, carts, or trains. Elsewhere, especially in more remote satellites, SS men conducted selections shortly before the treks departed, and murdered the weakest inmates.[73]

One of the largest massacres took place during the evacuation of Lieberose, a Sachsenhausen satellite camp that mainly held Jews from Poland and Hungary. On February 2, 1945, around 1,600 prisoners departed on foot toward the main camp, more than sixty miles away. Another 1,300 or so stayed behind. Their fate had been sealed in a telex a few days earlier, probably by the Sachsenhausen commandant, which had ordered the execution of the infirm. There was no shortage of SS volunteers. "Come on, let's go," one sentry said. "We're going Jew shooting, and will get some schnapps for it." The slaughter lasted for three days. There was some desperate defiance, with one prisoner stabbing the camp leader in the neck. But there was no way out. A few survivors, hidden under discarded uniforms and shoes, were later pulled out by another group of SS men and lynched.[74]

However, murder was not the SS default mode during the KL evacuations of January and February 1945. The officials were just as likely to leave exhausted prisoners behind as to kill them. During the partial evacuation of the Stutthof main camp in January 1945, for example, Commandant Hoppe issued written instructions that prisoners who were "sick and unable to march" should stay put; thousands of them watched as the others walked away.[75] In

Gross-Rosen, too, the SS left hundreds of sick prisoners behind in satellites.[76] Some officers shied away from last-minute murders for fear of Allied retribution.[77] Elsewhere, they simply ran out of time, surprised by the speed of the Red Army. Inside the deserted SS barracks, survivors later found signs of the hasty retreat: glasses filled with beer, half-eaten bowls of soup, board games abandoned midway.[78]

The Red Army liberated well over ten thousand prisoners in early 1945. Most of them, around seven thousand, were in the Auschwitz main camp, Birkenau, and Monowitz.[79] Here, more than a week had passed between the departure of the death marches and the arrival of the Soviets, who lost well over two hundred soldiers during battles in the vicinity of the camp complex. It was an extraordinary period of peril and promise for the remaining prisoners, the final chapter of their suffering, with the ending still unwritten. Dr. Otto Wolken later described these final days as probably the most difficult in all his years inside concentration camps. After most of the Auschwitz sentries had left, around January 20–21, the remaining prisoners became more audacious, cutting holes into the barbed wire, moving across different compounds, breaking into SS storerooms. The inmates tried to rule themselves; they looked after the sick, made fires, and handed out food. But it was too early to celebrate. An exuberant Soviet prisoner, who drunkenly fired into the Birkenau sky after he found some beer and weapons, was tracked down by a German patrol and shot. A group of French prisoners who had moved into the SS dining hall was also murdered. There were other threats, too, in addition to Nazi killers, including cold, hunger, and disease. And yet, the great majority of prisoners survived until January 27, 1945. When the first Soviet soldiers appeared at the gates of Birkenau, some prisoners ran toward them. "We hugged and kissed them," Otto Wolken said a few months later, "we cried with joy, we were saved."[80]

Elsewhere in the Auschwitz complex, however, fate took a last terrible twist. On the same day Birkenau was liberated, SS terror struck in the satellite camp Fürstengrube, just twelve miles farther north. The Camp SS had abandoned the compound eight days earlier, leaving some 250 sick prisoners to fend for themselves. On the afternoon of January 27, 1945, with survival already in sight, a group of SS men suddenly entered the camp and slaughtered almost all the inmates. Only some twenty prisoners lived to see the Red Army arrive; they had come through the last massacre in Auschwitz.[81]

Death on the Road

No one knows how many KL prisoners died during the evacuations of early 1945, on icy roads and crammed trains, in ditches and forests. It must have been several tens of thousands, among them an estimated fifteen thousand men, women, and children from the abandoned Auschwitz complex.[82] Although popular memory of these evacuations is dominated by death marches, most of the way to the KL farther inside the Reich was covered by rail. Conditions on these trains were immeasurably worse than during earlier evacuations from western camps such as Natzweiler. All the horrors of the KL were packed into the train carriages. With rolling stock in short supply, the German authorities used lots of open freight cars, which offered no protection against the elements. The suffering was greatly prolonged by all the delays. Although most trains eventually reached their destination, they often crawled for days along the congested and crumbling German railway network.[83] One of the deadliest transports left the Auschwitz satellite camp of Laurahütte on January 23, 1945. The train moved excruciatingly slowly, often forced to a complete standstill, and when it finally reached Mauthausen almost a week later, around one in seven prisoners on board were dead.[84]

For most of the prisoners, the ordeal of the evacuations did not begin on the trains, however, but on preceding death marches, which claimed the majority of victims in early 1945. The prisoners had received little food before they left. One Auschwitz survivor recalled that she got a tin of beef and two inedible loaves of bread. This was supposed to last for several days, but the starved had often devoured everything before they set off.[85] Soon prisoners were so exhausted that they walked in a trance; sometimes even friends no longer recognized each other.[86] But the marches did not erase all distinctions between captives. Some small support networks endured, with close friends and family helping each other as best they could, while those who walked alone were often the first to fall. Privileged prisoners also fared better, just as they had done inside the KL. Healthier and better fed, they wore proper shoes and warm clothes, while others staggered along in rags and wooden clogs, and soon collapsed.[87] Dispatched by Oswald Pohl to monitor the KL evacuations in the east, Rudolf Höss found it easy to chase the trail of individual treks: he just had to follow the dead.[88]

The death rates of the marches varied greatly, depending on factors such as available supplies and distances covered.[89] While illness and exhaustion were probably the main killers, shootings were endemic, too. Anyone suspected of escape was fair game, according to SS rules, even prisoners who had merely stepped out to defecate by the side of the road.[90] And although SS directives gave no clear guidance on the treatment of the sick, their murder was common practice, too. Most victims died a lonely death, felled by SS bullets after they had lost touch with the main column, though there were some large-scale massacres, as well; during a march from the Auschwitz satellite

Blechhammer, for example, the SS loaded the sick onto sledges and blew them up with hand grenades.[91]

Few of the killers were senior Camp SS officers, as most of the local top brass had already made their getaway. Despite their talk of standing tall against the Soviets, high-ranking Nazis made a habit of fleeing first. Rudolf Höss recounted bitterly that the Auschwitz commandant Richard Baer had saved himself in a comfortable SS limousine, with plenty of time to spare.[92] Other commandants, too, hurried away, leaving the supervision of the marches to their underlings. Many of them were NCOs who had risen to senior positions inside satellite camps. But these transport leaders could not be everywhere along the stretched columns, which meant that the decision to pull the trigger was often made by regular guards. "In practice each guard decided for himself who to shoot," one testified after the war. Some of these executioners were women, breaking one of the last gendered taboos of the Camp SS. But the great majority were men, including some elderly soldiers who had only recently joined.[93]

Fear of the Red Army drove many of these perpetrators in early 1945. Soviet troops were wreaking terrible revenge against the German population during their advance, and the Third Reich was awash with stories of massacres, skillfully exploited by the Nazi propaganda machine. Many ordinary Germans saw these crimes as payback for atrocities in the KL, which had "shown the enemy what they can do to us if they win." The guards themselves, meanwhile, were determined to keep ahead of the Red Army. If frail prisoners slowed the treks down, and if screams, slaps, and kicks could not drive them forward anymore, they used their guns.[94] The guards' desire to save their own necks prompted the largest massacre during this period of KL evacuations. In late January 1945, a death march of around three thousand Stutthof prisoners (mostly Jewish women) arrived in the town of Palmnicken in East Prussia. Trapped by the Baltic Sea on one side and the advancing Soviet troops on the other, the SS, eager to escape, escorted the prisoners to the nearby coast and mowed them down with machine guns; wounded survivors drowned or froze to death, their corpses washing up for days on local beaches.[95]

APOCALYPSE

In mid-March 1945, Oswald Pohl embarked on a frantic tour to check on conditions in the KL, on Himmler's orders. As he passed through a landscape littered with ruins, accompanied by Rudolf Höss and other WVHA officials, he must have realized that the end was near. But he did not slow the pace of his "breakneck tour," as Höss called it; "as far as I could I visited every camp," Pohl said later. In the end, he inspected half a dozen or more main camps within the prewar German borders.[96]

The situation inside these concentration camps, now bursting with ravaged prisoners from recently evacuated sites, had lately deteriorated dramatically; during the first three months of 1945, the Buchenwald SS recorded more dead inmates than during all of 1943 and 1944 combined. Although some crematoria were running day and night, the bodies of the dead were mounting up fast. In Dachau, the Camp SS started in February 1945 to bury thousands of prisoners in mass graves, on a hill near the main camp, because the incinerators could not keep up anymore. So many prisoners were dying, Nico Rost noted in his Dachau diary on February 25, 1945, that the survivors did not have time anymore to mourn their friends.[97]

Oswald Pohl witnessed all this carnage during his visits in March 1945. The worst camp, Pohl and his managers agreed, was Bergen-Belsen, where they saw masses of starving prisoners and corpses as Commandant Kramer led them through the grounds. The WVHA officials reacted by issuing various orders to the local SS, as they had done elsewhere on their tour. The hard-bitten Rudolf Höss offered practical advice about mass cremation, drawing on his own expertise. Pohl himself, meanwhile, gave worthless instructions about adding herbs, berries, and plants from nearby forests to the prisoner diet, and also used his last meetings with local KL officials, in Bergen-Belsen and the other camps, to discuss their evacuation plans, with mass murder still very much on SS minds.[98]

The Race Between Illness and War

Flossenbürg, January 5, '45

Dear Marianne! In this letter I will set out the whole truth to you for once. My health is fine. The life in the camp is dreadful. 1000 men in 200 beds. Manslaughter and whip—hunger are daily visitors. More than 100 kick the bucket every day—perish on the concrete in the latrine or lying outside. Beyond description the filth—lice a[nd] more . . . Talk to all [our] acquaintances about a donation of food—bread—cigarettes—margarine—spread. Your Hermann.

This plea by the German Communist Hermann Haubner was smuggled out of the camp and eventually reached his wife. But it did not save him. Haubner died on March 4, 1945, one of 3,207 fatalities in the Flossenbürg complex in the final month before the camp was abandoned.[99]

In the early months of 1945, the remaining concentration camps became disaster zones, including those that had so far been spared the worst. One immediate cause for the catastrophe was the huge rise in prisoner numbers. Overcrowding was nothing new, of course; Buchenwald had been packed to excess since 1942.[100] But nothing prepared the camps for the rush near the end, which began with the mass transports from sites closer to the front line in the second half of 1944. Many KL complexes were completely overcrowded by the end of the year, only to be hit by the second wave of evacuations in early 1945. All camps in the heartland of the Third Reich now registered record figures. Buchenwald remained the largest complex of all, with 106,421 prisoners on March 20, 1945; around thirty percent of them were crammed into the main camp, with the rest spread across eighty-seven satellites, many of them no less packed.[101]

The final few months came down to a "race between illness and war," as Arthur Haulot put it in his Dachau diary on January 31, 1945.[102] Would prisoners be saved in time by the Allies? Or would they perish from hunger and disease, like so many before them? Rations now dwindled to almost nothing. In camps like Ellrich, even bread, the staple of the prisoner diet, went missing. "It is dreadful, this hunger," the Belgian inmate Émile Delaunois wrote in his diary on March 8, 1945, adding two weeks later: "There are only *Muselmänner* left!" Almost one thousand prisoners—nearly one in six—died in Ellrich in March alone.[103]

This was not a natural disaster but a man-made one, the culmination of years of Camp SS terror. Overcrowding was a direct product of Nazi policy. Likewise, the dramatic shortages of supplies were linked to the SS conviction that inmates, as proven enemies of the German people, did not deserve better. While prisoners were dying of hunger in spring 1945, the Camp SS itself still received regular deliveries of high-quality provisions, including liver pâté and sausages. After liberation, former inmates found SS warehouses piled high with food, as well as shoes, coats, mattresses, and medicine.[104] Camp SS leaders showed little interest in systematically improving the prisoners' plight, preferring once more to blame the victims. When Oswald Pohl was told that some SS officials had requested better clothing for inmates, he was furious. Instead of pitying prisoners, Pohl thundered in November 1944, his men had better teach them how to look after their things, "if need be by a sound hiding."[105]

All the misery and despair ripped the fractious prisoner community further apart. Some camps descended into violent disorder. Starving prisoners ambushed inmates who carried food supplies to kitchens and barracks, only to be beaten back by others armed with clubs and sticks. Some did not stop short of murder, just for a bite to eat. On April 17, 1945, Ebensee prisoners killed a thirteen-year-old boy, who had just arrived from another Mauthausen satellite camp, and made off with the large piece of bread he had been holding.[106]

This boy was one of tens of thousands of KL prisoners who died soon after their transfer from another camp. After the horror of the trains and marches, the arrival at their destination had come as a relief to some.[107] But not for long. Gravely weakened, these newcomers largely found themselves without protection and connections, exposed to the full force of SS terror. This is what happened to many of those Jewish men who made the march from Lieberose to Sachsenhausen in February 1945. They had survived the "Jew-shooting" in their abandoned satellite camp and the ensuing death march, often barefoot and frostbitten, only to perish in Sachsenhausen. Upon arrival, the SS conducted a mass selection and murdered some four hundred victims. Many more were left to freeze and starve in an isolated area of the camp. On February 12, 1945, Odd Nansen watched a group of them delving into garbage bins and fighting over the scraps. They were beaten back by German Kapos, but soon tried again, their skeletal bodies smeared with blood.

When Nansen returned to his own Sachsenhausen barrack—tormented by his inability to help—he was greeted by a different picture. His fellow Norwegian prisoners still lived in relative comfort. They had enough food, thanks to the Red Cross parcels, as well as plenty of cigarettes, the unofficial camp currency. After their meals they settled down with a novel, talked, or played games, "unaffected by the death and destruction" outside, as Nansen noted. Some Norwegians saw the death struggle of the Jews from Lieberose as evidence of their depravity. "Those aren't human beings, they're swine!" one of them said to Nansen. "I've starved myself, but I could never sink to eating sheer filth!"[108]

The prisoner community remained deeply unequal, as did the inmates' survival chances. What was garbage to the prominent few was nourishment to the destitute, and not just in Sachsenhausen; when a German Kapo in Ebensee threw up in January 1945, because he had eaten too much goulash, a starved Russian prisoner devoured his vomit.[109] The vast inequities were summed up on March 21, 1945, by Nico Rost, then a Kapo in the Dachau infirmary, who collected lists of prisoners who had died in the main camp. There had been no deaths among the kitchen staff, he noted, as they could help themselves to whatever they needed. Most German prisoners also survived, he added, because they held better posts and received more food. Likewise, there were few deaths in the barracks holding Czech prisoners and priests, who received food packages from outside. "But everywhere else," Rost wrote, "bodies—bodies—bodies."[110]

Zones of Death

The deadliest spaces were special compounds for invalids in main camps and some satellites, where the SS left the doomed to die.[111] The Camp SS could build on previous experience here: ever since conditions had worsened early in World War II, it had isolated invalids in special sites to hasten their death. From late 1944, SS officials stepped up this policy of death through deprivation, as a local solution to illness and epidemics in their overcrowded camps, not least after the option of deporting prisoners to die in Auschwitz had fallen away.[112]

There were "shit blocks" for those depleted by diarrhea, lying in pools of urine and excrement. There were "death blocks" for typhus-ridden prisoners, sometimes surrounded by barbed wire to stop them from fleeing to other parts of the camp. There were "convalescent blocks," where gaunt prisoners were sprawled among indescribable filth. And there were the infirmaries, which were often little more than waiting rooms for the dying; still, desperate inmates begged for admission, some of them collapsing just outside the entrances.[113]

The largest zones of death were former quarantine compounds in main camps, which had grown rapidly during 1944, with many thousands of new arrivals temporarily housed in tents. Initially, the SS had used these compounds as transit camps, sending most inmates elsewhere for slave labor. But over time, it left more invalids behind, and as the prisoner population grew and disease spread, these spaces acquired a new function, as huge sites for isolating the sick and dying.

Among the worst such compounds was the "little camp" in Buchenwald, set up two years earlier in windowless horse stables separated from the main camp by barbed wire. By early April 1945, it held eighteen thousand prisoners. Many had only recently arrived from evacuated camps, in a state of shock and exhaustion. The misery of the adjoining main compound—vermin, disease, and starvation—was magnified in the "little camp," and between January and April 1945, around six thousand prisoners died inside. Among them was Shlomo Wiesel. His son, Elie, later said that Buchenwald, which had promised to be an improvement on Auschwitz, turned out to be much the same: "At first, the little camp was almost worse for me than Auschwitz."[114]

There were so many *Muselmänner* by the beginning of 1945 that the Camp SS designated entire satellite camps as collection sites; SS men sometimes called them "bite-the-dust camps."[115] In January 1945, for example, the Dora SS set up a satellite camp in the deserted garages of the Boelcke air force barracks on the edge of Nordhausen, not far from the main camp. There was no shortage of dying men and the new camp filled up fast; in less than three months, around twelve thousand Dora prisoners were forced inside, many of them survivors of the Auschwitz and Gross-Rosen evacuations. The weakest ones—unable to walk, stand, or speak—were left to die in one of the two-story garages; the concrete floors inside were hosed down, once in a while, to wash away some of the blood and feces. Prisoners soon called the Boelcke camp a "living crematorium," and for good reason. In the weeks before U.S. troops reached the camp on April 11, up to one hundred men died every day; in all, more than three thousand perished. Another 2,250 dying prisoners were herded into boxcars, one day in early March 1945, and sent away, never to be seen again. Their destination was Bergen-Belsen, which had become the largest zone of death in the KL system.[116]

Belsen

In the early months of 1945, veteran inmates of Bergen-Belsen watched in dismay as endless rows of cadaverous men, women, and children marched toward their compounds. Transport after transport brought more prisoners, whole armies of "wretched figures," as Hanna Lévy-Hass, who had been held there since the previous summer (following her arrest as a resistance fighter in Montenegro), wrote in her diary in February 1945. In just eight weeks, the camp more than doubled in size, from 18,465 prisoners on January 1, 1945, to 41,520 on March 1, and peaking at around 53,000 on April 15, the day British troops liberated Bergen-Belsen.[117] And as the camp grew, so did chaos, disease, and death, with devastating speed.

Set up as a camp for "exchange Jews" selected for possible prisoner swaps by the Nazi authorities, Bergen-Belsen had since taken on several new functions, putting it on the road to disaster. From spring 1944, as we have seen, the Camp SS used it as a holding camp for sick and dying men from other KL. Then, in summer 1944, it established a transit compound for thousands of women en route from occupied eastern Europe to German satellite camps. Around 2,500 of them stayed behind in Bergen-Belsen. Among them were two young German Jews, fifteen-year-old Anne Frank and her older sister, Margot, who had been deported from Auschwitz in late October 1944, where they had arrived several weeks earlier on the last RSHA train to leave the Netherlands (after evading the Nazi authorities for two years in a hideout in Amsterdam, together with their parents and four others). In Bergen-Belsen, the sisters were initially crammed into the tents of the transit compound, which offered no shelter against the cold and rain. After a storm blew several tents away on November 7, 1944, the Camp SS moved the women into barracks inside the "star camp."[118] By then, the situation of the so-called exchange Jews was sharply deteriorating, too. Although they were still held separately, the SS started to treat them like the other KL inmates. "The regimen in the camp gets worse every day," Hanna Lévy-Hass wrote in December 1944. "Have we not already reached the nadir of our suffering?"[119]

Much worse was to come, as mass transports in early 1945 completely overwhelmed the camp. While WVHA officials continued to use Bergen-Belsen as a destination for half-dead men from other KL, they also turned it into a reception camp for evacuation transports, initially from eastern camps like Auschwitz and Gross-Rosen, and later from camps deep inside the Reich, too.[120] On April 11, for example, a train came from the recently abandoned Dora satellite camp Woffleben. Around 150 prisoners had died during the weeklong journey (another 130 men escaped). Some 1,350 survivors were herded into Bergen-Belsen. One of them was Émile Delaunois, whom we met earlier. Just before the evacuation of Woffleben he had vowed "to do anything to regain my freedom as soon as possible." He did survive the last days in Bergen-Belsen, only to die shortly after liberation.[121]

The Bergen-Belsen SS hastily reassigned compounds and added new ones, including a subcamp on the grounds of nearby army barracks. Even so, the site was hopelessly overcrowded. The composition of the prisoner population changed, too. Most of the new prisoners were female, turning Bergen-Belsen into the only wartime camp (apart from Ravensbrück and Stutthof) that held considerably more women than men. And it was no longer a camp almost exclusively for Jews. Although Jews were still by far the largest group—accounting for around half the inmates in mid-April 1945—they were joined by prisoners from other backgrounds, among them many political prisoners from Poland and the Soviet Union.[122]

"What takes place here is the most horrendous in world history," the noted Dutch lawyer and Zionist leader Abel Herzberg wrote in his diary on March 17, 1945, more than a year after his arrival as an "exchange Jew."[123] Even before new prisoners glimpsed the horror that awaited them in Bergen-Belsen, they could smell it. A stench of decay and death—sickeningly familiar to prisoners from camps like Auschwitz—enveloped the compounds during the final weeks. "We are all full of lice, everything is dirty, filthy, and full of crap," sixteen-year-old Arieh Koretz, another "exchange Jew," noted in his diary on February 8, 1945. Thousands of inmates soiled themselves, and the whole camp, a prisoner doctor later said, came to resemble one huge latrine. At night, inmates faced more agony, with cold winds sweeping through broken roofs, windows, and doors. The barracks were often bare—no lights, straw sacks, covers, stoves, chairs—except for the mass of prisoners, dead and alive.[124] Disease was raging, too, with a devastating typhus epidemic gripping the camp. The greatest killer of all was hunger. "I have been working for five days now without bread," the twenty-four-year-old Dutch Jew Louis Tas wrote on March 25, 1945. "Last night insane hunger and dreams of food," he added the next day. There were *Muselmänner* everywhere, so emaciated that their bones made up more than half of their body weight.[125]

The prisoners' hope of survival vanished fast. "I am ill again and have given up all hope of getting out of here," Abel Herzberg wrote on March 7, 1945. "I am afraid of the pain, of the death-struggle."[126] Each morning, prisoners threw the bodies of those who had died the previous night out of the barracks, though not before they had ripped clothes and valuables from the stiff bodies. The corpses were then flung on trucks or carts, which dumped the dead in different corners of the camp; toward the end, prisoners were just left lying wherever they had died.[127]

Never in the history of the KL did so many prisoners die as fast of disease and deprivation as in Bergen-Belsen in March 1945. During this one month, when the camp held an average of around 45,500 prisoners, some 18,168 lost their lives.[128] Among the dead were Anne and Margot Frank. During their last days, the two sisters, ravaged by typhus and dysentery, had been huddled under a blanket in one of the infirmaries. When friends found them there, they pleaded with Anne to get up. But Anne, who had been looking after her dying sister, just replied: "Here the two of us can lie on a bunk, we are together and have peace."[129]

Camp SS leaders had not planned the Bergen-Belsen disaster. They expected weak prisoners to die, to be sure, but not at this rate.[130] As the situation spiraled out of control, Commandant Josef Kramer sent a frank letter to the WVHA on March 1, 1945, warning that conditions were "untenable." Shortages of supplies and massive overcrowding were causing a "catastrophe." Kramer demanded beds and blankets, as well as trucks to pick up food and equipment for delousing.[131] But his appeal rang hollow. Kramer was at pains to present himself as a responsible official, not just to his SS superiors but to future Allied judges, as well.[132] Previously, he had betrayed little of the urgency expressed in his letter to the WVHA. In fact, as a veteran Camp SS officer and radical anti-Semite, he had brought more suffering to the camp after his arrival in early December 1944. And when the full tragedy unfolded, Kramer and his men mostly watched from the sidelines, not least to protect themselves from disease. During March 1945, the sight of SS officials became rare inside the Bergen-Belsen compounds. "There are no more roll calls. Also no work," Abel Herzberg wrote on April 1, 1945. "There is only death."[133]

Mass Murder

Along with death by deprivation, the Camp SS relied on mass executions to decimate the weak. Lethal selections expanded across the remaining KL in the early months of 1945, probably in line with WVHA orders. The SS killed several tens of thousands of frail prisoners by shooting, lethal injection, and gas, determined to rid the camps of prisoners seen as health risks, drains on resources, and obstacles during evacuations.[134] Sometimes the SS chose its victims as they arrived in the camp.[135] Further selections followed in the compounds, especially inside the death zones. In Uckermark—a police camp for "deviant" girls and young women, which was largely taken over by the Ravensbrück SS in January 1945 to isolate the weakest and oldest women from the main camp and its satellites—the SS conducted daily selections. "We may be sick, but we are still human beings!" one wrote in despair on February 9, 1945. Those who were spared listened as the victims were driven off on SS trucks, their cries and screams growing fainter. The trucks stopped by the nearby Ravensbrück crematorium, where the doomed were forced into a hut that had been converted in January 1945 into a gas chamber. In all, some 3,600 out of the 8,000 (or more) Uckermark women were murdered there, perhaps half of them Jews.[136]

In addition to the sick, the Camp SS executed political prisoners and others it wanted to silence forever. These murders were part of a final killing frenzy that swept across the Third Reich as the regime collapsed. Driven by the same self-destructive desires as Hitler, a small band of fanatics targeted German defeatists, foreign workers, prisoners, and many more; if Nazi Germany was going to perish, so were these "community aliens."[137] Inevitably, the concentration camps, which were meant to hold the most dangerous enemies, stood at the center of the carnage. Hitler and other Nazi leaders had long envisaged a bloody reckoning with KL prisoners in case of defeat, and that moment had arrived in early 1945.[138] The casualties included selected "high-value" prisoners like Allied agents and prominent resistance fighters. Among those hanged in the final days by the Flossenbürg SS, for example, were thirteen

British secret agents, three French women accused of sabotage, and seven leading German opponents of the regime, including the theologian Dietrich Bonhoeffer.[139]

Initially, many such murders followed the top-down route established in 1939, with formal execution orders issued by the RSHA. Apparently, concentration camp commandants had been asked in early 1945 to report those prisoners they regarded as a threat, in case the camp had to be abandoned. The RSHA probably added further names to these lists from its database of dangerous inmates, and then gave the go-ahead for the executions.[140] As central government structures broke down, however, regional and local officials across Germany gained greater powers to kill on their own initiative, leading to a final escalation of violence.[141] In the KL, commandants received the official license to order prisoner executions, awarded powers they had long claimed for themselves anyway.[142]

Some of the doomed fought back, just as the Special Squad prisoners had done in Birkenau. The largest rebellion involved so-called "Bullet" prisoners in Mauthausen. Faced with a growing number of POW escapes, the Wehrmacht High Command had ordered back in March 1944 that fugitive enemy officers and NCOs (except for U.S. and British nationals) should be sent to Mauthausen upon recapture. The code name for the secret operation—Action "Bullet" (*Kugel*)—made clear that no one was supposed to survive. Over the coming months, some five thousand condemned men came to Mauthausen. Most were Soviet POWs who had fled from sites of Nazi slave labor. The Mauthausen SS executed some upon arrival, isolating the others in barrack 20, a quarantine block surrounded by a stone wall and electric fence. "It was the intention to have the inmates under me slowly starved to death," the responsible SS block leader later confessed, "or to have them perish through diseases." This is exactly what happened, and by late January 1945, only some six or seven hundred prisoners were still alive.[143]

On the night of February 1–2, 1945, most of the surviving "Bullet" prisoners, facing certain death, tried to escape from Mauthausen. Several conspirators strangled the senior Kapo, a German (or Austrian) political prisoner loyal to the SS. Then, armed with little more than rocks, wooden shoes, pieces of soap, and fire extinguishers, the men attacked the SS at nearby searchlights and guard towers, capturing a machine gun. Using clothes and wet blankets, which short-circuited the electric fence, over four hundred men climbed over the wall: the greatest mass escape in the history of the KL. The merciless pursuit of them across the region lasted for around two weeks. Most of the fugitives were captured within a day or two and executed on the spot; only a handful are known to have survived the "hare hunting," as the SS and some locals called it. "We really shot down those guys," one SS man boasted at the time.[144]

Elsewhere, the SS killed to rewrite history, by silencing witnesses to some of its most heinous crimes. This included numerous privileged KL prisoners, who paid with their lives for all the secrets they had learned.[145] And it also included some survivors of human experiments. One of the victims was young Georges Kohn, whom we last saw as he was deported from Auschwitz to Neuengamme in November 1944, together with nineteen other Jewish boys and girls. Here, they had soon fallen seriously ill, after an SS doctor infected them with tuberculosis and supervised operations on their glands. Georges was the weakest, stretched out lifelessly on his bunk. Still, the children had survived until the last days of the war. Then, on April 20, 1945, three days before his thirteenth birthday, the SS came for Georges and the others. The drowsy children were taken late at night to an empty school at Bullenhuser Damm in Hamburg, previously an SS satellite camp. In the cellar, they were drugged by the senior SS camp physician and hanged; afterward, the SS doctor had a coffee to steady himself and drove back to Neuengamme.[146]

The dedication of diehard SS men was undimmed. Although the Camp SS had undergone massive changes in recent years, its core was still made up of zealots. With the end of the war in sight, they redoubled their assault on prisoners.[147] Many of them had previously served in the occupied east and brought all they had learned about prisoner abuse and killing to the remaining KL. This was true, above all, for some of the one thousand former Auschwitz staff redeployed in early 1945, together with their most violent Kapos. "I must admit that I had been hardened by conditions in Auschwitz," an SS officer later said to justify his actions in Mauthausen, which absorbed around one hundred former Auschwitz SS men. Even more ended up in Dora, among them the new commandant, Richard Baer, who oversaw an immediate increase of violence. Another new commandant, Josef Kramer in Bergen-Belsen, had arrived via Auschwitz, as well, followed by more veterans of the camp. "They are all bastards, thugs, and sadists," Arieh Koretz noted in his diary.[148]

Rudolf Höss, meanwhile, was a frequent presence in Ravensbrück, where he appeared in late 1944 (his wife and family had moved next door) to supervise mass shootings and the construction of the new gas chamber. Höss must have felt at home there, surrounded as he was by familiar faces from Auschwitz, such as the new camp compound leader Johann Schwarzhuber (whom he had known since his Dachau days). These killing experts had not come to Ravensbrück by chance, but had evidently been dispatched by the

WVHA to decimate supposedly dangerous and sick prisoners. Even after its demise, then, Auschwitz cast a shadow over the KL camp system.[149]

Few Auschwitz alumni were more versed in mass murder than twenty-nine-year-old Otto Moll, the former chief of the Birkenau crematorium complex. The WVHA valued Moll's expertise and put him in charge, in early 1945, of a mobile killing unit made up of other Birkenau veterans. The unit participated in mass gassings in Ravensbrück, and was also behind the Lieberose massacre and executions in Sachsenhausen. In late February 1945, the WVHA then moved Moll to the south of Germany, to the Kaufering complex, where he continued his murderous spree; the inmates here simply knew him as the "henchman from Auschwitz."[150] Moll was an extreme case, however, and while he continued to rage, some of his colleagues turned away from murder.

The Camp SS had never spoken with one voice, and it sounded more disjointed than ever in early 1945. By then, domestic support for Hitler and the Nazi regime had largely collapsed.[151] The Camp SS was infected by the grim popular mood, not least because more and more ordinary Germans—customs officials, railway workers, members of the People's Storm (the ramshackle last-ditch Nazi militia), and other civilians—were drafted into guard units right at the end of the war, a sign of how frantic KL recruitment had become.[152] Resignation had already crept into Camp SS ranks in summer 1944, following the Allied landings in France and the gains of the Red Army in the east. "Soon you will be liberated," SS guards had told prisoners in Klooga. "And our lot is bad. They will slaughter us with no mercy."[153] Defeatism spread further over the coming months, until even the model camp at Sachsenhausen conspicuously stopped flying the Nazi flag above its entrance.[154] The growing sense of desperation was summed up by a guard in a Flossenbürg satellite camp, who asked the Jewish prisoners to pray for a German victory.[155]

Some SS staff scrambled to distance themselves from KL crimes. In the past, they had felt invincible.[156] But as the Thousand-Year Reich crumbled, they feared that the tables would turn. "I wish you all the best for the coming year," Elie Cohen recalls an Auschwitz guard saying at the end of 1944. "In that year I shall most likely find myself in your shoes and you in mine."[157] More and more Camp SS men simply stayed away, in the same way that Wehrmacht soldiers absconded from the army, feigning illness or deserting.[158] Some of the remaining SS staff put on a friendlier face. They made a calculated bid for prisoner sympathies, hoping that this would help them later on. One such attempt to buy "life insurance," as the prisoners called it, was made by the Mauthausen commandant Franz Ziereis, who suddenly posed as a friend of Jews. More than once in April 1945, he paraded a young Jewish boy through the camp, whom he had dressed in specially tailored clothes.[159] A few SS officers even engaged in acts of disobedience. The SS physician Franz Lucas, who had previously participated willingly in Auschwitz selections, apparently refused to do the same in Ravensbrück in early 1945. After the war, an SS colleague dismissed this change of heart as a cynical ploy to purchase a "return ticket" to postwar society.[160]

Camp SS leaders reacted furiously to the progressive breakdown of morale and discipline. In late February 1945, Oswald Pohl branded all those who entered into "personal relationships" with prisoners as "traitors," and threatened them with execution.[161] Commandants, wedded to the world of the KL, echoed this hard line. During a screening of the Nazi propaganda film *Kolberg*—a crude historical epic celebrating individual sacrifice for the nation—on April 20, 1945, Hitler's last birthday, the Neuengamme commandant Max Pauly vowed that anyone who sullied the SS uniform faced brutal punishment. His men did not doubt his words, for he had just handed over one of them—an officer whom Pauly disliked, possibly because of his reputation for greater civility to prisoners—to an SS court for dereliction of duty; he was executed four days later.[162]

Himmler's Endgame

In early 1945, Nazi leaders had to face up to defeat. The Allied coalition held firm and there were no miraculous reverses on the battlefield, as the Wehrmacht was routed and German arms production, in rapid decline since autumn 1944, collapsed. In his Berlin bunker, Hitler sank further into gloom and paranoia, ranting against all those he blamed for his downfall, from his own generals to the Jews. Hopeless as the situation was, however, Hitler did not deviate from his uncompromising course—total victory or total destruction. There would be no retreat, no capitulation, no negotiation.

Some of Hitler's lieutenants, by contrast, were hoping to save themselves and some of their powers. Planning their own endgame, Himmler and other Nazi leaders considered approaches to the West, hoping that the western Allies' fears of Soviet domination in Europe would prompt them to agree to a separate peace. But any such plans were delusional from the start. Even if the Allied policy of total German surrender had not been set in stone, Himmler would have been the most improbable of all associates: this was the man who had been featured on the front cover of *Time* magazine as the infamous butcher of Nazi Europe, pictured before a huge mound of corpses. Himmler's folly was exposed at the end of the war. Assuming that Hitler had effectively abdicated, he made a secret capitulation offer to the western powers through an emissary. The Allies rebuffed Himmler, brusquely and publicly. When Hitler heard the news on April 28, 1945, he dissolved into a last fit of rage, screaming about "the most shameful betrayal in human history." A few hours later, not long before his suicide, he expelled Himmler from the party.[163]

For Himmler, the pursuit of a deal with the western Allies ended in humiliation. For thousands of KL prisoners, however, it meant salvation, as they benefited from Himmler's efforts to transform himself into a respectable negotiation partner. He had first tried to pose as a pragmatic statesman back in 1944, when he approved the release of some Jewish prisoners. On June 30, 1944, following secret negotiations with Jewish organizations abroad, the SS dispatched a select group of 1,684 Jews from Budapest to Bergen-Belsen, where they were held under privileged conditions until their transport (in August and December) to Switzerland. The SS was looking for goods and money in return, though the deal was also driven by Himmler's desire for a peace agreement.[164]

Secret negotiations about prisoner releases intensified in early 1945. Although Himmler remained cautious, his search for an exit strategy made him seek closer contacts abroad. This coincided with growing efforts by foreign governments (such as Sweden and France) and organizations (such as the World Jewish Congress) to save prisoners, animated by reports about mass deaths in the KL. The rescue efforts were led by the International Committee of the Red Cross (ICRC), headed by the Swiss diplomat Carl J. Burckhardt, and by the Swedish Red Cross, represented by its vice president, Count Folke Bernadotte. There was a flurry of letters and meetings between January and April 1945, occasionally involving Himmler's shady masseur Felix Kersten as go-between.[165] The foreign envoys met with a rogues' gallery of the Third Reich, including the new RSHA boss Ernst Kaltenbrunner and his Gestapo chief Heinrich Müller, Camp SS managers like Rudolf Höss and Enno Lolling, and senior SS officers like Standartenführer Kurt Becher (a key figure during the occupation of Hungary in 1944, he had been appointed by Himmler in April 1945 as Reich commissioner for the KL, primarily to negotiate with the Allies and the Red Cross).[166]

As for Himmler himself, he appealed for sympathy from the foreign officials, whining that he was a much misunderstood man. Despite his terrible image, he insisted, he had always been a good shepherd, concerned only with prisoner well-being. To lend some credence to his story, he made a few tactical adjustments behind the scenes, ordering a temporary stop to corporal punishment and deadly human experiments.[167] Himmler and his men constructed an alternative reality of the KL to impress their foreign guests. On the occasion of a visit to Ravensbrück in April 1945, Commandant Suhren regaled an ICRC official with tales about the camps' educational mission. Such claims were echoed by Himmler. Reports about mass death and murder were just "atrocity propaganda," he assured his interlocutors. He also brushed aside concerns about conditions in Bergen-Belsen, claiming that a team of medical experts had everything under control.[168]

For all their contacts with the SS, the foreign rescuers initially had little to show. True, the ICRC continued its delivery of food parcels (especially for western European and Scandinavian prisoners), dropping off supplies directly at the camps.[169] But the negotiators were frustrated by German refusals to allow proper inspections and complained about broken promises by WVHA managers.[170] Above all, there was almost no movement on the critical issue of prisoner releases. Only in exceptional cases, Himmler decided in February 1945, could sick and elderly inmates from Denmark and Norway be handed over; between January and March, the Danish authorities received just some 140 freed prisoners.[171]

Himmler's most significant concession during this period concerned the move of Scandinavian prisoners to a special compound in Neuengamme. From mid-March 1945, buses and trucks of the Swedish Red Cross carried inmates from other KL to this camp. One of them was Odd Nansen. As he walked out of Sachsenhausen with fellow Norwegian prisoners, "it was as though we sprouted wings and flew out, to where the row of white buses stood." By the end of March, Nansen and more than 4,800 other Scandinavians enjoyed decent food, adequate conditions, and medical care in Neuengamme. Their joy meant more misery for others. To make room for the incoming prisoners, the SS had thrown inmates out of a so-called recuperation block. Some died within hours. More than two thousand others were taken away on buses—the very same white buses that had brought the Scandinavian prisoners—after the Swedish Red Cross reluctantly agreed to help transport these exhausted inmates to satellite camps (where many of them would perish). Some of the Scandinavian prisoners were deeply troubled by these developments. He was feeling a "gnawing sense of undeserving and unfairness," Odd Nansen wrote on March 31, 1945, "in our being preferred to other people who are worse off, and who are going under and dying while we live in plenty."[172]

Only in April 1945, with much of Germany already occupied, did the SS finally surrender a more substantial number of its prisoners. Desperate for an agreement with the Allies, Himmler put his hopes in the well-connected Count Bernadotte, a nephew of the Swedish king. They met three times that month, the last time on the night of April 23–24, when Himmler made his offer to capitulate on the Western Front (Bernadotte was the emissary who relayed it to the Allies). To help his cause, Himmler let more KL prisoners go. At first, the main beneficiaries were Scandinavians: the Danish and Swedish Red Cross spirited away almost eight thousand prisoners, including those held in Neuengamme. Odd Nansen completed his last diary entry in Germany on April 20, 1945, on "the bus to freedom"; after the prisoners crossed the border to Denmark, they were greeted by thousands lining the streets, waving flags and handing out flowers, bread, and beer. Himmler soon agreed to free further prisoners. The man responsible for the extermination of countless women and children now extended his "charity" to a few female prisoners, among them pregnant and seriously ill women, as well as mothers with children. In the final two weeks of war, the Danish and Swedish Red Cross picked up around 9,500 women, largely from Ravensbrück. Another two thousand or more were put onto ICRC trucks and taken to Switzerland. Most of the saved women came from Poland, others from France, Belgium, and elsewhere. "The camp behind us is getting smaller and smaller," the French prisoner Marijo Chombart de Lauwe wrote about her rescue from Mauthausen on April 22, 1945, "and I sit here with empty eyes, silent and dazed." It took time before they understood that they really were free.[173]

But releases remained the exception. The rescue of some twenty thousand men, women, and children in April and early May 1945 coincided with the suffering of hundreds of thousands more still trapped inside the KL system. When he made his tactical concessions, Himmler was determined to hold on to the great bulk of prisoners as bargaining chips for the elusive deal with the Allies—even if this meant the continuation of deadly KL evacuations.[174] This strategy was most transparent in his approach to Jewish prisoners, whose fate was raised repeatedly during discussions with the Red Cross. Himmler had thought for some time that improving the conditions for Jews might boost his stock in the West.[175] Now he took some symbolic steps. Around March 13, 1945, just before Pohl set off on his hectic tour of the last KL, Himmler apparently instructed him to tell commandants that the killing of Jews should cease. Himmler made similar promises to his foreign negotiation partners and talked to camp commandants directly about improving the treatment of Jews.[176] But his disingenuous intervention came far too late to make any difference. In Mauthausen, for example, Jewish prisoners were still more likely to die than any other group, despite sudden orders to give preferential treatment to sick Jews.[177]

Eager to buy credit in the West, Himmler was willing to let at least some more Jewish prisoners go. Rewriting his own genocidal past, he claimed to have always supported their orderly emigration from Germany. To prove his point, he agreed to release one thousand Jewish women from Ravensbrück to the Swedish Red Cross with immediate effect, following an extraordinary meeting on the night of April 20–21, 1945, with Norbert Masur, a representative of the World Jewish Congress who had come to Germany from Sweden, his safe conduct guaranteed by the SS.[178] Himmler never went beyond such tactical adjustments, however.[179] In general, he continued to regard Jewish prisoners as hostages for a deal with the West. "Look after these Jews and treat them well," Himmler is said to have told the Mauthausen commandant Ziereis in late March 1945, "that is my best capital."[180]

Himmler's hostage strategy also determined the fate of the remaining "exchange Jews" in Bergen-Belsen. Between April 7 and 10, 1945, just days before British troops reached the camp, the RSHA dispatched three trains with 6,700 Jews toward Theresienstadt, the last remaining ghetto, now redesignated as another exchange camp. Only one train reached its destination, after an odyssey of almost two weeks. The other two drifted for days through war-torn Germany like ghost trains, until they were liberated by the Allies; by then, several hundred prisoners on board were dead.[181]

THE FINAL WEEKS

By early April 1945 the KL system was in turmoil, caught up in the general maelstrom of doom and defeat. Himmler's kingdom of terror had shrunk fast since the start of the year, as the Allies penetrated deep into German territory; in all, the Camp SS lost some 230 satellite camps in the first three months of 1945.[182] Meanwhile, chaos and death had spread through the remaining camps. Even their much-vaunted war production had ground to a virtual standstill because of shortages and air raids, which constantly sent SS and prisoners running for cover. "The siren has diarrhea," a friend of Ágnes Rózsa joked in Nuremberg on February 19, 1945, only days before their camp was hit—one of several satellites destroyed by Allied bombs in the final months of war, causing yet more deaths.[183] In all, perhaps one hundred and fifty thousand KL prisoners perished between January and March 1945, during the evacuations and inside the remaining camps, resulting in the first sharp fall in inmate numbers for many years.[184]

But it would be a mistake to think that the Camp SS was finished. Although its grip was slipping fast, it had not yet lost complete control. And the size of its terror apparatus was still formidable. At the beginning of April 1945, the SS operated ten main concentration camps and almost four hundred satellites.[185] Around thirty to thirty-five thousand SS officials served in these

selection on arrival, Jewish women and children stand outside Birkenau before they are gassed, May 1944. (USHMM, courtesy of Yad Vashem)

oners from the privileged Canada Commando sort the belongings side the SS warehouses in Birkenau, May 1944. (USHMM, courtesy of

remaining camps.[186] And although the prisoner population had plummeted, the KL still held an estimated five hundred and fifty thousand inmates, far more than one year earlier.[187] These men, women, and children came from all across Europe, and most of them were held in satellite camps. Germans were in a smaller minority than ever, making up less than ten percent of the prisoner population.[188] By contrast, Jewish prisoners had grown into one of the largest groups. Their numbers in concentration camps within the Third Reich's prewar borders had increased rapidly in recent months, first with the transports of slave laborers to satellites, and then with the evacuations from the east. By early spring 1945, Jews made up perhaps thirty percent of the KL population.[189]

Only in April and early May 1945 did the KL system finally collapse. During a dramatic five weeks, the WVHA disbanded, and Allied forces reached the remaining satellites and the last main camps: Buchenwald and Dora (April 11), Bergen-Belsen (April 15), Sachsenhausen (April 22–23), Flossenbürg (April 23), Dachau (April 29), Ravensbrück (April 30), Neuengamme (May 2), Mauthausen-Gusen (May 5), and Stutthof (May 9).[190] In well over one hundred camps, the Allies found prisoners left by the SS, ranging from a handful of survivors in some satellites to fifty-three thousand in Bergen-Belsen. In total, an estimated two hundred and fifty thousand prisoners were liberated inside concentration camps during this period.[191]

Most camps, however, were empty when Allied troops arrived. The SS had evacuated the great majority of satellites and also reduced the prisoner population in most main camps. In Neuengamme, virtually no inmates were left inside when British soldiers entered the vast compound.[192] The deserted camps stood in sharp contrast to roads and trains outside, which were full of prisoners. Countless death transports crisscrossed the ever-shrinking Third Reich, often cut off from the remaining camps; tens of thousands of prisoners died before Allied troops reached them.

Historians have offered conflicting assessments of these last death transports. Some depict the KL system as remarkably resilient, even at the end, with prisoner treks operating as small concentration camps on the move.[193] Others argue that the transports should be viewed separately from the history of the KL, as a new stage of Nazi genocide.[194] Ultimately, neither position is fully persuasive. There was nothing stable about the KL system in spring 1945; seeing the treks as mobile camps ignores the manifest differences from life inside.[195] At the same time, the death transports are still very much part of the camps' history. The transports were dominated by Camp SS men, after all, who were already accustomed to murdering prisoners for escaping or for losing their strength. As for the prisoners themselves, their desperate physical state was a product of the camps, while the behavior they had learned inside, and the connections they had made there, proved invaluable on the road. In the final analysis, the death transports accelerated long-standing trends in the KL system. Its structure became even more dynamic, with prisoners perpetually on the move; perpetrators gained even more autonomy, killing with complete impunity; staff became even more diverse, as more men from outside were drafted in as guards; Kapos held even more sway, with some officially armed and co-opted as escorts; and terror became even more visible, with treks and trains moving all over Germany.[196]

"No Prisoners [Must] Fall Alive into Enemy Hands"

The mass evacuation of the KL in spring 1945 was no foregone conclusion. Amid growing panic, SS leaders considered several alternatives and sent contradictory signals to the bewildered local officials.[197] The most radical idea was a last bloodbath, condemning all prisoners to go down with the Third Reich. At a time when Hitler preached that it was better to reduce Germany to ruins than to leave anything to the enemy, there was some loose talk among SS leaders and local officials of razing the camps, too, together with all those inside. But just as Hitler's scorched-earth order was not implemented, the SS never came close to the total annihilation of all prisoners.[198]

At the other end of the scale stood mass releases. When it came to the evacuation of Nazi prisons, the Reich Ministry of Justice decided to free large numbers of inmates regarded as harmless.[199] But such a measure was unacceptable to Himmler and his officers. Mass releases would have destroyed the founding myth of the KL as the bulwark against Germany's most evil enemies. Ultimately, the RSHA only agreed to rather low-level releases, freeing several thousand political prisoners.[200] A few thousand more German inmates were pressed into ragtag military formations, but despite the hopes of Nazi grandees like Joseph Goebbels, these reluctant, ill-equipped soldiers made no discernible contribution to the defense of the fatherland.[201]

Yet another option was to abandon camps after selected prisoners had been moved out, leaving the great majority behind. There was some support for such an approach within the WVHA. After all, orderly mass evacuations were out of the question by spring 1945; the transport system was in meltdown and the last camps were bursting.[202] Himmler briefly toyed with this idea, too, and when it came to the final evacuation of the Buchenwald main camp, he ordered that the remaining inmates should be left to the Allies.[203] But he quickly changed his mind. On April 6, 1945, Commandant Pister received Himmler's new order to abandon the camp with immediate effect.

Rudolf Höss and Auschwitz SS men relax [...] of 1944. Front row, from left: adjutant Kar[...] (partially obscured); Höss; commandants [...] Josef Kramer; camp compound leader Fr[...] Mengele (partially obscured); and two ot[...]

Following the S[...] crematorium II[...]

A uniformed SS doctor (center [...] from Subcarpathian Rus to Au[...] immediate extermination (in [...] complex. (USHMM, courtesy of [...]

Male and female pri[...] of murdered Jews ou[...] Yad Vashem)

Covert prisoner photograph from inside the Birkenau gas chambers documenting the open-air cremation of murdered Jews, August 1944 (State Museum Auschwitz-Birkenau, Oświęcim)

SS photograph of so-called Special Squad prisoners inside Birkenau crematorium II or III in 1943 (State Museum Auschwitz-Birkenau, Oświęcim)

On the morning of July 18, 1942, SS leader Heinrich Himmler (front row, left) inspects the IG Farben construction site near Auschwitz-Monowitz, led by the civilian chief engineer, Max Faust (center), and Commandant Rudolf Höss (right). (State Museum Auschwitz-Birkenau, Oświęcim)

The head of the SS concentration camp system, Oswald Pohl (center), visits Auschwitz in 1944, accompanied by Commandant Richard Baer. Between them (in the background) is Karl Bischoff, the main SS architect of the crematorium complex. (USHMM)

Majdanek guards celebrate a birthday in a Lublin dance hall and restaurant in March 1944. (Landesarchiv North Rhine–Westphalia, Rhineland division, RWB 28432/3)

SS accommodation barracks in Neuengamme during the war: most regular guards lived regimented lives outside the barbed wire. (KZ-Gedenkstätte Neuengamme)

Slave labor for the war effort: directed by a civilian foreman, prisoners of the Farge satellite camp build a bombproof bunker for submarine production, circa 1944. (Staatsarchiv Bremen, collection Schmidt)

Armaments Minister Albert Speer (center, right) and the Gauleiter of Upper Austria, August Eigruber (center, left), with prisoners of a satellite camp in Linz, 1944 (bpk/Hanns Hubmann)

Covert photograph taken by a German civilian from his kitchen window in Cologne in October 1943. The prisoners came from Buchenwald and belonged to an SS Building Brigade clearing bomb damage.

(NS-Dokumentationszentrum, Cologne)

A prisoner from the Dora satellite camp pushes a cart toward the entrance of the deep tunnel system that housed V2 rocket production, summer 1944.

(bpk/Hanns Hubmann)

The dismal "little camp" in Buchenwald, captured in a covert photograph by a French prisoner in June 1944. Inmates slept in tents (center) or windowless stables (left); designed for around fifty horses, the stables held up to two thousand men. (Gedenkstätte Buchenwald)

Inside a hut at a Kaufering satellite camp (photographed after liberation). The SS crammed prisoners into such vermin-infested huts, which were covered with grass and earth. (U.S. National Archives)

A 1944 self-portrait of the young German Jew Peter Edel by the Auschwitz gate, illustrating how the camp had changed him. The caption reads "Who is this?" — "You!" — "Me?" — "Yes!" (State Museum Auschwitz-Birkenau, Oświęcim)

A 1943 drawing by an unidentified Auschwitz prisoner depicting the powers and privileges of so-called Kapos (State Museum Auschwitz-Birkenau, Oświęcim)

This covert photograph by a resident of a village on Lake Starnberg documents prisoners on a death march from Dachau on April 28, 1945. (akg-images/Benno Gantner)

Prisoners in the Below forest in late April 1945, on a death march from the abandoned Sachsenhausen camp. In the foreground someone carries a Red Cross food parcel. (ICRC, courtesy of Willy Pfister)

On April 30, 1945, a train with thousands of prisoners from the abandoned Leitmeritz satellite camp makes a stop in a Czech town, where locals defy the SS to distribute food and take pictures. (Museum of Central Bohemia, Roztoky u Prahy)

Georges Kohn, aged twelve, pictured here during medical experiments in Neuengamme, was hanged on April 20, 1945. He was one of countless victims of last-minute Camp SS murders. (KZ-Gedenkstätte Neuengamme)

A U.S. soldier outside a train full of dead prisoners, soon after the liberation of Dachau. The prisoners had departed from Buchenwald some three weeks earlier. (USHMM, courtesy of J. Hardman)

Soviet soldiers survey burned bodies at the Klooga satellite camp in Estonia. On September 19, 1944, shortly before the Red Army arrived, the SS had slaughtered the inmates and torched the camp. (USHMM, courtesy of Esther Ancoli-Barbasch)

Dachau prisoners welcome U.S. troops on April 29, 1945 (photographed from a watchtower). (USHMM, courtesy of *The New York Times*)

The liberation of a Bergen-Belsen death train near Magdeburg, April 13, 1945 (USHMM, courtesy of Dr. Gross)

Bergen-Belsen on April 18, 1945, three days after the arrival of British forces. Thousands of survivors died here in the following weeks. (Imperial War Museums, London)

Young survivors cook a meal in the Ebensee satellite camp two days after the May 6, 1945, liberation. (USHMM/U.S. National Archives)

Survivors of Buchenwald leave the Weimar train station for a children's home in France, June 1, 1945. One youth writes on the carriage: "Where are our parents? You murderers." (Gedenkstätte Buchenwald)

The execution of Rudolf Höss on the grounds of the former Auschwitz main camp on April 16, 1947 (Instytut Pamięci Narodowej, Warsaw, GK-14-4-6-11)

U.S. soldiers confront Weimar civilians with corpses near the Buchenwald crematorium, April 16, 1945—one of many explicit images to appear in the Allied press. (Gedenkstätte Buchenwald)

Postcard of Dachau as a residential settlement for refugees, circa 1955–60. Next to the main road (bottom, right) are the former prisoner barracks used as apartments. (KZ-Gedenkstätte Dachau)

Buchenwald had to be cleared to a very large extent, Himmler demanded, by taking the prisoners to Flossenbürg.[204] In the end, evacuation remained the SS default mode.[205]

During April 1945, the Camp SS forced hundreds of thousands of prisoners onto transports, as it moved to abandon eight main camps and well over 250 satellite camps. Some SS officials yielded to pressure from local industry and municipal authorities, who wanted the SS to take away slave laborers before the Allies arrived, to wash their own hands of any association with KL crimes.[206] Moreover, the SS principals saw good reasons for holding on to their inmates.[207] Himmler himself still regarded prisoners—especially Jews—as pawns in his gambit for a separate peace.[208] And the WVHA leaders still saw the KL as sites for vital armaments production. Refusing to accept the inevitable, Pohl and his managers worked frantically to keep the last factories running, while the relentless Hans Kammler hoped to make new miracle weapons; after the Dora underground complex was abandoned, Kammler wanted to produce antiaircraft missiles in another tunnel system, by taking blueprints, machines, and prisoners to Ebensee.[209] From the perspective of fanatics like Kammler, the idea of leaving able-bodied slaves behind in abandoned camps must have seemed like sabotage.

Most important, perhaps, SS leaders believed that they had to protect the German public. They remembered the scare stories of the 1918 revolution, when freed prison inmates were (wrongly) accused of terrible crimes.[210] Fears of a recurrence appeared to come true after the evacuation of Buchenwald. Although the Camp SS had managed to force some twenty-eight thousand prisoners out of the main camp at the last moment, following Himmler's revised orders, another twenty-one thousand were still left inside when U.S. troops arrived. Their liberation came as a great surprise to the German civilian authorities—the Weimar police president called the camp in the late afternoon of April 11 to speak to Commandant Pister, only to be informed by a gleeful inmate that Pister was no longer available—and the region was soon awash with reports of prisoners pillaging and raping the helpless population. These stories were largely baseless; years of pent-up fears among locals distorted minor incidents into atrocities. But there was no stopping the rumors, which even reached the Führerbunker in Berlin. Hitler was livid, and is said to have instructed Himmler that all KL prisoners who could march had to be forced out during evacuations.[211]

Himmler was spurred into action. Around April 15, 1945, he held a meeting with Camp SS officers, receiving Richard Glücks and other senior figures on his special train. Pointing to the alleged atrocities in Weimar, he evidently ordered the complete evacuation of the remaining KL.[212] Just a few days later, around April 18, 1945, Himmler reiterated his hard line in a telex to Flossen-bürg, brushing aside any suggestion of leaving inmates to the Allies: "There is no question of handing over the camp. No prisoners [must] fall alive into enemy hands. The prisoners in Weimar-Buchenwald abused the population in the cruelest way."[213] Similar instructions appear to have reached other main camps at the time.[214]

Himmler's uncompromising stance was hardened, no doubt, by recent accounts of Camp SS crimes in the foreign media. There had been earlier ex-posés, after the Allies reached sites like Majdanek, Natzweiler, and Auschwitz, including the first films shot in abandoned camps, but the echo abroad had still been muted.[215] Not so in April 1945, as graphic images from recently liberated camps flashed around the globe. The media attention initially cen-tered on Buchenwald, the first SS camp liberated in spring 1945 with large numbers of prisoners still inside.[216] Himmler was furious about these reports, which made a mockery of his ongoing efforts to paint himself as a humani-tarian. During his meeting with the representative of the World Jewish Con-gress on April 20–21, 1945, he complained bitterly about the Buchenwald "horror stories" in the foreign media. In the future, Himmler threatened, he might not leave any more prisoners behind.[217]

This was not the final word, however, as the local Camp SS did not, or could not, implement Himmler's order to the letter. Of all the main camps abandoned during the last three weeks of the war, only Neuengamme was almost completely cleared. In Flossenbürg, Sachsenhausen, and Ravensbrück, by contrast, the Camp SS left some invalids behind.[218] The same happened in numerous satellite camps.[219] So not all Camp SS men had understood Himm-ler's instruction—insofar as it reached them—as an automatic order to march all mobile prisoners out and kill the rest.[220]

In the last remaining camps, meanwhile, which persisted into the final days of the regime, the SS really had nowhere left to send all its prisoners. As a result, the Dachau main camp was only partially emptied, with U.S. troops liberating some thirty-two thousand inmates on April 29. And when SS offi-cials fled Mauthausen, a few days later, they left some thirty-eight thousand prisoners behind in the main camp and in Gusen.[221] In the last satellite camps (over eighty), too, the SS staff left most prisoners inside as they slipped away in early May. Still, until the Camp SS ran out of options, it generally tried to implement a policy of total (or near-total) evacuations.

The most striking exception to the rule was Bergen-Belsen, the only main camp formally turned over to the Allies. On April 11, 1945, Himmler autho-rized his representative, SS Standartenführer Kurt Becher, to leave the area around Bergen-Belsen to the British army. Perhaps Himmler wanted to make a grand gesture to the West, though he also had pragmatic reasons for abandoning the camp and its prisoners, since an evacuation would have run the risk of spreading typhus among the German population and troops. Following the conclusion of a local armistice, British forces rolled up to the main camp entrance on the afternoon of April 15, 1945. They were greeted by Josef Kramer—the only SS commandant not to flee—who officially handed over the camp. British soldiers were shocked when they entered. Despite desperate SS efforts to clear up the site, more than thirteen thousand bodies were strewn across the main compounds. Major Alexander Smith Allan recalled "a carpet of human bodies, mostly very emaciated, many of them unclothed, jumbled together." During an uneasy period of transition, some SS men initially helped to administer the camp; they even shot at prisoners. But as the full scale of the crimes emerged, British troops disarmed and detained the remaining SS staff. "The first person I arrested was Josef Kramer," Sergeant Norman Turgel said after the war. "I was very proud of being a Jew who arrested one of the most notorious gangsters in Nazi Germany."[222]

Abandoning the Camps

By spring 1945, the SS officials were experts in preparing for evacuations.[223] Often, they began by closing the satellites nearest to the front line, moving prisoners back to the main camp or to satellites designated as reception camps. Although the advance of the Allies frequently foiled these plans, and diverted prisoner transports elsewhere, some of the reception camps became vast sites. In the Neuengamme complex, the two camps Wöbbelin and Sandbostel took in almost fifteen thousand prisoners in April 1945; conditions inside were infernal and around four thousand inmates died before liberation. "We could smell the Wöbbelin camp before we saw it," the regional U.S. army commander later wrote.[224]

Another well-established SS routine was the eradication of incriminating evidence. Across the remaining camps, the officials destroyed documents, torture instruments, and other proof of SS crimes, including the gallows. The gas chambers in Sachsenhausen, Mauthausen, and Ravensbrück were dismantled, too, while prisoner corpses were hastily buried or burned. The aim was to make everything "look decent" before the arrival of the Allies, as the Ravensbrück commandant Fritz Suhren told inmates. In the Neuengamme main camp, the SS even forced prisoners to clean the barrack floors and windows, and paint some of the walls, expecting a coat of whitewash to cover years of barbarity.[225]

On the eve of the final evacuation, local Camp SS officials then decided the destiny of the remaining invalids. Many weakened inmates had perished over the preceding weeks and months. But the catastrophic conditions always created more *Muselmänner*, and their fate hung in the balance to the end. Individual Camp SS officials chose very different paths, just as their colleagues had done during earlier evacuations. Some forced the invalids to leave, providing that transport was available.[226] Elsewhere, SS men left the sick behind as the camp was cleared. And there were also some final massacres, following Himmler's maxim that no prisoners should fall into Allied hands.

The treatment of invalids was only one of the dilemmas facing the local Camp SS. As they realized that camps like Buchenwald and Dachau could only be partially emptied, SS officials had to decide which prisoners to take with them. In Dachau, they began by assembling Jews, and later added Germans and Soviets. In total, 8,646 inmates left on April 26, 1945; almost half came from the Soviet Union, Jews made up more than a third, and Germans the rest.[227] In Buchenwald, the SS started with Jews, as well, and then added others, among them Polish, Soviet, Czech, French, Belgian, and German inmates; more than half of the twenty-eight thousand prisoners who departed came from the "little camp."[228] Clearly, SS officials did not proceed at random during their selections for death transports. They targeted specific prisoners, especially those seen as high value or particularly dangerous, with Jewish "hostages" falling into both categories.[229]

Prisoners did anything to avoid the final death transports. Having dreamed for so long about leaving the camps, they were now desperate to stay until the Allies arrived. During the partial evacuation of Buchenwald and Dachau, some prisoners tried to obstruct and delay the SS. But most defiance was easily broken. "With a handful of SS men one can force prisoners to do anything deemed necessary," one Buchenwald inmate wrote despondently on April 9, 1945.[230]

The mastery of the SS often ended at the camp gates, however. While it was still powerful enough to force prisoners out, it was unable to keep its transports on track. With the German transport system torn apart, trains constantly stopped or changed direction. Journeys that should have lasted a day took weeks, and the longer they lasted, the more prisoners died. When the remnant of a train that had left Buchenwald on April 7, 1945, with around five thousand prisoners on board reached Dachau some three weeks later, it was packed with more than two thousand dead (these were the corpses U.S. soldiers found as they first entered the camp on April 29). Elsewhere, SS guards pushed survivors out of trains that had got stuck in the middle of nowhere, and continued on foot. But with many roads no longer passable or cut off, treks often split or got lost. Prisoners felt as though they walked in circles, always escaping from the nearest Allied troops.[231]

On the road, the SS transport leaders could expect no more guidance from their superiors. The communications network was collapsing, making contact with WVHA headquarters largely impossible. Soon, the WVHA disappeared altogether. Oswald Pohl left his office in Berlin in mid-April, shortly before the German capital was surrounded, and so did most of his men, including those in Office Group D; the last Camp SS managers, including Richard Glücks, fled from Oranienburg on April 20–21, 1945. After SS security guards locked the doors for a last time, the T-Building, the nerve center of the KL system since summer 1938, stood empty.[232] And just as Germany was divided in late April, so, too, was the Camp SS. WVHA managers fleeing from Berlin split into two groups, one heading north, the other south, and quickly lost touch with each other.[233]

With few exceptions, the final death transports were also supposed to move north or south, as the SS tried to hold on to its last prisoners.[234] Initially, most transports headed for the remaining main camps. Likewise, Camp SS managers assembled in KL that were still operational. In the north, the rump of WVHA Office Group D set up a temporary base at Ravensbrück. Oswald Pohl, meanwhile, moved south (apparently on Himmler's orders) and settled in his quarters on the Dachau plantation. Here he was joined by several other WVHA officers, including a few members of Office Group D and their families, as well as two former commandants, Richard Baer (Dora) and Hermann Pister (Buchenwald), and their staff. Just days before Dachau was liberated, Pohl presided over a last lavish supper for his men. Accustomed to an opulent life, he wanted to go out in style.[235]

In late April 1945, as the last main camps came into reach of Allied troops, some transports began to head for wholly imaginary sites. In the south, Nazi leaders like RSHA chief Kaltenbrunner dreamed of an impregnable Alp fortress on Austrian soil, with its own arms factories. Several Camp SS officials duly moved toward this make-believe site in Tyrol. Among them were Commandant Pister and his colleague Eduard Weiter, who had replaced Martin Weiss as commandant of Dachau. They fled from Dachau at the last moment on April 28 or 29, driving off in convoys loaded with food and alcohol. With Himmler's blessing, prisoner treks were heading south for the Ötz Valley, too, where a testing facility for fighter jets was being built. If necessary, Himmler ordered, the prisoners would have to live in holes in the ground; in the end, few even made it onto Austrian soil.[236]

The SS in northern Germany also had visions of a remote new camp.[237]

Camp SS leaders considered various sites, including German cities near the Baltic coast (Lübeck and Flensburg) and an island in the Baltic Sea (Fehmarn). There was even talk of taking prisoners to Norway, where the former Auschwitz camp compound leader Aumeier was setting up a camp staffed by guards from Sachsenhausen. Although there were no proper plans to speak of, a number of prisoner convoys duly headed toward the northern corner of Germany. Many were cut off by Allied troops, but the SS still assembled well over ten thousand prisoners from Neuengamme and Stutthof in Neustadt (outside Lübeck) at the beginning of May 1945. Most were held on board three ships (the freighters *Athen* and *Thielbek*, and the passenger ship *Cap Arcona*) in Neustadt bay. Inmates were crammed belowdecks without food, water, or air; each morning, the Soviet prisoner Aleksander Machnew recalled, they had to lift out the dead on ropes.[238]

Meanwhile, many Camp SS leaders gathered farther north, in Flensburg, the fanciful "Fortress North" that became a magnet for the die-hard elite of the Third Reich. It was the seat of the German caretaker government around Grand Admiral Karl Dönitz, the fanatical military commander who became Reich president after Hitler's suicide on April 30, 1945, and it drew the experts of Nazi terror, as well, including leading SS and RSHA officers. Senior WVHA staff arrived via Ravensbrück, after fleeing the camp around April 28, and were joined by other Camp SS veterans. It was an illustrious group. All department leaders of Office Group D were present—Rudolf Höss, Gerhard Maurer, Enno Lolling, and Wilhelm Burger—as was their nominal boss, Richard Glücks. Also gathered were several former commandants—Max Pauly (Neuengamme), Anton Kaindl (Sachsenhausen), Fritz Suhren (Ravensbrück), and Paul Werner Hoppe (Stutthof)—accompanied by some of their staff. Finally, there was Bertha Eicke and her family; as the widow of the legendary Theodor Eicke, she was as close to royalty as anyone in the Camp SS, and was looked after personally by Höss. What brought all of them to Flensburg was, above all, the presence of Heinrich Himmler, who had also made his way north and met his men around May 3–4, 1945. It was to be the final conference between Himmler and his Camp SS leaders.[239]

Lethal Transports

The final death transports of spring 1945 reproduced the suffering of earlier evacuations. Prisoners had no hope of respite on marches, even after treks pulled up for the night. Barns and sheds were so packed that sleep was often impossible, while those lying out in the open—in quarries, fields, or forest clearings—shivered in the cold and rain; there were frequent scuffles, as well,

with stronger inmates stealing food and blankets.[240] Occasionally, the Camp
SS regrouped along the way in provisional compounds. The largest such site
was set up on April 23, 1945, when the first columns of the Sachsenhausen
death march stopped near a village called Below. Even the most primitive
satellite camp was well equipped compared to the Below forest. At least sixteen thousand prisoners slept in muddy holes or tents made from branches.
During the day, they huddled around fires or walked a few steps to forage for
bark, roots, and beetles. It was days before prisoners received real nourishment, after trucks from the ICRC, which monitored the course of the death
march, arrived with food parcels. The distribution of milk, canned meat, and
fruit undoubtedly saved prisoner lives. But hundreds were dead by the time
the SS resumed the march on April 29–30, 1945.[241]

SS murders mounted up during these last transports. Because of the
growing reluctance of ordinary guards to cover themselves in blood just before the German defeat was sealed, Camp SS leaders entrusted the task of
killing stragglers to selected SS men stationed at the rear of death march columns. The so-called burial detail on one of the Flossenbürg death marches,
for example, was led by none other than Erich Muhsfeldt, the veteran of the
Majdanek and Birkenau crematorium, whom we last encountered waving
body parts at female guards. SS men like Muhsfeldt, who had long become inured to murder, occasionally taunted and tormented the exhausted prisoners
before shooting them.[242]

The fact that many of the hardened SS killers were anti-Semites, and many
of their victims Jews, has led some historians to describe the spring 1945
death transports as the last stage of the Holocaust: with the gas chambers
closed, Jewish prisoners were now exterminated by other methods.[243] There is
no doubt that Jews made up a large proportion of KL prisoners on these death
marches—somewhere between one-third and half—and a large proportion of
the dead.[244] And yet, the SS made no attempt to systematically kill all Jews
during evacuations. This time, there were no genocidal orders from above; on
the contrary, Himmler talked about Jews as hostages, which was one reason
why they were more likely than most prisoners to be moved out of camps as
the Allies approached. During the ensuing death transports, Jews were not
treated fundamentally differently from the other prisoners.[245] They often
marched together and shared a similar fate. In fact, with prisoner numbers
and uniforms mixed up or missing, and many Jews using the confusion of
the final weeks—when files were lost or destroyed—to conceal their identities, it was often impossible to tell them apart from other prisoner groups
anyway. In the end, survival depended primarily on luck and strength.[246]

Even when the SS specifically selected Jews for separate transports, it was not necessarily as a prelude to mass extermination. Many escorts of the train of "exchange Jews" that departed from Bergen-Belsen on April 10, 1945 were demoralized elderly ex-soldiers, and they largely left the prisoners in peace. Some shared food and cigarettes with them, while the transport leader tried to find additional supplies along the way. At times, the guards even allowed prisoners to leave the train and wander through the countryside to search for something edible—utterly unthinkable during earlier KL evacuations.[247]

All this leads to a crucial conclusion: the main purpose of the KL evacuations was not the murder of Jews or other prisoners.[248] Although mass death through exhaustion, hunger, disease, and bullets was an inevitable result, it was not the end itself. When it came to mass extermination, the SS still had more effective means at its disposal, as it demonstrated to devastating effect during occasional last-minute massacres.[249] Nonetheless, the transports proved lethal and many tens of thousands of prisoners died on German roads, trains, and ships during April and early May 1945—including some killed inadvertently by Allied forces, perhaps the most tragic chapter in the course of the evacuations.[250]

Prisoner deaths by friendly fire had increased with the escalation of bombing raids in 1944, as the Allies attacked various German factories using slave labor. One of the most lethal attacks came on August 24, 1944: following a U.S. raid on the Buchenwald armaments works, almost four hundred prisoners perished, including the former SPD chairman in the Reichstag, Rudolf Breitscheid. The SS also suffered more than one hundred casualties from the attack, including many relatives of SS men; Gerhard Maurer, the de facto leader of Office Group D, lost his wife and three children when a shelter was hit.[251] Other main KL were bombed, too, as were some satellites.[252] Prisoners had mixed feelings about these raids. They reveled in the vulnerability of their SS tormentors, and in the fact that Allied air supremacy would shorten the war. At the same time, they knew that their would-be liberators might kill them, as the bombs were blind to the difference between perpetrator and victim. When prisoners from the Dachau screw factory were hit in October 1944 by a hail of bombs, they thought "that this would be the end of us all," Edgar Kupfer wrote soon after in his secret diary, recovering from a broken foot in the infirmary.[253]

The threat to prisoner lives from the air increased in the first months of 1945, as Allied planes dropped more bombs than ever and low-flying aircraft began strafing soldiers and civilians. Among the targets was the notorious Oranienburg brick works, which were flattened on April 10, 1945, burying hundreds of inmates among the rubble. A raid on Nordhausen a few days earlier had claimed even more lives, killing 1,300 prisoners in the Boelcke death zone.[254] Many more casualties came outside the KL. Evacuation trains were particularly vulnerable. On the evening of April 8, 1945, for example, a U.S. attack on the freight depot at Celle partially destroyed a long train, which had arrived with almost 3,500 prisoners from Neuengamme and Buchenwald; several hundred were killed, many more badly wounded.[255]

The worst disaster came right at the end of the war, on May 3, 1945. During a major British aerial attack on German ships around Kiel and Lübeck, several missiles hit the *Thielbek* and *Cap Arcona* in Neustadt bay. An urgent warning from the Swiss Red Cross that both ships held inmates had not been passed on in time. Prisoners who survived the explosions and fires on board froze to death or drowned; some were shot by British fighter planes. "I had already swum a little," Anatolij Kulikow later testified, "but to keep swimming any farther was beyond my power." He was saved by other prisoners in a lifeboat, some of the five hundred survivors of what may be the largest naval catastrophe in history, having claimed over seven thousand lives.[256]

Ordinary Germans

At around four-thirty on the afternoon of April 26, 1945, the concentration camps came to Oberlindhart, a sleepy hamlet amid the rolling hills of Lower Bavaria. Centa Schmalzl, a fifty-two-year-old housekeeper on her brother's farm, was alone when a trek of around 280 prisoners slowly came into view, surrounded by a few dozen SS escorts. The agitated transport leader, an elderly SS man with a bright red face, told Schmalzl brusquely that they would stay for the night. He then demanded a bed for a woman he introduced as his wife and some food for his guards, who made themselves comfortable in the kitchen. Centa Schmalzl watched as the guards beat prisoners who begged for food. They also hit a local French laborer who tried to give water to the captives. After the SS had finally distributed a few potatoes among the starving prisoners, they locked them in a barn, though not for long. Following a nearby explosion, the panicking SS men forced them out again after midnight. Just before the column left, Centa Schmalzl heard shots from the barn. An SS man emerged and asked her to get rid of three corpses inside; the other prisoners marched away, disappearing into the night.[257]

This trek was part of a death march that had left Buchenwald on April 7 with more than three thousand prisoners, mostly Jews from the "little camp," and which had since split into different groups. Oberlindhart was one of countless crime scenes along the way, as the trek wound toward faraway Dachau.[258] Similar scenes took place all over Germany in spring 1945. In streets, squares, and stations, local Germans were confronted with death transports from the KL: they saw the beatings, heard the shots, and smelled the dead. SS terror had become ever more visible since the spread of satellite camps in late 1943. Now it fully spilled into the open, as prisoners appeared even in remote corners like Oberlindhart.[259]

The responses of ordinary Germans varied, as they had done during earlier encounters. One reaction was shock; even months later, some witnesses were unable to testify without breaking down.[260] Occasionally, dismayed locals left food and drink on the roads, or handed it directly to prisoners.[261] Others aided those who had fled. There were plenty of escapes during the transports as desperate prisoners used the growing chaos to steal away, often at the spur of the moment.[262] The prisoners were helped by the fact that many were wearing civilian clothing, after the WVHA had run out of prisoner uniforms months earlier.[263] To succeed, the fugitives often needed local Germans to turn a blind eye or to offer shelter.[264] On April 28, 1945, in a singular event in the history of the KL, some fifteen escaped prisoners even joined a local uprising by civilians in Dachau, the birthplace of the KL. Determined to hand over the town to U.S. troops without bloodshed, the small group of rebels stormed the town hall. SS men soon surrounded them, and although most rebels got away, six were shot dead.[265]

Far more common than popular support, however, was silence. The few German helpers were far outnumbered by the silent majority, which stood by or looked away as transports passed through. Such passivity could conceal different emotions, as we have seen, including curiosity, indifference, and resignation.[266] Above all, there was fear. Fear of the SS, which threatened locals willing to help prisoners and occasionally lashed out at them.[267] Fear of guilt by association, because civilians wanted nothing to do with SS crimes as the Allies were about to arrive; when a guard dragged away an exhausted prisoner in a village near Oberlindhart, a local woman beseeched him not to shoot his victim right outside her house.[268] And finally, there was the fear of the prisoners. The picture of KL inmates as dangerous criminals was firmly entrenched, and some locals and passing soldiers vented their disgust, shouting "traitors!" "bandits!" and "bastards!" as treks passed.[269] SS guards encouraged such hostility, reminding the locals: "These are criminals."[270]

Fear sometimes turned into paranoia and panic, with apocalyptic visions of escaped criminals attacking defenseless civilians. In reality, most prisoners on the run were careful to stay out of sight. But this did not stop the rumors about hordes of dangerous prisoners on the loose, which fed on similar anxieties about marauding bands of foreign workers. Local officials and newspapers sounded hysterical warnings, and there was plenty of talk about looting, rape, and murder, just as there had been after the evacuation of Buchenwald.[271] Galvanized into action, elderly men from the People's Storm, youngsters from the Hitler Youth, small-time party officials, and upstanding members of the local community reported escaped prisoners to the authorities or joined in manhunts, typical for the decentralization of Nazi terror toward the end of the Third Reich.[272]

Among the victims were prisoners who escaped from the train in Celle in the wake of the U.S. air raid on April 8, 1945. The following morning, German soldiers, policemen, and SS forces combed nearby gardens and woods, where most prisoners were hiding, and shot them at point-blank range. Local civilians took part, too. The massacre was masterminded by the local military commander, who claimed that prisoners were "plundering and murdering" all over town; in all, at least 170 prisoners were killed around Celle.[273] In numerous other German towns and villages, too, fugitive prisoners were murdered with the help of the local population. It was "a real bloodbath," one witness wrote after a similar pursuit, still stunned by the sudden killing frenzy that had come over some of his neighbors, who shot prisoners cowering in cellars, sheds, and barns.[274]

Some locals also participated in massacres of prisoners still under SS control. This is what happened on April 13, 1945, in Gardelegen, a small town north of Magdeburg. Several prisoner treks had recently reached the area, which was almost completely encircled by U.S. troops. Arguing that the prisoners would pose a grave threat to the population if liberated, the fanatical young Nazi Party district leader in Gardelegen pushed for mass murder. He was supported by other locals, whipped up by stories of outrages committed by fugitive prisoners. On the afternoon of April 13, the prisoners were marched from army barracks in the center of town to an isolated brick barn outside. The killers—a motley crew of SS men, paratroopers, and others—used torches and flamethrowers to ignite the petrol-soaked straw inside the barn, and threw grenades. The barn was soon ablaze. "The screams by the men who were burning alive grew louder, as did the groans," the Polish prisoner Stanisław Majewicz, one of around twenty-five survivors, later recalled. Those who tried to flee were cut down with machine guns. When U.S. troops reached the site on April 15, they found around a thousand charred corpses.[275]

News of this atrocity rapidly spread through the U.S. press, and Gardelegen has become a symbol of Nazi war crimes. But it was the exception, not the norm. Few local leaders were as bent on mass murder as those in Gardelegen. Just some twenty miles away, for instance, another Nazi Party official protected a trek of five hundred prisoners in his village. And even in Gardelegen, only a small number of citizens actively participated in the murder of prisoners. Many more Germans, here and elsewhere, had little desire to tie themselves to a lost cause.[276]

The KL and their prisoners always drew a range of responses from ordinary Germans. Popular opinion was never united, not at the beginning of the Third Reich, and not at the end, either. The wide spectrum of reactions was evident even in small villages like Oberlindhart. Most locals had watched in silence as the Buchenwald trek halted on April 26, 1945. A few called for mass executions; several others, among them the mayor, sheltered fugitives. The local drama continued even after the trek had left the village. Some fervent inhabitants denounced prisoners who had hidden in the barn of the Schmalzl family. But there was another twist: a local policeman took pity on the recaptured prisoners after they pleaded for their lives, and led them to a different farm, where they stayed until U.S. soldiers arrived the following day. They were finally free.[277]

The End

By early May 1945, even the most blinkered Nazi fanatic knew that the game was up. The Third Reich was in ruins, and many career SS men like Rudolf Höss felt that "with the Führer, our world has gone under, too." Their last hope was Heinrich Himmler. As Höss and the other Camp SS managers prepared to meet their leader in Flensburg on May 3–4, 1945, they probably expected a final battle cry. Would Himmler offer them another fantastic vision to cling to? Or would he order them to go down in a blaze of glory? But there was no last stand. All smiles, Himmler, who had been frozen out of the new Dönitz government, breezily announced that he had no more directives for the KL. Before he dismissed his men with a handshake, he issued one last order: the officials should disguise themselves and go into hiding, just as he planned to do himself.[278]

Even in defeat, the Camp SS leaders followed Himmler. Several men from Office Group D dressed in navy uniforms and took false identities. Gerhard Maurer became Paul Kehr, and Höss turned into Franz Lang. In disguise, Höss and Maurer, together with several other WVHA men, took jobs on small farms in rural northern Germany and initially evaded capture. Their former boss Richard Glücks, however, who had taken the jolly moniker Sonnemann (Sunnyman), had no hope of passing himself off as a farmhand. Glücks was a shadow of the sturdy figure he had been six years earlier, when he took over the KL system. His gradual loss of institutional power, evident not least in his increasingly rare meetings with Oswald Pohl, had been accompanied by a marked physical decline. Popping pills and drinking heavily, he was rumored to have lost his mind, and ended up in a German military hospital in Flensburg, more dead than alive. On May 10, 1945, just after the capitulation of the Third Reich, Glücks killed himself, biting on a capsule of potassium cyanide.[279]

Glücks's death was part of a wave of suicides that swept Germany in spring 1945. Nazi propaganda extolled suicide as the ultimate sacrifice. In truth, it was mostly fear and despair that led former Nazi officials to take their lives.[280] The roll call of SS suicides was led by Heinrich Himmler, who killed himself on May 23, 1945, in British captivity, two days after his arrest. Among the other Camp SS officers who died by their own hand were Enno Lolling and the last Dachau commandant, Eduard Weiter.[281] Most of the dead were hardbitten veterans, though some had felt more ambivalent about the KL system, among them Hans Delmotte, the young Auschwitz doctor who had broken down during his first selection of prisoners.[282] Like Himmler and Glücks, several Camp SS suicides used cyanide, which had been tested a few months earlier for this very purpose during a lethal prisoner trial in Sachsenhausen. A few others, like the Gross-Rosen commandant Arthur Rödl, departed in more dramatic style: a man with a long history of hands-on violence, Rödl chose a suitably gory death and blew himself up with a hand grenade.[283]

Most Camp SS officers, however, wanted to survive the Third Reich. They may have talked about heroic sacrifice and kamikaze missions, but in the end, they scrambled to save their skins.[284] The mass of SS guards did the same. In the remaining camps, the officials often stayed away from the compounds in the final days, plotting their getaway. When the moment came, they changed into civilian clothes and disappeared.[285] Likewise, SS escorts on death transports tried to evade capture at the last moment; if there were no regular clothes at hand, they put on prisoner uniforms.[286]

Before they made their escape, SS escorts had to decide the fate of the remaining prisoners on their transports. Some chose to kill. Early on May 3, 1945, for example, SS men ordered prisoners on a Buchenwald death march, which had reached a small forest near Traunstein in Bavaria, to line up and opened fire, killing fifty-eight men. Then the guards "threw away their weapons and made a quick getaway," testified the only survivor, who had lain injured under two dead comrades.[287] Elsewhere, SS escorts disappeared during brief stops or overnight, concerned only with saving themselves.[288] When the survivors of a Sachsenhausen death march awoke on May 2, 1945, by a forest clearing outside a small village near Schwerin, with all guards gone, they were dumbfounded. "We could not comprehend it, not believe it," the Austrian Jew Walter Simoni recalled after the war.[289] But the abandoned prisoners were not yet safe; they were "free people but not liberated," as one survivor later put it, still in danger of falling victim to Nazi fanatics. Bewildered and exhausted, some dazed prisoners actually continued their aimless march, even without SS escorts.[290] Only the arrival of the Allies finally put an end to the transports. We will never know how many prisoners gained their freedom in April and early May 1945 in German cities and villages, on trains, in forests, and on the open road, but their total number most probably exceeded one hundred thousand.[291]

Many more men, women, and children survived inside the last KL. During the final five weeks of the Third Reich, the Allies liberated an estimated one hundred and sixty thousand prisoners in main camps, most of them in Buchenwald, Bergen-Belsen, Dachau, and Mauthausen-Gusen. In addition, Allied troops found an estimated ninety thousand prisoners in over one hundred satellite camps, in some cases even after the official German capitulation. The great majority of liberated satellites were small, holding fewer than one thousand prisoners. But there were also huge ones like Ebensee, where U.S. troops encountered an estimated sixteen thousand survivors on May 6, 1945. Among them were Dr. Miklós Nyiszli, who had arrived in the Mauthausen complex on the death transport from Auschwitz in January 1945, and the Czech interpreter Drahomír Bárta, a longtime inmate of the camp. When the first U.S. soldiers appeared in Ebensee, Bárta noted in his diary, they were greeted by "indescribable scenes of joy and ecstasy."[292]

The final moments of captivity were full of confusion. The prisoners had long been suspended in a state of nervous exhaustion, between hope of liberation and fear of SS massacres, stray bullets, and bombs. "All that has kept us going for three weeks is the rumor that the war will only last for two or three more days," Ágnes Rózsa wrote on April 28, 1945, in the Flossenbürg satellite camp Holleischen, where she had arrived after the bombing of her old camp in Nuremberg. She endured more slave labor in a nearby munitions workshop, until it was hit by Allied bombs on May 3, 1945. Rózsa survived once more, but she was still in SS hands. "Our liberation is so close and so real," she wrote the following day. "That makes the thought that we have to die at the last minute . . . even more unbearable." When freedom finally came on the morning of May 5—with U.S. soldiers emerging from the surrounding forest—it came suddenly. Silence fell across the former farm that made up the Holleischen camp. Then there were shouts of "They are coming! They are here!" followed by wild screams from more than one thousand women inside.[293]

On occasion, the transition from terror to freedom came in a more orderly fashion. In Buchenwald, SS Commandant Pister told the camp elder, the German Communist Hans Eiden, early on April 11, 1945, that he would hand the camp over to him. Soon after, a final command went out over the loudspeakers, ordering SS members to move out immediately. By now, U.S.

troops were in the immediate vicinity; shots were ringing out as the SS fled, with the guards on the watchtowers the last to leave. In midafternoon, with the SS finally gone, prisoners emerged from hiding and went toward the main gate. Soon after, Eiden spoke over the public address system, confirming that "the SS has left the camp" and that an international committee of prisoners was in control. When the U.S. troops reached the main compound, a white flag greeted them on one of the towers.[294]

In Dachau, too, U.S. soldiers saw a white flag when they arrived on the afternoon of April 29, 1945, though here the flag had been raised by anxious SS men, not the prisoners. Although Dachau was not the last concentration camp to fall, its liberation symbolized the destruction of the Nazi terror machine. It was more than twelve years since the SS had set up its first makeshift camp on the site. Since then, Dachau had changed its appearance many times over and gained multiple functions: bulwark of the Nazi revolution, model camp, SS training ground, slave labor reservoir, human experimentation site, mass extermination ground, and center of a satellite camp network. Dachau was not the most deadly KL, but it was the most notorious at the time, inside Germany and abroad. "Dachau, Germany's most dreaded extermination camp, has been captured," *The New York Times* reported on its front page on May 1, 1945. Of the more than two hundred thousand prisoners who had passed through the Dachau complex since 1933, at least fourteen thousand had perished in the final months from January 1945, not counting all the unknown victims, like those of the death marches that continued for several days after the liberation of the main camp.[295]

The final hours in Dachau had been just as tense as in the other camps. By the morning of April 29, 1945, most SS men had fled, but the guards on the watchtowers still trained their machine guns on the prisoners. Detonations could be heard close by, planes roared across the overcast sky, and the howl of tank engines came and went. Then prisoners listened as small arms fire edged closer, with some guards shooting back. Finally, a U.S. officer, accompanied by two reporters, peered into the compound from the gatehouse and entered the empty roll call square. Within minutes, the square was bursting with ecstatic inmates, who embraced and kissed the liberators. "They grabbed us," the officer wrote the following day, "and tossed us into the air screaming at the top of their lungs."[296]

Before long, all of Dachau was in an uproar, with the news spreading fast across the compound. Even prisoners in the infirmary heard the revelry and began to celebrate. Among them was Edgar Kupfer, the intrepid chronicler of Dachau, who had become weaker and weaker in recent months. Now he watched from his bed as other sick prisoners struggled to their feet and went outside, or looked through the windows at the tumultuous scenes.[297]

Soon Kupfer was joined by Moritz Choinowski, who had been treated in the Dachau infirmary a few weeks earlier for an ear infection. It was almost a miracle that the fifty-year-old Polish-born Jew was still alive. His ordeal in the KL had begun years earlier, on September 28, 1939, when the Gestapo took him from his adopted hometown of Magdeburg to Buchenwald. That afternoon, Choinowski had handed over everything—his money, documents, suit, hat, shirt, socks, jumper, and trousers—and become a concentration camp inmate. "I stood there naked and received a convict uniform," he later wrote. His red-yellow triangle marked him out as a political prisoner (he had been an SPD supporter) and as a Jew. He survived the early war years in Buchenwald, despite several months in the lethal quarry and repeated corporal punishment (including three times "twenty-five blows"), and escaped the clutches of the murderous T-4 doctors. He survived his first mass selection in Auschwitz, soon after his arrival there on October 19, 1942, on a freight car with some four hundred other men from Buchenwald. He survived more selections over the coming two years in Auschwitz-Monowitz, at the height of the Holocaust, and also withstood more illness, starvation, and beatings, despite serious injuries. He survived the death transport from Auschwitz via the hell of Gross-Rosen, during which an SS bullet only just missed his head, hitting his ear instead, and arrived in Dachau on January 28, 1945. And he survived the final months of forced labor, even though he was now badly emaciated and sick, and contracted typhus, which claimed thousands of lives in Dachau in early 1945. Somehow Moritz Choinowski had survived all this, and on April 29, 1945, after more than two thousand days in the KL, he was free. "Is this possible?" he sobbed, as he hugged and kissed Edgar Kupfer in the Dachau infirmary. "And he cries," Kupfer continued in his diary, "and I think about how he has suffered, and I cannot hold back my tears."[298]

Epilogue

Liberation was a cathartic moment. Many inmates felt grief and rage for all they had lost, but also relief and euphoria. They were alive and the camps were gone. One could end the story here, with the embrace of Moritz Choinowski and Edgar Kupfer in Dachau encapsulating the suffering of prisoners and the hopes of survivors. But these hopes were often dashed, and this legacy of the camps is part of their history, too. In fact, some survivors never had any hope at all. Thousands of them were so sick they did not realize what had happened; as Choinowski and Kupfer hugged, prisoners nearby were dying and stared straight past the U.S. soldiers.[1] Others observed the jubilation with incomprehension. One teenage survivor of Dachau, who had lost his father only weeks earlier, recalled that he "watched the people sing and dance with joy, and they seemed to me as if they'd lost their minds. I looked at myself and couldn't recognize who I was."[2] Among the more ecstatic survivors, meanwhile, the initial excitement quickly waned as they emerged from the depths of the KL.

Take Moritz Choinowski himself. Released from an American-run hospital in Dachau in June 1945, he moved to a camp for displaced persons (DPs) and then, in early 1946, to a sparsely furnished room on the outskirts of Munich. For the next three years, he led a pitiful life. His body had been ruined by the camps; he could barely use his left arm and was in constant pain, not least from chronically infected scars left by SS whippings. Unable to work, he depended on welfare for his rent, food, heating, bedding, and clothes. "I have not received any shoes since 1946," he pleaded with an aid organization in

April 1948. He was all alone, assuming wrongly that his daughter and his ex-wife (their marriage had been annulled by a Nazi court because she was an "Aryan") had died in a devastating bombing raid on Magdeburg that destroyed their home. His last hope was to join his brother in the United States, which appeared to many DPs like the promised land. Tens of thousands of Holocaust survivors headed for North America in the late 1940s, after the United States temporarily relaxed its immigration restrictions, and in June 1949 Choinowski boarded the navy ship *General Muir* to cross the Atlantic. After spending some time with his brother in Detroit, he moved to Toledo, Ohio, where he married another survivor in 1952. But he could not remake his old life.

Before the Third Reich, Moritz Choinowski had been a vigorous self-made businessman, running a thriving tailor's store and workshop. Now he was weak and ailing, with the SS tattoo on his pale arm a constant reminder of who had destroyed his existence. He could only work occasionally, and then only with painkillers. Employed mainly by a local dry cleaner and tailor, he earned an average of $125 a month by the mid-1950s, barely enough to live. Meanwhile, his claims for reparations, submitted years earlier, had come to nothing, despite the efforts of his daughter in Germany, with whom he had finally reestablished contact in 1953 (she had last heard from him nine years earlier, in a postcard from Auschwitz). In April 1957, Choinowski appealed directly to the president of the Bavarian Reparations Office, which had dragged out his case, to "save me from my hardship." A few months later, he received a first payment, but he continued to live in humble circumstances. Despite his poor health he was grateful for having survived the camps, he told his daughter in one of his last letters, but he questioned what all the suffering had been for: "Humanity has learned nothing from the wars, on the contrary, almost all nations are arming once more for warfare and that will probably be the end for humanity." Choinowski died in Toledo Hospital on the evening of March 9, 1967, aged seventy-two.[3]

By that time, his former Dachau comrade Edgar Kupfer was living as a recluse on the Italian island of Sardinia. He had also struggled in the early years after liberation. The bombing raid on Dachau had left him with a badly damaged foot and he suffered from a depression that pushed him to the edge of suicide. He felt like a stranger in his native Germany, and in 1953, after a spell in Switzerland and Italy, he gained entry to the United States, like Choinowski before him. But he never settled. He was plagued by pain and by nightmares about the KL, and following a breakdown in 1960, the destitute fifty-six-year-old told an acquaintance: "My life here in America has not been blessed by fortune: bellboy in a hotel, security guard in a warehouse, dishwasher, professional Santa Claus, and finally here [in Hollywood] doorman in a large cinema."

Edgar Kupfer returned to Europe soon after and spent more than two decades in Italy, increasingly withdrawn and isolated. Bitter about the lack of interest in his chronicle of Dachau, he lived in abject poverty; again and again, he had to "tighten the belt, not to say starve," as he put it. He had received some reparation payments in the 1950s, after a lengthy struggle in the courts. From the 1960s, he also drew a pension from the German authorities, though it was only small because unsympathetic assessors had minimized his mental anguish. The indignity was compounded by the authorities' failure to ensure timely payments. After yet another late transfer, the normally reserved and formal Kupfer lost his composure. All these years after liberation and he still had to beg for every scrap. "Trust me, this life makes me sick," he wrote to the Stuttgart Office for Reparations in November 1979, adding: "It would probably be best if I took my life, then you would have one troublemaker less and the German state would only have to pay for my funeral, nothing more. But I am not sure if I want to give this satisfaction to those responsible." Kupfer eventually returned to Germany and died in a nursing home on July 7, 1991, in complete obscurity.[4]

All survivors had their own stories, some happier, some even more miserable than Kupfer and Choinowski. Whatever happened to them, they often faced similar hardships: the lasting pain of injury and illness, the search for a new home and job, the indifference of wider society, and the undignified struggle for compensation. And they were left with all the agonizing memories, the final cruelty of the camps. The memory of the crimes was far more torturous for survivors than for perpetrators, who often settled into quiet lives and forgot about the KL, as long as they could escape justice.[5] Survivors could not hope for such oblivion.

First Steps

A few hours after the liberation of Bergen-Belsen on the afternoon of April 15, 1945, Arthur Lehmann clambered across the demolished fence that had enclosed his prisoner sector and rushed to the nearby compounds for women in search of his wife, Gertrude. The SS had ripped them apart in Vught more than a year ago, having already deported their two children to their deaths in Auschwitz. Since then, Lehmann, a middle-aged German Jewish lawyer who emigrated to the Netherlands before the war, had survived an odyssey through the KL complex that finally brought him, via Auschwitz, Mauthausen, and Neuengamme, to Bergen-Belsen. In the days after liberation, he continued to search in vain for his wife. Later he learned that she had died just after the arrival of the British troops: "And so the day that brought me freedom brought her death."[6]

Gertrude Lehmann was one of an estimated twenty-five to thirty thousand prisoners who were freed in concentration camps in spring 1945, only to perish soon after; in all, at least ten percent of survivors had died by the end of May 1945.[7] Mortality was highest in the largest camps, where misery had multiplied at the end of the war. And none of the liberated camps was bigger or deadlier than Bergen-Belsen. British troops found fifty-three thousand prisoners across two sites, with most inmates, including Lehmann and his wife, held on the grounds of the main camp. Here typhus and other illnesses still raged, and the sick and starved had received no food or drink for days. "The dying just continued," Arthur Lehmann noted later.[8]

Emergency relief in the liberated KL fell to the individual Allied forces. The soldiers on the ground were poorly prepared for the humanitarian disaster. Whatever information had trickled down during the haphazard planning for the occupation—about the location of camps and conditions inside—was often outdated and inaccurate. Mostly, the troops did not even aim to liberate specific camps, they simply stumbled across them.[9] Their initial reaction was shock. They were overwhelmed by the sight of skeletal survivors and decomposing bodies, and by the stench of waste and death.[10] Meanwhile, a few predatory soldiers, particularly from the Red Army, used the initial chaos to assault female inmates. "That was the worst, half-dead as I was," testified Ilse Heinrich, who had survived as an "asocial" in Ravensbrück.[11]

With Allied commanders unable to provide immediate order and aid, as they scrambled for more staff and supplies, survivors took matters into their own hands. As soon as the Camp SS had departed, they stormed storerooms and depots; in Bergen-Belsen, Arthur Lehmann saw the night sky light up with fires of inmates cooking their first meals in freedom. But as some survivors celebrated, a few drunk on SS champagne, others felt the dark side of inmate self-help. As in the past, inmates fought over the spoils. The weakest often went empty-handed, while some of the stronger ones ate until they were sick. "Most [inmates] immediately gobbled down everything, and a new round of dying began," Lehmann recalled.[12] Survivors also looked beyond the camps in search of supplies, walking to nearby SS settlements, villages, and towns.

The need was greatest for all those prisoners liberated outside the KL, during death transports. Desperate for food, medication, and lodging, they could not count on help from passing Allied troops, and initially had to fend for themselves. For the most part, this meant asking locals, or taking from them.

After Renata Laqueur was freed from one of the Bergen-Belsen trains destined for Theresienstadt, she walked to the nearby town of Tröbitz, some ninety miles south of Berlin, which was teeming with Soviet tanks and soldiers. Laqueur entered a German home and demanded food; she ate in silence, watched by the nervous occupants. Then she went to the local shops, which were being ransacked by other survivors of the death train (the Soviet military later gave them official permission to plunder). Packing as much as she could on a stolen bicycle, she slowly made her way back to the train and her gravely ill husband: "Paul's face—as he saw the meat, bread and bacon, jam and sugar—was more than enough reward for all the effort and agony," she wrote a few months later.[13]

Many Germans dreaded encounters with freed prisoners. Some offered help and assistance, including the women of Tröbitz, who later carried Paul Laqueur and other invalids from the train to a makeshift hospital—though it is unclear whether they acted out of charity or calculation.[14] Many more stood back, looking at the survivors as a threat. A farmer from the village of Bergen, a couple of miles from the camp, spoke for many when he claimed that robberies by freed prisoners and slave laborers had spread "the greatest horror since the Thirty Years' War."[15] When it became clear that ordinary Germans had little to fear from feeble survivors, who were often just as scared, the early panic gave way to disgust, with complaints about dirty foreigners defecating everywhere, and bitter resentment about their supposed privileges and profiteering. This hostility grew out of long-standing social and racial prejudices, as well as the more immediate impact of defeat and occupation. Wrapped up in their own sense of victimhood, most locals had little room for compassion.[16]

Adverse reactions were not restricted to former members of the Nazi national community. Allied officials, too, showed little sympathy at times. Amid all the dirt and disease, they found it hard to see the humanity in survivors, who appeared to them (to use the words of a U.S. congressman visiting Buchenwald) like "absent-minded apes." They were particularly troubled by the survivors' behavior. Some liberators had expected docile charges and now decried the inmates' lack of hygiene, modesty, and morality. One British official in Bergen-Belsen complained that they made "an infernal mess of the camp," and another recoiled at inmates fighting "for every morsel" like a "swarm of angry monkeys."[17] In part, the lack of empathy stemmed from the discrepancy between the norms of civil society, internalized by the liberators, and the norms of the camp, deeply ingrained in survivors. "Organizing," for example, had been a basic rule of survival, and inmates naturally continued to "organize" (as they still called it) in the early days of liberation. When a baffled British soldier confronted two Polish boys, who carried a large sack of food during the early looting around Bergen-Belsen, and asked if they knew that stealing was wrong, one boy answered: "Steal? We aren't stealing, we're just taking what we want!"[18]

Such tensions eased after the relief effort gathered strength and conditions gradually improved. In the largest camps, however, the situation remained critical for several weeks after liberation, as Allied officials struggled with the SS legacy of overcrowding, starvation, and epidemics. In Dachau, as French inmates reported on May 8, 1945, some of the barracks, built for seventy-five men, were still packed with up to six hundred sick inmates, who wasted away with little medical help, their bodies entangled with the dead; by the end of the month, 2,221 Dachau survivors had perished.[19]

The greatest challenge was Bergen-Belsen, where British forces faced an "almost superhuman task," as Arthur Lehmann noted.[20] Early on, they focused on the provision of food and water. Although the war was still raging, the British authorities quickly secured extra supplies. And as more relief workers arrived in late April, among them a group of British medical students, a more orderly refeeding routine could commence, using different diets. "Signs of humanity returning," one student wrote in his diary on May 5. By then, a special unit had already completed the dusting of barracks and inmates with DDT, an antityphus measure that began here and elsewhere within days of liberation. Despite all these efforts, some thirteen thousand survivors of Bergen-Belsen had perished by the end of May 1945.[21]

The expansion of medical relief was accompanied by growing Allied control over the freed camps, though not all survivors welcomed this development. The greatest point of contention was the restriction on inmate movements. Several camps went into temporary lockdown, with the U.S. commander of Dachau threatening to shoot anyone who left without permission. The military authorities wanted to contain looting and infectious illnesses and prepare for orderly releases. The survivors, meanwhile, felt like free men caught behind KL wire.[22]

To maintain discipline, the military relied heavily on selected inmates, building on the existing structures (even terms like "block elders" remained in use in some camps). During the first days, organized inmate groups—often emerging from the prisoner underground—played the central role in many freed camps. With the blessing of the beleaguered liberators, they tried to distribute supplies, enforce discipline, and stop plunder. In Dachau, the camp elder proudly proclaimed the "self-administration of comrades" on May 1, 1945, which even envisaged the continuation of daily roll calls. Over in

Buchenwald, armed inmates from the camp police guarded SS officials. They also patrolled the infernal "little camp," seen by survivors outside as a source of illness and criminality, thereby prolonging the suffering of those still trapped inside; the compound resembled a "concentration camp that has not been liberated," a U.S. army report found on April 24, 1945.[23] Even as more power passed to the Allied commanders, organized inmates—often led by an international committee, as in Dachau, Buchenwald, and Mauthausen—remained a major force, working with the new administration and enforcing its calls for order. "No chaos, no anarchy!" read an appeal of the Dachau committee on May 8, 1945.[24]

The international committees were dominated by former political prisoners, who would shape the memory of the camps for years to come; most stood on the left of the political spectrum, leading to enthusiastic celebrations of the Day of Labor (May 1) inside the liberated camps. By contrast, social outsiders had no voice at all, and Jews were marginalized, too. Neither Allied commanders nor inmate leaders acknowledged them as a distinct group, at least not initially. In Dachau and Buchenwald, Jewish survivors had to fight for a place on the international committees. "We demand that Jewish affairs are dealt with by Jewish representatives," a young Pole wrote in his Buchenwald diary on April 16, 1945.[25]

This was not the only clash between inmates under the frayed banner of international solidarity. Unresolved political conflicts poisoned the atmosphere, and would continue to do so in Cold War Europe, with entrenched battles between survivor groups over commemoration. Even more pronounced were the tensions between the national groups, yet another legacy of the KL. Nationality became the main marker of the postliberation inmate community, with separate barracks, organizations, and newspapers; during the May 1 celebration, most former prisoners marched under their own country's flag. Conflicts soon flared up over old resentments and new problems, though they rarely turned as violent as in Ebensee, where Soviet and Polish survivors apparently shot at each other. Most precarious was the position of some German survivors, who faced intense hostility because of their comparatively privileged position in the wartime KL. "To be honest, we should be glad that they did not bash our heads in," a German inmate wrote in Dachau on April 30, 1945.[26]

Even the timing of releases was determined by the inmates' national background, at least in Dachau. Within days of the German surrender on May 7, 1945, U.S. forces started to transfer former prisoners to better-appointed SS barracks and buildings outside the camp compound, with one national group following another. The final communiqué of the international committee appeared on June 2, 1945: "We depart happy and full of joy from this hell: it is over."[27]

Other liberated camps were quickly cleared, too. In Bergen-Belsen, British forces moved all survivors out of the main camp within four weeks, one barrack at a time, before burning the empty huts to the ground. The last one was torched in a ceremony on May 21, 1945; soldiers and former prisoners watched as the wooden hut, a large picture of Hitler pinned to one of its walls, was consumed by flames. Sick survivors, meanwhile, had been washed and disinfected, and taken to a huge and reasonably well-equipped British hospital area nearby, with enough space for ten thousand patients. One of them was Arthur Lehmann. He was operated on twice, delirious with fever. But he slowly got better and took great pleasure in the hot baths and clean beds. Most important was the care of the medical staff, especially by the matron on his ward, who sometimes sat down by his side and listened to his story. "I told her about my wife and my children," he wrote the following year. "She stroked my head and told me that everything would be all right. And that made me believe it, too."[28]

Survivors

Trapped in the nightmare of the KL, prisoners had often daydreamed about a happy future. Some inmates longed for a peaceful life in the countryside, an Auschwitz prisoner wrote in 1942, whereas others imagined only parties and pleasure.[29] After liberation, such visions of quiet contentment or hedonism quickly faded in the cold light of postwar Europe. The great majority of survivors were hoping to return home, though few were certain what would await them there. Once they left the compounds, they had to confront the reality of rebuilding their existence, often from Allied field hospitals and assembly centers crowded with others displaced by Nazi terror. "I have to begin to live again, without wife and family," the Dutch Jew Jules Schelvis, who had lost his loved ones in Sobibor, wrote in a French military hospital on May 26, 1945, a few weeks after his liberation from a Natzweiler satellite camp.[30]

At the end of the war, the former territory of the Third Reich was awash with millions of uprooted men, women, and children. While some were making their own way home, the occupation forces discouraged such independent initiatives, concerned about obstructions of military movements, and about the spread of disease and social disorder. Instead, the Allies set a vast repatriation program in motion, moving fast to reduce the number of DPs in their care. Among the first to return were former KL prisoners.[31]

Although the way home was hard for all survivors of the concentration camps, it proved harder for some than for others. On the whole, western Europeans had better prospects. True, their journey through the war-torn landscape was arduous, traveling on packed trains and trucks, but it rarely lasted for longer than a few weeks. Renata Laqueur and her convalescing husband, for example, left a reception camp near Dresden on July 4, 1945; three weeks later, she was sitting on her sofa in Amsterdam, still wearing a Hitler Youth shirt she had "organized" in Tröbitz. By that time, Arthur Lehmann had been back in the Netherlands for a month, having been flown out from Germany because of his poor health (he weighed just eighty-two pounds). The quickest to be repatriated were probably French inmates, almost all of whom were back home by mid-June, where many received a hero's welcome. A large group arrived in Paris on May 1, 1945, and marched in formation down the Champs-Élysées—past a tearful crowd, as one of them recalled—to be greeted at the Arc de Triomphe by General de Gaulle, who used the occasion to cement the image of a united "other France" of Nazi resisters, which became the focus of early postwar French national memory; later that year, de Gaulle appointed one of the survivors, Edmond Michelet, as his minister of armed forces.[32]

The situation was very different for most eastern European survivors. Inside the former camp compounds, Soviet inmates heard alarming rumors about what would happen to them, prompting a Dachau bulletin (run by loyal Stalinists) to issue an emphatic denial: everyone will be welcomed home "with care and love," a Red Army captain promised. Even skeptics had little choice, however, as the western Allies, on whose territory most displaced Soviets lived, had agreed to repatriate them, even if it meant using force. Between spring and autumn 1945, tens of thousands of KL survivors arrived in Soviet filtration and assembly camps, where they were received with suspicion and hostility. Alleged cowards, deserters, and traitors were quickly drafted into forced labor or sentenced to the Gulag. "It is difficult for me to talk about it," recalled a Ukrainian survivor of Dachau, who had been sent to the coal mines in the Donets Basin upon his return. "We survived the concentration camps and then some of our comrades died here in these mines." Those who escaped punishment often faced prejudice in Soviet society and stayed silent about their experiences in the KL.[33]

Eastern European Jews also endured great adversity after they returned from the camps. Within weeks of being freed, many tens of thousands had come home (most of them to Hungary).[34] Their first goal was to find missing relatives, but all too often, hope turned to despair. Lina Stumachin, a survivor of several KL, walked back from Saxony to Poland as fast as her swollen legs would take her. "In my imagination," she said later, "I saw my house, and those that I had lost would come back to me." When she finally arrived in the spa town of Zakopane, where she had run a shop before the war, goats were grazing where her house had once stood. There was no sign of her husband or child, either: "I waited for long days and weeks for nothing."[35] There was little local support for survivors like Stumachin. The Nazis had eradicated traditional Jewish culture, together with most Polish Jews. Local Poles, meanwhile, often refused to return homes and other possessions they had taken over after the deportation of the Jewish owners (the same happened in Hungary and the Baltic States). A wave of anti-Jewish discrimination and violence soon drove many concentration camp survivors back to the west, mainly to the U.S. zone of occupied Germany, together with Jews who had sheltered on Soviet territory during the war.[36]

Almost all foreign KL survivors who still lived on German soil in 1946 came from eastern Europe, and some stayed in permanent DP camps until well into the 1950s. Many were organized in survivor committees—mostly along national lines—that documented their suffering and promoted their interests. Among those resisting repatriation were thousands of Ukrainian and Baltic nationals who had no desire to live under Soviet rule. The same was true for some Poles from areas swallowed up by the USSR. Other Poles worried about the growing Communist domination over their country, which would eventually claim the lives of survivors like Witold Pilecki, who had played a significant part in the Auschwitz prisoner underground; arrested by the Polish secret police, he was executed in 1948 for his anticommunist activities.[37]

Then there were those Jewish KL survivors without anywhere to return to. Most vulnerable were the children. Thomas (Tommy) Buergenthal was lucky, being reunited with his mother (herself a survivor of Auschwitz and Ravensbrück) in late 1946 in Göttingen, Germany. Many others never saw their parents again and stayed in orphanages. It was in one such home in Paris that Lina Stumachin worked, after she had left Zakopane and Poland for good. Looking after the orphans, she told an interviewer in September 1946, helped her to fill the emptiness in her life and to forget "that you once had your own home, your own family, that you once had your own child." As for the future, she wanted to accompany the orphans to Palestine. Other Jewish DPs also headed there, especially after the foundation of the state of Israel in 1948; even here, though, they faced a difficult start to their new lives, overshadowed by the past, poverty, and the mistrust of earlier Jewish settlers. Of course, by no means all survivors were Zionists, and many thousands were admitted to countries like Britain and the United States; among them was Buergenthal, who arrived in New York in 1951, now aged seventeen, and embarked on a distinguished legal career culminating in his appointment to the International Court of Justice in The Hague.[38]

Wherever they lived, and however successful they became, the survivors bore scars that never healed. "No one came out as he went in," wrote Eugen Kogon.[39] Most noticeable were the physical wounds. Former prisoners left the camps marked by illness and infirmity, and most never regained their full strength. When Hermine Horvath, who had been dragged to Auschwitz and Ravensbrück as a Gypsy, was interviewed in January 1958, she explained how infections, frostbite, and operations had left her unable to work. "I would like to start [my life] again from the beginning," she said, "if only I could be healthy"; she died two months later, just thirty-three years old. Many other survivors died by their own hand, sometimes decades after liberation, like Jean Améry, shining a glaring light on the mental scars left by the KL.[40]

The "memory of the offense" stayed with survivors for decades, Primo Levi wrote shortly before his own apparent suicide in 1987, "denying peace to the tormented."[41] Many were traumatized by what they had seen, what they had suffered, and what they had done. At the end of his anguished 1946 memoir, Miklós Nyiszli, the prisoner who had assisted Dr. Mengele in Auschwitz, swore that he would never again lift a scalpel.[42] More generally, former prisoners often felt that their survival was somehow undeserved, given the deaths of so many others. They suffered from apathy and anxiety, and their condition was further aggravated by the limited mental health provision of the 1950s and 1960s. The doctors only diagnosed his physical problems, one survivor complained at the time, "but what I need is a person who understands my trouble."[43]

Former inmates bore the burden of the camps in different ways. Some dedicated their lives to the legacy of the KL, by commemorating them in survivor associations and publications, by becoming politicians to right society's wrongs, or by pursuing the perpetrators. Barely recovered from his ordeal, which had left him close to death in Mauthausen, Simon Wiesenthal offered his services to the local U.S. commander on May 25, 1945, because "the crimes of these men [the Nazis] are of such magnitude that no effort can be spared to apprehend them"; this became Wiesenthal's mission until his death sixty years later.[44] Other survivors, too, helped to convict Camp SS men.[45] Others again, like David Rousset and Margarete Buber-Neumann, spoke out against political violence and terror more widely, even though their vigorous campaign against the Soviet Gulag in the late 1940s and 1950s lost them many friends on the left, including fellow survivors.[46]

Far more former prisoners withdrew into their private lives, returning to their careers, resuming their education, rebuilding families. Still, they often shared their experiences in private with other survivors (often spouses or close friends). This was true for several hundred Jewish children, almost all of them orphans, who were brought to Britain in 1945–46, settled there, and never lost touch. "We were better than blood brothers," recalled Kopel Kendall (born Kandelcukier) more than five decades later. "That saved me."[47]

Finally, there were those who wanted to erase the camps from their mind. This impulse was forcefully expressed by Shlomo Dragon in May 1945, at the end of a long testimony about his time in the Special Squad. "I desperately want to return to a normal life," he told Polish investigators, "and forget everything I experienced in Auschwitz." Like Dragon, some survivors tried to repress their memories and focused only on the present, often burying themselves in work.[48] But even when the past did not haunt them during the day, it came back at night. According to a 1970s survey of Auschwitz survivors, most of them frequently dreamed about the camps.[49] Shlomo Dragon himself, who emigrated to Israel with his brother in late 1949, suffered from nightmares, too. Only after many years of silence, enforced by the stigma surrounding the Special Squad, did the two brothers begin to speak about the inferno that was Birkenau.[50]

Other survivors had to confront the past in the courtroom, as they testified against their former tormentors. Not everyone had the will to do so. "If my nightmares could be used as evidence in court, I would no doubt be an important witness," wrote one Auschwitz survivor in 1960, as he declined the invitation of a German court to testify.[51] But many more did appear, driven by a desire for justice, as well as by a sense of duty, both to history and to the dead.[52] The experience was harrowing. As soon as they stepped onto the stand, they had to relive the worst moments of their lives. Asked by a judge in 1964 whether he was married, Lajos Schlinger replied: "Well, I have no wife. She stayed in Auschwitz."[53] The pressure of the courtroom, heightened by skeptical judges, hostile lawyers, and brazen defendants, proved too much for some. During the Nuremberg Doctors' Trial, one survivor leaped out of the witness box and hit one of the accused, who had tortured him during the Dachau seawater experiments. "This bastard has ruined my life," he screamed as guards led him away.[54] Former prisoners were also frustrated by their inability to recall crimes in sufficient detail. Most unnerving of all, though, was the outcome of many judicial investigations, especially in later years, when fewer cases came to court and sentences grew more lenient.[55] This was not the kind of justice that inmates had imagined as they clung to their lives inside the camps.

Justice

Prisoners often fantasized about revenge. Dreams of vengeance sustained them during their darkest days in the KL, and still gripped them in the face of death. Expecting to perish, one Birkenau Special Squad prisoner expressed his regret in autumn 1944 that he could not "take revenge as I would like to."[56] After liberation, some survivors released their pent-up thirst for vengeance. In the first hours of freedom, they humiliated, tortured, and killed SS personnel, and defiled their corpses; in Dachau, a U.S. official watched an emaciated inmate urinate on the face of a dead guard.[57] Since most SS staff had slipped away, however, it was hated Kapos who bore the brunt of mob violence. Many hundreds were battered, strangled, and trampled to death, including notorious figures like the former Auschwitz camp elder Bruno Brodniewicz. Fellow survivors felt that justice was being done; after all, the right to kill cruel Kapos had long been a basic law of the camp. "It was dreadful and inhumane, and still just," Drahomír Bárta wrote about a massacre at Ebensee, which may have claimed over fifty former prisoner functionaries.[58]

Despite the inmates' suffering and habituation to violence, such revenge killings remained relatively rare.[59] Many survivors were too weak, or found no targets for their fury; others, including some senior inmates, urged moderation. "We should not act as they [the Germans] acted toward us," one Buchenwald survivor counseled, otherwise "we would have been just like them in the end."[60] Equally important was the restraint exercised by the Allied forces. True, some soldiers stayed on the sidelines early on, happy for prisoners to exact revenge. In the heat of the moment, a few went even further and shot SS men and Kapos; overwhelmed by the sight of the corpses on the Dachau death train on April 29, 1945, some U.S. soldiers executed the first SS men they met and then mowed down dozens more, lined up against a wall, before an agitated officer intervened.[61] But this was an isolated incident. The Allies guarded the great majority of captured perpetrators and put a stop to further outbreaks of violence.[62] The accused would be judged not by their victims, but by the courts.

The punishment of Nazi criminals had been a major war aim, and the Camp SS was among the main targets in spring 1945. Soon after Allied troops had liberated the last large camps, American, British, and Soviet war crimes investigators arrived on the scene, and collected evidence for military trials. The most prominent court was established on a site that the SS had once revered—Dachau. In a highly symbolic move, the U.S. army turned the birthplace of the camp system into a center for war crimes trials (there were practical reasons, as well: the site was used since summer 1945 as a U.S. internment camp). Up to the end of 1947, the Dachau court prosecuted some one thousand defendants for KL crimes.[63]

The first of these Dachau trials began on November 15, 1945, inside a former slave labor workshop. In the dock were forty men from KL Dachau, led by Commandant Martin Weiss. Designed to dispense swift justice, the court found all the defendants guilty in less than a month and sentenced the vast majority to death. They were convicted for participating in a "common design" to commit war crimes against enemy civilians and POWs since January 1942 (the date of the Declaration of the United Nations), a legal construct that made them liable even if there was no evidence for their involvement in individual killings. This served as the legal model for later prosecutions in Dachau, which included principal trials of staff from other main camps liberated by U.S. troops (Mauthausen, Buchenwald, Flossenbürg, and Dora), as well as some 250 successor trials, mostly involving staff from attached satellite camps. Death sentences were carried out in Landsberg prison and the impenitent Commandant Weiss was one of the first to die, hanged in May 1946. "It is worth dying for your fatherland," he wrote in a farewell letter to his infant sons.[64]

While the U.S. court in Dachau was the most prolific, it was not the first Allied military court to convict concentration camp perpetrators. The earliest British case—against men and women accused of concerted war crimes in Bergen-Belsen—had been heard between September and November 1945 in Lüneburg. In the end, thirty defendants were convicted (fourteen were found innocent), of whom eleven were sentenced to death by hanging; one of those executed in Hameln prison on December 13, 1945, was Josef Kramer, the former commandant. Others followed over the coming months, as British military courts sentenced more perpetrators from main and satellite camps.[65] French military courts also prosecuted KL crimes; one of these trials led to the execution in June 1950 of the former Ravensbrück commandant Fritz Suhren, who had lived under a false name in Bavaria until he was recognized by his former secretary.[66] Soviet military tribunals, too, punished KL perpetrators. The most high-profile case was the Berlin trial of Sachsenhausen staff, which ended in November 1947 with life terms for fourteen defendants (the USSR had temporarily abandoned capital punishment), among them "Iron" Gustav Sorge and Wilhelm "Pistol" Schubert; within less than a year, six of the defendants, including the former commandant Anton Kaindl, had perished in Soviet labor camps.[67]

In addition to Allied courts in occupied Germany, former Camp SS staff faced justice in Poland, which had been the major site of KL crimes. In fact, it was a Polish special court, set up by the provisional Communist government, that presided over the first trial and execution: in late 1944, five men from Majdanek were publicly hanged next to the former crematorium. After the war was over, more proceedings followed. Numerous cases came before special courts, including a trial in Gdańsk that ended in summer 1946 in the public hanging of Stutthof officials, with eleven former prisoners, dressed in their old uniforms, acting as executioners. The most high-profile cases came before the new Polish Supreme National Tribunal in Krakow. On September 5, 1946, it condemned Amon Göth, the commandant of Plaszow, to death. On December 22, 1947, it convicted thirty-nine Auschwitz perpetrators; the twenty-three defendants who received the death penalty included Arthur Liebehenschel, Hans Aumeier, Maximilian Grabner, and Erich Muhsfeldt (Dr. Johann Paul Kremer's death sentence was later commuted because of his advanced age). And on April 2, 1947, it sentenced the Auschwitz commandant Rudolf Höss, who had been tracked down the previous year on a remote farm by a British war crimes unit. Two weeks later, Höss stood on a scaffold erected at the former Auschwitz main camp and gazed beyond a group of spectators across the grounds of the concentration camp he had established almost seven years earlier. In a typically bold gesture, he moved his head to adjust the noose. Then the trapdoor opened.[68]

Before Höss had left occupied Germany, as one of many hundreds of KL perpetrators extradited to Poland by the Allies, he testified before the Nuremberg International Military Tribunal for leading Nazi perpetrators. The concentration camps had already featured during the first of these trials against major war criminals: Hermann Göring was charged with setting up the KL system, the former RSHA chief Ernst Kaltenbrunner with helping to run it, and Albert Speer with directing forced labor inside (the SS, meanwhile, was declared a criminal organization). One of the most poignant moments came on November 29, 1945, when U.S. prosecutors showed a one-hour film about KL atrocities. Some of the defendants seemed shocked, for the first time, while public sentiment against them hardened. "Why can't we shoot the swine now?" one spectator exclaimed.[69]

The camps occupied an even more prominent place in subsequent Nuremberg tribunals. In the IG Farben trial (August 1947–July 1948), senior managers stood accused of exploiting prisoners from Auschwitz-Monowitz. Although the proceedings demonstrated that the complicity for KL crimes extended deep into "respectable" German society, the punishments were mild, as the judges were inclined to see the defendants as errant businessmen, not murderous slave drivers.[70] In the Doctors' Trial (November 1946–August 1947), the human experiments took center stage. Several defendants were sentenced to death, among them Dr. Hoven, the bungling Buchenwald physician, and

Professor Gebhardt, the man behind the Ravensbrück sulfonamide trials.[71] Finally, there was the WVHA case (April–November 1947) against senior SS managers of the camp system. Most of them received lengthy jail terms, and one was executed—Oswald Pohl. Prior to his death in June 1951, Pohl converted to Catholicism (like Rudolf Höss and Martin Weiss) and published a remarkable tract about his religious awakening, remarkable not for its contrition, but its utter lack of insight.[72]

Denial was the default mode of Camp SS captives.[73] In its most extreme form, it culminated in the claim that all had been well in the KL. "Dachau was a good camp," proclaimed Martin Weiss before his trial, and Josef Kramer protested that he had "never received any complaints from the prisoners"; former inmates who talked about abuse and torture were pernicious liars.[74] The core teachings of the Camp SS had not been forgotten, with the defendants still picturing prisoners as deviants and themselves as decent. "I have served as a professional soldier," declared Oswald Pohl from the scaffold.[75]

The self-image as regular soldiers, ubiquitous among KL defendants, was just another form of denial. After all, local initiatives by devoted Camp SS men—who aspired to the ideal of the fanatical "political soldier"—had done much to escalate terror inside. Now many defendants portrayed themselves as underlings without ideological convictions, just as Adolf Eichmann would do in Jerusalem several years later: they had only done their duty. While this tale of the obedient soldier was gender-specific, female SS defendants made a similar point. The former chief of the Ravensbrück bunker, for example, claimed in court that she had been "a small inanimate cog in a machine." Inevitably, defendants also turned on one another, shifting responsibility up and down the chain of command. True, some old accomplices stuck together, still committed to the ideal of SS comradeship. But these bonds, always brittle, frayed in court. After his former WVHA managers had blamed everything on him, Oswald Pohl was left to lament the demise of the SS motto "My honor is loyalty."[76]

Although denials of personal responsibility made little impression on Allied courts pursuing charges of common conspiracy, Camp SS defendants resorted to ever more outrageous lies. Mass murderers denied everything, like Otto Moll, the head of the Birkenau crematoria (he claimed to have worked only as a gardener) and leader of a mobile killing squad ("I didn't shoot anybody. I was a German soldier, not a murderer").[77] Senior officers feigned ignorance, too. Arthur Liebehenschel said that he had signed IKL directives without reading them and was unaware of any gassings in Auschwitz. His lies were so transparent that even his interrogator lost his cool. "You are like a lit-tle child," he chided one day. But Liebehenschel was undeterred. In a final plea for mercy to the Polish president, he denied all guilt, blamed his superiors, and suggested that he had always helped prisoners.[78]

Such falsehoods were more than desperate defense strategies. Of course, many defendants lied to save themselves. But the most devoted Camp SS members had become so used to the normality of evil that they continued to believe in the righteousness of their actions, justifying the murders of the sick as a humanitarian act and SS violence as a disciplinary measure. Even outsid-ers were still infused with this SS spirit. The veteran professor of tropical medicine Claus Schilling, at seventy-four probably the oldest accused at any of the Dachau trials, not only defended his murderous malaria experiments, he asked the court to let him complete his research, for the greater good of science and humanity. All he needed, he said, was a chair, a table, and a type-writer; he got the gallows instead.[79]

Hidden among the defendants' delusions and lies were occasional half truths. Only a few came close to making full confessions. Rudolf Höss was the most voluble witness, speaking and writing with surprising candor. At the same time, Höss remained committed to Nazi ideology, and his greatest regret was not his crimes, but his failure to have become a farmer.[80] If confessions were rare, remorse was even rarer. One reluctant penitent was the former Auschwitz camp compound leader Hans Aumeier. Arrested in June 1945 in Norway, he soon dropped his most obvious lies and gave a detailed account of the Holocaust; he also lectured unbelieving German army officers about SS deeds. Before the Polish court in 1947, Aumeier conceded his crimes and his hardening toward prisoners, which he put down to his long years in Dachau—where he first caught the eye of Theodor Eicke back in 1934—and to the daily mass extermination of Jews in Auschwitz. In his last plea for clemency, he wrote of his "feeling of greatest remorse." He was executed in early 1948, just like the unrepentant Liebehenschel.[81]

How, then, should we judge the early postwar trials of KL perpetrators? Given the immense difficulties facing Allied courts—the chaos in occupied Germany, the absence of legal precedent, the shortages of time, staff, and re-sources—it is easy to see why most commentators have reached a positive verdict.[82] After all, many leading Camp SS men were punished. They included most of the top WVHA officials, with Gerhard Maurer, the powerful man-ager of slave labor, the last to be tried; he was executed in Poland in 1953. In addition, they included most of the surviving wartime KL commandants. Between 1945 and 1950, fourteen former commandants were sentenced to death by military courts and executed (Hans Loritz hanged himself in British captivity in 1946); at the end of the decade, only seven wartime commandants were still alive.[83]

But these sentences cannot obscure the serious shortcomings of the Allied trials, as basic legal standards were sacrificed in the search for swift sentences. The hasty preparation caused procedural nightmares, including wrongful prosecutions and convictions, while numerous confessions were extracted through improper means.[84] Few of the accused could mount a meaningful defense, either, with some trials lasting no more than a day. Then there was the haphazard selection of defendants, especially among lower-ranking SS captives. Some were quickly sentenced, others waited for trials that never came—not to mention the Nazi doctors and engineers who were whisked away as technical experts by the Allies, despite their implication in KL abuses.[85]

There were also major inequities in sentencing. Several senior WVHA and IG Farben managers received far milder sentences than ordinary guards and sentries, even though they bore a greater share of the overall responsibility.[86] The timing of trials was crucial here. Initially, Allied judges aimed at strict deterrence and retribution, reflecting the clamor back home for the harsh punishment of KL perpetrators. But by 1947–48, when the former managers were tried, the early outrage had dissipated. As the Cold War turned divided Germany into a strategic ally of both East and West, sentencing for Nazi crimes became more lenient and more defendants were cleared altogether.[87]

The most troubling aspect of Allied trials was their failure to distinguish between SS officials and prisoner functionaries. From the beginning, the two were often tried together. Unfamiliar with the basic organizational structures of the camps, or unwilling to grasp the many "gray zones" inside, Allied jurists saw Kapos as part of the wider criminal conspiracy (and occasionally as SS members), helping to cement the caricature of Kapos that has endured to this day.[88] This approach led to some extraordinary scenes. In the first Belsen trial, for instance, a Jewish survivor, who had acted for two days as a lowly block elder, was forced to sit in the dock with career SS men like Commandant Kramer.[89] The number of Kapos on trial was high—in the U.S. proceedings at Dachau, almost ten percent of defendants were former KL inmates—and the sentences severe.[90] Indeed, former Kapos were often punished harder than the SS, probably because they had stuck more vividly in the minds of fellow prisoners than the more anonymous guards. They were less likely to be pardoned, as well; the last defendant from the Belsen trial to be released from prison was not an SS official but a Polish Kapo.[91]

Most Kapos had a mixed reputation among survivors, reflecting earlier divisions between prisoners. Since it was possible for the same person to be lauded as a hero by one group, and reviled as a henchman by another, any notion of perfect justice was illusory.[92] But even in the case of universally reviled Kapos, one has to ask whether their punishment fitted their crime. Take Christof Knoll, a particularly vicious Dachau overseer, who made an impassioned plea in December 1945. "A Kapo is a prisoner," he exclaimed in court, and enumerated the SS threats, abuses, and beatings he had suffered during almost twelve years in Dachau. After his death sentence, Knoll received unexpected support from Arthur Haulot, the Belgian political prisoner who now acted as president of the Dachau International Committee. Whatever the crimes of a Kapo like Knoll, Haulot explained in the name of fellow survivors, he was primarily a victim of the camp, and it was wrong to punish him as severely as an SS volunteer. The U.S. authorities were unmoved, and hanged Knoll in Landsberg in May 1946, together with another Kapo and twenty-six SS men.[93]

Even if one comes to a more positive conclusion about the Allied trials, there is the sobering fact that the great majority of KL perpetrators went unpunished.[94] Many cases dealt solely with crimes committed against Allied (or non-German) nationals between 1942 and 1945, letting off a large number of Camp SS officials.[95] Other suspects committed suicide in Allied captivity, like Dr. Ding, the man behind the Buchenwald typhus trials, and the Auschwitz chief physician Dr. Wirths, who hanged himself in September 1945, shortly after he described the gassing of Jews as an "unpleasant" but "acceptable solution" for illness and overcrowding.[96] Many more simply slipped through the net. Some fled overseas, among them Dr. Mengele, who used a similar escape route to Latin America as Adolf Eichmann and lived largely undisturbed until his death in February 1979, when he drowned at a Brazilian holiday resort.[97] Most fugitives stayed on the territory of the former Third Reich, and once the Allied war crimes trials ended in the early 1950s, their punishment depended, above all, on German and Austrian courts.

German courts had started in summer 1945 to prosecute violent Nazi crimes against German nationals, with Allied authorization, and the judges had heard hundreds of cases involving KL crimes by 1949, when the two rival German states were founded; in addition to SS men and Kapos accused of wartime crimes in satellite camps and on death marches, the courts pursued perpetrators from the early camps and the prewar KL. Some defendants were severely punished, including the verbose "euthanasia" physician Dr. Mennecke, who was sentenced to death in December 1946 (his old friend Dr. Steinmeyer had killed himself in May 1945). But one could see warning signals in the early postwar years, as well, such as superficial investigations and soft sentences.[98] The same applied to proceedings across the border, before Austrian Peoples' Courts. In 1952, for example, Innsbruck judges dismissed the murder charges against a Plaszow SS man after they discounted the "hate-filled" testimonies of former Jewish prisoners; it was "inconceivable," the court found, that the picture of daily violence the survivors had painted was actually true.[99] Such judgments reflected popular views of the KL at the time, though these views were never uncontested in postwar Austria and Germany.

Memory

Around midday on Monday, April 16, 1945, a large procession of one thousand or more men, women, and children set off from Weimar city center and slowly wound its way through the countryside, up the Ettersberg and past the gates of Buchenwald. They were assembled here on orders of the U.S. liberators, who led the locals through the camp. The Weimar citizens were spared none of the horrors, from the starved survivors in the barracks to the charred remains in the crematorium, while American officers lectured them about their guilt.[100] Similar scenes took place in other liberated camps in spring 1945, as the Allies forced ordinary Germans to confront the KL. This included the exhumation of mass graves inside camps and on the trails of death marches; locals had to dig up the dead, wash the corpses, and attend ceremonial burials. During the mass funeral of two hundred Wöbbelin victims, who were lined up in long rows on a nearby town square, a U.S. chaplain accused local citizens on May 7, 1945, of being "individually and collectively responsible for these atrocities" because of their support for Nazism.[101]

Concentration camps like Buchenwald and Wöbbelin were highly visible in the first weeks and months after the war. During a hard-hitting Allied reeducation campaign, graphic details flashed across occupied Germany, on posters, leaflets, and pamphlets, in newspapers, newsreels, and radio broadcasts. According to one observer, the whole country was "deluged with photographs of corpses." The campaign in occupied Germany climaxed in 1946, when well over one million viewers saw the harrowing twenty-two-minute U.S. documentary *Death Mills*, which also placed the blame on the shoulders of the wider population.[102] Further details emerged from survivor memoirs and perpetrator trials, which received significant media coverage.[103]

The public picture of the concentration camps was incomplete, however. The history and function of the KL remained hazy, while the perpetrators were largely depicted as beasts—especially women, whose violent acts were explained as a perversion of female nature. The media obsession with female perpetrators culminated in the 1947 Buchenwald trial in Dachau, where reports centered on the widow of the first commandant, Ilse Koch, even though she had held no SS rank and played only a peripheral part in the crimes (the U.S. authorities later reduced her life sentence to four years' imprisonment).[104]

The reactions of ordinary Germans to the KL crimes varied, as they had done throughout the Third Reich. Some continued to look away, preoccupied with their own lot. But it was hard to avoid the topic in 1945–46 and there was plenty of talk, arising from both Allied pressure and personal interest. Some Germans expressed shame and outrage, coupled with the demand for the harsh punishment of perpetrators.[105] On the other side of the debate stood those who dismissed stories about the atrocities as Allied propaganda, and defended the KL as well-run institutions for the detention and reeducation of dangerous outcasts, giving a new lease on life to Nazi propaganda.[106]

Most Germans probably found themselves somewhere in-between. They acknowledged that terrible things had happened, and sometimes expressed genuine revulsion, but they denied any responsibility. First, they claimed that the crimes had been carried out behind their backs by Nazi fanatics. This was the myth of the invisible camp, which expunged all memories of the pervasive (if partial) popular knowledge of the KL, from the open terror of the early camps to the death marches at the end. Second, many Germans relativized the crimes by equating the fate of prisoners with their own. This was the myth of German victimhood: both prisoners and ordinary Germans, it was said, had suffered under the Nazis and the war. Many Germans therefore bristled at charges of collective guilt, leading to an exculpatory campaign spearheaded by senior politicians and clergymen. As early as Sunday, April 22, 1945, just six days after the U.S.-led tour of Buchenwald, a proclamation read in Weimar churches declared that locals held "no blame whatsoever" for crimes that had been *"entirely unknown."*[107] These myths became entrenched in the late 1940s, aided by the Allies' abandonment of denazification, and formed a major part of early German postwar narratives about the Third Reich.[108]

In the young Federal Republic of Germany, the memory of the KL was initially marginalized, reflecting a wider social and political consensus to leave the Nazi past behind. It was time to move on, most Germans felt, and focus on rebuilding their lives and their country.[109] The widespread amnesia in the early 1950s benefited the remaining KL perpetrators. It emboldened calls for amnesties, amid mounting cries of Allied "victors' justice." Under pressure from the new West German government, a strategic ally in the escalating Cold War, the U.S. authorities released most SS prisoners; the last Camp SS defendant from the U.S. Dachau trials walked free in 1958. British and French courts also enacted amnesties (as did the Polish and Soviet authorities).[110] Some convicts returned to their old vocations. Professor Otto Bickenbach, for one, was allowed to practice as a physician after a tribunal accepted his claim that Natzweiler prisoners had volunteered for his deadly phosgene experiments. Many former Camp SS professionals, meanwhile, found new jobs: having been released in 1954, the Gross-Rosen commandant Johannes Hassebroek earned his living as a salesman.[111]

With little political pressure on the prosecution authorities, there were few systematic investigations, and convictions for Nazi crimes dropped dramatically; in 1955, just twenty-seven defendants were charged by West German courts, down from 3,972 in 1949. The trials were coming to an end, it seemed, and anyone who had not yet been sentenced would probably never face justice.[112] Crucially, most SS fugitives stayed under the radar by adjusting to the postwar norms of liberal society, pointing once more to the importance of socio-psychological causes of KL crimes; in a different environment, these former Camp SS perpetrators kept their heads down and led law-abiding lives.[113] While their behavior altered, their convictions often remained unchanged. Remnants of the core Camp SS networks survived, with former staff and their families held together by nostalgia for the past. Interviewed by the Israeli historian Tom Segev in 1975, the ex-commandant Hassebroek scoffed: "The only thing I regret is the collapse of the Third Reich."[114]

While the memory of the camps faded in the early Federal Republic, it did not disappear altogether. This was partly due to the contentious issue of reparations, which vexed leading West German politicians and industrialists during the 1950s and 1960s. Keen to draw a line under the past, the German authorities reluctantly offered direct compensation to some victims and made lump-sum payments to Israel, Western European states, and Jewish organizations (represented by the Claims Conference). Designed to help West Germany gain admission to the international community, rather than to help all victims, these measures resulted in a system riddled with inequities, injustices, and indignities (as we saw in the case of Edgar Kupfer and Moritz Choinowski). Those left completely empty-handed included many former slave laborers, as German industrialists argued that the Nazi regime had compelled them to deploy KL prisoners.[115] One survivor who challenged this falsehood was Norbert Wollheim, a German Jew who had survived working for IG Farben at Auschwitz-Monowitz. In 1951, he brought a civil case against the chemicals giant, which turned into a long-running political and legal drama, and ended in 1957 with an out-of-court settlement of close to thirty million DM paid to the Claims Conference (other big German corporations criticized the agreement, and successfully fought civil actions by survivors).[116]

Criminal trials also kept the KL in the public eye in the 1950s. The press still reported on proceedings, which now mostly concerned Kapos and low-level SS officials, such as Private Steinbrenner, the would-be murderer of Hans Beimler in Dachau, who was sentenced to life by a Munich court in 1952.[117] Toward the end of the decade, in particular, individual cases gained extensive media exposure, stimulating more critical engagement with the camps. This included the trial of Gustav Sorge and Wilhelm Schubert. Both had survived the Siberian coal mines and returned to West Germany in 1956. But they were not among those Nazi perpetrators embraced on their return from Soviet captivity. Quickly rearrested, they were tried once more, under the spotlight of the national and international press, and sentenced to life (for a second time) in early 1959.[118] Sorge died in prison in 1978, one of a few Camp SS convicts who faced up to the past ("We had lost our sense of right!" he once shouted at a psychologist). Schubert, by contrast, stayed true to his cause. Released in 1986, he built a shrine in his flat with an SS picture of himself surrounded by images of Hitler and other Nazi leaders; his funeral in 2006 drew a crowd of neo-Nazis.[119]

Popular attitudes in West Germany continued to change in the 1960s. This was due, in part, to the renewed interest in survivor memoirs. In 1960, the long-time chancellor Konrad Adenauer himself used the foreword to a memoir to criticize those compatriots who wanted to burnish the nation's image by burying memories of KL horrors committed by Germans.[120] Even more important were high-profile court proceedings that signaled a more systematic judicial approach, propelled by the creation of the Central Office for the Investigation of National Socialist Crimes in 1958. Most significant was the first Auschwitz trial in Frankfurt between December 1963 and August 1965. In the dock stood twenty defendants, headed by two of the former adjutants (Commandant Richard Baer, arrested in 1960, died of a heart attack before the trial). The accompanying media storm, with almost one thousand articles in national newspapers alone, as well as programs on radio and television, caught the attention of most Germans. "Damn it!" one reader wrote to a Frankfurt paper in December 1964, "give it a rest with your reporting about Auschwitz already."[121]

The West German proceedings resulted in imperfect justice, as perpetrators often benefited from the kind of legal protection they had denied their victims.[122] The trials also produced imperfect history lessons. Media reports were irregular, in particular in mammoth cases like the trial of Majdanek staff, which opened in Düsseldorf in November 1975 and concluded five years and seven months later, setting a record for the longest and most expensive

West German trial.[123] What is more, the reporting only scratched the surface. This was most obvious, perhaps, in the continued treatment of defendants as an abnormal species. Here, the tone had been set by the Allied proceedings and the early West German cases, including the second trial of Ilse Koch— dubbed by the press as the "red-headed green-eyed witch of Buchenwald"— who was rearrested after her release from U.S. detention and sentenced to life in 1951 by an Augsburg court (she later suffered from mental illness, convinced that former KL prisoners would abuse her in her cell, and committed suicide in 1967).[124]

Popular reactions to the West German trials of the 1960s and 1970s were mixed; the Auschwitz trial, in particular, briefly galvanized the opposition to further proceedings against Nazi perpetrators. At the same time, however, the cases confronted the population with more detailed images from the KL than ever before and gave a vital impetus to pedagogical and cultural initiatives, often led by a younger generation, which did much to generate a more differentiated memory culture.[125]

By the 1980s, the distorted picture of the KL, as painted in the early Federal Republic, had developed many cracks. In particular, the myth of the invisible KL lost its power after local activists uncovered the myriad links between SS camps and the wider population. Historians and campaigners also began to turn a spotlight onto victim groups who had been obscured in public memory. Just as there had been prisoner hierarchies in the Nazi period, there were survivor hierarchies after the war. From the start, social outsiders—including homosexuals and Gypsies—were pushed to the bottom, by prevailing prejudices and also by former political prisoners determined to dissociate themselves from more unpopular victim groups. As early as 1946, some "asocial" and "criminal" survivors joined together to protest against their marginalization in a short-lived journal of their own. Suffering in the camps, they announced, should not be measured by the color of a survivor's triangle. But they were not heard. Social outsiders were widely excluded from compensation and commemoration, and it took decades before they were recognized as KL victims.[126]

It would be wrong to paint the 1980s as a golden period. The Nazi past was still contentious in the Federal Republic and popular memory of the camps remained patchy. Few Germans fully understood the operation of the KL system or its dimensions; many main camps and almost all satellite camps remained obscure. There was also confusion over who had suffered inside and over who had run the camps, as one-dimensional perpetrator images persisted. Nonetheless, public memory had shifted significantly since the foundation of the Federal Republic. Above all, most Germans now accepted a moral obligation to commemorate the camps and their victims.[127]

It was a somewhat different story in the Austrian Republic across the border. Building on the myth of Austria as the first foreign victim of Nazi tyranny, the political and social elites evaded a full confrontation with Austria's Nazi past until well into the 1980s. While the West German legal apparatus coordinated its pursuit of KL perpetrators, Austria went the other way and effectively abandoned prosecutions in the early 1970s. One of the last trials, against two SS architects involved in the construction of the Birkenau gas and crematorium complex, ended in a travesty of justice in 1972. Not only did the jury find the defendants innocent, it awarded them damages. Most Austrians ignored this case and others like it, leaving the national Communist newspaper to fume about scandalous judgments that turned Austria into a "sanctuary for Nazi mass murderers."[128]

This chimed with the views of Communist leaders in the German Democratic Republic in Soviet-dominated Eastern Europe, who rarely passed up the chance to castigate others for letting Nazi criminals off the hook, all the better to burnish their own antifascist badge of honor. In reality, the number of trials in East Germany, extensive early on, had also declined sharply by the mid-1950s. GDR leaders wanted to move on, too, and released convicted criminals, while many former Nazi supporters were silently integrated into the new state. Prosecutions for KL crimes edged up again in the 1960s and became more coordinated, partly to keep step with West Germany. Among the defendants was Kurt Heissmeyer, the physician behind the tuberculosis trials on Georges Kohn and other children in Neuengamme, who had lived as a respected lung specialist in Magdeburg, tacitly protected by the local elites; he was sentenced to life in 1966 and died soon after. However, such proceedings were highly politicized and did little to stimulate a more direct confrontation with the Nazi past, as they gradually did in West Germany.[129]

Since the GDR proclaimed itself as the successor to the resistance against Nazism, concentration camps gained a central place in the national narrative. The Socialist Unity Party (SED) took ownership of their commemoration, drawing on self-glorifying accounts by Communist survivors like Rudi Jahn, who boasted in an early mass publication that Buchenwald had been a "headquarter in the fight to free Europe of Fascists." The conversion of such hyperbole into official history was facilitated by the influx of former KPD prisoners into state positions (though none reached the highest offices of state, unlike in Poland, where the Socialist Józef Cyrankiewicz, a major player in the Auschwitz underground, became prime minister in 1947). As living embodiments of the antifascist spirit, former Communist prisoners held a special status and were expected to bolster the official version of the camps, popularized in a spate of memoirs in the 1960s and 1970s (alleged renegades, meanwhile, were written out). The approved GDR account of the camps was also enacted during ceremonies at memorials, above all at Buchenwald, which was transformed into a shrine to the Communist resistance.[130]

Sites of Remembrance

On September 14, 1958, the GDR political elite celebrated one of its most solemn acts of state: the dedication of the Buchenwald national memorial complex. By the following year, the new memorial, which reminded some critics of monumental Nazi architecture, already drew more than six hundred thousand visitors, including children on mandatory school trips. It encompassed burial grounds, pylons, a huge bell tower, and a sculpture depicting inmates standing tall against the SS—an allusion to the mythical self-liberation of Buchenwald, the fictional focus of the official Communist narrative, which discounted the decisive role of U.S. liberators. Further national memorials followed in Ravensbrück (1959) and Sachsenhausen (1961). All three sites sought to legitimize the East German state by celebrating international solidarity and the heroics of the Communist prisoners; just as resistance fighters had supposedly overcome Nazism in the camps, the GDR would defeat contemporary incarnations of Fascism. During his speech in Buchenwald on September 14, 1958, Prime Minister Grotewohl promised to "fulfill the legacy of the dead heroes," a reference to the estimated fifty-six thousand victims of the KL. What he did not say was that another seven thousand or more prisoners had died in Buchenwald after the demise of the Third Reich, not as victims of the SS, but at the hands of the Soviet occupation forces.[131]

Between August 1945 and February 1950, Buchenwald had served as one of ten Soviet special camps on German soil. Red Army guards took over the Camp SS buildings, as they did in Sachsenhausen and Lieberose, which also became special camps. The old prisoner barracks filled up with new inmates, rounded up in ad hoc arrests and condemned by military tribunals or interned without trial. Most prisoners were middle-aged German men who had once belonged to the Nazi movement. But they were not detained as war criminals—few had been senior officials or violent perpetrators—but as alleged threats to the current Soviet occupation. They even included some former resisters against Nazism, like Robert Zeiler, a survivor of KL Buchenwald who found himself back inside the camp in 1947 on trumped-up charges as an alleged U.S. spy.

In general, there was nothing unusual about the temporary transformation of former KL sites into Allied internment camps. In the early postwar years, Dachau and Flossenbürg were used by the U.S. military, Neuengamme and Esterwegen by the British, Natzweiler by the French. But the western Allies quickly released most prisoners and held the remaining war crimes suspects under mostly adequate conditions. Not so the Soviet authorities, who neglected the special camps and their often harmless inmates. Indifference and ineptitude bred terrible conditions, with hunger, overcrowding, and illness resulting in mass death. Out of one hundred thousand prisoners taken to the three former concentration camps turned into Soviet special camps, well over twenty-two thousand perished inside.[132]

The use of former KL for Allied internment hampered early survivor efforts of on-site remembrance. In many camps, inmates had come together immediately after liberation to honor the dead. In Buchenwald, survivors held an impromptu service on the roll call square on April 19, 1945, gathering around a wooden obelisk (elsewhere, survivors built more permanent memorials). But the Buchenwald grounds were soon out of bounds, following the establishment of the special camp, and former inmates had to direct their commemorative efforts elsewhere. When the site was designated as a national memorial, in 1953, the initiative came not from survivors but from the SED, which elbowed the inmate association aside. By then, the appearance of the former concentration camp had already altered dramatically. Some parts had collapsed; some had been torn down; and some had been taken away by the Soviet troops and German locals, who departed with machines, pipes, and even with the windows of the crematorium. More alterations and demolition work followed to prepare the ground for the memorial and museum. By the time of the opening, much of the old camp was gone, replaced by the new GDR version of Buchenwald.[133]

KL memorials in other countries also reflected the commemorative concerns of the respective political authorities, who tried to stamp the dominant national narrative of the Nazi past onto these sites. True, survivor organizations played an important role, but the appearance of museums and monuments, and the speed of their construction, was largely determined by wider social forces.[134] In Auschwitz, for example, a state museum opened in 1947 in the former main camp under the auspices of the new Polish government, and it has been expanded and revamped ever since (the grounds of the former IG Farben plant at Dwory, by contrast, belong to the Polish chemicals giant Synthos and remain off-limits to commemoration and conservation). For decades, public memory in Auschwitz was dominated by national Polish narratives. As the main memorial of the Polish People's Republic, Auschwitz marked the patriotic resistance against Germany, national suffering, socialist solidarity, and Catholic martyrdom—themes that resonated with large sections of the Polish population. By contrast, the memory of Jewish prisoners, who made up the vast majority of the dead, was sidelined, as symbolized by the progressive decay of the Birkenau compound. Memory has become far more diverse in recent decades, linked in part to the fall of Communism at the end of the 1980s, though this did not put an end to political controversies over the memorial.[135] Such commemorative conflicts were grounded in the history of the camps themselves. The KL system had always fulfilled multiple functions, allowing individual interest groups to emphasize separate elements in their narratives.

This is evident in Mauthausen, too, where a vast memorial park has grown along the road to the former camp. Starting with a granite monument dedicated to French freedom fighters in 1949, more than a dozen national memorials followed, each mirroring aspects of public memory prevailing in the sponsoring state. As for the Austrian authorities, they opened a memorial in 1949, encompassing some restored KL buildings (though most prisoner barracks were sold off and dismantled). In keeping with the official Austrian account of the Nazi period, the memorial was primarily designed as a site of national martyrdom, with a Catholic chapel in the former laundry and a stone sarcophagus on the roll call square. A museum was not added until 1970, with an exhibition focusing on Austrian victimhood. Since then, commemoration in Mauthausen has changed, reflecting the growing engagement with the past since the 1980s. Memorials for forgotten victims have been added, remembering homosexuals (1984), Roma (1994), and Jehovah's Witnesses (1998), and a more nuanced history of the camp is told in a new visitor center (2003). Popular interest has sharply risen, with the number of visiting Austrian students expanding from just six thousand (1970) to over fifty-one thousand (2012).[136]

The memorial landscape in the neighboring German Federal Republic has also shifted since the early postwar years. The long and rocky path can be best illustrated by the development of Dachau, the birthplace of the KL system. Following the end of the U.S. military trials, the Bavarian authorities turned the former prisoner compound into a housing project for ethnic German refugees from Eastern Europe (other KL sites became DP camps, too, among them Bergen-Belsen and Flossenbürg). The Dachau prisoner barracks were used as apartments, the infirmary as a kindergarten, and the delousing block as a restaurant, later called "At the Crematorium." For years, the history of the KL was obscured by the settlement, and between 1953 and 1960 there was not even a rudimentary museum on the site. Most locals ignored the camp in their midst, or distorted its history. The Dachau mayor, who had already served as deputy mayor during the Nazi years, told a journalist in 1959 that many inmates had been rightly detained as criminals. Local politicians around other KL sites were equally reluctant to face the truth. In 1951, the Hamburg mayor opposed plans for a French memorial in Neuengamme, because "everything should be done to avoid opening old wounds and reawakening painful memories"; instead, the former KL grounds were used for decades as a prison, built with bricks from the Neuengamme SS works.

Only in the 1960s did Dachau become a major site of remembrance. Under pressure from survivors' organizations, the Bavarian state finally relocated the residents from the camp grounds, with the last ones leaving just before the opening of the state memorial in spring 1965. As elsewhere, this process was accompanied by major changes to the site. Against the wishes of survivors, the authorities razed many of the remaining KL buildings, leaving behind a vast, clean, and barren area. Fresh foundations indicated where the barracks had once stood. Around the former roll call square, two newly built huts were meant to illustrate everyday prisoner life and a museum charted the rise of Nazism and the history of the camp. This was still a partial history, though, foregrounding political prisoners. The same applied to a new monument on the square, erected by the main survivor association, which included a chain with colored triangles worn by different inmate groups: red (political prisoners), yellow (Jews), purple (Jehovah's Witnesses), and blue (returned emigrants). The colors denoting social outsiders, however, were all missing: there was no black (asocials), green (criminals), pink (homosexuals), or brown (Gypsies). At the far end of the site, meanwhile, several new buildings sprang up, with a large Catholic chapel and convent, a Jewish monument, and a Protestant church aiming to give religious meaning to the prisoners' suffering. The expanding Dachau memorial attracted more and more visitors, and by the early 1980s, annual figures had risen from around four hundred thousand (1965) to nine hundred thousand. The growing visibility of the site generated some hostility among local politicians, who still preferred to gloss over the past. Their opposition only abated from the 1990s, when Dachau and other German KL memorials entered a new phase of commemoration.[137]

Unification in 1990 had a major impact on German memory culture, above all in former East Germany. Over the coming years, the national concentration camp memorials were stripped of GDR propaganda and remodeled, not least by commemorating the Soviet special camps. This process proved particularly painful in Buchenwald, where clashes between the new curators and the Socialist-led KL survivor association degenerated into a public row over the actions of Communist Kapos.[138] But unification affected memory in western parts of Germany, as well. The suffering of German Communists and their fellow travelers, previously marginalized by the prevailing Cold War mind-set, gradually received greater recognition.[139] Similarly, the fate of Soviet KL prisoners came into sharper focus, and they also finally received some compensation as forced laborers, following a second wave of German reparations (though this came too late for most).[140]

The end of the Cold War intensified public engagement with the Third Reich more generally, not least to assuage anxieties outside Germany about a possible resurgence of radical nationalism. Since the 1990s, the German government has taken an active lead in the commemoration of Nazi crimes, from the designation of the Auschwitz liberation date as the Day of Remembrance for the Victims of National Socialism, to the construction of the Memorial to the Murdered Jews of Europe in the heart of Berlin. Similarly, the national government has started to support KL memorials directly, providing an important catalyst for changes in official commemoration.[141] Previously neglected sites, like Dora (in the shadow of Buchenwald) and Flossenbürg (in the shadow of Dachau), have been remade in recent years; in Flossenbürg, the former prisoner kitchen and laundry—used commercially by a private company until the 1990s—now house exhibitions about the camp.[142] And new monuments and museums on the sites of long-ignored satellite camps and death marches make the immense spread of the KL system more visible.[143] Even established memorials like Dachau have been redesigned once more in light of new research and changing public perceptions.

Dachau, March 22, 2013. It is a bright, cold spring day, much as it was exactly eighty years ago, when the concentration camp first opened. The site is easy to find, with plenty of signs pointing the way (until the 1980s, the city authorities kept its profile low). Anyone arriving by train can walk along a Path of Remembrance, adorned with multilingual panels, to the memorial. At the entrance stands a new visitor center, opened in a state ceremony in 2009, broadcast live, and attended by the Bavarian political establishment, which had long shunned the memorial. "We don't forget, we don't suppress, we don't relativize what happened here," the prime minister pledged. As prisoners did in the past, visitors pass through the doorway of the old SS gatehouse, following a path reopened in 2005 despite local opposition. The wrought-iron gates with the inscription ARBEIT MACHT FREI lead directly onto the roll call square, where several large visitor groups are gathered. It is a quiet day, like most Fridays, but there are still some 1,500 visitors. To the left of the square they see the two reconstructed barracks and the outlines of the others, bisected by the camp street that leads toward the crematorium. On the right stands the museum, overhauled in 2003. And straight ahead lie the offices of some thirty academic, archival, and pedagogic staff. Their task, the director says in a newspaper interview to mark Dachau's anniversary, "is to tell the history of this camp free from all political slant."[144] The memorial has clearly come a long way. This is far from suggesting a sense of closure, though. Commemoration will keep on changing, here and at other former KL sites. Neither will the history of the camps ever come to an end. Blind spots remain. New sources, approaches, and questions will make us reconsider what we thought we knew; on March 22, 2013, for example, none of the historians in Dachau could pinpoint with certainty the building where it had all begun eighty years earlier.

In the same way, our search for deeper meaning in the KL will go on, even though efforts to extract a single essence are destined to come up short. As we have seen, the concentration camps meant different things at different times of Nazi rule. Even Auschwitz cannot be reduced to its genocidal function alone, as the SS also used it to destroy the Polish resistance and to forge a closer collaboration with industry. Neither was its place as the most deadly site of the Nazi Final Solution preordained. It emerged only gradually over several fateful months in 1942, at a time when hundreds of thousands of Jews had already been killed elsewhere; the path of Auschwitz to the Holocaust was long and twisted.[145] And yet, the inadequacy of simple answers should not stop us from asking bigger questions about the nature of the concentration camps. The KL were patently products of modernity, for example, with their reliance on bureaucracy, transport, mass communication, and technology, as well as industrially manufactured barracks, barbed wire, machine guns, and gas canisters. But does that make them paradigms of the modern age, as some scholars have suggested, any more than, say, mass vaccination or universal suffrage? As the historian Mark Mazower pointedly asks: "What makes one choice of historical symbol . . . better than another?"[146] Then there is the question of the camps' origins. Of course, the KL were products of German history; they emerged and developed under specific national political and cultural conditions, and drew inspiration from the violent practices of Weimar paramilitaries, as well as the disciplinary traditions of the German army and prison service. But does that make them "typically German," as some prisoners argued?[147] It seems doubtful. After all, the men behind the KL system were far more invested in radical Nazi ideology than most ordinary Germans, who felt more ambivalent about the camps. More generally, the KL shared some generic features with repressive camps established elsewhere during the twentieth century. That said, their development still diverged from other totalitarian camps, raising perhaps the most important issue: How best to understand the course of the Nazi concentration camps?

As this integrated history has shown, there was nothing inevitable about the trajectory of the KL. Looking at the horrors of the wartime years, it is hard not to see them as the inevitable conclusion of the early camps. But there was no direct trail from Dachau in 1933 to Dachau in 1945. The concentration camps could well have taken a different direction, and in the mid-1930s, it even looked as if they might disappear. They endured because Nazi leaders, above all Adolf Hitler himself, came to value them as flexible instruments of lawless repression, which could easily adapt to the changing requirements of the regime. The specific character of individual camps owed much to the initiative of the local SS. But these officials operated within wider parameters set by their superiors, and in the end, the KL acted much like seismographs, closely attuned to the general aims and ambitions of the regime's rulers. The reason they oscillated so much was that the priorities of Nazi leaders changed over time, and as the regime radicalized, so did its camps.

Despite some sharp turns, however, the path of the concentration camps unfolded without sharp breaks. The successive stages of the camps might appear like different worlds, as we saw at the beginning of this book, but these worlds were connected nonetheless. The basic rules, organization, and ethos of the Camp SS were already in place by the mid-1930s, and remained largely unchanged thereafter. Similarly, pioneering SS programs of mass extermination, which claimed tens of thousands of infirm prisoners and Soviet POWs in 1941, left an important legacy for the Holocaust, including the use of Zyklon B in Auschwitz. The continuities between the different stages of the camps are personified by core SS professionals like Rudolf Höss, a man who learned about prisoner abuse in Dachau at the start of the Third Reich, graduated to systematic murder in Sachsenhausen early in the war, moved on to genocide in Auschwitz, and then oversaw the final slaughter in Ravensbrück. Throughout his career, new outrages broke new ground, and each transgression made the next one easier, inuring him, like other SS perpetrators, to acts that would have been unthinkable a little earlier. The KL system was a great transformer of values. Its history is a history of these mutations, which normalized extreme violence, torture, and murder. And this history will continue to be written and it will keep on living, and so will the memory of those who were its witnesses, its perpetrators, and its victims.

APPENDIX

Tables

TABLE 1. **Daily Inmate Numbers in the SS Concentration Camps, 1934–45**

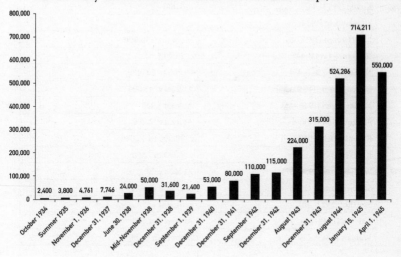

The figures for 1935, 1938, 1940, 1941, December 1942, December 1943, and April 1945 are estimates.

TABLE 2. Prisoner Deaths in SS Concentration Camps

Main KL complex and period of operation	Total number of deaths
Arbeitsdorf (1942)	6
Auschwitz (1940–45)	At least c. 1,100,000 (including at least c. 870,000 Jews murdered on arrival without registration as KL inmates)
Bergen-Belsen (1943–45)	c. 37,000
Bad Sulza (1936–37)	0
Berlin-Columbia (1934–36)	At least 3
Buchenwald (1937–45)	c. 56,000
Dachau (1933–45)	c. 39,000
Dora (1944–45)	c. 15,000 to 20,000
Esterwegen (1934–36)	28
Flossenbürg (1938–45)	c. 30,000
Gross-Rosen (1941–45)	At least c. 40,000
Herzogenbusch (1943–44)	c. 750
Kovno (1943–44)	c. 6,000
Lichtenburg (1934–39)	c. 25
Mauthausen (1938–45)	More than 90,000
Majdanek (1941–44)	c. 78,000
Natzweiler (1941–45)	19,000 to 20,000
Neuengamme (1940–45)	At least c. 43,000
Niederhagen (1941–43)	At least 1,235
Plaszow (1944–45)	At least c. 2,200
Ravensbrück (1939–45)	c. 30,000 to 40,000
Riga (1943–44)	c. 7,000 to 7,500
Sachsenburg (1934–37)	At least c. 30
Sachsenhausen (1936–45)	c. 35,000 to 40,000
Stutthof (1942–45)	c. 61,500
Vaivara (1943–44)	At least c. 4,500
Warsaw (1943–44)	More than 3,400
Total number of KL deaths	Over 1.7 million

Most figures are (often rough) estimates; the precise number of victims will never be known.

Sources: *OdT*, vol. 2, 27–30, 198–99; vol. 3, 65; vol. 4, 57; vol. 5, 339; vol. 6, 43, 195, 520; vol. 7, 24, 122, 145, 187, 261; vol. 8, 104, 134–42, 276–80; Piper, *Zahl*, 167; http://totenbuch.buchenwald.de; Schilde and Tuchel, *Columbia-Haus*, 51–57, 68; KZ-Gedenkstätte Dachau (ed.), *Gedenkbuch*,

9, 13; http://totenbuch.dora.de; Klausch, *Tätergeschichten*, 292–94; Association (ed.), *Mauthausen*, 10; Dieckmann, *Besatzungspolitik*, 1248–1327; Hördler and Jacobeit (eds.), *Lichtenburg*; idem (eds.), *Gedenkort*; Kranz, "Erfassung," 243; Strebel, *Ravensbrück*, 510; Helm, *If*; R. B. Birn to the author, March 28, 2014; D. Drywa to the author, April 8, 2014; F. Jahn to the author, May 6, 2014.

TABLE 3. **SS Ranks, with Army Equivalents**

SS	Army
Reichsführer SS	Field marshal general
Oberstgruppenführer	Colonel general
Obergruppenführer	General
Gruppenführer	Lieutenant general
Brigadeführer	Major general
Oberführer	Brigadier general
Standartenführer	Colonel
Obersturmbannführer	Lieutenant colonel
Sturmbannführer	Major
Hauptsturmführer	Captain
Obersturmführer	First lieutenant
Untersturmführer	Second lieutenant
Hauptscharführer	Sergeant major
Oberscharführer	Technical sergeant
Scharführer	Staff sergeant
Unterscharführer	Sergeant
Rottenführer	Corporal
Sturmmann	Private first class
SS-Mann (Schütze)	Private

Source: Zentner and Bedürftig (eds.), *Encyclopedia*, 753; Snyder (ed.), *Encyclopedia*, 280.

Notes

Abbreviations

AdsD	Archiv der sozialen Demokratie
AE	Allgemeine Erlaßsammlung
AEKIR	Archiv der Evangelischen Kirche im Rheinland, Düsseldorf
AEL	Arbeitserziehungslager (Work Education Camp[s])
AfS	*Archiv für Sozialgeschichte*
AG	Amtsgericht
AGFl	Archiv der KZ-Gedenkstätte Flossenbürg
AGN	Archiv der KZ-Gedenkstätte Neuengamme
AHR	*The American Historical Review*
AM	Archiv der KZ-Gedenkstätte Mauthausen
APMO	Archiwum Państwowe Muzeum w Oświęcimiu
AS	Archiv der Gedenkstätte Sachsenhausen
ASL	Archiv der Stadt Linz
BArchB	Bundesarchiv Berlin
BArchF	Bundesarchiv Filmarchiv
BArchK	Bundesarchiv Koblenz
BArchL	Bundesarchiv Ludwigsburg
BayHStA	Bayerisches Hauptstaatsarchiv
BDC	Berlin Document Center
BGVN	*Beiträge zur Geschichte der nationalsozialistischen Verfolgung in Norddeutschland*
Bl.	Blatt (folio)
BLA	Bayerisches Landesentschädigungsamt
BLHA	Brandenburgisches Landeshauptarchiv
BoA	Boder Archive online
BPP	Bayerische Politische Polizei
BStU	Behörde des Bundesbeauftragten für die Unterlagen des Staatssicherheitsdienstes der ehemaligen DDR

BwA	Archiv der Gedenkstätte Buchenwald
CEH	*Central European History*
CoEH	*Contemporary European History*
CSDIC	Combined Services Detailed Interrogation Centre
DaA	Archiv der Gedenkstätte Dachau
DAP	*Der Auschwitz-Prozeß* (DVD-Rom)
DAW	Deutsche Ausrüstungswerke GmbH (German Equipment Works)
DESt	Deutsche Erd- und Steinwerke GmbH (German Earth and Stone Works)
DH	*Dachauer Hefte*
DJAO	Deputy Judge Advocate's Office
DM	Deutsche Mark
DöW	Stiftung Dokumentationsarchiv des österreichischen Widerstandes
DP	Displaced Person
DV	Dienstvorschrift
EE	Eidesstattliche Erklärung
EHQ	*European History Quarterly*
ERH	*European Review of History*
EV	Einstellungsverfügung
FZH	Forschungsstelle für Zeitgeschichte, Hamburg
GDR	German Democratic Republic
Gestapa	Geheimes Staatspolizeiamt (Secret State Police Office)
Gestapo	Geheime Staatspolizei (Secret State Police)
GH	*German History*
GHI	German Historical Institute
GPD	German Police Decodes
GStA	Generalstaatsanwalt
GStA PK	Geheimes Staatsarchiv Preußischer Kulturbesitz
HGS	*Holocaust and Genocide Studies*
HHStAW	Hessisches Hauptstaatsarchiv
HIA	Hoover Institution Archives
HIS	Hamburger Institut für Sozialforschung
HLSL	Harvard Law School Library, Nuremberg Trials Project
HSSPF	Höhere SS und Polizeiführer (Higher SS and police leader[s])
HStAD	Landesarchiv NRW, Abteilung Rheinland
HvA	*Hefte von Auschwitz*
ICRC	International Committee of the Red Cross
IfZ	Institut für Zeitgeschichte, Munich
IKL	Inspektion der Konzentrationslager (Inspectorate of Concentration Camps)
IMT	*Trial of the Major War Criminals Before the International Military Tribunal*
ITS	International Tracing Service
JAO	Judge Advocate's Office
JCH	*Journal of Contemporary History*
JfA	*Jahrbuch für Antisemitismusforschung*
JMH	*The Journal of Modern History*
JNV	*Justiz und NS-Verbrechen*, Rüter and de Mildt (eds.)
JVL	Jewish Virtual Library online
KB	Kommandanturbefehl
KE	Kleine Erwerbungen
KL	Konzentrationslager (Concentration Camp[s])
KOK	Kriminaloberkommissar
KPD	Kommunistische Partei Deutschlands (German Communist Party)
Kripo	Kriminalpolizei (Criminal Police)
KTI	Kriminaltechnisches Institut (Criminal Technical Institute)

LaB	Landesarchiv Berlin
LBIJMB	Leo Baeck Institute Archives, Berlin
LBIYB	*Leo Baeck Institute Yearbook*
LG	Landgericht
LHASA	Landeshauptarchiv Sachsen-Anhalt
LK	Lagerkommandant(en) (Camp commandant[s])
LKA	Landeskriminalamt
LSW	Landesgericht für Strafsachen, Wien
LULVR	Lund University Library, Voices from Ravensbrück online
MdI	Minister/Ministerium des Innern (Minister/Ministry of the Interior)
MG	Manuscript Group
MPr	Ministerpräsident (Minister president)
MSchKrim	*Monatsschrift für Kriminalpsychologie und Strafrechtsreform*
NAL	National Archives, London
NARA	National Archives, Washington, D.C.
NCA	*Nazi Conspiracy*, Office of U.S. Chief Counsel (ed.)
NCC	*The Nazi Concentration Camps*, Wachsmann and Goeschel (eds.)
NCO	Noncommissioned Officer
n.d.	no date
ND	Nuremberg Document
NGC	*New German Critique*
NKVD	People's Commissariat of Internal Affairs
NLA-StAO	Niedersächsisches Landesarchiv, Staatsarchiv Oldenburg
NLHStA	Niedersächsisches Hauptstaatsarchiv
NMGB	Nationale Mahn- und Gedenkstätte Buchenwald
NN	Nacht und Nebel (Night and Fog)
NRW	Nordrhein-Westfalen
NSDAP	National Sozialistische Deutsche Arbeiter Partei (Nazi party)
NYPL	New York Public Library
ODNB	*Oxford Dictionary of National Biography*
OdT	*Ort des Terrors*, Benz and Distel (eds.)
OKW	Oberkommando der Wehrmacht (High Command of the Wehrmacht)
ORR	Oberregierungsrat
OStA	Oberstaatsanwalt
OT	Organisation Todt
PAdAA	Politisches Archiv des Auswärtigen Amtes
PMI	Prussian Minister of the Interior
POW	Prisoner of War
Publ.	Published
RaR	Review and Recommendations
RdI	Reichsministerium des Innern (Reich Ministry of the Interior)
RJM	Reichsministerium der Justiz (Reich Ministry of Justice)
RKPA	Reichskriminalpolizeiamt (Reich Criminal Police Office)
RM	Reichsmark
RMi	Reichsminister
RSHA	Reichssicherheitshauptamt (Reich Security Main Office)
SD	Sicherheitsdienst (Security Service)
SED	Sozialistische Einheitspartei Deutschlands (German Socialist Unity Party)
Sipo	Sicherheitspolizei (Security Police)
Sk	Staatskanzlei (State Chancellery)
SlF	Schutzhaftlagerführer (Camp compound leader)
SMAB	State Museum Auschwitz-Birkenau
SPD	Sozialdemokratische Partei Deutschlands (German Social Democratic Party)

SS	Schutzstaffel (Protection squad)
StA	Staatsanwaltschaft(en)
StAAm	Staatsarchiv Amberg
StAAu	Staatsarchiv Augsburg
StAL	Landesarchiv Baden-Württemberg, Staatsarchiv Ludwigsburg
StAMü	Staatsarchiv München
StANü	Staatsarchiv Nürnberg
StB	Standortbefehl
StW	Stadtarchiv Weimar
Texled	Gesellschaft für Textil- und Lederverwertung (Company for Textile and Leather Utilization)
ThHStAW	Thüringisches Hauptstaatsarchiv, Weimar
TS	Totenkopfstandarten (Death's Head regiments)
TWC	*Trials of War Criminals Before the Nuernberg Military Tribunals*
USHMM	United States Holocaust Memorial Museum
VfZ	*Vierteljahrshefte für Zeitgeschichte*
VöB	*Völkischer Beobachter*
VoMi	Volksdeutsche Mittelstelle (Ethnic German Liason Office)
VVN	Vereinigung der Verfolgten des Naziregimes
WG	*Werkstatt Geschichte*
WL	Wiener Library
WVHA	Wirtschafts-Verwaltungshauptamt (SS Business and Administration Main Office)
YIVO	YIVO Institute for Jewish Research
YUL	Yale University Library, Archives
YVA	Yad Vashem Archives
ZfG	*Zeitschrift für Geschichtswissenschaft*

See Sources for full bibliographic details.

Prologue

1. Dann, *Dachau*, quote on 22; Zarusky, "Erschießungen"; Abzug, *Inside*, 89–92; DaA, DA 20202, F. Sparks, "Dachau and Its Liberation," March 20, 1984; Greiser, *Todesmärsche*, 70, 502–503; KZ-Gedenkstätte Dachau, *Gedenkbuch*, 10; Marcuse, *Legacies*, 51; Weiß, "Dachau," 26–27, 31–32; "Dachau Captured by Americans Who Kill Guards, Liberate 32,000," *New York Times*, May 1, 1945. See also images in the USHMM photograph collection. The death train had set off on April 7, 1945, from Buchenwald, with 4,500 to 5,000 prisoners on board.

2. Hannah Arendt already made a similar point soon after the Second World War; Brink, *Ikonen*, 78. More generally, see Weiß, "Dachau"; *NCC*, ix.

3. DaA, ITS, Vorläufige Ermittlung der Lagerstärke (1971); BArchB, R 2/28350, Chronik der SS-Lageranlage Dachau, March 1, 1938; Zámečník, *Dachau*, 86–90, 99–105; Neurath, *Gesellschaft*, 23, 38–41, 44–48; Burkhard, *Tanz*, 83, 86–89; Steinbacher, *Dachau*, 90; *OdT*, vol. 1, 102–104; ibid., vol. 2, 248; Pressac, *Krematorien*, 8. Thirty of the thirty-four Dachau barracks were used for regular prisoner accommodation. The SS did consider building a crematorium in Dachau in 1937, but did not go ahead with the plan; Comité, *Dachau* (1978), 166 (my thanks to Dirk Riedel for the reference).

4. Seubert, "'Vierteljahr,'" 63–68, 89–90, quote on 90; Richardi, *Schule*, 40–55; Dillon, "Dachau," 27, 153; Tuchel, *Konzentrationslager*, 123–25; Zámečník, *Dachau*, 22–25; KZ-Gedenkstätte Dachau, *Gedenkbuch*, 9, 13; DaA, 550, M. Grünwiedl, "Dachauer Gefangene erzählen," summer 1934, 2–3; ibid., 3.286; C. Bastian, "22. März 1933," in

Mitteilungsblatt der Lagergemeinschaft Dachau, April 1965 (thanks to Chris Dillon for this reference); BArchB, R 2/28350, Chronik der SS-Lageranlage Dachau, March 1, 1938. The number of deaths in Dachau excludes some 2,500 survivors who died in the first three months after liberation.

5. DaA, 9438, A. Hübsch, "Insel des Standrechts" (1961), 95.

6. For the term "order of terror," Sofsky, *Ordnung*. Sofsky's study also begins by contrasting Dachau in 1933 and 1945, though in a rather different manner.

7. Figures based on *OdT*, vols. 2–8, counting camps under the IKL and the WVHA. I have not included the SS special camp Hinzert or the women's camp Moringen among the main camps.

8. For an early discussion of the centrality of the camps to Nazism, Arendt, *Origins*, 438.

9. The term "KL" remained the main SS abbreviation for concentration camps throughout the Third Reich. For popular references to "KL," see *The Times*, January 24, 1935, NCC, doc. 277. Prisoners also applied the term, though they more commonly used the harsher sounding "KZ," which became the standard abbreviation in postwar Germany (Kamiński, *Konzentrationslager*, 51; Kautsky, *Teufel*, 259; Kogon, *SS-Staat*, 1946, 4). Still, some survivors (Internationales Lagerkommitee Buchenwald, *KL BU*) and scholars (Herbert et al., *Konzentrationslager*) continued to use "KL." In this book, "KL," or concentration camp, normally refers to SS camps under the authority of the IKL (from 1934) and WVHA (from 1942); at times, I also use the generic term "camps" to refer to these sites.

10. There were an estimated four hundred and fifty thousand KL survivors in 1945 (chapter 11), in addition to perhaps one hundred thousand prisoners released from the KL between 1933 and 1944. For mortality figures, see table 2, appendix; Piper, *Zahl*, 143, 167. A small proportion of Jews murdered on arrival in Auschwitz died outside the gas chambers (chapter 9).

A brief note on terminology: The SS divided its prisoners into different categories according to their (presumed) background. These SS designations shaped the prisoner society and inevitably feature in this book. It is worth noting, however, that many prisoners would have described themselves differently. A number of Jewish prisoners, for example, did not see themselves as Jews (at least not before their arrest). Also, a generic SS term like "Russian prisoner" (which I have generally replaced with the broader term "Soviet prisoner") was often applied indiscriminately by the SS to Ukrainians, Russians, Belarusians, and some Poles.

11. Quote in Hitler speech, January 30, 1941, in Domarus, *Reden*, vol. 4, 1658. See also Welch, *Propaganda*, 229–35; Fox, *Film*, 171–84; Langbein, *Menschen*, 324; Evans, *Third Reich at War*, 145.

12. Hitler speech, January 30, 1940, in Domarus, *Reden*, vol. 3, 1459.

13. Quote in Himmler speech on the Day of the German Police, January 29, 1939, NCC, doc. 274. More generally, see Moore, "'What Concentration Camps.'"

14. Bauman, "Century." See also Kotek, Rigoulot, *Jahrhundert*; Wormser-Migot, *L'ère*.

15. Smith and Stucki, "Colonial." See also Sutton, "Reconcentration."

16. For German colonial camps, Hull, *Destruction*, 70–90 (who estimates over thirty-three thousand African captives); Kreienbaum, "'Vernichtungslager.'" On the supposed links to the KL, see especially Madley, "Africa," quote on 446. More generally, see Zimmerer, "War," 58–60; Kotek and Rigoulot, *Jahrhundert*, 32. For criticism of this thesis, see Wachsmann and Goeschel, "Before Auschwitz," 526–28. For a wider critique of supposed continuities between German colonial violence and Nazi extermination policy, see Gerwarth and Malinowski, "Hannah Arendt's Ghosts."

17. Quote in Bell, *Völkerrecht*, 723. From a German perspective, see Hinz, *Gefangen*; Stibbe, *Civilian Prisoners*; Jones, *Violence*. More generally, see Kramer, "Einleitung," 17–20, 29–30; Buggeln and Wildt, "Lager," 168–69.

18. Overy, "Konzentrationslager." On Spain, see Rodrigo, "Exploitation," especially page 557. For a visit by Spanish police officials to Sachsenhausen in 1940, Ley and Morsch,

Medizin, 390–91. For a visit by Himmler to Franco's camps in 1940, Preston, *Holocaust*, 494–95. For concentration camps in Fascist Italy, Guerrazzi, di Sante, "Geschichte."

19. This is reflected in books on both camp systems; Todorov, *Facing*; Kamiński, *Konzentrationslager*; Armanski, *Maschinen*.

20. Khlevniuk, *History*, figures on 328; Applebaum, *Gulag*; Overy, "Konzentrationslager," 44–50; Kramer, "Einleitung," 22, 30; Wachsmann, "Comparisons." For one of the so-called special settlements, see Werth, *Cannibal*.

21. For a contemporaneous claim, see "Life in a Nazi Concentration Camp," *New York Times Magazine*, February 14, 1937. In 1980s Germany, the inflammatory claim by the historian Ernst Nolte that the Gulag had set a precedent for Auschwitz triggered the so-called "historians' dispute"; Nolte, "Vergangenheit"; Evans, *Hitler's Shadow*.

22. Arendt, *Origins*, 445. For figures on deaths and releases in NKVD camps, see Khlevniuk, *History*, 308; Snyder, *Bloodlands*, xiii; Arch Getty et al., "Victims," 1041; Kramer, "Einleitung," 24. For other differences between SS and Soviet camps, see Wachsmann, "Comparisons."

23. Quotes in Aly, "*Endlösung*," 274; Ereignismeldung UdSSR Nr. 59, August 21, 1941, Anlage I, "Das Verschickungs- und Verbannungswesen in der UdSSR," in Boberach, *Regimekritik*, doc. rk1204. See also the recollections of Rudolf Höss in Broszat, *Kommandant*, 209.

24. StAMü, Staatsanwaltschaften Nr. 34479/1, Bl. 93–97: Lebenslauf H. Steinbrenner, n.d. (c. late 1940s), Bl. 95; StANü, EE by G. Wiebeck, February 28, 1947, ND: NO-2331, quote on page 5.

25. Klemperer, *LTI*, 42.

26. Figure correct as of July 2014.

27. For this and the previous paragraph, see Zelizer, *Remembering*, especially pages 63–154; Reilly, *Belsen*, 29–33, 55–66; Abzug, *Inside*, 30 (my thanks to Dan Stone for this reference), 128–40; Frei, "'Wir waren blind'"; Gallup, *Gallup Poll*, 472, 504 (the figure of one million dead was the median average of answers); Chamberlin, "Todesmühlen." For the muted coverage of the liberation of Auschwitz, see Weckel, *Bilder*, 47; Brink, *Ikonen*, 25. Quotes in O. White, "Invaders rip veil from Nazi horrors," *Courier-Mail* (Brisbane), April 18, 1945, in idem, *Conqueror's Road*, 188–91; "Dachau Gives Answer to Why We Fought," *45th Division News*, May 11, 1945. Important early books by prisoners include Beimler, *Mörderlager*; Seger, *Oranienburg*; Langhoff, *Moorsoldaten*. Works by relatives include Mühsam, *Leidensweg*; Litten, *Mutter*. My section on the KL in history draws partly on Wachsmann and Caplan, "Introduction," 2–6.

28. For criticism of these claims, Cesarani and Sundquist, *After the Holocaust*.

29. Kupfer used the pen name Kupfer-Koberwitz. For his life, see B. Distel, "Vorwort," in Kupfer-Koberwitz, *Tagebücher*, 7–15; ibid., 19–30. For the reasons behind his arrest, see also StAL, EL 350 I/Bü 8033, Fragebogen Wiedergutmachung, October 16, 1949; ibid., Erklärung A. Karg, May 23, 1950.

30. Quote in Perz, *KZ-Gedenkstätte*, 37. See also Niethammer, *Antifaschismus*, 198–206; Shephard, *Daybreak*, 92.

31. Jockusch, *Collect*, 3–10, 165–85. See also Cesarani, "Challenging," 16–18.

32. For example, see KPD Leipzig, *Buchenwald!*; Grossmann, *Jews*, 197.

33. P. Levi, "Note to the Theatre Version of *If This Is a Man*," 1966, in Belpoliti, *Levi*, 24. See also idem, *If*, 381; idem, *Drowned*, 138; Sodi, "Memory." As early as spring 1945, Levi wrote a brief account of medical conditions in Auschwitz, together with a fellow survivor; Levi and de Benedetti, *Auschwitz*.

34. For some figures, see Taft, *Victim*, 130–32. A small selection of early survivor accounts includes Nyiszli, *Auschwitz* (first published in Romania in 1946); Nansen, *Day* (first published in Norway in 1947); Szmaglewska, *Smoke* (first published in Poland in 1945); Burney, *Dungeon*; Millok, *A kínok*. For early German accounts, Peitsch, "*Deutschlands*."

35. Kautsky, *Teufel*; Frankl, *Psycholog*.

36. Probably the first history of a single camp is Kraus, Kulka, *Továrna*; for this pioneering Czech study of Auschwitz, see Van Pelt, *Case*, 219–23. For poems and fiction, see Borowski, *This Way* (includes stories first published between 1946 and 1948); Ka-Tzetnik, *Sunrise* (first published in 1946); Wiechert, *Totenwald*.

37. Kogon, *SS-Staat* (1946); Wachsmann, "Introduction," in Kogon, *Theory*, xvii. Among the pamphlets was a collection of testimonies by former Buchenwald inmates, published in 1945 with a print run of two hundred thousand copies; KPD Leipzig, *Buchenwald!* More generally, see Peitsch, *"Deutschlands,"* 101–102, 139, 204. For widely read survivor accounts elsewhere in Europe, Cesarani, "Challenging," 20–22.

38. NYPL, Collection Farrar, Straus & Giroux Inc. Records, Box 191, R. Straus, Jr., to R. Gutman, June 21, 1948.

39. Quotes in P. Levi, "Deportees. Anniversary," *Torino* XXXI (April 1955), in Belpoliti, *Levi*, 3–5; DaA, Nr. 27376, E. Kupfer to K. Halle, September 1, 1960. Survivor accounts published in the 1950s include Cohen, *Human*; Michelet, *Rue*; Kupfer-Koberwitz, *Als Häftling*; Antelme, *L'espèce*. See also the contributions to the *Auschwitz Journal* (*Przegląd Lekarski-Oświęcim*). For public disinterest, see, for example, DaA, Nr. 9438, A. Hübsch, "Insel des Standrechts" (1961), 207. For general background, Cesarani, "Introduction," 1, 5; idem, "Challenging," 28–30; Diner, *Remember*, 365–90.

40. Kupfer-Koberwitz, *Tagebücher*. For the second wave of memoirs, see Waxman, *Writing*, 116; Cesarani, "Introduction," 10; Hartewig, "Wolf," 941. For the reception of *Holocaust* in Germany, see Hickethier, "Histotainment," 307–308.

41. Schnabel, *Macht*; NMGB, *Buchenwald* (first published in 1959); Maršálek, *Mauthausen* (first published in 1974); Zámečník, *Dachau*. See also the influential Langbein, *Menschen* (first published in 1972); Naujoks, *Leben*.

42. For a survey, see Reiter, *"Dunkelheit."*

43. For example, see Mitscherlich and Mielke, *Diktat*; Helweg-Larsen et al., *Famine*. For early references in *The Lancet* and the *British Medical Journal*, see Cesarani, "Challenging," 24. See also the study of the New School for Social Research, abandoned in 1951; Goldstein et al., *Individuelles*, 10–11.

44. Broszat, "Konzentrationslager"; Pingel, *Häftlinge*. Other pioneering works include, in chronological order, Kühnrich, *KZ-Staat* (first published in 1960); Kolb, *Bergen-Belsen*; Billig, *L'Hitlérisme*; Wormser-Migot, *Le système*; Broszat, *Studien*; Feig, *Death Camps*.

45. For example, see Dicks, *Licensed*; des Pres, *Survivor*.

46. Broszat, "Einleitung."

47. P. Levi, "Preface to L. Poliakov's *Auschwitz*," 1968, in Belpoliti, *Levi*, 27–29; Milward, "Review."

48. Orth, *System*. For an overview of the state of research in the 1990s, see Herbert et al., *Konzentrationslager*.

49. A bibliography of German works (ranging from 1945 until 2000) includes over six thousand items, most of them published after 1980; Warneke, *Konzentrationslager* (my thanks to Peter Warneke for a copy).

50. For the last point, see Wachsmann, "Review." For an assessment of recent academic work, see idem, "Looking."

51. Megargee, *Encyclopedia*, vol. I; *OdT*, vols. 2–8.

52. Quote in Reichel, "Auschwitz," 331.

53. The reasons for the growth of collective memories of the Holocaust have been examined in many stimulating and controversial studies. For the United States, see Novick, *Holocaust*.

54. Silbermann and Stoffers, *Auschwitz*, 205, 211, 213–14.

55. For figures, see chapter 7, appendix (table 2), and Piper, *Zahl*, 167. For the term "demystify," see Mazower, "Foucault," 30.

56. For figures, see chapters 6, 9, 11; Friedländer, *Jahre*, 692; Piper, *Zahl*, 167.

57. For this point, see also Langer, *Preempting.*

58. Quote in Mauriac, "Preface," x. The argument that the worst crimes in the camps were linked to a specific German mind-set is inherent in Goldhagen, *Executioners.* For the camps and modernity, see Bauman, "Century"; Kotek and Rigoulot, *Jahrhundert.*

59. Sofsky, *Ordnung.*

60. For early criticism of Sofsky's static approach, see Weisbrod, "Entwicklung," 349; Tuchel, "Dimensionen," 373 (n. 12). Of course, sociologists have acknowledged since Max Weber's time that "ideal types" may never appear in this form in reality; Weber, *Wirtschaft und Gesellschaft,* in Directmedia, *Max Weber,* 1431.

61. Rózsa, "Solange," 297–99. Rózsa edited her diaries, and added to them, prior to their publication in 1971 in Bucharest.

62. Nansen, *Day,* 545. See also Mess, *"Sonnenschein,"* 56.

63. BoA, testimony H. Frydman, August 7, 1946; Wagner, *Produktion,* 453; Nyiszli, *Auschwitz,* 66; Segev, *Million,* 158.

64. Transcript in Chamberlin and Feldman, *Liberation,* 42–45, p. 44. See also Frei and Kantsteiner, *Holocaust,* 201.

65. Some survivors expressed skepticism about the ability of historians to illuminate the camps, related (in part) to their belief that only survivors understand what the camps were really like; Waxman, *Writing,* 176–79; Cargas, "Interview," 5; Debski, *Battlefield,* 62.

66. Friedländer, "Eine integrierte Geschichte"; idem, *Nazi Germany,* 1–2, quote on 1; Frei and Kantsteiner, *Holocaust,* 82.

67. This book includes a large number of direct quotations from prisoners and perpetrators. Many of these quotes come from contemporary documents. Others are taken from later sources, however, which poses methodological problems. On the one hand, few eyewitnesses were able to recall expressions they had heard months or years earlier with absolute precision. On the other hand, paraphrasing all such quotes would sacrifice immediacy; the tone and wording of orders, after all, was a crucial part of the SS strategy of domination. In the end, I have decided to use some "retrospective quotes," but only if source criticism—analyzing the internal consistency of the document and comparing it against others—led me to conclude that the words quoted were likely to be a close approximation of what had been said.

68. For the estimate, see Kárný, "Waffen-SS," 248 (referring to men only).

69. Quotes in Warmbold, *Lagersprache,* 302–303.

70. For a survey of recent research, see Roseman, "Beyond Conviction?"

71. Cited in Todorov, *Facing,* 123. See also Levi, "Preface to H. Langbein's *People in Auschwitz,*" 1984, in Belpoliti, *Levi,* 78–81. For early scholarly criticism of the view of SS perpetrators as pathological aberrations, see Steiner, "SS"; Dicks, *Licensed,* especially page 237.

72. See also Langbein, *Widerstand,* 8.

73. Kautsky, *Teufel,* 226.

74. The term "Kapo" was widely used in the KL. It was already employed before World War II (Neurath, *Gesellschaft,* 210) and became even more popular during the war years. In the historical literature, the term is often applied in a narrow sense, to designate prisoners in charge of labor details. Drawing on the work of some survivors (Kupfer-Koberwitz, *Tagebücher,* 467; Kautsky, *Teufel,* 160) and historians (Niethammer, *Antifaschismus,* 15), I propose a wider definition here, applying the term to all prisoners who gained direct or indirect power over fellow inmates by taking over an official function inside the camp.

75. Quotes in Arendt, *Origins,* 455; Siedlecki et al., *Auschwitz,* 4 (first published in 1946). See also Armanski, *Maschinen,* 188; Langer, *Holocaust Testimonies,* ix, 162–63; Browning, *Remembering,* 297; Löw et al., *Alltag.*

76. Researchers working on the ongoing USHMM encyclopedia of camps and ghettos project have identified more than forty-two thousand separate sites; "The Holocaust

just got more shocking," *New York Times*, March 1, 2013. Occasionally, these other sites were mistaken for concentration camps. The Theresienstadt (Terezín) ghetto, for example, is frequently described as a concentration camp (for background, see Hájková, "Prisoner Society," 14).

77. BArchK, All. Proz. 6/103, Bl. 16. For background, see Stangneth, *Eichmann*.

78. For the dispersal of documents, see Perz, *KZ-Gedenkstätte*, 39–42.

79. There are still no academic monographs on key programs of mass murder, such as Action 14f13 and Action 14f14 (see chapter 5). The same is true for some stages in the camps' history, most notably the early war years (see chapter 4). In addition, we are lacking monographs on several main camps established for Jewish prisoners in occupied eastern Europe (see chapters 6 and 7). There is also little systematic work on the headquarters of the Camp SS during the war (see chapter 8) and its interaction with local camps. Similarly, the fate of some prisoner groups, such as criminals and asocials, continues to be widely ignored (see chapter 3).

80. Tuchel, *Konzentrationslager*, 27. The three men who knew the most—Theodor Eicke, Richard Glücks, and Heinrich Himmler—were all dead by May 1945.

81. Winter, *Winter*, 53. See also Levi, *Drowned*, 6–7.

82. Levi, *Drowned*; Maršálek, *Gusen*, 33.

83. For the latter point, see Greiser, *Todesmärsche*, 141; Raim, *Dachauer*, 286; Erpel, "Trauma," 127.

84. Schrade, *Elf Jahre*, especially pages 9–14, 32–33. Strikingly, Schrade ignores the treatment of criminals and asocials throughout his memoir.

85. This accounts for the relatively small number of memoirs by Soviet prisoners; Zarusky, "'Russen,'" especially pages 105–107, 111. For one recent collection of memories, see Timofeeva, *Nepobedimaja*.

86. For data and documents produced by the Camp SS, see Kranebitter, "Zahlen," 98–117; Grotum, *Archiv*, 236–44.

87. The material I consulted includes documents from the Special Archive in Moscow (via digital copies held at the USHMM), opened to Western scholars in the early 1990s. I have also used records from the Tracing Service of the Red Cross in Bad Arolsen, which had been inaccessible to historians between the 1970s and 2006–07. Finally, I draw on British decryptions of secret German radio messages, held at the National Archives in Kew and declassified from the late 1990s. Data-protection rules require some prisoner and perpetrator names to be anonymized.

88. *OdT*, vol. 1, 279–83; Blatter, Milton, *Art*, 136–225.

89. Didi-Huberman, *Bilder*; "Francesc Boix."

90. Büge, *KZ-Geheimnisse*.

91. For diaries, see especially Laqueur, *Schreiben*. Thirty diaries survived in Bergen-Belsen alone, more than in any other KL; Rahe, "Einleitung," 18–19. For notes written in camps, see Świebocki, *Resistance*.

92. For some examples, see Świebocki, *London*.

93. Friedländer, *Jahre*, 23–24. See also his comments in Frei and Kantsteiner, *Holocaust*, 85–86, 252.

94. Many KL historians give preference to early testimony; Shik, "Erfahrung," 104–105; Buggeln, *Arbeit*, 536; Hayes, "Auschwitz," 347. On later oral histories, see Jureit and Orth, *Überlebensgeschichten*, especially pages 185–86.

95. Langbein, *Menschen*, 334–35; Browning, *Remembering*, 233–36. For other examples, see ibid., 237; Mailänder Koslov, *Gewalt*, 361–70; Fulbrook, *Small Town*, 306. More generally on the unreliability of some memoirs, see Cziborra, *KZ-Autobiografien*, especially pages 70–75.

96. For example, see Semprun and Wiesel, *Schweigen*, 15, 19.

97. For the last point, see the testimonies of Soviet prisoners and German criminals at the Frankfurt Auschwitz trials of the 1960s.

98. For methodological problems, see Orth, "Lagergesellschaft," 117–18.

99. For exceptions, see Segev, *Soldiers*.

100. Orth, *SS*, 15. Particular care should be taken with testimonies before Soviet and East German courts; Eschebach, "'Ich bin unschuldig'"; Pohl, "Sowjetische," 138.

101. Karin Orth's organizational history of the KL, for example, devotes only one-eighth of its text to the prewar period; Orth, *System*.

102. Caplan, "Detention," 26.

103. See also Wachsmann and Goeschel, "Before Auschwitz," 518.

104. Mommsen, "Cumulative Radicalization."

1. Early Camps

1. Beimler, *Mörderlager* (first published in 1933), quotes on pages 56–57. For other detail, Zámečník, *Dachau*, 30 (n. 44); DaA, A-1281, "Aus dem Dachauer Konzentrationslager," *Amperbote*, May 11, 1933; StAMü, StA 34453/1, Bl. 44–46: Zeugenvernehmung J. Hirsch, December 27, 1949 (my thanks to Chris Dillon for this and other references about Beimler); Dillon, "Dachau," 234–35.

2. Quote in Beimler, *Mörderlager*, 10. See also Seubert, "'Vierteljahr,'" 80.

3. Mühldorfer, *Beimler*, 78–114; Richardi, *Schule*, 7–8; Büro, *Reichstagshandbuch 1932*, 37; Herker-Beimler, *Erinnerungen*, 14, 26–27.

4. Quote in DaA, A-1281, "Aus dem Dachauer Konzentrationslager," *Amperbote*, May 11, 1933. More generally, see Dillon, "Dachau," 35–36, 51–53.

5. Quotes in StAMü, StA Nr. 34479/1, Bl. 93–97: Lebenslauf H. Steinbrenner, n.d. (c. late 1940s), Bl. 95; Beimler, *Mörderlager*, 28–29. See also ibid., 25–26, 31; DaA, 550, M. Grünwiedl, "Dachauer Gefangene erzählen," summer 1934, 6. Around May 1, 1933, Beimler was transported from Dachau to a Munich hospital; regarded by doctors as a "malingerer," he returned to Dachau on a police transport on May 4, 1933; DaA, 17.269, BPP, Betreff: Beimler Johann, May 1, 1933; ibid., 17.270, BPP, Vermerk, May 3, 1933.

6. StAMü, StA Nr. 34479/1, Bl. 93–97: Lebenslauf H. Steinbrenner, n.d. (c. late 1940s). More generally, see Evans, *Coming*, 159–60; Dillon, "Dachau," 36–37, 55.

7. The exact circumstances of Beimler's escape remain unclear (for an attempted reconstruction, Richardi, *Schule*, 14). The involvement of two SS men is mentioned by former guards and prisoners; StAMü, StA Nr. 34453/1, Bl. 44–46: Zeugenvernehmung J. Hirsch, December 27, 1949; ibid., Nr. 34465, Bl. 48–49: Zeugenvernehmung J. Nicolai, January 21, 1953; DaA, 550, M. Grünwiedl, "Dachauer Gefangene erzählen," summer 1934, 6–7.

8. Quote in StAMü, StA Nr. 34453/1, Bl. 44–46: Zeugenvernehmung J. Hirsch, December 27, 1949. See also DaA, 550, M. Grünwiedl, "Dachauer Gefangene erzählen," 6.

9. Quote in DaA, A-1281, "Aus dem Dachauer Konzentrationslager," *Amperbote*, May 11, 1933. See also DaA, 550, M. Grünwiedl, "Dachauer Gefangene erzählen," 6; Polizeifunknachrichten, May 10, 1933, in Michaelis and Schraepler, *Ursachen*, vol. 9, 364; Mühldorfer, *Beimler*, 123; Internationales Zentrum, *Nazi-Bastille*, 79.

10. For the quote by Nazi officials and further details, see PAdAA, Inland II A/B, R 99641, Bay. MdI to RdI, January 26, 1934. See also Mühldorfer, *Beimler*, 14–15, 125–29; DaA, A-1281, "28 Volksschädlinge verlieren deutsche Staatsangehörigkeit," November 4, 1933; Richardi, *Schule*, 15–17; Drobisch and Wieland, *System*, 170–71; Beimler, *Four Weeks*. For Beimler's postcard and quote, see interrogation Michael S., June 14, 1939, *NCC*, doc. 300.

11. Rubner, "Dachau," 56–57; Dillon, "Dachau," 154.

12. *Verhandlungen des Reichstags* (1938), quotes on 3. See also Domarus, *Hitler*, vol. 2, 664.

13. For example, see address by Himmler to the *Staatsräte*, March 5, 1936, *NCC*, doc. 78.
14. I am drawing here (and below) on Wachsmann and Goeschel, "Introduction."
15. For the term, see Aly, "Wohlfühl-Diktatur." More generally, see Gellately, "Social Outsiders," 57–58. For a judicious rejoinder, see Eley, "Silent Majority?," 553–61.
16. The dual thrust of the "national community" concept was emphasized early in Peukert, *Inside*, 209. More recently, see Wachsmann, "Policy," 122–23.
17. More generally on 1918, see Mason, "Legacy."
18. Quote in Broszat, "Konzentrationslager," 328.
19. Reichardt, *Kampfbünde*, 87–88, 99, 616, 698–99. For political violence in Berlin, see also Swett, *Neighbors*.
20. On the appeal of the NSDAP, see the classic study by Allen, *Seizure*. See also Weisbrod, "Violence."
21. For the Reichstag fire, see Hett, *Burning*, quote on 16 (my thanks to Ben Hett for sharing his manuscript). For older accounts, Kershaw, *Hubris*, 456–60, 731–32; Evans, *Coming*, 328–31.
22. For the lists, see Hett, *Crossing*, 178–79; idem, *Burning*, 35–36; Tuchel, *Konzentrationslager*, 96–97. The Prussian police leadership had issued orders for immediate measures against Communists—including protective custody—on the afternoon of February 27, 1933, a few hours before the burning of the Reichstag (Hett, *Burning*, 36–37). This rather strengthens the likelihood that some Nazi officials were involved in the fire.
23. Hett, *Crossing*, 158–59, quote on 159. See also Mühsam, *Leidensweg* (first published in 1935), 24; Mühldorfer, *Beimler*, 86; Suhr, *Ossietzky*, 201. On Litten, see also Bergbauer et al., *Denkmalsfigur*.
24. *VöB*, March 2, 1933. See also Tuchel, *Konzentrationslager*, 100.
25. For this and the previous paragraph, see Longerich, *Bataillone*, 165–79; Schneider, "Verfolgt"; Mayer-von Götz, *Terror*, 51–56, 62, 80–81, 118; Hett, *Burning*, 16, 155; Browder, *Enforcers*, 39, 77; Roth, "Folterstätten," 9–10; Helbing, "Amtsgerichtsgefängnis," 250–52. On Köpenick, see also Hördler, *SA-Terror*.
26. Quotes in Tuchel, *Konzentrationslager*, 52; Bracher, *Diktatur*, 229.
27. For this process, see Kershaw, "Working." More generally on Nazi governance, see idem, *Dictatorship*.
28. Quote in GStA PK, I. HA Rep. 84a, Nr. 3736, Göring to Oberpräsidenten et al., February 22, 1933. See also Tuchel, *Konzentrationslager*, 45–53; Gruchmann, *Justiz*, 320–21; Allen, *Seizure*, 157.
29. Graf, "Genesis"; Browder, *Enforcers*, 30–31, 78; Gellately, *Backing*, 17–18.
30. Quote in "Der neue Geist im Münchner Polizeipräsidium," *VöB*, March 15, 1933. For other senior Nazis holding police powers, see Wilhelm, *Polizei*, 39.
31. Wachsmann, "Dynamics," 18.
32. Lüerßen, "'Wir,'" 161, 467–71; Knop et al., "Häftlinge," 55; Baganz, *Erziehung*, 119–21; Krause-Vilmar, *Breitenau*, 49, 55, 65; Kienle, "Heuberg," 48–50; Mayer-von Götz, *Terror*, 92–95; Roth, "Folterstätten," 5; Evans, *Coming*, 334. Compared to the blanket arrests of Communists, the Nazi authorities were more selective when it came to the detention of Social Democrats and union officials, often concentrating on more senior figures.
33. Caplan, "Gender," 88; Kienle, "Gotteszell"; Mayer-von Götz, *Terror*, 102–103.
34. Herker-Beimler, *Erinnerungen*, 17, 21. See also Distel, "Schatten."
35. Average daily inmate numbers in German penal institutions increased from c. sixty-three thousand (1932) to c. ninety-five thousand (1933), though not all the new prisoners were political opponents; Wachsmann, *Prisons*, 69, 392–93.
36. BArchB, NS 19/4014, Bl. 158–204: Rede des Reichsführers SS vor Generälen der Wehrmacht, June 21, 1944, Bl. 170.

37. Quote in Fraenkel, *Dual State*, 3. The so-called Reichstag Fire Decree is reprinted in Hirsch et al., *Recht*, 89–90. For the decree, Raithel and Strenge, "Reichstagsbrand-verordnung." For extralegal detention before 1933, Caplan, "Political Detention," 26–28.

38. Drobisch and Wieland, *System*, 37–38, 104–105, 136; BArchB, R 43 II/398, Bl. 92: Übersicht Schutzhaft, n.d.; Tuchel, *Konzentrationslager*, 103, 107.

39. For some detail, see Drobisch and Wieland, *System*, 29, 31–36.

40. SA Gruppenführer Schmid to MPr Siebert, July 1, 1933, *NCC*, doc. 11. For confusing detention practices, see also Baganz, *Erziehung*, 69–73.

41. I use the term "early camp"—introduced by Karin Orth (*System*, 23–26)—in the most comprehensive way, to cover *all* places of extralegal detention, from SA torture chambers to protective custody wings in prisons. For an attempt to construct a typology of early Nazi camps, see Tuchel, *Konzentrationslager*, 42–45. For a critical assessment, see Wachsmann and Goeschel, "Introduction," xv.

42. For these terms, see Baganz, *Erziehung*, 58–61.

43. Tuchel, *Konzentrationslager*, 107; Gruchmann, *Justiz*, 573.

44. For this point, see also Caplan, "Political Detention," 30.

45. Ayaß, *Breitenau*, 14, 244, 250–51; Caplan, "Political Detention," 22, 29–30; *OdT*, vol. 2, 160–68.

46. Wachsmann, "Dynamics," 19; Baganz, *Erziehung*, 81–82; Drobisch and Wieland, *System*, 31, 45. In 1932, the average monthly number of adult inmates in Bavarian prisons and penitentiaries (excluding county jails) stood at 4,493; BayHStA, MJu 22663.

47. Herker-Beimler, *Erinnerungen*, 17–21; *OdT*, vol. 2, 169–70; Moore, "Popular Opinion," 68. For other institutions holding female protective custody prisoners in 1933, see Riebe, "Frauen," 125–27.

48. For cells in the Aichach prison, see StAMü, Strafanstalt Aichach Nr. 27, Letter, Margarete J., September 3, 1933.

49. LBIJMB, MF 425, L. Bendix, "Konzentrationslager Deutschland," 1937–38, vol. 1, 5–18. See also Bendix, *Berlin*. For other examples, see Kienle, "Gotteszell," 69–70; Krause-Vilmar, *Breitenau*, 118–19.

50. LBIJMB, MF 425, Bendix, "Konzentrationslager Deutschland," 1937–38, vol. 1, quotes on p. 8. See also Wachsmann, *Prisons*, 187; Mayer-von Götz, *Terror*, 60.

51. *OdT*, vol. 2, 212–13; Wisskirchen, "Schutzhaft," 139–41, 145–47; Rudorff, "Schutzhaft."

52. Wachsmann, *Prisons*, 172–73.

53. L. Pappenheim to District President Kassel, March 31, 1933, in Krause-Vilmar, *Breitenau*, 73. At the time, the German-Jewish SPD politician Ludwig Pappenheim was held in "protective custody" in Schmalkalden jail. He was murdered on January 4, 1934, by SA guards in Neusustrum early camp; ibid., 191–203.

54. Compare, for example, the violence Hans Litten suffered in the early camp Sonnenburg in April 1933 to his much milder treatment in Spandau prison a few weeks later; Hett, *Crossing*, 171–73.

55. For one example, see Roth, "Folterstätten," 14. More generally, see Wachsmann, *Prisons*, 59–61; Schilde, "Tempelhofer," 66.

56. Address by M. Lahts, September 4, 1933, *NCC*, doc. 13; Diercks, "Fuhlsbüttel." On paper, the Fuhlsbüttel camp came under the legal authorities until December 1933, when it was subordinated to the local police in all but economic matters (ibid., 273–74, 307). See also Guckenheimer, "Gefängnisarbeit," 112; Klee, *Personenlexikon*, 301.

57. Quotes in excerpts from secret notes by F. Solmitz, September 13–18, 1933, *NCC*, doc. 29. See also USHMM, RG-11.001M.20, reel 91, 1367-2-33, Bl. 2–3: Berichte aus Hamburg, n.d.; Jürgens, *Solmitz*; Diercks, "Fuhlsbüttel," 290; Drobisch and Wieland, *System*, 128.

58. For these calls, see Gruchmann, *Justiz*, 573–74.

59. IfZ, Fa 183/1, Bl. 269: Wagner to Frank, March 13, 1933. See also Bauer et al., *München*, 231.

60. For the diversity of early camps, see Benz and Distel, *Terror*; idem, *Herrschaft*; idem, *Gewalt*.

61. Baganz, *Erziehung*, 87–88.

62. For SA *Sturmlokale* of the Weimar years, see Reichardt, *Kampfbünde*, 449–62.

63. Quote in Mayer-von Götz, *Terror*, 56.

64. Across Saxony alone, for example, well over thirty such camps were set up in 1933; Baganz, *Erziehung*, 24, 78–81.

65. Mayer-von Götz, *Terror*, 19, 23–24, 56–60; Reichardt, *Kampfbünde*, 468–75. For details of the Berlin elections, see "Wahl zum Deutschen Reichstag in Berlin am 5.3.1933," sent by Landeswahlleiterin Berlin to the author, October 4, 2011.

66. USHMM, RG-11.001M.20, reel 91, 1367-2-33, Bl. 19–20: Bericht Justizrat Broh, n.d. For Broh, see Liebersohn and Schneider, *"My Life,"* 47. Broh's abuse escalated because of his Jewish origins.

67. This point has been made, above all, in Tuchel, *Konzentrationslager*, 38–42. See also idem, "Organisationsgeschichte," 12–13. For torture and "confessions," see Diercks, "Fuhlsbüttel," 286–87; Roth, "Folterstätten," 16–17; LG Nuremberg-Fürth, Urteil, November 29, 1948, *JNV*, vol. 3, 580–82.

68. Dörner, "Ein KZ."

69. Seger, "Oranienburg" (first published in 1934), quotes on pages 26–27. See also Drobisch, "Oranienburg," 18. For other camps, see Drobisch and Wieland, *System*, 108–14; Mayer-von Götz, *Terror*, 74, 121–32; Baganz, *Erziehung*, 159–71; Rudorff, "'Privatlager,'" 158–60.

70. For the figure, Morsch, *Oranienburg*, 220.

71. Améry, *Jenseits* (first published in 1966), 47.

72. Langhoff, *Moorsoldaten*, 162. For other examples, see ibid., 70, 77, 88–89, 195.

73. For background, see Goffman, *Asylums*.

74. For violence as a form of communication, see Keller, *Volksgemeinschaft*, 422.

75. Quotes in Burkhard, *Tanz*, 22. For other examples, see JVL, JAO, Review of Proceedings, *United States v. Weiss*, n.d. (1946), 29.

76. Mailänder Koslov, *Gewalt*, 418.

77. Seger, "Oranienburg," 57; Mayer-von Götz, *Terror*, 120.

78. Neurath, *Gesellschaft* (completed in 1943), 30–37.

79. Ibach, *Kemna*, 18. For the abuse of women, see Mayer-von Götz, *Terror*, 80, 101.

80. Mayer-von Götz, *Terror*, 125, 137–46. See also Bernhard, "Konzentrierte," 235–36.

81. For the Dachau case, see DaA, 550, M. Grünwiedl, "Dachauer Gefangene erzählen," summer 1934, 20; Zámečník, *Dachau*, 46. For other examples, see USHMM, RG-11.001M.20, reel 91, 1367-2-33, Bl. 19–20: Bericht Justizrat Broh, n.d.; Abraham, "Juda," 131–33.

82. Bendig, "Unter Regie," 100; Rudorff, "Misshandlung," 51–52; Moore, "Popular Opinion," 117; USHMM, RG-11.001M.20, reel 91, 1367-2-33, Bl. 2: Bericht aus Staaken, n.d.; Baganz, *Erziehung*, 133–35.

83. For exceptions, see Rudorff, "Misshandlung," 42.

84. Mayer-von Götz, *Terror*, 112–13; Baganz, *Erziehung*, 151.

85. StAMü, StA Nr. 34479/1, Bl. 93–97: Lebenslauf H. Steinbrenner, n.d. (c. late 1940s). See also Dillon, "Dachau," 57, 59, 141.

86. Some unemployed SA men did petition the authorities for employment in local camps; Moore, "Popular Opinion," 142.

87. Dillon, "Dachau," 45, 141; Baganz, *Erziehung*, 149; Stokes, "Das oldenburgische Konzentrationslager," 190–96; Reichardt, *Kampfbünde*, 330–31; Drobisch and Wieland, *System*, 54; Tooze, *Wages*, 48, table 1.

88. Mayer-von Götz, *Terror*, 117–18; Baganz, *Erziehung*, 152; Lüerßen, "'Moorsoldaten,'" 177. On remuneration, see Seubert, "'Vierteljahr,'" 73; BArchL, B 162/7998, Bl. 623–44: Vernehmung J. Otto, April 1, 1970, Bl. 623–24.

89. For the term "superfluous generation," see Peukert, *Weimar*, 18, 89–95. More generally, see Reichardt, *Kampfbünde*, 384–86, 703–707. For the guards' background, see Dillon, "Dachau," 29–30; Krause-Vilmar, *Breitenau*, 147–48; Diercks, "Fuhlsbüttel," 275; Lechner, "Konzentrationslager," 89–90.

90. Reichardt, *Kampfbünde*, 697–99, 712, 719; Drobisch and Wieland, *System*, 96.

91. Schäfer, *Konzentrationslager*, 21. More generally, see Dillon, "Dachau," 39–40; Reichardt, *Kampfbünde*, 617–24; Moore, "Popular Opinion," 48–50.

92. For flags, see Mayer-von Götz, *Terror*, 123. For the relation between total power and abuse more generally, see Zimbardo, *Lucifer*, 187.

93. Baganz, *Erziehung*, 97–98, quote on 189.

94. Ecker, "Hölle," 25. For some examples, see Stokes, "Das oldenburgische Konzentrationslager," 196; Ibach, *Kemna*, 22; Morsch, "Oranienburg—Sachsenhausen," 121–22.

95. Dillon, "Dachau," 47–51; Knop et al., "Häftlinge," 47–48; Wohlfeld, "Nohra," 116–17.

96. Dillon, "Dachau," 67–68. See also Wachsmann, *Prisons*, 36; ITS, ARCH/HIST/KL Kislau, Bl. 59–72: Wachvorschrift, July 12, 1933.

97. Seger, "Oranienburg," 28–30; Mayer-von Götz, *Terror*, 63, 65, 89, 93, 138.

98. Arendt, "Concentration Camps," 758.

99. For figures from individual camps, see Drobisch and Wieland, *System*, 127–31; Mayer-von Götz, *Terror*, 147–52.

100. Quotes in Mühsam, *Leidensweg*, 25; Suhr, *Ossietzky*, 203. More generally, Nürnberg, "Außenstelle"; Drobisch and Wieland, *System*, 55; Hett, *Crossing*, 161; Litten, *Mutter*, 18; Hohengarten, *Massaker*, 13.

101. Mühsam, *Leidensweg*, 26, 29; Drobisch and Wieland, *System*, 55; Hett, *Crossing*, 71, 162–63; Suhr, *Ossietzky*, 203; Wünschmann, "Jewish Prisoners," 39. For camp guards' hatred of intellectuals, see also Kautsky, *Teufel*, 75–76.

102. Quotes in Litten, *Mutter*, 22; Mühsam, *Leidensweg*, 30. See also ibid., 27–29; Suhr, *Ossietzky*, 203–205; Buck, "Ossietzky," 22; *Braunbuch* (first published in 1933), 287; Hett, *Crossing*, 163.

103. Quotes in Abraham, "Juda," 135. See also ibid., 135–36; Seger, "Oranienburg," 51–54 (stating that the two men were not abused on the day of their arrival); BArchB, R 43 II/398, Bl. 99: Gestapa to RK, September 27, 1933; Büro, *Reichstagshandbuch 1933*, 121; Danckwortt, "Jüdische 'Schutzhäftlinge,'" 154–55. On alerts about impending transports, see Lüerßen, "'Moorsoldaten,'" 169. For forced labor of prominent prisoners, see Kienle, "Heuberg," 54; Rudorff, "'Privatlager,'" 163.

104. Hans Litten, who embraced his Jewish roots, would have been officially classified as a "half Jew" under the later Nuremberg Laws (his mother was Protestant, his father had converted from Judaism to Protestantism); Hett, *Crossing*, 7.

105. Quote in Kraiker, Suhr, *Ossietzky*, 103.

106. For the estimate, see Wünschmann, "Jewish Prisoners," 86, 89.

107. The summer 1933 census recorded some five hundred thousand persons of Jewish faith in the German Reich, making up 0.77 percent of the population; Friedländer, *Nazi Germany*, 15, 338. Nazi statisticians put the figure higher, adding German Jews who had converted or had no religious affiliation.

108. Based on the assumption that up to two hundred thousand prisoners went through the early camps in 1933.

109. In 1932, not one KPD Reichstag deputy was Jewish; Friedländer, *Nazi Germany*, 106.

110. Saxon Ministry of the Interior to police departments, April 18, 1933, cited in Wünschmann, "Cementing," 583 (emphasis in the original). For the detention of Jewish lawyers, see Wünschmann, "Jewish Prisoners," 52.

111. SA-Gruppe Berlin-Brandenburg, Gruppenbefehl Nr. 28, May 24, 1933, cited in Mayer-von Götz, *Terror*, 99.

112. For the detention of German Jews on nonpolitical grounds, see Wünschmann, "'Natürlich,'" 100–103.

113. For the anti-Semitism of SA and SS men, see Reichardt, *Kampfbünde*, 631–43; Szende, *Zwischen*, 40–41.

114. Quote in Beimler, *Mörderlager*, 28. More generally, see Wünschmann, "Jewish Prisoners," 76, 82–83, 95.

115. Quote in report by R. Weinmann, November 13, 1933, *NCC*, doc. 30. More generally, Sofsky, *Violence*, 168.

116. Quote in StAMü, StA Nr. 34479/1, Bl. 93–97: Lebenslauf H. Steinbrenner, n.d. (c. late 1940s), Bl. 94. For the other examples, see Mühsam, *Leidensweg*, 27; Megargee, *Encyclopedia*, vol. I/A, 51.

117. Quotes in Abraham, "Juda," 136. For torture through forced labor in other early camps, see Endlich, "Lichtenburg," 30–31; Lüerßen, "'Moorsoldaten,'" 169; Meyer and Roth, "Zentrale," 207–208; *NCC*, doc. 30.

118. Wünschmann, "Jewish Prisoners," 89, 95–101. See also Meyer and Roth, "Zentrale," 191–92, 200.

119. Quotes in Dr. Mittelbach to Daluege, April 10, 1933, in Michaelis and Schraepler, *Ursachen*, vol. 9, 360–62; Litten, *Mutter*, 29. See also Mühsam, *Leidensweg*, 29–31; Hett, *Crossing*, 164, 171.

120. Quote in Graf, "Genesis," 424. See also ibid., 423–24; Tuchel, *Konzentrationslager*, 54–55, 57, 62–65; Drobisch and Wieland, *System*, 55.

121. Wohlfeld, "Nohra," 110–13, 119–20.

122. Drobisch and Wieland, *System*, 42, 135; Baganz, *Erziehung*, 218–21; Roth, "Folterstätten," 18.

123. Noakes and Pridham, *Nazism*, vol. 1, 171; Kershaw, *Hubris*, 501–502.

124. Drobisch and Wieland, *System*, 134.

125. Meyer and Roth, "Zentrale," 189–91; *NCC*, doc. 7.

126. For example, see Kienle, "Konzentrationslager"; Baganz, *Erziehung*, 108–13, 225.

127. For the figures, see Drobisch and Wieland, *System*, 66; Tuchel, *Konzentrationslager*, 155.

128. Prussia held 14,906 out of 26,789 prisoners on July 31, 1933; BArchB, R 43 II/398, Bl. 92.

129. MdI Preußen to Regierungspräsident Osnabrück, June 22, 1933, in Kosthorst and Walter, *Strafgefangenenlager*, vol. 1, 59–61.

130. Tuchel, *Konzentrationslager*, 60–69.

131. PMI to Provincial Administrations, October 14, 1933, *NCC*, doc. 14. See also Tuchel, *Konzentrationslager*, 71.

132. Nürnberg, "Außenstelle," 88.

133. Bendig, "'Höllen'"; Mühsam, *Leidensweg*, 32.

134. Mette, "Lichtenburg," 132–35.

135. For the Emsland camps, see below.

136. Hesse, "'Erziehung,'" 122–27. The circular of October 14, 1933, recognized only one more camp, the Provincial Institution Brauweiler; PMI to Provincial Administrations, October 14, 1933, *NCC*, doc. 14. For other camps under Prussian district administrators, Tuchel, *Konzentrationslager*, 76.

137. PMI to Provincial Administrations, October 14, 1933, *NCC*, doc. 14.

138. Jenner, "Trägerschaft," 125; Drobisch and Wieland, *System*, 135.

139. PMI to Provincial Administrations, October 14, 1933, *NCC*, doc. 14.

140. Tuchel, *Konzentrationslager*, 49–50, 73–76, 78–80. SS units also arrived in regional camps like Moringen and Brauweiler; Hesse, "'Erziehung,'" 122; Wisskirchen, "Schutzhaft," 140.

141. Tuchel, *Konzentrationslager*, 80. In Brauweiler, by contrast, the civilian director apparently kept the SS guards under control; Wisskirchen, "Schutzhaft," 140–41.

142. SA Gruppenführer Ernst to Preußisches MdI, September 8, 1933, in Michaelis and Schraepler, *Ursachen*, vol. 9, 367–68; HIA, DD 253/K 769, B. Köhler, "In eigener Sache," 1934, 96–97; Tuchel, *Konzentrationslager*, 77.

143. Tuchel, *Konzentrationslager*, 76–77, 92–93; Drobisch and Wieland, *System*, 68–69; Mayer-von Götz, *Terror*, 164–67.

144. Rudorff, "Misshandlung."

145. Göring to inspector of the Prussian secret state police, March 11, 1934, *NCC*, doc. 21.

146. Niederschrift der Reichsstatthalterkonferenz vom 22.3.1934, in Repgen and Booms, *Akten*, vol. I/2, 1200.

147. Tuchel, *Konzentrationslager*, 85–89, 95; Graf, "Genesis," 424.

148. The best accounts of the early Emsland camps are Lüerßen, "'Wir'"; Klausch, *Tätergeschichten*.

149. For this and the previous paragraph, Langhoff, *Moorsoldaten*, 118–31, 136–37, 165, quote on 130. See also Lüerßen, "'Wir,'" 52–55, 344–45; Abraham, "Juda," 147–48; Knoch, "Konzentrationslager," 292.

150. Lüerßen, "'Moorsoldaten,'" 157–61.

151. *OdT*, vol. 1, 211–12.

152. Tuchel, *Konzentrationslager*, 103.

153. Himmler speech at a Wehrmacht course, January 15 to 23, 1937, *NCC*, doc. 83. For this and the previous paragraph, see ibid., doc. 135; Lüerßen, "'Wir,'" 96–102; Wachsmann, *Prisons*, 98, 102–103; Patel, *Soldiers*, 296–300.

154. Quote in Langhoff, *Moorsoldaten*, 200–201. See also Lüerßen, "'Wir,'" 96, 102–105; Fackler, *"Lagers Stimme,"* 142, 245–51.

155. Lüerßen, "'Wir,'" 56–58, 76–86, 467–68; Klausch, *Tätergeschichten*, 30, 67–68, 266; Tuchel, *Konzentrationslager*, 80.

156. Klausch, *Tätergeschichten*, 163–66; Knoch, "'Stupider Willkür,'" 35–36.

157. For this and the previous paragraph, see Langhoff, *Moorsoldaten*, 171, 234–43; Abraham, "Juda," 148–52; Klausch, *Tätergeschichten*, 82–90, 95–97; Diekmann and Wettig, *Oranienburg*, 109; Schumacher, *M.d.R.*, 175–78. Quotes in LG Oldenburg, Anklage gegen Johannes K., 1948, in Kosthorst and Walter, *Strafgefangenenlager*, vol. 1, 68; NLA-StAO, 140–45, Nr. 1154, Vernehmung F. Ebert, June 11, 1949.

158. LG Oldenburg, Urteil 1949, in Kosthorst and Walter, *Strafgefangenenlager*, vol. 1, 79–84; Klausch, *Tätergeschichten*, 34. For the 1932 riot, see Evans, *Coming*, 285.

159. WL, P.III.h. no. 280, A. Benjamin, "KZ Papenburg und Lichtenburg," c. 1934, quote on 5. See also Klausch, *Tätergeschichten*, 95–99, 166; Mette, "Lichtenburg," 137; Abraham, "Juda," 157–61.

160. Klausch, *Tätergeschichten*, 108–14, 206–12, 230–31.

161. Ibid., 281–86.

162. Hett, *Crossing*, 200–201, 216–17; Buck, "Ossietzky," 22–23; Kraiker and Suhr, *Ossietzky*, 108; Suhr, *Ossietzky*, 208–211; Lüerßen, "'Moorsoldaten,'" 196.

163. Klausch, *Tätergeschichten*, 284–85.

164. Tuchel, *Konzentrationslager*, 142–43; NSDAP Reichsleitung, Rundschreiben, December 27, 1933, in IfZ, *Akten*, vol. 2, 42.

165. Quote in Breitman and Aronson, "Himmler-Rede," 344. In his speech, Himmler gives the date of his appointment as March 12. He was actually appointed on the evening of March 9, 1933; Longerich, *Himmler*, 158–59. For Heydrich, see Gerwarth, *Heydrich*.

166. Longerich, *Himmler*, especially pages 158–60, 759–63. More generally on Himmler's early political career, see Mües-Baron, *Himmler*.

167. "Ein Konzentrationslager für politische Gefangene," *Münchner Neueste Nachrichten*, March 21, 1933, partial translation *NCC*, doc. 5. See also BArchB, R 2/28350, Chronik der SS-Lageranlage in Dachau, March 1, 1938. For state prisoners in 1932, BayHStA, MJu 22663.

168. Tuchel, *Konzentrationslager*, 153–55; Drobisch and Wieland, *System*, 51. On August 1, 1933, Dachau held 2,218 of all 4,152 Bavarian protective custody prisoners; Aronson, *Heydrich*, 325.

169. Rubner, "Dachau," 56–59; Ecker, "Hölle," 30; DaA, 550, M. Grünwiedl, "Dachauer Gefangene erzählen," summer 1934, 4; Zámečník, *Dachau*, 51–52; Richardi, *Schule*, 65–66. For a map, Comité, *Dachau* (2005), CD-Rom.

170. Tuchel, *Konzentrationslager*, 125; Drobisch and Wieland, *System*, 51–52; Richardi, *Schule*, 54–56; Dillon, "Dachau," 51, 67, 139, 155.

171. StAMü, StA Nr. 34479/1, Bl. 93–97: Lebenslauf H. Steinbrenner, n.d. (c. late 1940s), Bl. 94. See also DaA, 550, M. Grünwiedl, "Dachauer Gefangene erzählen," summer 1934, 3.

172. Tuchel, "Kommandanten des KZ Dachau," 331–32; Internationales Zentrum, *Nazi-Bastille*, 20.

173. Richardi, *Schule*, 58; Orth, *SS*, 99.

174. Seubert, "'Vierteljahr,'" quotes on pages 90–91. See also Wünschmann, "Jewish Prisoners," 79–80.

175. Seubert, "'Vierteljahr,'" 103. See also Dillon, "Dachau," 156, 164.

176. Estimate based on figures in Seubert, "'Vierteljahr,'" 76–77; Drobisch and Wieland, *System*, 51.

177. Seubert, "'Vierteljahr,'" 81–92, quotes on pages 90, 120.

178. Wünschmann, "Jewish Prisoners," 83–84; idem, "Jüdische politische Häftlinge."

179. Special regulations for the Dachau camp, May 1933, *NCC*, doc. 8.

180. Seubert, "'Vierteljahr,'" 79, 91–96. For the quote, Himmler speech at SS Gruppenführer conference, February 18, 1937, *NCC*, doc. 98.

181. For this and the previous paragraph, Gruchmann, *Justiz*, 634–39; Richardi, *Schule*, 97–113; StAMü, StA Nr. 34479/1, Bl. 93–97: Lebenslauf H. Steinbrenner, n.d. (c. late 1940s), Bl. 95.

182. For the paragraphs on Eicke, see especially Segev, *Soldiers*, 137–55; Bürckel quote on 142; Tuchel, *Konzentrationslager*, 128–41. See also BArchB (ehem. BDC), SSO, Eicke, Theodor, 17.10.1892; Longerich, *Himmler*, 162–63; extracts of testimony of O. Pohl, 1947, *TWC*, vol. 5, 437; Koehl, *Black Corps*, 232; Bernhard, "Konzentrierte," 237. For a biography, focusing on the period until 1934, see Weise, *Eicke*. For Eicke's cigar, see MacLean, *Camp*, 306–307.

183. Dillon, "Dachau," 56, 59–60, 69, 157–59, 191, 198, 213, 235, quote on 197. According to his postwar testimony, Steinbrenner left Dachau around mid-July 1933, returning in autumn as an instructor and later an office worker in the Guard Troop; StAMü, StA Nr. 28791/28, Bl. 39–41: Vernehmungsniederschrift H. Steinbrenner, May 12, 1949.

184. Richardi, *Schule*, 179–80. For Wessel, see Siemens, *Making*.

185. Burkhard, *Tanz*, 37–40; Ecker, "Hölle," 34; Tuchel, *Konzentrationslager*, 143.

186. Disziplinar- u. Strafordnung Dachau, October 1, 1933, *IMT*, vol. 26, 291–96, ND: 778-PS, emphasis in the original. The translation draws on *NCC*, doc. 150. See also Drobisch and Wieland, *System*, 79–80.

187. Wünschmann, "Jewish Prisoners," 84.

188. Quote in Vermerk Dr. Stepp, December 6, 1933, *IMT*, vol. 36, 54–55, ND: 926-D. See also Gruchmann, *Justiz*, 640–45; Tuchel, *Konzentrationslager*, 141.

189. Meyer and Roth, "Zentrale," 202, 208. Figures covering the period between March 1933 and July 1934.

190. LKA Dresden, Vorläufige Bestimmungen, August 5, 1933, in Baganz, *Erziehung*, 377–86, p. 380.

191. Comité, *Dachau* (1978), 204; KZ-Gedenkstätte Dachau, *Gedenkbuch*, 19.

192. Zámečník, *Dachau*, 52–55.

193. *VöB*, August 11, 1932, *NCC*, doc. 2; *VöB*, March 13, 1921, *NCC*, doc. 1 (with a minor correction to the translation). The 1923 Nazi constitution, drafted before the failed beer hall putsch, also envisaged collection camps for opponents; Drobisch and Wieland, *System*, 13.

194. See also Tuchel, *Konzentrationslager*, 37. The following section draws partly on Wachsmann and Goeschel, "Before Auschwitz," especially pages 525, 529–32.

195. For example, see Arendt, "Concentration Camps," 748.

196. For one example, see Eicke order for Lichtenburg camp, June 2, 1934, *NCC*, doc. 148.

197. Compare "Grundsätze," esp. §48 and §139–43, and LKA Dresden, Vorläufige Bestim-mungen, August 5, 1933 (in Baganz, *Erziehung*, 377–86), especially IV and V.16.f. See also Lechner, "Kuhberg," 86; Hesse, "'Erziehung,'" 120.

198. Wachsmann, *Prisons*, 23, 409; Krohne, *Gefängniskunde*, 354–57; Hoelz, "Weißen Kreuz" (first published in 1929), 302. For Dachau, see Disziplinar- u. Strafordnung Dachau, October 1, 1933, *IMT*, vol. 26, 291–96, ND: 778–PS. In 1937, Himmler himself drew attention to the precedent of floggings in Prussian penitentiaries; speech at a Wehrmacht course, January 15 to 23, 1937, *NCC*, doc. 83.

199. One prisoner to prosper under this system was the later Auschwitz commandant Ru-dolf Höss, detained between 1924 and 1928; Wachsmann, *Prisons*, 26–27, 34–35, 38–39, 50.

200. Quote in special regulations for Dachau, May 1933, *NCC*, doc. 8. See also Beimler, *Mörderlager*, 29. For the stages system in other early camps, *NCC*, doc. 13; Baganz, *Erziehung*, 216.

201. Wachsmann, *Prisons*, 21–23, 28, 95–99, 102.

202. Caplan, "Political Detention." For personnel links between Weimar voluntary labor service camps and later SS camps, see Riedle, *Angehörigen*, 110–11.

203. Quote in Bendig, "'Höllen,'" 104. See also Mühsam, *Leidensweg*, 33.

204. Almost all men appointed as KL commandants between 1934 and 1939 had served in the First World War (one exception was Franz Ziereis, born in 1905) and at least four had been POWs (Heinrich Deubel, Karl Otto Koch, Hans Loritz, and Günther Tamaschke). For biographical summaries, see Tuchel, *Konzentrationslager*, 371–96.

205. Reichardt, *Kampfbünde*, 458–59, 566–70, 579–89, 702; Siemens, *Making*, 66–67.

206. Manuscript by P. M. Neurath, 1943, *NCC*, doc. 195.

207. Dillon, "Dachau," 122–23.

208. Quotes in BArchB, R 3001/21167, Bl. 62–69: KL Dachau, Dienstvorschriften für Begleit-personen, October 1, 1933. For roll calls, see Suderland, *Extremfall*, 190–94. For music, see Fackler, "Cultural Behaviour," 608, 614–15.

209. Report of a Jewish "reimmigrant," August 1936, *NCC*, doc. 243.

210. Quote in T. Eicke, special camp order for Esterwegen, August 1, 1934, *NCC*, doc. 149. See also BArchB, R 3001/21167, Bl. 62–69: KL Dachau, Dienstvorschriften für Begleit-personen, October 1, 1933, Bl. 63; Wachsmann, *Prisons*, 24.

211. Richardi, *Schule*, 65. This terminology only changed in 1937, not just in Dachau; Baganz, *Erziehung*, 257.

212. Springmann, "'Sport,'" 96–97. More generally, see Euskirchen, "Militärrituale," 128–34.

213. Wiedner, "Soldatenmißhandlungen."

214. Springmann, "'Sport,'" 89–95; *NCC*, doc. 209.

215. Quote in Sopade report, December 1936, *NCC*, doc. 192. See also Langhoff, *Moorsol-daten*, 139–40; Richardi, *Schule*, 73–74; Sofsky, *Ordnung*, 84–85.

216. Caplan, "Political Detention," 41. See also Raithel and Strenge, "Reichstagsbrandver-ordnung," 450.

217. *Hildesheimer Allgemeine Zeitung*, May 9, 1933, in Drobisch and Wieland, *System*, 27. More generally, see Moore, "Popular Opinion," 87, 113–14. For postwar memory, see Marcuse, *Dachau*, 74; *KL*, epilogue.

218. Quotes in *VöB* (Berlin edition), August 10, 1933; BArchF, BB (Nr. 5), Deutsche Wochenschau, 1933; Rudorff, "'Privatlager,'" 150; Moore, "Popular Opinion," 51, 44. More generally, ibid., 30–31, 36–39, 57; Drobisch and Wieland, *System*, 88–94.

219. For example, see Gellately, *Backing*, 60, 257.

220. Kershaw, *Hubris*, 456; idem, *Popular Opinion*, 73.

221. *Schleswig-Holsteinische Landeszeitung*, August 28, 1933, in Jenner, "Trägerschaft," 119.
222. On these difficulties, see Kershaw, *Popular Opinion*, 6.
223. See also Moore, "Popular Opinion," 129.
224. *Sonnenburger Anzeiger*, April 7, 1933, in Nürnberg, "Außenstelle," 86. For other examples, see Rudorff, "'Privatlager,'" 154–55; Borgstedt, "Kislau," 220–21. For photos of a public procession in Kislau, see Hesse and Springer, *Augen*, 55.
225. Seger, "Oranienburg," 55–56. See also *NCC*, doc. 65; Baganz, *Erziehung*, 185–87; Krause-Vilmar, *Breitenau*, 138–39.
226. Rudorff, "Misshandlung," 55; Mayer-von Götz, *Terror*, 154–55; Moore, "Popular Opinion," 132.
227. Aders, "Terror," 184; Moore, "Popular Opinion," 105–107. On contacts between towns and camps, see also Steinbacher, *Dachau*, 125–80.
228. Oberstes Parteigericht, Beschluss, April 1, 1935, in IfZ, *Akten*, vol. 1, 56. More generally on Kemna, see Mintert, "Konzentrationslager."
229. Langhoff, *Moorsoldaten*, 302.
230. Report of the Prussian Central State Prosecutor's Office, June 21, 1934, *NCC*, doc. 113.
231. Quotes in Asgodom, *"Halts Maul,"* 16; Steinbacher, *Dachau*, 150. Local variations were in use elsewhere; Rudorff, "'Privatlager,'" 166. More generally, see Hüttenberger, "Heimtückefälle," 478–79, 503; Kempowski, *Haben*, 24–26.
232. Litten, *Mutter*, 24.
233. Hett, *Crossing*, 163, 173. Some of Litten's letters went to his friends, not his mother. For regulations on letters, Krause-Vilmar, *Breitenau*, 138; Baganz, *Erziehung*, 171.
234. Seger, "Oranienburg," 70; Baganz, *Erziehung*, 171–72; Mayer-von Götz, *Terror*, 132; ITS, ARCH/HIST/KL Kislau, Bl. 59–72: Wachvorschrift, July 12, 1933, Bl. 67–68.
235. Litten, *Mutter*, 29. See also Mühsam, *Leidensweg*, 26–29, 36.
236. Quote in Mayer-von Götz, *Terror*, 133. For other cases of relatives forcing their way into camps, *NCC*, doc. 51; Drobisch and Wieland, *System*, 175.
237. Mühsam, *Leidensweg*, 29; Wollenberg, "Gleichschaltung," 267.
238. Cited in Drobisch and Wieland, *System*, 176.
239. For examples from 1934–35, ibid., 237–39.
240. Litten, *Mutter*, 22, 37, 59, 70.
241. Rudorff, "'Privatlager,'" 167; *NCC*, doc. 50.
242. Hett, *Crossing*, 187.
243. L. Ebert to Hindenburg, July 14, 1933, *NCC*, doc. 47. See also Gestapa to Hitler, September 27, 1933, in Repgen and Booms, *Akten*, vol. I/2, 840–41.
244. While some prisoners who left Oranienburg were transported to another camp, most were released; Knop et al., "Häftlinge," 56. More generally, see Tuchel, *Konzentrationslager*, 103; Mayer-von Götz, *Terror*, 158–59; Langhoff, *Moorsoldaten*, 24, 46. For mass releases for propaganda purposes, see Drobisch and Wieland, *System*, 133.
245. Quote in DaA, 550, M. Grünwiedl, "Dachauer Gefangene erzählen," summer 1934, p. 30. See also ibid., 5670, Grünwiedl to VVN, August 20, 1947; Richardi, *Schule*, 26–47.
246. Schneider, *Hakenkreuz*, especially pages 905–908.
247. K. G. Saur Verlag, *Tarnschriften*, doc. BTS-0064. More generally, see Gittig, *Tarnschriften*.
248. Drobisch and Wieland, *System*, 171.
249. Ehret, "Schutzhaft," 256; Stöver, *Berichte*, 38.
250. For background, see Johe, "Volk," 334.
251. Szalet, *Baracke*, 11.
252. "Bericht über die Lage in Deutschland," February 1934, in Stöver, *Berichte*, 69–70; Lüerßen, "'Wir,'" 157.
253. Union, *Strafvollzug*, 18–20; Mayer-von Götz, *Terror*, 162–64.

254. HStAD, Rep. 29, Nr. 302, Krankenanstalten Wuppertal-Barmen, Anamnese, October 5, 1933. More generally, Moore, "Popular Opinion," 115–19; Mayer-von Götz, *Terror*, 161.

255. For one case, see Mayer-von Götz, *Terror*, 151.

256. Quote in Moore, "Popular Opinion," 112. For other examples, see ibid., 103; *Deutschland-Berichte*, vol. 1 (1934), 233, 302.

257. Klemperer, *LTI*, 41.

258. For the Nazi vote, see Falter, *Wähler*.

259. Moore, "Popular Opinion," 162.

260. Quote in Fritzsche, *Life*, 31.

261. Quote in Mayer-von Götz, *Terror*, 155. See also Moore, "Popular Opinion," 78, 161–62.

262. Himmler speech to Reichsleiter and Gauleiter, October 6, 1943, in Smith and Peterson, *Geheimreden*, 168.

263. Drobisch and Wieland, *System*, 27.

264. Moore, "Popular Opinion," 159–60.

265. K. Tucholsky to W. Hasenclever, April 20, 1933, in Directmedia, *Tucholsky*, 11678.

266. *Braunbuch*, 270–302, quote on 270. See also Drobisch and Wieland, *System*, 168–71; Rabinbach, "*Antifascism*"; Milton, "Konzentrationslager," 142–43; Nürnberg, "Außenstelle," 89 (n. 25). For exile collections of eyewitness reports, *Deutschland-Berichte*; Stöver, *Berichte*.

267. Baganz, *Erziehung*, 241–44.

268. "Malice against Ebert's Son," *Manchester Guardian*, October 13, 1933. See also Klausch, *Tätergeschichten*, 90–91; Meyer and Roth, "'Wühler,'" 236.

269. Diekmann and Wettig, *Oranienburg*, 12.

270. Milton, "Konzentrationslager," 138–42, quote on 138. See also Dörner, "Ein KZ," 133–34.

271. Drobisch and Wieland, *System*, 180–81, quote on 180. See also Mühsam, *Leidensweg*, 41.

272. Moore, "Popular Opinion," 29–31, quote on 30. See also Heiß, *Deutschland*, 101. On German war crimes in 1914, see Kramer and Horne, *German Atrocities*.

273. *NCC*, 304.

274. For German foreign policy, see Kershaw, *Hubris*, 490–93.

275. Zámečník, *Dachau*, 91; Drobisch and Wieland, *System*, 88.

276. Baganz, *Erziehung*, 236–37.

277. Quotes in *The Times*, readers' letters, September 29, 1933, October 4, 1933, *NCC*, docs. 54 and 55.

278. Zámečník, *Dachau*, 96–97; Kersten, "'The Times.'"

279. Quotes in NAL, FO 371/16704, Bl. 363–65: report on a visit to Hohnstein, October 10, 1933. For Hohnstein, *OdT*, vol. 2, 129–34.

280. For example, Hett, *Crossing*, 189; German Foreign Ministry to embassies, July 1933, *NCC*, doc. 48.

281. Quotes in Favre, "'Wir,'" translation in *NCC*, doc. 56.

282. *Oranienburger Generalanzeiger*, March 28, 1933, in Longerich, "Straßenkampf," 30–31.

283. "Sie können sich nicht beklagen," *Kasseler Neueste Nachrichten*, June 23, 1933, in Krause-Vilmar, *Breitenau*, 104. More generally, see Moore, "Popular Opinion," 53–54, 66, 73, 77–78.

284. For films, see Drobisch, "Oranienburg," 19.

285. For a photo essay, see "Im Konzentrationslager Oranienburg bei Berlin," *Berliner Illustrirte Zeitung*, April 30, 1933. More generally, see Drobisch and Wieland, *System*, 88–92.

286. Moore, "Popular Opinion," 52–53. More generally, see Caplan, "Political Detention," 33.

287. *NS-Nachrichten für Nieder-Barnim*, August 19, 1933, *NCC*, doc. 49.

288. IfZ, Fa 199/29, Bl. 51: Schäfer to Hitler, March 24, 1934; ibid., Bl. 52: Dr. Meerwald to Schäfer, April 3, 1934; Drobisch and Wieland, *System*, 93; "Dokumentation der Ausstellung," 182. For Schäfer's book, see also P. Moore, "'What Happened.'"
289. Schäfer, *Konzentrationslager*, quotes on pages 25, 63, 40, 238–39.
290. For example, see Longerich, "Straßenkampf," 31; Wollenberg, "Gleichschaltung," 262–64.
291. Kershaw, *"Myth,"* 63; idem, *Hubris*, 494–95.
292. Ecker, "Hölle," 48; DaA, 550, M. Grünwiedl, "Dachauer Gefangene erzählen," summer 1934, 23–25. Not everywhere did intimidation work as well as in Dachau: in Sachsenburg, only twenty-seven percent of prisoners voted for the Nazis; Baganz, *Erziehung*, 181.
293. Bendig, "'Höllen,'" 107.
294. Schäfer, *Konzentrationslager*, 16.
295. Quotes in Longerich, "Straßenkampf," 31. See also "Konzentrationslager für Schutzhäftlinge in Bayern," *VöB*, March 21, 1933, in Comité, *Dachau* (1978), 43.
296. Bettelheim, "Individual," 426.
297. Klemperer, *Zeugnis*, vol. 1, 69.
298. Schäfer, *Konzentrationslager*, 23, 25, 27–28. For other examples, see Drobisch and Wieland, *System*, 92; Baganz, *Erziehung*, 237.
299. Wollenberg, "Gleichschaltung," 260.
300. For Dachau, see Steinbacher, *Dachau*, 186–87.
301. *Amper-Bote*, June 2, 1933, *NCC*, doc. 42 (with minor adjustment to translation). More generally, see Steinbacher, *Dachau*, 187–88.
302. Wollenberg, "Gleichschaltung," 263, 267–68; Wieland, "Bremischen," 282–87.
303. Dörner, "Konzentrationslager," 72; Longerich, "Straßenkampf," 31.
304. The decree is reprinted in Hirsch et al., *Recht*, 90–91. It was replaced on December 20, 1934, by the even more expansive Law against Malicious Attacks on State and Party. For background, see Dörner, *"Heimtücke,"* 17–25.
305. LaB, A Rep. 339, Nr. 702, Bl. 334–36: Sondergericht Berlin, Urteil, November 24, 1933. See also Hüttenberger, "Heimtückefälle," 478–79; Dörner, "Konzentrationslager," 71–73.
306. StAMü, StA Nr. 7457, Sondergericht München, Urteil, August 19, 1933. See also Drobisch and Wieland, *System*, 177.
307. Cited in Moore, "Popular Opinion," 110–11.
308. Moore, "Popular Opinion," 68–69.
309. Quote in "Life in Nazi Prison Camp," *Daily Telegraph*, March 19, 1934. See also "Baby Labelled 'Political Prisoner No. 58,'" *Daily Herald*, April 23, 1934; "Frau Seger Free," *Manchester Guardian*, May 25, 1933; IfZ, Fa 199/29, Bl. 69–71: ORR Volk to Reichskanzlei, April 30, 1934.
310. Quotes in Ecker, "Hölle," 15; Zámečník, *Dachau*, 45; Disziplinar- u. Strafordnung für Dachau, October 1, 1933, *IMT*, vol. 26, 291–96, ND: 778–PS, p. 294. See also Zámečník, *Dachau*, 43–46 (though Wilhelm Franz is wrongly identified here as a Jewish prisoner; Wünschmann, "Jewish Prisoners," 112).
311. Améry, *Jenseits*, 38, 54, 58. For a similar point in reference to Jewish victims, see Wildt, "Violent Changes;" K. Wünschmann, "Konzentrationslagererfahrungen," 56–57.
312. Mitteilungen des Gestapa, August 24, 1933, in Boberach, *Regimekritik*, doc. rk 21.
313. For example, see Kershaw, *Popular Opinion*, 79–80.
314. Eley, "Silent Majority?," 558.
315. See also Wachsmann, "Dynamics," 20.

2. The SS Camp System

1. For Röhm's murder, see especially StAMü, GStA beim OLG München Nr. 2116, LG München, Urteil, May 14, 1957, quote on page 46; the coup de grâce was undoubtedly delivered by Lippert, although the judges felt unable to establish this with absolute certainty. See also ibid., Nr. 6237, Vernehmung W. Kopp, May 27, 1953; ibid., StA Nr. 28791/40, Dr. Koch, Niederschrift, July 1, 1934; ibid., Nr. 28791/1, Bl. 13–16: Vernehmung Dr. Koch, January 25, 1949; ibid., Nr. 28791/3, Bl. 72–75: Vernehmung W. Noetzel, June 28, 1949. Eicke is said to have shot a Dachau prisoner in summer 1933 (Richardi, *Schule*, 187), but this would have been a rare case of him committing murder himself.

2. For this and the previous paragraph, see Kershaw, *Hubris*, 499–517. See also Longerich, *Himmler*, 180–84; Höhne, *Orden*, 90–124.

3. For the quote and Hitler's speech, see Kershaw, *Hubris*, 514. For the Dachau SS and the purge, see StAMü, StA Nr. 28791/3, Bl. 5–7: Vernehmung M. von Dall-Armi, May 5, 1949; ibid., Bl. 61–64: Vernehmung J. Hirsch, June 27, 1949; ibid., Bl. 103: Vernehmung M. Müller, July 19, 1949; ibid., Nr. 28791/6, Bl. 406–409: Vernehmung R. Dirnagel, June 3, 1953; ibid., Bl. 441–42: Vernehmung X. Hammerdinger, July 9, 1953; ibid., Nr. 28791/28, Bl. 36: Vernehmung T. Dufter, May 6, 1949; ibid., GStA beim OLG München Nr. 2116, LG München, Urteil, May 14, 1957, 18–19; Höhne, *Orden*, 101.

4. StAMü, StA Nr. 28791/28, Bl. 53–54: KOK Schmitt, Schlussbericht, June 17, 1949; Kershaw, *Hubris*, especially pages 159, 208–209.

5. StAMü, StA Nr. 28791/28, Bl. 39–41, 42–44: Vernehmung J. Steinbrenner, May 12, 1949, May 25, 1949; ibid., Nr. 28791/6, Bl. 398–402: Vernehmung J. Steinbrenner, June 1, 1953.

6. StAMü, StA Nr. 28791/3, Bl. 5–7: Vernehmung M. von Dall-Armi, May 5, 1949; ibid., Bl. 57–58: Vernehmung A. Pleiner, June 22, 1949; ibid., Nr. 28791/6, Bl. 398–402: Vernehmung J. Steinbrenner, June 1, 1953.

7. DaA, Nr. 24658, Bestattungsamt Munich, Ordner: Poliz. Opfer allg., n.d., Abschrift.

8. StAMü, StA Nr. 28791/46, GStA Munich, EV, January 28, 1952, p. 11; ibid., Nr. 28791/6, Bl. 403–405: Vernehmung W. Noetzel, June 2, 1953; ibid., Nr. 28791/28, Bl. 35: Vernehmung A. Stadler, May 5, 1949; BayHStA, StK 6299/2, Bericht des Politischen Polizeikommandeurs Bayerns, May 7, 1935 (I am grateful to Kim Wünschmann for this reference).

9. StAMü, StA Nr. 28791/3, Bl. 61–64: Vernehmung J. Hirsch, June 27, 1949; ibid., Bl. 68–69: Vernehmung H. Reis, June 21, 1949; ibid., Bl. 70: Vernehmung L. Schmidt, June 30, 1949.

10. StAMü, StA Nr. 28791/6, Bl. 441–42: Vernehmung X. Hammerdinger, July 9, 1953; ibid., Nr. 28791/3, Bl. 5–7: Vernehmung M. von Dall-Armi, May 5, 1949; ibid., Bl. 12–13: Vernehmung J. Lutz, May 11, 1949; ibid., Bl. 72–75: Vernehmung W. Noetzel, June 28, 1949; ibid., Bl. 92: Vernehmung J. Klampfl, July 15, 1949.

11. Domarus, *Hitler*, vol. 1, 405. For the murders on July 2 in Dachau, StAMü, StA Nr. 28791/46, GStA Munich, EV, January 28, 1952, p. 11.

12. Twenty-two victims are known by name; Zámečník, *Dachau*, 70. At least another three men are known to have been murdered not far from the camp, probably by Dachau SS men; StAMü, StA Nr. 28791/46, GStA Munich, EV, January 28, 1952, pp. 13–15.

13. StAMü, StA Nr. 28791/46, GStA Munich, EV, January 28, 1952, pp. 11–16; ibid., Nr. 28791/32, KOK Schmitt, Schlussbericht, June 20, 1949.

14. Kershaw, *Hubris*, 517–26. See also idem, *"Myth,"* passim.

15. USHMM, 1998.A.0247, reel 15, Bl. 184–93: statement H. Aumeier, December 15, 1947 (translation from Polish by Katharina Friedla). See also BArchB (ehem. BDC), SSO, Aumeier, Hans, 20.8.1906.

16. Eicke order for Lichtenburg, June 2, 1934, *NCC*, doc. 148.

17. Eicke to Himmler, August 10, 1936, *NCC*, doc. 152.

18. Endlich, "Lichtenburg," 32; Schilde and Tuchel, *Columbia-Haus*, 35, 123–25; StAMü, StA Nr. 28791/7, Vernehmung K. Launer, May 23, 1949.

19. StAMü, GStA beim OLG München Nr. 2116, LG München, Urteil, May 14, 1957, 56–59, quote on 55.

20. Quote in *IMT*, vol. 29, Rede bei der SS Gruppenführertagung in Posen, October 4, 1943, ND: 1919–PS, p. 145. See also Longerich, *Himmler*, 184; von Papen, *Papen*, 30–31. The exact date of Eicke's promotion in July 1934 is unknown; Tuchel, *Konzentrationslager*, 181.

21. Quote in Breitman and Aronson, "Himmler-Rede," 345.

22. Longerich, *Himmler*, 165–79, 192–96; Gerwarth, *Heydrich*, 102.

23. Tuchel, *Konzentrationslager*, 319.

24. The first nationwide rules for protective custody by the Reich Ministry of the Interior in April 1934 confirmed the central role of the Gestapo in imposing KL detention; Wachsmann, "Dynamics," 20–21.

25. Quote in Himmler to district president in Merseburg, June 15, 1934, in Tuchel, "Theodor Eicke," 65. For the dating of Himmler's instruction, BArchB (ehem. BDC), SSO, Eicke, Theodor, 17.10.1892, Lebenslauf, March 15, 1937.

26. Tuchel, *Konzentrationslager*, 162–63; Mette, "Lichtenburg," 144; BArchB (ehem. BDC), SSO, Eicke, Theodor, 17.10.1892, Eicke to Chef des SS-Amtes, June 2, 1934.

27. Eicke order for Lichtenburg, June 2, 1934, *NCC*, doc. 148.

28. BArchB (ehem. BDC), SSO, Schmidt, Bernhard, 18.4.1890, Eicke to Chef des SS-Amtes, June 21, 1934.

29. For Sachsenburg and Hohnstein, see Baganz, *Erziehung*, 251–52; *OdT*, vol. 2, 132. The takeover date of Esterwegen is unclear: the new commandant, Loritz, was appointed on July 9, 1934 (Riedel, *Ordnungshüter*, 98) but may have arrived earlier (Drobisch and Wieland, *System*, 189).

30. For Eicke's title, BArchB (ehem. BDC), SSO, Eicke, Theodor, 17.10.1892, Gesamtdienstbescheinigung, March 30, 1943.

31. Von Papen, *Papen*, 25–30; Tuchel, *Konzentrationslager*, 184–86; Mühsam, *Leidensweg*, 43–48; Kreiler, "Tod," 106; Hirte, *Mühsam*, 311.

32. *OdT*, vol. 2, 132, 180. For Himmler's involvement in closing Oranienburg, BArchB, NS 4/Sa 18, Bl. 118: KL Oranienburg to Bürgermeister Fuchs, July 14, 1934.

33. For Eicke's dominant role, see BArchB (ehem. BDC), SSO, Loritz, Hans, 21.12.1895, Kommandantur Dachau to H. Loritz, June 29, 1934.

34. Riedel, *Ordnungshüter*, 113. In Sachsenburg, the Dachau regulations were apparently introduced in 1935; Baganz, *Erziehung*, 266–69.

35. Riedel, *Ordnungshüter*, 85–116, quote on 116. In Dachau, Loritz had impressed Eicke as the head of the adjacent "SS-Hilfswerk," a camp for Austrian SS men.

36. IfZ, F 13/6, Bl. 369–82: R. Höss, "Theodor Eicke," November 1946, Bl. 372.

37. Himmler directive, December 10, 1934, *NCC*, doc. 72; Rürup, *Topographie*, 13; Tuchel, *Konzentrationslager*, 209–10, 220, 294, 347–48. Eicke and Heydrich reported to Himmler, both as SS officers and as state officials.

38. Himmler memorandum to the Gestapo, July 8, 1935, *NCC*, doc. 73; Sydnor, *Soldiers*, 21–22; BArchB, R 58/264, Bl. 50–52: Heydrich Anordnung, May 31, 1934. KL commandants could appeal to Himmler if they objected to a Gestapo release order; ITS, ARCH/HIST/KL Lichtenburg 2, Bl. 86: IKL to LK, November 6, 1936.

39. Tuchel, *Konzentrationslager*, 210, 223–25, 229, 238–40; Kaienburg, *Wirtschaftskomplex*, 59–60.

40. The five camps were Dachau, Lichtenburg, Esterwegen, Sachsenburg, and Columbia House (Berlin); see also map 2.

41. Herbert, "Gegnerbekämpfung," 60–61. See also memorandum by Reichsbank president Schacht, May 3, 1935, in Hockerts and Kahlenberg, *Akten*, 567–70; German ambassador to Great Britain report, January 26, 1935, *NCC*, doc. 278; Longerich, *Himmler*, 203; Gruchmann, *Justiz*, 545–47.

42. See PMI, circular, April 24, 1933, *NCC*, doc. 6; Krause-Vilmar, *Breitenau*, 107.

43. Tuchel, *Konzentrationslager*, 93–94; Kube, "Göring," 78.
44. Quote in Prussian MPr, announcement, December 9, 1933, *NCC*, doc. 18. See also Tuchel, *Konzentrationslager*, 104–105; Drobisch and Wieland, *System*, 136–37. For amnesties elsewhere in Germany in late 1933, see Baganz, *Erziehung*, 223–24.
45. For general background, see Pingel, *Häftlinge*, 25, 51.
46. Schumacher, *M.d.R.*, 302. Ebert survived and became a senior SED politician in the GDR.
47. Frick's views are reflected in RdI to Landesregierungen et al., April 12, 1934, in Repgen and Booms, *Akten*, vol. I/2, 1235–38. See also ibid., 1200; Gruchmann, *Justiz*, 547–49; FZH, 353-31, "Schutzhaft," *Frankfurter Zeitung*, March 13, 1934.
48. BayHStA, Staatskanzlei 6299/1, Frick to Sk Bayern, October 5, 1934; BArchB, R 43 II/398, Bl. 92: Übersicht Schutzhaft, n.d.; Langhoff, *Moorsoldaten*, 315.
49. Drobisch and Wieland, *System*, 140.
50. GStA PK, I. HA, Rep. 77, Nr. 484, Bl. 115: Hitler to Landesregierungen et al., August 7, 1934; Gruchmann, *Justiz*, 334–36.
51. BayHStA, Staatskanzlei 6299/1, Frick to Sk Bayern, October 5, 1934; Hett, *Crossing*, 205–207. For SS guards, ITS, ARCH/KL Sachsenburg 1, Bl. 6: Beurteilung A. Cieslok, September 7, 1934. For Esterwegen, see Lüerßen, "'Wir,'" 465.
52. GStAPK, I. HA, Rep. 90P, Nr. 137, Bl. 63: "Weitere Schutzhaftentlassungen," n.d. See also Tuchel, *Konzentrationslager*, 187.
53. Wachsmann, *Prisons*, 68–71, 112–18, 372–75, 392–93.
54. Quote in Sarodnick, "'Haus,'" 347. More generally, see Wachsmann, *Prisons*, 83–101, 375–76.
55. Wachsmann, *Prisons*, 101–11, 398–99. See also Knoch, "'Willkür,'" 39–44.
56. Wachsmann, *Prisons*, 168.
57. RJM proposal, n.d. (1935), *IMT*, vol. 26, ND: 785–PS, quotes on 308; Baganz, *Erziehung*, 286–89; Gruchmann, *Justiz*, 368–71.
58. Quote in Domarus, *Hitler*, vol. 1, 422. Hitler did not mention the Stettin camp by name. Among the executed men was the former commandant. More generally, see "Ein Interview Ministerpräsident Görings über die Sicherheit in Deutschland," *VöB*, April 22–23, 1934; Rudorff, "Misshandlung," 62–63; Gruchmann, *Justiz*, 348–52; RJM proposal, n.d. (1935), *IMT*, vol. 26, 311, ND: 785–PS.
59. Gruchmann, *Justiz*, 364–65; Tuchel, *Konzentrationslager*, 83, 163, 181–83, 387.
60. To coordinate the SS response, Himmler ordered commandants to inform him personally about unnatural prisoner deaths; BArchB, NS 4 Bu/12, Eicke to LK, May 24, 1935.
61. Himmler speech at the Reich Peasant Congress, November 12, 1935, in Noakes and Pridham, *Nazism*, vol. 2, 301–302. The Gestapo accused foreign newspapers of trying to create an "atmosphere for the abolition of the camps in Germany"; Gestapo to Foreign Ministry, March 12, 1935, *NCC*, doc. 263.
62. Eicke quote in Best to Göring, September 27, 1935, *NCC*, doc. 120. See also Gruchmann, *Justiz*, 647; Dillon, *Dachau*, chapter 4.
63. Gruchmann, *Justiz*, 564–70. See also BArchB, R 3001/alt R 22/1467, Bl. 74–75: Evangelische Kirche to RJM, May 4, 1935. For Eicke's view of Gürtner, BArchB (ehem. BDC), SSO, Eicke, Theodor, 17.10.1892, Lebenslauf, March 15, 1937.
64. Himmler to Göring, December 6, 1934, *NCC*, doc. 71.
65. See also Tuchel, *Konzentrationslager*, 212, 306.
66. Quotes in Himmler speech to *Staatsräte*, March 5, 1936, *NCC*, doc. 78 (the first quote was deleted from Himmler's manuscript). More generally, see Wachsmann, "Dynamics," 22; Longerich, *Himmler*, 204–207.
67. See especially Herbert, "Gegnerbekämpfung." For the quotes, idem, *Best*, 163, 178. See also Tuchel, *Konzentrationslager*, 297–307.
68. See also Thamer, *Verführung*, 376–78.
69. Himmler speech at a Wehrmacht course, January 15–23, 1937, *NCC*, doc. 83.

70. BayHStA, Staatskanzlei 6299/1, Bl. 174–77: Reichstatthalter to Bay. MPr, March 20, 1934. See also ibid., Bl. 215: Aktennotiz, March 12, 1934, March 15, 1934; Bauer et al., *München*, quote on page 230; BArchB, R 43 II/398, Bl. 92. More generally, see Fraenkel, *Dual State*, passim; Wachsmann, *Prisons*, 3, 379–83.

71. BayHStA, Staatskanzlei 6299/1, Bl. 132–41: MdI to Bay. MPr, April 14, 1934. See also Tuchel, *Konzentrationslager*, 303.

72. The overall number of protective custody prisoners in Bavaria fell from 3,500 (February 1934) to 2,343 (April 1934); Tuchel, *Konzentrationslager*, 155.

73. BayHStA, Staatskanzlei 6299/1, Bl. 23: Frick to Sk Bayern, October 5, 1934.

74. BayHStA, Staatskanzlei 6299/1, Bl. 9–12: Himmler to Sk Bayern, November 15, 1934.

75. Longerich, *Himmler*, 201.

76. Gestapa, Lagebericht Marxismus, August 23, 1935, in Boberach, *Regimekritik*, doc. rk 127; Tuchel, *Konzentrationslager*, 95, 106.

77. Frick to Bavarian Sk, January 30, 1935, NCC, doc. 114; Tuchel, *Konzentrationslager*, 307–308.

78. Figures for autumn 1934: Dachau: 1,744 (October 1934); Esterwegen: 150 (October 1934); Lichtenburg: 369 (August 8, 1934); Sachsenburg: less than 200 (October 1934). See Tuchel, *Konzentrationslager*, 155; Lüerßen, "'Wir,'" 465; Mette, "Lichtenburg," 154; Baganz, *Erziehung*, 254.

79. For isolated Hitler references to camps, see Domarus, *Hitler*, vol. 2, 527; ibid., vol. 3, 1459; ibid., vol. 4, 1658.

80. Speech on the Day of the German Police, January 29, 1939, NCC, doc. 274. Himmler added that such criticism came "especially [from] abroad." It was a common tactic by Nazi leaders to blame foreigners for spreading "atrocity stories," to avoid having to openly criticize Germans who did the same. For continuing unease about the KL in Germany, see Schley, *Nachbar*, 90–91; Gestapa II A 2, Bericht, June 27, 1938, in Kulka and Jäckel, *Juden*, doc. 2461.

81. Kershaw, *"Myth,"* especially pages 257–58.

82. For an early private conversation about the camps, see Fröhlich, *Tagebücher*, I/2/III, October 12, 1933.

83. Hitler had originally made these comments to a reporter of the *Daily Mail*; VöB, February 19, 1934, in Domarus, *Hitler*, vol. 1, 364–65.

84. GStAPK, I. HA, Rep. 77, Nr. 484, Bl. 115: Hitler to Landesregierungen et al., August 7, 1934; BayHStA, Staatskanzlei 6299/1, Frick to Sk Bayern, October 5, 1934. For foreign reports, "Prisoners in Germany," *The Times*, September 3, 1934.

85. Early on, Hitler repeatedly made tactical concessions to present himself as a man of moderation, not least to his national-conservative allies. For examples, see Repgen and Booms, *Akten*, vol. I/2, 840 (n. 1); Broszat, "Konzentrationslager," 350.

86. Cited in Broszat, "Konzentrationslager," 352. For Himmler's inspections, see BArchK, N 1126/7, Bl. 16: Himmler diary entries for February 15 and 16, 1935.

87. Tuchel, *Konzentrationslager*, 309–10.

88. Drobisch and Wieland, *System*, 82–87.

89. Tuchel, *Konzentrationslager*, 225–26, 324–25. For the timing of Hitler's decision, Eicke to Himmler, August 10, 1936, NCC, doc. 152. Its implementation took some time; Pohl to Grauert, December 4, 1935, NCC, doc. 75.

90. Eicke to Sauckel, June 3, 1936, in NMGB, *Buchenwald*, 55–56.

91. Tuchel, *Konzentrationslager*, 230, 258, 261; Drobisch and Wieland, *System*, 260.

92. Broszat, "Konzentrationslager," 353. In spring 1936, Himmler made a concession to the Reich Ministry of Justice regarding legal representation, but this had no practical implications; Longerich, *Himmler*, 209.

93. Baganz, *Erziehung*, 291–92; Gruchmann, *Justiz*, 373–74. This was not the first time Hitler intervened in such a case; ibid., 365–66.

94. For an exception, see the case of Friedrich Weissler, below.

95. For SS obstruction, BArchB, R 3001/21522, Bl. 9–18: AG-Rat Hans, Dienstliche Äusserung, July 26, 1938.

96. Tuchel and Schattenfroh, *Zentrale*, 89–92, 112, 118–25; Longerich, *Himmler*, 204, 207–209; Herbert, "Gegnerbekämpfung," 66–67, 72–73; Heydrich decree, January 16, 1937, *NCC*, doc. 84. As chief of police, Himmler was formally subordinated to Frick, as Reich minister of the interior.

97. Wachsmann, *Prisons*, 68–69, 212–15; Neliba, "Frick."

98. Kube, "Göring," 73–75.

99. Tuchel, *Konzentrationslager*, 309.

100. Quote in BArchB (ehem. BDC), SSO, Eicke, Theodor, 17.10.1892, Eicke to Himmler, August 10, 1936. See also ITS, HIST/SACH, Sachsenburg, Ordner 1, Bl. 7: KL Sachsenburg, Zusatzbefehl, August 10, 1935; ibid., Bl. 24: Wachtruppenbefehl, August 24, 1935; ibid., Bl. 33: Befehl, August 1935 (I am grateful to Stefan Hördler for sharing these and other documents).

101. Himmler to RJM, November 6, 1935, in Tuchel, *Inspektion*, 43.

102. For example Bormann to Wernicke, January 29, 1940 and November 26, 1940, in IfZ, *Akten*, vol. 1, 481, 539.

103. Tuchel, *Konzentrationslager*, 309–10, 324.

104. Quotes in BArchB, R 58/264: Bl. 142: Heydrich to Stapostellen, July 29, 1935. German police forces had stepped up arrests of Communist suspects since spring 1935, following Himmler's lead; Longerich, *Himmler*, 202–203; Tuchel, *Konzentrationslager*, 311–12.

105. BArchB, NS 19/1447, Bl. 17: Führervortrag, October 18, 1935. More generally, see Herbert, "Gegnerbekämpfung," 72.

106. See chapter 3.

107. *Deutsches Recht*, April 15, 1936, *NCC*, doc. 123.

108. For the term, see Hüttenberger, "Polycracy."

109. Prisoner figures for summer 1935: Columbia House 400 (estimate); Dachau 1,656 (July 1935); Esterwegen 322 (June 10, 1935); Lichtenburg 706 (June 10, 1935); Sachsenburg 678 (June 10, 1935). See Schilde, "Tempelhofer," 77; Tuchel, *Konzentrationslager*, 203; Drobisch and Wieland, *System*, 204.

110. Tuchel, *Konzentrationslager*, 339.

111. For some flash points, see Gruchmann, *Justiz*, 599–602.

112. In practice, this division was not always strictly enforced. The police sometimes dragged lawbreakers straight to the KL, and regular prisons still held hundreds of protective custody prisoners, at least in the mid-1930s; Wachsmann, *Prisons*, 171–72.

113. Wachsmann, *Prisons*, 171, 175–83, quote on 179.

114. GStA Jena to RJM, September 30, 1937, *NCC*, doc. 129.

115. Kershaw, *Nemesis*, 5–9; Domarus, *Hitler*, vol. 2, 632–33.

116. Morsch, "Formation," 87–89, 101; Kaienburg, *Wirtschaftskomplex*, 139–41.

117. *OdT*, vol. 2, 58. See also Georg et al., *"Why."*

118. Sachsenhausen Song, *NCC*, doc. 224. For background, see Fackler, *"Lagers Stimme,"* 336–38.

119. Kaienburg, *Wirtschaftskomplex*, 111–17, 129–33, 138–41, 191–93; Morsch, "Formation," 126–29, Heilmann quote on 127; Wachsmann, *Prisons*, 104; Danckwortt, "Jüdische 'Schutzhäftlinge,'" 156; Schilde, "Tempelhofer," 77–80. Another factor in favor of the new Sachsenhausen site was the presence of SS guards (from the Columbia House) stationed at the nearby Oranienburg castle. The Columbia House was later demolished to make way for the Tempelhof airport, one of the reasons behind its closure.

120. During this period, the last remaining early camps outside Eicke's IKL were taken over or redesignated: Bad Sulza, established in 1933 by the Thuringian Ministry of the Interior, was taken over by the IKL on April 1, 1936 (Wohlfeld, "Hotel"); Hamburg-Fuhlsbüttel became a police prison in 1936 (Diercks, "Fuhlsbüttel," 305); Kislau, an

early camp in Baden, operated as a "detention camp" until the late 1930s (Hörath, "Terrorinstrument," 529–30). Himmler's appointments diary for 1937 records nine meetings with Eicke (there may have been more); IfZ, F 37/19.

121. *OdT*, vol. 3, 301–303; Tuchel, *Konzentrationslager*, 335–38; Eicke to Himmler, July 24, 1937, *NCC*, doc. 89; Koch to Gommlich, July 28, 1937, in Schnabel, *Macht*, 125; Moore, "Popular Opinion," 223; Burkhard, *Tanz*, 138. Eicke visited the Ettersberg on May 18, Himmler on May 22; Wildt, "Terminkalender," 686–87 (n. 68).

122. The first prisoner transport to Buchenwald arrived from Sachsenhausen, which had also absorbed many former Sachsenburg prisoners. The last Sachsenburg prisoners left for Buchenwald on September 9, 1937. Bad Sulza officially closed on August 1, 1937. Lichtenburg closed as a men's camp on August 18, 1937. See *OdT*, vol. 3, 302; NMGB, *Buchenwald*, 698; Wohlfeld, "Hotel," 275; Baganz, *Erziehung*, 283; Endlich, "Lichtenburg," 20–21; Morsch, "Formation," 133–34; Hett, *Crossing*, 210–19.

123. The same was true for the surrounding SS buildings; *OdT*, vol. 3, 303.

124. Zámečník, *Dachau*, 86–88; Riedel, *Ordnungshüter*, 188–89.

125. For references to the "modern" camp, see Eicke to Sauckel, June 3, 1936, in Schnabel, *Macht*, 121–22; Himmler to RJM, February 8, 1937, *NCC*, doc. 85.

126. Morsch, "Sachsenhausen—ein neuer Lagertypus?"; Kaienburg, "Systematisierung." These continuities mean that the SS did not create an entirely new type of concentration camp in 1936–37; cf. Orth, *System*, 35–36.

127. On November 1, 1936, the KL apparently held 4,761 prisoners; German Foreign Ministry to diplomatic missions, December 8, 1936, *NCC*, doc. 82. For projections for the two camps, Kaienburg, *Wirtschaftskomplex*, 193; Eicke to Thür. MdI, October 27, 1936, in Schnabel, *Macht*, 123. On camp architecture, see Gabriel, "Biopolitik," especially page 207.

128. Himmler made this reference in regard to Sachsenhausen; Himmler to RJM, February 8, 1937, *NCC*, doc. 85. He had inspected the camp on January 20, 1937; IfZ, F 37/19, Himmler diary. For space restrictions in older KL, ITS, ARCH/HIST/KL Lichtenburg 2, Bl. 54: Helwig to IKL, April 18, 1937.

129. Morsch, "Formation," 102; *OdT*, vol. 3, 302–303.

130. *OdT*, vol. 1, 210–29; ibid., vol. 3, 303–305, 321; Neurath, *Gesellschaft*, 37–44; Naujoks, *Leben*, 48, 52, 68, 98–100; Morsch, "Formation," 93–101; Gabriel, "Biopolitik," 207, 210–11.

131. Steinbacher, *Dachau*, 174, 178–9, 205–206.

132. For example, see Künstler to Salpeter, March 9, 1939, *NCC*, doc. 292; Kaienburg, *Wirtschaftskomplex*, 130. Even Dachau, which had been on the same site since 1933, became more concealed; Steinbacher, *Dachau*, 132–34.

133. Steinbacher, *Dachau*, 93–100, 126–29, 137–44, 181; Schley, *Nachbar*, 43–63, 79–86; Kaienburg, *Wirtschaftskomplex*, 150–51, 181, 275–80; idem, *Wirtschaft*, 123–29; Moore, "Popular Opinion," 144–57. For Lichtenburg, LBIJMB, MF 425, L. Bendix, "Konzentrationslager Deutschland," 1937–38, vol. 4, 27; Decker, "Stadt," 210–11.

134. Most locals kept away anyway, nervous to even discuss the camps in public. See Steinbacher, *Dachau*, 181, 185; Litten, *Mutter*, 189–90; A. Bettany, Reader's Letter, *The Times*, April 21, 1945.

135. Speech on the Day of the German Police, January 29, 1939, *NCC*, doc. 274.

136. The slogan was added, with small variations, in Dachau, Sachsenhausen, Mauthausen, and other camps; Riedel, *Ordnungshüter*, 206; Naujoks, *Leben*, 135–36; Maršálek, *Mauthausen*, 66.

137. Riedel, "'Arbeit.'" In Gross-Rosen, the SS apparently also displayed the motto "Work Makes Free" at the entrance of the prisoner compound. In Buchenwald, the SS chose a different slogan, adding the words "To Each His Own" to the iron gates. For the significance of the main gate in the KL, see Sofsky, *Ordnung*, 75–77.

138. Naujoks, *Leben*, 136.

139. For a different view, dismissing all SS talk of "reform," see Sofsky, *Ordnung*, 317.

140. Quote in special camp order for Esterwegen, August 1, 1934, *NCC*, doc. 149. See also Longerich, *Himmler*, 327–64; Himmler to A. Lehner, May 18, 1937, *NCC*, doc. 226. For the use of Nazi camps to educate "national comrades," see Patel, "'Auslese'"; Buggeln and Wildt, "Lager," 227–33.

141. Several tens of thousands of KL prisoners were released in this period, including most Jewish men arrested after the November 1938 pogrom; see chapter 3.

142. Quotes in speech on the Day of the German Police, January 29, 1939, *NCC*, doc. 274; speech at a Wehrmacht course, January 15–23, 1937, *NCC*, doc. 83.

143. Quotes in speech at SS Gruppenführer conference, November 8, 1937, *NCC*, doc. 94. For German criminological thinking, see Wachsmann, *Prisons*, 22–27, 46–54; Wetzell, *Inventing*, 107–289.

144. Speech at a Wehrmacht course, January 15–23, 1937, *NCC*, doc. 83.

145. For example, see Sydnor, *Soldiers*, 30; Shirer, *Rise*, 271–72.

146. For a typical example, see Kogon, *Theory*.

147. AdsD, KE, E. Büge, Bericht, n.d. (1945–46), 208, last sentence in capital letters in original.

148. Quote in Eicke to commandant offices, December 2, 1935, *NCC*, doc. 151. In the historical literature, the term SS Totenkopfverbände is often used with reference to the SS Guard Troops only (Tuchel, *Konzentrationslager*, 225; Drobisch and Wieland, *System*, 256). However, SS men serving in the KL Commandant Staffs and the IKL (including Eicke) came under this rubric, too, and wore the skull and crossbones (IfZ, Fa 183, Bl. 30–31: SS-Hauptamt, Abzeichen der SS-Wachverbände, March 9, 1936; *Statistisches Jahrbuch 1938*, 83; MacLean, *Camp*, 312). For the origin of the term "Camp SS," Orth, *SS*, 12.

149. Broszat, *Kommandant*, 84. For the term "political soldier," see also Eicke order for Lichtenburg, June 2, 1934, *NCC*, doc. 148.

150. Reichardt, *Kampfbünde*, 570–74.

151. Himmler described himself as a soldier in his first interview as acting Munich Police President; "Der neue Geist im Münchner Polizeipräsidium," *VöB*, March 15, 1933.

152. *VöB*, March 4, 1943. For Eicke's death, see Sydnor, *Soldiers*, 271.

153. Quotes in Eicke to Himmler, August 10, 1936, *NCC*, doc. 152. See also Kühne, *Kameradschaft*, 271–79; Reichardt, *Kampfbünde*, 590–93, 671–73; Dillon, "Dachau," 94–97.

154. Eicke order for Lichtenburg, June 2, 1934, *NCC*, doc. 148.

155. Quote in regulations for Esterwegen, August 1, 1934, *NCC*, doc. 150. See also IfZ, F 13/6, Bl. 369–82: R. Höss, "Theodor Eicke," November 1946.

156. Eicke to commandant offices, December 2, 1935, *NCC*, doc. 151. See also Broszat, *Kommandant*, 84.

157. For masculinity and the Camp SS, Dillon, "Dachau," 98–126.

158. For Himmler inspections, see *OdT*, vol. 4, 20, 293–94; Drobisch and Wieland, *System*, 303–304; Baganz, *Erziehung*, 278. For meetings with Eicke, see Wildt, "Terminkalender," 685–86.

159. Quotes in Dicks, *Mass Murder*, 104. See also AS, J D2/43, Bl. 146–54: Vernehmung G. Sorge, May 6, 1957.

160. IfZ, F 13/6, Bl. 369–82: R. Höss, "Theodor Eicke," November 1946.

161. Drobisch and Wieland, *System*, 195, 256; Tuchel, *Konzentrationslager*, 218–20, 230–31.

162. IfZ, Fa 127/1, for the issues 1 to 6, covering the period from February to July 1937.

163. Kaienburg, *Wirtschaftskomplex*, 146–47, 160, 195. See also Tuchel, *Inspektion*, 50; Drobisch and Wieland, *System*, 256; Segev, *Soldiers*, 153.

164. Eicke order for Lichtenburg, June 2, 1934, *NCC*, doc. 148. For Nazi hostility to bureaucracies, Caplan, "Civil Service," especially page 49.

165. Eicke to Himmler, August 10, 1936, *NCC*, doc. 152.

166. Riedel, *Ordnungshüter*, 150; Morsch, *Sachsenburg*, 353.

167. For Max Weber's concept of charismatic leadership and its application to Nazi rule, Kershaw, *"Myth,"* 8–10.

168. Rudolf Höss, for one, believed that Eicke had fought gallantly on the battlefronts of the First World War and had later been sentenced to death by the French for resistance to the occupation of the Rhineland; IfZ, F 13/6, Bl. 369–82: R. Höss, "Theodor Eicke," November 1946.

169. Ibid.; Segev, *Soldiers*, 133–36; Dicks, *Mass Murder*, 104. Quote in Eicke order for Lichtenburg, June 2, 1934, *NCC*, doc. 148.

170. Quote in Segev, *Soldiers*, 149. See also BArchB (ehem. BDC), SSO, Eicke, Theodor, 17.10.1892, Eicke to Himmler, August 10, 1936; Dicks, *Mass Murder*, 99; Dillon, "Dachau," 97, 197.

171. Quote in Segev, *Soldiers*, 149. For Hassebroek, see Orth, *SS*, 118–24. For *Junkerschulen*, see Wegner, *Soldaten*, 149–71.

172. Quote in IfZ, MA 312, Rede bei SS Gruppenführerbesprechung, November 8, 1938. More generally, see Longerich, *Himmler*, 319–22.

173. For example, see Commandant's order, Buchenwald, August 30, 1937, *NCC*, doc. 168.

174. Ehrenwörtliche Verpflichtung, September 7, 1938, cited in Dillon, "Dachau," 140. Such declarations were still signed by Camp SS staff during the Second World War; Mailänder Koslov, *Gewalt*, 147.

175. Order of the SS Death's Head units, March 1, 1937, *NCC*, doc. 155. For an earlier warning by Himmler, BArchB, R 58/264, Bl. 69: Gestapa to Dienststellen, September 5, 1934.

176. Order of the SS Death's Head units, June 4, 1937, *NCC*, doc. 157. At times, Eicke also privately censured Camp SS men for prisoner abuse; Riedel, *Ordnungshüter*, 156.

177. Quote in BArchB, R 58/264, Bl. 69: Gestapa to Dienststellen, September 5, 1934.

178. *OdT*, vol. 1, 59–61.

179. For a vivid description, see IfZ, F 13/7, Bl. 397–420: R. Höss, "Lagerordnung für die Konzentrationslager," October 1946.

180. ITS, ARCH/HIST/KL Lichtenburg 2, Bl. 74: IKL to Kommandanturen, October 9, 1935.

181. Buggeln, *Arbeit*, 352.

182. StAMü, StA Nr. 34479/1, Bl. 93–97: Lebenslauf H. Steinbrenner, n.d. (c. late 1940s), Bl. 95; ibid., Nr. 34430, Bl. 21–22: LG München, Urteil, July 8, 1948.

183. Disziplinar- u. Strafordnung für Dachau, October 1, 1933, *IMT*, vol. 26, 291–96, ND: 778–PS; Drobisch and Wieland, *System*, 193.

184. Riedel, *Ordnungshüter*, 182; *NCC*, doc. 208; *OdT*, vol. 3, 335; Union, *Strafvollzug*, 26–27. Officially, prisoners were not supposed to be whipped on the naked body, though this rule was not always observed.

185. The status of this torture is disputed. It was not listed on some official SS forms for recording punishments (YVA, O-51/64, Bl. 16–17: Strafverfügung), which has led historians to assume that it was not officially sanctioned (*OdT*, vol. 3, 337). However, it was included in Eicke's punishment regulations from 1933–34, which formed the basis for official regulations in other KL (Disziplinar- u. Strafordnung für Dachau, October 1, 1933, *IMT*, vol. 26, 295, ND: 778–PS; USHMM, RG-11.001M.20, reel 91, 1367–2–19, KL Esterwegen, Disziplinar- u. Strafordnung, August 1, 1934).

186. Drobisch and Wieland, *System*, 210; Richardi, *Schule*, 136; Lüerßen, "'Wir,'" 125. For medieval roots, see Schmidt, "Tortur," 212–13.

187. Pretzel, "Vorfälle," 133–35, quote on 148–50. See also DaA, 9394, A. Lomnitz (later A. Laurence), "Heinz Eschen zum Gedenken," July 3, 1939; Richardi, *Schule*, 136–39; *NCC*, docs. 216 and 217; Kohlhagen, *Bock* (written in 1945), 20, 136–37.

188. Disziplinar- u. Strafordnung für Dachau, October 1, 1933, *IMT*, vol. 26; YVA, O-51/64, Bl. 16–17: Strafverfügung; *NCC*, doc. 217.

189. IfZ, F 13/6, Bl. 369–82: R. Höss, "Theodor Eicke," November 1946.

190. Neurath, *Gesellschaft*, 134–35; anonymous report, c. 1936, *NCC*, doc. 208.

191. Order of the SS Death's Head units, March 1, 1937, *NCC*, doc. 155.

192. Naujoks, *Leben*, 67.

193. For one example, see Riedel, *Ordnungshüter*, 189. More generally, see Kaienburg, "Systematisierung," 59–60.

194. See Fraenkel, *Dual State*.

195. M. Simon to Führer der Sturmbanne, June 10, 1938, in Merkl, *General*, 119. See also Zámečník, *Dachau*, 100–101.

196. The only other Sachsenhausen guard charged with the abuse of Weissler, Scharführer Guthardt, committed suicide before sentencing. LaB, A Rep. 358–02, Nr. 1540, Notiz, April 5, 1937; ibid., GStA Berlin to RJM, June 3, 1937; ibid., Justizpressestelle to GStA Berlin, November 17, 1938; Morsch, *Mord*, 71–77; *The Times*, Letters to the Editor, March 11, 1937, p. 12. Among the SS men who prospered was Oberscharführer Jarolin, who had been on duty in the bunker when Weissler was murdered; Riedle, *Angehörigen*, 69, 78; Zámečník, *Dachau*, 305–306; JVL, JAO, Review of Proceedings, *United States v. Weiss*, n.d. (1946), 22–24.

197. *Statistisches Jahrbuch 1937*, 51; *Statistisches Jahrbuch 1938*, 83.

198. IfZ, Fa 183, Bl. 30–31: SS-Hauptamt, Abzeichen der SS-Wachverbände, March 9, 1936. By late 1937, each KL employed, on average, 112 men in the Commandant Staff; *Statistisches Jahrbuch 1937*, 51 (excluding the women's camp Lichtenburg).

199. Service Regulations for Escorts, October 1, 1933, *NCC*, doc. 146; Orth, *SS*, 34–35; idem, "Personnel," 45–46; Kaienburg, *Wirtschaftskomplex*, 37–40, 62–64, 172–77; Burkhard, *Tanz*, 99–100, 103–104. From April 1937, there were three Death's Head regiments (SS-Totenkopfstandarten), stationed at Dachau, Sachsenhausen, and Buchenwald. A fourth was added in Mauthausen in 1938. Initially, there was no separate battalion in Flossenbürg.

200. Orth, *SS*, 35; Tuchel, *Konzentrationslager*, 143, 150; Riedle, *Angehörigen*, 43–47, 54, 130.

201. *Statistisches Jahrbuch 1937*, 51 (excluding Lichtenburg).

202. Longerich, *Himmler*, 312–13; Dillon, "Dachau," 112–13; IfZ, Fa 127/1, Bl. 4–5: Merkblatt für die Einstellung in die SS-TS, 1939.

203. Dillon, "Dachau," 142–47.

204. Quotes in Order of the Death's Head units, July 6, 1937, *NCC*, doc. 159; order of the SS Death's Head units, May 4, 1937, ibid., doc. 156; BArchB, NS 19/1925: Bl. 1–9: Eicke to Himmler, August 10, 1936; IfZ, MA 312, Himmler Rede bei der SS Gruppenführerbesprechung, November 8, 1938. See also Himmler speech at a Wehrmacht course, January 15–23, 1937, *NCC*, doc. 83.

205. *Statistisches Jahrbuch 1938*, 87. See also Dillon, "Dachau," 149.

206. Dillon, "Dachau," 142–46. See also *NCC*, doc. 159.

207. *Statistisches Jahrbuch 1938*, 87. Apparently, the great majority of applicants were admitted into the Camp SS; Riedle, *Angehörigen*, 75; Kaienburg, *Wirtschaftskomplex*, 58.

208. Dillon, "Dachau," 142, 150–52; IfZ, Fa 127/1, Bl. 4–5: Merkblatt für die Einstellung in die SS-TS, 1939; Steiner, "SS," 432.

209. Quote in Dicks, *Mass Murder*, 135. See also Sydnor, *Soldiers*, 25; Orth, *SS*, 76, 129–32; Dillon, "Dachau," 114–15, 145, 170; Kaienburg, *Wirtschaftskomplex*, 169–72; DAP, Vernehmung R. Baer, December 29, 1960, 3035.

210. Quote in *Neuer Vorwärts*, February 14, 1937, *NCC*, doc. 180. See also Dillon, "Dachau," 109–11, 115, 139–40, 161–63, 180–81; *OdT*, vol. 3, 40–41; Eicke to Himmler, August 10, 1936, *NCC*, doc. 152.

211. Quotes in *Arbeiter-Illustrierte Zeitung*, May 23, 1935, *NCC*, doc. 177; Eicke order, April 29, 1936, in ibid., doc. 153. For discontent among the Camp SS, see also LBIJMB, MF 425, L. Bendix, "Konzentrationslager Deutschland," 1937–38, vol. 4, 63–64.

212. Boehnert, "Sociography," 116, 239–40; Riedle, *Angehörigen*, 102–13.

213. *OdT*, vol. 1, 131–32; Riedle, *Angehörigen*, 134; Dillon, "Dachau," 140, 190. By 1942, KL commandants could personally transfer men from the Guard Troop to the Commandant Staff; NAL, HW 16/21, GPD Nr. 3, October 17, 1942.

214. Orth, *SS*, 105–15; Broszat, *Kommandant*, passim; BArchB (ehem. BDC), SSO, Höss, Rudolf, 25.11.1900. See now also Koop, *Rudolf*.

215. KL Dachau, Protokoll, April 18, 1934, in Friedlander and Milton, *Archives*, vol. XI/2, doc. 17. See also Riedle, *Angehörigen*, 72, 79–83; Dillon, "Dachau," 191–92; Morsch, "Formation," 170–74.

216. Based on a survey of serving SS commandants (1934–39), largely using the data in Tuchel, *Konzentrationslager*, 371–96. See also Orth, *SS*, 79–81.

217. Orth, *SS*, 39–40; *OdT*, vol. 1, 61–63. For more detail, see BArchB, NS 3/391, Bl. 4–22: Aufgabengebiete in einem KL, n.d. (1942), Bl. 4–9.

218. *OdT*, vol. 1, 59; ibid., vol. 3, 41.

219. *OdT*, vol. 1, 61.

220. BArchB, NS 3/391, Bl. 1–2: Zweck und Gliederung des Konzentrationslagers, n.d.; JVL, JAO, Review of Proceedings, *United States v. Weiss*, n.d. (1946), 86. Oranienburg had developed a rather similar organizational structure to Dachau in 1933 (*OdT*, vol. 1, 58).

221. Quote in Kogon, *Theory*, 53. See also Tuchel, "Registrierung"; *OdT*, vol. 1, 65–66; Orth, *SS*, 46–48, 66–71.

222. Hahn, *Grawitz*, 42–57, 96–106, 154–55; Orth, *SS*, 45; Morsch, "Formation," 166–67.

223. Orth, *SS*, 41–44, 71–75.

224. Quote in Broszat, *Kommandant*, 139. See also BArchB, NS 3/391, Bl. 4–22: Aufgabengebiete in einem KL, n.d. (1942), Bl. 17–21; Orth, *SS*, 40–41, 63; *OdT*, vol. 1, 66–68; DaA, 9438, A. Hübsch, "Insel des Standrechts" (1961), 268; StAMü, StA Nr. 34588/2, Bl. 95–106: Vernehmung K. Kapp, November 14–16, 1956, Bl. 98.

225. Quote in Broszat, *Kommandant*, 134. See also ibid., 84–85, 266; BArchB (ehem. BDC), SSO, Höss, Rudolf, 25.11.1900; Hördler, "Ordnung," 39, 44; Riedle, *Angehörigen*, 56.

226. Eicke to commandant offices, December 2, 1935, *NCC*, doc. 151.

227. ITS, ARCH/HIST/KL Lichtenburg 2, Bl. 104–15: Befehlsblatt SS-TV/IKL, April 1, 1937; Morsch, "Formation," 114–16, 120–22; Schwarz, *Frau*, 112–15; KZ-Gedenkstätte Flossenbürg, *Flossenbürg*, 50–51; Dillon, "Dachau," 111.

228. For one example, see Broszat, *Kommandant*, 103–104, 132–34.

229. Commandant's order for Buchenwald, August 3, 1937, August 30, 1937, *NCC*, docs. 167 and 168; BArchB, NS 31/372, Befehlsblatt SS-TV/IKL, June 1937, Bl. 69; ITS, HIST/SACH, Sachsenburg, Ordner 1, Bl. 73: Wachtruppenbefehl, October 21, 1935.

230. Naujoks, *Leben*, 64, 68, 131, quote on 150; instruction by Himmler, July 21, 1938, *NCC*, doc. 161; *OdT*, vol. 3, 33.

231. Quote in Dicks, *Mass Murder*, 103, "KZs" in the original. See also ibid., 138; Orth, *SS*, especially pages 151–52; Broszat, *Kommandant*, 49, 233–34; Warmbold, *Lagersprache*, 122–43. More generally, see Rouse, "Perspectives"; Gioia et al., "Organizational identity."

232. Riedel, *Ordnungshüter*, 175, 205–209; BArchB, R 2/28350, Chronik der SS-Lageranlage Dachau, March 1, 1938; Dillon, "Dachau," 105; Orth, *SS*, 88, 145.

233. Orth, *SS*, 151. See also Sofsky, *Violence*, 24–27; Kühne, *Belonging*, 91, 168–69.

234. Steinbacher, *Dachau*, 179–80; Dillon, "Dachau," 81–84.

235. Buggeln, *Arbeit*, 344–48; APMO, Proces Höss, Hd 6, Bl. 129–312: Vernehmung O. Wolken, April 17–20, 1945, Bl. 297.

236. For example, see Naujoks, *Leben*, 38–39.

237. The 1937 mortality figure is the combined monthly average across the three big camps (Dachau: forty-one deaths; Sachsenhausen: forty-four deaths, including prisoners who died in Berlin State Hospital; Buchenwald: fifty-three deaths between July and December 1937); KZ-Gedenkstätte Dachau, *Gedenkbuch*; AS, Totenbuch des KZ Sachsenhausen; http://totenbuch.buchenwald.de.

238. This estimate includes victims of the Röhm purge in Dachau. For suicides, see Goeschel, "Suicide," 630–32.

239. Quote in Broszat, *Kommandant*, 98. See also ibid., 97–98, 101; Sydnor, *Soldiers*, 27–28; *NCC*, doc. 174; ITS, HIST/SACH, Sachsenburg, Ordner 1, Bl. 22: Wachtruppenbefehl, August 21, 1935; Dillon, "Dachau," 178–80; Van Dam and Giordano, *KZ-Verbrechen*, 28.

240. Sofsky, *Ordnung*, 134; Neurath, *Gesellschaft*, 117.

241. Broszat, *Kommandant*, 81–83; IfZ, F 13/6, Bl. 369–82: R. Höss, "Theodor Eicke," November 1946, Bl. 370. In 1937, Eicke relaxed his orders: instead of the entire platoon, only selected long-term members (with two years or more of experience) of the Commandant Staff had to attend floggings; order of the SS Death's Head units, March 1, 1937, *NCC*, doc. 155.

242. Dicks, *Mass Murder*, 100–101.

243. For example, see Broszat, *Kommandant*, 85–86.

244. For example, see *NCC*, doc. 180; Lüerßen, "'Wir,'" 119–20; *DAP*, Vernehmung F. Hofmann, April 22, 1959, 3850.

245. For the quotes, see AS, J D2/43, Bl. 59–72: Vernehmung G. Sorge, April 23, 1957, Bl. 71; Lüerßen, "'Moorsoldaten,'" 195. More generally, see Dillon, "Dachau," 125, 190, 233, 241; Broszat, *Kommandant*, 83; Hördler, "Ordnung," 49; Trouvé, "Bugdalle," 33; Sofsky, *Ordnung*, 262–63; Springmann, "'Sport,'" 91–92.

246. For a discussion of Nazi violence as an end in itself, see Neitzel and Welzer, *Soldaten*, 88–94.

247. Quotes in Broszat, *Kommandant*, 102; Eicke to commandant offices, December 2, 1935, *NCC*, doc. 151. See also Segev, *Soldiers*, 122, 135; Orth, *SS*, 131–34; Riedle, *Angehörigen*, 237–39; Dicks, *Mass Murder*, 101; Dillon, "Dachau," 115, 118–19; Zimbardo, *Lucifer*, 221, 259. Dismissals from the Camp SS were common: during a six-month period in 1937, some two hundred men were sacked. A few SS men may have been bullied into killing themselves, which would explain the unusually high suicide rate among the Camp SS; Segev, *Soldiers*, 128.

248. Tuchel, "Kommandanten des KZ Dachau," 337–40; Dillon, "Dachau," 82–83, 200–201.

249. Orth, *SS*, 101; Tuchel, *Konzentrationslager*, 295.

250. For this and the previous paragraph, see Dillon, "Dachau," 183–84, 201–202, 214–15, guard quote on 202; Schilde and Tuchel, *Columbia-Haus*, 67–69, Eicke quote on 68; KZ-Gedenkstätte Dachau, *Gedenkbuch*, 19. More generally on comradeship, see Kühne, *Belonging*, 83.

251. Riedel, *Ordnungshüter*, 31–134. See also BArchB (ehem. BDC), SSO, Loritz, Hans, 21.12.1895, Loritz letter, June 19, 1934.

252. Riedel, *Ordnungshüter*, 141–42, 178–82, Loritz quotes on 142, 144; Dillon, "Dachau," 204, 222, Loritz quote on 203; Internationales Zentrum, *Nazi-Bastille*, prisoner quote on 36; IfZ, statement P. Wauer, May 21, 1945, ND: NO-1504.

253. Riedel, *Ordnungshüter*, 143–49, quote on 145; Tuchel, "Kommandanten des Konzentrationslagers Flossenbürg," 201–204; Dillon, "Dachau," 214–16, 226–27, 233, 237; *Nazi-Bastille*, 37; Hördler, "Ordnung," 78. For the Dachau death rate, see KZ-Gedenkstätte Dachau, *Gedenkbuch*.

254. For general background, see Orth, *SS*, 127. For Loritz's move to Sachsenhausen in late 1939, and his official appointment on March 11, 1940, see Riedel, *Ordnungshüter*, 217–29.

255. Orth, *SS*, 63 (n. 18); Dillon, "Dachau," 242–43; Tuchel, "Kommandanten des Konzen-

trationslagers Flossenbürg," 204; *NCC*, docs. 145 and 208. For Dachau as a springboard for future KL commandants, see also Hördler, "Ordnung," 58.

256. Riedle, *Angehörigen*, 50 (n. 50), 135, 157, 223; Morsch, "Formation," 169–70, 176; Kaienburg, *Wirtschaftskomplex*, 114–15.

257. BArchB (ehem. BDC), SSO, Koch, Karl, 2.8.1897; Morsch, *Sachsenburg*, 336–37; Segev, *Soldiers*, 187–89; Schilde and Tuchel, *Columbia-Haus*, 64–66; StAAu, StA Augsburg, KS 22/50, Vernehmung I. Koch, April 29, 1949.

258. Quote in Hackett, *Buchenwald*, 338.

259. IfZ, F 13/6, Bl. 369–82: R. Höss, "Theodor Eicke," November 1946, Bl. 378; Riedel, *Ordnungshüter*, 150–59.

260. Quote in BArchB (ehem. BDC), SSO, Künstler, Karl, 12.1.1901, Eicke to 1. SS-TS, January 5, 1939. More generally, see Tuchel, "Kommandanten der Konzentrationslagers Flossenbürg," 206–209; Hördler, "Ordnung," 76. Weiseborn's official cause of death was a heart attack, though there were persistent rumors among inmates that he had taken his own life. For network theories applied to Nazi perpetrators, see Berger, *Experten*.

261. Previously, there had been some variation. In some camps, prisoners already had short-cropped (or shaved) hair from 1933–34; elsewhere, they could still keep it longer (see photos in Morsch, *Sachsenburg*, 227–37). For the SS practice from 1936, ibid., 286, 304–307; DaA, Nr. 7566, K. Schecher, "Rückblick auf Dachau," n.d., 230–32; LBIJMB, MF 425, L. Bendix, "Konzentrationslager Deutschland," 1937–38, vol. 5, 3; Neurath, *Gesellschaft*, 68–69.

262. In some camps, winter uniforms had green, not blue, stripes; Schmidt, "Geschichte." The new uniforms were introduced at different times between 1937–38 (Dachau) and spring 1939 (Sachsenhausen); Zámečník, *Dachau*, 86; *OdT*, vol. 3, 51. For prisoner names and numbers, AdsD, KE, E. Büge, Bericht, n.d. (1945–46), 57; Baganz, *Erziehung*, 271.

263. For material benefits of some privileged prisoners, LBIJMB, MF 425, L. Bendix, "Konzentrationslager Deutschland," 1937–38, vol. 4, 33–34.

264. *OdT*, vol. 1, 91–95; Baganz, *Erziehung*, 165; DaA, Nr. 7566, K. Schecher, "Rückblick auf Dachau," n.d., 90. For the pioneering role of Dachau and Esterwegen, see Knoll, "Homosexuelle Häftlinge," 65; Lüerßen, "'Wir,'" 90–91.

265. Sofsky, *Ordnung*, 89.

266. DaA, 9438, A. Hübsch, "Insel des Standrechts" (1961), 77–78; Naujoks, *Leben*, 34; Freund, *Buchenwald!*, 121.

267. Naujoks, *Leben*, 34, 49, 62–63, 69, 76; Drobisch and Wieland, *System*, 294; Neurath, *Gesellschaft*, 44–49; Freund, *Buchenwald!*, 162–65. Quote in BArchB, NS 4/Bu 31, Bl. 20: A. Rödl, Allgemeine Anordnungen, October 9, 1937.

268. Some prisoners had lunch at their work sites. Others returned to the compound for a quick wash and roll call, and ate inside their quarters.

269. Neurath, *Gesellschaft*, 54–56, 69–78; Naujoks, *Leben*, 32, 69, 96; Drobisch and Wieland, *System*, 207; Kautsky, *Teufel*, 246; *NCC*, docs. 190–92; ITS, ARCH/KL Sachsenburg, Ordner 11, Bl. 82: Bekanntmachung, June 10, 1936. More generally on the SS administration of prisoner monies, see Grabowski, *Geld*, especially pages 29–51.

270. Neurath, *Gesellschaft*, 57–58, 239–42; Naujoks, *Leben*, 65–67; Kogon, *Theory*, 75–80; Freund, *Buchenwald!*, 163; Drobisch and Wieland, *System*, 297.

271. Fackler, *"Lagers Stimme,"* 151–69, 340–42, 356–61; Drobisch and Wieland, *System*, 297; Kautsky, *Teufel*, 219–22; Barkow et al., *Novemberpogrom*, 77.

272. Fackler, *"Lagers Stimme,"* 187–90; Zámečník, *Dachau*, 53–54; Steinbacher, *Dachau*, 165–70; Drobisch and Wieland, *System*, 215, 307–308. In the early camp Osthofen, Jews had occasional access to a rabbi; Wünschmann, "Jewish Prisoners," 118.

273. Quote in Hett, *Crossing*, 218. See also Seela, *Bücher*; Neurath, *Gesellschaft*, 238–39; Fackler, *"Lagers Stimme,"* 182; Seger, "Oranienburg," 37–38; Freund, *Buchenwald!*, 158.

274. Quotes in Neurath, *Gesellschaft*, 67; DaA, 9438, A. Hübsch, "Insel des Standrechts" (1961), 111. See also BArchB, NS 4/Na 6, Bl. 3–4: Eicke to LK, October 14, 1938; ibid., R 58/264, Bl. 293–97: Gestapo Munich to Stapoleitstellen et al., March 4, 1937; Baganz, *Erziehung*, 277; Internationales Zentrum, *Nazi-Bastille*, 58–59; Bettelheim, "Individual," 440–41.

275. Langhoff, *Moorsoldaten*, 175–95; Lüerßen, "'Wir,'" 131; Kautsky, *Teufel*, 221–22; Zámečník, *Dachau*, 55; Fackler, *"Lagers Stimme,"* 406–407.

276. BArchB, NS 19/4014, Bl. 158–204: Rede vor Generälen, June 21, 1944, Bl. 165. For a general discussion of Kapos, see Sofsky, *Ordnung*, 152–68.

277. For ghettos and labor camps, see Browning, *Remembering*, 116–17.

278. In the Gulag, the Soviet authorities had long relied on selected inmates to support them; Applebaum, *Gulag*, 329–37.

279. Interrogation W. Bartel, May 29, 1953, in Niethammer, *Antifaschismus*, 427. See also BLHA, Pr. Br. Rep. 29, Zuchthaus Brandenburg Nr. 691; Broszat, *Kommandant*, 72. For trusties in the 1920s, see also Hoelz, *"Weißen Kreuz."*

280. Langhoff, *Moorsoldaten*, 34–41, 140–42, quote on 142. Kurt's real name was Karl Schabrod; Drobisch and Wieland, *System*, 142. Similar elections took place in other early camps, including Dachau; StAMü, StA Nr. 34588/2, Bl. 39–40: Vernehmung K. Kapp, September 28, 1956; Wieland, "Bremischen," 286.

281. SS documents list around four hundred prisoner functionaries in late 1938, excluding work Kapos, who must have numbered more than one hundred; *OdT*, vol. 3, 331. See also Naujoks, *Leben*, 97.

282. SS quote in DaA, 5427, Richtlinien für Capos, n.d.; prisoner quote in Neurath, *Gesellschaft*, 224. See also StAMü, StA Nr. 34588/8, LG München, Urteil, October 14, 1960, p. 6.

283. Quotes in SS Buchenwald instructions, n.d., *NCC*, doc. 196. See also Kautsky, *Teufel*, 214–19.

284. For early camps, see Langhoff, *Moorsoldaten*, 219; Richardi, *Schule*, 196; Wünschmann, "Jewish Prisoners," 109–10. For the late 1930s, see Naujoks, *Leben*, 105–106; Freund, *Buchenwald!*, 37, 54, 72.

285. Naujoks, *Leben*, 117, 121–22, quote on 122. See also Neurath, *Gesellschaft*, 210–11, 227, 245; *NCC*, doc. 230; Pingel, *Häftlinge*, 57–58. In Mauthausen, unusually, the chief camp clerk is said to have been more influential than the camp elder; Fabréguet, "Entwicklung," 195–96.

286. Neurath, *Gesellschaft*, 222.

287. For the contemporaneous use of the term, see LBIJMB, MF 425, L. Bendix, "Konzentrationslager Deutschland," 1937–38, vol. 4, 34. For the uncritical use of this term today, see Sofsky, *Ordnung*, 152.

288. See also *OdT*, vol. 1, 120; Orth, "Lagergesellschaft," 110.

289. For one example, see DaA, Nr. 7566, K. Schecher, "Rückblick auf Dachau," n.d., 80.

290. Naujoks, *Leben*, 333–39.

291. Kogon, *Theory*, 37.

292. Naujoks, *Leben*, 53–54, 77; Schikorra, *Kontinuitäten*, 54, 55, 219.

293. Although the SS use of triangles was not standardized until 1937–38, political prisoners had often worn red stripes or badges before; *OdT*, vol. 1, 92, 95; Naujoks, *Leben*, 30; Endlich, "Lichtenburg," 48.

294. StANü, Auswärtiges Amt to Missionen et al., December 8, 1936, ND: NG-4048 (figures include Moringen, which did not come under the IKL). The figures are corroborated by internal Gestapo statistics; GStAPK, I. HA, Rep. 90A, Nr. 4442, Bl. 187–91, Schutzhaft, 1937.

295. More than a quarter of prisoners taken into protective custody by the Prussian Gestapo in December 1936 were accused of "Communist activities"; GStAPK, I. HA, Rep. 90A, Nr. 4442, Bl. 187–91, Schutzhaft, 1937.

296. For Gestapo warnings about former prisoners rejoining the resistance, see Gestapa, Lagebericht Marxismus, August 23, 1935, in Boberach, *Regimekritik*, doc. rk 127.

297. Himmler to Eicke, March 23, 1936, *NCC*, doc. 79. The automatic review of protective custody every three months was laid down in RdI to Landesregierungen et al., April 12, 1934, in Repgen and Booms, *Akten*, vol. I/2, 1235-38.

298. LBIJMB, MF 425, L. Bendix, "Konzentrationslager," 1937-38, vol. 5, 7-20, quote on 20. More generally, see Sopade report, May 1937, *NCC*, doc. 220.

299. Browder, *Enforcers*, 82; Gestapa, Lagebericht, October 3, 1935, in Boberach, *Regimekritik*, doc. rk 128.

300. NLHStA, Hann. 158 Moringen, Acc. 84/82, Nr. 6, Bl. 158.

301. Longerich, *Himmler*, 227-33. For the figures, see Moore, "Popular Opinion," 108-109; BArchB, R 3001/21467, Bl. 74: Evangelische Kirche to RJM, May 4, 1935.

302. Quote in Sydnor, *Soldiers*, 29 (n. 68). See also Wegner, *Soldaten*, 251, table 25.

303. Eicke quotes in W. Best to H. Göring, September 27, 1935, *NCC*, doc. 120. Lichtenberg was not arrested until 1941, after he spoke out once more for inmates in the camps. Following a prison term, he collapsed on a transport to Dachau and died in November 1943; Lüerßen, "'Wir,'" 142.

304. Naujoks, *Leben*, 50; Dillon, "Dachau," 107, 136-37.

305. Garbe, "Erst verhasst," 219-22; Wachsmann, *Prisons*, 125-27. More generally, see Garbe, *Widerstand*; Kater, "Bibelforscher."

306. Quotes in report by A. Winkler, 1938, *NCC*, doc. 229; AS, J D2/43, Bl. 146-54: Vernehmung G. Sorge, May 6, 1957, Bl. 147.

307. Quote in BArchB, NS 4/Bu32, Bl. 3: SlF to Kommandantur Buchenwald, November 17, 1938.

308. *OdT*, vol. 3, 46 (Rachuba died in Sachsenhausen in September 1942); Garbe, "Erst verhasst," 224-36; Pingel, *Häftlinge*, 90-91; Lüerßen, "'Wir,'" 211-13. In all, over four thousand Jehovah's Witnesses were taken to the KL during the Third Reich, mostly German citizens; around one in four perished (Garbe, "Erst verhasst," 235).

309. The number of men forced into the KL as homosexual has been estimated as between five thousand and fifteen thousand, with recent research pointing toward the lower figure; Röll, "Homosexuelle," 95. More generally, see Wachsmann, *Prisons*, 144-46; Longerich, *Himmler*, 242-50; Jellonnek, *Homosexuelle*.

310. Müller, "Homosexuelle," 74.

311. Knoll, "Homosexuelle," 62-66; Müller, "Homosexuelle," 75-78; idem, "'Wohl'"; Hackett, *Buchenwald*, 173.

312. Quote in O. Giering, Entschädigungsantrag, 1955, in Pretzel, "Vorfälle," 159-61. See also Ley and Morsch, *Medizin*, 290-97; Wachsmann, *Prisons*, 139-44, 146-49; Poller, *Arztschreiber*, 105-107. Giering was moved to a Berlin state prison in 1942 to serve a sentence for sex offenses allegedly committed in Sachsenhausen. He was released in May 1945.

313. For example, see Pretzel, "Vorfälle"; StAMü, StA Nr. 14719.

314. Quote in O. Giering, Entschädigungsantrag, 1955, in Pretzel, "Vorfälle," 159-61. See also Heger, *Männer*, 91; Kogon, *Theory*, 35; Burkhard, *Tanz*, 68-71; Zinn, "Homophobie," 85-94. For female prisoners, see Eschebach, "Homophobie." For a (wartime) case of a Kapo being falsely accused of sex crimes by rivals, see Kożdoń, ". . . ich kann," 87-89.

315. Naujoks, *Leben*, 8, 14-17, 27-34.

316. Neurath, *Gesellschaft*, 34-35.

317. Naujoks, *Leben*, 35-39, 55-56, 69-70, 115-17, quote on 56.

318. Quote in Suhr, *Ossietzky*, 215.

319. Naujoks, *Leben*, 45, 47-49, 103, 133, quote on 49.

320. Jahnke, "Eschen," 27-28; Drobisch and Wieland, *System*, 324-25.

321. Drobisch and Wieland, *System*, 149-50.

322. Kirsten and Kirsten, *Stimmen*, 47–50; Jahn, *Buchenwald!*, 89–94; Gedenkstätte Buchenwald, *Buchenwald*, 130–31; Freund, *Buchenwald!*, 112–15; Poller, *Arztschreiber*, 159–65.

323. For background, see Pingel, *Häftlinge*, 51–52.

324. Rubner, "Dachau," 67–68, quote on 67; Seger, "Oranienburg," 50–55, quote on 51; Riedel, "Bruderkämpfe"; Knop et al., "Häftlinge," 62–63; Langhoff, *Moorsoldaten*, 214–16, 235–37; Krause-Vilmar, *Breitenau*, 135–36.

325. Langhoff, *Moorsoldaten*, 240; Seger, "Oranienburg," 52; Klausch, *Tätergeschichten*, 95 (n. 380); Suhr, *Ossietzky*, 214–15; Morsch, "Formation," 143; Abraham, "Juda," 150–51.

326. *Deutschland-Berichte*, vol. 3, 1006; Pingel, *Häftlinge*, 109–10; Morsch, "Formation," 141–43; Naujoks, *Leben*, 17, 43–45; LBIJMB, MF 425, L. Bendix, "Konzentrationslager Deutschland," 1937–38, vol. 4, 56–58, 62, 82.

327. Herker-Beimler, *Erinnerungen*, 23–24. Moringen, the central Prussian site for women in protective custody, took in female prisoners from some other German states from 1934 (Riebe, "Frauen," 127). Since early 1936, long-term prisoners from Bavaria could be transferred to Moringen, too (IfZ, Fa 183/1, Bl. 354–55: Politische Polizei to Polizeidirektionen et al., February 13, 1936). For the influential role of the Moringen governor in this process, see Hörath, "Terrorinstrument," 526–27.

328. Caplan, "Einleitung," 42–44, 46; OdT, vol.2, 163–65; NLHStA, Hann. 158 Moringen, Acc. 84/82, Nr. 2, Bl. 144–47: Dienst- und Hausordnung, n.d. This is not to say that the Moringen director was a humanitarian: like other prison and workhouse governors, he subscribed to many of the prevailing racial and criminological stereotypes.

329. Herker-Beimler, *Erinnerungen*, 25. See also Riebe, "Frauen," 128–29; Hesse and Harder, *Zeuginnen*, 30–32, 50–52; Caplan, "Einleitung," 12, 55; Herz, "Frauenlager," 188–90.

330. Caplan, "Einleitung," 51–52; Herz, "Frauenlager," 130–31, 202.

331. Riebe, "Funktionshäftlinge," 52–53.

332. Hesse and Harder, *Zeuginnen*, 34, 40–50.

333. NLHStA, Hann. 158 Moringen, Acc. 84/82, Nr. 2, Bl. 103: Moringen to Gestapa, February 18, 1937; Hesse and Harder, *Zeuginnen*, 40–41.

334. Herz, "Frauenlager," 202, 220–21, quote on 220; Herker-Beimler, *Erinnerungen*, 27–28; Krammer, "Germans." Beimler was killed on December 1, 1936, outside Madrid, possibly by friendly fire.

335. Fahrenberg and Hördler, "Lichtenburg," 166–69; IfZ, F 37/19, Himmler diary, May 28, 1937. The prisoner transfers from Moringen to Lichtenburg occurred in stages between December 1937 and March 1938.

336. Hesse and Harder, *Zeuginnen*, 322–33; Fahrenberg and Hördler, "Lichtenburg," 170–71, 172–73, 176–78; Riebe, "Frauen," 136; Riebe, "Funktionshäftlinge," 54–55.

337. Fahrenberg and Hördler, "Lichtenburg," 173, 179; Hesse, Harder, *Zeuginnen*, 93–94, 117–19; Endlich, "Lichtenburg," 21; Riebe, "Frauen," 137; Hördler, "SS-Kaderschmiede," 109. Hesse and Harder mention a third victim, though there is no official confirmation. On corporal punishment, BArchB, NS 3/415, Bl. 1: KL Lichtenburg to IKL, March 14, 1939.

338. Hesse and Harder, *Zeuginnen*, 88, 122, quote on 333; Strebel, *Ravensbrück*, 44–47, 103–104; Endlich, "Lichtenburg," 21–22.

339. Hesse and Harder, *Zeuginnen*, 124–146, quote on 333; Strebel, *Ravensbrück*, 189.

340. Kaienburg, "Resümee," 171; Strebel, *Ravensbrück*, 84–88. It is not clear whether corporal punishment in Ravensbrück was first carried out before the war or in 1940; Fahrenberg and Hördler, "Lichtenburg," 180 (n. 54).

341. Koslov, *Gewalt*, 17–22, 99; Hördler, "SS-Kaderschmiede," 109–19.

342. Koslov, *Gewalt*, 93–111, 117, 132–33, 490–91; Strebel, *Ravensbrück*, 72–78; Hördler, "Ordnung," 92–93; Wolfram, "KZ-Aufseherinnen"; Toussaint, "Nach Dienstschluss."

343. Koslov, *Gewalt*, 149, 159–63, 175–94; Strebel, *Ravensbrück*, 91–98.

344. In September 1938, the daily number of KL prisoners stood at around 24,400, includ-

ing 800 women in Lichtenburg; NMGB, *Buchenwald*, 698; DaA, ITS, Vorläufige Ermittlung der Lagerstärke (1971); *OdT*, vol. 4, 22; Fahrenberg and Hördler, "Lichtenburg,"
169; AS, D 1 A/1020: Bl. 117 (my thanks to Monika Liebscher); Maršálek, *Mauthausen*,
109. In September 1939, there were 21,400 KL prisoners, including around 2,500
women in Ravensbrück; Pohl to Himmler, April 30, 1942, *IMT*, vol. 38, 363–65, ND:
129–R. My thanks to Stefan Hördler for confirming the Lichtenburg figures (also
below).

345. Caplan, "Gender," 99.

346. Arendt, "Concentration Camps," 760. This theory does not hold for the USSR, where
the camp system diminished substantially after Stalin's death. KL prisoner figures for
the end of 1937: Buchenwald 2,561; Dachau 2,462; Lichtenburg 200; Sachsenhausen
2,523. See NMGB, *Buchenwald*, 698; Drobisch and Wieland, *System*, 266, 271; Endlich,
"Lichtenburg," 23.

3. Expansion

1. Röll, *Sozialdemokraten*, 65, 80; Jahn, *Buchenwald!*, 53–56; StW, "Mörder Bargatzky
zum Tode verurteilt," *Allg. Thüringische Landeszeitung*, May 28, 1938. The spelling of
Bargatzky's name varies; I follow his birth certificate.

2. On Eicke and escapes, Broszat, *Kommandant*, 127–28; Dienstvorschriften Dachau,
October 1, 1933, *IMT*, vol. 26, 296, ND: 778–PS.

3. Röll, *Sozialdemokraten*, 70–73; BArchB, NS 19/1542, Bl. 3–4: Himmler to Gürtner,
May 16, 1938; *Deutschland-Berichte*, vol. 5, 869; Moore, "Popular Opinion," 200–201.

4. StW, "Mörder Bargatzky zum Tode verurteilt," *Allg. Thüringische Landeszeitung*, May
28, 1938; Röll, *Sozialdemokraten*, 65–66, 73–74.

5. BArchB, NS 19/1542, Bl. 8: Himmler to Gürtner, May 31, 1938.

6. BwA, 31/450, Bericht E. Frommhold, n.d. (1945), 41–42; Schrade, *Elf Jahre*, 146; Berke,
Buchenwald, 91–92; ITS, 1.1.5.3/BARE-BARR/00009874/0009. On foreign reports, see
Moore, "Popular Opinion," 201.

7. BArchB, NS 19/1542, Eicke to RFSS-Kommandohaus, June 3, 1938; ibid., Bl. 13: H. Pott-
hast to Dr. Brandt, June 4, 1938; Berke, *Buchenwald*, 91. The men taken for execution to
Dachau during the 1934 Röhm purge had not been inmates of the camp. For executions in the early modern period, see Evans, *Rituals*, 73–77.

8. "Er fiel für uns!," *Das schwarze Korps*, May 26, 1938. See also Dillon, "Dachau," 166–
67; Zeck, *Korps*.

9. Burkhard, *Tanz*, 119; DaA, 9438, A. Hübsch, "Insel des Standrechts" (1961), 82–83.

10. Jahn, *Buchenwald!*, 54–56; Röll, *Sozialdemokraten*, 68–70; BArchB, NS 19/1542, Bl. 3–4:
Himmler to Gürtner, May 16, 1938; Stein, *Juden*, 16.

11. Stein, *Juden*, 21.

12. *VöB*, May 17, 1938, cited in Gruchmann, *Justiz*, 652.

13. BArchB, NS 19/1542, Bl. 3–4: Himmler to Gürtner, May 16, 1938. See also ITS, 1.1.5.3/
BARE-BARR/00009874/0024, Eicke to Himmler, July 5, 1938; Stein, *Juden*, 15; Röll,
Sozialdemokraten, 70.

14. BwA, Totenbuch. In 1938, the IKL warned commandants about a new judicial office
investigating shootings; IKL to KL, July 27, 1938, *NCC*, doc. 132.

15. BArchB, NS 19/4004, Bl. 278–351: Rede bei der SS Gruppenführerbesprechung,
November 8, 1937, Bl. 293.

16. For the figures, Gedenkstätte Buchenwald, *Buchenwald*, 698; DaA, ITS, Vorläufige Ermittlung der Lagerstärke (1971); *OdT*, vol. 4, 22; Endlich, "Lichtenburg," 23; Morsch
and Ley, *Sachsenhausen*, 54.

17. Drobisch and Wieland, *System*, 289, 337.

18. *OdT*, vol. 3, 33.

19. Neugebauer, "Österreichertransport," quote on 201. See also Ungar, "Konzentrations-lager," 198–99; Kripoleitstelle Vienna, "Transporte von Schutzhäftlingen," April 1, 1938, in Neugebauer and Schwarz, *Stacheldraht*, 17; Wünschmann, "Jewish Prisoners," 173.

20. Riedel, *Ordnungshüter*, 197–98; DaA, 9438, A. Hübsch, "Insel des Standrechts" (1961), 113.

21. Röll, *Sozialdemokraten*, 66–67, 74–79, 80–81, quote on 77.

22. Zámečník, *Dachau*, 102; Poller, *Arztschreiber*, 193; Wünschmann, *Before Auschwitz*, chapter 6.

23. Wachsmann, "Policy," 133–35.

24. Many political prisoners believed that the Nazi regime wanted to humiliate and de-fame them by detaining them together with social outsiders (Kogon, *Theory*, 37). This claim was later taken over by historians in East and West Germany (Kühnrich, *KZ-Staat*, 58; Richardi, *Schule*, 226–27; Baganz, *Erziehung*, 61–62, 145–46). For a critical survey of the historiography, Ayaß, "Schwarze und grüne Winkel."

25. A 1990 scholarly survey of various KL victims still ignored "asocials" and "criminals"; Feig, "Non-Jewish Victims."

26. Herbert et al., "Konzentrationslager," 26–28; Herbert, "Gegnerbekämpfung"; Orth, *SS*, 148–50, 298.

27. For the different means used to detain social outsiders in the KL, see Hörath, "Terror-instrument."

28. "Der neue Geist im Münchner Polizeipräsidium," *VöB*, March 15, 1933.

29. Tuchel, *Konzentrationslager*, 157, 209, 312.

30. Zámečník, *Dachau*, 57; Rubner, "Dachau," 67.

31. Ayaß, "*Asoziale*," 19–41.

32. There were 2,592 inmates in Bavaria (including 142 workhouse prisoners from Rebdorf held at Dachau), 2,009 of them accused of political offenses; figures (mostly for April 10, 1934) in Tuchel, *Konzentrationslager*, 155–56; Drobisch and Wieland, *System*, 105. For the classification of Rebdorf prisoners as work-shy, see MdI to Ministry of Finance, August 17, 1934, *NCC*, doc. 232.

33. BayHStA, Staatskanzlei 6299/1, Bl. 174–77: Reichsstatthalter to MPr, March 20, 1934.

34. BayHStA, Staatskanzlei 6299/1, Bl. 132–41: MdI to MPr, April 14, 1934, translation in *NCC*, doc. 23.

35. For the view that Himmler's assault on social outsiders in Bavaria was exceptional, *OdT*, vol. 1, 55–56.

36. Ayaß, "*Asoziale*," 31–32, quote on 31; Drobisch and Wieland, *System*, 71; Hörath, "Ter-rorinstrument," 516–18, 525; Harris, "Role," 678; Diercks, "Fuhlsbüttel," 266, 278. For the influx of "beggars" into existing camps, see Stokes, "Eutiner," 619–20; Wollenberg, "Ahrensbök-Holstendorf," 228.

37. Wachsmann, *Prisons*, 49–54, 128–37.

38. Quotes in Prussian MdI decree, November 13, 1933, *NCC*, doc. 16. See also Wagner, *Volksgemeinschaft*, 198–200; Terhorst, *Vorbeugungshaft*, 74–80.

39. Wagner, *Volksgemeinschaft*, 200–204; Mette, "Lichtenburg," 141. On May 25, 1934, 257 of all 439 Lichtenburg prisoners were classified as "professional criminals."

40. Wagner, *Volksgemeinschaft*, 204–209; Roth, "Kriminalpolizei," 332–33; *OdT*, vol. 2, 541; Langhammer, "Verhaftungsaktion," 58; BArchB, R 3001/alt R 22/1469, Bl. 24: "Erfolg der Vorbeugungshaft," *Berliner Börsen-Zeitung*, October 24, 1935; ibid. (ehem. BDC), SSO, Loritz, Hans, 21.12.1895, Personal-Bericht, Stellungnahme Eicke, July 31, 1935.

41. Langhammer, "Verhaftungsaktion," 58–60; Hörath, "Terrorinstrument," 523.

42. Quote in Bavarian Gestapo to KL Dachau, July 10, 1936, *NCC*, doc. 97. See also ITS, ARCH/HIST/KL Dachau 4 (200), Bl. 15: KL Dachau to IKL, June 19, 1936; *IMT*, vol. 31, EE by M. Lex, November 16, 1945, ND: 2928–PS.

43. Police Directorate Bremen, November 23, 1935, *NCC*, doc. 253.

44. The SS classified another 950 prisoners as "political" and 85 as "returned emigrant Jews"; NAL, FO 371/18882, Bl. 386–90: Appendix A, Visit to Dachau, July 31, 1935. According to the German Foreign Office, 1,067 "professional criminals" and other "asocial elements" were detained in the KL on November 1, 1936 (excluding homosexuals), making up more than twenty-two percent of the prisoner population; StANü, Auswärtigs Amt to Missionen et al., December 8, 1936, ND: NG-4048.

45. Wachsmann, "Dynamics," 24.

46. Wagner, Volksgemeinschaft, 235–43.

47. Wagner, Volksgemeinschaft, 235, 254–57, quotes on 254; Langhammer, "Verhaftungsaktion," 60–63; Röll, Sozialdemokraten, 66. Himmler met Eicke on March 10, 1937, the day after the raids; IfZ, F 37/19, Himmler diary. Up to thirty women were arrested as "professional criminals" and taken to Moringen.

48. Wagner, Volksgemeinschaft, 254–55. More generally, see Herbert, Best, 174–75.

49. Speech at SS Gruppenführer conference, November 8, 1937, NCC, doc. 94.

50. Hörath, "Experimente," chapters 4 and 8. For the modern school of criminal law, see Wachsmann, Prisons, 20–22.

51. It has been suggested that Himmler wanted to gain more forced laborers for the construction and extension of the KL (Wagner, Volksgemeinschaft, 255). This is unlikely to have been a major factor, since well over half of the men arrested in March 1937 were taken to two camps (Lichtenburg and Sachsenburg) that were not slated for extension (both closed as men's camps later that year). For the figures, see Langhammer, "Verhaftungsaktion," 62.

52. Tooze, Wages, 260–68; Schneider, Hakenkreuz, 738–46.

53. IfZ, Fa 199/20, Sitzung des Ministerrats am 11.2.1937.

54. RJM minutes, February 15, 1937, NCC, doc. 127. Himmler met with Eicke on February 11 and 12, 1937; IfZ, F 37/19, Himmler diary.

55. Quote, from Himmler's February 23, 1937, decree, in Wagner, Volksgemeinschaft, 254.

56. German criminologists had long labeled social outsiders and criminals as "work-shy" (Hörath, "Experimente," chapters 4 and 8). This term took on greater economic meaning in the late 1930s.

57. RJM minutes, February 15, 1937, NCC, doc. 127. More generally, see Wachsmann, Prisons, 173.

58. For overcrowding, see Drobisch and Wieland, System, 286.

59. Langhammer, "Verhaftungsaktion," 73–74; NLHStA, 158 Moringen, Acc. 84/82, Nr. 8, Bl. 2: Krack, Aktenvermerk, October 6, 1937; Roth, "Kriminalpolizei," 335.

60. The German police held 2,752 "professional criminals and habitual sex offenders" in preventive detention on November 13, 1937 (BArchB, R 58/483, Bl. 120–21: Mitteilungsblatt des LKA). Little more than a year later, the figure had risen to around 4,000 (figure for December 31, 1938, referring to 12,921 prisoners in preventive police custody, among them 8,892 "asocials"; evidently, the remaining 4,029 prisoners were regarded as "criminals"; Tuchel, Konzentrationslager, 313).

61. Langhammer, "Verhaftungsaktion," 64; ITS, 1.1.5.1/0544–0682/0647/0027, Einlieferungsbuch; Röll, Sozialdemokraten, 68 (n. 163).

62. Drobisch and Wieland, System, 288.

63. For the transports, see Langhammer, "Verhaftungsaktion," 69. Only 198 "criminals" were left in Buchenwald when war broke out in September 1939; Stein, "Funktionswandel," 170.

64. Broszat, Kommandant, 58–61, 73, quotes on 61, 101. For violence against "criminals" in early camps, see Langhoff, Moorsoldaten, 292–304.

65. Report by A. Hübsch, 1961, NCC, doc. 240.

66. BArchB, KLuHafta Sachsenburg 2, Kommandantur-Befehl, April 14, 1937.

67. OdT, vol. 1, 92, 96.

68. AS, Totenbuch.

69. The figures exclude six men classified as preventive custody prisoners; BwA, Toten-buch. During the same period—August 1937 to July 1938—the SS recorded thirty-seven deaths among political prisoners.

70. Quote in Kogon, *Theory*, 31. For the term "BVer," ITS, 1.1.6.0, folder 25, doc. 82095206, *Wahrheit und Recht* 1 (May 1946). For the USSR, see Khlevniuk, *Gulag*, doc. 98; Barnes, "Soviet," 107–10.

71. For example, see Freund, *Buchenwald!*, 99–100, 103–105; Seger, "Oranienburg," 34, 47. For SS views, Himmler speech at a Wehrmacht course, January 15–23, 1937, *NCC*, doc. 83.

72. See also Orth, "Lagergemeinschaft," 114–16.

73. Of 2,752 "professional criminals and habitual sex offenders" in preventive detention on November 13, 1937, 1,679 were classified as burglars and thieves. Another 522 were classified as fraudsters and fences. Only some twenty percent were accused of crimes against the person: 495 so-called sex offenders (including homosexual men) and 56 robbers; BArchB, R 58/483, Bl. 120–21: Mitteilungsblatt des LKA. See also Langhammer, "Verhaftungsaktion," 61; Pretzel, "'Umschulung.'"

74. Wagner, "'Vernichtung,'" 104–105.

75. For "green" prisoners being held in the same barracks, *NCC*, doc. 220. More generally, see Naujoks, *Leben*, 52–55.

76. For a different view, see Neurath, *Gesellschaft*, 97–98.

77. For the tensions, see report by H. Schwarz, July 1945, *NCC*, doc. 231; Poller, *Arzt-schreiber*, 150.

78. The spring 1937 arrests were carried out on the basis of the Reichstag Fire Decree; Drobisch and Wieland, *System*, 286. For background of the December 1937 decree, see Wagner, *Volksgemeinschaft*, 258–59.

79. BArchB, R 58/473, Bl. 46–49: Erlaß des Reichs- und Preußischen MdI, December 14, 1937; partial translation in *NCC*, doc. 99.

80. The Duisburg police also suspected Müller of a recent theft and speculated that he might be guilty of other unnamed offenses; HStAD, BR 1111, Nr. 188, quote on Bl. 43, Krimineller Lebenslauf, n.d. (my thanks to Julia Hörath for her notes on this case).

81. Figure in Schmid, "Aktion," 36.

82. Ayaß, *"Asoziale,"* 151–59; Wagner, *Volksgemeinschaft*, 280–86.

83. Schmid, "Aktion," 32–34; Ayaß, *"Asoziale,"* 140–43. Ayaß stresses that protective custody prisoners (arrested by the Gestapo) and preventive police detention prisoners (arrested by the Kripo) could both be classified as "asocials" in the KL; Ayaß, *"Aso-ziale,"* 170.

84. Ayaß, *"Gemeinschaftsfremde,"* 114–15; Wagner, *Volksgemeinschaft*, 292–93. For female "asocials," see Schikorra, "Grüne," 108; idem, *Kontinuitäten*, 143; Caplan, "Gender," 89.

85. Barkow et al., *Novemberpogrom*, 46.

86. BArchB, R 58/473, Bl. 63–72: Richtlinien zum Erlaß zur vorbeugenden Verbrechens-bekämpfung, April 4, 1938.

87. Ayaß, *"Asoziale,"* 150–54; Wagner, *Volksgemeinschaft*, 279, 282–84, 288–89.

88. Heydrich to Kripo, June 1, 1938, *NCC*, doc. 103. For the use of the term "gypsy" by scholars of the Third Reich, see Zimmermann, *Rassenutopie*, 17–20; Fings, "Dünnes Eis," 25.

89. There were an estimated twenty to twenty-six thousand Gypsies living in Germany in 1933. For the above, see Zimmermann, *Rassenutopie*, 106–20; Wachsmann, "Policy," 142–43. See also Lewy, *Nazi Persecution*, 17–55.

90. LHASA, MD, Rep. C 29 Anh. 2, Nr. Z 98/1, quote on Bl. 4: Kripolizeistelle Magdeburg, Anordnung, June 16, 1938. Laubinger was released on August 25, 1939. My thanks to Christian Goeschel for these documents.

91. Herbert, *Best*, 163–68, 176–77.

92. Wagner, *Volksgemeinschaft*, 280–82, 286, 290; Ayaß, *"Asoziale,"* 141, 143–46, 156–58.

93. This is also stressed in Ayaß, *"Asoziale,"* 160–65, and Wagner, *Volksgemeinschaft,* 287–89.

94. Hörath, "'Arbeitsscheue Volksgenossen.'"

95. Heydrich to Kripo, June 1, 1938, *NCC,* doc. 103. See also Pingel, *Häftlinge,* 71–72.

96. Quotes in Picker, *Tischgespräche,* 600. See also Eicke to Greifelt, August 10, 1938, in Tuchel, *Inspektion,* 56.

97. Ayaß, *"Asoziale,"* 141–42, 148–49, 163. In 1938, Himmler also launched another attempt to poach inmates from state prisons (*NCC,* doc. 131) and workhouses (*NCC,* doc. 101).

98. *OdT,* vol. 1, 97. The situation was different in the Lichtenburg women's camp, where Jehovah's Witnesses outnumbered "asocials"; Schikorra, "Grüne," 108.

99. Schmid, "Aktion," 38–39.

100. On August 30, 1939, 2,873 of all 5,382 Buchenwald prisoners fell into the category "work-shy," which included "work-shy Jews" (Stein, "Funktionswandel," 170). On August 31, 1939, 3,313 of all 6,573 Sachsenhausen prisoners fell into the category "work-shy" (AS, D 1 A/1024, Bl. 264: Veränderungsmeldung). On prisoner markings, see *OdT,* vol. 1, 94, 97–98.

101. All men arrested in the April 1938 raids were taken to Buchenwald. The camp was also initially chosen as the destination for those arrested in the June 1938 raids (Heydrich to Kripo, June 1, 1938, in *NCC,* doc. 103).

102. Schmid, "Aktion," 36.

103. Broszat, *Kommandant,* 86, 97, quote on 93.

104. Barkow et al., *Novemberpogrom,* 49–50, quote on 50; Naujoks, *Leben,* 77–78.

105. Naujoks, *Leben,* 78–80; *OdT,* vol. 3, 22; Barkow et al., *Novemberpogrom,* 61–62.

106. For background, see Neurath, *Gesellschaft,* 42–44.

107. Pingel, *Häftlinge,* 85–86; Schikorra, *Kontinuitäten,* 143–44, 207, 210–17; Pretzel, "Vorfälle," 125; Ayaß, *"Asoziale,"* 168–69. For the term "Asos," see ITS, 1.1.6.0, folder 25, doc. 82095206, *Wahrheit und Recht* 1 (May 1946). For an inside view of life among the "asocials," see ibid., doc. 82095213, *Wahrheit und Recht* 2 (June 1946).

108. Poller, *Arztschreiber,* quotes on 187; Naujoks, *Leben,* 81–82; Wagner, *Volksgemeinschaft,* 288.

109. Friedlander, *Genocide,* 25–31; Burleigh, *Death,* 55–66.

110. Tuchel, *Konzentrationslager,* 289–91, quote on 289; BArchL, B 162/491, Bl. 66–79: Vernehmung W. Heyde, October 19, 1961, quote on 70. See also monthly report of the Buchenwald SS doctor, June 8, 1938, *NCC,* doc. 237; Naujoks, *Leben,* 107; DaA, 9438, A. Hübsch, "Insel des Standrechts" (1961), 109; Hahn, *Grawitz,* 161; Poller, *Arztschreiber,* 116; Schikorra, *Kontinuitäten,* 176.

111. DaA, Häftlingsdatenbank; BwA, Totenbuch; AS, Totenbuch; AGFl, Häftlingsdatenbank; AM, Zugangslisten und Totenbücher. I am very grateful to Albert Knoll, Sabine Stein, Monika Liebscher, Johannes Ibel, and Andreas Kranebitter for sending me this data on prisoner mortality, which I have drawn on in this and other sections in this chapter.

112. AS, Totenbuch. A small number of fatalities may have gone unrecorded in the Sachsenhausen "death ledger."

113. As note 111, above.

114. Quote in Kohlhagen, *Bock,* 24. For the figures, see AS, Totenbuch.

115. In all, there are 1,232 known fatalities, including 169 "asocial Jews"; see note 111, above.

116. BArchB, NS 19/4014, Bl. 158–204: Rede vor Generälen, June 21, 1944, Bl. 170. More generally, see Wachsmann, *Prisons,* 112, 192–94, 210.

117. There were some early reports on the detention of social outsiders (Moore, "Popular Opinion," 57–61), but the main media focus was on political opponents.

118. See also Moore, "Popular Opinion," 185.

119. "Konzentrationslager Dachau," *Illustrierter Beobachter*, December 3, 1936, 2014–17, 2028, partial translation in *NCC*, doc. 270. For a similar article from 1936, *NCC*, doc. 268.

120. Broadcast by Himmler, January 29, 1939, *NCC*, doc. 274; "Erfolg der Vorbeugungshaft," *Berliner Börsen-Zeitung*, October 24, 1935.

121. Wachsmann, *Prisons*, 18–19, 54–58. More generally, see Peukert, *Nazi Germany*, 222–23.

122. Kautsky, *Teufel*, 144. More generally, see Peukert, *Nazi Germany*, 198–99; Noakes, Pridham, *Nazism*, vol. 2, 574; Moore, "Popular Opinion," 207–208.

123. "Konzentrationslager Dachau," *Illustrierter Beobachter*, December 3, 1936, *NCC*, doc. 270. See also Moore, "Popular Opinion," 184–87; Gray, *About Face*. On the staging of photos for the article about Dachau, see *Deutschland-Berichte*, vol. 4, 694.

124. Peukert, "Alltag," 56. For the persistence of crime under the Nazis, see Wachsmann, *Prisons*, 69–70, 198, 221–22.

125. Gellately, *Backing*, 97–98; Moore, "Popular Opinion," 209; Kershaw, *Popular Opinion*, 74. For isolated press reports, Ayaß, *"Asoziale,"* 157, 164–65.

126. *Deutschland-Berichte*, vol. 2, 372; Klemperer, *Zeugnis*, vol. 1, 443.

127. Neurath, *Gesellschaft*, 25–26; Christ, "Wehrmachtsoldaten," 819; Steinbacher, *Dachau*, 151–52.

128. See also Moore, "Popular Opinion," 235, 239.

129. For media reports, see Milton, "Konzentrationslager," 137–38; Moore, "Popular Opinion," 203–204. For orders to scale back reports, see *NCC*, docs. 267 and 271. For occasional reminders, see *NCC*, docs. 266, 270, 274.

130. Quote in instruction to the German press, December 11, 1936, *NCC*, doc. 271.

131. For example, see ITS, ARCH/HIST/KL Lichtenburg 2, Bl. 104–15: Befehlsblatt SS-TV/IKL, April 1, 1937.

132. NAL, FO 371/18882, Bl. 386–90: Appendix A, Visit to Dachau, July 31, 1935, quote on 390.

133. *Manchester Guardian*, reader's letter, April 7, 1936, *NCC*, doc. 281.

134. Milton, "Konzentrationslager," passim; Drobisch and Wieland, *System*, 240–48.

135. Hett, *Crossing*, 228–34; Wünschmann, "Jewish prisoners," 41.

136. Quotes in Buck, "Ossietzky," 23–27, p. 26; report by C. Burckhardt, November 1935, *NCC*, doc. 279. See also Kraiker and Suhr, *Ossietzky*, 106–26.

137. Moore, "Popular Opinion," 177–78, quote on 178.

138. Milton, "Konzentrationslager," 140.

139. Evans, *Third Reich in Power*, 220–32; Gruchmann, *Justiz*, 77–78; Fröhlich, *Tagebücher*, I/5, March 3, 1938. The Berlin Special Court convicted Niemöller of lesser charges that would not have resulted in further detention.

140. IfZ, MA 312, Rede bei der SS Gruppenführerbesprechung, November 8, 1938.

141. Himmler speech at a Wehrmacht course, January 15–23, 1937, *IMT*, vol. 29, ND: 1992(A)-PS, especially pages 231–32; Kaienburg, *Wirtschaftskomplex*, 37–38, 51, 56, 197.

142. Kaienburg, *Wirtschaftskomplex*, 37–38. Previously, historians generally dated this development to the late 1930s.

143. Kaienburg, *Wirtschaftskomplex*, 38, 56–57, 62–63, 141–46, 169–77, 197–98; Dillon, "Dachau," 85, 162; Wachsmann, "Dynamics," 33; Merkl, *General*, 79; ITS, ARCH/HIST/KL Lichtenburg 2, Bl. 104–15: Befehlsblatt SS-TV/IKL, April 1, 1937; Hördler, "SS-Kaderschmiede," 105–106.

144. Quote in IfZ, MA 312, Rede bei der SS Gruppenführerbesprechung, November 8, 1938. See also Wegner, *Soldaten*, 79–112; Kaienburg, *Wirtschaftskomplex*, 65.

145. Quote in BArchB, NS 19/1652, Bl. 5–15: Geheime Kommandosache, Erlass, August 17, 1938, Bl. 11. See also Wegner, *Soldaten*, 112–23; Merkl, *General*, 127–37; Dillon, "Dachau," 186; Kaienburg, *Wirtschaftskomplex*, 66–68; Zámečník, *Dachau*, 101.

146. IfZ, F 13/6, Bl. 369–82: R. Höss, "Theodor Eicke," November 1946, Bl. 377. See also Segev, *Soldiers*, 129–30.

147. Eicke quotes in Segev, *Soldiers*, 130–31.

148. For the numbers, which include the relatively small number of Commandant Staff officials, BArchB, R 2/12164, Bl. 25–28: Best to RMi Finanzen, November 26, 1938; Kaienburg, *Wirtschaftskomplex*, 71–72. Following Charles Sydnor, historians have often used a significantly higher number, putting the strength of the Death's Head SS in mid-1939 at 22,033 men (Sydnor, *Soldiers*, 34). However, as Hermann Kaienburg points out (reference above), it is likely that this figure included Camp SS reservists, who were not stationed permanently at the KL but only underwent brief training courses in 1938–39.

149. Sydnor, *Soldiers*, 34.

150. *Brockhaus*, 1937, *NCC*, doc. 272.

151. "Sachsenhausen Song," *NCC*, doc. 224.

152. For an introduction, see Morris and Rothman, *Oxford History*.

153. Sofsky, *Ordnung*, 194.

154. Wohlfeld, "Nohra," 115; Ehret, "Schutzhaft," 251; Lechner, "Kuhberg," 94; Meyer and Roth, "Zentrale," 205; Wachsmann, *Prisons*, 95–96; Langhoff, *Moorsoldaten*, 40–41, 61, 71.

155. Krause-Vilmar, *Breitenau*, 122–24; Rudorff, "'Privatlager,'" 162–63; Seger, "Oranienburg," 34; Diercks, "Fuhlsbüttel," 280–81; Mayer-von Götz, *Terror*, 135–36.

156. Kienle, "Heuberg," 54. See also Rudorff, "'Privatlager,'" 163.

157. Special camp order by Eicke, August 1, 1934, *NCC*, doc. 149.

158. Quote in Kogon, *Theory*, 27. See also Jahn, *Buchenwald!*, 42–45; Stein, *Juden*, 10–12; *OdT*, vol. 3, 327–29; *NCC*, doc. 88. For death rates, see BwA, Totenbuch; AS, Totenbuch.

159. Kaienburg, *Wirtschaft*, 159–72, 356, 1017.

160. Naujoks, *Leben*, 36.

161. Ecker, "Hölle," 35; Kaienburg, *Wirtschaft*, 114–29; DaA, Nr. 7566, K. Schecher, "Rückblick auf Dachau," n.d., 74.

162. Kaienburg, *Wirtschaft*, 248–49.

163. Quotes in BArchB (ehem. BDC), SSO Pohl, Oswald, 30.6.1892, Lebenslauf, 1932; ibid., Pohl to Himmler, May 24, 1933. More generally, see Schulte, *Zwangsarbeit*, 32–37, 45; testimony O. Pohl, June 3, 1946, in Mendelsohn, *Holocaust*, vol. 17, 35–38.

164. Schulte, *Zwangsarbeit*, 45–69, 76–91, 148–52; Kaienburg, *Wirtschaft*, 107–113, 403–405; IfZ, F 13/6, Bl. 343–54: R. Höss, "Oswald Pohl," November 1946.

165. Schulte, *Zwangsarbeit*, 40–44.

166. Schulte, *Zwangsarbeit*, 46–48, 69–75, 99–103; Kaienburg, *Wirtschaft*, 123–27; IfZ, F 13/6, Bl. 343–54: R. Höss, "Oswald Pohl," November 1946; StANü, EE by H. Karl, June 21, 1947, p. 4, ND: NO-4007.

167. IfZ, F 13/6, Bl. 343–54: R. Höss, "Oswald Pohl," November 1946, quote on 346. See also Schulte, *Zwangsarbeit*, 69.

168. For example, see Schulte, *Zwangsarbeit*, 75.

169. BArchB, NS 19/1792, Bl. 226: Minutenprogramm für den 25.4.1939; ibid., Film 44564, Vernehmung O. Pohl, January 6, 1947, Bl. 6, 9; extracts of testimony of defendant Pohl, 1947, *TWC*, vol. 5, 559; IfZ, F 13/6, Bl. 343–54: R. Höss, "Oswald Pohl," November 1946; ibid., Bl. 369–82: R. Höss, "Theodor Eicke," November 1946; StANü, EE by H. Karl, June 21, 1947, p. 4, ND: NO-4007. For one such clash, see *NCC*, doc. 133.

170. Kaienburg, *Wirtschaft*, 25, 356–57, 373–76, 1091. For a different interpretation, which sees Himmler's initiative as primarily defensive (aimed at maintaining control over KL labor at a time of growing labor shortages in Germany), see Schulte, *Zwangsarbeit*, 108–11. Historians recognized the significance of the shift in the SS economy early; Georg, *Unternehmungen*, 42; Billig, *L'Hitlérisme*, 289–90.

171. Quote in Pohl to Hamburg treasurer, September 13, 1938, *NCC*, doc. 141. See also BArchB, NS 19/1919, Bl. 4–5: Himmler to Hildebrandt, December 15, 1939; Naasner, *SS-Wirtschaft*, 255–56.

172. For example, see Kaienburg, *Wirtschaft*, 434.

173. For this and the previous paragraph, see Jaskot, *Architecture*, 21–25, 36–37, 80–94; Kaienburg, *Wirtschaft*, 455–58, 460–61, 603–609, 1018; *OdT*, vol. 3, 388–89; Schulte, *Zwangsarbeit*, 111–19, 125; BArchB, Film 14428, Stabsamt, Besuchs-Vermerk, June 17, 1938.

174. For the trip, StANü, EE by H. Karl, June 21, 1947, pp. 6–7, ND: NO-4007, which dates it to May 1938. For the March dating, *OdT*, vol. 4, 18–19, 293.

175. *OdT*, vol. 4, 17–20, 293–94.

176. *OdT*, vol. 4, 19–22; KZ-Gedenkstätte Flossenbürg, *Flossenbürg*, 35.

177. *OdT*, vol. 4, 294, 298; Fabréguet, "Entwicklung," 194.

178. *OdT*, vol. 4, 19, 21, 296, 298; Hördler, "Ordnung," 93.

179. Police and SS also saw practical advantages of setting up a KL in the recently annexed Austrian territory; *OdT*, vol. 4, 293.

180. Jaskot, *Architecture*, 126–35; *OdT*, vol. 4, 20, 29, 299.

181. *OdT*, vol. 4, 26; Maršálek, *Mauthausen*, 123. Initially, the police did not take prisoners directly to Flossenbürg and Mauthausen, but transferred them from other KL.

182. For the plans, BArchB, NS 3/415, Bl. 3: Verwaltungschef SS to Bauleitung Flossenbürg, April 5, 1939.

183. Stein, "Funktionswandel," 169–70; Maršálek, *Mauthausen*, 27, 109–10; *OdT*, vol. 4, 22; Langhammer, "Verhaftungsaktion," 69.

184. Ibel, "Il campo," 235–36; Maršálek, *Mauthausen*, 109; *OdT*, vol. 4, 308, 315. It seems likely that there were numerous Gypsies among Mauthausen prisoners already in 1938; A. Hübsch, "Insel des Standrechts" (1961), 105–106.

185. In all, 105 "professional criminals" are known to have died in Flossenbürg and Mauthausen by the end of August 1939—compared to 82 known fatalities (January 1938–August 1939) in the three big camps for men; see note 111.

186. Quote in K. Wolff to H. Krebs, December 15, 1938, *NCC*, doc. 143. See also H. Krebs to Himmler, November 19, 1938, ibid., doc. 142.

187. USHMM, RG-11.001M.01, reel 17, 500–5–1, Bl. 98: Heydrich to RSHA et al., January 2, 1941.

188. Speech at a Wehrmacht course, January 15–23, 1937, *NCC*, doc. 83.

189. For other SS leaders, see Heydrich to Gürtner, June 28, 1938, *NCC*, doc. 131. Jewish prisoners, who ranked even lower than "professional criminals" in the SS hierarchy, would not have been numerous enough at the time to fill either of the new camps.

190. Siegert, "Flossenbürg," 440–41.

191. ITS, ARCH/KL Flossenbürg, Indiv. Unterlagen Männer, Josef Kolacek, Bl. 12: KL Flossenbürg to RKPA, November 30, 1938 (my thanks to Christian Goeschel for these and other documents). For the transport on July 1, 1938, see *OdT*, vol. 4, 22.

192. Maršálek, *Mauthausen*, 27, 85; *OdT*, vol. 4, 21, 24–27, 301–303.

193. Recollections A. Gussak, 1958, *NCC*, doc. 198.

194. Maršálek, *Mauthausen*, 146; AM, Zugangslisten und Totenbücher (the figures for 1938 may not be complete). Of all the sixty-seven "asocials" known to have perished in Mauthausen until the outbreak of war, fifty-seven had arrived on the March 21, 1939 transport from Dachau; it is unknown why so many prisoners of this transport perished so quickly.

195. DaA, 9438, A. Hübsch, "Insel des Standrechts" (1961), 105–106; Fabréguet, "Entwicklung," 196; Maršálek, *Mauthausen*, 123.

196. AGFl, Häftlingsdatenbank. The higher death rate in Mauthausen was linked in part to the unusually high mortality among prisoners who had arrived on the March 21, 1939 transport (see note 194, above).

197. ITS, ARCH/KL Flossenbürg, Indiv. Unterlagen Männer, Josef Kolacek.

198. Kaienburg, *Wirtschaft*, 647–51, 656; Allen, *Business*, 67–71.

199. Kaienburg, *Wirtschaft*, 647, 649–55; Trouvé, "Klinkerwerk," 65–67.

200. Trouvé, "Klinkerwerk," 46–47, 49–50, 54–57; AS, R 42/1, H. Gartsch, "Beiträge zum KZ Sachsenhausen, Klinkerwerk," n.d., 4–5.

201. For a different view, stressing the similarities to other labor details in Sachsenhausen, see Trouvé, "Klinkerwerk," 77.

202. Trouvé, "Klinkerwerk," 47, 56, 64–65; AS, R 42/1, H. Gartsch, "Beiträge zum KZ Sachsenhausen, Klinkerwerk," n.d., 4–5; Kaienburg, *Wirtschaft*, 650; WL, P.III.h. 758, B. Landau, "Die Hölle von Sachsenhausen," n.d., 27.

203. For suicides, see Trouvé, "Klinkerwerk," 58; AS, R 42/1, H. Gartsch, "Beiträge zum KZ Sachsenhausen, Klinkerwerk," n.d., 5.

204. Naujoks, *Leben*, 111; Trouvé, "Klinkerwerk," 57–58; Schlaak, "Wetter," 182.

205. AS, Totenbuch. The onset of the first period of prolonged frost in mid-December 1938 coincided with a sharp rise in the death rate.

206. Between December 1938 and March 1939, "asocial" prisoners made up eighty-two per-cent of all registered fatalities in Sachsenhausen; AS, Totenbuch. For "asocials" at the brick works, see Meyer, "Funktionalismus," 85; Trouvé, "Klinkerwerk," 60.

207. LaB, A. Rep. 358–02, Nr. 7468, Bl. 5: Erklärung Hermann R., March 21, 1939. See also ibid., Bl. 1–2: StA Berlin, Vermerk, March 21, 1939.

208. For the Sachsenhausen SS, see Meyer, "Funktionalismus," 84; Trouvé, "Klinkerwerk," 77.

209. Kaienburg, *Wirtschaft*, 655–56; Trouvé, "Klinkerwerk," 36–45; Allen, *Business*, 70–71; Khlevniuk, *Gulag*, 336.

210. Schulte, *Zwangsarbeit*, 122.

211. Kaienburg, *Wirtschaft*, 656–83, 762–63; Trouvé, "Klinkerwerk," 79–98. The plant was still unfinished in 1943, having lost millions of Reichsmark. On SS managers during the war, with different emphases, see Allen, *Business*, 85–86; Schulte, *Zwangsarbeit*, 159–67.

212. There are two confirmed deaths in Lichtenburg and four in Ravensbrück (during 1939); Hesse and Harder, *Zeuginnen*, 117–19; Strebel, *Ravensbrück*, 506.

213. For the mortality figures, see note 111.

214. According to largely accurate ITS figures, 388 Dachau prisoners died during the twenty months between January 1938 and August 1939 (the actual figure was closer to 415; DaA, Häftlingsdatenbank), compared to thirty-seven deaths over the preceding twenty months (May 1936 to December 1937); meanwhile, the average monthly pris-oner population rose from 2,157 to 4,845. DaA, ITS, Vorläufige Ermittlung der Lager-stärke (1971).

215. Hahn, *Grawitz*, 155–59; Morsch and Ley, *Medizin*, 53–54, 78; Naujoks, *Leben*, 110.

216. Quote in LBIJMB, MF 425, L. Bendix, "Konzentrationslager Deutschland," 1937–38, vol. 5, 21.

217. Special camp order by Eicke, August 1, 1934, *NCC*, doc. 149.

218. For example, see Poller, *Arztschreiber*, 89–90, 93–94, 98–102.

219. Morsch, "Formation," 167–69, 172; Boehnert, "SS Officer Corps," 116; Hahn, *Grawitz*, 163; Ley and Morsch, *Medizin*, 182–85; Naujoks, *Leben*, 107–109; Pukrop, "SS-Karrieren," 76, 86. The Soviet authorities executed Ehrsam in 1947.

220. LBIJMB, MF 425, L. Bendix, "Konzentrationslager Deutschland," 1937–38, vol. 5, 37–38, 63; Tuchel, *Konzentrationslager*, 287–88; Naujoks, *Leben*, 126–27.

221. See the case of Dr. Katz in Dachau (chapter 1).

222. *NCC*, doc. 186.

223. Naujoks, *Leben*, 105; Hahn, *Grawitz*, 159–60; Freund, *Buchenwald!*, 72.

224. Ley and Morsch, *Medizin*, 69; Poller, *Arztschreiber*, 59, 74, 77; Orth, *SS*, 45–46.

225. Schley, *Nachbar*, 64–66; Freund, *Buchenwald!*, 95–96; *OdT*, vol. 3, 325.

226. Quote in Freund, *Buchenwald!*, 84. See also Stein, *Juden*, 57–59.
227. DaA, Häftlingsdatenbank; ibid., ITS, Vorläufige Ermittlung der Lagerstärke (1971); BwA, Totenbuch; NMGB, *Buchenwald*, 698.
228. Between January 1938 and August 1939, 491 Jewish prisoners perished in Buchenwald, including Jews arrested as asocial or political opponents; BwA, Totenbuch.
229. Quote in Besprechung über die Judenfrage, November 12, 1938, *IMT*, vol. 28, 538, ND: 1816–PS. See also Steinweis, *Kristallnacht*.
230. For surveys, see Friedländer, *Nazi Germany*; Longerich, *Holocaust*, 29–130.
231. A first monograph on the topic is now forthcoming; Wünschmann, *Before Auschwitz*.
232. See also Matthäus, "Verfolgung," 66–68.
233. Lagebericht Stapostelle Magdeburg, August 5, 1935, in Kulka and Jäckel, *Juden*, doc. 1018. Although the overall number of Jews dragged to the camps for "race defilement" in 1935 is unknown, it was not insignificant; in Breslau alone, the police sent twenty male Jewish "race defilers" to the KL during July; Stapostelle Regierungsbezirk Breslau, Bericht für Juli 1935, ibid., doc. 1007.
234. Quotes in BArchB, R 58/264, Bl. 161: Gestapa to Stapostellen, September 1935; Informationen des Gestapa, February 25, 1938, in Boberach, *Regimekritik*, doc. rk 1706. See also Matthäus, "Verfolgung," 72. The Gestapo also arrested some men after terms of judicial imprisonment for "race defilement"; Wachsmann, *Prisons*, 180. More generally, see Friedländer, *Nazi Germany*, 120–22, 137–43; Longerich, *Holocaust*, 54–61.
235. Longerich, *Holocaust*, 67–69, 105–107, 126–27.
236. IfZ, Fa 183/1, Bl. 336: Grauert to Landesregierungen, February 9, 1935; Bavarian Political Police decree, March 7, 1935, *NCC*, doc. 95.
237. Wünschmann, "Cementing," 589–94; idem, "Jewish Prisoners," 140–42. See also Matthäus, "Verfolgung," 76; *OdT*, vol. 1, 95, 103. For the threat of lifelong detention, see also *NCC*, doc. 110. Such threats also served the wider aim, Hitler later acknowledged, of preventing other "asocial" émigrés from returning to Germany; Picker, *Tischgespräche*, 513–14.
238. Matthäus, "Verfolgung," 68–77, quote on 80; *OdT*, vol. 1, 98.
239. Wünschmann, "Jewish Prisoners," 65, 156–58. See also Morsch, "Formation," 135.
240. Report of a Jewish "reimmigrant," 1936, *NCC*, doc. 243; Lüerßen, "'Wir,'" 204.
241. LaB, A Rep. 358-02, Nr. 1540, GStA Berlin to RJM, June 3, 1937. More generally, see Broszat, *Kommandant*, 166.
242. Quote in Kogon, *Theory*, 77. This was one of three official camp songs recognized by the Buchenwald commandant in summer 1939; Stein, *Juden*, 66. More generally, see Lüerßen, "'Wir,'" 204–205.
243. *NCC*, doc. 243; Neurath, *Gesellschaft*, 115; Broszat, *Kommandant*, 169.
244. Quotes in Union, *Strafvollzug*, 29. For the use of the term "4711" in Esterwegen, Dachau, and Buchenwald, see Lüerßen, "'Wir,'" 124, 204; Burkhard, *Tanz*, 61–62; Gedenkstätte, *Buchenwald*, 78.
245. Quote in Morsch, "Formation," 148. See also Naujoks, *Leben*, 40.
246. LG Bonn, Urteil, February 6, 1959, *JNV*, vol. 15, quote on 473. More generally, see Kogon, *Theory*, 83.
247. Figures in Wünschmann, "Jewish Prisoners," 162.
248. Such Kapo posts were normally restricted to the supervision of other Jewish prisoners (Morsch, "Formation," 149; Jahnke, "Eschen"), though there were exceptions (LBIJMB, MF 425, L. Bendix, "Konzentrationslager Deutschland," 1937–38, vol. 4, 31).
249. Herz, "Frauenlager," 179–80.
250. BArchB, R 58/264, Bl. 263: Politischer Polizeikommandeur to Politische Polizeien, August 1[8] 1936; Wünschmann, "Jewish Prisoners," 141.
251. Given Himmler's keen interest in Jewish KL prisoners, he must have approved this major initiative, perhaps on the occasion of his visit to Dachau on February 16, 1937;

IfZ, F 37/19, Himmler diary. For more detail on the policy, BArchB, R 58/264, Bl. 285: Heydrich to Stapoleitstellen et al., February 17, 1937. Heydrich only referred to Jewish prisoners in protective custody and so-called instructive custody (that is, returning émigrés), but the new policy of concentrating Jews in Dachau presumably applied to Jewish men in preventive police custody, as well.

252. Wünschmann, "Cementing," 589.

253. Wünschmann, "Jewish Prisoners," 158, 166. On January 1, 1938, 2,457 prisoners were held in Dachau; DaA, ITS, Vorläufige Ermittlung der Lagerstärke (1971).

254. Dillon, "Dachau," 239. See also Burkhard, Tanz, 95–100; NCC, docs. 210 and 220.

255. ITS, ARCH/HIST/KL Dachau 4 (200), Bl. 43: LK Dachau, Führungsbericht Leo L., July 6, 1938.

256. Wünschmann, "Jewish Prisoners," 164–65; Broszat, Kommandant, 167; Eicke order of the IKL, March 1, 1937, NCC, doc. 155. The Dachau SS appears to have imposed similar isolation on Jews in 1935 and 1936.

257. Quote in Broszat, Kommandant, 169. See also ibid., 168; Eicke order of the IKL, March 1, 1937, NCC, doc. 155. On Jews as hostages, see Burrin, Hitler.

258. Quote in Hett, Crossing, 226. See also ibid., 220; "Die Erpresser von Dachau," Neuer Vorwärts, December 19, 1937; Wünschmann, "Jewish Prisoners," 164.

259. Burkhard, Tanz, 89–94; DaA, 9394, A. Lomnitz, "Heinz Eschen zum Gedenken," July 3, 1939; Litten, Mutter, 226.

260. NLHStA, 158 Moringen, Acc. 105/96, Nr. 104: G. Glogowski to H. Krack, August 26, 1937 (my thanks to Kim Wünschmann for sharing this document).

261. DaA, 9394, A. Lomnitz, "Heinz Eschen zum Gedenken," July 3, 1939; Litten, Mutter, 209–10, 225–29; Jahnke, "Eschen," 29–33; Hett, Crossing, 221–24, 227–28, 236–45; Königseder, "Regimegegner," 357–60; Wünschmann, "Jewish Prisoners," 164. For the mortality figures, see DaA, Häftlingsdatenbank.

262. Barkai, " 'Schicksalsjahr.' "

263. Evans, Third Reich in Power, 574–79, 657–61; Friedländer, Nazi Germany, 241–68; Longerich, Holocaust, 98–109.

264. Wünschmann, "Jewish Prisoners," 173. See also Neugebauer, "Österreichertransport," 195–98; Riedel, Ordnungshüter, 195.

265. Quotes in Riedel, Ordnungshüter, 196; Eichmann minute, May 30, 1938, NCC, doc. 102. More generally, see Wünschmann, "Jewish Prisoners," 182–83; Cesarani, Eichmann, 62–64; Schmid, "Aktion," 34. Several hundred more Austrian Jews arrived in Dachau on "mixed" transports with other prisoners.

266. By June 1938, there were some 2,500 Jewish prisoners in the packed Dachau camp, crammed into several barracks of the new compound. For the above, see Wünschmann, "Jewish Prisoners," 174–75, 186; A. Hübsch, "Insel des Standrechts" (1961), 88–93; M. Simon to Führer der Sturmbanne, June 10, 1938, in Merkl, General, 119.

267. Quote in Gruner, Jewish Forced Labor, 3.

268. Quote in Heydrich to Kripo, June 1, 1938, NCC, doc. 103. More generally, see Wünschmann, "Cementing," 595–97; idem., "Jewish Prisoners," 193–200, 205; Berkowitz, Crime.

269. Barkow et al., Novemberpogrom, 46; Stein, Juden, 18; Wünschmann, "Jewish Prisoners," 206; Dirks, " 'Juni-Aktion.' " For Jewish communities, see SD-Hauptamt II 112, Lagebericht, October 8, 1938, in Kulka and Jäckel, Juden, doc. 2509. For a full-length study, see Faludi, ed.,"Juni-Aktion."

270. Schmid, "Aktion," 36–37; Stein, Juden, 15; idem., "Funktionswandel," 169; Wünschmann, "Jewish Prisoners," 193.

271. Quotes in Wünschmann, "Jewish Prisoners," 202; Stein, Juden, 22. See also ibid., 19–24; Barkow et al., Novemberpogrom, 43–91; Report of the Amsterdam Jewish Central Information Office, July 1938, NCC, doc. 246.

272. Report of the Amsterdam Jewish Central Information Office, July 1938, NCC, doc. 246;

Stein, *Juden*, 24–26; idem, "Funktionswandel," 169; BwA, Totenbuch. Although they accounted for less than twenty percent of the Buchenwald prisoner population, Jews made up more than forty percent of victims in this period.

273. Quote in summary of reports by released prisoners and lawyers, late July 1938, in Barkow et al., *Novemberpogrom*, 77.

274. Dachau held around twice as many Jewish prisoners as Buchenwald in summer 1938. Between eighteen and twenty-six Jewish prisoners (the figures are not conclusive) died from June to August 1938 in Dachau, compared to at least ninety-two in Buchenwald. See DaA, Häftlingsdatenbank; BwA, Totenbuch.

275. Historians have speculated that the authorities decided to move Jewish prisoners out of Dachau at the time of the "Sudeten Crisis" to make room for prisoners expected from Czechoslovakia. In autumn 1938, following the Munich agreement, some two thousand prisoners from the Sudetenland were indeed deported to Dachau. See Wünschmann, "Jewish Prisoners," 189; Stein, *Juden*, 31–33.

276. Stein, *Juden*, 33; Neurath, *Gesellschaft*, 43.

277. BwA, Totenbuch; Stein, *Juden*, 26.

278. I am drawing closely on Wachsmann, "Policy," 139–40. See also Steinweis, *Kristallnacht*, 16–17, 36–48; Evans, *Third Reich in Power*, 580–86. For the quote, Fröhlich, *Tagebücher*, I/6, November 10, 1938, 180.

279. Fröhlich, *Tagebücher*, I/6, November 10, 1938, 181.

280. Police orders in *IMT*, vol. 25, 377–78, ND: 374–PS.

281. "Dr. Adler" quote in WL, B. 216, January 1939; the author's real name is unknown (WL to the author, May 14, 2012). See also Steinweis, *Kristallnacht*, 92–97; Wünschmann, "Jewish Prisoners," 212–13. According to one estimate, up to thirty-six thousand Jews were arrested during and after the pogrom; Pollmeier, "Verhaftungen," 168. On the Frankfurt *Festhalle*, see Gerhardt and Karlauf, *Nie mehr*, 232.

282. Kulka and Jäckel, *Juden*, docs. 2607, 2628, 2633, 2856; Steinweis, *Kristallnacht*, 92–93.

283. Quotes in Regierungspräsident Niederbayern und Oberpfalz, Monatsbericht, December 8, 1938, in Kulka and Jäckel, *Juden*, doc. 2582; SD-Unterabschnitt Württemberg-Hohenzollern, Lagebericht, February 1, 1939, ibid., doc. 2778. For other critical voices, see ibid., doc. 2624; *NCC*, doc. 296. On support for the detention of Jews, see Kulka and Jäckel, *Juden*, docs. 2587, 2631. More generally, see Longerich, *"Davon,"* 124–35; Evans, *Third Reich in Power*, 590–91.

284. Quotes in WL, B. 216, anonymous report, January 1939, translation in *NCC*, doc. 249; Stein, *Juden*, 41. See also ibid., 43; Freund, *Buchenwald!*, 36; Barkow et al., *Novemberpogrom*, 574, 608.

285. Around 6,000 Jews arrived in Sachsenhausen (November 1938); 9,828 in Buchenwald (November 10–14); 10,911 in Dachau (November 10–December 22). No Jewish men were sent to Mauthausen and Flossenbürg. See Pollmeier, "Verhaftungen," 171; Stein, *Juden*, 41; Riedel, *Ordnungshüter*, 198. The SD reported that around twenty-five thousand Jewish men had been taken to the KL after the pogrom; SD-Hauptamt II 1, Jahreslagebericht 1938, in Kulka and Jäckel, *Juden*, doc. 2766.

286. According to Werner Best, the camps had held twenty-four thousand prisoners just before the pogrom; his figure of sixty thousand prisoners after the pogrom is too high; BArchB, R 2/12164, Bl. 25–28: Best to RMi Finanzen, November 26, 1938.

287. Figure for late September 1938 in Fahrenberg and Hördler, "Lichtenburg," 169.

288. Hackett, *Buchenwald*, 250.

289. *NCC*, doc. 247; *OdT*, vol. 3, 22; Naujoks, *Leben*, 91–92.

290. Quote in WL, B. 216, anonymous report, January 1939, translation in *NCC*, doc. 249. See also Stein, *Juden*, 43–45; Wünschmann, "Jewish Prisoners," 213–14; Richarz, *Leben*, 330–31; Hackett, *Buchenwald*, 249.

291. Quotes in *NCC*, doc. 249; Freund, *Buchenwald!*, 38, 41. See also Stein, *Juden*, 44–46, 55–56; Richarz, *Leben*, 331–32; Barkow et al., *Novemberpogrom*, 523–24.

292. Quote in Naujoks, *Leben*, 93. See also Wünschmann, "Jewish Prisoners," 216–17; Pollmeier, "Verhaftungen," 176; Trouvé, "Klinkerwerk," 75.

293. *NCC*, docs. 247–49; Stein, *Juden*, 22; Trouvé, "Klinkerwerk," 75; Richarz, *Leben*, 329; Burkhard, *Tanz*, 117.

294. Quote in Sopade report, May 1937, *NCC*, doc. 220. For abuses of Jewish prisoners by fellow inmates, see Barkow et al., *Novemberpogrom*, 67, 75.

295. Wünschmann, "Cementing," 580–81, 588, 592.

296. For example, see Stein, *Juden*, 50.

297. WL, B. 216, anonymous report, January 1939, translated in *NCC*, doc. 249.

298. Quoted in Wünschmann, "Konzentrationslagererfahrungen," 53.

299. Stokes, "Das oldenburgische Konzentrationslager," 207; Meyer and Roth, "Zentrale," 210; Rudorff, "Misshandlung," 46–47.

300. For Eicke, see BArchB, Film 44564, Vernehmung O. Pohl, January 6, 1947, p. 6; Tuchel, *Konzentrationslager*, 266; *NCC*, doc. 155. For other examples of SS corruption, see Internationales Zentrum, *Nazi-Bastille*, 54–56; Hackett, *Buchenwald*, 129; Riedel, *Ordnungshüter*, 204–14; Decker, "Stadt Prettin," 214.

301. Quote in Verordnung über eine Sühneleistung der Juden, November 12, 1938, in Hirsch et al., *Recht*, 371–72. More generally, see Bajohr, *Parvenüs*, 101–20.

302. HLSL, Anklageschrift gegen Koch und andere, 1944, pp. 20–24, ND: NO-2366; BArchB (ehem. BDC), SSO, Morgen, Konrad, 8.6.1909, Bl. 854–64: Ermittlungsergebnis, December 5, 1943. For SS corruption in Dachau and Sachsenhausen after the pogrom, Naujoks, *Leben*, 92–93; Riedel, *Ordnungshüter*, 200–202.

303. Quote in Broszat, *Kommandant*, 170. See also Hackett, *Buchenwald*, 248; Stein, *Juden*, 46.

304. Jewish prisoners who died in the KL in late 1938 had overwhelmingly been arrested after the outbreak of the pogrom. No deaths of Jewish men were recorded in Mauthausen and Flossenbürg during this period, since neither camp held Jews at the time (Wünschmann, "Jewish Prisoners," 189, n. 736). For the figures, see note 111 (above) and KZ-Gedenkstätte Dachau, *Gedenkbuch*. Several hundred "November Jews" died from injuries sustained in the KL following their release; Wünschmann, "Jewish Prisoners," 215.

305. WL, B. 216, anonymous report, January 1939, translation in *NCC*, doc. 297.

306. Quote in H. Nathorff, manuscript, 1939–40, in Gerhardt and Karlauf, *Nie mehr*, 206–25, p. 225. See also Kaplan, *Dignity*, 129–44; Longerich, *Holocaust*, 114–17, 125–27; Distel, "'Warnung,'" 986; Wachsmann, "Policy," 141.

307. See also Dillon, *Dachau*, chapter 4; Stein, *Juden*, 65.

308. Wünschmann, "Jewish Prisoners," 217–20, Heydrich quote on 217; Riedel, *Ordnungshüter*, 202–203; Loritz quote on 203. See also Stein, *Juden*, 48–50, 64–65, 70; *NCC*, docs. 249, 283, 301; ITS, ARCH/KL Buchenwald, Ordner 185 A, Bl. 2: Judenaktion vom 10.11.38.

309. For the figures, see Wünschmann, *Before Auschwitz*; Friedländer, *Nazi Germany*, 241, 245, 316–17 (excluding Jews living in the Czech Protectorate and the Sudetenland).

310. Prisoner figures for the end of 1938: Buchenwald 11,028; Dachau 8,971; Flossenbürg 1,475; Lichtenburg c. 800 (figure for late November 1938); Mauthausen 994; Sachsenhausen 8,309. See Gedenkstätte Buchenwald, *Buchenwald*, 698; Drobisch and Wieland, *System*, 266, 271–72; *OdT*, vol. 4, 26; Maršálek, *Mauthausen*, 123.

311. In the first eight months of 1938, 11,631 new prisoners came to Dachau and Buchenwald; in the first eight months of 1939, 4,041 new prisoners arrived in both two camps; NMGB, *Buchenwald*, 698; DaA, ITS, Vorläufige Ermittlung der Lagerstärke (1971). For Austrian Gypsies, see Zimmermann, *Rassenutopie*, 117–18; Danckwortt, "Sinti und Roma," 81.

312. Quote in Eicke to LK, March 10, 1939, *NCC*, doc. 162. See also Drobisch and Wieland, *System*, 289, 308–309; ITS, OuS Archiv, 1.1.6.0, folder 0004/200, Bl. 47: IKL to KL

Dachau, April 13, 1939; ibid., Bl. 51: IKL to KL Dachau, April 18, 1939; ibid., Bl. 52: Sipo to KL Dachau, April 18, 1939; BArchB, R 58/264, Bl. 376–77: Heydrich to Stapostellen, April 5, 1939; HStAD, BR 1111, Nr. 188.

313. Pohl to Himmler, April 30, 1942, *IMT*, vol. 38, 363, ND: 129–R.

314. BArchB, R 2/12164, Bl. 25–28: Best to RM Finanzen, November 26, 1938; ibid., Bl. 29–32: Haushalt, December 30, 1938; IfZ, Fa 127/1, Heydrich to Pohl, January 1939; ibid., W. Best, Vermerk, December 3, 1938.

315. For example, see Evans, *Third Reich in Power*, 591; Pingel, *Häftlinge*, 94.

316. See note 111. Ninety prisoners are known to have died in the KL between January and May 1938, compared to 354 prisoners between June and August 1938.

317. In Buchenwald, "asocial" Jews were more likely to die in June 1938 than "pogrom" Jews in November 1938; Stein, *Juden*, 20, 41; BwA, Totenbuch. For prisoner perceptions at the time, see WL, B. 216, anonymous report, January 1939.

318. For the figures, see note 111.

319. Several historians imply that all, or almost all, KL fatalities in this period were Jewish men arrested after the pogrom (e.g., Fritzsche, *Life*, 138). In fact, "November Jews" made up just under half of the dead: in all, 969 prisoners are known to have died in the KL between November 1938 and January 1939; at most, 453 of them were "November Jews." For the figures, see note 111.

320. In Sachsenhausen, more "asocial" prisoners (141) than Jews (60) perished between November 1938 and January 1939. For the figures, see note 111.

321. By contrast, Karin Orth assumed that the release of Jewish prisoners resulted in a sharp fall in prisoner mortality; Orth, *System*, 53.

322. Of the 566 prisoners who died in KL between February and April 1939, 369 were classified as asocial (among them were seven "asocial" Jews). For the figures, see note 111 above.

323. For the figures, see note 111 (figures for 1939 cover the period June to August).

324. Gedenkstätte Buchenwald, *Buchenwald*, 91; Naujoks, *Leben*, 122; Applebaum, *Gulag*, 68.

325. Quote in Naujoks, *Leben*, 122.

326. Poller, *Arztschreiber*, 121–24, quotes on 123–24; Röll, *Sozialdemokraten*, 94.

4. War

1. Quote in Domarus, *Hitler*, vol. 3, 1315. See also ibid., 1311–14, 1318. Hitler got the timing wrong: Germany had started the war at 4:45 a.m. For KL prisoners, see Naujoks, *Leben*, 139; Schrade, *Elf Jahre*, 197.

2. Speech to commanders in chief, August 22, 1939, in *Akten*, D/7, p. 172, ND: 1014–PS. See also Baumgart, "Ansprache"; LaB, B Rep. 057–01, Nr. 3865, Bl. 171–80: Vernehmung E. Schäfer, September 14, 1965.

3. For this and the previous paragraph, see LaB, B Rep. 057–01, Nr. 3870, Bl. 1051–65: Vernehmung K. Hoffmann, August 15, 1969; ibid., Bl. 1072–1101: OStA Düsseldorf, Verfügung, August 26, 1969; M. Crombach, Lebenslauf, 1953, in AS, Projektordner Sender Gleiwitz; Runzheimer, "Grenzzwischenfälle"; Schrade, *Elf Jahre*, 194–96. Müller quote in " 'Grossmutter Gestorben,' " 72–73. At least one more corpse was left behind during the mock attack on Gleiwitz; this victim was not a KL prisoner but a local sympathizer of the Polish cause.

4. Figures in appendix, table 2; Beevor, *World War*, 946.

5. Fröhlich, *Tagebücher*, I/5, May 30, 1938, 325.

6. Broszat, *Kommandant*, 104.

7. The new main camps were Auschwitz, Gross-Rosen, Majdanek, Natzweiler, Neuengamme, Niederhagen, and Stutthof. Inmate figures in appendix, table 1.

8. For a different view, see Gellately, *Backing*, 261.

9. Rossino, *Hitler*, 227–29.

10. Wildt, *Generation*, 421–28, quote on 426; Rossino, *Hitler*, 53–57.

11. Rossino, *Hitler*; Böhler, *Auftakt*; Mallmann and Musial, *Genesis*. On atrocities against Jews, see Pohl, "Judenpolitik," 22–25.

12. Sydnor, *Soldiers*, 37–63, 87–312; idem, "Theodor Eicke," 155; Merkl, *General*, 137–43; Kaienburg, *Wirtschaftskomplex*, 74–77, 89; Kárný, "Waffen-SS," 242; Orth, *SS*, 157; Leleu, *Waffen-SS*, 541–677. After Eicke's death, the command of the SS Death's Head division fell to Max Simon, another prewar Camp SS veteran; Merkl, *General*.

13. Merkl, *General*, 159–60; Zámečník, *Dachau*, 113–15.

14. Orth, *SS*, 163, 171–72.

15. For this and the previous paragraph, see BArchB (ehem. BDC), SSO, Glücks, Richard, 22.4.1889; ibid., RS (ehem. BDC), B 5195, quote on Bl. 2748: Glücks to Rasse- und Siedlungshauptamt, November 19, 1935; Tuchel, *Inspektion*, 58; idem., *Konzentrationslager*, 339; IfZ, F 13/7, Bl. 383–88: R. Höss, "Richard Glücks," November 1946; Hördler, "Ordnung," 49; Moors and Pfeiffer, *Taschenkalender*, 375. Glücks's appointment came in October 1939 (Kaienburg, *Wirtschaftskomplex*, 77), and was officially confirmed on November 15, 1939. His direct subordination to Himmler apparently ended on December 31, 1941 (in staffing matters, the IKL was officially subordinated to the SS Leadership Main Office, founded on August 15, 1940); Tuchel, *Konzentrationslager*, 228.

16. Quotes in IfZ, F 13/7, Bl. 389–92: R. Höss, "Arthur Liebehenschel," November 1946; BArchB (ehem. BDC), SSO, Liebehenschel, Arthur, 25.11.01, R. Baer, Stellungnahme, July 3, 1944. See also ibid., R.u.S. Fragebogen, August 28, 1944; ibid., Film 44837, Vernehmung A. Liebehenschel, September 18, 1946; Tuchel, *Konzentrationslager*, 382; Cherish, *Kommandant*, 28. For Glücks's view, see BArchB (ehem. BDC), SSO, Höss, Rudolf, 25.11.1900, Glücks to Wander, January 14, 1941. In the mid-1930s, Liebehenschel had spent more than two years as Lichtenburg adjutant; Hördler, "SS-Kaderschmiede," 92.

17. Orth, *SS*, 60, 81; Sofsky, *Ordnung*, 121.

18. Orth, *SS*, 95–96, 99, 136–37, 181–89, 233–40.

19. Quote in IfZ, F 13/7, Bl. 387: Rudolf Höss, "Richard Glücks," November 1946. See also Orth, *SS*, 164. Orth suggests that Glücks hardly interfered with commandants, which pushes this point too far.

20. A draft was circulated to the KL in February 1940, followed by the completed version one year later; apparently, there were only a few changes to Eicke's prewar rules. BArchB, NS 4/Ma 1, Bl. 2: Glücks to LK, February 22, 1940; Himmler, DV für KL, 1941, ND: 011–USSR, *IMT*, vol. 39, pp. 262–64 (extracts); Tuchel, *Inspektion*, 100.

21. Quote in IfZ, F 13/7, Bl. 389: R. Höss, "Arthur Liebehenschel," November 1946.

22. Schulte, "London"; BArchB, NS 3/391, Bl. 4–22: Aufgabengebiete in einem KL, n.d. (1942), Bl. 5–6, 15.

23. Quote in Broszat, *Kommandant*, 204.

24. For an LK conference, see BArchB, NS 4/Na 103, Bl. 57: Glücks to LK, September 7, 1940. For informal get-togethers, StAAu, StA Augsburg, KS 22/50, Vernehmung I. Koch, April 29, 1949, p. 11.

25. From 1940, protective custody orders were completed by regional Gestapo offices, rather than centrally in Berlin; Wildt, *Generation*, 348.

26. For example, see BArchB, NS 3/425, Bl. 56: Glücks to LK, February 3, 1942; Heiber, *Reichsführer!*, docs. 109a, 184, 227; Longerich, *Himmler*, 511.

27. Moors and Pfeiffer, *Taschenkalender*, 172–73, 229, 232, 244, 325, 330, 366, 394; Schulte, "Konzentrationslager," 144.

28. Kárný, "Waffen-SS," 248; Kaienburg, *Wirtschaftskomplex*, 82.

29. IfZ, Fa 127/3, Bl. 418: SS-Hauptamt to TS et al., September 2, 1939; Kaienburg, *Wirtschaftskomplex*, 210.

30. Broszat, *Kommandant*, 104–105.

31. *Das Schwarze Korps*, December 21, 1939, in Overesch et al., *Dritte Reich*, CD-Rom, doc. 220.

32. Wegner, *Soldaten*, 124–29; Buchheim, "SS," 178; Tuchel, "Wachmannschaften," 139; Maršálek, *Mauthausen*, 190. Even the private letters of Camp SS officials were officially classified as field post, as if they were fighting at the front.

33. Buchheim, "SS," 178; idem, "Befehl," 269; Kaienburg, *Wirtschaftskomplex*, 73, 80–81, 210. See also IfZ, Fa 127/1, Bl. 165–70: T. Eicke, Einberufung der Verstärkung der TS, August 30, 1939; Tuchel, "Wachmannschaften," 138–40, 144–45.

34. Poller, *Arztschreiber*, 208.

35. Riedle, *Angehörigen*, 75; IfZ, F 13/6, Bl. 369–82: R. Höss, "Theodor Eicke," November 1946, Bl. 380; Kaienburg, *Wirtschaftskomplex*, 178–79.

36. Poller, *Arztschreiber*, 210. See also Gostner, *1000 Tage*, 137–38.

37. Quote in Zámečník, "Aufzeichnungen," 175.

38. Quotes in BArchB, NS 31/372, Bl. 116: Glücks to TS, January 22, 1940. See also BArchB, R 187/598, Erklärung E. Hinz, September 6, 1940.

39. For example, see BArchB, NS 4/Na 9, Bl. 88–89: KB, September 5, 1941.

40. Mailänder Koslov, *Gewalt*, 140; Browning, "One Day," 179.

41. K. Heimann to Herr Dostert, November 22, 1939, in Schnabel, *Macht*, 158, 165.

42. BArchB, NS 4/Bu 33, Sonderbefehl, August 31, 1939.

43. Ibid., KB, Nr. 130, November 22, 1939; ibid., KB, Nr. 128, November 9, 1939.

44. Ibid., KB, Nr. 124, October 20, 1939. See also ibid., Sonderbefehl, August 31, 1939.

45. Ibid., KB, Nr. 128, November 9, 1939.

46. Ibid., KB, Nr. 124, October 20, 1939; ibid., KB, Nr. 128, November 9, 1939.

47. Ibid., KB, Nr. 128, November 9, 1939; ibid., Sonderbefehl, August 31, 1939.

48. Ibid., KB, Nr. 130, November 22, 1939. For Koch's use of informants, see BArchB (ehem. BDC), SSO, Morgen, Konrad, 8.6.1909, Bl. 854–64: Ermittlungsergebnis, December 5, 1943.

49. BArchB, NS 4/Bu 33, KB, Nr. 128, November 9, 1939. See also ibid., KB, Nr. 126, October 31, 1939.

50. LG Bonn, Urteil, February 6, 1959, *JNV*, vol. 15, 600–601.

51. For this and the previous paragraphs, see HLSL, Anklageschrift gegen Koch und andere, 1944, ND: NO-2366; BArchB (ehem. BDC), SSO, Morgen, Konrad, 8.6.1909, Bl. 854–64: Ermittlungsergebnis, December 5, 1943. See also Kogon, *SS-Staat* (1947), 268–69; Stein and Stein, *Buchenwald*, 52–55. For Pister, see Orth, *SS*, 191–97.

52. Koch became commandant of Majdanek (see below).

53. Wachsmann, *Prisons*, 192–94.

54. Cited in Domarus, *Hitler*, vol. 3, 1316.

55. Wildt, *Generation*, passim.

56. Tuchel and Schattenfroh, *Zentrale*, 125–30; Röll, *Sozialdemokraten*, 124–34.

57. In Buchenwald, around one in seven political prisoners in the early war years was classified as a "recidivist"; *OdT*, vol. 3, 313.

58. Quotes in IfZ, Dc 17.02, Bl. 136: RKPA to Kripoleitstellen, July 7, 1939; ibid., Bl. 147: RdI to Landesregierungen et al., September 12, 1939; ibid., Bl. 157: RSHA to Kripoleitstellen, October 18, 1939.

59. Wagner, *Volksgemeinschaft*, 333.

60. IfZ, Dc 17.02, Bl. 143: RKPA to Kripoleitstellen, September 7, 1939.

61. Zámečník, *Dachau*, 116; Sládek, "Standrecht," 327; Jochmann, *Monologe*, 197.

62. Van Dam and Giordano, *KZ-Verbrechen*, quote on 215–16; *OdT*, vol. 3, 34–35; Pingel, *Häftlinge*, 100, 267. Despite this brutality, Czech prisoners initially received some privileges, probably on racial grounds; most important, they were not forced to work.

63. Ruppert, "Spanier"; Landauer, "Spanienkämpfer"; Maršálek, *Mauthausen*, 111–13.

64. Borodziej, *Geschichte*, 191–201; Noakes and Pridham, *Nazism*, vol. 3, 323–36.

65. Longerich, *Politik*, 251–92.

66. Rossino, *Hitler*, 21–22. A few months later, Oswald Pohl expected forty thousand Polish prisoners working inside Germany; Niederschrift über die Besprechung beim Reichsstatthalter am 23.1.1940, in Johe, *Neuengamme*, 52–53.

67. August, *"Sonderaktion,"* 7.

68. Broszat, "Konzentrationslager," 404; BArchB, R 58/825, Bl. 1–2: Amtschefbesprechung am 7.9.1939; Külow, "Jüdische Häftlinge," 180.

69. Herbert, *Fremdarbeiter*, 67–95. See also Wachsmann, *Prisons*, 205–206.

70. Quote in AdsD, KE, E. Büge, Bericht, n.d. (1945–46), 75. See also Kosmala, "Häftlinge," 96; Zámečník, *Dachau*, 172–73; Escher, "Geistliche," 302–303; Eisenblätter, "Grundlinien," 173.

71. By August 1940, around one-third of all Sachsenhausen prisoners were Polish (AdsD, KE, E. Büge, Bericht, n.d. [1945–46], 112). In Neuengamme, Poles even outstripped Germans by spring 1941 (Kaienburg, *"Vernichtung,"* 155).

72. Quote in Buber-Neumann, *Dictators*, 209. See also Strebel, *Ravensbrück*, 139.

73. BArchB, NS 19/4004, Bl. 278–351: Rede bei der SS Gruppenführerbesprechung, November 8, 1938, Bl. 293.

74. IfZ, Heißmeyer, Vorschlag für endgültige Standortfestlegung, n.d. (November 1939), ND: NO-1995.

75. Quote in BArchB, NS 19/1919, Bl. 4–5: Himmler to Hildebrandt, December 1939. See also ibid., Bl. 1: Glücks to Wolff, December 16, 1939; ibid., Bl. 10: Himmler to Heißmeyer, January 15, 1940; IfZ, Fa 183, Bl. 42: Himmler to Heydrich, Glücks, February 26, 1940. See also Orth, *System*, 68–69.

76. Quote in BArchB, Film 14429, Glücks to Himmler, January 30, 1940.

77. Steinbacher, *"Musterstadt,"* 26–28, 66–78; Dwork and Van Pelt, *Auschwitz*, 17–65; BArchB, NS 19/1919, Bl. 25–27: Glücks to Himmler, February 21, 1940; IfZ, Fa 183, Bl. 46: Heißmeyer to Himmler, January 25, 1940.

78. Steinbacher, *"Musterstadt,"* 28, 68–69. The area was not entirely unused (as has been suggested). In February 1940, a building company of the German army was still stationed there; BArchB, NS 19/1919, Bl. 25–27: Glücks to Himmler, February 21, 1940.

79. Steinbacher, *Auschwitz*, 22–23. See also USHMM, RG-11.001M.03, reel 32, 502-1-192, Neubauleitung Auschwitz to Hauptamt Haushalt u. Bauten, June 7, 1941; ibid., Erläuterungsbericht, November 19, 1940. The decision for Auschwitz was welcome news for the German police in Kattowitz, which had lobbied for a camp to ease the overcrowding in local jails and prisons; Konieczny, "Bemerkungen."

80. Strzelecka, "Polen," 21–24; Wildt, *Generation*, 483–84.

81. Quote in Kielar, *Anus Mundi*, 17. See also Strzelecka, "Polen," 11, 26–27; Lasik, "Organizational," 199–200.

82. Broszat, *Kommandant*, 134–36, 268–69, quote on 141. See also Orth, *SS*, 176–77; Rees, *Auschwitz*, 48.

83. For a critical SS assessment, see USHMM, RG-11.001M.03, reel 34, 502-1-218, Erläuterungsbericht, August 11, 1941.

84. Czech, *Kalendarium*, 68; Strzelecka and Setkiewicz, "Construction," 63–67.

85. Schulte, "London," 220–26 (Auschwitz figure for January 6, 1942). The Mauthausen complex (including Gusen) held well over fifteen thousand prisoners; Maršálek, *Mauthausen*, 126.

86. Among the Polish prisoners were some Jews arrested for infractions of the myriad Nazi rules; Fulbrook, *Small Town*, 164–65, 171–72, 217–18.

87. I am not including the Hinzert camp here. This camp, initially set up to discipline German workers at the Westwall (the line of fortifications on Germany's western border

684 Notes to pages 204-207

built from May 1938), had quickly gravitated toward the orbit of the KL system. It was designated an SS Special Camp in October 1939, and Himmler placed it under the control of the IKL in July 1940; the guards became members of the Death's Head SS and more foreign political prisoners arrived. But while it resembled the other KL in some respects, Hinzert—a small regional camp, holding some eight hundred prisoners on average—never fully became one. As a result of its special status, it was often excluded from the correspondence between IKL and KL. See *OdT*, vol. 5, 17–42; Orth, *System*, 94–95.

88. Kaienburg, *"Vernichtung,"* 152–56, quote on 153; Schulte, *"Konzentrationslager,"* 146.

89. Sprenger, *Groß-Rosen*, 44–46, 88–89, 100–103; Konieczny, "Groß-Rosen," 309–12; Moors and Pfeiffer, *Taschenkalender*, 366.

90. Steegmann, *Struthof*, 44–45, 323. See also BArchB, NS 4/Na 9, Bl. 75–76: KB, April 28, 1941. Natzweiler had not operated as a Sachsenhausen satellite camp from August 1940 (cf. Orth, *System*, 85).

91. BArchB, NS 3/1346, Bl. 56–76: DESt Geschäftsbericht 1940, Bl. 71; Steegmann, *Struthof*, 64 (2,428 prisoners on December 31, 1943).

92. John-Stucke, "Niederhagen." After the Niederhagen main camp closed, a few dozen prisoners stayed behind as part of a Buchenwald satellite commando. See also Schulte, *SS*; idem, "London," 224.

93. Three main KL (Gross-Rosen, Neuengamme, Niederhagen) had started out as satellite camps of Sachsenhausen, and the other two (Auschwitz and Natzweiler) had close links, too.

94. Tuchel, *Konzentrationslager*, 197–99; 389–90. The new commandant in Neuengamme, Eisfeld, was in a similar position to Rödl; Broszat, *Kommandant*, 132, 261; Kaienburg, *"Vernichtung,"* 152–53.

95. At first, prisoners arrived in the new camps via more established ones. Neuengamme only became an *Einweisungslager* (receiving prisoners directly from the police) in late 1940, Gross-Rosen in early 1942, Natzweiler in August 1942; Kaienburg, *"Vernichtung,"* 155; idem, "Funktionswandel," 259; Konieczny, "Groß-Rosen," 312; Orth, *System*, 85.

96. Quote in Hitler order, June 25, 1940, in Dülffer et al., *Hitlers Städte*, 36 (according to Speer, the order was signed on June 28, and backdated). For this and the previous paragraph, Speer to Reichsschatzmeister, February 19, 1941, in ibid., 64–79; ibid., 22–24; Speer, *Erinnerungen*, 185–88; Kershaw, *Nemesis*, 299–300; Van der Vat, *Nazi*, 94–95.

97. Kaienburg, *Wirtschaft*, 763, 768. See also BArchB, NS 3/1346, Bl. 56–76: DESt Geschäftsbericht 1940, Bl. 73.

98. Ansprache an das Offizierskorps der Leibstandarte-SS, September 7, 1940, *IMT*, vol. 29, 98–110, quote on 108, ND: 1919–PS.

99. Kaienburg, *Wirtschaft*, 26–27; Schulte, *Zwangsarbeit*, 176–78.

100. Schulte, *Zwangsarbeit*, 159–67.

101. BArchB, NS 4/Bu 31, Bl. 13: IKL to LK, April 19, 1941; Kaienburg, *Wirtschaft*, 27.

102. Kaienburg, *Wirtschaft*, 857–78; Schulte, *Zwangsarbeit*, 125–31.

103. Seidl, *"Himmel"*; Kaienburg, *Wirtschaft*, 771–92.

104. Kaienburg, *Wirtschaft*, 840–55. See also BArchB (ehem. BDC), SSO, Höss, Rudolf, 25.11.1900, Glücks to Wander, January 14, 1941.

105. Wagner, *IG Auschwitz*, 37–73; Hayes, *Industry*, xii–xvi, 347–54; Schmaltz, "IG Farbenindustrie." Wagner and Hayes disagree about the significance of the ready availability of KL labor for the decision by IG Farben to build its nearby factory.

106. BArchB, NS 3/1346, Bl. 56–76: DESt Geschäftsbericht 1940; Moors and Pfeiffer, *Taschenkalender*, 173, 229, 232, 325, 366; Kaienburg, *Wirtschaft*, 660; Maršálek, *Mauthausen*, 248; Witte et al., *Dienstkalender*, 165.

107. Kaienburg, *"Vernichtung,"* 97–112, 149–56, 190–99.
108. BArchB, NS 3/1346, Bl. 56–76: DESt Geschäftsbericht 1940; Sprenger, *Groß-Rosen*, 41–44, 88–89; Kaienburg, *Wirtschaft*, 695–96, 715–18; Jaskot, *Architecture*, 69–70; Moors and Pfeiffer, *Taschenkalender*, 330.
109. BArchB, NS 3/1346, Bl. 56–76: DESt Geschäftsbericht 1940; Kaienburg, *Wirtschaft*, 616, 626, 635, 660, 664, 671, 727–45; Maršálek, *Gusen*, 3–5. The Lungitz brick works were also attached to Gusen.
110. Quote in BArchB, NS 4/Na 103, Bl. 58: "Ein Weg zur Freiheit," n.d. (1940). See also ibid., Bl. 57: Glücks to LK, September 7, 1940; ibid., NS 3/1346, Bl. 56–76: DESt Geschäftsbericht 1940, Bl. 60.
111. Kaienburg, *Wirtschaft*, 672, 1060.
112. The creation of the DAW, for example, promised a financial windfall; Kaienburg, *Wirtschaft*, 858, 867–70.
113. StANü, Chef Amt D II, Häftlingssätze, February 24, 1944, ND: NO-576. See also Schulte, *Zwangsarbeit*, 117–19.
114. BArchB, NS 3/1346, Bl. 56–76: DESt Geschäftsbericht 1940; Kaienburg, *Wirtschaft*, 633, 681; Schulte, *Zwangsarbeit*, 440; Allen, *Business*, 85–86.
115. Kaienburg, *Wirtschaft*, 613, 637; Schulte, *Zwangsarbeit*, 119; Fabréguet, *Mauthausen*, 272–73.
116. Quotes in Levi, *If*, 95–96.
117. Quotes in Marszałek, *Majdanek*, 105; Caplan, "Gender," 95. *Muselmann* was a common German word for Muslim, widely used in the nineteenth century (*Herders Conversations-Lexikon* [1809–11], in Directmedia, *Lexika*, 51214; *Pierer's Universal-Lexikon* [1857–65], ibid., 212659). There are different theories as to why this term was applied to the living dead in the KL; Wesołowska, *Wörter*, 115–21. For the term *Muselweiber*, ibid., 120; Kremer, "Tagebuch," 219.
118. Ryn and Kłodziński, "Grenze."
119. On postwar representations, see Körte, "Stummer Zeuge." For a prominent example, see Agamben, *Remnants*, 82.
120. Quote in Szalet, *Barracke*, 97. See also Naujoks, *Leben*, 262; Maršálek, *Mauthausen*, 67.
121. For smells, see also Gigliotti, *Train Journey*, 156–57.
122. BArchB, NS 4/Bu 18, Bl. 21, 34, 37. The figure for October includes some 2,200 inmates from the temporarily closed KL Dachau. The Buchenwald figures do not include prisoners in work details absent during the roll call.
123. 6,563 prisoners (late August 1939) became 12,168 (end of 1939); AS, R 214, M 58.
124. NMGB, *Buchenwald*, 698–99.
125. BArchB, R 3001/alt R 22/1442, Bl. 125: RM Ernährung u. Landwirtschaft to Landesregierungen et al., January 16, 1940; Naujoks, *Leben*, 139; Kaienburg, "Systematisierung," 63 (n. 19).
126. Quote in IfZ, statement P. Wauer, May 21, 1945, ND: NO-1504. See also Maršálek, *Mauthausen*, 57–58.
127. DaA, 9438, A. Hübsch, "Insel des Standrechts" (1961), 222. See also August, *"Sonderaktion,"* 244.
128. LG Cologne, Urteil, April 20, 1970, *JNV*, vol. 33, p. 701. For similar cases, see LG Bonn, Urteil, February 6, 1959, *JNV*, vol. 15, 586, 596.
129. Zámečník, *Dachau*, 147; Naujoks, *Leben*, 161–62; DaA, 9438, A. Hübsch, "Insel des Standrechts" (1961), 228.
130. DaA, 9438, A. Hübsch, "Insel des Standrechts" (1961), 185.
131. AdsD, KE, E. Büge, Bericht, n.d. (1945–46), 77.
132. For a general overview, see Helweg-Larsen et al., *Famine*.
133. Naujoks, *Leben*, 159–67; Schlaak, "Wetter," 180. The IKL eventually allowed prisoners some additional clothes from home, but this came too late for many; BArchB, NS 3/425, Bl. 34: IKL to LK, September 24, 1941.

134. AdsD, KE, E. Büge, Bericht, n.d. (1945–46), 112, 138.

135. Ziółkowski, *Anfang*, 27. See also Szalet, *Baracke*, 322; Helweg-Larsen et al., *Famine*, 124–60; DaA, 9438, A. Hübsch, "Insel des Standrechts" (1961), 220–21.

136. For example, see AdsD, KE, E. Büge, Bericht, n.d. (1945–46), 138. More generally, see Süß, *"Volkskörper,"* 223–24, 233. The largest KL, Mauthausen, was hit at least twice by typhus epidemics in the early war years; Maršálek, *Mauthausen*, 47.

137. In December 1940, less than four percent of Buchenwald inmates were inside the infirmary; BArchB, NS 4/Bu 143, Schutzhaftlager-Rapport, December 2, 1940. Apparently, the Camp SS operated quotas determining how many inmates were allowed inside infirmaries. An SS doctor in Sachsenhausen who tried to change this practice in 1940 was thwarted and soon left the camp; Naujoks, *Leben*, 162, 209–10.

138. Quotes in DaA, 9438, A. Hübsch, "Insel des Standrechts" (1961), 259, 282.

139. Urbańczyk, "Sachsenhausen," 221–22.

140. Hohmann and Wieland, *Konzentrationslager*, 45–46; Naujoks, *Leben*, 162–64; Zámečník, *Dachau*, 162–66.

141. Dante, *Divine Comedy*, 241–42.

142. Quote in "The Stone Quarry," 1945, in Hackett, *Buchenwald*, 184. See also ibid., 51. For prisoner and SS references to Dante, see Levi, *If*, 115–21; SMAB, *Inmitten*, 263; Świebocki, *Resistance*, 260; Kremer, "Tagebuch," 211.

143. For one revealing case study of the SS quarry in Gross-Rosen, see Kaienburg, *Wirtschaft*, 708–15.

144. Ibid., 713.

145. Quotes in USHMM, RG-11.001M.01, reel 17, 500–5–1, Bl. 98: Chef Sipo und SD to RSHA et al., January 2, 1941; YUL, MG 1832, Series II—Trials, 1945–2001, box 10, folder 50, Bl. 1320–23: statement J. Niedermayer, February 6, 1946. More generally, see Pingel, *Häftlinge*, 81, 260 (n. 74); Dillon, *Dachau*, chapter 4; Maršálek, *Mauthausen*, 34; Kaienburg, *"Vernichtung,"* 41–42. For the *Mordhausen* reference, see Gross, *Zweitausend*, 298. Female prisoners were not affected by the classification, as there was still only one KL for women in the early war years; BArchB, NS 4/Bu 31, Bl. 3: RSHA to Sipo, July 30, 1942.

146. Prisoner files were supposed to include the classifications (BArchB, NS 4/Na 6, Bl. 12–13: Glücks to LK, July 7, 1942; ibid., Bl. 14: Liebehenschel to LK, September 4, 1942). Over time, further camps were added and the status of some camps changed. Gross-Rosen, for example, another KL with a notorious quarry, was later moved from stage two to three (BArchB, NS 4/Bu 31, Bl. 1: IKL to LK, n.d. (autumn 1942).

147. There were 3,809 registered dead in Sachsenhausen and 1,772 in Buchenwald; StANü, Pohl to Himmler, September 30, 1943, Anlage, ND: PS-1469; *OdT*, vol. 3, 347.

148. In early 1941, Auschwitz I was declared a stage 1 camp and Auschwitz II a stage 2 camp (USHMM, RG-11.001M.01, reel 17, 500–5–1, Bl. 98: Chef Sipo und SD to RSHA et al., January 2, 1941). This is perplexing, since Auschwitz was not officially divided into separate camps until autumn 1943 (see chapter 7). In any case, the Auschwitz camp as a whole was officially moved to stage 2 around autumn 1942 (BArchB, NS 4/Bu 31, Bl. 1: IKL to LK, n.d.). More generally on classifications during the second half of the war, see StANü, testimony O. Pohl, June 13, 1946, pp. 13–14, ND: NO-4728.

149. Piper, "Exploitation," 80–88; Strzelecka and Setkiewicz, "Construction," 67.

150. LG Cologne, Urteil, October 30, 1967, *JNV*, vol. 26, 751–61, quote on 756. For the figure, AM Datenbank (my thanks to Andreas Kranebitter, also for other details from the Mauthausen prisoner database used in this chapter).

151. Weiss-Rüthel, *Nacht*, 65–67, quote on 66; Kaienburg, *Wirtschaftskomplex*, 301–20; Trouvé, "Klinkerwerk," 122–35; LG Cologne, Urteil, April 20, 1970, *JNV*, vol. 33, 708–709, quote on 709.

152. For Gusen, see LG Cologne, Urteil, October 30, 1967, *JNV*, vol. 26, 752.

153. Quote in AS, 62/1, "Sachsenhausen. Mahnung und Verpflichtung," n.d., 160. See also Naujoks, *Leben*, 166–67; AdsD, KE, E. Büge, Bericht, n.d. (1945–46), 26.

154. Quotes in Vermerk H. Müller, September 8, 1939, in Engelmann, *"Sie blieben,"* 76; Heinen to his wife, ibid., 127–28; Broszat, *Kommandant*, 107. See also ibid., 106; Morsch, *Mord*, 153–55; Wysocki, "Lizenz," 238; Gürtner note, October 14, 1939, in Broszat, "Perversion," 411.

155. Hitler Proklamation, September 3, 1939, in Domarus, *Hitler*, vol. 3, 1341.

156. Gruchmann, *Justiz*, 676. See also Gürtner note, September 28, 1939, in Broszat, "Perversion," 408–409, ND: NG-190.

157. Kershaw, "Working." It is likely that Hitler had kept his initial instructions to Himmler rather general; Gürtner note, October 14, 1939, in Broszat, "Perversion," 411.

158. Quote in BArchB, R 58/243, Bl. 202–204: Chef der Sipo to Stapo(leit)stellen, September 3, 1939. See also IfZ, Himmler, Durchführungsbestimmungen für Exekutionen, January 6, 1943, ND: NO-4631; Broszat, *Kommandant*, 105.

159. BArchB, R 58/243, Bl. 209 and 215: Heydrich to Stapo(leit)stellen, September 7, 1939, and September 20, 1939.

160. Morsch, *Mord*, 158–61, quote on 158.

161. Gürtner note, September 28, 1939, in Broszat, "Perversion," 408–409, ND: NG-190; Gruchmann, *Justiz*, 677–78; Wachsmann, *Prisons*, 401–403. On the death penalty, see Evans, *Rituals*, 689–737.

162. Gruchmann, *Justiz*, 679–81; Gürtner note, October 14, 1939, in Broszat, "Perversion," 411.

163. Broszat, "Perversion," 400, 412–15; Gruchmann, *Justiz*, 686, 689.

164. Morsch, *Mord*, 79–85, quote on 83; IfZ, statement P. Wauer, May 21, 1945, ND: NO-1504; Naujoks, *Leben*, 142–43; Hohmann and Wieland, *Konzentrationslager*, 22.

165. Quote in USHMM, RG-06.025*26, File 1551, Bl. 249–67: Interrogation K. Eccarius, December 20, 1946, Bl. 263. See also AS, J SU 1/61, Anklageschrift UDSSR, October 19, 1947; ibid., D 30A, Bd. 8/2 A, Bl. 126–29: E. Eggert, "Meine Erlebnisse im Zellenbau Sachsenhausen," n.d.; ibid., D 1 A/1024, Bl. 387: Veränderungsmeldung; LG Munich, Urteil, December 22, 1969, *JNV*, vol. 33, 309–45; ITS, ARCH/HIST/KL Dachau 4 (200), Bl. 59: Glücks to LK, February 25, 1939; BArchB, R 3001/alt R 22/1467, Bl. 314–17: Besprechung mit den GStA am 23.1.1939.

166. Broszat, *Kommandant*, 107–109, quote on 107. For secret Camp SS statistics on executions, see Glücks to 1. Lagerärzte, December 28, 1942, in NMGB, *Buchenwald*, 257–58.

167. The first detailed regulations were apparently passed on October 17, 1940; IfZ, H. Müller to HSSPF, January 14, 1943, ND: NO-4631.

168. Camp SS executioners also occasionally operated outside the KL. In August 1942, for example, Flossenbürg SS men traveled to three Bavarian towns to execute Polish forced workers; NAL, HW 16/11, Flossenbürg to IKL, August 24, 1942; StAAm, StA Weiden Nr. 81/8, Bl. 1624–29: LG Weiden, Beschluss, July 15, 1955.

169. IfZ, Himmler, Durchführungsbestimmungen für Exekutionen, January 6, 1943, ND: NO-4631; ibid., MA 414, Bl. 6117: WVHA-D to LK, June 27, 1942; JVL, JAO, Review of Proceedings, *United States v. Prince zu Waldeck*, November 15, 1947, 58; Evans, *Rituals*, passim.

170. For example, see AdsD, KE, E. Büge, Bericht, n.d. (1945–46), 125.

171. Among the dead were 33 Poles executed in Sachsenhausen on November 9, 128 or more executed in Mauthausen (in six actions between November 12 and 25), and 40 in Auschwitz on November 22; AdsD, KE, E. Büge, Bericht, n.d. (1945–46), 123; LG Cologne, Urteil, October 30, 1967, *JNV*, vol. 26, 691; KL Auschwitz to IKL, November 22, 1940, in *HvA* 2 (1959), 131. More generally, see Broszat, *Polenpolitik*, passim.

172. Morsch, *Mord*, 93–95; Naujoks, *Leben*, 214–17; AdsD, KE, E. Büge, Bericht, n.d. (1945/6),

123, 150; AS, J D2/43, Bl. 86–98: Vernehmung G. Sorge, April 26, 1957; ibid., Ordner Nr. 10, Vernehmung R. Rychter, November 14, 1946.

173. In Flossenbürg, 184 Polish prisoners were executed (between February 6 and September 8, 1941) "on the order of the Reichsführer SS"; StAAm, StA Weiden Nr. 81/1, Bl. 185–87, 192–97: Augenscheinprotokoll, September 15 and 24, 1953.

174. For background, see Madajczyk, *Okkupationspolitik*, 187–89; Majer, *"Non-Germans,"* 453–54; Broszat, *Kommandant*, 154.

175. Majer, *"Non-Germans,"* 449–69, 512–19; Strebel, *Ravensbrück*, 284. In the incorporated territories, summary police courts were temporarily suspended between 1940 and 1942.

176. Steinbacher, "'Mord,'" 274–80. The first recorded session of the Auschwitz court was on January 25, 1943; Piper, *Mass Murder*, 46.

177. On the last point, see NAL, HW 16/11, Glücks to Hinzert, September 1, 1942; BArchL, B 162/7999, Bl. 768–937: StA Koblenz, EV, July 25, 1974, Bl. 906.

178. Kershaw, *Nemesis*, 271–75; Domarus, *Hitler*, vol. 3, 1415.

179. Kershaw, *"Myth,"* 146.

180. Apel, *Frauen*, 143–44, quote on 144; Szalet, *Baracke*, 193–99; LG Cologne, May 28, 1965, *JNV*, vol. 21, 112–13.

181. Kautsky, *Teufel*, 36; Hackett, *Buchenwald*, 252–53; Poller, *Arztschreiber*, 133–34; HLSL, Anklageschrift gegen Koch, ND: NO-2366, pp. 53–54; Stein, *Juden*, 93–95; LG Frankfurt a. M., Urteil, February 27, 1970, *JNV*, vol. 22, 785–87.

182. LG Frankfurt a. M., Urteil, February 27, 1970, *JNV*, vol. 22, 785. The term "willing executioners" was popularized by Goldhagen, *Executioners*.

183. HLSL, Anklageschrift gegen Koch, 1944, ND: NO-2366, pp. 53–54; LG Frankfurt a. M., Urteil, February 27, 1970, *JNV*, vol. 22, 787–88; BArchB, NS 4/Bu 18, Bl. 56.

184. Quote in HLSL, Anklageschrift gegen Koch, 1944, ND: NO-2366, p. 53. See also ibid., 57–65; Hackett, *Buchenwald*, 170–71, 196–204; LG Bayreuth, Urteil, July 3, 1958, *JNV*, vol. 14, 809–16; Anklage gegen Sommer, in Van Dam and Giordano, *KZ-Verbrechen*, 21–27.

185. Röll, *Sozialdemokraten*, 89–102; LG Nürnberg-Fürth, Urteil, October 21, 1953, *JNV*, vol. 11, 455–63.

186. Naujoks, *Leben*, 176–79. Of the 680 Sachsenhausen prisoners who died in January 1940, around 160 perished between January 18 and 20, many of them as victims of Höss's action (AdsD, KE, E. Büge, Bericht, n.d. [1945–46], 111; AS, Totenbuch; StANü, Pohl to Himmler, September 30, 1943, Anlage, ND: PS-1469).

187. In Mauthausen, lethal injections probably commenced sometime between autumn 1939 and summer 1940; Maršálek, *Mauthausen*, 162; Hördler, "Ordnung," 108–109.

188. Riedle, *Angehörigen*, 163–79; LG Bonn, Urteil, February 6, 1959, *JNV*, vol. 15, 416–21, 653–54; IfZ, statement P. Wauer, May 21, 1945, ND: NO-1504, p. 7. More generally, see Mann, *Dark Side*, 212–39; Orth, *SS*, 87–90. The cart driver Gustav Hermann had found fame in the 1920s as "Iron Gustav" by driving from Berlin to Paris; his feat inspired a novel by Hans Fallada (*Der eiserne Gustav* [Berlin, 1938]).

189. Prisoner quote in NAL, WO 208/3596, CSDIC, SIR Nr. 727, August 11, 1944; Sorge quotes in LG Cologne, Urteil, April 20, 1970, *JNV*, vol. 33, 628. See also LG Cologne, Urteil, May 28, 1965, *JNV*, vol. 21, 93–94; Kogon, *Theory*, 52; BArchB, NS 3/391, Bl. 4–22: Aufgabengebiete in einem KL, n.d. (1942), Bl. 20–21.

190. Riedle, *Angehörigen*, 204–14, quote on 208; LG Bonn, Urteil, February 6, 1959, *JNV*, vol. 15, 421–22, 655–56; AdsD, KE, E. Büge, Bericht, n.d. (1945–46), 87.

191. Quote in Naujoks, *Leben*, 179. See also LG Munich, Urteil, January 20, 1960, *JNV*, vol. 16, 277–85; Trouvé, "Bugdalle."

192. AS, J D2/43, Bl. 146–54: Vernehmung G. Sorge, May 6, 1957, quote on 147.

193. For example, see AdsD, KE, E. Büge, Bericht, n.d. (1945–46), 97–98.

194. Quote in Hohmann and Wieland, *Konzentrationslager*, 26. See also LG Bonn, Urteil, February 6, 1959, *JNV*, vol. 15, 474–75.

195. LG Bonn, Urteil, February 6, 1959, *JNV*, vol. 15, 535, 538, 601–602, quote on 571.

196. For the SS court system, see Vieregge, *Gerichtsbarkeit*, 6–17, 247–48; Longerich, *Himmler*, 501–505; Gruchmann, *Justiz*, 654–58. In theory, regular courts retained the right to prosecute alleged crimes among KL prisoners themselves. In practice, such prosecutions were very rare. For some exceptions, see Eiber, "Kriminalakte," 32–33.

197. Quote in LG Cologne, Urteil, April 20, 1970, *JNV*, vol. 33, 626.

198. Kautsky, *Teufel*, 35–36; DaA, 9438, A. Hübsch, "Insel des Standrechts" (1961), 248.

199. Browning, *Origins*, 309–30.

200. Quote in LG Cologne, Urteil, April 20, 1970, *JNV*, vol. 33, 627.

201. For Sorge, see Riedle, *Angehörigen*, 184.

202. AS, J D2/43, Bl. 146–54: Vernehmung G. Sorge, May 6, 1957, quote on 152.

203. Kershaw, "Working."

204. DaA, 9438, A. Hübsch, "Insel des Standrechts" (1961), 245.

205. Buchenwald: 802 dead (BwA, Totenbuch); Dachau: 243 (DaA, Häftlingsdatenbank); Flossenbürg: 12 (AGFl, Häftlingsdatenbank); Mauthausen: 15 (AM, Zugangslisten und Totenbücher); Sachsenhausen: 243 (AS, Totenbuch); Lichtenburg: 0 (Fahrenberg and Hördler, "Lichtenburg," 173).

206. Buchenwald: 1,838 dead (BwA, Totenbuch); Dachau: at least 1,574 (DaA, Gedenkbuch, 19); Flossenbürg: 242 (StAAm, StA Weiden Nr. 81/1, Bl. 185–87); Mauthausen-Gusen: 3,846 (Maršálek, *Mauthausen*, 146); Neuengamme: 430 (Kaienburg, *"Vernichtung,"* 473); Ravensbrück: 36 (Strebel, *Ravensbrück*, 506); Sachsenhausen: 3,809 (StANü, Pohl to Himmler, September 30, 1943, Anlage, ND: PS-1469); Auschwitz: there is no exact data, but a figure of 2,500 is a reasonable guess. For the Mauthausen percentage, see Kranebitter, *Zahlen*.

207. For emaciated corpses, see NMGB, *Buchenwald*, 177–78. More generally on causes of death in the KL, see Buggeln, *Arbeit*, 200–203.

208. AdsD, KE, E. Büge, Bericht, n.d. (1945–46), 128–29, 139–40; HLSL, Anklageschrift gegen Koch, 1944, ND: NO-2366, p. 51; Kamieński, "Erinnerung," 130.

209. Pressac, *Krematorien*, 4–15; *OdT*, vol. 4, 30.

210. In larger KL such as Mauthausen and Auschwitz, registry offices were set up in 1941 (Lasik, "Structure," 180; Maršálek, *Mauthausen*, 150). In some smaller camps, with lower death rates, registry offices were not set up until later in 1942 (StAAm, StA Weiden Nr. 81/1, Bl. 192–97: Augenscheinprotokoll, September 24, 1953; Sprenger, *Groß-Rosen*, 221).

211. Pingel, *Häftlinge*, 99–100; Fabréguet, *Mauthausen*, 168.

212. Strebel, *Ravensbrück*, 180.

213. Wachsmann, "Introduction," in Buber-Neumann, *Dictators*, vii–xxii.

214. Buber, *Dictators*, 186–93, quote on 192.

215. For reform, see IfZ, Himmler to Pohl, November 15, 1942, ND: PS-1583.

216. Ibid.; BArchB, NS 3/426, Bl. 16: Glücks to LK, January 20, 1943.

217. Strebel, *Ravensbrück*, 189–93, 250; Buber, *Dictators*, 190.

218. IfZ, Geschäftsbericht Texled, June 28, 1941, ND: NO-1221, quote on 11; Kaienburg, *Wirtschaft*, 939–77; Allen, *Business*, 72–78; Strebel, *Ravensbrück*, 213–28. The SS paid a daily rate of ten Pfennig for unskilled female labor, compared to thirty Pfennig for men.

219. Quote in Koegel to Eicke, March 14, 1939, NCC, doc. 258. See also Strebel, *Ravensbrück*, 56–65; Segev, *Soldiers*, 232–36.

220. Heike, "Langefeld," 10–16; Buber-Neumann, *Flamme*, 30–43; Buber, *Dictators*, 263–65; Strebel, *Ravensbrück*, 67–68.

221. Mailänder Koslov, *Gewalt*, 157, 483.

222. Strebel, *Ravensbrück*, 283–84. Initially, almost all the dead were Polish women accused of resistance by summary courts.

223. Calculations based on Strebel, *Ravensbrück*, 180, 293, 506, 509. Strebel argues that the death rate among men was unusually high because this subcamp was classed as a punishment camp until late 1942 (Strebel, "'Unterschiede,'" 120). However, its death rate was in fact lower than in some other KL. For the crematorium, see *OdT*, vol. 4, 476.

224. Strebel, *Ravensbrück*, 105–108, 185, 250; Buchmann, *Frauen*, 8–9.

225. Quotes in Buber-Neumann, *Dictators*, 164; Rózsa, "Solange," 186 (referring to Auschwitz in 1944). See also Amesberger et al., *Gewalt*, 70–85; Caplan, "Gender," 93–94; Strebel, *Ravensbrück*, 269–71; Suderland, *Extremfall*, 298.

226. Strebel, *Ravensbrück*, 140, 251; Buchmann, *Frauen*, 9; Schikorra, Kontinuitäten, 131.

227. Apel, *Frauen*, 47–48, 138–52, 339–44.

228. Böhler, *Auftakt*, 158.

229. Kees, "'Greuel,'" 87–126, quote on 106 (n. 69); Krzoska, "'Blutsonntag'"; Wildt, *Generation*, 432–47; Weckbecker, *Freispruch*, 442–45; Sydnor, *Soldiers*, 40.

230. Quotes in Domarus, *Hitler*, vol. 3, 1360.

231. *Deutschland-Berichte*, vol. 6, 1031–32.

232. Szalet, *Baracke*, 28–31; Külow, "Jüdische," 180–82.

233. Stein, *Juden*, 83–84. See also BArchB, NS 4/Bu 18, Bl. 48.

234. Quote in BwA, 5244–16, Bericht J. Ihr, n.d., 1. See also Stein, *Juden*, 83–88.

235. Quote in WL, P. III.g. No. 998, F. Rausch, "Allen Gewalten zum Trotz," 1959, 3. See also BArchB, NS 4/Bu 18, Bl. 53–54.

236. Hackett, *Buchenwald*, 184–86, 271–76.

237. Gedenkstätte Buchenwald, *Buchenwald*, 118.

238. BwA, 31/450, Bericht E. Frommhold, n.d. (1945), 71–72.

239. Stein, *Juden*, 88.

240. For this and the previous paragraph, see Szalet, *Baracke*, especially pages 31–42, quotes on 31, 64; Meyer, "Nachwort"; Külow, "Häftlinge," 182–83, 198; LG Cologne, Urteil, May 28, 1965, *JNV*, vol. 21, 113. Szalet's papers are held at the Leo Baeck Institute (New York), AR 10587.

241. LG Cologne, Urteil, April 20, 1970, *JNV*, vol. 33, 658; LG Bonn, Urteil, February 6, 1959, *JNV*, vol. 15, 563; Szalet, *Baracke*, 222.

242. Szalet, *Baracke*, 320. See also Külow, "Häftlinge," 191–92.

243. Quote in LG Cologne, Urteil, April 20, 1970, *JNV*, vol. 33, 627. More generally, see Wünschmann, *Before Auschwitz*, chapter 6.

244. Buber, *Dictators*, 265; Heike, "Langefeld," 15. See also Zámečník, "Aufzeichnungen," 181.

245. BArchB, R 58/1027, Bl. 128: RSHA, Vermerk, April 23, 1940.

246. For releases after April 1940, see Strebel, *Ravensbrück*, 175; Stein, *Juden*, 65.

247. Szalet, *Baracke*, quote on 417.

248. Ibid.; Meyer, "Nachwort." Szalet and his daughter left for Shanghai on May 10, 1940, and later settled in the United States.

249. Stein, *Juden*, 82.

250. Quote in LG Bonn, Urteil, February, 6, 1959, *JNV*, vol. 15, 482. See also Sprenger, *Groß-Rosen*, 125; *OdT*, vol. 1, 105; YVA, O-51/64.

251. Quote in Kwiet, "'Leben,'" 236. More generally, see Stein, *Juden*, 74–82; Naujoks, *Leben*, 210; AdsD, KE, E. Büge, Bericht, n.d. (1945–46), 139; LG Bonn, Urteil, February 6, 1959, *JNV*, vol. 15, 564–65, 578–79, 588–89.

252. Seidl, *"Himmel,"* 169–70; Zámečník, *Dachau*, 120–24. Zámečník worked on Freiland II in 1941.

253. Quote in Zámečník, "Aufzeichnungen," 173.

254. Quote in ibid., 175-76.
255. AM Datenbank. According to SS figures, 2,064 Jews were taken to this KL between 1939 and 1942; by the end of 1942, 1,985 had died; BArchB, NS 19/1570, Bl. 12-28: Inspekteur für Statistik, Endlösung der Judenfrage (1943), Bl. 24.
256. Browning, *Origins*, 203; Hilberg, *Vernichtung*, vol. 2, 610; Moore, *Victims*, 71-72; Stein, *Juden*, 96. For the use of the term "hostages," see Befehlshaber Sipo und SD, Meldungen aus den Niederlanden, Jahresbericht 1942, in Boberach, *Regimekritik*, doc. rk 1593, Bl. 420673.
257. Testimony M. Nebig, 1945, in Hackett, *Buchenwald*, 250-51 (Nebig stayed in Buchenwald and survived the war). See also Perz, "'Vernichtung,'" 97; Stein, *Juden*, 99-100; ITS, KL Buchenwald GCC 2/193, Ordner 168, KL Buchenwald to Hauptamt Haushalt und Bauten, May 21, 1941; ibid., KL Buchenwald to Deutsche Reichsbahn, May 16, 1941.
258. Quotes in AM, Totenbuch (my thanks to Andreas Kranebitter for the copy); testimony A. Kuszinsky and L. Neumeier, 1945, in Hackett, *Buchenwald*, 251-52. See also AM, Datenbank; Maršálek, *Mauthausen*, 85 (with the erroneous date June 14, 1941).
259. For example, see August, "Sonderaktion," 269; Hackett, *Buchenwald*, 251.
260. For such isolated calls, see NSDAP Kreisleitung Kitzingen-Gerolzhofen, Stimmungs-Bericht, September 4 and 11, 1939, in Kulka and Jäckel, *Juden*, docs. 2986, 2988.
261. Gruner, *Forced Labor*; Corni, *Ghettos*.
262. Moore, *Victims*, 82-83; NAL, FO 371/26683-0033, Memorandum for Political Intelligence Department, Holland, December 16, 1941; LG Munich, Urteil, February 24, 1967, *JNV*, vol. 25.
263. Maršálek, *Mauthausen*, 219, 260-61, 275 (confusing the first names of the two escapees). Just seven prisoners fled from Mauthausen in 1940.
264. Maršálek, *Mauthausen*, 145-47, 218-20, 303-304; idem, *Gusen*, 5-6, 14, 39; Fabréguet, *Mauthausen*, 167-69; *OdT*, vol. 4, 371-72. The figures for the average monthly mortality refer to the period April 1940 to June 1941.
265. Quote in BArchB (ehem. BDC), SSO, Chmielewski, Karl, 16.7.1903, Personalbericht 1940. See also ibid., Lebenslauf, n.d.; LG Ansbach, Urteil, April 11, 1961, *JNV*, vol. 17, 153-231; *OdT*, vol. 4, 373.
266. Naujoks, *Leben*, 192-94.
267. Siegert, "Flossenbürg," 458; JVL, DJAO, RaR, *United States v. E. Ziehmer*, January 16, 1948.
268. Kielar, *Anus Mundi*, 99. See also Strzelecka, "Polen."
269. Piper, *Zahl*, 153-54. This figure includes neither prisoner corpses taken straight to the crematorium, nor the thousands of Soviet POWs who perished during this period (see chapter 5).
270. Quote in Gedenkstätte Buchenwald, *Buchenwald*, 76. See also ibid., 74; Zimmermann, *Rassenutopie*, 121-22; Broszat, *Kommandant*, 31; BwA, 31/450, Bericht E. Frommhold, n.d. (1945), 67.
271. Quote in "Der Steinbruch." See also AM Datenbank; Kranebitter, *Zahlen*; Maršálek, *Mauthausen*, 305; idem, *Gusen*, 15; Pingel, *Häftlinge*, 101-102; Fabréguet, *Mauthausen*, 169; Sofsky, *Ordnung*, 142. More generally, see Pike, *Spaniards*.
272. Snyder, *Bloodlands*, 123-41, 150-51; Maršálek, *Mauthausen*, 304-305; Pingel, *Häftlinge*, 98; Naujoks, *Leben*, 196-97, 201-203.
273. Quote in Kupfer-Koberwitz, *Häftling*, 273. See also Maršálek, *Mauthausen*, 309.
274. Szalet, *Baracke*, 95, 285, quote on 388.
275. Ibid., 120-21, 125, 198, 290, 349, 351.
276. August, "Sonderaktion," 137.
277. In Mauthausen, the reasonably well-equipped infirmary was reserved for Germans, while foreign inmates were left to die in the so-called special ward (*Sonderrevier*); Maršálek, *Mauthausen*, 159-62.

278. AdsD, KE, E. Büge, Bericht, n.d. (1945–46), 31–32, 37.

279. Quote in StAMü, StA Nr. 34398, KL Dachau, Vernehmung G. Brandt, June 10, 1940. See also ibid., LG Munich, Vernehmung P. Höferle, June 10, 1940; ibid., LG Munich, Urteil, November 4, 1940. Ordinarily, prisoner deaths at the hands of other inmates were not reported to the legal authorities. For reasons that remain unclear, the Dachau SS made an exception in the case of Brüggen, who was found guilty of homicide by the Munich District Court and sentenced to eight years in a penitentiary. For background, see Eiber, "Kriminalakte," 20–21, 32.

280. AdsD, KE, E. Büge, Bericht, n.d. (1945–46), 98–99.

5. Mass Extermination

1. Mennecke to his wife, letters of April 2, 4, 5, and 6, 1941, in Chroust, *Mennecke*, 183–85, 192; ibid., 1–14; Kersting, *Anstaltsärzte*, 286–96; Ley and Morsch, *Medizin*, 309–10; Klee, *"Euthanasie,"* 226; idem, *Was sie taten*, 301 (n. 19); Burleigh, *Death*, 222; StANü, Pohl to Himmler, September 30, 1943, ND: 1469–PS.

2. Quotes in Mennecke to his wife, April 4, 1941, in Chroust, *Mennecke*, 185. See also ibid., 185, 191–96; Hohmann and Wieland, *Konzentrationslager*, 27. In 1965, a GDR court sentenced Hebold to life imprisonment; he died in jail in 1975; Klee, *Personenlexikon*, 234–35.

3. Quotes in AS, P 3 Hüttner, Johann/1, part 1 and 2, Interview J. Hüttner, n.d. (early 1970s; my thanks to Monika Liebscher for this document); BStU, MfS HA IX/11 ZUV 45 Bd. 1, Bl. 362–64: Vernehmung O. Hebold, October 23, 1964, Bl. 363. See also AdsD, KE, E. Büge, Bericht, n.d. (1945–46), 141; Naujoks, *Leben*, 247–49; Ley and Morsch, *Medizin*, 317.

4. Hohmann and Wieland, *Konzentrationslager*, 27; Naujoks, *Leben*, 247–48; AdsD, KE, E. Büge, Bericht, n.d. (1945–46), 141.

5. Quote in BStU, MfS HA IX/11 ZUV 45 Bd. 1, Bl. 358–61: Vernehmung O. Hebold, August 12, 1964, Bl. 360. See also Mennecke to his wife, April 7, 1941, in Chroust, *Mennecke*, 195.

6. Naujoks, *Leben*, 248–49, quote on 249; Ley, "'Aktion,'" 235 (n. 16); Hohmann and Wieland, *Konzentrationslager*, 27. My thanks to Astrid Ley for the dates of these transports.

7. Mennecke to his wife, April 7, 1941, March 18, 1942, in Chroust, *Mennecke*, 195, 335; BArchL, B 162/7995, Bl. 271–304: Aussage F. Mennecke, January 16–17, 1947, Bl. 289–91.

8. Quote in Friedlander, *Genocide*, 93. More generally, see ibid., passim; Burleigh, *Death*; Schmuhl, "Bouhler."

9. Witte et al., *Dienstkalender*, 111 (n. 46); In 't Veld, *SS*, 323; Moors and Pfeiffer, *Taschenkalender*, 244.

10. Glücks's order is summarized in StANü, KL Buchenwald, Hauptabteilung I/5 to Koch, October 28, 1940, ND: NO-2102. The security police described Dachau as a place for prisoners who were old and partially able to work on the plantation; IfZ, RSHA, AE, 2. Teil, Bl. 204–205: Heydrich to RSHA et al., January 2, 1941.

11. ITS, KL Sachsenhausen GCC 10/84, Ordner 93; AdsD, KE, E. Büge, Bericht, n.d. (1945–46), 112, 136; USHMM, RG-06.025*26, File 1558, Bl. 157–75: Vernehmung G. Sorge, December 19, 1946, Bl. 173.

12. Stein, "Vernichtungstransporte," quotes on 35; ITS, KL Buchenwald GCC 2/191, Ordner 164, Transport nach Dachau, October 24, 1940.

13. DaA, 9438, A. Hübsch, "Insel des Standrechts" (1961), quotes on 252–53.

14. DaA, ITS, Vorläufige Ermittlung der Lagerstärke (1971).

15. Zámečník, *Dachau*, 162–64, quote on 163 (diary entry for February 4, 1941).
16. Quotes in Stein, "Vernichtungstransporte," 35.
17. AdsD, KE, E. Büge, Bericht, n.d. (1945–46), 112.
18. This was largely a result of the terrible conditions inside. In addition, the Dachau SS partially subverted Glücks's orders by sending some of "their" invalids to other camps; Stein, "Vernichtungstransporte," 35 (n. 19).
19. LG Frankfurt a. M., Urteil, May 27, 1970, *JNV*, vol. 34, 215.
20. Quote in DaA, 9438, A. Hübsch, "Insel des Standrechts" (1961), 253.
21. For the term "cumulative radicalization," see Mommsen, "Radicalization."
22. Goerdeler, "Zeit" (written in November 1940).
23. Himmler talked about "euthanasia" with Brack on January 13, 1941 (Witte et al., *Dienstkalender*, 107). For the discussion with Bouhler, LG Frankfurt a. M., Urteil, May 27, 1970, *JNV*, vol. 34, 215.
24. Friedlander, *Genocide*, 68, 142–43; Berger, *Experten*, 41, 300–301.
25. LG Frankfurt a. M., Urteil, May 27, 1970, *JNV*, vol. 34, 273; Witte et al., *Dienstkalender*, 141.
26. LG Frankfurt a. M., Urteil, May 27, 1970, *JNV*, vol. 34, 215.
27. Quotes in August, "Auschwitz," 72, citing notes by M. Grabner; StANü, WVHA to LK, March 26, 1942, ND: 1151-P-PS. See also ibid., EE by Dr. J. Muthig, April 16, 1947, ND: NO-2799; LG Cologne, Urteil, October 30, 1967, *JNV*, vol. 26, 722; HLSL, EE by Dr. W. Hoven, October 1946, ND: NO-429.
28. StANü, Aussage W. Neff, December 17, 1946, ND: NO-2637; StAMü, StA Nr. 34868/18, Vernehmung H. Schwarz, July 11, 1960; ibid., Vernehmung W. Leitner, October 17, 1961; Zámečník, *Dachau*, 215. For quotas, see StANü, SlF to Kommandantur Gross-Rosen, December 16, 1941, ND: 1151-G-PS.
29. For most of the dates, see Ley, "'Aktion,'" 235–40, with corrections and additions from Chroust, *Mennecke*, 265–70, 318–21. The list of camps is not complete. According to an IKL document of November 12, 1941 (see StANü, IKL to LK, December 10, 1941, ND: 1151-C-PS), return visits by T-4 doctors to Dachau, Sachsenhausen, Auschwitz, and Mauthausen were scheduled before the end of the year. At least the visit to Mauthausen appears to have taken place; in addition, T-4 doctors were also scheduled to visit Niederhagen, sometime in early 1942.
30. In addition to Nitsche and Heyde, the doctors included Dr. Mennecke, Dr. Steinmeyer, Dr. Wischer, Dr. Lonauer, Dr. Renno, Dr. Robert Müller, Dr. Schmalenbach, Dr. Ratka, Dr. Gorgass, and Dr. Hebold. For personal details, see Klee, *"Euthanasie,"* 227–29, 242–43.
31. For visits to asylums, see Klee, *"Euthanasie,"* 242–48; Chroust, *Mennecke*, 6.
32. Mennecke to his wife, November 19, 1941, in Chroust, *Mennecke*, 203–204; BArchL, B 162/7995, Bl. 271–304: Aussage F. Mennecke, January 16–17, 1947, Bl. 296.
33. For example Zámečník, "Aufzeichnungen," 185–86.
34. For example Mennecke to his wife, November 20, 1941, in Chroust, *Mennecke*, 205.
35. Quotes in HLSL, Meldebogen 1, ND: 1151-A-PS. For the early use of the form, during selections in Buchenwald in summer 1941, BArchL, B 162/7996, Bl. 360–64: Vernehmung R. Gottschalk, November 14, 1960.
36. StAMü, StA Nr. 34868/18, Vernehmung K. Zimmermann, February 25, 1960; Mennecke to his wife, November 26, 1941, in Chroust, *Mennecke*, 243; Zámečník, "Aufzeichnungen," 185.
37. Quotes in Mennecke to his wife, September 3, 1941, and November 20, 1941, in Chroust, *Mennecke*, 199, 205. Calculations based on Mennecke to his wife, April 7, 1941, November 22, 1941, in ibid., 195, 222. Selections also sped up because Camp SS officials now completed more details on forms before the arrival of T-4 doctors; StANü, IKL to LK, December 10, 1941, ND: 1151-C-PS.
38. For the exemption of some veterans from the "euthanasia" action, see Friedlander,

Genocide, 81. The T-4 forms used in the KL asked about war injuries (HLSL, Meldebogen 1, ND: 1151–A-PS); consequently, some T-4 doctors questioned prisoners as to whether they had been wounded; StAMü, StA Nr. 34868/18, Vernehmung H. Schwarz, July 11, 1960; StANü, Aussage W. Neff, December 17, 1946, ND: NO-2637.

39. LG Frankfurt a. M., Urteil, May 27, 1970, *JNV*, vol. 34, 217. For the standard "euthanasia" form, see Klee, *"Euthanasie,"* 176.

40. This procedure of the "euthanasia" program (Friedlander, *Genocide*, 83) was also applied to 14f13; BArchL, B 162/7996, Bl. 360–64: Vernehmung R. Gottschalk, November 14, 1960.

41. StANü, testimony Dr. Mennecke, n.d., ND: NO-2635, pp. 7, 14.

42. StANü, Pflegeanstalt Bernburg to KL Gross-Rosen, March 3, 1942, ND: 1151–J-PS.

43. BArchL, B 162/1281, Bl. 18–23: Vernehmung Walter M., October 23, 1964.

44. NAL, HW 16/18, KL Flossenbürg to IKL, May 12, 1942.

45. LG Frankfurt a. M., Urteil, May 27, 1970, *JNV*, vol. 34, 219–21, 233, 245, 248–49, 261, 275; LG Cologne, Urteil, October 30, 1967, ibid., vol. 26, 718; Friedlander, *Genocide*, 95–97; Trunk, "Gase," 27–30.

46. For this view, see Lifton, *Doctors*, 419; Todorov, *Facing*, 241. Lifton draws on the Mennecke papers, but appears to disregard some of the evidence. For similar criticism, see Burleigh, *Death*, 224.

47. His letters (and the replies from his wife) are reprinted in Chroust, *Mennecke*. His verbosity proved his undoing: after the war, the letters were used as evidence against him in court and contributed to his death sentence.

48. Mennecke to his wife, November 28, 1941, in Chroust, *Mennecke*, 248.

49. BArchL, B 162/7996, Bl. 310–20: Vernehmung E. Mennecke, June 1–2, 1960.

50. Mennecke to his wife, November 21, 1940 (wrongly dated 1941), in Chroust, *Mennecke*, 177.

51. Mennecke to his wife, December 2, 1941, and November 29, 1941, in ibid., 269, 253.

52. Around two thousand prisoners perished in Dachau during the first half of 1941. DaA, ITS, Vorläufige Ermittlung der Lagerstärke (1971); Kimmel, "Dachau," 385.

53. Mennecke to his wife, September 3 and 4, 1941, in Chroust, *Mennecke*, 197–200; Ley, "'Aktion,'" 241 (n. 35); BArchL, B 162/491, Bl. 229–50: LG Limburg, Vernehmung W. Heyde, November 20, 1961, Bl. 244.

54. Quote in Zámečník, "Aufzeichnungen," 185. For other camps, see Kłodzinski, "'Aktion,'" 138, 142.

55. StAMü, StA Nr. 34868/18, Vernehmung K. Krämer, August 27, 1960.

56. LG Frankfurt a. M., Urteil, May 27, 1970, *JNV*, vol. 34, 217.

57. For the "euthanasia" program, see Friedlander, *Genocide*, 89–96.

58. Friedlander, *Genocide*, 106–107.

59. Mennecke to his wife, April 2 and 4, 1941, in Chroust, *Mennecke*, 183, 185; Bezirksgericht Cottbus, Urteil, July 12, 1965, in Rüter, *DDR-Justiz*, vol. 2, 730.

60. Stein, "Vernichtungstransporte," 38.

61. Kogon et al., *Massentötungen*, 66; BArchL, B 162/7996, Bl. 360–64: Vernehmung R. Gottschalk, November 14, 1960.

62. Stein, *Juden*, 110.

63. For this and the previous two paragraphs, see Mennecke to his wife, November 19–22, 1941, November 25, 1941, January 5, 1942, January 6, 1942, January 12, 1942, January 14, 1942, in Chroust, *Mennecke*, 202–10, 221–27, 236–41, 284–90, 312–16, 318–30, quotes on 207, 208 (partially underlined in original). See also Ley, "'Aktion,'" 238–39; Strebel, *Ravensbrück*, 323–36.

64. In November 1941 and January 1942, the Ravensbrück SS apparently presented 334 men (forty-two percent of all male prisoners) and 810 women (twelve percent of all fe-

male prisoners) to Mennecke; Chroust, *Mennecke*, 205, 208–209, 222; Ley, "'Aktion,'" 239 (n. 26, with slightly different calculations).

65. Quotes in Mennecke to his wife, November 25, 1941, in Chroust, *Mennecke*, 237; F. Itzkewitsch to his son, June 29, 1941, in Stein, *Juden*, 107. See also ibid., 100–110; idem, "Vernichtungstransporte," 39–40, 43–45, 49–50; BArchL, B 162/7996, Bl. 360–64: Vernehmung R. Gottschalk, November 14, 1960; Kłodzinski, "'Aktion,'" 139–40.

66. Kłodzinski, "'Aktion,'" 143–44; StAMü, StA Nr. 34868/18, Vernehmung F. Eberlein, November 30, 1961.

67. Quotes in BArchL, B 162/7996, Bl. 360–64: Vernehmung R. Gottschalk, November 14, 1960; Stein, "Vernichtungstransporte," 50.

68. For example, see August, "Auschwitz," 81–83.

69. LG Frankfurt a. M., Urteil, May 27, 1970, *JNV*, vol. 34, 217, 220; Kłodzinski, "'Aktion,'" 141–42. For the efforts by a Dachau Kapo to save some "invalids" from the transports, see StAMü, StA Nr. 34433, LG Munich, Urteil, December 30, 1948.

70. Of the 510 Gusen prisoners gassed in Hartheim in August 1941, four hundred seventy-five came from Poland or Spain; ITS, ARCH/KL Mauthausen, Ordner 231. See also Maršálek, *Gusen*, 15.

71. Ley, "'Aktion,'" 238.

72. In Ravensbrück, "asocial" men made up four percent of the prisoner population but fourteen percent of the victims of Action 14f13 (Strebel, *Ravensbrück*, 302, 332). In Sachsenhausen, 115 of 269 men taken to Sonnenstein in June 1941 were classed as professional criminals, far exceeding their share among the prisoner population (Külow, "Häftlinge," 194).

73. HLSL, Meldebogen 1, ND: 1151–A-PS; StANü, IKL to LK, December 10, 1941, ND: 1151–C-PS; Zámečník, "Aufzeichnungen," 185–86. For the impact of "criminality" and "asociality" on T-4 selections in asylums, see LG Frankfurt a. M., Urteil, May 27, 1970, *JNV*, vol. 34, 196.

74. Mennecke to his wife, April 7, 1941, in Chroust, *Mennecke*, 195.

75. Many men sent as invalids from other KL to Dachau in 1940 were Jews. The transports from Sachsenhausen in September 1940 contained almost half of all the Jewish prisoners in the camp (Külow, "Häftlinge," 198). And a transport from Buchenwald on October 24, 1940, included 169 Jews among its 371 prisoners (ITS, KL Buchenwald GCC 2/191, Ordner 164, Transport nach Dachau, October 24, 1940).

76. Friedlander, *Genocide*, 263–83. For the classification of working Jewish prisoners as unemployed, BArchB, NS 4/Bu 143, Unbeschäftigte, October 14, 1940; ibid., Unbeschäftigte, January 6, 1941; ibid., Unbeschäftigte, January 4, 1941.

77. BwA, KL Buchenwald, Transportliste, July 14, 1941; ibid., Transport II, July 15, 1941; BArchB, NS 4/Bu 143, Schutzhaftlager-Rapport, July 6, 1941.

78. As note 77, above. On average, the Buchenwald Jews gassed in Sonnenstein in mid-July 1941 were over fifty years old.

79. Testimony Dr. Mennecke, January 16–17, 1947, in Mitscherlich and Mielke, *Medizin*, 215–16, and BArchL, B 162/7995, Bl. 271–304. When Mennecke came to Buchenwald in November 1941, he expected that 1,200 Jews would be examined (note 82, below)— almost all the approximately 1,400 Jews in the camp at the time (BArchB, NS 4/Bu 143, Schutzhaftlager-Rapport, November 30, 1941).

80. Longerich, *Holocaust*, 219–304.

81. The extension of Action 14f13 may well have caused the flurry of confusing orders Mennecke received in Ravensbrück in November, just before he went to Buchenwald; Strebel, *Ravensbrück*, 324–25.

82. Mennecke to his wife, November 26, 1941, in Chroust, *Mennecke*, 243; BArchB, NS 4/Bu 143, Schutzhaftlager-Rapport, November 30, 1941.

83. Quote in Mennecke to his wife, November 26, 1941, in Chroust, *Mennecke*, 243.

84. Stein, *Juden*, 117; Schulte, "London," 221.

85. HLSL, LK Gross-Rosen to Pflegeanstalt Bernburg, March 6, 1942, ND: 1151–K-PS; ITS, OuS Archiv, 1.1.5.1., Ordner 679, Lagerarzt Buchenwald to Pflegeanstalt Bernburg, February 2, 1942.

86. This caused some disagreements with the Camp SS. In Gross-Rosen, the SS held back forty-two Jewish men earmarked by T-4 for the gas chambers, because they were still fit for work; HLSL, LK Gross-Rosen to WVHA, March 26, 1942, ND: 1151–N-PS.

87. Testimony Dr. Mennecke, January 16–17, 1947, in Mitscherlich and Mielke, *Medizin*, 215–16, and BArchL, B 162/7995, Bl. 271–304.

88. HLSL, ND: NO-3060; Hördler, "Ordnung," 103. For Mennecke's ambitions, see his letter to his wife, April 7, 1941, in Chroust, *Mennecke*, 195.

89. Quotes on photos in HLSL, ND: NO-3060. See also Strebel, *Ravensbrück*, 325; Stein, *Juden*, 117.

90. Quote on photo in HLSL, ND: NO-3060. See also ITS, docs. 6891552–6891562; BwA, Nachtrag zur Veränderungsmeldung vom 12. März 1942. Radinger was a "second-time-rounder." He had first been arrested in June 1938 and was detained in Dachau and Buchenwald until his release in August 1939. He was rearrested in June 1940 and taken back to Buchenwald in August 1940.

91. Dates in Ley, "'Aktion,'" 240; Römmer, "'Sonderbehandlung.'"

92. Action 14f13 claimed the lives of at least 269 prisoners from Sachsenhausen; 575 from Auschwitz; 571 from Buchenwald; 295 from Neuengamme; around 1,000 from Ravensbrück (estimate; Mennecke is known to have examined c. 1,150 prisoners in November 1941 and January 1942). For these figures, see Ley, "'Aktion,'" 235–36, 239–40. In addition, Action 14f13 claimed 127 prisoners from Gross-Rosen (HLSL, LK Gross-Rosen to WVHA, March 26, 1942, ND: 1151–N-PS) and 209 prisoners from Flossenbürg (NAL, HW 16/18, KL Flossenbürg to IKL, May 12, 1942). Action 14f13 also claimed 2,013 men from Dachau, in two waves of transports to Hartheim (1,452 men between January 15 and March 3, 1942, and 561 men between May 4 and June 11, 1942; ITS, KL Dachau GCC 3/92 II E, Ordner 152, Invaliden-Transporte KL Dachau, May 18, 1945). It has been argued that this second wave of transports from Dachau was not really part of Action 14f13, including instead prisoners selected autonomously by Dachau SS doctors (Ley, "'Aktion,'" 238). This seems unlikely, since the transports fall into the period of the main Action 14f13, and since a second round of T-4 selections had been scheduled for Dachau in this period (StANü, IKL to LK, December 10, 1941, ND: 1151–C-PS). Furthermore, Action 14f13 claimed c. 1,380 prisoners from Mauthausen, deported to Hartheim in three waves in August 1941, December 1941, and January–February 1942 (Maršálek, *Mauthausen*, 222–23, 225, 227). Given the overall course of Action 14f13 and the fact that a return to Mauthausen by the T-4 commission was imminent toward the end of 1941 (StANü, IKL to LK, December 10, 1941, ND: 1151–C-PS), the deportations to Hartheim in late 1941/early 1942 must have formed part of Action 14f13 rather than marking an independent initiative by the local Camp SS (cf. Ley, "'Aktion,'" 237).

  The real number of victims was higher still, since the number of murdered Niederhagen prisoners is unknown (*OdT*, vol. 7, 23). Also, further T-4 selections may have been carried out in late 1941 or early 1942 in Auschwitz and Sachsenhausen (StANü, IKL to LK, December 10, 1941, ND: 1151–C-PS).

93. StANü, WVHA to LK, March 26, 1942, ND: 1151–P-PS. By now, the IKL was officially called Office Group D of the WVHA (see chapters 6 and 8). However, I will continue to use the term Camp Inspectorate in this chapter to avoid confusion.

94. On paper, the program continued into 1943; as late as April 1943, Glücks still referred to selections by T-4 doctors (DaA, 3220, WVHA to LK, April 27, 1943). However, there is no evidence for any visits after spring 1942 (Ley, "'Aktion,'" 234, 240).

95. See also Orth, *System*, 133–34.

96. The Sachsenhausen SS sent 232 prisoners to Bernburg in October 1942 (Ley and

Morsch, *Medizin*, 320). The Dachau SS sent over 500 prisoners to Hartheim between August and December 1942 (ITS, KL Dachau GCC 3/92 II E, Ordner 152, Invaliden-Transporte KL Dachau, May 18, 1945, September 20, 1968). Sonnenstein and Bernburg stopped operating in 1942, Hartheim did not operate in 1943 (Ley, "'Aktion,'" 234).

97. Stein, *Juden*, 110–12; Hackett, *Buchenwald*, 76–77.

98. LG Ansbach, Urteil, April 11, 1961, *JNV*, vol. 17, 174–78; LG Hagen, Urteil, October 29, 1968, ibid., vol. 30. For more detail, see Orth, *System*, 134–37.

99. Quote in NAL, WO 235/307, Examination of Dr. Rosenthal, January 21, 1947, 25. See also Strebel, *Ravensbrück*, 243, 248–49; Klee, *Auschwitz*, 22–23; Hördler, "Ordnung," 139–41; Kaienburg, "Funktionswandel," 265; HLSL, Anklageschrift gegen Koch, 1944, ND: NO-2366, p. 58.

100. This is what happened in Mauthausen. See Maršálek, *Mauthausen*, 46, 94; YUL, MG 1832, Series II—Trials, 1945–2001, Box 10, folder 50, Bl. 1326–27: statement J. Niedermayer, February 11, 1946.

101. The SS sometimes still used the code name "Action 14f13" for these murders; NAL, HW 16/11, Maurer to LK Dachau, October 29, 1942.

102. Quotes in HLSL, Anklageschrift gegen Koch, 1944, ND: NO-2366, pp. 47, 69. Several Camp SS officials testified after the war that they had received orders to murder sick, infirm, and infectious prisoners; YVA, Tr-10/1172, LG Düsseldorf, Urteil, June 30, 1981, 78; IfZ, EE by F. Entress, April 14, 1947, ND: NO-2368.

103. Quote in BArchB, NS 3/425, Bl. 119: WVHA to LK, November 4, 1942. On the afternoon of October 29, 1942, the IKL informed the Dachau commandant about the plan to move most "infirmary patients" from other KL to Dachau, and made clear the murderous intentions behind this order (NAL, HW 16/11, Maurer to LK Dachau, October 29, 1942). The first of these transports was in fact already under way. Early the same day, the Buchenwald SS had cabled Dachau that a group of 181 "debilitated and invalid prisoners" was about to depart (NAL, HW 16/11, KL Buchenwald to KL Dachau, October 29, 1942). The old program of deporting "invalids" to Dachau had never been fully abandoned, it seems, although the number of transports had declined in the wake of mass killings elsewhere (for one transport in summer 1942, see NAL, HW 16/21, GPD Nr. 3, Pister to WVHA-D, August 24, 1942).

104. The former Sachsenhausen commandant Kaindl testified that more than five thousand invalid prisoners were sent from his camp to Dachau for extermination between 1942 and 1944; BStU, MfS HA IX/11, ZUV 4/23, Bl. 320–46: Vernehmungsprotokoll, September 16, 1946, Bl. 344.

105. Tired of corpses spilling out of the trains, the Dachau SS complained to the IKL, which duly banned transfers of prisoners who were about to die. BArchB, NS 3/425, Bl. 119: WVHA to LK, November 4, 1942.

106. Zámečník, "Aufzeichnungen," 206–10, quote on 210; Kupfer-Koberwitz, *Tagebücher*, 31–32, 36, 41.

107. Zámečník, "Aufzeichnungen," 213–14; DaA, A 3675, testimony F. Blaha.

108. For a direct link between "invalid transports" and the construction of the Dachau gas chamber, see Rascher to Himmler, August 9, 1942, in Comité, *Dachau* (1978), 161. By contrast, it is highly unlikely that the gas chamber was built for the mass murder of Soviet POWs (cf. Zámečník, *Dachau*, 297–98), since their systematic killing actually ended around the time the construction began. For background, see Distel, "Gaskammer."

109. For Mauthausen, see Maršálek, *Mauthausen*, 174; YUL, MG 1832, Series II—Trials, 1945–2001, Box 10, folder 50, Bl. 1326–27: statement J. Niedermayer, February 11, 1946.

110. Overy, *Russia's War*, 72–85; Kershaw, *Nemesis*, 388–93.

111. Halder diary, in Noakes and Pridham, *Nazism*, vol. 3, 483.

112. Gerlach, *Krieg*, 15–30; Aly and Heim, *Vordenker*, 365–76.

113. Jochmann, *Monologe*, 60; OKW, Kriegsgefangenenwesen, June 16, 1941, ND: PS-888, in Jacobsen, "Kommissarbefehl," doc. 23, pp. 510–12.

114. Quote in Rosenberg to Keitel, February 28, 1942, in Michaelis and Schraepler, *Ursachen*, vol. 17, 350. More generally, see Gerlach, *Krieg*, 30–56.

115. OKW, Richtlinien für Behandlung politischer Kommissare, June 6, 1941, in Jacobsen, "Kommissarbefehl," doc. 12, pp. 500–503. See also ibid., 457–58; Neitzel and Welzer, *Soldaten*, 122, 199; Römer, *Kommissarbefehl*, passim.

116. Quotes in RSHA, Einsatzbefehl Nr. 8, July 17, 1941, in Jacobsen, "Kommissarbefehl," doc. 24, pp. 512–16.

117. Quote in Keller and Otto, "Kriegsgefangene," 22. See also Otto, *Wehrmacht*, 61–69, 111.

118. For figures, see Gestapo Regensburg to RSHA, January 19, 1942, *IMT*, vol. 38, 452–54, ND: 178–R. For Jews, see Nolte, "Vernichtungskrieg"; Römer, *Kommissarbefehl*, 299.

119. Keller and Otto, "Kriegsgefangene," 20.

120. Otto, *Wehrmacht*, 110–11.

121. Gestapo Munich, Überprüfung der russischen Kriegsgefangenen, November 15, 1941, *IMT*, vol. 38, 424–28, ND: 178–R.

122. RSHA, Einsatzbefehl Nr. 8, July 17, 1941, in Jacobsen, "Kommissarbefehl," doc. 24, pp. 512–16.

123. Quote in RSHA, Einsatzbefehl Nr. 9, July 21, 1941, in Jacobsen, "Kommissarbefehl," doc. 26, pp. 517–19. See also Otto, *Wehrmacht*, 33–38.

124. Otto, *Wehrmacht*, 9, 71; StANü, EE by P. Ohler, August 15, 1947, ND: NO-4774; BArchL, B 162/16613, Bl. 15–32: Vernehmung Erwin S., October 11, 1965. Some POW transports were carried out by bus or truck, not train.

125. AdsD, KE, E. Büge, Bericht, n.d. (1945–46), 171.

126. Müller to Gestapoleitstellen et al., November 9, 1941, *IMT*, vol. 27, 42–44, ND: 1165–PS.

127. Quote in Johe, "Volk," 339–40. For reactions elsewhere, see Steinbacher, *Dachau*, 184–85.

128. Quote in Müller to Gestapoleitstellen et al., November 9, 1941, *IMT*, vol. 27, 42–44, ND: 1165–PS.

129. Keller and Otto, "Kriegsgefangene," 33, 41; Ibel, "Kriegsgefangene," 120; Römer, *Kommissarbefehl*, 567. For further KL executions of "commissars" in 1942–43, LaB, B Rep. 057–01, Nr. 296, GStA Berlin, Abschlussvermerke, November 1, 1970, 142–44, 224–27.

130. There are no reports of executions in Natzweiler, while executions in Neuengamme remained highly exceptional (Otto, *Wehrmacht*, 268). Although it has been suggested that no women were selected in POW camps on German soil (Strebel, "Feindbild," 164), there are reports of female prisoners being executed alongside male "commissars" in Dachau (Zámečník, "Aufzeichnungen," 186).

131. Figures in *OdT*, vol. 3, 64.

132. Orth, *System*, 124–26; Riedel, *Ordnungshüter*, 257–58; AS, JD 21/66 T1, Vernehmung G. Sorge, August 5, 1946 (my thanks to Jörg Wassmer for this document). The meeting cannot have taken place before early August (cf. Orth) because Eicke was recuperating until then in a Berlin hospital; BArchB (ehem. BDC), SSO, Eicke, Theodor, 17.10.1892, Universitätsklinik to Himmler, August 4, 1941.

133. BArchB (ehem. BDC), SSO, Eicke, Theodor, 17.10.1892, Totenkopfdivision to Reichsführer SS, July 7, 1941. More generally, see Sydnor, *Soldiers*, 152–66.

134. Quote in BArchB (ehem. BDC), SSO, Eicke, Theodor, 17.10.1892, Himmler to Frau Eicke, March 2, 1943. See also Witte et al., *Dienstkalender*, 199–200; Hördler, "Ordnung," 111; IfZ, F 13/6, Bl. 369–82: R. Höss, "Theodor Eicke," November 1946, Bl. 380–81; Tuchel, *Inspektion*, 50.

135. Quote in AS, J D2/43, Bl. 86–98: Vernehmung G. Sorge, April 26, 1957, Bl. 89. For Eicke's injuries, see BArchB (ehem. BDC), SSO, Eicke, Theodor, 17.10.1892, Universitätsklinik to Himmler, August 4, 1941.

136. Sorge testimony in Dicks, *Licensed*, 102.

137. LG Cologne, Urteil, May 28, 1965, *JNV*, vol. 21, 125–26; AS, J D2/43, Bl. 86–98: Vernehmung G. Sorge, April 26, 1957; ibid., JD 21/66 T1, Vernehmung G. Sorge, August 5, 1946; BArchL, B 162/4627, OStA Cologne, Anklageschrift, November 18, 1963, 146; USHMM, RG-06.025*26, File 1558, Bl. 157–75: Vernehmung G. Sorge, December 19, 1946, Bl. 165.

138. BArchL, B 162/4627, OStA Cologne, Anklageschrift, November 18, 1963, 158; ibid., B 162/16613, Bl. 95–104: Vernehmung G. Link, November 17, 1964, Bl. 101.

139. Naujoks, *Leben*, 266–67.

140. AdsD, KE, E. Büge, Bericht, n.d. (1945–46), 165; Hohmann and Wieland, *Konzentrationslager*, 33; Witte et al., *Dienstkalender*, 199; Hördler, "Ordnung," 111–12.

141. AS, JD 21/66 T1, Vernehmung G. Sorge, August 5, 1946; USHMM, RG-06.025*26, File 1560, Bl. 243–58: Vernehmung M. Knittler, December 20, 1946, Bl. 248. See also the SS photos of POWs taken in September 1941 in Sachsenhausen; Morsch, *Mord*, 172–73; Naujoks, *Leben*, 277.

142. Dwork and Van Pelt, *Auschwitz*, 260.

143. AdsD, KE, E. Büge, Bericht, n.d. (1945–46), 165–66; Naujoks, *Leben*, 266; USHMM, RG-06.025*26, File 1560, Bl. 243–58: Vernehmung M. Knittler, December 20, 1946, Bl. 247–48.

144. For this and the previous paragraph, see LG Cologne, Urteil, May 28, 1965, *JNV*, vol. 21, 126–27, 134; LG Bonn, Urteil, February 6, 1959, in ibid., vol. 15, 451–52; AdsD, KE, E. Büge, Bericht, n.d. (1945–46), 165; BArchL, B 162/4627, OStA Cologne, Anklageschrift gegen M., November 18, 1963, 151; BStU, MfS HA IX/11 ZUV 4, Bd. 24, Bl. 101–105: M. Saathoff, "Erklärungen zu meiner Zeichnung," September 6, 1946; ibid., Bl. 115–25: Gegenüberstellungsprotokoll, June 21, 1946; ibid., Bl. 207–30: Vernehmungsprotokoll P. Sakowski, August 3, 1946. During the 1934 Röhm purge, the Dachau Camp SS had also covered the sound of shots with loud music; Internationales Zentrum, *Nazi-Bastille*, 100–101.

145. BStU, RHE-West 329/1, Bl. 282–88: Vernehmungsprotokoll F. Ficker, August 22, 1946 (my thanks to Kim Wünschmann for checking this document); LG Bonn, Urteil, February 6, 1959, *JNV*, vol. 15, 452.

146. BStU, MfS HA IX/11 ZUV 4, Bd. 24, Bl. 207–30: Vernehmungsprotokoll P. Sakowski, August 3, 1946, Bl. 224.

147. USHMM, RG-06.025*26, File 1558, Bl. 157–75: Vernehmung G. Sorge, December 19, 1946, Bl. 167–68; AdsD, KE, E. Büge, Bericht, n.d. (1945–46), 222.

148. For the dating, see Orth, *System*, 128–29.

149. Quote in DöW, Nr. 5547, Vernehmungsprotokoll F. Ziereis, May 24, 1945, 6. See also LG Cologne, Urteil, May 28, 1965, *JNV*, vol. 21, 131; BArchL, B 162/16613, Bl. 15–32: Vernehmung Erwin S., October 11, 1965, Bl. 18, 20; AdsD, KE, E. Büge, Bericht, n.d. (1945–46), 215; Friedlander, *Genocide*, 66, 224.

150. Witte et al., *Dienstkalender*, 208.

151. For background, see Beer, "Gaswagen," 407; Browning, *Origins*, 353; Hilberg, *Vernichtung*, vol. 2, 937.

152. Quote in DöW, Nr. 5547, Vernehmungsprotokoll F. Ziereis, May 24, 1945, 6. "Politruk" is an abbreviation for the political instructors of Red Army units; McCauley, *Longman*, 221. For Mauthausen, see Speckner, "Kriegsgefangenenlager," 46.

153. LG Kassel, Urteil, October 20, 1953, *JNV*, vol. 11, 432–51; LG Waldshut, Urteil, June 13, 1953, in ibid., vol. 10, 746–72. It has been suggested that the Buchenwald execution chamber was built from early August 1941, simultaneous with the Sachsenhausen installation (*OdT*, vol. 3, 337–38). This seems highly unlikely. According to a well-informed former Buchenwald prisoner, the neck-shooting apparatus was not installed until mid-October 1941 (Polak, *Dziennik*, 89). After the war, a former SS man confirmed that the Buchenwald killings were carried out "in accordance with the system used at Oranienburg" (JVL, DJAO, *United States v. Berger*, RaR, February 20, 1948, 10).

154. DA, 37.144, Vernehmung J. Thora, October 20, 1950; Hammermann, "Kriegsgefangene," 96–97. 102–107; Zámečník, "Aufzeichnungen," 186.

155. Otto, *Wehrmacht*, 40–41, 111–12; Hammermann, "Kriegsgefangene," 110.

156. Zámečník, "Aufzeichnungen," 188.

157. Siegert, "Flossenbürg," 465–66; Otto, *Wehrmacht*, 93–94. For the start of the killings in Flossenbürg, Stapostelle Regensburg to Stapoleitstelle Munich, January 17, 1942, *IMT*, vol. 38, 449–51.

158. Otto, *Wehrmacht*, 93; Siegert, "Flossenbürg," 465–66.

159. Otto, *Wehrmacht*, 87–90. There is some ambiguity about the date. While several former prisoners and historians prefer September 3, 1941 (e.g., Czech, *Kalendarium*, 117), September 5, 1941, is more likely, as it is mentioned in two near-contemporous documents (Kłodziński, "Vergasung," 271; Piper, *Mass Murder*, 120).

160. Kłodziński, "Vergasung"; Dwork and Van Pelt, *Auschwitz*, 174–75.

161. The first murders of Soviet "commissars" in Auschwitz had occurred around late August 1941, with the SS shooting its victims in the gravel pit or outside block 11 (Broszat, *Kommandant*, 188, 240). The suggestion that several hundred POWs arrived as early as July 1941 (Brandhuber, "Kriegsgefangenen," 15–16; Smoleń, "Kriegsgefangene," 131) is probably incorrect (Hałgas, "Arbeit," 167; Otto, *Wehrmacht*, 90, n. 17).

162. Several Auschwitz officials saw the Sonnenstein gas chambers in late July 1941; Czech, *Kalendarium*, 105–106.

163. Kalthoff and Werner, *Händler*, 152, 156, 173; Dwork and Van Pelt, *Auschwitz*, 292–93; Morsch, "Tötungen," 260–62.

164. Czech, *Kalendarium*, 115–17; Broszat, *Kommandant*, 188; IfZ, Interview with Dr. Kahr, September 19, 1945, p. 3, ND: NO-1948. Fritzsch had begun his Camp SS career in Dachau in 1934; *DAP*, p. 220.

165. Kłodziński, "Vergasung"; Kogon et al., *Massentötungen*, 282–85; Broszat, *Kommandant*, 188–89; Trunk, "Gase," 37, 40.

166. Broszat, *Kommandant*, 189–90, 241.

167. Kłodziński, "Vergasung," 272–74, quote on 274.

168. Dwork and Van Pelt, *Auschwitz*, 293; Piper, *Mass Murder*, 128.

169. Some historians have dated this action to September 16, 1941 (Czech, *Kalendarium*, 122), though September 13, 1941, is a more likely date (*DAP*, Aussage Lebedev, October 1, 1964, 19870).

170. Quote in Broszat, *Kommandant*, 189. See also ibid., 241; *DAP*, 12705–07.

171. Otto, *Wehrmacht*, 92; Czech, "Calendar," 139.

172. Quote in Broszat, *Kommandant*, 190.

173. Perz and Freund, "Tötungen," 248–55; Maršálek, *Mauthausen*, 198–200. Ziereis may have been inspired to build a gas chamber by the killings in nearby Hartheim, rather than the Auschwitz experiments; Hördler, "Ordnung," 119.

174. Maršálek, *Vergasungsaktionen*, 16–17; *OdT*, vol. 4, 323; Freund and Perz, "Tötungen," 257–58; BArchB, R 58/871, Bl. 7: Rauff letter, March 26, 1942.

175. Beer, "Entwicklung"; Morsch, "Tötungen," 262–64; Kalthoff and Werner, *Händler*, 188.

176. Morsch, "Tötungen," 264–74.

177. Möller, "'Zyklon B.'" The Camp SS also constructed gas chambers in Majdanek (summer 1942), Natzweiler (April 1943), and Stutthof (June 1943); Kranz, "Massentötungen"; Orski, "Vernichtung"; Schmaltz, "Gaskammer."

178. The other exception was Majdanek (see chapter 6). In Mauthausen, too, the gas chamber was used continuously until 1945, though on a far smaller scale; Hördler, "Ordnung," 377.

179. Broszat, *Kommandant*, 189–90, 240–41.

180. A well-placed former prisoner estimated that five thousand or more Soviet POWs were gassed in the Auschwitz crematorium in 1941–42 (Piper, *Mass Murder*, 129, n. 405). This figure probably includes Soviet POWs who had initially been taken to Auschwitz

for forced labor (see below). The figure of Soviet POWs executed as "commissars," following Gestapo selections, was smaller, probably more in the region of two thousand (Otto, *Wehrmacht*, 268).

181. In Dachau alone, some forty SS men are said to have participated in each mass shooting; Affidavit J. Jarolin, n.d. (c. autumn 1945), in JVL, JAO, Review of Proceedings, *United States v. Weiss*, n.d. (1946), 22–25.

182. Hördler, "Ordnung," 125.

183. For Schubert, see LG Bonn, Urteil, February 6, 1959, *JNV*, vol. 15, 452.

184. Affidavit J. Jarolin, n.d. (c. autumn 1945), in JVL, JAO, Review of Proceedings, *United States v. Weiss*, n.d. (1946), 23; Musial, "Konterrevolutionäre," 200–209; BArchL, B 162/16613, Bl. 15–32: Vernehmung Erwin S., October 11, 1965, Bl. 20; ibid., Nr. 4627, OStA Cologne, Anklageschrift, November 18, 1963, 146; Neitzel and Welzer, *Soldaten*, 135–36. For praise for SS executioners more generally, see IfZ, Himmler, Durchführungsbestimmungen für Exekutionen, January 6, 1943, ND: NO-4631.

185. For background, see G. Sorge testimony in Dicks, *Licensed*, 103.

186. Quote in Gruner, *Verurteilt*, 90. See also JVL, DJAO, *United States v. Berger*, RaR, February 20, 1948, 14; Zámečník, "Aufzeichnungen," 183; Neitzel and Welzer, *Soldaten*, 14–15, 101.

187. Quote in DA, 37.144, Vernehmung J. Thora, October 20, 1950.

188. LG Cologne, Urteil, May 28, 1965, *JNV*, vol. 21, 127–28; JVL, DJAO, *United States v. A. Berger*, RaR, February 20, 1948, 8–11; Riedle, *Angehörigen*, 241 (n. 355). For epidemics in POW camps, see Gerlach, *Krieg*, 34–35, 49.

189. Naujoks, *Leben*, 273–74; Major Meinel to Kommandeur der Kriegsgefangenen im Wehrkreis VII, January 13, 1942, *IMT*, vol. 38, 439–40, ND: 178–R; Siegert, "Flossenbürg," 465; Zámečník, "Aufzeichnungen," 188; LG Cologne, Urteil, May 28, 1965, *JNV*, vol. 21, 143; LG Kassel, Urteil, October 20, 1953, *JNV*, vol. 11, 443–44; BArchL, B 162/4627, OStA Cologne, Anklageschrift, November 18, 1963, 160. For task forces, see Klee et al., *"Schöne Zeiten,"* 64–70.

190. Quotes in LG Bonn, Urteil, February 6, 1959, *JNV*, vol. 15, 453; BArchL, B 162/16613, Bl. 15–32: Vernehmung Erwin S., October 11, 1965, Bl. 21. See also LG Kassel, Urteil, October 20, 1953, *JNV*, vol. 11, 443; Naujoks, *Leben*, 274; Kühne, *Kameradschaft*, 272–73.

191. For example, see Riedle, *Angehörigen*, 239–40.

192. For the practice of excusing SS men from executions (though not specifically in the context of 14f14), see Langbein, *Menschen*, 326–27.

193. StAMü, StA Nr. 28791/3, Bl. 114: Vernehmung K. Minderlein, July 25, 1949; Hammermann, "Kriegsgefangene," 107–108.

194. IfZ, Himmler, Durchführungsbestimmungen für Exekutionen, January 6, 1943, ND: NO-4631.

195. Quotes in BArchL, B 162/16613, Bl. 15–32: Vernehmung Erwin S., October 11, 1965, Bl. 16; Vernehmung F. Ficker, August 22, 1946, in Orth, *SS*, 174. See also Hördler, "Ordnung," 125–26.

196. Quote in BStU, MfS HA IX/11 ZUV 4, Bd. 24, Bl. 207–30: Vernehmungsprotokoll P. Sakowski, August 3, 1946, Bl. 223. See also BArchL, B 162/4627, OStA Cologne, Anklageschrift, November 18, 1963, 152.

197. JVL, JAO, Review of Proceedings, *United States v. Weiss*, n.d. (1946), 28; BArchL, B 162/16613, Bl. 15–32: Vernehmung Erwin S., October 11, 1965, Bl. 21.

198. AS, J D2/43, Bl. 146–54: Vernehmung G. Sorge, May 6, 1957, Bl. 153; BArchB, NS 4/Na 9, Bl. 78: KB Nr. 3/41, May 26, 1941.

199. For alcohol and murders during the Holocaust, see Browning, *Männer*, 103, 122.

200. Quote in Riedle, *Angehörigen*, 241.

201. Quote in BArchB, NS 4/Gr 3, Bl. 35: Liebehenschel to LK, November 14, 1941. See also Orth, *SS*, 175–76. Himmler discussed military decorations with his intimate Karl

Wolff on November 14, 1941 (Witte et al., *Dienstkalender*, 260), the same day the telex from Liebehenschel went to the commandants.

202. Riedel, *Ordnungshüter*, 273–75; Morsch, *Mord*, 179; Hammermann, "Kriegsgefangene," 109–10; AdsD, KE, E. Büge, Bericht, n.d. (1945–46), 222.

203. Riedle, *Angehörigen*, 241.

204. Zámečník, "Aufzeichnungen," 187; DaA, 6170, A. Carl to H. Schwarz, December 3, 1967.

205. Quote in Morsch, *Mord*, 175.

206. Hohmann and Wieland, *Konzentrationslager*, quote on 35; Naujoks, *Leben*, 274–75.

207. The best analysis of the historiography of the Third Reich is still Kershaw, *Dictatorship*.

208. Jäckel, *Weltanschauung*, 29–54; Kershaw, *Nemesis*, 775–76.

209. Schulte, *Zwangsarbeit*, 260–61, quote on 261.

210. Quote in Picker, *Tischgespräche*, 93. See also ibid., 94–95; Jochmann, *Monologe*, 63, 90.

211. H. Johst, *Ruf des Reiches—Echo des Volkes* (Munich, 1940), translated in Van Pelt, "Site," 101–103. See also Longerich, *Himmler*, 33–65; Düsterberg, *Johst*.

212. Erlaß zur Festigung deutschen Volkstums, October 7, 1939, *IMT*, vol. 26, 255–57, ND: 686–PS.

213. Aly, *"Endlösung,"* 29–203; Aly and Heim, *Vordenker*, 125–256.

214. Schulte, *Zwangsarbeit*, 261.

215. Witte et al., *Dienstkalender*, 179.

216. For background, see Aly and Heim, *Vordenker*, 394–440; Roth, "'Generalplan Ost'"; Madajczyk, *Generalplan Ost*.

217. Schulte, *Zwangsarbeit*, 296–99, 311, 345; Allen, *Business*, 158, 176.

218. Quotes in BArchB, NS 19/2065, Bl. 8–9: Himmler to Pohl, January 31, 1942. See also ibid., Bl. 2–3 Pohl to Himmler, (mid) December 1941; ibid., Bl. 20–32: Kammler, Aufstellung von SS Baubrigaden, February 10, 1942; ibid., Bl. 36–37: Himmler to Pohl, March 23, 1942.

219. BArchB, NS 19/2065, Bl. 8–9: Himmler to Pohl, January 31, 1942.

220. Maršálek, *Mauthausen*, 189.

221. BArchB, NS 4/Na 103, Bl. 147–49: Glücks to LK, September 29, 1941. More generally, see Allen, *Business*, 117–22; Schulte, *Zwangsarbeit*, 381–84. The KL labor representatives, who now reported to their local commandant and the IKL, remained marginal figures. See BArchB, NS 4/Na 103, Bl. 140–42: Burböck to SlF E, November 28, 1941; Schulte, *Zwangsarbeit*, 385–86.

222. IfZ, Himmler to Pohl et al., December 5, 1941, ND: NO-385. See also BArchB, NS 19/2065, Bl. 8–9: Himmler to Pohl, January 31, 1942.

223. IfZ, Dienstanweisung für SlF E, November 7, 1941, ND: 3685–PS, underlined in the original. See also BArchB, NS 4/Na 103, Bl. 26: WVHA to LK, April 14, 1942.

224. Even before the war, Himmler had envisaged a role for the Camp SS in the internment of POWs; Himmler to Hess, July 23, 1938, in IfZ, *Akten*, vol. 3, 230.

225. Streit, *Kameraden*, 192–95; Herbert, *Fremdarbeiter*, 132–40; Keller, *Kriegsgefangene*, 158–72; Gruchmann, *Krieg*, 120.

226. Keller and Otto, "Kriegsgefangene," 23.

227. Witte et al., *Dienstkalender*, 208–10. For Himmler's conversation with Pohl about "prisoners" on September 15, 1941, missing from this publication of his official diary, see BArchB, Film 3570.

228. Witte et al., *Dienstkalender*, 215; IKL to LK Flossenbürg, September 15, 1941, in Tuchel, *Inspektion*, 73.

229. Streit, *Kameraden*, 220–21. The initial OKW order on September 25 had earmarked up to one hundred thousand POWs for a project around Lublin.

230. Otto, *Wehrmacht*, 187–88, quote on 188; Hördler, "Ordnung," 113; Schulte, "Kriegsgefangenen-Arbeitslager," 82–83; USHMM, RG-11.001M.03, reel 19, 502–1–13, H. Kammler, Bericht des Amtes II, December 1941, p. 4; IKL to LK Flossenbürg,

September 15, 1941, in Tuchel, *Inspektion*, 73 (similar messages must have gone out to other KL).

231. At first, Majdanek was called a POW camp, even though it was subordinated to the IKL and belonged to its system of concentration camps; it was officially designated as a KL on February 16, 1943. See Kranz, "KL Lublin," 363-69; Kranz, "Konzentrationslager," 237-39; *OdT*, vol. 7, 33-36, 39; Schulte, *Zwangsarbeit*, 332-36; White, "Majdanek"; IfZ, Himmler Vermerk, n.d., ND: NO-3031. For the SS economy in Lublin, see Kaienburg, *Wirtschaft*, 529-63. Frank quote in Präg and Jacobmeyer, *Diensttagebuch*, 219.

232. The interest zone was designed to protect the SS and to provide it with opportunities for farming and fishing. For the above, see Steinbacher, *"Musterstadt*,*"* 238-39; Schulte, *Zwangsarbeit*, 336-38; Strzelecka and Setkiewicz, "Construction," 70-74, 80-81; USHMM, RG-11.001M.76, reel 421, folder 156, Erläuterungsbericht zum Vorentwurf, October 30, 1941, p. 6; ibid., Vorgang für die Erstellung eines Kriegsgefangenen-lagers, October 9, 1941, pp. 1-2. Many historians have argued that Himmler ordered the construction of Birkenau earlier, on March 1, 1941. But Steinbacher and Schulte show convincingly that this did not happen until September 1941.

233. Michael Thad Allen suggests that the new Auschwitz crematorium (in the works since October 1941, and later built as crematorium II in Birkenau) was designed from the start to include a gas chamber, a decision he links to the Nazi Final Solution (Allen, "Devil"; idem, "Not Just a 'Dating Game,' " 186-87). This is contradicted by the research of Robert Jan van Pelt, who argues that the transformation of crematorium II to allow for gassings did not occur until 1942 (Dwork and Van Pelt, *Auschwitz*, 269-71, 321-24). Even if Allen's thesis were to prove correct, however, this would not suggest that the SS planned (in autumn 1941) to use this gas chamber to murder the Jews of Europe (Schulte, "Auschwitz," 571).

234. Schulte, *Zwangsarbeit*, 338-39, 362; Steinbacher, *"Musterstadt"*; Dwork and Van Pelt, *Auschwitz*; Wegner, *Soldaten*, 46, 62.

235. Stutthof was referred to as a KL by Glücks on January 7, 1942, but was only formally taken over the following month. See Orski, "Organisation"; Kaienburg, *Wirtschaft*, 516-22; *OdT*, vol. 6, 477-80; Witte et al., *Dienstkalender*, 271 (n. 84). For the 1940 discussions, see IfZ, Fa 183, Bl. 53-55: IKL to Himmler, January 30, 1940; BArchB, NS 19/1919, Bl. 25-27: IKL to Himmler, February 21, 1940; ibid., NS 19/3796, Bl. 2: IKL to Himmler, April 30, 1940. The initial rejection of Stutthof was probably linked to the decision to establish a camp on former Polish soil in Auschwitz.

236. Kaienburg, *Wirtschaft*, 519-23; *OdT*, vol. 6, 479, 483-85; IfZ, Maurer, Besichtigung von Stutthof, December 11, 1941, ND: NO-2147.

237. On January 6, 1942, there were 9,884 prisoners in Auschwitz, not counting Soviet POWs; Schulte, "London," 222.

238. Quotes in *DAP*, Vernehmung N. Wassiljew, October 23, 1964, 22443-44; Wassiljew was registered under the name Iwanow (ibid., 22437-38). See also ibid., Vernehmung A. Pogoschew, October 23, 1964, 22641-47; ibid., Vernehmung P. Stjenkin, October 29, 1964, 23066; Brandhuber, "Kriegsgefangenen," 19; Czech, *Kalendarium*, 126.

239. Quotes in *DAP*, Vernehmung N. Wassiljew, October 23, 1964, 22446, 22533. See also Brandhuber, "Kriegsgefangenen," 18-20; Hałgas, "Arbeit," 167-69; Kielar, *Anus Mundi*, 101-103. More generally, see Smoleń, "Kriegsgefangene"; Strzelecka, "Quarantine."

240. Figures in Czech, *Kalendarium*, 126-34; Schulte, "London," table 7, p. 222.

241. Otto, *Wehrmacht*, 188-89; Keller and Otto, "Sowjetische Kriegsgefangenen," 25-27; Kranz, "Erfassung," 242 (n. 67). Apparently, no transports went to Niederhagen, Natzweiler, or Ravensbrück, which were also not copied into key IKL correspondence (e.g., BArchB, NS 4/Gr 2, Bl. 6-7: IKL to LK, October 23, 1941).

242. Quotes in NARA, RG 549, 000-50-9, Box 440A, statement B. Lebedev, April 22, 1945 (Lebedev dated his arrival to October 19, 1941). See also AdsD, KE, E. Büge, Bericht, n.d. (1945-46), 182; Otto, *Wehrmacht*, 189.

243. Sprenger, *Groß-Rosen*, 190–92; Streim, *Behandlung*, 116. It is unclear if the prisoners were barred because the barracks were not ready yet, or because their clothes had not been disinfected.

244. Mailänder Koslov, *Gewalt*, 230–31.

245. Quote in Świebocki, *Resistance*, 346. See also Hałgas, "Arbeit," 170–71; Brandhuber, "Kriegsgefangenen," 23–25; Dwork and Van Pelt, *Auschwitz*, 272.

246. Ibel, "Kriegsgefangene," 132–33.

247. Sprenger, *Groß-Rosen*, 190–94, quote on 194; Keller and Otto, "Kriegsgefangene," 25.

248. *DAP*, Vernehmung N. Wassiljew, October 23, 1964, 22412–14, quote on 22415; Hałgas, "Arbeit," 168, 171.

249. Quote in Broszat, *Kommandant*, 159. See also USHMM, RG-06.025*26, File 1558, Bl. 157–75: Vernehmung G. Sorge, December 19, 1946, Bl. 167; Hałgas, "Arbeit," 169; LG Cologne, Urteil, May 28, 1965, *JNV*, vol. 21, 126; Vernehmung A. Joseph, December 1, 1958, in Van Dam and Giordano, *KZ-Verbrechen*, 210.

250. For one example, see BArchB, NS 4/Fl 388, Bl. 54: Lagerarzt to Kommandantur, February 15, 1942.

251. Marszałek, *Majdanek*, 123.

252. For Himmler's views, see Süß, *"Volkskörper,"* 229 (n. 72).

253. *DAP*, Vernehmung N. Wassiljew, October 23, 1964, 22416, 22457–58, 22465–67, 22489–91, 22501.

254. *OdT*, vol. 4, 322; ibid., vol. 7, 51; Mailänder Koslov, *Gewalt*, 298–99.

255. Brandhuber, "Kriegsgefangenen," 21–22, quote on 22; Smoleń, "Kriegsgefangene," 142–45; Otto, *Wehrmacht*, 193–95.

256. BArchB, NS 3/425, Bl. 45–46: IKL to LK, November 15, 1941; Hammermann, "Kriegsgefangene," 99.

257. For the murder of Jews, see Longerich, *Holocaust*, 314–15, 429.

258. Majdanek held 112 Soviet POWs on January 16, 1942; Schulte, "London," table 10, p. 224.

259. Quote in Broszat, *Kommandant*, 157. By January 6, 1942, Auschwitz held 2,095 Soviet POWs (Schulte, "London," table 7, p. 222), which means that at least 7,900 of the men who had arrived in October 1941 were now dead. For the other figures, see Brandhuber, "Kriegsgefangenen," 33, 35.

260. AdsD, KE, E. Büge, Bericht, n.d. (1945–46), 175.

261. Sprenger, *Groß-Rosen*, 194.

262. Iwaszko, "Reasons," 22–23; Brandhuber, "Kriegsgefangenen," 20; Hałgas, "Arbeit," 169. German prisoners (except for Jews) in Auschwitz were not normally tattooed; see Strzelecka, "Women," 182, also for other exceptions. In the weeks after the November 1938 pogrom, Jews in Dachau and Buchenwald had their prisoner numbers stamped on their arms; *NCC*, doc. 247; Stein, *Juden*, 45.

263. Bischoff quote in Dwork and Van Pelt, *Auschwitz*, 177. See also Piper, *Mass Murder*, 128; Brandhuber, "Kriegsgefangenen," 26; Hałgas, "Arbeit," 172.

264. Quote in AdsD, KE, E. Büge, Bericht, n.d. (1945–46), 181.

265. RSHA to KL, October 11, 1941, cited in Otto, *Wehrmacht*, 199, underlined in the original.

266. Himmler Rede bei der SS Gruppenführertagung in Posen, October 4, 1943, *IMT*, vol. 29, 121–22, ND: 1919-PS; Mailänder Koslov, *Gewalt*, 230–31.

267. Quote in AdsD, KE, E. Büge, Bericht, n.d. (1945–46), 95. For Knittler's crimes, see USHMM, RG-06.025*26, File 1560, Bl. 243–58: Vernehmung M. Knittler, December 20, 1946, Bl. 252–53.

268. For this belief among the Camp SS, see Broszat, *Kommandant*, 159.

269. BArchB, NS 4/Gr 2, Bl. 6–7: IKL to LK, October 23, 1941; ibid., NS 4/Fl 389, Bl. 11: IKL to SlF E, November 29, 1941; ibid., NS 4/Na 103, Bl. 126: IKL to SlF E, October 27, 1941.

270. IKL to LK Flossenbürg, September 15, 1941, in Tuchel, *Inspektion*, 73.
271. Quote in Himmler Rede bei der SS Gruppenführertagung in Posen, October 4, 1943, *IMT*, vol. 29, 123. See also Dwork and Van Pelt, *Auschwitz*, 262–68; Streit, *Kameraden*, 197.
272. Apparently, there were already plans in late autumn 1941 for further transports of Soviet POWs to the KL; Keller and Otto, "Sowjetische Kriegsgefangene," 26–27.
273. Streit, *Kameraden*, 191–208; Keller, *Kriegsgefangene*, 215–17, 322–23; Gerlach, *Krieg*, 42–43, 52–53; Herbert, *Fremdarbeiter*, 137–43.
274. USHMM, RG-11.001M.76, reel 421, folder 156, Kammler to Himmler, December 19, 1941.
275. BArchB (ehem. BDC), SSO, Koch, Karl, 2.8.1897, Koch to SS und Polizeigericht VI Krakow, August 2, 1942.
276. Kranz, "KL Lublin," 369; Kaienburg, *Wirtschaft*, 536–37.
277. Quote in "Bericht von Rudolf Vrba," 200. See also Brandhuber, "Kriegsgefangenen," 25–26; Strzelecka and Setkiewicz, "Construction," 86.
278. Figures in Schulte, "Kriegsgefangenen-Arbeitslager," 89; idem, "London," 220–24; Sprenger, *Groß-Rosen*, 194; *OdT*, vol. 3, 35; Kaienburg, *"Vernichtung,"* 156. According to the available figures, there were around five to six thousand Soviet POWs in the KL in spring 1942. Not all were survivors of the October 1941 transports; among them were also some "commissaris" temporarily spared execution.
279. *DAP*, Vernehmung N. Wassiljew, October 23, 1964, 22564–66.
280. The other main KL in early 1942 were Buchenwald, Dachau, Flossenbürg, Gross-Rosen, Mauthausen, Neuengamme, Niederhagen, Ravensbrück, and Sachsenhausen.
281. *OdT*, vol. 3, 29; Pingel, *Häftlinge*, 301 (n. 174).

6. Holocaust

1. Himmler's itinerary (also used below) in Witte et al., *Dienstkalender*, 491–93.
2. Langbein, *Menschen*, 327; Strzelecka and Setkiewicz, "Construction," 106–107; Longerich, *Himmler*, 34–66; Kaienburg, *Wirtschaft*, 841–42.
3. Wagner, *IG Auschwitz*, 80–81; BArchB, Film 44564, Interrogation O. Pohl, January 25, 1947, p. 17.
4. Strebel, *Ravensbrück*, 352.
5. Broszat, *Kommandant*, 243, quote on 275; Czech, *Kalendarium*, 250–51; Strzelecka and Setkiewicz, "Construction," 86–88. For Himmler's presence during a mass killing in Auschwitz, see also Langbein, *Menschen*, 327–28; Adler et al., *Auschwitz*, 204.
6. Longerich, *Himmler*, 552.
7. Broszat, *Kommandant*, 276–78, quote on 278; Laqueur and Breitman, *Mann*, 9–11; Mulka to Führer des Standortes Auschwitz, July 17, 1942, in Frei et al., *Kommandanturbefehle*, 154–55.
8. Broszat, *Kommandant*, 278–79; testimony S. Dubiel, August 7, 1946, in Bezwińska and Czech, *KL Auschwitz*, 287–92.
9. Himmler order, March 3, 1942, cited in WVHA Befehl, March 13, 1942, in Tuchel, *Inspektion*, 88; Witte et al., *Dienstkalender*, 369–71; Schulte, *Zwangsarbeit*, 201. The official transfer of the IKL from the nominal control of Jüttner's SS Leadership Main Office to the WVHA took place on March 16, 1942; Pohl to Glücks, March 11, 1942, in Tuchel, *Inspektion*, 89.
10. Longerich, *Himmler*, 590–92; Arad, *Belzec*, 46–47; Witte et al., *Dienstkalender*, 491–93; Berger, *Experten*, 91; Browning, "Final Hitler Decision." Late on July 18, Himmler also met with Pohl, who had been unable to accompany him to Auschwitz.
11. Broszat, *Kommandant*, 279; BArchB (ehem. BDC), SSO, Höss, Rudolf, 25.11.1900, Bl. 258: WVHA to SS-Personalhauptamt, July 27, 1942. Several other Auschwitz SS men

involved in the Holocaust were also decorated or promoted after Himmler's visit; Hördler, "Ordnung," 152.

12. Hilberg, "Auschwitz"; Piper, *Zahl*, table D; Arad, *Belzec*, 370–76; *OdT*, vol. 8, 359–60.

13. In a path-breaking essay, Robert Jan van Pelt coined the phrase of Auschwitz as a "site in search of a mission"; Van Pelt, "Site." While this phrase captures the dynamic nature of the camp and its changes in function, it is still overly teleological, implying that the Holocaust was the true mission of Auschwitz. However, earlier missions—the brutal repression of the Polish opposition, say, or the lethal imprisonment of Soviet POWs—had been no less real to the Camp SS.

14. Most recently, *OdT*, vol. 5, 140.

15. For this and the previous paragraphs on the genesis of the Holocaust, see Longerich, *Holocaust*; Browning, *Origins*; Pohl, *Holocaust*; Friedländer, *Jahre*. On the death camps, see Berger, *Experten*; Montague, *Chełmno*; Krakowski, *Todeslager*; *OdT*, vol. 8, 301–28.

16. Arad, *Belzec*; Berger, *Experten*, 71, for the reference to the Warsaw ghetto.

17. Paradigmatically, Arad, *Belzec*.

18. For Majdanek, see Witte and Tyas, "Document." For Auschwitz, see Perz and Sand-kühler, "Auschwitz." As the latter two authors point out, the link between the KL and Operation Reinhard is confirmed by the itinerary of Pohl's visit to Auschwitz in September 1942. Here, the barracks used for sorting and storing the property of murdered Jews (Canada I) are referred to as "Disinfestation & Effect Chamber/Action Reinhard," while the gas chambers at bunker 2 are referred to as "Station 2 of Action Reinhardt [*sic*]"; USHMM, RG-11.001M.03, reel 19, folder 19, Besichtigung durch SS Obergruppenführer Pohl am 23.9.1942. For another example, see NAL, HW 16/21, GPD Nr. 3, October 22, 1942.

19. Quotes in Browning, "Final Hitler Decision," 7; IfZ, F 13/6, Bl. 359–68: R. Höss, "Globocnik," January 1947. More generally, see Pohl, *"Judenpolitik"*; Longerich, *Himmler*, especially pages 361–64.

20. For this paragraph, see Berger, *Experten*, quote on 41; Arad, *Belzec*; Kogon et al., *Massentötungen*, 146–86; Rieß, "Wirth." The T-4 organization of the Chancellery of the Führer was also involved in the management of the death camps.

21. According to SS statistics intercepted by British intelligence, 2,024 prisoners were classified as Jews in January 1942. However, these statistics only covered around seventy-five to eighty percent of all KL prisoners; Schulte, "London," 210, 227. Also, the statistics did not account for Jews among Soviet POWs.

22. Wannsee conference minutes, in Noakes and Pridham, *Nazism*, vol. 3, 535–41, quote on 538. See also Longerich, *Politik*, 466–72; Friedländer, *Jahre*, 367–71; Haus der Wannsee-Konferenz, *Wannsee-Konferenz*; Berger, *Experten*, 79. For the term "annihilation through labor" (not used in the official minutes), see Wachsmann, "'Annihilation.'"

23. For IKL awareness of the poor health and high mortality of Soviet POWs in the KL, see BArchB, NS 4/Gr 9, Bl. 63: Glücks to LK, January 23, 1942; KL Gross-Rosen to IKL, January 27, 1942, referenced in Sprenger, *Groß-Rosen*, 194.

24. IfZ, Fa 183, Bl. 61: Himmler to Glücks, January 26, 1942. See also Van Pelt, "Site," 148–49; Allen, "Anfänge," 568–69; Schulte, *Zwangsarbeit*, 356–62.

25. Quotes in Jochmann, *Monologe*, 229; Witte et al., *Dienstkalender*, 326–27.

26. ITS, KL Buchenwald GCC 2/313, Ordner 519, IKL to LK, January 19, 1942; ibid., IKL to all [LK], January 26, 1942. The only camps excluded from the initial IKL order were the small KL Natzweiler and Stutthof. Few, if any, of the selected Jewish prisoners had been sent to Majdanek by the time the order was rescinded; on February 3, 1942, there were no registered Jewish prisoners in Majdanek; Schulte, "London," 224.

27. IfZ, Fa 183, Bl. 61: Himmler to Glücks, January 26, 1942. Deportations of Jews from the Greater German Reich resumed in mid-March 1942, but none of the transports over the coming weeks went to the KL; Longerich, *Politik*, 483–86.

28. Longerich, *Politik*, 491–95.
29. Initially, there may have been plans to select some skilled prisoners among the Jews deported to Auschwitz and Majdanek, and transfer them to other KL earmarked for armaments works; StANü, K.-O. Saur, Niederschrift über Besprechung, March 17, 1942, ND: NO-569.
30. Pressac, *Krematorien*, 31–34, 45–48; Pressac and Van Pelt, "Machinery," 199, 210–12.
31. Witte et al., *Dienstkalender*, 367–69; Strebel, *Ravensbrück*, 342–43.
32. NAL, HW 16/17, GPD Nr. 3, March 10, 1942.
33. NARA, RG 549, 000–50–11 Ravensbruck CC (Box 522), testimony J. Langefeld, December 26 and 31, 1945; Strebel, *Ravensbrück*, 344; Strzelecka, "Women," 172; USHMM, RG-11.001M.03, reel 19, 502–1–6, WVHA to Bauinspektion Posen, March 18, 1942.
34. Czech, *Kalendarium*, 189–93.
35. For this and the previous paragraph, see testimony of S. Jankowski (also known as Alter Feinsilber), April 16, 1945, in SMAB, *Inmitten*, 25–57, quote on 32. See also YIVO, RG 294.1, MK 488, series 20, folder 542, Bl. 7–17: testimony V. Walder, n.d. (1945–49).
36. Longerich, *Politik*, 584; Hayes, "Auschwitz."
37. Piper, *Zahl*, 187, 195. A further one thousand Slovak Jews arrived in May via Majdanek; Czech, *Kalendarium*, 215.
38. Quote in ITS, KL Buchenwald GCC 2/313, Ordner 519, IKL to LK, January 19, 1942. This order was issued in relation to Jewish KL prisoners earmarked for deportation to Majdanek. See also IfZ, Verwaltung Auschwitz to WVHA, March 25, 1942, ND: NO-2146.
39. SS statistics summarized in APMO, Proces Höss, Hd 6, Bl. 114–20: O. Wolken, Kommentar, n.d. (c. spring 1945).
40. Grotum, *Archiv*, 255–56; Longerich, *Politik*, 492.
41. Strzelecka and Setkiewicz, "Construction," 86–87; testimony of S. Jankowski, April 16, 1945, in SMAB, *Inmitten*, 32–33; Schulte, "Kriegsgefangenen-Arbeitslager," 87; Czech, *Kalendarium*, 206.
42. For this and the previous paragraph, see Strzelecka and Setkiewicz, "Construction," 78–79; Strzelecka, "Women," 172; Strebel, *Ravensbrück*, 349–51; WL, P.III.h. No. 1174a, Vernehmung R. Kagan, December 8–10, 1959; APMO, Oswiadczenia, vol. 124, Bl. 152–66: testimony of M. Schvalbova, June 8, 1988; Broszat, *Kommandant*, 172–73; IfZ, RSHA, AE, 2. Teil, Runderlaß RSHA, July 10, 1942.
43. Figures in Schulte, "London," 222; Strebel, *Ravensbrück*, 349.
44. Several historians have argued that sporadic murders of nonworking Silesian Jews had begun earlier, with small groups sent to Auschwitz for extermination from late 1941. Sybille Steinbacher has provided the most detailed account in her otherwise excellent study of Auschwitz. Starting in late 1941, she argues, selections were carried out among Jews in forced labor camps run by SS Oberführer Schmelt (mostly in Upper Silesia); those selected as "unfit for work" were sent to Auschwitz and murdered in crematorium I (Steinbacher, *"Musterstadt,"* 276–77; on the Schmelt camps, see ibid., 138–53). However, her sources do not fully bear out this conclusion. One source refers to a transport to Auschwitz in late *1940*, another to small transports from *mid-1941* (BArchL, B 162/20513, Bl. 83: Vermerk, October 11, 1967; ibid., Bl. 47–54: Vernehmungsniederschrift Hirsch B., September 21, 1961). As for the assumed murder of a transport of Jews from Beuthen (Upper Silesia) on February 15, 1942, in crematorium I, this information is based on erroneous data in the Auschwitz chronicle (Czech, *Kalendarium*, 174–75); there was no such transport at the time (Gottwaldt and Schulle, *"Judendeportationen,"* 393).

Christopher Browning also dates the first gassings of Jews "no longer capable of work" in crematorium I to autumn 1941 (Browning, *Origins*, 357). In addition to Steinbacher's work, Browning relies on another piece of evidence: the postwar account of SS man Hans Stark. Testifying before German legal officials, Browning recounts, Stark stated that small groups of Jews were brought to Auschwitz on trucks in October 1941 and gassed there (Browning, *Origins*, 527, n. 211). Stark was among the accused of the first Frankfurt Auschwitz trial, where he was sentenced to ten years in prison. In his first pretrial interrogation, Stark did indeed state that he had participated in the gassing of small groups of Jewish men, women, and children, deported to Auschwitz for immediate extermination in crematorium I in autumn 1941 (*DAP*, Vernehmung H. Stark, April 23, 1959, 4537–50). However, in a subsequent interrogation Stark corrected himself, stating that the date he had given previously was wrong. He was unaware of any gassings in autumn 1941, he now said, adding that the murders of Jewish men, women, and children he had described could only have occurred *after* he returned to Auschwitz in spring 1942 from a period of study leave (the Frankfurt court found that Stark had been on leave until March 15, 1942; *DAP*, 36765). Stark gained no advantage from changing these dates, as he still admitted his participation in the gassings. Most likely, therefore, he corrected what he regarded as a genuine mistake (*DAP*, Vernehmung H. Stark, July 24, 1959, 4578–79). During his later trial testimony in 1964, Stark reiterated that the first transports of Jews gassed in crematorium I as "unfit for work" had arrived in April–May 1942. He also admitted to his participation in the gassing of a group of 150 to 200 Polish and Jewish men and women in October 1941. However, these victims had not been selected as "unfit for work" as part of the Nazi Final Solution. Rather, Stark testified, they had been sentenced to death by court martial (*DAP*, Aussage H. Stark, January 16, 1964, 4813–26). This seems plausible, given the practice of mass executions in Auschwitz in late 1941 at the behest of Summary Courts.

45. Browning, *Origins*, 421, though with different dating (see above).
46. Schulte, "Vernichtungslager," 65.
47. Orth, "Höß"; Gerlach, "Eichmann"; Wojak, *Memoiren*.
48. Quotes by Eichmann in his postwar talks with W. Sassen, in BArchK, All. Proz. 6/97, Bl. 24–25. See also ibid., Bl. 22–27; ibid., 6/106, Bl. 23; State of Israel, *Trial*, vol. 7, 371–72; Broszat, *Kommandant*, 199.
49. Broszat, *Kommandant*, 191, 238. The former Auschwitz camp compound leader Aumeier testified that Eichmann (whom he wrongly called Hildebrand) appeared at the time when the first RSHA transports arrived; NAL, WO 208/4661, statement of H. Aumeier, July 25, 1945, p. 2.
50. Quote by Eichmann in his postwar talks with W. Sassen, in BArchK, All. Proz. 6/99, Bl. 31.
51. For the date of Pohl's visit, see USHMM, RG-11.001M.03, reel 19, folder 19, R. Höss, Bericht über Schlussbesprechung des Hauptamtschefs am 23.9.1942; NARA, RG 549, 000–50–11 Ravensbrück CC (Box 522), testimony of J. Langefeld, December 26 and 31, 1945.
52. Witte et al., *Dienstkalender*, 397–98; Longerich, *Himmler*, 582–83.
53. Piper, *Zahl*, 183; Steinbacher, "*Musterstadt*," 286–87, 290; Gottwaldt and Schulle, "*Judendeportationen*," 393–94; Fulbrook, *Small Town*, 2, 31, 222–24.
54. Broad, "Erinnerungen," 170–73, quote on 172; *DAP*, Aussage F. Müller, January 5, 1964, 20489–20507, quote on 20494. See also Müller, *Eyewitness*, 30–39; Van Pelt, *Case*, 224–25; Piper, *Mass Murder*, 128–33; *DAP*, Vernehmung H. Stark, April 23, 1959, 4517–62; NAL, WO 208/4661, statement of H. Aumeier, July 25, 1945, p. 6.
55. For the perspective of the SS, see Broad, "Erinnerungen," 173; NAL, WO 208/4661, statement of H. Aumeier, July 25, 1945, pp. 6–7 (with erroneous dates).
56. Pressac and Van Pelt, "Machinery," 212; Pressac, *Krematorien*, 49; Piper, *Mass Murder*, 134.
57. For the May date, see Pressac, *Krematorien*, 49. This seems the most plausible dating, given the broader historical context. By contrast, many historians favor an earlier date, March 20, 1942, for the first gassing in bunker 1, relying on the work of Danuta Czech. However, the two sources used by Czech (*Kalendarium*, 186–87) do not support her conclusions, a concern also raised by Schulte ("Vernichtungslager," 64, n. 121). The first of Czech's sources, the so-called memoirs of Rudolf Höss, is notoriously unreliable as

regards dates. The second source, the account by Pery Broad, actually contradicts Czech's dating, as Broad only arrived in Auschwitz in April 1942 and initially served with the Guard Troop, which would not have allowed him to closely observe murders in the Birkenau bunkers. It was only from around June 1942, after Broad was transferred to the political department (which *was* closely involved with the gassings) that he could have watched the extermination process close-up (*DAP*, Vernehmung P. Broad, April 30, 1959, 3424–25). Gassings in crematorium I apparently stopped in autumn 1942 (Piper, *Mass Murder*, 133).

58. Piper, *Mass Murder*, 131–32; Friedler et al., *Zeugen*, 64; Broad, "Erinnerungen," 173; Müller, *Eyewitness*, 16–17; NAL, WO 208/4661, statement of H. Aumeier, July 25, 1945, p. 5. Structural faults eventually forced the SS to dismantle the old chimney in June 1942 and build a new one; Pressac, *Krematorien*, 49–50.

59. Himmler quote in Friedländer, *Jahre*, 378. See also Dannecker, Vermerk, June 15, 1942, in Klarsfeld, *Vichy*, 379–80; Longerich, *Himmler*, 586–91; idem, *Politik*, 495–96; Cesarani, *Eichmann*, 139–40. For the continuing focus on forced labor, see NAL, HW 16/19, GPD Nr. 3, WVHA-D to Auschwitz, June 17, 1942.

60. Broszat, *Kommandant*, 237; interrogation R. Höss, April 1, 1946, in Mendelsohn, *Holocaust*, vol. 12, 81.

61. Höss quote in USHMM, RG-11.001M.03, reel 20, folder 26, Vermerk, Besprechung mit Kammler, May 22, 1943.

62. Kalthoff and Werner, *Händler*, 148–51. See also UN War Crimes Commission, *Law Reports*, 95. For the Zyklon B production overseen by Degesch, and its distribution, see Hayes, *Cooperation*, 272–300.

63. Witte et al., *Dienstkalender*, 461–62.

64. IfZ, F 13/7, Bl. 383–88: R. Höss, "Richard Glücks," November 1946.

65. State of Israel, *Trial*, vol. 7, 392; BArchK, All. Proz. 6/99, Bl. 31; ibid., 6/101, Bl. 36; YVA, M-5/162, D. Wisliceny, Betrifft: Adolf Eichmann, October 27, 1946.

66. O. Pohl testimony, June 4, 1946, extract in *NCA*, supplement B, 1590.

67. APMO, D-AUI-1/3a, Bl. 58: Führer vom Dienst, June 16–17, 1942; ibid., Proces Höss, Hd 6, Bl. 114–20: O. Wolken, Kommentar, n.d. (c. spring 1945).

68. An inspection of the crematorium by a high-ranking SS officer on June 17 or 18, 1942, is attested by Filip Müller (Kraus and Kulka, *Todesfabrik*, 131–32). Like Wolken (see previous note), Müller believed that the SS officer was Heinrich Himmler. But by the time Himmler visited Auschwitz in mid-July, Müller had already left the cremation commando in the main camp (*DAP*, Aussage F. Müller, October 5, 1964, 20507).

69. For bunker 2, see Piper, *Mass Murder*, 134–36; Van Pelt, *Case*, 267; Pressac and Van Pelt, "Machinery," 213–14; Broszat, *Kommandant*, 242.

70. Quote in NAL, HW 16/19, GPD Nr. 3, KL Auschwitz to Glücks, June 24, 1942. See also ibid., WVHA-D to KL Auschwitz, June 24, 1942; ibid., Liebehenschel to KL, June 18, 1942.

71. Piper, *Zahl*, 183–97; Longerich, *Politik*, 521. In addition, it is likely that around 1,700 Jews were deported from Germany to Auschwitz in July 1942; Gottwaldt and Schulle, "*Judendeportationen*," 395–96.

72. Piper, *Zahl*, 191, 198, and table D; Gottwaldt and Schulle, "*Judendeportationen*," 397–98; Longerich, *Himmler*, 710–12; Ahnert, Vermerk, September 1, 1942, in Klarsfeld, *Vichy*, 447–48; NAL, HW 16/21, GPD Nr. 3, WVHA to Auschwitz, August 22 and 24, 1942.

73. Piper, *Zahl*, table D and 15; Steinbacher, "*Musterstadt*," 295–302.

74. For Westerbork, see Boas, *Boulevard*; Hillesum, *Letters*. For the Slovakian camps, from an SS perspective, see YVA, M-5/162, Verhör D. Wisliceny, May 7, 1946.

75. For Drancy, see Wellers, *L'Étoile*.

76. Quotes in Stuldreher, "Konzentrationslager," 328; WL, P.III.h. No. 573, A. Lehmann, "Das Lager Vught," n.d., 5. See also *OdT*, vol. 7, 133–50; Van Pelt, "Introduction."

77. For this and the previous paragraph, see WL, P.III.h. No. 573, A. Lehmann, "Das Lager

Vught," n.d., quote on 15; Deen, *"Wenn,"* quote on 21; Koker, *Edge,* 20, 104, 198, 256, 294, 340, 369, quote on 341; Stuldreher, "Herzogenbusch"; *OdT,* vol. 7, 133–50.

78. Figures for ghettos in BArchB, NS 19/1570, Bl. 12–28: Inspekteur für Statistik, Endlö-sung der Judenfrage. These figures are not always accurate and should be used with some caution. For the Schmelt camps in Silesia and parts of the Sudetenland, see Ru-dorff, "Arbeit"; Steinbacher, *"Musterstadt,"* 138–53.

79. Around two hundred thousand Jews were deported to Auschwitz during 1942; Piper, *Zahl,* table D. In early January 1943, 11,112 Jewish men and 1,540 Jewish women were still alive in Auschwitz; Schulte, "London," 223.

80. Berger, *Experten,* 177, 254–55.

81. Pohl, "Holocaust," 152–54.

82. SMAB, *Inmitten,* 62, 70–71; Langfus, "Aussiedlung," 80, 87 (n. 9), 104–105, 114, 117–120; Friedler et al., *Zeugen,* 204–207, 374, 380; Greif, *Wir weinten,* 56.

83. Langfus, "Aussiedlung," quotes on 121. See also Steinke, *Züge,* 58; Gigliotti, *Train,* 101–10; Greif, *Wir weinten,* 57. More generally on profiteering during the Holocaust in Poland, see Gross, *Golden Harvest.*

84. Quotes in Langfus, "Aussiedlung," 81, 114; Fulbrook, *Small Town,* 288; Bacharach, *Dies,* 99. See also Friedländer, *Jahre,* 549–50; Dörner, *Die Deutschen,* 324–25; Koker, *Edge,* 256–57; Hájková, "Prisoner Society," 283–84.

85. RSHA, Richtlinien zur Durchführung der Evakuierung von Juden, February 20, 1943, in Gottwaldt and Schulle, *"Judendeportationen,"* 373–79; NAL, HW 16/21, Höss to Eichmann, October 7, 1942.

86. Quotes in Broad, "Erinnerungen," 174; Van Pelt, *Case,* 240. See also *DAP,* Vernehmung H. Stark, April 23, 1959, 4540–41; Iwaszko, "Reasons," 17; Citroen and Starzyńska, *Auschwitz,* 57–90.

87. For this and the previous paragraph, see Langfus, "Aussiedlung," 121–22, quotes on 122; Greif, *Wir weinten,* 57–58; Czech, *Kalendarium,* 352. More generally on the ar-rival of deportation trains, see Adler et al., *Auschwitz,* 59–62; Gradowski, "Tagebuch," 156–57; Friedler et al., *Zeugen,* 145; Gigliotti, *Train,* 179, 185–90. SS men acted more brutally when they expected Jews to resist; Fulbrook, *Small Town,* 303–304.

88. Czech (*Kalendarium,* 241) dates the first selection to July 4, 1942. Even after selections at the ramp became routine, some transports were taken to Birkenau transit com-pounds and selected there instead; Piper, *Mass Murder,* 109.

89. Piper, *Zahl,* 183, 190, 193, 198; Czech, *Kalendarium,* 347–70; Broszat, *Kommandant,* 208.

90. Quote in Broad, "Erinnerungen," 188. During the first months, the responsibility for selections apparently fell to camp compound leaders. From around spring 1943, it lay with SS doctors; Dirks, *"Verbrechen,"* 101–104; Wagner, *IG Auschwitz,* 174; *DAP,* Vernehmung H. Stark, April 23, 1959, 4540–41. However, some prisoners testified to the participation of doctors prior to spring 1943 (e.g., Greif, *Wir weinten,* 58). For labor action leaders, BArchB, Film 44840, Interrogation G. Maurer, March 13, 1947, p. 9.

91. The SS had not encountered children, women, or old men during the selections among Soviet "commissars" in 1941.

92. Quote in Van Pelt, *Case,* 238.

93. Kubica, "Children," 205, 217, 289; Buser, *Überleben,* 116–21; Pohl, *Holocaust,* 106–107; the figures exclude deportations from Theresienstadt (see chapters 7 and 9). I use the term "children" for all those under the age of eighteen.

94. Strzelecka, "Women," 171; IfZ, EE by F. Entress, April 14, 1947, ND: NO-2368; APMO, Proces Höss, Hd 6, Bl. 46–50, O. Wolken, "Frauen u. Kinderschicksale," February 18, 1945.

95. Lengyel, *Chimneys,* 27 (first published in 1947).

96. Gerlach and Aly, *Kapitel,* 290; men could claim to be slightly older than forty.

97. For example, see Wiesel, *Nacht,* 50–53 (first published in 1958).

98. Langer, "Dilemma," quote on 224. See also Shik, "Erfahrung," 108.

99. NAL, HW 16/21, Höss to Eichmann, October 7, 1942; Steinbacher, *Musterstadt,* 278.

100. Broszat, *Kommandant,* 205–206, quote on 205.

101. Broad, "Erinnerungen," quote on 188; Dirks, *"Verbrechen,"* 102.

102. Broszat, *Kommandant,* 246; IfZ, F 13/8, Bl. 480–85: R. Höss, "Dr. Grawitz," January 1947.

103. IfZ, F 13/6, Bl. 355–58: R. Höss, "Gerhard Maurer," November 1946; Broszat, *Kommandant,* 246; testimony of R. Höss, April 2, 1946, in Mendelsohn, *Holocaust,* vol. 12, 109.

104. Broszat, *Kommandant,* 208, 246.

105. Piper, *Mass Murder,* 143.

106. Langfus, "Aussiedlung," 123; Czech, *Kalendarium,* 352; Greif, *Wir weinten,* 58; APMO, Proces Höss, Hd 5, Bl. 24–38: testimony of Dr. B. Epstein, April 7, 1945; Lewental, "Gedenkbuch," 204; BoA, testimony of H. Frydman, August 7, 1946.

107. Quotes in Delbo, *Auschwitz,* 7 (in Delbo's text, the last phrase precedes the first one); IfZ, F 13/8, Bl. 480–85: R. Höss, "Dr. Grawitz," January 1947, Bl. 485. See also Friedler et al., *Zeugen,* 71; Piper, *Mass Murder,* 136–37.

108. Quotes in IfZ, G 20/2, testimony of J. P. Kremer, July 18, 1947; LSW, Bl. 44–66: Vernehmung S. Dragon, May 10, 11, and 17, 1946. See also Friedler et al., *Zeugen,* 71–73; Broad, "Erinnerungen," 173. The two wooden barracks were completed after mid-August 1942.

109. Pressac and Van Pelt, "Machinery," 213–14; NAL, WO 208/4661, statement of H. Aumeier, July 25, 1945, p. 9.

110. For this and the previous paragraph, see LSW, Bl. 44–66: Vernehmung S. Dragon, May 10, 11, and 17, 1946, Bl. 45–46; Friedler et al., *Zeugen,* 92–98, 206; Greif, *Wir weinten,* 60–63; Hördler, "Ordnung," 142; Schmid, "Moll," 125–28; Czech, *Kalendarium,* 356. Earlier on December 9, 1942, the SS had murdered all prisoners of the old Special Squad, following a spate of escapes.

111. Greif, *Wir weinten,* 49–58; Czech, *Kalendarium,* 352; Piper, *Zahl,* 204.

112. Quotes in LSW, Bl. 44–66: Vernehmung S. Dragon, May 10, 11, and 17, 1946, Bl. 47, 51. For "dentists," see also Friedler et al., *Zeugen,* 176.

113. Pressac and Van Pelt, "Machinery," 215–16; Van Pelt, *Case,* 255; Friedler et al., *Zeugen,* 88; "Bericht Tabeau," 154.

114. Van Pelt, *Case,* 80, 214, 352, 465–66; Pressac and Van Pelt, "Machinery," 216–19, 223–24; Piper, *Mass Murder,* 164–73; Fröbe, "Kammler," 310–11. Another reason why SS planners regarded the new crematoria complex as more effective was related to the chemical reaction of Zyklon B. During the long winter months, cyanide took longer to evaporate in the unheated bunkers 1 and 2. By contrast, the new crematoria IV and V could be preheated with the help of stoves, while the ovens above the gas chambers of crematoria II and III had a similar effect (I am grateful to Robert Jan van Pelt for clarifying this point).

115. For this and the previous paragraph, see Friedler et al., *Zeugen,* 88–92, quote on 91; Broszat, *Kommandant,* 243–44; Arad, *Belzec,* 170–71; NAL, WO 208/4661, statement of H. Aumeier, July 25, 1945, pp. 3–4; USHMM, RG-11.001M.03, reel 43, folder 336, W. Dejaco, Dienstfahrt nach Litzmannstadt, September 17, 1942; Strzelecki, "Utilization," 412–13; Broad, "Erinnerungen," 166; Montague, *Chelmno,* 114–19. Between September 1942 and March–April 1943, smaller transports of Jews still went to Chelmno, before the camp was closed down, only to be briefly reopened in June–July 1944; *OdT,* vol. 8, 310–17.

116. Pressac and Van Pelt, "Machinery," 223, 232–36; Van Pelt, *Case,* 450–51. For Topf & Sons, see Knigge, *Techniker;* Schüle, *Industrie.*

117. Bischoff to WVHA, June 28, 1943, in Kogon et al., *Massentötungen,* 219; Van Pelt, *Case,* 342–50. In addition, 340 corpses could still be burned in the old crematorium I.

118. Broad, "Erinnerungen," 181.

119. Broszat, *Kommandant*, quote on 199; USHMM, RG-11.001M.03, reel 20, folder 26, Besuch des Hauptamtschefs in Auschwitz, August 17, 1943; deposition H. Tauber, May 24, 1945, in Piper, *Mass Murder*, appendix 3, 255.
120. P. Levi, "A Past We Thought Would Never Return," *Corriere della Sera*, May 8, 1974, in Belpoliti, *Levi*, 31–34, p. 33.
121. Bauman, *Modernity*, 7–9.
122. Quotes in KL Auschwitz to WVHA, February 20, 1943, in Kogon et al., *Massentötungen*, 222; *DAP*, Vernehmung H. Stark, July 24, 1959, 4581–82; IfZ, G 20/1, Das Oberste Volkstribunal, Urteil, December 22, 1947, p. 108. See also Van Pelt, *Case*, 296; Kagan, "Standesamt," 153; BArchL, B 162/7999, Bl. 768–937: StA Koblenz, EV, July 25, 1974, Bl. 895; ibid., B 162/7998, Bl. 623–44: Vernehmung J. Otto, April 1, 1970, Bl. 641; testimony of defendant Sommer, *TWC*, vol. 5, 677–78. The Birkenau SS apparently kept a separate record of corpses burned; deposition of H. Tauber, May 24, 1945, in Piper, *Mass Murder*, appendix 3, 262.
123. For one example, see Kotek and Rigoulot, *Jahrhundert*, 416.
124. Pressac and Van Pelt, "Machinery," 233–39. Faults and breakdowns forced the quick closure of crematorium IV.
125. For some thoughts on the mechanical nature of Nazi genocide, see Bauman, *Modernity*, 83–116.
126. *DAP*, Aussage R. Böck, August 3, 1964, 14149–50; Kogon et al., *Massentötungen*, 228; Kremer, "Tagebuch," 222.
127. Deposition of H. Tauber, May 24, 1945, in Piper, *Mass Murder*, appendix 3, 251–57; Friedler et al., *Zeugen*, 164–65.
128. Quote in Langfus, "Aussiedlung," 126.
129. On the historiography, see Marrus, "Jewish Resistance."
130. Quotes in Bettelheim, "Foreword," 7, 12. See also Wünschmann, "'Scientification,'" 112 (n. 5).
131. For this and the previous paragraph, see Friedler et al., *Zeugen*, 150, 158, quote on 147; Greif, *Wir weinten*, xxxi–ii; Müller, *Eyewitness*, 75–80.
132. Quote in Greif, *Wir weinten*, 32.
133. Borowski, "This Way," 89 (first published in 1946).
134. Quotes in Unbekannter Autor, "Einzelheiten" (1943–44), 180, 183.
135. Bettelheim, "Foreword," 12.
136. YVA, 03/2874, protocol I. Gönczi, January 11, 1966; Longerich, *Politik*, 492–93.
137. Marszałek, *Majdanek*, 74–75; Schwindt, *Majdanek*, 103–11.
138. *OdT*, vol. 7, 42, 47–48; Schulte, "London," 224; Glücks to Pohl, July 15, 1942, in Marszałek, *Majdanek*, 155.
139. For this and the previous paragraph, see Lenard, "Flucht," quotes on 150, 161. Lenard's trail disappears after summer 1944. See also *OdT*, vol. 7, 56–59, 62; Mailänder Koslov, *Gewalt*, 86–90; Marszałek, *Majdanek*, 97–99; Hördler, "Ordnung," 128, 133; HLSL, Anklageschrift gegen Koch, 1944, p. 2, ND: NO-2366; YVA, 03/2874, protocol I. Gönczi, January 11, 1966; Ambach and Köhler, *Lublin-Majdanek*, quote on 187.
140. Quote in USHMM, RG-11.001M.76, reel 421, folder 157, WVHA-C/III, Dienstreise zur Zentralbauleitung Lublin, January 20, 1943. For mortality figures, see Kranz, "Erfassung," 234, 241.
141. Marszałek, *Majdanek*, quote on 136–37; Mailänder Koslov, *Gewalt*, 288–93; *OdT*, vol. 7, 51; YVA, Tr-10/1172, LG Düsseldorf, Urteil, June 30, 1981, 78.
142. Arad, *Belzec*, 56–58; White, "Majdanek"; Marszałek, *Majdanek*, 14–15; Berger, *Experten*, 82. In some cases, Jews were even selected *in* Sobibor and Treblinka for slave labor in Majdanek; ibid., 391.
143. Schwindt, *Majdanek*, 158–67, 289; Kranz, "Massentötungen," 220–22; Mailänder Koslov, *Gewalt*, 310–12. The first gassings probably took place some weeks before the completion of the killing complex.

144. *OdT*, vol. 8, 354–55; Arad, *Belzec*, 370–71. There were only sporadic killings of Jews in Belzec in 1943; Berger, *Experten*, 190.

145. Witte and Tyas, "Document," 471–72; Kranz, "Erfassung," 234.

146. Quotes in testimony of R. Awronska, in Ambach and Köhler, *Lublin-Majdanek*, 101. See also Schwindt, *Majdanek*, 290; *OdT*, vol. 7, 54; Marszałek, *Majdanek*, 150; Longerich, *Politik*, 539; Mailänder Koslov, *Gewalt*, 322–23; Kranz, "Massentötungen," 225; idem, "Erfassung," 243.

147. Quotes in BArchB (ehem. BDC), SSO, Florstedt, Hermann, 18.2.1895, Glücks to SS-Personalhauptamt, March 5, 1943; "Bericht Vrba" (1944), 282. See also Conway, "Augenzeugenberichte," 269; *OdT*, vol. 7, 61–65. For most of its life, Majdanek held ten thousand prisoners or less; ibid., 50.

148. Arad estimates that around 135,000 of 1.7 million Jews murdered in the Globocnik death camps came from outside Poland and the Soviet Union; Arad, *Belzec*, 149, 379. See also Hayes, "Auschwitz," 339; BArchK, All. Proz. 6/106, Bl. 24.

149. Quote in IfZ, F 13/6, Bl. 359–68: R. Höss, "Globocnik," January 1947. See also Black, "Globocnik," 112; Berger, *Experten*, 85.

150. Berger, *Experten*, 252–53; Piper, *Zahl*, tables D and 15.

151. Arad, *Belzec*, 30, 69, 84; Pohl, "Holocaust," 153; Berger, *Experten*, 224–25; YVA, TR-10/1069, vol. 8, Bl. 78–88: Vernehmung Erich B., December 10, 1962; Strzelecka and Setkiewicz, "Construction," 73; BArchB (ehem. BDC), SSO Pohl, Oswald, 30.6.1892, Pohl to Himmler, April 5, 1944; Schulte, "London," 223.

152. Quote in YVA, O.3/4039, Bl. 1921–29: Vernehmung E. Rosenberg, February 11, 1961, Bl. 1921–22. See also Arad, *Belzec*, 23–88; Berger, *Experten*, 52, 78, 96, 110–11, 129, 144–46, 207, 210–13; Krakowski, *Todeslager*, passim.

153. Friedlander, *Genocide*, 279–302; Berger, *Experten*, 190.

154. YVA, TR-10/1069, vol. 6, Bl. 74–76: Vernehmung Karl F., April 10, 1962, quotes on 74; Arad, *Belzec*, 105–13; Berger, *Experten*, 300–301.

155. Perz and Sandkühler, "Auschwitz," 291–93; Berger, *Experten*, 180–81.

156. To fully exploit his labor camps, Globocnik set up the limited company Osti (Ostindustrie GmbH) in a joint venture with the WVHA; Kaienburg, *Wirtschaft*, 550–51.

157. See, for example, the involvement of the Gauleiter of Upper Austria, August Eigruber, in Mauthausen; YUL, MG 1832, Series II—Trials, 1945–2001, Box 10, folder 50, Affidavit A. Eigruber, February 19, 1946.

158. YVA, Globocnik to Himmler, January 5, 1944, p. 12, ND: 4024–PS.

159. Schwindt, *Majdanek*, 75–76; Kranz, "Konzentrationslager Majdanek," 239–41; idem, "Massentötungen," 220.

160. BArchB (ehem. BDC), SSO, Florstedt, Hermann, 18.2.1895, SS Personalhauptamt to SS Oberabschnitt Fulda-Werra, September 14, 1943; IfZ, F 13/6, Bl. 359–68: R. Höss, "Globocnik," January 1947.

161. IfZ, F 13/6, Bl. 359–68: R. Höss, "Globocnik," January 1947, quotes on 364, 367.

162. Affidavit of R. Höss, April 5, 1946, *IMT*, vol. 33, 275–79, ND: 3868–PS, quotes on 277; Broszat, *Kommandant*, 256–57.

163. Hilberg, *Vernichtung*, vol. 2, 955; Arad, *Belzec*, 100–104; Berger, *Experten*, 98.

164. Quote in IfZ, F 13/6, Bl. 359–68: R. Höss, "Globocnik," January 1947, Bl. 366.

165. For this view, see Orth, *System*, 199.

166. Quote in Himmler to Pohl et al., October 2, 1942, in Heiber, *Reichsführer!*, 189–90 (another publication dates the letter to October 9, 1942; *TWC*, vol. 5, 616–17). See also Longerich, *Himmler*, 684–88; Pohl, "Holocaust," 156–57, also used below.

167. Kárný, "Waffen-SS," 246.

168. Paserman, "Bericht," quotes on 151–52. See also *OdT*, vol. 8, 91–109; Finder, "Jewish Prisoner Labour"; Longerich, *Himmler*, 684–85; Snyder, *Bloodlands*, 286–92; Friedländer, *Jahre*, 550–53. Himmler had first ordered the establishment of a KL in Warsaw back in October 1942, to bring its ghetto workshops under SS control. This order was

never implemented, however, and once Himmler decided to liquidate the ghetto, the function of the proposed camp changed.

169. IfZ, Himmler to Pohl et al., June 21, 1943, ND: NO-2403. More generally, see Snyder, *Bloodlands*, 189–94, 228; Dieckmann, *Besatzungspolitik*, vol. 1, 451; ibid., vol. 2, 1248–49.

170. Quote in USHMM, RG-11.001M.05, reel 75, 504–2–8, Einsatzgruppe A, Vermerk, October 1, 1941. See also ibid., Stahlecker to RSHA, August 21, 1941 and October 6, 1941; Angrick and Klein, *"Endlösung,"* 207–11.

171. *OdT*, vol. 8, 17–87; Angrick and Klein, *"Endlösung,"* 391–405, 420; IfZ, F 37/2, Himmler diary, entries for March 13, 14, and 16, 1943.

172. Quote in BArchB (ehem. BDC), SSO, Aumeier, Hans, 20.8.1906, Glücks, Personal-Antrag, August 22, 1944. See also *OdT*, vol. 8, 131–83.

173. Quote in unknown correspondent to M. Lubocka, August 27, 1943, in Harshav, *Last Days*, 660. See also Dieckmann, *Besatzungspolitik*, vol. 2, especially pages 1268–1321; idem, "Ghetto"; IfZ, Himmler to Pohl et al., June 21, 1943, ND: NO-2403; *OdT*, vol. 8, 185–208. Jürgen Matthäus suggests that Kovno was not subordinated to the WVHA (*OdT*, vol. 8, 200). This conclusion rests on a misunderstanding of the role of the regional SS economic officer (see below). The WVHA certainly regarded Kovno as one of its KL (e.g., BArchB, NS 4/Na 9, Bl. 9–11).

174. *OdT*, vol. 1, 223; ibid., vol. 8, 18, 106, 133, 200; Dieckmann, "Ghetto," 454; idem, *Besatzungspolitik*, vol. 2, 1282, 1287–96; Megargee, *Encyclopedia*, I/B, 1230.

175. SS economic officers were attached to regional higher SS and police leaders, with whom they shared reports from local KL commandants; Schulte, *Zwangsarbeit*, 313–20; Allen, *Business*, 180–81; *OdT*, vol. 8, 132.

176. Steinbacher, *"Musterstadt,"* 305; Rudorff, "Arbeit," 35–36; *OdT*, vol. 5, 186–91; *OdT*, vol. 6, 204.

177. Quote in BArchB (ehem. BDC), SSO Pohl, Oswald, 30.6.1892, Aktenvermerk, September 7, 1943. See also YVA, Globocnik to Himmler, January 5, 1944, ND: 4024–PS (here reference to Pohl order of October 22, 1943).

178. Schelvis, *Sobibor*, 145–72; Pohl, "Zwangsarbeiterlager," 427–28; Berger, *Experten*, 254; Friedländer, *Jahre*, 588; Longerich, *Himmler*, 687.

179. For this and the previous paragraph, see Mailänder Koslov, *Gewalt*, 205, 302–308, 324–26, quote on 305; *OdT*, vol. 7, 52–53; Ambach and Köhler, *Lublin-Majdanek*, 85, 98, 183.

180. *OdT*, vol. 7, 48–49; Kranz, "Massentötungen," 226.

181. Kaienburg, *Wirtschaft*, 540–48, 551–52; Berger, *Experten*, 261–64; Goldhagen, *Executioners*, 300–311; YVA, Globocnik to Himmler, January 5, 1944, ND: 4024–PS.

182. Kaienburg, *Wirtschaft*, 559–61; Longerich, *Himmler*, 686; Pohl, "Zwangsarbeiterlager," 429–31; Friedländer, *Jahre*, 614–15. Himmler was thwarted by the Warthegau Gauleiter Greiser in his efforts to turn the Lodz ghetto into a KL.

183. For this and the previous paragraph, see BArchL, B 162/1124, Bl. 2351–2418: Dr. A. Biberstein, "Das Lager Plaszow," n.d., quotes on 2396, 2398; *OdT*, vol. 8, 239–87; Megargee, *Encyclopedia*, vol. 1/B, 862–66.

184. Fröhlich, *Tagebücher*, II/4, June 2, 1942, 432. See also Witte et al., *Dienstkalender*, 572–73; APMO, Proces Maurer, 6, Bl. 52–56: EE by A. Kaindl, June 15, 1946, ND: NI-280; AdsD, KE, E. Büge, Bericht, n.d. (1945–46), 157–58; BStU, MfS HA IX/11 ZUV 4, Bd. 24, Bl. 190–96: Vernehmungsprotokoll H. Hempel, August 23, 1946; Wein, "Krankenrevier," 51 (n. 27).

185. For the figures, see above and Schulte, "London." For the nationality of Jewish prisoners, e.g., BArchB, NS 4/Bu 143, Rapport, October 17, 1942.

186. BArchL, B 162/7999, Bl. 768–937: StA Koblenz, EV, July 25, 1974, Bl. 894; Witte et al., *Dienstkalender*, 573 (n. 155); Longerich, *Himmler*, 644.

187. Quote in HLSL, WVHA to LK, October 5, 1942, ND: 3677–PS. See also ITS, DE ITS

1.1.0.6, RSHA to Stapo(leit)stellen, November 5, 1942, ND: NO-2522. As these documents show, some SS and police leaders wrongly thought of Auschwitz as being located outside the German Reich.

188. Buggeln, *System*, 47–48.
189. Sprenger, *Groß-Rosen*, 130.
190. Külow, "Häftlinge," 197–98, quote on 197. See also Piper, *Mass Murder*, 105; Czech, *Kalendarium*, 325, 328–29; Kwiet, "Leben," 238.
191. BArchB, NS 19/1570, Bl. 12–28: Inspekteur für Statistik, Endlösung der Judenfrage, Bl. 24. Of course, not all Jews inside the KL were identified by the German authorities (Kogon, *Theory*, 2006, 192), despite the use of prisoner informants (NAL, HW 16/11, Buchenwald to Auschwitz, October 19, 1942).
192. NAL, HW 16/21, GPD Nr. 3, Pister to WVHA, October 29, 1942.
193. WL, P.III.h. No. 228, Bericht E. Federn, n.d. Federn was liberated from Buchenwald in April 1945.
194. For this and the previous paragraph, see de Rudder, "Zwangsarbeit," 206–19, quote on 212 (n. 36); Burger, *Werkstatt*, 89–198 (the source for the film *The Counterfeiters*, 2007); Witte et al., *Dienstkalender*, 475; Hohmann and Wieland, *Konzentrationslager*, 38–39.
195. Quote in Bauer, *Jews*, 252.
196. *OdT*, vol. 7, quotes on 188. See also Wenck, *Menschenhandel*, 33–93.
197. For the POW camp, see Stiftung, *Bergen-Belsen*, 41–141.
198. *OdT*, vol. 1, 220–21; *OdT*, vol. 7, 188–93; WVHA to LK, June 29, 1943, in Kolb, *Bergen-Belsen*, 208–209. See also Wenck, *Menschenhandel*, passim.
199. Quotes in WL, P.III.h. No. 555, F. Heilbut, "Bergen-Belsen," n.d. (1945–49), p. 3; S. H. Herrmann, "Austauschlager Bergen-Belsen," 1944, in Niedersächsische Landeszentrale, *Bergen-Belsen*, 53. See also Wenck, *Menschenhandel*, 58–70, 147–55, 180–81, 220–28; *OdT*, vol. 7, 190–97.
200. Wenck, *Menschenhandel*, 248–60; Niedersächsische Landeszentrale, *Bergen-Belsen*, 36–37; *OdT*, vol. 7, 191–96; Buser, *Überleben*, 267.

7. Anus Mundi

1. Quotes in IfZ, G 20/2, Aussage J. P. Kremer, July 18, 1947; Kremer, "Tagebuch," 213. See also Czech, *Kalendarium*, 295; *DAP*, Vernehmung J. P. Kremer, June 4, 1964, 9857. More generally, see Lewental, "Gedenkbuch," 215–20; Vaisman, *Auschwitz*, 27–32 (written in 1945).
2. Quote in Kremer letter, September 5, 1942, cited in Langbein, *Menschen*, 391. See also Kremer, "Tagebuch," 209–29; Rawicz, "Dokument."
3. Kremer, "Tagebuch," quotes on 212, 217. See also NAL, HW 16/66, "II. Concentration Camps," November 27, 1942; Czech, *Kalendarium*, 209; Schwarz, *Frau*, 175–76.
4. Mailänder Koslov, *Gewalt*, 218–22, 484–85.
5. Kremer, "Tagebuch," quotes on 222, 214, 218. See also Czech, *Kalendarium*, 336; IfZ, G 20/1, Das Oberste Volkstribunal, Urteil, December 22, 1947, 135–36; Klee, *Auschwitz*, 407–408; Rawicz, "Document," 13.
6. For the loot, and its value, see Kremer, "Tagebuch," 219–28. In 1943, a married SS Untersturmführer without children earned around 2,640 Reichsmark annually (after tax); Buggeln, *Arbeit*, 401.
7. *DAP*, Vernehmung K. Morgen, March 9, 1964, 5560–61.
8. StN, Pohl to Himmler, September 30, 1943, ND: PS-1469; Lasik, "Historical-Sociological," 274; Schulte, "London," 223 (using the Auschwitz figures for September 1 and October 1 to calculate the average for September 1942).
9. NAL, HW 16/6, Part 2, Bl. 534–35: report on German police, September 26, 1942;

Glücks to 1. Lagerärzte, December 28, 1942, in NMGB, *Buchenwald*, 257–58 (the figure of 12,832 includes 99 prisoners officially executed). The estimate of Jews murdered on arrival in August 1942 is largely based on Czech, *Kalendarium*, 263–92.

10. Piper, *Zahl*, 164.

11. Grotum, *Archiv*, quote on 297.

12. Dirks, *"Verbrechen,"* 97–99.

13. IfZ, F 13/6, Bl. 343–54: R. Höss, "Oswald Pohl," November 1946, quote on 350; ibid., F 13/8, Bl. 462–66: R. Höss, "Dr. Ing. Kammler," n.d. (1946–47).

14. StN, Pohl to Himmler, September 30, 1943, ND: PS-1469.

15. BArchB (ehem. BDC), SSO Pohl, Oswald, 30.6.1892, Pohl to Himmler, April 5, 1944. See also IfZ, G 20/1, Das Oberste Volkstribunal, Urteil, December 22, 1947, 104–105; BArchB, NS 4/Na 9, Bl. 8.

16. APMO, Proces Höss, Hd 6, Bl. 129–312: Vernehmung O. Wolken, April 17–20, 1945, Bl. 202; YVA, 033/989, anonymous testimony (by W. Simoni), n.d. (1947), pp. 2, 7. There were some brick barracks in Birkenau, too; Iwaszko, "Housing," 54.

17. For this and the previous two paragraphs, see BoA, interview N. Epstein-Kozlowski, August 31, 1946; Boder, *Interview*; Rosen, *Wonder*; Matthäus, "Displacing Memory"; Czech, *Kalendarium*, 531.

18. For example, see Naasner, *Machtzentren*, 15–17.

19. For the debate about ideology versus economics, see Wagner, "Work." For reservations about the universal applicability of the concept of "annihilation through labor," see Browning, *Remembering*, 153.

20. Ambach and Köhler, *Lublin-Majdanek*, 94; *OdT*, vol. 7, 63.

21. Strzelecka, "Women," 193.

22. For this and the previous paragraph, see Wagner, *IG Auschwitz*, 62–107, 129, 162, 180–81, 286, 331–33; Schmaltz, "IG Farbenindustrie." Quotes in Levi, *If*, 78. Schmaltz argues that general plans for the establishment of a KL at the IG Farben site were probably already made in late 1941 or early 1942; even if this is correct, the final decision was not reached until summer 1942.

23. Quotes in WL, P.III.h. No. 198, F. Pagel, "Eines der Vielen Tausende[n] von Schicksalen," autumn 1955, p. 9; Levi, *If*, 78, 143. See also ibid., 142–47; Wagner, *IG Auschwitz*, 114, 141–63; Kwiet, "Leben", 238–39.

24. Quotes in Kautsky, *Teufel*, 254; Levi, *If*, 43; APMO, Proces Höss, Hd 5, Bl. 24–38: testimony Dr. B. Epstein, April 7, 1945 (translation from Polish by K. Friedla). See also Wagner, *IG Auschwitz*, 97–100, 125–33, 165, 280–81.

25. LG Osnabrück, Urteil, February 10, 1953, *JNV*, vol. 10, 347–91, quote on 357.

26. LG Frankfurt, Urteil, June 14, 1968, *JNV*, vol. 29, 421–523, quote on 514.

27. Setkiewicz, "Häftlingsarbeit," quotes on 599.

28. APMO, Proces Maurer, 7, Bl. 56–64: Auszüge aus IGF Auschwitz-Wochenberichten, ND: NI-15256, quote on 63 (February 10, 1943); Dirks, *"Verbrechen,"* 125–33, quote on 129; Wagner, *IG Auschwitz*, 166–67, 173–92, 217–18, 289.

29. *DAP*, Aussage S. Baretzki, November 20, 1964, 25627–35, quote on 25634.

30. APMO, Proces Höss, Hd 2a, Bl. 20–21: Untersturmführer Kinna, Bericht zu dem Transport nach Auschwitz, December 16, 1942.

31. Maršálek, *Mauthausen*, 46, 94; Kaienburg, "Funktionswandel," 265.

32. APMO, Proces Höss, Hd 2a, Bl. 20–21: Untersturmführer Kinna, Bericht zu dem Transport nach Auschwitz, December 16, 1942.

33. Historians and survivors of Auschwitz generally date the shift in SS policy to spring or summer 1943 (e.g., Piper, *Mass Murder*, 103; Strzelecka, "Hospitals," 322; APMO, Proces Höss, Hd 6, Bl. 129–312: Vernehmung O. Wolken, April 17–20, 1945, Bl. 203), though it may in fact have occurred in late 1942 (see previous note). For Majdanek, see *OdT*, vol. 7, 55.

34. Interview with L. Lady, September 19, 1947, in Tych et al., *Kinder*, 182.

35. Glücks to LK, July 28, 1942, cited in Greiser, "'Sie starben,'" 106. See also Strzelecka, "Quarantine."

36. For one example, see APMO, Proces Höss, Hd 6, Bl. 38–45: O. Wolken, "Lager-Bilder," n.d. (c. spring 1945), Bl. 43.

37. Quote in BArchL, B 162/2985, Bl. 2029–31: Vernehmung Sarah A., October 3, 1973. See also ibid., Nr. 26150, Bl. 541–657: LG Düsseldorf, Urteil, August 14, 1985, Bl. 579–80; *OdT*, vol. 8, 48; Piper, *Mass Murder*, 110–12.

38. Testimony of D. Medryk, in Ambach and Köhler, *Lublin-Majdanek*, 162–67; Langbein, *Menschen*, 409.

39. YVA, 033/8, "Was is forgekom in di lagern fon estonia," December 1944; Klüger, *weiter*, 118.

40. Quote in USHMM, RG-11.001M.03, reel 20, folder 26, Besprechung mit Amtsgruppenchef Kammler, May 22, 1943.

41. NAL, WO 208/4661, statement of H. Aumeier, July 25, 1945, p. 5.

42. Strzelecka, "Hospitals," 311–12; "Bericht Tabeau," 132–36.

43. Vaisman, *Auschwitz*, 21.

44. Hördler, "Ordnung," 142.

45. BArchL, B 162/26150, Bl. 541–657: LG Düsseldorf, Urteil, August 14, 1985, Bl. 596–606. The infirmary for men could hold around sixty prisoners; ibid., 591.

46. Ibid., 594–95, 612–17, quote on 617. See also ibid., Nr. 26148, Bl. 174–82: Vernehmung Ewald A., February 12, 1980, Bl. 181; ibid., Bl. 148–54: Aussage Jindrich S., November 6, 1979, and April 18, 1980; *OdT*, vol. 8, 28, 41.

47. Lewental, "Gedenkbuch," 210.

48. WL, P.III.h. No. 158, R. Lasker-Allais, "Auschwitz," n.d. (before November 1955), p. 7.

49. Langbein, *Menschen*, 90, citing Jean Améry's work.

50. Levi, "Grey Zone," 37.

51. NARA, M-1174, roll 3, Bl. 1441–65: examination E. Mahl, December 6, 1945, quote on 1447.

52. For this and the previous paragraph, see Piper, *Mass Murder*, 180–90, 251; Kilian, "'Handlungsräume'"; Friedler et al., *Zeugen*, 121, 136–38, 198–200, 372; Nyiszli, *Auschwitz*, 44; SMAB, *Inmitten*, 264; ITS, document ID 5618957.

53. C. Herman to his wife and daughter, November 6, 1944, in SMAB, *Inmitten*, 262. See also Friedler et al., *Zeugen*, 377.

54. Friedler et al., *Zeugen*, 134–35; Greif, *Wir weinten*, 190–93; Piper, *Mass Murder*, 190.

55. Nyiszli, *Auschwitz*, 43–44; Kilian, "'Handlungsräume,'" 127; Piper, *Mass Murder*, 190–92. Other Special Squad members lived in crematorium IV.

56. Levi, "Grey Zone," 38. See also Greif, "Sanity," 50–53; Nyiszli, *Auschwitz*, 60.

57. Friedler et al., *Zeugen*, 136; Vaisman, *Auschwitz*, 42.

58. Quotes in "Bericht Vrba," 229. See also Lewental, "Gedenkbuch," 246; Levi and de Benedetti, *Auschwitz Report*, 73.

59. Quote in Unbekannter Autor, "Einzelheiten," 182.

60. Müller, *Eyewitness*, 47–48; Lewental, "Gedenkbuch," 215.

61. Kilian, "'Handlungsräume,'" 121; Friedler et al., *Zeugen*, 7; Greif, *Wir weinten*, xli. Recent research by historians like Greif and Kilian has done much to change undifferentiated judgments about the Special Squad.

62. Greif, "Sanity," 38–41, quote on 41; Lewental, "Gedenkbuch," quote on 211.

63. Deposition of H. Tauber, May 24, 1945, in Piper, *Mass Murder*, appendix 3, pp. 250, 258; Nyiszli, *Auschwitz*, 84.

64. Lewental, "Gedenkbuch," 212.

65. Quote in Langer, "Dilemma," 224.

66. Levi, "Grey Zone," quote on 37; Lewental, "Gedenkbuch," 209, 213, 224; Nyiszli, *Auschwitz*, 61, 134.

67. Quote in Unbekannter Autor, "Notizen," 185. The State Museum in Oświęcim honored

the wishes of the unknown prisoner by using his title for its edition of writings by Special Squad prisoners discovered on the grounds of the camp; SMAB, *Inmitten*.

68. *OdT*, vol. 7, 48–49. The number of female prisoners was also exceptionally high in the two camps for Jews in western Europe, Herzogenbusch and Bergen-Belsen.

69. Czech, *Kalendarium*, 691; Strzelecka, "Women," 180–81.

70. StANü, Pohl to Himmler, September 30, 1943, ND: PS-1469.

71. Piper, *Zahl*, 158–62.

72. StANü, Pohl to Himmler, September 30, 1943, ND: PS-1469; Kranz, "Erfassung," 240. The passage above is based on Majdanek and Auschwitz. There are, as yet, no detailed statistics from the KL for Jews set up in eastern Europe in 1943–44.

73. BArchB, NS 3/426, Bl. 94: Runderlass, Chef Sipo und SD, May 6, 1943; Wachsmann, *Prisons*, 93.

74. NAL, WO 208/4200, CSDIC, SR Report, statement Obergefreiter Till, September 25, 1944; Lengyel, *Chimneys*, 112.

75. Quote in NAL, WO 309/1699, deposition of J. Schwarzhuber, January 23, 1946. See also APMO, Proces Höss, Hd 6, Bl. 129–312: Vernehmung O. Wolken, April 17–20, 1945, Bl. 254; ibid., Oswiadczenia, vol. 124, Bl. 152–66: testimony of M. Schvalbova, June 8, 1988; Kubica, "Children," 240, 267–73; *OdT*, vol. 8, 139; WL, P.III.h. No. 1007, E. Wuerth-Tscherne to Zentralstelle der baltischen Flüchtlinge, April 5, 1949.

76. Lengyel, *Chimneys*, 111.

77. Kielar, *Anus Mundi*, 122.

78. Shik, "Mother-Daughter," 117.

79. WL, P.III.b. No. 1164, N. Rosenberg, "Zwangsarbeiter fuer Siemens-Schuckert," January 1960, 2; "Bericht Vrba," 285; Lévy-Hass, *Vielleicht*, 10–11; Sommer, *KZ-Bordell*, 194–95.

80. WL, P.III.h. No. 782, E. Zwart, "Incidents in Birkenau," n.d. (before February 1958), pp. 8–9; ibid., No. 271, interview with L. Reig, June 2, 1956, p. 3 (my thanks to Jeff Porter for the translation); APMO, Proces Höss, Hd 6, Bl. 51–62: O. Wolken, "Chronik des Lagers Auschwitz II," n.d. (c. spring 1945), Bl. 60; Delbo, *Auschwitz*, 117.

81. *OdT*, vol. 8, 159–61, 260; WL, P.III.h. No. 1007, E. Wuerth-Tscherne to Zentralstelle der baltischen Flüchtlinge, April 5, 1949; Rolnikaite, *Tagebuch*, 189.

82. For example, see Kielar, *Anus Mundi*, 127.

83. Quote in P. Levi, "Films and Swastikas," *La Stampa*, February 12, 1977, in Belpoliti, *Levi*, 37–38. See also Kootz, "Nachwort," 193–94; Mailänder Koslov, "Meshes."

84. Frankl, *Ja*, 67; Cohen, *Human*, 73–74; Sommer, *KZ-Bordell*, 196–98.

85. YVA, 033/989, anonymous testimony (by W. Simoni), n.d. (1947), p. 8. See also Bass, "Love," 344.

86. Rózsa, "'Solange,'" quote on 187. On menstruation, see Amesberger et al., *Gewalt*, 85–88; Flaschka, "'Pretty,'" 81.

87. Shik, "Erfahrung," 110–13; Hughes, "Forced Prostitution," 249; Sommer, *KZ-Bordell*, 198–201.

88. Langbein, *Menschen*, 452; Hájková, "Barter," 516.

89. Semprun and Wiesel, *Schweigen*, 35. For a discussion of the thesis that the Holocaust was unique, see Stone, "Historiography."

90. Gradowski, "Tagebuch," quotes on 162, 166. Gradowski may have arrived on December 8, 1942; Friedler et al., *Zeugen*, 376.

91. Quote in Cohen, *Abyss*, 84.

92. YVA, 03/5787, interview with M. Zelikovitz, 1985, quotes on 4 (translation from Hebrew by Kim Wünschmann).

93. Cited in Unger, "Encounter," 280.

94. *OdT*, vol. 7, 46; Grotum, *Archiv*, 255–57; Kubica, "Children," 206.

95. Interview with J. Erner, n.d. (1945–46), in Tych et al., *Kinder*, 106; Interview with Z. Minc, April 28, 1947, ibid., 200; Rolnikaite, *Tagebuch*, 189–93; Buser, *Überleben*, 158–79; Kubica, "Children," 246–47.

96. Kubica, "Children," 249–50; Lenard, "Flucht," 164.

97. LG Ulm, Urteil, September 8, 1969, *JNV*, vol. 33, 209. See also *OdT*, vol. 8, 170–73.

98. Quote in APMO, Proces Höss, Hd 6, Bl. 38–45: O. Wolken, "Lager-Bilder," n.d. (spring 1945), Bl. 43.

99. Ambach and Köhler, *Lublin-Majdanek*, 87, 127, 153, 167, 197, Mitron quote on 125; *OdT*, vol. 7, 55–56.

100. Shik, "Mother-Daughter," 124.

101. Stargardt, *Witnesses*, 216–17, 378; Heberer, *Children*, 300.

102. J. Avram testimony, 1955, in Heberer, *Children*, 177–80, quote on 179. For "camp mothers," see Amesberger et al., *Gewalt*, 251–52. It is not clear if the term "camp fathers" was used at the time, though it seems likely. Otto Wolken, for example, referred to an Italian boy he saved (see chapter 10) as "my son in the camp"; APMO, Proces Höss, Hd 6, Bl. 129–312: Vernehmung O. Wolken, April 17–20, 1945, Bl. 260.

103. Shik, "Mother-Daughter," 112–21.

104. Buser, *Überleben*, 133, 215–16.

105. BArchL, B 162/5109, Bl. 1885–90: letter Molly I., October 27, 1964, quote on 1889. Molly I. joined her daughter on the deportation train to Auschwitz and survived the camps, liberated in Bergen-Belsen in April 1945. More generally, see *OdT*, vol. 8, 138–39, 152–55.

106. *OdT*, vol. 1, 20–21.

107. For this and the previous paragraph, see Kárný, "Familienlager"; Strzelecka and Setkiewicz, "Construction," 84–85, 96–97; Kubica, "Children," 240; "Bericht Vrba," 252.

108. Keren, "Family Camp"; Stargardt, *Witnesses*, 215–16; Kárný, "Familienlager," 134, 172–73, 194–97, 204; Kubica, "Children," 230, 289; Vrba, *Forgive*, 190–92; Heberer, *Children*, 168, 312; Czech, *Kalendarium*, 731, 734–37.

109. Steiner and Steiner, "Zwillinge," quote on 127; Kárný, "Familienlager," 214–23; Czech, *Kalendarium*, 811.

110. Buggeln, *Arbeit*, 262, 550.

111. *DAP*, Aussage S. Baretzki, February 18, 1965, 29242–43; Buser, *Überleben*, 150, 188; Stargardt, *Witnesses*, 216.

112. USHMM, RG-11.001M.03, reel 19, folder 19 (labelled 17 on microfilm), Besichtigung durch SS Obergruppenführer Pohl am 23.9.1942.

113. BArchB, NS 19/14, Bl. 131–33: Pohl to Himmler, September 16, 1942; Perz and Sandkühler, "Auschwitz," 292; Schulte, "London," 223.

114. Witte et al., *Dienstkalender*, 557–58.

115. USHMM, RG-11.001M.03, reel 19, folder 19, R. Höss, Besprechungen im "Haus der Waffen-SS," September 24, 1942.

116. Ibid., Besichtigung durch SS Obergruppenführer Pohl am 23.9.1942; Kremer, "Tagebuch," 217.

117. Quotes in USHMM, RG-11.001M.03, reel 19, folder 19, R. Höss, Bericht über Schlussbesprechung des Hauptamtschefs am 23.9.1942. See also Friedler et al., *Zeugen*, 89. Though the visit to bunker 2 was on Pohl's agenda, it is not clear whether it took place; there is no mention in Höss's summary of the places Pohl saw; USHMM, RG-11.001M.03, reel 19, folder 19, Besichtigung durch SS Obergruppenführer Pohl am 23.9.1942.

118. Ibid. In the end, the brothel was not opened until 1944; Sommer, *KZ-Bordell*, 45.

119. Broszat, *Kommandant*, 145.

120. IfZ, F 13/8, Bl. 486–87: R. Höss, "Dr. Lolling," November 1946; ibid., Bl. 467: R. Höss, "Karl Bischoff," n.d. (1946–47); ibid., F 13/7, Bl. 393–96: R. Höss, "Hartjenstein," November 1946; Broszat, *Kommandant*, 137 (note 2), 138 (note 1).

121. USHMM, 1998.A.0247, reel 15, Bl. 184–93: statement H. Aumeier, December 15, 1947; Dicks, *Licensed*, 122.

122. IfZ, KL Auschwitz to WVHA, March 25, 1942, ND: NO-2146; BArchB (ehem. BDC), SSO Pohl, Oswald, 30.6.1892, Pohl to Himmler, April 5, 1944.

123. Pohl to LK et al., April 30, 1942, *IMT*, vol. 38, 365–67, ND: 129–R; Perz, "Wehrmacht," 69.

124. Quote in BArchB (ehem. BDC), SSO, Koch, Karl, 2.8.1897, Glücks to Pohl, August 28, 1942.

125. BArchL, B 162/5222, Bl. 28–39: Vernehmung Hans K., May 22, 1962. See also Lasik, "SS Garrison," 329.

126. Mailänder Koslov, *Gewalt*, 195–201, 224–29.

127. Tuchel, "Wachmannschaften," 140–41; IfZ, F 13/6, Bl. 369–82: R. Höss, "Theodor Eicke," November 1946, Bl. 382.

128. Leleu, *Waffen-SS*, 54–87, 169–89, 1090. For brief overviews, see Heinemann, "*Rasse*," 341–49, 539–42; Longerich, *Himmler*, 621–22, 693–701.

129. Tuchel, "Wachmannschaften," 142–43; Mailänder Koslov, *Gewalt*, 130–31.

130. Some also came from western Europe, from countries such as Holland, France, and Denmark; *OdT*, vol. 7, 137; Buggeln, *Arbeit*, 457–60.

131. Tuchel, "Wachmannschaften," 144; Hördler, "Ordnung," 163–64.

132. Hördler, "Wehrmacht," 13; idem, "Ordnung," 168–69; Golczewski, "Kollaboration," 179–80; Arad, *Belzec*, 19–22; Pohl, "Trawniki-Männer"; Black, "Foot Soldiers." One of the transferred Trawniki men was Ivan Demjanjuk, a former Sobibor guard, who arrived in Flossenbürg in autumn 1943. After several decades of investigations, trials, and appeals, Demjanjuk was sentenced to five years' imprisonment by a Munich court in 2011, one year before his death; Volk, *Urteil*; Benz, "John Demjanjuk."

133. Stiller, "Zwangsgermanisierung," 118.

134. For example, see BArchB, R 187/598, KL Buchenwald, KB 5/43, May 12, 1943.

135. Quote in BArchB, NS 4/Au 1, Meldung an die Lagerführung Birkenau, July 13, 1944. On dismissals, and on the further fate of SS Private Marschall (who was sent back to sentry duty as a disciplinary measure), see Hördler, "Ordnung," 178–79. For SS appeals to comradeship, see Tuchel, "Wachmannschaften," 148.

136. Leleu, *Waffen-SS*, 271–77.

137. Buggeln, *Arbeit*, 424; Mailänder Koslov, *Gewalt*, 269; Stiller, "Zwangsgermanisierung," 121; Golczewski, "Kollaboration," 180; Riedle, *Angehörigen*, 84–85.

138. BArchB, NS 3/426, Bl. 101: WVHA to LK, 10 July 1943; IfZ, F 13/6, Bl. 359–68: R. Höss, "Globocnik," January 1947, Bl. 364–65.

139. For example, see Langbein, *Menschen*, 438–39.

140. Buggeln, *Arbeit*, 427–28.

141. WL, P.III.h. No. 228, Bericht E. Federn, n.d.; ibid., No. 418, E. Clemm, Erfahrungsbericht über Auschwitz, November 27, 1945.

142. For example, see Langbein, *Menschen*, 469–70.

143. Sprenger, *Groß-Rosen*, 211–12; BArchL, B 162/7999, Bl. 924: KL Gross-Rosen to WVHA-D, June 16, 1944; ibid., Bl. 925: KL Gross-Rosen to WVHA-D, August 26, 1944.

144. Mailänder Koslov, *Gewalt*, 20–21, 124–25, 258–66, 273, 280–81, 486–87.

145. From early 1944, Pohl prevented commandants from punishing female guards with detention; StN, WVHA to LK, January 17, 1944, ND: NO-1549.

146. Broszat, *Kommandant*, 177.

147. NARA, RG 549, 000–50–11 Ravensbrück CC (Box 522), testimony of J. Langefeld, December 26 and 31, 1945; Broszat, *Kommandant*, 177–78; Strebel, *Ravensbrück*, 70–71; Heike, "Langefeld," 13–14; Hördler, "SS-Kaderschmiede," 119. More generally, see Schwartz, "Eigensinn."

148. Mailänder Koslov, *Gewalt*, 210–11, 240, 282–86. See also Tillion, *Ravensbrück*, 147; Schwarz, *Frau*, 170–76; Mühlenberg, *SS-Helferinnenkorps*, 322–25, 418–20.

149. Mailänder Koslov, *Gewalt*, 439. See also ibid., 435-39; Hördler, "Ordnung," 142; Kielar, *Anus Mundi*, 348-49.

150. Mailänder Koslov, *Gewalt*, 218, 411-24, 441-50, 487-88.

151. For example, see YVA, Tr-10/1172, LG Düsseldorf, Urteil, June 30, 1981, pp. 238-39.

152. BArchL, B 162/5109, Bl. 1859-69: Protokoll Efim K., September 19, 1962; ibid., Bl. 1853-58: Protokoll Zelik G., November 5, 1962.

153. Quotes in BArchL, B 162/5109, Bl. 1854: Protokoll Zelik G., November 5, 1962; ibid., Nr. 5120, Bl. 2423: Vernehmungsniederschrift Sima S., October 14, 1965. See also ibid., Nr. 5117, Bl. 1670-75: Protokoll Zusman S., September 9, 1962; *OdT*, vol. 8, 133, 139, 172. Pannicke could not be traced after the war and was never prosecuted; ibid., 143.

154. Mühlhäuser, *Eroberungen*. See also Berger, *Experten*, 344-46; Sémelin, *Säubern*, 315-19; Weitz, *Century*, 227-33; Gourevitch, *We Wish*, 115.

155. Shik, "Sexual Abuse"; Amesberger et al., *Gewalt*, 142-46; Langbein, *Menschen*, 457-58. The suggestion that KL guards could rape with impunity (e.g., Hedgepeth and Saidel, "Introduction," 9, n. 6) is incorrect. For the official SS ban on sexual relations with prisoners, see KB Nr. 5/43, February 18, 1943, in Frei et al., *Kommandanturbefehle*, 224. There has been plenty of speculation about an illicit relationship between Rudolf Höss and a female Auschwitz prisoner, but the evidence is patchy; Sommer, *KZ-Bordell*, 205, 414 (n. 123).

156. Quote in Ambach and Köhler, *Lublin-Majdanek*, 202.

157. *DAP*, Aussage R. Böck, August 3, 1964, 14194.

158. Langbein, *Menschen*, 421.

159. For example, see Ambach and Köhler, *Lublin-Majdanek*, 151, 181.

160. Schmid, "Moll."

161. Broszat, *Kommandant*, 197.

162. Quote in Kohlhagen, *Bock*, 87 (written in 1945). See also Langbein, *Menschen*, 474, 480-81; Dirks, "*Verbrechen*," 168-69; Mailänder Koslov, *Gewalt*, 292-93.

163. Ambach and Köhler, *Lublin-Majdanek*, 96; Lasik, "Garrison," 337. Such offers by superiors were not unprecedented during the Holocaust; Browning, *Männer*, 22, 105.

164. IfZ, F 13/8, Bl. 488-91: R. Höss, "Dr. Eduard Wirths," November 1946; Lifton and Hackett, "Doctors," 310-11; Lifton, *Doctors*, 384-414; Langbein, *Menschen*, 411-32; Beischl, *Wirths*, 93-113, 217-225, 229.

165. For parallels with German soldiers during the Nazi war of extermination, see Werner, "'Hart.'"

166. Broszat, *Kommandant*, 197-201, quote on 198; Stangneth, *Eichmann*, quote on 359; Langbein, *Menschen*, 331, 363-64.

167. Langbein, *Menschen*, 473-74, 476-78.

168. For example, see Mailänder Koslov, *Gewalt*, 338-39.

169. Quotes in Kremer, "Tagebuch," 213-14. See also Broad, "Erinnerungen," 166, 176; Berger, *Experten*, 119, 197, 332-33.

170. Interrogation A. Hradil, August 13, 1963, in Friedler et al., *Zeugen*, 70.

171. BArchL, B 162/1124, Bl. 2288-2316: Volksgerichtshof Krakow, Urteil, September 5, 1946; BArchB (ehem. BDC), SSO, Göth, Amon, 11.12.1908.

172. Orth, *SS*, 202, 300.

173. The compound leaders were Karl Fritzsch, Hans Aumeier, Franz Johann Hofmann, and Franz Hössler; Lasik, "Organizational," 154-55, 199-201. For Hofmann, see LG Hechingen, Urteil, March 18, 1966, *JNV*, vol. 23, 372.

174. BArchL, B 162/2985, Bl. 2032-34: Vernehmung Calelzon B., September 7, 1973. See also *OdT*, vol. 8, 65, 73, 83; Riedle, *Angehörigen*, 193-94.

175. LG Bonn, Urteil, February 6, 1959, *JNV*, vol. 15, 420; LG Cologne, Urteil, May 28, 1965, ibid., vol. 21, 87, 95; LG Munich, Urteil, December 22, 1969, ibid., vol. 33, 313; LG Ansbach, Urteil, April 11, 1961, ibid., vol. 17, 154.

176. Most prisoners in the protective custody compound moved on after a few months, either released or transferred to a harsher camp inside the German prewar borders. See *OdT*, vol. 7, 133–50; Stuldreher, "Konzentrationslager."

177. Riedle, *Angehörigen*, 193; WL, P.III.h. No. 573, A. Lehmann, "Das Lager Vught," n.d., pp. 6, 30.

178. Stuldreher, "Herzogenbusch," quote on 327; LG Munich, Urteil, December 22, 1969, *JNV*, vol. 33, 313.

179. Orth, "Lagergesellschaft," 127–28. His successor as commandant, Adam Grünewald, also lost his job, after ten female prisoners suffocated in a cell in January 1944. Despite a cover-up, their deaths became known locally, causing Rauter to step in once more. In March 1944, Grünewald was sentenced to forty-two months in prison by the SS and Police Court in Den Haag (The Hague); BArchB (ehem. BDC), SSO, Grünewald, Adam, 20.10.1902, Feldurteil, March 6, 1944.

180. Testimony of Zakis, in Ambach and Köhler, *Lublin-Majdanek*, 96–98, quote on 98.

181. Mallmann and Paul, "Sozialisation," 15; Mailänder Koslov, *Gewalt*, 236–37.

182. Todorov, *Facing*, 158–61; Wagner, *IG Auschwitz*, 128.

183. Mailänder Koslov, *Gewalt*, 89.

184. Broad, "Erinnerungen," 178.

185. For example, see Welzer, *Täter*, 215–16.

186. Orth, "Höβ," 55; Broszat, *Kommandant*, 43–45.

187. *DAP*, Aussage S. Baretzki, October 1, 1964, 19660–68.

188. USHMM, 1998.A.0247, reel 15, Bl. 184–93: statement H. Aumeier, December 15, 1947, Bl. 189. See also Broszat, *Kommandant*, 197; Himmler speech to generals, May 5, 1944, in Noakes and Pridham, *Nazism*, vol. 3, 618.

189. Mailänder Koslov, *Gewalt*, 206–24, 229–35, 252–53, 333, 414.

190. Kagan, "Standesamt," 148. See also *DAP*, 44709; NAL, HW 16/66, "II. Concentration Camps," November 27, 1942.

191. NAL, WO 208/4661, statement H. Aumeier, July 25, 1945, p. 5.

192. For example, see Welzer, *Täter*, 202–203.

193. Mailänder Koslov, *Gewalt*, 327, 484, 489.

194. Kremer, "Tagebuch," 211–29.

195. Quote in WL, P.III.h. No. 418, E. Clemm, Erfahrungsbericht über Auschwitz, November 27, 1945, p. 3.

196. Schwarz, *Frau*, 128–30; Lifton, *Doctors*, 309–11; Langbein, *Menschen*, 405–406. Delmotte shot himself in 1945, apparently when he was about to be taken into Allied custody.

197. Broszat, *Kommandant*, 9, 174–75, 202, quotes on 201; BArchK, All. Proz. 6/97, Bl. 25; Langbein, *Menschen*, 351; testimony S. Dubiel, August 7, 1946, in Bezwińska and Czech, *KL Auschwitz*, 288–91. For Höss's life in Auschwitz, see also Setkiewicz, *Życie*, 103–16.

198. KB Nr. 16/42, September 3, 1942, in Frei et al., *Kommandanturbefehle*, 169; Rundschreiben, February 10, 1943, ibid., 220; Rundschreiben, April 19, 1943, ibid., 248; StB Nr. 11/44, April 4, 1944, ibid., 432; StB Nr. 19/44, July 14, 1944, ibid., 470; StB Nr. 30/44, December 11, 1944, ibid., 520. See also Steinbacher, *"Musterstadt,"* 188–89; Czech, *Kalendarium*, 296; Merziger, *Satire*, 148–49, 342–44; Bahro, *SS-Sport*. In 1944, the actor Johannes Riemann toured both Stutthof and Auschwitz (Frei et al., *Kommandanturbefehle*, 426; Hördler, "Ordnung," 186).

199. WL, P.III.h. No. 782, E. Zwart, "Incidents in Birkenau," n.d. (before February 1958), pp. 5–6. See also Langbein, *Menschen*, 435–37; WL, P.III.h. No. 1174a, LG Frankfurt, Vernehmung R. Kagan, December 8–10, 1959, p. 7; Fackler, "'Lagers Stimme,'" 484–89; Gilbert, *Music*, 175–90. Memoirs of prisoners from the Birkenau orchestra include Fénelon, *Musicians*; Lasker-Wallfisch, *Inherit*; Menasche, *Birkenau*.

200. KB Nr. 5/41, April 18, 1941, in Frei et al., *Kommandanturbefehle*, 31; StB Nr. 7/44, February 14, 1944, ibid., 406; Steinbacher, *"Musterstadt,"* 189; Dirks, *"Verbrechen,"* 150–51, 163–64.

201. There were also brothels for Ukrainian guards at some KL deeper inside the Reich (these guards were banned from municipal German brothels); some women abused here were KL prisoners. See Sommer, *KZ-Bordell*, 44–47, 95–97, 440 (n. 5); Vossler, *Propaganda*, 351.

202. Steinbacher, *"Musterstadt,"* 183–84, 205–45. See also Dwork and Van Pelt, *Auschwitz*, passim; Dirks, *"Verbrechen,"* 163; Wagner, *IG Auschwitz*, 73; KB Nr. 5/41, April 18, 1941, in Frei et al., *Kommandanturbefehle*, 31.

203. Steinbacher, *"Musterstadt,"* 184–86; Schwarz, *Frau*, 115–19, 150, 158–60. See also StB Nr. 9/43, April 10, 1943, in Frei et al., *Kommandanturbefehle*, 242; StB Nr. 12/43, April 15, 1943, ibid., 245–46; StB Nr. 33/43, August 21, 1943, ibid., 328–29.

204. Dirks, *"Verbrechen,"* 154–55, 165–66; Schwarz, *Frau*, 118–19; Steinbacher, *"Musterstadt,"* 185–86; Langbein, *Menschen*, 511; KB Nr. 10/41, May 28, 1941, in Frei et al., *Kommandanturbefehle*, 43. Women in the service of the Camp SS were mostly unmarried.

205. Lifton, *Doctors*, 395–99, quote on 398; Schwarz, *Frau*, 102, 168–69.

206. BArchB, NS 3/391, Bl. 4–22: Aufgabengebiete in einem KL, n.d. (1942), Bl. 7; KB Nr. 8/42, April 29, 1942, in Frei et al., *Kommandanturbefehle*, 130.

207. Schwarz, *Frau*, 141–42.

208. For example, see Van Pelt, *Case*, 238; BArchB, NS 4/Sa 2, Bl. 10–12: KL Sachsenhausen, Tatbericht, June 18, 1942.

209. Testimony S. Dubiel, August 7, 1946, in Bezwińska and Czech, *KL Auschwitz*, quote on 290; Langbein, *Menschen*, 353.

210. StB Nr. 7/43, March 30, 1943, in Frei et al., *Kommandanturbefehle*, 239; StB Nr. 9/44, March 8, 1944, ibid., 420; StB Nr. 30/44, December 11, 1944, ibid., 519–20.

211. Affidavit R. Höss, April 5, 1946, *IMT*, vol. 33, 275–79, ND: 3868–PS, p. 278; Schwarz, *Frau*, 151.

212. For example, see KB Nr. 25/43, June 11, 1943, in Frei et al., *Kommandanturbefehle*, 292.

213. StB Nr. 25/43, July 12, 1943, in Frei et al., *Kommandanturbefehle*, 306. See also Langbein, *Menschen*, 516; Dirks, *"Verbrechen,"* 166–68; Schwarz, *Frau*, 124; *DAP*, Vernehmung E. Bednarek, November 29, 1960, 3130.

214. Schwarz, *Frau*, 103, 146–47, 151–52, 279–80.

215. Quote in Segev, *Soldiers*, 195.

216. Testimony S. Dubiel, August 7, 1946, in Bezwińska and Czech, *KL Auschwitz*, 288–91; Schwarz, *Frau*, 142; Langbein, *Menschen*, 352; Strzelecki, "Plundering," 168.

217. Longerich, *Himmler*. More generally on Nazism and morality, see Welzer, *Täter*, 18–75; Koonz, *Conscience*; Weikart, *Ethic*.

218. See contribution by Dan Diner in Frei and Kantsteiner, *Holocaust*, 103–104.

219. Rede bei der SS Gruppenführertagung in Posen, October 4, 1943, *IMT*, vol. 29, ND: 1919–PS, quotes on 145–46; IfZ, F 37/5, Himmler diary, October 4, 1943. More generally, see Orth, "'Anständigkeit.'"

220. Rede bei der SS Gruppenführertagung in Posen, October 4, 1943, *IMT*, vol. 29, ND: 1919–PS, quotes on 146. An audio recording of the speech is archived at NARA.

221. Bajohr, *Parvenüs*, 96–97, 162–63, quote on 162; Perz and Sandkühler, "Auschwitz," 296; Scheffler, "Praxis," 232–34; BArchB, NS 19/1916, Bl. 124–31: Kriminalstatistik für das 1. Vierteljahr 1943. More generally, see Dean, *Robbing*.

222. Strzelecki, "Plundering," 147–48; K. E. Möckel, "Aktion 'R,'" July 7, 1947, extract in Perz and Sandkühler, "Auschwitz," 304.

223. Strzelecki, "Plundering," 149; idem, "Utilization," 404–406, 408–411; Czech, *Kalendarium*, 790. For the rumors about soap, see Strzelecki, "Utilization," 415; Neander, "'Seife.'"

224. USHMM, RG-11.001M.03, reel 37, folder 275, Zentralbauleitung Auschwitz to WVHA-C, June 9, 1942; ibid., reel 19, folder 19, Besichtigung durch SS Obergruppenführer Pohl am 23.9.1942; Strzelecki, "Plundering," 149–52; Broszat, *Kommandant*, 253.

225. K. Hart, *I Am Alive* (London, 1961), extract in Adler et al., *Auschwitz*, 82–84, quote on 82. See also Strzelecki, "Plundering," 137–38, 151; K. E. Möckel, "Aktion 'R,'" July 7, 1947, extract in Perz and Sandkühler, "Auschwitz," 304–305; testimony K. Morla, n.d., cited in ibid., 297–98.

226. YVA, Globocnik to Himmler, January 5, 1944, ND: 4024–PS, pp. 11–12; K. E. Möckel, "Aktion 'R,'" July 7, 1947, extract in Perz and Sandkühler, "Auschwitz," 305; Broszat, *Kommandant*, 254.

227. Strzelecki, "Utilization," 407–12; WVHA to LK, January 4, 1943, in Schnabel, *Macht*, 262–63.

228. Frank to SS Administration in Lublin and Auschwitz, September 26, 1942, *TWC*, vol. 5, 695–97, ND: NO-724; Pohl to Himmler's office, February 6, 1943, ibid., 699–703, ND: NO-1257; YVA, Globocnik to Himmler, January 5, 1944, ND: 4024–PS, p. 13. See also Lumans, *Auxiliaries*, especially page 203.

229. Judgment U.S. Military Tribunal II, November 3, 1947, *TWC*, vol. 5, 958–1064, quote on 988.

230. Quotes in Hildebrandt to Himmler, n.d. (1943), in Schnabel, *Macht*, 248; BArchK, All. Proz. 6/102, Bl. 53. See also WVHA to Himmler, November 29, 1944, in ibid., 249; BArchB, Film 44840, Vernehmung G. Maurer, March 21, 1947, pp. 1–4; StN, EE by K. Sommer, January 22, 1947, ND: NO-1578, pp. 2–3; de Rudder, "Zwangsarbeit," 221–25; NAL, HW 16/21, GPD Nr. 3, WVHA-D to KL Auschwitz, October 22, 1942; ibid., HW 16/22, GPD Nr. 3, WVHA-D to KL Auschwitz, December 18, 1942.

231. Testimony O. Pohl, June 3, 1946, in *NCA*, supplement B, 1582–85; K. E. Möckel, "Aktion 'R,'" July 7, 1947, extract in Perz and Sandkühler, "Auschwitz," 306; ibid., 291; BArchB, Film 44563, Vernehmung O. Pohl, September 26, 1946, 57–60. Having been suspected of dishonesty before, Globocnik was evidently at pains to demonstrate his integrity.

232. Hayes, *Cooperation*, esp. 181–84. By no means all deliveries of precious metals were sent for processing; dozens of caches were recovered in their original state by the U.S. army in 1945.

233. WVHA-A to Himmler, October 8, 1942, in Tuchel, *Inspektion*, 151. See also Strzelecki, "Utilization," 400.

234. Strzelecki puts the value of loot in Auschwitz alone at a minimum of hundreds of millions of Reichsmark; Strzelecki, "Plundering," 169. More generally, see Kaienburg, *Wirtschaft*, 1079.

235. For overall Nazi gains, see Aly, *Volksstaat*, 311–27; Dean, *Robbing*, 391–95.

236. Marszałek, *Majdanek*, 92; YVA, Globocnik to Himmler, January 5, 1944, ND: 4024–PS, p. 23.

237. Bajohr, *Parvenüs*, 189–90.

238. Wagner, *Volksgemeinschaft*, 316–29.

239. Gross, *Golden Harvest*.

240. Arad, *Belzec*, 92, quote on 161–62; Bajohr, *Parvenüs*, 120–36.

241. Kautsky, *Teufel*, 94.

242. For example, see Langbein, *Menschen*, 442.

243. Quote in Mailänder Koslov, *Gewalt*, 254. See also Perz and Sandkühler, "Auschwitz," 295–97; Kilian, "'Handlungsräume,'" 135–36; Broad, "Erinnerungen," 176; *DAP*, Urteil LG Frankfurt August 19–20, 1965, 37195–96.

244. *OdT*, vol. 8, 262; Paserman, "Bericht," 154.

245. Greif, *Wir weinten*, 277–78. For envy of the Canada Commando, see also BoA, testimony of G. Kaldore, August 31, 1946.

246. Rózsa, "'Solange,'" 133; Kautsky, *Teufel*, 253.

247. Quote in Harshav, *Last Days*, 696, diary entry, July 19, 1944.
248. Levi, *If*, 84–85, quote on 84; Wagner, *IG Auschwitz*, 138–39.
249. Lenard, "Flucht," 145.
250. Kielar, *Anus Mundi*, 131; Ambach and Köhler, *Lublin-Majdanek*, 149, 160, 190.
251. Testimony O. Wolken, 1945, in Adler et al., *Auschwitz*, 120.
252. Maršálek, *Mauthausen*, 53; Marszałek, *Majdanek*, 137; BArchL, B 162/21846, Bl. 167–254: W. Neff, "Recht oder Unrecht," n.d., Bl. 219–20; *OdT*, vol. 8, 261; NAL, WO 235/309, Aussage L. Ramdohr, August 21, 1946, pp. 1–2.
253. BArchB (ehem. BDC), SSO, Aumeier, Hans, 20.8.1906, KL Auschwitz, Aktenvermerk, November 30, 1943; ibid., Vernehmungsniederschrift, January 17, 1944.
254. Langbein, *Menschen*, 457–58; Schwarz, *Frau*, 167–68; *OdT*, vol. 5, 196; Citroen and Starzyńska, *Auschwitz*, 162–63; Hördler, "Ordnung," 144; Broad, "Erinnerungen," 168.
255. Orth, "Kommandanten," 760.
256. BArchB, NS 4/Sa 2, Bl. 22–26: K. Wendland to Gestapo, April 1942, quote on 23; ibid., Bl. 10–12: KL Sachsenhausen, Tatbericht, June 18, 1942; ibid., Bl. 14–20: RKPA, Vernehmung H. Loritz, June 20, 1942; AdsD, KE, E. Büge, Bericht, n.d. (1945–46), 214–15.
257. Riedel, *Ordnungshüter*, 273–86; *OdT*, vol. 2, 493–95; BArchB, NS 4/Sa 2, Bl. 22–26: K. Wendland to Gestapo, April 1942; ibid., Bl. 27: Loritz to Pohl, June 24, 1942.
258. BArchB, NS 4/Sa 2, Bl. 14–20: RKPA, Vernehmung H. Loritz, June 20, 1942; ibid., Bl. 27: Loritz to Pohl, June 24, 1942; IfZ, statement P. Wauer, May 21, 1945, ND: NO-1504, p. 5.
259. Bajohr, *Parvenüs*, 164–66. For Himmler's spending, see his recently unearthed private correspondence; www.welt.de/himmler/.
260. On Loritz's career, see Riedel, *Ordnungshüter*, passim.
261. BArchB, Film 44563, Vernehmung O. Pohl, January 2, 1947, pp. 4–7 (Pohl largely disputed this episode); Dillon, "Concentration Camp SS," 84.
262. For WVHA awareness, see BArchB, NS 3/426, Bl. 82: WVHA-D to LK, June 12, 1943.
263. Orth, "Kommandanten," 760; BArchB (ehem. BDC), SSO, Piorkowski, Alex, 11.10.1904, Himmler to Piorkowski, May 31, 1943.
264. Riedel, *Ordnungshüter*, 288–326; *OdT*, vol. 2, 494.
265. BArchB (ehem. BDC), SSO, Koch, Karl, 2.8.1897, KL Lublin to WVHA-D, July 15, 1942; ibid., Stab Reichsführer SS to SS Personalhauptamt, July 25, 1942; ibid., Koch to SS und Polizeigericht Krakow, August 2, 1942; ibid., SS Polizeigericht Berlin, EV, February 17, 1943; Mailänder Koslov, *Gewalt*, 345–50; Marszałek, *Majdanek*, 136 (with incorrect dates and figures); Witte et al., *Dienstkalender*, 493.
266. Quote in BArchB (ehem. BDC), SSO, Koch, Karl, 2.8.1897, Himmler to Berger, March 12, 1943. See also ibid., Brandt to Berger, March 24, 1943; Himmler to Pohl, March 5, 1943, in Heiber, *Reichsführer!*, 245–47.
267. HLSL, Anklageschrift gegen Koch, 1944, ND: NO-2366; BArchB (ehem. BDC), SSO, Koch, Karl, 2.8.1897, Weuster to Jüttner, August 25, 1943. The first SS investigation of Koch, begun in 1941, had been shut down by Himmler in July 1943.
268. Weingartner, "Law"; BArchB (ehem. BDC), SSO, Morgen, Konrad, 8.6.1909, Chef des Hauptamtes SS-Gericht to Himmler, August 3, 1944; testimony K. Morgen, August 7, 1946, *IMT*, vol. 20, 488–89; Gross, *Anständig*, 145–48.
269. For a perceptive analysis of Morgen's postwar testimony, and its uncritical use by some historians, see Wittmann, *Beyond Justice*, 160–74.
270. For example, see testimony of K. Morgen, August 7–8, 1946, *IMT*, vol. 20, 490, 504–505, 511. The USSR chief prosecutor counted Morgen among the "famous perjurers" of the trial; ibid., vol. 22, 323.
271. HLSL, Anklageschrift gegen Koch, 1944, pp. 46–47, 74–75, ND: NO-2366.
272. Ibid., quote on 35.
273. BArchB (ehem. BDC), SSO, Morgen, Konrad, 8.6.1909, K. Morgen, Ermittlungsbericht,

December 5, 1943; ibid., ZBV-Gericht Kassel, Anklageverfügung gegen G. Michael, December 5, 1943. It is not clear if or when Michael was sentenced.

274. BArchL, B 162/4782, Anklageschrift gegen H. Hackmann, November 15, 1974, pp. 120–23. See also ibid., B 162/7998, Bl. 746–47: Zentrale Stelle to StA Koblenz, May 14, 1970; BArchB (ehem. BDC), SSO, Hackmann, Hermann, 11.11.1913; Hördler, "Ordnung," 50. Released from U.S. custody in 1955, Hackmann was later tried in Düsseldorf and sentenced in 1981 to ten years in prison for crimes in Majdanek.

275. HLSL, Anklageschrift gegen Koch, 1944, pp. 38–39, 48, ND: NO-2366; IfZ, F 65, Bl. 57–68: Dr. Morgen, Die Unrechtsbekämpfung in Konzentrationslagern, December 21, 1945 (here comments by Wiebeck); ibid., Bl. 10–20: Cernely to RKPA, June 30, 1944, Bl. 19.

276. HLSL, Anklageschrift gegen Koch, 1944, pp. 40–46, ND: NO-2366; StAAu, Vernehmungsniederschrift I. Koch, April 29, 1949, pp. 13–14; BArchB, Film 2922, Bl. 2699424: Polizeipräsident Weimar to Hauptamt SS-Gericht, March 26, 1945; NARA, RG 549, 000–50–9, Box 437, Interrogation H. Schmidt, March 2, 1947; Weingartner, "Law," 292–93.

277. Testimony G. Reinecke, August 7, 1946, IMT, vol. 20, 436; testimony K. Morgen, August 7, 1946, ibid., 488; IfZ, F 65, Bl. 10–20: Cernely to RKPA, June 30, 1944, Bl. 11.

278. BArchB (ehem. BDC), SSO, Morgen, Konrad, 8.6.1909, Chef des Hauptamtes SS-Gericht to Himmler, August 3, 1944; ibid., Morgen to Breithaupt, February 2, 1944; Weingartner, "Law," 289; IfZ, F 65, Bl. 57–68: Dr. Morgen, "Unrechtsbekämpfung in Konzentrationslagern," December 21, 1945, Bl. 67; ibid., Bl. 111–12: Morgen to RKPA, June 16, 1944. Cases of fraud and theft in the KL were also pursued by other authorities, including the local SS, the RSHA, and the WVHA (e.g., OdT, vol. 8, 110; OdT, vol. 6, 652–58). Among the larger cases was a police investigation of sleaze in Sachsenhausen, which began in November 1943; according to a well-informed survivor, two SS men were shot in autumn 1944 for stealing clothes and valuables that had found their way to the camp from Auschwitz and Majdanek (IfZ, F 65, Bl. 10–20: Cernely to RKPA, June 30, 1944, Bl. 10; Weiss-Rüthel, Nacht, 128, 160–61; Banach, Elite, 171; Riedle, Angehörigen, 244–45).

279. In addition to Buchenwald, Morgen's commission worked in Auschwitz, Majdanek, Plaszow, Sachsenhausen, and Dachau. After the war, Morgen also claimed credit for investigations in Herzogenbusch and Warsaw, though he was not instrumental in either case; IfZ, F 65, Bl. 57–68: Dr. Morgen, "Unrechtsbekämpfung in Konzentrationslagern," December 1, 1945, Bl. 66; ibid., Bl. 111–12: Morgen to RKPA, June 16, 1944.

280. Quotes in IfZ, F 65, Bl. 111–12: Morgen to RKPA, June 16, 1944.

281. BArchB (ehem. BDC), SSO, Florstedt, Hermann, 18.2.1895, Glücks to SS Personalhauptamt, March 5, 1943; ibid., Terminnotiz, November 10, 1943; ibid., Film 2922, Bl. 2699424: Polizeipräsident Weimar to Hauptamt SS-Gericht, March 26, 1945. There are unconfirmed reports that Florstedt was executed before the end of the war; Orth, SS, 208 (n. 13).

282. BArchL, B 162/1124, Bl. 2288–2316: Volksgerichtshof Krakow, Urteil, September 5, 1946, Bl. 2312–13; OdT, vol. 8, 271. Göth was sentenced to death in Krakow in September 1946 and executed.

283. DAP, Aussage H. Bartsch, March 13, 1964, 5798 [with wrong date], 5820, 5857; ibid., Aussage G. Wiebeck, October 1, 1964, 19700–701.

284. Quote in StB Nr. 51/43, November 16, 1943, in Frei et al., Kommandanturbefehle, 359. Such draconian threats were not unusual. In May 1944, Auschwitz camp staff had to acknowledge in writing that they knew that "I will be punished by death if I take any sort of Jewish property"; Strzelecki, "Plundering," 167.

285. DAP, Aussage H. Bartsch, March 13, 1964, 5799; Langbein, Menschen, 339; Perz and Sandkühler, "Auschwitz," 297; Strzelecki, "Plundering," 167.

286. IfZ, F 65, Bl. 111–12: Morgen to RKPA, June 16, 1944, quote on 112; ibid., Bl. 72–74: Erklärung G. Wiebeck, March 22, 1954.

287. Tuchel, "Registrierung"; Lasik, "Organizational," 170–92; Langbein, *Menschen*, 371–73; IfZ, G 20/1, Das Oberste Volkstribunal, Urteil, December 22, 1947, p. 108; BArchB, RS B5261, Lebenslauf M. Grabner, n.d. (1939).

288. IfZ, G 20/1, Das Oberste Volkstribunal, Urteil, December 22, 1947, p. 111.

289. StB Nr. 54/43, December 1, 1943, in Frei et al., *Kommandanturbefehle*, 371; *DAP*, Vernehmung F. Hofmann, April 22, 1959, 3880.

290. *DAP*, Aussage G. Wiebeck, October 1, 1964, 19700–701; ibid., Aussage H. Bartsch, March 13, 1964, 5866. Morgen later claimed that Grabner was charged with murder in two thousand cases (testimony K. Morgen, August 7–8, 1946, *IMT*, vol. 20, 507). However, another member of Morgen's team testified that Grabner was charged with fewer than two hundred killings (*DAP*, Aussage H. Bartsch, March 13, 1964, 5864–65). Morgen's team also issued charges for illicit prisoner killings against two Buchenwald officials, the camp doctor Waldemar Hoven and the bunker supervisor Martin Sommer, though neither man was convicted before the end of the war.

291. *DAP*, Aussage G. Wiebeck, October 1, 1964, 19700–703, Boger quote on 19703; ibid., Aussage W. Hansen, November 27, 1964, 26002–3; ibid., Aussage W. Boger, July 5, 1945, 3253–56.

292. The case of Adam Grünewald, the Herzogenbusch commandant convicted by an SS court in 1944 after prisoners suffocated in a detention cell (see note 179, above), illustrates Himmler's attitude. As the highest SS authority, Himmler immediately came to the rescue of Grünewald, who did not have to serve his prison sentence, was awarded a week's holiday, and then joined the SS Death's Head division. See BArchB (ehem. BDC), SSO, Grünewald, Adam, 20.10.1902.

293. *DAP*, Aussage W. Boger, July 5, 1945, 3256–57; Langbein, *Menschen*, 374–75; Broad, "Erinnerungen," 194.

294. *DAP*, Aussage W. Boger, July 5, 1945, 3252.

295. For example, see Hackett, *Buchenwald*, 126, 341.

296. Czech, *Kalendarium*, 672.

297. IfZ, F 65, Bl. 111–12: Morgen to RKPA, June 16, 1944; BArchB (ehem. BDC), SSO, Morgen, Konrad, 8.6.1909, SS-Richter beim Reichsführer SS to Chef des Hauptamtes SS-Gericht, August 26, 1944; Longerich, *Himmler*, 311.

298. For the last point, see Himmler to Bormann, February 10, 1944, in Heiber, *Reichsführer!*, 316.

299. IfZ, F 65, Bl. 10–20: Cernely to RKPA, June 30, 1944.

300. StN, EE by G. Wiebeck, February 28, 1947, ND: NO-2331; Schmeling, *Erbprinz*, 98; testimony of G. Reinecke, August 7, 1946, *IMT*, vol. 20, 439; *DAP*, Aussage K. Morgen, March 9, 1964, 5592.

301. Schulte, *Zwangsarbeit*, 40–41; Schwarz, *Frau*, 93 (n. 15); *OdT*, vol. 2, 340–41; Witte et al., *Dienstkalender*, 643.

302. Bindemann, "Koserstrasse 21"; Koch, *Himmlers*, 75–77, 81; StN, testimony O. Pohl, June 13, 1946, ND: NO-4728, p. 7.

303. See also Bajohr, *Parvenüs*, 192.

304. Zámečník, "Aufzeichnungen," 240.

305. *OdT*, vol. 2, 340–41; Schulte, *Zwangsarbeit*, 32. See also chapter 8, below.

306. *OdT*, vol. 4, 535–38; Koch, *Himmlers*, 78–80; BArchB, Film 44563, Vernehmung O. Pohl, September 17, 1946, p. 8. One of Pohl's SS companies (DVA) had bought the estate for farming experiments, and Pohl rented the manor house at a favorable rate.

307. Zámečník, "Aufzeichnungen," 225, 229, 240. See also BArchB (ehem. BDC), SSO Pohl, Oswald, 30.6.1892, Fragebogen zur Berichtigung der Führerkartei, October 1936; ibid., Film 44563, Vernehmung O. Pohl, January 2, 1947, p. 2.

308. Zámečník, "Aufzeichnungen," 199–200, 212, quote on 240.

8. Economics and Extermination

1. Pohl to LK et al., April 30, 1942, *IMT*, vol. 38, 365–67, ND: 129–R, quotes on 366, taken from Pohl's summary of the conference on April 24–25, 1942. See also Pohl to Himmler, April 30, 1942, in ibid., 363–65; testimony O. Pohl, 1947, *TWC*, vol. 5, 434; BArchB, Film 44563, Vernehmung O. Pohl, January 2, 1947, p. 11. Contrary to what Pohl implied in his April 30, 1942, summary of the conference for Himmler, handing responsibility for forced labor to the commandants was no major departure from previous practice but restated an earlier order by Glücks (which had spelled the end of the brief SS experiment with local labor representatives formally overseeing KL labor deployment); BArchB, NS 4/Na 103, Bl. 2–4: Glücks to LK, February 20, 1942.

2. For grumbling, see Judgment of the U.S. Military Tribunal, November 3, 1947, *TWC*, vol. 5, 981. The April 1942 WVHA conference was also attended by KL plant managers.

3. For example, see IfZ, F 13/6, Bl. 343–54: R. Höss, "Oswald Pohl," November 1946, Bl. 352–53; IfZ, ZS-1590, interrogation of G. Witt, November 19, 1946, pp. 11–12. During 1942, Pohl saw Himmler on average almost once a month; Witte et al., *Dienstkalender*.

4. BArchL, B 162/7998, Bl. 623–44: Vernehmung J. Otto, April 1, 1970, Bl. 630–31; Tuchel, *Konzentrationslager*, 28. In January 1943, for example, Himmler asked for a survey of the prisoner population of Auschwitz and Majdanek since the beginning; NAL, HW 16/23, GPD Nr. 3, WVHA-D to Auschwitz and Majdanek, January 26, 1943.

5. Himmler's official diary lists visits to Ravensbrück (March 3, 1942), Dachau (May 1, 1942, and November 13, 1942), Auschwitz (July 17–18, 1942), and Sachsenhausen (September 29, 1942); Witte et al., *Dienstkalender*.

6. Zámečník, "Aufzeichnungen," quote on 197–98.

7. Longerich, *Himmler*, 701–25.

8. Müller, "Speer," 275–81; Kroener, "'Menschenbewirtschaftung,'" 777–82, 804; Naasner, *Machtzentren*, 445–55. More generally, see Tooze, *Wages*, 513–89.

9. BArchB, Film 44564, Vernehmung O. Pohl, February 5, 1947, p. 5.

10. Schulte, *Zwangsarbeit*, 200–201; Witte et al., *Dienstkalender*, 371. Himmler's initial order for setting up the WVHA did not encompass the IKL (Befehl Reichsführers SS, January 19, 1942, in Naasner, *SS-Wirtschaft*, 225–26), so its addition was clearly an afterthought. The IKL was officially incorporated on March 16, 1942; R. Glücks, Stabsbefehl Nr. 1, March 16, 1942, in Tuchel, *Inspektion*, 90–91.

11. Quote in WVHA, Befehl Nr. 10, March 13, 1942, in Tuchel, *Inspektion*, 88. See also BArchB, NS 19/2065, Bl. 36–37: Himmler to Pohl, March 23, 1942.

12. StANü, K.-O. Saur, Niederschrift über Besprechung, March 17, 1942, ND: NO-569; Protocol Hitler-Speer conference on March 19, 1942, in Boelcke, *Rüstung*, 74–82. See also Buggeln, *System*, 15.

13. Quotes in BArchB (ehem. BDC), SSO Pohl, Oswald, 30.6.1892, "Warum bin ich Nationalsozialist," January 24, 1932; ibid., E. Pohl to Himmler, July 4, 1943. See also IfZ, F 13/6, Bl. 343–54: R. Höss, "Oswald Pohl," November 1946; Witte et al., *Dienstkalender*, 381. Himmler's office diary for 1941–42 records just three meetings with Glücks.

14. Schulte, *Zwangsarbeit*, 201–208, 447; Allen, *Business*, 154–58; Judgment of the U.S. Military Tribunal, November 3, 1947, *TWC*, vol. 5, 993, 997–1000, 1004–1008, 1023–31, 1043–47; BArchB, Film 44563, Vernehmung O. Pohl, September 26, 1946 (p. 79), December 17, 1946 (p. 36); Naasner, *SS-Wirtschaft*, 242–43; Kaienburg, *Wirtschaft*, 20.

15. Testimony O. Pohl, June 3, 1946, in Mendelsohn, *The Holocaust*, vol. 17, 47.

16. Liste Stab/Amtsgruppe D, September 6, 1944, in Tuchel, *Inspektion*, 200–203; Kaienburg, *Wirtschaftskomplex*, 348.

17. BArchB, Film 44840, Vernehmung G. Maurer, June 26, 1947, p. 1; testimony Sommer, *TWC*, vol. 5, 345–46, 678; Fernsprechverzeichnis, January 15, 1945, in Tuchel,

Inspektion, 204–207. For the SS mess hall, see IfZ, ZS-1154, Vernehmung H. C. Lesse, November 16 and 19, 1946.

18. Liste Stab/Amtsgruppe D, September 6, 1944, in Tuchel, *Inspektion*, 200–203. It is likely that a few women, not listed here, worked as SS telegraph and radio operators; Mühlenberg, *SS-Helferinnenkorps*, 322. For the above, see also StANü, G. Rammler report, January 30, 1946, ND: NO-1200, p. 8.

19. R. Glücks, Stabsbefehl Nr. 1, March 16, 1942, in Tuchel, *Inspektion*, 90–91. According to a well-informed WVHA-D official, an additional office for troop instruction was added later; StANü, G. Rammler report, January 30, 1946, ND: NO-1200, p. 9.

20. BArchL, B 162/7998, Bl. 623–44: Vernehmung J. Otto, April 1, 1970, Bl. 639; ibid., Nr. 7999, Bl. 768–937: StA Koblenz, EV, July 25, 1974, Bl. 786–89; Broszat, *Kommandant*, 204–207. For a floorplan of the T-Building, Tuchel, *Inspektion*, 208–209.

21. BArchL, B 162/7999, Bl. 768–937: StA Koblenz, EV, July 25, 1974, Bl. 895; testimony O. Pohl, June 3, 1946, in *NCA*, supplement B, 1582.

22. Quote in testimony O. Pohl, June 13, 1946, in *NCA*, supplement B, 1604. See also BArchL, B 162/7997, Bl. 615–19: Vernehmung W. Biemann, December 9, 1969, Bl. 618.

23. BArchL, B 162/7997, Bl. 525–603: Vernehmung K. Sommer, June 30, 1947; BArchB, Film 44563, Vernehmung O. Pohl, September 26, 1946, p. 42; ibid., Film 44840, Vernehmung G. Maurer, March 14, 1947 (quote on p. 1) and March 19, 1947; ibid., NS 4/Na 6, Bl. 30: Glücks to LK, January 13, 1944; Allen, *Business*, 183–84; Schulte, *Zwangsarbeit*, 390–91.

24. MacLean, *Camp*, 276–77; BArchB, Film 44840, Vernehmung G. Maurer, March 19, 1947, pp. 11–13; ibid., Film 44563, Vernehmung O. Pohl, September 26, 1946, pp. 47–48.

25. LG Münster, Urteil, February 19, 1962, *JNV*, vol. 18, 271; BArchL, B 162/7996, Bl. 325–38: Vernehmung J. Muthig, March 18, 1960, Bl. 333; IfZ, F 13/8, Bl. 486–87: R. Höss, "Dr. Enno Lolling," November 1946.

26. StANü, G. Rammler report, January 30, 1946, ND: NO-1200; Hahn, *Grawitz*, 238–40.

27. Hahn, *Grawitz*, 237–38. Appointments of KL doctors also went through the SS Leadership Main Office (and later the Reich doctor SS); ibid., 375.

28. IfZ, F 13/8, Bl. 486–87: R. Höss, "Dr. Enno Lolling," November 1946, quote on 487; IfZ, Interview with Dr. Kahr, September 19, 1945, ND: NO-1948, p. 4.

29. R. Glücks, Stabsbefehl Nr. 1, March 16, 1942, in Tuchel, *Inspektion*, 90–91; BArchB, Film 44563, Vernehmung O. Pohl, September 26, 1946, p. 85. For more detail, see Bartel and Drobisch, "Aufgabenbereich."

30. There was a gap of eight months between the two appointments (September 1, 1942, to May 1, 1943), during which the post was apparently unoccupied; Schulte, *Zwangsarbeit*, 464; BArchB (ehem. BDC), SSO, Kaindl, Anton, 14.7.1902, Dienstlaufbahn; BArchL, B 162/7997, Bl. 525–603: Vernehmung K. Sommer, June 30, 1947, Bl. 544.

31. Quotes in BArchB (ehem. BDC), SSO, Burger, Wilhelm, 19.5.1904, R. Höss, Dienstleistungszeugnis, May 7, 1943. See also Schulte, *Zwangsarbeit*, 464; APMO, Dpr-ZO, 29/2, LG Frankfurt, Urteil, September 16, 1966; Lasik, "Organizational," 230.

32. Broszat, *Kommandant*, 171, 202–204, 210; StANü, G. Rammler report, January 30, 1946, ND: NO-1200, p. 3; Fernsprechverzeichnis, January 15, 1945, in Tuchel, *Inspektion*, 204–207.

33. BArchB (ehem. BDC), SSO, Kaindl, Anton, July 14, 1902, Dienstlaufbahn; Buggeln, *Arbeit*, 116.

34. For example, see *OdT*, vol. 6, 66–69.

35. MacLean, *Camp*, 286.

36. Kaienburg, *Wirtschaft*, quote on 1047–48; Orth, *SS*, 210–11. More generally on Pohl's recruitment policy, see Allen, *Business*.

37. Eicke order for Lichtenburg, June 2, 1934, *NCC*, doc. 148.

38. Wildt, *Generation*, especially page 861. For the term "fighting administration," used by Heydrich, see ibid., 858.

39. Schwarz, *Frau*, 251–53.

40. BArchB, Film 44564, Vernehmung O. Pohl, February 5, 1947, quote on 3; testimony O. Pohl, June 3, 1946, in Mendelsohn, *Holocaust*, vol. 17, 45.

41. Cf. Kaienburg, *Wirtschaft*, 410–12.

42. For the appointments of Liebehenschel, Lolling, and Kaindl, see BArchB (ehem. BDC), SSO, Kaindl, Anton, 14.7.1902, WVHA-A to Chef des SS-Personalhauptamtes, March 16, 1942. Kaindl had served in the IKL as the head of administration from October 1, 1941; Liebehenschel as chief of staff since May 1, 1940; Lolling as chief physician since June 1, 1941.

43. Quote in IfZ, Himmler to Pohl, May 29, 1942, ND: NO-719.

44. Affidavit G. Maurer, May 22, 1947, *TWC*, vol. 5, 602; testimony O. Pohl, 1947, in ibid., 430.

45. APMO, Proces Maurer, 5a, Bl. 115–16: EE by H. Pister, March 3, 1947, ND: NO-2327; BArchB, Film 44840, Vernehmung G. Maurer, March 20, 1947, pp. 22–24.

46. Judgment of the U.S. Military Tribunal, November 3, 1947, *TWC*, vol. 5, 993, 1022; BArchB, Film 44840, Vernehmung G. Maurer, March 18, 1947, p. 13; StANü, G. Rammler report, January 30, 1946, ND: NO-1200, p. 10.

47. For the historiography, see Paul, "Psychopathen," esp. 13–37.

48. Himmler to Pohl, March 5, 1943, in Heiber, *Reichsführer!*, 245–47, quote on 246.

49. Pohl inspected Auschwitz in early April 1942 (chapter 6), on September 23, 1942 (chapter 7), on August 17, 1943 (USHMM, RG-11.001M.03, reel 20, folder 26, Besuch des Hauptamtschefs, August 17, 1943), and on June 16, 1944 (ibid., RG-11.001M.03, reel 19, folder 21, Aktenvermerk, Besuch des Hauptamtschefs, June 20, 1944).

50. IfZ, F 13/6, Bl. 343–54: R. Höss, "Oswald Pohl," November 1946, quote on 352.

51. BArchB (ehem. BDC), SSO, Glücks, Richard, 22.4.1889, Dienstlaufbahn. There is no evidence of any serious tensions between Pohl and Glücks.

52. Previously, much of the initiative had been left to Pohl's then-external apparatus, even after the establishment of an IKL office for labor in autumn 1941. For the IKL administrative structure, see Tuchel, *Konzentrationslager*, 231.

53. The Representative for the Labor Action Burböck was sacked in spring 1942 and left the Camp SS. As for Maurer, he was seconded to the V2 production between January and March 1945, during which time Hans Moser headed D II. See Schulte, *Zwangsarbeit*, 389–90, 464, 472–73.

54. Allen, *Business*, especially pages 13, 24–26, 32.

55. BArchB (ehem. BDC), SSO, Maurer, Gerhard, 9.12.1907; ibid., Film 44840, Vernehmung G. Maurer, March 13, 1947, pp. 1–3.

56. BArchB, Film 44563, Vernehmung O. Pohl, October 7, 1946, p. 18; ibid., Film 44840, Vernehmung G. Maurer, May 13, 1947 (pp. 6–7) and June 19, 1947 (p. 5); IfZ, F 13/6, Bl. 355–58: R. Höss, "Gerhard Maurer," November 1946.

57. Buggeln, *Arbeit*, 109–10; Wagner, *Produktion*, 292–96; Lasik, "Organizational," 216–17; Strebel, *Ravensbrück*, 201; BArchB, NS 3/391, Bl. 4–22: Aufgabengebiete in einem KL, n.d. (1942), Bl. 19–20; ibid., Film 44840, Vernehmung G. Maurer, March 20, 1947, pp. 24–25. The labor action leaders—often experts in their field who moved from one camp to the next—were fully absorbed into the organizational chart of the KL in 1942. Their new offices (III/E or IIIa) for work deployment were nominally part of department III (camp compound), but in practice acted largely independently, reporting to the commandant or, higher up the chain, directly to Maurer's department. The offices oversaw all aspects of the local organization of forced labor, including the formation of prisoner commandos and transports, the supervision during work by SS officials and Kapos, and the establishment of new work sites.

58. NAL, HW 16/21, GPD Nr. 3, WVHA-D to KL Auschwitz, October 27, 1942. For the meeting, which took place on October 28, 1942, see Müller, "Speer," 448.

59. BArchB, Film 44837, Vernehmung A. Liebehenschel, October 7, 1946, quote on 11; StANü, EE by K. Sommer, April 4, 1947, ND: NO-2739; BArchB, B 162/7998, Bl. 623–44: Vernehmung J. Otto, April 1, 1970, Bl. 632; IfZ, F 13/6, Bl. 355–58: R. Höss, "Gerhard Maurer," November 1946; Schulte, *Zwangsarbeit*, 390; Allen, *Business*, 183.

60. IfZ, F 13/6, Bl. 343–54: R. Höss, "Oswald Pohl," quote on 353.

61. BArchB, NS 3/425, Bl. 74: WVHA-D to LK, May 6, 1942. The letter was signed by Glücks and drafted by Liebehenschel, but given the level of Pohl's engagement with the KL at the time, he must have been involved.

62. LG Cologne, Urteil, April 20, 1970, *JNV*, vol. 33, 640, 643. More generally, see Hördler, "Ordnung," 51, 137.

63. In May 1942, Himmler ordered that SS leaders under thirty years of age should be moved from the KL to the front line (camp compound leaders were exempt); NAL, HW 16/18, GPD Nr. 3, May 13, 1942. More generally, see Sydnor, *Soldiers*, 208–35; Broszat, *Kommandant*, 276.

64. Trouvé, "Bugdalle," 37–41; LG Bonn, Urteil, February 6, 1959, *JNV*, vol. 15, 422.

65. Most changes were set out in a letter by Pohl to Himmler on July 28, 1942 (*TWC*, vol. 5, 303–306, ND: NO-1994), in which he included the SS special camp Hinzert as a fifteenth KL (its commandant remained unchanged). Some parts of the plan were later amended. In his letter, Pohl had earmarked Kaindl for Dachau and Weiss for Sachsenhausen, but he later reversed the order. Also, Pohl's initial choice of commandant for Flossenbürg, Hans Hüttig, remained on SS service in Norway (he had left his post as Natzweiler commandant in January 1942; *OdT*, vol. 6, 36); as a result, the Flossenbürg camp compound leader Fritzsch temporarily acted as commandant until Zill was appointed in October 1942 (*OdT*, vol. 4, 38). For Himmler's acceptance of Pohl's proposals, see BArchB (ehem. BDC), SSO, Koch, Karl, 2.8.1897, Stab Reichsführer SS to Pohl, August 13, 1942. More generally, see Orth, *SS*, 213–14.

66. BArchB, Film 44563, Vernehmung O. Pohl, October 28, 1946, quotes on 10–11.

67. For example, see Orth, *SS*, 205–206, 210, 250.

68. For Kramer, see Orth, *SS*, 103–104, 137; Segev, *Soldiers*, 67–73.

69. Orth, *SS*, 157, 211, 214. Other wartime commandants who had served in the SS Death's Head division were Johannes Hassebroek, Friedrich Hartjenstein, Adam Grünewald, and Richard Baer.

70. BArchB (ehem. BDC), SSO, Kaindl, Anton, 14.7.1902; Pohl to Himmler, July 28, 1942, *TWC*, vol. 5, 305, ND: NO-1994; Sydnor, *Soldiers*, 50.

71. The connection between the reshuffle and the functional change of the camps is emphasized in Orth, *SS*, 206. However, the motive for the dismissals cannot be reduced to the economic reorientation alone. For example, it seems likely that a man like Hans Loritz—generally regarded in SS circles as a capable manager—would have kept his job had he not been caught up in an embarrassing corruption scandal.

72. BArchB (ehem. BDC), SSO, Künstler, Karl, 12.1.1901; Tuchel, "Kommandanten des Konzentrationslagers Flossenbürg," 207–209. Künstler was sent to the SS Division Prinz Eugen and is said to have been killed in April 1945.

73. For example, see Tuchel, "Kommandanten des Konzentrationslagers Flossenbürg," 214; idem, "Kommandanten des KZ Dachau," 345–49.

74. Orth, *SS*, 211–13; Sprenger, *Groß-Rosen*, 93–94.

75. See chapter 7.

76. BArchB (ehem. BDC), SSO, Kaindl, Anton, 14.7.1902. For other new commandants like Suhren, Hoppe, and Kramer, see Orth, *SS*, 103–104, 115–24, 144–45, 157, 215–16; Strebel, *Ravensbrück*, 59.

77. If economic motives had been all-decisive, Pohl would have made more of this in his communications with Himmler; Pohl to Himmler, July 28, 1942, *TWC*, vol. 5, 303–306, ND: NO-1994.

78. See also Orth, *SS*, 253.

79. For persistent dreams of settlement and cities, see Himmler to Kaltenbrunner, July 21, 1944, in Heiber, *Reichsführer!*, 343–45; Kershaw, *Nemesis*, 777–78.

80. StANü, K.-O. Saur, Niederschrift über Besprechung, March 17, 1942, ND: NO-569.

81. Pohl to Himmler, April 30, 1942, *IMT*, vol. 38, ND: 129–R.

82. APMO, Proces Maurer, 8a, Bl. 137–38: Himmler to Pohl, July 7, 1942, ND: NO-598; BArchB, NS 19/14, Bl. 131–33: Pohl to Himmler, September 16, 1942 (quotes on 131–32). See also Kaienburg, *Wirtschaft*, 498–99.

83. StANü, K.-O. Saur, Niederschrift über Besprechung, March 17, 1942, ND: NO-569; BArchB, NS 19/14, Bl. 131–33: Pohl to Himmler, September 16, 1942; Buggeln, *System*, 15–22; Naasner, *Machtzentren*, 302–303.

84. *OdT*, vol. 7, 107–30, quote on 108. For brief surveys, see Orth, *System*, 169–71; Megargee, *Encyclopedia*, vol. 1/A, 198–201; Kaienburg, *"Vernichtung,"* 236. More generally, see Mommsen and Grieger, *Volkswagenwerk*; Siegfried, *Leben*. In the literature, the closure of the camp is linked to a decision by Speer in mid-September. However, the decision clearly came earlier (Pohl to Himmler, July 28, 1942, *TWC*, vol. 5, 303–306, ND: NO-1994).

85. BArchB, NS 19/14, Bl. 131–33: Pohl to Himmler, September 16, 1942, quote on 131.

86. APMO, Proces Maurer, 8a, Bl. 137–38: Himmler to Pohl, July 7, 1942, ND: NO-598; Kaienburg, *Wirtschaft*, 498–99; Schulte, *Zwangsarbeit*, 214–16.

87. Himmler to Pohl, March 5, 1943, in Heiber, *Reichsführer!*, 245–47. On June 17, 1943, Hitler and Himmler discussed weapons production involving one hundred and forty thousand KL prisoners; BArchB, Film 4141, Vortrag beim Führer, June 17, 1943.

88. *OdT*, vol. 4, 40–42, 48; Kaienburg, *Wirtschaft*, 618–22; BArchB, Film 44563, Vernehmung O. Pohl, July 31, 1946, p. 6, ND: NI-389. For DESt armaments production in other KL, see *OdT*, vol. 4, 374, 392–94; Perz, "Arbeitseinsatz," 541–43; Schulte, *Zwangsarbeit*, 228–29.

89. Rede bei der SS Gruppenführertagung in Posen, October 4, 1943, *IMT*, vol. 29, ND: 1919–PS, quote on 144.

90. Schulte, *Zwangsarbeit*, 221–32; Kaienburg, *Wirtschaft*, 687–88; Allen, *Business*, 240–42; NAL, HW 16/21, GPD Nr. 3, Maurer to KL Mauthausen, October 6, 1942.

91. APMO, Proces Maurer, 10, Bl. 50–52: Pohl to Brandt, April 19, 1943.

92. Schulte, *Zwangsarbeit*, 216–18; Kaienburg, *Vernichtung*, 239–42; Strebel, *Ravensbrück*, 384–418.

93. Kaienburg, *Wirtschaft*, 28, 1035, quote on 500; Naasner, *Machtzentren*, 302, 306–307; Kroener et al., "Zusammenfassung," 1010–11.

94. Buggeln, *Arbeit*, 38.

95. BArchB, NS 19/14, Bl. 131–33: Pohl to Himmler, September 16, 1942; protocol conference Hitler-Speer, September 20–22, 1942, in Boelcke, *Rüstung*, 187–88; Naasner, *Machtzentren*, 303–306, 452; Schulte, *Zwangsarbeit*, 218–21. As a sop to the SS, its troops were to receive a small proportion of weapons produced by its prisoners.

96. Kaienburg, *Wirtschaft*, 434–36; idem, *"Vernichtung,"* 243; Schulte, *Zwangsarbeit*, 212–13. For other early joint ventures between industry and the SS, see *OdT*, vol. 3, 205–206; *OdT*, vol. 4, 437–40.

97. Fröbe, "KZ-Häftlinge," 640, 668–69; Orth, *System*, 180; Buggeln, *Arbeit*, 42; idem, *System*, 18–19, 54; Schalm, *Überleben*, 72–74.

98. Werner, *Kriegswirtschaft*, 168–90; Schalm, *Überleben*, 80, 95–98; *OdT*, vol. 2, 425–30.

99. Buggeln, *System*, 57–61; Orth, *System*, 175–79; *OdT*, vol. 3, 245–48. For a detailed account, see Budraß, "Schritt."

100. Schröder, "Konzentrationslager," 52–63; Megargee, *Encyclopedia*, vol. 1/B, 1143–45; Fröbe, "KZ-Häftlinge," 664; Buggeln, *Arbeit*, 71–74.

101. Fings, *Krieg*, 48–68, 84–103, 188. For bomb disposal squads, see also Wachsmann, *Prisons*, 232; IfZ, RSHA, AE, 2. Teil, Runderlaß Chef Sipo und SD, September 25, 1940; AdsD, KE, E. Büge, Bericht, n.d. (1945–46), 197, 203, 205.

102. Buggeln, *Arbeit*, 42; idem, *System*, 53; Orth, *System*, 180; StANü, Pohl to Himmler, September 30, 1943, Anlage, ND: PS-1469.

103. *OdT*, vol. 1, quote on 189; Fröbe, "KZ-Häftlinge," 667–69; Schulte, *Zwangsarbeit*, 394, 397.

104. Pohl to LK et al., April 30, 1942, *IMT*, vol. 38, 365–67, ND: 129–R; BArchB, Film 44564, EE by O. Pohl, March 21, 1947; IfZ, Maurer to LK, November 21, 1942, ND: PS-3685. On rare occasions local commandants still went ahead and made their own deals.

105. BArchB, Film 44840, Vernehmung G. Maurer, August 12, 1947, pp. 1–3; extract testimony of Sommer, June 30 to July 2, 1947, *TWC*, vol. 5, 595–96; BStU, MfS HA IX/11 ZUV 4, Bd. 24, Bl. 235–51: Vernehmung P. Rose, December 10, 1946.

106. Orth, *System*, 181.

107. StANü, WVHA-D II, Häftlingssätze, February 24, 1944, ND: NO-576.

108. Kaienburg, *Wirtschaft*, 29–30, 1078; Naasner, *Machtzentren*, 399–402; BArchB, Film 44840, Vernehmung G. Maurer, March 18, 1947, pp. 18–19; StANü, EE by K. Sommer, January 22, 1947, ND: NO-1578, p. 5.

109. See also Kaienburg, *"Vernichtung,"* 236–47.

110. Buggeln, "Slaves?" For the revisionist view, see Spoerer and Fleischhacker, "Forced Laborers," 176; Sofsky, *Ordnung*, 193–99.

111. Kupfer-Koberwitz, *Tagebücher*, quote on 75. More generally, see Buggeln, "Slaves?," 103.

112. BArchB, NS 19/2065, Bl. 36–37: Himmler to Pohl, March 23, 1942.

113. Quotes in Schulte, *Zwangsarbeit*, 351.

114. BArchB, NS 19/2065, Bl. 36–37: Himmler to Pohl, March 23, 1942.

115. BArchB, NS 4/Na 6, Bl. 9–10: Glücks to LK, February 12, 1942; IfZ, Maurer to LK, June 24, 1942, ND: PS-3685; Kaienburg, *"Vernichtung,"* 326–27; Wagner, *Ellrich*, 62.

116. *OdT*, vol. 4, 43; Kaienburg, *Wirtschaft*, 432. See also chapter 4.

117. BArchB, NS 19/2065, Bl. 36–37: Himmler to Pohl, March 23, 1942.

118. Sommer, *KZ-Bordell*, 112–14.

119. Himmler to Pohl, March 5, 1943, in Heiber, *Reichsführer!*, 245–47; IfZ, F 37/2, Himmler diary, entry February 26, 1943.

120. Quotes in IfZ, O. Pohl, DV für Gewährung von Vergünstigungen, May 15, 1943 (extracts), ND: NO-400. See also Strebel, *Ravensbrück*, 198; Sommer, *KZ-Bordell*, 76–80.

121. Wachsmann, *Prisons*, 95.

122. Wagner, *IG Auschwitz*, 221.

123. Buggeln, *Arbeit*, 302; Sommer, *KZ-Bordell*, 81.

124. Wagner, *IG Auschwitz*, 221.

125. ITS, KL Flossenbürg GCC 5/88, Ordner 87, Aufstellung der ausbezahlten Häftlingsprämien, September 4, 1943; extracts testimony of Sommer, June 30 to July 2, 1947, *TWC*, vol. 5, 598; Kaienburg, *"Vernichtung,"* 406–409; Sommer, *KZ-Bordell*, 84; Sprenger, *Groß-Rosen*, 181–82; KB Nr. 6/44, April 22, 1944, in Frei et al., *Kommandanturbefehle*, 439.

126. WL, P.III.b. No. 1164, N. Rosenberg, "Zwangsarbeiter für Siemens-Schuckert," January 1960.

127. Himmler to Pohl, March 5, 1943, in Heiber, *Reichsführer!*, quote on 246; Sommer, *KZ-Bordell*, 78, 80, 161–65; BArchB, NS 3/426, Bl. 84: WVHA-D to LK, June 15, 1943.

128. Borowski, "Auschwitz," 122. See also Sommer, *KZ-Bordell*, 174–89; Hughes, "Forced Prostitution," 204–205.

129. Sommer, *KZ-Bordell*, 81–82, 126, 174, 239, 242–44, 251; Hughes, "Forced Prostitution," 209; Gross, *Zweitausend*, 207–208; Wagner, *Produktion*, 418. Some main camps (including Majdanek and Gross-Rosen) never had a brothel. And contrary to some suggestions, there was apparently no systematic SS policy of "curing" homosexuals by sending them to camp brothels; Sommer, *KZ-Bordell*, 250–51.

130. Quotes in APMO, Proces Maurer, 5a, Bl. 150: Dr. Rascher, Bericht über KL-Dirnen,

November 5, 1942, ND: NO-323; LULVR, interview No. 239, March 20, 1946. See also Sommer, *KZ-Bordell*, 101, 107–108, 234–37, 259–60, 278.

131. Sommer, *KZ-Bordell*, 77, 83; Weiss-Rüthel, *Nacht*, 143.

132. Ovrashko survived the KL; Gedenkstätte Sachsenhausen, *Gegen das Vergessen* (CD-Rom).

133. NMGB, *Buchenwald*, 699–700.

134. Estimates based on Schulte, "London"; *OdT*, vol. 3, 29; ibid., vol. 4, 45; ibid., vol. 6, 513; ibid., vol. 7, 48–49, 190–91; ibid., vol. 8, 25, 103–104, 134; NMGB, *Buchenwald*, 699–700; StANü, Pohl to Himmler, September 30, 1943, Anlage, ND: PS-1469; Maršálek, *Mauthausen*, 126; Strebel, *Ravensbrück*, 182, 293, 349; KZ-Gedenkstätte Neuengamme, *Ausstellungen*, 22; Steegmann, *Struthof*, 50, 64; Sprenger, *Groß-Rosen*, 168–71, 225; DaA, ITS, Vorläufige Ermittlung der Lagerstärke (1971); Koker, *Edge*, 301 (n. 556); Czech, *Kalendarium*, 691; Kaienburg, *Neuengamme*, 315; Dieckmann, *Besatzungspolitik*, vol. 2, 1317; Stiftung, *Bergen-Belsen*, 163. The composite figures sent by Pohl to Himmler in September 1943 need to be treated with some caution, especially those for late 1942, which are evidently too low (see also Kárný, "'Vernichtung,'" 143).

135. The SS special camp Hinzert is not included here.

136. Pohl to Himmler, April 30, 1942, *IMT*, vol. 38, 363–65, ND: R-129.

137. The number of deported Jews rose from around 197,000 (1942) to 270,000 (1943); Piper, *Zahl*, table D.

138. Picker, *Tischgespräche*, 474.

139. Quotes in Hillgruber, *Staatsmänner*, vol. 1, 611; Jochmann, *Monologe*, 126; Picker, *Tischgespräche*, 282–83, 617; Fröhlich, *Tagebücher*, II/4, May 30, 1942, 405.

140. The speech was recorded by Goebbels; Fröhlich, *Tagebücher*, II/4, May 24, 1942, 361.

141. Wagner, *Volksgemeinschaft*, 316–29, 338–43; Roth, "Kriminalpolizei," 326–28, 341–47; Strebel, *Ravensbrück*, 117–21; Longerich, *Himmler*, 658.

142. Zimmermann, "Entscheidung"; Fings, "'Wannsee-Konferenz'"; Czech, *Kalendarium*, 423.

143. LHASA, MD, Rep. C 29 Anh. 2, Nr. Z 98/1, Bl. 27: Bürgermeister Quedlinburg, Umzugs-Abmeldebestätigung, March 1, 1943; SMAB, *Memorial Book*, 7.

144. For this and the previous paragraph, see Rede bei der SS Gruppenführertagung in Posen, October 4, 1943, *IMT*, vol. 29, ND: 1919–PS, Himmler quote on 133; Spoerer, *Zwangsarbeit*, 37–39, 50, 66, 80, 89, 93–95, 116–44, 179; Herbert, *Fremdarbeiter*, 246, 301–306. See also Gellately, *Gestapo*, 226–27; Wachsmann, *Prisons*, 225–26; Kárný, "Waffen-SS," 257; Buggeln, *System*, 46; Wildt, "Funktionswandel," 85. For Gestapo camps, see Lotfi, *KZ*; Thalhofer, *Entgrenzung*.

145. Walter, "Kinder," 185–86; Spoerer, *Zwangsarbeit*, 79; Spoerer and Fleischhacker, "Forced Laborers," 199, table 9; BArchB, NS 3/426, Bl. 29: WVHA-D to LK, February 2, 1943; ibid., Bl. 30: RSHA, Richtlinien, January 29, 1943. More generally, see Steinert, *Deportation*.

146. Zarusky, "'Russen,'" 127.

147. Kupfer-Koberwitz, *Tagebücher*, 101.

148. Longerich, *Himmler*, 672–82; Wachsmann, *Prisons*, 271–74; Tillion, *Ravensbrück*, 192–97; Nacht- und Nebel-Erlaβ, August 4, 1942, extract in Schnabel, *Macht*, 157–58.

149. Schulte, "London," 220–22; Stein, "Funktionswandel," 179. In Mauthausen, by contrast, the major influx of foreigners did not come until 1944; Kranebitter, "Zahlen," 137.

150. IfZ, Himmler to Pohl, May 29, 1942, ND: NO-719.

151. For example, see Glücks to Lagerärzte, December 28, 1942, in NMGB, *Buchenwald*, 257–58.

152. For this and the previous two paragraphs, see Wachsmann, *Prisons*, 208–17, 223–26,

284–98, 392–93, quote on 285; StANü, Pohl to Himmler, September 30, 1943, Anlage, ND: PS-1469; Jochmann, *Monologe*, 271–72.

153. Marszałek, *Majdanek*, 71, 167; Czech, *Kalendarium*, 386–87, 395–96; Wachsmann, *Prisons*, 200–201.

154. Himmler to all Hauptamtschefs, December 29, 1942, in Heiber, *Reichsführer!*, 218–20; Kershaw, *Nemesis*, 538–50.

155. Reference to Pohl's letter in BArchB, NS 3/426, Bl. 13: Chef Sipo und SD to Pohl, December 31, 1942. More generally, see BStU, MfS HA IX/11 ZUV 4/23, Bl. 320–46: Vernehmungsprotokoll A. Kaindl, September 16, 1946, Bl. 322.

156. Witte et al., *Dienstkalender*, 643; Himmler to Pohl, December 15, 1942, in Heiber, *Reichsführer!*, 216.

157. For the order, which refers specifically to Polish resisters, see Himmler to Pohl, mid-December 1942, in Pilichowski et al., *Obozy*, ill. 135–36; Kaienburg, "*Vernichtung*," 304.

158. USHMM, RG-11.001M.05, reel 75, 504–2–8, Müller to Befehlshaber der Sipo et al., December 17, 1942, underlined in the original.

159. Müller to Himmler, December 16, 1942, *IMT*, vol. 27, 251–53, ND: 1472–PS.

160. USHMM, RG-11.001M.05, reel 75, 504–2–8, Müller to Befehlshaber der Sipo et al., December 17, 1942.

161. Himmler to HSSPF in Russia et al., January 6, 1943, in Heiber, *Reichsführer!*, quote on 225; Himmler to Oberg, January 18, 1943, ibid., quote on 223; Himmler to Krüger, January 1943, *TWC*, vol. 5, 618–19; Longerich, *Himmler*, 669–71, 678–80.

162. Schulte, "London," 223; Piper, *Zahl*, table D.

163. Foreign workers from the Soviet Union, for example, were only supposed to be released from the KL in exceptional cases; BA Berlin, NS 3/426, Bl. 41: WVHA-D to LK, February 26, 1943.

164. StANü, Pohl to Himmler, September 30, 1943, Anlage, ND: PS-1469.

165. BArchB, NS 3/426, Bl. 13: Chef Sipo und SD to Pohl, December 31, 1942.

166. Glücks to Lagerärzte, December 28, 1942, in NMGB, *Buchenwald*, 257–58. See also Himmler to Pohl, mid-December 1942, in Pilichowski et al., *Obozy*, ill. 135–36; IfZ, Dienstanweisung für SlF E, November 7, 1941, ND: PS-3685; BArchB, DO 1/32593, WVHA-D to LK, December 2, 1942.

167. BArchB, NS 3/426, Bl. 14: Glücks to LK, January 20, 1943; Himmler to Pohl, mid-December 1942, in Pilichowski et al., *Obozy*, ill. 135–36.

168. APMO, IZ-13/89, Bl. 168–72: Pohl to LK, October 26, 1943.

169. Ibid.

170. Pohl, "Zwangsarbeiterlager," 425; Spoerer, *Zwangsarbeit*, 97–99.

171. Himmler to Pohl, mid-December 1942, in Pilichowski et al., *Obozy*, ill. 135–36; Buggeln, *Arbeit*, 131.

172. Himmler to Pohl, December 15, 1942, in Heiber, *Reichsführer!*, 216.

173. Quotes in APMO, IZ-13/89, Bl. 168–72: Pohl to LK, October 26, 1943. See also Kaienburg, "*Vernichtung*," 318–19, 352; idem, "Systematisierung," 66 (n. 25).

174. BArchB, NS 3/425, Bl. 118: Himmler to RSHA and WVHA-D, October 29, 1942. Although Himmler's order was restricted to relatives, the Red Cross soon dispatched packages, too; Favez, *Red*, 69–71, 94–99.

175. Quotes in Laqueur, *Schreiben*, 48; NAL, WO 235/305, Bl. 135–42: Examination of H. Dziedziecka, December 10, 1946, Bl. 137. See also Helweg-Larsen et al., *Famine*, 47–48, 98, 141, 351; Kosmala, "Häftlinge," 108.

176. For one estimate, see Wagner, *Produktion*, 464–65.

177. *OdT*, vol. 7, 66; Favez, *Red*, 70, 75; Strebel, *Ravensbrück*, 196; Mettbach, Behringer, "Wer," 37.

178. Kupfer-Koberwitz, *Tagebücher*, 344–45, entry August 9, 1944.

179. Buggeln, *Arbeit*, 132–35; Kaienburg, "*Vernichtung*," 317–18; Kaienburg, *Wirtschaft*, 949. In state prisons, which came under the same regulations, no more than one-third of all prisoners received extra rations by summer 1942; ThHStAW, GStA OLG Jena, Nr. 430: Arbeitstagung am 30.6 und 1.7.1942, Bl. 258.

180. Himmler to Pohl, mid-December 1942, in Pilichowski et al., *Obozy*, ill. 135–36.

181. See also Keller and Otto, "Kriegsgefangene," 31–32.

182. See chapter 7.

183. StANü, WVHA to LK, April 27, 1943, ND: NO-1007. In some camps, Action 14f13 apparently continued in some fashion, following Himmler's intervention. After the war, the Ravensbrück camp doctor testified that a physician from Berlin had picked out "mentally disturbed" prisoners, who were later gassed in Hartheim; Strebel, *Ravensbrück*, 337.

184. Glücks to Lagerärzte, December 28, 1942, in NMGB, *Buchenwald*, 257–58.

185. Ley and Morsch, *Medizin*, 69, 100; Ley, "Kollaboration," 123, 126, 132; Hahn, *Grawitz*, 160 (placing the shift in SS practice around 1941); Strzelecka, "Hospitals," 314, 320, 328; Kaienburg, "*Vernichtung*," 372–75; Wagner, *Produktion*, 298.

186. Kaienburg, "*Vernichtung*," 323–24.

187. Quote in Hohmann and Wieland, *Konzentrationslager*, 39.

188. Maršálek, *Mauthausen*, 160–66; Kaienburg, "*Vernichtung*," 374.

189. APMO, Proces Höss, Hd 6, Bl. 51–62: O. Wolken, "Chronik Auschwitz II (B II a)," n.d. (c. spring 1945), Bl. 53. Transports of sick prisoners from other KL to Auschwitz started no later than autumn 1942; NAL, HW 16/66, "II. Concentration Camps," November 27, 1942; AdsD, KE, E. Büge, Bericht, n.d. (1945/46), 143.

190. Kaienburg, "*Vernichtung*," 327–28; APMO, IZ-13/89, Bl. 168–72: Pohl to LK, October 26, 1943; Zámečník, *Dachau*, 251; BStU, MfS HA IX/11, ZUV 4, Akte 23, Vernehmungsprotokoll A. Kaindl, August 20, 1946, Bl. 246; BArchB, NS 3/426, Bl. 16: Glücks to LK, January 20, 1943; KB Nr. 4/44, February 22, 1944, in Frei et al., *Kommandanturbefehle*, 412–13.

191. BArchB, NS 3/426, Bl. 121: WVHA-D to LK, July 27, 1943; ibid., Bl. 122–28: Aufgaben und Pflichten der Wachposten, n.d. (1943), Bl. 125; Sprenger, *Groß-Rosen*, 179–80.

192. Wagner, *IG Auschwitz*, 223; *OdT*, vol. 3, 349; Gedenkstätte Buchenwald, *Buchenwald*, 58–59.

193. Bessmann and Buggeln, "Befehlsgeber," 530.

194. For the historiography, see Schulte, *Zwangsarbeit*, 395–96 (n. 79).

195. Maurer to LK, June 7, 1942, in Schnabel, *Macht*, doc. D 69.

196. Gustloff-Werke to LK Buchenwald, June 16, 1942, in Schnabel, *Macht*, doc. D 72.

197. Pohl to LK, November 22, 1943, *TWC*, vol. 5, 370–72, emphasis in the original (mistakenly dated January 22 in this printed version). See also Wagner, *Produktion*, 381.

198. StANü, Pohl to Himmler, September 30, 1943, Anlage, ND: PS-1469; ibid., Himmler to Pohl, October 8, 1943.

199. Broszat, "Konzentrationslager," 438, 443; Pingel, *Häftlinge*, 183.

200. Kárný, "'Vernichtung.'" More generally, see Orth, *System*, 219–20 (though Orth herself indirectly uses figures from Pohl's report, via the works of Broszat and Pingel; ibid., 217, n. 208; 219, n. 219); Piper, *Zahl*, 160; Kagan, "Standesamt," 155; BArchB, NS 4/Na 6, Bl. 29: WVHA-D to LK, September 20, 1943.

201. Kárný suggests that Pohl's figures masked an increase in the relative number of deaths; "'Vernichtung,'" 145.

202. Buggeln, *Arbeit*, 41–42; idem, *System*, 72.

203. Piper, *Zahl*, 158–62.

204. Langbein, *Menschen*, 74. See also Piper, "Exploitation," 134; Hayes, "Auschwitz," 336; Pilecki, *Auschwitz*, quote on 278.

205. StANü, Pohl to Himmler, September 30, 1943, Anlage, ND: PS-1469.

206. Strebel, *Ravensbrück*, 524; *OdT*, vol. 4, 44–46; Freund, "Mauthausen," 261; Kranebitter, *Zahlen*, 196–97 (with the most recent figures for Mauthausen).

207. Wachsmann, *Prisons*, 288–98; Pingel, *Häftlinge*, 186.

208. See also Buggeln, *Arbeit*, 42.

209. Quote in HLSL, Rascher to Himmler, April 5, 1942, ND: 1971-PS-a. See also Ebbinghaus, Roth, "Medizinverbrechen," 127–31; Knoll, "Humanexperimente"; Klee, *Auschwitz*, 220; Weindling, *Victims*, chapter 9; Rascher to Himmler, May 15, 1941, ND: 1602-PS, in Mitscherlich and Mielke, *Medizin*, 20–21. My thanks to Albert Knoll for identifying Siegmund Wassing.

210. HLSL, Himmler to Rascher, April 13, 1942, ND: 1971-PS-b; BArchL, B 162/21846, Bl. 167–254: W. Neff, "Recht oder Unrecht," n.d., Bl. 222–23; Witte et al., *Dienstkalender*, 414; BArchB, Film 44563, O. Pohl, "Medizinische Versuche," July 23, 1946, p. 2.

211. Schmidt, *Brandt*, 257–96, quote on 294; Weindling, *Victims*, table 9 (my thanks to Prof. Weindling for sharing his manuscript). For categorizing the different medical experiments, see *OdT*, vol. 1, 167; Freyhofer, *Medical Trial*.

212. *OdT*, vol. 1, 165–67; Cocks, "Old as New," 178–79; Roelcke, "Introduction," 14.

213. Benz, "Rascher," 193–96; Danckwortt, "Wissenschaft," 140–41.

214. Stoll, "Sonntag," 920–24; Ley and Morsch, *Medizin*, 329–35.

215. Weindling, *Victims*, tables 6 and 7.

216. NAL, HW 16/22, GPD Nr. 3, November 26, 1942.

217. Quote in Stoll, "Sonntag," 924.

218. For these terms, see Klee, *Auschwitz*, 380; Sachse, "Menschenversuche," 7; Tillion, *Ravensbrück*, 182; NARA, RG 549, 000–50–9, Box 437, Nebe to Mrugowsky, February 29, 1944.

219. Hahn, *Grawitz*, 460; Schmidt, *Brandt*, 256–57.

220. Pohl to Brandt, August 16, 1943, in Heiber, *Reichsführer!*, 284.

221. Benz, "Rascher," 192.

222. Kater, *"Ahnenerbe,"* 255–57; Hahn, *Grawitz*, 401–402.

223. Hahn, *Grawitz*, 225, 280–83, 372–75, 403–404.

224. Himmler to Rascher, October 24, 1942, in Heiber, *Reichsführer!*, 205–206; Benz, "Rascher," 204; Schmidt, "Medical Ethics," 601–602; Wolters, *Tuberkulose*, 94–100.

225. For this and the previous paragraph, see Benz, "Rascher," 191–210. See also Hahn, *Grawitz*, 60–61.

226. For this and the previous paragraph, see Ebbinghaus and Roth, "Medizinverbrechen," 136–46, Michalowski quote on 142; StAMü, StA Nr. 34433, Bl. 115–16: Vernehmungsniederschrift G. Tauber, August 17, 1948, Polish prisoner quote on 115; BArchL, B 162/21846, Bl. 167–254: W. Neff, "Recht oder Unrecht," n.d., Bl. 225–27, 235–36; Mitscherlich and Mielke, *Medizin*, 51–61.

227. BArchL, B 162/21846, Bl. 167–254: W. Neff, "Recht oder Unrecht," n.d., Bl. 241–42, quote on 221; Mitscherlich and Mielke, *Medizin*, 65–66.

228. APMO, Proces Maurer, 5a, Bl. 150: Dr. Rascher, Bericht über KL-Dirnen, November 5, 1942, ND: NO-323; IfZ, Himmler to Pohl, November 15, 1942, ND: NO-1583; Kater, *"Ahnenerbe,"* 236.

229. Quote in Himmler to Rascher, October 24, 1942, in Heiber, *Reichsführer!*, 205–206.

230. Mitscherlich and Mielke, *Medizin*, 61–65; Holzhaider, "'Schwester Pia,'" 368–69; Schalm, *Überleben*, 187.

231. Himmler to Rascher, October 24, 1942, in Heiber, *Reichsführer!*, 205–206, quote on 206; IfZ, Himmler to Pohl, November 15, 1942, ND: PS-1583; APMO, Proces Maurer, 5a, Bl. 150: Dr. Rascher, Bericht über KL-Dirnen, November 5, 1942, ND: NO-323; Witte et al., *Dienstkalender*, 612; *DAP*, Vernehmung F. Hofmann, April 22, 1959, 3858; JVL, JAO, Review of Proceedings, *United States v. Weiss*, n.d. (1946), 17–18; Kater, *"Ahnenerbe,"* 236–37; Longerich, *Himmler*, 760–61.

232. Benz, "Rascher," 210–12; Mitscherlich and Mielke, *Medizin*, 70–71; BArchL, B 162/21846, Bl. 67–100: Kripo München, Abschlussbericht, June 25, 1944, Bl. 90–96.

233. Kater, *"Ahnenerbe,"* 239–43; NARA, M-1174, roll 3, Bl. 1441–65: Examination of E. Mahl,

December 6, 1945; BArchL, B 162/21846, Bl. 53–57: Kripo München, Zwischenbericht, May 26, 1944; ibid., Kripo München, Abschlussbericht, June 25, 1944; DaA, Nr. 7566, K. Schecher, "Rückblick auf Dachau," n.d., 249.

234. Benz, "Versuche," 93–95.

235. Hulverscheidt, "Menschen"; Klee, *Auschwitz*, 117–25; Weindling, *Victims*, chapter 10.

236. JVL, JAO, Review of Proceedings, *United States v. Weiss*, n.d. (1946), 17, 45.

237. Testimony of W. Karołewska, in Mitscherlich and Mielke, *Medizin*, 141–43; Klier, *Kaninchen*, 69; Schmidt, *Justice*, 182–83.

238. For this and the previous paragraph, see Mitscherlich and Mielke, *Medizin*, 131–39; Hahn, *Grawitz*, 458–62; *OdT*, vol. 1, 171–73; Schmidt, "'Scars,'" 31–32; Strebel, *Ravensbrück*, 256–58. More generally, see Ebbinghaus and Roth, "Kriegswunden."

239. Schmaltz, *Kampfstoff-Forschung*, 521–54, 562, quote on 550.

240. Wolters, *Tuberkulose*; Ley and Morsch, *Medizin*, 338–61.

241. Weindling, *Epidemics*, 352–63; idem, *Victims*, chapter 10; Kogon, *Theory*, 149–53; *OdT*, vol. 1, 169–70; Hahn, *Grawitz*, 326–29; Hackett, *Buchenwald*, 73; Gedenkstätte Buchenwald, *Buchenwald*, 200–201; Werther, "Menschenversuche"; HLSL, Anklageschrift gegen Koch, 1944, ND: NO-2366, pp. 65–67; BArchB (ehem. BDC), SSO, Hoven, Waldemar, 10.2.1903. For an overview of the Buchenwald typhus experiments, see also Allen, *Laboratory*, chapter 11. In addition to prisoners infected for the trials, the Buchenwald SS used inmates who had already caught typhus. For wider context, see Süss, "Volkskörper," 226–27, 236–37.

242. Ley and Morsch, *Medizin*, 361–70.

243. Kubica, "Crimes," 319, 328–29, Wirths's quote on 328; Keller, *Günzburg*, 20–35; Klee, *Auschwitz*, 459, 471–72.

244. For this and the previous paragraph, see Keller, *Günzburg*, 17–18, 39, 73–94; Kubica, "Crimes," 318.

245. Klee, *Auschwitz*, 473–75, 480–82, 489, quote on 475; Kubica, "Crimes," 325–26; Keller, *Günzburg*, 41–42.

246. For this and the previous paragraph, see Kubica, "Crimes," 318, 321–25, 326; Keller, *Günzburg*, 40–41, 83–84; Klee, *Auschwitz*, 477–79, 488–90; Piekut-Warszawska, "Kinder," 227–29. Quote in WL, P.III.h. No. 161, E. Herskovits to Familie Karo, May 21–23, 1945.

247. For this and the previous three paragraphs, see Strzelecka, "Experiments"; Hahn, *Grawitz*, 275–78; Lifton and Hackett, "Nazi Doctors," 306–308; Beischl, *Wirths*, 117–46; Eichmüller, *Keine Generalamnestie*, 135–42; Witte et al., *Dienstkalender*, 480; Schilter, "Schumann," 101–104; Clauberg to Himmler, June 7, 1943, in Heiber, *Reichsführer!*, 159–60; Weindling, "Opfer," 91–92; idem, *Victims*, chapter 14; Weinberger, *Fertility Experiments* (Dr. Schumann also carried out some experiments in Ravensbrück in 1944). Quotes in Fragebogen Chopfenberg, n.d., in Schnabel, *Macht*, 277; APMO, Proces Maurer, 5a, Bl. 163–68: EE by C. Balitzki, November 22, 1946, ND: NO-819.

248. Klee, *Auschwitz*, 356–66, 371–78, Hirt quote on 359; Steegemann, *Struthof*, 384–86, 395–400; H.-J. Lang, "Die Spur der Skelette," *Spiegel Online*, accessed January 8, 2010; Kater, *"Ahnenerbe,"* 245–55; Kogon et al., *Massentötungen*, 274–76; Heinemann, *"Rasse,"* 535–39. Only in 2003 were all victims identified by name.

249. See also Hahn et al., "Medizin," 17.

250. Hahn, *Grawitz*, 500.

251. BArchL, B 162/7997, Bl. 525–603: Fall IV, Nuremberg, June 30, 1947, Bl. 580.

252. Benz, "Rascher," 202, 208; Kater, *"Ahnenerbe,"* 234, 263.

253. APMO, Proces Höss, Hd 2/1, Bl. 10–15: M. Stoppelman, "Meine Erlebnisse in Auschwitz," n.d. (c. spring 1945), prisoner doctor quotes on 15; Klee, *Auschwitz*, 63, 92, 488, Verschuer quote on 458–59; Sachse, "Menschenversuche," 10–14; Keller, *Günzburg*, 39, 41, 88, 92; Hulverscheidt, "Menschen," 122.

254. Mitscherlich and Mielke, *Medizin*, 54–61, 151; Klee, *Auschwitz*, 235–43; Hahn,

Grawitz, 328–29, 458–59; Kater, *"Ahnenerbe,"* 262; Ebbinghaus and Roth, "Medizinverbrechen," 137; Neumann, "Heeressanitätsinspektion," 129.

255. Klee, *Auschwitz*, 284–321, quotes on 279, 285; Maršálek, *Mauthausen*, 176–77 (with the spelling Helmut Vetter).

256. Cocks, "Old as New," 180, 190; Evans, *Third Reich in Power*, 445–46; Kater, *"Ahnenerbe,"* 262; idem., "Criminal," 79–81.

257. Mitscherlich and Mielke, *Medizin*, 96–102; NARA, RG 549, 000–50–9, Box 437, Himmler to chief of the Sipo, February 27, 1944; Klee, *Auschwitz*, 126, 310–12.

258. Kater, *"Ahnenerbe,"* quotes on 243–44; Mitscherlich and Mielke, *Medizin*, 132.

259. Wachsmann, *Prisons*, 316–17, quote on 317.

260. Nyiszli, *Auschwitz* (written in 1946), quotes on 51, 57, 101; Klee, *Auschwitz*, 489–90; Evans, "Introduction."

261. Steiner and Steiner, "Zwillinge," quote on 128.

262. Quotes in HLSL, Grawitz to Himmler, June 28, 1944, ND: NO-179; Benz, "Rascher," 204. See also BArchL, B 162/21846, Bl. 167–254: W. Neff, "Recht oder Unrecht," n.d., Bl. 219–20; Weindling, *Victims*, tables 3, 4, and 5.

263. Schwarberg, *SS-Arzt*, 7–9, 152; Weindling, "Opfer," 90.

264. The WVHA had already contemplated such a move before, in autumn 1942 and summer 1943, though these early plans for moving many thousands of Jews from Auschwitz to arms factories deep inside the Third Reich had come to nothing; BArchB, NS 19/14, Bl. 131–33: Pohl to Himmler, September 16, 1942; Maurer to Höss, September 4, 1943, in Tuchel, *Inspektion*, 128; Herbert, "Arbeit," 222–24. Quote in HLSL, WVHA to LK, October 5, 1942, ND: 3677–PS.

9. Camps Unbound

1. For this and the previous paragraphs, see Wagner, *Produktion*, 184–94, 376, 459, 485–86, Van Dijk quote on 189; idem, *Mittelbau-Dora*, 48; Michel, *Dora*, 66–75; Sellier, *Dora*, 58–61; Eisfeld, *Mondsüchtig*, 120; NARA, M-1079, roll 5, Vernehmung W. Hein, April 16, 1945; ibid., roll 6, examination of C. Jay, August 7, 1947; ibid., examination of H. Iwes, August 12, 1947, quote on 299; testimony of K. Kahr, April 10, 1947, *TWC*, vol. 5, 396. My thanks to Jens-Christian Wagner for further details on the sleeping tunnels.

2. For this and the previous paragraph, see Wagner, *Mittelbau-Dora*, 31–37, 161; Wagner, *Produktion*, 89; Neufeld, *Rocket*, 176, 184–204; Eisfeld, *Mondsüchtig*, 112–18; IfZ, F 37/3, Himmler diary, entries June 28 and 29, 1943.

3. Himmler to Pohl, December 17, 1943, cited in Wagner, *Produktion*, 89. More generally, see Fröbe, "Arbeitseinsatz," 352–56.

4. Freund, *Zement*, 449–57; Wagner, *Produktion*, 87–88; *OdT*, vol. 4, 354–60, 416–20. Further underground projects were under way in existing KL; ibid., 375.

5. Buggeln, "Building"; idem, *Arbeit*, 239; idem, *Bunker*; *OdT*, vol. 5, 372–76.

6. IfZ, Burger to Loerner, August 15, 1944, ND: NO-399; ibid., Fa 183, Bl. 6–7, n.d.; Schulte, *Zwangsarbeit*, 402, table 6.

7. Hördler, "Ordnung," quote on 298; Buggeln, *System*, 95.

8. Karin Orth (*System*, 243) coined the term "concentration camps of the relocation projects."

9. Wagner, *Produktion*, 244–59, 386; Fings, *Krieg*, 14, 316.

10. Wiedemann, "Rózsa"; Jochem, "Bedingungen," 64–69; Gerlach and Aly, *Kapitel*, 18, 31–35, 53. At the time, Rózsa was known under her married name, Schapira.

11. Nansen, *Day*, 410; Zámečník, "Aufzeichnungen," 220, 224; AdsD, KE, E. Büge, Bericht, n.d. (1945–46), 103, 159; StANü, EE by K. Roeder, February 20, 1947, ND: NO-2122.

12. Quote in Kupfer-Koberwitz, *Dachauer*, 349 (entry for August 14, 1944). See also YIVO,

RG 294.1, MK 488, series 20, folder 541, Bl. 1279–86: testimony J. Levine, n.d. (1945–46); Nansen, *Day*, 512–13; NAL, WO 208/3596, CSDIC, SIR Nr. 727, August 11, 1944.

13. Estimate in Buggeln, *System*, 135.

14. Boelcke, *Rüstung*, Hitler quote on 338; Wagner, *Produktion*, 89–96; Raim, *Dachauer*, 28–35, 37–41; Süß, *Tod*, 13–14.

15. Fröbe, "Arbeitseinsatz," 357–58; Kroener, "'Menschenbewirtschaftung,'" 912–18; Kooger, *Rüstung*, 283–84; Wagner, *Produktion*, 94, 97; Uziel, *Arming*, 1–2.

16. Wagner, *Produktion*, 90–91, 101–104; Fröbe, "Kammler," 312–14; idem., "Arbeitseinsatz," 358–59.

17. Perz, *Projekt Quarz*; *OdT*, vol. 4, 405–408.

18. For this and the two previous paragraphs, see Fröbe, "Kammler." See also Wagner, *Produktion*, 106–10, Kammler quote on 103; Wagner, *Mittelbau-Dora*, 41–44, Speer quotes on 44; BArchB, Film 44563, Vernehmung O. Pohl, December 17, 1946, p. 14; IfZ, F 13/8, Bl. 462–66: R. Höss, "Dr. Ing. Kammler," n.d. (1946–47); Broszat, *Kommandant*, 271–75; Fings, *Krieg*, passim; Schley, *Buchenwald*, 62–63; Buchheim, "Befehl," 241; Kogon, *Theory*, 97–98; Eisfeld, *Mondsüchtig*, 120; *OdT*, vol. 3, 539–44; Hördler, "Ordnung," 255; Megargee, *Encyclopedia*, vol. 1/A, 402–405.

19. Raim, *Dachauer*, 41–60; *OdT*, vol. 2, 360–73, 389–95; Wagner, *Produktion*, 101, 110; Müller, "Speer," 448–55; Buggeln, "'Menschenhandel'"; Schalm, *Überleben*, 76, 154. Although the OT was officially led by Speer in his capacity as armaments minister, the powerful head of the OT, Xaver Dorsch, often acted independently.

20. *OdT*, vol. 6, 461–67; Megargee, *Encyclopedia*, vol. 1/A, 782–83.

21. Glauning, *Entgrenzung*, 101–19; Megargee, *Encyclopedia*, vol. 1/B, 1012–14; Bütow and Bindernagel, *KZ*, 77–90, 106–11, 223; Wagner, *Produktion*, 111–16; Freund, *Zement*, 451. Up to forty thousand KL prisoners may have been deployed (at any one time) for the Geilenberg Staff; Buggeln, *System*, 131–33.

22. Testimony of O. Pohl, 1947, *TWC*, vol. 5, 445–46. Pohl spoke of approximately 600,000 KL prisoners at the end of 1944 (he meant only those prisoners classified as working). Of these, he estimated that 230,000 to 250,000 had been employed by private industry, around 170,000 by the Special Staff Kammler, another 40,000 to 50,000 by Kammler's construction inspectorates (as part of WVHA-C), and 15,000 in Kammler's construction and railway brigades.

23. Quotes in Fröhlich, *Tagebücher*, II/11, February 29, 1944, p. 366; BArchB, NS 19/4014, Bl. 158–204: Rede des Reichsführers SS vor Generälen, June 21, 1944, Bl. 166, 162. See also Rede bei der SS Gruppenführertagung in Posen, October 4, 1943, *IMT*, vol. 29, ND: 1919-PS, pp. 144–45.

24. BArchB (ehem. BDC), SSO Pohl, Oswald, 30.6.1892, Pohl to Himmler, April 5, 1944.

25. Kaienburg, *"Vernichtung,"* 320–21; Buggeln, *Arbeit*, 131–33, 141.

26. For example, see Glauning, *Entgrenzung*, 249–55, 405–406.

27. Wagner, *Produktion*, 389–90; Wagner, *IG Auschwitz*, 265–69.

28. For example, see Buggeln, *Arbeit*, 309–10.

29. Estimates in Spoerer, "Unternehmen," 68–69. See also idem, *Zwangsarbeit*, 186.

30. Spoerer, "Unternehmen," 70, 88–90; Buggeln, *System*, 58; Wagner, *Produktion*, 76, 394; Hayes, "Ambiguities," 14–16.

31. Orth, *System*, 248–49; Wagner, *Produktion*, 580; Schulte, *Zwangsarbeit*, 406–409, 413.

32. Schulte, *Zwangsarbeit*, 399–403.

33. Quotes in Strebel, *Ravensbrück*, 439. See also Roth, "Zwangsarbeit"; Hördler, "Ordnung," 326; Spoerer, *Zwangsarbeit*, 111; Wagner, *IG Auschwitz*, 144, 219; Fröbe, "KZ-Häftlinge," 652–54.

34. Ibel, "Digitalisierung"; Römmer, "Digitalisierung," 10–12.

35. Naasner, *Machtzentren*, 454; Kershaw, *End*, 79.

36. Wagner, *Produktion*, 116–18, 237, 240; Kroener et al., "Zusammenfassung," 1003–1006, 1016–17; Raim, *Dachauer*, 138–41.

37. Kaienburg, *Wirtschaft*, 1043-44, 1095. By contrast, many industrialists had a more rational agenda: they wanted to save their machines and plants into the postwar period; Fröbe, "Arbeitseinsatz," 371-72; Wagner, *Produktion*, 117-18.

38. Hayes, *Industry*, 367; Wagner, *IG Farben*, 263, 295.

39. Glauning, *Entgrenzung*, 218-20; Wagner, *Produktion*, 116.

40. Neufeld, *Rocket*, 264. See also Wagner, *Produktion*, 202-207, 220, 288.

41. Wagner, *Produktion*, 288; Kogon, *Theory*, 98-99.

42. Hördler, "Ordnung," 9-11, 329-30, 338-40; Orth, *System*, 260-62.

43. Freund, "Mauthausen," 263; Maršálek, *Mauthausen*, 161-62; LG Frankfurt, Urteil, May 27, 1970, *JNV*, vol. 34, 219, 229; Kogon et al., *Massentötungen*, 77-78; Friedlander, *Genocide*, 149-50; Hördler, "Ordnung," 346-58, 373. The murders in Hartheim were not a continuation of Action 14f13, as Hördler suggests, but of more limited character, largely restricted to sick prisoners from nearby Mauthausen.

44. Hördler, "Ordnung," 316, 398.

45. *OdT*, vol. 7, 48-49; Kranz, "Erfassung," 230; idem., "KL Lublin," 376; Marszałek, *Majdanek*, 77, 133.

46. Quote (attributed to Richard Glücks) in NAL, WO 235/19, statement of J. Kramer, May 22, 1945, p. 10. See also Wenck, *Menschenhandel*, 338-43; *OdT*, vol. 7, 200-202.

47. Quotes in NARA, M-1079, roll 6, examination of C. Jay, August 7, 1947, Bl. 62; Zeugenaussage J. H. Mulin, May 5, 1945, in Niedersächsische Landeszentrale, *Bergen-Belsen*, 89-90. See also *OdT*, vol. 7, 200-201; Wenck, *Menschenhandel*, 340; Wagner, *Produktion*, 493.

48. Broszat, *Kommandant*, 205, 208, 263-66, quote on 264; StANü, EE by K. Sommer, January 22, 1947, ND: NO-1578.

49. *OdT*, vol. 4, 45; IfZ, Fa 183, Bl. 6.

50. IfZ, Burger to Loerner, August 15, 1944, ND: NO-399; ibid., Fa 183, Bl. 6-7, n.d.; Schulte, *Zwangsarbeit*, 402, table 6; Strebel, *Ravensbrück*, 349. The Buchenwald figure includes prisoners in Ohrdruf (listed separately in the SS table). The exclusion of female prisoners from Dora appears to have been deliberate, perhaps to avoid disruption to high-profile production commandos; my thanks to Jens-Christian Wagner for this point.

51. Roth, "'Asozialen,'" 449-53; Wachsmann, *Prisons*, 221-22, 319-20; Longerich, *Himmler*, 718-19; *OdT*, vol. 1, 162-63; Röll, *Sozialdemokraten*, 185-90. Soldmann died just weeks after liberation in spring 1945.

52. Lotfi, *KZ*, 235-36; Kroener, "'Menschenbewirtschaftung,'" 929; Kaienburg, "*Vernichtung*," 302-303 (n. 37); Herbert, *Fremdarbeiter*, 356.

53. Longerich, *Himmler*, 725-26.

54. Sellier, *Dora*, 56; Strebel, *Ravensbrück*, 151-52.

55. Borodziej, *Geschichte*, 249-51; Snyder, *Bloodlands*, 298-309; Strebel, *Ravensbrück*, 143-44; *OdT*, vol. 8, 109-14; IfZ, Burger to Loerner, August 15, 1944, ND: NO-399. Quotes in LULVR, interview No. 357, June 13, 1946.

56. Buggeln, *System*, 139; Pohl, "Holocaust," 159-60.

57. Browning, *Remembering*, 153-54, 218; Karay, *Death*.

58. Pohl, "Holocaust," 159; Piper, *Zahl*, 185-86; Friedländer, *Jahre*, 658-61.

59. Friedländer, *Jahre*, 636-42; Longerich, *Himmler*, 711-13, 726-27; Piper, *Zahl*, table D; Levi and de Benedetti, *Auschwitz*, 32-35; Czech, *Kalendarium*, 730.

60. Kárný, "Theresienstädter," 213-15; Piper, *Zahl*, 192; Friedländer, *Jahre*, 667.

61. Cesarani, *Eichmann*, 159-73; Pohl, "Holocaust," 158; Longerich, *Himmler*, 714-15; Gerlach and Aly, *Kapitel*, 276, 375.

62. Quote in WL, P.III.h. No. 233, E. Fejer, "Bericht aus der Verfolgungszeit," January 1956, p. 7. More generally, see Gerlach and Aly, *Kapitel*, 271-73, 355-67; Pohl, "Holocaust," 158.

63. Fröbe, "Arbeitseinsatz," 360-61, quote on 361; idem, "Kammler," 314; Gerlach and Aly, *Kapitel*, 163-71, 251-52, 375; Wagner, *Produktion*, 98-99; Cesarani, *Eichmann*, 162.

64. In addition, over fifteen thousand Jewish prisoners are likely to have died in Monowitz during 1944; Wagner, *IG Auschwitz*, 281.

65. For the last point, see Pohl, "Holocaust," 158. Between May and July 1944, some 430,000 to 435,000 Jews arrived from Hungary, and another 35,000 from elsewhere, bringing the total number of deported Jews in this period to 465,000 or more. This compares to 456,450 Jews deported to Auschwitz between May 1942 and April 1944; Gerlach and Aly, *Kapitel*, 276, 375; Piper, *Zahl*, table D.

66. Interrogation of R. Höss, April 2, 1946, in Mendelsohn, *Holocaust*, vol. 12, 121–27; Höss testimony and quote, January 1947, in Van Pelt, *Case*, 262; YVA, M-5/162, affidavit D. Wislieceny, November 29, 1945, p. 4; Stangneth, "Aufenthaltsorte," 4; BArchK, All. Proz. 6/101, Bl. 29.

67. StB Nr. 14/44, May 8, 1944, in Frei et al., *Kommandanturbefehle*, 445–46.

68. StANü, EE by K. Sommer, April 4, 1947, ND: NO-2739, p. 3.

69. For Liebehenschel's reputation, see Orth, *SS*, 245–46.

70. Quote in BArchB (ehem. BDC), SSO, Liebehenschel, Arthur, 25.11.01, Stellungnahme R. Baer, July 3, 1944. See also ibid., Brandt to Pohl, June 26, 1944; ibid., Pohl to Brandt, June 6, 1944; ibid., RS, Liebehenschel, Arthur, 25.11.01, Fernspruch, October 3, 1944; ibid., Ärztlicher Untersuchungsbogen, August 29, 1944; IfZ, F 13/7, Bl. 389–92: R. Höss, "Arthur Liebehenschel," November 1946; ibid., F 13/8, Bl. 468–71: R. Höss, "Richard Baer," November 1946; Orth, *SS*, 243–46. Liebehenschel was finally allowed to marry in autumn 1944, because his fiancée was about to give birth, but he never forgave Pohl; BArchB, Film 44837, Vernehmung A. Liebehenschel, September 18, 1946, p. 33.

71. Hördler, "Ordnung," 64, 268–70.

72. Quotes in BArchK, All. Proz. 6/106, Bl. 25; ibid., 6/101, Bl. 29. See also ibid., 6/97, Bl. 22; ibid., 6/99, Bl. 4; Gerlach and Aly, *Kapitel*, 275, 296–97; Höss testimony, January 1947, in Van Pelt, *Case*, 262; Piper, *Zahl*, table D.

73. Gerlach and Aly, *Kapitel*, 276, 285–86, 289–96, 375 (these figures contradict the often-repeated suggestion that no more than ten percent of Hungarian Jews were selected as fit for slave labor in Auschwitz; most recently, Longerich, *Holocaust*, 408). See also Braham, "Hungarian Jews," 463–64; Dirks, *"Verbrechen,"* 111; StANü, EE by K. Sommer, April 4, 1947, ND: NO-2739, p. 3; Strzelecka and Setkiewicz, "Construction," 91, 98–99; Browning, *Survival*, 234–35, 240; WL, P.III.h. No. 562, Protokoll Dr. Wolken, April 1945, p. 13.

74. StB Nr. 14/44 (May 8, 1944), StB Nr. 15/44 (May 11, 1944), StB Nr. 20/44 (July 29, 1944), all in Frei et al., *Kommandanturbefehle*, 445–46, 475; Hördler, "Ordnung," 65. Baer had led the old main camp (Auschwitz I) since May 11, 1944.

75. Iwaszko, "Reasons," 17; LSW, Bl. 44–66: Vernehmung S. Dragon, May 10, 11, and 17, 1946, Bl. 59; Van Pelt, *Case*, 187, 262; Citroen and Starzyńska, *Auschwitz*, 78; Vaisman, *Auschwitz*, 39; WL, P.III.h. No. 867, "Eine polnische Nicht-Jüdin in Auschwitz," August 17, 1957, p. 8; "Bericht von Czesław Mordowicz," summer 1944, 303; Gilbert, *Music*, 177–78; Gutman, *Auschwitz Album*.

76. Pressac and Van Pelt, "Machinery," 237–38; Piper, *Mass Murder*, 178, 184–86, 193; Van Pelt, *Case*, 188, 256, 262; LSW, Bl. 44–66: Vernehmung S. Dragon, May 10, 11, and 17, 1946, Bl. 56, 58; USHMM, RG-11.001M.03, reel 19, folder 21, Aktenvermerk, Besuch des Hauptamtschefs, June 20, 1944. The Camp SS later erected a large empty barrack to obscure the open-air cremations; Perz and Sandkühler, "Auschwitz," 295.

77. Schmid, "Moll," 129–32; APMO, Proces Höss, Hd 6, Bl. 38–45: O. Wolken, "Lager-Bilder," n.d. (c. spring 1945), Bl. 44; LSW, Bl. 44–66: Vernehmung S. Dragon, May 10, 11, and 17, 1946, Bl. 52; NARA, RG 549, 000–50–9, Box 440A, statement P. Lazuka, April 23, 1945; Aussage S. Jankowski, April 16, 1945, in SMAB, *Inmitten*, 49–50; Höss testimony, January 1947, in Van Pelt, *Case*, 262–63.

78. *DAP*, Vernehmung S. Baretzki, February 18, 1965, 29223–38, quote on 29237; Strzelecka

and Setkiewicz, "Construction," 98–99; Strzelecka, "Women," 174; Langbein, *Menschen*, 66–67; Rózsa, "Solange," 100–108.

79. Iwaszko, "Reasons," 40–41.

80. Piper, *Zahl*, 103; Bauer, "Gypsies," 453.

81. See chapter 8.

82. For this and the previous three paragraphs, see Zimmermann, *Rassenutopie*, 326–38, 340, letter quote on 335; Winter, *Winter*, 45–53, quote on 47; Guttenberger, "Zigeunerlager," quote on 132; Langbein, *Menschen*, 52, 271–73; Kubica, "Children," 289; WL, P.III.h. No. 795, "Gipsy-Camp Birkenau," January 1958; ibid., No. 664, ". . . Juden und Zigeuner," September 1957; Fings, " 'Wannsee-Konferenz,' " 333; Strzelecka and Setkiewicz, "Construction," 84–85, 90–91, 93–94; Szymański et al., " 'Spital' "; Grotum, *Archiv*, 261; Piper, " 'Familienlager,' " 297; Świebocki, "Sinti," 332, 341.

83. Drawing on the testimony of a Polish political prisoner, several historians suggest that the local Camp SS—keen to empty the Gypsy camp for incoming Hungarian Jews—entered on May 16, 1944, but were driven back by the prisoners, leading the SS to abandon its first attempt to exterminate the remaining Gypsies (Zimmermann, *Rassenutopie*, 340; Lewy, *Nazi Persecution*, 163; Czech, *Kalendarium*, 774–75). However, this account is not corroborated by former inmates from the Gypsy camp (testimonies by Paul Morgenstern, Aron Bejlin, and Max Friedrich, all in *DAP*; accounts by Winter and Guttenberger, cited above).

84. Quotes in *DAP*, Vernehmung J. Glück, August 20, 1964, 15108; WL, P.III.h. No. 795, "Gipsy-Camp Birkenau," January 1958, p. 8. See also Strzelecka and Setkiewicz, "Construction," 91; Zimmermann, *Rassenutopie*, 336; Winter, *Winter*, 83–84.

85. Broszat, *Kommandant*, quote on 163; *DAP*, Vernehmung A. Bejlin, August 28, 1964, 16314–18, quote on 16318; ibid., Vernehmung J. Mikusz, April 26, 1965, 32386; APMO, Proces Höss, Hd 6, Bl. 46–50, O. Wolken, "Frauen u. Kinderschicksale," February 18, 1945, Bl. 49; ibid., Hd 5, Bl. 24–38: testimony of Dr. B. Epstein, April 7, 1945; Zimmermann, *Rassenutopie*, 343–44; Świebocki, *Resistance*, 42; Hördler, "Ordnung," 63; Broad, "Erinnerungen," 186.

86. See Świebocki, "Sinti," 332–35, quote (from 1943) on 335; Zimmermann, *Rassenutopie*, 339–47; WL, P.III.h. No. 795, "Gipsy-Camp Birkenau," January 1958, p. 8; Winter, *Winter*, 85–88; Wagner, *Ellrich*, 71–73; idem, *Produktion*, 648; idem, "Sinti," 103.

87. Quotes in BArchB, Film 14428, Pohl to Himmler, April 5, 1944, underlined in original (letter drafted by Maurer); ibid., Himmler to Pohl, April 22, 1944. For Alderney and Loiblpass, see *OdT*, vol. 5, 347–49; ibid, vol. 4, 400–404.

88. Glauning, *Entgrenzung*, 121–23.

89. Schalm, "Außenkommandos," 58–59.

90. WVHA figure in BArchB (ehem. BDC), SSO, Glücks, Richard, 22.4.1889, O. Pohl, Vorschlagsliste, January 13, 1945. According to the data in *OdT*, there were 557 satellite camps in January 1945 (my thanks to Chris Dillon for compiling these figures for me).

91. Satellite camps held prisoners on permanent sites outside the main KL, but remained administratively attached to it. They differed from outside labor details, whose prisoners returned to the main camp in the evenings; Buggeln, *Arbeit*, 105.

92. This point has been made by, among others, Sabine Schalm, who proposes a separate term (satellite commando) for small camps with fewer than 250 prisoners; Schalm, *Überleben*, 45–50.

93. For an influential typology of satellite camps, see Freund, "Mauthausen," 225.

94. Buggeln, *Arbeit*, 152–55; Wagner, *Produktion*, 480; Megargee, *Encyclopedia*, vol. 1/A, 346–48.

95. Wagner, *Ellrich*, 57.

96. Fings, *Krieg*, 247–70.

97. For a different interpretation, seeing the emergence of a new period of order and ratio-nalization of the KL system in 1944, see Hördler, "Ordnung."

98. Buggeln, *Arbeit*, 105–106, 113–14, 118, 121–23; Wagner, *Produktion*, 472; Hördler, "Ordnung," 253–54, 263.

99. Strebel, *Ravensbrück*, 450.

100. Stein, "Funktionswandel," 170, 178, 184.

101. Buggeln, *Arbeit*, 45; idem, *System*, 117–18, 133.

102. *OdT*, vol. 8, 48–49; Buggeln, *Arbeit*, 164–65; Hördler, "Ordnung," 333.

103. Wagner, *Produktion*, 498, 537; Schalm, *Überleben*, 309.

104. Buggeln, *Arbeit*, 117–21, 136, 152, 159–62, 396–99, 407–408, 416–17; idem, "Schulung," 189–90; Glauning, *Entgrenzung*, 149–58, 404; Wagner, *Ellrich*, 124, 127–28; idem, *Produktion*, 328; Freund, "Mauthausen," 270; BArchL, B 162/7995, Bl. 214–44: Vernehmung J. Hassebroek, March 16–22, 1967, Bl. 222.

105. Buggeln, *Arbeit*, 394.

106. Hördler, "Ordnung," 160–61.

107. BArchB (ehem. BDC), SSO, Harbaum, August, 25.3.1913, Bl. 119: R. Glücks, Personal-Antrag, April 24, 1944 (the figure of 22,000 WVHA-D staff given here does not include female guards, presumably, as they were not SS members); IfZ, Fa 183, Bl. 6–7, n.d. (the often-cited figure of 39,969 Camp SS guard personnel on January 1, 1945, is incom-plete, as it omits thousands of men transferred to the KL from the military; Buggeln, *Arbeit*, 392–93).

108. Perz, "Wehrmacht," 70–80; Buggeln, *Arbeit*, 392–93. See also IfZ, Fa 127/2, Bl. 276: Himmler to Pohl et al., May 11, 1944; BArchB (ehem. BDC), SSO, Harbaum, August, 25.3.1913, Bl. 119: R. Glücks, Personal-Antrag, April 24, 1944; Glauning, *Entgrenzung*, 167–68; Wagner, *Produktion*, 332, 336–37; Ellger, *Zwangsarbeit*, 212–13; Hördler, "Ordnung," 176. I am using the term "soldier" broadly, to encompass seamen and airmen.

109. Glauning, *Entgrenzung*, 168–69, 173, 176; Buggeln, *Arbeit*, 436; Wagner, *Produktion*, 332; Riedle, *Angehörigen*, 47.

110. Wagner, *Produktion*, 335–38, prisoner quote on 335; AGN, Ng. 7.6., H. Behncke to his family, September 1, 1944, quote on 35. For Vierke's case, see USHMM, RG-11.001M.20, reel 89, folder 127.

111. Historians still debate to what extent women drafted as KL guards could refuse to serve in these positions; Mailänder Koslov, *Gewalt*, 119–25, 133–35. For the figures, see IfZ, Fa 183, Bl. 6–7, n.d.

112. Strebel, *Ravensbrück*, 102; Buggeln, *Arbeit*, 462; Perz, "Wehrmacht," 76; Oppel, "Eß-mann," 87.

113. Hördler, "Ordnung," 9, 161; Buggeln, *Arbeit*, 393, 667; Orth, *SS*, 54.

114. Bornemann, *Geheimprojekt*, 190–98, Pauler quotes on 197, 192; AGN, Ng. 7.6.; Heike, "Lagerverwaltung," 235.

115. Bornemann, *Geheimprojekt*, Pauler quote on 198; AGN, Ng. 7.6., H. Behncke to his wife, n.d., quote on 66; BArchB, Film 44563, Vernehmung O. Pohl, July 15, 1946; Perz, "Wehrmacht," 81; Wagner, *Produktion*, 321, 334–36; Hördler, "Wehrmacht," 14; Bug-geln, *Arbeit*, 433.

116. Glücks to LK, December 18, 1944, in Wagner, *Mittelbau-Dora*, 109. See also Glauning, *Entgrenzung*, 167; Wagner, *Produktion*, 335–36, 345. For SS complaints about female guards, see Lasik, "SS Garrison," 290; Sprenger, "Aufseherinnen," 27; Schwarz, "Frauen," 807.

117. Hördler, "Ordnung," 23, 33–34, 181–90; idem, "Wehrmacht," 17–18; Buggeln, "Schu-lung."

118. Perz, "Wehrmacht," 82; Wagner, *Produktion*, 324; Fings, *Krieg*, 82–83 (on police reserv-ists). For a more skeptical note, see Hördler, "Wehrmacht," 18–19.

119. Quote in Jansen, "Zwangsarbeit," 93.

120. BArchL, B 162/5109, Bl. 1859-69: Erklärung Efim K., September 19, 1962, quote on 1865. For the correct spelling of the camp, see *OdT*, vol. 8, 150 (n. 2). Several other Jewish prisoners also recalled acts of kindness by German soldiers; BArchL, B 162/2985, Bl. 2032-34: Vernehmung Calelzon B., September 7, 1973; BoA, testimony G. Kaldore, August 31, 1946; Eichhorn, "Sabbath," 209-10.

121. For this and the previous two paragraphs, see Buggeln, *Arbeit*, 395-96, 399, 404-407, 417-19, 437-38, 442, 482-83, 667; idem, "Lebens- und Arbeitsbedingungen," 50; Wagner, *Produktion*, 343-44, Pauler quote on 339; AGN, Ng. 7.6., H. Behncke to his wife, January 28 and April 2, 1945, quotes on 167 and 260. See also Schalm, *Überleben*, 153-55; Hördler, "Ordnung," 178; *OdT*, vol. 4, 51; Fröbe, "Mineralölindustrie," 175.

122. Buggeln, *Arbeit*, 142-43, quote on 143; Freund, "Mauthausen," 267-68; Fröbe, "Arbeitseinsatz," 365-67; idem, "KZ-Häftlinge," 656-57; Wagner, *Produktion*, 362-71, 380, 476, 487, 500; *OdT*, vol. 5, 477-79.

123. For Gandersheim, see Antelme, *Menschengeschlecht*, quotes on 115; Megargee, *Encyclopedia*, vol. 1/A, 346-48; *OdT*, vol. 3, 374-76. More generally, see Buggeln, *Arbeit*, 17, 156, 213, 224-25, 283-95, 328.

124. Wagner, *Produktion*, 366-67, 469, 483, 493-97.

125. There was a second, much smaller satellite camp in town (Ellrich-Bürgergarten); *OdT*, vol. 7, 301.

126. Sellier, *Dora*, quote on 201; Wagner, *Produktion*, 478-79, 487-89; idem, *Ellrich*, 56, 59-66.

127. Tauzin, 1945, cited in Sellier, *Dora*, 208; Wagner, *Produktion*, 382-83, 479; idem, *Ellrich*, 90-96.

128. Quotes in YVA, O 15 E/1761, Protokoll V. Jakubovics, July 9, 1945; Bornemann, *Geheimprojekt*, 191. See also Wagner, *Produktion*, 382, 470-71, 476-77, 487; idem, *Ellrich*, 59, 96-98; Sellier, *Dora*, 210-12.

129. NARA, M-1079, roll 11, Aussage O. Brinkmann, June 30, 1947, quote on Bl. 1069; Wagner, *Ellrich*, 118-19, 127-36; Bornemann, *Geheimprojekt*, 188; JVL, DJAO, RaR, *United States v. Andrea*, April 15, 1948, 46-50.

130. Quotes in YVA, O 15 E/1761, Protokoll V. Jakubovics, July 9, 1945; Wagner, *Ellrich*, 89. See also ibid., 100, 104-109; idem, *Produktion*, 314, 382, 477, 488.

131. The more pressing the completion of a project, the worse the conditions; Buggeln, *Arbeit*, 239-40, 243, 256-60.

132. YVA, O 15 E/647, Protokoll J. Jakobovics, July 2, 1945. See also *OdT*, vol. 6, 286-87, 457-59.

133. Herbert, "Arbeit." For the term, see Burleigh and Wippermann, *Racial State*.

134. Orth, *System*, 240; Zimmermann, "Arbeit," 747.

135. Above all, see the pioneering work by Jens-Christian Wagner (*Produktion*). More recently, see Buggeln, *Arbeit*, 282; Kranebitter, "Zahlen," 148.

136. Wagner, *Produktion*, 402, quote on 579; idem, *Ellrich*, 110-11; idem, "Sinti."

137. Buggeln, *Arbeit*, 333.

138. Buggeln, *Arbeit*, 241, 245.

139. Renouard, *Hölle*, 39; Wagner, *Produktion*, 403, 579; idem, *Ellrich*, 112; Buggeln, *Arbeit*, 245, 497-98, 550.

140. Quote in Buggeln, *Arbeit*, 314 (n. 104). For Jews in mixed satellite camps, see Freund, "Häftlingskategorien," 880; idem, *Toten*, 380-83; Wagner, *Produktion*, 405-407.

141. Raim, *Dachauer*, 154-55, 192-246; idem, "KZ-Außenlagerkomplexe." See also Ervin-Deutsch, "Nachtschicht"; YIVO, RG 294.1, MK 488, series 20, folder 549, Bl. 718-27: testimony of S. Heller, July 10, 1945; YVA, O 15 E/534, protokoll S. Fülöp, July 1, 1945, quote on 2; Hördler, "Ordnung," 251; LG Augsburg, Urteil, June 28, 1950, *JNV*, vol. 6, 653-60. Other lethal construction camps (primarily) for Jews included Magdeburg-Rothensee, the Riese complex, Hanover-Ahlem, and Stempeda.

142. Buggeln, *Arbeit*, 216, 251, 296, 329-30; Wagner, *Produktion*, 370, 407-408.

143. Kupfer-Koberwitz, *Tagebücher*, 356.

144. Schalm, *Überleben*, 205.

145. Strebel, *Ravensbrück*, 426–27; Perz, "Wehrmacht," 78; Fröbe, "KZ-Häftlinge," 667–68.

146. Strebel, *Ravensbrück*, 428–29, 441–43; Hördler, "Ordnung," 289–92, 341.

147. Buggeln, *Arbeit*, 217, 317–18; Rudorff, *Frauen*, 386.

148. While sewing and cooking could bring obvious benefits, so could carpentry and similar trades (more male preserves). Also, since many male prisoners had served in the army, they may have become more easily accustomed to the military regimen inside the KL; Buggeln, *Gewalt*, 513–15; Debski, *Battlefield*, 82–83.

149. For the debate on this issue, see Buggeln, *Arbeit*, 280, 508, 513; Ellger, *Zwangsarbeit*, 315. Like Lawrence Langer, I am not convinced that survivor testimonies show a significant gendered difference in the levels of mutual support. Even if this was the case, however, it could simply be a reflection of male survivors' reluctance to talk about their reliance on emotional support from other men.

150. Strebel, *Ravensbrück*, 522; Ellger, *Zwangsarbeit*, 134, 315–16; Buggeln, *Arbeit*, 226.

151. Debski, *Battlefield*, 84; Rudorff, *Frauen*, 390; Buggeln, *Arbeit*, 278, 280–81, 394–95, 467–68; idem, *System*, 126–27. See also chapter 10, below.

152. Satellite camps for women were still normally led by a male camp leader, and the sentries in the Guard Troop were usually male, too; Ellger, *Zwangsarbeit*, 190, 214, 311; Buggeln, *Arbeit*, 464.

153. Pfingsten and Füllberg-Stolberg, "Frauen," 921; Buggeln, *Arbeit*, 466–67; Sprenger, "Aufseherinnen," 29–30; Rudorff, *Frauen*, 389–90.

154. Ellger, *Zwangsarbeit*, 215–16, 306–307, 312, 316, quote on 216.

155. For Neuengamme, see Buggeln, *Arbeit*, 333. The term "race" is used here in the way it was ascribed by the SS authorities.

156. Raim, *Dachauer*, 193–94, 200; idem, "KZ-Außenlagerkomplexe," 75–76; Schalm, *Überleben*, 195–96; YIVO, RG 294.1, MK 488, series 20, folder 549, Bl. 718–27: testimony Dr. S. Heller, July 10, 1945.

157. For Jewish women in production, see Zimmermann, "Arbeit," 746–47.

158. Rudorff, *Frauen*, 386–91.

159. Seidel, "Frauen," 155–56; *OdT*, vol. 3, 495–500.

160. Rózsa, "Solange," 98, 121, 125, 133, 141, 144, 157–61, 225, quotes on 107, 188; Jochem, "Bedingungen," 83–91; *OdT*, vol. 4, 213–16.

161. Buggeln, *Arbeit*, 275; Ellger, *Zwangsarbeit*, 95; *OdT*, vol. 6, 301–303, 410–12.

162. Fröhlich, *Tagebücher*, II/12, April 27, 1944, p. 202.

163. Browning, *Remembering*, 153–54. See also the case of Jewish "forgers" in Sachsenhausen and "hostages" in Bergen-Belsen (chapter 6, above).

164. See also Buggeln, *Arbeit*, 658.

165. Rózsa, "Solange," 159.

166. Wagner, *Produktion*, 534–55, Güntsche quote on 534.

167. Steinbacher, *Dachau*, quote on 184; Zámečník, "Aufzeichnungen," 210–11.

168. ITS, 1.1.6.0, folder 55, KL Dachau, Auszug aus der DV der KL Bewachung, n.d. (1942?).

169. Some of these satellite camps had already emerged before the war; for example, see *OdT*, vol. 3, 388–92, 587–90.

170. G. Meier to LK Flossenbürg, June 18, 1942, in KZ-Gedenkstätte Flossenbürg, *Flossenbürg*, quote on 171; Strebel, *Ravensbrück*, 207; Wachsmann, *Prisons*, 95. In 1942, the charge was three Reichsmark per male prisoner per day, and two Reichsmark per female prisoner; IfZ, WVHA to Kommandanturen, August 17, 1942, ND: PS-3685.

171. Schley, *Nachbar*, 71–75.

172. Bringmann, *Neuengamme*, quote on 43; Fings, *Krieg*, 161–62. For prisoner uniforms, see Schmidt, "Geschichte und Symbolik," 292–93.

173. Steinbacher, "*Musterstadt*," 193.

174. E. Mercker, "Granitbrüche Flossenbürg" (1941), oil on canvas, displayed in the exhibi-

tion *Histories in Conflict*, Haus der Kunst, Munich, June 2012–January 2013. The Camp SS also still conducted staged visits for state and party officials, as well as for foreign dignitaries; for example, see Wein, "Krankenrevier."

175. Fröhlich, *Tagebücher*, II/4, June 13, 1942, pp. 510–18.

176. Schley, *Nachbar*, 108–109; Horwitz, *Shadow*, 93, 109; Wagner, *Produktion*, 157–58; Glauning, *Entgrenzung*, 332–33; Marcuse, *Legacies*.

177. Dörner, *Die Deutschen*, 606.

178. Kremer, "Tagebuch," September 2, 1942, 211.

179. Neitzel, *Abgehört*, 283; Tyas, "Intelligence," 12.

180. Czech, *Kalendarium*, 380; NAL, HW 16/23, GPD Nr 3, Glücks to Höss, January 22, 1943. More generally, see Steinbacher, *"Musterstadt,"* 249–52.

181. Dörner, *Die Deutschen*, 325; Steinbacher, *"Musterstadt,"* 247–49; Frei, *1945*, 156–57; Broszat, *Kommandant*, 247.

182. Klemperer, *Zeugnis*, vol. 2, 47, 268, 306, 313, 378, quote on 259.

183. Dörner, *Die Deutschen*, 398, 416, 605–608; Fritzsche, *Life*, 240, 262–64.

184. BArchB, NS 4/Bu 31, Bl. 15: WVHA to LK, July 11, 1942; ibid., NS 3/426, Bl. 40: WVHA-D to LK, February 25, 1943.

185. BArchB, NS 3/426, Bl. 76: Himmler to Glücks, May 26, 1943; Grotum, *Archiv*, 219.

186. RSHA circular, October 26, 1939, in *NCA*, vol. 1, 962.

187. Dörner, *Die Deutschen*, 39–40, 355–56, quote on 355; LG Cologne, Urteil, April 20, 1970, *JNV*, vol. 33, 646.

188. BArchB, NS 3/391, Bl. 4–22: Aufgabengebiete in einem KL, n.d. (1942), Bl. 8; ibid., NS 4/Bu 31, Bl. 19: Verhalten beim Briefe-Schreiben, n.d.; ibid., NS 4/Na 6, Bl. 24: WVHA to LK, April 12, 1943; Wagner, *Produktion*, 463. Among the barred groups were Soviet POWs and so-called NN prisoners; Lasik, "Organizational," 168. For a ban on letters by Jewish inmates in summer 1944, see Sprenger, *Groß-Rosen*, 165.

189. C. Herman to his wife and daughter, November 6, 1944, in SMAB, *Inmitten*, quote on 259. For other examples, see Bárta, "Tagebuch," 50–51; S. Sosnowski to his wife, October 27, 1940, in Geehr, *Letters*, 44–45.

190. Quotes in Maršálek, *Mauthausen*, 50; A. Bala to J. Esztsadnika, July 1943, in Bacharach, *Worte*, 328.

191. J. Pogonowski to his family, April 21, 1943, in Piper, *Briefe*, 44–45.

192. IfZ, RSHA, AE, 2. Teil, Bl. 202: Runderlaß Chef Sipo und SD, October 24, 1939.

193. BArchB, NS 19/1570, Bl. 12–28: Inspekteur für Statistik, Endlösung der Judenfrage, Bl. 24.

194. *OdT*, vol. 3, 39; Strebel, *Ravensbrück*, 175.

195. Niethammer, *Antifaschismus*, 36 (n. 36); Roth, "'Asozialen,'" 449; Strebel, *Ravensbrück*, 174–75; KZ-Gedenkstätte Flossenbürg, *Flossenbürg*, 46; Eisenblätter, "Grundlinien," 167; August, *"Sonderaktion,"* 7, 42–46. None of the arrested Jewish professors from Krakow were freed.

196. BArchB, NS 3/391, Bl. 4–22: Aufgabengebiete in einem KL, n.d. (1942), Bl. 16–17; Maršálek, *Mauthausen*, 251; Weiss-Rüthel, *Nacht*, 175; Gostner, *1000 Tage*, 169.

197. Glücks to Lagerärzte, December 28, 1942, in NMGB, *Buchenwald*, 257–58, figures for July to November 1942.

198. BArchB, NS 4/Bu 143, Schutzhaftlager-Rapport, November 6, 1943.

199. *OdT*, vol. 1, 163; Hett and Tuchel, "Reaktionen," 382–83.

200. Klausch, *Antifaschisten*, 27–75.

201. Himmler quotes in "Dokumentation. Die Rede Himmlers," 378; Himmler to Dirlewanger et al., February 19, 1944, in Heiber, *Reichsführer!*, document 299, p. 319. Other quotes in ITS, 1.1.6.0, folder 25, *Wahrheit und Recht* 2 (June 1946), doc. 82095211; Ley and Morsch, *Medizin*, 304. See also ibid., 302–305; Klausch, *Antifaschisten*, 68, 75–104, 120–21, 136–37, 398–400; Heger, *Männer*, 141.

202. Eberle, "'Asoziale,'" quote on 266; Klausch, *Antifaschisten*, 105–21, 401.

203. Quote in Kupfer-Koberwitz, *Tagebücher*, 390. See also Klausch, *Antifaschisten*, 140–270, 327–96, 404–15.

204. Rede vor Generälen, May 24, 1944, in Smith and Peterson, *Geheimreden*, 203.

205. Fabréguet, "Entwicklung," 207, figure for March 1945.

206. Wagner, *Produktion*, 549.

207. Cited in Sellier, *Dora*, 137.

208. Kaienburg, "KZ Neuengamme," 46; Wagner, *IG Auschwitz*, 119, 233; Wagner, *Produktion*, 379–80, 550–51.

209. Renouard, *Hölle*, 43–44, 163; Fröbe et al., "Nachkriegsgeschichte," 577–78.

210. Ellger, *Zwangsarbeit*, 304; Wysocki, "Häftlingsarbeit," 58. On the oscillation between compliance and noncompliance, see Lüdtke, "Appeal," 49.

211. Levi, *If*, 88.

212. Buggeln, *Arbeit*, 262–63, 618; Kielar, *Anus Mundi*, 382.

213. ITS, KL Auschwitz OCC2/35a, Ordner 57, Vernehmungsniederschrift, October 4, 1944.

214. Megargee, *Encyclopedia*, vol. 1/A, 718–20; ibid., vol. 1/B, 872–73; *OdT*, vol. 8, 289–94; ibid., vol. 6, 262–65. This case became famous through Thomas Keneally's book *Schindler's Ark* (London, 1982) and Steven Spielberg's film *Schindler's List* (1993).

215. Levi, *If*, 126.

216. Antelme, *Menschengeschlecht*, quotes on 69–70; Todorov, *Facing*, 243.

217. For background, see Wagner, *Produktion*, 560–62; Buggeln, *Arbeit*, 593–94, 610.

218. Füllberg-Stolberg, "Frauen," quote on 328.

219. Mittelwerk GmbH, Umgang mit Häftlingen, December 30, 1943, in Wagner, *Mittelbau-Dora*, 120.

220. For example, see Kaienburg, "KZ Neuengamme," 47.

221. BArchL, B 162/30170, Bl. 368: LK Sachsenhausen, Anordnung, February 2, 1942, underlined in the original. See also Wysocki, "Häftlingsarbeit," 61.

222. Wagner, *Produktion*, 178–80, 503, 554; Fings, "Public Face," 118.

223. Quotes in Kempowski, *Haben*, 117.

224. Horwitz, *Shadow*, 83–98, quote on 94; *OdT*, vol. 4, 416–17.

225. Glauning, *Entgrenzung*, 332–38, 346–52, quote on 336; Riexinger and Ernst, *Vernichtung*, 59, 67–68; Kaienburg, "KZ Neuengamme," 49; Wagner, *Produktion*, 536–45; Maršálek, *Mauthausen*, 93; AGN, Ng. 7.6., H. Behncke to his family, September 30, 1944; ibid., E. Behncke to her family, November 25, 1944.

226. Bütow and Bindernagel, *KZ*, 9, 115, 175.

227. Calculation based on *OdT*, vol. 2, 396–450. For bomb-clearing squads, ibid., 421.

228. Fings, "Public Face," quote on 117; Delbo, *Auschwitz*, 183–85.

229. Renouard, *Hölle*, 29; Kielar, *Anus Mundi*, 366; Riexinger and Ernst, *Vernichtung*, 60.

230. For example, see Zámečník, "Aufzeichnungen," 233–34.

231. Ellger, *Zwangsarbeit*, 177, 294, quote on 306; Steinbacher, *Dachau*, 175–77; Horwitz, *Shadow*, 111; Raim, *Dachauer*, 270.

232. Bringmann, *Neuengamme*, 43; Glauning, *Entgrenzung*, 343–45.

233. Quote in Horwitz, *Shadow*, 114. See also ibid., 93; Wagner, *Produktion*, 560–61; Glauning, *Entgrenzung*, 345; Fings, "Public Face," 118; Buggeln, *Arbeit*, 623.

234. Quote in Kirsten and Kirsten, *Stimmen*, 133. See also ibid., 306.

235. Horwitz, *Shadow*, 175–76.

236. Wagner, *Produktion*, 538–39, 547–49, 556–60; Schley, *Nachbar*, 109; *OdT*, vol. 6, 68.

237. Fings, "Public Face," 118.

238. Quote in Zámečník, "Aufzeichnungen," 226. See also Dörner, *Deutschen*, 321–22, 328; NAL, WO 208/3596, C.S.D.I.C., S.I.R. 727, Information from Lt. Marcinek, August 11, 1944.

239. BArchB, NS 19/4014, Bl. 158–204: Rede vor Generälen, June 21, 1944, quotes on 166.

240. "Dokumentation. Die Rede Himmlers," 393; Kupfer-Koberwitz, *Tagebücher*, 346; Loeffel, *"Sippenhaft"*; Vermehren, *Reise*, 152–53.

241. German opposition leaflet (1941), in Kulka and Jäckel, *Juden*, doc. 3282; Goerdeler, "Ziel" (autumn 1941), 898; Hamerow, *Road*, 325.

242. For one example, see Steinbacher, *"Musterstadt,"* 315.

243. Raim, *Dachauer*, 269; Fings, "Public Face," 118; Horwitz, *Shadow*, 93.

244. Quote in Kempowski, *Haben*, 108.

245. Kautsky, *Teufel*, 235–40. More generally, see Buggeln, *Arbeit*, 619.

246. WL, P.III.h. No. 198, F. Pagel, "Eines der Vielen Tausende[n] von Schicksalen," autumn 1955; Wagner, *IG Auschwitz*, 89, 139. For the story of another British POW who is said to have briefly changed places with a Jewish prisoner in Monowitz, see Avey, *Man*.

247. Fings, *Krieg*, 220–28, 242–43, Maurer quote on 226, Knöller quote (from October 1944) on 242, underlined in the original; Klein, *Jehovas*, 129–30; Kogon, *SS-Staat* (1946), 336–37; Whatmore, "Exploring."

248. RSHA, Meldung staatspolizeilicher Ereignisse, September 17, 1941, in Boberach, *Regimekritik*, doc. rk584; Meldungen aus Frankreich, March 5, 1943, ibid., doc. rk 1059; Parteikanzlei, Auszüge aus Berichten der Gauleitungen et al., May 8, 1943, in Kulka and Jäckel, *Juden*, doc. 3594.

249. NAL, FO 371/34523–005, Press Reading Bureau Stockholm to Political Intelligence Department London, July 22, 1943.

250. Quotes in Höss to Glücks, July 12, 1940, cited in Steinbacher, *"Musterstadt,"* 200; S. Kłodziński to T. Lasocka-Estreicher, November 19, 1942, in Świebocki, *Resistance*, 334–35. See also ibid., 145–53, 171–90.

251. Świebocki, *Resistance*, 272–92.

252. For Polish underground reports on the extermination of Jews in Auschwitz and Majdanek, see Friedrich, "Judenmord," 113–17.

253. Breitman, *Secrets*, 88–89, 112–13.

254. Quotes in NAL, HW 16/66, "II. Concentration Camps," November 27, 1942. See also ibid., HW 16/6, Part 2, Bl. 534–35: report on German police, September 26, 1942. More generally, see ibid., HW 16/11; ibid., HW 16/17–19. Some decoded statistics of KL prisoner numbers have been compiled in an invaluable article; Schulte, " 'London.' "

255. For the last point, see Breitmann, *Secrets*, 113.

256. Breitman et al., *U.S. Intelligence*, 31–32.

257. NAL, FO 371/34523–005, Press Reading Bureau Stockholm to Political Intelligence Department London, July 22, 1943; ibid., FO 371/34389–0008, Berne to Foreign Office, October 6, 1943.

258. "German Brutality in Prison Camp," *The Times*, June 11, 1941, 3; Świebocki, *Resistance*, 304–14; Breitman, *Secrets*, 116–21, 231; Gilbert, *Auschwitz*, 51–52, 92; Laqueur, *Secret*, 200. More generally, see Fleming, *Auschwitz*. For another early account of Auschwitz, published by the Polish underground in December 1942 (English translation 1944), see Kunert, *Auschwitz*.

259. *Hansard*, December 17, 1942, vol. 385, cc2082–7; Breitman, *Secrets*, 229–31; Laqueur, *Secret*, 169, 196, 201–204; Van Pelt, *Case*, 131–34.

260. Breitman et al., *Intelligence*, 33–37.

261. Tyas, "Intelligence," 12; Neitzel, *Abgehört*, 283.

262. "Bericht von Czesław Mordowicz," quote on 302–303; Gilbert, *Auschwitz*, 231–32.

263. Świebocki, *Resistance*, 224–27, 298–99, 315–19; idem, *London*, 25–46, 57–67, 75–76; Vrba, *Forgive*. For the unabridged report, see "Bericht Vrba." More generally on the U.S. media and the Holocaust, see Lipstadt, *Beyond Belief*.

264. Wiesel, *All Rivers*, 74.

265. Westermann, "Royal Air Force"; Gilbert, *Auschwitz*, 236–37, 245–48.

266. Neufeld, "Introduction," 8–9; Feingold, "Bombing"; Gilbert, *Auschwitz*, 301–306; Mahoney, "American." For the role of the USSR, see Herf, "Nazi Extermination Camps"; Orbach and Solonin, "Indifference."

267. Neufeld, "Introduction." See also Weinberg, "Allies"; Gilbert, *Auschwitz*, 307; Mahoney, "American," 440–41; Overy, *Bombing War*, passim; Horwitz, *Shadow*, 115–16; APMO, Proces Höss, Hd 6, Bl. 51–62: O. Wolken, "Chronik des Lagers Auschwitz II," n.d. (c. spring 1945), Bl. 58–59.

268. Conway, "Augenzeugenberichte," 279. For the debate as to whether Jewish leaders in Hungary, who knew of the Vrba-Wetzler report, should have done more to warn Hungarian Jews, see idem, "Vrba-Wetzler report"; Bauer, "Anmerkungen."

269. Gallup, *Poll*, 472.

270. Dörner, *Die Deutschen*, 204, 209, 415; Kempowski, *Haben*, 123.

271. For knowledge of Allied reports in the KL, DaA, 9438, A. Hübsch, "Insel des Standrechts" (1961), 246; Zámečník, "Aufzeichnungen," 240.

10. Impossible Choices

1. Haulot, "Lagertagebuch," 183.

2. For example, see Lévy-Hass, *Vielleicht*, 54–57.

3. Brzezicki et al., "Funktionshäftlinge," 236; Adler, "Selbstverwaltung," 228.

4. Jureit and Orth, *Überlebensgeschichten*, 190–91, quote on 87; Cohen, *Human*, 281; Wagner, *Produktion*, 458; Adler, "Selbstverwaltung," 229–30. For the wording, see the description of the state of nature in T. Hobbes, *The Leviathan* (London, 1651).

5. Kupfer-Koberwitz, *Häftling*, 302–305, quote on 273; Langbein, *Menschen*, 160; Zámečník, *Dachau*, 147–48.

6. For a discussion of the "moral life in the concentration camps," see Todorov, *Facing*.

7. J. Pogonowski to his family, September 25, 1942, in Piper, *Briefe*, quote on 23–24.

8. Ibid., quote on 24.

9. For the former view, see Sofsky, "Grenze," 1159. For the latter view, see text below and Aharony, "Arendt."

10. Rózsa, "Solange," 227.

11. Świebocki, *Resistance*, quote on 14; Strebel, *Ravensbrück*, 530; Zámečník, *Dachau*, 320; Tuchel, "Möglichkeiten," 224.

12. For background, see Langbein, *Widerstand*, 57–58; Pingel, *Häftlinge*, 20; Tuchel, "Selbstbehauptung," 939; Browning, *Survival*, 297; Van Pelt, "Resistance"; Świebocki, *Resistance*, 14–17; Peukert, *Inside*, 81–85; Kershaw, *Nazi Dictatorship*, 183–217.

13. Pollak, *Grenzen*, quote on 47; Browning, *Survival*, 297.

14. Antelme, *Menschengeschlecht*, 65; Fröbe, "Exkurs."

15. Levi, *If*, 46–47. More generally, drawing on the work of Pierre Bourdieu, see Suderland, *Territorien*.

16. Erpel, "Trauma," 129–31.

17. Delbo, *Auschwitz*, 187–88; Todorov, *Facing*, 97–103, 107–108; SMAB, *Forbidden Art*; Blatter and Milton, *Art*, 142, 187. By no means all intellectual prisoners found solace in the life of the mind; Améry, *Jenseits*, 15–36.

18. Adler, *Theresienstadt*.

19. "Bericht Tabeau," 112.

20. Levi, "Intellectual," 117. For the term "selfhood," see Brubaker and Cooper, "'Identity,'" 7 (my thanks to Anna Hájková for drawing this article to my attention).

21. Pingel, "Social life." See also idem, "Destruction," 172.

22. Wiesel, *Rivers*, 80–81.

23. For example, see Gerlach and Aly, *Kapitel*, 398.

24. On parent-child relationships, see Shik, "Mother-Daughter," 115, 122; Sonnino, *Nacht*, 86–87; Buser, *Überleben*, 273–75.

25. Jureit and Orth, *Überlebensgeschichten*, 65; Luchterhand, "Prisoner."

26. Świebocki, *Resistance*, 44–45; Goldstein et al., *Individuelles*, 45; Pollak, *Grenzen*, 170.

27. Buber-Neumann, *Milena*, 22, 273, 284, 289, quote on 20; Buber, *Dictators*, 213, 238–39, 277–78, 293–94, 309. See also Darowska, *Widerstand*.
28. Rózsa, "Solange," quotes on 212; Ellger, *Zwangsarbeit*, 279–89.
29. For one example, see *OdT*, vol. 1, 246.
30. Levi, *If*, 63, 144, 161, 393, quote on 144; Shik, "Weibliche Erfahrung," 113–17.
31. Kolb, *Bergen-Belsen*, quote on 258; Fröbe, "Arbeit," quote on 243; Suderland, *Extremfall*, 308–15.
32. Pollak, *Grenzen*, 50.
33. Walter, "Kinder," 190; Langbein, *Menschen*, 102.
34. Todorov, *Facing*, 82; Shik, "Weibliche Erfahrung," 115. For the term "groupness," and its definition, see Brubaker and Cooper, "'Identity,'" 19–21.
35. Ryn and Kłodziński, "Grenze," quote on 127.
36. Wiesel, *Nacht*, quote on 153; idem, *Rivers*, 92–95.
37. Buber, *Dictators*, 294.
38. For pioneering scholarship on this aspect, see Pingel, *Häftlinge*; Pollak, *Grenzen*, esp. 54, 105.
39. Apel, *Frauen*, 203, 213, 309; Strebel, *Ravensbrück*, 103–104, 543–44, 550; Rolnikaite, *Tagebuch*, 214–15; Gilbert, *Music*, 107–15; Morsch, *Sachsenhausen-Liederbuch*.
40. Mankowitz, *Life*, 32–37.
41. See also Pingel, *Häftlinge*.
42. StAMü, StA Nr. 34588/1, Bl. 210–12: Vernehmung H. Stöhr, July 21, 1956; Langbein, *Widerstand*, 94.
43. Quote in Poller, *Arztschreiber*, 75.
44. Hartewig, "Wolf," quotes on 947; Langbein, *Widerstand*, 128–30.
45. Niethammer, *Antifaschismus*, 51–55, 57, 284, 298–99, 519, quotes on 85 (Busse) and 426 (Bartel); Hackett, *Buchenwald*, quote (Žák) on 298; Wagner, *Produktion*, 401–402. For other camps, see Buggeln, *Arbeit*, 125; Heger, *Männer*, 146.
46. Buber, *Dictators*, 195, quote on 257; Langbein, *Widerstand*, 117–23, 130–31, 146; Niethammer, *Antifaschismus*, 268, 288, 293, 305; Kaienburg, "'Freundschaft?,'" 30–31; Röll, *Sozialdemokraten*, 231–44.
47. Wiesel, *Rivers*, 82–83.
48. Rahe, "Bedeutung," 1009, 1014, 1016.
49. Świebocki, *Resistance*, 339; Strebel, *Ravensbrück*, 549–50; Rahe, "Bedeutung," 1018; Lanckorońska, *Michelangelo*, 238.
50. Obenaus, "Kampf," 860; Rahe, "Bedeutung," 1010, 1015; Jaiser, "Sexualität," 130–31; Waxman, *Writing*, 69–70.
51. Améry, *Jenseits*, 27–28; Levi, "Intellectual," 118. For the religious thought of orthodox Jews during World War II, see Greenberg, "Introduction."
52. Escher, "Geistliche," 302–305, 309–10; Gruner, *Verurteilt*, 88; JVL, JAO, Review of Proceedings, *United States v. Weiss*, n.d. (1946), 63.
53. Rahe, "Bedeutung," 1011; Wagner, *IG Auschwitz*, 135–36; Gutterman, *Bridge*, 185–86.
54. Lenard, "Flucht," quote on 157; WL, P.III.h. No. 573, A. Lehmann, "Das Lager Vught," n.d., p. 22.
55. Levi, *If*, 135–36, quote in 136.
56. *OdT*, vol. 6, 499; Greenberg et al., *Wrestling*, 58–60.
57. Kautsky, *Teufel*, 153–59, quote on 194; Goldstein et al., *Individuelles*, 51; Raim, *Dachauer*, 262–63; Nomberg-Przytyk, *Auschwitz*, 19; Levi, *If*, 51, 55, 74; idem, "Communicating," 78.
58. Lenard, "Flucht," quote on 158; Glicksman, "Social," 948.
59. Quote in LaB, B Rep 058, Nr. 3850, Bl. 71–72: Zeugenaussage Herbert F., May 10, 1947. See also Langbein, *Menschen*, 96–98; Vaisman, *Auschwitz*, 16–17; BoA, testimony of I. Rosenwasser, August 22, 1946; Kautsky, *Teufel*, 193–95.
60. Buggeln, *Arbeit*, 371, quote on 267.

61. Warmbold, *Lagersprache*, 275; Kautsky, *Teufel*, 195.

62. Adler et al., *Auschwitz*, 102; Langbein, *Widerstand*, 195. For caring in the camps, see also Todorov, *Facing*, 84, 118.

63. Strebel, *Ravensbrück*, 553–54.

64. BoA, testimony of G. Kaldore, August 31, 1946.

65. Levi, *If*, 44. The language of the largest prisoner group normally gained some dominance inside different barracks and camps; Langbein, *Menschen*, 96; Raim, *Dachauer*, 252. For the figures, see NMGB, *Buchenwald*, 707; BArchB, NS 4/Bu 143, Schutzhaftlager-Rapport, April 15, 1944.

66. For social life in Nazi captivity more generally, see Hájková, "Prisoner Society."

67. Kosmala, "Häftlinge," 101, 105; Daxelmüller, "Kulturelle," 989–90.

68. Rózsa, "Solange," 113–14, 146, 176.

69. Gilbert, *Music*, 151–58, quote on 152. For a collection of Jewish songs, see Kaczerginski, *Lider*.

70. Kosmala, "Häftlinge," 109–11.

71. *OdT*, vol. 1, 95.

72. Langbein, *Widerstand*, 167–69; Golczewski, "Kollaboration"; Zarusky, "'Russen,'" 125, 128–29. The Camp SS generally referred to Soviet citizens as "Russians," though Ukrainian prisoners occasionally wore a "U" on their triangle, not an "R" (Tillion, *Ravensbrück*, 218). POWs deported to the KL from 1941 were the exception, as they were often classified as "Soviet Prisoners of War."

73. Suderland, *Extremfall*, 316. See also Tillion, *Ravensbrück*, 218; Rovan, *Geschichten*, 85.

74. Buggeln, *Arbeit*, 500; Wagner, *Produktion*, 399; AdsD, KE, E. Büge, Bericht, n.d. (1945–46), 136–37.

75. Nansen, *Day*, 411, 449, 517, quotes on 430, 432.

76. Siedlecki et al., *Auschwitz*, 4.

77. See also Debski, *Battlefield*, 195–203.

78. Nansen, *Day*, quote on 504; Langbein, *Widerstand*, 105–106, 109; Buber, *Dictators*, 308; Vermehren, *Reise*, 202–203.

79. Michel, *Dora*, 76; Sellier, *Dora*, 110; Lanckorońska, *Michelangelo*, 243–44.

80. Kielar, *Anus Mundi*, quote on 269; Langbein, *Widerstand*, 154.

81. AdsD, KE, E. Büge, Bericht, n.d. (1945–46), 204; BArchB, NS 3/426, Bl. 16: WVHA to LK, January 20, 1943. In spring 1944, the RSHA ordered that female German prisoners should no longer be sent to the camp on account of its "high mortality rate"; USHMM, RG-11.001M.05, reel 75, folder 8, RSHA to WVHA, April 12, 1944.

82. Broszat, *Kommandant*, 156. See also Wagner, *Produktion*, 398; BArchB, NS 3/426, Bl. 107: WVHA to LK, July 14, 1943 (referring to female prisoners).

83. Buber, *Dictators*, 297.

84. Hájková, "Prisoner Society," chapter 2; Pingel, *Häftlinge*, 180; *OdT*, vol. 3, 320 (with a slightly erroneous calculation); Freund, *Toten*, 403.

85. Quotes in Warmbold, *Lagersprache*, 287; Vrba, "Warnung," 14. See also Levi, "Grey Zone," 24–25; idem, *If*, 34; Obenaus, "Kampf," 850–51; Klüger, *weiter*, 113; Sofsky, *Ordnung*, 171.

86. Langbein, *Menschen*, 90–91; Levi, *If*, 126.

87. On the historiography, see Hansen and Nowak, "Über Leben."

88. Wesołowska, *Wörter*, 85, 155–91, quotes on 164, 233, 235, 236; Warmbold, *Lagersprache*, 122–32.

89. Levi, "Communicating," 75.

90. Maršálek, *Mauthausen*, 349.

91. Warmbold, *Lagersprache*, 318.

92. Quotes in Warmbold, *Lagersprache*, 132, 135; Maršálek, *Mauthausen*, 350; Wesołowska, *Wörter*, 234; Bárta, "Tagebuch," 64.

93. Rousset, *Kingdom*, quote on 172; Warmbold, *Lagersprache*, 317.

94. Warmbold, *Lagersprache*, 257, 262–71, quote on 264; Zámečník, "Aufzeichnungen," quote on 204; Kogon, *Theory*, 239, quote on 72; Frankl, *Ja*, 54, 76–78; Unger, "Encounter," 280.

95. Kielar, *Anus Mundi*, 154–60, 225–27, 233–34, 244, 264, 278, 351, 366–73.

96. Langbein, *Menschen*, 151.

97. *OdT*, vol. 4, 495.

98. Maršálek, *Mauthausen*, 47; Wagner, *Produktion*, 460; Langbein, *Menschen*, 155–56; Hájková, "Prisoner Society," 232.

99. Gilbert, *Music*, 130–32, 159–60, 175–76; Fackler, "'Lagers Stimme,'" 485–87, 499.

100. Rost, *Goethe*, 25, 223, 244, quote on 44; the diary was edited before publication. See also Laqueur, *Schreiben*, 134–39; Seela, *Bücher*, 79–91.

101. Kielar, *Anus Mundi*, 352–54; Kogon, *Theory*, 133–34; Wagner, *Produktion*, 461; text above, chapter 3.

102. Sommer, *KZ-Bordell*, 134; Langbein, *Menschen*, 328; BArchB, NS 3/426, Bl. 69: WVHA to LK, May 22, 1943.

103. Nansen, *Day*, 477; Borowski, *This Way*, 83–84; Pingel, *Häftlinge*, 180.

104. Bárta, "Tagebuch," 63.

105. BoA, testimony (in German) of I. Rosenwasser, August 22, 1946.

106. Figures in Hördler, "Ordnung," 161; chapter 3, above.

107. *OdT*, vol. 5, 185, 213, 287; Freund, "Mauthausen," 271; Langbein, *Widerstand*, 101; Strzelecka and Setkiewicz, "Construction," 65; Langbein, *Menschen*, 174, 181.

108. Freund, *Toten*, 406–407; Brzezicki et al., "Funktionshäftlinge," 234.

109. Quote in Renouard, *Hölle*, 46.

110. Strebel, *Ravensbrück*, 235; Selbmann, *Alternative*, 326; Wagner, *IG Auschwitz*, 114.

111. Kogon, *Theory*, 55; Hackett, *Buchenwald*, 117–20; Piper, "Exploitation," 78–79; Sofsky, *Ordnung*, 155–56.

112. Wagner, *Produktion*, 348; StANü, EE by K. Roeder, February 20, 1947, ND: NO-2122.

113. Quote in K. Keim, "Bericht," spring 1945, in Niethammer, *Antifaschismus*, 220. See also Kogon, *Theory*, 58–59; Wagner, *Produktion*, 434; Strebel, "Arm," 37, 46.

114. JVL, JAO, Review of Proceedings, *United States v. Weiss*, n.d. (1946), quote on 72; Ambach and Köhler, *Lublin-Majdanek*, 150, 155, 178–79, 190, 204; LK Gross-Rosen, Exekution der Transportjüdin Scheer, November 13, 1944, in Tuchel, *Inspektion*, 111.

115. JVL, DJAO, *United States v. Becker*, RaR, n.d. (1947), 30–31.

116. For Kapos replaced by SS men, see BArchB, NS 4/Na 9, Bl. 113: Kommandanturbefehl, June 13, 1942.

117. Rousset, *Kingdom*, quote on 134; WL, P.III.h. No. 198, F. Pagel, "Eines der Vielen Tausende[n] von Schicksalen," autumn 1955, p. 9; BoA, interview A. Kimmelmann, August 27, 1946; Kautsky, *Teufel*, 258–60; Maršálek, *Mauthausen*, 69; DaA, Nr. 7566, K. Schecher, "Rückblick auf Dachau," n.d., 232; Buggeln, *Arbeit*, 27, 490, 532; Kupfer-Koberwitz, *Tagebücher*, 466, 468, 472–73; Wagner, *IG Auschwitz*, 113.

118. Paserman, "Bericht," 149.

119. *OdT*, vol. 1, 222; Rousset, *Kingdom*, 133; Sellier, *Dora*, 152; Wagner, *IG Auschwitz*, 127; Kielar, *Anus Mundi*, 195.

120. Wolf, "Judgement," quote on 630; Jansen, "Zwangsarbeit," 91; LaB, B Rep 058, Nr. 3850, Bl. 153–60: Schwurgericht Berlin, Urteil, March 1, 1948, Bl. 155; NARA, M-1079, roll 5, Bl. 454–65: testimony Willi Z., June 17, 1947.

121. Quote in APMO, Proces Maurer, 10a, Bl. 132: KL Auschwitz, Vernehmungsniederschrift, November 26, 1943. On Kalvo (also spelled Calvo), see also Czech, *Kalendarium*, 496; ITS, doc. 496950#1, KL Auschwitz, Häftlingspersonalbogen, n.d. (1943); Recanati, *Memorial Book*, 104. It is possible that the incident refers to another prisoner, called Juda Kalvo (or Calvo), who had arrived on the same transport: ITS, doc. 505749#1, KL Auschwitz, Vernehmungsniederschrift, November 26, 1943.

122. Shik, "Sexual Abuse"; Heger, *Männer*, 58, 63–64, 66, 79; Jaiser, "Sexualität," 128; Buser,

Überleben, 193–94. More generally, see Sommer, *KZ-Bordell*, 201; Wagner, *Produktion*, 412; Zinn, "Homophobie," 89–90; Hájková, "Barter."

123. Frister, *Mütze*, 295–300; APMO, Proces Höss, Hd 6, Bl. 129–312: Vernehmung O. Wolken, April 17–20, 1945, Bl. 215–16; Buser, *Überleben*, 194–95.

124. Levi, *If*, 113–14; Sofsky, *Ordnung*, 173–74; Maršálek, *Mauthausen*, 53.

125. LG Frankfurt, Urteil, June 14, 1968, *JNV*, vol. 29, 448–49, 484; Wagner, *IG Auschwitz*, 121–22.

126. Kupfer-Koberwitz, *Tagebücher*, 411; NARA, M-1204, roll 6, examination of A. Ginschel, October 4 and 7, 1946, Bl. 4619–20; Frankl, *Ja*, 93.

127. Quote in AdsD, KE, E. Büge, Bericht, n.d. (1945–46), 104.

128. StAMü, StA Nr. 34588/8, LG Munich, Urteil, October 14, 1960, pp. 3–8; ibid., Nr. 34588/7, Bl. 160–72: LG Munich, Beschluss, May 27, 1960; ibid., Nr. 34588/2, Bl. 95–106: Vernehmung K. Kapp, November 14–16, 1956. Kapp's time in Dachau was interrupted by a spell in Mauthausen, where he became a Kapo in the quarry. In 1943 he was transferred from Dachau to help establish the satellite camp Augsburg-Haunstetten and the main camp Warsaw.

129. Testimonies in StAMü, StA Nr. 34588/1; ibid., Nr. 34588/2. See also Zámečník, "Aufzeichnungen," 204–205.

130. Buber, *Dictators*, 216. See also LG Cologne, Urteil, April 20, 1970, *JNV*, vol. 33, 673; Sofsky, *Ordnung*, 160–61.

131. Buggeln, *Arbeit*, 348, 529; Rousset, *Kingdom*, 152; Deutsches Rundfunkarchiv, DW 4025830, "Das Lager," Deutsche Welle, November 20, 1968, Kamiński testimony at 8 minutes and 35 seconds (my thanks to René Wolf for a copy of this program).

132. Koker, *Edge*, 289.

133. Zámečník, "Aufzeichnungen," 204–205, 225–26; Kaienburg, "'Freundschaft?,'" 34; Langbein, *Menschen*, 217–18.

134. Zarusky, "'Tötung,'" 81–82; Pingel, *Häftlinge*, 192–93.

135. StAMü, StA Nr. 34588/1, Bl. 218–19: Zeugenvernehmung E. Zapf, July 24, 1956; ibid., Nr. 34588/2, Bl. 11–13: Zeugenvernehmung H. Schwarz, August 20, 1956.

136. Wagner, *Produktion*, 439, 448; NARA, M-1079, roll 6, examination of C. Jay, August 7, 1947, Bl. 66–67. Thomas and Szymczak were shot in April 1945, shortly before the evacuation of the camp.

137. Kirsten and Kirsten, *Stimmen*, 203–207; Naujoks, *Sachsenhausen*, 198.

138. For example, see Ambach and Köhler, *Lublin-Majdanek*, 155.

139. BArchB, NS 19/4014, Bl. 158–204: Rede vor Generälen, June 21, 1944, Bl. 165. For revenge fantasies, see Szalet, *Baracke 38*, 354.

140. Wagner, *IG Auschwitz*, 120; Sofsky, *Ordnung*, 162–63.

141. StAMü, StA Nr. 34588/1, Bl. 29: Zeugenvernehmung A. Daschner, March 2, 1956; ibid., Nr. 34588/7, Bl. 14–16: Vernehmung F. Olah, July 24, 1959.

142. Sofsky, *Ordnung*, 164.

143. StAMü, StA Nr. 34588/7, Bl. 40–43: Vernehmung E. Oswald, September 2, 1959; ibid., Nr. 34588/8, LG Munich, Urteil, October 14, 1960, 21–23; ibid., Nr. 34588/2, Bl. 59–60: Vernehmung P. Hussarek, October 22, 1956.

144. Ibid., Nr. 34588/2, Bl. 95–106: Vernehmung K. Kapp, November 14–16, 1956; ibid., Nr. 34588/1, Bl. 130–32: Vernehmung K. Kapp, May 11–12, 1956.

145. For this paradox, see also Sofsky, *Ordnung*, 167.

146. Wagner, *IG Auschwitz*, 119; Kaienburg, "'Freundschaft?,'" 32; Kautsky, *Teufel*, 198–201.

147. Quotes in StAMü, StA Nr. 34588/8, LG Munich, Urteil, October 14, 1960, p. 21; ibid., Nr. 34588/2, Bl. 59–60: Vernehmung P. Hussarek, October 22, 1956.

148. StAMü, StA Nr. 34588/8, LG Munich, Urteil, October 14, 1960, p. 20–21; ibid., Nr. 34588/2, Bl. 41: Vernehmung W. Neff, October 8, 1956.

149. StAMü, StA Nr. 34588/8, LG Munich, Urteil, October 14, 1960.

150. See also Kaienburg, "'Freundschaft?,'" 43.

151. BoA, testimony (in German) Irena Rosenwasser, 22.8.1946. See also *JVL*, JAO, Review of Proceedings, *United States v. Weiss*, n.d. (1946), 108; LG Augsburg, Urteil, June 28, 1950, JNV, vol. 6, 654–55.

152. For example, see Rousset, *Kingdom*, 151–52.

153. Kielar, *Anus Mundi*, 304.

154. Rousset, *Kingdom*, 135. During wartime, the SS appointed up to three camp elders in each camp; Kogon, *Theory*, 54.

155. Kautsky, *Teufel*, 160.

156. Maršálek, *Mauthausen*, 55; 127. See also Adler, "Selbstverwaltung," 225; Wagner, *Ellrich*, 76.

157. There are no exact figures for Germans in the KL system as a whole. Speaking to the Gauleiter on August 3, 1944, Heinrich Himmler, who was well informed about the composition of the KL prisoner population, indicated that some eighteen percent of all inmates were German. In a speech to army generals some six weeks earlier, Himmler put the figure at ten percent. See "Dokumentation. Die Rede Himmlers," 393; BArchB, NS 19/4014, Bl. 158–204: Rede vor Generälen, June 21, 1944, Bl. 161. In Buchenwald, the proportion of German prisoners had fallen to less than ten percent by summer 1944; Stein, "Funktionswandel," 180. For Germans as senior Kapos, see Buggeln, *Arbeit*, 131.

158. For the perspective of foreign KL prisoners, see Rousset, *Kingdom*, 148–49.

159. Quote in Rede bei der SS Gruppenführertagung in Posen, October 4, 1943, *IMT*, vol. 29, p. 122, ND: 1919–PS.

160. In autumn 1943, almost three-quarters of the fifty Buchenwald block elders were veterans (with prisoner numbers under five thousand) and all, or almost all, of them were German; ITS, KL Buchenwald GCC 2/versch., Ordner 492, Bl. 109: Aufstellung der Blockältesten, October 21, 1943. On the official language of the KL, see Hansen and Nowak, "Über Leben," 116, 124.

161. Müller, "Homosexuelle," 85–87; Röll, "Homosexuelle," 99–100; Zinn, "Homophobie," 83–84.

162. *OdT*, vol. 7, 208; Michelsen, "Homosexuelle," 128; Mußmann, "Häftlinge," 136; Wagner, *Produktion*, 410–12; Heger, *Männer*, 124–25.

163. Czech, "Prisoner Administration," 365; *OdT*, vol. 6, 497; ibid., vol. 7, 46; Kielar, *Anus Mundi*, 276–77.

164. Strebel, *Ravensbrück*, 139, 238–39; Schikorra, *Kontinuitäten*, 222–23; Erpel, *Vernichtung*, 49; Tillion, *Ravensbrück*, 215, 221–22.

165. For example, see Wagner, *IG Auschwitz*, 123.

166. "Bericht Vrba," 269, 290; Kárný, "Familienlager," 169; Marszałek, *Majdanek*, 82.

167. On main camps, see Siegert, "Flossenbürg," 36; Kolb, *Bergen-Belsen*, 75–77; Apel, *Frauen*, 231–32, 348. On satellite camps, see ibid., 349; Raim, *Dachauer*, 246–47; Ellger, *Zwangsarbeit*, 177–89; Glauning, *Entgrenzung*, 189–90. On camps and ghettos, see Raim, "KZ-Außenlagerkomplexe," 78; *OdT*, vol. 8, 260–61; Rabinovici, *Jews*, 200–201. For the use of the term "gray zone" in the context of Nazi terror, see especially Levi, "Grey Zone."

168. Wagner, *Produktion*, 398, 435; Buggeln, *Arbeit*, 127, 522.

169. Strebel, *Ravensbrück*, 237; Oertel, *Gefangener*, 201.

170. Kautsky, *Teufel*, 8–9, 141–45, 160–61, quotes on 142–43. Published in 1946, Kautsky's book was completed in late 1945; ibid., 13.

171. Though classified as a Jew for most of his imprisonment, Kautsky—a former union official and the son of the leading German Social Democrat Karl Kautsky—saw himself primarily as a political prisoner.

172. Quote in "Arbeit unter Berufsverbrechern," spring 1945, in Niethammer, *Antifaschismus*, 228. See also Eiden, "Buchenwald," 221; Eberle, "'Asoziale,'" 254–55.

173. Quotes in Siegert, "Flossenbürg," 459. In Ravensbrück, "green" prisoners were apparently underrepresented among female block elders; Strebel, *Ravensbrück*, 235.

174. Levi, *If*, 97–98; idem, "Resistance," 1965, in Belpoliti, *Levi*, 18.

175. Even among the state prisoners handed over as "asocial" to the SS in 1942–43, violent criminals were far outnumbered by small-time thieves; Wachsmann, *Prisons*, 132–37, 284–96.

176. Renouard, *Hölle*, 30, 160; Tillion, *Ravensbrück*, 180.

177. LaB, B Rep 058, Nr. 3850, Bl. 153–60: Schwurgericht Berlin, Urteil, March 1, 1948; ibid., Bl. 53–55: Vernehmung B. Frohnecke, March 28, 1947. Quote in ibid., Bl. 10: Vernehmung Heinz J., November 22, 1946.

178. For example, see Kwiet, "'Leben,'" 237; BoA, interview with J. Bassfreund, September 20, 1946.

179. Most recently, see *OdT*, vol. 5, 135–36.

180. LG Frankfurt, Urteil, June 14, 1968, *JNV*, vol. 29, 446–47, 500–503; Wagner, *IG Auschwitz*, 114–15, 120–21. Other notorious Kapos include Arno Böhm (Nr. 8), the camp elder of the family camp, Bruno Brodniewicz (Nr. 1), the first Auschwitz camp elder, and his deputy Leo Wietschorek (Nr. 30); Kárný, "Familienlager," 168; Strzelecka and Setkiewicz, "Construction," 65.

181. HHStAW, Abt. 461, Nr. 37656, Bd. 32, Vernehmung J. Lechenich, April 25, 1968, quote on 10; LG Frankfurt, Urteil, June 14, 1968, *JNV*, vol. 29, 484; Strzelecka and Setkiewicz, "Construction," 65; Czech, *Kalendarium*, 318; Świebocki, *Resistance*, 158.

182. *DAP*, Vernehmung O. Küsel, August 3, 1964, 13909–18, 13953–54; Świebocki, *Resistance*, 36–37; Langbein, *Menschen*, 180–81. Other Kapos pictured in a positive light include Hans Bock (Nr. 5) and Kurt Pachala (Nr. 24); Strzelecka and Setkiewicz, "Construction," 65; Czech, *Kalendarium*, 233, 383; *DAP*, Mitschrift beisitzender Richter, 7646 (May 14, 1964).

183. Quote in Gutterman, *Bridge*, 154.

184. *OdT*, vol. 3, 333; Hartewig, "Wolf," 952–54; Langbein, *Widerstand*, 36; Neurath, *Gesellschaft*, 223–24. Even in Gross-Rosen, a camp often described as controlled by "greens," important Kapo posts went to German political prisoners; Spenger, *Groß-Rosen*, 140, 290.

185. Niethammer, *Antifaschismus*, 38–41.

186. DaA, 14.444, *Die Vergessenen*, Nr. 3, July 1946, pp. 2, 6, 17–18, quote on 7; ibid., 9438, A. Hübsch, "Insel des Standrechts" (1961), 186–87, 200, 223, 236; Gross, *Zweitausend*, 237–38.

187. Langbein, *Widerstand*, 139–41; Niethammer, *Antifaschismus*, 299.

188. On "green" blocks, see StAMü, StA Nr. 34588/1, Bl. 29: Aussage A. Daschner, March 2, 1956; ITS, KL Buchenwald GCC 2/versch., Ordner 492, Bl. 109: Aufstellung der Blockältesten, October 21, 1943. The spatial separation of "green" and "red" prisoners reflected SS orders; IfZ, WVHA-D to LK, September 22, 1943, ND: PS-3685.

189. Wagner, *Produktion*, 436; Buggeln, *Arbeit*, 527; Fings, *Krieg*, 174.

190. Siedlecki et al., *Auschwitz*, 9. See also Levi, *If*, 98.

191. Buggeln, *Arbeit*, 557–58.

192. Quote in BArchB, NS 19/4014, Bl. 158–204: Rede vor Generälen, June 21, 1944, Bl. 168. See also Sofsky, *Ordnung*, 158–59; Broszat, *Kommandant*, 126; Buggeln, *Arbeit*, 237.

193. Quote in NAL, HW 16/11, WVHA-D to Flossenbürg, November 4, 1942. See also Naujoks, *Leben*, 333–40; Selbmann, *Alternative*, 358–71.

194. BArchL, B 162/7996, Bl. 360–64: Vernehmung R. Gottschalk, November 14, 1960.

195. Quote in Gross, *Zweitausend*, 238. Gross, a former priest who supported the dissident Confessing Church, had arrived in Dachau in 1940; Laqueur, *Schreiben*, 104–107.

196. Quote in Tauke, "Häftlingskrankenbauten," 36. See also Ley, "Kollaboration."

197. Lifton, *Doctors*, 218–21; Dirks, *"Verbrechen,"* 132–33.

198. Cohen, *Abyss*, 90–91, 100.

199. For injections, see Ambach and Köhler, *Lublin-Majdanek*, 179, 190.

200. BArchL, B 162/21846, Bl. 167–254: W. Neff, "Recht oder Unrecht," n.d.; Klee, *Auschwitz*, 220–22.

201. Lifton, *Doctors*, 215–16, quote on 221; Cohen, *Abyss*, quote on 97. See also Fabréguet, *Mauthausen*, 197–98.

202. *DAP*, Aussage J. Weis, November 6, 1964, quote on 24264; ibid., Mitschrift beisitzender Richter, November 6 and 12, 1964, 24269–75.

203. Quote in Langbein, *Menschen*, 245.

204. Adler et al., *Auschwitz*, 105.

205. Hartewig, "'Wolf,'" quote on 946; Niethammer, *Antifaschismus*, 517. Thiemann's confession did not harm his career in the GDR, where he reached senior positions in the Stasi.

206. BArchL, B 162/21846, Bl. 167–254: W. Neff, "Recht oder Unrecht," n.d., 221, 227–28, 231, quote on 245; StAMü, StA Nr. 34433, Bl. 206–12: LG München, Protokoll der Sitzung, December 30, 1948. More generally, see Lifton, *Doctors*, 223; Niethammer, *Antifaschismus*, 309.

207. Lifton, *Doctors*, 242–53; WL, P.III.h. No. 562, Protokoll Dr. Wolken, April 1945, pp. 2–3; JVL, JAO, Review of Proceedings, *United States v. Weiss*, n.d. (1946), 101.

208. Adler et al., *Auschwitz*, 105–106; Strebel, *Ravensbrück*, 240–41.

209. Zámečník, *Dachau*, 327–31; APMO, Proces Höss, Hd 6, Bl. 129–312: Vernehmung O. Wolken, April 17–20, 1945, Bl. 260–61.

210. Ibid., Bl. 279–83; Świebocki, *Resistance*, 56–57; Czech, *Kalendarium*, 792; Adler et al., *Auschwitz*, 295. Luigi had been brought up a Catholic, the son of an Italian mother and an Italian-Jewish father.

211. J. Pogonowski to his family, July 14, 1942, in Piper, *Briefe*, quote on 16; Langbein, *Widerstand*, 59–60; Todorov, *Facing*, 54; Świebocki, *Resistance*, 17–26.

212. Quote in Ryn and Kłodziński, "Tod," 290.

213. See also Buggeln, *Arbeit*, 501–505.

214. *OdT*, vol. 1, 250–51; Zarusky, "'Tötung,'" 81; Zámečník, *Dachau*, 334–42; Semprun and Wiesel, *Schweigen*, 40.

215. Niethammer, *Antifaschismus*, 212; Strebel, *Ravensbrück*, 555; Zámečník, *Dachau*, 328–29.

216. Niven, *Buchenwald*, 18–39, 206–208; Heberer, *Children*, 189. Zweig was one of twelve prisoners struck from the original transport list and replaced by others. For a fictionalized account, see Apitz, *Nackt* (first published 1959). In 2012, Zweig sued the director of the Buchenwald memorial to stop him from referring to his case as a "victim swap"; "KZ-Überlebender wehrt sich gegen Begriff des 'Opfertauschs,'" *Süddeutsche Zeitung*, February 25, 2012. On adult prisoners protecting children more generally, see Buser, *Überleben*, 105, 183–91, 275–77.

217. For this and the previous paragraph, see Kogon, *Theory*, 206–15 (referring to forty-three, not thirty-seven, Allied agents), quotes on 214, 215; Hessel testimony in Kirsten and Kirsten, *Stimmen*, 183–87; Sellier, *Dora*, 324; ODNB, articles 37063 and 35501; Hackett, *Buchenwald*, 241–42. For Yeo-Thomas, see also Seaman, *Bravest*.

218. Świebocki, *Resistance*, 257, 267–92, quote on 278; Pilecki, *Auschwitz*, 11, 17, 23.

219. Lewental, "Gedenkbuch," quotes on 222, 248; Friedler et al., *Zeugen*, 243–44.

220. Didi-Huberman, *Bilder*, 20–34; Friedler et al., *Zeugen*, 214–18; Stone, "Sonderkommando"; Deposition of H. Tauber, May 24, 1945, in Piper, *Mass Murder*, 268. Other photographs taken by Special Squad prisoners have never been found.

221. Broad, "Erinnerungen," 192.

222. APMO, Proces Maurer, 5a, Bl. 113: WVHA-D to LK, March 31, 1944, ND: NO-1554; Naujoks, *Leben*, 131.

223. Wagner, *Produktion*, 446–49. For one case, which resulted in the execution of twenty-seven Sachsenhausen prisoners, see LG Münster, Urteil, February 19, 1962, *JNV*, vol. 18, 293–94.

224. NARA, M-1079, roll 6, examination of H. Iwes, August 12, 1947, Bl. 299; Langbein, *Widerstand*, 68.

225. Bárta, "Tagebuch," 94; JVL, JAO, Review of Proceedings, *United States v. Weiss*, n.d. (1946), 70–71.

226. Quote in Buggeln, *Arbeit*, 325. See also Schalm, *Überleben*, 308; Wagner, *Produktion*, 450; Świebocki, *Resistance*, 17.

227. DaA, 9438, A. Hübsch, "Insel des Standrechts" (1961), 209.

228. Warmbold, *Lagersprache*, 286; Langbein, *Widerstand*, 59.

229. Quotes in AdsD, KE, E. Büge, Bericht, n.d. (1945–46), 97; ITS, doc. 4105401#1.

230. For example, see APMO, Proces Höss, Hd 5, Bl. 24–38: testimony of Dr. B. Epstein, April 7, 1945, Bl. 32–33.

231. Hesse and Harder, *Zeuginnen*, 146–205; Strebel, *Ravensbrück*, 535–36; *OdT*, vol. 1, 247–48; Witte et al., *Dienstkalender*, 316. Other Jehovah's Witnesses took a less extreme stance and worked to the satisfaction of the SS.

232. For another example, see Wagner, *Dora*, 423–25.

233. Sobolewicz, *Jenseits*, 213–21, quote on 219; *OdT*, vol. 4, 203–206.

234. Quotes in LULVR, interview No. 117, January 13, 1946; report by N. Iwanska, in Tillion, *Ravensbrück*, 185. See also Strebel, *Ravensbrück*, 534.

235. Jagoda et al., "'Nächte,'" 200.

236. Buggeln, *Arbeit*, 280–81; Świebocki, *Resistance*, 232.

237. Maršálek, *Mauthausen*, 261; BArchB, NS 4/Bu 143, Schutzhaftlager-Rapport, September 15, 1944.

238. Kaienburg, "KZ Neuengamme," 39.

239. Quote in NAL, WO 208/3596, CSDIC, SIR 716, August 9, 1944.

240. Piper, *Briefe*, 13, 46, 52; Świebocki, *Resistance*, 197, 243–44.

241. Świebocki, *Resistance*, 199–202, quote on 199; Pilecki, *Auschwitz*, quote on 205. Three of the four men survived.

242. Davis, "Introduction"; Kwiet, "'Leben,'" 239–41; Kaplan, *Dignity*, 228.

243. Świebocki, *Resistance*, 245.

244. NAL, WO 208/3596, CSDIC, SIR 716, August 9, 1944; ibid., CSDIC, SIR 741, August 10, 1944. For a similar case, see Langbein, *Menschen*, 494–500.

245. The fate of another 331 known escapees from the Auschwitz complex remains unknown; Świebocki, *Resistance*, 232–33. Prisoners killed during mutinies are not normally included in these figures.

246. Himmler to Pohl and Glücks, February 8, 1943, in Heiber, *Reichsführer!*, 236–37; BArchB, NS 3/426, Bl. 87: WVHA-D to LK, June 20, 1943.

247. IfZ, F 13/7, Bl. 383–88: R. Höss, "Richard Glücks," November 1946, Bl. 385–86.

248. WVHA-D to LK, January 6, 1944, in Tuchel, *Inspektion*, 193.

249. BArchB, NS 3/426, Bl. 122–28: Aufgaben und Pflichten der Wachposten, n.d. (1943); APMO, Proces Maurer, 5a, Bl. 126–41: Bilderbuch "Falsch-Richtig" für die Posten im KL-Dienst, n.d., Bl. 140.

250. JVL, DJAO, *United States v. Becker*, RaR, n.d. (1947), 29; Fröbe, "Arbeit," 174 (n. 28); BArchB, NS 3/426, Bl. 135: WVHA-D to LK, August 12, 1943.

251. NAL, WO 235/301, Bl. 185–87: deposition of A. Lütkemeyer, November 4, 1946.

252. For interrogations, see BArchL, B 162/7999, Bl. 918–19: WVHA-D to LK, January 26, 1944; ibid., Nr. 7994, Bl. 139–42: WVHA-D, Richtlinien zur Bekanntgabe an die Leiter der politischen Abteilungen, March 1944, ND: NO-1553.

253. AdsD, KE, E. Büge, Bericht, n.d. (1945–46), 90; WL, P.III.h. No. 1174a, Vernehmung R. Kagan, December 8–10, 1959.

254. For one example, see Angrick and Klein, *"Endlösung,"* 429.

255. BArchL, B 162/7999, Bl. 768–937: StA Koblenz, EV, July 25, 1974, Bl. 919–20.

256. Fackler, "Panoramen," 251–59, quotes on 252, 254; Maršálek, *Mauthausen*, 257; NAL, HW 16/19, GPD Nr. 3, KL Mauthausen to WVHA-D, June 23, 1942.

257. Quote in NAL, WO 208/3596, CSDIC, SIR Nr. 727, August 11, 1944.

258. For example, see Nansen, *Day*, 487.

259. Quote in Gostner, *KZ*, 114. See also Maršálek, *Mauthausen*, 217.

260. Broszat, *Kommandant*, 152–53; Albin, *Gesucht*, 220–21.

261. Czech, *Kalendarium*, 88, 107, 111; Todorov, *Facing*, 54–55. The Catholic Church later canonized Kolbe; the prisoner he had saved survived the war.

262. Piper, *Briefe*, 5, 13 (apparently, Pogonowski hanged himself before the Camp SS could do so; ibid., 6, 55).

263. Paserman, "Bericht," 158.

264. StAMü, StA Nr. 34588/8, LG Munich, Urteil, October 14, 1960, p. 18.

265. Quotes in AdsD, KE, E. Büge, Bericht, n.d. (1945–46), 99; AS, Häftlingsdatenbank.

266. Świebocki, *Resistance*, 203; Loewy, "Mutter"; Gałek and Nowakowski, *Episoden*.

267. For this and the previous paragraph, see Kagan, "Mala"; Czech, *Kalendarium*, 303, 805, 878–79; Kielar, "Edek"; idem., *Anus Mundi*, 242, 297–98; Świebocki, *Resistance*, 259–61; *DAP*, Aussage Steinberg, September 28, 1964, 19448; BoA, testimony of H. Frydman, August 7, 1946 (also for the quote). My account of the escape draws primarily on the 1947 testimony of Raya Kagan, a former Auschwitz prisoner who had had access to SS files in the political office.

268. Wagner, *Mittelbau-Dora*, 95.

269. Langbein, *Menschen*, 135; Nansen, *Day*, 500; Świebocki, *Resistance*, 40; Broad, "Erinnerungen," 143–44.

270. Unbekannter Autor, "Einzelheiten," 179.

271. Quotes in Borowski, *This Way*, 146; Hördler, "Ordnung," 271. For the most common version of Schillinger's death, see Friedler et al., *Zeugen*, 154–57. Other accounts in Lewental, "Gedenkbuch," 195; Chatwood, "Schillinger." For the SS response, see APMO, Proces Höss, Hd 6, Bl. 51–62: O. Wolken, Chronik des Lagers Auschwitz II, n.d. (c. spring 1945).

272. Friedler et al., *Zeugen*, 271–73 (with a different numbering for the crematoria). See also Müller, *Eyewitness*, 155–56; Lewental, "Gedenkbuch," 241.

273. S. Gradowski, letter, September 6, 1944, in SMAB, *Inmitten*, 137–39.

274. Friedler et al., *Zeugen*, 240–42, 248–51, 258–63, 266–68. See also Lewental, "Gedenkbuch," 239–40; Gutman, "Aufstand"; Arad, *Belzec*, 286–364, esp. 299. For the possible link to liquidation of the family camp, see Van Pelt, "Resistance."

275. Lewental, "Gedenkbuch," quote on 229; Świebocki, *Resistance*, 81–82, 134–35, 237–41.

276. *DAP*, Aussage F. Müller, October 5, 1964, 20543; Lewental, "Gedenkbuch," 228, 238–41; Friedler et al., *Zeugen*, 273–74, 278.

277. Müller, *Eyewitness*, quote on 157; Friedler et al., *Zeugen*, 272–75.

278. For this and the previous paragraph, see Friedler et al., *Zeugen*, 275–81, quote on 292; Fulbrook, *Small Town*, quote on 316; Lewental, "Gedenkbuch," 241–43; Gutman, "Aufstand," 216–19.

279. Friedler et al., *Zeugen*, 274–79; BArchB (ehem. BDC), SSO Pohl, Oswald, 30.6.1892, Pohl to Himmler, April 5, 1944; StB Nr. 26/44, October 12, 1944, in Frei et al., *Kommandanturbefehle*, 499. The escapes from Treblinka and Sobibor were also aided by better planning and large numbers of participants. In total, up to 400 prisoners evaded the SS and police pursuit, and 120 to 130 survived until the end of the war; Arad, *Belzec*, 363–64.

280. Pressac and Van Pelt, "Machinery," 234; Czech, *Kalendarium*, 891–921; Friedler et al., *Zeugen*, 285; Adler, *Theresienstadt*, 185–95; Piper, *Zahl*, 192; Kárný, "Herbsttransporte."

281. S. Gradowski, letter, September 6, 1944, in SMAB, *Inmitten*, quote on 138; Friedler et al., *Zeugen*, 376.

282. Lewental, "Gedenkbuch," 247–49.

283. Figures in Friedler et al., *Zeugen*, 299, 307.

11. Death or Freedom

1. For this and the previous two paragraphs, see Nansen, *Day*, 553–68, quotes on 562–63; Buergenthal, *Lucky Child*, 64–105; Kubica, "Children," 282; Strzelecki, "Liquidation," 31.

2. Figures in Knop and Schmidt, "Sachsenhausen," 23.

3. Blatman, *Death*, 11.

4. IfZ, Burger to Loerner, August 15, 1944, ND: NO-399; ibid., Fa 183, Bl. 6–7, n.d.; Neander, *Mittelbau*, 86–87.

5. In Mauthausen, over twenty thousand new inmates were registered between January and April 1945, in addition to existing prisoners from other, abandoned KL; Fabréguet, *Mauthausen*, 126; idem, "Entwicklung," 207; *OdT*, vol. 4, 314.

6. Keller, *Volksgemeinschaft*.

7. Zámečník, "Aufzeichnungen," 224; Nansen, *Day*, 482.

8. Kautsky, *Teufel*, 182–83; Rózsa, "Solange," 137, 204; Kupfer-Koberwitz, *Tagebücher*, 403–404.

9. Bessel, *Germany*, 31–34, 46–47, 130–31; Kershaw, *End*, 129–61.

10. Marszałek, *Majdanek*, quote on 240; Mess, *"Sonnenschein,"* 64, 66, 76; Rózsa, "Solange," 222; Kielar, *Anus Mundi*, 347.

11. Nansen, *Day*, 561–68, quote on 563; Levi, *Periodic Table*, 140; Gross, *Fünf Minuten*, 118; Kupfer-Koberwitz, *Tagebücher*, 431, 442–43; Overesch, "Ernst Thapes," 641.

12. This is assuming that some 750,000 prisoners went through the KL system in 1945. Other historians have estimated a death rate of between one-third and half of the prisoner population; Orth, *System*, 335, 349; Neander, "Vernichtung," 54; Bauer, "Death Marches," 2–3.

13. A similar estimate (c. 450,000 survivors) was put forward by the French historian Joseph Billig; Spoerer and Fleischhacker, "Forced Laborers," 193. For a far too high estimate (700,000 or more survivors), see Gellately, *Backing*, 219.

14. Morsch and Ley, *Sachsenhausen*, 142; Morsch, "Einleitung," 8.

15. Quotes in Buergenthal, *Child*, 112, 211. On luck, see also P. Levi, "Preface," 1965, in Belpoliti, *Levi*, 12–16; Bettelheim, *Surviving*, 101.

16. Strzelecki, "Liquidation," 19–20, 41–48; Czech, *Kalendarium*, 860, 989; Pressac and Van Pelt, "Machinery," 239.

17. In addition to individual countries honoring the date, the UN General Assembly has designated January 27 the International Day of Commemoration in memory of the victims of the Holocaust; www.un.org/en/holocaustremembrance.

18. Müller, *Weltkrieg*, 314–18; Kershaw, *End*, 61.

19. *OdT*, vol. 7, 146–47, 156–84.

20. Steegmann, *Struthof*, 98, 141, 159–65; *OdT*, vol. 6, 48–190; Müller, *Weltkrieg*, 318–21. The evacuation of the satellite camps on the left bank of the Rhine appears to have continued until October 1944.

21. Strebel, *Ravensbrück*, quote on 171; Steegmann, *Struthof*, 98, 103, 161; *OdT*, vol. 6, 41; Neander, *Mittelbau*, 139–40.

22. Evans, *Third Reich at War*, 618–24; Kershaw, *End*, 92.

23. *OdT*, vol. 7, 66–68, 86–87, 91, 95, 97; ibid., vol. 8, 109–13; Marszałek, *Majdanek*, 239–44.

24. *OdT*, vol. 8, 272–80, 292–98.

25. *OdT*, vol. 8, 51–54, 66–87; Megargee, *Encyclopedia*, vol. 1/B, 1230–32; Harshav, *Last Days*, 699. Some prisoners of the Riga complex were taken to Libau on the west coast of Latvia, where a few remained until February 1945; *OdT*, vol. 8, 81.

26. Dieckmann, *Besatzungspolitik*, vol. 2, 1299–1321, quote on 1320; Blatman, *Death*, 60–61; Friedländer, *Jahre*, 614; *OdT*, vol. 8, 202, 210–31.

27. *OdT*, vol. 8, 135, 140–42, 149–77; Gruchmann, *Krieg*, 205–10. Quotes in Harshav, *Last Days*, 667, 702, 703; LULVR, interview No. 422, July 28, 1946, p. 10, Gdansk in the original.

28. YVA, 033/8, "Was is forgekom in di lagern fon estonia," December 1944, quote on 5 (translation by Kim Wünschmann); BArchL, B 162/5116, Bl. 1716–21: Aussage Benjamin A., July 5, 1961; ibid., Bl. 1835–42: Vernehmung W. Werle, June 5, 1962; ibid., Nr. 5120, Bl. 2234–52: Vernehmungsniederschrift Nissan A., July 15, 1965; ibid., Bl. 2256–

62: Vernehmungsniederschrift Benjamin A., September 21, 1965; WL, P.III.h. No. 1012, B. Aronovitz, "Die grausame 'Liquidierung' des Klooga-Camps," September 1949; *OdT*, vol. 8, 135, 164; Gruchmann, *Krieg*, 210; Angrick and Klein, *"Endlösung,"* 429.

29. *OdT*, vol. 8, 169.

30. For similar motives during later KL evacuations, see Blatman, *Death*, 179, 425–27.

31. Dieckmann, *Besatzungspolitik*, 1297–98, quote on 1286; *OdT*, vol. 8, 48–51, 68, 78, 80–81, 85, 215–19, 227, 267–68.

32. *OdT*, vol. 8, 27–28, 51–52, 74, 77–78, 81–85; WL, P.III.h. No. 286, letter, H. Voosen, October 1945; Maršálek, *Mauthausen*, 174. At times, Krebsbach appears to have acted as commandant of Riga; Hördler, "Ordnung," 53.

33. *OdT*, vol. 8, 141, 149, 154, 160–61.

34. For one example, see *OdT*, vol. 8, 54.

35. *OdT*, vol. 8, 140, 151, 168, 172–73, 180; YVA, 033/8, "Was is forgekom in di lagern fon estonia," December 1944, p. 4; BArchL, B 162/5120, Bl. 2234–52: Vernehmungsniederschrift Nissan A., July 15, 1965, Bl. 2241–42.

36. Paserman, "Bericht," quote on 160; *OdT*, vol. 8, 112–13, 124; Mix, "Räumung," 272–73; Blatman, *Death*, 64; DaA, 6589/I, statement A. Kramer, November 1, 1945, p. 115.

37. Historians have tended to describe the early evacuations as orderly and a far cry from the chaotic later death marches; Neander, *Mittelbau*, 85–88; *OdT*, vol. 1, 298. For postwar research on the death marches, see Winter and Greiser, "Untersuchungen."

38. Wenck, *Menschenhandel*, 345–46; *OdT*, vol. 7, 91; ibid., vol. 8, 273; Marszałek, *Majdanek*, 243; Neander, "Vernichtung," 46–48, 59. For the destruction of evidence, see Hoffmann, *"Aktion 1005"*; Hördler, "Ordnung," 206–207.

39. For this and other factors, see also Blatman, *Death*, 72.

40. Bericht I. Rotschild, January 25, 1946, in Tych et al., *Kinder*, 219–24; *OdT*, vol. 8, 79–81.

41. *OdT*, vol. 6, 493, 505, 513; ibid., vol. 8, 53, 202; Hördler, "Ordnung," 208–14. Stutthof also received transports of Jewish prisoners from other sites of Nazi detention in 1944.

42. Bericht I. Rotschild, January 25, 1946, in Tych et al., *Kinder*, quote on 223–24; *OdT*, vol. 6, 485, 505, 513; ibid., vol. 8, 53; Rolnikaite, *Ich*, 258; Orth, *System*, 229–30; Hördler, "Ordnung," 212, 218; Megargee, *Encyclopedia*, vol. I/B, 1425.

43. Hördler, "Ordnung," 214, 222, 230, 242, 245. There is much to learn from Hördler's important study, though I am not persuaded by the argument that the Stutthof killings were unaffected by the impending evacuations. Preparations for the evacuation of Stutthof were being made from autumn 1944 (Orth, *System*, 295–96; *OdT*, vol. 6, 514) and prisoner killings in this period must have been part of this process, just like they were in other KL under threat of occupation.

44. For this and the previous paragraph, see Hördler, "Ordnung," 133, 214–17, 224, 231, 235, 241, quote on 233–34. See also Bericht I. Rotschild, January 25, 1946, in Tych et al., *Kinder*, 224; Orski, "Vernichtung"; *OdT*, vol. 6, 501–502, 506; Rolnikaite, *Ich*, 260–66.

45. Czech, *Kalendarium*, 923–24; Kielar, *Anus Mundi*, 352.

46. Gilbert, *Auschwitz*, 324–26; "Germans Plan Mass Execution," *The Times*, October 11, 1944, p. 4; *DAP*, Aussage S. Kłodziński, May 22, 1964, 8470; Broad, "Erinnerungen," 183; Dirks, *"Verbrechen,"* 171–72.

47. Friedler et al., *Zeugen*, 285; Czech, *Kalendarium*, 921; Hoffmann, *"Aktion 1005,"* 293–94. Chelmno had briefly resumed the mass extermination of Jews in summer 1944; Kershaw, *End*, 123.

48. Quote in Hördler, "Ordnung," 410.

49. Nyiszli, *Auschwitz*, 144.

50. Most historians accept the existence of a Himmler "stop" order, at least for Birkenau; Orth, *System*, 259, 274–75; Gerlach and Aly, *Kapitel*, 401; Pressac and Van Pelt, "Machinery," 239.

51. APMO, Dpr-ZO, 29/2, LG Frankfurt, Urteil, September 16, 1966, p. 60.

52. Czech, *Kalendarium*, 941.

53. Friedländer, *Jahre*, 657; *OdT*, vol. 7, 68.

54. For the Mauthausen plans, see Perz and Freund, "Auschwitz"; Hördler, "Ordnung," 381–85.

55. Czech, *Kalendarium*, 860, 921–22, 929, 932, 948; IfZ, Fa 183, Bl. 6–7, n.d.

56. Strzelecki, "Liquidation," 22–23; *OdT*, vol. 6, 493.

57. Gutterman, *Bridge*, quote on 146; Sprenger, *Groß-Rosen*, 224–26, 286–92; *OdT*, vol. 6, 202–17; Rudorff, *Frauen*, 87–101; Orth, *System*, 279–80; Konieczny, "Groß-Rosen," 320.

58. Bessel, *1945*, esp. 23–28, 35–36; Kershaw, *End*, 167, 175; Evans, *Third Reich at War*, 681–82, 711–12.

59. IfZ, Fa 183, Bl. 6–7, n.d.

60. Blatman, *Death*, 52–57; Orth, *System*, 272–73; Neander, *Mittelbau*, 89–96.

61. Orth, *System*, 276; IfZ, F 13/8, Bl. 468–71: R. Höss, "Richard Baer," November 1946.

62. Orth, *System*, 273–74; Kolb, *Bergen-Belsen*, 305–306; Greiser, *Todesmärsche*, 39–42; Neander, "Vernichtung," 50.

63. Blatman, *Death*, 81. For a similar approach by the German prison authorities in 1944–45, see Wachsmann, *Prisons*, 324.

64. Kershaw, *End*, 176, 229.

65. Czech, *Kalendarium*, quotes on 967; Levi, *If*, 161; Friedler et al., *Zeugen*, 299; Strzelecki, "Liquidation," 27; Müller, *Eyewitness*, 166.

66. Strzelecki, "Liquidation," 27, 40.

67. Strzelecki, "Liquidation," 27–28, 31–33, 36–37.

68. *OdT*, vol. 6, 217–18, 223–473; Sprenger, *Groß-Rosen*, 292–301; Bessel, *1945*, 72–76.

69. Figures in *OdT*, vol. 6, 531–792.

70. *OdT*, vol. 6, 514–20, 607–609, 611–16, 670–72, 674–76, 687–89, 703–706, 737–39, 772–74; Orth, *System*, 282–87, 332–33; Bericht I. Rotschild, January 25, 1946, in Tych et al., *Kinder*, 224.

71. An estimated twenty thousand prisoners were moved from the Sachsenhausen complex to other KL; Blatman, *Death*, 163–64.

72. Neander, "Vernichtung," 46; idem, *Mittelbau*, 87, 138; Blatman, *Death*, 62, 80, 83, 103.

73. Blatman, *Death*, 99–103, 114–15; *OdT*, vol. 6, 284, 302, 733–35.

74. Weigelt, "'Komm,'" quote on 184. See also Knop and Schmidt, "Sachsenhausen," 27; *OdT*, vol. 3, 224–29; Hördler, "Ordnung," 397–99; BStU, MfS HA IX/11, RHE 15/71, vol. 6, Bl. 97–99: Zeugenaussage Fritz M., June 18, 1964; ibid., RHE 15/71, Bd. 3, Bl. 113–16: H. Simon, Bericht über Lieberose, March 3, 1950; USHMM, RG-06.025*26, File 1558, Bl. 157–75, interrogation of G. Sorge, December 19, 1946, Bl. 171–72.

75. Orth, *System*, quote on 284; *OdT*, vol. 6, 514–16. Other examples in ibid., 267, 299, 339.

76. *OdT*, vol. 6, passim.

77. Broad, "Erinnerungen," 195.

78. Levi, *If*, 171.

79. Strzelecki, "Liquidation," 48. Another five hundred prisoners survived in Auschwitz satellite camps, and several hundred more in Gross-Rosen satellite camps. In addition, thousands of prisoners escaped from death marches.

80. APMO, Proces Höss, Hd 6, Bl. 129–312: Vernehmung O. Wolken, April 17–20, 1945, quote on 310; Strzelecki, "Liquidation," 45–47; Czech, *Kalendarium*, 994 (my thanks to Dan Stone for this reference); Adler et al., *Auschwitz*, 128; Levi, *If*, 162–79.

81. Megargee, *Encyclopedia*, vol. 1/A, 240–41; *OdT*, vol. 5, 224.

82. Estimates in Strzelecki, "Liquidation," 27, 40; Orth, *System*, 286.

83. Neander, *Mittelbau*, 128, 136; Steinke, *Züge*, 62; Bessel, *1945*, 77.

84. *OdT*, vol. 5, 440–41; Megargee, *Encyclopedia*, vol. 1/A, 261–62; WL, P.III.h. No. 416, A. Lehmann, "Die Evakuations-Transporte," n.d. (1946?).

85. LULVR, interview No. 139, January 16, 1946.

86. LBIJMB, MM 32, P. Heller, "Tagebuchblätter aus dem Konzentrationslager," October 1945, p. 7; BoA, interview with Dr. L. Frim, September 25, 1946.

87. Blatman, *Death*, 87, 116, 431. See also NARA, M-1204, reel 4, Bl. 2373–97: examination of M. Pinkas, August 19–20, 1946, Bl. 2385; Vaisman, *Auschwitz*, 61; Laqueur, *Bergen-Belsen*, 115.

88. Broszat, *Kommandant*, 219.

89. Blatman, *Death*, 12, 432; Neander, *Mittelbau*, 140. When general conditions were better and prisoners healthier, a large proportion survived even lengthier death marches; *OdT*, vol. 6, 223–25.

90. APMO, Oswiadczenia, vol. 89, Bl. 131–35: testimony J. Wygas, July 10, 1978; Orth, *System*, 276–77, 285.

91. BArchL, B 162/20519, Bl. 186–95: Aussage Moszek G., February 25, 1947; Blatman, *Death*, 85–86; Neander, *Mittelbau*, 141–42.

92. IfZ, F 13/8, Bl. 468–71: R. Höss, "Richard Baer," November 1946; Neander, *Mittelbau*, 137–38; Blatman, *Death*, 103; Bessel, *1945*, 88–89.

93. Blatman, *Death*, 96, 370–72, 378–80, 418, quote on 193. See also Greiser, *Todesmärsche*, 97, 108; *OdT*, vol. 6, 253.

94. Orth, *System*, 278–79; Blatman, *Death*, 76–79, 92; Kershaw, *End*, 114–16, 181–82. Quote in Stuttgart SD report, November 6, 1944, in Noakes, *Nazism*, vol. 4, 652. The killing of frail prisoners was also intended as a warning to others not to fall behind.

95. Blatman, *Death*, 117–25; Henkys, "Todesmarsch."

96. Quotes in testimony O. Pohl, June 7, 1946, in *NCA*, supplement B, 1595; Broszat, *Kommandant*, 211. See also ibid., 217; StANü, Erklärung R. Höß, March 14, 1946, p. 6, ND: NO-1210; IfZ, ZS-1590, interrogation of G. Witt, November 19, 1946, p. 20. The full itinerary is unknown. According to Höss, it included Neuengamme, Bergen-Belsen, Buchenwald, Dachau, and Flossenbürg. Pohl said that he also went to Mauthausen, Sachsenhausen, and Ravensbrück (testimony above, dated June 7, 1946, and StANü, testimony of O. Pohl, June 13, 1946, p. 19, ND: NO-4728).

97. Rost, *Goethe*, 234; *OdT*, vol. 3, 347 (figure for deaths among men); Strebel, *Ravensbrück*, 523; KZ-Gedenkstätte Dachau, *Gedenkbuch*, 11; Buggeln, *Arbeit*, 210–13; Orth, *System*, 314; NARA, M-1174, roll 3, Bl. 1441–65: examination E. Mahl, December 6, 1945, Bl. 1461.

98. StANü, Erklärung R. Höß, March 14, 1946, p. 6, ND: NO-1210; ibid., testimony of Oswald Pohl, June 13, 1946, p. 18–20, ND: NO-4728; Orth, *System*, 303–304; Erpel, *Vernichtung*, 73; NAL, WO 253/163, Trial of War Criminals, Curiohaus, April 2, 1946, p. 55–56.

99. H. Haubner to his wife, January 5, 1945, in KZ-Gedenkstätte Flossenbürg, *Flossenbürg*, 185. See also *OdT*, vol. 4, 53.

100. *OdT*, vol. 3, 321–22.

101. Stein, "Funktionswandel," 188.

102. Haulot, "Lagertagebuch," 185.

103. Wagner, *Ellrich*, 97, 108, quotes on 96, 98; Sellier, *Dora*, 212–13. See also Cohen, *Human*, 55–56; Strebel, *Ravensbrück*, 194.

104. Kupfer-Koberwitz, *Tagebücher*, 331, 372; JVL, JAO, Review of Proceedings, *United States v. Weiss*, n.d. (1946), 132, 138; Güldenpfenning, "Bewacher," 72.

105. Wagner, *Produktion*, 472–73, quote on 473.

106. Vogel, *Tagebuch*, 93; Rousset, *Kingdom*, 160; Bárta, "Tagebuch," 94, 138; Kolb, *Bergen-Belsen*, 147.

107. For example, see LBIJMB, MM 32, P. Heller, "Tagebuchblätter aus dem Konzentrationslager," October 1945, p. 11.

108. For this and the previous paragraph, see Nansen, *Day*, 541–48, quotes on 541, 548; *OdT*, vol. 3, 227; BStU, MfS HA IX/11, RHE 15/71, vol. 4, Bl. 23–28: Vernehmung Wojciech C., January 17, 1969.

109. Bárta, "Tagebuch," 81–82, 182.

110. Rost, *Goethe*, quote on 253.

111. Orth, *System*, 260–62; Wagner, *Produktion*, 494.

112. Hördler, "Schlussphase," 223–24; idem, "Ordnung," 410; Erpel, *Vernichtung*, 94.

113. Quotes in Rost, *Goethe*, 237; YIVO, RG 104, MK 538, reel 6, folder 749, testimony F. Uhl, January 4, 1947; Nansen, *Day*, 578 (Nansen also uses the phrase "waiting room of death"). More generally, see Siegert, "Flossenbürg," 474–75; Bárta, "Tagebuch," 92–94; Szita, *Ungarn*, 120–21.

114. For this and the previous paragraph, see Semprun and Wiesel, *Schweigen*, 7–8, quote on 11; Greiser, "'Sie starben'"; Hördler, "Schlussphase," 235–37; *OdT*, vol. 3, 323–25; ibid., vol. 4, 49–50, 300–301; Hackett, *Buchenwald*, 318–19.

115. Megargee, *Encyclopedia*, vol. 1/A, quote on 784; Raim, *Überlebende*, 17; Hördler, "Ordnung," 337.

116. Wagner, *Produktion*, 264–65, 271–72, 475, 482, 495–96, 506–509, quote on 496; idem, *Ellrich*, 104, 153–54; *OdT*, vol. 7, 320–21; NARA, M-1079, roll 7, Bl. 1849–67: examination of H. Maienschein, September 18, 1947, Bl. 1857–58.

117. Lévy-Hass, *Vielleicht*, 53–54, quote on 53; *OdT*, vol. 7, 204; Stiftung, *Bergen-Belsen*, 217.

118. Wenck, *Menschenhandel*, 343–47; *OdT*, vol. 7, 202–203; Kolb, *Bergen-Belsen*, 112–17; Lasker-Wallfisch, *Inherit*, 159; Gutman, *Enzyklopädie*, 472–76.

119. Lévy-Hass, *Vielleicht*, quotes on 43–44; Wenck, *Menschenhandel*, 268–71; Koretz, *Bergen-Belsen*, 127.

120. Wenck, *Menschenhandel*, 347–361.

121. Wagner, *Ellrich*, 162–63, quote on 157–58; *OdT*, vol. 7, 340–41. By early April 1945, Delaunois had been transferred from Ellrich to Woffleben (my thanks to Jens-Christian Wagner for this information).

122. Wenck, *Menschenhandel*, 351–61; *OdT*, vol. 7, 190, 204–207. In early 1945, women made up eighty-five percent of the prisoner population in the Ravensbrück complex, and sixty-four percent in Stutthof; IfZ, Fa 183, Bl. 6–7, n.d.

123. Herzberg, *Between*, 203; Van Pelt, "Introduction," 41.

124. Koretz, *Bergen-Belsen*, quote on 155; Kolb, *Bergen-Belsen*, 137–40; Wenck, *Menschenhandel*, 349, 371–74; Obenaus, "Räumung," 517; WL, P.III.h. No. 839, Dr. P. Arons, "Faelle von Kannibalismus," December 1957.

125. Vogel, *Tagebuch*, 99–102, 109, quotes on 113; Wenck, *Menschenhandel*, 349–50, 371–72; Koretz, *Bergen-Belsen*, 161; MacAuslan, "Aspects," 37.

126. Herzberg, *Between*, 201–202, quote on 201.

127. WL, P.III.h. No. 494, A. Lehmann, "Im Lager Bergen Belsen," 1946; Wenck, *Menschenhandel*, 373–74; Koretz, *Bergen-Belsen*, 165.

128. Niedersächsische Landeszentrale, *Bergen-Belsen*, 164–65.

129. Testimony of L. Jaldati, ibid., quote on 130; Shephard, *Daybreak*, 17.

130. At one stage, Oswald Pohl apparently considered closing the camp to further transports, but this plan came to nothing. Testimony O. Pohl, June 7, 1946, in *NCA*, supplement B, 1604; NAL, WO 235/19, statement of J. Kramer, May 22, 1945, p. 13.

131. Kramer to Glücks, March 1, 1945, in Niedersächsische Landeszentrale, *Bergen-Belsen*, 160–63.

132. My assumption that Kramer wrote his letter with an eye on postwar exculpation rests on the text (which includes a telling reference to the catastrophe in Bergen-Belsen as something for which "surely no one wants to take responsibility"), and on the fact that Kramer apparently left a copy among the private papers in his apartment.

133. Herzberg, *Between*, quote on 207; Kolb, *Bergen-Belsen*, 137–38, 141, 145, 195–97; Lévy-Hass, *Vielleicht*, 58.

134. Hördler, "Schlussphase," 234–35, 239; Erpel, *Vernichtung*, 78; Strebel, *Ravensbrück*, 466. On WVHA orders, see Orth, *System*, 288–89, 298–99; Blatman, *Death*, 213; Strebel, *Ravensbrück*, 464. In Sachsenhausen and Ravensbrück alone, ten thousand or more prisoners were murdered; Orth, *System*, 299; Tillion, *Ravensbrück*, 367. More

generally, see Hördler, "Ordnung," 135, 203, 360–61 (though with less emphasis on the significance of the impending evacuations).

135. For one example, see Maršálek, *Mauthausen*, 106.

136. Many of the victims were recent arrivals. Another two thousand victims were gassed following selections elsewhere in the Ravensbrück complex. See Buchmann, *Frauen*, quote on 32; Strebel, *Ravensbrück*, 475–88; Erpel, *Vernichtung*, 74, 85–88; Hördler, "Ordnung," 310; Tillion, *Ravensbrück*, 279–99, 367–92; LULVR, interview No. 449, May 7, 1946. More generally on Uckermarck, see Strebel, *Ravensbrück*, 356–83, 460–61, 468–75; Erpel, *Vernichtung*, 80–85.

137. Keller, *Volksgemeinschaft*; Bessel, *1945*, 48–66; Kershaw, *End*, 392; Wachsmann, *Prisons*, 319–23; Wegner, "Ideology."

138. Fröhlich, *Tagebücher*, II/4, May 24, 1942, p. 361; Wachsmann, *Prisons*, 210–11.

139. *OdT*, vol. 4, 54; Siegert, "Flossenbürg," 478–80; KZ-Gedenkstätte Flossenbürg, *Flossenbürg*, 206–11.

140. Orth, *System*, 296–98; StANü, Erklärung H. Pister, July 2, 1945, p. 37, ND: NO-254.

141. Keller, *Volksgemeinschaft*.

142. NAL, HW 16/15, GPD Headlines, April 7, 1945.

143. Quotes in Müller to Stapo(leit)stellen, March 4, 1944, in Maršálek, *Mauthausen*, 263–65; YUL, MG 1832, Series II—Trials, 1945–2001, Box 10, folder 50, Bl. 1320–23: statement J. Niedermayer, February 6, 1946. See also Kaltenbrunner, *Flucht*, 11–12, 21–99; Maršálek, *Mauthausen*, 266–67; LaB, B Rep. 057-01, Nr. 296, GStA Berlin, Abschlußvermerke, November 1, 1970, pp. 178–85. Kaltenbrunner argues that the first victims of Action "Bullet" in February 1944 were eastern European civilian workers, not POWs.

144. JVL, DJAO, *United States v. Altfuldisch*, RaR, March 1946, quote on 42; Maršálek, *Mauthausen*, 267–70; ASL, Kam 5539, L4, Bl. 37–44: Bericht V. Ukrainzew, n.d.; Horwitz, *Shadow*, 124–43; Kaltenbrunner, *Flucht*, 99–168.

145. Wagner, *Produktion*, 448; Maršálek, *Mauthausen*, 322, 330.

146. Schwarberg, *SS-Arzt*, 34–55. The execution order may have come from the WVHA.

147. Wagner, *Produktion*, 356; Bárta, "Tagebuch," 83.

148. Koretz, *Bergen-Belsen*, quote on 158; YUL, MG 1832, Series II—Trials, 1945–2001, Box 10, folder 50, Bl. 1330–32: statement of F. Entress, January 26, 1946, quote on 1331 (Entress took up his Mauthausen post in 1943, after almost two years in Auschwitz); Lasik, "SS-Garrison," 382; Wagner, *Produktion*, 272–73, 307–308; idem, *Ellrich*, 153; Orth, *SS*, 247, 255–60; Hördler, "Ordnung," 70, 158.

149. Hördler, "Schlussphase," 229–32; idem, "Ordnung," 147–57, Erpel, *Vernichtung*, 86; Strebel, *Ravensbrück*, 61, 467–68; Broszat, *Kommandant*, 222. The significance of transfers from Auschwitz should not be exaggerated, however; plenty of SS men from other KL were also well versed in mass murder.

150. Schmid, "Moll," 133–38, quote on 134; Hördler, "Schlussphase," 228–29, 242–43; idem, "Ordnung," 365–66. Relentless to the end, Moll shot dozens of exhausted prisoners during the death march from Kaufering in late April 1945.

151. Evans, *Third Reich at War*, 467, 651–53, 714–15; Kershaw, *Nemesis*, 764–66; idem, *End*, 389; Bessel, *1945*, 2, 42, 65.

152. Buggeln, *Arbeit*, 447–55; Wagner, *Produktion*, 341–42. For the People's Storm guarding evacuation treks, see Blatman, *Death*, 304, 397; Greiser, *Todesmärsche*, 112.

153. Quote in Harshav, *Last Days*, 694. See also AGN, Ng. 7.6., H. Behncke to his wife, August 28, 1944; Kupfer-Koberwitz, *Tagebücher*, 314; Nansen, *Day*, 492.

154. Weiss-Rüthel, *Nacht*, 181.

155. Rózsa, "Solange," 152.

156. Langbein, *Menschen*, 482.

157. Cohen, *Abyss*, quote on 105; Rózsa, "Solange," 212; Naujoks, *Leben*, 342.

158. *OdT*, vol. 4, 297; Bessel, *1945*, 18–19; Kershaw, *End*, 220.

159. Rózsa, "Solange," 296, quote on 217; Maršálek, *Mauthausen*, 325; Glauning, *Entgrenzung*, 241–42; Freund, "Mauthausenprozess," 38; Burger, *Werkstatt*, 189.

160. *DAP*, Aussage S. Baretzki, February 18, 1965, quote on 29219; Strebel, *Ravensbrück*, 245, 466–67; Hördler, "Ordnung," 150–51. The 1965 sentence against Dr. Lucas in the Frankfurt Auschwitz trial—three years' and three months' penitentiary—was later annulled.

161. APMO, Proces Maurer, 5a, Bl. 114: WVHA, Chefbefehl Nr. 7, February 27, 1945.

162. NAL, WO 253/163, examination of M. Pauly, April 2, 1946, p. 60; Orth, *SS*, 260–61; Buggeln, *Arbeit*, 642–44; Welch, *Propaganda*, 189–97.

163. For this and the previous paragraph, see Kershaw, *Nemesis*, 751–828, quote on 819; idem, *End*, 79; Longerich, *Himmler*, 740–52; *Time. The Weekly Newsmagazine*, October 11, 1943.

164. Wenck, *Menschenhandel*, 272–335; Longerich, *Himmler*, 728–30; Bauer, *Jews*, 145–238. In November 1944, Himmler also agreed to repatriate 200 Danish policemen and 140 sick Norwegian students; Stræde, "'Aktion,'" 179–81; Erpel, *Vernichtung*, 124.

165. Kersten's later testimony should be approached with great care; Fleming, "Herkunft"; Neander, *Mittelbau*, 99; Wenck, *Menschenhandel*, 362–63. For Burckhardt and Bernadotte, see Favez, *Red*, 284–85; Erpel, *Vernichtung*, 128–29.

166. Erpel, *Vernichtung*, passim; Bauer, *Jews*, 249–50; Hördler, "Ordnung," 26, 314.

167. NAL, WO 235/19, statement J. Kramer, May 22, 1945, p. 13; APMO, Proces Maurer, 5a, Bl. 117–20: H. Pister, "Strafen für Häftlinge," July 21, 1945, ND: NO-256; Heiber, *Reichsführer!*, 387 (n. 2).

168. Longerich, *Himmler*, 746–49; Jacobeit, "*Ich*," 82–83.

169. Favez, *Red*, 99, 258, 261, 265; Zweig, "Feeding," 845–50. Such efforts were hampered by shortages of suitable vehicles and the breakdown of the transport network.

170. Erpel, *Vernichtung*, 104–105, 111; Favez, *Red*, 268.

171. Stræde, "'Aktion,'" 176, 183; Erpel, *Vernichtung*, 131.

172. Nansen, *Day*, 570–82, quotes on 572, 582; Grill, "Skandinavierlager," 196–206; Erpel, *Vernichtung*, 131–34; Obenaus, "Räumung," 519–44.

173. Nansen, *Day*, quote on 592; Jacobeit, "*Ich*," 32–35, 40, 77, de Lauwe quote on 41; Erpel, *Vernichtung*, 114–19, 128–29, 134–54; Bernadotte, *Fall*, 45–46, 53, 58–59; Stræde, "'Aktion,'" 182–84; Grill, "Skandinavierlager," 206–15; Longerich, *Himmler*, 749–50; Hertz-Eichenrode, *KZ*, vol. 1, 125–28; Maršálek, *Mauthausen*, 323.

174. See also Longerich, *Himmler*, 752.

175. Favez, *Red*, 265–66; Breitman et al., *Intelligence*, 111.

176. Orth, *System*, 302–303; Erpel, *Vernichtung*, 138; StANü, Erklärung H. Pister, July 2, 1945, p. 15, ND: NO-254; StANü, Erklärung R. Höß, March 14, 1946, p. 6, ND: NO-1210; ibid., testimony O. Pohl, June 13, 1946, p. 20, ND: NO-4728; NAL, FO 188/526, report N. Masur, April 1945.

177. Fabréguet, *Mauthausen*, 186–87; Maršálek, *Mauthausen*, 325.

178. Longerich, *Himmler*, 746–49; NAL, FO 188/526, report N. Masur, April 1945; Erpel, *Vernichtung*, 148.

179. This makes it hard to take seriously Himmler's alleged offer in November 1944 of negotiating the release of six hundred thousand Jews; Bauer, *Jews*, 225.

180. Quote in Maršálek, *Mauthausen*, 136. Pohl also said that Himmler had wanted to use Jews "for bargaining purposes in the peace negotiations"; testimony O. Pohl, June 7, 1946, in *NCA*, supplement B, 1596.

181. Wenck, *Menschenhandel*, 362–71; WL, P.III.h. No. 842, J. Weiss, P. Arons, "Bergen-Belsen," June 20, 1945; Hájková, "Prisoner Society," 5, 279.

182. Calculation based on *OdT*, vols. 2–8 (I am grateful to Chris Dillon for pulling these figures together, which I have used throughout this section).

183. Rózsa, "Solange," 180, 184, 187, 196, 199–200, 225, 240–41, quote on 238. See also Buggeln, *Arbeit*, 294; Greiser, *Todesmärsche*, 77.

184. The number of KL prisoners fell from 715,000 (mid-January 1945) to around 550,000 (beginning of April), which would mean a "loss" of 165,000 prisoners. The total "loss" is closer to 200,000, since the KL still admitted new inmates. Several tens of thousands of them had been released or liberated or escaped. But the great majority of "lost" prisoners—perhaps 150,000—had perished.

185. For satellites, see note 182 above.

186. Aussage A. Harbaum, March 19, 1946, *IMT*, vol. 35, 493, ND: 750–D.

187. Estimate based on Wenck, *Menschenhandel*, 362; Stein, "Funktionswandel," 187; DaA, ITS, Vorläufige Ermittlung der Lagerstärke (1971); Wagner, *Produktion*, 648; *OdT*, vol. 5, 331; ibid., vol. 6, 48–190, 223–473; Strebel, *Ravensbrück*, 182; Maršálek, *Mauthausen*, 127; USHMM, *Encyclopedia*, vol. 1/B, 1423, 1471; AS, JSU 1/101, Bl. 84: Veränderungsmeldung, April 1, 1945 (my thanks to Monika Liebscher for this reference); AGFl to the author, May 17, 2011.

188. See figures in Comité, *Dachau* (1978), 207; Wagner, *Produktion*, 648; Stein, "Funktionswandel," 187–88; *OdT*, vol. 4, 52–53, 316; ibid., vol. 5, 331.

189. Figures for some camps in *OdT*, vol. 4, 316; ibid., vol. 7, 265; Comité, *Dachau* (1978), 206 (my thanks to Dirk Riedel for this reference); Stein, "Funktionswandel," 187. The total number of Jewish prisoners was somewhat higher than SS figures suggest, as a number of Jews succeeded in hiding their identities.

190. *OdT*, vols. 2–7.

191. In April and early May, an estimated 90,000 prisoners were liberated from satellite camps, and around 155,000 from main camps. See data in *OdT*, vols. 2–7; USHMM, *Encyclopedia*, vol. I.

192. *OdT*, vol. 5, 339; KZ-Gedenkstätte Neuengamme, *Ausstellungen*, 129. The SS fully evacuated well over 260 satellite camps in April and May 1945 (see note 182 above).

193. Greiser, *Todesmärsche*, 136–37.

194. Blatman, *Death*, 7, 10, 411.

195. In addition to frequent escapes on transports, many daily routines in camps—with fixed schedules revolving around forced labor—were absent on trains and marches.

196. For Kapos as escorts, see NARA, M-1204, roll 6, Bl. 4607–87: examination of A. Ginschel, October 4 and 7, 1946.

197. Greiser, *Todesmärsche*, 52; Erpel, *Vernichtung*, 140–44; Blatman, *Death*, 155.

198. Many historians have argued that Hitler issued a general order in March 1945 to destroy every camp and its prisoners as the Allies approached. However, the source basis for this supposed order is unsatisfactory; Neander, *Mittelbau*, 97–106, 289–308. For Hitler's "scorched earth" order, see Kershaw, *Nemesis*, 784–86.

199. Wachsmann, *Prisons*, 323–24, 331.

200. Released prisoners included some German priests, long-term inmates (including Margarete Buber-Neumann), and Polish women arrested after the 1944 Warsaw Uprising. Strebel, *Ravensbrück*, 460, 498–500; Distel, "29. April," 5.

201. Klausch, *Antifaschisten*, 316–26; Fröhlich, *Tagebücher*, II/15, March 1, 1945; ITS, KL Dachau GCC 3/998–12 II H, folder 162, Freiwillige für den Heeresdienst, March 5, 1945.

202. For WVHA support, see Glücks to KL Buchenwald, April 7, 1945, in Tuchel, *Inspektion*, 215; Broszat, *Kommandant*, 280. Many historians suggest that Himmler himself ordered an end to all KL evacuations in mid-March (Neander, *Mittelbau*, 106–109; Orth, *System*, 302–308; Blatman, *Death*, 137, 154, 199–200). This supposition is largely based on the account of Himmler's masseur Felix Kersten, a notoriously unreliable witness (see above, note 165). A supposed Himmler order is also mentioned in postwar accounts of former SS officers like Walter Schellenberg and Rudolf Höss (IfZ, ED 90/7, W. Schellenberg, "Memorandum," n.d., Bl. 30; IfZ, G 01/31, Zeugenaussage R. Höss, *IMT*, April 15, 1946). But the former's testimony is unreliable and self-serving (Breitman et al., *Intelligence*, 113–14, 447), while the latter is inconsistent on this point (cf.

Broszat, *Kommandant*, 280). All considered, it seems unlikely that Himmler issued a blanket stop-order. The former head of the KL system, Oswald Pohl, made no mention of such an order in his extensive postwar testimony. Also, KL evacuations continued without interruption after Himmler's supposed order (see below). Most likely, Himmler had made some promises to his foreign interlocutors—perhaps about ending *all* evacuations—but never intended to keep them (he lied persistently during meetings with foreign representatives in spring 1945; NAL, FO 188/526, Report N. Masur, April 1945).

203. StANü, Erklärung H. Pister, July 2, 1945, p. 34, ND: NO-254; Greiser, *Todesmärsche*, 52. Following Himmler's orders, the Buchenwald commandant apparently promised some German prisoners that the KL would not be evacuated; Overesch, "Ernst Thapes," 638. Around the same time, the WVHA may have given similar instructions not to evacuate Flossenbürg; Zámečník, "Kein Häftling," 224–25.

204. Pister to WVHA-D, April 6, 1945, in Tuchel, *Inspektion*, 214; NAL, HW 16/15, GPD Headlines, April 6, 1945; Greiser, *Todesmärsche*, 57.

205. Between mid-March and mid-April 1945, the SS evacuated well over 160 satellite camps across nine of the ten remaining KL complexes; see note 182 above.

206. Buggeln, *Arbeit*, 626–34, 655–57.

207. For the following, see also Neander, *Mittelbau*, 152–61.

208. This was the main reason why the SS forced Jewish KL prisoners from Buchenwald satellites (and elsewhere) onto transports to Theresienstadt; Greiser, *Todesmärsche*, 55–56; Blatman, *Death*, 177.

209. Broszat, *Kommandant*, 218; Fröbe, "Kammler," 316; Wagner, *Produktion*, 277.

210. Wachsmann, *Prisons*, 325; Neander, *Mittelbau*, 160–61.

211. Blatman, *Death*, 153–54; Greiser, *Todesmärsche*, 57, 76; StANü, Erklärung H. Pister, July 2, 1945, p. 41, ND: NO-254; Broszat, *Kommandant*, 280; IfZ, G 01/31, Zeugenaussage R. Höss, April 15, 1946, p. 14; Overesch, *Buchenwald*, 81–82.

212. StANü, Erklärung H. Pister, July 2, 1945, pp. 40–41, ND: NO-254; Orth, *System*, 310–11.

213. DaA, 21.079, Hauptsturmführer Schwarz, "The raport [*sic*] about my way to Flossenbürgk [*sic*]," April 24(?), 1945. This is a poor English translation (probably by former prisoners) of the German original, which has been lost. I have followed the translation, with a few corrections of grammar and idiom (notably "abused" instead of "mishandled"). For an analysis of this much-misunderstood order, see Zámečník, "Kein Häftling"; Zámečník's version of Himmler's telex includes a sentence ("The camp must be evacuated immediately") that is not part of the English translation (of the lost German original).

214. Zámečník, "Kein Häftling," 229; Orth, *System*, 326; NAL, WO 309/408, deposition of M. Pauly, March 30, 1946, p. 2.

215. Abzug, *Inside*, 3–8; *OdT*, vol. 1, 315; Van Pelt, *Case*, 154–57; Klemperer, *Zeugnis*, vol. 2, 648; Zelizer, *Remembering*, 49–61; Struk, *Photographing*, 138–49.

216. Frei, "'Wir waren blind'"; Abzug, *Heart*, 21–59.

217. NAL, FO 188/526, report N. Masur, April 1945. Himmler made similar complaints to Bernadotte (Bernadotte, *Fall*, 51) and also complained about adverse reports about Bergen-Belsen following liberation.

218. *OdT*, vol. 3, 67; ibid., vol. 4, 55–57, 513.

219. For example, see *OdT*, vol. 3, 79; ibid., vol. 4, 225, 242, 530; ibid., vol. 6, 244.

220. Himmler may have made such a "concession" himself; Zámečník, "Kein Häftling," 220; Greiser, *Todesmärsche*, 58–59.

221. Maršálek, *Mauthausen*, 127.

222. Flanagan and Bloxham, *Remembering*, quotes on 9, 13; Wenck, *Menschenhandel*, 374–82; Kolb, *Bergen-Belsen*, 157–64, 225–27; Shephard, *Daybreak*, 33–42; Reilly, *Belsen*, 22–28; Niedersächsische Landeszentrale, *Bergen-Belsen*, 175–80; Orth, *SS*, 265. At least

one satellite camp, Amersfoort, also officially surrendered (on April 19, 1945); *OdT*, vol. 7, 153.

223. It was now more than a year since the first KL in Eastern Europe had closed.

224. Hertz-Eichenrode, *KZ*, vol. 1, quote on 340; Baganz, "Wöbbelin"; Volland, "Stalag"; Greiser, *Todesmärsche*, 78–80; Knop and Schmidt, "Sachsenhausen," 25; Buggeln, *Arbeit*, 635–36; Schalm, *Überleben*, 102; Blatman, *Death*, 142, 166, 214.

225. Jacobeit, *"Ich,"* quote on 162; Greiser, *Todesmärsche*, 82; Perz and Freund, "Tötungen," 258–59; Morsch, "Tötungen," 275; Hertz-Eichenrode, *KZ*, vol. 1, 197; Buggeln, *Arbeit*, 637; APMO, Proces Maurer, 5a, Bl. 117–20: H. Pister, "Strafen für Häftlinge," July 21, 1945, ND: NO-256.

226. Greiser, *Todesmärsche*, 83–84; Blatman, *Death*, 299; Obenaus, "Räumung," 527–28.

227. Distel, "29. April," 6–7; Zarusky, "Dachau," 51; Zámečník, *Dachau*, 382–84. Another 137 prominent German and foreign prisoners, assembled from other KL, left by bus.

228. Greiser, *Todesmärsche*, 64–76, 240, 500–508; idem, "'Sie starben,'" 112.

229. See also Greiser, *Todesmärsche*, 73, 241.

230. Overesch, "Ernst Thapes," 646, quote on 644; Greiser, *Todesmärsche*, 71–73, 243–44; Distel, "29. April," 7.

231. Greiser, *Todesmärsche*, 91–95, 146, 206, 502–503; Neander, *Mittelbau*, 88, 128–51; Blatman, *Death*, 143, 177, 208–209; Kielar, *Anus Mundi*, 388; Bessel, *1945*, 63, 85, 92–93. In addition to trains and marches, the SS occasionally used boats; Orth, *System*, 334.

232. StANü, G. Rammler report, January 30, 1946, ND: NO-1200; ibid., EE by K. Sommer, January 22, 1947, ND: NO-1578; BArchB, Film 44563, Vernehmung O. Pohl, September 26, 1946, p. 51; Schulte, *Zwangsarbeit*, 426–28.

233. IfZ, F 13/6, Bl. 343–54: R. Höss, "Oswald Pohl," November 1946, Bl. 354.

234. First described in detail in Orth, *System*, 313–35.

235. StANü, Erklärung R. Höss, March 14, 1946, ND: NO-1210; ibid., G. Rammler report, January 30, 1946, ND: NO-1200; ibid., testimony O. Pohl, June 13, 1946, ND: NO-4728; ibid., EE by G. Wiebeck, February 28, 1947, ND: NO-2331; IfZ, F 13/6, Bl. 343–54: R. Höss, "Oswald Pohl," November 1946, Bl. 354; Orth, *SS*, 264–65.

236. Orth, *System*, 317–19, 328–29; Wildt, *Generation*, 726–27; *OdT*, vol. 2, 459–61; JVL, JAO, Review of Proceedings, *United States v. Weiss*, n.d. (1946), p. 77; BArchL, B 162/7998, Bl. 623–44: Vernehmung J. Otto, April 1, 1970, Bl. 626; StANü, Erklärung H. Pister, July 2, 1945, p. 41–42, ND: NO-254; Tuchel, "Die Kommandanten des KZ Dachau," 347–48.

237. For a different view, see Buggeln, *Arbeit*, 655.

238. Orth, *System*, 322, 325–26, 329–35. See also Lange, "Neueste Erkenntnisse"; *OdT*, vol. 6, 518–19; Hertz-Eichenrode, *KZ*, vol. 1, 262; NAL, WO 208/4661, statement H. Aumeier, June 29, 1945, p. 13.

239. Orth, *SS*, 267–68; StANü, Erklärung R. Höss, March 14, 1946, ND: NO-1210; ibid., G. Rammler report, January 30, 1946, ND: NO-1200; Wildt, *Generation*, 731–34; Kershaw, *End*, 352, 400; Hördler, "Ordnung," 154; Broszat, *Kommandant*, 222, 281–82; Hillmann, "'Reichsregierung.'"

240. Greiser, *Todesmärsche*, 151–52; Kaplan, "Marsch," 26.

241. Several hundred prisoners were released or handed to the ICRC during the stop at Below forest. See *OdT*, vol. 3, 291–93; Zeiger, "Todesmärsche," 66–68; Orth, *System*, 323; Farré, "Sachsenhausen." The site may also have held some female prisoners from Ravensbrück; Blatman, *Death*, 169–70.

242. LG Cologne, Urteil, October 30, 1967, *JNV*, vol. 26, 797–98; Greiser, *Todesmärsche*, 164; Lasik, "Organizational," 184 (n. 80); Neander, *Mittelbau*, 143; JVL, DJAO, *United States v. Becker*, RaR, n.d. (1947), pp. 49–50; NARA, RG 549, 000–50–9, Box 438, statement S. Melzewski, September 6, 1945. For the reluctance of other guards, see Blatman, *Death*, 110, 114, 420; Greiser, *Todesmärsche*, 99–100, 154, 272–73; Jacobeit, *"Ich,"* 84.

243. Goldhagen, *Executioners*, 332, 363, 367, 371. See also Rothkirchen, "'Final Solution'"; Bauer, "Death Marches," 4, 8. For criticism of this thesis, see Blatman, *Death*, esp. 416; Sprenger, "KZ Groß-Rosen," 1120; Greiser, *Todesmärsche*, 27–29; Buggeln, *Arbeit*, 625.

244. Estimate in Greiser, *Todesmärsche*, 27–28. See also Blatman, *Death*, 194; Kolb, "Kriegsphase," 1135.

245. For the opposite argument, see Goldhagen, *Executioners*, 345.

246. Blatman, *Death*, 417. See also Greiser, *Todesmärsche*, 136, 139–40; BoA, testimony of B. Warsager, September 1, 1946; de Rudder, "Zwangsarbeit," 230–31. The WVHA introduced new insignia for Jews in November 1944, with a yellow stripe over a triangle, though this was rarely used in practice; Hördler, "Ordnung," 272.

247. Laqueur, *Bergen-Belsen*, 106, 112–13, 121.

248. For the opposite view, see Bauer, *Jews*, 241; Sofsky, *Violence*, 104–107; idem, "Perspektiven," 1160–63.

249. See also Neander, *Mittelbau*, 164–65.

250. Some eight to twelve thousand Buchenwald inmates and eight thousand Neuengamme inmates perished on death transports; Greiser, *Todesmärsche*, 9; Buggeln, *Arbeit*, 635, 653.

251. Gedenkstätte Buchenwald, *Buchenwald*, 204–206; Röll, *Sozialdemokraten*, 139–56; *VöB*, September 1, 1944; IfZ, F 13/6, Bl. 355–58: R. Höss, "Gerhard Maurer," November 1946; Kirsten and Kirsten, *Stimmen*, 188–92.

252. For example, see *OdT*, vol. 2, 285; ibid., vol. 4, 459.

253. Kupfer-Koberwitz, *Tagebücher*, quote on 383; Antelme, *Menschengeschlecht*, 89; Langbein, *Menschen*, 149.

254. Kaienburg, *Wirtschaft*, 683; Wagner, *Produktion*, 280–81; Bessel, *Germany 1945*, 12, 24.

255. Strebel, *Celle*.

256. Hertz-Eichenrode, *KZ*, vol. 1, 53–55, 265–74, quote on 272; Lange, "Neueste Erkenntnisse"; Garbe, "'Cap Arcona.'"

257. NARA, RG 549, 000–50–9, Box 438, statement C. Schmalzl, September 11, 1945; ibid., statement X. Triebswetter, September 11, 1945; ibid., statement S. Melzewski, September 6, 1945.

258. Greiser, *Todesmärsche*, 284, 500–502; NARA, RG 549, 000–50–9, Box 438, statement X. Triebswetter, September 11, 1945.

259. Horwitz, *Shadow*, 144–51; Greiser, *Todesmärsche*, 262–68.

260. For example, see NARA, M-1174, roll 2, Bl. 762: examination of G. Neuner, November 26, 1945. See also Horwitz, *Shadow*, 151; Zarusky, "Dachau," 58.

261. Laqueur, *Bergen-Belsen*, 120–28; Herzberg, *Between*, 213; Horwitz, *Shadow*, 152–53; Greiser, *Todesmärsche*, 269–70.

262. For example, see YVA, O 15 E/1761, Protokoll V. Jakubovics, July 9, 1945.

263. Buggeln, *Arbeit*, 145–48; WVHA-D to WVHA-B, August 15, 1944, ND: NO-1990, *TWC*, vol. 5, 388–92.

264. Jacobeit, "Ich," 113–15; Greiser, *Todesmärsche*, 190–93, 197, 273–75; Wagner, *Produktion*, 555; Blatman, *Death*, 429–31.

265. Zarusky, "'Tötung,'" 85; Distel, "29. April," 8. See also Holzhaider, *Sechs.*

266. Greiser, *Todesmärsche*, 125, 161; Erpel, *Vernichtung*, 176–77; Neander, *Mittelbau*, 135–36.

267. Horwitz, *Shadow*, 146–47, 153; NARA, M-1174, roll 2, Bl. 762–70: examination of T. Weigl, November 26, 1945.

268. NARA, RG 549, 000–50–9, Box 438, statement X. Triebswetter, September 11, 1945; Greiser, *Todesmärsche*, 125, 160.

269. Maršálek, *Mauthausen*, quotes on 296; Dietmar, "Häftling X," 131. See also Greiser, *Todesmärsche*, 260–61; Neander, *Mittelbau*, 161–62; Blatman, *Death*, 399, 401–402.

270. JVL, JAO, Review of Proceedings, *United States v. Weiss*, n.d. (1946), quote on 68; Greiser, *Todesmärsche*, 160; Horwitz, *Shadow*, 154.

271. Blatman, *Death*, 270-71, 396-400, 405, 418-19. See also Neander, *Mittelbau*, 135; Schulze, *Zeiten*, 291; Herbert, *Fremdarbeiter*, 330-31, 338-39.

272. Blatman, *Death*, 394-405, 419; Greiser, *Todesmärsche*, 115-23, 132, 167.

273. Most of the survivors were forced on a death march toward Bergen-Belsen. See Strebel, *Celle*, 52-123, quote on 61; Bertram, "8. April 1945."

274. ASL, Kam 5539, L4, Bl. 26-29: Schwertberger Postenchronik, 1945, quote on 28.

275. Obenaus, "Räumung," quote on 542; Blatman, *Death*, 272-342; Neander, *Mittelbau*, 466-73; Gring, "Massaker."

276. Blatman, *Death*, 343-46; Bessel, *1945*, 45, 65.

277. Greiser, *Todesmärsche*, 126-27, 199-201, 274.

278. Broszat, *Kommandant*, 222-23, 281-82, quote on 222; StANü, Erklärung R. Höss, March 14, 1946, ND: NO-1210; Kershaw, *End*, 359-60; Orth, *SS*, 268-69.

279. IfZ, F 13/7, Bl. 388: R. Höss, "Richard Glücks," November 1946; Broszat, *Kommandant*, 224-25; *DAP*, Aussage W. Boger, July 5, 1945, 3251; Naasner, *SS-Wirtschaft*, 334; IfZ, ZS-1590, interrogation G. Witt, November 19, 1946, 9; BArchB, Film 44840, Vernehmung G. Maurer, March 13, 1947, pp. 3-5.

280. Goeschel, *Suicide*, 149-66.

281. Longerich, *Himmler*, 757; BArchL, B 162/7996, Bl. 381-85: Liste von SS-Führern und Unterführern, November 6, 1967; *OdT*, vol. 2, 486. Hans Kammler is also said to have killed himself (Fröbe, "Kammler," 316-17), though there are rumors that he was captured and taken to a U.S. detention center (Karlsch, "Selbstmord").

282. Delmotte shot himself soon after fleeing Dachau in 1945; Langbein, *Menschen*, 559; Lifton, *Doctors*, 311.

283. Sigl, *Todeslager*, 84; Raim, "Westdeutsche Ermittlungen," 223.

284. For this mind-set, see Broszat, *Kommandant*, 222-23.

285. Rózsa, "Solange," 278-79; Maršálek, *Mauthausen*, 331-32; Kaplan, "Marsch," 34.

286. Greiser, *Todesmärsche*, 102; JVL, JAO, Review of Proceedings, *United States v. Weiss*, n.d. (1946), p. 67.

287. Greiser, *Todesmärsche*, quote on 177.

288. Blatman, *Death*, 207; Neander, *Mittelbau*, 150.

289. YVA, 033/989, anonymous testimony (by W. Simoni), n.d. (1947), 40.

290. Kaplan, "Marsch," 31-33, quote on 31; Zeiger, "Todesmärsche," 68; WL, P.III.h. No. 804, M. Flothuis, "Arbeit für die Philips-Fabrik," January 1958, p. 16.

291. Perhaps 150,000 prisoners died in the last five weeks of the war (out of around 550,000 KL prisoners at the start of April). Of the remaining c. 400,000 prisoners, maybe 250,000 were liberated inside, around 20,000 were released abroad, and thousands more released inside Germany. This would mean that well over one hundred thousand men, women, and children found freedom during marches and train transports.

292. Bárta, "Tagebuch," quote on 96; Freund, "KZ Ebensee," 22, 31; Freund, *Toten*, 337; Evans, "Introduction," xvi. Among the last satellites to be reached by Allied troops were the small Mauthausen camp St. Lambrecht on May 11, 1945, and the even smaller Flossenbürg camp Schlackenwerth the following day; *OdT*, vol. 4, 250-52, 429-33.

293. Rózsa, "Solange," 302-22, quotes on 290, 316, 323; *OdT*, vol. 4, 151-54.

294. Overesch, *Buchenwald*, 60-85, quote on 68; Greiser, *Todesmärsche*, 76.

295. "Dachau Captured by Americans Who Kill Guards, Liberate 32,000," *New York Times*, May 1, 1945; KZ-Gedenkstätte Dachau, *Gedenkbuch*, 9, 13, 19; Rost, *Goethe*, 302.

296. Quote in W. Cowling to his parents, April 30, 1945, in Dann, *Dachau*, 21-24. See also Zámečník, *Dachau*, 390-96; Distel, "29. April," 8-11; Rost, *Goethe*, 304-305; Antelme, *Menschengeschlecht*, 401.

297. Kupfer-Koberwitz, *Tagebücher*, 419, 425, 444–45.
298. Quotes in Kupfer-Koberwitz, *Tagebücher*, 445; Ballerstedt, "Liebe," 207. See also Czech, *Kalendarium*, 322, 328–29; Stein, *Juden*, 126; Zámečník, *Dachau*, 365–67; ITS, docs 5278997#1, 5323555#1, 5364738#1, 5376484#1, 9896136#1, 9918546#1, 9934351#1, 9943226#2 (my thanks to Susanne Urban for these documents); BLA, EG 74002, EE by M. Choinowski, March 1, 1946 and June 16, 1958; ibid., Bay. Hilfswerk, Fürsorge-bericht, April 24, 1949; ibid., Antrag M. Choinowski, June 23, 1958.

Epilogue

1. Antelme, *Menschengeschlecht*, 401–402; BoA, interview with J. Bassfreund, September 20, 1946. On the postwar use of the term "survivor," Reinisch, "Introduction." For the liberation of the camps, see now also Stone, *Liberation* (my thanks to Dan Stone for sharing an early draft).
2. Testimony of P. H., February 1946, in Heberer, *Children*, 384.
3. For this and the previous paragraph, see BLA, EG 74002. Additional information in R. König to M. Choinowski, n.d. (late 1953) (copy in possession of the author); ITS, Doc. No. 90343219#1; Shephard, *Road*, 364–79; Cohen, *Case*, 30. Quotes in BLA, EG 74002, M. Choinowski, Antrag auf Erteilung eines Bezugsscheins, April 14, 1948; ibid., M. Choinowski to Landesentschädigungsamt, April 20, 1957; M. Choinowski to R. König, May 10, 1965 (copy in possession of the author; my thanks to Rita von Borck for this letter and other information).
4. For the quotes in this and the previous paragraph, see DaA, Nr. 27376, E. Kupfer to K. Halle, September 1, 1960; StAL, EL 350 I/Bü 8033, E. Kupfer to Landesamt für Wiedergutmachung, November 28, 1979. For Kupfer's postwar life, see StAL, EL 350 I/Bü 8033; Distel, "Vorwort," 15–17; ITS, doc. 81062064#1.
5. Todorov, *Facing*, 263; Orth, *SS*, 273–95.
6. WL, P.III.h. No. 494, A. Lehmann, "Im Lager Bergen Belsen," 1946, quote on 4; ibid., No. 573, A. Lehmann, "Das Lager Vught," n.d., 33; ibid., No. 416, A. Lehmann, "Die Evakuations-Transporte," n.d. (1946); Koker, *Edge*, 369–70.
7. My calculation is based on an estimated 250,000 prisoners being liberated from the KL during the final five weeks of Nazi rule.
8. WL, P.III.h. No. 494, A. Lehmann, "Im Lager Bergen Belsen," 1946, quote on 5; Stiftung, *Bergen-Belsen*, 217; Reilly, *Belsen*, 25–26; report G. Hughes, June 1945, in Niedersächsische Landeszentrale, *Bergen-Belsen*, 186–93.
9. Shephard, *Road*, 69–72; idem, *Daybreak*, 28–32; Zweig, "Feeding," 843–45; Zelizer, *Remembering*, 64.
10. Abzug, *Inside*, passim.
11. Quote in Strebel, *Ravensbrück*, 503. See also Gutterman, *Bridge*, 225–26; Erpel, *Vernichtung*, 193–94; WL, P.III.h. No. 864, G. Deak, "Wie eine junge Frau Auschwitz und den Todes-Marsch überlebt hat," March 1958, p. 18; ibid., No. 828, T. Krieg, "Der 'Totenzug' von Bergen-Belsen nach Theresienstadt," December 1957, p. 8. For mass rapes of German women by Soviet soldiers during the occupation more generally, see Grossmann, *Jews*, 48–71; Beevor, *Berlin*.
12. WL, P.III.h. No. 494, A. Lehmann, "Im Lager Bergen Belsen," 1946, quote on 5; Helweg-Larsen et al., *Famine*, 255–62; Reckendrees, "Leben," 101–102; Vaisman, *Auschwitz*, 65–66; Kielar, *Anus Mundi*, 402; Goldstein et al., *Individuelles*, 188; YVA, M-1/E 121, Aussage M. Weiss, June 24, 1946, p. 8; MacAuslan, "Aspects," 50–55. The problem of overeating was exacerbated by well-meaning soldiers who handed out excessive amounts of rich food, upsetting the inmates' already damaged digestive system.
13. Laqueur, *Bergen-Belsen*, 129–32, quote on 132; Greiser, *Todesmärsche*, 201, 207–14.
14. Laqueur, *Bergen-Belsen*, 136.

15. Quote in Schulze, *Zeiten*, 299. See also Meyer, *Kriegsgefangenen*, 80.

16. Schulze, *Zeiten*, 91, 120–21, 295–96, 299–300; Meyer, *Kriegsgefangenen*, 81–85; Vogel, *Tagebuch*, 166; Greiser, *Todesmärsche*, 281.

17. Quotes in Abzug, *Inside*, 132; Reilly, *Belsen*, 41; MacAuslan, "Aspects," 74. See also Shephard, *Road*, 67, 101–102; Flanagan and Bloxham, *Remembering*, 65–66.

18. Quote in letter by A. Horwell, May 1945, in Flanagan and Bloxham, *Remembering*, 65. For the use of the term "organize," see Laqueur, *Bergen-Belsen*, 131; YVA, 033/989, anonymous testimony (by W. Simoni), n.d. (1947), p. 41.

19. Rovan, *Geschichten*, 293–97; Zámečník, *Dachau*, 398.

20. WL, P.III.h. No. 494, A. Lehmann, "Im Lager Bergen Belsen," 1946, p. 5.

21. MacAuslan, "Aspects," 65, 69–82, 106–107, 110–11, quote on 75. See also Reilly, *Belsen*, 26–28, 33–40; Flanagan and Bloxham, *Remembering*, 21–40; Kolb, *Bergen-Belsen*, 315; Stiftung, *Bergen-Belsen*, 253.

22. Benz, "Befreiung." See also Overesch, "Ernst Thapes," 657, 661–63, 670; Greiser, *Todesmärsche*, 280; Erpel, *Vernichtung*, 195.

23. Quotes in ITS, 1.1.6.0/folder 21, Bl. 2–3: Lagerälteste to Blockältesten, May 1, 1945; E. Fleck and E. Tenenbaum, "Buchenwald," April 24, 1945, in Niethammer, *Antifaschismus*, 196. See also Greiser, "'Sie starben,'" 122–23; Benz, "Befreiung," 39–42, 47, 53; Maršálek, *Mauthausen*, 338–39; Freund, *Zement*, 434–35.

24. Quote in Benz, "Befreiung," 51. In Belsen, the prisoner organization was weaker; Kolb, *Bergen-Belsen*, 165.

25. Szeintuch, "'Tkhias Hameysim,'" quote on 215 (translation by Kim Wünschmann); Poljan, "'Menschen,'" 87; Mankowitz, *Life*, 39; Königseder and Wetzel, *Lebensmut*, 19–20.

26. Gross, *Fünf Minuten*, 214, 217, 244, 263–64, quote on 216; Overesch, "Ernst Thapes," 666–68; idem, *Buchenwald*, 121; Freund, *Zement*, 429; Hammermann, "'Dachau.'"

27. Benz, "Befreiung," quote on 61; Poljan, "'Menschen,'" 86–87.

28. WL, P.III.h. No. 494, A. Lehmann, "Im Lager Bergen Belsen," 1946, quote on 6; MacAuslan, "Aspects," 134–59; D. Sington report, 1948, in Niedersächsische Landeszentrale, *Bergen-Belsen*, 202–203.

29. J. Pogonowski to his family, n.d. (November 1942?), in Piper, *Briefe*, 36–39.

30. Hördler, "Ordnung," quote on 313; Schelvis, *Sobibor*, 2.

31. Bessel, *1945*, 255–62; Shephard, *Road*, 63–64; Judt, *Postwar*, 29.

32. Laqueur, *Bergen-Belsen*, 139; WL, P.III.h. No. 494, A. Lehmann, "Im Lager Bergen Belsen," 1946, p. 5; Sellier, *Dora*, 333; Judt, *Postwar*, 29–30; Rovan, *Geschichten*, 256–76. On France, see also Koreman, "Hero's Homecoming"; Dreyfus, "Aufnahme"; Bauerkämper, *Gedächtnis*, 227–28; Michelet, *Freiheitsstraße*.

33. Poljan, "'Menschen,'" quote on 84; Distel and Zarusky, "Dreifach," quote on 101; Shephard, *Road*, 78–83; Erpel, *Vernichtung*, 211–14.

34. Shephard, *Road*, 100–101; Gerlach and Aly, *Kapitel*, 409.

35. BoA, interview with L. Stumachin, September 8, 1946.

36. Gross, *Fear*. See also Zaremba, "Nicht"; Königseder and Wetzel, *Lebensmut*, 47–57; Shephard, *Road*, 185–87; Michael, *Davidstern*; Szita, *Ungarn*, 211, 216; Ellger, *Zwangsarbeit*, 254–55.

37. Königseder, "Aus dem KZ," 226–28, 231; Shephard, *Road*, 83–94, 200–211; Holian, *Between*, 213–36; Pilecki, *Auschwitz*, liii–liv; Debski, *Battlefield*, 245; Lowe, *Savage*, 212–29. For background, see Stone, *Goodbye*.

38. Quotes in BoA, interview with L. Stumachin, September 8, 1946. See also Buergenthal, *Child*, 134–65; Segev, *Million*, 118–19, 153–86.

39. Kogon, *Theory*, 300.

40. Quote in WL, P.III.h. No. 795, "Gipsy-Camp Birkenau," January 1958. See also Pilichowski, *Verjährung*, 166–69; Cohen, *Human*, 63–81; Langbein, *Menschen*, 549–50; Helweg-Larsen et al., *Famine*, 418.

41. Levi, "Memory," 12. More generally, see Langer, *Holocaust*.

42. Nyiszli, *Auschwitz*, 158; Evans, "Introduction," xvii. He died of a heart attack in 1956.

43. Helweg-Larsen et al., *Famine*, quote on 436; Delbo, *Auschwitz*, 257–67; Leys, *Guilt*; Niederland, *Folgen*, 8–9, 229–35; Jureit and Orth, *Überlebensgeschichten*, 166–70.

44. Freund, "Mauthausenprozess," quote on 43. More generally, see Pick, *Wiesenthal*; Segev, *Wiesenthal*.

45. For example, see Stengel, *Langbein*.

46. Wachsmann, "Introduction" (2009), xviii–xxii; Todorov, *Hope*, 148–58.

47. Quote in author's interview with K. Kendall, June 1996. See also Gilbert, *Boys*, 140–41, 203–204, 385; Jureit and Orth, *Überlebensgeschichten*, 56–57; Ellger, *Zwangsarbeit*, 261.

48. LSW, Bl. 44–66: Vernehmung S. Dragon, May 10, 11, and 17, 1946, quote on 66; Fings, *Krieg*, 297; Jureit and Orth, *Überlebensgeschichten*, 170; Niederland, *Folgen*, 170.

49. Jagoda et al., "'Nächte,'" 222.

50. Greif, *Wir weinten*, 50, 122–24.

51. Langbein, *Menschen*, quote on 540; Fröbe et al., "Nachkriegsgeschichte," 547.

52. Lichtenstein, *Majdanek*, 82–85.

53. DAP, Aussage L. Schlinger, September 14, 1964, quote on 17788; Renz, "Tonband-mitschnitte."

54. Schmidt, *Justice*, quote on 237. The ex-prisoner was sentenced to three months' imprisonment for dishonoring the tribunal, though later freed on bail.

55. DA, A 3233, A. Carl to H. Schwarz, November 19, 1967; Lasker-Wallfisch, *Inherit*, 128.

56. Letter M. Nadjary, November 1944, in SMAB, *Inmitten*, 270–73; Nadjary survived and emigrated to the United States. See also Bacharach, *Worte*, 60–65; Roseman, "'. . . but of revenge,'" 79–82; Langbein, *Menschen*, 133; Stoop, *Geheimberichte*, 52; LBIJMB, MF 425, L. Bendix, "Konzentrationslager Deutschland," 1937–38, vol. 4, 59, 64.

57. Bohnen, "Als"; Gutterman, *Bridge*, 224.

58. Bárta, "Geschichte," quote on 161; Freund, *Zement*, 419–20; Liblau, *Kapos*, 144; Niethammer, *Antifaschismus*, 65; Wagner, *Produktion*, 445; Szita, *Ungarn*, 192–93; Goldstein et al., *Individuelles*, 84; Stiftung, *Bergen-Belsen*, 231; Cramer, *Belsen*, 88–89.

59. There were fewer than eighty vigilante killings in the first days after the liberation of Buchenwald (which held over twenty thousand inmates); Abzug, *Inside*, 52.

60. Quote in Heberer, *Children*, 381. See also BoA, interview with I. Unikowski, August 2, 1946; Gutterman, *Bridge*, 224; Todorov, *Facing*, 216–20.

61. The best account of the events is Zarusky, "Erschießungen."

62. Kielar, *Anus Mundi*, 405; BoA, interview with B. Piskorz, September 1, 1946.

63. Hammermann, "Kriegsgefangenenlager"; Jardim, *Mauthausen*, 22; Sigel, *Interesse*, 38. For the early arrival of war crimes investigators, see Wickert, "Aufdeckung"; DaA, A 3675, testimony Colonel Chavez, n.d.; Jardim, *Mauthausen*, 62–63; Cramer, *Belsen*, 47–92.

64. Quote in Orth, *SS*, 286. See also Sigel, *Interesse*, passim; Jardim, *Mauthausen*, 10–50; Yavnai, "U.S. Army." Of the thirty-six defendants sentenced to death, eight later had their sentences commuted.

65. Cramer, *Belsen*. See also Jardim, *Mauthausen*, 36–37; *OdT*, vol. 1, 348–49.

66. Form, "Justizpolitische," 58–61; Paetow, "Ravensbrück-Prozess."

67. *OdT*, vol. 1, 350–51; Eiber, "Nürnberg," 45–48; Morsch, *Sachsenburg*, 46; Sigl, *Todeslager*.

68. Prusin, "Poland's Nuremberg." See also Struk, *Photographing*, 119–23; BArchL, B 162/1124, Bl. 2288–316: Volkstribunal Krakow, Urteil, September 5, 1946; IfZ, G 20/1, Volkstribunal Krakow, Urteil, December 22, 1947; Marszałek, *Majdanek*, 248; Harding, *Hanns*, 240–45; Rudorff, "Strafverfolgung," 337–38, 346. After his release from Polish captivity in 1958, Dr. Kremer was tried once more in West Germany, but did not serve any of his ten-year sentence, as it was set off against the time he had served in Poland. He died later in the 1960s; Rawicz, "Dokument," 11–16.

69. Weckel, *Bilder*, 115–23, 219–26, quote on 222; Indictment, n.d. (October 1945), *IMT*, vol. 1, 27–92; Orth, *SS*, 282; Broszat, *Kommandant*, 226–27; Rudorff, "Strafverfolgung," 333.

70. The harshest penalty was eight years in prison. See Lindner, "Urteil"; Wagner, *IG Auschwitz*, 297–311. Not all managers with links to the KL system were as fortunate: the owner of the Zyklon B supplier Tesch & Stabenow and his second-in-command were sentenced to death by a British court in March 1946; UN War Crimes Commission, *Law Reports*, 93–103.

71. Weindling, *Nazi Medicine*; Schmidt, *Justice*.

72. Schulte, "Zentrum"; Von Kellenbach, *Mark*, 88–97; Orth, *SS*, 282–86.

73. For Camp SS defense strategies (also used below), see Jardim, *Mauthausen*, 115–67; Cramer, *Belsen*, 193–234; Hammermann, "Verteidigungsstrategien."

74. Quotes in JVL, JAO, Review of Proceedings, *United States v. Weiss*, n.d. (1946), p. 136; NAL, WO 235/19, statement J. Kramer, May 22, 1945, p. 14.

75. Von Kellenbach, *Mark*, quote on 95; Cramer, *Belsen*, 260.

76. Wolfangel, "'Nie,'" quote on 76; Von Kellenbach, *Mark*, quote on 91 (my translation); Hammermann, "Verteidigungsstrategien," 90–95; Cramer, *Belsen*, 199–201; Kretzer, *NS-Täterschaft*, 336–37; Roseman, "Beyond Conviction?"

77. NARA, M-1174, roll 3, Bl. 1428–36: examination of O. Moll, December 5–6, 1945, Bl. 1431, 1434. Initially, Moll had worked in agriculture in Auschwitz, but he was soon transferred to the gas chambers (Hördler, "Ordnung," 152). He was hanged in May 1946.

78. BArchB, Film 44837, Vernehmung A. Liebehenschel, September 18, 1946, quote on 26; USHMM, 1998.A.0247, reel 15, NTN 169, Bl. 52–53: Gnadengesuch A. Liebehenschel, December 24, 1947; IfZ, G 20/1, Volkstribunal Krakow, Urteil, December 22, 1947, p. 102.

79. JVL, JAO, Review of Proceedings, *United States v. Weiss*, n.d. (1946), 106; Sigel, *Interesse*, 71–75. See also Jardim, *Mauthausen*, 107; Cramer, *Belsen*, 201–208; Hammermann, "Verteidigungsstrategien," 86, 91, 95.

80. Broszat, *Kommandant*, 76–79, 229–35; Orth, *SS*, 282–83; Prusin, "Poland's Nuremberg," 11–12.

81. Quote in USHMM, 1998.A.0247, NTN 169, Bl. 60: Gnadengesuch Aumeier, December 24, 1947. See also ibid., reel 15, Bl. 184–93: statement of H. Aumeier, December 15, 1947; Hördler, "Ordnung," 49; APMO, Proces Liebehenschel, ZO 54, Bl. 19–29: interrogation H. Aumeier, August 10, 1945; ibid., Bl. 33–39: questionnaire H. Aumeier; NAL, WO 208/4661, statement H. Aumeier, July 25, 1945; Langbein, *Menschen*, 559–60.

82. Sigel, *Interesse*, 196; Greiser, *Todesmärsche*, 449; Cramer, *Belsen*, 390–91.

83. Schulte, *Zwangsarbeit*, 434; Tuchel, *Inspektion*, 217–18; Orth, "SS-Täter," 55–56; Riedel, *Ordnungshüter*, 338. Probably the most senior WVHA official to get away, escaping from Allied captivity in 1946, was August Harbaum, Glücks's former deputy.

84. Jardim, *Mauthausen*, 82–83, 165–67, 206–207, 213–14, 216; Greiser, "Dachauer," 166; Cramer, *Belsen*, 245–46; Pohl, "Sowjetische," 138.

85. Jardim, *Mauthausen*, 96, 102, 202; Hammermann, "Verteidigungsstrategien," 88–89; Eisfeld, *Mondsüchtig*, 164–73; Klee, *Auschwitz*, 90, 253. More generally, see Jacobsen, *Paperclip*.

86. Just one example: Obersturmbannführer Mummenthey, the former head of DESt in charge of all SS quarries, was sentenced to life in November 1947 and released early in 1953, while Rottenführer Klimowitsch, a regular sentry who had patrolled the Mauthausen quarry, was sentenced to death in May 1946 and executed; Schulte, *Zwangsarbeit*, 473; JVL, DJAO, *United States v. Altfuldisch*, RaR, March 1946, p. 46.

87. Sigel, *Interesse*, 160, 194; idem, "Dachauer," 77; Bryant, "Militärgerichtsprozesse," 120–22; Wagner, *Produktion*, 568. According to a U.S. poll in late 1944, most respondents demanded that Germans guilty of KL murders should be executed, preferably "in poison gas chambers, by hanging, electrocution, or by firing squad"; Gallup, *Poll*, 472.

88. Kretzer, *NS-Täterschaft*, 131–33; JVL, JAO, Review of Proceedings, *United States v. Weiss*, n.d. (1946), p. 162; Sigel, *Interesse*, 57; Jardim, *Mauthausen*, 47.

89. Cramer, *Belsen*, 114–15. The prisoner was found not guilty.

90. Yavnai, "U.S. Army," 62–63. Israeli judges often handed out lighter sentences in trials of former KL Kapos during the 1950s and 1960s; Ben-Naftali and Tuval, "Punishing."

91. Cramer, *Belsen*, 115, 249, 257. See also Raim, *Dachauer*, 248; Bessmann and Buggeln, "Befehlsgeber," 540.

92. Brzezicki et al., "Funktionshäftlinge," 238; Wagner, *IG Auschwitz*, 200, 321–22.

93. NARA, M-1174, roll 3, examination of L. Knoll, December 7, 1945, quote on 1593 ("capo" in the original); JVL, JAO, Review of Proceedings, *United States v. Weiss*, n.d. (1946), pp. 107–108, 155–56; Zámečník, *Dachau*, 154–55; Sigel, *Interesse*, 57–63, 75. Knoll was also known by the first names Christian and Ludwig.

94. Between 1945 and 1953, just 673 of around 6,400 surviving Auschwitz SS officials were known to have been tried by Polish courts, which conducted most Auschwitz trials; Lasik, "Apprehension."

95. Eiber, "Nürnberg," 43–44; Jardim, *Mauthausen*, 30–32, 112–13.

96. Beischl, *Wirths*, 212–16, quote on 228; Klee, *Personenlexikon*, 112.

97. Keller, *Günzburg*, 60; Stangneth, *Eichmann*, 377. More generally, see Schneppen, *Odessa*; Stahl, *Nazi-Jagd*.

98. Raim, *Justiz*, 647–53, 1007–39; Wieland, "Ahndung," 15–51, 57; Eichmüller, "Strafverfolgung"; Eschebach, "Frauenbilder." Mennecke was sentenced primarily for his part in the general "euthanasia" program; he died before the death penalty was executed; LG Frankfurt, Urteil, December 21, 1946, *JNV*, vol. 1, 143–44; Klee, *Personenlexikon*, 403, 601.

99. Kuretsidis-Haider, "Österreichische," quote on 257.

100. Schley, *Nachbar*, 1–3.

101. Hertz-Eichenrode, *KZ*, vol. 1, 344–52, quote on 351; *OdT*, vol. 5, 546; Greiser, *Todesmärsche*, 297–315; Wagner, *Produktion*, 565; Raim, *Dachauer*, 276–77; Erpel, *Vernichtung*, 200; Perz, *KZ-Gedenkstätte*, 34–35.

102. Brink, *Ikonen*, 23–78, quote on 46; Weckel, *Bilder*, 151–72, 418–56; Peitsch, "*Deutschlands*," 107.

103. Cramer, *Belsen*, 271; Erpel, "Ravensbrück-Prozesse"; Urban, "Kollektivschuld."

104. Greiser, "Dachauer," 170; JVL, DJAO, *United States v. Prince zu Waldeck*, RaR, November 15, 1947, p. 95. See also Heschel, "Atrocity"; Kretzer, *NS-Täterschaft*; Jaiser, "Grese."

105. Brink, *Ikonen*, 84, 89; Weckel, *Bilder*, 517–18; Neitzel, *Abgehört*, 313–15.

106. Peitsch, "*Deutschlands*," 102–103; Schulze, *Zeiten*, 76, 286; Marcuse, *Legacies*, 80–81.

107. Schley, *Nachbar*, quotes on 4, emphasis in the original; Knigge, "Schatten," 156; Weckel, *Bilder*, 170–72, 493, 528; Chamberlin, "Todesmühlen"; Brink, *Ikonen*, 84–93; Peitsch, "*Deutschlands*," 96, 131, 142; Steinbacher, *Dachau*, 220; Johe, "Volk," 332; Rüther, *Köln*, 908–10. More generally, see Frei, *Vergangenheitspolitik*; Moeller, *War Stories*; Marcuse, *Legacies*.

108. Stone, *Goodbye*, chapters 1 and 2.

109. Marcuse, *Legacies*, 151–57; Kansteiner, "Losing," 108–12.

110. Sigel, *Interesse*, 159–93; Jardim, *Mauthausen*, 208–11; Urban, "Kollektivschuld."

111. Klee, *Auschwitz*, 385–88; Segev, *Soldiers*, 228.

112. Eichmüller, *Keine Generalamnestie*, 226, 425, 428–30.

113. Steiner, "SS," 432–33, 441; Mallmann and Paul, "Sozialisation," 19–20.

114. Orth, *SS*, quote on 291; Mailänder Koslov, *Gewalt*, 230–31, 299, 488; Steiner, "SS," 441; Schwarz, *Frau*, 162; Dicks, *Licensed*.

115. Goschler, *Schuld*; idem, "Wiedergutmachungspolitik."

116. Wollheim instructed his lawyer in 1958 to end the legal proceedings; Rumpf, *Fall Wollheim*. For an unsuccessful civil case, see Irmer, "'Stets.'"

117. Distel, "Morde," 113. Steinbrenner was released in 1962 and committed suicide two years later.

118. Van Dam and Giordano, *KZ-Verbrechen*; Gregor, *Haunted*, 250–55; Eichmüller, *Keine Generalamnestie*, 155, 174–81, 214–19, 430; "Charge of Killing 11,000 Prisoners," *The Times*, October 14, 1958; LG Bonn, Urteil, February 6, 1959, *JNV*, vol. 15.

119. Dicks, *Licensed*, quote on 100; AEKIR, 7 NL 016 Nr. 95, Sorge to Schlingensiepen, March 3, 1965, January 4, 1970, March 1, 1970; Riedle, *Angehörigen*, 203, 219.

120. K. Adenauer, "Geleitwort," in Michelet, *Freiheitsstrasse*, 5–6.

121. Pendas, *Frankfurt*, 20–21, 249–52, quote on 256; Wittmann, *Beyond*, 3, 174–90; Orth, *SS*, 289–90; Weinke, *Verfolgung*, 82–93, 333; Horn, *Erinnerungsbilder*; Wolf, "'Mass Deception.'"

122. Some cases, including the 1970s proceedings against the Auschwitz sterilization doctor Horst Schumann, collapsed because the defendants were judged too ill (Schilter, "Schumann," 106–107). Others never came to court because the offenses were judged to fall under the statute of limitations, as in the case of a lengthy investigation of former WVHA-D managers, finally abandoned in 1974 (BArchL B 162/7999, Bl. 768–937: StA Koblenz, EV, July 25, 1974).

123. Zimmermann, *NS-Täter*, 169–93.

124. Przyrembel, "Transfixed," quote on 396; LG Augsburg, Urteil, January 15, 1951, *JNV*, vol. 8; StAMü, Justizvollzugsanstalten Nr. 13948/2, Vermerk, ORR Meyer, February 1967. The focus of later trials on the bestial behavior of defendants was a result of homicide falling under the statute of limitations in 1960, which meant that prosecutors had to prove "bloodlust" or "base motives" to secure a murder conviction; Pendas, *Frankfurt*, 56–61; Wittmann, *Beyond*, 36–53.

125. Gregor, *Haunted*, 265; Pendas, *Frankfurt*, 253–54; Wittmann, *Beyond*, 271–72.

126. Marcuse, *Legacies*, 335–71; DaA, 14.444, *Die Vergessenen*, Nr. 3, July 1946; Ayaß, "Schwarze"; Baumann, "Winkel-Züge"; von dem Knesebeck, *Roma*; Mussmann, *Homosexuelle*. The failure of the 1946 journal owed something to the political extremism of one of its founders, Karl Jochheim-Armin, a former member of Otto Strasser's Nazi breakaway Schwarze Front, who remained a far-right activist until his death in 1984; *Schwarze Front* 3 (2008); Eiber, *"Ich wusste,"* 128–29.

127. Silbermann and Stoffers, *Auschwitz*; Paul, "Täter," 33–67.

128. Kuretsidis-Haider, "Österreichische Prozesse," 250–52, 263–65, quote on 252; idem, "Verfolgung"; Uhl, "Victim"; Allen, "Realms."

129. Wieland, "Ahndung," 60–90; Bauerkämper, *Gedächtnis*, 132–37, 195–97; Weinke, *Verfolgung*, 344–54; Diercks, "Gesucht"; Stone, *Goodbye*, chapter 1.

130. KPD Leipzig, *Buchenwald!*, quote on 96; Niethammer, *Antifaschismus*, passim; Goschler, *Schuld*, 407–11; Overesch, *Buchenwald*, 101; Langbein, *Menschen*, 22; Hartewig, "Wolf," 941–43; Gring, "'zwei Feuern'"; Schiffner, "Cap Arcona-Gedenken"; Borodziej, *Polens*, 270.

131. Overesch, *Buchenwald*, 62–63, 78–81, 261–328, quote on 326. See also *OdT*, vol. 1, 317–18; Niven, *Buchenwald*, 56–71; Reichel, *Politik*, 101–106; Endlich, "Orte," 354–58; Knigge, "Schatten," 165–69; Marcuse, *Legacies*, ill. 74; idem, "Afterlife," 200.

132. For this and the previous paragraph, see Greiner, *Terror*. See also Ritscher et al., *Speziallager*, 7–10, 64, 70–73, 216–17; Wachsmann, *Prisons*, 357–58; *OdT*, vol. 6, 44. For abuses in British captivity, see Cobain, *Cruel*.

133. Overesch, *Buchenwald*, 261–300; idem, "Ernst Thapes," 658; Reichel, *Politik*, 102–103; Niven, *Buchenwald*, 56–71.

134. Marcuse, "Afterlife," 203.

135. Huener, *Auschwitz*. See also Citroen and Starzyńska, *Auschwitz*; Kucia and Olszewski, "Auschwitz." For other Polish KL memorials, see Marcuse, "Afterlife," 191–94.

136. Perz, *KZ-Gedenkstätte*. My thanks to Andreas Kranebitter for the 2012 figure.

137. For this and the previous paragraph, see Marcuse, *Legacies*; idem, "Afterlife," 189–90, 195–99; Prenninger, "Riten," quote on 192; Endlich, "Orte," 359; Reichel, *Politik*, 124.

138. For a brief survey, see Niven, *Buchenwald*, 201–204.

139. For one example, see Hett, *Crossing*, 258–59. More generally, see Wachsmann and Steinbacher, *Linke*.

140. Goschler, "Wiedergutmachungspolitik," 79–84. For reparations for forced laborers from 2000, idem, *Entschädigung*; Hense, *Verhinderte Entschädigung*.

141. Reichel et al., "'Zweite Geschichte,'" 19–20; Schmid, "Deutungsmacht," 206–209; Siebeck, "'Raum,'" 75–76; Endlich, "Orte," 367–69.

142. Skriebeleit, "Ansätze," 19–20.

143. Garbe, "Wiederentdeckte."

144. My thanks to Dirk Riedel for showing me around on March 22, 2013. I am also grateful to other staff at the Dachau memorial—Albert Knoll, Rebecca Ribarek, and Ulrich Unseld—for their assistance that day. Quotes in H. Holzhaider, "Zeugnis wider das Vergessen," *Süddeutsche Zeitung*, May 2 and 3, 2009; G. Hammermann, "Bezug zur Gegenwart," ibid., March 22, 2013. For signage, see Marcuse, *Legacies*, ill. 77.

145. For the use of these terms in Holocaust historiography, see Schleunes, *Twisted Road*; Browning, *Fateful Months*. More generally on Auschwitz, see Pressac and Van Pelt, "Machinery," 213.

146. For his critique of Giorgio Agamben's work, see Mazower, "Foucault," quote on 31. For a survey of the debate about modernization, see Stone, *Histories*, 113–59.

147. Quote in Debski, *Battlefield*, 206.

Sources

Archives

Archiv der Evangelischen Kirche im Rheinland, Düsseldorf
Archiv der Gedenkstätte Buchenwald
Archiv der Gedenkstätte Dachau
Archiv der Gedenkstätte Sachsenhausen
Archiv der KZ-Gedenkstätte Neuengamme
Archiv der sozialen Demokratie, Bonn
Archiv der Stadt Linz
Archiwum Państwowe Muzeum w Oświęcimiu
Bayerisches Hauptstaatsarchiv, Munich
Bayerisches Landesentschädigungsamt, Munich
Behörde des Bundesbeauftragten für die Unterlagen des Staatssicherheitsdienstes der ehemaligen DDR, Berlin
Brandenburgisches Landeshauptarchiv, Potsdam
Bundesarchiv, Abteilung Filmarchiv, Berlin
Bundesarchiv, Berlin
Bundesarchiv, Koblenz
Bundesarchiv, Ludwigsburg
Deutsches Rundfunkarchiv, Frankfurt am Main
Forschungsstelle für Zeitgeschichte, Hamburg
Geheimes Staatsarchiv Preußischer Kulturbesitz, Berlin
Hessisches Hauptstaatsarchiv, Wiesbaden
Hoover Institution Archives, Stanford
Institut für Zeitgeschichte, Munich
International Tracing Service, Bad Arolsen
Landesarchiv Baden-Württemberg, Staatsarchiv Ludwigsburg
Landesarchiv Berlin
Landesarchiv NRW, Abteilung Rheinland, Düsseldorf
Landesgericht für Strafsachen, Vienna

Landeshauptarchiv Sachsen-Anhalt, Magdeburg
Leo Baeck Institute Archives, Berlin
National Archives, London
National Archives, Washington, D.C.
New York Public Library
Niedersächsisches Hauptstaatsarchiv, Hanover
Niedersächsisches Landesarchiv, Staatsarchiv Oldenburg
Politisches Archiv des Auswärtigen Amtes, Berlin
Staatsarchiv Augsburg
Staatsarchiv München
Staatsarchiv Nürnberg
Stadtarchiv Weimar
Stiftung Dokumentationsarchiv des österreichischen Widerstandes, Vienna
United States Holocaust Memorial Museum, Washington, D.C.
Wiener Library, London
Yad Vashem Archives, Jerusalem
Yale University Library, New Haven
YIVO Institute for Jewish Research, New York

Electronic Sources

Boberach, H. (ed.), *Regimekritik, Widerstand und Verfolgung in Deutschland und den besetzten Gebieten* (Munich, 1999–2001), in K. G. Saur Verlag, *National Socialism, Holocaust, Resistance and Exile, 1933–1945*, online database.
Boder Archive, Voices of the Holocaust, http://voices.iit.edu
Die Toten des KZ Mittelbau-Dora 1943–1945, http://totenbuch.dora.de
Directmedia (ed.), *Kurt Tucholsky. Werke–Briefe–Materialien*, CD-ROM (Berlin, 2007).
——, *Legendäre Lexika*, DVD-ROM (Berlin, 2006).
——, *Max Weber: Gesammelte Werke*, CD-ROM (Berlin, 2004).
Fritz Bauer Institut, SMAB (eds.), *Der Auschwitz-Prozeß*, DVD-Rom (Berlin, 2004).
Gedenkstätte Sachsenhausen (ed.), *Gegen das Vergessen*, CD-ROM (Munich, 2002).
Harvard Law School, Nuremberg Trials Project, http://nuremberg.law.harvard.edu
Heinrich Himmler's private letters, serialized on www.welt.de/himmler/
IfZ (ed.), *Akten der Partei-Kanzlei der NSDAP*, 6 vols. (Munich, 1983–92), in K. G. Saur Verlag, *National Socialism, Holocaust, Resistance and Exile, 1933–1945*, online database.
Jewish Virtual Library, www.jewishvirtuallibrary.org
K. G. Saur Verlag (ed.), *Tarnschriften 1933 bis 1945* (Munich, 1997), in idem., *National Socialism, Holocaust, Resistance and Exile, 1933–1945*, online database.
Konzentrationslager Buchenwald. Die Toten, 1937–1945, http://totenbuch.buchenwald.de
Kulka, O. D. & Jäckel, E. (eds.), *Die Juden in den geheimen NS-Stimmungsberichten 1933–1945*, CD-Rom (Düsseldorf, 2004).
Lund University Library, Voices from Ravensbrück, www.ub.lu.se/collections/digital-collections.
Overesch, M., F. Saal, W. Herda, and Y. Artelt (eds.), *Das Dritte Reich. Daten, Bilder, Dokumente*, CD-Rom (Berlin, 2004).
Oxford Dictionary of National Biography, www.oxforddnb.com
Warneke, P., *Nationalsozialistische Konzentrationslager im Spiegel deutschsprachiger Printmedien* (unpublished electronic file, in the possession of the author).

Printed Sources

Abraham, M., "Juda verrecke. Ein Rabbiner im Konzentrationslager," in *Oranienburg*, eds. Diekmann and Wettig, 117–67.

Abzug, R. H., *Inside the Vicious Heart: Americans and the Liberation of Nazi Concentration Camps*, New York, 1985.

Aders, G., "Terror gegen Andersdenkende. Das SA-Lager am Hochkreuz in Köln-Porz," in *Instrumentarium*, eds. Benz and Distel, 179–88.

Adler, H. G., "Selbstverwaltung und Widerstand in den Konzentrationslagern der SS," *VfZ* 8 (1960), 221–36.

——, *Theresienstadt 1941–1945*, Göttingen, 2005.

Adler, H. G., H. Langbein and E. Lingens-Rainer (eds.), *Auschwitz. Zeugnisse und Berichte*, Hamburg, 1994.

Agamben, G., *Remnants of Auschwitz*, New York, 2002.

Aharony, M., "Hannah Arendt and the Idea of Total Domination," *HGS* 24 (2010), 193–224.

Akten zur deutschen auswärtigen Politik, Baden-Baden, 1956, vol. D/7.

Albin, K., *Steckbrieflich Gesucht*, Oświęcim, 2000.

"Alle Kreise der Hölle. Erinnerungen ehemaliger Häftlinge faschistischer Konzentrationslager aus der Ukraine, 1942–45," *Jahrbuch für die Forschungen zur Geschichte der Arbeiterbewegung* 3 (2005), 153–63.

Allen, A., *The Fantastic Laboratory of Dr. Weigl*, New York, 2014.

Allen, M. T., "Anfänge der Menschenvernichtung in Auschwitz, Oktober 1941," *VfZ* 51 (2003), 565–73.

——, "Not just a 'dating game': Origins of the Holocaust at Auschwitz in the Light of Witness Testimony," *GH* 25 (2007), 162–91.

——, "Realms of Oblivion: The Vienna Auschwitz Trial," *CEH* 40 (2007), 397–428.

——, *The Business of Genocide: The SS, Slave Labor, and the Concentration Camps*, Chapel Hill, 2002.

——, "The Devil in the Details: The Gas Chambers of Birkenau, October 1941," *HGS* 16 (2002), 189–216.

Allen, W. S., *The Nazi Seizure of Power*, 2nd ed., London, 1989.

Aly, G., "Die Wohlfühl-Diktatur," *Der Spiegel* 10 (2005), 56–62.

——, *"Endlösung." Völkerverschiebung und der Mord an den europäischen Juden*, Frankfurt a. M., 1995.

——, *Hitlers Volksstaat. Raub, Rassenkrieg und nationaler Sozialismus*, Frankfurt a. M., 2005.

Aly, G., and S. Heim, *Vordenker der Vernichtung. Auschwitz und die deutschen Pläne für eine neue europäische Ordnung*, Frankfurt a. M., 1993.

Ambach, D., and T. Köhler, *Lublin-Majdanek. Das Konzentrations- und Vernichtungslager im Spiegel von Zeugenaussagen*, Düsseldorf, 2003.

Améry, J., *Jenseits von Schuld und Sühne*, Munich, 1988.

Amesberger, H., K. Auer, and K. Halbmayr, *Sexualisierte Gewalt. Weibliche Erfahrungen in NS-Konzentrationslagern*, Vienna, 2004.

Angrick, A., and P. Klein, *Die "Endlösung" in Riga. Ausbeutung und Vernichtung 1941–1944*, Darmstadt, 2006.

Antelme, R., *Das Menschengeschlecht*, Frankfurt a. M., 2001.

——, *L'espèce humaine*, Paris, 1957.

Apel, L., *Jüdische Frauen im Konzentrationslager Ravensbrück 1939–1945*, Berlin, 2003.

Apitz, B., *Nackt unter Wölfen*, Berlin, 1998.

Applebaum, A., *Gulag: A History of the Soviet Camps*, London, 2003.

Arad, Y., *Belzec, Sobibor, Treblinka*, Bloomington, 1999.

Arch Getty, J., G. Rittersporn, and V. Zemskov, "Victims of the Soviet Penal System in the Pre-war Years," *AHR* 98 (1993), 1017–49.

Arendt, H., *The Origins of Totalitarianism*, San Diego, 1994.

———, "The Concentration Camps," *Partisan Review* 15 (1948), 743–63.

Armanski, G., *Maschinen des Terrors*, Münster, 1993.

Aronson, S., *Reinhard Heydrich und die Frühgeschichte von Gestapo und SD*, Stuttgart, 1971.

Asgodom, S. (ed.), *"Halts Maul—sonst kommst nach Dachau!" Frauen und Männer aus der Arbeiterbewegung berichten über Widerstand und Verfolgung unter dem Nationalsozialismus*, Cologne, 1983.

Association for Remembrance and Historical Research in Austrian Concentration Camp Memorials (ed.), *The Mauthausen Concentration Camp 1938–1945*, Vienna, 2013.

August, J., "Das Konzentrationslager Auschwitz und die 'Euthanasie'-Anstalt Pirna-Sonnenstein," in *Sonnenstein*, ed. Kuratorium, 51–94.

———, (ed.), *"Sonderaktion Krakau." Die Verhaftung der Krakauer Wissenschaftler am 6. November 1939*, Hamburg, 1997.

Avey, D., *The Man Who Broke into Auschwitz*, London, 2011.

Ayaß, W., *"Asoziale" im Nationalsozialismus*, Stuttgart, 1995.

———, *Das Arbeitshaus Breitenau*, Kassel, 1992.

——— (ed.), *"Gemeinschaftsfremde." Quellen zur Verfolgung "Asozialer" 1933–1945*, Koblenz, 1998.

———, "Schwarze und grüne Winkel. Die nationalsozialistische Verfolgung von 'Asozialen' und 'Kriminellen,'" *BGVN* 11 (2009), 16–30.

Baberowski, J., and A. Doering-Manteuffel, *Ordnung durch Terror. Gewaltexzesse und Vernichtung im nationalsozialistischen und im stalinistischen Imperium*, Bonn, 2006.

Bacharach, W. Z. (ed.), *Dies sind meine letzten Worte. Briefe aus der Shoah*, Göttingen, 2006.

Baganz, C., *Erziehung zur "Volksgemeinschaft"? Die frühen Konzentrationslager in Sachsen 1933–34/37*, Berlin, 2005.

———, "Wöbbelin. Das letzte Außenlager des KZ Neuengamme als Sterbelager," in *Häftlinge*, eds. Garbe and Lange, 105–16.

Bahro, B., *Der SS-Sport. Organisation, Funktion, Bedeutung*, Paderborn, 2013.

Bajohr, F., *Parvenüs und Profiteure. Korruption in der NS-Zeit*, Frankfurt a. M., 2001.

Ballerstedt, M., "Liebe wider Rassenwahn," in *Unerwünscht, Verfolgt, Ermordet*, ed. M. Puhle, Magdeburg, 2008, 201–13.

Banach, J., *Heydrichs Elite. Das Führerkorps der Sicherheitspolizei und des SD, 1936–1945*, Paderborn, 1998.

Barkai, A., "'Schicksalsjahr 1938.' Kontinuität und Verschärfung der wirtschaftlichen Ausplünderung der deutschen Juden," in *Der Judenpogrom 1938*, ed. W. H. Pehle, Frankfurt a. M., 1988, 94–117.

Barkow, B., R. Gross, and M. Lenarz (eds.), *Novemberpogrom 1938. Die Augenzeugenberichte der Wiener Library, London*, Frankfurt a. M., 2008.

Barnes, S., "Soviet Society Confined," Ph.D. dissertation, Stanford University, 2003.

Bárta, D., "Tagebuch aus dem Konzentrationslager Ebensee, 1943–1945," in *Drahomír*, eds. Freund and Pawlowsky, 35–96.

———, "Zur Geschichte der illegalen Tätigkeit und der Widerstandsbewegung der Häftlinge im Konzentrationslager Ebensee," in *Drahomír*, eds. Freund and Pawlowsky, 97–167.

Bartel, W., and K. Drobisch, "Der Aufgabenbereich des Leiters des Amtes D IV des Wirtschafts-Verwaltungshauptamtes der SS," *ZfG* 14 (1966), 944–56.

Bass, F., "Love and Concentration Camps," *Theresienstädter Studien und Dokumente* 13 (2006), 340–47.

Bauer, R., H. G. Hockerts, B. Schütz, W. Till, and W. Ziegler, eds., *München—"Hauptstadt der Bewegung,"* Munich, 2002.

Bauer, Y., "Anmerkungen zum "Auschwitz-Bericht" von Rudolf Vrba," *VfZ* 45 (1997), 297–307.

———, "Gypsies," in *Anatomy*, eds. Gutman and Berenbaum, 441–55.

———, *Jews for Sale? Nazi-Jewish Negotiations, 1933–1945*, New Haven, 1994.

———, *Rethinking the Holocaust*, New Haven, 2001.

———, "The Death-Marches, January–May, 1945," *Modern Judaism* 3 (1983), 1–21.

Bauerkämper, A., *Das umstrittene Gedächtnis. Die Erinnerung an Nationalsozialismus, Faschismus und Krieg in Europa seit 1945*, Paderborn, 2012.

Bauman, Z., "A Century of Camps?," in *The Bauman Reader*, ed. P. Beilharz, Oxford, 2001, 266–80.

———, *Modernity and the Holocaust*, Ithaca, N.Y., 1992.

Baumann, I., "Winkel-Züge: 'Kriminelle' KZ-Häftlinge in der westdeutschen Nachkriegsgesellschaft," in *Praxis*, eds. Frei et al., 290–322.

Baumgart, W., "Zur Ansprache Hitlers vor den Führern der Wehrmacht am 22. August 1939: Eine quellenkritische Untersuchung," *VfZ* 16 (1968), 120–49.

Beccaria Rolfi, L., *Zurückkehren als Fremde. Von Ravensbrück nach Italien: 1945–1948*, Berlin, 2007.

Beer, M., "Die Entwicklung der Gaswagen beim Mord an den Juden," *VfZ* 35 (1987), 403–17.

Beevor, A., *Berlin*, London, 2003.

———, *The Second World War*, London, 2014.

Beimler, H., *Four Weeks in the Hands of Hitler's Hell-Hounds*, London, 1933.

———, *Im Mörderlager Dachau. Vier Wochen in den Händen der braunen Banditen*, Berlin, 1976.

Beischl, K., *Dr. med. Eduard Wirths und seine Tätigkeit als SS-Standortarzt im KL Auschwitz*, Würzburg, 2005.

Bell, J. (ed.), *Völkerrecht im Weltkrieg*, Berlin, 1927.

Belpoliti, M. (ed.), *Primo Levi: The Black Hole of Auschwitz*, Cambridge, U.K., 2005.

Ben-Naftali, O., and Y. Tuval, "Punishing International Crimes Committed by the Persecuted. The *Kapo* Trials in Israel (1950s–1960s)," *Journal of International Criminal Justice* 4 (2006), 128–78.

Bendig, V., "Unter Regie der SA. Das Konzentrationslager Börnicke und das Nebenlager Meissnerhof im Osthavelland," in *Instrumentarium*, eds. Benz and Distel, 97–101.

———, "'Von allen Höllen vielleicht die grausamste.' Das Konzentrationslager in Brandenburg an der Havel 1933–1934," in *Instrumentarium*, eds. Benz and Distel, 103–109.

Bendix, R., *From Berlin to Berkeley*, New Brunswick, 1986.

Benz, A., "John Demjanjuk und die Rolle der Trawnikis," in *Bewachung*, eds. Benz and Vulesica, 159–69.

Benz, A., and M. Vulesica (eds.), *Bewachung und Ausführung. Alltag der Täter in nationalsozialistischen Lagern*, Berlin, 2011.

Benz, W., and B. Distel (eds.), *Der Ort des Terrors*, 9 vols., Munich, 2005–09.

———, *Terror ohne System. Die ersten Konzentrationslager im Nationalsozialismus 1933–1935* (Berlin, 2001).

———, *Herrschaft und Gewalt. Frühe Konzentrationslager 1933–1939*, Berlin, 2002.

———, *Instrumentarium der Macht. Frühe Konzentrationslager 1933–1937*, Berlin, 2003.

Benz, W., and A. Königseder (eds.), *Das Konzentrationslager Dachau*, Berlin, 2008.

Benz, W., "Dr. med. Sigmund Rascher. Eine Karriere," *DH* 4 (1988), 190–214.

———, "Medizinische Versuche im KZ Dachau," in *Dachau*, eds. Benz and Königseder, 89–102.

———, "Zwischen Befreiung und Heimkehr. Das Dachauer Internationale Häftlings-Komitee und die Verwaltung des Lagers im Mai und Juni 1945," *DH* 1 (1985), 39–61.

Bergbauer, K., S. Fröhlich, and S. Schüler-Springorum, *Denkmalsfigur. Biographische Annäherung an Hans Litten, 1903–1938*, Göttingen, 2008.

Berger, S., *Experten der Vernichtung. Das T4-Reinhardt-Netzwerk in den Lagern Belzec, Sobibor und Treblinka*, Hamburg, 2013.

"Bericht von Czesław Mordowicz und Arnošt Rosin," in *London*, ed. Świebocki, 295–309.

"Bericht von Jerzy Tabeau," in *London*, ed. Świebocki, 107–79.

"Bericht von Rudolf Vrba und Alfred Wetzler," in *London*, ed. Świebocki, 181–293.

Berke, H., *Buchenwald. Eine Erinnerung an Mörder*, Salzburg, 1946.

Berkowitz, M., *The Crime of My Very Existence: Nazism and the Myth of Jewish Criminality*, Berkeley, 2007.

Berliner Illustrirte Zeitung.

Bernadotte, F., *The Fall of the Curtain*, London, 1945.

Bernhard, P., "Konzentrierte Gegnerbekämpfung im Achsenbündnis. Die Polizei im Dritten Reich und im faschistischen Italien 1933 bis 1943," *VfZ* 62 (2011), 229–62.

Bertram, M., "8. April 1945. Celle—ein Luftangriff, ein Massenmord und die Erinnerung daran," in *Häftlinge*, eds. Garbe and Lange, 127–44.

Bessel, R., *Germany 1945: From War to Peace*, London, 2009.

Bessmann, A., and M. Buggeln, "Befehlsgeber und Direkttäter vor dem Militärgericht. Die britische Strafverfolgung der Verbrechen im KZ Neuengamme und seinen Außenlagern," *ZfG* 53 (2005), 522–42.

Bettelheim, B., "Foreword," in *Auschwitz*, Nyiszli, 5–14.

——, "Individual and Mass Behavior in Extreme Situations," *Journal of Abnormal and Social Psychology* 38 (1943), 417–52.

——, *Surviving the Holocaust*, London, 1986.

Bezwińska, J., and D. Czech (eds.), *KL Auschwitz in den Augen der SS*, Katowice, 1981.

Billig, J., *L'Hitlérisme et le système concentrationnaire*, Paris, 1967.

Bindemann, M., D. König, and S. Trach, "Koserstrasse 21. Die Villa Pohl," in *Dahlemer Erinnerungsorte*, eds. J. Hoffmann, A. Megel, R. Parzer, and H. Seidel, Berlin, 2007, 17–18.

Black, P., "Foot Soldiers of the Final Solution: The Trawniki Training Camp and Operation Reinhard," *HGS* 25 (2011), 1–99.

——, "Odilo Globocnik—Himmlers Vorposten im Osten," in *Braune Elite*, eds. Smelser et al., vol. 2, 103–15.

Blatman, D., *The Death Marches: The Final Phase of Nazi Genocide*, Cambridge, Mass., 2011.

Blatter, J., and S. Milton, *Art of the Holocaust*, London, 1982.

Blondel, J.-L., S. Urban, and S. Schönemann (eds.), *Freilegungen. Auf den Spuren der Todesmärsche*, Göttingen, 2012.

Boas, J., *Boulevard des Misères: The Story of Transit Camp Westerbork*, Hamden, 1985.

Bock, G. (ed.), *Genozid und Geschlecht*, Frankfurt a. M., 2005.

Boder, D. P., *I Did Not Interview the Dead*, Urbana, 1949.

Boehnert, G. C., "A Sociography of the SS Officer Corps, 1925–1939," Ph.D. dissertation, University of London, 1977.

Boelcke, W. (ed.), *Deutschlands Rüstung im Zweiten Weltkrieg*, Frankfurt a. M., 1969.

Böhler, J., *Auftakt zum Vernichtungskrieg. Die Wehrmacht in Polen 1939*, Bonn, 2006.

Bohnen, E. A., "Als sich das Blatt gewendet hatte. Erinnerungen eines amerikanischen Militär-Rabbiners an die Befreiung Dachaus," *DH* 1 (1985), 204–206.

Borgstedt, A., "Das nordbadische Kislau. Konzentrationslager, Arbeitshaus und Durchgangslager für Fremdenlegionäre," in *Herrschaft*, eds. Benz and Distel, 217–29.

Bornemann, M., *Geheimprojekt Mittelbau*, Bonn, 1994.

Borodziej, W., *Geschichte Polens im 20. Jahrhundert*, Munich, 2010.

Borowski, T., "Auschwitz, Our Home, A Letter," in *Auschwitz*, eds. Siedlecki et al., 116–49.

——, "This Way for the Gas, Ladies and Gentlemen," in *Auschwitz*, eds. Siedlecki et al., 83–98.

——, *This Way for the Gas, Ladies and Gentlemen*, London, 1967.

Bracher, K. D., *Die deutsche Diktatur*, Cologne, 1979.

Braham, R. L., "Hungarian Jews," in *Anatomy*, eds. Gutman and Berenbaum, 456–68.

Brandhuber, J., "Die sowjetischen Kriegsgefangenen im Konzentrationslager Auschwitz, *HvA* 4 (1961), 5–46.

Braunbuch über Reichstagsbrand und Hitlerterror, Frankfurt a. M., 1973.

Breitman, R., *Official Secrets: What the Nazis Planned, What the British and Americans Knew*, London, 1999.

Breitman, R., and S. Aronson, "Eine unbekannte Himmler-Rede vom Januar 1943," *VfZ* 38 (1990), 337–48.

Breitman, R., N. Goda, T. Naftali, and R. Wolfe, *U.S. Intelligence and the Nazis*, New York, 2005.

Bringmann, F., *KZ Neuengamme. Berichte, Erinnerungen, Dokumente*, Frankfurt a. M., 1982.

Brink, C., *Ikonen der Vernichtung. Öffentlicher Gebrauch von Fotografien aus nationalsozialistischen Konzentrationslagern nach 1945*, Berlin, 1998.

Broad, P., "Erinnerungen," in *KL Auschwitz*, eds. Bezwińska and Czech, 133–95.

Broszat, M., "Einleitung," in *Studien*, ed. Broszat, 7–9.

—— (ed.), *Kommandant in Auschwitz. Autobiographische Aufzeichnungen des Rudolf Höß*, 14th ed., Munich, 1994.

——, "Nationalsozialistische Konzentrationslager 1933–1945," in *Anatomie*, eds. Buchheim et al., 323–445.

——, *Nationalsozialistische Polenpolitik 1939–1945*, Frankfurt a. M., 1965.

—— (ed.), *Studien zur Geschichte der Konzentrationslager*, Stuttgart, 1970.

—— (ed.), "Zur Perversion der Strafjustiz im Dritten Reich," *VfZ* 6 (1958), 390–442.

Broszat, M., E. Fröhlich, and A. Grossmann (eds.), *Bayern in der NS-Zeit*, 6 vols., Munich, 1977–83.

Browder, G. C., *Hitler's Enforcers: The Gestapo and the SS Security Service in the Nazi Revolution*, New York, 1996.

Browning, C., "A Final Hitler Decision for the 'Final Solution'? The Riegner Telegram Reconsidered," *HGS* 10 (1996), 3–10.

——, *Fateful Months: Essays on the Emergence of the Final Solution*, New York, 1985.

——, *Ganz normale Männer. Das Reserve-Polizeibatallion 101 und die "Endlösung" in Polen*, Reinbek, 1996.

——, "One Day in Józefów," in *The Path to Genocide*, ed. Browning, Cambridge, U.K., 1995, 169–83.

——, *Remembering Survival. Inside a Nazi Slave-Labor Camp*, New York, 2010.

——, *The Origins of the Final Solution*, London, 2004.

Brubaker, F., and F. Cooper, "Beyond 'Identity,'" *Theory and Society* 29 (2000), 1–47.

Bryant, M., "Die US-amerikanischen Militärgerichtsprozesse gegen SS-Personal, Ärzte und Kapos des KZ Dachau 1945–1948," in *Dachauer*, eds. Eiber and Sigel, 109–25.

Brzezicki, E., A. Gawalewicz, T. Hołuj, A. Kępiński, S. Kłodziński, and W. Wolter, "Die Funktionshäftlinge in den Nazi-Konzentrationslagern. Eine Diskussion," in *Auschwitz*, ed. HIS, vol. 1, 231–39.

Buber, M., *Under Two Dictators*, London, 1949.

Buber-Neumann, M., *Die erloschene Flamme. Schicksale meiner Zeit*, Munich, 1976.

——, *Milena. Kafkas Freundin*, Berlin, 1992.

——, *Under Two Dictators*, London, 2009.

Buchheim, H., "Befehl und Gehorsam," in *Anatomie*, eds. Buchheim et al., 213–320.

——, "Die SS—das Herrschaftsinstrument," in *Anatomie*, eds. Buchheim et al., 13–212.

Buchheim, H., et al., *Anatomie des SS-Staates*, Munich, 1994.

Buchmann, E., *Frauen im Konzentrationslager*, Stuttgart, 1946.

Buck, K., "Carl von Ossietzky im Konzentrationslager," *DIZ Nachrichten* 29 (2009), 21–27.

Budraß, L., "Der Schritt über die Schwelle," in *Zwangsarbeit während der NS-Zeit in Berlin und Brandenburg*, eds. W. Meyer and K. Neitmann, Potsdam, 2001, 129–62.

Buergenthal, T., *A Lucky Child: A Memoir of Surviving Auschwitz as a Young Boy*, London, 2010.

Büge, E., *1470 KZ-Geheimnisse*, Berlin, 2010.

Buggeln, M., *Arbeit & Gewalt. Das Außenlagersystem des KZ Neuengamme*, Göttingen, 2009.

——, "Building to Death: Prisoner Forced Labour in the German War Economy—The Neuengamme Subcamps, 1942–1945," *EHQ* 39 (2009), 606–32.

——, *Bunker "Valentin." Marinerüstung, Zwangsarbeit und Erinnerung*, Bremen, 2010.

——, *Das System der KZ-Außenlager*, Bonn, 2012

——, "Die weltanschauliche Schulung der KZ-Wachmannschaften in den letzten Kriegsmonaten," in *Bewachung*, eds. Benz and Vulesica, 177–90.

——, "'Menschenhandel' als Vorwurf im Nationalsozialismus," in *Rüstung, Kriegswirtschaft und Zwangsarbeit im "Dritten Reich,"* eds. A. Heusler, M. Spoerer, and H. Trischler, Munich, 2010, 199–218.

——, *Slave Labour in Nazi Concentration Camps*, Oxford, 2014.

——, "Unterschiedliche Lebens- und Arbeitsbedingungen in den Außenlagern des KZ Neuengamme unter Wehrmachts- und unter SS-Bewachung?," *BGVN* 13 (2012), 40–51.

——, "Were Concentration Camp Prisoners Slaves?," *International Review of Social History* 53 (2008), 101–29.

Buggeln, M., *Das System der KZ-Außenlager*, Bonn, 2012.

Buggeln, M., and M. Wildt, "Lager im Nationalsozialismus. Gemeinschaft und Zwang," in *Welt*, eds. Greiner and Kramer, 166–202.

Burger, A., *Des Teufels Werkstatt*, Berlin, 1985.

Burkhard, H., *Tanz mal Jude! Von Dachau bis Shanghai*, Nuremberg, 1967.

Burleigh, M., *Death and Deliverance: "Euthanasia" in Germany 1900–1945*, Cambridge, U.K., 1994.

Burleigh, M., and W. Wippermann, *The Racial State: Germany 1933–1945*, Cambridge, U.K., 1991.

Burney, C., *The Dungeon Democracy*, London, 1945.

Burrin, P., *Hitler and the Jews*, London, 1994.

Büro des Reichstags (ed.), *Reichstagshandbuch, VI. Wahlperiode*, Berlin, 1932.

——, *Reichstagshandbuch 1933*, Berlin, 1933.

Buser, V., *Überleben von Kindern und Jugendlichen in den Konzentrationslagern Sachsenhausen, Auschwitz und Bergen-Belsen*, Berlin, 2011.

Bütow, T., and F. Bindernagel, *Ein KZ in der Nachbarschaft*, Cologne, 2004.

Caplan, J., "Einleitung," in *Herz.* ed. Caplan, 11–87.

—— (ed.), *Gabriele Herz. Das Frauenlager von Moringen*, Berlin, 2006.

——, "Gender and the Concentration Camps," in *Concentration Camps*, eds. Wachsmann and Caplan, 82–107.

—— (ed.), *Nazi Germany*, Oxford, 2008.

——, "Political Detention and the Origin of the Concentration Camps in Nazi Germany, 1933–35/6," in *Nazism*, ed. Gregor (2005), 22–41.

——, "Recreating the Civil Service: Issues and Ideas in the Nazi Regime," in *Government, Party and People in Nazi Germany*, ed. Noakes, Exeter, 1980, 34–56.

Cargas, H. J., "An Interview with Elie Wiesel," *HGS* 1 (1986), 5–10.

Cesarani, D., "Challenging the 'Myth of Silence,'" in *Holocaust*, eds. Cesarani and Sundquist, 15–38.

——, *Eichmann: His Life and Crimes*, London, 2004.

——, 'Introduction' in *Holocaust*, eds. Cesarani and Sundquist, 1–14.

Cesarani, D., and E. Sundquist (eds.), *After the Holocaust: Challenging the Myth of Silence*, London, 2012.

Chamberlin, B., "Todesmühlen. Ein früher Versuch zur Massen-'Umerziehung' im besetzten Deutschland 1945–1946," *VfZ* 29 (1981), 420–36.

Chamberlin, B., and M. Feldman (eds.), *The Liberation of the Nazi Concentration Camps*, Washington, D.C., 1987.

Chatwood, K., "Schillinger and the Dancer," in *Sexual Violence*, eds. Hedgepeth and Saidel, 61–74.

Cherish, B. U., *The Auschwitz Kommandant*, Stroud, 2009.

Christ, M., "Was wussten Wehrmachtsoldaten über Konzentrationslager und Kriegsverbrechen? Die geheimen Abhörprotokolle aus Fort Hunt (1942–1946)," *ZfG* 60 (2012), 813–30.

Chroust, P. (ed.), *Friedrich Mennecke. Innenansichten eines medizinischen Täters im Nationalsozialismus*, Hamburg, 1987.

Citroen, H., and B. Starzyńska, *Auschwitz-Oświęcim*, Rotterdam, 2011.

Cobain, I., *Cruel Britannia: A Secret History of Torture*, London, 2012.

Cocks, G., "The Old as New: The Nuremberg Doctors' Trial and Medicine in Modern Germany," in *Medicine and Modernity*, eds. G. Cocks and M. Berg, Cambridge, U.K., 2002, 173–91.

Cohen, B., *Case Closed: Holocaust Survivors in Postwar America*, New Brunswick, 2007.

Cohen, E., *Human Behaviour in the Concentration Camp*, London, 1954.

——, *The Abyss: A Confession*, New York, 1973.

Comité International de Dachau (ed.), *Konzentrationslager Dachau 1933–1945*, Munich, 1978.

—— (ed.), *Konzentrationslager Dachau 1933 bis 1945*, Munich, 2005.

Conway, J., "Frühe Augenzeugenberichte aus Auschwitz," *VfZ* 27 (1979), 260–84.

——, "The Significance of the Vrba-Wetzler Report on Auschwitz-Birkenau," in *Forgive*, ed. Vrba, 398–431.

Corni, G. *Hitler's Ghettos*, London, 2002.

Cramer, J., *Belsen Trial 1945: Der Lüneburger Prozess gegen Wachpersonal der Konzentrationslager Auschwitz und Bergen-Belsen*, Göttingen, 2011.

Czech, D., "A Calendar of the Most Important Events in the History of the Auschwitz Concentration Camp," in *Auschwitz*, eds. Długoborski and Piper, vol. 5, 119–231.

——, "The Auschwitz Prisoner Administration," in *Anatomy*, eds. Gutman and Berenbaum, 363–78.

——, *Kalendarium der Ereignisse im Konzentrationslager Auschwitz-Birkenau 1939–1945*, Reinbek, 1989.

Cziborra, P., *KZ-Autobiografien. Geschichtsfälschungen zwischen Erinnerungsversagen, Selbstinszenierung und Holocaust-Propaganda*, Bielefeld, 2012.

Danckwortt, B., "Jüdische 'Schutzhäftlinge' im KZ Sachsenhausen 1936 bis 1938," in *Häftlinge*, eds. Morsch and zur Nieden, 140–63.

——, "Sinti und Roma als Häftlinge im KZ Ravensbrück," *BGVN* 14 (2012), 81–98.

——, "Wissenschaft oder Pseudowissenschaft? Die 'Rassenhygienische Forschungsstelle' am Reichsgesundheitsamt," in *Medizin*, eds. Hahn et al., 140–64.

Dann, S. (ed.), *Dachau 29 April 1945*, Lubbock, 1998.

Dante, *The Divine Comedy*, Oxford, 1993.

Darowska, L., *Widerstand und Biografie. Die widerständige Praxis der Prager Journalistin Milena Jesenská gegen den Nationalsozialismus*, Bielefeld, 2012.

Davis, N., "Introduction," in *Auschwitz*, ed. Pilecki, xi–xiii.

Daxelmüller, C., "Kulturelle Formen und Aktivitäten als Teil der Überlebens- und Vernichtungsstrategie in den Konzentrationslagern," in *Konzentrationslager*, eds. Herbert et al., vol. 2, 983–1005.

De Rudder, A., "Zwangsarbeit im Zeichen des Völkermordes 1942 bis 1945," in *Häftlinge*, eds. Morsch and zur Nieden, 200–242.

Dean, M., *Robbing the Jews: The Confiscation of Jewish Property in the Holocaust, 1933–1945*, New York, 2008.

Debski, T., *A Battlefield of Ideas: Nazi Concentration Camps and Their Polish Prisoners*, New York, 2001.

Decker, A., "Die Stadt Prettin und das Konzentrationslager Lichtenburg," in *Lichtenburg*, eds. Hördler and Jacobeit, 205–28.

Deen, H., *"Wenn mein Wille stirbt, sterbe ich auch." Tagebuch und Briefe*, Reinbek, 2007.

Delbo, C., *Auschwitz and After*, New York, 1995.

"Der Steinbruch in Mauthausen," *Tranvia* Nr. 28 (March 1993), 14–15.

Des Pres, T., *The Survivor*, New York, 1976.

Deutschland-Berichte der Sozialdemokratischen Partei Deutschlands (Sopade), 7 vols., Frankfurt a. M., 1980.

Dicks, H. V., *Licensed Mass Murder: A Socio-psychological Study of Some SS Killers*, London, 1972.

Didi-Huberman, G., *Bilder trotz allem*, Munich, 2007.

Dieckmann, C., "Das Ghetto und das Konzentrationslager in Kaunas 1941–1944," in *Konzentrationslager*, eds. Herbert et al., vol. 1, 439–71.

——, *Deutsche Besatzungspolitik in Litauen 1941–1944*, 2 vols., Göttingen, 2011.

Diefenbacher, M., and G. Jochem (eds.), *"Solange ich lebe, hoffe ich." Die Aufzeichnungen des ungarischen KZ-Häftlings Ágnes Rózsa*, Nuremberg, 2006.

Diekmann, I., and K. Wettig (eds.), *Konzentrationslager Oranienburg*, Potsdam, 2003.

Diercks, H., "Fuhlsbüttel—das Konzentrationslager in der Verantwortung der Hamburger Justiz," in *Terror*, eds. Benz and Distel, 261–308.

——, "Gesucht wird. Dr. Kurt Heißmeyer," *BGVN* 9 (2005), 102–15.

Dietmar, U., *"Häftling X,"* Weimar, 1946.

Dillon, C., *Dachau and the SS*, Oxford, 2015.

——, "The Dachau Concentration Camp SS, 1933–1939," Ph.D. dissertation, Birkbeck, University of London, 2010.

——, "'We'll meet again in Dachau': The Early Dachau SS and the Narrative of Civil War," *JCH* 45 (2010), 535–54.

Diner, D. (ed.), *Ist der Nationalsozialismus Geschichte?*, Frankfurt a. M., 1987.

Diner, H., *We Remember with Reverence and Love: American Jews and the Myth of Silence after the Holocaust, 1945–1962*, New York, 2009.

Dirks, C., "The 'Juni-Aktion' (June Operation) in Berlin," in *Jews in Berlin*, eds. B. Meyer, H. Simon, and C. Schütz, Chicago, 2009, 22–35.

——, *"Die Verbrechen der anderen." Auschwitz und der Auschwitz-Prozess der DDR: Das Verfahren gegen den KZ-Arzt Dr. Horst Fischer*, Paderborn, 2006.

Distel, B., "Der 29. April 1945. Die Befreiung des Konzentrationslagers Dachau," *DH* 1 (1985), 3–11.

——, "Die Gaskammer in der 'Baracke X' des Konzentrationslagers Dachau und die 'Dachau-Lüge,'" in *Studien*, eds. Morsch and Perz, 337–42.

——, "Die letzte ernste Warnung vor der Vernichtung. Zur Verschleppung der 'Aktionsjuden' in die Konzentrationslager nach dem 9. November 1938," *ZfG* 46 (1998), 985–90.

——, "Im Schatten der Helden. Kampf und Überleben von Centa Beimler-Herker und Lina Haag," *DH* 3 (1987), 21–57.

——, "Staatlicher Terror und Zivilcourage. Die ersten Morde im Konzentrationslager Dachau," in *Die Linke*, eds. Wachsmann and Steinbacher, 104–16.

——, "Vorwort," in Kupfer-Koberwitz, *Tagebücher*, 7–18.

Distel, B., and J. Zarusky, "Dreifach geschlagen—Begegnung mit sowjetischen Überlebenden," *DH* 8 (1992), 88–102.

Długoborski, W. (ed.), *Sinti und Roma im KL Auschwitz-Birkenau 1943–44*, Oświęcim, 1998.

Długoborski, W., and F. Piper (eds.), *Auschwitz: 1940–1945*, 5 vols., Oświęcim, 2000.

"Dokumentation der Ausstellung," in *Oranienburg*, ed. Morsch, 129–218.

"Dokumentation. Die Rede Himmlers vor den Gauleitern am 3. August 1944," *VfZ* 1 (1953), 363–94.

Domarus, M., *Hitler: Reden und Proklamationen 1932–1945*, 4 vols., Wiesbaden, 1973.

Dörner, B., "Das Konzentrationslager Oranienburg und die Justiz," in *Oranienburg*, ed. Morsch, 67–77.

——, *Die Deutschen und der Holocaust*, Berlin, 2007.

——, "Ein KZ in der Mitte der Stadt. Oranienburg," in *Terror*, eds. Benz and Distel, 123–38.

——, *"Heimtücke." Das Gesetz als Waffe: Kontrolle, Abschreckung und Verfolgung in Deutschland 1933–1945*, Paderborn, 1998.

Dreyfus, J.-M., "Die Aufnahme der deportierten Widerstandskämpfer nach 1945 und ihre Wiedereingliederung in die französische Gesellschaft," in *Das Konzentrationslager Dachau*, eds. A. Bernou-Fieseler and F. Théofilakis, Munich, 2006, 83–93.

Drobisch, K., "Oranienburg—eines der ersten nationalsozialistischen Konzentrationslager," in *Oranienburg*, ed. Morsch, 13–22.

Drobisch, K., and G. Wieland, *System der NS-Konzentrationslager 1933–1939*, Berlin, 1993.

Dülffer, J., J. Thies, and J. Henke (eds.), *Hitlers Städte. Baupolitik im Dritten Reich*, Cologne, 1978.

Düsterberg, R., *Hanns Johst. Der Barde der SS*, Paderborn, 2004.

Dwork, D., and R. J. van Pelt, *Auschwitz: 1270 to the Present*, New York, 1997.

Ebbinghaus, A., and K. Dörner (eds.), *Vernichten und Heilen. Der Nürnberger Ärzteprozess und seine Folgen*, Berlin, 2001.

Ebbinghaus, A., and K. H. Roth, "Medizinverbrechen vor Gericht. Die Menschenversuche im Konzentrationslager Dachau," in *Dachauer*, eds. Eiber and Sigel, 126–59.

———, "Kriegswunden—Die kriegschirurgischen Experimente in den Konzentrationslagern und ihre Hintergründe," in *Vernichten*, eds. Ebbinghaus and Dörner, 177–218.

Eberle, A.," 'Asoziale' und 'Berufsverbrecher': Dachau als Ort der 'Vorbeugehaft,'" in *Dachau*, eds. Benz and Königseder, 253–68.

Ecker, F., "Die Hölle Dachau," in *Konzentrationslager*, 13–53.

Ehret, R., "Schutzhaft im Schloss Neu-Augustusburg," in *Instrumentarium*, eds. Benz and Distel, 239–59.

Eiber, L. (ed.), *"Ich wußte, es wird schlimm." Die Verfolgung der Sinti und Roma in München 1933–1945*, Munich, 1993.

———, "Kriminalakte 'Tatort Konzentrationslager Dachau.' Verbrechen im KZ Dachau und Versuche zu ihrer Ahndung bis zum Kriegsende," in *Dachauer*, eds. Eiber and Sigel, 12–40.

———, "Nach Nürnberg. Alliierte Prozesse in den Besatzungszonen," in *Recht*, eds. Finger et al., 38–51.

Eiber, L., and R. Sigel (eds.), *Dachauer Prozesse. NS-Verbrechen vor amerikanischen Militärgerichten in Dachau 1945–1948*, Göttingen, 2007.

Eichhorn, D. M., "Sabbath-Gottesdienst im Lager Dachau. Bericht des US-Militärrabbiners über die erste Maiwoche 1945," *DH* 1 (1985), 207–18.

Eichmüller, A., "Die Strafverfolgung von NS-Verbrechen durch westdeutsche Justizbehörden seit 1945," *VfZ* 4 (2008), 621–40.

———, *Keine Generalamnestie. Die Strafverfolgung von NS-Verbrechen in der frühen Bundesrepublik*, Munich, 2012.

Eiden, H., "Das war Buchenwald. Tatsachenbericht," in *Eh' die Sonne lacht. Hans Eiden—Kommunist und Lagerältester im KZ Buchenwald*, ed. H. Gobrecht, Bonn, 1995, 207–64.

Eisenblätter, G., "Grundlinien der Politik des Reichs gegenüber dem Generalgouvernement, 1939–1945," Ph.D. dissertation, Frankfurt University, 1969.

Eisfeld, R., *Mondsüchtig. Wernher von Braun und die Geburt der Raumfahrt aus dem Geist der Barbarei*, Hamburg, 2000.

Eley, G., "Hitler's Silent Majority? Conformity and Resistance Under the Third Reich (Part 2)," *Michigan Quarterly Review* 42 (2003), 550–83.

Ellger, H., *Zwangsarbeit und weibliche Überlebensstrategien. Die Geschichte der Frauenaußenlager des Konzentrationslagers Neuengamme 1944/45*, Berlin, 2007.

Endlich, S., "Die Lichtenburg 1933–1939. Haftort politischer Prominenz und Frauen-KZ," in *Herrschaft*, eds. Benz and Distel, 11–64.

———, "Orte des Erinnerns—Mahnmale und Gedenkstätten," in *Nationalsozialismus*, eds. Reichel et al., 350–77.

Engelking, B., and H. Hirsch, *Unbequeme Wahrheiten. Polen und sein Verhältnis zu den Juden*, Frankfurt a. M., 2008.

Engelmann, H., *"Sie blieben standhaft." Der antifaschistische Widerstandskampf in Dessau unter Führung der Kommunistischen Partei Deutschlands*, Dessau, 1983.

Erpel, S., "Die britischen Ravensbrück-Prozesse 1946–1948," in *Gefolge*, ed. Erpel, 114–28.

——, "Dokumentiertes Trauma. Zeugenaussagen polnischer Überlebender des Frauen-Konzentrationslagers Ravensbrück in einer schwedischen Befragung 1945/46," in *Nationalsozialismus*, eds. Fank and Hördler, 121–34.

—— (ed.), *Im Gefolge der SS. Aufseherinnen des Frauen-KZ Ravensbrück*, Berlin, 2007.

——, *Zwischen Vernichtung und Befreiung: Das Frauen-Konzentrationslager Ravensbrück in der letzten Kriegsphase*, Berlin, 2005.

Ervin-Deutsch, L., "Nachtschicht im Arbeitslager III in Kaufering," *DH* 2 (1993), 79–122.

Eschebach, I., "Gespaltene Frauenbilder. Geschlechtsdramaturgien im juristischen Diskurs ostdeutscher Gerichte," in *"Bestien,"* eds. Weckel and Wolfrum, 95–116.

—— (ed.), *Homophobie und Devianz*, Berlin, 2012.

——, "Homophobie, Devianz und weibliche Homosexualität im Konzentrationslager Ravensbrück," in *Homophobie*, ed. Eschebach, 65–78.

——, "'Ich bin unschuldig.'" Vernehmungsprotokolle als historische Quellen. Der Rostocker Ravensbrück-Prozeß 1966," *WG* 4 (1995), 65–70.

Escher, C., "Geistliche im KZ Dachau," in *Dachau*, eds. Benz and Königseder, 301–10.

Euskirchen, M., "Militärrituale. Die Ästhetik der Staatsgewalt," Ph.D. dissertation, Free University Berlin, 2004.

Evans, R. J., *In Hitler's Shadow: West German Historians and the Attempt to Escape from the Nazi Past*, London, 1989.

——, "Introduction," in *Auschwitz. A Doctor's Eyewitness Account*, M. Nyiszli, London, 2012, v–xxii.

——, *Rituals of Retribution: Capital Punishment in Germany, 1600–1987*, London, 1997.

——, *The Coming of the Third Reich*, London, 2003.

——, *The Third Reich at War*, London, 2008.

——, *The Third Reich in Power*, London, 2005.

Fabréguet, M., "Entwicklung und Veränderung der Funktionen des Konzentrationslagers Mauthausen 1938–1945," in *Konzentrationslager*, eds. Herbert et al., vol. 1, 193–214.

——, *Mauthausen: Camp de concentration national-socialiste en Autriche rattachée*, Paris, 1999.

Fackler, G., "Cultural Behaviour and the Invention of Traditions: Music and Musical Practices in the Early Concentration Camps, 1933–6/7," *JCH* 45 (2010), 601–27.

——, *"Des Lagers Stimme." Musik im KZ*, Bremen, 2000.

——, "'Des Lagers Stimme'—Musik im KZ," in *Rieser Kulturtage* 14 (2002), 479–506.

——, "Panoramen von Macht und Ohnmacht. KZ-Bilder als ikonisierte Erinnerung und historisches Dokument," in *Der Bilderalltag*, eds. H. Gerndt and M. Haibl, Münster, 2005, 251–74.

Fahrenberg, H., and N. Hördler, "Das Frauen-Konzentrationslager Lichtenburg," in *Lichtenburg*, eds. Hördler and Jacobeit, 166–89.

Falter, J., *Hitlers Wähler*, Munich, 1991.

Faludi, C. (ed.) *"Die Juni-Aktion" 1938. Eire Dokumentation zur Radikalisierung der Judenverfolgung*, Frankfurt a. M. 2013.

Fank, P., and S. Hördler (eds.), *Der Nationalsozialismus im Spiegel des öffentlichen Gedächtnisses*, Berlin, 2005.

Farré, S., "From Sachsenhausen to Schwerin," in *Freilegungen*, eds. Blondel et al., 282–99.

Favez, J.-C., *The Red Cross and the Holocaust*, Cambridge, U.K., 1999.

Favre, M., "'Wir können vielleicht die Schlafräume besichtigen.' Originalton einer Reportage aus dem KZ Oranienburg (1933)," *Rundfunk und Geschichte* 24 (1998), 164–70.

Feig, K., *Hitler's Death Camps: The Sanity of Madness*, New York, 1979.

——, "Non-Jewish Victims in the Concentration Camps," in *A Mosaic of Victims: Non-Jews Persecuted and Murdered by the Nazis*, ed. Berenbaum, London, 1990, 161–78.

Feingold, H. L., "Bombing Auschwitz and the Politics of the Jewish Question during World War II," in *Bombing*, eds. Neufeld and Berenbaum, 193–203.

Fénelon, F., *The Musicians of Auschwitz*, London, 1979.

Finder, G. N., "Jewish Prisoner Labour in Warsaw after the Ghetto Uprising, 1943–1944," *Polin. Studies in Polish Jewry* 17 (2004), 325–51.

Finger, J. et al. (eds.), *Vom Recht zur Geschichte. Akten aus NS-Prozessen als Quelle der Zeitgeschichte*, Göttingen, 2009.

Fings, K., "Dünnes Eis. Sinti, Roma und Deutschland," *BGVN* 14 (2012), 24–34.

——, "Eine 'Wannsee-Konferenz' über die Vernichtung der Zigeuner?," *JfA* 15 (2006), 303–33.

——, *Krieg, Gesellschaft und KZ. Himmlers SS–Baubrigaden*, Paderborn, 2005.

——, "The Public Face of the Camps," in *Concentration Camps*, eds. Wachsmann and Caplan, 108–26.

Flanagan, B., and D. Bloxham, *Remembering Belsen: Eyewitnesses Record the Liberation*, London, 2005.

Flaschka, M., "'Only Pretty Women Were Raped': The Effect of Sexual Violence on Gender Identities in Concentration Camps," in *Sexual Violence*, eds. Hedgepeth and Saidel, 77–93.

Fleming, G., "Die Herkunft des 'Bernadotte-Briefs' an Himmler vom 10. März 1945," *VfZ* 26 (1978), 571–600.

Fleming, M., *Auschwitz, the Allies and Censorship of the Holocaust*, Cambridge, U.K., 2014.

Form, W., "Justizpolitische Aspekte west-alliierter Kriegsverbrecherprozesse 1942–1950," in *Dachauer*, eds. Eiber and Sigel, 41–66.

Fox, J., *Film Propaganda in Britain and Nazi Germany*, Oxford, 2007.

Fraenkel, E., *The Dual State: A Contribution to the Theory of Dictatorship*, New York, 1969.

"Francesc Boix," *Tranvia* 28 (1993), 15–16.

Frankl, V., *Ein Psycholog erlebt das KZ*, Vienna, 1946.

——, *From Death-Camp to Existentialism*, Boston, 1959.

——, *Man's Search for Meaning*, Boston, 1963.

——, *. . . trotzdem Ja zum Leben sagen. Und ausgewählte Briefe (1945–1949)*, Vienna, 2005.

Frei, N., *1945 und Wir. Das Dritten Reich im Bewußtsein der Deutschen*, Munich, 2005.

——, *Vergangenheitspolitik. Die Anfänge der Bundesrepublik und die NS-Vergangenheit*, Munich, 1996.

——, "'Wir waren blind, ungläubig und langsam': Buchenwald, Dachau und die amerikanischen Medien im Frühjahr 1945," *VfZ* 35 (1987), 385–401.

Frei, N., and W. Kantsteiner (eds.), *Den Holocaust erzählen*, Göttingen, 2013.

Frei, N., S. Steinbacher, and B. Wagner (eds.), *Ausbeutung, Vernichtung, Öffentlichkeit. Neue Studien zur nationalsozialistischen Lagerpolitik*, Munich, 2000.

——, *Die Praxis der Wiedergutmachung*, Göttingen, 2009.

——, *Standort- und Kommandanturbefehle des Konzentrationslagers Auschwitz 1940–1945*, Munich, 2000.

Freund, F., *Arbeitslager Zement. Das Konzentrationslager Ebensee und die Raketenrüstung*, Vienna, 1989.

——, "Das KZ Ebensee," in *Drahomír Bárta*, eds. Freund and Pawlowsky, 16–32.

——, "Der Dachauer Mauthausenprozess," *Jahrbuch des Dokumentationsarchivs des österreichischen Widerstands*, Vienna, 2001, 35–66.

——, *Die Toten von Ebensee*, Vienna, 2010.

——, "Häftlingskategorien und Sterblichkeit in einem Außenlager des KZ Mauthausen," in *Konzentrationslager*, eds. Herbert et al., vol. 2, 874–86.

——, "Mauthausen. Zu Strukturen von Haupt- und Außenlagern," *DH* 15 (1999), 254–72.

Freund, F., and V. Pawlowsky (eds.), *Drahomír Bárta. Tagebuch aus dem KZ Ebensee*, Vienna, 2005.

Freund, J., *O Buchenwald!*, Klagenfurt, 1945.

Freyhofer, H., *The Nuremberg Medical Trial: The Holocaust and the Origin of the Nuremberg Medical Code*, New York, 2004.

Friedlander, H., *The Origins of Nazi Genocide*, Chapel Hill, 1995.

Friedlander, H., and S. Milton (eds.), *Archives of the Holocaust*, 22 vols., New York, 1990–95.

Friedländer, S., *Die Jahre der Vernichtung*, Munich, 2006.

——, "Eine integrierte Geschichte des Holocaust," in *Nachdenken über den Holocaust*, ed. Friedländer, Munich, 2007, 154–67.

——, *Nazi Germany & the Jews: The Years of Persecution 1933–39*, London, 1998.

Friedler, E., B. Siebert, and A. Kilian, *Zeugen aus der Todeszone. Das jüdische Sonderkommando in Auschwitz*, Munich, 2005.

Friedrich, K. P., "Der nationalsozialistische Judenmord in polnischen Augen. Einstellungen in der polnischen Presse 1942–1946/47," Ph.D. dissertation, University Cologne, 2002.

Fritzsche, P., *Life and Death in the Third Reich*, Cambridge, Mass., 2008.

Fröbe, R., "Arbeit für die Mineralölindustrie. Das Konzentrationslager Misburg," in *Konzentrationslager*, eds. Fröbe et al., vol. 1, 131–275.

——, "Der Arbeitseinsatz von KZ-Häftlingen und die Perspektive der Industrie, 1943–1945," in *Europa und der "Reichseinsatz"*, ed. U. Herbert, Essen, 1991, 351–83.

——, "Exkurs. René Baumer—Ein Zeichner im KZ," in *Konzentrationslager*, eds. Fröbe et al., vol. 1, 109–30.

——, "Hans Kammler. Technokrat der Vernichtung," in *SS*, eds. Smelser and Syring, 305–19.

——, "KZ-Häftlinge als Reserve qualifizierter Arbeitskraft," in *Konzentrationslager*, eds. Herbert et al., vol. 2, 636–81.

Fröbe, R., C. Füllberg-Stolberg, C. Gutmann, R. Keller, H. Obenaus, and H. H. Schröder, *Konzentrationslager in Hannover. KZ-Arbeit und Rüstungsindustrie in der Spätphase des Zweiten Weltkriegs*, 2 vols., Bremen, 1985.

——, "Zur Nachkriegsgeschichte der hannoverschen Konzentrationslager," in ibid., vol. 2, 545–85.

Fröhlich, E. (ed.), *Die Tagebücher von Joseph Goebbels*, part I: 1924–1941, 4 vols. (Munich, 1987); part II: 1941–1945, 15 vols. (Munich, 1993–96).

Fulbrook, M., *A Small Town Near Auschwitz*, Oxford, 2012.

Füllberg-Stolberg, C., "Frauen im Konzentrationslager: Langenhagen und Limmer," in *Konzentrationslager*, eds. Fröbe et al., vol. 1, 277–329.

Füllberg-Stolberg, C., M. Jung, R. Riebe, and M. Scheitenberger (eds.), *Frauen in Konzentrationslagern. Bergen-Belsen, Ravensbrück* (Bremen, 1994).

Gabriel, R., "Nationalsozialistische Biopolitik und die Architektur der Konzentrationslager," in *Auszug aus dem Lager*, ed. L. Schwarte, Berlin, 2007, 201–19.

Gabriel, R., E. Mailänder Koslov, M. Neuhofer, and E. Rieger (eds.), *Lagersystem und Repräsentation. Interdisziplinäre Studien zur Geschichte der Konzentrationslager*, Tübingen, 2004.

Gałek, M., and M. Nowakowski, *Episoden aus Auschwitz. Liebe im Schatten des Todes*, Oświęcim, 2009.

Gallup, G. H., *The Gallup Poll: Public Opinion, 1935–1971*, vol. 1, New York, 1972.

Garbe, D., "'Cap Arcona'-Gedenken," *BGVN* 10 (2007), 167–72.

——, "Erst verhasst, dann geschätzt. Zeugen Jehovas als Häftlinge im KZ Dachau," in *Dachau*, eds. Benz and Königseder, Berlin, 2008, 219–36.

——, "Wiederentdeckte Geschichte," in *Häftlinge*, eds. Garbe and Lange, 295–307.

——, *Zwischen Widerstand und Martyrium. Die Zeugen Jehovas im "Dritten Reich,"* Munich, 1993.

Garbe, D., and C. Lange (eds.), *Häftlinge zwischen Vernichtung und Befreiung. Die Auflösung des KZ Neuengamme und seiner Außenlager durch die SS im Frühjahr 1945*, Bremen, 2005.

Gedenkstätte Buchenwald (ed.), *Konzentrationslager Buchenwald 1937–1945*, Göttingen, 2004.

Geehr, R. S. (ed.), *Letters from the Doomed: Concentration Camp Correspondence 1940–1945*, Lanham, 1992.

Gellately, R., *Backing Hitler: Consent and Coercion in Nazi Germany*, Oxford, 2001.

——, "Social Outsiders and the Consolidation of Hitler's Dictatorship, 1933–1939," in *Nazism*, ed. Gregor, 2005, 56–74.

——, *The Gestapo and German Society: Enforcing Racial Policy 1933–1945*, Oxford, 1991.

Georg, E., *Die wirtschaftlichen Unternehmungen der SS*, Stuttgart, 1963.

Georg, K., K. Schilde, and J. Tuchel, *"Why is the world still silent?!" Häftlinge im Berliner Konzentrationslager Columbia-Haus 1933–1936*, Berlin, 2013.

Gerhardt, U., and T. Karlauf (eds.), *Nie mehr zurück in dieses Land. Augenzeugen berichten über die Novemberpogrome 1938*, Berlin, 2011.

Gerlach, C., *Krieg, Ernährung, Völkermord. Forschungen zur deutschen Vernichtungspolitik im Zweiten Weltkrieg*, Hamburg, 1998.

——, "The Eichmann Interrogations in Holocaust Historiography," *HGS* 15 (2001), 428–52.

Gerlach, C., and G. Aly, *Das letzte Kapitel. Der Mord an den ungarischen Juden*, Stuttgart, 2002.

Gerwarth, R., *Reinhard Heydrich. Biographie*, Munich, 2011.

Gerwarth, R., and S. Malinowski, "Hannah Arendt's Ghosts: Reflections on the Disputable Path from Windhoek to Auschwitz," *CEH* 42 (2009), 279–300.

Gigliotti, S., *The Train Journey: Transit, Captivity, and Witnessing in the Holocaust*, New York, 2010.

Gilbert, M., *Auschwitz and the Allies*, London, 2001.

——, *The Boys: Triumph over Adversity*, London, 1997.

Gilbert, S., *Music in the Holocaust: Confronting Life in the Nazi Ghettos and Camps*, New York, 2005.

Gioia, D. A., M. Schultz, and K. Corley, "Organizational Identity, Image and Adaptive Instability," *Academy of Management* 25 (2000), 63–81.

Gittig, H., *Illegale antifaschistische Tarnschriften 1933–1945*, Leipzig, 1972.

Glauning, C., *Entgrenzung und KZ-System. Das Unternehmen "Wüste" und das Konzentrationslager Bisingen 1944–45*, Berlin, 2006.

Glicksman, W., "Social Differentiation in the German Concentration Camps," in *The Nazi Holocaust*, ed. M. Marrus, Westport, Conn., 1989, vol. 6/2, 924–51.

Goerdeler, C., "Das Ziel," in *Politische Schriften und Briefe Carl Friedrich Goerdelers*, eds. S. Gillmann and H. Mommsen, Munich, 2003, vol. 2, 873–944.

——, "Die Zeit," in ibid., 823–28.

Goeschel, C., "Suicide in Nazi Concentration Camps, 1933–39," *JCH* 45 (2010), 628–48.

——, *Suicide in Nazi Germany*, Cambridge, U.K., 2009.

Goffman, E., *Asylums: Essays on the Social Situation of Mental Patients and Other Inmates*, Chicago, 1971.

Golczewski, F., "Die Kollaboration in der Ukraine," in *Beiträge zur Geschichte des Nationalsozialismus* 19 (2003), 151–82.

Goldhagen, D. J., *Hitler's Willing Executioners: Ordinary Germans and the Holocaust*, London, 1997.

Goldstein, J., I. Lukoff, and H. Strauss, *Individuelles und kollektives Verhalten in Nazi-Konzentrationslagern*, Frankfurt a. M., 1991.

Goschler, C. (ed.), *Die Entschädigung von NS-Zwangsarbeit am Anfang des 21. Jahrhunderts*, 4 vols., Göttingen, 2012.

——, *Schuld und Schulden. Die Politik der Wiedergutmachung für NS-Verfolgte seit 1945*, Göttingen, 2005.

——, "Wiedergutmachungspolitik—Schulden, Schuld und Entschädigung," in *Nationalsozialismus*, eds. Reichel et al., 62–84.

Gostner, E., *1000 Tage im KZ. Ein Erlebnisbericht aus den Konzentrationslagern Dachau, Mauthausen und Gusen*, Innsbruck, c. 1945.

Gottwaldt, A., N. Kampe, and P. Klein (eds.), *NS-Gewaltherrschaft. Beiträge zur historischen Forschung und juristischen Aufarbeitung*, Berlin, 2005.

Gottwaldt, A., and D. Schulle, *Die "Judendeportationen" aus dem Deutschen Reich 1941–1945*, Wiesbaden, 2005.

Gourevitch, P., *We Wish to Inform You That Tomorrow We Will Be Killed with Our Families: Stories from Rwanda*, London, 1999.

Grabowski, H. L., *Das Geld des Terrors. Geld und Geldersatz in deutschen Konzentrationslagern und Ghettos 1933 bis 1945*, Regenstauf, 2008.

Gradowski, S., "Tagebuch," in *Inmitten*, ed. SMAB, 139–72.

Graf, C., "The Genesis of the Gestapo," *JCH* 22 (1987), 419–35.

Gray, R. T., *About Face: German Physiognomic Thought from Lavater to Auschwitz*, Detroit, 2004.

Greenberg, G., "Introduction," in *Wrestling*, eds. Katz et al., 11–26.

Gregor, N., *Haunted City: Nuremberg and the Nazi Past*, New Haven, 2008.

—— (ed.), *Nazism*, Oxford, 2000.

—— (ed.), *Nazism, War and Genocide: Essays in Honour of Jeremy Noakes*, Exeter, 2005.

Greif, G., "Between Sanity and Insanity: Spheres of Everyday Life in the Auschwitz-Birkenau Sonderkommando," in *Gray Zones*, eds. Petropoulos and Roth, 37–60.

——, *Wir weinten tränenlos . . . Augenzeugenberichte der jüdischen "Sonderkommandos" in Auschwitz*, Cologne, 1995.

Greiner, B., *Verdrängter Terror. Geschichte und Wahrnehmung sowjetischer Speziallager in Deutschland*, Bonn, 2010.

Greiner, B., and A. Kramer (eds.), *Welt der Lager*, Hamburg, 2013.

Greiser, K., "Die Dachauer Buchenwald-Prozesse," in *Dachauer*, eds. Eiber and Sigel, 160–73.

——, *Die Todesmärsche von Buchenwald*, Göttingen, 2008.

——, "'Sie starben allein und ruhig, ohne zu schreien oder jemand zu rufen.' Das 'Kleine Lager' im Konzentrationslager Buchenwald," *DH* 14 (1998), 102–24.

Grill, M., "Das Skandinavierlager in Neuengamme und die Rückführung der skandinavischen Häftlinge mit den 'weißen Bussen,'" in *Häftlinge*, eds. Garbe and Lange, 185–213.

Gring, D., "Das Massaker von Gardelegen," in *Häftlinge*, eds. Garbe and Lange, 155–65.

——, "'[. . .] immer zwischen zwei Feuern.' Eine Annäherung an die Biographie des kommunistischen Funktionshäftlings Karl Semmler," *BGVN* 4 (1998), 97–105.

Gross, J. (with I. Gross), *Golden Harvest: Events at the Periphery of the Holocaust*, New York, 2012.

Gross, J., *Fear: Anti-Semitism in Poland after Auschwitz*, New York, 2007.

Gross, K. A., *Fünf Minuten vor Zwölf. Dachauer Tagebücher des Häftlings Nr. 16921*, Munich, n.d.

——, *Zweitausend Tage Dachau. Berichte und Tagebücher des Häftlings Nr. 16921*, Munich, 1946.

Gross, R., *Anständig geblieben. Nationalsozialistische Moral*, Frankfurt a. M., 2010.

Grossmann, A., *Jews, Germans, and Allies: Close Encounters in Occupied Germany*, Princeton, 2007.

"'Grossmutter Gestorben.' Interview mit dem ehemaligen SS-Sturmbannführer Helmut Naujocks," *Der Spiegel* 17 (1963), Nr. 46, 71–77.

Grotum, T., *Das digitale Archiv. Aufbau und Auswertung einer Datenbank zur Geschichte des Konzentrationslagers Auschwitz*, Frankfurt a. M., 2004.

Gruchmann, L., *Justiz im Dritten Reich. Anpassung und Unterwerfung in der Ära Gürtner*, 2nd ed., Munich, 1990.

——, *Totaler Krieg. Vom Blitzkrieg zur bedingungslosen Kapitulation*, Munich, 1991.

"Grundsätze für den Vollzug von Freiheitsstrafen vom 7. Juni 1923," *Reichsgesetzblatt*, II.

Gruner, M., *Verurteilt in Dachau*, Augsburg, 2008.

Gruner, W., *Jewish Forced Labor Under the Nazis*, New York, 2006.

Guckenheimer, E., "Gefängnisarbeit in Hamburg seit 1622," *MSchKrim*, Beiheft 3 (1930), 103–21.

Guerrazzi, A. O., and C. Di Sante, "Die Geschichte der Konzentrationslager im faschistischen Italien," in *Faschismus in Italien und Deutschland*, eds. Reichardt and Nolzen, Göttingen, 2005, 176–200.

Güldenpfenning, L., "Gewöhnliche Bewacher. Sozialstruktur und Alltag der Konzentrationslager-SS Neuengamme," *BGVN* 7 (2003), 66–78.

Gutman, Y., "Der Aufstand des Sonderkommandos," in *Auschwitz*, eds. Adler et al., 213–19.

———(ed.), *Enzyklopädie des Holocaust*, 4 vols., Munich, 1995.

Gutman, Y., and M. Berenbaum (eds.), *Anatomy of the Auschwitz Death Camp*, Bloomington, 1998.

Gutman, Y., and B. Gutman (eds.), *Das Auschwitz Album*, Göttingen, 2005.

Gutmann, C., "KZ Ahlem. Eine unterirdische Fabrik entsteht," in *Konzentrationslager*, eds. Fröbe et al., vol. 1, 331–406.

Guttenberger, E., "Das Zigeunerlager," in *Auschwitz*, eds. Adler et al., 131–34.

Gutterman, B., *A Narrow Bridge to Life: Jewish Forced Labor and Survival in the Gross-Rosen Camp System, 1940–1945*, New York, 2008.

Hackett, D. A. (ed.), *The Buchenwald Report*, Boulder, 1995.

Hahn, J., *Grawitz, Genzken, Gebhardt. Drei Karrieren im Sanitätsdienst der SS*, Münster, 2008.

Hahn, J., S. Kavčič, and C. Kopke (eds.), *Medizin im Nationalsozialismus und das System der Konzentrationslager*, Frankfurt a. M., 2005.

———, "Medizin und Konzentrationslager—eine Annäherung," in *Medizin*, eds. Hahn et al., 9–25.

Haibl, M., "'Baumhängen.' Zu Authentizität und Wirklichkeit einer Fotografie," *DH* 14 (1998), 278–88.

Hájková, A., "Prisoner Society in the Terezín Ghetto, 1941–1945," Ph.D. dissertation, University of Toronto, 2013.

———, "Sexual Barter in Times of Genocide," *Signs* 38 (2013), 503–33.

Hałgas, K., "Die Arbeit im 'Revier' für sowjetische Kriegsgefangene in Auschwitz," in *Auschwitz Hefte*, ed. HIS, vol. 1, 167–72.

Hamerow, T. S., *On the Road to the Wolf's Lair: German Resistance to Hitler*, Cambridge, Mass., 1999.

Hammermann, G., "'Dachau muß in Zukunft das Mahnmal des deutschen Gewissens werden.' Zum Umgang mit der Geschichte der frühen politischen Häftlinge," in *Die Linke im Visier*, eds. Wachsmann and Steinbacher, 229–58.

———, "Das Internierungs- und Kriegsgefangenenlager Dachau 1945–1948," in *Dachau*, eds. Benz and Königseder, 125–46.

———, "Sowjetische Kriegsgefangene im KZ Dachau," in *Einvernehmliche Zusammenarbeit?*, ed. Ibel, 91–118.

———, "Verteidigungsstrategien der Beschuldigten in den Dachauer Prozessen und im Internierungslager Dachau," in *Dachauer*, eds. Eiber and Sigel, 86–108.

Hansen, I., and K. Nowak, "Über Leben und Sprechen in Auschwitz. Probleme der Forschung über das Lagersprache der polnischen politischen Häftlinge von Auschwitz," in *Kontinuitäten*, eds. Heß et al., 115–41.

Harding, T., *Hanns and Rudolf: The German Jew and the Hunt for the Kommandant of Auschwitz*, London, 2013.

Harris, V., "The Role of the Concentration Camps in the Nazi Repression of Prostitutes, 1933–39," *JCH* 45 (2010), 675–98.

Harshav, B. (ed.), *The Last Days of the Jerusalem of Lithuania: Herman Kruk*, New Haven, 2002.

Hartewig, K., "Wolf unter Wölfen? Die prekäre Macht der kommunistischen Kapos im Konzentrationslager Buchenwald," in *Konzentrationslager*, eds. Herbert et al., vol. 2, 939–58.

Haulot, A., "Lagertagebuch Januar 1943–Juni 1945," *DH* 1 (1985), 129–203.

Haus der Wannsee-Konferenz (ed.), *Die Wannsee-Konferenz und der Völkermord an den europäischen Juden*, Berlin, 2006.

Hayes, P., "Auschwitz, Capital of the Holocaust," *HGS* 17 (2003), 330–50.

——, *From Cooperation to Complicity: Degussa in the Third Reich*, Cambridge, U.K., 2004.

——, *Industry and Ideology: IG Farben in the Nazi Era*, 2nd ed., Cambridge, U.K., 2001.

——, "The Ambiguities of Evil and Justice: Degussa, Robert Pross, and the Jewish Slave Laborers at Gleiwitz," in *Gray Zones*, eds. Petropoulos and Roth, 7–25.

Heberer, P., *Children During the Holocaust*, Lanham, 2011.

Hedgepeth, S., and R. Saidel (eds.), *Sexual Violence Against Jewish Women During the Holocaust*, Hanover, N.H., 2010.

——, "Introduction," in *Sexual Violence*, eds. Hedgepeth and Saidel, 1–10.

Heger, H., *Die Männer mit dem Rosa Winkel*, Hamburg, 1972.

Heiber, H. (ed.), *Reichsführer! Briefe an und von Himmler*, Munich, 1970.

Heike, I., "Johanna Langefeld—Die Biographie einer KZ-Oberaufseherin," *WG* 12 (1995), 7–19.

——, "Lagerverwaltung und Bewachungspersonal," in *Frauen*, eds. Füllberg-Stolberg et al., 221–39.

Heinemann, I., *"Rasse, Siedlung, deutsches Blut." Das Rasse- & Siedlungshauptamt der SS und die rassenpolitische Neuordnung Europas*, Göttingen, 2003.

Heiß, F., *Deutschland zwischen Nacht und Tag*, Berlin, 1934.

Helbing, I., "Das Amtsgerichtsgefängnis Köpenick in seiner Funktion als frühes Konzentrationslager während der 'Köpenicker Blutwoche,'" in *Transformation*, eds. Klei et al., 247–60.

Helm, S., *If This Is a Woman: Inside Ravensbrück*, London, 2015.

Helweg-Larsen, P., H. Hoffmeyer, J. Kieler, E. Thaysen, J. Thaysen, P. Thygesen, and M. Wulff, *Famine Disease in German Concentration Camps*, Copenhagen, 1952.

Henkys, R., "Ein Todesmarsch in Ostpreußen," *DH* 20 (2004), 3–21.

Hense, A., *Verhinderte Entschädigung. Die Entstehung der Stiftung "Erinnerung, Verantwortung und Zukunft" für die Opfer von NS-Zwangsarbeit und "Arisierung,"* Münster, 2008.

Herbert, U., "Arbeit und Vernichtung. Ökonomisches Interesse und Primat der 'Weltanschauung' im Nationalsozialismus," in *Nationalsozialismus*, ed. Diner, 198–236.

——, *Best: Biographische Studien über Radikalismus, Weltanschauung und Vernunft*, Bonn, 1996.

——, *Fremdarbeiter. Politik und Praxis des "Ausländer-Einsatzes" in der Kriegswirtschaft des Dritten Reiches*, Berlin, 1986.

——, "Von Auschwitz nach Essen. Die Geschichte des KZ-Außenlagers Humboldtstraβe," *DH* 2 (1993), 13–34.

——, "Von der Gegnerbekämpfung zur 'rassischen Generalprävention,'" in *Konzentrationslager*, vol. 1, ed. Herbert et al., 60–86.

Herbert, U., K. Orth, and C. Dieckmann (eds.), *Die nationalsozialistischen Konzentrationslager—Entwicklung und Struktur*, 2 vols., Göttingen, 1998.

——, "Die nationalsozialistischen Konzentrationslager. Geschichte, Erinnerung, Forschung," in *Konzentrationslager*, vol. 1, eds. Herbert et al., 17–40.

Herf, J., "The Nazi Extermination Camps and the Ally to the East: Could the Red Army and Air Force Have Stopped or Slowed the Final Solution?," in *Lessons and Legacies VII*, ed. Herzog, Evanston, 2006, 269–82.

Herker-Beimler, C., *Erinnerungen einer Münchner Antifaschistin*, Munich, 2002.

Hertz-Eichenrode, K. (ed.), *Ein KZ wird geräumt. Häftlinge zwischen Vernichtung und Befreiung*, 2 vols., Bremen, 2000.

Herz, G., "Das Frauenlager von Moringen," in *Herz*, ed. Caplan, 89–244.

Herzberg, A., *Between Two Streams: A Diary from Bergen-Belsen*, London, 1997.

Heschel, S., "Does Atrocity Have a Gender? Feminist Interpretations of Women in the SS," in *Lessons and Legacies VI*, ed. Diefendorf, Evanston, 2004, 300–321.

Heß, C., J. Hörath, D. Schröder, and K. Wünschmann (eds.), *Kontinuitäten und Brüche. Neue Perspektiven auf die Geschichte der NS-Konzentrationslager*, Berlin, 2011.

Hesse, H., "Von der 'Erziehung' zur 'Ausmerzung.' Das Konzentrationslager Moringen 1933–1945," in *Instrumentarium*, eds. Benz and Distel, 111–46.

Hesse, H., and J. Harder, ". . . *und wenn ich lebenslang in einem KZ bleiben müßte . . .*" *Die Zeuginnen Jehovas in den Frauenkonzentrationslagern Moringen, Lichtenburg und Ravensbrück*, Essen, 2001.

Hesse, K., and P. Springer (eds.), *Vor aller Augen. Fotodokumente des nationalsozialistischen Terrors in der Provinz*, Essen, 2002.

Hett, B., *Burning the Reichstag*, Oxford, 2014.

——, *Crossing Hitler: The Man Who Put the Nazis on the Witness Stand*, New York, 2008.

Hett, U., and J. Tuchel, "Die Reaktionen des NS-Staates auf den Umsturzversuch vom 20. Juli 1944," in *Widerstand gegen den Nationalsozialismus*, eds. P. Steinbach and J. Tuchel, Bonn, 1994, 377–89.

Hickethier, K., "Nur Histotainment? Das Dritte Reich im bundesdeutschen Fernsehen," in *Nationalsozialismus*, eds. Reichel et al., 300–317.

Hilberg, R., "Auschwitz and the Final Solution," in *Anatomy*, eds. Gutman and Berenbaum, 81–92.

——, *Die Vernichtung der europäischen Juden*, 3 vols., Frankfurt a. M., 1990.

Hillesum, E., *Letters from Westerbork*, New York, 1986.

Hillgruber, A. (ed.), *Staatsmänner und Diplomaten bei Hitler*, 2 vols., Frankfurt a. M., 1967.

Hillmann, J., "Die 'Reichsregierung' in Flensburg," in *Kriegsende 1945 in Deutschland*, eds. J. Hillmann and J. Zimmermann, Munich, 2002, 35–65.

Hinz, U., *Gefangen im Großen Krieg. Kriegsgefangenschaft in Deutschland 1914–1921*, Essen, 2006.

Hirsch, M., D. Majer, and J. Meinck (eds.), *Recht, Verwaltung und Justiz im Nationalsozialismus*, Cologne, 1984.

Hirte, C., *Erich Mühsam. Eine Biographie*, Freiburg, 2009.

HIS (ed.), *Die Auschwitz-Hefte*, 2 vols., Hamburg, 1994.

Hockerts, H. G., and F. Kahlenberg (eds.), *Akten der Reichskanzlei. Regierung Hitler*, vol. II/1, Boppard a. R., 1999.

Hoelz, M., *Vom "Weißen Kreuz" zur roten Fahne*, Frankfurt a. M., 1984.

Hoffmann, J., "*Das kann man nicht erzählen.*" *"Aktion 1005" Wie die Nazis die Spuren ihrer Massenmorde in Osteuropa beseitigten*, Hamburg, 2008.

Hohengarten, A., *Das Massaker im Zuchthaus Sonnenburg vom 30./31. Januar 1945*, Luxemburg, 1979.

Hohmann, J., and G. Wieland (eds.), *Konzentrationslager Sachsenhausen bei Oranienburg 1939 bis 1944. Die Aufzeichnungen des KZ-Häftlings Rudolf Wunderlich*, Frankfurt a. M., 1997.

Höhne, H., *Der Orden unter dem Totenkopf. Die Geschichte der SS*, Augsburg, 1997.

Holian, A., *Between National Socialism and Soviet Communism: Displaced Persons in Postwar Germany*, Ann Arbor, 2011.

Holzhaider, H., *Die Sechs vom Rathausplatz*, Munich, 1982.

——, "'Schwester Pia.' Nutznießerin zwischen Opfern und Tätern," in *Dachau*, eds. Benz and Königseder, 363–76.

Hörath, J., "'Arbeitsscheue Volksgenossen.' Leistungsbereitschaft als Kriterium der Inklusion und Exklusion," unpublished manuscript, 2013.

——, "Experimente zur Kontrolle und Repression von Devianz und Delinquenz. Die Einweisung von 'Asozialen' und 'Berufsverbrechern' in die Konzentrationslager 1933 bis 1937/38," Ph.D. dissertation, Free University Berlin, 2012.

——, "Terrorinstrument der 'Volksgemeinschaft'?," *ZfG* 60 (2012), 513–32.

Hördler, S. (ed.), *SA-Terror als Herrschaftssicherung. "Köpenicker Blutwoche" und öffentliche Gewalt im Nationalsozialismus*, Berlin, 2013.

Hördler, S., "Die Schlussphase des Konzentrationslagers Ravensbrück," *ZfG* 56 (2008), 222–48.

———, "Ordnung und Inferno. Das KZ-System im letzten Kriegsjahr," Ph.D. dissertation, Humboldt University, Berlin, 2011.

———, "SS-Kaderschmiede Lichtenburg," in *Lichtenburg*, eds. Hördler and Jacobeit, 75–129.

———, "Wehrmacht und KZ-System," *BGVN* 13 (2012), 12–23.

Hördler, S., and S. Jacobeit (eds.), *Dokumentations- und Gedenkort KZ Lichtenburg*, Münster, 2009.

———, *Lichtenburg. Ein deutsches Konzentrationslager* (Berlin, 2009).

Horn, S., *Erinnerungsbilder. Auschwitz-Prozess und Majdanek-Prozess im westdeutschen Fernsehen*, Essen, 2009.

Horwitz, G., *In the Shadow of Death: Living Outside the Gates of Mauthausen*, London, 1991.

Huener, J., *Auschwitz, Poland, and the Politics of Commemoration, 1945–1979*, Athens, Ohio, 2003.

Hughes, J., "Forced Prostitution: The Competing and Contested Uses of the Concentration Camp Brothel," Ph.D. dissertation, Rutgers, 2011.

Hull, I., *Absolute Destruction: Military Culture and the Practices of War in Imperial Germany*, Ithaca, 2005.

Hulverscheidt, M., "Menschen, Mücken und Malaria—Das wissenschaftliche Umfeld des KZ-Malariaforschers Claus Schilling," in *Medizin*, eds. Hahn et al., 108–26.

Hüttenberger, P., "Heimtückefälle vor dem Sondergericht München," in *Bayern*, vol. 4, eds. Broszat et al., 435–526.

———, "National Socialist Polycracy," in *Nazism*, ed. Gregor (2000), 194–98.

Ibach, K., *Kemna. Wuppertaler Lager der SA 1933*, Wuppertal, 1948.

Ibel, J., "Digitalisierung der Häftlingskartei des SS-Wirtschafts-Verwaltungshauptamtes," *BGVN* 10 (2007), 172–76.

——— (ed.), *Einvernehmliche Zusammenarbeit? Wehrmacht, Gestapo, SS und sowjetische Kriegsgefangene*, Berlin, 2008.

———, "Il campo di concentramento di Flossenbürg," in *Il Libro dei Deportati*, vol. 3, eds. Mantelli and Tranfaglia, Milan, 2010.

———, "Sowjetische Kriegsgefangene im KZ Flossenbürg," in *Zusammenarbeit?*, ed. Ibel, 119–57.

In 't Veld, N. (ed.), *De SS en Nederland*, 'S-Gravenhage, 1976.

Ingrao, C., *The SS Dirlewanger Brigade*, New York, 2011.

Internationales Lagerkommitee Buchenwald, *KL BU*, Weimar, n.d.

Internationales Zentrum für Recht und Freiheit in Deutschland (ed.), *Nazi-Bastille Dachau. Schicksal und Heldentum deutscher Freiheitskämpfer*, Paris, 1939.

Irmer, T., "'Stets erfolgreich abgewehrt?' Die deutsche Industrie und die Auseinandersetzung um Entschädigung von NS-Zwangsarbeit nach 1945," in *Zwangsarbeit im Nationalsozialismus und die Rolle der Justiz*, eds. H. Kramer, K. Uhl, and J.-C. Wagner, Nordhausen, 2007, 119–31.

Iwaszko, T., "Reasons for Confinement in the Camp and Categories of Prisoners," in *Auschwitz*, eds. Długoborski and Piper, vol. 2, 11–43.

———, "The Housing, Clothing and Feeding of Prisoners", in *Auschwitz*, eds. Długoborski and Piper, vol.2, 51–63.

Jäckel, E., *Hitlers Weltanschauung*, Stuttgart, 1991.

Jacobeit, S. (ed.), *"Ich grüße Euch als freier Mensch." Quelledition zur Befreiung des Frauen-Konzentrationslagers Ravensbrück im April 1945*, Berlin, 1995.

Jacobsen, A., *Operation Paperclip: The Secret Intelligence Program That Brought Nazi Scientists to America*, New York, 2014.

Jacobsen, H.-A., "Kommissarbefehl und Massenexekutionen sowjetischer Kriegsgefangener," in *Anatomie*, eds. Buchheim et al., 449–544.

Jagoda, Z., S. Kłodziński, and J. Masłowski, "'Die Nächte gehören uns nicht . . .' Häftlingsträume in Auschwitz und im Leben danach," *Auschwitz-Hefte*, ed. HIS, vol. 2, 189–239.

Jah, A., C. Kopke, A. Korb, and A. Stiller (eds.), *Nationalsozialistische Lager. Neue Beiträge zur NS-Verfolgungs- und Vernichtungspolitik und zur Gedenkstättenpädagogik*, Münster, 2006.

Jahn, R. (ed.), *Das war Buchenwald! Ein Tatsachenbericht*, Leipzig, n.d.

Jahnke, K. H., "Heinz Eschen—Kapo des Judenblocks im Konzentrationslager Dachau bis 1938," *DH* 7 (1991), 24–33.

Jaiser, C., "Irma Grese. Zur Rezeption einer KZ-Aufseherin," in *Gefolge*, ed. Erpel, 338–46.

——, "Repräsentationen von Sexualität und Gewalt in Zeugnissen jüdischer und nicht-jüdischer Überlebender," in *Genozid*, ed. Bock, 123–48.

Jansen, C., "Zwangsarbeit für das Volkswagenwerk. Häftlingsalltag auf dem Laagberg bei Wolfsburg," in *Ausbeutung*, eds. Frei et al., 75–107.

Jardim, J., *The Mauthausen Trial: American Military Justice in Germany*, Cambridge, Mass., 2012.

Jaskot, P., *The Architecture of Oppression: The SS, Forced Labor and the Nazi Monumental Building Economy*, London, 2000.

Jellonnek, B., *Homosexuelle unter dem Hakenkreuz. Die Verfolgung der Homosexuellen im Dritten Reich*, Paderborn, 1990.

Jenner, H., "In Trägerschaft der Inneren Mission. Das Konzentrationslager Kuhlen," in *Terror*, eds. Benz and Distel, 111–27.

Jochem, G., "Bedingungen und Umfeld des Einsatzes der ungarischen Sklavenarbeiterinnen in Nürnberg," in *"Solange,"* eds. Jochem and Diefenbacher, 63–93.

Jochmann, W. (ed.), *Adolf Hitler. Monologe im Führerhauptquartier 1941–1944*, Hamburg, 1980.

Jockusch, L., *Collect and Record!: Jewish Holocaust Documentation in Early Postwar Europe*, Oxford, 2012.

Johe, W., "Das deutsche Volk und das System der Konzentrationslager," in *Das Unrechtsregime*, ed. Büttner, Hamburg, 1986, vol. 1, 331–46.

—— (ed.), *Neuengamme. Zur Geschichte der Konzentrationslager in Hamburg*, Hamburg, 1982.

John-Stucke, K., "Konzentrationslager Niederhagen/Wewelsburg," in *Konzentrationslager*, ed. Schulte, 97–111.

Jones, H., *Violence Against Prisoners of War in the First World War*, Cambridge, U.K., 2011.

Judt, T., *Postwar: A History of Europe since 1945*, London, 2007.

Jureit, U., and K. Orth, *Überlebensgeschichten. Gespräche mit Überlebenden des KZ-Neuengamme*, Hamburg, 1994.

Jürgens, C., *Fritz Solmitz. Kommunalpolitiker, Journalist, Widerstandskämpfer und NS-Verfolgter aus Lübeck*, Lübeck, 1996.

Kaczerginski, S., *Lider fun di getos un lager*, New York, 1948.

Kagan, R., "Das Standesamt Auschwitz," in *Auschwitz*, eds. Adler et al., 145–58.

——, "Mala," in *Auschwitz*, eds. Adler et al., 209–12.

Kaienburg, H., *Das Konzentrationslager Neuengamme 1938–1945*, Bonn, 1997.

——, *Der Militär- und Wirtschaftskomplex der SS im KZ-Standort Sachsenhausen-Oranienburg*, Berlin, 2006.

——, "Die Systematisierung der Gewalt. Das KZ Sachsenhausen als neues Zentral- und Musterlager," in *Konzentrationslager*, ed. Kaienburg, 51–71.

——, *Die Wirtschaft der SS*, Berlin, 2003.

——, "'Freundschaft? Kameradschaft? . . . Wie kann das dann möglich sein?' Solidarität, Widerstand und die Rolle der 'roten Kapos' in Neuengamme," *BGVN* 4 (1998), 18–50.

——, "Funktionswandel des KZ-Kosmos? Das Konzentrationslager Neuengamme 1938–1945," in *Konzentrationslager*, eds. Herbert et al., vol. 1, 259–84.

—— (ed.), *Nationalsozialistische Konzentrationslager 1933–1945. Die Veränderung der Existenzbedingungen*, Berlin, 2010.

——, "Resümee," in *Konzentrationslager*, ed. Kaienburg, 163–84.

——, "'. . . sie nächtelang nicht ruhig schlafen ließ.' Das KZ Neuengamme und seine Nachbarn," *DH* 12 (1996), 34–57.

——, *"Vernichtung durch Arbeit." Der Fall Neuengamme*, Bonn, 1990.

Kaltenbrunner, M., *Flucht aus dem Todesblock. Der Massenausbruch sowjetischer Offiziere aus dem Block 20 des KZ Mauthausen und die "Mühlviertler Hasenjagd,"* Innsbruck, 2012.

Kalthoff, J., and M. Werner, *Die Händler des Zyklon B. Tesch & Stabenow. Eine Firmengeschichte zwischen Hamburg und Auschwitz,* Hamburg, 1998.

Kamieński, B., "Erinnerung an die Sonderaktion Krakau," in *"Sonderaktion,"* ed. August, 121–41.

Kamiński, A., *Konzentrationslager 1896 bis heute,* Munich, 1990.

Kansteiner, W., "Losing the War, Winning the Memory Battle," in *Politics,* eds. Kansteiner et al., 102–46.

Kansteiner, W., C. Fogu, and R. Lebow (eds.), *The Politics of Memory in Postwar Europe,* Durham, NC, 2006.

Kaplan, I., "Marsch aus den Kauferinger Lagern," in *Überlebende,* ed. Raim, 19–36.

Kaplan, M., *Between Dignity and Despair: Jewish Life in Nazi Germany,* New York, 1998.

Karay, F., *Death Comes in Yellow,* Amsterdam, 1996.

Karlsch, R., "Ein inszenierter Selbstmord. Überlebte Hitlers 'letzter Hoffnungsträger,' SS-Obergruppenführer Hans Kammler, den Krieg?," *ZfG* 62 (2014), 485–505.

Kárný, M., "Das Theresienstädter Familienlager (BIIb) in Birkenau," *HvA* 20 (1997), 133–237.

——, "Die Theresienstädter Herbsttransporte 1944," *Theresienstädter Studien und Dokumente* 2 (1995), 7–37.

——, "'Vernichtung durch Arbeit.' Sterblichkeit in den NS-Konzentrationslagern," in *Sozialpolitik und Judenvernichtung,* eds. G. Aly, S. Heim, M. Kárný, P. Kirchberger, and A. Konieczny, Berlin, 1987, 133–58.

——, "Waffen-SS und Konzentrationslager," in *Jahrbuch für Geschichte* 33 (1986), 231–61.

Kater, M. H., "Criminal Physicians in the Third Reich," in *Medicine and Medical Ethics in Nazi Germany,* eds. Nicosia and Huener, New York, 2002, 77–92.

——, *Das "Ahnenerbe" der SS 1935–1945,* 2nd ed., Munich, 1997.

——"Die ernsten Bibelforscher im Dritten Reich," *VfZ* 17 (1969), 181–218.

Katz, S., S. Biderman, and G. Greenberg (eds.), *Wrestling with God,* Oxford, 2007.

Ka-Tzetnik, *Sunrise over Hell,* London, 1977.

Kautsky, B., *Teufel und Verdammte,* Zurich, 1946.

Kees, T., "'Polnische Greuel.' Der Propagandafeldzug des Dritten Reiches gegen Polen," MA dissertation, University of Trier, 1994.

Keller, R., *Sowjetische Kriegsgefangene im Dritten Reich 1941/42,* Göttingen, 2011.

Keller, R., and R. Otto, "Sowjetische Kriegsgefangene in Konzentrationslagern der SS," in *Zusammenarbeit?,* ed. Ibel, 15–43.

Keller, S., *Günzburg und der Fall Josef Mengele. Die Heimatstadt und die Jagd nach dem NS-Verbrecher,* Munich, 2003.

——, *Volksgemeinschaft am Ende. Gesellschaft und Gewalt 1944/45,* Munich, 2013.

Kempowski, W., *Haben Sie davon gewusst? Deutsche Antworten,* Munich, 1999.

Keren, N., "The Family Camp," in *Anatomy,* eds. Gutman and Berenbaum, 428–40.

Kershaw, I., *Hitler: 1889–1936; Hubris,* London, 1998.

——, *Hitler: 1936–1945; Nemesis,* London, 2000.

——, *The End: Germany 1944–45,* London, 2012.

——, *The "Hitler Myth": Image and Reality in the Third Reich,* Oxford, 1989.

——, *The Nazi Dictatorship,* 4th ed., London, 2000.

——, *Popular Opinion and Political Dissent in the Third Reich,* 2nd ed., Oxford, 2002.

——, "Working Towards the Führer," *CoEH* 2 (1993), 103–18.

Kersten, L., "'The Times' und das KZ Dachau," *DH* 12 (1996), 104–22.

Kersting, F.-W., *Anstaltsärzte zwischen Kaiserreich und Bundesrepublik,* Paderborn, 1996.

Khlevniuk, O. V., *The History of the Gulag,* New Haven, 2004.

Kielar, W., *Anus Mundi. Fünf Jahre Auschwitz,* Frankfurt a. M., 1979.

——, "Edek und Mala," *HvA* 5 (1962), 121–32.

Kienle, M., "Das Konzentrationslager Heuberg in Stetten am kalten Markt," in *Terror*, eds. Benz and Distel, 41–63.

———, "Gotteszell—das frühe Konzentrationslager für Frauen in Württemberg," in *Terror*, eds. Benz and Distel, 65–77.

Kilian, A., "'Handlungsräume' im *Sonderkommando* Auschwitz," in *Lagersystem*, eds. Gabriel et al., 119–39.

Kimmel, G., "Das Konzentrationslager Dachau," in *Bayern*, eds. Broszat et al., vol. 2, 349–413.

Kirsten, H., and W. Kirsten (eds.), *Stimmen aus Buchenwald. Ein Lesebuch*, Göttingen, 2003.

Klarsfeld, S., *Vichy—Auschwitz*, Nördlingen, 1989.

Klausch, H.-P., *Antifaschisten in SS-Uniform*, Bremen, 1993.

———, *Tätergeschichten. Die SS-Kommandanten der frühen Konzentrationslager im Emsland*, Bremen, 2005.

Klee, E., *Auschwitz, die NS-Medizin und ihre Opfer*, Frankfurt a. M., 1997.

———, *Das Personenlexikon zum Dritten Reich*, Frankfurt a. M., 2003.

———, *"Euthanasie" im NS-Staat. Die "Vernichtung lebensunwerten Lebens,"* Frankfurt a. M., 1983.

———, *Was sie taten—Was sie wurden*, Frankfurt a. M., 1986.

Klee, E., W. Dreßen, and V. Rieß (eds.), *"Schöne Zeiten." Judenmord aus der Sicht der Täter und Gaffer*, Frankfurt a. M., 1988.

Klei, A., et al. (eds.), *Die Transformation der Lager*, Bielefeld, 2011.

Klein, E., *Jehovas Zeugen im KZ Dachau*, Bielefeld, 2001.

Klemperer, V., *Ich will Zeugnis ablegen bis zum letzten*, 2 vols., Berlin, 1995.

———, *LTI*, Leipzig, 1995.

Klier, F., *Die Kaninchen von Ravensbrück*, Munich, 1994.

Kłodziński, S., "Die 'Aktion 14f13,'" in *Aktion T-4. 1939–1945*, ed. G. Aly, Berlin, 1987, 136–46.

———, "Die erste Vergasung von Häftlingen und Kriegsgefangenen im Konzentrationslager Auschwitz," in *Auschwitz Hefte*, ed. HIS, vol. 1, 261–75.

Klüger, R., *weiter leben. Eine Jugend*, Göttingen, 1992.

Knigge, V., "Im Schatten des Ettersberges," in *". . . mitten im deutschen Volke." Buchenwald, Weimar und die nationalsozialistische Volksgemeinschaft*, eds. Knigge and Baumann, Göttingen, 2008, 151–75.

——— (ed.), *Techniker der "Endlösung." Topf & Söhne—Die Ofenbauer von Auschwitz*, Weimar, 2005.

Knoch, H., "Das Konzentrationslager," in *Orte der Moderne*, eds. Knoch and Geisthövel, Frankfurt a. M., 2005, 290–99.

———, "'Stupider Willkür ausgeliefert.' Organisationsformen und Gewaltpraktiken in den emsländischen Konzentrations- und Strafgefangenenlagern 1933–1940," in *Konzentrationslager*, ed. Kaienburg, 25–50.

Knoll, A., "Homosexuelle Häftlinge im KZ Dachau," in *Homosexuelle*, ed. Mußmann, 59–71.

———, "Humanexperimente der Luftwaffe im KZ Dachau," *BGVN* 13 (2012), 139–48.

Knop, M., H. Krause, and R. Schwarz, "Die Häftlinge des Konzentrationslagers Oranienburg," in *Oranienburg*, ed. Morsch, 47–66.

Knop, M., and M. Schmidt, "Das KZ Sachsenhausen in den letzten Monaten vor der Befreiung," in *Befreiung*, eds. Morsch and Reckendrees, 22–34.

Koch, P.-F. (ed.), *Himmlers graue Eminenz—Oswald Pohl und das Wirtschafts-Verwaltungshauptamt der SS*, Hamburg, 1988.

Koehl, R. L., *The Black Corps: The Structure and Power Struggles of the Nazi SS*, Madison, Wis., 1983.

Kogon, E., *Der SS-Staat. Das System der deutschen Konzentrationslager*, Munich, 1946.

———, *Der SS-Staat. Das System der deutschen Konzentrationslager*, Berlin, 1947.

———, *The Theory and Practice of Hell*, New York, 2006.

Kogon, E., H. Langbein, and A. Rückerl (eds.), *Nationalsozialistische Massentötungen durch Giftgas*, Frankfurt a. M., 1983.

Kohlhagen, E., *Zwischen Bock und Pfahl. 77 Monate in den deutschen Konzentrationslagern*, Berlin, 2010.

Koker, D., *At the Edge of the Abyss: A Concentration Camp Diary, 1943-1944*, Evanston, 2012.

Kolb, E., *Bergen-Belsen*, Hanover, 1962.

Konieczny, A., "Bemerkungen über die Anfänge des KL Auschwitz," *HvA* 12 (1970), 5-44.

———, "Das KZ Groß-Rosen in Niederschlesien," in *Konzentrationslager*, eds. Herbert et al., vol. 1, 309-26.

Königseder, A., "Als prominenter Regimegegner vernichtet. Der Dachau-Häftling Hans Litten," in *Dachau*, eds. Benz and Königseder, 351-61.

———, "Aus dem KZ befreit, aber ohne Staatsbürgerschaft. Displaced Persons," *DH* 23 (2007), 224-35.

Königseder, A., and J. Wetzel, *Lebensmut im Wartesaal. Die jüdischen DPs (Displaced Persons) im Nachkriegsdeutschland*, Frankfurt a. M., 2004.

Konzentrationslager. Ein Appell an das Gewissen der Welt, Karlsbad, 1934.

Kooger, B., *Rüstung unter Tage. Die Untertageverlagerung von Rüstungsbetrieben und der Einsatz von KZ-Häftlingen in Beendorf und Morsleben*, Berlin, 2004.

Koonz, C., *The Nazi Conscience*, Cambridge, Mass., 2003.

Koop, V., *Rudolf Höß. Der Kommandant von Auschwitz*, Cologne, 2014.

Kootz, J., "Nachwort," in *Zurückkehren*, Beccaria Rolfi, 181-99.

Koreman, M., "A Hero's Homecoming: The Return of the Deportees to France, 1945," *JCH* 32 (1997), 9-22.

Koretz, A., *Bergen-Belsen. Tagebuch eines Jugendlichen*, Göttingen, 2011.

Körte, M., "Stummer Zeuge. Der 'Muselmann' in Erinnerung und Erzählung," in *Vom Zeugnis zur Fiktion*, ed. Segler-Messner, Frankfurt a. M., 2006, 97-110.

———, "Die letzte Kriegsphase. Kommentierende Bemerkungen," in *Konzentrationslager*, eds. Herbert et al., vol. 2, 1128-38.

Kosmala, B., "Polnische Häftlinge im Konzentrationslager Dachau 1939-1945," *DH* 21 (2005), 94-113.

Kosthorst, E., and B. Walter (eds.), *Konzentrations- und Strafgefangenenlager im Dritten Reich. Beispiel Emsland*, 3 vols., Düsseldorf, 1983.

Kotek, J., and P. Rigoulot, *Das Jahrhundert der Lager*, Berlin, 2001.

Kożdoń, W., " . . . ich kann dich nicht vergessen." *Erinnerungen an Buchenwald*, Berlin, 2006.

KPD Leipzig (ed.), *Das war Buchenwald! Ein Tatsachenbericht*, Leipzig, n.d., 1945.

Kraiker, G., and E. Suhr, *Carl von Ossietzky*, Reinbek, 1994.

Krakowski, S., *Das Todeslager Chelmno/Kulmhof. Der Beginn der "Endlösung,"* Göttingen, 2007.

Kramer, A., "Einleitung," in *Welt*, eds. Greiner and Kramer, 7-42.

Kramer, A., and J. Horne, *German Atrocities 1914: A History of Denial*, New Haven, 2001.

Krammer, A., "Germans Against Hitler: The Thaelmann Brigade," *JCH* 4 (1969), No. 2, 65-81.

Kranebitter, A., "Zahlen als Zeugen. Quantitative Analysen zur 'Häftlingsgesellschaft' des KZ Mauthausen-Gusen," M.A. dissertation, University of Vienna, 2012.

———, *Zahlen als Zeugen. Soziologische Analysen zur Häftlingsgesellschaft des KZ Mauthausen*, Vienna, 2014.

Kranz, T., "Das KL Lublin—zwischen Planung und Realisierung," in *Konzentrationslager*, eds. Herbert et al., vol. 1, 363-89.

———, "Das Konzentrationslager Majdanek und die 'Aktion Reinhardt,'" in *"Aktion Reinhardt." Der Völkermord an den Juden im Generalgouvernement 1941-1944*, ed. B. Musial, Osnabrück, 2004, 233-55.

———, "Die Erfassung der Todesfälle und die Häftlingssterblichkeit im KZ Lublin," *ZfG* 55 (2007), 220-44.

——, "Massentötungen durch Giftgase im Konzentrationslager Majdanek," in *Studien*, eds. Morsch and Perz, 219–27.

Kraus, O., and E. Kulka, *Továrna na smrt*, Prague, 1946.

Krause-Vilmar, D., *Das Konzentrationslager Breitenau*, Marburg, 1998.

Kreienbaum, J., "'Vernichtungslager' in Deutsch-Südwestafrika? Zur Funktion der Konzentrationslager im Herero- und Namakrieg (1904–1908)," *ZfG* 58 (2010), 1014–26.

Kreiler, K., "Vom zufälligen Tod eines deutschen Anarchisten," in *Oranienburg*, ed. Morsch, 95–107.

Kremer, J. P., "Tagebuch," in *KL Auschwitz*, eds. Bezwińska and Czech, 197–281.

Kretzer, A., *NS-Täterschaft und Geschlecht. Der erste britische Ravensbrück-Prozess 1946/47 in Hamburg*, Berlin, 2009.

Kroener, B. R., "'Menschenbewirtschaftung,' Bevölkerungsverteilung und personelle Rüstung in der zweiten Kriegshälfte (1942–1944)," in *Reich*, ed. Militärgeschichtliches Forschungsamt, 777–1001.

Kroener, B. R., R.-D. Müller, and H. Umbreit, "Zusammenfassung," in *Reich*, ed. Militärgeschichtliches Forschungsamt, 1003–22.

Krohne, K., *Lehrbuch der Gefängniskunde*, Stuttgart, 1889.

Krzoska, M., "Der 'Bromberger Blutsonntag' 1939. Kontroversen und Forschungsergebnisse," *VfZ* 60 (2012), 237–48.

Kube, A., "Hermann Göring—Zweiter Mann im 'Dritten Reich,'" in *Elite*, eds. Smelser et al., vol. 1, 69–83.

Kubica, H., "Children and Adolescents in Auschwitz," in *Auschwitz*, eds. Długoborski and Piper, vol. 2, 201–90.

——, "The Crimes of Josef Mengele," in *Anatomy*, eds. Gutman and Berenbaum, 317–37.

Kucia, M., and M. Olszewski, "Auschwitz im polnischen Gedächtnis," in *Wahrheiten*, eds. Engelking and Hirsch, 111–15.

Kühne, T., *Belonging and Genocide: Hitler's Community, 1918–1945*, New Haven, 2010.

——, *Kameradschaft. Die Soldaten des nationalsozialistischen Krieges und das 20. Jahrhundert*, Göttingen, 2006.

Kühnrich, H., *Der KZ-Staat 1933–1945*, 2nd ed., Berlin, 1980.

Külow, K., "Jüdische Häftlinge im KZ Sachsenhausen 1939 bis 1942," in *Häftlinge*, eds. Morsch and zur Nieden, 180–99.

Kunert, A. (ed.), *Auschwitz: Natalia Zarembina*, Warsaw, 2005.

Kupfer-Koberwitz, E., *Als Häftling in Dachau*, Bonn, 1956.

——, *Dachauer Tagebücher. Die Aufzeichnungen des Häftlings 24814*, Munich, 1997.

Kuratorium Gedenkstätte Sonnenstein (ed.), *Sonnenstein. Von den Krankenmorden auf dem Sonnenstein zur "Endlösung der Judenfrage" im Osten*, Pirna, 2001.

Kuretsidis-Haider, C., "Die strafrechtliche Verfolgung von NS-Verbrechen durch die österreichische Justiz," in *Recht*, eds. Finger et al., 74–83.

——, "Österreichische Prozesse zu Verbrechen in Konzentrations- und Vernichtungslagern," in *Dachauer*, eds. Eiber and Sigel, 237–71.

Kuwalek, R., *Das Vernichtungslager Belzec*, Berlin, 2013.

Kwiet, K., "'Ich habe mich durchs Leben geboxt!' Die unglaubliche Geschichte des Bully Salem Schott," in *Jüdische Welten*, eds. M. Kaplan and B. Meyer, Göttingen, 2005, 231–47.

KZ-Gedenkstätte Dachau (ed.), *Gedenkbuch für die Toten des Konzentrationslagers Dachau*, Dachau, 2011.

KZ-Gedenkstätte Flossenbürg (ed.), *Konzentrationslager Flossenbürg 1939–1945*, Flossenbürg, 2008.

KZ-Gedenkstätte Neuengamme (ed.), *Die Ausstellungen*, Bremen, 2005.

Lanckorońska, K., *Michelangelo in Ravensbrück: One Woman's War Against the Nazis*, Cambridge, Mass., 2007.

Landauer, H., "Österreichische Spanienkämpfer in deutschen Konzentrationslagern," *DH* 8 (1992), 170–79.

Langbein, H., *Menschen in Auschwitz*, Vienna, 1980.

——, *... nicht wie die Schafe zur Schlachtbank. Widerstand in den nationalsozialistischen Konzentrationslagern*, Frankfurt a. M., 1980.

Lange, W., "Neueste Erkenntnisse zur Bombardierung der KZ-Schiffe in der Neustädter Bucht am 3. Mai 1945," in *Häftlinge*, eds. Garbe and Lange, 217–29.

Langer, L., *Preempting the Holocaust*, New Haven, 2000.

——, *Holocaust Testimonies: The Ruins of Memory*, New Haven, 1991.

——, "The Dilemma of Choice in the Deathcamps," in *Holocaust: Religious and Philosophical Implications*, eds. J. Roth and M. Berenbaum, St. Paul, 1989, 222–32.

Langfus, L., "Aussiedlung," in *Inmitten*, ed. SMAB, 73–129.

Langhammer, S., "Die reichsweite Verhaftungsaktion vom 9. März 1937," *Hallische Beiträge zur Zeitgeschichte* 1 (2007), 55–77.

Langhoff, W., *Die Moorsoldaten. 13 Monate Konzentrationslager*, Zurich, 1935.

Laqueur, R., *Bergen-Belsen Tagebuch 1944/1945*, Hanover, 1989.

——, *Schreiben im KZ. Tagebücher 1940–1945*, Hanover, 1991.

Laqueur, W., *The Terrible Secret*, London, 1980.

Laqueur, W., and R. Breitman, *Der Mann, der das Schweigen brach*, Frankfurt a. M., 1987.

Lasik, A., "Historical-Sociological Profile of the Auschwitz SS," in *Anatomy*, eds. Gutman and Berenbaum, 271–87.

——, "Organizational Structure of Auschwitz Concentration Camp," in *Auschwitz*, eds. Długoborski and Piper, vol. 1, 145–279.

——, "The Apprehension and Punishment of the Auschwitz Concentration Camp Staff," in *Auschwitz*, eds. Długoborski and Piper, vol. 5, 99–117.

——, "The Auschwitz SS Garrison," in *Auschwitz*, eds. Długoborski and Piper, vol. 1, 281–337.

Lasker-Wallfisch, A., *Inherit the Truth 1939–1945: The Documented Experiences of a Survivor of Auschwitz and Belsen*, London, 1996.

Lechner, S., "Das Konzentrationslager Oberer Kuhberg in Ulm," in *Terror*, eds. Benz and Distel, 79–103.

Leleu, J.-L., *La Waffen-SS: Soldats politiques en guerre*, Paris, 2007.

Lenarczyk, W., A. Mix, J. Schwartz, and V. Springmann (eds.), *KZ-Verbrechen*, Berlin, 2007.

Lenard, D., "Flucht aus Majdanek," *DH* 7 (1991), 144–73.

Lengyel, O., *Five Chimneys: A Woman Survivor's True Story of Auschwitz*, London, 1984.

Levi, P., "Communicating," in *Drowned*, Levi, 68–82.

——, *If This Is a Man; The Truce*, London, 1987.

——, *The Drowned and the Saved*, London, 1989.

——, "The Grey Zone," in *Drowned*, Levi, 22–51.

——, "The Intellectual in Auschwitz," in *Drowned*, Levi, 102–20.

——, "The Memory of the Offence," in *Drowned*, Levi, 11–21.

——, *The Periodic Table*, London, 1986.

Levi, P., and L. de Benedetti, *Auschwitz Report*, London, 2006.

Lévy-Hass, H., *Vielleicht war das alles erst der Anfang. Tagebuch aus dem KZ Bergen-Belsen 1944–1945*, Berlin, 1979.

Lewental, S., "Gedenkbuch," in *Inmitten*, ed. SMAB, 202–51.

Lewy, G., *The Nazi Persecution of the Gypsies*, Oxford, 2001.

Ley, A., "Die 'Aktion 14f13' in den Konzentrationslagern," in *Studien*, eds. Morsch and Perz, 231–43.

——, "Kollaboration mit der SS zum Wohle von Patienten? Das Dilemma der Häftlingsärzte in Konzentrationslagern," *ZfG* 61 (2013), 123–39.

Ley, A., and G. Morsch, *Medizin und Verbrechen. Das Krankenrevier des KZ Sachsenhausen 1936–1945*, Berlin, 2007.

Leys, R., *From Guilt to Shame: Auschwitz and After*, Princeton, 2007.

Liblau, C., *Die Kapos von Auschwitz*, Oświęcim, 1998.

Lichtenstein, H., *Majdanek—Reportage eines Prozesses*, Frankurt a. M., 1979.

Liebersohn, H., and D. Schneider, *"My Life in Germany Before and After January 30, 1933." A guide to a manuscript collection at Houghton Library, Harvard University*, Philadelphia, 2001.

Lifton, R. J., *The Nazi Doctors: Medical Killing and the Psychology of Genocide*, New York, 1986.

Lifton, R. J., and A. Hackett, "Nazi Doctors," in *Anatomy*, eds. Gutman and Berenbaum, 301–16.

Lindner, S., "Das Urteil im I.G.-Farben-Prozess," in *NMT*, eds. Priemel and Stiller, 405–33.

Lipstadt, D., *Beyond Belief: The American Press & the Coming of the Holocaust 1933–1945*, New York, 1986.

Litten, I., *Eine Mutter kämpft gegen Hitler*, Rudolstadt, 1985.

Loeffel, R., *"Sippenhaft*, Terror and Fear in Nazi Germany: Examining One Facet of Terror in the Aftermath of the Plot of 20 July 1944," *CoEH* 16 (2007), 51–69.

Loewy, H., "Die Mutter aller Holocaust-Filme?," in *Gefolge*, ed. Erpel, 277–95.

Longerich, P., *"Davon haben wir nichts gewusst!" Die Deutschen und die Judenverfolgung 1933–1945*, Munich, 2006.

——, *Die braunen Bataillone. Geschichte der SA*, Munich, 1989.

——, *Heinrich Himmler. Biographie*, Munich, 2008.

——, *Holocaust*, Oxford, 2010.

——, *Politik der Vernichtung. Eine Gesamtdarstellung der nationalsozialistischen Judenverfolgung*, Munich, 1998.

——, "Vom Straßenkampf zum Anstaltsterror," in *Oranienburg*, ed. Morsch, 23–38.

Lorska, D., "Block 10 in Auschwitz," in *Auschwitz Hefte*, ed. HIS, vol. 1, 209–12.

Lotfi, G., *KZ der Gestapo*, Frankfurt a. M., 2003.

Löw, A., D. Bergen, and A. Hájková (eds.), *Alltag im Holocaust*, Munich, 2013.

Lowe, K., *Savage Continent: Europe in the Aftermath of World War II*, London, 2012.

Luchterhand, E., "Prisoner Behavior and Social System in the Nazi Concentration Camps," *International Journal of Social Psychiatry* 13 (1967), 245–64.

Lüdtke, A., "The Appeal of Exterminating 'Others': German Workers and the Limits of Resistance," *JMH* 64 (1992), 46–67.

Lüerßen, D., " 'Moorsoldaten' in Esterwegen, Börgermoor, Neusustrum. Die frühen Konzentrationslager im Emsland 1933 bis 1936," in *Herrschaft*, eds. Benz and Distel, 157–210.

——, " 'Wir sind die Moorsoldaten.' Die Insassen der frühen Konzentrationslager im Emsland 1933 bis 1936," Ph.D. dissertation, University of Osnabrück, 2001.

Lumans, V. O., *Himmler's Auxiliaries: The Volksdeutsche Mittelstelle and the German National Minorities of Europe 1933–45*, Chapel Hill, 1993.

MacAuslan, O. R., "Aspects of the Medical Relief of Belsen Concentration Camp," MPhil dissertation, Birkbeck, University of London, 2012.

MacLean, F. L., *The Camp Men*, Atglen, 1999.

Madajczyk, C., *Die Okkupationspolitik Nazideutschlands in Polen 1939–1945*, Cologne, 1988.

—— (ed.), *Vom Generalplan Ost zum Generalsiedlungsplan*, Munich, 1994.

Madley, B., "From Africa to Auschwitz: How German South West Africa Incubated Ideas and Methods Adopted and Developed by the Nazis in Eastern Europe," *EHQ* 35 (2005), 429–64.

Mahoney, K. A., "An American Operational Response to a Request to Bomb Rail Lines to Auschwitz," *HGS* 25 (2011), 438–46.

Mailänder Koslov, E., "Der Düsseldorfer Majdanek-Prozess (1975–1981). Ein Wettlauf mit der Zeit?," *BGVN*, vol. 9 (2005), 74–88.

——, *Female SS Guards and Workday Violence: The Majdanek Concentration Camp, 1942–1944*, Lansing, 2015.

———, *Gewalt im Dienstalltag. Die SS-Aufseherinnen des Konzentrations- und Vernichtungslagers Majdanek 1942–1944*, Hamburg, 2009.

———, "Meshes of Power: The Concentration Camp as Pulp or Art House in Liliana Cavani's *The Night Porter*," in *Nazisploitation! The Nazi Image in Low-Brow Cinema and Culture*, eds. D. H. Magilow, K. T. Vander Lugt, and E. Bridges, London, 2012, 175–95.

Majer, D., *"Non-Germans" Under the Third Reich: The Nazi Judicial and Administrative System in Germany and Occupied Eastern Europe, with Special Regard to Occupied Poland, 1939–1945*, Baltimore, 2003.

Mallmann, K.-M., and B. Musial (eds.), *Genesis des Genozids. Polen 1939–1941*, Darmstadt, 2004.

Mallmann, K.-M., and G. Paul (eds.), *Die Gestapo im Zweiten Weltkrieg*, Darmstadt, 2000.

——— (eds.), *Karrieren der Gewalt. Nationalsozialistische Täterbiographien*, Darmstadt, 2004.

———, "Sozialisation, Milieu und Gewalt. Fortschritte und Probleme der neueren Täterforschung," in *Karrieren*, eds. Mallmann and Paul, 1–32.

Mankowitz, Z. W., *Life Between Memory and Hope: The Survivors of the Holocaust in Occupied Germany*, Cambridge, U.K., 2002.

Mann, M., *The Dark Side of Democracy: Explaining Ethnic Cleansing*, Cambridge, U.K., 2005.

Marcuse, H., "The Afterlife of the Camps," in *Concentration Camps*, eds. Wachsmann and Caplan, 186–211.

———, *Legacies of Dachau: The Uses and Abuses of a Concentration Camp, 1933–2001*, Cambridge, U.K., 2001.

Marrus, M., "Jewish Resistance to the Holocaust," *JCH* 30 (1995), 83–110.

Maršálek, H., *Die Geschichte des Konzentrationslagers Mauthausen*, 3rd ed., Vienna, 1995.

———, *Die Vergasungsaktionen im Konzentrationslager Mauthausen*, Vienna, 1988.

———, *Konzentrationslager Gusen. Kurze dokumentarische Geschichte eines Nebenlagers des KZ Mauthausen*, Vienna, 1968.

Marszałek, J., *Majdanek. Geschichte und Wirklichkeit des Vernichtungslagers*, Hamburg, 1982.

Mason, T., "The Legacy of 1918 for National Socialism," in *German Democracy and the Triumph of Hitler*, eds. A. Nicholls and E. Matthias, London, 1971, 215–39.

Matthäus, J., "Displacing Memory: The Transformations of an Early Interview," in *Approaching an Auschwitz Survivor*, ed. J. Matthäus, New York, 2009, 49–72.

———, "Verfolgung, Ausbeutung, Vernichtung. Jüdische Häftlinge im System der Konzentrationslager," in *Häftlinge*, eds. Morsch and zur Nieden, 64–90.

Mauriac, F., "Preface," in *Ravensbrück*, M. Maurel, London, 1959, ix–xi.

Mayer-von Götz, I., *Terror im Zentrum der Macht. Die frühen Konzentrationslager in Berlin 1933/34–1936*, Berlin, 2008.

Mazower, M., "Foucault, Agamben: Theory and the Nazis," *boundary 2* 35 (2008), Nr. 1, 23–34.

———, *Hitler's Empire: Nazi Rule in Occupied Europe*, London, 2009.

McCauley, M., *The Longman Companion to Russia Since 1914*, London, 1998.

Megargee, G. P. (ed.), *Encyclopedia of Camps and Ghettos 1933–1945*, vol. I, Bloomington, 2009.

Menasche, A., *Birkenau: Memoirs of an Eyewitness: How 72,000 Greek Jews Perished*, New York, n.d., c. 1947.

Mendelsohn, J. (ed.), *The Holocaust*, 18 vols., New York, 1982.

Merkl, F. J., *General Simon. Lebensgeschichten eines SS-Führers*, Augsburg, 2010.

Merziger, P., *Nationalsozialistische Satire und "Deutscher Humor,"* Stuttgart, 2010.

Mess, K. (ed.), *". . . als fiele ein Sonnenschein in meine einsame Zelle." Das Tagebuch der Luxemburgerin Yvonne Useldinger aus dem Frauen-KZ Ravensbrück*, Berlin, 2008.

Mettbach, A., and J. Behringer, *"Wer wird die nächste sein?" Die Leidensgeschichte einer Sintezza, die Auschwitz überlebte*, Frankfurt a. M., 1999.

Mette, S., "Schloss Lichtenburg. Konzentrationslager für Männer von 1933 bis 1937," in *Lichtenburg*, eds. Hördler and Jacobeit, 130–65.

Meyer, H.-G., and K. Roth, "'Wühler, Saboteure, Doktrinäre.' Das Schutzhaftlager in der Turenne-Kaserne Neustadt an der Haardt," in *Instrumentarium*, eds. Benz and Distel, 221–38.

——, "Zentrale staatliche Einrichtung des Landes Hessen. Das Konzentrationslager Osthofen," in *Instrumentarium*, eds. Benz and Distel, 189–219.

Meyer, S., *Ein Kriegsgefangenen- und Konzentrationslager in seinem Umfeld. Bergen-Belsen von "außen" und von "innen" 1941-1950*, Stuttgart, 2003.

Meyer, W., "Funktionalismus, Intentionalismus und 'Machtsystem eigener Art.' Anmerkungen zur Erklärung der heterogenen Existenzbedingungen der KZ-Häftlinge," in *Konzentrationslager*, ed. Kaienburg, 73–87.

——, "Nachwort," in *Baracke*, Szalet, 461–98.

Michael, H., *Zwischen Davidstern und Roter Fahne*, Berlin, 2007.

Michaelis, H., and E. Schraepler (eds.), *Ursachen und Folgen. Vom deutschen Zusammenbruch 1918 und 1945 bis zur staatlichen Neuordnung Deutschlands*, 26 vols., Berlin, 1958-1978.

Michel, J., *Dora*, London, 1979.

Michelet, E., *Die Freiheitsstraße. Dachau 1943-1945*, 2nd ed., Stuttgart, 1961.

——, *Rue de la Liberté*, Paris, 1955.

Michelsen, J., "Homosexuelle im Konzentrationslager Neuengamme," in *Homosexuelle*, Mußmann, 126–32.

Militärgeschichtliches Forschungsamt (ed.), *Das Deutsche Reich und der Zweite Weltkrieg*, vol. 5/2, Stuttgart, 1999.

Millok, S., *A kínok útja Budapesttöl Mauthausenig*, Budapest, 1945.

Milton, S., "Die Konzentrationslager der dreißiger Jahre im Bild der in- und ausländischen Presse," in *Konzentrationslager*, eds. Herbert et al., vol. 1, 135–47.

Milward, A., "Review of Billig, *Les Camps*," *JMH* 48 (1976), 567–68.

Mintert, D. M., "Das frühe Konzentrationslager Kemna und das sozialistische Milieu im Bergischen Land," Ph.D. dissertation, Ruhr University Bochum, 2007.

Mitscherlich, A., and F. Mielke (eds.), *Das Diktat der Menschenverachtung. Eine Dokumentation*, Heidelberg, 1947.

—— (eds.), *Medizin ohne Menschlichkeit. Dokumente des Nürnberger Ärzteprozesses*, Frankfurt a. M., 1978.

Mix, A., "Die Räumung des Konzentrationslagers Warschau," *Theresienstädter Studien und Dokumente* 13 (2006), 251–87.

Moeller, R. G., *War Stories: The Search for a Usable Past in the Federal Republic of Germany*, Berkeley, 2001.

Möller, R., "Die beiden 'Zyklon B'-Mordaktionen im Konzentrationslager Neuengamme 1942," in *Studien*, eds. Morsch and Perz, 288–93.

Mommsen, H., "Cumulative Radicalization and Self-Destruction of the Nazi Regime," in *Nazism*, ed. Gregor (2000), 191–94.

Mommsen, H., and M. Grieger, *Das Volkswagenwerk und seine Arbeiter im Dritten Reich*, Düsseldorf, 1996.

Montague, P., *Chełmno and the Holocaust*, London, 2012.

Moore, B., *Victims & Survivors: The Nazi Persecution of the Jews in the Netherlands 1940-1945*, London, 1997.

Moore, P., "'And What Concentration Camps Those Were!': Foreign Concentration Camps in Nazi Propaganda, 1933–39," *JCH* 45 (2010), 649–74.

——, "German Popular Opinion on the Nazi Concentration Camps, 1933–1939," Ph.D. dissertation, Birkbeck, University of London, 2010.

——, "'What Happened in Oranienburg': Weimar Paramilitaries and Nazi Terror in Werner Schäfer's Anti-Brown Book," forthcoming.

Moors, M., and M. Pfeiffer (eds.), *Heinrich Himmlers Taschenkalender 1940*, Paderborn, 2013.

Morris, N., and D. J. Rothman (eds.), *The Oxford History of the Prison*, New York, 1995.

Morsch, G., "Einleitung," in *Befreiung*, eds. Morsch and Reckendrees, 7–12.

——, "Formation and Construction of the Sachsenhausen Concentration Camp," in *Sachsenburg*, ed. Morsch, 87–201.

—— (ed.), *From Sachsenburg to Sachsenhausen*, Berlin, 2007.

—— (ed.), *Konzentrationslager Oranienburg*, Berlin, 1994.

—— (ed.), *Mord und Massenmord im Konzentrationslager Sachsenhausen 1936–1945*, Berlin, 2005.

——, "Oranienburg—Sachsenhausen, Sachsenhausen—Oranienburg," in *Konzentrationslager*, eds. Herbert et al., vol. 1, 111–34.

——, "Sachsenhausen—ein neuer Lagertypus? Das Konzentrationslager bei der Reichshauptstadt in der Gründungsphase," *ZfG* 56 (2008), 805–22.

——, (ed.), *Sachsenhausen-Liederbuch*, Berlin, 1995.

——, "Tötungen durch Giftgas im Konzentrationslager Sachsenhausen," in *Studien*, eds. Morsch and Perz, 260–76.

Morsch, G., and A. Ley, *Das Konzentrationslager Sachsenhausen 1936–1945*, Berlin, 2008.

——, *Medizin und Verbrechen. Das Krankenrevier des KZ Sachsenhausen 1936–1945*, Berlin, 2007.

Morsch, G., and B. Perz (eds.), *Neue Studien zu nationalsozialistischen Massentötungen durch Giftgas*, Berlin, 2011.

Morsch, G., and A. Reckendrees (eds.), *Befreiung Sachsenhausen 1945*, Berlin, 1996.

Morsch, G., and S. zur Nieden (eds.), *Jüdische Häftlinge im Konzentrationslager Sachsenhausen 1936 bis 1945*, Berlin, 2004.

Mües-Baron, K., *Heinrich Himmler—Aufstieg des Reichsführers SS (1900–1933)*, Göttingen, 2011.

Mühldorfer, F. (ed.), *Hans Beimler. Im Mörderlager Dachau*, Cologne, 2012.

Mühlenberg, J., *Das SS-Helferinnenkorps*, Hamburg, 2011.

Mühlhäuser, R., *Eroberungen. Sexuelle Gewalttaten und intime Beziehungen deutscher Soldaten in der Sowjetunion 1941–1945*, Hamburg, 2010.

Mühsam, K., *Der Leidensweg Erich Mühsams*, Berlin, 1994.

Müller, F., *Eyewitness Auschwitz: Three Years in the Gas Chambers*, Chicago, 1999.

Müller, J., "Homosexuelle in den Konzentrationslagern Lichtenburg und Sachsenhausen," in *Homosexuelle*, ed. Mußmann, 72–93.

——, "'Wohl dem, der hier nur eine Nummer ist.' Die *Isolierung* der Homosexuellen," in *Homosexuelle*, eds. Müller and Sternweiler, 89–108.

Müller, J., and A. Sternweiler (eds.), *Homosexuelle Männer im KZ Sachsenhausen*, Berlin, 2000.

Müller, R.-D., "Albert Speer und die Rüstungspolitik im totalen Krieg," in *Reich*, ed. Militärgeschichtliches Forschungsamt, 275–773.

——, *Der Zweite Weltkrieg, 1939–1945*, Stuttgart, 2004.

Musial, B., *"Konterrevolutionäre sind zu erschießen." Die Brutalisierung des deutsch-sowjetischen Krieges im Sommer 1941*, Berlin, 2000.

Mußmann, O., "Häftlinge mit rosa Winkel im KZ Mittelbau-Dora," in *Homosexuelle*, ed. Mußmann, 133–38.

—— (ed.), *Homosexuelle in Konzentrationslagern*, Berlin, 2000.

Naasner, W. (ed.), *SS-Wirtschaft und SS-Verwaltung*, Düsseldorf, 1998.

——, *Neue Machtzentren in der deutschen Kriegswirtschaft 1942–1945*, Boppard a. R., 1994.

Nansen, O., *Day After Day*, London, 1949.

Naujoks, H., *Mein Leben im KZ Sachsenhausen*, Cologne, 1987.

Neander, J., *Das Konzentrationslager Mittelbau in der Endphase der NS-Diktatur*, Clausthal-Zellerfeld, 1997.

——, "'Seife aus Judenfett'—Zur Wirkungsgeschichte einer urban legend," unpublished paper, 28th conference of the German Studies Association, Washington, D.C., October 2004.

——, "Vernichtung durch Evakuierung?," in *Häftlinge*, eds. Garbe and Lange, 45–59.

Neitzel, S., *Abgehört. Deutsche Generäle in britischer Kriegsgefangenschaft 1942–1945*, Berlin, 2007.

Neitzel, S., and H. Welzer, *Soldaten. Protokolle vom Kämpfen, Töten und Sterben*, Frankfurt a. M., 2012.

Neliba, G., "Wilhelm Frick—Reichsinnenminister und Rassist," in *Elite*, eds. Smelser et al., vol. 2, 80–90.

Neufeld, M. J., "Introduction to the Controversy," in *Bombing*, eds. Neufeld and Berenbaum, 1–10.

——, *The Rocket and the Reich*, Cambridge, Mass., 1999.

Neufeld, M. J., and M. Berenbaum (eds.), *The Bombing of Auschwitz: Should the Allies Have Attempted It?*, New York, 2000.

Neugebauer, W., and P. Schwarz, *Stacheldraht, mit Tod geladen . . . Der erste Österreichertransport in das KZ Dachau 1938*, Vienna, 2008.

Neugebauer, W., "Der erste Österreichertransport in das KZ Dachau 1938," in *Dachau*, eds. Benz and Königseder, 193–206.

Neumann, A., "Die Heeressanitätsinspektion und die Militärärztliche Akademie und die Konzentrationslager," in *Medizin*, eds. Hahn et al., 127–39.

Neurath, P. M., *Die Gesellschaft des Terrors*, Frankfurt a. M., 2004.

Niederland, W. G., *Folgen der Verfolgung. Das Überlebenden-Syndrom*, Frankfurt a. M., 1980.

Niedersächsische Landeszentrale für politische Bildung (ed.), *Konzentrationslager Bergen-Belsen*, 2nd ed., Göttingen, 2002.

Niethammer, L. (ed.), *Der "gesäuberte" Antifaschismus. Die SED und die roten Kapos von Buchenwald*, Berlin, 1994.

Niven, B., *The Buchenwald Child: Truth, Fiction, and Propaganda*, Rochester, N.Y., 2007.

NMGB (ed.), *Buchenwald: Mahnung und Verpflichtung*, 4th ed., Berlin, 1983.

Noakes, J., and G. Pridham (eds.), *Nazism: 1919–1945*, 4 vols., Exeter, 1998–2001.

Nolte, E., "Vergangenheit, die nicht vergehen will," in *"Historikerstreit." Die Dokumentation der Kontroverse um die Einzigartigkeit der nationalsozialistischen Judenvernichtung*, Munich, 1987, 39–47.

Nolte, H.-H., "Vernichtungskrieg: Vergessene Völker. Review neuer Literatur," *AfS* (online) 53 (2013).

Nomberg-Przytyk, S., *Auschwitz: True Tales from a Grotesque Land*, Chapel Hill, 1985.

Novick, P., *The Holocaust and Collective Memory*, London, 2000.

Nürnberg, K., "Außenstelle des Berliner Polizeipräsidiums. Das 'staatliche Konzentrationslager' Sonnenburg bei Küstrin," in *Herrschaft*, eds. Benz and Distel, 83–100.

Nyiszli, M., *Auschwitz: A Doctor's Eye-witness Account*, London, 1973.

Obenaus, H., "Der Kampf um das tägliche Brot," in *Konzentrationslager*, eds. Herbert et al., vol. 2, 841–73.

——, "Die Räumung der hannoverschen Konzentrationslager im April 1945," in *Konzentrationslager*, Fröbe et al., vol. 2, 493–544.

Oertel, O., *Als Gefangener der SS*, Oldenburg, 1990.

Office of U.S. Chief Counsel for Prosecution of Axis Criminality (ed.), *Nazi Conspiracy and Aggression*, Washington, D.C., 1948.

Oppel, S., "Marianne Eßmann. Von der Kontoristin zur SS-Aufseherin," in *Gefolge*, ed. Erpel, 81–88.

Orbach, D., and M. Solonin, "Calculated Indifference: The Soviet Union and Requests to Bomb Auschwitz," *HGS* 27 (2013), 90–113.

Orski, M., "Die Vernichtung von Häftlingen des Konzentrationslagers Stutthof durch das Giftgas Zyklon B," in *Studien*, eds. Morsch and Perz, 294–303.

——, "Organisation und Ordnungsprinzipien des Lagers Stutthof," in *Konzentrationslager*, eds. Herbert et al., vol. 1, 285–308.

Orth, K., *Das System der nationalsozialistischen Konzentrationslager. Eine politische Organisationsgeschichte*, Hamburg, 1999.

——, "Die 'Anständigkeit' der Täter. Texte und Bemerkungen," *Sozialwissenschaftliche Informationen* 25 (1996), 112–15.

——, "Die Kommandanten der nationalsozialistischen Konzentrationslager," in *Konzentrationslager*, eds. Herbert et al., vol. 2, 755–86.

——, *Die Konzentrationslager-SS. Sozialstrukturelle Analysen und biographische Studien*, Munich, 2004.

——, "Egon Zill—ein typischer Vertreter der Konzentrationslager-SS," in *Karrieren*, eds. Mallmann and Paul, 264–73.

——, "Gab es eine Lagergesellschaft? 'Kriminelle' und politische Häftlinge im Konzentrationslager," in *Ausbeutung*, eds. Frei et al., 109–33.

——, "Rudolf Höß und die 'Endlösung der Judenfrage.' Drei Argumente gegen deren Datierung auf den Sommer 1941," *WG* 18 (1997), 45–57.

——, "SS-Täter vor Gericht. Die strafrechtliche Verfolgung der Konzentrationslager-SS nach Kriegsende," in *"Gerichtstag halten über uns selbst . . ." Geschichte und Wirkung des ersten Frankfurter Auschwitz-Prozesses*, ed. I. Wojak, Frankfurt a. M., 2001, 43–60.

——, "The Concentration Camp Personnel," in *Concentration Camps*, eds. Wachsmann and Caplan, 44–57.

Otto, R., *Wehrmacht, Gestapo und sowjetische Kriegsgefangene im deutschen Reichsgebiet 1941/42*, Munich, 1998.

Overesch, M. (ed.), *Buchenwald und die DDR*, Göttingen, 1995.

——, "Ernst Thapes Buchenwalder Tagebuch von 1945," *VfZ* 29 (1981), 631–72.

Overy, R., "Das Konzentrationslager. Eine internationale Perspektive," *Mittelweg 36* (2011), Nr. 4, 40–54.

——, *Russia's War: A History of the Soviet War Effort: 1941–1945*, London, 1998.

——, *The Bombing War: Europe 1939–1945*, London, 2013.

Paetow, V., "Der französische Ravensbrück-Prozess gegen den Lagerkommandanten Fritz Suhren und den Arbeitseinsatzführer Hans Pflaum," in *Kontinuitäten*, eds. Heß et al., 204–22.

Paserman, O., "Bericht über das Konzentrationslager Warschau," *DH* 23 (2007), 146–61.

Patel, K. K., "'Auslese' und 'Ausmerze.' Das Janusgesicht der nationalsozialistischen Lager," *ZfG* 54 (2006), 339–65.

——, *Soldiers of Labor: Labor Service in Nazi Germany and New Deal America, 1933–1945*, New York, 2005.

Paul, G., "Von Psychopathen, Technokraten des Terrors und 'ganz gewöhnlichen' Deutschen", in idem., ed., *Die Täter der Shoah*, Göttingen, 2002, 13–90.

Peitsch, H., *"Deutschlands Gedächtnis an seine dunkelste Zeit." Zur Funktion der Autobiographik in den Westzonen Deutschlands und den Westsektoren von Berlin 1945 bis 1949*, Berlin, 1990.

Pendas, D. O., *The Frankfurt Auschwitz Trial, 1963–1965: Genocide, History, and the Limits of the Law*, New York, 2010.

Perz, B., "Der Arbeitseinsatz im KZ Mauthausen," in *Konzentrationslager*, eds. Herbert et al., vol. 2, 533–57.

——, *Die KZ-Gedenkstätte Mauthausen 1945 bis zur Gegenwart*, Innsbruck, 2006.

——, *Projekt Quarz. Steyr-Daimler-Puch und das Konzentrationslager Melk*, Vienna, 1991.

——, "'Vernichtung durch Arbeit' im KZ Mauthausen (Lager der Stufe III) 1938–1945," in *Konzentrationslager*, ed. Kaienburg, 89–104.

——, "Wehrmacht und KZ-Bewachung," *Mittelweg 36* (1995), Nr. 5, 69–82.

Perz, B., and F. Freund, "Auschwitz neu?," *DH* 20 (2004), 58–70.

——, "Tötungen durch Giftgas im Konzentrationslager Mauthausen," in *Studien*, eds. Morsch and Perz, 244–59.

Perz, B., and T. Sandkühler, "Auschwitz und die 'Aktion Reinhard' 1942–45. Judenmord und Raubpraxis in neuer Sicht," *Zeitgeschichte* 26 (1999), 283–316.

Petropoulos, J., and J. K. Roth (eds.), *Gray Zones: Ambiguity and Compromise in the Holocaust and Its Aftermath*, New York, 2005.

Peukert, D., "Alltag und Barbarei. Zur Normalität des Dritten Reiches," in *Nationalsozialismus*, ed. Diner, 51–61.

——, *Inside Nazi Germany*, London, 1987.

——, *The Weimar Republic*, London, 1993.

Pfingsten, G., and C. Füllberg-Stolberg, "Frauen in Konzentrationslagern—geschlechtsspezifische Bedingungen des Überlebens," in *Konzentrationslager*, eds. Herbert et al., vol. 2, 911–38.

Pick, H., *Simon Wiesenthal: A Life in Search of Justice*, Boston, 1996.

Picker, H. (ed.), *Hitlers Tischgespräche im Führerhauptquartier*, Berlin, 1997.

Piekut-Warszawska, E., "Kinder in Auschwitz: Erinnerungen einer Krankenschwester," in *Auschwitz Hefte*, ed. HIS, vol. 1, 227–29.

Pike, D. W., *Spaniards in the Holocaust: Mauthausen, the Horror on the Danube*, London, 2000.

Pilecki, W., *The Auschwitz Volunteer: Beyond Bravery*, Los Angeles, 2012.

Pilichowski, C., *Es gibt keine Verjährung*, Warsaw, 1980.

—— (ed.), *Obozy hitlerowskie na ziemiach polskich 1939–1945*, Warsaw, 1979.

Pingel, F., *Häftlinge unter SS-Herrschaft. Widerstand, Selbstbehauptung und Vernichtung im Konzentrationslager*, Hamburg, 1978.

——, "Social Life in an Unsocial Environment," in *Concentration Camps*, eds. Wachsmann and Caplan, 58–81.

——, "The Destruction of Human Identity in Concentration Camps," *HGS* 6 (1991), 167–84.

Piper, F., *Die Zahl der Opfer von Auschwitz*, Oświęcim, 1993.

——, "'Familienlager' für Juden und 'Zigeuner' im KL Auschwitz-Birkenau," in *Sinti*, ed. Długoborski, 293–99.

—— (ed.), *Illegale Briefe aus Auschwitz von Janusz Pogonowski*, Oświęcim, 1999.

——, *Mass Murder*, vol. 3 of *Auschwitz*, eds. Długoborski and Piper.

——, "The Exploitation of Prisoner Labor," in *Auschwitz*, eds. Długoborski and Piper, vol. 2, 71–136.

Pohl, D., "Die großen Zwangsarbeitslager der SS- und Polizeiführer für Juden im Generalgouvernement 1942–1945," in *Konzentrationslager*, eds. Herbert et al., vol. 1, 415–38.

——, "Die Trawniki-Männer im Vernichtungslager Belzec 1941–1943," in *NS-Gewaltherrschaft*, eds. Gottwaldt et al., 278–89.

——, *Holocaust*, Freiburg i. Br., 2000.

——, "Sowjetische und polnische Strafverfahren wegen NS-Verbrechen—Quellen für den Historiker?," in *Recht*, eds. Finger et al., 132–41.

——, "The Holocaust and the Concentration Camps," in *Concentration Camps*, eds. Wachsmann and Caplan, 149–66.

——, *Von der "Judenpolitik" zum Judenmord. Der Distrikt Lublin des Generalgouvernements 1939–1944*, Frankfurt a. M., 1993.

Polak, E., *Dziennik buchenwaldzki*, Warsaw, 1983.

Poljan, P., "'Bereits Menschen, keine Häftlinge mehr.' Die Dachauer Lagergesellschaft nach der Befreiung im Spiegel des *Sowjetischen Bulletins*," *DH* 21 (2005), 82–93.

Pollak, M., *Die Grenzen des Sagbaren. Lebensgeschichten von KZ-Überlebenden als Augenzeugenberichte und als Identitätsarbeit*, Frankfurt a. M., 1988.

Poller, W., *Arztschreiber in Buchenwald*, Hamburg, 1946.

Pollmeier, H., "Die Verhaftungen nach dem November-Pogrom 1938 und die Masseninternierung in den 'jüdischen Barracken' des KZ Sachsenhausen," in *Häftlinge*, eds. Morsch and zur Nieden, 164–79.

Präg, W., and W. Jacobmeyer (eds.), *Das Diensttagebuch des deutschen Generalgouverneurs in Polen 1939–1945*, Stuttgart, 1975.

Prenninger, A., "Riten des Gedenkens. Befreiungsfeiern in der KZ-Gedenkstätte Mauthausen," in *Lagersystem*, eds. Gabriel et al., 183–205.

Pressac, J.-C., *Die Krematorien von Auschwitz*, Munich, 1995.

Pressac, J.-C., and R.-J. van Pelt, "The Machinery of Mass Murder at Auschwitz," in *Anatomy*, eds. Gutman and Berenbaum, 183–245.

Preston, P., *The Spanish Holocaust*, London, 2013.

Pretzel, A., "Vorfälle im Konzentrationslager Sachsenhausen vor Gericht in Berlin," in *Homosexuellenverfolgung*, eds. Pretzel and Roßbach, 119–68.

———, "'. . . zwecks Umschulung auf unbestimmte Zeit.' Als *Berufsverbrecher* in Vorbeugungshaft," in *Homosexuelle*, eds. Müller and Sternweiler, 79–88.

Pretzel, A., and G. Roßbach (eds.), *Wegen der zu erwartenden hohen Strafe . . . Homosexuellenverfolgung in Berlin 1933–1945*, Berlin, 2000.

Priemel, K. C., and A. Stiller (eds.), *NMT. Die Nürnberger Militärtribunale zwischen Geschichte, Gerechtigkeit und Rechtschöpfung*, Hamburg, 2013.

Prusin, A. V., "Poland's Nuremberg: The Seven Court Cases of the Supreme National Tribunal, 1946–1948," *HGS* 24 (2010), 1–25.

Przyrembel, A., "Transfixed by an Image: Ilse Koch, the 'Kommandeuse of Buchenwald,'" *GH* 19 (2008), 369–99.

Pukrop, M., "Die SS-Karrieren von Dr. Wilhelm Berndt und Dr. Walter Döhrn," *WG* 62 (2012), 76–93.

Rabinbach, A., "*Staging Antifascism*: The Brown Book of the Reichstag Fire and Hitler Terror," *NGC* 35 (2008), 97–126.

Rabinovici, D., *Eichmann's Jews: The Jewish Administration of Holocaust Vienna, 1938–1945*, London, 2011.

Rahe, T., "Die Bedeutung von Religion und Religiosität in den nationalsozialistischen Konzentrationslagern," in *Konzentrationslager*, eds. Herbert et al., vol. 2, 1006–22.

———, "Einleitung," in Koretz, *Bergen-Belsen*, 9–22.

Raim, E., *Die Dachauer KZ-Außenkommandos Kaufering und Mühldorf*, Munich, 1991.

———, "Die KZ-Außenlagerkomplexe Kaufering und Mühldorf," in *Dachau*, eds. Benz and Königseder, 71–88.

———, *Justiz zwischen Diktatur und Demokratie. Wiederaufbau und Ahndung von NS-Verbrechen in Westdeutschland 1945–1949*, Munich, 2013.

——— (ed.), *Überlebende von Kaufering*, Berlin, 2008.

———, "Westdeutsche Ermittlungen und Prozesse zum KZ Dachau und seinen Außenlagern," in *Dachauer*, eds. Eiber and Sigel, 210–36.

Raithel, T., and I. Strenge, "Die Reichstagsbrandverordnung," *VjZ* 48 (2000), 413–60.

Rawicz, J., "Ein Dokument der Schande (Vorwort zu Kremers Tagebuch)," *HvA* 13 (1971), 5–23.

Recanati, A. (ed.), *A Memorial Book of the Deportation of the Greek Jews*, Jerusalem, 2006.

Reckendrees, A., "Das Leben im befreiten Lager," in *Befreiung*, eds. Morsch and Reckendrees, 100–110.

Rees, L., *Auschwitz: The Nazis & the "Final Solution,"* London, 2005.

Reichardt, S., *Faschistische Kampfbünde. Gewalt und Gemeinschaft im italienischen Squadrismus und in der deutschen SA*, 2nd ed., Cologne, 2009.

Reichel, P., "Auschwitz," in *Deutsche Erinnerungsorte. Eine Auswahl*, eds. E. François and H. Schulze, Munich, 2005, 309–31.

———, *Politik mit der Erinnerung. Gedächtnisorte im Streit um die nationalsozialistische Vergangenheit*, Frankfurt a. M., 1999.

Reichel, P., H. Schmid, and P. Steinbach (eds.), *Der Nationalsozialismus—Die zweite Geschichte* (Munich, 2009).

———, "Die 'zweite Geschichte' der Hitler-Diktatur. Zur Einführung," in *Nationalsozialismus*, eds. Reichel et al., 7–21.

Reilly, J., *Belsen: The Liberation of a Concentration Camp*, London, 1998.

Reinisch, J., "Introduction: Survivors and Survival in Europe after the Second World War," in *Justice, Politics and Memory in Europe after the Second World War*, eds. S. Bardgett, D. Cesarani, J. Reinisch, and J.-D. Steinert, London, 2011, 1–16.

Reiter, A., *"Auf daß sie entsteigen der Dunkelheit." Die literarische Bewältigung von KZ-Erfahrung*, Vienna, 1995.

Renouard, J.-P., *Die Hölle gestreift*, Hanover, 1998.

Renz, W., "Tonbandmitschnitte von NS-Prozessen als historische Quelle," in *Recht*, eds. Finger et al., 142–53.

Repgen, K., and H. Booms (eds.), *Akten der Reichskanzlei. Regierung Hitler*, vol. I, Boppard a. R., 1983.

Richardi, H.-G., *Schule der Gewalt. Das Konzentrationslager Dachau*, Munich, 1995.

Richarz, M. (ed.), *Jüdisches Leben in Deutschland*, Stuttgart, 1988.

Riebe, R., "Frauen in Konzentrationslagern 1933–1939," *DH* 14 (1998), 125–40.

——, "Funktionshäftlinge in Frauenkonzentrationslagern 1933–1939," *BGVN* 4 (1998), 51–56.

Riedel, D., " 'Arbeit macht frei.' Leitsprüche und Metaphern aus der Welt der Konzentrationslager," *DH* 22 (2006), 11–29.

——, "Bruderkämpfe im Konzentrationslager Dachau. Das Verhältnis zwischen kommunistischen und sozialdemokratischen Häftlingen," in *Die Linke*, eds. Wachsmann and Steinbacher, 117–40.

——, *Ordnungshüter und Massenmörder im Dienst der "Volksgemeinschaft." Der KZ-Kommandant Hans Loritz*, Berlin, 2010.

Riedle, A., *Die Angehörigen des Kommandanturstabs im KZ Sachsenhausen*, Berlin, 2011.

Rieß, V., "Christian Wirth—der Inspekteur der Vernichtungslager," in *Karrieren*, eds. Mallmann and Paul, 239–51.

Riexinger, K., and D. Ernst, *Vernichtung durch Arbeit. Rüstung im Bergwerk*, Tübingen, 2003.

Ritscher, B., G. Hammermann, R.-G. Lüttgenau, W. Röll, and C. Schölzel (eds.), *Das sowjetische Speziallager Nr. 2, 1945–1950*, Göttingen, 1999.

Rodrigo, J., "Exploitation, Fascist Violence and Social Cleansing: A Study of Franco's Concentration Camps from a Comparative Perspective," *ERH* 19 (2012), 553–73.

Roelcke, V., "Introduction," in *Twentieth Century Ethics of Human Subjects Research*, eds. Roelcke and G. Maio, Wiesbaden, 2004, 11–18.

Röll, W., "Homosexuelle Häftlinge im Konzentrationslager Buchenwald 1937 bis 1945," in *Homosexuelle*, ed. Mußmann, 94–104.

——, *Sozialdemokraten im Konzentrationslager Buchenwald 1937–1945*, Göttingen, 2000.

Rolnikaite, M., *Ich muss erzählen. Mein Tagebuch 1941–1945*, Berlin, 2002.

Römer, F., *Der Kommissarbefehl. Wehrmacht und NS-Verbrechen an der Ostfront 1941/42*, Paderborn, 2008.

Römmer, C., "Digitalisierung der WVHA-Häftlingskartei," unpublished project report, 2009.

——, " 'Sonderbehandlung 14f13,' " *BGVN* 11 (2009), 209–11.

Roseman, M., "Beyond Conviction? Perpetrators, Ideas and Action in the Holocaust in Historiographical Perspective," in *Conflict, Catastrophe, and Continuity*, eds. F. Biess, M. Roseman, and H. Schissler, New York, 2007, 83–103.

——, " '. . . but of revenge not a sign': Germans' Fear of Jewish Revenge after World War II," *JfA* 22 (2013), 79–95.

Rosen, A., *The Wonder of Their Voices: The 1946 Holocaust Interviews of David Boder*, New York, 2010.

Rossino, A., *Hitler Strikes Poland: Blitzkrieg, Ideology and Atrocity*, Lawrence, Kans., 2003.

Rost, N., *Goethe in Dachau*, Berlin, n.d.

Roth, K.-H., " 'Generalplan Ost'—'Gesamtplan Ost,' " in *Der "Generalplan Ost,"* eds. Rössler and Schleiermacher, Berlin, 1993, 25–95.

——, "Zwangsarbeit im Siemens-Konzern (1938–1945)," in *Konzentrationslager und deutsche Wirtschaft 1939–1945*, ed. H. Kaienburg, Opladen, 1996, 149–68.

Roth, T., "Die 'Asozialen' im Blick der Kripo," in *Wessen Freund und wessen Helfer?*, eds. H. Buhlan and W. Jung, Cologne, 2000, 424–63.

——, "Die Kölner Kriminalpolizei," in ibid., 299–366.

——, "Frühe Haft- und Folterstätten in Köln 1933/34," in *Konzentrationslager*, ed. Schulte, 3–24.

Rothkirchen, L., "The 'Final Solution' in Its Last Stages," *Yad Vashem Studies* 8 (1970), 7–29.

Rouse, J. E., "Perspectives on Organizational Culture," *Public Administration Review* 50 (1990), 479–85.

Rousset, D., *L'univers concentrationnaire*, Paris, 1946.

——, *The Other Kingdom*, New York, 1947.

Rovan, J., *Geschichten aus Dachau*, Munich, 1999.

Rózsa, Á., "Solange ich lebe, hoffe ich," in *"Solange,"* eds. Diefenbacher and Jochem, 95–352.

Rubner, W., "Dachau im Sommer 1933," in *Konzentrationslager*, 54–76.

Rudorff, A., "Arbeit und Vernichtung *reconsidered*. Die Lager der Organisation Schmelt für polnische Jüdinnen und Juden aus dem annektierten Teil Oberschlesiens," *Sozial.Geschichte Online* 7 (2012), 10–39.

——, "Die Strafverfolgung von KZ-Aufseherinnen in Polen," *ZfG* 61 (2013), 329–50.

——, *Frauen in den Außenlagern des Konzentrationslagers Groß-Rosen*, Berlin, 2014.

——, "Misshandlung und Erpressung mit System. Das Konzentrationslager 'Vulkanwerft' in Stettin-Bredow," in *Instrumentarium*, eds. Benz and Distel, 35–69.

——, "'Privatlager' des Polizeipräsidenten mit prominenten Häftlingen. Das Konzentrationslager Breslau-Dürrgoy," in *Instrumentarium*, eds. Benz and Distel, 147–70.

——, "Schutzhaft im Gewahrsam der Justiz. Das Zentralgefängnis Gollnow bei Stettin," in *Instrumentarium*, eds. Benz and Distel, 27–34.

Rumpf, J. R., *Der Fall Wollheim gegen die I.G. Farbenindustrie AG in Liquidation*, Frankfurt a. M., 2010.

Runzheimer, J., "Die Grenzzwischenfälle am Abend vor dem deutschen Angriff auf Polen," in *Sommer 1939*, eds. W. Benz and H. Graml, Stuttgart, 1979, 107–47.

Ruppert, A., "Spanier in deutschen Konzentrationslagern," *Tranvia* Nr. 28 (March 1993), 5–9.

Rürup, R. (ed.), *Topographie des Terrors*, 10th ed., Berlin, 1995.

Rüter, C. F. (ed.), *DDR-Justiz und NS-Verbrechen. Sammlung ostdeutscher Strafurteile wegen nationalsozialistischer Tötungsverbrechen*, 15 vols., Amsterdam, 2002–2010.

Rüter, C. F., and D. W. de Mildt (eds.), *Justiz und NS-Verbrechen. Sammlung deutscher Strafurteile wegen nationalsozialistischer Tötungsverbrechen*, 49 vols., Amsterdam, 1968–81, 1998–2012.

Rüther, M., *Köln im Zweiten Weltkrieg*, Cologne, 2005.

Ryn, Z., and S. Kłodziński, "An der Grenze zwischen Leben und Tod. Eine Studie über die Erscheinung des 'Muselmanns' im Konzentrationslager," in *Auschwitz Hefte*, ed. HIS, vol. 1, 89–154.

——, "Tod und Sterben im Konzentrationslager," in *Auschwitz Hefte*, ed. HIS, vol. 1, 281–328.

Sachse, C., "Menschenversuche in Auschwitz. überleben, erinnern, verantworten," in *Die Verbindung nach Auschwitz*, ed. Sachse, Göttingen, 2003, 7–34.

Sarodnick, W., "'Dieses Haus muß ein Haus des Schreckens werden . . .' Strafvollzug in Hamburg 1933 bis 1945," in *"Für Führer, Volk und Vaterland . . ." Hamburger Justiz im Nationalsozialismus*, ed. Justizbehörde Hamburg, Hamburg, 1992, 332–81.

Schäfer, W., *Konzentrationslager Oranienburg. Das Anti-Braunbuch über das erste deutsche Konzentrationslager*, Berlin, n.d., 1934.

Schalm, S., "Außenkommandos und Außenlager des KZ Dachau," in *Dachau*, eds. Benz and Königseder, 53–70.

———, *Überleben durch Arbeit? Außenkommandos und Außenlager des KZ Dachau 1933–1945*, Berlin, 2009.

Scheffler, W., "Zur Praxis der SS- und Polizeigerichtsbarkeit im Dritten Reich," in *Klassenjustiz und Pluralismus*, eds. G. Doeker and W. Steffani, Hamburg, 1973, 224–36.

Schelvis, J., *Sobibor: A History of a Nazi Death Camp*, Oxford, 2007.

Schiffner, S., "Cap Arcona-Gedenken in der DDR," in *Häftlinge*, eds. Garbe and Lange, 309–24.

Schikorra, C., "Grüne und schwarze Winkel—geschlechterperspektivische Betrachtungen zweier Gruppen von KZ-Häftlingen 1938–40," *BGVN* 11 (2009), 104–10.

———, *Kontinuitäten der Ausgrenzung. "Asoziale" Häftlinge im Frauen-Konzentrationslager Ravensbrück*, Berlin, 2001.

Schilde, K., "Vom Tempelhofer Feld-Gefängnis zum Schutzhaftlager. Das 'Columbia-Haus' in Berlin," in *Herrschaft*, eds. Benz and Distel, 65–81.

Schilde, K., and J. Tuchel, *Columbia-Haus. Berliner Konzentrationslager 1933–1936*, Berlin, 1990.

Schilter, T., "Horst Schumann—Karriere eines Arztes im Nationalsozialismus," in *Sonnenstein*, ed. Kuratorium, 95–108.

Schlaak, P., "Das Wetter in Berlin von 1933 bis 1945," *Berlinische Monatsschrift* 9 (2000), Nr. 9, 177–84.

Schleunes, K. A., *The Twisted Road to Auschwitz: Nazi Policy Towards German Jews, 1933–39*, Urbana, 1970.

Schley, J., *Nachbar Buchenwald. Die Stadt Weimar und ihr Konzentrationslager 1937–1945*, Cologne, 1999.

Schmaltz, F., "Die Gaskammer im Konzentrationslager Natzweiler," in *Studien*, eds. Morsch and Perz, 304–15.

———, "Die IG Farbenindustrie und der Ausbau des Konzentrationslagers Auschwitz 1941–1942," *Sozial. Geschichte* 21 (2006), 33–67.

———, *Kampfstoff Forschung im Nationalsozialismus. Zur Kooperation von Kaiser-Wilhelm-Instituten, Militär und Industrie*, Göttingen, 2005.

Schmeling, A., *Josias Erbprinz zu Waldeck und Pyrmont. Der politische Weg eines hohen SS-Führers*, Kassel, 1993.

Schmid, Hans, "Otto Moll—'der Henker von Auschwitz,'" *ZfG* 54 (2006), 118–38.

Schmid, H.-D., "Die Aktion 'Arbeitsscheu Reich' 1938," *BGVN* 11 (2009), 31–42.

Schmid, Harald, "Deutungsmacht und kalendarisches Gedächtnis—die politischen Gedenktage," in *Nationalsozialismus*, eds. Reichel et al., 175–216.

Schmidt, B., "Geschichte und Symbolik der gestreiften KZ-Kleidung," Ph.D. dissertation, University of Oldenburg, 2000.

Schmidt, P., "Tortur als Routine. Zur Theorie und Praxis der römischen Inquisition in der frühen Neuzeit," in *Das Quälen des Körpers*, eds. P. Burschel, G. Distelrath, and S. Lembke, Cologne, 2000, 201–15.

Schmidt, U., *Justice at Nuremberg. Leo Alexander and the Nazi Doctors' Trial*, Houndmills, 2006.

———, *Karl Brandt: The Nazi Doctor*, London, 2007.

———, "Medical Ethics and Nazism," in *The Cambridge World History of Medical Ethics*, eds. R. Baker and L. McCullough, Cambridge, U.K., 2009, 595–608.

———, "'The Scars of Ravensbrück': Medical Experiments and British War Crimes Policy, 1945–1950," *GH* 23 (2005), 20–49.

Schmuhl, H.-W., "Philipp Bouhler—Ein Vorreiter des Massenmordes," in *Braune Elite*, eds. Smelser et al., vol. 2, 39–50.

Schnabel, R., *Macht ohne Moral*, 2nd ed., Frankfurt a. M., 1958.

Schneider, M., *Unterm Hakenkreuz. Arbeiter und Arbeiterbewegung 1933 bis 1939*, Bonn, 1999.

———, "Verfolgt, unterdrückt und aus dem Land getrieben: Das Ende der Arbeiterbewegung im Frühjahr 1933," in *Die Linke*, eds. Wachsmann and Steinbacher, 31–51.

Schneppen, H., *Odessa und das Vierte Reich*, Berlin, 2007.

Schrade, C., *Elf Jahre: Ein Bericht aus deutschen Konzentrationslagern*, Göttingen, 2014.

Schröder, H. H., "Das erste Konzentrationslager in Hannover. Das Lager bei der Akkumulatorenfabrik in Stöcken," in *Konzentrationslager*, eds. Fröbe et al., vol. 1, 44–108.

Schüle, A., *Industrie und Holocaust. Topf & Söhne—Die Ofenbauer von Auschwitz*, Göttingen, 2010.

Schulte, J. E., "Auschwitz und der Holocaust," *VfZ* 52 (2004), 569–72.

———, "Die Konzentrationslager 1939 bis 1941," in *Taschenkalender*, eds. Moors and Pfeiffer, 141–54.

———, "Die Kriegsgefangenen-Arbeitslager der SS 1941/42: Größenwahn und Massenmord," in *Zusammenarbeit*, ed. Ibel, 71–90.

———, *Die SS, Himmler und die Wewelsburg*, Paderborn, 2009.

———, "Im Zentrum der Verbrechen. Das Verfahren gegen Oswald Pohl und weitere Angehörige des SS-Wirtschafts-Verwaltungshauptamtes," in *NMT*, eds. Priemel and Stiller, 67–99.

——— (ed.), *Konzentrationslager im Rheinland und in Westfalen 1933–1945*, Paderborn, 2005.

———, "London war informiert. KZ-Expansion und Judenverfolgung," in *Hitlers Kommissare*, eds. R. Hachtmann and W. Süß, Göttingen, 2006, 207–27.

———, "Vom Arbeits- zum Vernichtungslager. Die Entstehungsgeschichte von Auschwitz-Birkenau 1941/42," *VfZ* 50 (2002), 41–69.

———, *Zwangsarbeit und Vernichtung. Das Wirtschaftsimperium der SS*, Paderborn, 2001.

Schulze, R. (ed.), *Unruhige Zeiten. Erlebnisberichte aus dem Landkreis Celle 1945–1949*, Munich, 1991.

Schumacher, M. (ed.), *M.d.R. Die Reichstagsabgeordneten in der Weimarer Republik in der Zeit des Nationalsozialismus*, Düsseldorf, 1994.

Schwarberg, G., *Der SS-Arzt und die Kinder. Bericht über den Mord vom Bullenhuser Damm*, Munich, 1982.

Schwartz, J., "Geschlechtsspezifischer Eigensinn von NS-Täterinnen am Beispiel der KZ-Oberaufseherin Johanna Langefeld," in *Frauen als Täterinnen im Nationalsozialismus*, ed. V. Schubert-Lehnhardt, Gerbstedt, 2005, 56–82.

Schwarz, G., *Eine Frau an seiner Seite. Ehefrauen in der "SS-Sippengemeinschaft*," Berlin, 2001.

———, "Frauen in Konzentrationslagern—Täterinnen und Zuschauerinnen," in *Konzentrationslager*, eds. Herbert et al., vol. 2, 800–821.

Schwindt, B. *Das Konzentations- und Vernichtungslager Majdanek*, Wurzburg, 2005

Seaman, M., *Bravest of the Brave*, London, 1997.

Seela, T., *Bücher und Bibliotheken in nationalsozialistischen Konzentrationslagern*, Munich, 1992.

Seger, G., "Oranienburg. Erster authentischer Bericht eines aus dem Konzentrationslager Geflüchteten," in *Oranienburg*, eds. Diekmann and Wettig, 15–89.

Segev, T., *Simon Wiesenthal. Die Biographie*, Munich, 2010.

———, *Soldiers of Evil: The Commandants of the Nazi Concentration Camps*, London, 2000.

———, *The Seventh Million: The Israelis and the Holocaust*, New York, 1991.

Seidel, I., "Jüdische Frauen in den Außenkommandos des Konzentrationslagers Buchenwald," in *Genozid*, ed. Bock, 149–68.

Seidl, D., *"Zwischen Himmel und Hölle." Das Kommando "Plantage" des Konzentrationslagers Dachau*, Munich, 2008.

Selbmann, F., *Alternative, Bilanz, Credo*, Halle, 1975.

Sellier, A., *A History of the Dora Camp*, Chicago, 2003.

Sémelin, J., *Säubern und Vernichten. Die politische Dimension von Massakern und Völkermorden*, Hamburg, 2007.

Semprun, J., and E. Wiesel, *Schweigen ist unmöglich*, Frankfurt a. M., 1997.

Setkiewicz, P., "Häftlingsarbeit im KZ Auschwitz III-Monowitz," in *Konzentrationslager*, eds. Herbert et al., vol. 2, 584–605.

—— (ed.), *Życie prywatne esesmanów w Auschwitz*, Oświęcim, 2012.

Seubert, R., "'Mein lumpiges Vierteljahr Haft...' Alfred Anderschs KZ-Haft und die ersten Morde von Dachau," in *Alfred Andersch Revisited*, eds. J. Döring and M. Joch, Berlin, 2011, 47–146.

Shephard, B., *After Daybreak: The Liberation of Belsen, 1945*, London, 2006.

——, *The Long Road Home: The Aftermath of the Second World War*, London, 2010.

Shik, N., "Mother-Daughter Relationships in Auschwitz-Birkenau, 1942–1945," *Tel Aviver Jahrbuch für deutsche Geschichte*, vol. 36, Göttingen, 2008, 108–27.

——, "Sexual Abuse of Jewish Women in Auschwitz-Birkenau," in *Brutality and Desire*, ed. D. Herzog, New York, 2009, 221–47.

——, "Weibliche Erfahrung in Auschwitz-Birkenau," in *Genozid*, ed. Bock, 103–22.

Shirer, W. L., *The Rise and Fall of the Third Reich*, London, 1991.

Siebeck, C., "'Im Raum lesen wir die Zeit?' Zum komplexen Verhältnis von Geschichte, Ort und Gedächtnis (nicht nur) in KZ-Gedenkstätten," *Transformation*, eds. Klei et al., 69–97.

Siedlecki, J., K. Olszewski, and T. Borowski, *We Were in Auschwitz* (New York, 2000).

Siegert, T., "Das Konzentrationslager Flossenbürg," in *Bayern*, eds. Broszat and Fröhlich, vol. 2, 429–92.

Siegfried, K.-J., *Das Leben der Zwangsarbeiter im Volkswagenwerk 1939–1945*, Frankfurt a. M., 1988.

Siemens, D., *The Making of a Nazi Hero: The Murder and Myth of Horst Wessel*, London, 2013.

Sigel, R., "Die Dachauer Prozesse und die deutsche Öffentlichkeit," in *Dachauer*, eds. Eiber and Sigel, 67–85.

——, *Im Interesse der Gerechtigkeit. Die Dachauer Kriegsverbrecherprozesse 1945–1948*, Frankfurt a. M., 1992.

Sigl, F., *Todeslager Sachsenhausen*, Berlin, 1948.

Silbermann, A., and M. Stoffers, *Auschwitz. Nie davon gehört? Erinnern und Vergessen in Deutschland*, Berlin, 2000.

Skriebeleit, J., "Ansätze zur Neukonzeption der KZ-Gedenkstätte Flossenbürg," in *Konzentrationslager. Geschichte und Erinnerung*, eds. P. Haustein, R. Schmolling, and J. Skriebeleit, Ulm, 2001, 15–25.

——, *Erinnerungsort Flossenbürg*, Göttingen, 2009.

Sládek, O., "Standrecht und Standgericht. Die Gestapo in Böhmen und Mähren," in *Gestapo im Zweiten Weltkrieg*, eds. Mallmann and Paul, 317–39.

SMAB (ed.), *Forbidden Art: Illegal Works by Concentration Camp Prisoners*, Oświęcim, 2012.

——, *Inmitten des grauenvollen Verbrechens. Handschriften von Mitgliedern des Sonderkommandos*, Oświęcim, 1996.

——, *Memorial Book: The Gypsies at Auschwitz-Birkenau*, Munich, 1993.

Smelser, R., and E. Syring (eds.), *Die SS. Elite unter dem Totenkopf*, Paderborn, 2000.

Smelser, R., E. Syring, and R. Zitelmann (eds.), *Die braune Elite*, 2 vols., 4th ed., Darmstadt, 1999.

Smith, B. F., and A. F. Peterson, *Heinrich Himmler. Geheimreden 1933 bis 1945*, Frankfurt a. M., 1974.

Smith, I. R., and A. Stucki, "The Colonial Development of Concentration Camps (1868–1902)," *Journal of Imperial and Commonwealth History* 39 (2011), 417–37.

Smoleń, K., "Sowjetische Kriegsgefangene im KL Auschwitz," in *Sterbebücher von Auschwitz*, ed. J. Dębski, Munich, 1995, 127–47.

Snyder, L. (ed.), *Encyclopedia of the Third Reich*, London, 1976.

Snyder, T., *Bloodlands: Europe Between Hitler and Stalin*, London, 2010.

Sobolewicz, T., *Aus dem Jenseits zurück*, Oświęcim, 1993.

Sodi, R., "The Memory of Justice: Primo Levi and Auschwitz," *HGS* 4 (1989), 89–104.

Sofsky, W., "An der Grenze des Sozialen. Perspektiven der KZ-Forschung," in *Konzentrationslager*, eds. Herbert et al., vol. 2, 1141–69.

———, *Die Ordnung des Terrors. Das Konzentrationslager,* Frankfurt a. M., 1997.

———, *Violence: Terrorism, Genocide, War,* London, 2003.

Sommer, R., *Das KZ-Bordell: Sexuelle Zwangsarbeit in nationalsozialistischen Konzentrationslagern,* Paderborn, 2009.

Sonnino, P., *Die Nacht von Auschwitz,* Reinbek, 2006.

Speckner, H., "Kriegsgefangenenlager—Konzentrationslager Mauthausen und 'Aktion K,'" in *Zusammenarbeit?,* ed. Ibel, 45–57.

Speer, A., *Erinnerungen,* Frankfurt a. M., 1969.

Spoerer, M., "Profitierten Unternehmen von KZ-Arbeit? Eine kritische Analyse der Literatur," *Historische Zeitschrift* 268 (1999), 61–95.

———, *Zwangsarbeit unter dem Hakenkreuz,* Stuttgart, 2001.

Spoerer, M., and J. Fleischhacker, "Forced Laborers in Nazi Germany: Categories, Numbers and Survivors," *Journal of Interdisciplinary History* 33 (2002), 169–204.

Sprenger, I., "Aufseherinnen in den Frauenaußenlagern des Konzentrationslagers Groß-Rosen," *WG* 12 (1995), 21–33.

———, "Das KZ Groß-Rosen in der letzten Kriegsphase," in *Konzentrationslager,* eds. Herbert et al., vol. 2, 1113–27.

———, *Groß-Rosen. Ein Konzentrationslager in Schlesien,* Cologne, 1996.

Springmann, V., "'Sport machen.' Eine Praxis der Gewalt im Konzentrationslager," in *KZ-Verbrechen,* eds. Lenarczyk et al., 89–101.

Stahl, D., *Nazi-Jagd. Südamerikas Diktaturen und die Ahndung von NS-Verbrechen,* Göttingen, 2013.

Stangneth, B. "Dienstliche Aufenthaltsorte Adolf Eichmanns, 12.3.1938 bis 8.05.1945," unpublished manuscript, Berlin, 2010.

———, *Eichmann vor Jerusalem. Das unbehelligte Leben eines Massenmörders,* Zurich, 2011.

Stargardt, N., *Witnesses of War: Children's Lives Under the Nazis,* London, 2005.

State of Israel Ministry of Justice (ed.), *The Trial of Adolf Eichmann,* vol. 7, Jerusalem, 1995.

Statistisches Jahrbuch der Schutzstaffel der NSDAP 1937.

Statistisches Jahrbuch der Schutzstaffel der NSDAP 1938.

Steegmann, R., *Das Konzentrationslager Natzweiler-Struthof und seine Außenkommandos am Rhein und Neckar 1941–1945,* Berlin, 2010.

———, *Struthof. Le KL-Natzweiler et ses kommandos,* Strasbourg, 2005.

Stein, H., "Die Vernichtungstransporte aus Buchenwald in die 'T4'-Anstalt Sonnenstein 1941," in *Sonnenstein,* ed. Kuratorium, 29–50.

———, "Funktionswandel des Konzentrationslagers Buchenwald im Spiegel der Lagerstatistiken," in *Konzentrationslager,* eds. Herbert et al., vol. 1, 167–92.

———, *Juden in Buchenwald 1937–1942,* Weimar, 1992.

Stein, H., and S. Stein, *Buchenwald, Ein Rundgang durch die Gedenkstätte,* Weimar, 1993.

Steinbacher, S., *Auschwitz: A History,* London, 2005.

———, *Dachau: Die Stadt und das Konzentrationslager in der NS-Zeit,* Frankfurt a. M., 1994.

———, *"Musterstadt" Auschwitz. Germanisierungspolitik und Judenmord in Ostoberschlesien,* Munich, 2000.

———, "'. . . nichts weiter als Mord.' Der Gestapo-Chef von Auschwitz und die bundesdeutsche Nachkriegsjustiz," in *Ausbeutung,* eds. Frei et al., 265–98.

Steiner, J., and Z. Steiner, "Zwillinge in Birkenau," in *Auschwitz,* eds. Adler et al., 126–28.

Steiner, J. M., "The SS Yesterday and Today: A Sociopsychological View," in *Survivors, Victims, and Perpetrators,* ed. J. E. Dimsdale, Washington, D.C., 1980, 405–56.

Steinert, J.-D., *Deportation und Zwangsarbeit. Polnische und sowjetische Kinder im nationalsozialistischen Deutschland und im besetzten Osteuropa 1939–1945,* Essen, 2013.

Steinke, K., *Züge nach Ravensbrück. Transporte mit der Reichsbahn 1939–1945,* Berlin, 2009.

Steinweis, A., *Kristallnacht 1938,* Cambridge, Mass., 2009.

Stengel, K., *Hermann Langbein. Ein Auschwitz-Überlebender in den erinnerungspolitischen Konflikten der Nachkriegszeit,* Frankfurt a. M., 2012.

Stibbe, M., *British Civilian Prisoners of War in Germany*, Manchester, 2008.

Stiftung niedersächsischer Gedenkstätten (ed.), *Bergen-Belsen. Katalog der Dauerausstellung*, Göttingen, 2009.

Stiller, A., "Zwischen Zwangsgermanisierung und 'Fünfter Kolonne.' 'Volksdeutsche' als Häftlinge und Bewacher in den Konzentrationslagern," in *Lager*, eds. Jah et al., 104–24.

Stokes, L., "Das Eutiner Schutzhaftlager 1933/34. Zur Geschichte eines 'wilden' Konzentrationslager," *VfZ* 27 (1979), 570–625.

———, "Das oldenburgische Konzentrationslager in Eutin, Neukirchen und Nüchel 1933," in *Terror*, eds. Benz and Distel, 189–210.

Stoll, K., "Walter Sonntag—ein SS-Arzt vor Gericht," *ZfG* 50 (2002), 918–39.

Stone, D., *Goodbye to All That? The Story of Europe since 1945*, Oxford, 2014.

———, *Histories of the Holocaust*, Oxford, 2010.

———, "The Historiography of Genocide: Beyond 'Uniqueness' and Ethnic Competition," *Rethinking History* 8 (2004), 127–42.

———, "The Sonderkommando Photographs," *Jewish Social Studies* 7 (2001), 132–48.

———, *The Liberation of the Camps*, New Haven, 2015.

Stoop, P. (ed.), *Geheimberichte aus dem Dritten Reich*, Berlin, 1990.

Stöver, B. (ed.), *Berichte über die Lage in Deutschland. Die Meldungen der Gruppe Neu Beginnen aus dem Dritten Reich 1933–1936*, Bonn, 1996.

Stræde, T., "Die 'Aktion Weiße Busse,'" in *Häftlinge*, eds. Garbe and Lange, 175–84.

Strebel, B., *Celle April 1945 Revisited*, Bielefeld, 2008.

———, *Das KZ Ravensbrück. Geschichte eines Lagerkomplexes*, Paderborn, 2003.

———, "Feindbild 'Flintenweib.' Weibliche Kriegsgefangene der Roten Armee im KZ Ravensbrück," in *Zusammenarbeit?*, ed. Ibel, 159–80.

———, "'Himmelweite Unterschiede.' Über die Existenzbedingungen im KZ Ravensbrück 1939–1945," in *Konzentrationslager*, ed. Kaienburg, 105–23.

———, "Verlängerter Arm der SS oder schützende Hand? Drei Fallbeispiele von weiblichen Funktionshäftlingen im KZ Ravensbrück," *WG* 12 (1995), 35–49.

Streim, A., *Die Behandlung sowjetischer Kriegsgefangener im "Fall Barbarossa,"* Heidelberg, 1981.

Streit, C., *Keine Kameraden. Die Wehrmacht and die sowjetischen Kriegsgefangenen, 1941–1945*, Stuttgart, 1978.

Struk, J., *Photographing the Holocaust*, London, 2004.

Strzelecka, I., "Die ersten Polen im KL Auschwitz," *HvA* 18 (1990), 5–67.

———, "Experiments," in *Auschwitz*, eds. Długoborski and Piper, vol. 2, 347–69.

———, "Quarantine on Arrival," in ibid., 45–50.

———, "The Hospitals at Auschwitz Concentration Camp," in ibid., 291–346.

———, "Women in the Auschwitz Concentration Camp," in ibid., 171–200.

Strzelecka, I., and P. Setkiewicz, "The Construction, Expansion and Development of the Camp and Its Branches," in *Auschwitz*, eds. Długoborski and Piper, vol. 1, 63–138.

Strzelecki, A., "Plundering the Victims' Property," in *Auschwitz*, eds. Długoborski and Piper, vol. 2, 137–70.

———, "The Liquidation of the Camp," in ibid., vol. 5, 9–85.

———, "Utilization of the Victims' Corpses," in ibid., vol. 2, 399–418.

Stuldreher, C.J.F., "Das Konzentrationslager Herzogenbusch—ein 'Musterbetrieb der SS'?," in *Konzentrationslager*, eds. Herbert et al., vol. 1, 327–48.

Suderland, M., *Ein Extremfall des Sozialen*, Frankfurt a. M., 2009.

———, *Territorien des Selbst: Kulturelle Identität als Ressource für das tägliche Überleben im Konzentrationslager*, Frankfurt a. M., 2004.

Suhr, E., *Carl von Ossietzky: Eine Biographie*, Cologne, 1988.

Süß, D., *Tod aus der Luft. Kriegsgesellschaft und Luftkrieg in Deutschland und England*, Bonn, 2011.

Süß, W., *Der "Volkskörper" im Krieg. Gesundheitspolitik, Gesundheitsverhältnisse und Krankenmord im nationalsozialistischen Deutschland 1939–1945*, Munich, 2003.

Sutton, J., "Reconcentration During the Philippine-American War (1899–1902)," unpublished paper, Oxford Workshop on the Colonial Development of Concentration Camps, All Soul's College, November 2010.

Swett, P. E., *Neighbors & Enemies: The Culture of Radicalism in Berlin, 1929–1933*, Cambridge, U.K., 2004.

Świebocki, H. (ed.), *London wurde informiert. Berichte von Auschwitz-Flüchtlingen*, Oświęcim, 1997.

———, *The Resistance Movement*, vol. 4 of *Auschwitz*, eds. Piper and Długoborski.

———, "Sinti und Roma im KL Auschwitz in der Berichterstattung der polnischen Widerstandsbewegung," in *Sinti*, ed. Długoborski, 330–41.

Sydnor, C., *Soldiers of Destruction: The SS Death's Head Division 1933–1945*, London, 1989.

———, "Theodor Eicke. Organisator der Konzentrationslager," in *SS*, eds. Smelser and Syring, 147–59.

Szalet, L., *Baracke 38. 237 Tage in den "Judenblocks" des KZ Sachsenhausen*, Berlin, 2006.

Szeintuch, Y., "'Tkhias Hameysim,'" *Chulyot* 10 (2006), 191–218.

Szende, S., *Zwischen Gewalt und Toleranz. Zeugnisse und Reflexionen eines Sozialisten*, Frankfurt a. M., 1975.

Szita, S., *Ungarn in Mauthausen*, Vienna, 2006.

Szmaglewska, S., *Smoke over Birkenau*, Oświęcim, 2008.

Szymański, T., T. Śnieszko, and D. Szymańska, "Das 'Spital' im Zigeuner-Familienlager in Auschwitz-Birkenau," in *Auschwitz Hefte*, ed. HIS, vol. 1, 199–207.

Taft, M., *From Victim to Survivor: The Emergence and Development of the Holocaust Witness, 1941–1949*, London, 2013.

Tauke, O., "Gestaffelte Selektion. Die Funktion der Häftlingskrankenbauten in den Lagern des KZ Mittelbau-Dora," in *Medizin*, eds. Hahn et al., 26–45.

Terhorst, K.-L., *Polizeiliche planmäßige Überwachung und polizeiliche Vorbeugungshaft im Dritten Reich*, Heidelberg, 1985.

Thalhofer, E., *Entgrenzung der Gewalt. Gestapo-Lager in der Endphase des Dritten Reiches*, Paderborn, 2010.

Thamer, H.-U., *Verführung und Gewalt. Deutschland 1933–1945*, Munich, 1986.

The Times (London).

Tillion, G., "A la recherche de la vérité," in *Les Cahiers du Rhône*, Neuchâtel, 1946, 11–88.

———, *Frauenkonzentrationslager Ravensbrück*, Lüneburg, 1998.

Timofeeva, N. P. (ed.), *Nepobedimaja sila slabykh: Koncentracionnyj lager Ravensbrjuk v pamjati i sud'be byvshikh zakljuchennyk*, Voronezh, 2008.

Todorov, T., *Facing the Extreme: Moral Life in the Concentration Camps*, London, 2000.

———, *Hope and Memory*, London, 2003.

Tooze, A., *The Wages of Destruction: The Making and Breaking of the Nazi Economy*, London, 2006.

Toussaint, J., "Nach Dienstschluss," in *Gefolge*, ed. Erpel, 89–100.

Trial of the Major War Criminals Before the International Military Tribunal, 42 vols., Nuremberg, 1947–49.

Trouvé, C., "Das Klinkerwerk Oranienburg (1938–1945)—ein Außenlager des Konzentrationslagers Sachsenhausen," Ph.D. dissertation, TU Berlin, 2004.

———, "Richard Bugdalle, SS-Blockführer im Konzentrationslager Sachsenhausen. Stationen einer Karriere," in *Tatort KZ*, eds. U. Fritz, S. Kavčič, and N. Warmbold, Ulm, 2003, 20–42.

Trunk, A., "Die todbringenden Gase," in *Studien*, eds. Morsch and Perz, 23–49.

Tuchel, J., *Die Inspektion der Konzentrationslager 1938–1945*, Berlin, 1994.

———, "Die Kommandanten des Konzentrationslagers Flossenbürg—Eine Studie zur Personalpolitik der SS," in *Die Normalität des Verbrechens*, eds. J. Tuchel, H. Grabitz, and K. Bästlein, Berlin, 1994, 201–19.

———, "Die Kommandanten des KZ Dachau," in *Dachau*, eds. Benz and Königseder, 329–49.

——, "Die Wachmannschaften der Konzentrationslager 1939 bis 1945—Ergebnisse und offene Fragen der Forschung," in *NS-Gewaltherrschaft*, eds. Gottwaldt et al., 135–51.

——, "Dimensionen des Terrors: Funktionen der Konzentrationslager in Deutschland 1933–1945," in *Lager, Zwangsarbeit, Vertreibung und Deportation*, eds. D. Dahlmann and G. Hirschfeld, Essen, 1999, 371–89.

——, *Konzentrationslager. Organisationsgeschichte und Funktion der "Inspektion der Konzentrationslager,"* Boppard a. R., 1991.

——, "Möglichkeiten und Grenzen der Solidarität zwischen einzelnen Häftlingsgruppen im nationalsozialistischen Konzentrationslager," in *Strategie des Überlebens*, eds. R. Streibel and H. Schafranek, Vienna, 1996, 220–35.

——, "Organisationsgeschichte der 'frühen' Konzentrationslager," in *Instrumentarium*, eds. Benz and Distel, 9–26.

——, "Registrierung, Mißhandlung und Exekution. Die 'Politischen Abteilungen' in den Konzentrationslagern," in *Gestapo im Zweiten Weltkrieg*, eds. Mallmann and Paul, 127–40.

——, "Selbstbehauptung und Widerstand in nationalsozialistischen Konzentrationslagern," in *Der Widerstand gegen den Nationalsozialismus*, eds. J. Schmädeke and P. Steinbach, Munich, 1985, 938–53.

——, "Theodor Eicke im Konzentrationslager Lichtenburg," in *Lichtenburg*, eds. Hördler and Jacobeit, 59–74.

Tuchel, J., and R. Schattenfroh, *Zentrale des Terrors. Prinz-Albrecht-Straße 8: Hauptquartier der Gestapo*, Frankfurt a. M., 1987.

Tyas, S., "Allied Intelligence Agencies and the Holocaust: Information Acquired from German Prisoners of War," *HGS* 22 (2008), 1–24.

Tych, F., A. Eberhardt, A. Kenkmann, and E. Kohlhaas (eds.), *Kinder über den Holocaust. Frühe Zeugnisse 1944–1948*, Berlin, 2008.

Uhl, H., "From Victim Myth to Co-Responsibility Thesis," in *Politics*, eds. Kansteiner et al., 40–72.

UN War Crimes Commission (ed.), *Law Reports of Trials of War Criminals*, vol. 1, London, 1947.

Unbekannter Autor, "Einzelheiten," in *Inmitten*, ed. SMAB, 177–84.

——, "Notizen," in *Inmitten*, ed. SMAB, 184–85.

Ungar, G., "Die Konzentrationslager," in *Opferschicksale*, ed. DöW, Vienna, 2013, 191–209.

Unger, M., "The Prisoner's First Encounter with Auschwitz," *HGS* 1 (1986), 279–95.

Union für Recht und Freiheit (ed.), *Der Strafvollzug im III. Reich*, Prague, 1936.

Urban, M., "Kollektivschuld durch die Hintertür? Die Wahrnehmung der NMT in der westdeutschen Öffentlichkeit, 1946–1951," in *NMT*, eds. Priemel and Stiller, 684–718.

Urbańczyk, S., "In Sachsenhausen und in Dachau," in *Sonderaktion*," ed. August, 212–36.

Uziel, D., *Arming the Luftwaffe: The German Aviation Industry in World War II*, Jefferson, N.C., 2012.

Vaisman, S., *In Auschwitz*, Düsseldorf, 2008.

Van Dam, H. G., and R. Giordano (eds.), *KZ-Verbrechen vor deutschen Gerichten*, vol. 1, Frankfurt a. M., 1962.

Van der Vat, D., *The Good Nazi: The Life and Lies of Albert Speer*, London, 1998.

Van Pelt, R. J., "A Site in Search of a Mission," in *Anatomy*, eds. Gutman and Berenbaum, 93–156.

——, *The Case for Auschwitz: Evidence from the Irving Trial*, Bloomington, Ind., 2002.

——, "Introduction," in *Edge*, Koker, 3–71.

——, "Resistance in the Camps," in *Jewish Resistance to the Nazis*, ed. P. Henry, Washington, D.C., 2014.

Verhandlungen des Reichstags, vol. 459, Berlin, 1938.

Vermehren, I., *Reise durch den letzten Akt. Ein Bericht*, Hamburg, 1947.

Vieregge, B., *Die Gerichtsbarkeit einer "Elite." Nationalsozialistische Rechtsprechung am Beispiel der SS- und Polizei-Gerichtsbarkeit*, Baden-Baden, 2002.

Vogel, L., *Tagebuch aus einem Lager*, Göttingen, 2002.

Volk, R., *Das letzte Urteil. Die Medien und der Demjanjuk-Prozess*, Munich, 2012.

Völkischer Beobachter.

Volkov, S., "Antisemitism as a Cultural Code: Reflections on the History and Historiography of Antisemitism in Imperial Germany," *LBIYB* 23 (1978), 25–46.

Volland, K., "Das Stalag X B Sandbostel als Auffanglager für KZ-Häftlinge," in *Häftlinge*, eds. Garbe and Lange, 117–25.

Von dem Knesebeck, J., *The Roma Struggle for Compensation in Post-War Germany*, Hatfield, 2011.

Von Götz, I., "Terror in Berlin—Eine Topographie für das Jahr 1933," in *SA-Gefängnis Papestraße*, eds. von Götz and P. Zwaka, Berlin, 2013, 27–46.

Von Götz, I., and C. Kreutzmüller, "Spiegel des frühen NS-Terrors. Zwei Foto-Ikonen und ihre Geschichte," *Fotogeschichte* 34 (2014), Nr. 131, 73–75.

Von Kellenbach, K., *The Mark of Cain: Guilt and Denial in the Post-war Lives of Nazi Perpetrators*, New York, 2013.

Von Papen, F., *Ein von Papen spricht . . . : über seine Erlebnisse im Hitler-Deutschland*, Amsterdam, c. 1939.

Vossler, F., *Propaganda in die eigene Truppe. Die Truppenbetreuung in der Wehrmacht 1939–45*, Paderborn, 2005.

Vrba, R., "Die mißachtete Warnung: Betrachtungen über den Auschwitz-Bericht von 1944," *VfZ* 44 (1996), 1–24.

——, *I Cannot Forgive*, Vancouver, 1997.

Wachsmann, N., "'Annihilation Through Labor': The Killing of State Prisoners in the Third Reich," *JMH* 71 (1999), 624–59.

——, "Comparisons and Connections: The Nazi Concentration Camps in International Context," in *Rewriting German History*, eds. J. Rüger and N. Wachsmann, London, 2015 (forthcoming).

——, *Hitler's Prisons: Legal Terror in Nazi Germany*, New Haven, 2004.

——, "Introduction," in *Under Two Dictators*, Buber-Neumann, 2009, vii–xxii.

——, "Introduction," in *Theory*, Kogon, xi–xxi.

——, "Looking into the Abyss: Historians and the Nazi concentration camps," *EHQ* 36 (2006), 247–78.

——, "Review of Benz, Distel, *Ort des Terrors*," *sehepunkte* 5 (2005), Nr. 11.

——, "The Dynamics of Destruction: The Development of the Concentration Camps, 1933–45," in *Concentration Camps*, eds. Wachsmann and Caplan, 17–43.

——, "The Policy of Exclusion: Repression in the Nazi State, 1933–39," in *Nazi Germany*, ed. Caplan, 122–45.

Wachsmann, N., and J. Caplan (eds.), *Concentration Camps in Nazi Germany: The New Histories*, London, 2010.

——, "Introduction," in *Concentration Camps*, eds. Wachsmann and Caplan, 1–16.

Wachsmann, N., and C. Goeschel, "Before Auschwitz: The Formation of the Nazi Concentration Camps, 1933–39," *JCH* 45 (2010), 515–34.

——, "Introduction," in *Nazi Concentration Camps*, eds. Wachsmann and Goeschel, ix–xxvii.

—— (eds.), *The Nazi Concentration Camps, 1933–1939: A Documentary History*, Lincoln, Neb., 2012.

Wachsmann, N., and S. Steinbacher (eds.), *Die Linke im Visier. Zur Errichtung der Konzentrationslager 1933*, Göttingen, 2014.

Wagner, B. C., *IG Auschwitz. Zwangsarbeit und Vernichtung von Häftlingen des Lagers Monowitz 1941–1945*, Munich, 2000.

Wagner, J.-C., *Ellrich 1944/45. Konzentrationslager und Zwangsarbeit in einer deutschen Kleinstadt*, Göttingen, 2009.

—— (ed.), *Konzentrationslager Mittelbau-Dora 1943–1945*, Göttingen, 2007.

——, *Produktion des Todes. Das KZ Mittelbau-Dora*, Göttingen, 2004.

——, "Sinti und Roma als Häftlinge im KZ Mittelbau-Dora," *BGVN* 14 (2012), 99–107.

——, "Work and Extermination in the Concentration Camps," in *Concentration Camps*, eds. Wachsmann and Caplan, 127–48.

Wagner, P., *Volksgemeinschaft ohne Verbrecher. Konzeptionen und Praxis der Kriminalpolizei in der Zeit der Weimarer Republik und des Nationalsozialismus*, Hamburg, 1996.

——, "'Vernichtung der Berufsverbrecher'. Die vorbeugende Verbrechensbekämpfung der Kriminalpolizei bis 1937", in *Konzentrationslager*, eds. Herbert et al., vol.1, 87–110.

Walter, V., "Kinder und Jugendliche als Häftlinge des KZ Dachau," in *Dachau*, eds. Benz and Königseder, 183–92.

Warmbold, N., *Lagersprache. Zur Sprache der Opfer in den Konzentrationslagern Sachsenhausen, Dachau, Buchenwald*, Bremen, 2008.

Waxman, Z., *Writing the Holocaust: Identity, Testimony, Representation*, Oxford, 2006.

Weckbecker, G., *Zwischen Freispruch und Todesstrafe. Die Rechtsprechung der nationalsozialistischen Sondergerichte Frankfurt/Main und Bromberg*, Baden-Baden, 1998.

Weckel, U., *Beschämende Bilder. Deutsche Reaktionen auf alliierte Dokumentarfilme über befreite Konzentrationslager*, Stuttgart, 2012.

Weckel, U., and E. Wolfrum (eds.), *"Bestien" und "Befehlsempfänger." Frauen und Männer in NS-Prozessen nach 1945*, Göttingen, 2003.

Wegner, B., *Hitler's Politische Soldaten. Die Waffen-SS, 1933–1945*, Paderborn, 2006.

——, "The Ideology of Self-Destruction: Hitler and the Choreography of Defeat," *Bulletin of the German Historical Institute London* 26 (2004), No. 2, 18–33.

Weigelt, A., "'Komm, geh mit! Wir gehn zum Judenerschiessen . . .' Massenmord bei der Auflösung des KZ-Aussenlagers Lieberose im Februar 1945," *DH* 20 (2004), 179–93.

Weikart, R., *Hitler's Ethic: The Nazi Pursuit of Evolutionary Progress*, Houndmills, 2011.

Wein, D., "Das Krankenrevier im Konzentrationslager Sachsenhausen in seiner Funktion als Vorführobjekt," in *Medizin*, eds. Hahn et al., 46–65.

Weinberg, G. L., "The Allies and the Holocaust," in *Bombing*, eds. Neufeld and Berenbaum, 15–26.

Weinberger, R. J., *Fertility Experiments in Auschwitz-Birkenau*, Saarbrücken, 2009.

Weindling, P. J., "Die Opfer von Humanexperimenten im Nationalsozialismus," in *Geschlecht und "Rasse" in der NS-Medizin*, eds. I. Eschebach and A. Ley, Berlin, 2012, 81–99.

——, *Epidemics and Genocide in Eastern Europe, 1890–1945*, Oxford, 2000.

——, *Nazi Medicine and the Nuremberg Trials*, New York, 2006.

——, *Victims and Survivors of Nazi Human Experiments*, London, 2015.

Weingartner, J. J., "Law and Justice in the Nazi SS: The Case of Konrad Morgen," *CEH* 16 (1983), 276–94.

Weinke, A., *Die Verfolgung von NS-Tätern im geteilten Deutschland*, Paderborn, 2002.

Weisbrod, B., "Entwicklung und Funktionswandel der Konzentrationslager 1937/38 bis 1945," in *Konzentrationslager*, eds. Herbert et al., 349–60.

——, "Violence and Sacrifice: Imagining the Nation in Weimar Germany," in *The Third Reich Between Vision and Reality*, ed. H. Mommsen, Oxford, 2001, 5–21.

Weise, N., *Eicke. Eine SS-Karriere zwischen Nervenklinik, KZ-System und Waffen-SS*, Paderborn, 2013.

Weiß, H., "Dachau und die internationale Öffentlichkeit," *DH* 1 (1985), 12–38.

Weiss-Rüthel, A., *Nacht und Nebel. Ein Sachsenhausen-Buch*, Berlin, 1949.

Weitz, E. D., *A Century of Genocide: Utopias of Race and Nation*, Princeton, 2003.

Welch, D., *Propaganda and the German Cinema 1933–1945*, 2nd ed., London, 2001.

Wellers, G., *L'Étoile jaune à l'heure de Vichy: De Drancy à Auschwitz*, Paris, 1973.

Welzer, H., *Täter. Wie aus ganz normalen Menschen Massenmörder werden*, Frankfurt a. M., 2005.

Wenck, A.-E., *Zwischen Menschenhandel und "Endlösung." Das Konzentrationslager Bergen-Belsen*, Paderborn, 2000.

Werner, C., *Kriegswirtschaft und Zwangsarbeit bei BMW*, Munich, 2006.

Werner, F., "'Hart müssen wir hier draußen sein.' Soldatische Männlichkeit im Vernichtungskrieg 1941–1944," *Geschichte und Gesellschaft* 34 (2008), 5–40.

Werth, N., *Cannibal Island: Death in a Siberian Gulag*, Princeton, 2007.

Werther, T., "Menschenversuche in der Fleckfieberforschung," in *Vernichten*, eds. Ebbinghaus and Dörner, 152–73.

Wesołowska, D., *Wörter aus der Hölle. Die "lagerszpracha" der Häftlinge von Auschwitz*, Krakow, 1998.

Westermann, E. B., "The Royal Air Force and the Bombing of Auschwitz: First Deliberations, January 1941," *HGS* 15 (2001), 70–85.

Wetzell, R., *Inventing the Criminal: A History of German Criminology 1880–1945*, Chapel Hill, 2000.

Whatmore, H., "Exploring KZ 'Bystanding' within a West-European Framework," in *Kontinuitäten*, eds. Heß et al., 64–79.

——, "Living with the Nazi KZ Legacy," in Klei et al. (eds.), *Transformation*, 47–67.

White, E. B., "Majdanek: Cornerstone of Himmler's SS Empire in the East," *Simon Wiesenthal Center Annual* 7 (1990), 3–21.

White, O., *Conqueror's Road: An Eyewitness Report of Germany 1945*, Cambridge, U.K., 2003.

Wickert, C., "Die Aufdeckung der Verbrechen durch die sowjetische Regierungskommission im Sommer 1945 und ihre Folgen," in *Befreiung*, eds. Morsch and Reckendrees, 120–27.

Wiechert, E., *Der Totenwald*, Zurich, 1946.

Wiedemann, M., "Ágnes Rózsa. Eine biographische Skizze," in *"Solange,"* eds. Diefenbacher and Jochem, 13–15.

Wiedner, H., "Soldatenmißhandlungen im Wilhelminischen Kaiserreich (1890–1914)," *AfS* 22 (1982), 159–99.

Wieland, G., "Die Ahndung von NS-Verbrechen in Ostdeutschland 1945–1990," in *DDR-Justiz*, ed. Rüter, vol. 15, 13–94.

Wieland, L., "Die Bremischen Konzentrationslager Ochtumsand und Langlütjen II," in *Herrschaft*, eds. Benz and Distel, 275–94.

Wiesel, E., *All Rivers Run to the Sea: Memoirs*, London, 1997.

——, *Die Nacht. Erinnerung und Zeugnis,* Munich, 2008.

Wildt, M., "Funktionswandel der nationalsozialistischen Lager," *Mittelweg 36* (2011), No. 4, 76–86.

——, *Generation des Unbedingten. Das Führungskorps des Reichssicherheitshauptamtes*, Hamburg, 2002.

——, "Himmlers Terminkalender aus dem Jahr 1937," *VfZ* 52 (2004), 671–91.

——, "Violent Changes of Society—Social Changes through Violence," unpublished paper, conference "German Society in the Nazi Era," GHI London, March 2010.

Wilhelm, F., *Die Polizei im NS-Staat*, Paderborn, 1997.

Winter, M. C., and K. Greiser, "Untersuchungen zu den Todesmärschen seit 1945," in *Freilegungen*, eds. Blondel et al., 73–84.

Winter, W., *Winter Time: Memoirs of a German Sinto Who Survived Auschwitz*, Hatfield, 2004.

Wisskirchen, J., "Schutzhaft in der Rheinprovinz. Das Konzentrationslager Brauweiler 1933–1934," in *Herrschaft*, eds. Benz and Distel, 129–56.

Witte, P., A. Angrick, C. Dieckmann, C. Gerlach, P. Klein, D. Pohl, M. Voigt, and M. Wildt (eds.), *Der Dienstkalender Heinrich Himmlers 1941/42*, Hamburg, 1999.

Witte, P., and S. Tyas, "A New Document on the Deportation and Murder of Jews During 'Einsatz Reinhardt' 1942," *HGS* 15 (2001), 468–86.

Wittmann, R., *Beyond Justice: The Auschwitz Trial*, Cambridge, Mass., 2005.

Wohlfeld, U., "Das Konzentrationslager Nohra in Thüringen," in *Terror*, eds. Benz and Distel, 105–21.

——, "Im Hotel 'Zum Großherzog.' Das Konzentrationslager Bad Sulza 1933–1937," in *Instrumentarium*, eds. Benz and Distel, 261–75.

Wojak, I., *Eichmanns Memoiren. Ein kritischer Essay*, Frankfurt a. M., 2001.

Wolf, R., "'Mass Deception Without Deceivers?' The Holocaust on East and West German Radio in the 1960s," *JCH* 41 (2006), 741–55.

Wolfangel, E., "'Nie anders, als ein willenloses Rädchen.' Margarete Mewes: Aufseherin und Leiterin des Zellenbaus im KZ Ravensbrück (1939–1945)," in *Gefolge*, ed. Erpel, 72–80.

Wolfram, L., "KZ-Aufseherinnen. Parteigängerinnen der NSDAP?," in *Gefolge*, ed. Erpel, 39–47.

Wollenberg, J., "Das Konzentrationslager Ahrensbök-Holstendorf im oldenburgischen Landesteil Lübeck," in *Terror*, eds. Benz and Distel, 223–50.

——, "Gleichschaltung, Unterdrückung und Schutzhaft in der roten Hochburg Bremen. Das Konzentrationslager Bremen-Mißler," in *Herrschaft*, eds. Benz and Distel, 245–73.

Wolters, C., *Tuberkulose und Menschenversuche im Nationalsozialismus*, Stuttgart, 2011.

Wormser-Migot, O., *L'ère des camps*, Paris, 1973.

——, *Le système concentrationnaire Nazi (1933–45)*, Paris, 1968.

Wünschmann, K., *Before Auschwitz: Jewish Prisoners in the Prewar Concentration Camps*, Cambridge, Mass., 2015.

——, "Cementing the Enemy Category. Arrest and Imprisonment of German Jews in Nazi Concentration Camps, 1933–8/9," *JCH* 45 (2010), 576–600.

——, "Die Konzentrationslagererfahrungen deutsch-jüdischer Männer nach dem Novemberpogrom 1938," in "*Wer bleibt, opfert seine Jahre, vielleicht sein Leben." Deutsche Juden 1938–1941*, eds. S. Heim, B. Meyer, and F. Nicosia, Göttingen, 2010, 39–58.

——, "Jewish Prisoners in Nazi Concentration Camps, 1933–1939," Ph.D. dissertation, Birkbeck, University of London, 2012.

——, "Jüdische politische Häftlinge im frühen KZ Dachau," in *Die Linke*, eds. Wachsmann and Steinbacher, 141–67.

——, "'Natürlich weiß ich, wer mich ins KZ gebracht hat und warum ...' Die Inhaftierung von Juden im Konzentrationslager Osthofen 1933/34," in *Die Erinnerung an die nationalsozialistischen Konzentrationslager*, eds. A. Ehresmann, P. Neumann, A. Prenninger, and R. Schlagdenhauffen, Berlin, 2011, 97–111.

——, "The 'Scientification' of the Concentration Camp," *LBIYB* 58 (2013), 111–26.

Wysocki, G., "Häftlingsarbeit in der Rüstungsproduktion," *DH* 2 (1986), 35–67.

——, "Lizenz zum Töten. Die 'Sonderbehandlungs'-Praxis der Stapo-Stelle Braunschweig," in *Gestapo im Zweiten Weltkrieg*, eds. Mallmann and Paul, 237–54.

Yavnai, L., "US Army War Crimes Trials in Germany, 1945–1947," in *Atrocities on Trial*, eds. P. Heberer and J. Matthäus, Lincoln, Neb., 2008, 49–71.

Zámečník, S., "Das 'Baumhängen' und die umstrittenen Fotografien aus der Sicht des ehemaligen Häftlings," *DH* 14 (1998), 289–93.

—— (ed.), "Die Aufzeichnungen von Karel Kašák," *DH* 11 (1995), 167–251.

——, *Das war Dachau*, Luxemburg, 2002.

——, "Kein Häftling darf lebend in die Hände des Feindes fallen. Zur Existenz des Himmler-Befehls vom 14./18. April 1945," *DH* 1 (1985), 219–31.

Zaremba, M., "Nicht das endgültige Urteil," in *Wahrheiten*, eds. Engelking and Hirsch, 251–59.

Zarusky, J., "Die Erschießungen gefangener SS-Leute bei der Befreiung des KZ Dachau," in *Dachau*, eds. Benz and Königseder, 103–24.

——, "Die 'Russen' im KZ Dachau. Bürger der Sowjetunion als Opfer des NS-Regimes," *DH* 23 (2007), 105–39.

———, "'. . . gegen die Tötung der Menschen und die Abtötung alles Menschlichen.' Zum Widerstand von Häftlingen im Konzentrationslager Dachau," in *Der vergessene Widerstand*, ed. J. Tuchel, Göttingen, 2005, 63–96.

———, "Von Dachau nach nirgendwo. Der Todesmarsch der KZ-Häftlinge im April 1945," in *Spuren des Nationalsozialismus*, ed. Bayerische Landeszentrale für politische Bildungsarbeit, Munich, 2000, 42–63.

Zeck, M., *Das Schwarze Korps. Geschichte und Gestalt des Organs der Reichsführung*, Tübingen, 2002.

Zeiger, A., "Die Todesmärsche," in *Befreiung*, eds. Morsch and Reckendrees, 64–72.

Zelizer, B., *Remembering to Forget: Holocaust Memory Through the Camera's Eye*, Chicago, 1998.

Zentner, C., and F. Bedürftig (eds.), *The Encyclopedia of the Third Reich*, New York, 1997.

Zimbardo, P., *The Lucifer Effect*, New York, 2008.

Zimmerer, J., "War, Concentration Camps and Genocide in South-West Africa: The First German Genocide," in *Genocide in German South-West Africa*, eds. Zimmerer and Zeller, Monmouth, 2008, 41–63.

Zimmermann, M., "Arbeit in den Konzentrationslagern," in *Konzentrationslager*, eds. Herbert et al., vol. 2, 730–51.

———, "Die Entscheidung für ein Zigeunerlager in Auschwitz-Birkenau," in *Zwischen Erziehung und Vernichtung*, ed. M. Zimmermann, Stuttgart, 2007, 392–424.

———, *Rassenutopie und Genozid. Die nationalsozialistische "Lösung der Zigeunerfrage,"* Hamburg, 1996.

Zimmermann, V., *NS-Täter vor Gericht. Düsseldorf und die Strafprozesse wegen nationalsozialistischer Gewaltverbrechen*, Düsseldorf, 2001.

Zinn, A., "Homophobie und männliche Homosexualität in Konzentrationslagern," in *Homophobie*, ed. Eschebach, 79–96.

Ziółkowski, M., *Ich war von Anfang an in Auschwitz*, Cologne, 2006.

Zweig, R. W., "Feeding the Camps: Allied Blockade Policy and the Relief of Concentration Camps in Germany, 1944–1945," *The Historical Journal* 41 (1998), 825–51.

Acknowledgments

I want to thank everyone who has helped, over the last ten years, to make this book possible.

The following institutions provided essential backing during different periods of research and writing: the Arts & Humanities Research Council (AHRC), the British Academy, the Leverhulme Trust, and the Harry Frank Guggenheim Foundation. I am profoundly grateful for their grants and fellowships, and to the colleagues who supported my applications: Richard Bessel, Jane Caplan, Sir Richard Evans, Norbert Frei, Mary Fulbrook, Neil Gregor, Sir Ian Kershaw, Jeremy Noakes, and Richard Overy.

Equally indispensable was the help of the staff in memorials, libraries, and archives. I owe a very big word of thanks to Albert Knoll and Dirk Riedel (Dachau), Andreas Kranebitter (Vienna/Mauthausen), Johannes Ibel (Flossenbürg), Monika Liebscher (Sachsenhausen), Wojciech Płosa (Oświęcim), and Sabine Stein (Buchenwald), who all went well beyond the call of duty, and answered my frequent questions and requests with unfailing patience and unrivaled knowledge. In addition, I want to acknowledge the special assistance I received from Maren Ballerstedt (Stadtarchiv Magdeburg); Na'ama Shik, Daniel Uziel, and the late David Bankier (Yad Vashem); Robert Bierschneider (StAMü); Danuta Drywa (Sztutowo); Andreas Eichmüller, Edith Raim, and Jürgen Zarusky (IfZ); Christine Schmidt (WL); Gunter Friedrich (StANü); Karoline Georg and Johannes Tuchel (Gedenkstätte Deutscher Widerstand); Sabine Gresens (BArchB); Gabriele Hammermann and Julia Rosche (Dachau); Regine Heubaum and Jens-Christian Wagner (Dora); Cordula Hundertmark

(Ravensbrück); Annette Kraus and Jörg Skriebeleit (Flossenbürg); Astrid Ley and Günter Morsch (Sachsenhausen); Reimer Möller (Neuengamme); Margret Schmidt and Susanne Urban (ITS, Bad Arolsen); Jan Erik Schulte (Wewelsburg); Agnieszka Sieradzka (Oświęcim); and Bianca Welzing-Bräutigam (LaB).

My huge debt to fellow historians is evident from the bibliography. Many other experts were kind enough to share additional documents and ideas, and the book has benefited greatly from their input. I want to thank Carina Baganz, Antony Beevor, Ruth Bettina Birn, Marc Buggeln, Gabriel Finder, Klaus Gagstädter, Gideon Greif, Wolf Gruner, Susanne Heim, Sarah Helm, Ulrich Herbert, Ben Hett, Jörg Hillmann, Stefan Hördler, Franziska Jahn, Tomaz Jardim, Padraic Kenney, Angelika Königseder, Tamar Lewinsky, Andreas Mix, Pieter Romijn, Andreas Sander, Stefanie Schüler-Springorum, Patrik Schwarz, Rolf Seubert, Dan Stone, Friedrich Veitl, Robert Jan van Pelt, Rita von Borck, Irene von Götz, Peter Warneke, Paul Weindling, Michael Wildt, and René Wolf. I also want to acknowledge the support of my colleagues and friends at Birkbeck, including John Arnold, Catharine Edwards, David Feldman, Matt Innes, Jessica Reinisch, Jan Rüger, Julian Swann, and Frank Trentmann; above all, I must thank Christian Goeschel, who tracked down key documents on the prewar camps as an AHRC postdoctoral fellow.

I have been most fortunate to receive expert research assistance from four of my doctoral students, who have all gone on to write outstanding studies of Nazi terror: Chris Dillon, Julia Hörath, Paul Moore, and Kim Wünschmann. Kim also helped with some translations, as did Jeff Porter, Katharina Friedla, and Shaun Morcom. And I want to thank David Dunning, Amelia Nell, and Ina Sondermann for their administrative help.

I am greatly indebted to those colleagues and friends who generously took the time to read the manuscript and make suggestions for changes and corrections. For their notes on individual sections, I want to express my sincere thanks to Marc Buggeln, Wolfgang Burgmair, Christoph Dieckmann, Julia Hörath, Tomaz Jardim, Michael Metzger, Elissa Mailänder Koslov, Anna Hájková, Dieter Pohl, Jessica Reinisch, Dirk Riedel, Jan Rüger, Ulf Schmidt, Robert Jan van Pelt, Jens-Christian Wagner, and Matthias Weber. And I am immensely grateful to Jane Caplan, Chris Dillon, Paul Moore, Michael Wachsmann, and Kim Wünschmann, who commented on the entire text. The book would be much poorer without their sound advice.

It has been a real privilege to work with Eric Chinski, my editor at FSG, who was extremely encouraging every step of the way and made countless crucial improvements to the manuscript. I also want to acknowledge the exceptional support by Andrew Wylie and James Pullen at the Wylie Agency, who believed in the book from the start. The lengthy passage of the text from my computer to the printers was eased by the extremely efficient work and good cheer of Scott Auerbach, Gabriella Doob, Frieda Duggan, Peng Shepherd, and everyone else at FSG. Jeff Ward did a first-rate job with the maps, and Pon Ruiter and his team suggested several important last-minute corrections.

Closest to home, Basti, Christa, Michael, and Gabi helped in every way they could, Gerald did me a big favor with the photos, and Mike was an invaluable counselor and friend, as always. Tracey accompanied me once again during a long research project about a grim subject—from the first germ of the idea to the end—and gave me all the support and love to see it through. And Josh reminded me, every day during writing, that there was a much better world out there, away from my desk. I am so very grateful to them all.

Index

Page numbers in *italics* refer to illustrations.